A PRACTICAL TOOL

For many years the French language has been a subject of study in high school and college throughout the English-speaking world. Today it is more than a subject of study; it is a practical tool of communication in almost every corner of the globe. It is second only to English itself as a universal tongue.

Whether one travels abroad as a tourist, an exchange student, a business agent or an employee of the government, a good speaking acquaintance with the French language is an asset of great personal value. Even for the stay-at-home whose travels are purely literary, the ability to read French may become an unfailing source of profit and enjoyment.

For a thorough, up-to-date mastery of the language, nothing can be more useful than a thoroughly up up-to-date French-English, English-French Dictionary. That is exactly what is provided here. Within the covers of this book are all the translated words and phrases needed to understand, read, and speak both languages. Many of the new words have never before appeared in any French-English dictionary.

Features of special value to every user of this dictionary are a complete guide to French pronunciation and a brief but comprehensive guide to French grammar.

Also included is another feature, a **Traveler's Conversation Guide**, which lists in English and translates into good idiomatic French hundreds of the most commonly used questions, phrases, expressions, and road signs of practical value to tourists. With the help of this Guide, one can travel with greater convenience and enjoyment wherever the French language is spoken.

Richard Switzer, Ph.D., is Professor of French and Chairman of the Department of French and Italian at the University of Wisconsin, Madison. He was formerly in the French department at the University of Chicago and prior to that taught French in the Department of Romance Languages, Northwestern University, Evanston, Illinois.

Herbert S. Gochberg, Ph.D., is Professor of French at the University of Wisconsin. He was previously in the French department at the University of Chicago.

World-wide
FRENCH
DICTIONARY

French-English   English-French
(AMERICAN ENGLISH)

COMPILED BY
RICHARD SWITZER, Ph.D.
AND
HERBERT S. GOCHBERG, Ph.D.

FAWCETT PREMIER • NEW YORK

A Fawcett Premier Book
Published by Ballantine Books
Copyright © 1961 by Fawcett Publishing Company, Chicago

ISBN 0-449-30005-6

This edition published by arrangement with
Follett Publishing Company

Printed in Canada

First Fawcett Premier Edition: October 1965
First Ballantine Books Edition: December 1983
Twenty-ninth Printing: August 1991

CONTENTS

PRONUNCIATION GUIDES

1. **Ordinary Vowels.** French vowels are pronounced much more precisely and cleanly than English vowels. This is due, in part, to the fact that in English the muscles involved in speech are usually very relaxed. In French these muscles are markedly tense during articulation. While it is impossible to give faithful comparisons between the sounds of English and French, the following examples provide useful approximations of French sound patterns.

French Spelling	Examples	English Sound
a, a + s, à, â	pas, là, âme	*father, bah*
è, ê, ai, ei, -ais, e followed by two consonants	père, bête, peine, laid, selle, parlais	*send*
é, final er, -et, -ez, -ai	été, aller, palet, donnez, parlai	*pay*
e	le, petit	*per*
i, y	mine, y	*machine*
i (as semi-vowel)	rien	*year*
o, ô, -ot, au, eau	rose, vôtre, complot, gauche, beau	*open*
o, au	donner, auto	*love*
œ, œu, eu, ue	œil, bœuf, heure, orgueil	*hurt*
oi	loi	*swat*
ou	vous	*soon*
u	vu, puis	*No example

2. **Nasal Vowels.** Nasalization occurs during speech when sound is accompanied by air being expelled through the mouth *and* nose. In general, vowels followed by *n* or *m* are nasalized, except when followed by a vowel or another *n* or *m*. In French the words pin and pain are nasalized, but not peine and penne.

French Spelling	Examples	English Sound
an, am, en, em	pan, champ, enfant, emploi	*tong*
in, im, ain, aim, ein, yn, ym, en	pin, impie, pain, faim, ceinture, syndicat; sympathie, bien	*tang*
on, om	bon, pompier	*only*
un, um	un, parfum	*lung*

* Vowel may be reproduced by uttering the sound of *ee*, as in *seen*, with the lips rounded.

3. Consonants. Listed below are French consonants which differ from English in one or more respects.

French Spelling	Examples	English Sound
c (before a, o, u)	canne, corps, cube	can
c (before e, i, y)	cent, cire, cygne	ceiling
ç	français	ceiling
ch	chien	share
g (before a, o, u)	garçon, gober, légume	gone
g (before e, i, y)	gens, gifler, gyroscope	azure
gn	cogner	onion
gu (before e, i)	guerre, gui	gone
h	halte	Always silent

Although all **h**'s are silent in French, a distinction is made between the *mute* h and the *aspirate* h. The latter is indicated by an asterisk (*h) in this dictionary. *Aspirate* h prevents linking and elision. *Mute* h: l'heure; aspirate h: le haut monde.

il (final), ill (between vowels)	travail, travailler	player
j	juger	azure
q (final)	coq	cock
qu	quel	kill
r	raison, carotte	*No example
s (between vowels)	raison	pose
s (other cases)	seigneur, masseur, censure, pasteur	sing, missile
th	théâtre	test
ti (before vowels)	patience, nation	missile
w	wagon, watt	very, watt
y	fuyant	yes

SILENT LETTERS

e is silent when its elimination does not form a group of three consonants; -ent is silent when it is final in a third person plural verb. Final consonants are usually silent.

*The trilled r, formed in the front of the mouth with the tip of tongue, is heard in some parts of France. The Parisian French r, in contrast, comes from well back in the mouth. The sound is caused by friction between the back of the tongue and the soft palate, accompanied by vibration of the vocal chords.

ELISION

Monosyllables ending in e and the word la elide to l' before a word beginning with a vowel or a silent h. si contracts before il.

$$\text{si plus il} = \text{s'il} \qquad \text{le plus homme} = \text{l'homme}$$

LINKING

An otherwise silent final consonant is pronounced in careful speech when the following word begins with a vowel and is closely linked grammatically.

STRESS ACCENT

French words have no fixed accent. A slight accent is placed on the last pronounced syllable before a pause in speaking.

INTONATION

The voice tends to rise on the accentuated syllable in a given word group, and on the next-to-last syllable of a sentence. It then falls on the last syllable.

USEFUL FRENCH GRAMMAR GUIDES.

ARTICLES

1. Definite Article

Masc. le (l' before vowel)	*Fem.* la (l' before vowel)	*Pl.* les
le garçon the boy	la dame the lady	les pommes (the)
l'arbre the tree	l'école the school	apples

2. Indefinite Article

Masc. un	*Fem.* une	*Pl.* des
un homme a man	une fête a holiday	des amis (some) friends

3. Partitive Construction. In French the definite article is often used with the preposition de to express the partitive. In some cases, de alone signifies a partitive construction. The definite article used by itself may refer to specific objects or to a whole category of objects. The following examples will be helpful:

Avez-vous du pain?	Have you any bread?
Je n'ai pas de pain.	I haven't any bread.
Il a des amis.	He has (some) friends.
L'homme est riche.	The man is rich.
Le lait est blanc.	Milk is white.
Les hommes sont des animaux.	Men are animals.

4. Contractions with Articles

$$\text{à plus } le = \text{au} \qquad \text{à plus } les = \text{aux} \qquad \text{de plus } le = \text{du} \qquad \text{de plus } les = \text{des}$$

GENDER OF NOUNS AND ADJECTIVES

Nouns in French are masculine or feminine. The gender of a noun is predetermined by history and usage. Modifying words will be of the same gender and number as the noun.

8

Un bon ami (*m.*)	A good friend
La main droite (*f.*)	The right hand

Some nouns, because of the nature of the reference, may be either masculine or feminine.

Un élève, une élève a pupil	Un enfant a child, a boy
	Une enfant a child, a girl

The feminine of most adjectives and nouns is indicated by adding -e to the masculine form.

grand, grande   ami, amie

Most adjectives ending in -e in the masculine remain invariable in the feminine.

Un champ fertile   Une terre fertile

Other regular patterns of gender are as follows:

Masculine	Feminine	Masculine	Feminine
beau	belle	lion	lionne
chameau	chamelle	ancien	ancienne
heureux	heureuse	pieux	pieuse
sec	sèche	blanc	blanche
danseur	danseuse	reveur	reveuse
acteur	actrice	moteur	motrice
neuf	neuve	veuf	veuve

PLURALS

Most words add -s to indicate the plural.

Singular le grand garçon	*Plural* les grand garçons
la petite fille	les petites filles

Masculine words ending in -s or -x remain unchanged in the plural.

Singular le chapeau gris	*Plural* les chapeaux gris
le moment heureux	le moment heureux

Most words ending in -al, -au, -eu, and -eau form the plural ending in -x.

Singular	Plural	Singular	Plural
cheval	chevaux	beau	beaux
feu	feux	château	châteaux

UNSTRESSED PRONOUNS

1. Direct Object Pronouns

me	me; myself	la	her; it
te	you; yourself	nous	us; ourselves
se	himself; herself; themselves	vous	you; yourself; yourselves
le	him; it	les	them

2. Indirect Object Pronouns

me	to me; to myself	lui	to him, her
te	to you; to yourself	nous	to us; to ourselves
se	to himself, herself; to themselves; to each other	vous	to you; to yourself; to yourselves
	leur	to them	

3. The unstressed words **y** (to it, to them, there) and **en** (of it, of them, from it, some, any) appear in the same part of the sentence as the unstressed pronouns.

9

The position of pronouns in normal French word order is at times similar to English usage. In many instances, however, the position varies, particularly in the use of the unstressed pronouns. In declarative, interrogative and all negative sentences, these pronouns appear *before* the verb. The examples below will be helpful:

Je vous parle.	I am speaking to you.
Il le voit.	He sees him.
Y êtes-vous allé?	Did you go there?
Je n'en vois pas.	I don't see any.
Nous nous habillons.	We are dressing (ourselves).
Elles se sont parlé.	They spoke to each other.
Je lui ai donné le livre.	I gave him the book. (her)
Je le lui ai donné.	I gave it to him. (to her.)
Les avez-vous?	Do you have them?
Je leur en parlerai.	I'll speak to them about it.
Elle me l'a vendu.	She sold it to me.
Nous les y verrons.	We'll see them there.

ADVERBS

Most adverbs are derived from corresponding adjective forms by adding the suffix -ment to the feminine form of the adjective.

Adjective	*Adverb*
heureux	heureusement
cruel	cruellement
final	finalement

Some adverbs follow a variant of the above pattern.

Adjective	*Adverb*
négligent	négligemment
évident	évidemment
constant	constamment

INTERROGATION

Interrogation is indicated in French in several ways, just as in English. The use of the interrogative pronouns, adjectives, and adverbs; the inversion of verb and subject; the addition of a questioning phrase at the beginning or end of the sentence; a simple change in the inflection of the voice—all are signs of interrogation.

Qui êtes-vous?	Who are you?
Quel est son nom?	What is his name?
Qu'a-t-elle fait?	What has she done?
Comment le sait-il?	How does he know (it)?
Qu'est-ce qui est tombé?	What fell?
Pourquoi ne me parlez-vous pas?	Why don't you speak to me?
Est-ce que c'est vrai?	Is it true?

NEGATION

Verbs are made negative in French by the use of ne before the verb and one of several negative words after the verb. In some cases, ne may appear without an accompanying sign of negation, but for the most part both signs are found.

Je ne sais pas.	I don't know.
Je ne sais danser.	I don't know how to dance.
Il ne lui écrit jamais.	He never writes to her.
Il n'a rien vu.	He saw nothing.
Je ne la verrai plus.	I won't see her any more.
Elle n'aime personne.	She loves no one.

10

When negative signs such as **personne** and **rien** are used as subjects of the sentence, the following order is found:

Personne ne le sait.   No one knows it.

The use of **ne . . . que** (only) follows the same pattern as the above.

Je ne vois que deux choses.   I only see two things.

REGULAR VERBS

In each of these conjugations, the endings refer to 1st, 2nd, and 3rd person, singular and plural.

1. -er Verbs. Example: donner

Present participle, donnant; *Past participle*, donné
Present donne, -es, -e, -ons, -ez, -ent
Future donnerai, -as, -a, -ons, -ez, -ont
Conditional donnerais, -ais, -ait, -ions, -iez, -aient
Present subjunctive donne, -es, -e, -ions, -iez, -ent
Imperfect donnais, -ais, -ait, -ions, -iez, -aient
Past definite donnais, -as, a, -âmes, -âtes, -èrent

2. -ir Verbs. Example: finir

Present participle finissant; *Past participle* fini
Present finis, -is, -it, -issons, -issez, -issent
Future finirai, -as, -a, -ons, -ez, -ont
Conditional finirais, -ais, -ait, -ions, -iez, -aient
Present subjunctive finisse, -es, -e, -ions, -iez, -ent
Imperfect finnissais, -ais, -ait, -ions, -iez, -aient
Past definite finis, -is, -it, -îmes, -îtes, -irent

3. -re Verbs. Example: rendre

Present participle rendant; *Past participle* rendu
Present rends, -ds, -d, -dons, -dez, -dent
Future rendrai, -as, -a, -ons, -ez, -ont
Conditional rendrais, -ais, -ait, -ions, -iez, -aient
Present subjunctive rende, -es, -e, -ions, -iez, -ent
Imperfect rendais, -ais, -ait, -ions, -iez, -aient
Past definite rendis, -is, -it, -îmes, -îtes, -irent

4. Examples of Compound Verb Tenses

Present Perfect	J'ai donné	I gave, have given
(Past Indefinite)	Il a fini	He finished, has finished
	Il est allé	He went, has gone
Past Perfect	Nous avions vendu	We had sold
(Pluperfect)	Ils avaient parlé	They had spoken
	Elle etait arrivée	She had arrived
Future Perfect	Vous aurez obéi	You will have obeyed
	Je serai venu	I will have come
	Tu auras rendu	You will have given back
Past Conditional	Elles auraient pleuré	They would have cried
	Vous auriez beni	You would have blessed
	Elle serait devenue	She would have become
Past Anterior	Il eut fendu	He had split
	Vous eûtes étudié	You had studied
	Je fus tombé	I had fallen
Perfect Subjunctive	Elle ait bondi	She jumped, has jumped
	Nous ayons tordu	We twisted, have twisted
	Vous soyez resté	You remained, have remained

11

The following list deals with the frequently used irregular verbs. Only the basic pattern of irregularity is given. Where forms and tenses do not deviate from regular patterns, they are not listed; it may be assumed that they are like regular forms.

absoudre like résoudre; *p.p.* absous
accueiller like cueillir
acquérir *p.p.* acquis; *pres.* acquiers -s, -t, acquérons, -ez, acquièrent *fut.* acquerrais; *pres. subj.* acquières, -es, -e, acquérions, -iez, acquièrent
admettre like mettre
aller *pres.* vais, vas, va, allons, -ez, vont; *fut.* irai; *pres. subj.* aille, -es, -e, allions, -iez, aillent
apercevoir like recevoir
apparaître like connaître
appartenir like tenir
apprendre like prendre
asseoir *p.p.* assis; *pres.* asseieds, -ds, -d, asseyons, -ez, -ent; *fut.* assiérai
assortir like sortir
atteindre like craindre

avoir *pres. p.* ayant; *p.p.* eu; *pres.* ai, as, a, avons, -ez, ont; *fut.* aurai; *pres. subj.* aie, -es, -e, aient
battre *pres.* bats, -ts, -t, -ttons, -ttez, -ttent
boire *p.p.* bu; *pres.* bois, -s, -t, buvons, -ez, boivent; *pres. subj.* boive, -es, -e, buvions, -iez, boivent
bouillir *pres. p.* bouillant; *pres.* bous, -s, -t, -illons, -illez, -illent
commettre like mettre
comprendre like prendre
concevoir like recevoir
conclure *p.p.* conclu; *pres.* conclus, -s, -t, -ons, -ez, -ent
concourir like courir
conduire *p.p.* conduit; *pres.* conduis, -s, -t, -sons, -sez, -sent; *past def.* conduisis
confire like suffire
connaître *p.p.* connu; *pres.* connais, -ait, -aissons, -aissez, -aissent
conquérir like acquérir
consentir like mentir
construire like conduire
contenir like tenir
contredire like dire
convaincre like vaincre
convenir like venir
coudre *pres. p.* cousant; *p.p.* cousu; *pres.* couds, -ds, -d, -sons, -sez, -sent
courir *p.p.* couru; *pres.* cours, -s, -t, -ons, -ez, -ent; *fut.* courrai
couvrir like ouvrir

craindre *p.p.* craint; *pres.* crains, -s, -t, craignons, -ez, -ent
croire *p.p.* cru; *pres.* crois, -s, -t, croyons, -ez, croient; *pres. subj.* croie, -es, -e, croyions, -iez, croient
croître *p.p.* crû; *pres.* crois, -s, -t, croissons, -ez, -ent, *past def.* crûs; *imp. subj.* crusse
cueiller *pres.* cueille, -es, -e, ons, -ez, -ent; *fut.* cueillerai
cuire like conduire
decévoir like recevoir
découvrir like ouvrir
décrire like écrire
dédire like dire
déduire like conduire
défaire like faire
dépeindre like craindre
détruire like conduire

devoir *p.p.* dû; *pres.* dois, -s, -t, devons, -ez, doivent; *fut.* devrais *pres. subj.* doive, -es, e, devions, diez, doivent; *past def.* dus
dire *p.p.* dit; *pres.* dis, -s, -t, -sons, -tes, -sent
discourir like courir
disparaître like connaître
dissoudre like résoudre; *p.p.* dissous
dormir *pres.* dors, -s, -t, -mons, -mez, -ment
écrire *p.p.* écrit; *pres.* écris, -s, -t, -vons, -vez, -vent; *past def.* écrivis
élire like lire
endormir like dormir
entreprendre like prendre
envoyer *pres.* envoie, -es, -e, envoyons, -ez, envoient; *fut.* enverrai; *pres. subj.* envoie, -es, -e, envoyions, -iez, envoient
être *pres. p.* étant; *p.p.* été; *pres.* suis, es, est, sommes, êtes, sont; *fut.* serai; *pres. subj.* sois, -s, -t, soyons, ez, soient
étreindre like craindre
exclure like conclure
faire *p.p.* fait; *pres.* fais, -s, -t, -sons, -tes, font; *fut.* ferai; *pres. subj.* fasse; *past def.* fis
falloir *p.p.* fallu; *pres.* (3rd per. sing. only) faut; *fut.* faudra; *pres. subj.* faille
feindre like craindre

12

frire *p.p.* frit; *pres.* fris, -s, -t, -ons, -ez, -ent

fuir *pres.* fuis, -s, -t, fuyons, -ez, fuient; *pres. subj.* fuie, -es, -e, fuyions, -iez, fuient

geindre like craindre

haïr *p.p.* haï; *pres.* hais, -s, -t, haïssons, -ez, -ent

inscrire like écrire

instruire like conduire

joindre like craindre

lire *p.p.* lu; *pres.* lis, -s, -t, -sons, -sez, -sent

maintenir like tenir

mentir *pres.* mens, -s, -t, -tons, -tez, -tent

mettre *p.p.* mis; *pres.* mets, -ts, -t, -ttons, -ttez, -ttent

moudre *pres. p.* moulant, *p.p.* moulu; *pres.* mouds, -ds, -d, -lons, -les, -lent

mourir *p.p.* mort; *pres.* meurs, -s, -t, mourons, -ez, meurent; *fut.* mourrai; *pres. subj.* meure, -es, -e, mourions, -iez, meurent; *past def.* mourus

mouvoir *p.p.* mû; *pres.* meus, -s, -t, mouvons, -ez, meuvent; *fut.* mouvrais; *pres. subj.* meuve; *past def.* mus

naître *p.p.* né; *pres.* nais, naît, naissons, -ez, -ent; *past def.* naquis

muire like conduire

obtenir like tenir

offrir like ouvrir

ouvrir *p.p.* ouvert; *pres.* ouvre, -es, -e, -ons, -ez, -ent; *past def.* ouvris

paître like connaître

paraître like connaître

parcourir like courir

partir *pres.* pars, -s, -t, -tons, -tez, -tent

parvenir like venir

peindre like craindre

permettre like mettre

plaindre like craindre

plaire *p.p.* plu; *pres.* plais, -ais, -aît, -aisons, -aisez, -aisent

pleuvoir *pres. p.* pleuvant; *p.p.* plu; *pres.* (3rd. per. sing. only) pleut; *fut.* pleuvra

poursuivre like suivre

pouvoir *p.p.* pu; *pres.* peux, -x, -t, pouvons, -ez, peuvent; *fut.* pourrai; *pres. subj.* puisse

prédire like dire

prendre *p.p.* pris; *pres.* prends, -ds, -d, prenons, -ez, -nent; *pres. subj.* prenne, -es, prenions, -iez, prennent

prescrire like écrire

produire like conduire

promettre like mettre

recevoir *p.p.* reçu; *pres.* reçois, -s, -t, recevons, -ez, reçoivent; *fut.* recevrai; *pres. subj.* reçoive, -es, -e, recevions, -iez, reçoivent

reconnaître like connaître

réduire like conduire

repentir like mentir

résoudre *pres. p.* résolvant; *p.p.* résolu, résous; *pres.* résous, -s, -t, résolvons, -ez, -ent; *pres. subj.* résolve

rire *p.p.* ri; *pres.* ris, -s, -t, -ons, -ez, -ent

rompre *pres.* romps, -s, -t, -ons, -ez, -ent

satisfaire like faire

savoir *p.p.* su; *pres.* sais, -s, -t, savons, -ez, -ent; *fut.* saurai; *pres. subj.* sache

secourir like courir

séduire like conduire

sentir like mentir

servir *pres.* sers, -s, -t, -vons, -vez, -vent

sortir *pres.* sors, -s, -t, -tons, -tez, -tent

souffrir like ouvrir

soumettre like mettre

sourire like rire

soutenir like tenir

suffire *pres.* suffis, -s, -t, -sous, -sez, -sent

suivre *pres.* suis, -s, -t, -vons, -vez, -vent

surprendre like prendre

taire like plaire (without circumflex)

teindre like craindre

tenir *p.p.* tenu; *pres.* tiens, -s, -t, tenons, -ez, tiennent; *fut.* tiendrai; *pres. subj.* tienne, -es, -e, tenions, -iez, tiennent

traduire like conduire

tressaillir like cueillir

vaincre *p.p.* vaincu; *pres.* vaincs, -cs, -c, vainquons, -ez, -ent; *past def.* vainquis

valoir *p.p.* valu; *pres.* vaux, -x, -t, valons, -ez, -ent; *fut.* vaudrai; *pres. subj.* vaille, -es, -e, valions, -iez, vaillent

venir like tenir (compound tenses conjugated with être as auxiliary verb)

vêtir *p.p.* vêtu; *pres.* vêts, -ts, -t, -tons, -tez, -tent; *past def.* vêtis

vivre *p.p.* vécu; *pres.* vis, -s, -t, -vons, -vez, -vent

voir *p.p.* vu; *pres.* vois, -s, -t, voyons, -ez, voient; *fut.* verrai; *pres. subj.* voie, -es, -e, voyions, -iez, voient; *past def.* vis

vouloir *p.p.* voulu; *pres.* veux, -x, -t, voulons, -ez, veulent; *fut.* voudrais; *pres. subj.* veuille, -es, -e, voulions, -iez, veuillent

ABBREVIATIONS

a.	adjective	math.	mathematics
adv.	adverb	mech.	mechanics
agr.	agriculture	med.	medicine
anat.	anatomy	mil.	military art
arch.	architecture	min.	mining
art.	article	mus.	music
ast.	astronomy	*n.*	noun
auto.	automobile	naut.	nautical
avi.	aviation	*past def.*	past definite
biol.	biology	phot.	photography
bot.	botany	phy.	physics
chem.	chemistry	*pl.*	plural
coll.	colloquial	poet.	poetry
com.	commerce	pol.	politics
cond.	conditional	*p.p.*	past participle
conj.	conjunction	*prep.*	preposition
dent.	dentistry	*pres.*	present
eccl.	ecclesiastic	*pres. p.*	present participle
elec.	electricity	print.	printing
ent.	entomology	*pron.*	pronoun
f.	feminine	rad.	radio
fig.	figuratively	rail.	railway
fut.	future	rhet.	rhetoric
geol.	geology	*sing.*	singular
gram.	grammar	*subj.*	subjunctive
imp.	impersonal	theat.	theatre
imper.	imperfect	*v.*	verb
infin.	infinitive	vet.	veterinary
interj.	interjection	*vi.*	verb intransitive
interr.	interrogative	*vt.*	verb transitive
m.	masculine	zool.	zoology

14

French-English

A

à *prep.* to, at, in, with

abaisse-langue *m.* tongue depressor

abaissement *m.* lowering, falling; drop; abasement

abaisser *vt.* to lower; abase; s'— to humble oneself; resort, stoop, cringe

abandon *m.* abandonment, neglect; abandon; à l'— uncared for, at random

abandonner *vt.* to abandon, give up; s'— to resign oneself; give way, yield

abasourdi *a.* astounded, amazed; —ssement *m.* bewilderment, consternation

abasourdir *vt.* astound, stupefy, amaze

abat *m.* sudden shower; pluie d'— drenching rain

abâtardir *vt.* corrupt, debase, bastardize

abat-jour *m.* lamp shade; shutter, blind, skylight

abattage *m.* slaughter; (coll.) reprimand; felling (trees)

abattant *m.* flap; — *a.* depressing

abattement *m.* prostration; dejection

abattis *m.* giblets, feet; slaughtered animals; felling

abattoir *m.* stockyard; slaughterhouse

abattre *vt.* to fell; demolish; slaughter; depress; s'— to alight; (avi.) crash; calm down, abate; become depressed

abattu *a.* depressed, humbled

abbaye *f.* abbey

abbé *m.* abbot; priest, superior; ecclesiastic

abbesse *f.* abbess

abcéder *vi.* to abscess

abcès *m.* abscess

abdication *f.* abdication

abdiquer *vt.* to abdicate; resign

abdomen *n.* abdomen

abdominal *a.* abdominal

abécédaire *m.* child's first speller, reader or primer

abeille *f.* bee

aberration *f.* aberration, alienation

abêtir *vt.* to stupefy, blunt

abhorrer *vt.* to abhor, detest, loathe

abîme *m.* abyss, chasm

abimer *vt.* to damage, ruin, spoil; s'— to spoil; be engulfed

abject *a.* abject

abjuration *f.* abjuration, renunciation

abjurer *vi.* to abjure, renounce

ablatif *m.* ablative

ablution *f.* ablution, purification

abnégation *f.* abnegation, sacrifice

aboiement *m.* barking, baying

abois *m. pl.*, aux — at bay; mettre aux — to make desperate

abolir *vt.* to abolish, repeal, suppress

abolition *f.* abolition; -iste abolitionist

abomination *f.* abomination

abominer *vt.* to abominate, detest

abondamment *adv.* abundantly

abondance *f.* abundance, wealth; parler d'— to speak extemporaneously

abondant *a.* plentiful, abundant, abounding

abonder *vi.* to abound, be plentiful

abonné *m.* subscriber

abonnement *m.* subscription; (rail.) commuter ticket; season ticket

abonner *vt.* to enter a subscription (for someone); s'— a to subscribe to

abonnir *vt.* to improve, correct

abonnissement *m.* improvement

abord *m.* approach; -s *pl.* outskirts; d'— at first

abordable *a.* accessible, receptive, approachable

aborder *vt.* to approach, accost; undertake; — *vi.* (naut.) to land

aborigène *a. & m.* aboriginal, native

abortif *a.* abortive

abot *m.* hobble; fetter for horse

aboucher *vt.* s'— confer; bring together

about *m.* end of wood piece (to be added to another), butt end

aboutement *m.* abutment; placing end to end

abouter *vt.* to place end to end

aboutissement *m.* result, outcome; (med.) heading of an abcess

aboyer *vi.* to bark, yelp

abrasion *f.* abrasion

abrégé *m.* resumé, digest, abridgment; en — briefly

abrègement *m.* abridgment; abridging

abréger *vt.* to shorten; abbreviate

abreuer *vt.* to water; soak; flood

abreuvoir *m.* trough for water

abri *m.* shelter; protection; à l'— (de) under cover of, sheltered from; sans — homeless

abricot *m.* apricot; -ier *m.* apricot tree

abriter *vt.* to shelter, protect

15

abroger vt. to abrogate

abruti m. stupid person, fool; —a. stupid

abrutir vt. to stupefy

abrutissement m. stupefaction, degradation

absent a. absent; absent-minded, wondering

absentéisme m. absenteeism

absenter v., s'— to be away, step out

abside f. apse

absinthe f. (liqueur) absinthe; wormwood

absolu a. absolute, unlimited

absolument adv. absolutely; completely

absolution f. absolution

absolutisme m. absolutism

absorbant a. absorbing; absorbent

absorber vt. to absorb; s'— to be absorbed

absorption f. absorption

absoudre vt. to absolve; forgive; remit

abstenir v., s'— to abstain

abstention f. abstention

abstinence f. abstinence; abstention

abstinent a. abstinent, abstemious

abstraction f. abstraction; faire — de consider independently

abstraire vt. to abstract, consider separately

abstrait a. abstract; engrossed; inattentive

absurde a. absurd; silly; preposterous

absurdité f. absurdity; nonsense

abus m. abuse, misuse; mistake; breach

abuser vt. to take advantage, impose; misuse; — vt. to deceive; s'— to be mistaken

abusif a. abusive; contrary to rule or law; improper

Abyssinie f. Abyssinia

abyssinien a. Abyssinian

acacia m. acacia

académicien m. academician

académie f. academy; school; university; learned society

académique a. academic

acajou m. mahogany

acariâtre a. quarrelsome; nagging

accablant a. overwhelming; annoying

accablement m. dejection, discouragement

accablé a. worn out; overwhelmed; (fig.) weighed down

accabler vt. to discourage; wear out; crush, overwhelm

accalmie f. (naut.) calm, lull, respite

accaparer vt. to corner (the market); monopolize

accéder vi. to agree; accede; to have access to

accélérateur m. accelerator; —a. accelerative

accélération f. acceleration

accélérer vi. to accelerate

accent m. accent; tone; emphasis, stress

accentuer vt. to accent, accentuate, stress

acceptabilité f. acceptability

acceptable a. acceptable

acceptation f. acceptance

accepter vt. to accept, agree

acception f. meaning, acceptation

accès m. approach; access; attack, fit; par — by fits and starts

accessible a. accessible

accession f. accession, adhesion, union

accessoire m. & a. accessory

accident m. accident; — de terrain unevenness of ground

accidenté a. rough, uneven; varied

accidentel a. accidental, unexpected

accidenter vt. (coll.) to involve in an accident; to make uneven

accise f. excise tax

acclamation f. acclamation

acclamer vt. to acclaim, hail

acclimatation f. acclimation

acclimater vt. to acclimate

accointance f. acquaintance; familiarity

accointer vt. to make acquainted; s'— to become friendly

accolade f. embrace; accolade; knighting; (print.) bracket, brace

accoler vt. to fasten; join, link

accommodage m. preparation or dressing; hairdressing

accommodant a. accommodating, easygoing, obliging; courteous

accommodement m. agreement, compromise, settlement; reconciliation

accommoder vt. to adjust; fix up; fix over; arrange; s'— to adjust, adapt; make oneself comfortable; compromise; come to terms with

accompagnateur m. accompanist

accompagnement m. accompaniment; tir d'— m. (mil.) covering-fire

accompagner vt. to accompany, be with, come with, go with

accompli a. accomplished; fulfilled; perfect

accomplir vt. to accomplish, do; complete

accomplissement m. accomplishment, achievement; completion

accord m. accord; agreement; (mus.) chord; harmony, tune; d'— in agreement; agreed, all right; être d'— to agree; tomber d'— to come to an agreement, agree

accordé m. bridegroom, fiancé

accordéon m. accordion

accorder vt. to reconcile; accord; tune; s'— agree, be in agreement; be in tune, harmonize

accore a. abrupt, sheer; vertical (coast); — m. (naut.) prop used during boat construction

accort a. gracious, compliant

accoster vt. to approach; accost

accoter v., s'— à to lean against

accotoir m. support; prop; stanchion

accouchement m. delivery (birth); lying-in

accoucher vi. to give birth; — vt. to attend someone giving birth; deliver (baby)

accoucheur m. obstetrician

accoucheuse f. midwife

accoudoir m. armrest, sill; (arch.) rail

accouplement m. coupling; joining; pairing

accoupler vt. to couple, join, pair

accourcie f. shortcut

accourcir vt. to shorten; hasten

accourir vi. to rush up to, flock together

accoutrement m. bizarre attire; garb

accoutrer vt. to dress up ridiculously, to rig out

accoutumance f. habit, custom

accoutumé a. accustomed; customary, usual

accoutumer vt. to accustom; s'— get used to, become accustomed to

accréditer vt. to accredit; give credence to

accroc m. tear, rip; difficulty; hindrance, hitch

accrocher vt. to hang up; bump; catch (by hook), hook; embarrass; s'— hold on, cling, grab; clinch (in boxing)

accroire (faire) vt. to believe; enfaire — impose on; s'en faire — be self-conceited

accroissement m. growth, increase

accroître vi. to grow; — vt. to increase, enhance

accroupir v., s'— to crouch, squat

accroupissement m. crouching, cowering

accueil m. reception; welcome

accueillant a. cordial, hospitable, gracious

accueillir vt. to receive, welcome, greet

accul m. blind alley

acculer vt. to drive back, corner

accumulateur m. battery, cell

accumulation f. accumulation

accumuler vt. to accumulate

accusateur a. accusing; — m. accuser; — public m. attorney-general

accusatif a. & m. accusative

accusation f. accusation, indictment

accusé m. accused; defendant; notice; — de réception receipt; — a. accentuated, marked

accuser vt. to accuse; reveal; announce; accentuate, heighten

acerbe a. bitter, sour, sharp, astringent

acerbité f. acerbity; bitterness, sharpness

acéré a. sharp, keen

acescent a. becoming acid

acétique a. acetic

acétone f. acetone

acétylène m. acetylene

achalander vt. to supply or attract customers; to stock, supply

acharné a. stubborn, tenacious, persistant; desperate

acharnement m. tenacity, obstinacy, rancor

acharner v., s'— to be tenacious; persist

achat m. purchase; — vt. faire des —s to buy

achée f. worms used for bait

acheminement m. progress; direction

acheminer vt. to send, forward; s'— to go ahead, move

acheter vt. to buy, purchase

acheteur m. purchaser, buyer

achevé a. finished; perfect; accomplished

achèvement m. finish(ing), completion; finished quality

achever vt. to finish, complete; finish off, dispatch

achoppement m. obstacle; pierre d'— f. stumbling block

achopper v., s'— to stumble

acide m. & a. acid

acidité f. acidity

acidulé a. acid, acidulated; bonbon — m. drop; fruit-flavored hard candy

acier m. steel; — fondu cast steel; — trempé tempered steel; cœur d'— hard heart; fil d'— steel wire

aciérer vt. to convert to steel

aciérie f. steel mill

acmé f. acme

acné f. acne

acompte m. part payment, payment on account, installment

Açores f. pl. Azores

à-coup m. jerk, jolt

acoustique a. acoustic(al); cornet — m. ear trumpet; — f. acoustics; — m. speaking-tube

acquéreur m. purchaser

acquérir vt. to acquire, win

acquiescement m. acquiescence, consent

acquiescer vi. to acquiesce, consent, agree

acquis a. acquired; — m. acquired knowledge or experience

acquisition f. acquisition

acquit m. receipt; release; par — de conscience to ease one's conscience; pour — paid

acquittement m. (com.) payment in full; legal acquittal

acquitter vt. to acquit, discharge; (com.) receipt; s'— discharge, fulfill

acre m. acre

âcre a. acrid, sharp, bitter

âcreté f. bitterness, sharpness

acrimonie f. acrimony

acrimonieux a. acrimonious

acrobate m. & f. acrobat; rope-dancer

acrobatie f. acrobatics; stunt

acrobatique a. acrobatic

acropole f. acropolis

acrostiche m. acrostic

acte m. act, action; title; deed; certificate; — de naissance birth certificate; —s pl. proceedings

acteur m. actor

actif a. active; — m. credit (side of ledger), asset; (gram.) active voice

action f. action; act; functioning; lawsuit; (mil.) engagement; (com.) share of stock

actionnaire m. & f. stockholder, shareholder

actionné a. active, busy

actionner vt. to put in motion; begin a court action, sue

activer vt. to activate; make active

activeur m. activator

activité f. activity; en — active

actrice f. actress

actuaire m. actuary; Roman scribe

actualité f. something real; present, thing of the moment; —s pl. newsreel; news items

actuel a. present, current

actuellement *adv.* at present, now, today, really

acuité *f.* acuteness, keenness

adaptateur *m.* adaptor

adapter *vt.* to adapt, adjust; s'— adapt oneself

addenda *m.* addition(s)

additif *m. & a.* additive

addition *f.* addition; (restaurant) check

additionnel *a.* additional

additionner *vt.* to add up; adulterate, cut (with water)

adénoïde *a.* adenoids; **végétations** –s *f. pl.* adenoids

adent *m.* notch, groove; dovetail, mortise

adepte *n.* partisan; expert; adept

adéquat *a.* equivalent; adequate

adhérence *f.* adherence

adhérent *a.* adherent; adhesive; — *m.* supporter; adherent; subscriber to a belief

adhérer *vi.* to adhere, stick, cling; subscribe, belong

adhésif *a. & m.* adhesive

adhésion *f.* adhesion; adherence

adieu *m.* farewell

adipeux *a.* adipose

adjacent *a.* adjacent, adjoining

adjectif *a.* adjectival, adjective; — *n.* adjective

adjectivement *adv.* adjectively

adjoindre *vt.* to adjoin, join on, add

adjoint *a. & m.* assistant, deputy, adjunct

adjonction *f.* addition, annex

adjudant-chef *m.* master sergeant, sergeant-major

adjudicataire *m. & f.* highest bidder; beneficiary of adjudication

adjudication *f.* adjudication; knocking down (at auction sale); contract; mettre en — contract for

adjuger *vt.* to adjudicate, award, knock down at auction

adjurer *vt.* to adjure; entreat; bind *or* command under oath

admettre *vt.* to admit, allow

administrateur *m.* administrator; director

administratif *a.* administrative

administration *f.* administration; management; direction

administrer *vt.* to administer, manage, direct

admirateur *a.* admiring; — *n.* admirer

admiratif *a.* admiring

admiration *f.* admiration

admirer *vt.* to admire; wonder

admissibilité *f.* admissibility

admissible *a.* admissible

admission *f.* admission

admonestation *f.* admonition

admonester *vt.* to admonish

admonition *f.* admonition

adolescence *f.* adolescence

adolescent *a. & m.* adolescent

adonner *v.*, s'— à give oneself over to, devote oneself to

adopter *vt.* to adopt

adoption *f.* adoption

adorateur *m.* adorer

adoration *f.* adoration, worship

adorer *vt.* to adore, worship

adosser *vt.* to place back to back, lean back against; s'— to lean (back)

adoucir *vt.* to soften, moderate; sweeten; relieve, ease; appease; s'— to become mild, soften

adoucisseur *m.* water softener

adrénaline *f.* adrenalin

adresse *f.* address; skill; adroitness

adresser *vt.* to address; s'— (à) to address oneself to; apply to; speak to

adroit *a.* skillful, clever, adroit

aduler *vt.* to adulate

adulte *m. & a.* adult

adultération *f.* adulteration

adultère *m.* adultery; — *a.* adulterous

adultérer *vt.* to adulterate

advenir *v.* to happen, come about; become

adverbe *m.* adverb

adverbial *a.* adverbial

adversaire *m.* adversary, opponent

adverse *a.* contrary; adverse

adversité *f.* adversity, affliction

aération *f.* aeration, renewal of air

aéré *a.* airy, well-aired

aérer *vt.* to air, ventilate; aerate

aérien *a.* aerial; **ligne** –ne *f.* airline

aérodrome *m.* airport

aérodynamique *f.* aerodynamics; — *a.* aerodynamic

aérofrein *m.* airbrake

aérogare *f.* airline terminal

aérographe *m.* airbrush

aéronaute *m.* aeronaut

aéronautique *f.* aeronautics; — *a.* aeronautic

aéronef *n.* airship, aircraft

aéroplane *m.* airplane

aéroport *m.* airport

aéroporté *a.* airborne

aéropostal *a.* relating to airmail

aérostat *m.* balloon, dirigible

aérotransporté *a.* airborne

affabilité *f.* affability, kindness

affable *a.* affable, courteous

affadir *vt.* to dull; make insipid

affadissement *m.* state of becoming faded; dulling, loss of taste

affaiblir *vt.* to weaken; s'— to grow weak; droop

affaiblissement *m.* weakening

affaire *f.* business, lawsuit; matter, deal; –s belongings; business; **chiffre d'**—s *m.* receipts (total business); **homme d'**–s *m.* business man; **avoir** — à to have to deal with

affairé *a.* busy

affairement *m.* activity, bustle

affairer *v.* s'— to be busy, hustle and bustle

affaissement *m.* collapse, depression, weakness

affaisser *v.* s'— to collapse, sink

affaîter *vt.* to train falcons

affamé *a.* starved, famished; greedy

affamer *vt.* to starve

affectation *f.* affectation; pretense; designation

affecter *vt.* to affect; feign; assume; (mil.) draft; designate; s'— to be moved

affectif *a.* affective; emotional

affection *f.* affection; mental state; (med.) ailment; -né *a.* affectionate

affectionner *vt.* to be fond of; take an interest in

affecteux *a.* affectionate

affermer *vt.* to rent by lease

affermir *vt.* to strengthen; harden; s'— to become firmer

affété *a.* affected

affichage *m.* posting on billboards

affiche *f.* poster, bill; -r *vt.* to post, advertise; make a show of

afficheur *m.* bill poster

affidavit *m.* affidavit

affidé *a.* trustworthy; — *m.* confederate; spy

affier *vt.* give one's word

affilé *a.* sharp; avoir la langue bien -e to have a sharp tongue, gossip; d'—e *adv.*

affiler *vt.* to sharpen

affilier *vt.* to affiliate, associate closely

affiloir *m.* hone; steel; knife sharpener

affiner *vt.* to refine; improve

affinité *f.* affinity; tendency to combine

affiquets *m. pl.* gew-gaws; knickknacks

affirmatif *a.* affirmative, positive

affirmation *f.* affirmation; assertion

affirmer *vt.* to affirm, assert; s'— assert oneself

affleurer *vt.* to make even; be even with

affliction *f.* affliction

affligé *a.* afflicted; sad; vexed

affligeant *a.* sad, distressing, bad (news)

affliger *vt.* to afflict; grieve, sadden, trouble

affluence *f.* affluence; abundance; crowd; heures d'— *f. pl.* rush hours

affluent *m. & a.* tributary

affluer *vt.* to flow; abound

afflux *m.* influx

affolement *m.* panic, distress; infatuation

affolé *a.* maddened, panic-stricken; infatuated

affoler *vt.* to madden, panic; infatuate; s'— to be panic-stricken; be madly in love with

affouiller *vt.* to undermine; wash away

affranchir *vt.* to emancipate, free; to stamp (letter)

affranchissement *m.* postage; liberation, emancipation

affres *f. pl.* anguish; dread

affrètement *m.* chartering, freighting

affréter *vt.* to charter, freight

affreux *a.* frightful; horrible

affriander *vt.* to make appetizing; lure; entice

affrioler *vt.* to attract; allure

affront *m.* insult; disgrace; reproach

affronter *vt.* to face; brave; s'— be in opposition

affubler *vt.* to fit out bizarrely; muffle

affût *m.* gun carriage; hunting post; être à l'— be on watch; lie in wait

affûter *vt.* to sharpen tools

affûtiau *m.* trifle; knickknack

Afghan *m. & a.* Afghan

afin, — que *conj.* so that, in order that; — de *prep.* in order to

Africain *m. & a.* African

Afrique *f.* Africa

afro-asiatique *a.* Afro-Asian

agaçant *a.* irritating, annoying

agacement *m.* annoyance, irritation

agacer *vt.* to irritate, annoy; egg on

âge *m.* age; period, epoch; — viril manhood; d'un certain — middle-aged; bas — infancy; entre deux -s of middle age; fleur de l'— prime of life; moyen — Middle Ages; quel — avez-vous? how old are you?

âgé *a.* old, aged; of age

agence *f.* agency; bureau

agencement *m.* arrangement; -s *pl.* fixtures

agencer *vt.* to adjust, arrange; equip

agenda *m.* memorandum book; appointment book

agenouillé *a.* kneeling

agenouiller *v.*, s'— to kneel

agenouilloir *m.* kneeling stool, kneeler

agent *m.* agent; — de change stockbroker; — de police policeman

agglomération *f.* agglomeration; settlement (of people)

aggloméré *m.* briquette, compressed fuel

agglutiner *vt.* to unite; s'— agglutinate, to cake

aggraver *vt.* to aggravate, worsen

agile *a.* agile, nimble

agilité *f.* agility

agioteur *m.* (com.) speculator

agir *vi.* to art: operate; (com.) manage; prosecute; il s'agit de it is a question of

agitateur *m.* agitator; stirrer, stirring-rod

agitation *f.* agitation

agité *a.* agitated; upset; restless

agiter *vt.* to agitate, shake, stir; disturb; debate

agneau *m.* lamb

agneler *vi.* to lamb

agnelin *m.* lamb's skin (with wool)

agnès *f.* innocent girl, ingénue

agnostique *m. & a.* agnostic

agonie *f.* agony, death throes

agonir *vt.* abuse; (coll.) insult highly

agonisant *a. & m.* dying; dying person

agoniser *vt.* to lie dying; be at death's door

agrafe *f.* clasp, hook, clip, clamp; — et porte hook and eye

agrafer *vt.* to clasp, hook, fasten

agrafeuse *f.* stapler

agraire *a.* agrarian

agrandir *vt.* to enlarge; s'— to grow, expand

agrandissement *m.* enlargement; aggrandizement

agrandisseur *m.* (phot.) enlarger

agrarien *m. & a.* agrarian

agréable *a.* pleasant, agreeable

agréer *vt.* to accept; approve; allow; — *vi.* to suit, be acceptable

agrégation *f.* degree required for teaching in a lycée; aggregation, aggregate

agrégé *m.* holder of the agrégation

agréger vt. to admit (to a society); accept; incorporate

agrément m. charm; ornamentation; pleasure; note d'— f. (mus.) grace-note

agrémenter vt. to embellish, adorn; trim

agrès m. pl. gymnasium equipment; (naut.) gear; rigging

agresser vt. to attack, commit aggression on

agresseur m. aggressor

agressif a. aggressive

agression f. aggression

agressivité f. aggressiveness

agreste a. rustic; rural

agricole a. agricultural; comices -s m. pl. county fairs

agriculteur m. farmer

agriculture f. agriculture

agriffer v., s'— to hang, grip by claws

agripper vt. to snatch, grab; s'— to clutch at; come to grips

agronomie f. agronomy

agrouper vt. to group

aguerrir vt. to train in war, season, inure

aguet m. watch, watching; -s pl., être aux -s to be on the lookout

ahaner vi. to groan, pant; sigh

aheurtement m. stubbornness, obstinacy

ahuri a. astounded

ahurir vt. to astound, amaze

ahurissement m. stupefaction

aiche, éche f. bait

aide f. help, aid; — m. & f. helper, aide, assistant; à l'—! interj. help!; à l'— de by means of

aide-mémoire m. reminder; memory aid

aider vt. to aid, help, assist

aïeul m. grandfather; -e f. grandmother; -s m. pl. grandfathers, grandparents

aïeux m. pl. ancestors

aigle m. eagle

aiglefin m. haddock

aiglon m. eaglet

aigre a. sour; sharp; harsh; — m. sourness, mustiness

aigre-doux a. bittersweet; sweet and sour

aigrefin m. adventurer, swindler; haddock

aigrelet a. somewhat bitter

aigrette f. aigrette; crest; cluster of feathers, diamonds, etc.

aigreur f. bitterness; (med.) heartburn

aigrir vt. to embitter; turn sour; make ill-humored

aigu a. acute, sharp; bitter, intense; piercing, shrill

aiguillage m. (rail.) switch; switching

aiguille f. needle; (clock) hand; pointer, indicator; (rail.) switch; magnetic needle

aiguiller vt. (rail.) to switch; direct

aiguilleur m. switchman

aiguillon m. goad; stinger; thorn; stimulus

aiguiser vt. to sharpen, stimulate

ail m. garlic

aile f. wing; blade; (auto.) fender

ailé a. winged

aileron m. wing tip; (avi.) aileron; fin

ailette f. wing; fin; blade

ailleurs adv. elsewhere; d'— besides, furthermore; par — besides; otherwise

aimable a. pleasant, kind, amiable

aimant m. magnet

aimanter vt. to magnetize

aimer vt. to love, like; — bien to like, be fond of

aine f. groin

aîné a. elder, eldest

aînesse f. seniority; primogeniture

ainsi adv. & conj. so, thus; — que just as; et — de suite and so forth

air m. air; tune, melody, appearance; manner; avoir l'— to seem; au grand —, en plein — outdoors, open air

airain m. bronze, brass

aire f. area; floor; surface; eyrie; wind direction

airelle f. cranberry

aisance f. ease; lieu d'— m. toilet

ais m. stave, board

aise f. comfort, ease; à l'— comfortable; mal à l'— uncomfortable; indisposed; — a. happy, content

aisé a. easy; well-off

aisselle f. armpit

aisément adv. easily

ajour m. opening; openwork

ajournement m. (mil.) deferment; postponement; legal summons

ajourner vt. to adjourn, postpone, defer

ajouter vt. to add; supply; interpolate

ajuster vt. to adjust; fix; aim at; fix up, ornament, dress

alambic m. (chem.) still

alambiquer vt. to distill; (fig.) make overly subtle

alanguir vt. to make languid, feeble

alarme f. alarm

alarmer v., s'— de to become alarmed at

alarmiste m. & a. alarmist

Albanais n. & a. Albanian

Albanie f. Albania

albâtre m. alabaster

albatros m. albatros

album m. album, scrapbook; coloring book

albumen m. albumen

albumine f. albumen, egg white

alcaloïde m. alkaloid

alchimie f. alchemy

alchimiste m. alchemist

alcool m. alcohol; -ique m. & a. alcoholic

alcoolisme m. alcoholism

alcôve f. alcove

aléa m. chance, hazard

aléatoire a. risky; contingent (law); -ment adv. by chance

alène f. awl

à l'entour adv. in the vicinity; around

alentours m. pl. vicinity, neighborhood

alerte f. alarm, warning; — a. alert, brisk, watchful

alerter vt. to alert, warn

aléser vt. to bore (tube, gun, etc.), grind

alevin m. fish fry; young fish

aleviner vt. to stock with young fish

algarade f. unmotivated attack; insult

algèbre f. algebra

algébrique a. algebraic

Alger m. Algiers

Algérie f. Algeria; -n m. & a. Algerian

algérois *a.* of Algiers

algue *f.* seaweed; alga

aliboron *m.* jackass

aliéné *m.* deranged person, lunatic; — *a.* mad

aliéner *vt.* to give over, transfer; alienate

alignée *f.* line, row

alignement *m.* alignment

aligner *vt.* to align; (com.) balance an account

aliment *m.* food, nourishment

alimentaire *a.* alimentary; subsistance; pension — *f.* alimony; régime — *m.* diet

alimentation *f.* feeding; nourishment; provisionment

alimenter *vt.* to feed; maintain

alinéa *m.* indentation, paragraph

alité *a.* bedridden, confined to bed

allaitement *m.* nursing, nourishing on milk

allaiter *vt.* to suckle, nurse

allant *a.* active; — *m. pl.* activities, comings and goings

allécher *vt.* to entice; attract

allée *f.* walk, alley, path; going

allégation *f.* allegation; statement

alléger *vt.* to lighten; relieve

allègre *a.* gay, lively

alléguer *vt.* to allege

alléluia *m.* hallelujah

Allemagne *f.* Germany

Allemand *n. & a.* German

aller *vi.* to go, ride; — à to fit; suit: — bien to be well; — mal to be ill; s'en — go away; billet d'— et retour *m.* round-trip ticket

allergie *f.* allergy

allergique *a.* allergic

alliage *m.* alloy; mixture

alliance *f.* alliance; union; wedding ring

allié *a.* allied; — *m.* ally; in-law, relative by marriage

allier *vt.* to alloy; ally; join; mix

alligator *m.* alligator

allitération *f.* alliteration

allocation *f.* allowance, subsidy; item

allocution *f.* address, speech

allonge *f.* extension; elongating piece; hook for hanging meat; boxing reach

allonger *vt.* to lengthen; extend; s'— to lie down; grow longer

allongement *m.* lengthening

allouer *vt.* to allocate, allow

allumage *m.* lighting; ignition, spark

allume-gaz *m.* gas stove lighter

allumer *vt.* to light; fire; ignite; turn on; s'— catch fire

allumette *f.* match

allumoir *m.* lighter

allure *f.* gait; bearing; speed

allusif *a.* allusive, containing an allusion

allusion *f.* allusion

alluvial *a.* alluvial

almanach *m.* almanac, calendar

aloès *m.* aloes

aloi *m.* purity, quality

alors *adv.* then; — que *conj.* while, whereas; — même que even though,

even when

alose *f.* shad

alouette *f.* lark

alourdir *vt.* to make heavy; s'— to become heavy

alourdissant *a.* oppressive

alourdissement *m.* heaviness; dullness

aloyau *m.* sirloin of beef

alpaga *m.* alpaca

alpage *m.* mountain pasture

Alpes *f. pl.* Alps

alpestre *a.* Alpine

alphabet *m.* alphabet

alphabétique *a.* alphabetical

alpin *a.* Alpine

alpinisme *m.* mountain climbing

alpiniste *m.* mountain climber

Alsace *f.* Alsace

Alsacien *n. & a.* Alsatian

altérable *a.* alterable

altération *f.* alteration, falsification

altercation *f.* altercation; dispute

altérer *vt.* to spoil; tamper with; distort; make thirsty

altéré *a.* altered; avid

alternance *f.* alternation

alternatif *a.* alternating

alternation *f.* alternation; succession

alternative *f.* alternative

alterner *vi.* to alternate

altesse *f.* (titre) highness

altier *a.* haughty

altièrement *adv.* haughtily, proudly

altimètre *m.* altimeter

altitude *f.* altitude

alto *m.* alto; viola; alto horn

altruisme *m.* altruism

altruiste *n.* altruist; — *a.* altruistic

alumelle *f.* plane (tool)

aluminium *m.* aluminum

alun *m.* alum

alvéole *m.* cell of honeycomb; socket of tooth; compartment, pigeonhole

alvéolé *a.* honey-combed

alvin *a.* abdominal; flux — *m.* diarrhea

amabilité *f.* amiability; kindness

amadou *m.* tinder

amadouer *vt.* to wheedle, coax

amaigrir *vt.* to make thin; — *vi.* to become thin

amaigrissant *a.*, régime — *m.* weight-reducing diet

amaigrissement *m.* reducing, dieting; emaciation

amalgamation *f.* amalgamation

amalgame *m.* amalgam, mixture

amalgamer *vt.* to amalgamate; blend

amande *f.* almond

amandier *m.* almond tree

amant *m.* lover

amarrage *m.* (naut.) mooring

amarre *f.* (naut.) hawser, painter, cable

amarrer *vt.* to moor; make fast

amaryllis *f.* amaryllis

amas *m.* heap, pile, accumulation

amasser *vt.* to heap up, pile up, amass

amateur *m.* amateur, fan; devotee; connoisseur

Amazone *f.* Amazon; horsewoman; riding

habit; monter en — ride side-saddle

ambages f. pl., parler sans — to stop beating around the bush

ambassade f. embassy

ambassadeur m. ambassador

ambassadrice f. ambassador's wife

ambiance f. atmosphere, environment

ambiant a. surrounding

ambidextre a. ambidextrous

ambigu a. ambiguous; — m. cold buffet; — comique comic play

ambiguïté f. ambiguity

ambitieux a. ambitious

ambitionner vt. to have ambitions to

ambivalence f. ambivalence

amble m. trot, amble

ambre m. amber; — gris ambergris

ambré a. amber-colored

ambulance f. ambulance

ambulancier m. ambulance attendant

ambulant a. itinerant; traveling; marchand — peddler; — m. railway post office

ambulatoire a. ambulatory; movable

âme f. soul, spirit, life

amélioration f. improvement, amelioration

améliorer vt. to improve, ameliorate

aménagement m. arrangement; preparation; furnishings

aménager vt. to prepare; fix up; arrange; outfit

amende f. fine, penalty; faire — honorable apologize courteously

amendement m. amendment; improvement; fertilizer

amender vt. to improve; amend; s'— reform

amène a. affable

amener vt. to bring; introduce, bring in; lead to

aménité f. amenity, pleasantness

amenuiser vt. to thin, make thin

amer a. bitter; — m. landmark

américain a. & m. American

américaine f. bicycle relay race; surrey

américaniser vt. to Americanize

américanisme m. Americanism; American studies

Amérindien m. & a. Indian (of America)

Amérique f. America

amerrir vi. to land on the water

amertume f. bitterness

améthyste f. amethyst

ameublement m. furniture

ameuter vt. to gather hunting hounds; stir up

ami m. friend; sweetheart; — a. friendly

amiable a. amicable; à l'— adv. amicably

amiante m. asbestos

amibe f. amoeba

amibiase f. amoebic dysentery

amibien a. amoebic

amical a. friendly

amicale f. club, group

amict m. amice

amidon m. starch

amidonnage m. starching

amidonner vt. to starch

amincir vt. to make thin

aminé a. amino

amiral m. admiral

amirauté f. admiralty

amitié f. friendship; liking; —s pl. regards

ammoniaque f. ammonia

amnésie f. amnesia

amnésique m. & f. amnesia victim

amnistie f. amnesty, pardon

amnistier vt. to amnesty, pardon

amoindrir vt. to lessen, reduce, diminish

amollir vt. to soften; weaken; s'— to grow softer

amollissement m. softening

amonceler vt. to heap up, pile up

amoncellement m. heap, pile

amont m. upper portion of a river; en — upstream

amorce f. fuse, detonator; bait; beginning

amorcer vt. to prime a gun; bait; start

amorphe a. amorphous

amortir vt. to deaden, muffle, dull; amortize, redeem

amortissable a. redeemable

amortissement m. amortization; deadening, damping; depreciation; (arch.) final, crowning ornament; caisse d'— f. sinking fund

amortisseur m. shock absorber

amour m. love; passion

amouracher v., s'— (de) to become infatuated (with)

amourette f. love affair

amoureux a. in love; amorous; — m. lover; suitor

amour-propre m. self-esteem, pride, vanity

amovible a. movable; removable

ampère m. ampere; —mètre m. ammeter

amphibie a. amphibious; — m. amphibian

amphibologique a. ambiguous, equivocal

amphigouri m. hodge-podge; nonsense

amphithéâtre m. amphitheater; lecture hall

amphore f. amphora

ample a. wide, vast; ample, full; roomy, spacious; —ur f. fullness

ampliation f. amplification, expansion; duplicate

amplificateur m. amplifier; (phot.) enlarger; — a. enlarging, amplifying

amplification f. amplification; enlarging

amplifier vt. to amplify; enlarge; magnify

amplitude f. amplitude, extent

ampoule f. blister; sealed phial; ampule; (elec.) light bulb

ampoulé a. pompous, high-flown; blistered

amputé m. amputee

amputer vt. to amputate

amulette f. amulet, charm

amusement m. amusement, fun, entertainment

amuser vt. to entertain; amuse; s'— to have a good time

amusette f. plaything; toy; small amusement

amygdale f. tonsil

amygdalite f. tonsilitis

an m. year; jour de l'— New Year's day; par — yearly

ana *m.* collection of ancedotes and sayings

anachorète *m.* hermit

anachronique *a.* anachronistic

anachronisme *m.* anachronism

anagramme *f.* anagram

anal *a.* anal

analogie. *f* analogy

analogique *a.* analogical

analogue *a.* analogous; — *m.* analogue

analphabète *n. & a.* illiterate

analphabétisme *m.* illiteracy

analysable *f.* analysable

analyse *f.* analysis; résumé, summary

analyser *vt.* to analyse

analytique *a.* analytical

ananas *m.* pineapple

anarchie *f.* anarchy

anarchique *a.* anarchical

anarchiste *m. & f.* anarchist

anathématiser *vt.* to curse, anathematize

anathème *m.* anathema

anatomie *f.* anatomy

anatomique *a.* anatomical

anatoxine *f.* antitoxin

ancêtre *m.* ancestor

anche *f.* (mus.) reed

anchois *m.* anchovy

ancien *a.* old, former; ancient; — élève *m.* alumnus; -nement *adv.* formerly

ancienneté *f.* seniority; age, antiquity

ancrage *m.* anchorage

ancre *f.* anchor; -r *vt.* to anchor

Andalou *m. & a.* Andalusian

Andalousie *f.* Andalusia

Andes *f. pl.* Andes

andin *a.* of the Andes

Andorre *f.* Andorra

andouille *f.* pork, tripe sausage; (coll.) idiot, fool

andouiller *m.* antler

andouillette *f.* small pork, tripe sausage

âne *m.* ass, donkey; fool

anéantir *vt.* to destroy, annihilate

anéantissement *m.* destruction, annihilation

anémie *f.* anemia

anémié *a.* anemic

anémique *a.* anemic

anémomètre *m.* anemometer

anémone *f.* anemone

ânerie *f.* huge blunder; gross ignorance

anesthésie *f.* anesthesia

anesthésier *vt.* anesthetize

anesthésique *a. & m.* anesthetic

anesthésiste *m.* anesthetist

ange *m.* angle; être aux —s to be delighted

angélique *a.* angelic; — *f.* angelica

angélus *m.* angelus

angine *f.* quinsy, tonsillitis; angina

Anglais *m.* Englishman; English; — *a.* English; -e *f.* Englishwoman; English dance; -es *f. pl.* long curls; filer à l'-e to take French leave; pommes à l'-e *f. pl.* boiled potatoes

angle *m.* angle; corner

Angleterre *f.* England

anglican *a.* Anglican

angliciser *vt.* Anglicize

anglophile *m. & a.* Anglophile, admirer

of anything English

Anglo-Saxon *m. & a.* Anglo-Saxon

angoisse *f.* anguish, agony

angoisser *vt.* to anguish; afflict

anguille *f.* eel; nœud d'— *m.* slipknot

angulaire *a.* angular; pierre — *f.* cornerstone

anguleux *a.* angular

anicroche *f.* small obstacle, snag

ânier *m.* mule driver, muleteer

animadversion *f.* reproof, blame

animal *m.* animal, beast; — *a.* animal

animateur *m.* animator; organizer

animation *f.* animation; movement, life

animé *a.* animated; lively; dessin — *m.* cartoon (movies)

animer *vt.* to animate, enliven; move, encourage

animosité *f.* animosity

anion *m.* anion

anis *m.* anise; -ette *f.* (liqueur) anisette

ankylose *f.* stiffness of the joints

ankylosé *a.* stiff

ankyloser *vt.* to stiffen; s'— to stiffen; rust

annales *f. pl.* annals

anneau *m.* ring; link

année *f.* year

annelé *a.* ringed, annulated

annexe *f.* annex; supplement

annexer *vt.* to annex; append

annexion *f.* annexation

annihilation *f.* annihilation

annihiler *vt.* to annihilate

anniversaire *m.* birthday; anniversary

annonce *f.* advertisement; announcement

annoncer *vt.* to announce; predict; s'— to give promise of being

annonceur *m.* advertizer, sponsor

Annonciation *f.* Annunciation

annotateur *m.* annotator

annotation *f.* annotation

annoter *vt.* to annotate

annuaire *m.* directory (phone); yearbook; annual

annuel *a.* yearly, annual

annuité *f.* annuity; yearly payment

annulaire *a.* annular

annulation *f.* annulment

annuler *vt.* to annul, cancel

anoblir *vt.* to ennoble

anodin *a.* soothing; harmless; — *m.* anodyne

anomal *a.* irregular, abnormal

anomalie *f.* anomaly, irregularity

ânonner *vi.* to speak haltingly; stutter

anonymat *m.* anonymity

anonyme *a.* anonymous; — *n.* anonymity

anophèle *m.* anopheles, mosquito

anorak *m.* hooded jacket; rainproof sport jacket

anormal *a.* abnormal

anse *f.* handle; inlet, bay

antagonisme *m.* antagonism

antagoniste *n.* antagonist; — *a.* antagonistic; opposite

antan *m.* yore, yesteryear

antarctique *a.* antarctic

antécédent *a.* previous, prior, antecedent; — *m.* antecedent; -s *pl.* past history

Antéchrist m. Antichrist
antedéluvien a. antediluvian
antenne f. antenna; aerial
antérieur a. anterior; front; previous, earlier
anthologie f. anthology
anthracite f. anthracite, hard coal
anthropoïde n. & a. anthropoid
anthropologie f. anthropology
anthropologue m. anthropologist
anthropophage m. cannibal; — a. cannibalistic
anthropophagie f. cannibalism
antiaérien a. antiaircraft
antibiotique m. antibiotic
antibrouillard a. anti-fog; phare — m. fog light
antichambre f. antichamber, waiting room
antichar a. (mil.) antitank
anticipation f. anticipation
anticiper vt. to anticipate, forestall
anticlérical a. anticlerical
anticorps m. antibody
antidater vt. to antedate
antienne f. anthem
antigel m. antifreeze
antihistaminique m. antihistamine
antillais a. of the West Indies
Antilles f. pl. West Indies
antilope f. antelope
antimite m. moth repellant
antimoine m. antimony
antimoral a. immoral
antinomie f. antinomy, contradiction
antinomique a. contradictory
antipathie f. antipathy, repugnance
antipathique a. antipathetic
antiquaille f. rubbish, junk
antiquaire m. antiquary; antique dealer
antique a. antique, ancient
antiquité f. antiquity; antique
antirabique a. antirabies
antiradar a. anti-radar
antirouille m. rust preventative
antisémite m. & f. antisemite
antisémitisme m. antisemitism
antiseptique m. & a. antiseptic
antisocial a. antisocial
antitétanique a. antitetanous
antithèse f. antithesis
antitoxine f. antitoxin
antivol m. antitheft device, burglar alarm
antonyme m. antonym
antre m. cavern, lair, den
anus m. anus
Anvers m. Antwerp
anxiété f. anxiety
anxieux a. anxious, concerned, uneasy
aorte f. aorta
août m. August
apaiser vt. to appease; calm; s'— to abate, calm down
apanage m. lot, portion
aparté m. (theat.) aside
apathie f. apathy
apathique a. apathetic
apatride a. stateless
apercevoir vt. to perceive, see; s'— de to discover, realize

aperçu m. brief account; first glimpse; par — rough guess
apéritif m. apéritif, appetizer, small, before-dinner drink
apeuré a. frightened
aphasie f. aphasia
aphone a. soundless, voiceless
aphonie f. aphony, loss of speech
aphorisme m. aphorism
aphte m. mouth canker; cold sore
aphteux a. cankerous; fièvre aphteuse f. hoof and mouth disease
apiculteur m. beekeeper
apitoiement m. pity, compassion
apitoyer vt. to cause pity, move to pity; s'— sur to sympathize with
aplanir vt. to level, smooth; plane
aplatir vt. to flatten; s'— to become flat; lie flat, fall flat
aplomb m. balance, poise; plumb; assurance; d'— level, even, plumb
apocalypse f. Apocalypse, Revelations; (fig.) obscure text or allegory
apocalyptic a. obscure; allegorical; apocalyptic
apocope f. (gram.) apocope, elision; (med.) amputation
apocryphe a. apocryphal
apode a. apodal, footless
apogée m. apogee, zenith
apologétique a. apologetic
apologie f. justification, defense, apology
apologue m. apologue, fable
apoplectique a. apopleptic
apoplexie f. stroke; apoplexy
apostasie f. apostasy; back sliding
apostat m. & a. apostate
aposter vt. to station; place in ambush
apostille f. annotation, postscript, endorsement
apostiller vt. to annotate, endorse; add postscript
apostolique a. apostolic
apostrophe f. apostrophe
apothéose f. apotheosis
apothicaire m. apothicary, pharmacist
apôtre m. apostle
apparaître vi. to appear; become apparent
apparat m. pomp, show
apparaux m. pl. fittings (of a ship)
appareil m. appliance, machine; apparatus; telephone; — photographique camera; — plâtré (med.) cast
appareiller vi. to set sail; prepare to leave; — vt. to equip; match (with); out
apparemment adv. apparently
apparence f. appearance, semblance
apparent a. apparent; —é a. related
apparenter v., s'— to be related
apparier vt. to match, pair (off)
apparition f. apparition; appearance
appartement m. apartment
appartenance f. appurtenance
appartenant a. belonging, pertaining to
appartenir vt. to belong; appertain
appas m. pl. charms
appât m. bait, lure, attraction
appâter vt. to lure; fatten; feed (baby or invalid)

appauvrir *vt.* to impoverish; s'— to become poor

appauvrissement *m.* impoverishment

appeau *m.* bird call; lure, decoy

appel *m.* appeal; call; roll call; telephone buzzer

appelant *m.* decoy; appellant (law)

appelé *m.* draftee

appeler *vt.* to call; call up; invoke, summon; — *vi.* appeal (law); s'— to be named; je m'appelle my name is

appellation *f.* appellation; brand name; — contrôlée registered trademark

appendice *m.* appendix

appendicite *f.* appendicitis

appentis *m.* lean-to

appesantir *vt.* to make heavy; s'— to insist

appétissant *a.* appetizing

appétit *m.* appetite; desire

applaudir *vt.* to applaud; approve

applaudissements *m. pl.* applause

application *f.* application; diligence

applique *f.* ornamentation; wall candlestick, wall bracket

appliqué *a.* diligent, studious

appliquer *vt.* to apply; adapt; s'— to apply; apply oneself

appoint *m.* (com.) balance

appointements *m. pl.* salary

appointer *vt.* to pay a salary; sharpen; settle a case at law

appontage *m.* landing (on the deck of an aircraft carrier)

appontement *m.* crane; dock

apponter *vi.* to land on the deck of an aircraft carrier

apport *m.* contribution, share

apporter *vt.* to bring; procure, use

apposer *vt.* to apply, affix, put

appréciable *a.* appreciable

appréciation *f.* appreciation; appraising, estimate, evaluation

apprécier *vt.* to appreciate; appraise, value, evaluate, estimate

appréhender *vt.* to apprehend; dread, fear

appréhension *f.* apprehension

apprendre *vt.* to learn; find out, hear; teach, show

apprenti *m.* apprentice

apprentissage *m.* apprenticeship

apprêt *m.* preparing, cooking and seasoning; affectation; —s *pl.* preparation

apprêter *vt.* to prepare; s'— prepare oneself

appris *a.*, mal — ill-bred

apprivoiser *vt.* to tame; make sociable

approbateur *a.* approving

approbation *f.* approval, approbation

approchable *a.* accessible

approchant *a.* somewhat like, approximately

approche *f.* approach; —s *pl.* access

approché *a.* approximate

approcher *vt.* to bring near; — *vi.* to come close; s'— to approach

approfondi *a.* thorough, deep

approfondir *vt.* to deepen; examine thoroughly; s'— to deepen

appropriation *f.* appropriation

approprier *vt.* to make appropriate, conform; s'— to appropriate

approuver *vt.* to approve (of); agree to

approvisionnement *m.* supply, provisions; provisioning

approvisionner *vt.* to provision; s'— to buy provisions; take in supplies

approximatif *a.* approximate

approximation *f.* approximation

appui *m.* support; prop; ledge, sill

appui-bras *m.* armrest

appui-livres *m.* bookends

appui-tête *m.* headrest

appuyer *vt. & vi.* to press; lean; support; s'— to lean, depend; insist

âpre *a.* rough, harsh; bitter, sharp; eager

après *prep.* after; next to; d'— according to; from, after; — *adv.* afterward, later, et —? so?, so what?; then what?

après-demain *m.* day after tomorrow

après-dîner *m.* period after dinner, evening

après-guerre *f.* postwar period

après-midi *m. or f.* afternoon

âpreté *f.* bitterness; harshness, roughness

à-propos *m.* opportuneness; aptness

apte *a.* apt, proper, suited, suitable

aptitude *f.* aptitude, capacity, qualification

apurement *m.* audit, verification

apurer *vt.* to verify, audit

apyre *a.* fireproof

aquafortiste *m.* etcher

aquaplane *m.* aquaplane, surfboard; aquaplaning

aquarelle *f.* watercolor

aquarelliste *n.* water-color artist

aquatique *a.* aquatic

aqueduc *m.* aqueduct

aqueux *a.* aqueous, watery

aquifère *a.* water-bearing

aquilin *a.* aquiline

aquilon *m.* north wind; cold blast

ara *m.* macaw

Arabe *m.* Arabian; — *a.* Arabian, Arabic

Arabie *f.* Arabia; — Soudite, — Saoudite, — Séoudite Saudi Arabia

arable *a.* arable

arachide *f.* peanut

araignée *f.* spider; toile d'— *f.* spider web

araser *vt.* to level

aratoire *a.* agricultural

arbalète *f.* crossbow

arbalétier *m.* crossbowman; rafters

arbitrage *m.* arbitration

arbitraire *a.* arbitrary

arbitre *m.* arbiter; umpire, referee; libre — free will (philosophy)

arbitrer *vt.* to arbitrate; referee

arborer *vt.* show off; — un drapeau hoist a flag

arbousier *m.* arbutus

arbre *m.* tree; (mech.) shaft; — moteur driveshaft

arbrisseau *m.* shrub

arbuste *m.* shrub, bush

arc *m.* bow; arch; arc

arcade *f.* archway; série d'—s *f.* arcade

arcane *m.* mystery

arcature *f.* blind arcade; row of arcades

arc-boutant *m.* flying buttress
arceau *m.* arched opening; small arch
arc-en-ciel *m.* rainbow
archaïque *a.* archaic
archange *m.* archangel
arche *f.* arch; ark
archéologie *f.* archeology
archéologue *m.* archeologist
archer *m.* bowman, archer
archet *m.* (mus.) bow
archevêché *m.* archdiocese; archbishop's palace
archevêque *m.* archbishop
archi- *prefix* arch-
archipel *m.* archipelago
architecte *m.* architect
architectural *a.* architectural
architecture *f.* architecture
archives *f. pl.* archives
archiviste *m. & f.* archivist
arçon *m.* saddle bow; saddle; wool carder
arctique *a.* arctic
ardemment *adv.* ardently
ardent *a.* ardent; burning; fiery
ardeur *f.* ardor; heat; fire; zeal
ardillon *m.* tongue of a belt buckle
ardoise *f.* slate; score
ardu *a.* arduous; steep; difficult
are *m.* 100 square meters (about 120 square yards)
arène, -s *f. s. or pl.* arena, bull ring
aréner *vi.* to sink, settle
aréneux *a.* sandy
arête *f.* fishbone; ridge; edge; angle; — du nez bridge of the nose
argent *m.* silver; money
argenté *a.* silver; silver-plated; silvery
argenter *vt.* to plate with silver
argenterie *f.* silver plate, silverware
argentifère *a.* silver-bearing
argentin *a.* silvery; tinkling
argenture *f.* silvering; l'— des glaces silvering on mirrors
argile *f.* clay
argileux *a.* of clay, clayey
argonaute *m.* argonaut; nautilus
argot *m.* slang; -ique *a.* slangy
argousin *m.* prison guard
arguer *vt.* to infer; — *vi.* to argue
argument *m.* argument, summary, reasoning
argumentation *f.* argumentation; arguing
argumenter *vt.* to argue
argus *m.* spy; argus
argutie *f.* subtlety; quibbling
aride *a.* arid, dry, barren
aridité *f.* aridity
ariette *f.* air, song
aristocrate *m. & f.* aristocrat; — *a.* aristocratic
aristocratie *f.* aristocracy
aristocratique *a.* aristocratic
aristotélicien *a.* Aristotelian
arithméticien *m.* arithmetician
arithmétique *f.* arithmetic; — *a.* arithmetical
arlequin *m.* Harlequin
arlésien *a.* from Arles
armagnac *m.* brandy of Armagnac
armateur *m.* ship outfitter, shipowner

armature *f.* armature; (arch.) steel framework, iron braces; (mus.) signature
arme *f.* arm, weapon; -s portatives small arms; maître d'—s *m.* fencing master; place d'—s *f.* parade ground; salle d'—s *f.* fencing school
armé *a.* armed; béton — reinforced concrete
armée *f.* army
armement *m.* armament; arming; equipping; loading; cocking
Arménie *f.* Armenia; -n *m. & a.* Armenian
armer *vt.* to arm; (naut.) to fit out; commission; reinforce; equip, outfit; load; cock; — *vi.* arm oneself
armistice *m.* armistice
armoire *f.* wardrobe; cupboard
armoiries *f. pl.* arms (heraldic), coat of arms
Armor *m.* (Celtic) Brittany
armorial *m.* armorial, book of heraldry
Armoricain *m. & a.* Breton
armure *f.* armor; (mus.) signature
armurier *m.* armorer, gunsmith
aromate *m.* aromatic substance
aromatique *a.* aromatic
aromatiser *vt.* to perfume; flavor
arôme *m.* aroma, flavor
aronde *f.* swallow; queue d'— *f.* dovetail
arpège *m.* arpeggio
arpent *m.* acre (= approximately 1½ American acres); -er *vt.* to survey, measure
arpenteur *m.* surveyor
arqué *a.* arched; bowed
arquebuse *f.* musket
arquer *vt.* to arch, bend, bow; curve; — *vi.* bend, sag
arrache-clou *m.* claw hammer
arrache-pied, d'— *adv.* uninterruptedly
arracher *vt.* to tear out; uproot, pull a tooth
arracheuse *f.* digger (potatoes, sugar beets)
arrangement *m.* arrangement; settlement; —s *m.* terms
arranger *vt.* to arrange, fix, settle; s'— to manage; agree, come to an agreement
arrangeur *m.* arranger
arrérages *m. pl.* arrears; money due
arrestation *f.* arrest, custody
arrêt *m.* stop; decree; verdict (law), sentence; arrest; mandat d'— *m.* arrest warrant; chien d'— *m.* hunting dog, pointer
arrêté *m.* decree, order; police decision
arrêter *vt.* to arrest; stop; settle; close (an account); determine, fix; engage; point (dog); s'— to stop
arrêtoir *m.* stop, catch
arrhes *f. pl.* deposit, security
arrière *m.* back; stern; rear; vent — *m.* tail wind; en — *adv.* back, backwards; behind; en — de *prep.* behind
arrière- *prefix* rear-; after-; great- (relationship by blood)
arriéré *m.* arrears; — *a.* backward; overdue
arriéré *m.* arrearage; — *a.* deferred; behind

arriere-ban *m.* reserve
arriere-bouche *f.* pharynx
arrière-boutique *f.* back room of a shop
arrière-garde *f.* rear guard
arrière-goût *m.* aftertaste
arrière-pays *m.* hinterland, back country
arrière-pensée *f.* ulterior motive
arrière-plan *m.* background
arriérer *vt.* to delay; s'— stay behind
arrière-saison *f.* end of autumn
arrière-train *m.* rear; hindquarters
arrimer *vt.* to stow away
arrimeur *m.* stevedore
arrivage *m.* arrival of goods *or* ships
arrivée *f.* arrival, coming, approach
arriver *vi.* to arrive; happen; succeed; — à to reach, attain; manage to
arrivisme *m.* social climbing
arrogamment *adv.* arrogantly
arrogant *a.* arrogant
arroger *v.*, s'— to claim, assume with presumption
arrondir *vt.* to round off, make round; enlarge
arrondissement *m.* administrative district; ward
arrosage *m.* sprinkling; watering; basting; tuyau d'— *m.* garden hose
arroser *vt.* to water; baste; drain an area
arroseur *m.* sprinkler
arrosoir *m.* watering can; shower head
arrondir *vt.* to make round; increase; double
arsenic *m.* arsenic
art *m.* art; cunning; beaux -s fine arts
artère *f.* artery
artérial *a.* arterial
artériosclérose *f.* hardening of the arteries
artésian *a.* artesian; from Artois
arthrite *f.* arthritis
arthritique *a. & n.* arthritic
artichaut *m.* artichoke
article *m.* article; item; — de fond editorial
articulation *f.* articulation; joint; enumerated legal facts
articulé *a.* articulated; articulate
articuler *vt.* to affirm, declare; articulate
artifice *m.* artifice, trick; feu d'— *m.* fireworks
artificiel *a.* artificial
artificier *m.* maker of fireworks
artificieux *a.* sly, artful, full of artifice
artillerie *f.* artillery; ordnance
artilleur *m.* artilleryman
artisan *m.* craftsman, artisan
artiste *m. & f.* artist; — *a.* artistic
artistique *a.* artistic
arum *m.* calla lily; arum
aryen *a.* Aryan
as *m.* ace; expert
ascendant *m.* influence; -s *pl.* ancestry, lineage; — *a.* ascending
ascenseur *m.* elevator
ascension *f.* ascent; Assumption
ascète *m. & f.* ascetic
ascétique *a.* ascetic
ascétisme *m.* asceticism
asdic *m.* sonar, submarine detector
aseptique *a.* aseptic

Asiatique *m. & f. & a.* Asiatic
Asie *f.* Asia; — Mineure Asia Minor
asile *m.* asylum, refuge, shelter
aspect *m.* aspect, appearance, sight; look
asperge *f.* asparagus
aspergès *m.* sprinkler for holy water; time of sprinkling with such water
asperger *vt.* to sprinkle
aspérité *f.* asperity, roughness
asphalte *m.* asphalt
asphalter *vt.* to asphalt
asphyxie *f.* asphyxia
asphyxier *vt.* to asphyxiate
aspirant *m.* officer candidate; candidate
aspirateur *m.* vacuum cleaner; aspirator; — de buée *f.* ventilator
aspiration *f.* aspiration; intake
aspiré *m.* aspirate; — *a.* aspirated
aspirer *vi.* to aspire; — *vt.* to aspirate; take in; inhale
aspirine *f.* aspirin
assaillant *m.* assailant; aggressor
assaillir *vt.* to assail, attack
assainir *vt.* to make healthy, purify
assaisonnement *m.* seasoning, condiment; dressing
assaisonner *vt.* to season, flavor
assassin *m.* murderer; — *a.* murderous
assassinat *m.* assassination, murder
assassiner *vt.* to assassinate, murder
assaut *m.* assault, attack; bout
assécher *vt.* to drain, dry up
assemblage *m.* collection; assembly, assemblage; joining, joint (in carpentry)
assemblée *f.* assembly; meeting
assembler *vt.* to assemble; join; gather; s'— to meet, assemble
asséner *vt.* to strike a blow
assentiment *m.* assent, agreement, approval
asseoir *vt.* to seat; place, lay; s'— to sit down, be seated
assermenté *a.* sworn
assertion *f.* assertion
asservir *vt.* to enslave; s'— à to obey
asservissement *m.* slavery
assez *adv.* enough; rather; sufficiently
assidu *a.* assiduous; -ité *f.* assiduity
assidûment *adv.* assiduously; punctually
assiéger *vt.* to besiege
assiette *f.* plate; dish; position; seat; balance
assignation *f.* assignation; (com.) assignment; summons
assigner *vt.* to summon; assign; subpoena
assimiler *vt.* to assimilate; compare
assis *a.* seated, sitting; place -e *f.* seat
assise *f.* layer, stratum; -s *pl.* criminal court sessions
assistance *f.* audience; spectators; aid, assistance; — judiciare public defender's office; — sociale social work, welfare work
assistant *m.* assistant; bystander; -s *pl.* audience; -e sociale *f.* social worker
assister *vt.* to help; — à *vi.* to attend, be present at
association *f.* association; partnership
associé *m.* associate, partner
associer *vt.* to associate; s'— to enter into

partnership; join in: be associated with
assoiffé *a.* thirsting. greedy
assolement *m.* crop rotation
assoler *vt.* to rotate crops
assombrir *vt.* to darken; **s'—** to get gloomy
assommant *a.* boring; crushing. telling
assommer *vt.* to knock down: kill; bore
assommoir *m.* blunt instrument, bludgeon: (coll.) bar, dive
Assomption *f.* Assumption
assorti *a.* matching
assortiment *m.* assortment; set; matching
assortir *vt.* to match
assoupir *vt.* to make sleepy; lull; **s'—** to doze off, fall asleep
assouplir *vt.* to make supple
assouplissement *m.* suppleness, docility
assourdir *vt.* to deafen; muffle
assourdissant *a.* deafening
assouvir *vt.* to gratify, satiate, surfeit
asujettir *vt.* subdue, subjugate; oblige; **s'—** to submit
asujettissement *m.* submission; subduing, subjugation
assumer *vt.* to assume, take on oneself
assurance *f.* assurance; insurance
assuré *a.* assured, confident; secure; firm, steady; insured
assurément *adv.* certainly, assuredly; confidently
assurer *vt.* to assure; secure; insure; **s'—** to make sure
Assyrie *f.* Assyria; **—n** *m.* & *a.* Assyrian
aster *m.* aster
astérie *f.* starfish
astérisque *m.* asterisk
astéroïde *m.* asteroid
asthmatique *m.* & *a.* asthmatic
asthme *m.* asthma
asticot *m.* maggot, worm
astigmatisme *m.* astigmatism
astiquer *vt.* to polish; clean up
astrakan *m.* Persian lamb
astre *m.* star
astreindre *vt.* to oblige, force, compel; **s'—** (à) to force oneself
astringent *a.* & *m.* astringent
astrologie *f.* astrology
astrologue *m.* astrologer
astronaute *m.* & *f.* space traveller
astronautique *f.* space travel
astronef *m.* space ship, rocket ship
astronome *m.* astronomer
astronomie *f.* astronomy
astronomique *a.* astronomical
astrophysigne *f.* astrophysics
astuce *f.* astuteness, guile, wile
astucieux *a.* astute, crafty
asymétrique *a.* asymetrical
atavique *a.* atavistic
atelier *m.* workshop; studio
atermoyer *vi.* to stall, delay
athée *m.* atheist; **—** *a.* atheistic
athéisme *m.* atheism
athénée *m.* secondary school
athlète *m.* athlete
athlétique *a.* athletic
athlétisme *m.* track, athletics (sports)
Atlantide *f.* Atlantis

atlantique *a.* Atlantic
atmosphère *f.* atmosphere
atmosphérique *a.* atmospheric
atome *m.* atom; iota, speck
atomique *a.* atomic
atomiser *vt.* to atomize; subject to radiation; destroy with an atomic bomb
atomiseur *m.* atomizer
atomiste *m.* & *f.* atom scientist
atonal *a.* atonal
atonalité *f.* atonality
atone *a.* atonic, unaccented; atonal; dull
atours *m. pl.* women's finery
atout *m.* trump; sans — no trump
âtre *m.* hearth, fireplace
atroce *a.* atrocious
atrocité *f.* atrocity
atrophie *f.* atrophy
atrophier *vi.* to atrophy, waste away
attabler *v.*, **s'—** to sit down at the table
attache *f.* fastener, tie, clip; leash; tether
attaché *m.* attaché
attacher *vt.* to attach, fasten, join, tie; **s'—** (à) to grow fond (of); apply oneself (to)
attaquant *m.* attacker; aggressor
attaque *f.* attack; fit; **—r** *vt.* to attack
attardé *a.* late; behind; delayed
attarder *vt.* to delay; **s'—** to linger
atteindre *vt.* to reach, attain; strike, hit; wound
atteinte *f.* attack; blow; reach; injury
attelage *m.* team; pair; harnessing; coupling
atteler *vt.* to harness, yoke; hitch; couple
attelle *f.* splint
attenant *a.* adjoining, next
attendant *adv.*, **en —** meanwhile; for the moment; **en — que** *conj.* until
attendre *vt.* to wait for, expect; **s'—** (à) to expect
attendrir *vt.* to make tender; move, affect, touch; **s'—** to be moved
attendu *prep.* in view of; **— que** *conj.* since, whereas
attentat *m.* criminal attack or attempt; outrage
attente *f.* expectation; waiting; hope
attenter *vi.* to make an attempt
attentif *a.* attentive; careful
attention *f.* attention, care; **—!** *interj.* watch out!; faire — to pay attention, be careful
atténuant *a.* extenuating; attenuating
atténuer *vt.* to attenuate; diminish, reduce
atterrage *m.* (naut.) landfall; landing
atterrer *vt.* to crush, overwhelm; demolish
atterrir *vi.* (avi.) to land
atterrissage *m.* (avi.) landing
atterrissement *m.* alluvion; descent (balloon)
attestation *f.* attestation, testimony
attester *vt.* to attest (to); witness
attiédir *vt.* to make lukewarm; **s'—** to become lukewarm
attifer *vt.* to deck out, ornament
attirail *m.* paraphernalia, gear
attirance *f.* attraction, temptation
attirant *a.* attracting, attractive
attirer *vt.* to attract, lure; **s'—** to bring

upon oneself

attiser vt. to stir up; excite

attitré a. official

attitude f. posture, attitude, position

attractif a. attractive

attraction f. attraction; —s pl. shows, entertainment

attrait m. charm, attraction

attrape f. snare; trick

attrape-mouches m. flypaper; flycatcher (bird)

attrape-nigaud m. booby trap

attraper vt. to catch; take in; trick

attrayant a. attractive

attribuer vt. to attribute, ascribe

attribut m. attribute

attribution f. attribution; sphere, power

attrister vt. to sadden; s'— to become sad

attrouper vt. to assemble

aubaine f. windfall

aube f. dawn; board; paddle; (eccl.) alb; roue à —s f. paddlewheel

aubépine f. hawthorn

auberge f. inn; — de la jeunesse youth hostel

aubergine f. eggplant

aubergiste m. & f. innkeeper

aucun pron. & a. no one, none; no; any

aucunement adv. not at all, by no means, in no way

audace f. boldness, audacity

audacieux a. audacious, bold; impudent

au-dehors adv. outside

au-delà adv. beyond; — de prep. beyond

au-dessous adv. below, under; — de prep. below, under

au-dessus adv. above, over; — de above, over

au-devant adv., aller — to go, meet; anticipate

audience f. hearing; audience

audio-visuel a. audio-visual

auditeur m. listener, hearer; —s pl. audience

auditif a. audial, auditory, auditive

audition f. hearing; audition; (mus.) recital

auditionner vt. to listen to; audition

auditoire m. audience

auge f. trough; hod

augmentation f. increase; salary raise

augmenter vt. to augment; increase; raise; enlarge; — vi. increase; rise

augure m. omen; de bon — auspicious

augurer vt. to augur; foresee

auguste a. august

aujourd'hui adv. today, nowadays; d'— en huit in a week, a week from today

aumône f. alms, charity

aumônier m. chaplain

aune f. ell (= 45 inches); measure, standard; — m. alder

auparavant adv. before, previously

auprès prep., — de near, close to; next to, with; compared with; — adv. nearby

auquel pron. to whom, to which

auréole f. halo; glory, aureola

auréomycine f. aureomycin

auriculaire a. aural, auricular; doigt — m. little finger

auricule f. auricle; outer ear

aurifier vt. to fill a tooth with gold

aurore f. dawn; — boréale aurora borealis

ausculter vt. (med.) to auscultate

aussi adv. also, too; — . . . que as . . . as; — conj. therefore, so

aussitôt adv. immediately; — que as soon as

austère a. austere, stern, severe

austérité f. austerity

austral a. southern

Australie f. Australia; —n m. & a. Australian

autan m. south wind; storm

autant adv. as much, as many; d'— as much as; d'— plus, (moins) all the more (less); d'— plus que all the more because

autel m. altar

auteur m. author; creator; cause

authenticité f. authenticity

authentifier vt. to authenticate

authentique a. authentic; sincere

auto f. automobile, auto, car

autobiographie f. autobiography

autobus m. bus

autocar m. intercity bus, sightseeing bus

autochenille f. caterpillar-tread vehicle

autochtone a. native

autoclave m. pressure cooker; sterilizer

autocopier vt. to duplicate, ditto

autocrate m. autocrat

autocratie f. autocracy

autocratique a. autocratic

autocritique f. self-criticism

autocuiseur m. pressure cooker

autodestruction f. self-destruction

autodétermination self-determination

autodidacte a. self-taught

autodrome m. race track (auto.)

auto-école f. driving school

autogène a. welded

autogire m. autogiro

autographe m. & a. autograph

autographier vt. to autograph

automate m. automaton

automatique a. automatic; — f. automation

automatiser vt. to introduce automation in

automatisme m. automation

automnal a. autumnal

automne m. or f. autumn

automobilisme m. driving, motoring

automobiliste m. motorist

automoteur a. self-propelling; train — m. diesel-powered train

autonome a. autonomous

autonomie f. autonomy

autoplastie f. skin grafting

autoportrait m. self-portrait

autopropulsion f. self-propulsion

autopsie f. autopsy

autopsier vt. to perform an autopsy on

autorail m. railway diesel car

autorisation f. authorisation

autoriser vt. to authorize, empower

autoritaire a. & m. authoritarian

autoroute f. highway; expressway

autorité f. authority; —s pl. officials

authorities

auto-stop *m.* hitchhiking; **faire l'—** to hitchhike

autostrade *f.* superhighway, expressway

autour *adv.* about, around; **— de** *prep.* about, around

autre *a.* other, another; different; **—part elsewhere; d'—** part on the other hand; **de temps à —** from time to time, occasionally; **l'un et l'—** both; **l'un ou l'—** either; **ni l'un ni l'—** neither

autrefois *adv.* formerly, once

autrement *adv.* otherwise; differently

Autriche *f.* Austria

autrichien *a. & m.* Austrian

autruche *f.* ostrich

autrui *pron.* others

auvent *m.* shed; cover, roof; penthouse

auvergnat *a.* from Auvergne

auxiliaire *a. & n.* auxiliary

avachir *v.*, **s'—** to become deformed; become flabby

aval *m.* guarantee; downstream portion of a river; **en —** downstream

avaler *vt.* to swallow

avaliser *vt.* to guarantee, co-sign

avaliseur *m.* co-signer

à-valoir *m.* part-payment

avance *f.* head start, lead; advance; loan; **d'—** in advance; **en —** early

avancé *a.* advanced; **heure -e** *f.* late hour

avancement *m.* advancement, advancing; furthering; progress; projection

avancer *vt.* to advance; hasten; further; promote; extend, put out; **— vi.** advance, move forward, progress; to be fast (clock)

avanie *f.* public insult; affront

avant *prep. & adv.* before; **— (de)** before; **en —** forward; **que** *conj.* before; **— m.** front portion; (naut.) bow

avantage *m.* advantage; profit

avantager *vt.* to favor; give an advantage

avantageux *a.* profitable, advantageous; vain

avant-bras *m.* forearm

avant-coureur *m.* forerunner

avant-dernier *f.* next-to-last

avant-garde *f.* vanguard

avant-goût *m.* foretaste

avant-guerre *f.* prewar period; **d'—** *a.* prewar

avant-hier *adv.* day before yesterday

avant-port *m.* outer port

avant-poste *m.* outpost

avant-projet *m.* preliminary consideration (of a plan or project)

avant-propos *m.* foreword

avant-scène *f.* proscenium; stagebox

avant-veille *f.* second day previous, two days before

avare *a.* miserly, stingy

avaricieux *a.* avaricious, stingy, miserly

avarie *f.* damage; loss; deterioration

avarié *a.* spoiled, damaged

avec *prep.* with; **d'—** from

aveline *f.* filbert

avenant *a.* coming; becoming; in keeping

avènement *m.* succession; coming; advent

avenir *m.* future; **à l'—** henceforth

avent *m.* (eccl.) Advent

aventure *f.* adventure, intrigue; **bonne —** fortune telling; **à l'—** *adv.* at random

aventurer *vt.* to venture, risk; **s'—** to venture

aventureux *a.* adventurous; risky

aventurier *m.* adventurer

avérage *m.* average

avéré *a.* verified, established

avérer *v.*, **s'—** to appear, prove

averse *f.* shower, downpour

averti *a.* informed; on guard; experienced

avertir *vt.* to warn; inform, notify

avertissement *m.* warning; notice; preface

avertisseur *a.* warning; **— m.** warning device; horn; alarm

aveu *m.* confession, avowal, admission

aveugle *a.* blind; **— m. & f.** blind person

aveuglement *m.* blinding; (fig.) blindness

aveuglément *adv.* blindly

aveugler *vt.* to blind

aveuglette, à l'— *adv.* blindly, gropingly; at random

aveulir *vt.* to weaken; enervate

aviateur *m.* aviator

aviation *f.* aviation; air force

avide *a.* greedy; eager, avid

avidité *f.* avidity, eagerness

avilir *vt.* to vilify; lower in value; **s'—** to lower oneself, stoop to; become lower in value

avilissement *m.* vilification

aviné *a.* drunk (from wine)

avion *m.* airplane; **par —** by air mail

aviron *m.* oar; rowing; **donner un coup d'—** lend a helping hand

avis *m.* advice; opinion; notice; **à mon —** in my opinion; **changer d'—** to change one's mind

avisé *a.* prudent; shrewd, wary

aviser *vt.* to notify; warn; notice; **— à** *vi.* to take care of, see to; **s'—** (de) to take into one's head (to)

avivage *m.* polishing, brightening; revival

aviver *vt.* to sharpen; irritate; make brighter

avocat *m.* lawyer; advocate; **poire d'—** *f.* avocado

avocatier *m.* avocado tree

avoine *f.* oats

avoir *vt.* to have; get; **— chaud (froid, raison, tort)** to be hot (cold, right, wrong); **qu'avez-vous?** what's the matter?; **y — v.**, **il y a** there is, there are, it is; ago; **— m.** property, possessions; credit (ledger)

avoisiner *vt.* to neighbor, be near, border on

avorter *vi.* to miscarry; go wrong, fail

avorton *m.* miscarriage; abortion; abortive offspring

avoué *m.* attorney, lawyer

avouer *vt.* to avow, confess, admit

avril *m.* April

axe *m.* axis; axle; Axis

axillaire *a.* axillary

axiomatique *a.* axiomatic

axiome *m.* axiom

axonge *f.* lard

azalée *f.* azalea

azotate m. nitrate

azote m. nitrogen; —ux a. nitrous

azotique a. nitric

aztèque a. Aztec

azur m. azure

azuré a. azure, bluish

azyme a. unleavened

B

baba m. rumcake

babeurre m. buttermilk

babil m. babble, babbling; baby talk

babillard a. babbling; talkative; — m. chatterbox; tattler

babiller vi. to babble, chatter about nothing

babine f. heavy lip; chop; se lécher les —s to lick one's chops

babiole f. bauble, toy, trinket

bâbord m. (naut.) port side

babouche f. heelless slipper

babouin m. baboon

Babylone n. Babylon

Babylonien m. & a. Babylonian

baby-parc m. playpen

bac m. ferry; vat, tank; box, bin; (coll.) bachelor's degree

baccalauréat m. bachelor's degree

baccara m. baccarat

bâche f. tarpaulin; tank; hotbed frame

bachelier m. lycée graduate

bachot m. small boat; (coll.) bachelor's degree

bacillaire a. caused by a bacillus

bacille m. bacillus

bâcle f. bolt, bar of a door

bâcler vt. to botch, patch together; bolt, bar; block, obstruct

bactérie f. microbe, bacterium

bactériologie f. bacteriology

bactériologue m. bacteriologist

badaud m. loafer; stroller

badigeon m. whitewash

badigeonner vt. to whitewash; fill with plaster; (med.) paint the throat

badin a. playful, joking, fooling

badinage m. banter, fooling, playfulness

badine f. switch, wand, rod

badiner vi. to joke, play, be playful; trifle, fool; — vt. tease

badminton m. badminton

bafouer vt. to make fun of; scoff at; ridicule without pity

bafouiller vi. & vt. (coll.) to stammer; (fig.) speak disconnectedly

bâfrer vt. & vi. (coll.) to devour, guzzle

bagage m. baggage; plier — to pack up and go; —s m. pl. baggage, luggage

bagarre f. riot, brawl, fight

bagatelle f. trifle; (fig.) something frivolous

bagnard m. prisoner, convict

bagne m. penitentiary; penal servitude

baguage m. banding (tree)

bague f. ring; jeu de —s merry-go-round

baguenauder vi. to trifle, waste time

baguer vt. to ring, band (tree); baste (cloth)

baguette f. switch, rod; drum stick; wand; long thin loaf of bread

baguier m. jewel box

bahut m. trunk, chest; (coll.) school

bai a. bay horse

baie f. berry; bay, gulf; (arch.) bay

baignade f. swimming; swimming place

baigner vt. to soak, bathe

baignoire f. bathtub; (theat.) orchestra box

bail m. (pl. baux) lease

bâillant a. yawning; open, ajar

bâillement m. yawn; opening; gap

bâilleur m. bondsman

bâiller vi. to yawn, gape; be ajar

bailli m. bailiff

bâillon m. gag

bâillonner vt. to gag; muzzle; (fig.) silence

bain m. bath; costume de — bathing suit, swim suit; —s pl. baths; spa, hot springs, resort

bain-marie m. water bath; double boiler

baïonnette f. bayonet

baisemain m. hand-kissing

baiser m. kiss; — vt. to kiss (hand, brow); (fig.) compliment

baissant a. setting (sun); falling; failing

baisse f. fall, decline, drop

baisser vt. to lower; — vi. to fall, drop, go down; sink; se — to stoop; bow down; — m. fall, falling; setting (of sun)

bajoue f. jowl

Bakélite f. Pakelite (trademark)

bal m. ball, dance

balader v., se — to wander, stroll; go for a ride

baladeuse f. cart; trailer, portable light, trouble light

baladin m. buffoon; actor

balafre f. gash; slash; scar; —r vt. to gash; scar

balai m. broom; (elec.) brush; carpet sweeper; — à laver mop

balance f. scales; balance; balance sheet

balancement m. rocking; hesitation; poising

balancer vt. to balance; swing, rock; weigh for and against — vi. to hesitate; fluctuate, waver; swing

balancier m. pendulum; beam; balance wheel; coin-press lever

balançoire f. seesaw, teeter-totter; swing

balayer vt. to sweep

balayette f. whisk broom

balayeur m. street cleaner, street sweeper

balayeuse f. carpet sweeper; street-cleaning truck

balayures f. pl. sweepings

balbutier vi. to stutter, stammer, mumble

balbuzard m. buzzard

balcon m. balcony

baldaquin m. canopy, tester

baleine f. whale; whalebone, stay

baleinier m. whaling ship

baleinière f. whaleboat

balise f. buoy, marker, beacon

baliser vt. to mark with buoys or lights

balistique a. ballistic; — f. ballistics

baliverne f. nonsense, stupidity, humbug

balkanique a. Balkan

Balkans m. pl. Balkans

ballant a. swinging, slack (rope), dangling
ballast m. ballast
balle f. ball; bullet; husk; — traçante tracer bullet
ballerine f. ballerina
ballet m. ballet
ballon m. balloon; ball; — d'essai trial balloon
ballonner vi. to swell, puff up
ballot m. bundle; bale; package of merchandise
ballottage m. balloting; indecisive first ballot
ballotter vt. to agitate; — vi. to move about; to be shaken
ballottine f. chicken loaf
balnéaire a. bathing; station — f. resort
balourd a. dull, heavy; stupid,
balsa m. balsa wood
Balte, Baltique n. & a. Baltic
balustrade f. balustrade, railing
balustre m. baluster
bambin m. little child
bambou m. bamboo
ban m. proclamation; cheer; -s pl. (eccl.) banns
banal a. banal, trite, commonplace
banalité f. triviality, triteness; overused expression
banane f. banana
bananier m. banana tree
banc m. bench; seat; pew; shoal
bancal a. bow-legged, bandy-legged
bandage m. bandage, truss; winding
bande f. band; strip; group; cushion (billiards)
bandeau m. headband; blindfold; en –x hair parted in the middle
bandelette f. band, headband, fillet
bander vt. to bandage; bind; blindfold; wind; se — to band together, join together
banderole f. streamer, pennant
bandit m. bandit
bandoulière f. sling; bandoleer; en — a. over the shoulder
banian m. banyan tree
banlieue f. suburbs; de — a. suburban
banlieusard m. suburbanite
banne f. basket, hamper; tarpaulin; awning
bannière f. banner, flag
bannir vt. to banish, exile
bannissement m. banishment, exile
banque f. bank; — du sang blood bank
banqueroute f. bankruptcy
banqueroutier m. bankrupt person
banqueter vi. to banquet, feast
banquette f. seat (train, bus); bank (earth or sand)
banquier m. banker
banquise f. ice pack, floe
banquiste m. charlatan
baptême m. christening, baptism; nom de — christian name
baptiser vt. to christen, baptize
baptismal a. baptismal
baptiste m. & f. Baptist
baptistère m. baptistry
baquet m. tub, washtub

bar m. bar; bass, perch
baragouiner vt. & vi. (coll.) to jabber; pronounce badly
baraque f. hut, shack; hovel
baratte f. churn; -r vt. to churn
Barbade f. Barbados
barbare a. barbarous, cruel; barbaric; — m. barbarian
barbarie f. barbarity; orgue de — m. barrel organ, organ-grinder's organ
barbarisme m. barbarism
barbe f. beard; se faire la — to shave; rire dans sa — laugh up one's sleeve
barbelé a. barbed; fil de fer — m. barbed wire
barbet m. water spaniel
barbiche f. goatee
barbier m. barber
barbillon m. barb
barbiturique m. & a. barbiturate
barbon m. old man; greybeard; (coll.) old fogy
barbouiller vt. to daub, smear, dirty; mess up, bungle
barbu a. bearded
barbue f. brill
barde m. bard; — f. fat used for larding
bardeau m. shingle; lath
barder vt. to lard; armor
bardot m. mule; laughing stock
barème m. tables of figures
barguette f. flat boat used as a ferry
barguigner vi. to hesitate; hesitate to take part
baricant m. small barrel
baril m. barrel, small cask
barillet m. small barrel; revolver cylinder; spring case
bariolage m. medley of colors
bariolé a. speckled; multicolored
barman m. bartender
baromètre m. barometer
barométrique a. barometric
baron m. baron; -ne f. baronness
baroque a. irregular; baroque
barque f. bark (small boat)
barrage n. (mil.) barrage; dam; barrier; (sports) play-off
barre f. bar; helm; stroke; dividing line
barreau m. bar; rung
barrer vt. to bar; cross out
barrette f. biretta; bar; barrette, slide; pin
barricade f. barricade; -r vt. to barricade
barrière f. barrier; starting gate; fence
barrique f. cask; hogshead
barrir vi. to trumpet (elephant)
baryton m. baritone; baritone horn
baryum m. barium
bas (basse) a. low; vulgar, cheap; — m. stocking, hose; lower part, bottom; foot; — adv. softly; down, low; en — downstairs, below
basalte m. basalt
basane f. sheep skin
basané a. tanned, sunburned, swarthy
bas-côté m. church side aisle; highway shoulder
bascule f. scale; balance; seesaw
basculer vi. to swing, rock, seesaw; dim (headlights)

base f. base, basis, foundation
baser vt. to base, found
bas-fond m. hole; hollow; shoal; —s pl. dregs
basilic m. sweet basil
basilique f. basilica
basique a. basic
Basque m. & f. & a. Basque
bas-relief m. bas-relief
basse f. (mus.) bass; tuba
basse-cour f. poultry yard; backyard
basse-fosse f. dungeon
bassesse f. baseness, lowness, meanness
bassin m. basin; dock; (anat.) pelvis
bassine f. pan (round and shallow)
bassiner vt. to sprinkle, water; warm; (coll.) bore, weary
bassinet m. small basin
bassinoire f. bedwarmer; (coll.) bore
basson m. bassoon, bassoonist
bastille f. fort, fortress
bastion m. bastion
bastonnade f. beating
bas-ventre m. abdomen
bat m. bat
bât m. pack saddle
bataclan m. paraphernalia
bataille f. battle, fight
batailler vi. to battle
batailleur a. quarrelsome, fighting
bataillon m. battalion
bâtard m. bastard; medium-sized loaf of bread — a. not pure bred; inferior
bâtarde f. cursive writing
bâtardeau m. temporary dam
bateau m. boat
bateau-maison m. houseboat
bateau-mouche m. Parisian excursion boat
batelée f. boatload
bateler vt. to transport by boat; — vi. to perform tricks, juggle
bateleur m. trickster, juggler, tumbler
batelier m. boatman
bâter vt. to saddle (a pack animal)
bâti m. frame; basted garment; basting thread
bâtiment m. building; ship
bâtir vt. to build; baste (clothing)
bâtisse f. masonry; building
bâtisseur m. builder
batiste f. batiste
bâton m. stick, cudgel; baton
bâtonner vt. to beat; cross out
bâtonnier m. dean of lawyers (in France)
battage m. beating, threshing; churning
battant m. bell clapper; part of door or furniture that swings on a hinge; porte à deux —s double door; — a. pelting, driving; porte — swinging door
batte f. bat; mallet
battement m. beating; throbbing, pulsing, pulsation; shuffling (cards)
batterie f. battery; (mus.) percussion; — de cuisine kitchen utensils
batteuse f. threshing machine
battoir m. paddle
battre vt. to beat, strike; mint; defeat; clap; shuffle cards; se — to fight
baudet m. donkey, ass; sawhorse; (fig.)
idiot
baudrier m. shoulder belt, sword belt
bauge f. lair, den
baume m. balm, balsam
bauxite f. bauxite
bavard a. talkative, gossipy
bavarder vi. to chatter, gossip
Bavarois m. & a. Bavarian
bave f. slobber, drool; drivel
baver vi. to drool, slobber
bavette f. bib; tailler une — to chat
Bavière f. Bavaria
bavoir m. bib
bavocher vi. to be smeared, poorly printed
bavure f. seam (of a mold)
bayer vi. to gape, stare
bazar m. bazaar; variety store
béant a. agape, gaping, yawning
béat a. smug, complacent, sanctimonious
béatification f. beatification
béatifier vt. to beatify
béatitude f. beatitude
beau, bel (belle) a. fine, fair, beautiful, handsome; vous avez — faire no matter what you do
beaucoup adv. much, many; de — by far
beau-fils m. son-in-law; stepson
beau-frère m. brother-in-law
beau-père m. father-in-law; stepfather
beauté f. beauty
beaux-arts m. pl. fine arts
beaux-parents m. pl. father-in-law and mother-in-law; (coll.) in-laws
bébé m. baby
bec m. beak, bill; spout; point
bécane f. old locomotive, switch engine
bécarre m. (mus.) natural
bécasse f. woodcock
bécassine f. snipe
bec-de-cane m. door handle; door bolt (like a beak)
bec-de-corbeau m. wire cutters
bec-de-lièvre m. harelip
bêche f. spade; -r vt. & vi. to dig, spade
bêchoir m. hoe
becqueter vt. to peck (at)
bedeau m. beadle
Bédouin m. & a. Bedouin
bée a. open; bouche — agape; flabbergasted; — f. large opening
beffroi m. belfry
bégayer vi. to stutter; stammer
bégaiement m. stammering
bégonia m. begonia
begue a. stuttering, stammering
bégueter vi. to bleat
béguin m. hood, cap; infatuation
beige a. beige; unbleached
beignet m. fritter; doughnut
béjaune m. novice, beginner; one having no knowledge of a matter at hand
bêler vi. to bleat
belette f. weasel
Belge n. & a. Belgian
Belgique f. Belgium
bélier m. ram
bélitre m. scoundrel
belladone f. belladonna
belinogramme m. wire photo
belinographe m. wire photo transmitter

belle *adv.* l'échapper — to have a narrow escape

belle-de-jour *f.* morning glory

belle-fille *f.* daughter-in-law; stepdaughter

belle-mère *f.* mother-in-law; stepmother

belle-sœur *f.* sister-in-law

belliciste *m.* warmonger

belligérance *f.* belligerance

belligérant *m. & a.* belligerant

belligueux *a.* warlike

bémol *m.* (mus.) flat

bémoliser *vt.* (mus.) to flat

bénédicité *m.* grace before meals

bénédictin *m.* (liquer) benedictine; -e *f.* benedictine nun

bénédiction *f.* benediction

bénéfice *m.* benefice; profit; advantage

bénéficiaire *a.* beneficiary

bénéficier *vt.* to benefit, profit

benêt *a.* stupid; — *m.* simpleton

bénévole *a.* kind; well-intentioned

Bengale *m.* Bengal

Bengali *n. & a.* Bengal

bénignité *f.* benignness; kindness; mildness

bénin (bénigne) *a.* benign; benignant; mild, gentle; kind

bénir *vt.* to bless, consecrate

bénitier *m.* holy-water font

benjamin *m.* youngest child, favorite child

benne *f.* hamper; hopper; body (dump truck); mine elevator

benoît *a.* indulgent

benzine *f.* benzine

benzoate *m.* benzoate

béquille *f.* crutch; -r *vi.* to walk with crutches

béquillon *m.* cane, crutch

bercail *m.* (eccl.) fold

berceau *m.* cradle; arbor; (arch.) tunnel vault; (mech.) motor support

bercelonnette *f.* cradle, bassinet

bercer *vt.* to rock; soothe; (fig.) lull to sleep

berceuse *f.* lullaby; rocking chair; rocking cradle

béret *m.* beret

berge *f.* steep bank, edge

berger *m.* shepherd

bergère *f.* shepherdess; armchair

bergerie *f.* fold, sheepfold; pastoral poetry

béribéri *m.* beri-beri

berlingot *m.* hard candy (caramel)

berkélium *m.* berkelium

berline *f.* carriage; sedan; mine truck

berne *f.* banter; en — at half mast

berner *vt.* to toss in a blanket; fool; haze

bernacle, bernache *f.* barnacle

berrichon *a.* (from Berry)

béryl *m.* beryl

béryllium *m.* beryllium

besace *f.* beggar's bag; wallet

besicles *f. pl.* spectacles

besogne *f.* work, task; -r *vi.* to work

besogneux *a.* needy

besoin *m.* need, want; necessity; misery; avoir — de have need of; au — if necessary

bessemer *m.* Bessemer converter

bestialité *f.* bestiality

bestiaux *m. pl.* cattle, livestock

bestiole *f.* little animal

bétail *m.* cattle, livestock

bêtatron *m.* betatron

bête *f.* animal; beast; — *a.* stupid, foolish

bêtifier *vt.* to make stupid

bêtise *f.* stupidity; nonsense

béton *m.* concrete; — armé reinforced concrete

bétonner *vt.* to make of concrete

bétonnière *f.* cement mixer

bette *f.* beet

betterave *f.* beet; — sucrière sugar beet

betting *m.* odds (racing)

beuglement *m.* bellow, bellowing; lowing

beugler *vi.* to low, bellow

beurre *m.* butter; -r *vt.* to butter

beurrée *f.* slice of bread and butter

beurrier *m.* butter dish

beuverie *f.* drinking party

bévatron *m.* bevatron

bévue *f.* blunder, big mistake, gaff

biais *m.* bias, slant; — *a.* oblique; en — at an angle, askew

biaiser *vi.* to go at an angle; hedge

bibelot *m.* knicknack, trinket

biberon *m.* nursing bottle; drinker

Bible *f.* Bible

bibliobus *m.* mobile library

biblographe *m.* bibliographer

bibliographie *f.* bibliography

bibliographique *a.* bibliographical

bibliophile *m.* bibliophile

bibliothécaire *m. & f.* librarian

bibliothèque *f.* library; book shelves, bookcase

biblique *a.* Biblical

bicamérisme *m.* (pol.) two-house system

bicéphale *a.* two-headed

biceps *m.* biceps

biche *f.* hind, darling

bichlamar *m.* pidgin English

bichon *m.* lapdog

bichonner *vt.* to curl; (fig.) caress

bicoque *f.* shack, hut

bicorne *a.* two-cornered

bicyclette *f.* bicycle

bidet *m.* nag, horse; sawhorse; sitz-bath

bidon *m.* can (for liquids); canteen

bief *m.* millrace; section of a canal (between two locks)

bielle *f.* (mach.) connecting rod, tie rod

bien *adv.* well; rightly; indeed; properly; quite; much, many; — que although; si — que so that; tant — que mal indifferently, so-so; — *m.* good; fortune; estate; welfare

bien-aimé *m.* beloved

bien-être *m.* well-being

bienfaisance *f.* charity, beneficence

bienfaisant *a.* charitable; beneficial

bienfait *m.* benefit, favor

bienfaiteur *m.* benefactor

bien-fonds *m.* real property, real estate

bienheureux *a.* very happy; blessed

biennal *a.* biennial

bienséance *f.* propriety, convention

bienséant *a.* proper, appropriate, fitting

bientôt *adv.* soon; shortly; à — goodbye, see you soon

bienveillance *f.* kindness, benevolence

bienveillant *a.* kind, benevolent

bienvenu *a.* welcome; -e *f.* welcome

bière *f.* coffin; bier

biffer *vt.* to cross out; cancel

bifteck *m.* beefsteak

bifurcation *f.* fork in a road; (rail.) junction; turnoff

bifurquer *vt. & vi.* to fork; bifurcate

bigame *a.* bigamous; — *m.* bigamist

bigamie *f.* bigamy

bigarreau *m.* white-heart cherry

bigarrer *vt.* to speckle

bigarrure *f.* mixture of colors or designs

bigle *f.* beagle hound; — *a.* squint-eyed

bigler *vi.* to squint

bigot *a.* bigotted, very devout, excessively devout; hypercritical; — *m.* bigot; devotee; hypocrite

bigoterie *f.* bigotry

bigoudi *m.* small hair curler

bihebdomadaire *a.* semi-weekly

bijou *m.* jewel, gem, stone

bijouterie *f.* jewelry; jeweler's shop

bijoutier *m.* jeweler

bilan *m.* balance sheet

bilatéral *a.* bilateral

bile *m.* bile, gall; (fig.) anger

biliaire *a.* biliary, bilious

bilieux *a.* bilious; choleric

bilingue *a.* bilingual

billard *m.* billiards; billiard table; billiard parlor

bille *f.* billiard ball; child's marble; log; block of wood; rolling pin; (mech.) ball; stylo à — *m.* ballpoint pen

billet *m.* note; bill; ticket; card; — d'aller et retour round-trip ticket; — simple one-way ticket; — de correspondance transfer

billevesée *f.* nonsense; fantasy

billon *m.* copper coin

billot *m.* block; chopping block

bimensuel *a.* semi-monthly

bimestriel *a.* bimonthly

bimoteur *a.* bimotor, two-engine

binaire *a.* binary

bine, binette *f.* hoe

binocle *m.* pince-nez, eye glasses (nose)

biochimie *f.* biochemistry

biographe *m.* biographer

biographie *f.* biography

biographique *a.* biographical

biologie *f.* biology

biologique *a.* biological

biologue *m.* biologist

biopsie *f.* biopsy

bipède *a.* two-footed; — *n.* biped

biplace *m. & f. & a.* two-seater

biplan *m.* biplane

Birman *m. & a.* Burmese; -ie *f.* Burma

bis *adv.* encore; (mus.) repeat, twice; house numbers(A,½); — *a.* gray-brown; pain — bread of low quality

bis aïeul *m.* great-grandfather; -e *f.* great-grandmother

bisannuel *a.* biennial

biscornu *a.* two-horned; odd; (fig.) bizarre

biscotte *f.* rusk

biscuit *m.* cooky, wafer, cracker; unglazed porcelain

bise *f.* cold wind; north wind

biseau *m.* beveled edge; bevelling tool

biseauter *vt.* to bevel; mark cards (to cheat)

biser *vt.* redye; — *vi.* spoil, degenerate; get brown (cereals)

bismuth *m.* bismuth

bisque *f.* rich, creamy soup

bissac *m.* bag, wallet

bisser *vt.* to give or ask for an encore

bissextile *a.*, année — *f.* leap year

bistouri *m.* scalpel

bistre *a.* bistre, black-brown; -r *vt.* to brown

bisulfite *m.* bisulfate

bisut(h) *m.* freshman

bitume *m.* asphalt; bitumen; — *vt.* to asphalt

bitumineux *a.* bituminous

bivouac *m.* bivouac, bivouac area

bizarre *a.* odd; strange, bizarre

bizarrerie *f.* oddness, whim; oddity

blackbouler *vt.* to blackball

blafard *a.* pale, pasty

blague *f.* tobacco pouch; joke; sans —? really?

blaguer *vi.* to joke; hoax

blagueur *m.* jokester, joker

blaireau *m.* badger; shaving brush

blâmable *a.* censurable, blameworthy

blâme *m.* blame; disapproval

blâmer *vt.* to find fault with; blame

blanc (blanche) *a.* white; blank; innocent; clean; (print.) space free of type; fer — *m.* tin; — *m.* white, whiteness (linen); — de chaux whitewash

blanchâtre *a.* whitish

blanche *f.* (mus.) half note

blancheur *f.* whiteness

blanchir *vt. & vi.* to whiten, bleach; wash; scald (raw food)

blanchissage *m.* laundering, washing

blanchisserie *f.* laundry

blanchisseuse *f.* laundress

blanc-manger *m.* blancmange pudding

blanquette *f.*, — de veau veal in white sauce

blasé *a.* bored

blason *m.* coat of arms; heraldry

blasphématoire *a.* blasphemous

blasphème *m.* blasphemy

blasphémer *vi.* to blaspheme

blatte *f.* cockroach

blé *m.* wheat; grain; — noir buckwheat

blême *a.* wan, livid, pale

blêmir *vi.* to turn pale

blèse *a.* lisping

bléser *vi.* to lisp

blessant *a.* offensive, mortifying; injurious

blesser *vt.* to wound, hurt, offend; injure

blessure *f.* wound; injury

blet *a.* overripe

blettir *vi.* to overripen

bleu *a.* blue; — *m.* blue; bruise; coveralls; (coll.) draftee; bluing; petit — letter sent by pneumatic tube

bleuâtre *a.* bluish
bleuet *m.* cornflower
bleuir *vt.* to make blue; — *vi.* to become blue
bleuté *a.* bluish
blindage *m.* armor plate
blindé *a.* armor-plated, armored
bloc *m.* block; lump; tablet, pad of paper; bloc; en — in a lump, in large quantities
blocaille *f.* rubble
blockhaus *m.* blockhouse
bloc-notes *m.* writing pad, note pad
blocus *m.* blockade
blond *a.* blond; fair
bloquer *vt.* to blockade; block, obstruct
blottir *v.*, se — to nestle; crouch; huddle
blouse *f.* blouse; smock; jacket
blouson *m.* jacket (sport or military)
bluette *f.* spark, flash
bluffer *vi. & vi.* to bluff
blutage *m.* act of bluing
bluter *vt.* to sift flour
blutoir *m.* sifter
boa *m.* boa
bobine *f.* bobbin; spool; reel; coil; roll
bobiner *vt.* to roll, spool, wind
bocage *m.* grove, small woods
bocager *a.* wooded
bocal *m.* bottle (druggist's), jar; fishbowl
bock *m.* beer, glass of beer
bœuf *m.* ox; beef; steer; — bourguignon beef in wine sauce
boggie *m.* (rail.) truck, bogie
Bohême *m.* Bohemia; Bohémien *m. & a.* Bohemian
bohème *m.* (fig.) Bohemia; — *a. & n.* Bohemian; person living from day to day
bohémien *a. & m. & f.* bohemian; gypsy; vagabond; unconventional in habits
boire *vt.* to drink; swallow an insult; absorb; — un coup to have a drink; — *m.* drink, drinking
bois *m.* wood; forest; antlers; — de lit bedstead; — contreplaqué plywood; — fondu plastic wood
boisé *a.* wooded; panelled
boiserie *f.* woodwork; panelling, wainscoting
boisseau *m.* bushel
boisson *f.* beverage, drink
boîte *f.* box; can, tin; — de nuit night club
boiter *vi.* to limp
boiteux *a.* lame
boîtier *m.* watch case
boitte *f.* fish bait
bol *m.* bowl; bolus, large pill
bolchevisme *m.* Bolshevism
boléro *m.* bolero; bolero jacket
bolide *m.* meteorite; (fig.) racing car
Bolivie *f.* Bolivia; -n *m. & a.* Bolivian
bombance *f.* feasting
bombarde *f.* mortar; ancestor of oboe
bombarder *vt.* to bombard, bomb
bombardier *m.* bomber (plane); bombardier
bombe *f.* bomb, shell; feast; — glacée molded ice cream; faire la — to have a gay time
bombé *a.* arched, rounded

bomber *vt.* to make round; — *vi.* to become round
bon *a.* good; kind; sound; wholesome; valid; fir; à quoi —? what's the use (of)?; à la —ne heure! fine!; well done; de -ne heure early; — *m.* (com.) bond, coupon
bonace *f.* calm sea; calm
bonasse *a.* simple; innocent; good-natured; -ment *ads.* simply; simple-mindedly
bonbec *m.* gossip
bonbon *m.* candy
bonbonne *f.* demijohn
bonbonnière *f.* candy dish
bond *m.* bound, leap; bounce
bonde *f.* bung hole; bung; plug; sluice gate
bondé *a.* crowded, jammed
bondir *vi.* to bound, leap; bounce
bondon *m.* bung; plug
bonheur *m.* happiness; good fortune, luck; par — luckily
bonhomie *f.* kindness; credulity
bonhomme *m.* fellow, good-natured man
boni *m.* surplus; bonus
bonification *f.* improvement; discount
bonifier *vt.* to improve; give a discount to
boniment *m.* misleading talk, empty talk; quack's show
bonite *f.* bonito
bonjour *m.* good day, good morning, hello
bonne *f.* maid, servant girl
bonnement *ads.* honestly; truly; tout — simply; plainly
bonnet *m.* cap; woman's hat; gros — (fig. & coll.) important person
bonneterie *f.* hosiery, knitwear
bonsoir *m.* good evening; good night
bonté *f.* goodness, kindness
borborygme *m.* growling of the stomach
bord *m.* edge, brink; shore; à — on board; — de la mer seashore; faux — *m.* (naut.) list; hors — outboard
bordage *m.* boards, planking; bulwarks; curb
bordeaux *m.* Bordeaux wine, claret
bordée *f.* (naut.) broadside, volley; tack; watch
bordel *m.* brothel
bordelais *a.* from Bordeaux; sauce -e *f.* Bordeau wine sauce
border *vt.* to border, edge; tuck in (bed); — un lit make a bed
bordereau *m.* itemised account; memorandum, note
bordure *f.* border; curb
bore *m.* boron
boréal *a.* northern
borgne *a.* one-eyed; suspicious (in appearance)
borinage *m.* soft coal mining *or* miner
borique *a.* boric
borne *f.* boundary, limit, milestone
borné *a.* limited, narrow
borner *vt.* to bound, limit
bosquet *m.* small wood, grove
bosse *f.* hump, bump, hunch
bosseler *vt.* to emboss
bossu *a.* hunchbacked
bot *a.*, clubfooted; — *m.* clubfooted person; pied — *m.* clubfoot

botanique f. botany; — a. botanical

botte f. boot; bunch, bundle; sword thrust

botteler vt. to bunch, tie in bunches

botter vt. to shoe, put on shoes; to boot, kick

bottier m. bootmaker (to order)

bottine f. high shoe (with buttons or elastic)

boubouler vi. to hoot like an owl

bouc m. billy-goat; — émissaire scapegoat

boucan m. smokehouse; (coll.) noise, tumult; —er vt. to smoke meat

boucanier m. buccaneer

boucharde f. roller; hammer (having points on the head)

bouche f. mouth; muzzle of a gun; opening; — d'incendie fire hydrant

bouchée f. mouthful; patty filled with creamed food

boucher m. butcher

boucher vt. to cork; block, stop up

boucherie f. butcher shop; slaughter, butchery

bouche-trou m. stopgap

bouchon m. cork, stopper

boucle f. buckle; curl; bend; loop, bow; — d'oreille earring

boucler vt. to buckle; curl, loop; tie; — vi. to curl; buckle

bouclier m. shield

bouddhisme m. Buddhism

bouddhiste m. Buddhist

bouder vi. to pout, sulk

boudeur a. pouting

boudin m. blood sausage; spring (coach); flange

boudiner vt. to twist

boudoir m. boudoir

boue f. mud, filth; (fig.) humiliation, abjection

bouée f. buoy; — de sauvetage life preserver

boueur m. garbage collector

boueux a. muddy

bouffant a. puffed

bouffe a. comical; opéra — light opera

bouffée f. puff; gust

bouffer vt. to puff; (coll.) gulp down food; — vi. to swell, puff

bouffette f. bow of ribbon; tassel (on harness)

bouffi a. swollen, puffed, bloated

bouffir vt. & vi. to expand, swell, bloat

bouffissure f. swelling; extreme vanity

bouffon m. clown; — a. comic, burlesque

bouffonnerie f. buffoonery, burlesque

bouge m. (coll.) burlesque; den; evil place; bulge

bougeoir m. short candlestick

bouger vi. to budge, stir, move

bougie f. candle; sparkplug; probe

bougran m. buckram

bouillabaisse f. fish stew

bouillant a. boiling; (fig.) ardent

bouilleur m. still (liquor); small nuclear reactor

bouilli m. boiled meat

bouillie f. cooked cereal, pap; pulp

bouillir vi. to boil; bubble

bouilloire f. teakettle

bouillon m. broth; à gros —s at a rolling boil

bouillonnement m. boiling; (fig.) agitation

bouillonner vi. to boil up

bouillotte f. hot-water bottle

boulanger m. baker; — vi. to bake bread

boulangerie f. bakery

boule f. ball

bouleau m. birch

bouledogue m. bulldog

bouler vt. to roll like a ball; (coll.) to muff, fail at; send (someone) packing

boulet m. cannon ball

boulette f. little ball, pellet; — de viande meatball

bouleversement m. upset, upheaval

bouleverser vt. to overthrow; upset

boulier m. kind of abacus

boulingrin m. lawn (edged with trees); bowling green

boulodrome m. bowling alley, bowling green

boulon m. metal bolt; —ner vt. to bolt

boulot a. fat, round; — m. (coll.) work; cylindrical loaf of bread

bouquet m. bunch, bouquet; clump; aroma (of wine); large shrimp; hare

bouquetier m. vase

bouquetière f. flower seller

bouquiner vi. to shop for old books

bouquiniste m. dealer in old books

bourbe f. mire, mud, slush

bourbeux a. muddy

bourbier m. mire; difficulty

bourde f. fib; sham; (coll.) error, stupidity

bourdon m. bumblebee; great bell; bourdon; pilgrim's staff; faux — drone

bourdonnement m. buzz, buzzing

bourdonner vi. to buzz, hum

bourg m. large village, small town

bourgade f. little village

bourgeois m. bourgeois; commoner; — a. middle-class

bourgeoisie f. middle class, bourgeoisie

bourgeon m. bud; pimple; —ner vi. to bud

bourgeonnement m. budding

bourgeron m. smock

bourguignon a. from Burgundy

Bourgogne f. Burgundy; — m. Burgundy wine

bourlinguer vi. to roll (ship); (coll.) gad about, travel

bourrade f. sharp blow; poke

bourrage m. stuffing; cramming

bourrasque f. squall; fit, attack, spasm

bourre f. wad; stuffing

bourreau m. executioner

bourreler vt. to torment, torture

bourrelet m. pad; weather stripping

bourrer vt. to stuff, pad, cram; beat, drub

bourrique f. she-ass; (coll.) stupid person

bourru a. rough; brusque; unfermented (wine)

bourse f. purse, bag; scholarship; stock exchange; —s pl. scrotum

boursier m. scholarship student; purse maker; stock dealer

boursouflé a. swollen, puffed up; bombastic

boursoufler vt. to swell, bloat, puff up

bousculer vt. to jostle; throw into disorder

bouse f. dung

bousiller vt. to bungle

boussole f. compass

boustifaille f. feasting; good food

bout m. end, tip; bit, piece; pousser à — to push to the limit; être à — to be exhausted; venir à — de to succeed in

boutade f. outburst, fit; whim

boutefeu m. firebrand; (fig.) trouble maker

bouteille f. bottle; — isolante vacuum bottle

boutique f. shop

boutiquier m. shopkeeper

bouton m. button, knob, handle; bud; pimple; — d'or buttercup

boutonner vt. to button; — vi. to bud

boutonneux a. pimply

boutonnière f. buttonhole

bouture f. cutting (from a plant)

bouturer vi. to take root; — vt. to root (cuttings)

bouvier m. cowherd

bouvillon m. young steer

bouvreuil m. bullfinch

bovin a. bovine

bow-window m. bay window

boxe f. boxing; -r vi. to box; -ur m. boxer

boy m. houseboy

boyau m. gut, intestine, bowel; narrow passage; tube

boycotter vt. to boycott

bracelet m. bracelet; — de caoutchouc rubber band

bracelet-montre m. wristwatch

braconnage m. poaching

braconner vi. & vt. to poach

braconnier m. poacher

braguette f. fly (pants); codpiece

Brahmane m. Brahman

brai m. resin, pitch

braille m. Braille

brailler vi. to bawl, yell

braiment m. bray

braire vi. to bray

braise f. embers, coals

braiser vt. to braise

brancard m. stretcher; shaft

brancardier m. stretcher-bearer

branche f. branch, bough

brancher vt. to connect, plug in; — vi. perch

branchies f. pl. gills

brande f. broom (plant); brand

brandebourg m. braid; facing

brandevin m. brandy

brandir vt. to brandish; wave

brandon m. torch; firebrand

branlant a. shaking, tottering; loose

branle m. impetus; oscillation; mettre en — to put in motion; -r vt. & vi. to shake, oscillate

braquer vt. to aim, point

bras m. arm; shaft; handle; — dessus — dessous arm in arm

braser vt. to braise, solder

brasero m. brazier, charcoal burner

brasier m. brazier; very hot charcoal fire

brasiller vt. to grill over charcoal; — vi. to spark, sparkle

brassage m. brewing; mixing

brassard m. brassard, armband

brasse f. (naut.) fathom; breast stroke (swimming)

brassée f. armful; stroke (swimming)

brasser vt. to brew; mix completely; (naut.) brace

brasserie f. brewery; bar, café

brasseur m. brewer; — d'affaires (fig.) one with many irons in the fire

brassière f. baby shirt; shoulder strap; breast support; — de sauvetage life-jacket

bravache m. braggart; bold front, false bravery; bully

bravade f. bravado

brave a. worthy; honest; courageous, brave

braver vt. to brave, face, defy

bravoure f. bravery; intrepidity

brebis f. ewe; — galeuse black sheep

brèche f. breach; gap

brèche-dent a. snaggle-toothed; missing one front tooth

bréchet m. breastbone (of a bird)

bredouille f. (fig.) sheepishness (as a result of returning empty-handed)

bredouiller vi. to stutter, sputter

bref (brève) a. brief, short; — adv. in short; — m. (eccl.) pastoral letter of the Pope

brelan m. three-of-a-kind; gaming house

breloque f. trinket, watch charm; battre la — to work irregularly; (fig.) go off the track

brème f. bream; flat calm-water fish

Brésil m. Brazil

Brésilien m. & a. Brazilian

Bretagne f. Brittany

bretelle f. sling, strap; (mil.) line of defense; -s pl. suspenders

Breton m. & a. Breton

bretzel m. pretzel

breuvage m. brew, potion; beverage

brevet m. diploma; license; patent

brevetable a. patentable

breveté a. certified, approved, licensed

breveter vt. to patent

bréviaire m. (eccl.) breviary

bribe f. scrap, bit; oddments

bric-à-brac m. bric-a-brac, odds and ends

brick m. brig (ship)

bricole f. trifle; strap, harness; something without importance

bricoler vi. to putter; — vt. (coll.) to cook up

bricoleur m. putterer

bride f. bridle; strap; clamp; à — abattue at full speed

brider vt. to bridle, check

bridge m. bridge (cards, teeth)

bridger vi. to play bridge

bridgeur m. bridge player

brièvement adv. briefly

brièveté f. brevity

brigade f. brigade; général de — m. brigadier general

brigadier m. corporal (cavalry)

brigand m. robber, brigand

brigue f. plot; —r vt. to plot to obtain.

brigueur m. plotter, schemer

brillamment adv. brilliantly

brillant a. brilliant; sparkling; — m. brilliance; diamond

brillantine f. brillantine

briller vi. to shine, sparkle, glitter

brimade f. hazing

brimborion m. small object of little value

brimer vt. to haze

brin m. bit, sprig; — d'herbe blade of grass

brindille f. twig; sprig

brio m. spirit

brioche f. brioche; rich, light roll

brique f. brick

briquet m. lighter; pierre à — f. flint

briquetage m. brickwork

briqueteur m. bricklayer

briquetier m. brickmaker

briquette f. fuel briquette

brisant m. breakers, reef

brise f. breeze

brisé a. broken; folding; jagged; chaise –e f. folding chair; pâte –e f. puff paste

brise-bise m. weather stripping; café curtains

brise-glace m. ice breaker

brise-jet m. deflector

brise-lames m. breakwater

briser vt. to break, shatter, crush

brisque f. service stripe (army)

bristol m. cardboard

brisure f. break; joint

britannique a. British

broc m. jug

brocanteur m. secondhand dealer

brocard m. taunt, gibe

brocart m. brocade

brocatelle f. imitation brocade; variegated marble

broche f. brooch (jewelry); spit; spindle; peg

broché a. brocaded; livre — m. paperbound book

brocher vt. to brocade; bind in paper; sew a binding; be slipshod (in working); nail the shoe of a horse

brochet m. pike (fish)

brochette f. skewer

brocheuse f. stapler

brochure f. pamphlet, brochure

brocoli m. broccoli

brodequin m. buskin; torture boot

broder vt. to embroider; –ie f. embroidery

brome m. bromine

bromure f. bromide

broncher vi. to stumble, falter; flinch; budge

bronches m. pl. bronchial tubes

bronchite f. bronchitis

bronzer vt. to tan; bronze

brook m. brook; waterjump (steeplechase)

broque m. broccoli

broquette f. tack

brossage m. brushing

brosse f. brush; –r vt. to brush

brou m. walnut shell

brouet m. thin broth, stew

brouette f. wheelbarrow

brouillage m. radio jamming

brouillard m. fog, mist

brouille f. quarreling, falling out

brouillé a. confused, mixed up; on the outs with; œufs –s m. pl. scrambled eggs

brouiller vt. to mix up, tangle, confuse; se — to have a falling out, quarrel; become confused

brouillon m. mischief-making; rough draft; muddled person; — a. muddled

broussailles f. pl. brush, underbrush

broussailleux a. overgrown; thick, heavy;

brousse f. brush

brouter vt. to graze

broyer vt. to grind, crush, pulverize

bru f. daughter-in-law

brucelles f. pl. tweezers

brugnon m. clingstone peach

bruine f. drizzle; –r vi. to drizzle

bruire vi. to sound, make a confused noise, rustle

bruissement m. rustling

bruit m. noise; rumor; uproar; fuss, ado

brûlé a. burned; — m. smell of something, burned

brûle-gueule m. short pipe

brûle-parfums m. incense burner

brûle-pourpoint adv. à — point-blank; (fig.) brusquely

brûler vt. to burn; singe; sting; — vi. to burn; se — la cervelle to blow out one's brains

brûleur m. burner

brûloir m. roaster

brûlure f. burn; scald

brumailleux a. misty

brume f. mist, fog; –x vi. to be foggy

brumeux a. misty, foggy

brun a. brown; dark; — m. brown; –e f. twilight

brunâtre a. brownish

brunet a. brownish; –te f. brunette

bruni a. burnished; — m. polish

brunir vt. to burnish; brown, tan; — vi. become dark; tan

brusque a. abrupt, brusque, blunt

brusquer vt. to treat roughly; be abrupt with

brut a. rough, raw; rude; crude; dry

brutal a. brutal, brutish; coarse

brutaliser vt. to treat roughly

brutalité f. brutality, brutishness; cruelty

Bruxelles, Brussels; choux de — m. pl. Brussels sprouts

bruyamment adv. noisily; clamorously

bruyant a. noisy, loud

bruyère f. heath; (bot.) heather; briar

buanderie f. laundry room

buandière f. laundress

bubonique a. bubonic; peste —f. bubonic plague

bûche f. firewood, log; (fig.) stupid person; — de Noël, log-shaped Christmas cake

bûcher vi. to chop wood; work hard; — m. woodshed; stake; pyre

bûcheron m. woodcutter

bûchette f. stick of wood

bûcheur *m.* hard worker, eager beaver (U.S. coll.)

bucolique *a.* bucolic

budgétaire *a.* budgetary

buée *f.* steam; mist, vapor

buffet *m.* buffet; refreshment room; sideboard

buffle *m.* buffalo

building *m.* very large, modern building

buis *m.* boxwood

buisson *m.* bush; thicket

buissonier *a.* hidden in bushes; (fig.) faire l'école —ère to play hooky

bulbe *f.* bulb

bulbeux *a.* bulbous

Bulgare *n. & a.* Bulgarian

Bulgarie *f.* Bulgaria

bulle *f.* bubble; (eccl.) papal bull; papier — *m.* wrapping paper

bulletin *m.* bulletin; ballot; — de bagages baggage check; — scolaire report card

bure *f.* monk's cloth; mine shaft

bureau *m.* office; writing desk; bureau; officers

bureaucrate *m.* bureaucrat

bureaucratie *f.* bureaucracy

bureaucratique *a.* bureaucratic

burette *f.* cruet; burette; oilcan

burin *m.* engraving; burin, engraving tool

burlesque *a.* comical

busc *m.* metal stay, whalebone

buse *f.* buzzard; millrace; shaft, tube

business *m.* work; complicated business

busqué *a.* arched; aquiline

buste *m.* bust (sculpture)

but *m.* mark, aim, purpose, design; goal; de — en blanc *adv.* abruptly; point-blank

butane *m.* butane

buté *a.* obstinate, unmoving, set

butée *f.* abutment

buter *vi.* to abut; — contre bump into, stumble on; — *vt.* to prop, support

butin *m.* booty; prize

butiner *vi.* to pillage; — *vt.* to gather nectar

butoir *m.* buffer

butor *m.* (fig.) lout, good-for-nothing

butte *f.* bluff; hill; en — à exposed to

butter *vt.* to heap earth around (asparagus, celery)

buvable *a.* drinkable

buvard *m.* blotter

buvette *f.* bar; taproom

buveur *m.* drinker; drunkard

Byzance *f.* Byzantium

Byzantin *m. & a.* Byzantine

C

ça *pron.* (coll.) that; c'est — that's it

çà *adv.* here; — et là here and there

cabale *f.* plot, cabal

cabaler *vi.* to plot, cabal

cabalistique *a.* cabalistic; mysterious

cabane *f.* cabin; hut; kennel

cabanon *m.* cabin; padded cell

cabas *m.* basket

cabestan *m.* capstan

cabillaud *m.* fresh cod

cabine *f.* boat cabin; booth; beach cabana

cabinet *m.* closet; study; lawyer's office; cabinet; collection; —s *pl.* toilets, bathrooms

câble *m.* cable

câbler *vt.* to twist; cord; send a cable

câblier *m.* cable-layer

câblogramme *m.* cable

cabochard *a.* obstinate

caboche *f.* hobnail; (coll.) big head

cabochon *m.* upholstery nail

cabot in *m.* strolling comedian; ham actor

cabrer *vt.* put into a passion; se — *vi.* to rear up

cabri *m.* kidskin

cabriole *f.* caper

cabrioler *vi.* to caper

cabriolet *m.* gig; place de — *m.* cabstand

cacao *m.* cocoa

cacaouète, cacaouette, cacauète *f.* peanut

cache *f.* cache, hiding place

cache-cache *m.* hide-and-go-seek

cachemire *m.* cashmere

cache-nez *m.* scarf, muffler

cacher *vt.* to hide, conceal

cache-radiateur *m.* radiator cover

cache-sexe *m.* loin cloth, shorts

cachet *m.* seal, distinctive mark; fee

cacheter *vt.* to seal; close an envelope

cachette *f.* hiding place; en — *adv.* secretly

cachot *m.* dungeon; cell

cacophonie *f.* cacophony

cadastre *m.* land-survey register

cadavre *m.* cadaver, corpse

cadeau *m.* gift, present

cadenas *m.* padlock; -ser *vt.* to padlock

cadencer *vt.* to cadence; put into rhythm

cadet *a.* younger, junior; — *m.* younger son; caddie (golf)

cadmium *m.* cadmium

cadrage *m.* framing

cadran *m.* dial; — solaire sundial

cadre *m.* frame; limit(s); (mil.) cadre

cadrer *vi.* to conform, agree, tally

caduc *a.* old, decrepit; null and void

caducée *m.* (med.) caduceus, symbol of Hermes

caducité *f.* decrepitude

cafard *m.* hypocrite; (coll.) melancholy; cockroach

café *m.* coffee; coffee shop, café

caféier *m.* coffee plant

caféière *f.* coffee plantation

caféine *f.* caffeine

cafetière *f.* coffeepot

cage *f.* cage; stair well; casing

cagnard *a.* indolent, lazy

cagneux *a.* knock-kneed

cagot *m. & a.* bigot; bigoted

cagoule *f.* hood, cowl

cahier *m.* notebook

cahot *m.* jerk, bump, jolt

cahoter *vi.* to jerk, bump, jolt

cahoteux *a.* bumpy

cahute *f.* hut

caille *f.* quail

caillé *m.* curdled milk, curds

caillebotis *m.* (mil.) duckboard; wooden trellis

cailler *vt. & vi.* to curdle, clot
caillot *m.* blood clot
caillou *m.* pebble
cailloutage *m.* paving with pebbles, gravelling
caillouteux *a.* pebbly
cailloutis *m.* mass of broken stones, gravel
caiman *m.* crocodile
caisse *f.* chest; till; cashier's desk; chassis, body; — d'épargne savings bank; grosse — bass drum
caissier *m.* cashier
caisson *m.* caisson, ammunition wagon; maladie des —s *f.* (med.) the bends
cajoler *vt.* to wheedle, cajole
cajolerie *f.* wheedling, cajolery
calamine *f.* calamine; sludge
calamiteux *a.* calamitous
calandre *f.* mangle, roller
calcaire *a.* calcareous, chalky; — *m.* limestone; eau — *f.* hard water
calcédoine *f.* chalcedony
calciner *vt.* to burn, reduce to powder
calcium *m.* calcium
calcul *m.* calculation; calculus; (med.) stone
calculateur *m.* calculator; — *a.* calculating
calculer *vt.* to calculate; machine à — *f.* adding machine
cale *f.* wedge; (naut.) hold; — sèche dry dock
calé *a.* smart
calebasse *f.* gourd
calèche *f.* old-style open carriage
caleçon *m.* undershorts; swimming trunks
calembour *m.* pun
calendrier *m.* calendar
caler *vt.* to prop up; give in; stop; stall, jam
calfater *vt.* to caulk
calfeutrer *vt.* to stop up; se — to shut oneself up
calibre *m.* caliber, quality; cylinder diameter (gun)
calibrer *vt.* to calibrate
calice *m.* chalice; calyx
calicot *m.* calico
calife *m.* caliph
californium *m.* californium
califourchon, (à) *adv.* astride, astraddle
câlin *a.* coaxing, cajoling
câliner *vt.* to coax; cajole
calla *f.* calla lily
calleux *a.* callous; callused
calligraphie *f.* calligraphy, penmanship
callosité *f.* callus
calmant *m.* (med.) sedative
calmar *m.* squid
calme *a. & n.* calm, calmness
calmer *vt.* to calm, appease, quiet; se — to calm down
calomnie *f.* calumny, slander
calorifère *m.* radiator; heater
calorifuge *a.* heat-retaining; insulating
calot *m.* cap, policeman's hat
calotte *f.* skullcap; (coll.) blow on the head
calotter *vt.* to hit on the head
caliquer *vt.* to trace, copy
calumet *m.* pipe, peace pipe
calvados *m.* applejack

calvaire *m.* Calvary; Stations of the Cross
calviniste *n. & a.* Calvinist
calvitie *f.* baldness
camarade *m. & f.* comrade, friend
camaraderie *f.* companionship
camard *a.* snub-nosed
Cambodge *m.* Cambodia
cambouis *m.* sludge; axle grease
cambrer *vt.* to curve, arch
cambrioler *vt.* to burgle
cambrioleur *m.* burglar
cambrure *f.* arch; curve
cambuse *f.* (naut.) storeroom; canteen
came *f.* cam
camée *m.* cameo
caméléon *m.* chameleon
camélia *m.* camellia
camelot *m.* peddler; paper boy
camelote *f.* junk, rubbish
camembert *m.* cheese of Camembert
caméra *f.* camera (movies, pictures) television camera
camion *m.* truck; paint bucket
camion-citerne *m.* tank truck
camionnage *m.* trucking
camionnette *f.* light truck; — sanitaire mobile health unit
camionneur *m.* truck driver, teamster
camisole *f.* camisole; — de force strait jacket
camomille *f.* camomile
camouflage *m.* camouflage
camoufler *vt.* to camouflage
camp *m.* camp; camp site; ficher le — (coll.) to clear out
campagnard *m.* country dweller; — *a.* rustic
campagne *f.* country; countryside; campaign
campé *a.* built, constructed; established
campement *m.* encampment
camper *vt. & vi.* to encamp
campeur *m.* camper
camphre *m.* camphor
camus *a.* flat-nosed
Canada *m.* Canada
Canadien *n. & a.* Canadian
canadienne *f.* mackintosh, jacket; canoe with raised ends
canaille *f.* rabble; scoundrel
canal *m.* canal; irrigation drain
canalisation *f.* canalization; canal-system
canapé *m.* sofa; canapé
canard *m.* duck; rumor; newspaper; sugar soaked in alcohol
canari *m.* canary
cancan *m.* can-can (dance); gossip
cancaner *vi.* to quack; gossip
cancer *m.* cancer; -eux *a.* cancerous
candélabre *m.* candelabrum; sconce
candeur *f.* candor, innocence
candi *m.* rock candy; — *a.* candied
candidat *m.* candidate
candidature *f.* candidacy
candide *a.* naïve, innocent
candir *v.*, se — to crystallize; go to sugar
cane *f.* female duck
caneton *m.* duckling
canette *f.* cane; beer bottle
canevas *m.* canvas

canezou *m.* lace blouse, usually sleeveless
caniche *f.* poodle
canicule *f.* dog days
canif *m.* penknife
canin *a.* canine; dent -e *f.* canine tooth
cannaie *f.* sugar-cane plantation
canne *f.* cane; reed; — à pêche fishing rod
canneler *vt.* to flute (a column)
cannelle *f.* cinnamon; spigot
cannelure *f.* fluting (of a column)
canner *vt.* to cane a chair
cannibale *n.* cannibal
canoë *m.* canoe
canon *m.* cannon; barrel of a gun; — *m.* (eccl.) decree; — *a.* canon; droit — *m.* canon law
cañon *m.* canyon
canonial, canonique *a.* canonical
canoniser *vt.* to canonize
canonnade *f.* volley, barrage
canonner *vt.* to fire cannons on
canonnier *m.* cannoneer
canonnière *f.* popgun; gunboat
canot *m.* rowboat, dinghy; — de sauvetage lifeboat
canotier *m.* rower; sailor hat, straw hat
cantaloup *m.* cantaloupe
cantate *f.* cantata
cantatrice *f.* professional singer
cantine *f.* canteen
cantique *m.* canticle, hymn
canton *m.* canton, district
cantonade *f.*, à la — *adv.* (theat.) in (to) the wings
cantonnement *m.* cantonment, billet(ing)
cantonner *vt.* to billet; district
canular *m.* practical joke
canule *f.* tube of a syringe
caoutchouc *m.* rubber
caoutchoutier *a.* rubber
cap *m.* cape, headland; (naut.) course
capacité *f.* capacity; ability; aptitude
cape *f.* cape; rire sous — to laugh up one's sleeve
capillaire *a.* capillary; vaisseau — *m.* capillary
capitaine *m.* captain
capital *m.* capital; stock; — *a.* capital; main, principal
capitale *f.* chief city, capital; capital letter
capitaliste *m.* capitalist; — *a.* capitalistic
capitation *f.* poll tax
capiteux *a.* heady wine or beer
capitonner *vt.* to stuff, upholster
capitulation *f.* capitulation, surrender
capituler *vt.* to capitulate
capon *a.* shameful, bashful; — *m.* coward, sneak
caporal *m.* corporal; shag (tobacco)
capot *m.* (auto.) hood; cover; casing; — *a.* trickless (cards); confused
capotage *m.* (auto.) overturning
capote *f.* hooded cloak; (mil.) greatcoat; (auto.) top of convertible
capoter *vi.* (auto.) to turn over; (naut.) capsize
câpre *f.* (bot.) caper
caprice *m.* caprice, whim
capricieux *a.* capricious
capsule *f.* capsule; bottle cap; pod; percussion cap

capsuler *vt.* to cap a bottle; — *vi.* to misfire
capter *vt.* to obtain, get hold of insidiously; to tap, bring in a water supply; (rad.) to tune in
captieux *a.* insidious; specious
captif *a. & n.* captive
captivant *a.* captivating
captiver *vt.* to captivate
captivité *f.* captivity
capture *f.* capture; -r *vt.* to capture
capuchon *m.* hood; cover; cap
capucine *f.* nasturtium; Capuchin nun
caque *f.* keg, barrel
caquet *m.* cackling; gossip, slander
caquetage *m.* cackling; gossiping
caqueter *vi.* to cackle; gossip
car *conj.* for, because; — *m.* sightseeing bus
carabe *m.* beetle
carabine *f.* carbine, rifle
carabinier *m.* cavalryman, rifleman; Italian policeman
caraco *m.* loose bodice; jacket
caractère *m.* character; feature; nature
caractériser *vt.* to characterize; distinguish
carafe *f.* decanter, bottle, carafe
carafon *m.* small carafe
Caraïbe *n. & a.* Carib; Mer — *f.* Caribbean Sea
carambolage *m.* jostling, bumping
caramboler *vi.* to carom (billiards)
caramel *m.* drop, chewy candy; — mou caramel
caraméliser *vt.* to caramelize
carapace *f.* turtle shell, carapace
caravane *f.* caravan; convoy; house trailer
caravansérail *m.* caravansary
caravelle *f.* (naut.) caravel
carbonate *m.* carbonate
carbonation *f.* carbonation
carbone *m.* carbon; papier — *m.* carbon paper
carboné *a.* carbonated
carbonique *a.* carbonic
carboniser *vt.* to carbonize
carbonnade *f.* charcoal-grilled meat
carborundum *m.* carborundum
carburant *m.* motor fuel
carburateur *m.* (auto.) carburetor
carbure *m.* carbide
carburéacteur *m.* jet fuel
carcan *m.* pillory
carcasse *f.* carcass; skeleton
cardamome *m.* cardamon
cardan *m.* (mech.) universal joint
carder *vt.* to card wool or flax
cardiaque *a.* cardiac; — *n.* heart patient
cardinal *m. & a.* cardinal
cardiogramme *m.* cardiograph
carême *m.* Lent
carême-prenant *m.* Shrovetide
carence *f.* lack; failure
carène *f.* hull
caréner *vt.* to careen
caresse *f.* caress; endearment
caresser *vt.* to caress, fondle

cargaison f. cargo, shipload
cargo m. freighter, cargo ship
cari m. curry powder
caricature f. caricature
caricaturer vt. to caricature
caricaturiste m. caricaturist
carie f. caries, decay; -r vt. to decay
carillonner vi. to chime
carlingue f. (avi.) cockpit
carmin m. & a. carmine
carnage m. carnage
carnassier a. carniverous
canassière f. bag for game
carnation f. flesh coloring; flesh color
carnaval m. carnival
carné a. flesh-colored; meaty
carnet m. notebook; ticket book; — de chèques checkbook
carnier m. hunting sack
carnivore a. carnivorous
carolingien a. Carolingian
carotide f. & a. carotid
carotte f. carrot; sampling (of rock from a mine)
carpe f. carp
carpette f. rug, mat
carquois m. quiver (for arrows)
carre f. shape; crown; breadth
carré a. square; sensible; firm; obstinate; — m. square; patch; — de papier slip of paper
carreau m. tile; flagstone; diamond (at cards); pane of glass; à -x checked; faire les -x wash the windows
carrefour m. crossroads
carrelage m. tiling, flooring
carreler vt. to tile
carrément adv. squarely; frankly
carrer vt. to square
carrier m. quarry worker
carrière f. career, course; race; quarry; open-pit mine
carriole f. cart
carrossable a. passable for vehicles
carrosse m. coach, carriage
carrosserie f. (auto.) body
carrousel m. cavalry parade; carousel
carrure f. width (of shoulders)
cartable m. cardboard portfolio; briefcase
carte f. card; map; chart; menu; jeu de -s m. deck of cards; — blanche free hand; — grise automobile registration
cartel m. wall clock; cartel, monopoly, trust; challenge
carte-lettre f. correspondence card
carter m. case, casing; (auto.) crankcase; bicycle-chain guard
cartésien a. cartesian, relative to Descartes
cartilagineux a. cartilagenous
cartographe m. cartographer, mapmaker
cartomancie f. fortune telling with cards
carton m. cardboard; cardboard box; cartoon
carton-pâte m. papier-mâché
cartonnage m. cardboard construction; cardboard binding
cartonner vt. to bind in cardboard
cartonnier m. cardboard file; chest of cardboard drawers

cartouche f. cartridge; cartouche; — chargée à balle rifle cartridge; — chargée à plomb shotgun shell
cartouchière f. cartridge bag
cas m. case, circumstance; matter; en tout — in any case. in any event; faire peu de — de to pay little attention to; consider unimportant
casanier m. homebody; — a. retired, domestic
casaque f. jacket; jockey's jacket
cascade f. cascade, waterfall
cascader vi. to cascade
case f. compartment; square, box; hut, cabin; — postale post-office box
caséine f. caseine
casemate f. underground fortification
caser vt. to get someone settled in a job; to put in order; se — to get settled, be established
caserne f. (mil.) barracks
caserner vt. to lodge in barracks
casier m. set of pigeonholes; cabinet of small drawers; — judiciaire police record
casque m. helmet; headpiece, headphones
casquette f. cap
cassant a. brittle; rigid
cassation f. reversal of a court decision; breaking of a noncommissioned officer; cour de — f. supreme court
casse f. breakage; type case; cassis
cassé a. broken, broken-down; hesitant voice
casse-cou m. daredevil; dangerous point in a road
casse-croûte m. snack
casse-noisette, casse-noix m. nutcracker
casser vt. to break, crack; reverse; reduce in rank
casserole f. saucepan
casse-tête m. club; cudgel; (fig.) work requiring close application
cassette f. strongbox
cassis m. black currant; black-currant liqueur; dip in a road
cassolette f. incense burner
cassonade f. brown sugar
cassoulet m. stew with white beans
cassure f. fracture, crack
castagnettes f. pl. castanets
caste f. caste, class
castor m. beaver
castrat m. something castrated
castration f. castration
castrer vt. to castrate
casuel a. chance, accidental; — m. supplementary income
casuiste m. casuist
cataclysme m. cataclysm
catacombes f. pl. catacombs
catafalque m. bier
catalepsie f. catalepsy
cataleptique a. cataleptic
catalogue m. catalog
cataloguer vt. to catalog
catalyse f. catalysis
catalyseur m. catalyst
catalytique a. catalytic
cataplasme m. poultice

catapulte *f.* catapult

cataracte *f.* cataract, waterfall

catarrhe *m.* catarrh

catastrophique *a.* catastrophic

catch *m.* wrestling

catcheur *m.* wrestler

catéchisme *m.* catechism

catégorie *f.* category

catégorique *a.* categorical

caterpillar *m.* caterpillar tread

cathartique *a.* cathartic

cathédrale *f.* cathedral

cathode *f.* cathode

catholique *m.* & *a.* Catholic

cati *m.* glaze, gloss

catir *vt.* to glaze

Caucasien *m.* & *a.* Caucasian

cauchemar *m.* nightmare

cause *f.* cause; source; reason; à — de on account of (law), for the sake of

causer *vt.* to cause; — *vi.* chat

causerie *f.* chat, talk; gossiping; unpretentious conference, informal lecture

causeur *a.* chatty, having art of conversation

causeuse *f.* love seat

caustique *m.* & *a.* caustic

cautérisation *f.* cauterization

cautériser *vt.* to cauterize

caution *f.* bail, security; (fig.) guarantee

cautionnement *m.* bail

cautionner *vt.* to provide bail for, bail out

cavalcade *f.* cavalcade; parade

cavalerie *f.* cavalry

cavalier *m.* horseman, rider; cavalier; gentleman; knight (chess); — *a.* cavalier; unceremonious; piste cavalière *f.* bridle path

cave *f.* cellar; crypt

caveau *m.* cellar

caver *vt.* to dig, excavate

caverne *f.* cavern; cave, den

caverneux *a.* cavernous

caviar *m.* caviar

caviarder *vt.* to cross out; censor

cavité *f.* cavity, hollow

cawcher, kasher *a.* kosher

ce, (cet) *a. m.* this, that; — *pron.* it, that, this; he, she; — qui, — que what, that which

céans *adv.* herein

ceci *pron.* this; the latter

cécité *f.* blindness

céder *vt.* & *vi.* to cede, yield, give up

cédille *f.* (gram.) cedilla

cédrat *m.* citron, citron tree

cèdre *m.* cedar

cédule *f.* rate, schedule

ceindre *vt.* to buckle on, gird; encircle

ceinture *f.* belt; waist, waistline; circle

ceinturer *vt.* to belt, gird

cela *pron.* that, it; this; the former

célébrant *m.* priest officiating at Mass

célébration *f.* celebration; solemn commemoration

célèbre *a.* celebrated, famous

célébrer *vt.* to celebrate; commemorate

célébrité *f.* celebrity

celer *vt.* to hide, conceal

céleri *m.* celery root; celery; — en branches celery stalks

célérité *f.* rapidity, promptness

céleste *a.* celestial, heavenly

célibat *m.* celibacy

célibataire *a.* unmarried; — *m.* bachelor

celle *pron.* the one, she; -ci this one; the latter; -là that one; the former

cellier *m.* storeroom; wine cellar

cellulaire *a.* cellular

cellule *f.* cell, cellule; — photo-électrique (phot.) exposure meter

celluloïd *m.* celluloid

celte *a.* & *m.* celt; celtic

celui *pron. m.* he, the one; -ci the one, this one; — -là the former; that one

cénacle *m.* group, club, circle

cendre *f.* ashes; couleur de — ashen

cendrée *f.* shot, buckshot; cinder track

cendrier *m.* ash tray

Cendrillon *f.* Cinderella

Cène *f.* Last Supper

cénobite *m.* cenobite

cénotaphe *m.* cenotaph

cens *m.* census; minimum tax for voting qualification

censé *a.* supposed, reputed; -ment *adv.* supposedly, reputedly

censeur *m.* censor, censurer; auditer

censurable *a.* censurable; blameworthy

censure *f.* censorship; censure; audit (govt.)

censurer *vt.* to censor; censure, criticize, find fault with

cent *a.* & *m.* one hundred; pour — per cent

centenaire *m.* centenary

centennal *a.* centennial

centiare *m.* 1/100 are, 1 square meter

centième *a.* & *m.* hundredth

centigramme *m.* centigram

centilitre *m.* centiliter

centime *m.* centime

centimètre *m.* centimeter

centipède *m.* centipede

central *a.* central; middle; main, principal; — *m.* center

centraliser *vt.* to centralize

centre *m.* center; middle

centrer *vt.* to center; focus, adjust

centrifuge *a.* centrifugal

centripète *a.* centripetal

centuple *m.* hundredfold (100 times); au — *adv.* a hundredfold

cep *m.* vine, vine stock

cèpe *m.* edible mushroom

cependant *adv.* meanwhile; — *conj.* however; but; still, yet

céramique *a.* ceramic; — *f.* ceramics; ceramic piece; ceramic tile

cerbère *m.* watchdog; guard

cerceau *m.* hoop, ring; -x *m. pl.* pin feathers

cercle *m.* circle, ring; club, group; dial

cercler *vt.* to ring, encircle

cercueil *m.* coffin

céréale *a.* & *f.* cereal plant

cérébral *a.* cerebral

cérémonial *a.* ceremonial; — *m.* ceremonial, ceremony

cérémonie *f.* ceremony, formality; faire

des —s to stand on ceremony

cérémonieux a. ceremonious; formal

cerf m. stag

cerf-volant m. kite

cerisaie f. cherry orchard

cerise f. cherry; — a. & m. cherry-colored, cerise

cerisier m. cherry tree

cerne m. annual ring (of a tree); circle, ring

cerner vt. to surround, ring, encircle; avoir les yeux cernés to have rings under one's eyes

certain a. certain, sure; some; —ement adv. certainly; of course

certes adv. indeed; certainly

certificat m. certificate

certification f. certification

certifier vt. to certify; authenticate

certitude f. certainty

cérumen m. ear wax

céruse f. lead carbonate, white lead

cerveau m. brain; mind

cervelet m. cerebellum

cervelle f. brain, brains; mind

cervical a. cervical, of the neck

ces a. pl. these, those

césar m. Caesar, occidental emperor

césarienne a. (med.) Caesarean (operation)

cesse f. cessation, rest; sans — unceasingly, incessantly, continually

cesser vt. & vi. to cease, stop, discontinue (com.) stop payment

cession f. relinquishing, giving up

cessez-le-feu n. cease-fire

c'est-à-dire conj. that is to say, in other words

césure f. caesura

cette a. f. this, that

ceux pron., m. pl. these, those, the ones

Ceylan m. Ceylon

chablis m. Chablis wine

chacal m. jackal

chacun pron. each; everyone

chadburn m. public address system (ship)

chagrin m. grief, sorrow; worry; goat leather; sheepskin; —é a. sad, worried, upset

chagriner vt. to grieve; worry

chah m. shah

chaîne f. chain; (naut.) cable; mountain range; fabric warp

chaînette f. small chain; point de — chain-stitch

chaînon m. link of a chain

chair f. flesh; pulp; meat; — de poule goose flesh

chaire f. pulpit; professorship, chair

chaise f. chair, seat; — longue reclining chair

chaland n. river or canal barge

Chaldée f. Chaldea

Chaldéen m. & a. Chaldean

châle m. shawl

chalet m. cottage, chalet; — de nécessité public toilet

chaleur f. heat, warmth; zeal

chaleureux a. warm, heated

châlit m. bedstead

chaloupe f. launch

chalumeau m. straw, reed; — oxyacétylénique acetylene torch

chalut m. seine, net

chalutier m. trawler

chamailler v., se — to squabble

chamarrer vt. to deck, ornament

chambellan m. chamberlain

chambre f. room; chamber; — à coucher bedroom; — à air (auto.) inner tube

chambré a. at room temperature (wine); chambered; honeycombed

chambrée f. roommates (army)

chameau m. camel

chamois m. chamois, shammy; — a. buff, chamois

champ m. field; ground; scope; range; subject; — de courses race track; — de tir firing range; — libre clear field

Champagne f. (province) Champagne; — m. champagne

champêtre a. rural

champignon m. mushroom (edible or inedible)

champignonner vi. to mushroom

championnat m. championship

chance f. chance; luck, good luck, good fortune; avoir de la — to be lucky, be fortunate

chancelant a. staggering; wavering; unsteady

chanceler vi. to stagger, waver

chancelier m. chancellor

chancellerie f. chancery; chancellery

chanceux a. risky; lucky

chancre m. canker

chandail m. sweater

chandelier m. candlestick

chandelle f. candle, taper; prop, stay; — de glace icicle

change m. exchange; agent de — stockbroker; cours du — rate of exchange; donner le — à to throw off the track

changeable a. changeable; exchangeable

changeant a. changing, changeable

changement m. change; turn; alteration

changer vt. to change; exchange; turn; alter; — vi. change; — d'avis change one's mind

changeur m. changer

chanoine m. (eccl.) canon

chanson f. song

chansonnier m. song writer; song book

chant m. singing, song; chant; canto; crowing (rooster)

chantage m. blackmail

chanter vt. & vi. to sing; praise

chanteur m., chanteuse f. singer, vocalist; blackmailer

chantier m. workshop; woodyard; shipyard

chantonner vt. & vi. to sing softly; hum

chantoung m. shantung

chantourner vt. to cut out; cut in profile, silhouette

chantre m. singer; poet

chanvre m. hemp; couleur de — flax color

chaos m. chaos, confusion, disorder

chaotique a. chaotic

chape f. cover, covering; coping; (eccl.)

cope; cap; tire tread

chapeau m. hat; cap; cover

chapelet m. rosary, beads

chapelier m. hatmaker, hat seller, hatter

chapelle f. chapel; choir

chapellerie f. hat trade, hats; hat shop

chapelure f. bread crumbs

chaperon m. hood, riding hood; chaperon; coping

chaperonner vt. to chaperon

chapiteau m. capital of a column; top

chapitre m. chapter; item, subject

chapitrer vt. to reprimand, lecture someone

chapon m. capon; head of garlic

chaque a. each, every

char m. chariot; cart; (mil.) tank

charabia m. gibberish

charançon m. weevil

charbon m. coal, ember; (med.) carbuncle; — de bois charcoal; carbon

charbonnage m. coal mining; coal mine

charbonnier m. charcoal-burner; coal-dealer

charcuter vt. to butcher, botch; mangle

charcuterie f. delicatessen

charcutier m. owner of a delicatessen; pork shop

chardon m. thistle

chardonneret m. goldfinch

charge f. load, burden; charge; commission; duty, responsibility; — prep. à — de provided that

chargé a. loaded, laden; full; overcast; lettre —e f. registered letter; — m. assistant, deputy; — d'affaires diplomatic representative

chargement m. loading, lading; charging; cargo

charger vt. to load, burden; entrust; charge; se — de to be responsible for, to take it upon oneself to

chargeur m. loader; stoker; shipper

chariot m. wagon; baby walker; typewriter carriage; — élévateur fork-lift; le grand — Ursa Major; le petit — Ursa Minor

charitable a. charitable

charité f. charity, love of neighbor

charivari m. noise; cacophony

charlatan m. charlatan, quack

charlatanisme m. charlatanism, quackery

charlemagne m., king (cards); faire — to quit while winning

charmant a. charming

charme m. charm, spell

charmer vt. to charm, bewitch; delight

charmeur m. charmer

charmille f. bower, arbor

charnel a. carnal; sensual

charnière f. hinge

charnu a. fleshy, pulpy; plump

charogne f. carrion

charpente f. framework; bois de — m. lumber

charpenter vt. to square (off); construct; frame; shape, cut

charpenterie f. carpentry

charpentier m. carpenter

charpie f. lint

charretée f. cartload

charretier m. driver of a cart

charrette f. cart

charriage m. cartage

charrier vt. to cart, haul

charroi m. cartage

charron m. cartmaker

charrue f. plow

charte f. charter

chartiste m. & f. student of the École des Chartes

chartreuse f. chartreuse liqueur; Carthusian monastery

chas m. eye of a needle

chasse f. hunting; chase; pursuit; — d'eau flush of water

châsse f. shrine; reliquary; (coll.) frame of eyeglasses

chasse-clou m. tool for countersinking; nail puller

chasse-mouches m. fly swatter

chasse-neige m. snowplow

chasse-pierres m. cowcatcher (train)

chasser vt. to hunt; put to flight, drive out; discharge, dismiss, fire; — vi. hunt

chasseresse f. huntress

chasseur m. hunter; bellhop; busboy; fighter plane; fighter pilot; — a. hunting

châssis m. frame, chassis; window frame; hotbed

châssis-presse m. (phot.) printing frame

chasteté f. chastity

chasuble f. chasuble

chat m., chatte f. cat; darling; — en poche pig-in-a-poke

châtaigne f. chestnut

châtaignier m. chestnut tree

châtain a. chestnut color, brown

château m. castle, fort; estate, manor; palace

chateaubriand, châteaubriant m. grilled beef steak

châtelain m. lord of a manor; —e f. lady of a manor; decorative chain

châtelet m. small château

chat-huant m. screech owl

châtier vt. to chastise, punish

châtiment m. punishment, chastisement

chatoiement m. sparkle; play of colors

chaton m. kitten; setting; set stone; (bot.) catkin

chatouillement m. tickling

chatouiller vt. to tickle

chatouilleux a. ticklish; sensitive, touchy

chatoyer vi. to shine, glisten like cat's eye

châtrer vt. to castrate

chatterie f. cajoling, coaxing

chatterton m. friction tape, insulating tape

chaud a. hot, warm; il fait — it is warm (weather); — m. heat, warmth; avoir — to be warm (of body)

chaud-froid m. jellied poultry (chicken) covered with jellied mayonnaise

chaudière f. large kettle, steam boiler

chaudron m. caldron, boiler

chaudronnier m. boilermaker

chauffage m. fuel; heating; stoking

chauffe f. heating; stoking

chauffe-assiette m. hot plate

chauffe-bain *m.* bathroom water heater

chauffe-eau *m.* water heater

chauffe-lit *m.* bed warmer

chauffe-pieds *m.* foot warmer

chauffe-plat *m.* dish warmer

chauffer *vt.* to heat, warm; — *vi.* get warm; overheat

chaufferette *f.* chafing dish; car heater; foot warmer

chauffeur *m.* driver, chauffeur; stoker

chaume *m.* stubble; thatch;

chaumière *f.* thatched cottage

chausse *f.* professor's robe insignia; -s *pl.* breeches

chaussée *f.* causeway; road, pavement

chausse-pied *m.* shoehorn

chausser *vt.* to put on footwear; se — put on one's shoes

chaussette *f.* sock

chausson *m.* slipper, pump; gym shoe; stocking; savate, French boxing; — aux pommes apple turnover

chaussure *f.* shoes, footwear; shoe

chauve *a.* bald

chauve-souris *f.* (zool.) bat

chauvin *a.* chauvinist(ic); — *m.* chauvinist

chaux *f.* lime; blanchir à la — to white-wash; lait de —, blanc de — whitewash; pierre à — *f.* limestone

chef *m.* chief, head, leader; chef; (mus.) conductor; sports captain; — de gare stationmaster

chef-d'œuvre *m.* masterpiece

chef-lieu *m.* chief town of a department

cheik *m.* sheik

chelem (schelem) *m.* slam (at cards)

chemin *m.* way, path, road; means; — de fer railroad, railway; — de traverse crossroad

chemineau *m.* tramp, vagabond, vagrant

cheminée *f.* fireplace; mantelpiece; chimney

cheminer *vi.* to walk, trudge, tramp

cheminot *m.* railway employee

chemise *f.* shirt; chemise; cover, folder; book jacket; -tte *f.* short-sleeved shirt

chemisier *m.* shirtmaker; tailored blouse

chenal *m.* channel

chenapan *m.* bandit, good-for-nothing

chêne *m.* oak

chêneau *m.* rain spout

chêne-liège *m.* cork oak

chenet *m.* andiron

chenil *m.* dog kennel

chenille *f.* caterpillar; chenille; caterpillar tread

chenillé *a.* with a caterpillar tread

chenu *a.* hoary; white with age

chèque *m.* check; toucher un — to cash a check

chéquier *m.* checkbook

cher (chère) *a.* dear; beloved; expensive; high; — *adv.* dear(ly), a great deal

chercher *vt.* to look for, seek; try; aller — to go and get; envoyer — to send for

chercheur *m.* seeker; researcher

chère *f.*, faire bonne — to live well

chéri (chérie) *a.* cherished, dear; — *n.* dear, darling

chérir *vt.* to cherish

cherté *f.* dearness, expensiveness

chérubin *m.* cherub

chétif *a.* puny, sickly; poor; wretched

cheval *m.* (*pl.* chevaux) horse; à — on horseback; — de course race horse; — de race thoroughbred

chevaleresque *a.* chivalrous

chevalerie *f.* chivalry; knighthood

chevalet *m.* sawhorse; easel; frame, stand; violin bridge

chevalier *m.* knight; rider; — d'industrie adventurer; swindler

chevalière *f.* signet ring

chevalin *a.* horse; boucherie -e *f.* horse-meat shop

cheval-vapeur *m.* horsepower

chevauchée *f.* ride on horseback; cavalcade

chevaucher *vi.* to ride a horse; overlap, cross; — *vt.* ride, straddle

chevelu *a.* hairy; long-haired

chevelure *f.* head of hair

chevet *m.* headboard; bolster; livre de — *m.* favorite book, constant reference; table de — *f.* bedside table

cheveu *m.* (*pl.* cheveux) hair of the head

cheville *f.* ankle; peg; pin, bolt; skewer

cheviller *vt.* to pin, bolt together

chèvre *f.* goat; derrick

chevreau *m.* kid, kidskin

chèvrefeuille *m.* honeysuckle

chevrette *f.* kid, goat; andiron; tripod

chevreuil *m.* roebuck; peau de — *f.* buck-skin

chevron *m.* stripe, chevron; rafter

chevronné *a.* experienced; chevroned

chevrotant *a.* trembling, tremulous

chevrotine *f.* buckshot

chez *prep.* at, to, in one's house; among, with; — soi at home

chez-soi *m.* home

chiasse *f.* metal scum, dross; flyspecks

chic *m.* style; — *a.* stylish, smart, fashionable; un — type a good egg (U.S. coll.)

chicane, chicanerie *f.* chicanery; quibbling, quarrel

chicaner *vt. & vi.* to quibble (with)

chiche *a.* stingy; lacking; pois — *m.* chickpea; dwarf pea

chichon *m.* romaine lettuce

chicorée *f.* chicory; curly endive

chicot *m.* stump, stub

chien *m.* dog; gun hammer; — d'arrêt pointer; — couchant setter; — de garde watchdog; temps de — *m.* bad weather

chienlit *m.* mask; disguise

chien-loup *m.* wolf hound

chienne *f.* bitch

chienner *vi.* to whelp

chiffe *f.* rag; (fig.) man without character

chiffon *m.* rag; scrap; chiffon

chiffonnade *f.* shredded greens

chiffonner *vt.* to crimple, rumple, wrinkle; to ruffle, anger

chiffonnier *m.* ragpicker; chest of drawers

chiffre *m.* figure, number; total; code; monogram

chiffrer *vt.* to number, mark; code, put into code; — *vi.* to calculate

chignole f. punch; (coll.) jalopy
chignon m. chignon, bun of hair
Chili m. Chile
chimère f. chimera, fancy
chimérique a. chimerical; fancied, fanciful
chimie f. chemistry
chimique a. chemical; produit — m. chemical
chimiste m. chemist
chimpanzé m. chimpanzee
Chine f. China; encre de — f. India ink
Chinois m. & a. Chinese
chinoiserie f. oriental objet d'art; -s pl. complications
chiot m. pup
chique f. chigger; quid of tobacco
chiquenaude f. flip, flick
chiromancie f. palm reading
chirurgical a. surgical
chirugie f. surgery; -n m. surgeon
chiure f. flyspeck
chlorate m. chlorate
chlore m. chlorine
chlorer vt. to chlorinate
chlorhydrique a. hydrochloric
chloroformer, chloroformiser vt. to chloroform
chlorophylle f. chlorophyll
chlorose f. anemia; (med.) chlorosis, green sickness; yellowing of plant leaves
chlorure m. chloride
chlorurer vt. to chlorinate, chlorinize
choc m. shock, collision; clash; clink of glasses
chocolat m. chocolate
chocolaterie f. chocolate factory
chocolatière f. chocolate pot
chœur m. choir; chorus
choir vi. to fall
choisi a. choice, select
choisir vt. to choose, select, pick
choix a. choice, option, selection; — a. de — choice, prime, best, first-class
choléra m. cholera; (coll.) evil person
cholestérol m. cholesterol
chômage m. unemployment; en — unemployed
chômé a. nonworking
chômer vi. to be unemployed
chômeur m. unemployed worker
chope f. beer mug, stein
chopine f. small mug; half-liter measure
chopper vi. to stumble; blunder
choquant a. shocking
choquer vt. to shock; strike against, knock; clink; se — to collide; be shocked
choral a. choral; — m. religious chant; -e f. choral group, chorus
chorégraphie f. choreography
choriste m. & f. member of the chorus
chorus m. chorus; faire — to repeat in chorus
chose f. thing; matter, case; autre — something else, another thing, another matter; quelque — something
chou m. cabbage; cream puff; dear, darling; — de Bruxelles Brussels sprout
chou-fleur m. cauliflower
chou-rave m. kohlrabi

choucroute f. sauerkraut; — garnie sauerkraut with sausages, ham
chouette f. owl
chow-chow m. chow dog
choyer vt. to pamper
chrême m. holy oil
chrestomathie f. anthology
chrétien (chrétienne) a. & n. Christian
chrétienté f. Christianity, Christendom
Christ m. Christ; Christus; crucifix
christianiser vt. to christianize
christianisme m. Christianity
chromatique a. chromatic
chrome m. chromium; chrome
chromer vt. to chrome-plate
chromosome m. chromosome
chronique a. chronicle; — a. chronic
chroniqueur m. chronicler; reporter
chronologique a. chronological
chronomètre m. chronometer; stop watch
chronométrer vt. to time
chronométreur m. timekeeper
chrysalide f. chrysalis, pupa
chrysanthème m. chrysanthemum
chuchotement m. whisper, whispering
chuchoter vt. & vi. to whisper
chuchoterie f. whispering; gossip
chuchoteur m. whisperer; —a. whispering
chut! interj. sh! quiet!
chute f. fall, downfall; drop; — d'eau cataract
chuter vt. to quiet; shush
Chypre f. Cyprus
ci adv. here; par —, par là here and there
ci-après adv. hereafter
ci-bas adv. below
cible f. target
ciboire m. ciborium
ciboule f. scallion; -tte f. chive
cicatrice f. scar
cicatriser vt. & vi. to scar; heal
cicérone m. guide
ci-dessous adv. hereafter; underneath
ci-dessus adv. aforesaid
ci-devant a. former; — adv. formerly
cidre m. cider; — bouché, — mousseux sparkling cider
ciel m. (pl. cieux) sky, heaven
cierge m. wax candle, church candle
cigale f. grasshopper; cicada
cigare m. cigar
cigogne f. stork
ciguë f. hemlock
ci-inclus a. enclosed
ci-joint a. herewith, enclosed
cil m. eyelash
cilice m. hair shirt
ciller vt. & vi. to blink, wink
cime f. top, summit
ciment m. cement; concrete; -er vt. to cement
cimeterre m. scimitar
cimetière m. cemetery
ciné m. movies
cinéaste m. movie technician
ciné-club m. film group, film club
cinégraphiste m. scenarist
cinéma m. movie theater; movies; cinema
cinémascope m. cinemascope
cinémathèque f. film library

cinématographique *a.* film, motion-picture, cinematographic

cinéphile *m. & f.* movie lover, movie fan

cinéprojecteur *m.* motion-picture projector

cinérama *m.* cinerama

cinétique *a.* kinetic; — *f.* kinetics

Cingalais *m. & a.* Cingalese, of Ceylon

cinglant *a.* biting, cutting; scathing

cingler *vt.* to cut, bite, sting; lash: — *vi.* to sail

cinq *a. & m.* five

cinquantaine *f.* fifty, about fifty; avoir la — be fifty years old

cinquante *a.* fifty

cinquantenaire *m.* fiftieth (golden) anniversary

cinquantième *a. & m.* fiftieth

cinquième *a. & m.* fifth

cintre *m.* arch, curve; hanger

cintrer *vt.* to arch, bend, curve

cirage *m.* shoe polish; wax; polishing, waxing

circoncire *vt.* to circumcise

circoncision *f.* circumcision

circonférence *f.* circumference

circonflexe *a.* circumflex

circonlocution *f.* circumlocution

circonscription *f.* circumscription, district

circonscrire *vt.* to circumscribe, circle; limit

circonspect *a.* circumspect, cautious

circonspection *f.* circumspection, caution, prudence

circonstance *f.* circumstance; case, situation: — *a.* de — occasional; improvised

circonstancié *a.* detailed

circonstanciel *a.* circumstantial; (gram.) adverbial

circonvenir *vt.* to circumvent

circuit *m.* circuit; lap (sports)

circulaire *a. & f.* circular

circulation *f.* circulation; traffic; movement; action

circulatoire *a.* circulatory

circuler *vi.* to circulate; move about; pass from one to another

cire *f.* wax; -r *vt.* to wax; polish

ciré *a.* waxed, polished; toile -e *f.* oilcloth

cireur *m.* polisher, waxer; bootblack

cireuses *f.* (mech.) floor waxer

cireux *a.* waxy

ciron *m.* mite, tiny animal infesting food

cirque *m.* circus

cirrhose *f.* cirrhosis

cirrus *m.* cirrus cloud

cisaille(s) *f.* (pl.) shears (for metal, branches); cuttings, metal shearings

cisailler *vt.* to shear

ciseau *m.* chisel; -x *pl.* scissors, shears, chisels

ciseler *vt.* to chisel; cut, carve; chase; emboss, tool

citadelle *f.* citadel

citadin *m.* townsman, citizen

citation *f.* citation; quotation; summons, subpoena

cité *f.* city; fortified city; group of apartment buildings; — universitaire university dormitories; —s ouvrières housing project

citer *vt.* to quote; cite; summon, subpoena

citerne *f.* cistern

cithare *f.* zither

citoyen *m.*, citoyenne *f.* citizen

citoyenneté *f.* citizenship

citrate *m.* citrate

citrique *a.* citric

citron *m.* lemon; — *a.* lemon-colored — pressé, lemonade

citronnade *f.* lemonade, lemon drink

citronnelle *f.* citronella

citronnier *m.* lemon tree

citrouille *f.* gourd; pumpkin

cive *f.* scallion

civet *m.* stew; — de lièvre jugged hare

civette *f.* civet cat

civière *f.* stretcher, litter; bier

civil *a.* civil; civic; polite; droit — *m.* civil rights, common law; — *m.* civilian

civilisateur *a.* civilizing

civilisation *f.* civilization

civiliser *vt.* to civilize; se — to become civilized

civilité *f.* civility, politeness

civique *a.* civic; civil

civisme *m.* civic pride, civic duty

clabauder *vi.* to clamor, bawl

claie *f.* wicker work; trellis; screen

clair *a.* clear, bright; evident, plain; light; pale; — *m.* light, brightness, highlight; — de lune moonlight

clairet *a.* light; pale

claire-voie *f.* skylight; lattice; (arch.) clerestory

clairière *f.* clearing

clair-obscur *m.* chiaroscuro (art)

clairon *m.* bugle; bugler

claironner *vi.* to sound the bugle; — *vt.* to announce

clairsemé *a.* scattered; sparse, thin

clairvoyance *f.* clairvoyance, second sight

clairvoyant *a.* clear-sighted; clairvoyant

clamer *vt.* to cry out

clameur *f.* clamor, outcry

clamp *m.* surgical clamp

clan *m.* clan, tribe

clandestin *a.* clandestine; secret

clapet *m.* (mech.) valve

clapier *m.* rabbit warren; hutch

clapotement *m.* lapping, splashing

clapoter *vi.* to lap, splash (water)

claque *f.* (theat.) claque; slap; — *m.* opera hat

claquemurer *vt.* to shut up, confine; s'— to shut oneself up at home

claquer *vt.* to clap; slap; bang; click; crack; snap; chatter (teeth); — *vt.* slap; applaud

claqueur *m.* member of the claque

clarifier *vt.* to clarify; se — become clear

clarine *f.* cowbell

clarinette *f.* clarinet

clarté *f.* clearness, clarity, brightness; light

classe *f.* class, order, rank; school

classement *m.* classification; filing

classer *vt.* to class, classify; sort; file

classeur *m.* sorter; file, filing cabinet

classification *f.* classification

classifier *vt.* to classify; sort

classique *a.* classic(al); livre — *m.* school-book, textbook; — *m.* classic; classicist

claudication *f.* limp, limping

clause *f.* clause, stipulation

claustration *f.* confinement; cloistering

clavecin *m.* harpsichord

claveciniste *m. & f.* harpsichordist

clavette *f.* (mech.) retaining pin

clavicule *f.* clavicle, collarbone

clavier *m.* keyboard; key ring

clayère *f.* oyster bed

clé, clef *f.* key; wrench; clue; (mus.) clef; donner un tour de — à to lock; fermer à — to lock; sous — locked, under lock and key

clémence *f.* clemency, leniency, mercy; mildness

clément *a.* lenient, merciful; mild

clenche, clenchette *f.* latch

cleptomane *m. & f.* kleptomaniac

cleptomanie *f.* kleptomania

clerc *m.* cleric; clergyman; clerk; scholar

clergé *m.* clergy

clérical *a.* (eccl.) clerical

cléricalisme *m.* clericalism

cliché *m.* stencil; negative; (print.) cut; cliché; photograph, picture; (coll.) banality

clicher *vt.* to stereotype

client *m.* client; customer; patient

clientèle *f.* customers, clientele; practice

clignement *m.* blinking; wink, winking

cligner *vt. & vi.* to wink; blink

clignotant *m.* (auto.) direction signal

clignotement *m.* twinkling, flickering; blinking

clignoter *vi.* to twinkle; flicker; wink; blink

climat *m.* climate

climatisation *f.* air-conditioning

climatisé *a.* air-conditioned

climatiser *vt.* to air-condition

clin d'œil *m.* twinkling of an eye

clinicien *m.* clinician

clinique *a.* clinical; — *f.* hospital

clinquant *m.* tinsel; foil; gaudiness, showiness

clip *m.* clip, pin (jewelry)

clique *f.* group, band, clique; drum and bugle corps; —s *pl.* wooden shoes

cliquet *m.* pawl, ratchet

cliqueter *vi.* to click; clink; jingle

cliquetis *m.* click(ing); clink(ing); jingling

clisse *f.* draining rack; wicker bottle-wrapping

cliver *vt.* to cleave, cut a gem

cloaque *f.* cesspool; sewer

cloche *f.* bell; glass-bell; blister (skin) — de sauvetage escape hatch (submarine)

clochement *m.* limp, limping

clocher *vi.* to limp

clocher *m.* steeple; bell tower, belfry

cloche-pied *adv.* à — hopping

clocheton *m.* small steeple, spire

clochette *f.* small bell

cloison *f.* partition, wall; — étanche ship's watertight door

cloisonner *vt.* to partition

cloître *m.* cloister; monastery

cloîtrer *vt.* to cloister; confine

clopiner *vi.* to limp

cloque *f.* blister

cloquer *vt. & vi.* to blister

clore *vt.* to close, shut; enclose; conclude, end

clos *a.* closed; concluded; — *m.* closing, end; enclosure

clôture *f.* fence, enclosure; closing; closure; conclusion

clôturer *vt.* to fence, enclose; conclude, end

clou *m.* nail; boil; — de girofle clove

clouer *vt.* to nail, tack; pin, hold down

clouter *vt.* to trim with nails; passage clouté *m.* crosswalk

club *m.* club, society

clystère *m.* enema

coadjuteur *m.* coadjutor

coagulation *f.* coagulation

coaguler *vt.* to coagulate, congeal; se — to clot, coagulate, congeal

coaliser *v.,* se — to form a coalition

coalition *f.* coalition; combination

coassement *m.* croak of a frog

coasser *vi.* to croak

coauteur *m.* coauthor

coaxial *a.* coaxial

cobalt *m.* cobalt

cobaye *m.* guinea pig

cobra *m.* cobra

cocaïne *f.* cocaine

cocaïnomane *m. & f.* cocaine addict

cocarde *f.* cockade

cocasse *a.* funny, ridiculous

coccinelle *f.* wood louse; lady bug (U.S.)

coche *m.* coach, stagecoach, 2-door sedan; barge; — *f.* notch

cocher *m.* coachman, driver; — *vt.* to check; notch; tally

cochère, porte — *f.* carriage entrance

cochon *m.* hog, pig; (fig.) swine; — de lait suckling pig; — d'Inde guinea pig

cockpit *m.* (avi.) cockpit

cocktail *m.* cocktail; cocktail party

coco *m.,* noix de — *f.* coconut

cocon *m.* cocoon

cocorico *m.* crow (of a cock)

cocotier *m.* coconut palm

cocotte *f.* saucepan, casserole; (coll.) hussy, street walker

code *m.* code; law

codéine *f.* codeine

codicille *m.* codicil

codifier *vt.* to codify; code

coefficient *m.* coefficient; factor

coéquipier *m.* teammate

coercitif *a.* coercive

coercition *f.* coercion

cœur *m.* heart; feeling(s); courage; center, middle; à contre — against one's will; avoir mal au — to be sick to one's stomach; donner mal au — to nauseate

coffre *m.* chest, box, trunk, coffer

coffre-fort *m.* safe, strongbox

coffrer *vt.* to place in safety; (coll.) lock up, jail

coffret *m.* small box; — à bijoux jewel case

cognac *m.* brandy from Cognac

cognassier *m.* quince tree

cognée *f.* axe, hatchet

cogner *vt.* to hammer, knock; bump; — *vi.* knock; bump

cohérence *f.* coherence

cohérent *a.* coherent

cohéritier *m.* joint heir

cohésion *f.* cohesion, cohesiveness

cohorte *f.* cohort

cohue *f.* crowd, throng

coi, (coite) *a.* calm, quiet, peaceful

coiffer *vt.* to put on a head covering; cap; to dress the hair; se — to arrange one's hair or hat.

coiffeur *m.* hairdresser; barber

coiffeuse *f.* hairdresser; dressing table

coin *m.* corner; nook; quiet place, spot; wedge

coincer *vt.* to wedge; se — *vi.* to jam, stick

coïncidence *f.* coincidence

coïncider *vi.* to coincide

coing *m.* quince

col *m.* collar; neck; (geog.) mountain pass

coléoptère *m.* beetle

colère *f.* anger; en — angry; mettre en— to anger; se mettre en — become very angry, lose one's temper

coléreux *a.* quick-tempered

colibri *m.* hummingbird

colifichet *m.* trinket

colimaçon *m.* snail; en — spiral

colin-maillard *m.* blindman's buff

colique *f.* colic

colis *m.* package, parcel

côlite *f.* colitis

collaborateur *m.*, collaboratrice *f.* collaborator; contributor; associate

collaboration *f.* collaboration

collaborer *vi.* to collaborate; contribute

collage *m.* pasting, gluing, mounting; collage; sizing; (coll.) common-law marriage

collant *a.* tight-fitting; sticky

collatéral *a.* & *m.* collateral

collation *f.* light meal; collation; conferring

collationner *vi.* to have a snack; — *vt.* to collate; confer

colle *f.* glue, paste

collecteur *m.* collector; (elec.) commutator; tuyau — sewage collector

collectif *a.* collective; joint, cooperative

collection *f.* collection, collecting

collectionner *vt.* to collect

collectionneur *m.* collector

collectivisme *m.* collectivism

collectivité *f.* collectivity

collège *m.* secondary school; college

collégial *a.* collegiate; (eccl.) of the chapter (canon); —e *f.* collegiate church

collègue *m.* colleague

coller *vt.* to paste, glue; stick; press; — *vi.* stick; cling

collerette *f.* cloth collar; metal flange; ring, pipe joint

collet *m.* collar; flange; neck; snare

colleter *vt.* to collar; s'— wrestle, scuffle with

collier *m.* necklace; harness collar; metal ring; (fig.) coup de — great effort

colline *f.* hill

collision *f.* collision

colonnade *f.* collonade

colloque *m.* conversation; conference

collusion *f.* collusion

colocataire *m.* & *f.* co-tenant

colombe *f.* dove

colombophile *m.* & *f.* pigeon raiser, pigeon fancier

colon *m.* colonist; settler

côlon *m.* (anat.) colon

colonial *a.* & *m.* colonial; soldier of colonial army

colonialisme *m.* colonialism

colonie *f.* colony; settlement

colonisation *f.* colonization

coloniser *vt.* to colonize; settle

colonne *f.* column, pillar

colophane *f.* colophony, rosin

coloration *f.* color, coloring

coloré *a.* colored; ruddy

colorer, colorier *vt.* to color

coloris *m.* coloring

colossal *a.* colossal, huge

colosse *m.* colossus, giant

colporter *vt.* to peddle; spread news

colporteur *m.* peddler

columbarium *m.* columbarium

comateux *a.* comatose

combat *m.* battle, fight, combat, struggle; hors de — out of action

combattant *m.* combatant; (ancien) — ex-serviceman, veteran

combattre *vt.* & *vi.* to fight

combien *adv.* how much, how many

combinaison *f.* combination; coveralls; (chem.) compound; machination; — s *f. pl.* lady's undergarment

combiné *m.* compound; — *a.* combined, joint

combiner *vt.* to combine, unite; contrive

comble *m.* top, summit; roofing; limit, end; — *a.* full, packed

combler *vt.* to fill; heap; overwhelm

combustible *a.* inflammable; — *m.* fuel

combustion *f.* combustion

comédie *f.* comedy

comédien *m.* actor; –ne *f.* actress

comédon *m.* blackhead

comestible *m.* food, provision; — *a.* edible

comète *f.* comet

comique *a.* comic(al), funny; — *m.* comic, comedian; comic author; comedy

comité *m.* committee

commandant *m.* commander; major; commanding officer

commande *f.* order for goods; control, lever; control panel; fait sur — made to order

commandement *m.* command, order; commandment

commander *vt.* & *vi.* to command, order; control

commandeur *m.* (mil.) cavalry commander

commanditaire *m.* backer, financier

commandite *f.* joint-stock company

commanditer *vt.* to back, finance

commando *m.* (mil.) detachment, detail; commando group

comme *adv.* as, like; how; sort of; — *conj.*

as, since

commémoraison f. commemoration (of a saint)

commémoratif a. commemorative; memorial

commémoration f. commemoration

commémorer vt. to commemorate

commençant m. beginner

commencement m. beginning

commencer vt. & vi. to begin, commence

comment adv. how; —! interj. what!

commentaire m. comment, commentary; —s pl. memoirs

commentateur m. commentator; author of commentaries

commenter vt. to comment on; annotate

commérage m. gossip

commerçant m. merchant, businessman; — a. commercial, business

commercer vi. to deal, trade, do business

commercial a. commercial, business; —e f. station wagon

commère f. gossip, busybody

commettre vt. to commit; do, make

commis m. clerk; grand — de l'État high official; — voyageur traveling salesman

commisération f. commiseration, pity

commissaire m. commissioner; commissar; purser

commissaire-priseur m. appraiser; auctioneer

commissariat m. commissariat; function of a commissioner; — de police police station

commission f. commission; committee, board; errand; (com.) payment for selling

commissionnaire m. factor; agent; messenger

commissionner vt. to delegate; authorize

commode f. chest of drawers; — a. convenient, comfortable, spacious; accommodating

commodité f. comfort, convenience, accommodation

commotion f. concussion (brain); commotion; shock

commuer vt. to commute (law)

commun a. common, ordinary, usual; commonplace; en — in common; cooperative(ly)

communal a. common; communal

communauté f. community

commune f. township, commune

communiant m. (eccl.) communicant

communicant a. communicating

communicatif a. communicative

communication f. communication; message; phone call; fausse — wrong number

communier vi. to take communion; commune

communiqué m. press release; official communication

communiquer vt. & vi. to communicate

communisant m. communist sympathizer

communisme m. communism

communiste m. & f. communist

commutation f. commutation

commutateur m. (elec.) switch, commutator

commutatrice f. (elec.) transformer

compact a. compact, solid

compagne f. female companion; spouse

compagnie f. company

compagnon m. companion, associate; worker, co-worker

comparable a. comparable

comparaison f. comparison

comparaître vi. (law) to appear

comparatif a. & m. comparative

comparé a. comparative; compared

comparer vt. to compare

comparoir vi. to appear in court

comparse m. & f. (theat.) supernumerary

compartiment m. compartment; division

comparution f. court appearance

compas m. compass; calipers; (fig.) standard

compassé a. stiff, set; formal; regularized

compasser vt. to measure with compass; weigh, consider

compatibilité a. compatible; — f. compatability

compatir vi. to sympathize

compatissant a. compassionate; sympathetic

compatriote m. fellow countryman

compensateur a. compensating; equalising; — m. compensator; equalizer

compensation f. compensation; equalisation; adjustment; chambre de — f. clearing house

compenser vt. to compensate, make up for; equalize; adjust

compérage m. gossip; plotting

compétence f. competence; competency; (fig.) jurisdiction

compétent a. competent; reliable

compilateur m. compiler

compilation f. compilation, compiling

compiler vt. to compile

complainte f. lament

complaire vi. to please; se — à take pleasure in, delight in

complaisance f. kindness, goodness, obligingness; complacency

complaisant a. obliging; compliant; complacent

complément m. complement

complémentaire a. complementary

complet (complète) a. complete; full; — m. man's suit; au — full; au grand — in force; at full strength

compléter vt. to complete; finish

complexe a. complex, complicated; (math.) compound; — m. complex

complexion f. constitution, disposition

complexité f. complexity

complice m. & f. accomplice, accessory

complicité f. complicity

compliment m. compliment

complimenter vt. to compliment; congratulate

compliqué a. complicated, intricate

compliquer vt. to complicate; se — become complicated

complot m. plot, conspiracy

comploter vt. to plot, conspire

comploteur m. plotter, conspirator

componction *f.* compunction

comportement *m.* behavior

comporter *vt.* to permit; comprise; se — to behave

composant *a. & m.* component

composé *a.* composed; compound, composite; — *m.* compound

composer *vt. & vi.* to compose; compound; write; set (type); se — de consist of, be composed of

compositeur *m.* composer; compositor

composition *f.* composition; composing; compound; typesetting

compost *m.* compost

composteur *m.* (print.) composing stick

compotier *m.* compote dish; dish for sauce

compréhensible *a.* comprehensible

compréhensif *a.* comprehensive; understanding

compréhension *f.* comprehension, understanding

comprendre *vt.* to understand; include, comprise; se faire — make oneself understood

compresse *f.* compress

compresseur *m.* compressor; rouleau — *m.* steam roller

compression *f.* compression; repression

comprimé *m.* tablet, pill; — *a.* compressed

comprimer *vt.* to compress; repress

compris *a.* understood, included; y — including

compromettre *vt. & vi.* to compromise; expose, put in embarrassment *or* peril

compromis *m.* compromise, mutual agreement

comptabilité *f.* accounting, bookkeeping

comptable *m.* accountant, bookkeeper; — *a.* accountable

comptant *a.* counted on, prompt; argent — *m.* ready money, cash

compte *m.* account, computation; value; profit; à — on account; à bon — cheap; — rendu *m.* report; review; se rendre — de to realize, be aware of; tenir — de take into account, bear in mind

compte-fils *m.* magnifier

compte-gouttes *m.* medicine dropper

compter *vt.* to count; number; expect; — *vi.* count, rely; sans — to say nothing of, not to mention, not counting

compte-tours *m.* revolution counter

compteur *m.* meter; speedometer; counter; comptometer

comptoir *m.* counter; cashier's desk

compulser *vt.* to subpoena records; to examine records

computation *f.* computation

computer *vt.* to compute

comte *m.* count, earl

comté *m.* county, earldom

comtesse *f.* countess

concasser *vt.* to crush

concasseur *m.* stone crusher, crushing machine

concéder *vt.* to concede, grant, admit

concentration *f.* concentration

concentré *a.* concentrated; (fig.) taciturn

concentrer *vt.* to concentrate, condense, repress; se — concentrate

concentrique *a.* concentric

concept *m.* concept, idea

conception *f.* conception; idea; image

concernant *prep.* concerning, about

concerner *vt.* to concern

concert *m.* concert; harmony; de — avec together with, hand in hand with

concertant *a.* performing together

concerté *a.* concerted

concerter *vt.* to plan, concert

concession *f.* concession; grant

concevable *a.* conceivable

concevoir *vt.* to conceive; imagine, understand

concierge *m. & f.* doorkeeper, janitor

concile *m.* (eccl.) council

conciliateur *a.* conciliating, conciliatory

conciliation *f.* conciliation; reconciliation

concilier *vt.* to conciliate; reconcile

concis *a.* concise, short

concision *f.* conciseness, brevity

concitoyen *m.* fellow citizen

conclave *m.* conclave

concluant *a.* conclusive

conclure *vt.* to conclude; decide; end, finish; drive *or* strike a bargain

conclusif *a.* conclusive

conclusion *f.* conclusion; decision; end, ending

concombre *m.* cucumber

concordance *f.* concordance; (gram.) agreement

concordat *m.* concordat, agreement

concorde *f.* harmony, concord, agreement

concorder *vi.* to agree

concourir *vi.* to compete; converge; cooperate

concours *m.* competitive examination; concourse; assistance, aid; concurrence

concret *a.* concrete

concupiscence *f.* lust

concuremment *adv.* concurrently; jointly

concurrence *f.* competition; concurrence

concurrencer *vt.* to rival; compete with

concurrent *a.* competitive; — *m.* competitor

concussion *f.* extortion, embezzlement

condamnable *a.* blameworthy

condamnation *f.* condemnation; blame, censure; legal sentence *or* judgment

condamner *vt.* to condemn, sentence; blame, censure, criticize

condensateur *m.* condenser

condensation *f.* condensation; gas liquidation; condensing

condensé *m.* resumé

condenser *vt.* to condense, liquify gas; se — condense (fig.) to group, assemble

condenseur *m.* condenser

condescendance *f.* condescension

condescendre *vi.* to condescend

condiment *m.* condiment, seasoning, spice

condisciple *m.* fellow student

condition *f.* condition, state; circumstance(s); position; rank; status; station; à — on approval; à — que on condition that; sans — unconditional

conditionnel *a.* conditional; — *m.* (gram.) conditional

conditionner *vt.* to condition

condolèance *f.* condolence

conducteur *m.*, conductrice *f.* leader; driver; motorman; (elec.) conductor; overseer, foreman; — *a.* conducting; driving

conduire *vt.* to conduct, lead; drive; se — to behave; permis de — *m.* driver's license

conduit *m.* conduit, pipe, main

conduite *f.* conduct, behavior; driving; direction, supervision; flue; main; tubing

cône *m.* cone

confection *f.* making; manufacturing; ready-made clothes

confectionner *vt.* to make; manufacture

confédération *f.* confederation, confederacy

confédérer *vt.* to confederate

conférence *f.* lecture; conference

conférencier *m.* lecturer

conférer *vt.* to compare; confer, bestow; — *vi.* confer, discuss

confesser *vt.* to confess; se — (eccl.) to confess

confesseur *m.* (eccl.) confessor

confession *f.* confession

confiance *f.* confidence; reliance; trust; (digne) de — reliable, trustworthy

confiant *a.* confiding; confident

confidamment *adv.* confidently, in confidence

confidence *f.* confidence, trust; secrecy; secret

confident *m.*, confidente *f.* trusted friend, confidant

confidentiel *a.* confidential

confier *vt.* to confide; trust, entrust; se — à to put one's trust in

configuration *f.* configuration

confiner *vt.* to confine; — *vi.* to border, verge on

confins *m. pl.* confines, limits

confire *vt.* to preserve, pickle, candy

confirmation *f.* confirmation

confirmer *vt.* to confirm

confiserie *f.* confectionary

confiseur *m.* confectioner

confisquer *vt.* to confiscate

confit *a.* preserved; candied

confiture *f.* jam, preserve(s)

confiturière *f.* jam dish; dealer in preserves

conflagration *f.* conflagration

conflit *m.* conflict, clash, struggle

confluence *f.* confluence

confluer *vi.* to meet, come together

confondre *vt.* to confound, mingle, confuse, mistake; disconcert, upset; se — to mix, blend

conformation *f.* conformation

conforme *a.* conformable, consistent; — à corresponding to; according to; copie — *f.* true copy

conformément *adv.* in conformity; — à in accordance with, according to

conformer *vt.* to form; conform; se — to conform, comply

conformiste *m. & f.* conformist

conformité *f.* conformity; similarity

confort *m.* comfort

confortable *a.* comfortable

confrère *m.* colleague

confrérie *f.* brotherhood

confronter *vt.* to confront, compare

confus *a.* confused; embarassed; blurred; overcome

confusément *adv.* confusedly; vaguely

confusion *f.* confusion; embarrassment

congé *m.* leave, furlough; dismissal; vacation; jour de — *m.* holiday

congédiement *m.* dismissal

congédier *vt.* to discharge, dismiss

congélation *f.* freezing; congealing, coagulation

congeler *vt.* to congeal, freeze

congère *f.* snowdrift

congestion *f.* congestion; accumulation in blood vessels

congestionné *a.* flushed face

congestionner *vt.* to congest; se — to become congested

conglomérat *m.* conglomerate

conglomérer *vt.* to conglomerate

congre *m.* conger eel

congrégation *f.* congregation

congrès *m.* congress

congressiste *m.* delegate

congru *a.* precise; sufficient; suitable

conifère *a.* coniferous; — *m.* conifer

conique *a.* conic(al)

conjecturer *vt.* to conjecture, guess

conjoindre *vt.* to join in marriage; unite

conjoint *a.* joined, joint; married

conjoncteur *m.* automatic switch

conjonctif *a.* (gram.) conjunctive; relative; (anat.) connective

conjonction *f.* conjunction; connection, joining, union

conjoncture *f.* contingency, conjuncture, juncture

conjugaison *f.* conjugation

conjugal *a.* conjugal; vie –e *f.* marriage, married life

conjuguer *vt.* to join; (gram.) to conjugate

conjurateur *m.* conjurer

conjuration *f.* conspiracy, plot; exorcism

conjuré *m.* conspirator, plotter

conjurer *vt.* to implore, beg, beseech; conspire, plot

connaissance *f.* knowledge; acquaintance; consciousness; faire la — de to meet, become acquainted with a person; perdre — to lose consciousness; sans — unconscious

connaissement *m.* bill of lading

connaisseur *m.* connoisseur, judge, expert

connaître *vt.* to know; be acquainted with; se — à, se — en be an expert in, be a good judge of

connecter *vt.* (elec.) to connect

connecteur *m.* (elec.) connector

connexe *a.* connected; related

connexion *f.* connection; relation

connexité *f.* relationship, connection

connivence *f.* connivance

connu *a.* known, well-known

conque *f.* conch; conch shell; (anat.) concha

conquérant *a.* conquering; — *m.* conqueror

conquérir *vt.* to conquer; gain

conquête *f.* conquest; acquired property, acquisition

consacré *a.* consecrated; hallowed; sacred; time-honored

consacrer *vt.* to consecrate; ordain; sanctify; dedicate, devote

consanguin *a.* related on the father's side

consciemment *adv.* consciously

conscience *f.* conscience, consciousness; conscientiousness; avoir — de to be aware of, be conscious of; avoir de la — be conscientious; en — *adv.* in truth

consciencieux *a.* conscientious

conscient *a.* conscious, aware

conscrit *m.* recruit, conscript, draftee

consécration *f.* consecration; dedication

consécutif *a.* consecutive

conseil *m.* counsel, advice; council, committee; — d'administration board of directors; — d'Etat legislative advisory group; — de guerre court-martial; — de révision draft board; — de prud'hommes labor-management arbitration committee; — des ministres cabinet; — général local (departmental) legislature

conseiller *m.* counsellor; councillor; adviser

conseiller *vt.* to counsel, advise, recommend

consensus *m.* consensus

consentement *m.* consent; approval

consentir *vi.* to consent, agree, approve; — *vt.* to grant; approve

conséquemment *adv.* consequently

conséquence *f.* consequence, conclusion, result; importance; inference

conséquent *a.* consistent; (coll.) important; par — consequently

conservateur *a.* preserving; conservative; — *m.* keeper; curator; librarian; conservative

conservation *f.* conservation, preservation; keeping

conservatisme *m.* conservatism

conservatoire *m.* conservatory, school of music

conserve *f.* preserved food, canned food; de — preserved; canned; -s *pl.* preserves, canned goods

conserver *vt.* to conserve, preserve; keep, hold, maintain; se — to keep, remain preserved

conserverie *f.* canning factory *or* industry

considérable *a.* considerable; extensive, large; important

considérant *m.* motive

considération *f.* consideration; regard, respect

considérer *vt.* to consider; regard

consignataire *m.* (com.) consignee; legal trustee

consignation *f.* (com.) consignment

consigne *f.* (mil.) order, instructions; password; (rail.) checkroom

consigner *vt.* to consign; confine; deposit money; check baggage

consistance *f.* consistency; stability

consistant *a.* firm, set

consister *vi.* to consist

consolateur *a.* consoling; — *m.* consoler

console *f.* bracket; console table; console organ

consoler *vt.* to console, comfort

consolider *vt.* to consolidate; se — to heal

consommateur *m.* consumer; café customer

consommation *f.* consummation; consumption; drink, beverage

consommé *a.* consummate, perfect; — *m.* consommé

consommer *vt.* to consummate; consume

consomptif *a.* consumptive

consonance *f.* consonance

consonne *f.* (gram.) consonant

consort *a.* consort; prince — *m.* prince consort; -s *m. pl.* interested parties

consortium *m.* association, company, group

conspirateur *m.* conspirator, plotter

conspirer *vt. & vi.* to conspire, plot

conspuer *vt.* to degrade publicly

constable *m.* constable, policeman

constamment *adv.* constantly

constance *f.* constancy; perseverance

constant *a.* constant; unchanging, steady; uniform; (math.) invariable

constat *m.* official declaration, examination

constatation *f.* proof; statement, declaration; authentication

constater *vt.* to declare; take note of; certify; establish

constellé *a.* spangled, star-spangled

consteller *vt.* to bespangle

consterner *vt.* to consternate, dismay

constipant *a.* constipating

constipation *f.* constipation

constituant *a.* constituent, component; — *m.* voter, constituent

constituer *vt.* to constitute, set up; make, take; — prisonnier to take prisoner, take into custody

constitutif *a.* constituent

constitution *f.* constitution; composition

constitutionnalité *f.* constitutionality

constitutionnel *a.* constitutional

constricteur *a. & m.* constrictor

constriction *f.* constriction; compression of diameter

constructeur *m.* constructor; builder, engineer

constructif *a.* constructive

construction *f.* construction, building; — mécanique mechanical engineering

construire *vt.* to construct; build; (gram.) to construe

consulaire *a.* consular

consulat *m.* consulate; consulship

consultant *a.* consulting; — *m.* consultant

consultation *f.* consultation

consulte *f.* (pol. & eccl.) consultation

consulter *vt.* to consult

consumer *vt.* to consume, destroy; use up

contact *m.* contact; touch; connection, switch

contacter *vt.* to contact, come in contact with

contagieux *a.* contagious

container *m.* case

contamination *f.* contamination

contaminer *vt.* to contaminate

conte *m.* tale, story

contemplateur *m.* contemplator

contemplatif *a.* contemplative

contemplation *f.* contemplation; meditation, thought

contempler *vt.* to contemplate; meditate

contemporain *a. & m.* contemporary

contempteur *a.* contemptuous

contenance *f.* countenance; content(s), capacity

contenant *m.* container

contenir *vt.* to contain; restrain

content *a.* content, satisfied, happy, glad

contentement *m.* contentment, satisfaction

contenter *vt.* to content, satisfy; se — de to be content with, be satisfied with

contentieux *a.* contentious

contention *f.* contention; contest

contenu *m.* contents

conter *vt.* to relate, tell

contestable *a.* disputable, debatable

contestation *f.* dispute

conteste, sans — *adv.* incontestably

contester *vt. & vi.* to dispute, contest

conteur *m.* storyteller

contexte *m.* context

contexture *f.* structure, arrangement

contigu (contiguë) *a.* adjoining, adjacent, contiguous

contiguïté *f.* contiguity

continence *f.* continence

continent *m.* continent; —al *m.* continental

contingence *f.* contingency

contingent *a.* contingent; — *m.* contingent; quota

continu *a.* continual, continuous

continuel *a.* continual; continuous

continûment *adv.* continually; continuously

continuer *vt. & vi.* to continue

continuité *f.* continuity

contondant *a.* blunt

contorsion *f.* contortion

contorsionner *vt.* to contort

contorsionniste *m. & f.* contortionist

contour *m.* outline, contour

contourné *a.* twisted; affected

contournement *m.* detour, bypass

contourner *vt.* to outline, shape; bypass, skirt; twist, distort; — la loi to get around the law

contractant *m.* person contracting; — *a.* contracting

contracte *a.* contracted, agreed

contracté *a.* contracted (made shorter)

contracter *vt.* to contract; acquire; se — to contract, narrow

contractuel *a.* contractual; stipulated by contract

contradiction *f.* contradiction

contradictoire *a.* contradictory

contraindre *vt.* to compel, restrain, constrain, force

contraint *a.* constrained, forced

contrainte *f.* restraint; force, constraint

contraire *a.* contrary, opposite; against; au — on the contrary

contrarier *vt.* to thwart; vex, annoy; go against

contrariété *f.* contrariness; annoyance

contraste *m.* contrast

contraster *vt. & vi.* to contrast

contrat *m.* contract, agreement

contravention *f.* violation, misdemeanor; traffic ticket

contre *prep.* against; contrary to; near by; — *adv.* against; near by; — *m.* counter, opposite; le pour et le — the pros and cons; par — on the other hand

contre-amiral *m.* rear admiral

contre-appel *m.* second appeal

contre-attaque *f.* counterattack

contre-attaquer *vt.* to counterattack

contre-avions *a.* antiaircraft

contrebalancer *vt.* to counterbalance

contrebande *f.* contraband; smuggling

contrebandier *m.* smuggler

contrebas, en — *adv.* downwards

contrebasse *f.* double bass; tuba; double bass player

contrebassiste, contrebassier *m.* double bass player

contrebasson *m.* contrabassoon

contre-boutant *m.* buttress

contre-bouter, contre-buter *vt.* to buttress

contrecarrer *vt.* to foil, thwart; oppose

contre-chant *m.* counter theme

contrecœur *m.* back of a fireplace; fireplace plaque; (rail.) guard rail; à — *adv.* unwillingly, reluctantly

contrecoup *m.* rebound; backfire; result

contredanse *f.* contredanse, country dance

contrée *f.* country, region

contre-écrou *m.* lock nut

contre-épaulette *f.* epaulette without fringe

contre-espion *m.* counterspy

contre-espionnage *m.* counterespionnage

contrefaçon *f.* counterfeit; forgery; counterfeiting; plagiarism

contrefacteur *m.* forger, counterfeiter

contrefaction *f.* counterfeiting

contrefaire *vt.* to counterfeit, forge, imitate; disguise

contre-feu *m.* reverse fire (fire fighting)

contre-fil *m.* opposite direction

contrefort *m.* buttress; spur; foothill(s); reinforcement

contre-haut, en — *adv.* up, upwards, above

contre-jour *m.* (photo.) light from opposite side of an object, à — *adv.* against the light

contremaître *m.* foreman; (naut.) petty officer

contremander *vt.* to countermand

contremarque *f.* countersign; pass-out check

contrepartie *f.* counterpart; return match (sports)

contre-pas *m.* rapid half-step; change in step (marching)

contre-plaqué *a.* laminated; bois — *m.* plywood

contre-plaquer *vt.* to laminate, manufac-

ture plywood
contrepoids *m.* counterweight, counterbalance
còntre-poil *m.* opposite direction; à —
adv. against the grain
contrepoint *m.* (mus.) counterpoint
contre-pointer *vt.* to quilt
contrepoison *m.* antidote
contrer *vt.* to counter; — *vi.* to double
(at cards)
contre-rail *m.* guard rail
contre-révolution *f.* counterrevolution
contre-révolutionnaire *a. & m. & f.* coun-
terrevolutionary
contresens *m.* misinterpretation
contresigner *vt.* to countersign
contretemps *m.* mishap; delay; (mus.)
syncopation; à — inopportunely
contre-torpilleur *m.* destroyer (navy)
contrevenant *m.* lawbreaker; noncon-
former
contrevenir *vt.* to break a law; act con-
trarily
contrevent *m.* window shutter
contribuable *m. & f.* taxpayer
contribuer *vi.* to contribute
contribution *f.* contribution; tax
contrister *vt.* to sadden
contrit *a.* contrite, grieved
contrôle *m.* inspection, verification; audit-
ing; ticket-taking
contrôler *vt.* to supervise; check; inspect-
audit; verify; control, restrain
contrôleur *m.* ticket collector; auditor; in;
spector; comptroller
controuvé *a.* made-up, invented, imagined
controversable *a.* controversial
controverse *f.* controversy; discussion
controverser *vt.* to debate; controvert
contumace *f.* contempt of court; nonap-
pearance; default
contus *a.* bruised; —ion *f.* contusion, bruise
contusionner *vt.* to bruise
convaincant *a.* convincing
convaincre *vt.* to convince; convict
convalescent *a. & m. & f.* convalescent
convenable *a.* suitable, proper, appropriate, becoming
convenance *f.* suitability; expediency;
propriety, convention; conformity
convenir *vi.* to agree; fit, suit
convention *f.* convention; agreement; de
— conventional
conventionnel *a.* conventional
convenu *a.* agreed, arranged, settled
convergeance *f.* convergence
converger *vi.* to converge
conversation *f.* conversation
converser *vi.* to converse, talk
converti *m.* convert
convertibilité *f.* convertibility
convertible *a.* (law) convertible
convertir *vt.* to convert; se — (en) to
become converted; turn into, change
into
convertissable *a.* convertible
convertisseur *m.* converter; transformer
convexe *a.* convex
convexité *f.* convexity
conviction *f.* conviction; belief

convié *m.* one guest
convier *vt.* to invite
convive *m.* guest; table companion
convocation *f.* convocation; convening
convoi *m.* funeral procession; convoy
convoiter *vt.* to covet, want, desire
convoiteur *a.* covetous
convoitise *f.* covetousness; cupidity; immoderate desire
convoquer *vt.* to convoke; summon
convoyer *vt.* to convoy
convoyeur *a.* convoying, escorting; — *m.*
escort, convoy; conveyor
convulser *vt.* to convulse
convulsif *a.* convulsive
convulsionner *vt.* to convulse
coopérateur *m.* co-operator; member of a
co-operative
coopératif *a.* co-operative
coopération *f.* co-operation
coopérer *vi.* to co-operate
coordination *f.* co-ordination
coordonnateur *m.* co-ordinator; — *a.* co-
ordinating
coordonné *a.* co-ordinate; co-ordinated;
—es *f. pl.* co-ordinates
copeau *m.* chip, wood shaving
copie *f.* copy; imitation; reproduction; —
conforme true copy, authenticated
copy
copier *vt.* to copy, imitate; reproduce
copieux *a.* copious; hearty
copilote *m.* copilot
copiste *m.* copyist; copier; clerk; faute de
— *f.* clerical error
coposséder *vt.* to own jointly
copra(h) *m.* copra
copte *m. & f.* Copt; — *a.* coptic
copulatif *a.* co-ordinating
coq *m.* rooster, cock; weathervane; sea
cook; — de bruyère grouse; poids —
bantamweight (boxing)
coq-à-l'âne *m.* confused speech; farce,
cock-and-bull story
coque *f.* shell; cocoon; hull; œuf à la — *m.*
soft-boiled egg
coquelicot *m.* (bot.) poppy
coqueluche *f.* whooping cough
coquerie *f.* galley, ship's kitchen
coqueriquer *vi.* to crow
coquet *a.* coquettish; natty
coqueter *vi.* to flirt
coquetier *m.* egg cup; egg and chicken
wholesaler
coquetière *f.* egg cooker
coquette *f.* coquette, flirt
coquetterie *f.* flirtation, coquetry
coquillage *m.* shellfish; shell
coquille *f.* shell; case, casing; typographical error; — Saint-Jacques creamed
scallops; huitres en — *f. pl.* scalloped
oysters
coquin *m.* rogue, rascal; — *a.* roguish
cor *m.* horn; French horn; corn (foot); —
de chasse hunting horn
corail *m.* coral
corbeau *m.* raven; crow
corbeille *f.* basket; wedding presents; —
à papier wastepaper basket
corbillard *m.* hearse

cordage *m.* rope; string

corde *f.* cord, rope, line; string; thread; wire; chord

cordé *a.* heart-shaped

cordeau *m.* string, lace

cordée *f.* cord (of wood); group of mountain climbers (roped tog.…er)

cordelier *m.* Franciscan friar

corder *vt.* to cord; make into rope; string

cordial *a.* cordial, warm, hearty; stimulating; — *m.* cordial; stimulant

cordialité *f.* cordiality

cordier *m.* ropemaker

cordon *m.* strand; cord; ribbon; tape; door pull; cordon; — bleu expert chef; — de soulier shoelace

cordonnerie *f.* shoemaking; shoe repairing

cordonnier *m.* shoemaker

Corée *f.* Korea; -n *m. & a.* Korean

coriace *a.* tough, leathery

Corinthe *f.* Corinth; raisin de — *m.* currant

corinthien *a.* Corinthian

cormoran *m.* cormorant

cornac *m.* elephant boy; guide

corne *f.* horn; dog-ear a page; — à souliers shoehorn

corné *a.* horny

cornée *f.* cornea

corneille *f.* crow

cornemuse *f.* bagpipes

corner *vt. & vi.* to blare out; (auto.) to blow the horn

cornet *m.* horn; trumpet; cornet; paper cone; — acoustique ear trumpet; — à pistons cornet with valves; glace en — ice-cream cone

cornette *f.* nun's headdress

corniche *f.* cornice; ledge

cornichon *m.* gherkin, pickle

Cornouailles *f. pl.* Cornwall

cornouiller *m.* dogwood

cornu *a.* horned

cornue *f.* (chem.) retort

corollaire *m.* corollary

coronaire *a.* coronary

corporatif *a.* corporate

corporel *a.* corporal; corporeal; bodily

corps *m.* body; substance; corpse; corps; font (type); — à — hand-to-hand; — simple (chem.) element; — composé (chem.) compound; prendre — to develop, take shape; saisir au — to arrest (law)

corps-à-corps *m.* hand-to-hand combat; clinch (boxing)

corpulent *a.* corpulent, fat

corpuscule *m.* corpuscle

correct *a.* correct; accurate; right; proper

correcteur *m.* corrector; proofreader

correctif *a.* corrective

correction *f.* correction, correcting; correctness, propriety; proofreading; punishment; reprimand

correctionnel *a.* relating to a misdemeanor; -le *f.* misdemeanor court

corrélatif *a.* correlative

corrélation *f.* correlation

correspondance *f.* correspondence; interchange, transfer

correspondant *a.* corresponding; — *m.* correspondent

correspondre *vi.* to correspond; communicate

corriger *vt.* to correct; proofread; punish

corroborer *vt.* to corroborate

corrodant *a. & m.* corrosive

corroder *vt.* to corrode

corrompre *vt.* to corrupt; spoil; bribe

corrompu *a.* corrupt; spoiled

corrosif *a. & m.* corrosive

corroyer *vt.* to plane (wood); solder, weld; prepare (leather)

corrupteur *a.* corrupting; — *m.* corrupter

corruption *f.* corruption; corruptness; bribery

corsage *m.* bust, bodice; blouse

corsaire *m.* corsair, pirate

Corse *f.* Corsica; — *m. & f. & a.* Corsican

corsé *a.* full-bodied; (fig.) scabrous

corselet *m.* bodice

cortege *m.* cortege, train, retinue, procession; funeral

cortisone *f.* cortizone

corvée *f.* drudgery; unpleasant task; hard labor; tenue de — *f.* (mil.) fatigues

corvette *f.* corvette; capitaine de — lieutenant commander

cosignataire *m. & f.* cosigner

cosinus *m.* (math.) cosine

cosmétique *a. & m.* cosmetic

cosmique *a.* cosmic

cosmopolite *a.* cosmopolitan

cosmos *m.* cosmos

cosse *f.* pod, husk, shell

costume *m.* costume, dress, suit

costumer *vt.* to costume

cosy *m.* cosy corner; studio bed

cote *f.* number; quota; mark; classification; (com.) price, quotation

côte *f.* rib; seacoast; hill; chop; — à — side by side

côté *m.* side; way; à — near, by, on one side; à — de beside, next to; d'un — on one hand; de l'autre — on the other hand; on the other side; across; de — aside, to one side; du — de in the direction of

coteau *m.* hill, hillside; slope

côtelé *a.* ribbed cloth; corded; corduroy

côtelette *f.* chop, cutlet

coter *vt.* to mark; number; classify; quote a price; assess

coterie *f.* group, set, coterie

cothurne *m.* buskin

côtier *a.* coastal

cotisation *f.* share; dues, fee; assessment

cotiser *vi.* to pay one's share

coton *m.* cotton

cotonnade *f.* cotton goods

cotonner *vt.* to pad, stuff with cotton; (se) — *vi.* to become fluffy, downy

cotonnerie *f.* cotton field; cotton raising; cotton factory

cotonneux *a.* fluffy; downy

cotonnier *a.* cotton; relating to cotton; — *m.* cotton plant

côtoyer *vt.* to border on; stay close to, hug (the shore)

cotre *m.* (naut.) cutter

cotte *f.* short skirt; — à bretelles overalls; — de mailles coat of mail

cou *m.* neck; couper le — à to behead

couard *a.* cowardly; — *m.* coward

couardise *f.* cowardice

couchage *m.* bedding; coating; sac de — *m.* sleeping bag

couchant *a.* setting; — *m.* sunset, west; decline

couche *f.* bed; confinement; layer, coat;. fausse — miscarriage

couché *a.* lying; in bed

coucher *vt.* to put to bed; put down, lay down; — en joue to aim at; se — to go to bed; lie down; — *m.* setting of sun; going to bed; bed, lodging

couchette *f.* berth; crib

coucou *m.* cuckoo; (bot.) daffodil

coude *m.* elbow; bend; angle; coup de — *m.* nudge, poke

cou-de-pied *m.* instep

couder *vt.* to bend like an elbow

coudoyer *vt.* to elbow, jostle

coudre *vt. & vi.* to sew; machine à — *f.* sewing machine

couenne *f.* rind; skin; birthmark

couette *f.* (coll.) feather bed; grating (on escape valve); strainer

cougar *m.* cougar

coulage *m.* pouring; leaking; (naut.) scuttling; waste

coulant *a.* flowing, smooth; nœud — *m.* slipknot

coulé *a.* cast *or* poured metal

coulée *f.* flow; casting; pouring

couler *vi.* to flow, run; leak; founder, sink; — *vt.* pour; sink, scuttle

couleur *f.* color; paint; complexion; suit at cards

couleuvre *f.* snake, serpent

coulisse *f.* groove; slide; (theat.) wing à — sliding

coulisseau *m.* slide, runner

couloir *m.* passage, corridor; lobby

coup *m.* blow, throw, stroke; knock, tap, rap; thrust; shot; attempt, coup; — de feu gun shot; — de froid chill, cold; — d'œil glance, look; — de sang (med.) stroke; — de téléphone telephone call; — de tête butt; rash action; — de vent gust of wind; encore un — once again; en venir aux —s to come to blows; sur le — on the spot, right off, outright; tout à — suddenly, all of a sudden; tout d'un — at one shot; at once

coupable *a.* guilty; culpable; sinful, wrong; — *m. & f.* culprit, guilty one

coupant *a.* sharp, cutting; — *m.* sword edge

coupe-de-poing *m.* brass knuckles (U.S.); fist blow

coupe *f.* cut, cutting; haircut; cross section; cup, champagne glass

coupé *a.* cut, broken; — *m.* (auto.) coupe

coupe-circuit *m.* circuit-breaker; fuse

coupe-coupe *m.* machete

coupe-feu *m.* fire break

coupe-fil *m.* wirecutters

coupe-gorge *m.* hazard, danger spot

coupe-jarret *m.* assassin

coupe-légumes *m.* vegetable cutter

coupe-ongles *m.* nail clippers

coupe-papier *m.* paper knife

couper *vt.* to cut; cross; interrupt, cut off, break; turn off; trump cards; cut wine, water down; se — to cut oneself; intersect

couperet *m.* chopper, cleaver; guillotine blade

couperose *f.* (med.) acne; (chem.) blue vitriol

coupeur *m.* cutter

coupe-vent *m.* windbreaker

couple *m.* couple, pair; — *f.* couple; yoke; brace

coupler *vt.* to couple, connect, join

couplet *m.* stanza, verse

coupleur *m.* coupler

coupoir *m.* cutter, cutting tool

coupole *f.* cupola

coupon *m.* remnant, cutting; coupon

coupure *f.* cut, slit; cutting, clipping; banknote (under 1000 francs)

cour *f.* court; yard; courtship; faire la — à to court

courage *m.* courage, bravery, valor; (fig.) heart, spirit

courageux *a.* courageous, brave

courailler *vi.* to run around, run from side to side

couramment *adv.* fluently; easily; currently

courant *a.* current, running; present; prix — *m.* price list; — *m.* current, flow, stream; course; — d'air draft; être au — de to know about, be informed about

courbature *f.* aching, stiffness

courbaturé *a.* aching, stiff

courbe *f.* curve; — *a.* curved, crooked, bent

courber *vt.* to bend, bow; curve; — *vi.* to bend, sag, droop; se — to bend, stoop

courbure *f.* curve, curvature, bend

courette *f.* small courtyard

coureur *m.* runner, racer; wanderer; adventurer; — de spectacles playgoer

courge *f.* gourd, squash

courgette *f.* zucchini

courir *vi.* to run; race; — *vt.* to run, run after, hunt, pursue; run, take a risk

courlis *m.* plover

couronne *f.* crown; coronet; wreath

couronnement *m.* coronation; crowning

couronner *vt.* to crown; cap; (fig.) honor, pay

courrier *m.* courier; mail; column, section of a newspaper

courriériste *m.* columnist, feature editor

courroie *f.* strap; drive-belt

courroucer *vt.* to irritate; anger

courroux *m.* anger, wrath

cours *m.* course; current, stream; way; price, rate; lecture; au — de during, in the course of; — du change rate of exchange; en — de route on the way, along the way

course *f.* running; racing; race; trip; errand; flight, course, path; champ de —s racetrack; faire des —s to go shopping

coursier *m.* messenger; steed

coursive f. passageway to ship cabin
court a. short; concise; brief; — adv. short; à — de short of; — m. tennis court
courtage m. brokerage; fee, commission
courtaud a. short, stocky
court-circuit m. short circuit
courtepointe f. quilt
courtier m. broker; jobber; agent
courtisan m. courtier; —e f. courtesan
courtiser vt. to court; woo
courtois a. courteous, polite; courtly
courtoisie f. courtesy, politeness
couru a. sought after; (fig. & coll.) sure thing
couseuse f. seamstress; sewing machine
cousin m., cousine f. cousin; — germain(e) first cousin
cousinage m. relatives
coussin m. cushion
coussinet m. small cushion; (mech.) bearing
coût m. cost, price
couteau m. knife
coutelas m. cutlass
coutellerie f. cutlery
coûter vi. to cost; — cher to be expensive
coûteux a. costly, expensive
coutil m. twill, duck; mattress ticking
coutume f. custom, habit; common law
coutumier a. customary, usual; droit — m. common law
couture f. sewing; seam; suture; scar
couturer vt. to seam, scar
couturier m. designer of women's clothes
couturière f. seamstress, dressmaker
couvaison f. incubation period
couvée f. brood of chickens; group of eggs under brood hen; (coll.) all the family
couvent m. convent; monastery
couver vt. to hatch; sit on; — vi. to smolder; brew; develop
couvercle m. cover, lid, cap
couvert m. table place setting; cover charge; shelter, cover; mettre le — to set the table; ôter le — to clear the table; — a. covered; shady, wooded; clothed, clad; overcast (weather)
couverture f. cover; wrapper; blanket
couveuse f. brood hen; incubator
couvre-feu m. curfew
couvre-lit m. bedspread, coverlet
couvre-pieds m. bedspread; quilt
couvreur m. roofer
couvrir vt. to cover; clothe; se — to put one's hat on; clothe oneself
coyote m. coyote
crabe m. crab
crachat m. spit; sputum
cracher vt. & vi. to spit out
crachin m. light drizzle
crachoir m. spittoon
crachoter vi. to spit frequently
craie f. chalk
craindre vt. to fear, be afraid of
crainte f. fear; de — de for fear of; de — que for fear that
craintif a. timid; fearful
cramoisi a. crimson
crampe f. cramp
crampillon m. small hook

crampon m. clamp; crampon; stud
cramponner vt. to clamp; (coll.) to pester, bother
cran m. cog, tooth, catch; notch
crâne m. skull; — a. bold, swaggering
crâner vi. to swagger
crânerie f. bravado; daring
cranien a. cranial
cranter vt. to notch, tally; cog
crapaud m. toad
crapule f. mob, rabble; lewdness; filth
crapuleux a. lewd; foul, filthy
craqueler vt. to crack
craquelure f. crack
craquement m. cracking, snapping
craquer vi. to crack; creak; crackle; crunch
crasse f. filth; squalor; stinginess; — a. crass
crasseux a. dirty, filthy; stingy
cratère m. crater
cravacher vt. to whip
cravate f. necktie; cravat, scarf
crayeux a. chalky
crawl(e) m. crawl (swimming stroke)
crayon m. pencil; crayon; stick; — hémostatique styptic pencil
crayonnage m. pencil sketch, pencil drawing
crayonner vt. to draw, sketch
créance f. trust, credit; credence; debt
créancier m. creditor
créateur m., créatrice f. creator; inventor, author; — a. creative
création f. creation, creating; establishment, establishing
créature f. creature; creation
crécelle f. rattle
crèche f. crib, manger; nursery school
crédence f. credenza, buffet
crédibilité f. credibility; probability
crédit m. credit; credence; prestige, repute; à — on credit
créditer vt. to credit
créditeur m. creditor
credo m. creed, belief
crédule a. credulous
crédulité f. credulity
créer vt. to create; produce; engender
crémaillère f. pothook; pendre la — to have a housewarming
crémation f. cremation
crématoire a. pertaining to cremation
crème f. cream; custard, pudding; cream soup; — fouettée whipped cream
crémer vt. to cremate
crémerie f. dairy; grocery; creamery
crémeux a. creamy
crémier m. dairyman, grocer
crénelé a. notched (as coin edge), toothed; crenate; crenellated; milled
créneler vt. to crenelate; cog; notch
créole a. & n. creole, French-colonial born
créosol m. creosol
créosote f. creosote
crêpe f. pancake; — m. crepe, crape; mourning band
crépitation f., crépitement m. crepitation; crackling
crépiter vi. to crackle

crépu *a.* fuzzy, frizzy; crinkled

crépusculaire *a.* twilight, crepuscular

crépuscule *m.* twilight

cresson *m.* watercress

crête *f.* crest, comb; ridge

crétin *m.* cretin; idiot

crétois *a. & n.* Cretan

creuser *vt.* to dig, excavate; look deeply into, study carefully; se — la tête to rack one's brains

creuset *m.* crucible; melting pot

creux (creuse) *a.* hollow; deep; sunken; — *m.* hollow; pit; hole

crevaison *f.* bursting; (auto.) puncture, blowout

crevasse *f.* crevice, chink, crack, crevasse

crevasser *vt.* to crack; to chap hands

crève-cœur *m.* heartbreak

crever *vt.* to break; burst; (coll.) die; — *vt.* to burst; puncture

crevette *f.* shrimp; prawn

cri *m.* cry, shout; dernier — latest thing, latest style

criaillement *m.* shrill sound; shouting, shrieking

criailler *vi.* to shout; bawl; whine; nag

criaillerie *f.* shouting; bawling; whining; nagging

criant *a.* outrageous, crying

criard *a.* noisy, shrill; loud color

crible *m.* sieve; screen

criblé *a.* riddled; pitted face; saddled with debts

cribler *vt.* to sift; riddle

cribleur *m.*, cribleuse *f.* sifter (machine)

cricri *m.* cricket; chirping

criée *f.* auction, public selling

crier *vi.* to proclaim; shout, cry out; scream; squeal; chirp; creak; — *vt.* shout, cry; peddle

crieur *m.* shouter, crier; peddlar; town crier

crime *m.* crime

criminalité *f.* crime rate; criminality

criminel *a.* criminal; guilty; — *m.* criminal

criminologie *f.* criminology

crin *m.* horsehair

crinière *f.* mane

crinoline *f.* crinoline, hoop skirt

crique *f.* cove; creek

criquet *m.* locust; cricket

crise *f.* crisis; attack, fit; problem

crispant *a.* irritating, annoying

crispation *f.* puckering, shriveling; tic, twitching; clenching; fidgeting

crisper *vt.* to contract; clench; make fidgety

crissement *m.* grating, rasping, grinding; squeaking

crisser *vt. & vi.* to grate, rasp, grind; squeak

cristal *m.* crystal; glass; — taillé cut glass

cristallin *a.* crystalline; clear, transparent

cristallisation *f.* crystalization

cristalliser *vt. & vi.* to crystallize

critère, critérium *m.* criterion; standard; test

critiquable *a.* censurable

critique *f.* criticism, critique; — *m.* critic; — *a.* critical

critiquer *vt.* to criticize

croasser *vi.* to croak; caw

croate *a. & n.* Croatian

Croatie *f.* Croatia

croc *m.* hook; fang; tusk

croc-en-jambe *m.* trip, fall; faire un — à to trip

croche *f.* (mus.) eighth-note

crocher *vt.* to hook

crochet *m.* small hook; (print.) square bracket; sharp turn; fang; pick, key

crocheter *vt.* to pick a lock; crochet

crochu *a.* hooked; crooked

crocodile *m.* crocodile

crocus *m.* crocus

croire *vt. & vi.* to believe, think; — à to believe in; en — to take someone's word for it

croisade *f.* crusade

croisé *a.* crossed; twilled; double-breasted; mots —s *m. pl.* crossword puzzle; — *m.* crusader; twill

croisée *f.* crossing; casement window; crossed filaments in a bomb sight

croisement *m.* crossing; cross; intersection

croiser *vt.* to cross; to fold arms; meet; pass; — *vi.* to cruise; se — to cross, meet, intersect

croisette *f.* small cross

croiseur *m.* cruiser

croisière *f.* cruise

croissance *f.* growth

croissant *a.* growing; increasing; — *m.* crescent moon; crescent roll

croître *vi.* to grow; increase

croix *f.* cross, crucifix; — ou pile heads or tails

croquant *a.* crisp, crunchy; tasty

croque-mitaine *m.* bugaboo, bugbear, bogyman

croque-mort *m.* funeral attendant

croquer *vt. & vi.* to crunch, munch; sketch

croquette *f.* croquette

croquis *m.* rough sketch; draft, outline

crosse *f.* crook, club, stick; gun butt; crozier

crotale *m.* rattlesnake

crotte *f.* mud; dung

crotter *vt.* to dirty; cover with mud

crottin *m.* horse manure

croulant *a.* crumbling, falling, tottering

crouler *vi.* to crumble, totter; collapse, fall

croupe *f.* croup, crupper, rump

croupetons, à — *adv.* squatting

croupier *m.* croupier

croupion *m.* rump

croupir *vi.* to stagnate; wallow

croustade *f.* crusty food

croustillant *a.* crisp, crusty

croustiller *vi.* to crunch

croustilleux *a.* risqué

croûte *f.* crust; rind; scab; casser la — to have a snack; faire — to form a crust

crouton *m.* piece of crust; crouton

croyable *a.* credible, believable

croyance *f.* belief

croyant *a.* believing; — *m.* believer

cru *m.* place of origin of a wine; vintage;

— *a.* raw; rough; crude
cruauté *f.* cruelty
cruche *f.* pitcher, jug
cruchon *m.* small pitcher
crucial *a.* cruciform; crucial
crucifiement *m.* crucifixion
crucifier *vt.* to crucify
crucifix *m.* crucifix
crucifixion *f.* crucifixion
cruciforme *a.* cross-shaped, cruciform
crudité *f.* crudeness; crudity; rawness; roughness, coarseness
crue *f.* rise, rising, flood
cruel *a.* cruel
cruellement *adv.* cruelly
crûment *adv.* roughly; crudely; harshly
crustacé *m.* crustacean
crypte *f.* crypt
cryptogénétique *a.* of unknown origin
cryptogramme *m.* cryptogram
cryptographie *f.* cryptography
Cuba *m.* Cuba
cubage *m.* cubic volume, capacity, space
Cubain *n. & a.* Cuban
cube *m.* cube; block
cuber *vt.* (math.) to cube
cubique *a.* cubic, cubical
cubisme *m.* cubism
cubital *a.* cubital
cubitus *m.* (anat.) ulna
cueillage *m.* gathering, picking; harvest time
cueillaison *f.* gathering, picking
cueilleur *m.* gatherer, picker, fruitpicker
cueillir *vt.* to gather, pluck, pick; (coll.) grab, take
cuillerée *f.* spoonful
cuilleron *m.* bowl of a spoon
cuir *m.* leather, hide; — chevelu scalp; — verni patent leather; — vert untanned leather; rawhide
cuirasse *f.* armor, plate; cuirass
cuirassé *m.* battleship
cuirasser *vt.* to armor; protect; se — to steel oneself
cuire *vt. & vi.* to cook
cuisant *a.* biting, stinging, smarting
cuisine *f.* kitchen; cuisine, cooking; food; faire la — to do the cooking
cuisiner *vt.* to cook; (coll.) doctor, falsify; question, grill
cuisinier *m.* cook
cuisinière *f.* cook; stove, range
cuisse *f.* thigh; drumstick
cuisseau *m.* leg of veal
cuisson *f.* cooking; firing; burning
cuissot *m.* leg of game
cuistre *m.* (coll.) pedant
cuite *f.* firing (ceramics)
cuivre *m.* copper; — jaune brass
cuivré *a.* copper-colored; bronzed; brassy
cuivrer *vt.* to copper; bronze; — *vi.* to blare, sound
cuivreux *a.* cuprous
cuivrique *a.* cupric
cul *m.* posterior, bottom; rump
culasse *f.* gun breech; bolt; (mech.) cyl-

inder head
culbute *f.* fall, tumble; somersault
culbuter *vt.* to overturn, overthrow, knock over — *vi.* to tumble; somersault
cul-de-sac *m.* dead-end street
culée *f.* abutment
culinaire *a.* culinary
culminant *a.* culminating, culminant; point — *m.* height, zenith
culminer *vi.* to culminate
culot *m.* base, bottom; dottle; (coll.) youngest child
culotte *f.* breeches; panties; shorts; rump meat
culotter *vt.* to color; — une pipe to cure a pipe
culpabilité *f.* guilt, culpability
cultivable *a.* suitable for farming; arable
cultivateur *m.* farmer; grower; plow, cultivator
cultivé *a.* cultivated; cultured person
cultiver *vt.* to cultivate; grow; farm; raise
cultural *a.* agricultural
culture *f.* cultivation, tillage; culture
culturel *a.* cultural
cumin *m.* cumin
cumul *m.* accumulation
cumulatif *a.* cumulative
cumuler *vt.* to accumulate
cumulus *m.* cumulus
cunéiforme *a.* cuneiform
cupide *a.* greedy
cupidité *f.* greed, cupidity
Cupidon *m.* Cupid
cuprifère *a.* copper-bearing
curable *a.* curable
curaçao *m.* curaçao, orange-peel liqueur
curage *m.* cleansing
curare *m.* curare
curatelle *f.* guardianship, trusteeship
curateur *m.* guardian, trustee
curatif *a.* curative
cure *f.* care; (med.) treatment; ministry; presbytery, rectory
curé *m.* parish priest
cure-dent *m.* toothpick
curée *f.* quarry (hunting); spoils
cure-pipe *m.* pipe cleaner
curer *vt.* to cleanse; pick; dredge
curieux *a.* curious; interested; indiscreet; inquisitive; odd
curiosité *f.* curiosity; inquisitiveness; curio; oddness; -s *pl.* sights; visiter les -s to go sightseeing
curium *m.* curium
curseur *m.* slide, runner
cursif *a.* cursory; handwritten
cursive *f.* handwriting
cutané *a.* cutaneous; pertaining to the skin
cuticule *f.* cuticle
cuve *f.* vat, tank for fermenting grapes
cuveau *m.* small vat or tank
cuver *vt. & vi.* to ferment wine
cuvette *f.* basin, pan
cuvier *m.* washtub
cyanose *f.* (med.) cyanosis
cyanure *m.* cyanide
cyclable *a.*, piste — *f.* bicycle path

cycle *m.* cycle; bicycle
cyclique *a.* cyclic, cyclical
cyclisme *m.* cycling, bicycling
cycliste *m. & f.* cyclist, bicyclist
cycloïde *f.* cycloid
cyclomoteur *m.* bicycle with auxiliary motor
cyclone *m.* cyclone
cyclope *m.* cyclops; giant
cyclotron *m.* cyclotron
cygne *m.* swan
cylindre *m.* cylinder; drum; roller
cylindrer *vt.* to roll; mangle
cylindrique *a.* cylindrical
cymbale *f.* cymbal
cynique *a.* cynical; — *m.* cynic
cynisme *m.* cynicism
cyprès *m.* cypress
cyste *m.* cyst
cytologie *f.* cytology
cytoplasme *m.* cytoplasm

D

dactyle *m.* dactyl
dactylique *a.* dactylic
dactylo, dactylographe *m. & f.* typist
dactylographie *f.* typing, typewriting
dactylographié *a.* typed, typewritten
dactylographier *vt.* to typewrite
dada *m.* hobbyhorse; (coll.) hobby; obsession
dadais *m.* idiot, stupid fellow
dague *f.* dagger
daguerréotype *m.* daguerrotype
dahlia *m.* dahlia
daigner *vt.* to deign, condescend
daim *m.* deer; buckskin; suede
dais *m.* canopy
dallage *m.* floor tile; flagstone surface
dalle *f.* flagstone, slab of marble, tile
daller *vt.* to tile, pave
dalmate *a. & n.* Dalmatian
dalot *m.* scupper
daltonien *a.* color-blind
daltonisme *m.* color blindness
Damas *m.* Damascus
damas *m.* damask; damson plum
damassé *a.* damask; Damascus steel
dame *f.* lady; queen (at cards); jeu de —s *pl.* game of checkers; pion du jeu de —s checkers man
damier *m.* chessboard, checkerboard
damnation *f.* damnation
damné *a.* damned
damner *vt.* to damn
damoiseau *m.* dandy; fop
dancing *m.* dance hall; public dance, ball
dandiner *vt.* to dandle; (fig.) pamper; se — to waddle
Danemark *m.* Denmark
danger *m.* danger; risk, peril
dangereux *a.* dangerous
danois *a.* Danish; — *m.* Dane; Danish language
dans *prep.* in, into, at, within; from, out of
dansant *a.* dancing; soirée —e *f.* dance; thé — *m.* tea dance
danse *f.* dance, dancing

danser *vt. & vi.* to dance
danseur *m.*, danseuse *f.* dancer, ballet dancer
dard *m.* dart; forked tongue; pain, sting
darder *vt.* to shoot, throw, flash
dardillon *m.* small dart
darne *f.* slice of fish
datation *f.* dating
date *f.* calendar date; sans — undated
dater *vt. & vi.* to date
datif *a. & m.* (gram.) dative
datte *f.* (bot.) date
dattier *m.* date palm
daube *f.* braising; bœuf en — braised beef
dauber *vt. & vi.* to braise; make fun of
dauphin *m.* dolphin; Dauphin
davantage *adv.* more, any more; more time
davier *m.* (naut.) davit; (dent.) forceps
de *prep.* of; from; by; with; in; — *art.* some, any
dé *m.* thimble; die; domino; golf tee; —s *m. pl.* dice
déambuler *vi.* to stroll, saunter
débâcle *m.* debacle, disaster; rout; collapse, downfall
déballer *vt.* to unpack
déballeur *m.* peddler
débandade *f.* dispersal; à la — in disorder
débander *vt.* to unbend, relax; unbandage; se — to disband, disperse
débaptiser *vt.* to change the name of
débarbouiller *vt.* to wash someone's face; se — to wash one's face; clear up (weather)
débarcadère *m.* landing place; wharf
débardage *m.* unloading
débarder *vt.* to unload
débardeur *m.* stevedore
débarquement *m.* landing; arrival; unloading
débarquer *vt.* to land, disembark; unload; — *vi.* to land, disembark, get off
débarras *m.* riddance
débarrasser *vt.* to clear; rid, disencumber; relieve; se — de to get rid of
débarrer *vt.* to unbar
débat *m.* debate; discussion; dispute
débattre *vt.* to discuss; debate; se — to struggle
débauche *f.* debauchery
débauché *a.* debauched
débaucher *vt.* to debauch; corrupt; lead astray
débile *a.* weak, sick
débilitant *a.* debilitating
débilité *f.* debility, weakness
débiliter *a.* to debilitate
débit *m.* debit; sale; store, shop; flow, output
débitant *m.* retailer
débiter *vt.* to retail, sell; deliver; produce; speak, pronounce, utter; debit
débiteur *m.* debtor; teller, speaker
déblayer *vt.* to clear away
débloquer *vt.* to unblock
déboire *m.* unpleasant aftertaste
déboisement *m.* deforestation
déboiser *vt.* to deforest

déboîtement *m.* (med.) dislocation

déboîter *vt.* to disconnect; dislocate

débonnaire *a.* easy-tempered, kind, good-natured, weak

débordant *a.* overflowing; blooming; protruding

débordé *a.* overflowing; (coll.) rushed, busy, snowed under

débordement *m.* overflowing; outburst

déborder *vt. & vi.* to overflow, run over; protrude; trim (adorn)

débouché *m.* outlet, exit

déboucher *vt.* to uncork; open; clear; — *vi.* to flow; open on; emerge

déboucler *vt.* to unbuckle; uncurl

débourser *vt.* to disburse, lay out

debout *adv.* standing up, upright; alive; à dormir — boring; se tenir — to stand

déboutonner *vt.* to unbutton

débraillé *a.* untidy, unkempt; loose

débrayage *m.* (auto.) clutch

débrayer *vt.* to disengage from gear; disconnect

débrider *vt.* to unbridle; stop

débris *m. pl.* remains; ruins; debris

débrouillard *a. & m.* resourceful, (coll.) smart person

débrouiller *vt.* to disentangle; clear up; decipher; se — to clear up; get along, manage

début *m.* beginning; debut; coming out

débutant *m.* beginner; new performer —e *f.* beginner in society

débuter *vi.* to begin; do, appear for the first time

deçà *prep. & adv.* on this side

décacheter *vt.* to unseal

décadence *f.* decay, decline, decadence

décadent *a.* decadent

décaféiné *a.* decaffeinated, caffeine-free

décaisser *vt.* to uncrate; pay out, disburse

décalcomanie *f.* decalcomania, transfer

décaler *vt.* to change, shift

décalitre *f.* decaliter

décalogue *m.* Ten Commandments

décalque *m.* tracing, transfer

décalquer *vt.* to trace, transfer

décamètre *m.* ten meters

décamper *vi.* to decamp

décanat *m.* office of dean, deanship

décanter *vt.* to decant, pour (off)

décaper *vt.* to scour, clean

décapitation *f.* decapitation

décapiter *vt.* to behead, decapitate

décapotable *a.* (auto.) convertible

décatir *vt.* to remove cloth shine by steaming

décathlon *m.* decathlon

décavé *a.* (coll.) broke, ruined, cleaned out

décédé *a.* deceased, departed

décéder *vi.* to decease, die

déceler *vt.* to disclose, betray

décélération *f.* deceleration

décembre *m.* December

décemment *adv.* decently

décence *f.* decency; propriety

décennal *a.* decennial

décent *a.* decent; proper

décentralisation *f.* decentralization

décentraliser *vt.* to decentralize

déception *f.* disappointment; deception

décerner *vt.* to award, confer

décès *m.* decease, death; acte de — *m.* death certificate

décevant *a.* disappointing; deceptive

décevoir *vt.* disappoint; to deceive

déchaînement *m.* unchaining; outburst, wave

déchaîner *vt.* to unchain; let loose; se — to break out

décharge *f.* discharge; discharging, unloading; rebate; release; acquittal (at law)

déchargement *m.* discharging, unloading

décharger *vt.* to unload, discharge; unburden; fire a gun; se — to discharge; go off; se — de to get rid of; relieve oneself of

déchargeur *m.* unloader

décharné *a.* skinny; emaciated; gaunt

déchaussé *a.* barefoot

déchausser *vt.*, se — to take off one's shoes

déchéance *f.* forfeiture; downfall; term, expiration

déchet *m.* loss; waste

déchiffrable *a.* legible, readable, decipherable

déchiffrer *vt.* to decipher; decode; read, make out

déchiqueté *a.* jagged, torn

déchirant *a.* heartrending

déchirement *m.* tearing; rift; sorrow

déchirer *vt.* to tear; rend

déchirure *f.* tear, rip, rent

déchloruré *a.* salt-free

déchoir *vi.* to fall; go down; decline in condition

déchu *a.* fallen; forfeited; expired

décibel *m.* decibel

décidé *a.* decided; resolved, determined

décidément *adv.* decidedly, positively; firmly, resolutely

décider *vt.* to decide; persuade; determine; se — to resolve, decide

décigramme *m.* ½ gram

décilitre *m.* ⅒ liter

décimal *a.* decimal; —e *f.* decimal

décimer *vt.* to decimate

décisif *a.* decisive; positive, firm; critical, crucial

décision *f.* decision; resolution

déclamation *f.* declamation; declaiming

déclamer *vt.* to declaim; rant, harangue

déclaration *f.* declaration; affadavit; statement; announcement

déclarer *vt.* to declare, proclaim; state, assert; notify

déclassé *m.* social outcast; — *a.* socially lowered; obsolete

déclasser *vt.* to lower in rank, class; demote; make obsolete; disarrange; declassify

déclencher *vt.* to unleash; (fig.) set in motion, release; trigger (mech.) disengage

déclic *m.* catch; trigger

déclin *m.* decline, decay; wane; ebb; fall

déclinaison *f.* (gram.) declension; (ast.) declination

décliner vt. to decline; shun, refuse; — vi. decline, diminish, fall, wane

déclive a. sloping; —f. slope

décliver vi. to slope, incline

déclivité f. slope, incline

décoder vt. to decode

décoiffer vt. to undo, disarrange (the hair)

décollage m. unsticking; (avi.) take-off

décollation f. decapitation, beheading

décoller vt. to unstick; loosen; — vi. (avi.) to take off

décolleté a. in a low-cut dress

décolorer vt. to fade; bleach; discolor

décombres m. pl. rubbish, refuse, debris

décommander vt. to cancel, countermand

décomposer vt. to decompose; se — to become decomposed; decay, rot; become distorted

décomposition f. decomposition

décompression f. decompression

décomprimer vt. to decompress

décompter vt. to deduct

déconcertant a. disconcerting

déconcerter vt. to disconcert; baffle, confound; upset

déconfit a. baffled, confused

décongeler vt. to defrost, thaw

déconseiller vt. to dissuade; advise against

déconsidérer vt. to discredit

décontenancer vt. to discountenance, upset, mortify

déconvenue f. disappointment

décor m. decoration; scenery, setting

décorateur m. decorator; (theat.) designer

décoratif a. decorative

décoration f. decoration; scenery; medal, ribbon

décorer vt. to decorate, adorn

décorum m. decorum; propriety, decency

découdre vt. to unsew, unstitch, rip; gore

découler vi. to flow, proceed; drip, trickle

découper vt. to carve; cut up; couteau à — m. carving knife; scie à — f. jigsaw; se — sur to stand out against

découpler vt. to uncouple

découpure f. cutting out; clipping, cut-out; indentation

découragé a. discouraged

décourageant a. discouraging

découragement m. discouragement

décourager vt. to discourage; se — to become discouraged

découronner vt. to dethrone; untop a tree

décours m. wane, ebb, decline

décousu a. unsewed, unstitched, ripped; rambling, incoherent; disjointed; loose

découvert m. deficit; overdraft; mettre à — to reveal, expose; — a. uncovered, open

découverte f. discovery

découvreur m. discoverer

découvrir vt. to uncover; discover; disclose; expose; show; se — to take off one's hat; be discovered, be revealed; come to light

décrasser vt. to scour, cleanse; (auto.) remove carbon

décréditer vt. to discredit

décrépi a. dilapidated

décrépit a. decrepit; dilapidated

décret m. decree

décréter vt. to decree

décri m. disrepute

décrier vt. to decry, disparage

décrire vt. to describe

décrocher vt. to unhook; lift the receiver (telephone); disconnect

décroiser vt. to uncross

décroissance f. decrease; decline

décroître vi. to decrease; decline; diminish

décrotter vt. to clean; scrape clean

décrotteur m. bootblack

décrottoir m. scraper; doormat

décrue f. fall, drop, subsiding

décuple a. tenfold

dédaigner vt. to disdain, scorn

dédaigneux a. disdainful, scornful

dédain m. disdain, scorn

dédale m. labyrinth, maze, confusion

dedans adv. in, within; — m. inside

dédicace f. dedication

dédicacer vt. to dedicate; autograph a book

dédicatoire a. dedicatory

dédier vt. to dedicate; inscribe

dédire v., se — de to take back, go back on, retract

dédit m. retraction; forfeit

dédommagement m. indemnity, damages, compensation

dédommager vt. to indemnify, compensate

dédouaner vt. to clear through customs

dédoublement m. dividing, sectioning into two parts; duality; duplication

dédoubler vt. to divide; remove lining; unfold; se — to divide; unfold

déduction f. deduction; discount

déduire vt. to deduct; discount; deduce

déesse f. goddess

défaillance f. failing; failure; weakness; lapse; faint

défaillant a. failing; weakening; faint

défaillir vi. to fail, faint; grow weak

défaire vt. to unmake, undo; defeat; rid of; untie; unpack; se — de to get rid of

défait a. lean; worn; pale

défaite f. defeat

défaitiste a. & n. defeatist

défalquer vt. to deduct, take away

défaut m. defect; fault, failing; default; lack, want; à — de, au — de for want of

défaveur f. disfavor

défavorable a. unfavorable

défavoriser vt. to handicap, put at a disadvantage

défectif a. (gram.) defective verb

défection f. defection; faire — to defect

défectueux a. defective

défectuosité f. defectiveness; defect

défendeur m. defendant (at law)

défendre vt. to defend; protect; prohibit, forbid; se — to defend oneself; protect oneself; deny; keep, refrain

défense f. defense; prohibition; — de fumer no smoking, smoking prohibited; légitime — self-defense (at law); —s pl. elephant tusks

défenseur m. defender; protector; defense

counsel (law)

défensif a. defensive

déférence f. deference; consideration, respect

déférent a. deferent; respectful

déférer vt. to confer, award; hand over (at law); refer; swear (in); — vi. to defer, comply

déferler vt. to unfurl; set sail; — vi. to break (waves)

défeuiller vt. to remove the leaves from

défi m. defiance; challenge

défiance f. diffidence; distrust, mistrust

défiant a. mistrustful, distrustful; suspicious

déficeler vt. to untie

déficit m. deficit

déficience f. lack, deficiency

déficitaire a. unbalanced, with a deficit

défier vt. to defy; challenge; se — de to mistrust, distrust, be suspicious of, beware of

défigurer vt. to disfigure, deform

défilé m. defile, narrow passage; pass; parade, procession

défiler vi. to parade, march (by)

défini a. definite; well-defined

définir vt. to define; se — to become clear

définissable a. definable

définitif a. definitive; final; permanent; definite

définition f. definition

définitivement adv. finally; permanently; once and for all, for good; definitely

déflation f. deflation; deflating

défloraison f. time of falling of flowers, falling of petals

défoncé a. battered; crumpled; bumpy

défoncer vt. to smash in; break up

déformation f. deformation; warping

déformer vt. to deform, distort; warp; se — to become deformed, lose shape; warp

défraichi a. shopworn; faded

défrayer vt. to defray

défricher vt. (agr.) to clear ground

défriser vt. to uncurl

défroncer vt. remove the wrinkles from

défunt a. deceased, late

dégagé a. disengaged, free; nonchalant

dégagement m. disengagement; clearing, freeing from obligation; release; relief; redeeming (pawned article); exit

dégager vt. to disengage, free; clear; release; relieve; redeem; se — to free oneself; clear oneself; appear, emerge, come out

dégaine f. (coll.) gait; ridiculous attitude

dégainer vt. to draw a sword; unsheathe

déganter vt. to unglove; se — to take off one's gloves

dégarnir vt. to strip, take apart; remove, take away; se — to lose (hair, leaves); be depleted, emptied, stripped

dégâts m. pl. damage

dégauchir vt. to straighten

dégel m. thaw; -er vt. & vi. to thaw

dégénération f. degeneration; deterioration

dégénéré a. degenerate

dégénérer vi. to degenerate; decline

dégivrer vt. to deice; defrost

dégivreuse f. defroster

déglacer vt. to thaw; defrost

dégonfler vt. to deflate; reduce; se — to lose air, go flat; diminish, subside

dégorger vt. to disgorge; clear, open; scour; — vi. to flow into; overflow

dégourdi a. lively; sharp, alert

dégourdir vt. to revive, quicken; warm, take the chill from; se — to stretch one's limbs; get warm

dégoût m. disgust; dislike

dégoûtant a. disgusting; disagreeable, unpleasant

dégoûter vt. to disgust; se — de to become disgusted with; be fed up with

dégouttant a. trickling; dripping

dégoutter vi. to drip, trickle

dégradation f. degradation; erosion; defacement; wear; damage

dégrader vt. to degrade; damage, deface; se — to degrade oneself, lower oneself; become dilapidated

dégrafer vt. to unhook, unclasp, undo

dégraisser vt. to remove fat from; scour, clean, dry-clean

dégraisseur m. cleaner, dry cleaner

degré m. degree; stair step

dégriser vt. to sober up; (fig.) to disillusion

déguenillé a. ragged, in rags

déguerpir vi. to move out; clear out; faire — to evict

déguisement m. disguise

déguiser vt. to disguise; hide, conceal

dégustation f. tasting, art of tasting

déguster vt. to taste; sip, savor

dehors adv. out, outdoors, outside; — m. outside; external appearance

déifier vt. to deify

déisme m. deism

déité f. deity

déjà adv. already

déjeter vt. to warp; make uneven

déjeuner vi. to lunch; petit — breakfast; — vi. to breakfast; lunch

déjouer vt. to baffle; frustrate, foil

delà prep. & adv. beyond, on the other side; au — (de) beyond

délabré a. broken, dilapidated

délabrer vt. to ruin, dilapidate

délacer vt. to unlace

délai m. delay; interval; respite; (com.) time extension; sans — immediately

délaissement m. legal abandonment, desertion; loneliness; helplessness

délassement m. rest, relaxation

délaisser vt. to abandon, forsake; relinquish

délasser vt. to rest, relax

délavé a. faded, washed out; soaked

délayer vt. to dilute, thin, water

délébile a. erasable

délectable a. delectable

délectation f. delight, pleasure

délecter vt. to delight; se — à to delight in, enjoy

délégation f. delegation

délégué m. delegate

déléguer vt. to delegate

délester vt. to unburden, relieve

délétère a. deleterious; harmful; poisonous

délibération f. deliberation

délibéré a. deliberate

délibérer vt. & vi. to deliberate; resolve

délicat a. delicate; sensitive; fine; difficult; dainty; touchy; tactful

délicatesse f. delicacy; daintiness; nicety; fineness; difficulty

délice m. delight; —s f. pl. delight, pleasure

délicieux a. delicious; delightful

délié a. slender, slim; sharp; glib

délier vt. to untie, release; se — to come loose

délinéer vt. to delineate

délinquant m. delinquent, offender

délirant a. delirious

délire m. delirium, frenzy

délirer vi. to be delirious; rave

délit m. offense, wrong; misdemeanor

délivrance f. deliverance, rescue; delivery

délivre m. afterbirth, placenta

délivrer vt. to deliver, free; rescue; se — de to free oneself from; get rid of

déloger vi. to move out; go away; — vt. to eject, dislodge, drive out

déloyal a. disloyal, unfaithful; unfair; foul, unsporting

déloyaute f. disloyalty; treachery; foul play

déluge m. deluge, flood

déluré a. lively

démagnétiser vt. to demagnetize

démagogie f. demagogy

démagogue m. demagog

démailler vt. to undo links or mesh

démailloter vt. to unswathe

demain adv. & m. tomorrow; à — goodby, until tomorrow, see you tomorrow

demande f. question, claim; request; demand; application; petition; proposal, offer

demander vt. to ask, ask for; claim; request; want, require, need; demand

demandeur m. plaintiff (at law)

démangeaison f. itch, itching; desire

démanger vi. to itch

démarcation f. demarcation

démarche f. step, pace; gait; measure; procedure

démarquer vt. to remove the mark; imitate; reduce, put on sale

démarrer vt. & vi. (naut.) to cast off; (auto.) start; (coll.) leave

démarreur m. (auto.) starter

démasquer vt. to unmask

démêlé m. dispute, strife

démêler vt. to disentangle, separate comb out; clear up; make out, see

démembrement m. dismemberment

démembrer vt. to dismember; divide up

déménagement m. moving, removal; voiture de — f. moving van

déménager vi. to move, change residence; (fig.) (coll.) to become childish

déménageur m. mover of household goods

démence f. insanity, madness

démener v., se — to struggle, be agitated

dément a. & m. lunatic

démenti m. denial, contradiction

démentir vt. to deny; contradict; belie

démériter m. lack of merit

démériter vi. to lose esteem, lose favor

démesure f. lack of measure, lack of moderation, excess

démesuré a. excessive; immoderate; inordinate

démettre vt. to dislocate; se — (de) to resign (from)

démeubler vt. to remove the furniture from

demeurant adv., au — furthermore, besides, moreover

demeure f. dwelling, residence; delay (law)

demeurer vi. to live; stay, remain; delay

demi a. half; — m. half; football halfback; à — half, by half

demi-cercle m. semicircle

demi-dieu m. demigod

demi-finale f. semi-final (sports)

demi-frère m. half brother; stepbrother

demi-heure f. half hour

demi-jour m. half-light; gray; twilight

démilitarisé a. demilitarized

demi-lune f. half-moon

demi-mesure f. half measure

demi-monde m. shady society

demi-mot m. adv., entendre à —, comprendre à — to take a hint

déminer vt. to demine, clear of mines

demi-pension f. partial board (two meals per day)

demi-pensionnaire m. & f. boarder (for breakfast and supper)

demi-place f. half price; half fare

demi-saison f. periods between winter and summer (spring and fall); vêtements de — m. pl. spring or fall clothing

demi-sœur f. half sister; stepsister

demi-solde f. army pension; — m. pensioned officer

démission f. resignation

démissionner vi. to resign

demi-tasse f. small coffee cup (after-dinner size)

demi-teinte f. medium shade (color)

demi-ton m. (mus.) half tone

demi-tour m. half turn; about-face; faire — to turn back, turn around

démobilisation f. demobilization

démobiliser vt. to demobilize

démocrate m. & f. democrat

démocratie f. democracy

démocratique a. democratic

démodé a. out of style; obsolete, old-fashioned

demoiselle f. young lady; dragonfly; — d'honneur bridesmaid; nom de — m. maiden name

démolir vt. to demolish

démolition f. demolition

démon m. demon, devil

démonétiser vt. to devalue, depreciate

démoniaque a. demoniac(al), devilish

démonstrateur m. demonstrator

démonstratif a. demonstrative

démonstration f. demonstration

démontable a. collapsible; detachable; portable

démonter vt. to dismantle; unhorse; upset

démontrable *a.* demonstrable

démontrer *vt.* to demonstrate

démoralisant, démoralisateur *a.* demoralizing

démoraliser *vt.* to demoralize

démuni *a.* out, sold out; unprovided; deprived

dénationaliser *vt.* to denationalize

dénaturer *vt.* to denature; make unnatural; pervert

dénégation *f.* denial

déni *m.* denial at law, refusal

dénicher *vt.* to dislodge; discover

denier *m.* money; penny, denier (of fibers); interest money

dénier *vt.* to deny, refuse

dénigrer *vt.* to disparage

dénombrement *m.* enumeration; census

dénombrer *vt.* to enumerate, count

dénominateur *m.* denominator

dénomination *f.* denomination; name

dénommer *vt.* to name

dénoncer *vt.* to denounce

dénonciateur *m.* denouncer; informer; — *a.* revealing

dénonciation *f.* denunciation

dénoter *vt.* to denote

dénouement *m.* untying; end, ending, outcome, result

dénouer *vt.* to untie, undo, clear up

denrée *f.* commodity, product; —s *pl.* provisions; produce

dense *a.* dense; thick; close

densité *f.* density

dent *f.* tooth; notch; cog; prong; coup de — *m.* bite; —s de lait baby teeth; mal de —s *m.* toothache; avoir mal aux —s to have a toothache

dentaire *a.* dental

dental *a.* dental (phonetics)

dent-de-lion *f.* dandelion

denté *a.* notched; cogged; toothed

dentelle *f.* lace, lacework

dentelure *f.* notching; perforation

dentier *m.* row of teeth; denture

dentifrice *m.* dentifrice; pâte — *f.* toothpaste

dentine *f.* dentine

dentiste *m.* dentist

dénuder *vt.* to strip, denude

dénué *a.* devoid, lacking; out, without

dénuement *m.* destitution, want, poverty

dénuer *vt.* to deprive, strip

déodoriser *vt.* to deodorize

dépannage *m.* repair service

dépanner *vt.* to repair a breakdown

dépanneur *m.* (auto.) repair man

dépanneuse *f.* wrecker, tow truck

dépaqueter *vt.* to unpack; unwrap

dépareiller *vt.* to remove one of a pair; spoil a pair

déparer *vt.* to strip; remove adornment from

départ *m.* departure; start; division, separation

département *m.* department, administrative department

départemental *a.* departmental

départir *vt.* to divide; se — de to depart from; part with, to cease, desist

dépasser *vt.* to go beyond, overreach, overstep; overtake; transcend; exceed

dépaysé *a.* out of place

dépecer *vt.* to carve, cut in pieces

dépêche *f.* dispatch; telegram

dépêcher *vt.* to dispatch; se — to hurry, hasten

dépeindre *vt.* to paint, portray, depict

dépendance *f.* dependence, dependency

dépendant *a.* dependent

dépendre *vi.* to depend on; result; belong; — *vt.* to unhang, take down

dépens *m. pl.* (com.) cost; costs (law); aux — de at the expense of

dépense *f.* expense, expenditure; pantry

dépenser *vt.* to spend, expend

dépensier *a. & m.* extravagant; spendthrift

dépérir *vi.* to waste away; pine; decline; die out

dépeupler *vt.* to depopulate; unstock

dépilatoire *a.* hair-removing, depilatory

dépiler *vt.* to remove hair from

dépister *vt.* to track, hunt down

dépit *m.* spite; vexation

dépiter *vt.* to vex; spite

déplacé *a.* misplaced, out of place

déplacement *m.* moving; travelling; displacement

déplacer *vt.* to move; displace; transfer

déplaire *vi.* to displease; offend

déplaisant *a.* unpleasant

déplaisir *m.* displeasure

déplanter *vt.* to dig up for transplanting

dépliant *m.* folder, brochure

déplier *vt.* to unfold

déplisser *vt.* to remove the pleats or wrinkles from

déploiement *m.* deployment; unfolding

déplorable *a.* deplorable

déplorer *vt.* to deplore

déployé *a.* unfolded; rire à gorge —e to laugh heartily

déployer *vt.* to unfold; display; unfurl; deploy

déplumer *vt.* to pluck the feathers from

dépolariser *vt.* to depolarize

dépolir *vt.* to take off the polish; verre dépoli *m.* frosted glass

dépopulation *f.* depopulation

déportation *f.* deportation

déportements *m. pl.* misdeeds

déporter *vt.* to deport; — *vi.* to swerve

déposant *m.* depositor; deponent (law), witness; — *a.* testifying

dépose *f.* removal

déposer *vt. & vi.* to depose; deposit; give testimony

dépositaire *m. & f.* depository

déposition *f.* deposition

déposséder *vt.* to dispossess

dépôt *m.* deposit; storehouse, warehouse, trust

dépouille *f.* spoil; remains; cast-off skin; —s *pl.* booty

dépouiller *vt.* to strip, skin an animal; examine, study

dépourvu *a.* unprovided for, destitute, lacking; au — *adv.* unawares

dépravation *f.* depravity, corruption

dépraver *vt.* to deprave

déprécier *vt.* to depreciate, disparage

déprédation f. depradation, pillage

déprendre v., se — to separate, detach oneself

dépression f. depression

déprimer vt. to depress; disparage

depuis prep. since, for; — longtemps for a long time; — adv. since; — que conj. since

dépurer vt. to purify

députation f. deputation

député m. deputy

députer vt. to send as representative

déraciner vt. to root out, uproot

dérailler vi. to be derailed; go off the track

déraison f. unreasonableness, folly

déraisonnable a. unreasonable

déraisonner vi. to be unreasonable

dérangement m. derangement; break-down

déranger vt. to derange; put out of order; disturb

déraper vi. to detach; skid; aweigh (anchor)

dératé m. lively individual; courir comme un — to run like a deer

derechef adv. again, anew

déréglé a. out of order; disorderly

dérèglement m. disorder; irregularity

dérégler vt. to put out of order

dérider vt. to unwrinkle; (fig.) to cheer up

dérision f. derision; tourner en — to ridicule, deride

dérisoire a. derisive, ridiculous

dérivatif m. & a. derivative

dérivation f. derivation; drift; diversion

dérive f. drift; à la — adrift

dérivé a. derivative

dériver vi. to derive; — vt. to divert

dermatologie f. dermatology

dermatologiste m. dermatologist

dernier a. last; preceding; final

dernièrement adv. recently, lately

dernier-né m. youngest (in a family)

dérobée f., à la — secretly

dérober vt. to rob, steal; hide, conceal; se — to steal away; disappear; hide

dérogation f. derogation

déroger vi., — à to depart from, not conform to; detract from

dérouiller vt. to remove the rust from; limber up; polish

dérouler vt. to unroll, unfold

déroute f. rout, disorder

dérouter vt. to rout

derrière prep. & adv. behind; — m. back, rear; behind

derviche m. dervish

dès prep. from, since, starting with; — que conj. as soon as

désabonner v., se — to cancel a subscription

désabuser vt. to disabuse, undeceive

désaccord m. disagreement, discord

désaccorder vt. to cause discord in

désaffecter vt. to deconsecrate, eliminate the original function of

désaffection f. loss of affection

désagréable a. disagreeable, unpleasant

désagrégation f. dissolution, separation; breaking up

désagréger vt. to separate, break up

désagrément m. unpleasantness

désaltérer vt. to quench one's thirst

désamorcer vt. to disarm a bomb; (elec.) cut the current

désappointement m. disappointment

désappointer vt. to disappoint; dull

désapprendre vt. to unlearn, forget

désapprobateur a. disapproving

désapprobation f. disapproval

désapprouver vt. to disapprove (of)

désarçonner vt. to unsaddle, unseat, throw from horse; (fig. & coll.) to disconcert; confuse in a discussion

désarmement m. disarmament

désarmer vt. to disarm; appease

désarroi m. disorder, confusion

désastre m. disaster

désastreux a. disastrous

désavantage m. disadvantage

désavantager vt. to put at a disadvantage, handicap

désavantageux a. disadvantageous

désaveu m. disavowal, denial

désavouer vt. to disavow

desceller vt. to unseal

descendance f. descent, descendants

descendant a. descending; — m. descendant

descendre vi. to descend, come down-stairs; — à un hotel stay at a hotel; — vt. to bring down; (coll.) depose; (avi.) bring down an enemy plane

descente f. descent; decline; hernia; — de lit bedside rug

descriptible a. describable

descriptif a. descriptive

désemballer vt. to unpack, unwrap

désemparé a. disconcerted

désemparer vi., sans — immediately; continuously

désenchanter vt. to disillusion, disenchant

désencombrer vt. to free, disencumber

désengager vt. to release from a commitment

désennuyer vt. to divert, cheer

désensabler vt. to free from the sand

désensibiliser vt. to desensitize

désentortiller vt. to straighten; sort

déséquilibrer vt. to unbalance

désert m. desert, wilderness; — a. deserted, solitary, abandoned

déserter vt. & vi. to desert

déserteur m. deserter

désertion f. desertion

désespérance f. despair, loss of hope

désespéré a. desperate, hopeless

désespérer vi. to despair; — vt. to be the despair of

désespoir m. despair

déshabillé m. housecoat

déshabiller vt. to undress; se — to undress, get undressed

déshérité a. disinherited; downtrodden

déshériter vt. to disinherit

déshonnête a. improper, unseemly

déshonneur m. dishonor, disgrace

déshonorer vt. to dishonor

déshydrater vt. to dehydrate

désignation f. designation

désigner *vt.* to designate, point out; appoint

désillusion *f.* disappointment, disillusion

désillusionner *vt.* to disillusion

désinence *f.* (gram.) ending of word

désinfecter *vt.* to disinfect

désinfection *f.* disinfection

désintégration *f.* disintegration

désintégrer *vt.* to disintegrate

désintéressé *a.* disinterested; unselfish

désintéressement *m.* impartiality; unselfishness

désintéresser *vt.* to indemnify; buy out (a partner)

désinviter *vt.* to withdraw an invitation

désinvolte *a.* unconstrained; impertinent

désinvolture *f.* ease, gracefulness

désir *m.* desire, wish

désirable *a.* desirable

désirer *vt.* to desire, wish for

désireux *a.* desirous, anxious

désister *v., se — to desist; se — de* to waive, renounce

désobéir *vi.* to disobey

désobéissance *f.* disobedience

désobligeant *a.* disobliging

désobliger *vt.* to displease

désodorisant *m.* deodorant

désodoriser *vt.* to clear of odor, deodorize

désœuvré *a.* idle, unoccupied

désœuvrement *m.* idleness, lack of occupation

désolant *a.* distressing, sad

désolation *f.* desolation; desolateness; grief

désolé *a.* very sorry; desolate

désoler *vt.* to desolate, ruin, destroy

désopilant *a.* very funny, hilarious

désordonné *a.* disordered; disorderly; untidy

désordonner *vt.* to disorder

désordre *m.* disorder, confusion

désorganiser *vt.* to disorganize

désorienter *vt.* to mislead; cause to become lost

désormais *adv.* henceforth

désoxyder *vt.* to deoxidize

despote *m.* despot; — *a.* despotic

despotisme *m.* despotism

dessaisir *vt.* to dispossess

dessécher *vt.* to dry; wither

dessein *m.* design, purpose; scheme, plan; à — on purpose; sans — unintentionally; aimlessly

desseller *vt.* to unsaddle

desserrer *vt.* to loosen

desserte *f.* sideboard

dessertir *vt.* to remove a gem from its setting

desservant *m.* parish priest

desservir *vt.* to serve; clear the table; harm, be of disservice to

dessiller *vt.* to open the eyes

dessin *m.* drawing; plan; pattern

dessinateur *m.* designer; draftsman

dessiner *vt.* to draw, design, sketch

dessouler *vt. & vi.* to sober up

dessous *prep. & adv.* under, below; underneath, undermost; au — (de) below; — *m.* underpart; wrong side

dessus *prep. & adv.* on, upon, uppermost;

au — (de) above, beyond; — *m.* upper part; advantage

destin *m.* destiny, fate

destinataire *m.* receiver, addressee, consignee

destinée *f.* destiny, doom, fate

destiner *vt.* to destine; intend

destitué *a.* destitute, devoid

destituer *vt.* to dismiss, discharge

destitution *f.* destitution, dismissal

destrier *m.* charger, war horse

destructeur *a.* destructive; — *m.* destroyer

destructif *a.* destructive

désuet *a.* obsolete

désuétude *f.* obsolescence, disuse

désunion *f.* lack of harmony, discord; misunderstanding

désunir *vt.* to separate, unjoin

détaché *a.* loose, indifferent, detached

détachement *m.* detachment

détacher *vt.* to detach, loosen; clean, remove spots from

détail *m.* detail; (com.) retail; au — (com.) at retail

détaillant *m.* retailer

détailler *vt.* to cut up; detail; retail

détartrer *vt.* remove tartar from teeth

detaxer *vt.* to remove the tax from, exempt from tax

détecter *vt.* to detect

détecteur *m.* detector

détective *m.* detective; (phot.) box camera

déteindre *vi.* to fade *or* run (colors)

dételer *vt.* to unharness; give up, cease

détendre *vt.* to relax, loosen; take down

détenir *vt.* to detain, withhold; hold, possess

détente *f.* trigger; (fig.) relaxation; expansion

détention *f.* detention, custody

détenu *m.* prisoner

déterger *vt.* to clean

détérioration *f.* deterioration

détériorer *vt.* to deteriorate

déterminant *a.* determining; — *m.* determinant

déterminatif *a.* determining

détermination *f.* determination

déterminé *a.* determined; definite

déterminer *vt.* to determine, settle, decide; cause

déterminisme *m.* determinism

déterrer *vt.* to disinter; unearth, discover

détersif *m.* detergent

détestable *a.* detestable

détestation *f.* detestation

détester *vt.* to detest, abhor, hate

détonant *a. & m.* explosive

détonateur *m.* detonating cap

détonation *f.* detonation, explosion

détoner *vi.* to explode

détonner *vi.* to sing *or* play off key; to clash

détordre *vt.* to untwist

détorquer *vt.* to distort, misrepresent

détorsion *f.* distortion

détortiller *vt.* to untwist

détour *m.* turning, roundabout way; evasion, excuse, subterfuge; turn, bend; prendre des —s to beat about the bush

détourné *a.* off the beaten track; isolated; secret

détournement *m.* diverting, turning away; embezzlement

détourner *vt.* to turn aside; divert, change; avert

détracteur *m.* detractor; — *a.* detracting

détraquer *vt.* to lead astray, distract, divert; break, put out of commission; se — to break down

détrempe *f.* distemper (art)

détremper *vt.* to dilute; soften, remove the temper

détresse *f.* distress; danger

détriment *m.* detriment

détritus *m.* waste, rubbish, debris

détroit *m.* strait, channel

détromper *vt.* to undeceive

détrôner *vt.* to dethrone

détrousser *vt.* to undo; rob

détruire *vt.* to destroy, ruin

dette *f.* debt

deuil *m.* mourning, mourning clothes

deutérium *m.* deuterium

deux *a.* two; tous les — both

deuxième *a.* second

deux-points *m.* colon

dévaler *vi.* to go down(ward)

dévaliser *vt.* to rob

dévaloriser *vt.* to devaluate

dévaluation *f.* devaluation

dévaluer *vt.* to devaluate

devancer *vt.* to go before, precede; anticipate

devancier *m.* predecessor; —s *pl.* ancestors

devant *m.* front, forepart; aller au — de to go and meet; — *prep. & adv.* in front of, before

devanture *f.* store window; window display

dévastateur *m.* devastator; — *a.* devastating

dévastation *f.* devastation

dévaster *vt.* to devastate

déveine *f.* bad luck

développement *m.* development

développer *vt.* to develop; unfold

devenir *vi.* to become; grow, turn

dévergondage *m.* shamelessness; excesses

dévergonder *v.,* se — to become dissolute, commit excesses, be shameless

dévernir *vt.* to remove the varnish

déverrouiller *vt.* to unbolt

devers *prep.* towards; par — in the possession of; in the eyes of

dévers *a.* out of alignment

déverser *vt.* to slope, bank; pour, divert; — *vi.* lean; become lopsided

dévêtir *vt.* to undress; divest

déviation *f.* deviation, deflection; detour

dévider *vt.* to wind onto

dévier *vt.* to turn aside; — *vi.* to make a detour; deviate

deviner *vt.* to divine, guess

devinette *f.* riddle

dévisager *vt.* to stare at

devise *f.* motto; —s *pl.* foreign currency

deviser *vi.* to chat

dévisser *vt.* to unscrew

dévoiler *vt.* to unveil, discover

devoir *vt. & vi.* to owe, be indebted to; be bound, be obliged; must, ought; be necessary; — *m.* duty, obligation, task

dévorateur *a.* devouring

dévorer *vt.* to devour; (fig.) consume

dévot *a.* devout; pious; bigoted

dévouement *m.* devotion; religious devotion

dévouer *vt.* to devote, dedicate

dévoyé *m. & a.* stray

dextérité *f.* dexterity

diabète *m.* (med.) diabetes

diabétique *a. & n.* diabetic

diable *m.* devil; hand truck for baggage

diablerie *f.* deviltry

diablotin *m.* little devil

diabolique *a.* diabolic(al)

diaconesse *f.* deaconess

diacre *m.* deacon

diacritique *a.* diacritic(al)

diadème *m.* diadem

diagnose *f.* (med.) diagnosis

diagnostique *a.* diagnostic

diagnostiquer *vt.* to diagnose

diagramme *m.* diagram

dialectal *a.* dialectical

dialecte *m.* dialect

dialectique *a.* dialectic; — *f.* dialectics

dialogue *m.* dialog

dialoguer *vi.* to converse

diamant *m.* diamond

diamantaire, diamantin *a.* diamond-like

diamétral *a.* diametrical

diamètre *m.* diameter

diane *f.* (mil.) reveille

diantre *interj.* devil, dickens

diapason *m.* diapason

diaphane *a.* transparent

diaphragme *m.* diaphragm

diapositif *m.,* **diapositive** *f.* (phot.) transparency

diaprer *vt.* to ornament, color with many hues

diarrhée *f.* diarrhea

diastolique *a.* (med.) diastolic

diathermie *f.* diathermy

diatomée *f.* diatom

diatonique *a.* (mus.) diatonic

dichromatique, a. dichromatic

dictateur *m.* dictator

dictatorial *a.* dictatorial

dictature *f.* dictatorship

dictée *f.* dictation

dicter *vt.* to dictate

diction *f.* diction

dictionnaire *m.* dictionary

dicton *m.* saying, proverb

didactique *a.* didactic

dièrèse *f.* diaeresis

dièse *a. & m.* (mus.) sharp

diesel *m.* diesel engine

diéser *vt.* (mus.) to sharp

diète *f.* diet

diéticien *m.* dietician

diététique *f.* dietetics

Dieu *m.* God; — merci! thank God!; plût à —! God grant it!; à — ne plaise! God forbid!

diffamation *f.* defamation

diffamatoire *a.* defamatory

diffamer *vt.* to defame, slander; libel
différemment *adv.* differently
différence *f.* difference
différenciation *f.* differentiation
différencier *vt.* to distinguish
différend *m.* difference, source of argument
différentiel *a. & m.* differential
différer *vt.* to defer, put off; — *vi.* to differ
difficile *a.* difficult; hard
difficulté *f.* difficulty
difficultueux *a.* difficult
difforme *a.* deformed
difformité *f.* deformity
diffracter *vt.* to diffract
diffraction *f.* diffraction
diffus *a.* diffuse; wordy
diffuser *vt.* to diffuse, spread
diffusion *f.* diffusion; spreading
digérer *vt. & vi.* to digest; stomach; simmer
digest *m.* digest, abridgment, résumé
digestif *m.* (med.) digestive; liqueur, brandy; — *a.* digestive
digestion *f.* digestion
digitaline *f.* (med.) digitalis
digne *a.* worthy (of); dignified
dignitaire *m.* dignitary
dignité *f.* dignity, title, rank
digression *f.* digression
digue *f.* dike
dilacérer *vt.* to lacerate
dilapidation *f.* dilapidation
dilapider *vt.* to dilapidate; embezzle; squander
dilation *f.* dilation, expansion
dilater *vt.* to dilate, expand, widen
dilatoire *a.* dilatory
dilemme *m.* dilemma
dilettante *m.* dilettante, amateur
diligemment *adv.* diligently
diligence *f.* diligence; haste; stagecoach
diluer *vt.* to dilute
diluvien *a.* diluvian; diluvial
dimanche *m.* Sunday
dîme *f.* tithe
diminuer *vt. & vi.* to diminish
diminutif *a.* diminutive
dinde *f.* hen turkey; (fig.) goose; foolish woman
dindon *m.* tom turkey; —neau *m.* young turkey
dîner *m.* dinner; — *vi.* to dine
dinette *f.* family supper; children's evening meal
dîneur *m.* dinner guest; diner
dinosaure, dinosaurien *m.* dinosaur
diocèse *m.* diocese
diphthérie *f.* diphtheria
diphthongue *m.* diphthong
diphtonguer *vt.* to diphthongize
diplomate *m.* diplomat
diplomatie *f.* diplomacy
diplomatique *a.* diplomatic
diplôme *m.* diploma
diplômé *a.* graduate, licensed
dipsomanie *f.* compulsive drinking
dire *vt.* to tell, say, relate; think; mean; pour ainsi — as it were; vouloir — to

mean; — *n.* words, statement
directeur *m.* director, manager
direction *f.* direction; management; steering gear
directionnel *a.* directional
directive *f.* directive
directoire *m.* directory
directorat *m.* directorship
dirigeable *m.* dirigible
diriger *vt.* to direct, manage, guide, lead, supervise
discernable *a.* discernible, perceptible
discernement *m.* discernment
discerner *vt.* to discern
disciple *m.* disciple
disciplinaire *a.* disciplinary; — *m.* disciplinarian
discipliner *vt.* to discipline
discobole *m.* discus thrower
discontinu *a.* discontinuous
discontinuation *f.* discontinuation
discontinuer *vt.* to interrupt, discontinue
discontinuité *f.* interruption, discontinuity
disconvenance *f.* disproportion, disparity; unsuitableness
disconvenir *vi.* to disagree
discophile *m. & f.* amateur record collector *or* maker
discordant *a.* discordant
discorde *f.* discord
discorder *vi.* to be out of harmony, not to harmonize; clash
discothèque *f.* collection of phonograph records, record library
discourir *vi.* to discourse
discours *m.* discourse; speech
discourtois *a.* discourteous
discourtoisie *f.* discourtesy, impoliteness
discrédit *m.* discredit; disfavor
discréditer *vt.* to discredit
discret *a.* discreet; prudent; quiet
discrétion *f.* discretion
discrétionnaire *a.* discretionary
discrimination *f.* discrimination
disculper *vt.* to clear, exonerate
discussion *f.* argument, debate; discussion
discutable *a.* moot, debatable
discuter *vt.* to discuss, argue, debate
disert *a.* fluent, eloquent
disette *f.* want, poverty; famine
diseur (diseuse) *m. & f.* speaker, teller; — de bonne aventure fortune teller
disgrâce *f.* disgrace, disfavor
disgracié *a.* fallen from favor
disgracieux *a.* ungraceful, awkward; disagreable; rude
disjoindre *vt.* to disjoin, disjoint
disjoncteur *m.* circuit breaker
disjonctif *a.* disjunctive
disloquer *vt.* to dislocate
disparaître *vi.* to disappear
disparate *a.* incongruous; unmatched; — *f.* incongruity, sharp contrast
disparité *f.* disparity
disparition *f.* disappearance
dispendieux *a.* costly, expensive
dispensaire *m.* dispensary, clinic
dispensation *f.* dispensing, dispensation
dispense *f.* dispensation; exemption

dispenser *vt.* to dispense; excuse, exempt
disperser *vt.* to disperse, scatter
dispersion *f.* dispersion, dispersal
disponibilités *f. pl.* available funds
disponible *a.* available; free, unoccupied
dispos *a.* well-disposed; in good condition
disposé *a.* disposed, inclined
disposer *vt. & vi.* to dispose; — de to have at one's disposal
dispositif *m.* apparatus; terms; assembly of machinery pieces
disposition *f.* disposition; arrangement; -s *pl.* preparation
disproportionné *a.* disproportionate
dispute *f.* dispute, quarrel
disputer *vt. & vi.* to dispute, quarrel, argue
disqualification *f.* disqualification
disquaire *m.* record seller, record dealer
disqualifier *vt.* to disqualify
disque *m.* disk, discus; phonograph record; (rail.) safety signal; — longue durée long-playing record
dissection *f.* dissection
dissemblable *a.* unsimilar, different
dissémination *f.* dissemination
disséminer *vt.* to disseminate
dissension *f.* dissension, discord
dissentiment *m.* difference of opinion
disséquer *vt.* to dissect
dissertation *f.* dissertation; essay on a certain subject
disserter *vi.* to expound
dissident *a.* dissident
dissimulateur *m.* dissembler; — *a.* dissembling, hiding
dissimulation *f.* dissimulation, dissembling
dissimulé *a.* secretive, deceptive
dissimuler *vt. & vi.* to conceal; hide; dissemble
dissipation *f.* dissipation
dissiper *vt.* to dissipate; disperse
dissociation *f.* dissociation
dissocier *vt.* to dissociate, separate
dissolu *a.* dissolute
dissolution *f.* dissolution; dissoluteness; dissolving
dissonance *f.* disssonance
dissonant *a.* dissonant
dissoudre *vt.* to dissolve
dissuader *vt.* to dissuade
distance *f.* distance; interval
distancer *vt.* to outdistance; to stagger (racing); to disqualify (racing)
distant *a.* distant
distendre *vt.* to distend
distension *f.* distension
distillat *m.* distillate
distillateur *m.* distiller
distillation *f.* distillation
distiller *vt.* to distill; -ie *f.* distillery
distinct *a.* distinct, clear
distinctif *a.* distinctive
distinction *f.* distinction
distingué *a.* distinguished
distinguer *vt.* to distinguish; single out
distordre *vt.* to distort, twist
distors *a.* distorted, twisted
distorsion *f.* distortion
distraction *f.* distraction, abstraction;

absent-mindedness; amusement
distraire *vt.* to distract, divert
distrait *a.* inattentive, absent-minded
distribuer *vt.* to distribute
distributeur *a.* distributing; — *m.* distributor
distribution *f.* distribution; (theat.) cast
district *m.* district
dit *a.* said, appointed, fixed; prendre pour — to take for granted; — *m.* saying
dito *adv.* ditto
diurétique *a. & m.* diuretic
diurne *a.* daily; day-blooming; active in daylight
divaguer *vi.* to go astray, wander, ramble
divan *m.* divan, couch
divergence *f.* divergency, divergence
divergent *a.* divergent
diverger *vi.* to diverge
divers *a.* diverse; various; different
diversifier *vt.* to diversify, vary
diversion *f.* diversion
diversité *f.* diversity
divertir *vt.* to divert, entertain; se — to have a good time
divertissement *m.* recreation, pastime, diversion
dividende *m.* dividend
divin *a.* divine; heavenly
divination *f.* divination, soothsaying
diviniser *vt.* to deify
divinité *f.* divinity
diviser *vt.* to divide; separate
diviseur *m.* divider; (math.) divisor, factor
divisible *a.* divisible
division *f.* division; dividing; section; disagreement; hyphen
divorcer *vi.* to divorce, be divorced
divulguer *vt.* to divulge
dix *a.* ten
dix-huit *a.* eighteen
dixième *a.* tenth
dix-neuf *a.* nineteen
dix-sept *a.* seventeen
dizaine *f.* about ten
djinn *m.* jinni, genie
do *m.* (mus.) do; first scale syllable; French key of C
docile *a.* docile, submissive
docilité *f.* docility
dock *m.* dock
docker *m.* dock worker
docte *a.* learned, scholarly
docteur *m.* doctor
doctorat *m.* doctor's degree, doctorate
doctrinal *a.* doctrinal
doctrine *f.* doctrine, dogma
document *m.* document; written proof
documentaire *a. & m.* documentary; documentative, educational film
documentation *f.* documentation
documenter *vt.* to document
dodeliner *vi.* to sway, rock; — *vt.* to dandle a baby, balance gently
dogmatique *a.* dogmatic
dogmatiser *vi.* to pontificate; speak in a pre-emptory tone
dogmatisme *m.* dogmatism
dogme *m.* dogma, tenet

dogue *m.* bullgod; watchdog

doigt *m.* finger; — du pied toe; montrer du — to point at

doigter *vt.* to finger, strum, play

doigtier *m.* finger guard

doit *m.* (com.) debit

doléance *f.* complaint; grievance

dolent *a.* sad, doleful; painful

dolmen *m.* dolmen (archeology)

domaine *m.* domain; estate; property

dôme *m.* dome

domestication *f.* domestication

domesticité *f.* domesticity

domestique *m. & f.* domestic, servant; — *a.* domestic

domestiquer *vt.* to tame, domesticate

domicilier *vt.* to domicile; se — to establish residence

dominant *a.* dominant; -e *f.* dominant trait

dominateur *a.* dominant, dominating

dominer *vt.* to dominate, rule, control; overlook; — *vi.* to rule, prevail

dominical *a.* dominical; Sunday; oraison -e *f.* Lord's prayer

domino *m.* domino; robe; disguise

dommage *m.* damage, loss; c'est — it is a pity

dommageable *a.* damaging; damageable

domptable *a.* conquerable; tamable, trainable

dompter *vt.* to tame; subdue, vanquish, conquer

dompteur *m.* conqueror; animal trainer

don *m.* gift, present; (fig.) knack, talent

donataire *m. & f.* recipient, beneficiary

donateur *m.* donor

donation *f.* donation, gift

donc *conj.* then, thus, therefore, so

donjon *m.* castle keep; isolated tower for castle watchman; tiered metal tower (modern battleship)

donne *f.* card deal

donnée *f.*, -s *pl.* information; data

donner *vt. & vi.* to give; impart; grant; deal cards; — sur to open onto, look out on

donneur *m.* donor; dealer at cards

dont *pron.* whose, of which, of whom

donzelle *f.* woman of easy virtue

dorade, daurade *f.* goldfish

dorénavant *adv.* henceforth

dorer *vt.* to gild; to glaze pastry

doreur *m.* gilder

dorique *a.* Doric

dorlotement *m.* coddling, pampering

dorloter *vt.* to pamper, coddle

dormant *a.* sleeping; dormant

dormeur *m.* sleeper

dormir *vi.* to sleep; à — debout boring, dull

dortoir *m.* dormitory

dorure *f.* gilding; application of pastry glaze

dos *m.* back; — du nez bridge of the nose

dosage *m.* dose, dosage

dossier *m.* chair back; file, folder; dossier

dot *f.* dowry

dotation *f.* endowment

doter *vt.* to endow; furnish with a dowry

douaire *m.* widow's dowry

douairière *f.* dowager

douane *f.* custom house, duty, customs

douanier *m.* customs officer; — *a.* concerning customs

doublage *m.* lining; doubling; dubbing (movie film)

double *m.* double; spare; copy; — *a.* double

doublé *m.* plated metal; metal plating (gold *or* silver); bank shot (billiards); — *a.* lined

doublement *adv.* doubly

doubler *vt.* to double; line; pass (a car); hasten; begin over; dub (a film)

doublon *m.* doubloon

doublure *f.* lining; (theat.) understudy

doucement *adv.* softly; slowly

doucereux *a.* unpleasantly sweet

douceur *f.* sweetness; softness, gentleness; docility

douche *f.* shower bath; (med.) douche

doucir *vt.* to polish, rub

doué *a.* gifted, endowed

douer *vt.* to bestow, endow

douille *f.* socket; cartridge shell; casing

douillet *a.* soft, delicate; (fig.) oversensitive

douleur *f.* pain, sorrow

douloureux *a.* painful; sorrowful

doute *m.* doubt; suspicion; skepticism; mettre en — to doubt, question; sans — without doubt, probably; of course

douter *vi.* to doubt; se — de to suspect

douteur *a.* doubting

douteux *a.* doubtful; dubious, suspicious

douve *f.* moat; plank, stave

doux (douce) *a.* sweet; soft, smooth; fresh; quiet; mild; timid

douzaine *f.* dozen

douze *a.* twelve

douzième *a.* twelfth

doxologie *f.* doxology

doyen *m.* dean

doyenneté *f.* seniority

dragée *f.* Jordan almond; buckshot; sugar-coated pill

drageon *m.* (bot.) sucker, shoot (tree root)

dragon *m.* dragon; (mil.) dragoon

drague *f.* dredge; seine; minesweeping apparatus; — à vapeur steam shovel

draguer *vt.* to dredge

dragueur *m.* dredge (boat); minesweeper

drain *m.* drain pipe; (med.) drain

drainage *m.* drainage

drainer *vt.* to drain

dramatique *a.* dramatic

dramatiser *vt.* to dramatize

dramaturge *m.* dramatist

drame *m.* drama, play

drap *m.* cloth; bed sheet; -ie *f.* drapery

drapeau *m.* flag

draper *vt.* to drape

drapier *m.* cloth merchant, cloth manufacturer; draper

drelin *m.* sound of ringing, ting-a-ling (bell)

dressage *m.* training of animals

dresser *vt.* to raise; build; train animals; set up; trim; — les oreilles prick up ears; se — to stand, straighten up, rise; sit up

dresseur m. animal trainer

dressoir m. sideboard, buffet; dresser

drisse f. halyard, rope

drogue f. drug; chemical

droguer vt. to drug; physic

droguerie f. drug business

droguiste m. druggist

droit m. right, justice; prerogative, privilege; law; tax; de — by rights, rightfully; — a. right; straight; just; honest; upright; — adv., tout — straight ahead

droite f. right; à — to the right

droitier a. right-hand(ed)

droiture f. integrity

drolatique a. droll, funny, amusing

drôle a. droll, funny; odd, peculiar

drôlesse f. wench, hussy

dromadaire m. dromadary

dru a. vigorous, heavy; — adv. thickly, heavily

dû a. & m. due; what is owed

dualisme m. dualism

dualité f. duality

duc m. duke; horned owl

duché m. duchy

duchesse f. duchess; (coll.) woman with airs; 18th century couch; Duchess pear

ductile a. ductile

duègne f. duenna, chaperon

duel m. duel

duelliste m. duelist

dulcifier vt. to sweeten; neutralize

dûment adv. duly

dune f. dune

dunette f. (naut.) poop

duo m. (mus.) duet

duodécimal a. duodecimal

duodénum m. duodenum

dupe f. dupe; — a. duped

duper vt. to dupe; fool

duperie f. deception, trickery

duplicata m. duplicate

duplicateur m. duplicator, duplicating machine

duplication f. duplication

duplicité f. duplicity

duquel pron. of which, of whom, whose

dur a. & adv. hard; tough, difficult

durabilité f. durability

durable a. durable, lasting

durant prep. during

durcir vt. & vi. to harden

durcissement m. hardening; stiffening

durée f. duration

durer vi. to last, endure

dureté f. hardness, toughness; cruelty

durillon m. callus, corn

duvet m. down; fuzz

duveté a. downy

duveteux a. downy

dynamique a. dynamic

dynamisme m. dynamism

dynamite f. dynamite; -r vt. to dynamite

dynamo f. dynamo

dynastie f. dynasty

dynastique a. dynastic

dyne f. dyne

dysenterie f. dysentery

dyspepsie f. dispepsia, indigestion

E

eau f. water; — de Cologne cologne; — douce soft water; fresh water; cours d' — m. stream; jet d' — m. fountain

eau-de-vie f. brandy; spirits

eau-forte f. nitric acid; etching

ébahir vt. to stupify, amaze

ébahissement m. astonishment, amazement

ébats m. pl. frolics, revels

ébattre v., s' — to frolic, revel

ébaubir v., s' — to be astonished

ébauche f. rough draft, sketch

ébaucher vt. to sketch, make a rough draft of

ébène f. ebony

ébenier m. ebony tree

ébéniste m. cabinetmaker

éberluer vt. to astonish

éblouir vt. to dazzle; bewitch

éblouissement m. dazzlement; glare

ébouillanter vt. to scald

éboulement m. landslide; cave-in (earth)

ébouler vt. to cause to fall; to crumble; s' — to tumble down

ébouriffant a. amazing

ébouriffer vt. to disorder, mess up; amaze

ébrancher vt. to prune

ébranlement m. shaking; shock

ébranler vt. to shake, shock; set in motion; s' — to waver, shake

ébrécher vt. to breach; notch; — sa fortune cut into one's fortune

ébriété f. inebriation

ébroer v. s' — to snort

ébruiter vt. to spread about; make public

ébullition f. boiling; boiling point

éburnéen a. ivory

écaille f. scale, shell; tortoise shell

écailler vt. & vi. to scale fish

écale f. shell, hull

écaler vt. to shell, hull

écarlate f. & a. scarlet

écarquiller vt. to spread, open wide

écart m. stepping aside; swerving; discard; digression; à l' — adv. aside; secluded; aloof à l' — de prep. far from

écarté a. lonely, secluded

écartèlement m. quartering

écarteler vt. to quarter

écartement m. removal, separation

écarter vt. to put aside; separate; avert

ecchymose f. bruise, black-and-blue mark

ecclésiastique a. & m. ecclesiastic

écervelé a. brainless, flighty; — m. scatterbrain

échafaud m. scaffold; platform

échafaudage m. scaffolding

échafauder vt. to put up a scaffold; plan, set up, build up

échalote f. (bot.) shallot

échancrer vt. to hollow out; indent

échange m. exchange; libre — free trade

échanger vt. to exchange, barter

échanson m. cupbearer

échantillon m. sample, specimen

échappatoire f. way out; loophole

échappée *f.* escape; space, short period; à l' — stealthily

échappement *m.* escapement (watch); leak, leakage, escape; exhaust

échapper *vt.* to escape; avoid; s' — to escape; leave

écharde *f.* splinter

écharpe *f.* scarf; sash; sling; en — *adv.* diagonally

écharper *vt.* to slash, cut up

échasse *f.* stilt

échauder *vt.* to scald

échauffement *m.* heating; overexcitement

échauffer *vt.* to warm; excite; s' — to get warm; grow angry

échauffourée *f.* blunder; riot; rash project

échéance *f.* expiration, falling due; tomber à — to fall due

échéant *a.* falling due; le cas — if such should be the case

échec *m.* check; failure; -s *pl.* chess; chessmen; — et mat checkmate

échelle *f.* ladder, scale; stocking run; —

échelon *m.* rung; echelon

échelonnement *m.* spreading out

échelonner *vt.* to spread out; space out; (mil.) arrange in echelon

écheniller *vt.* to exterminate caterpillars

écheveau *m.* skein

échevelé *a.* dishevelled, tangled

écheveler *vt.* to dishevel

échine *f.* spine; backbone

échiner *vt.* to break the back of; beat; s' — to tire oneself out

échiquier *m.* chessboard; exchequer

écho *m.* echo

échoir *vi.* to fall due; happen

échopper *vt.* to gouge, scoop out

échotier *m.* gossip columnist, newsmonger

échouer *vt. & vi.* (naut.) to run aground, strand; be stranded; fail; faire — to wreck

échu *a.* expired

éclabousser *vt.* to splash, splatter

éclaboussure *f.* splash, splatter

éclair *m.* lightning flash; eclair (pastry)

éclairage *m.* lighting, lamps; (fig.) point of view

éclaircie *f.* bright spot (sky); clearing (forest)

éclaircir *vt.* to clear, thin, brighten; explain, elucidate

éclaircissement *m.* clearing up; explanation

éclairer *vt. & vi.* to light, illuminate, enlighten

éclaireur *m.* scout

éclaireuse *f.* girl scout

éclat *m.* splinter; brightness; splendor; explosion; peal of thunder; (fig.) glory

éclatant *a.* glittering, brilliant

éclatement *m.* explosion, bursting

éclater *vi.* to split, burst; sparkle, glitter; break out, blow up

éclectique *a. & n.* eclectic

éclectisme *m.* eclecticism

éclipser *vt.* to eclipse; s' — to be eclipsed, vanish

éclisse *f.* splinter; (med.) splint

éclisser *vt.* (med.) to use a splint

éclopé *a.* lame, crippled

éclore *vi.* to be hatched; blossom; open

éclosion *f.* blooming; manifestation; advent; hatching

écluse *f.* floodgate; canal lock

écluser *vt.* to close by a lock; — un bateau to take a boat through a lock

écœurer *vt.* to sicken; dishearten; cause aversion

école *f.* school; — maternelle nursery school; — mixte school for boys *and* girls

écolier *m.* schoolboy

écolière *f.* schoolgirl

écologie *f.* ecology

éconduire *vt.* to show out; get rid of

économat *m.* treasurer's office; bureau of economies

économe *a.* economical; — *m. & f.* housekeeper; accounts keeper; treasurer

économie *f.* economy; saving

économique *a.* economic(al)

économiser *vt.* to economize, save

économiste *m.* economist

écope *f.* (naut.) bailing scoop

écoper *vt.* (naut.) to bail out

écorce *f.* bark (tree), rind, peel; outside

écorcer *vt.* to peel

écorcher *vt.* to flay; scrape; scorch

écorchure *f.* scrape, abrasion

écorner *vt.* to dog-ear; curtail, reduce

écornifleur *m.* parasite, moocher

écossais *a.* Scotch, Scottish; — *n.* Scot, Scotsman

Écosse *f.* Scotland

écosser *vt.* to shell

écot *m.* share, part, portion; tree stump

écoulement *m.* drain, discharge; sale

écouler *vt.* to sell; s' — to flow out, drain off; elapse, go by

écourter *vt.* to shorten; crop

écoute *f.* listening post; monitor; être aux -s to be listening (in); be eavesdropping

écouter *vt.* to listen (to); pay attention

écouteur *m.* listener; telephone receiver; earphone

écoutille *f.* hatch

écran *m.* fire screen; (phot.) filter

écrasant *a.* crushing

écrasement *m.* crushing; defeat, disaster

écraser *vt.* to crush; s' — to crash; flock over

écrémer *vt.* to skim milk

écrémeuse *f.* cream separator

écrevisse *f.* crayfish

écrier *v., s'* — to cry out, exclaim

écrin *m.* jewel box, casket

écrire *vt.* to write, compose; write down

écrit *m.* writing, written word, written examination; — *a.* written

écriteau *m.* sign, placard

écritoire *f.* writing set; desk set

écriture *f.* handwriting; document; account

Écriture *f.*, l' — sainte Scriptures

écrivailleur *m.* scribbler, hack writer

écrivain *m.* writer, author of books

écrou *m.* screw nut; lever l' — to liberate

écrouelles *f. pl.* scrofula

écrouer *vt.* to imprison

écroulement m. fall, collapse; (fig.) complete ruin

écrouler v., s' — to collapse, crumble

écroûter vt. to remove the crust from

écru a. unbleached; raw silk

ectoplasme m. ectoplasm

écu m. shield; crown (coin); —s pl. (fig.) money

écueil m. reef, rock

écuelle f. bowl, basin

éculer vt. to wear down a heel

écumant a. foaming; fuming

écume f. foam; froth; scum; (fig.) dregs (of humanity); — de mer meerschaum

écumer vt. to skim; — vi. to foam

écumeux a. scummy; foamy, frothy

écumoire f. skimmer

écurage m. scouring

écurer vt. to scour, cleanse

écureuil m. squirrel

écurie f. stable; string of horses (same owner)

écusson m. shield (heraldry); escutcheon; bud (grafting)

écuyer m. horseman, squire

écuyère f. horsewoman

eczéma m. eczema

éden m. Garden of Eden; paradise

édenté a. toothless

édicule m. small building on the street, shelter

édifiant a. edifying

édification f. erecting, building; edification

édifier vt. to edify; build, found

édile m. town councillor

édit m. edict

éditer vt. to edit; publish

éditeur m. editor, publisher; —a. publishing

édition f. edition; publishing

éditorial a. & m. editorial

édredon m. eiderdown; feather quilt

éducation f. upbringing; education; breeding

édulcorer vt. to sugar-coat; water down; make inoffensive

éduquer vt. to rear, bring up

effacement m. effacement, erasing, obliteration

effacer vt. to efface, erase; s' — to be obliterated; stand aside; (fig.) to bow to superiority

effarement m. fright

effarer vt. to frighten

effaroucher vt. to scare away; frighten, alarm

effectif m. effective force; (mil.) complement; manpower; size; — a. effective, actual

effectivement adv. actually, in fact

effectuer vt. to effect, accomplish

efféminé a. effeminate

effervescence f. effervescence, excitement

effervescent a. effervescent

effet m. effect, result; impression; —s pl. belongings; —s publics public bonds; en — indeed

effeuillaison f. falling of leaves

effeuiller vt. to strip of leaves, petals

efficace a. effective, efficacious

efficacité f. efficiency, effectiveness, efficacy

efficience f. effectiveness; efficiency

effigie f. effigy

effilé a. slender; — m. fringe

effiler vt. to unravel; taper

effilocher vt. to unravel

efflanqué a. lean, skinny, thin

effleurer vt. to graze, touch lightly

effluve m. effluvium, emanation

effondrement m. collapse, collapsing, destruction

effondrer vt. to break open; break up ground s' — to sink down, cave in

efforcer s., s' — to strive, try to do one's best

effort m. effort, work; stress, strain

effraction f. housebreaking, burglary

effranger vt. to unravel the edges

effrayant a. frightful, dreadful

effrayer vt. to frighten; s' — to be frightened

effréné a. unbridled; frantic

effroi m. fright, terror

effronté a. bold, shameless,. impudent

effronterie f. impudence, insolence, effrontery

effroyable a. frightful

effusion f. effusion; outpouring; — de sang bloodshed

égal a. equal; alike; indifferent; even, level; — m. equal; cela m'est — it's all the same to me, I don't care, all right

égaler vt. to equal, match, value the same

égalisation f. equalisation, equalizing

égaliser vt. to equalize, make even

égalitaire a. equalitarian

égalité f. equality; evenness

égard m. respect, consideration; à l' — de in reference to, toward; en — à considering that

égaré a. stray, lost

égarement m. losing, misplacing; deviation; straying, wandering; mental disorder

égarer vt. to mislead; mislay; bewilder; s' — to go astray, wander

égayer vt. to cheer up; s' — to make merry

égéen a. Aegean

églantier m. (plant), églantine f. (flower) eglantine; sweetbrier, wild rose

église f. church

égocentrique a. egocentric

égoïne f. handsaw

égoïsme m. selfishness

égoïste a. selfish; — m. egotist

égorger vt. to cut the throat (of), slaughter

égotisme m. egotism

égotiste m. & f. egotist

égout m. drainage; sewer

égoutier m. sewer worker

égoutter vt. & vi. to drain

égouttoir m. draining rack

égratigner vt. to scratch

égratignure f. scratch

égrener vt. to shell; pick off (grapes); gin

égrillard a. fancy-free

égrugeoir m. mortar

égruger vt. to pound, pulverize

égueuler *vt.* to break the neck of

Égypte *f.* Egypt

égyptien *m. & a.* Egyptian

égyptologie *f.* Egyptology

éhonté *a.* shameless

éjaculation *f.* ejaculation

éjaculer *vt.* to ejaculate

éjecter *vt.* to eject

éjection *f.* ejection

élaboration *f.* elaboration

élaborer *vt.* to elaborate

élaguer *vt.* to prune, trim; (fig.) to curtail (literary work)

élan *m.* impetus, impulse; bound; outburst; elk

élancé *a.* slender, slim

élancement *m.* twinge; yearning

élancer *vi.* to throb; dart; s' — to rush upon; shoot forward *or* up

élargir *vt.* to widen; free

élasticité *f.* elasticity

élastique *a.* elastic; — *m.* elastic, rubber band

électeur *m.* elector, voter

électif *a.* elective

élection *f.* election

électoral *a.* electoral

électricien *m.* electrician

électricité *f.* electricity

électrification *f.* electrification

électrifier *vt.* to electrify

électrique *a.* electric, electrical

électriser *vt.* to electrify

électro-aimant *m.* electromagnet

électrocardiogramme *m.* cardiogram

électrochoc *m.* shock treatment

électrocuter *vt.* to electrocute

électrocution *f.* electrocution

électrode *f.* electrode

électrodynamique *a.* electrodynamic; — *f.* electrodynamics

électro-encéphalogramme *m.* electroencephalogram

électrolyse *f.* electrolysis

électromagnétique *a.* electromagnetic

électromètre *m.* electrometer

électron *m.* electron

électronique *a.* electronic

électroscope *m.* electroscope

électrostatique *a.* electrostatic

élégamment *adv.* elegantly

élégance *f.* elegance

élégant *a.* elegant, stylish

élégie *f.* elegy

élément *m.* element; (elec.) cell -s *pl.* natural forces

élémentaire *a.* elementary, basic

éléphant *m.* elephant

éléphantesque *a.* enormous

élevage *m.* animal husbandry; ranching

élévation *f.* elevation

élève *m. & f.* pupil

élevé *a.* high; brought up; bien — wellbred, well-mannered; mal — ill-bred

élever *vt.* to raise, bring up; s' — to rise, arise

éleveur *m.* animal raiser

elfe *m.* elf

élider *vt.* to elide

éligibilité *f.* eligibility

éligible *a.* eligible

élimer *vt.* to wear out

élimination *f.* elimination

éliminatoire *a.* preliminary (sports)

éliminer *vt.* to eliminate; cancel

élire *vt.* to elect

élisabéthain *a.* Elizabethan

élision *f.* elision

élite *f.* élite; choice

élixir *m.* elixir

elle *pron.* she, her, it; -s *pl.* they

elle-même *pron.* herself, itself

ellipse *f.* ellipse

elliptique *a.* elliptical

élocution *f.* elocution

éloge *m.* eulogy, praise

élogieux *a.* full of praise

éloigné *a.* distant, faraway, remote; removed

éloignement *m.* absence, remoteness; aversion; postponement

éloigner *vt.* to remove; drive away; defer; s' — to move off, away, deviate

élongation *f.* elongation

éloquemment *adv.* eloquently

éloquence *f.* eloquence

éloquent *a.* eloquent

élu *n.* chosen one; -s *pl.* elect

élucidation *f.* elucidation

élucider *vt.* to elucidate

éluder *vt.* to elude

émaciation *f.* emaciation

émacié *a.* emaciated

émail *m.* enamel, glaze

émailler *vt.* to enamel

émailleur *m.* enameller

émanation *f.* emanation

émancipation *f.* emancipation

émanciper *vt.* to emancipate

émaner *vi.* to emanate

émarger *vi.* to note in the margin, initial to prove reading; trim; receive pay

émasculer *vt.* to emasculate

emballage *m.* packing, crating

emballer *vt.* to pack, wrap; crate; excite

emballeur *m.* packer

embarcadère *m.* wharf; (rail.) platform

embarcation *f.* small boat, launch

embardée *f.* lurch; (naut.) yaw; (auto.) swerve

embarquement *m.* embarcation; shipment

embarquer *vt. & vi.* to embark

embarras *m.* obstruction; difficulty; perplexity; confusion

embarrasser *vt.* to trouble; perplex; confuse; embarass

embaucher *vt.* to hire

embauchoir *m.* shoe tree

embaumement *m.* embalming

embaumer *vt.* to embalm; perfume

embellir *vt. & vi.* to embellish; become beautiful

embellissement *m.* embellishment

embêtement *m.* annoyance

embêter *vt.* (coll.) to bother, annoy

emblée, d' — *adv.* first, on the spot; without difficulty

emblématique *a.* emblematic

emblème *m.* emblem

embobiner *vt.* to wind (up), put on a

spool or reel

emboîter vt. to fit in; copy, take after; set a bone; — le pas à fall into step with

embonpoint m. plumpness

embouche f. pasture

embouché a., mal — foulmouthed

embouchoir m. (mus.) instrument mouthpiece

embouchure f. mouth of a river; mouthpiece

embourber vt. to stick in the mud, implicate

embout m. handle (cane, umbrella)

embouteillage m. bottling up; bottleneck; traffic jam

embouteiller vt. to bottle up; (fig.) to block

embranchement m. branch, division; road junction

embrasement m. conflagration, burning

embraser vt. to set on fire

embrassade f. embrace

embrasse f. curtain tieback; armrest

embrassement m. embrace; kiss

embrasser vt. to embrace; kiss

embrasure f. opening; port

embrayage m. clutch; coupling, engaging

embrayer vt. to connect, engage; (auto.) to let in the clutch

embrocher vt. to spit (meat cookery)

embrouiller vt. to tangle, mix up; s' — to get confused; become intricate

embroussaillé a. bushy; complex, tangled

embrumé a. misty, hazy

embrun m. spray; fog

embryologie f. embryology

embryon m. embryo

embryonnaire a. embryonic

embûche f. trap

embuscade f. ambush

embusqué m. soldier at the rear; person lying in ambush

embusquer vt. to ambush, trap

émeraude f. emerald

émergence f. emergence

émerger vi. to emerge

émeri m. emery

émerillonné a. lively

émérite a. eminent, experienced; emeritus

émerveillement m. wonderment

émerveiller vt. to astonish, amaze

émétique a. emetic

émetteur m. radio transmitter

émettre vt. to emit, issue; transmit, broadcast

émeute f. riot

émietter vt. to crumble

émigration f. emigration

émigré m. emigrant; refugee; emigrated nobleman (history)

émigrer vi. to emigrate

émincé m. minced meat, mincemeat

émincer vt. to slice thinly; hash

éminemment adv. eminently

éminence f. eminence

éminent a. eminent; distinguished

émissaire m. emissary

émission f. emission, issue; transmission, broadcast

emmagasiner vt. to store up, stockpile

emmailloter vt. to swathe, swaddle

emmêler vt. to entangle, mat; disturb

emménagement m. moving in, installation

emménager vt. to move into

emmener vt. to take away, lead away

emmenthal m. Swiss cheese from Emmethal

emmitoufler vt. to muffle up

emmurer vt. to wall up

émoi m. emotion, agitation, turmoil

émoluments m. pl. emoluments

émonder vt. to prune, trim

émotif a. emotive; emotional

émotion f. emotion, feeling; excitement

émotionnable a. emotional

émotionner vt. to move, thrill; s' — to get excited

émouchoir m. fly swatter

émoudre vt. to sharpen, grind

émoulage m. grinding, sharpening

émoulu a. sharpened; frais — de fresh from, just out of

émousser vt. to dull (senses), blunt; weaken

émouvoir vt. to move, affect; rouse; s' — to be moved

empailler vt. to cover, stuff, pack (with straw)

empailleur m. taxidermist

empaler vt. to impale

empan m. span (measure)

empanacher vt. to plume

empaqueter vt. to package

emparer v., s' — de to take possession of, seize

empâter vt. to make sticky; destroy harmony

empattement m. foundation, platform; (auto.) wheelbase

empaumer vt. to take in hand; overcome

empêchement m. obstacle, hindrance

empêcher vt. to hinder, prevent; s' — de to keep from, help, refrain from

empêcheur m. preventer; — de danser en rond (coll.) wet blanket

empeigne f. top leather of shoes

empennage m. stabilising fins; feathers on an arrow

empenné a. plumed, feathered

empereur m. emperor

empeser vt. to starch

empester vt. to infect, make foul; — vi. to reek, smell

empêtrer vt. to bind, involve, hinder

emphase f. overemphasis; bombast

emphatique a. emphatic, bombastic

empiècement m. yoke (clothing)

empierrer vt. to pave with stone (road); ballast (tracks, roads, etc.)

empiètement m. incursion, usurpation

empiéter vi., — sur to usurp; encroach on

empiler vt. to pile up, stack

empire m. empire, rule; mastery

empirer vt. to make worse; aggravate; — vi. grow worse

empirique a. empirical

empirisme m. empiricism

emplacement m. place, location, site

emplâtre m. (med.) plaster, salve; (fig.)

apathetic person

emplette f. purchase; aller faire des —s to go shopping

emplir vt. to fill up

emploi m. use; employment; — du temps schedule; mode d' — instructions for use

employé m. employee; clerk; white-collar worker

employer vt. to employ; use; s' — to occupy oneself

employeur m. user, employer

empocher vt. to pocket

empoigner vt. to grasp; seize; arrest

empois m. starch

empoisonnement m. poisoning

empoisonner vt. to poison; ruin; make bitter; (coll.) bore, annoy

empoisonneur m. poisoner, (coll.) bore, annoying person

empoissonner vt. to stock with fish

emporté a. quick-tempered, hasty

emporte-pièce m. punch tool

emportement m. temper, anger

emporter vt. to take away, carry away; prevail; s' — to lose control of oneself

empoter vt. to pot (plant)

empourprer v., s' — to turn crimson; flush

empreindre vt. to imprint, stamp

empreinte f. imprint; — digitale fingerprint

empressé a. bustling, eager

empressement m. eagerness, zeal, readiness

empresser v., s' — to be eager; hasten

emprise f. seizure; influence

emprisonnement m. imprisonment

emprisonner vt. to imprison

emprunt m. loan, borrowing

emprunté a. feigned; constrained

emprunter vt. to borrow; (fig.) plagiarize

emprunteur m. borrower

ému a. moved; affected

émulation f. emulation

émule m. emulator; rival

émulsion f. emulsion

émulsionner vt. to emulsify

en prep. in, into; at; by; — pron. of him, of her, of it, of them; some, any; — adv. from it, thence

enamourer v., s' — (de) to fall in love (with)

encadrement m. frame, framework

encadrer vt. to frame

encager vt. to cage

encaisse f. cash in hand; cash balance

encaissé a. banked, with high banks

encaissement m. taking in of money; boxing, crating; embankment

encaisser vt. to pack, box; deposit; take in

encan m. auction

encanailler vt. to degrade; s' — to lose caste

encapuchonner vt. to hood

encart, encartage m. insert

encarter vt. to insert

en-cas m. snack, potluck meal; emergency supply

encastrement m. groove; fitting

encastrer vt. to fit in, imbed

encaustique f. furniture wax, floor wax

encaustiquer vt. to wax

encaver vt. to put away, store (in a cellar)

enceindre vt. to surround, gird, encircle; enclose

enceinte f. enclosure; — a. pregnant

encens m. incense

encenser vt. to incense, perfume

encensoir m. incense burner

encéphalite f. encephalitis

encerclement m. encirclement

encercler vt. to encircle

enchaînement m. chain(ing); series

enchaîner vt. to chain; connect

enchanter vt. to enchant, delight; charm

enchanteur a. enchanting; — m. enchanter

enchâsser vt. to enclose; fit in; enshrine; set a jewel

enchère f. bid, bidding; vente aux —s f. auction sale

enchérir vt. to raise prices; — vi. go up in price; — sur outdo, exceed

enchevêtrer vt. to bind; entangle

enchifrener vt. to stop up, stuff up (with a cold)

enclave f. enclave; enclosed land

enclaver vt. to enclose; dovetail

enclin a. inclined, prone

enclos m. enclosure

enclume f. anvil

encoche f. notch; —s pl. thumb index

encocher vt. to notch, nick

encoignure f. corner building; corner furniture

encollage m. size (glue); sizing

encoller vt. to size

encolure f. neck opening; collar size; horse collar

encombre, encombrement m. encumbrance; hindrance; cumbersomeness; congestion

encombrer vt. to encumber, clog

encontre, à l' — prep. counter to

encore adv. yet; still; — une fois again

encorner vt. to horn; gore

encourageant a. encouraging

encourager vt. to encourage

encourir vt. to incur

encrasser vt. to make dirty, soil; clog

encre f. ink; — de Chine India ink

encrer vt. to ink

encroûter vt. to crust; plaster (walls); (fig.) make stupid

encrier m. inkwell

encyclique f. encyclical

encyclopédie f. encyclopedia

encyclopédique a. encyclopedic

endémique a. endemic

endenter vt. to tooth, cog; mesh

endetter vt. to put into debt; s' — to go into debt

endiablé a. bedeviled

endimancher v., s' — to put on Sunday clothes; get dressed up

endive f. French endive

endocrinologie f. endocrinology

endoctrinement m. indoctrination

endoctriner vt. to indoctrinate

endolorir vt. to make painful, cause pain in

endommagement *m.* damage
endommager *vt.* to damage, injure
endormi *a.* asleep, sleepy
endormir *vt.* to put to sleep; lull; s' — to fall asleep
endos, endossement *m.* endorsement
endosser *vt.* to endorse; take on
endosseur *m.* endorser
endroit *m.* place, spot; right side of cloth
enduire *vt.* to spread, cover, coat
enduit *m.* layer, coat, plastering
endurable *a.* endurable, bearable, tolerable
endurant *a.* patient
endurci *a.* hardened, inveterate, calloused
endurcir *vt.* to harden
endurcissement *m.* hardening
endurer *vt.* to endure, suffer, bear, tolerate
en entier *adv.* fully, in detail
énergie *f.* energy
énergique *a.* energetic
énergumène *m. & f.* enthusiast, avid fanatic, madman
énervant *a.* weakening, debilitating; nerve-racking
énervement *m.* enervation
énerver *vt.* to enervate
enfance *f.* childhood; children; dotage; première — infancy
enfant *m. & f.* child; — naturel illegitimate child; — trouvé foundling
enfantement *m.* childbirth; (fig.) creation
enfanter *vt.* to give birth to
enfantillage *m.* childishness
enfantin *a.* childish; juvenile; infantile
enfariner *vt.* to flour, cover with flour
enfer *m.* hell
enfermé *m.* mustiness
enfermer *vt.* to shut up, lock up; enclose
enferrer *vt.* to pierce; s' — to be caught
enfiévrer *vt.* to make feverish; inflame
enfilade *f.* file, string, series
enfiler *vt.* to thread (needle); string (beads); (fig.) put on (clothes); pierce; start down a street
enfin *adv.* after all, at last, finally; in short
enflammer *vt.* to inflame; s' — to catch fire; become inflamed
enfler *vt. & vi.* to swell, bloat; (fig.) exaggerate
enflure *f.* swelling
enfoncé *a.* sunken, deep
enfoncement *m.* hollow; recess; breaking down; breaking in
enfoncer *vt. & vi.* to thrust, drive in; break open; sink; s' — to plunge; sink
enfouir *vt.* to bury; hide
enfourcher *vt.* to climb on; straddle
enfourchure *f.* crotch (tree *or* trousers)
enfourner *vt.* to put in the oven
enfreindre *vt.* to violate, break, infringe on
enfuir *v.*, s' — to run away; elope
enfumé *a.* smoked; smoky
enfumer *vt.* to smoke, blacken
engagé *m.* (mil.) volunteer, enlisted man
engageant *a.* engaging, prepossessing
engagement *m.* commitment, obligation; pawning; promise; hiring; enlistment; (mil.) engagement

engager *vt.* to pawn; pledge; hire; (mech.) engage; enter into; s' — to commit oneself; enlist
engainer *vt.* to sheathe, envelop
engazonner *vt.* to sod
engeance *f.* breed; race
engelure *f.* chilblain
engendrer *vt.* to engender
engin *m.* engine; machinery; device
englober *vt.* to unite; comprise
engloutir *vt.* to swallow up, engulf
engloutissement *m.* swallowing (up)
engluer *vt.* to glue; lime; catch; take in
engorgement *m.* obstruction
engorger *vt.* to obstruct; block
engouement *m.* infatuation
engouer *v.*, s' — to become infatuated
engouffrer *vt.* to engulf
engourdi *a.* dull, numbed
engourdir *vt.* to numb; lull
engourdissement *m.* numbness
engrais *m.* fertilizer, manure; enriched fodder
engraisser *vt.* to fatten; fertilize; — vi. to grow fat
engramme *m.* engram
engrenage *m.* gear, system of gears
engrener *vt.* to engage gears
engueuler *vt.* (coll.) to bawl out; insult
enhardir *vt.* to make bold; s' — to venture, be bold enough
enharnacher *vt.* to harness; (fig.) to deck out
énigmatique *a.* enigmatic
énigme *f.* riddle; enigma
enivrant *a.* intoxicating
enivrement *m.* intoxication
enivrer *vt.* to intoxicate; (fig.) carry away; s' — to get drunk
enjambée *f.* stride
enjamber *vt. & vi.* to stride over, straddle; encroach
enjeu *m.* stake, bet
enjoindre *vt.* to enjoin, call on; order
enjôler *vt.* to coax, cajole, wheedle
enjôleur *a.* coaxing, cajoling
enjoliver *vt.* to make pretty, ornament, embellish
enjoué *a.* cheerful, lively, playful
enjouement *m.* cheerfulness
enlacer *vt.* to entwine; clasp; hem in
enlaidir *vt.* to make ugly; disfigure; — vi. to grow ugly
enlèvement *m.* removal; kidnapping; elopement
enlever *vt.* to remove; take away; abduct
enliser *vt.* to swallow up in sand, suck in
enluminer *vt.* to illuminate a manuscript
ennemi *m.* enemy; — *a.* hostile
ennoblir *vt.* to make noble, ennoble, dignify
ennui *m.* boredom, worry
ennuyeux *a.* annoying; boring, tiresome
ennuyer *vt.* to annoy; worry; bore; s' — to be bored, weary
énoncé *m.* terms, data; statement
énoncer *vt.* to state, announce
énonciation *f.* enunciation; stating, announcing
enorgueillir *vt.* to make proud; s' — de

to pride oneself on
énorme *a.* enormous
énormément *adv.* enormously; a great deal
énormité *f.* enormity
enquérir *v.*, s' — de to inquire about
enquête *f.* inquiry, investigation
enquêter (sur) *vt.* to investigate
enraciner *vt.* to implant s' — to take root
enragé *m.* enthusiast; madman; — *a.* mad; enthusiastic; inveterate
enrager *vt.* to madden; — *vi.* to be mad
enrayer *vt.* to halt, stop, brake; suspend
enregimenter *vt.* to regiment
enregistrement *m.* recording, registering, transcribing; transcription
enregistrer *vt.* to register, record
enrhumer *v.*, s' — to catch cold
enrichir *vt.* to enrich; adorn; develop
enrichissement *m.* enrichment
enrober *vt.* to cover, coat; wrap
enrôler *vt.* to enroll; enlist
enrouement *m.* hoarseness
enrouer *v.*, s' — to become hoarse
enrouler *vt.* to roll up
ensabler *vt.* to cover with sand; run aground
ensacher *vt.* to bag
ensanglanter *vt.* to stain with blood
enseignant *a.* teaching; — *m.* teacher
enseigne *f.* distinctive sign; insignia designating particular firm; ensign; — *m.* ensign (rank)
enseignement *m.* teaching; education
enseigner *vt.* to teach, show
ensemble *adv.* together; — *m.* whole, entirety; d' — comprehensive; combined
ensemencer *vt.* to sow
ensevelir *vt.* to bury; shroud
ensevelissement *m.* burial, interment
ensiler *vt.* to put in a silo
ensoleillé *a.* sunny
ensommeillé *a.* sleepy
ensorceler *vt.* to bewitch
ensorcellement *m.* enchantment, charm, spell; sorcery
ensuite *adv.* afterwards, then, after
ensuivre *v.*, s' — to result; follow; be the consequence
entacher *vt.* to soil, stain, taint
entailler *vt.* to notch, nick, gash
entamer *vt.* to cut; open; begin
entassement *m.* heaping, piling up, accumulation
entasser *vt.* to heap up, accumulate
ente *f.* plant graft; handle
entendement *m.* understanding, judgment
entendre *vt.* to hear; understand; mean; s' — to be heard; understand each other; get along
entendu *a.* heard, understood; c'est — all right, agreed
entente *f.* understanding; agreement
enter *vt.* to graft; s' — to be related by blood
entériner *vt.* to ratify
entérique *a.* enteric
entérite *f.* enteritis

enterrement *m.* funeral, burial, interment
enterrer *vt.* to bury, inter
on-tête *m.* heading, headline; letterhead
entêté *a.* obstinate, headstrong
entêtement *m.* obstinacy
entêter *v.*, s' — to persist, be obstinate
enthousiasme *m.* enthusiasm
enthousiasmer *vt.* to fill with enthusiasm; s' — to be enthusiastic about
enthousiaste *m. & f.* enthusiast; fanatic; — *a.* enthusiastic
entichement *m.* infatuation
enticher *v.*, s' — to become infatuated
entier *a.* entire, whole, intact; — *m.* totality
entièrement *adv.* completely, entirely, wholly
entité *f.* entity
entomologie *f.* entomology
entomologiste *m.* entomologist
entonner *vt.* to intone; begin to sing
entonnoir *m.* funnel
entorse *f.* sprain
entortiller *vt.* to twist, wind; warp, deform
entour *m.* à l' — (de) around, in the vicinity (of); -s *pl.* vicinity, surrounding area
entourage *m.* surroundings; set, circle, associates
entourer *vt.* to surround
entraccuser *v.*, s' — to accuse each other, accuse one another
entracte *m.* intermission, interval
entradmirer *v.*, s' — to admire each other, admire one another
entraide *f.* mutual aid
entraider *v.*, s' — to help one another
entrailles *f. pl.* entrails, bowels; feeling
entr'aimer *v.*, s' — to love each other, love one another
entrain *m.* spirit, gusto
entraînement *m.* carrying away; enthusiasm; training
entraîner *vt.* to drag, carry away; lead astray; entail
entraîneur *m.* trainer
entrave *f.* shackle; hindrance
entraver *vt.* to shackle; hinder
entre *prep.* between, among
entre- *prefix* inter-; partially; reciprocally, mutually
entrebâiller *vt.* to open partially, open slightly
entrebâilleur *m.* doorstop
entrecôte *f.* ribsteak, beef rib
entrecouper *vt.* to interrupt; intersect
entre-deux *m.* space between; partition
entrée *f.* entry, entrance, admission; course (usually fish or eggs) preceding main course; porte d' — *f.* front door
entrefaites *f. pl.*, sur ces — meanwhile
entrefermer *vt.* to close partially
entrefilet *m.* note, item in a newspaper
entregent *m.* tact, confidence; resourcefulness
entrejambes *m.* crotch; longueur d' — length from crotch to heel
entrelacer *vt.* to interlace
entrelarder *vt.* to lard
entre-ligne *m.* space between the lines

entremêler vt. to mix, mingle; intersperse
entremets m. dessert, sweet
entremetteur m., entremetteuse f. go-between
entremettre v., s' — to intervene
entremise f. intervention, mediation
entrepont m. (naut.) between decks
entreposer vt. to place in a warehouse
entrepôt m. warehouse
entreprenant a. enterprising
entreprendre vt. to undertake; contract for
entrepreneur m. contractor
entreprise f. enterprise, contract(ing)
entrer vi. to enter, come in
entreregarder v., s' — to look at each other, look at one another
entresol m. mezzanine floor
entre-temps adv. meanwhile; — m. interval
entretenir vt. to maintain, support; entertain, converse with
entretien m. maintenance; conversation
entre-tuer v., s' — to kill each other, kill one another
entrevoir vt. to glimpse; foresee
entrevue f. interview
entrouvrir vt. to open partially
énumérer vt. to enumerate
envahir vt. to invade
envahissement m. invasion
envaser vt. to fill with mud
enveloppe f. envelope, wrapper, casing
enveloppement m. enveloping
envelopper vt. to envelop, wrap up
envenimer vt. to poison, ruin
envergure f. wingspread; spread; scope, power
envers m. wrong side, reverse; à l' — inside out; upside down; — prep. towards
envi, à l' — (de) adv. vying (with)
envie f. desire, longing; envy; birthmark, hangnail; avoir — de to feel like, want to
envier vt. to envy, be jealous of; covet
envieux a. envious
environ adv. about, approximately; -s m. pl. outskirts, vicinity
environner vt. to surround
envisager vt. to envisage
envoi m. dispatch; consignment, shipment; envoy (poetry)
envol m., envolée f. flight; take-off
envoler v., s' — to fly away, take off
envoûtement m. voodoo, spell
envoûter vt. to dominate; to harm by a wax image used to cause a person to suffer (voodoo)
envoyé m. envoy
envoyer vt. to send
enzyme m. enzyme
épagneul m. spaniel
épais a. thick
épaisseur f. thickness
épaissir vt. & vi. to thicken
épanchement m. pouring out; effusion
épancher vt. to pour out, pour forth; s' — to open up, overflow
épandre vt. to scatter, spread

épanouir v., s' — to bloom; beam
épanouissement m. blossoming
épargne f. saving, thrift; caisse d' — f. savings bank
épargner vt. to spare, save
éparpillement m. scattering
éparpiller vt. to scatter
épars a. scattered, sparse
épatant a. amazing; (coll.) wonderful
épaté a. flattened; flat-nosed
épaule f. shoulder
épaulement m. breastworks
épauler vt. to help; put against the shoulder; put behind breastworks
épaulette f. epaulette; shoulder strap
épave f. wreck, wreckage; stray; (fig.) debris in general
épée f. sword
épéiste m. fencer, swordsman
épeler vt. to spell
épellation f. spelling
éperdu a. distracted; desperate
éperdument adv. desperately, wildly, madly
éperlan m. smelt
éperon m. spur
éperonner vt. to spur
épervier m. sparrow hawk; fishnet
épeuré a. fearful, frightened
éphémère a. ephemeral; — m. May fly
épi m. ear, head of grain; tuft, cowlick; cluster
épice f. spice; pain d' — gingerbread
épicer vt. to spice
épicerie f. grocery
épicier m. grocer
épicurien a. Epicurean
épidémie f. epidemic
épidémique a. epidemic
épiderme m. epidermis
épier vt. to watch, spy on
épieu m. pike
épiglotte f. epiglottis
épigramme f. epigram
épigraphe f. epigraph; quotation, motto
épilepsie f. epilepsy
épileptique m. & f. & a. epileptic
épiler vt. to pluck hair; depilitate
épilogue m. epilogue
épiloguer vt. to criticize, harp (on); split hairs
épinard m. spinach
épine f. thorn; spine
épinette f. spinet, clavichord
épineux a. thorny; difficult
épingle f. pin; — de sûreté safety pin
épingler vt. to pin; (fig., coll.) to pin down
épinière a. & f. spinal
Épiphanie f. Epiphany
épique a. epic
épiscopal a. episcopal, of the bishop
épiscopat m. bishopric; body of bishops; episcopacy
épisode m. episode
épisodique a. episodic
épisser vt. to splice
épissure f. splice
épistémologie f. epistemology
épistolaire a. epistolary
épistolier m. letter writer

épitaphe *f.* epitaph
épithète *f.* epithet
épitoge *f.* shoulder band (equivalent of French doctor's hood)
épitomé *m.* digest, abridgment
épitre *f.* epistle, letter
éploré *a.* weeping, sad
éployé *a.* outspread
éplucher *vt.* to peel, pare, clean; (fig.) examine closely
épluchoir *m.* paring knife
épluchure *f.* peeling, waste
épode *f.* epode
épointer *vt.* to dull the point of
éponge *f.* sponge
éponger *vt.* to sponge
épopée *f.* epic poem, epic
époque *f.* epoch, period
épouiller *vt.* to delouse
épousailles *f. pl.* wedding
épouse *f.* wife, spouse
épouser *vt.* to marry; espouse
époussetage *m.* dusting
épousseter *vt.* to dust
époussette *f.* duster
épouvantable *a.* dreadful, frightful, appalling
épouvantail *m.* scarecrow
épouvante *f.* fright, terror
épouvanter *vt.* to terrify, frighten
époux *m.* husband; — *pl.* married couple
éprendre *v., s'* — de to fall in love with
épreuve *f.* trial, proof, test; (phot.) print
épris (de) *a.* in love (with)
éprouver *vt.* to try; experience
éprouvette *f.* test tube, gauge
epsomite *f.* Epsom salts
épucer *vt.* to deflea
épuisant *a.* exhausting
épuisement *m.* exhaustion
épuiser *vt.* to exhaust; drain; wear out; use up
épuration *f.* purification, purifying, refining
épurer *vt.* to purify, filter
équanimité *f.* equanimity
équarrir *vt.* to square off; cut up, quarter
équateur *m.* equator
Équateur *m.* Ecuador
équation *f.* equation
équatorial *a.* equatorial
Équatorien *m. & a.* Ecuadorian
équerre *f.* T-square, angle iron
équestre *a.* equestrian
équidistant *a.* equidistant
équilatéral *a.* equilateral
équilibrage *m.* balancing
équilibre *m.* equilibrium; balance
équilibrer *vt.* to poise, balance
équilibriste *m. & f.* acrobat, tight-rope performer
équin *a.* equine
équinoxe *m.* equinox
équipage *m.* (naut.) crew; retinue; apparel, equipment
équipe *f.* team; travail d' — *m.* teamwork
équipée *f.* wild time, mad frolic
équipement *m.* equipment
équiper *vt.* to equip, fit out, man
équipier *m.* member of a team

équitable *a.* equitable
équitation *f.* horseback riding
équité *f.* equity, justice
équivalence *f.* equivalent, equivalence
équivalent *a.* equivalent
équivaloir *vt.* to be equivalent to
équivoque *f.* ambiguity; misunderstanding; — *a.* ambiguous; doubtful
équivoquer *vi.* to be ambiguous, be equivocal
érable *m.* maple; sucre d' — maple sugar
érafler *vt.* to graze, scratch
éraflure *f.* graze, scratch
éraillé *a.* bloodshot; frayed
ère *f.* era, epoch
érectile *a.* erectile
érection *f.* erection
éreinter *vt.* to exhaust; break from fatigue
érémitique *a.* ascetic, pertaining to hermits
erg *m.* erg
ergot *m.* rooster's spur; (agr.) ergot
ergotage *m.*, ergoterie *f.* quibbling, hairsplitting
ergoter *vi.* to quibble
ériger *vt.* to erect, raise
ermitage *m.* hermitage
ermite *m.* hermit
éroder *vt.* to erode
érosif *a.* erosive
érosion *f.* erosion
érotique *a.* erotic
érotisme *m.* eroticism
errant *a.* wandering; stray; errant
erratique *a.* erratic
errements *m. pl.* erring ways, habits
errer *vi.* to wander
erreur *f.* error, mistake; delusion
erroné *a.* erroneous
éructation *f.* belch
éructer *vi.* to belch
érudit *a.* learned; — *m.* scholar
érudition *f.* erudition
éruptif *a.* eruptive
éruption *f.* eruption
ès *prep.* in; docteur — lettres *m.* doctor of letters
escabeau *m.* stool; stepladder
escabelle *f.* stool; stepstool
escadre *f.* (navy) squadron
escadrille *f.* escadrille; small squadron
escadron *m.* (army) squadron
escalade *f.* scaling
escalader *vt.* to scale
escale *f.* (naut., avi.) port of call, stop; vol sans — *m.* nonstop flight
escalier *m.* staircase, stairs
escalope *f.* cutlet
escamotable *a.* concealable; retractable
escamoter *vt.* to hide, conceal; make away with; (fig.) side step a question
escarbille *f.* cinder, clinker
escarboucle *f.* carbuncle
escarcelle *f.* purse
escargot *m.* snail
escarmouche *f.* skirmish
escarmoucher *vt.* to skirmish
escarole *f.* escarole
escarpe *f.* scarp, escarpment; — *m.* thief, cutthroat

escarpé a. steep

escarpement m. escarpment; steep incline

escarpin m. pump (shoe)

escarpolette f. swing

escarre f. scab

esche f. bait

escient, à bon — with full knowledge

esclaffer v., s' — to burst out laughing

esclandre m. scandal

esclavage m. slavery; bondage

esclave m. & f. slave

escompte m. (com.) discount; rebate

escompter vt. (com.) to discount

escopette f. blunderbuss

escorte f. escort; (naut.) convoy

escorter vt. to escort, convoy

escouade f. squad

escrime f. fencing

escrimer vi. to fence

escrimeur m. fencer

escroc m. crook, swindler

escroquer vt. to swindle, cheat

escroquerie f. swindle, fraud

ésotérique a. esoteric

espace m. space, room; interval; time lapse

espacer vt. to space; separate

espadon m. swordfish

espadrille f. tennis shoe; beach sandal

Espagne f. Spain

Espagnol m. Spaniard

espagnol a. Spanish

espagnolette f. window catch

espalier m. row of espaliered trees

espèce f. species, kind; —s pl. cash

espérance f. hope, expectation

espéranto m. esperanto

espérer vt. & vi. to hope, expect

espiègle a. mischievous; — m. & f. mischievous person

espièglerie f. prank, mischievousness

espionnage m. espionage, spying

espionner vt. to spy (on)

esplanade f. esplanade, promenade

espoir m. hope

esprit m. spirit; mind; wit, intelligence

esquif m. skiff

esquimau a. & n. Eskimo

esquisse f. sketch; outline, rough plan

esquisser vt. to sketch, outline

esquiver vt. to avoid; — de la tête to duck; s' — to steal away

essai m. test, trial; assaying metal; attempt

essaim m. swarm; host, multitude

essaimage m. swarming

essaimer vt. to swarm

essarter vt. to clear

essarts m. pl. clearing(s)

essayage m. fitting; testing; trying on, trying out

essayer vt. to try, attempt; try on; try out, test

essayiste m. essayist

essence f. essence; gasoline

essentiel a. essential; most important, basic, fundamental; — m. most important thing; gist

esseulé a. left alone, abandoned

essieu m. axle

essor m. flight; soaring; (fig.) development

essorer vt. to dry; wring

essoreuse f. dryer; wringer

essoufflé a. breathless

essoufflement m. breathlessness

essuie-glace m. windshield wiper

essuie-main(s) m. towel

essuie-pieds m. doormat

essuie-plume m. penwiper

essuyer vt. to wipe, dry; suffer, endure, undergo

est m. east

estacade f. stockade

estafette f. runner, messenger

estafier m. armed servant; bully

estaminet m. bar, café

estampe f. print, engraving

estampille f. trademark; seal; impression; tax stamp

ester vi. to appear in court

esthète m. esthete

esthéticienne f. beauty shop attendant

esthétique a. esthetic; — f. esthetics

estimateur m. estimator, appraiser

estimation f. evaluation; estimation

estime f. esteem, estimation

estimer vt. to esteem; estimate; value; deem

estival a. summer

estivant m. summer resident

estiver vi. to spend the summer

estomac m. stomach

Estonie f. Esthonia

estrade f. platform for chairs

estragon m. tarragon

estropié a. crippled

estropier vt. to cripple

estuaire m. estuary

estudiantin a. student, pertaining to students

esturgeon m. sturgeon

et conj. and; — . . . — both . . . and

étable f. cattle shed; sty

établer vt. to stable; place in a stall

établi m. workbench

établir vt. to establish; create

établissement m. establishment; institution

étage m. story, floor; stage; condition

étagère f. set of shelves; whatnot

étai m. prop, stay, support

étain m. tin

étal m. butcher's block

étalage m. display, show

étalagiste m. window dresser, window trimmer

étaler vt. to display, show

étalon m. standard; stallion

étalonner vt. to verify, control, test; standardize; scale, graduate, calibrate

étamer vt. to tin; tin-plate; silver (a mirror)

étamine f. stamen; cheesecloth; etamine

étampe f. punch, stamp, die

étamper vt. to punch, stamp

étanche a. watertight

étancher vt. to stop; appease

étang m. pond

étape f. stage, stop

état m. state, condition; estate; — civil vital statistics
étatiser vt. to nationalize, put under state control
étatisme m. state control
état-major m. staff, headquarters
étau m. vise
étayer vt. to prop, stay
été m. summer
éteignoir m. candle snuffer
éteindre vt. to extinguish, put out; calm; fade; s' — to go out; become extinct
éteint a. extinguished, out, extinct
étendard m. standard, flag
étendoir m. clothesline, drying room
étendre vt. to extend, spread, stretch; s' — to stretch out; extend
étendu a. extended; stretched (out); adulterated, watered; vast, extensive
étendue f. extent, expanse, range, scope
éternel a. eternal
éterniser vt. to drag out, make last a long time
éternité f. eternity
éternuement m. sneeze, sneezing
éternuer vi. to sneeze
étêter vt. to top, remove the top of
éteule f. stubble
éther m. ether
éthéré a. ethereal
Ethiopie f. Ethiopia
éthiopien a. & m. Ethiopian
éthique a. ethical; — f. ethics
ethnique a. ethnic
ethnographie f. ethnography
ethnologie f. ethnology
ethnologue m. & f. ethnologist
éthyle m. ethyl
éthylène m. ethylene
étiage m. low-water point; low water
étincelant a. sparkling, glittering
étinceler vi. to sparkle, glitter
étincelle f. spark, flash
étincellement m. sparkling, glittering; twinkling
étioler v., s' — to wither away
étique a. lean, emaciated
étiqueter vt. to label, ticket, mark
étiquette f. label; etiquette
étirer vt. to lengthen, elongate
étoffe f. material, fabric
étoile f. star
étoiler vt. to bespangle
étole f. stole
étonnamment adv. astonishingly
étonnant a. astonishing
étonnement m. astonishment
étonner vt. to astonish; s' — to be astonished
étouffant a. stifling; sweltering
étouffée f. cuire à l' — to braise
étouffement m. suffocation; choking
étouffer vt. & vi. to stifle, suffocate, choke, smother
étouffoir m. piano damper; stuffy room
étoupe f. oakum, hemp fiber
étourderie f. inadvertance; oversight, stupidity
étourdi a. thoughtless, scatterbrained
étourdir vt. to stun, daze; deaden

étourdissement m. dizziness; numbing
étourneau m. starling
étrange a. strange
étranger m. foreigner; stranger, outsider; à l' — abroad; — a. strange, foreign
étrangeté f. strangeness
étrangler vt. & vi. to strangle; choke; strangulate
étrangleur m. strangler
être vi. to be, exist; — à belong to; y — understand; m. being, existence
étreindre vt. to embrace; grip
étreinte f. grasp; embrace
étrenner vt. to use for the first time
étrier m. stirrup
étrille f. currycomb
étriller vt. to curry; thrash; ransom
étriper vt. to gut, clean
étriquer vt. to make too narrow
étroit a. narrow; strict
étroitement adv. closely, intimately; strictly
étroitesse f. narrowness; closeness; — d'esprit narrow-mindedness
Étrusque m. & f. & a. Etruscan
étude f. study, research; study hall; lawyer's office; (mus.) etude
étudiant m. student
étudié a. studied, calculated
étudier vt. to study
étui m. case, box
étuve f. steam room; drying oven; sterilizer
étuver vt. to stew; steam; heat
étymologie f. etymology
étymologique a. etymological
étymologiste m. etymologist
eucalyptus m. eucalyptus
eucharistie f. eucharist
eugénique f., eugénisme m. eugenics
eunuque m. eunuch
euphémisme m. euphemism
euphonie f. euphony
eurasien a. & m. Eurasian
Europe f. Europe
Européen m. & a. European
euthanasie f. euthanasia
eux pron., m. pl. them, they
évacuation f. evacuation
évacuer vt. to evacuate; vacate
évader v., s' — to escape; break loose
évaluation f. evaluation
évaluer vt. to value, appraise
évangélique a. evangelical
évangéliser vt. to evangelise
évangeliste m. evangelist
évangile m. Gospel
évanouir v., s' — to faint; vanish
évanouissement m. faint; disappearance; (rad.) fading
évaporation f. evaporation
évaporé a. flighty, fickle
évaporer vt. to evaporate
évaser vt. to enlarge, widen
évasif a. evasive
évasion f. escape, evasion; (fig.) distraction
évêché m. bishopric, diocese; bishop's palace
éveil m. alertness; warning; awakening;

wakefulness
éveillé a. awake, alert
éveiller vt. to awaken, wake up
événement m. event; outcome
évent m. vent
éventail m. fan
éventer vt. to fan, ventilate, air; sense, suspect; s' — to get stale; fan oneself
éventrer vt. to disembowel; rip open
éventualité f. eventuality
éventuel a. possible; eventual
évêque m. bishop
évertuer v., s' — to strive, exert oneself
évidement m. hollowing out; hollowness
évidemment adv. evidently, obviously
évidence f. evidence
évident a. obvious, evident
évider vt. to hollow out
évier m. kitchen sink
évincer vt. to evict; oust
éviter vt. to avoid; dodge
évocateur a. evocative
évocation f. evocation; recollection
évocatoire a. evocative
évoluer vi. to evolve; revolve
évolution f. evolution
évoquer vt. to evoke
exacerber vt. to exacerbate
exact a. exact; correct; punctual
exaction f. exacting; exaction
exactitude f. exactness, correctness; punctuality
exagération f. exaggeration
exagérer vt. to exaggerate
exalté a. exalted
exalter vt. to exalt; excite
examen m. examination; survey; — de conscience self-examination
examinateur m. examiner
examiner vt. to examine
exaspérant a. exasperating
exaspération f. exasperation
exaspérer vt. to exasperate
exaucer vt. to grant prayer or request; — un vœu to fulfill a desire
excavateur m. steam shovel
excaver vt. to excavate
excédant a. excessive
excédent m. excess, surplus
excéder vt. to exceed; wear out
excellemment adv. excellently
excellence f. excellence; Excellency
exceller vt. to excel
excentricité f. eccentricity
excentrique a. eccentric
excepté prep. except, save
excepter vt. to except
exceptionnel a. exceptional
excès m. excess; abuse; (phot.) — de pose overexposure
excessif a. excessive; unreasonable
exciper (de) vi. to allege; take exception to
exciser vt. to excise, cut off
excitabilité f. excitability
excitant m. stimulant; — a. stimulating
excitateur a. exciting
excitation f. excitement
exciter vt. to excite, arouse, stimulate
exclamation f. exclamation; point d'— m. exclamation point

exclamer v., s'— to exclaim
exclure vt. to reject; exclude; (fig.) to be incompatible
exclusif a. exclusive
exclusivité f. exclusivity, exclusiveness; en -- first-run movies
excommunier vt. to excommunicate
excorier vt. to excoriate
excrément m. excrement
excréter vt. to excrete
excrétion f. excretion
excroissance f. growth, tumor
excursionner vi. to take a trip, go on an excursion
excuse f. excuse; —s pl. apology; faire ses —s to apologize
excuser vt. to.excuse; apologize for; s'— excuse oneself, apologize
exécrable a. execrable
exécration f. execration
exécrer vt. to execrate
exécutant m. performer
exécuter vt. to execute, perform
exécuteur m. executor
exécutif a. executive
exécution f. execution
exégèse f. exegesis
exemplaire m. copy, sample; — a. exemplary
exemple m. example; precedent; par — for example; indeed!
exempter vt. to exempt
exemption f. exemption
exercé a. practiced, experienced
exercer vt. to exercise; train; exert; s'— to practice
exercice m. exercise, practice; drill
exfolier vt. to scale, exfoliate
exhalaison f. exhalation, vapor
exhalation f. exhalation, exhaling
exhaler vt. to exhale; breathe out; give off
exhaussement m. raising; rise
exhausser vt. to raise; s'— to rise
exhaustif a. exhaustive
exhaustion f. exhaust
exhiber vt. to exhibit, display, show
exhibition f. exhibition; show, showing, exposition, display
exhibitionniste m. & f. exhibitionist
exhorter vt. to exhort, urge, encourage
exhumation f. exhumation
exhumer vt. to exhume, disinter; unearth, dig up
exigeant a. exacting, hard to please, demanding
exigence f. exigence, exigency, requirement, demand
exiger vt. to exact, require, demand
exigible a. required, due, exigible
exigu a. very small, tiny; slim, scanty
exiguïté f. smallness; scantiness; relative poverty
exil m. exile, banishment
exilé m. exiled person
exiler vt. to exile, banish
existant a. existent, existing, extant; living; present; available
existence f. existence; life, living; being; (com.) stock, inventory
existentialiste m. & f. existentialist

existentiel *a.* existential; pertaining to existence

exister *vi.* to exist, be; live

exode *m.* exodus

exonération *f.* exoneration; exemption

exonérer *vt.* to exonerate; exempt

exorable *a.* exorable, flexible

exorciser *vt.* to exorcize

exorcisme *m.* exorcism; exorcizing

exotique *a.* exotic

expansif *a.* expansive

expansion *f.* expansion; expansiveness

expatrié *m.* expatriate, exile

expatrier *vt.* to expatriate

expectant *a.* expectant

expectative *f.* expectancy, expectation; prospect

expectoration *f.* expectoration; sputum

expectorer *vt.* to expectorate

expédient *a.* expedient; — *m.* expedient; resource; device

expédier *vt.* to expedite; send off; dispatch; clear, get through

expéditeur *m.* sender, shipper

expéditif *a.* expeditious

expédition *f.* expedition; shipment, consignment; dispatch; copy

expéditionnaire *a.* expeditionary; — *m.* sender; shipper; forwarding agent

expérience *f.* experience; experiment

expérimental *a.* experimental

expérimentateur *m.* experimenter

expérimentation *f.* experimentation

expérimenté *a.* experienced; peu — inexperienced

expérimenter *vt.* to try, test; — *vi.* to experiment

expert *a.* expert; trained; skilled; competent; — *m.* expert; appraiser

expert-comptable *m.* certified public accountant

expertise *f.* expert appraisal or evaluation

expertiser *vt.* to appraise

expiable *a.* expiable

expiation *f.* expiation, atonement

expier *vt.* to expiate, atone for

expirant *a.* expiring, dying

expiration *f.* expiration; termination; exhaling

expirer *vi.* to expire; die; terminate; exhale

explétif *a. & m.* expletive

explicable *a.* explainable, explicable

explicatif *a.* explanatory

explication *f.* explanation, interpretation; accounting

explicite *a.* explicit

expliciter *vt.* to make explicit

expliquer *vt.* to explain; comment on, interpret; account for; s'— to explain oneself; have an argument

exploit *m.* exploit, deed; (law), writ summons

exploitable *a.* exploitable, workable

exploitant *m.* operator of an enterprise; cultivator; developer; — *a.,* huissier — *m.* process server

exploitation *f.* exploitation; working, cultivation; improvement; development

exploiter *vt.* to exploit; operate; work; cultivate; develop

explorateur *m.* explorer; — *a.* exploratory

exploratif *a.* exploratory

exploration *f.* exploration, exploring

explorer *vt.* to explore; examine; probe

exploser *vi.* to explode, blow up

explosible *a.* explosive

explosif *a. & m.* explosive

explosion *f.* explosion, exploding, blowing up; outburst

exportateur *m.* exporter

exporter *vt.* to export

exposant *m.* exhibitor; petitioner; (math.) exponent

exposé *a.* exposed; open; subject to, liable; — *m.* statement, account

exposer *vt.* to expose; exhibit, display, show; explain

exposition *f.* exposition; exhibition, display, showing; exposure; salle d'— *f.* showroom

exprès (**expresse**) *a.* express, explicit; par — special delivery; — *adv.* on purpose, intentionally, expressly

express *m.* local-express train

expressément *adv.* expressly, clearly

expressif *a.* expressive

expression *f.* expression; show, display; term, language, words; squeezing, extracting

expressivement *adv.* expressively

exprimable *a.* expressible

exprimer *vt.* to express; show; squeeze out, extract

expropriation *f.* expropriation

exproprier *vt.* to expropriate

expugnable *a.* pregnable

expulser *vt.* to expel; evict; eject, throw out

expulsion *f.* expulsion; eviction; ejection; deportation

expurger *vt.* to expurgate

exquis *a.* exquisite; of extreme beauty

exsangue *a.* bloodless, anemic

exsuder *vt. & vi.* to exude

extase *f.* ecstasy, rapture; trance

extasier *v.,* s'— to go into ecstasy, go wild, be wild

extatique *a.* ecstatic

extenseur *m.* stretcher, expander; extensor muscle

extensible *a.* extendable, expandable

extensif *a.* extensive; tensile

extension *f.* extension; stretching; spread, expansion; extent

exténuation *f.* extenuation; exhaustion

exténuant *a.* extenuating, exhausting

exténuer *vt.* to extenuate; exhaust; s'— to exhaust oneself

extérieur *a.* exterior, external; outside; foreign; — *m.* exterior, outside; outward appearance; surface

extérieurement *adv.* externally; outwardly; superficially, on the surface

exterminateur *m.* exterminator

extermination *f.* extermination

exterminer *vt.* to exterminate; wipe out

externat *m.* day school

externe *a.* external, exterior, outside; — *m.* nonresident pupil; (med.) nonresident assistant interne

extincteur m. fire extinguisher

extinction f. extinction; extinguishing; slaking; abolition; loss

extirpateur m. uprooter, extirpator; remover

extirpation f. uprooting, extirpation; removal

extirper vt. to extirpate, uproot; remove

extorquer vt. to extort

extorqueur m. extortionist

extorsion f. extortion

extra ads. extra, additional; — m. (pl.) extra(s)

extracteur m. extractor

extraction f. extraction; pulling out; origin, ancestry, birth

extrader vt. to extradite

extradition f. extradition

extra-fin a. superfine, very fine

extraire vt. to extract, draw out; pull out; pull a tooth

extrait m. extract, excerpt; abstract

extra-légal a. extralegal

extraordinaire a. extraordinary, out of the ordinary

extrapoler vt. to extrapolate

extra-sensoriel a. extrasensory

extravagance f. extravagance; exorbitance; foolishness

extravagant a. extravagant; exorbitant; foolish

extravaguer vi. to rave, talk nonsense

extrême a. extreme; excessive; severe; farthest; — m. extreme

extrêmement adv. extremely, very highly

extrême-onction f. (eccl.) extreme unction

Extrême-Orient m. Far East

extrémist m. & f. extremist

extrémité f. extremity; tip, end; urgency; dying moment; extreme

extrinsèque a. extrinsic

extroverti m. extrovert

exubérance f. exuberance

exubérant a. exuberant, luxuriant

exultation f. exultation

exulter vi. to exult, rejoice

ex-voto m. (eccl.) votive offering; ex-voto

F

fable f. fable, story; laughing stock

fablier m. collection of fables

fabricant m. manufacturer

fabricateur m. fabricator; forger

fabrication f. manufacturing, manufacture; fabrication; forging

fabrique f. manufacture; factory; paper mill

fabriquer vt. to manufacture, produce, make; fabricate; forge

fabuleux a. fabulous

façade f. façade, front

face f. front, face; aspect; side; en — de opposite; faire — à to face, confront, meet; pile ou — heads or tails

face-à-main m. lorgnette

facétie f. prank, joke, trick

facétieux a. facetious

facette f. facet

facetter vt. to cut in facets

fâché a. angry; sorry

fâcher vt. to anger; afflict, grieve; se — to get angry; be offended

fâcheux a. tiresome, annoying; troublesome; unfortunate

faciès m. facies; appearance, facial aspect

facile a. easy; facile; glib

facilité f. facility; ease, easiness; aptitude; glibness

faciliter vt. to facilitate

façon f. fashion; fashioning, making, creation; way, manner; fuss, ceremony; à la — de like; de — que so that; de cette — in this way, thus; de toute — in any event, in any case; faire des —s to stand on ceremony; sans —(s) without fuss or ceremony; unceremoniously

faconde f. glibness, fluency

façonner vt. to fashion, make; shape, form

façonnier a. overly fussy

facsimilé m. facsimile, reproduction, duplicate

factage m. delivery, delivery service

facteur m. (math.) factor; mailman, postman; agent; maker, manufacturer

factice a. imitation, factitious

factieux a. factious

factionnaire m. sentry; picket

factorielle f. (math.) factorial

factotum m. factotum; jack-of-all-trades; handyman

facturation f. billing, invoicing

facture f. (com.) invoice, bill; workmanship, make; making, manufacture

facturer vt. to invoice

facturier m. invoice book; billing clerk

facultatif a. optional

faculté f. faculty; ability, capacity; option; school within a university

fadaise f. silliness, foolishness, nonsense

fade a. insipid, tasteless, flat

fadeur f. insipidity; lack of taste, flatness

fagot m. faggot, bundle of sticks

fagotin m. small faggot, small bundle

faible a. feeble, weak; faint; poor; low; thin; — m. foible, weakness

faiblesse f. weakness; feebleness; failing, frailty; faint

faiblir vi. to weaken, fail; abate, diminish

faïence, (faïencerie) f. earthenware, pottery

faille f. (geol.) fault, crack, break

faillibilité f. fallibility

faillible a. fallible

faillir vi. to fail; go bankrupt; be on the point of; — faire quelque chose almost to do something

faillite f. failure, bankruptcy; faire — to go bankrupt

faim f. hunger; avoir — to be hungry; hunger

fainéant a. lazy; — m. loafer, idler; good-for-nothing

fainéanter vi. to idle, loaf, do nothing

fainéantise f. laziness, loafing, idleness

faire vt. to make; do; perform, execute, accomplish; be, come to, amount to; say, remark; play (music), act, pretend; matter, be of importance; see to, attend to, arrange; cause something to be done, have someone do something; have something done; — le mort play dead; — son droit study law; — une malle pack a trunk; — une pièce clean a room; — une promenade take a walk, go for a walk; cela ne fait rien it doesn't matter, never mind; il fait beau it's nice out (weather); il fait chaud it's warm, hot; il fait froid it's cold; il fait mauvais the weather is bad; il fait du soleil it's sunny; il fait du vent it's windy; se — become, grow; develop, be formed; get used to, adjust to; be, happen; — m. making, doing

faire-part m. notification, notice

faisable a. feasible, practical

faisan m., —(de) f. pheasant

faisceau m. bundle, bunch, cluster

faiseur m. maker, doer

fait a. made, done; matured, ripe; — m. fact; feat, act, deed; mettre au — to inform, bring up to date; sur le — in the act

fait-divers m. news item

faite m. top, summit; ridge; (fig.) in highest point

faix m. load, burden, weight

falaise f. cliff

fallacieux a. fallacious

falloir v. to be necessary; to be lacking; il faut — it is necessary, one must, one should; it takes; il me faut I must, I have to; I need; comme il faut proper, properly; il s'en faut de beaucoup, tant s'en faut far from it; peu s'en faut almost, nearly

falot a. pale, colorless; quaint; — m. lamp, lantern, light

falsificateur m. falsifier, forger

falsifier vt. to falsify; adulterate; forge

famé a. noted; bien — of good repute

famélique a. famished, starving, starved

fameux a. famous; distinguished; wonderful, excellent

familial a. of the family; domestic

familiariser vt. to familiarize; se — avec to become accustomed to, familiarize oneself with; become familiar with

familiarité f. familiarity; intimacy

familier a. familiar, intimate; of the family, domestic; colloquial

familièrement adv. familiarly, in a familiar manner

famille f. family; soutien de — m. breadwinner

famine f. famine; starvation

fanal m. light, lantern, beacon; headlight

fanatique a. & n. fanatic

fanatiser vt. to make fanatic, make a fanatic of

fanatisme m. fanaticism

fanchon f. scarf, kerchief

faner vt. to fade; pitch (hay); se — to fade, wither

fanfare f. fanfare, flourish; brass band, military band

fanfaron a. boasting, bragging; — m. braggart

fanfaronnade f. boasting, bragging

fanfaronner vi. to boast, brag, swagger

fanfreluche f. frill; trifle

fange f. mire, mud, dirt, filth; vice

fangeux a. muddy, dirty, filthy

fanion m. pennant, flag

fanon m. fetlock, dewlap, wattle; pendant; whalebone; (eccl.) maniple; —s pl. streamers of a bishop's mitre

fantaisie f. fantasy; fancy, imagination; whim, caprice; vagary; de — fancy; imaginary

fantaisiste a. fanciful, whimsical, imaginary

fantasmagorique a. fantastic, grotesque, weird

fantasque a. whimsical; temperamental; odd

fantassin m. foot soldier

fantastique a. fantastic; fanciful; unbelievable; weird

fantoche m. puppet, marionette

fantôme m. phantom, spectre, ghost, spirit

faon m. fawn

faonner vi. to fawn

faquin m. rascal, scoundrel

farce f. farce; trick, joke; stuffing (for food)

farceur m. joker, buffoon

farcir vt. to stuff (in cooking)

fard m. rouge; cosmetics, makeup; embellishment; pretense

fardeau m. burden, load, weight

farder vt. to make up; disguise, mask; se — to put on make-up

farfouiller vt. & vi. to search, look around, rummage

farine f. flour, meal; — lactée malted milk

farineux a. starchy, mealy; covered with flour

farouche a. wild, savage; cruel; timid, shy

fascicule m. cluster, bunch; section, part of a publication

fascinant, fascinateur a. fascinating

fasciner vt. to fascinate; charm; bewitch

fascisme m. Fascism

fasciste m. & f. Fascist

faste m. pomp; ostentation

fastidieux a. tedious, tiresome; dull

fastueux a. ostentatious; pompous; sumptuous

fat a. conceited, vain

fatal a. fatal; mortal; inevitable

fatalisme m. fatalism

fataliste a. fatalistic; — m. & f. fatalist

fatalité f. fatality, fate

fatidique a. fateful

fatigant a. fatiguing, tiring, tiresome

fatigue f. fatigue, weariness; strain, wear

fatiguer vt. to fatigue, tire; strain, overwork; — vi. to labor, strain; se — to get tired

fatras m. rubbish, trash, jumble

fatuité f. conceitedness

faubourg m. suburb

faubourien a. suburban

faucher vt. to mow, cut down; reap

faucheuse f. harvester, mower, reaper

faucille f. sickle

faucon m. falcon; hawk

fauconnerie f. falconry

faufil m. thread for basting

faufiler vt. to baste, tack; weave in and out; slip in; se — thread one's way; slip in or out, sneak in or out; curry favor

faune m. faun; — f. (zool.) fauna

faussaire m. & f. forger

faussement adv. falsely

fausser vt. to falsify; bend, warp; force (a lock); se — to bend, warp, crack, break down

fausset m. falsetto

fausseté f. falseness, falsehood, untruth

faute f. fault; error, mistake; blame; fowl (in sports); lack, need, want; faire — to be lacking; — de for lack of, for want of; sans — without fail

fauteuil m. armchair; chair; (theat.) seat

fauteur m. instigator, agitator

fautif a. faulty; offending

fauvette f. warbler

faux f. scythe

faux m. falsehood, lie; forgery, imitation; — (fausse) a. false, untrue; imitation; counterfeit, forged; wrong

faux-col m. removable collar

faux-filet m. steak

faux-fuyant m. evasion, subterfuge

faux-monnayeur m. counterfeiter

faux-semblant m. pretext

faveur f. favor; preference; liking, good graces; billet de — m. complimentary ticket, pass

favori m. favorite; —s m. pl. side whiskers; — (favorite) a. favorite

favoriser vt. to favor; encourage, promote; like

favoritisme m. favoritism

fébrile a. feverish, febrile

fébrilité f. feverishness

fécal a. fecal

fèces f. pl. feces, stool

fécond a. fecund, fertile, productive, fruitful; rich

féconder vt. to fecundate, impregnate

fécondité f. fecundity, fertility; richness

fécule f. flour-like consistency; — de maïs cornstarch

féculent a. starchy; — m. starchy food

fédéral a. federal

fédéraliser vt. to federalize

fédéraliste a. & n. federalist

fédératif a. federated, confederate

fédération f. federation

fédérer vt. to federate

fée f. fairy; conte de —s m. fairy tale

féerie f. fairyland; enchantment; fantasy

féerique a. fairy; magic

feindre vt. to feign, pretend, simulate

feinte f. feint, pretense, pretending; limp

feinter vi. to feint

feldspath m. felspar

fêlé a. cracked; crazy

fêler vt. to crack

félicitations f. pl. congratulations

félicité f. felicity, happiness

féliciter vt. to congratulate

félin a. & m. feline

félonie f. treason

fêlure f. crack, chink; break, fracture

femelle f. & a. female

féminin a. feminine; — m. (gram.) feminine

féminisme m. feminism

femme f. woman, wife; female; — de charge housekeeper; — de chambre chambermaid

fémur m. femur

fenaison f. harvesting of hay

fendille f. crack, break, fissure

fendiller vt. to crack; se — to crack, peel

fendoir m. cleaver, chopper

fendre vt. to split; crack; cleave; rend

fenêtre f. window

fenil m. hayloft

fenouil m. fennel

fente f. crack, split, crevice, fissure; slot; lunge

féodal a. feudal

féodalité f. feudalism

fer m. iron; (fig.) sword, blade; coup de — m. pressing, ironing; — à cheval horseshoe; — à friser curling iron; — à marquer branding iron; — à repasser flatiron; — à souder soldering iron; — de fonte cast iron; — forgé wrought iron; marquer au — to brand; —s irons, chains

ferblanterie f. tinware

ferblantier m. tinsmith

férié a., jour — m. public holiday

férir vt. to strike; se — be struck with, stricken with; fall in love with

ferler vt. to furl

fermage m. tenant farming

ferme a. firm, fixed, steady; — adv. fast; hard; firmly; with assurance

ferme f. farm; (theat.) flat (scenery mounted on frame)

fermé a. closed; exclusive, restricted

fermentation f. fermentation, ferment

fermenter vi. to ferment

fermer vt. to shut, close; turn off; — vi. shut, close; — à clef to lock

fermeté f. firmness, steadiness

fermeture f. closing; shutting; fastening, lock; bolt of a gun; lockout; — éclair zipper

fermier m. farmer

fermoir m. fastener, snap, clasp

féroce a. ferocious, savage, wild

férocité f. ferocity, wildness

ferraille f. scrap iron; junk

ferrailler vi. to rattle

ferré a. ironclad, ironshod; hobnailed (shoe sole); (coll.) good, well versed; route —e f. paved road; voie —e f. railway

ferrer vt. to shoe (horse); equip, fit with iron; pave

ferret m. tab, tag

ferreux a. ferrous

ferrique a. ferric

ferronnerie f. wrought iron; ironworks

ferroviaire a. railroad, railway, train

ferrure f. iron fittings

fertilisant a. fertilizing; — m. fertilizer

fertiliser vt. to fertilize; enrich

fertilité f. fertility, fruitfulness; richness

féru a. in love; wrapped up, obsessed

férule f. stick, cane, rod
fervent a. fervent, ardent; — m. devotee
ferveur f. fervor; ardor
fesse f. buttock
fessée f. spanking
fesse-mathieu m. miser, skinflint; usurer
fesser vt. to spank
festin m. feast, banquet
festiner vt. & vi. to feast
festivité f. festivity
feston m. festoon; scallop (sewing, edging)
festonner vt. to festoon; scallop
festoyer vt. & vi. to feast
fête f. feast, festival; holiday; saint's day; birthday; festivity; jour de — m. holiday
fête-Dieu f. (eccl.) Corpus Christi
fêter vt. to celebrate; entertain
fétiche m. fetish
fétide a. fetid, repulsive
fétidité f. fetidness
fétu m. straw; (fig.) something of no value
feu m. (pl. feux) fire, burning; flame; match, light; — de joie bonfire; — d'artifice fireworks; — rouge red light; au —! fire!; à petit — on a slow fire; by inches; armes à — f. pl. firearms; coup de — m. gunshot; mettre — à to set fire to; prendre — to catch fire; faire — to fire; faire du — to make a fire; faire long — hang fire
feu a. late, defunct
feudataire m. vassal
feuillage m. foliage
feuillaison f. appearance of leaves
feuille f. leaf; sheet; page; paper, newspaper
feuillée f. foliage; —s pl. (mil.) latrine
feuiller vt. to produce leaves
feuilleté a. laminated, foliated; — m. puff pastry
feuilleter vt. to leaf through; turn the pages of; foliate, form into leaves or thin layers
feuilleton m. serial; roman — serialized novel
feuillette f. small leaf; leaflet
feuillu a. leafy; — m. foliage
feutre m. felt; felt hat
feutré a. soft, quiet, velvet-like; muffled
feutrer vt. to cover with felt; make into felt
fève f. lima bean
février m. February
fi interj. fie! for shame!; — m., faire — de dislike, scorn
fiacre m. horse-drawn cab, hack
fiançailles f. pl. engagement, betrothal
fiancé a. engaged, betrothed; — m. fiancé, bridegroom; —e f. fiancée, bride
fiancer v., se — to become engaged
fibre f. fiber, grain, thread
fibreux a. fibrous; stringy
ficeler vt. to tie (up); wrap and tie
ficelle f. string, cord, twine
fiche f. index card, note card; case history; (elec.) plug; pin; microscope slide
ficher vt. to drive, thrust in; (coll.) cheat, trick; throw out; se — de to laugh at.

make fun of; care nothing about
fichier m. file, card file; filing cabinet
fichu m. scarf, shawl, kerchief
fictif a. fictitious, invented, imaginary
fiction f. fiction, invention, story
fidéicommis m. trust (law)
fidèle a. faithful, true, loyal
fidélité f. fidelity, faithfulness; loyalty
fiduciaire a. fiduciary; paper money; — m. fiduciary, trustee
fief m. fief, fee
fiel m. gall; bitterness, malice
fielleux a. galling, bitter
fiente f. droppings, manure, dung
fier (fière) a. proud; haughty
fier vt. to entrust; se — à to rely upon, trust, depend on, count on
fier-à-bras m. braggart, swaggerer
fièrement adv. proudly
fierté f. pride; dignity
fièvre f. fever; heat; temperature
fiévreux a. feverish, fevered
fifre m. fife
figement m. clotting, coagulation, congealing
figer vt. to coagulate, congeal; curdle; thicken, solidify; se — to clot, coagulate; become frozen
figue f. fig; — de Barbarie prickly pear
figuier m. fig tree
figurant n. (theat.) extra; —e f. ballet dancer
figuratif a. figurative
figuration f. figuration; (theat.) extras
figure f. face; figure, form, shape
figuré a. figured; figurative
figurer vt. to represent; portray; — vi. to figure; se — to imagine
fil m. thread; line; cutting edge; grain (of wood); — de fer wire; — de l'eau current, stream
filasse f. tow; oakum
filature f. spinning
file f. file, row, line; à la — in file; in succession, on and on
filé m. thread
filer vt. to spin; draw out, prolong; follow, shadow; — vi. pass, go by; move along, get going; leave; — à l'anglaise to take French leave
filet m. net; fillet; thread; bit, small amount, trickle; snaffle (harness part)
fileter vt. to stretch, draw metal; thread a screw
fileur m. spinner
filial a. filial; —e f. branch, subsidiary
filiation f. filiation; relationship; ancestry
filigrane m. filigree; watermark
fille f. daughter; girl; (eccl.) sister; fille d'honneur bridesmaid; maid of honor; jeune — girl; vieille — old maid, spinster
fillette f. young girl, little girl
filleul m. godson; —e f. goddaughter
film m. film; — fixe filmstrip
filmer vt. to film
filoche f. netting
filon m. vein, lode, strike
filou m. pickpocket; cheat, thief

filouter *vt.* to rob, cheat

fils *m.* son; junior (after a name); the younger

filtrant *a.* filtering; filterable; bout — *m.* filter tip

filtrat *m.* filtrate

filtration *f.* filtration, filtering

filtre *m.* filter; strainer; individual coffee-maker (strainer type)

filtrer *vt.* to filter, strain; — *vi.* to filter through; drip, leak

fin *f.* end, extremity, conclusion, close; aim, purpose; en — de compte in the end, as it turned out; to get to the point; sans — endless

fin *a.* fine; delicate, small, thin; clear, pure; ingenious; clever, subtle

final *a.* final, last, concluding

finalement *adv.* finally, lastly

finaliste *m. & f.* finalist

finalité *f.* finality

financement *m.* financing

financer *vt.* to finance, back

financier *a.* financial; — *m.* financier

finasser *vi.* to finesse, use finesse

finasserie *f.* finesse, shrewdness

finaud *a.* clever, shrewd, cunning

finesse *f.* fineness; finesse; delicacy, artifice; artfulness; ingenuity, subtlety; shrewdness

fini *a.* finished, ended, over, done, concluded; skilled, experienced; finite

finir *vt.* to finish, end, conclude; — *vi.* finish, end; en — avec be done with, get something over with; — de finish, stop

finissage *m.* finishing, final step, finishing touch

finisseur *m.* finisher

finlandais *a.* Finnish; — *m.* Finn

Finlande *f.* Finland

fiole *f.* phial, flask, bottle

fioriture *f.* flourish, curlicue

firmament *m.* firmament, heavens, sky

firme *f.* firm, house, company; imprint

fisc *m.* treasury, internal revenue

fiscal *a.* fiscal; pertaining to revenue

fiscaliser *vt.* to tax, make subject to tax

fiscalité *f.* tax collecting

fissurer *vt.* to fissure, split, cleave

fistule *f.* fistula

fixatif *m.* fixative

fixation *f.* fixation; fixing, setting, placing; determining

fixe *a.* fixed, steady, set; prix — set price; — *m.* regular salary

fixer *vt.* to fix; make firm, set, hold; stare at

fixité *f.* fixity

flaccidité *f.* flaccidity; flabbiness

flacon *m.* flask, bottle, decanter; flagon

flagellant *m.* flagellant

flagellation *f.* flagellation; flogging, whipping

flageller *vt.* to flagellate; flog, whip

flageoler *vi.* to quiver, tremble, buckle

flageolet *m.* (mus.) flageolet, flute; kidney bean

flagorner *vt.* to flatter, be obsequious toward

flagrance *f.* flagrancy

flagrant *a.* flagrant; en — délit in the act

flair *m.* scent; perspicacity; flair, knack

flairer *vt.* to smell, scent, sniff; sense

flamand *a. & m.* Flemish

flamant *m.* flamingo

flambant *a.* flaming

flambé *a.* flamed with brandy

flambeau *m.* torch, brand; light; candle; candlestick

flambée *f.* fire, blaze

flambement *m.* collapse, buckling

flamber *vi.* to flame, blaze; collapse, buckle, fall in; — *vt.* to singe, char

flamboyant *a.* flaming; flamboyant

flamboyer *vi.* to blaze

flamme *f.* flame; love

flammèche *f.* spark, ember

flan *m.* custard

flanc *m.* flank, side; (fig.) womb

flanchet *m.* meat flank

Flandre *f.* Flanders

flanelle *f.* flannel

flâner *vi.* to stroll, idle, loiter

flânerie *f.* idling, loitering; strolling

flâneur *m.* idler; loiterer; stroller

flanquer *vt.* to flank; throw; — à la porte throw out, kick out

flaque *f.* puddle

flash *m.* (photo.) flash attachment, flash bulb

flasque *a.* flaccid; flabby; — *f.* powder flask

flatter *vt.* to flatter, caress; please

flatterie *f.* flattery

flatteur *a.* flattering; pleasing; — *m.* flatterer

flatueux *a.* flatulent

flatulence *f.* flatulence

fléau *m.* scourge; flail; (fig.) plague

flèche *f.* arrow; church spire; pole; rise; dip

fléchette *f.* dart

fléchir *vt. & vi.* to bend; submit; give way

flegmatique *a.* phlegmatic; stolid

flegme *m.* phlegm

fiet *m.* flounder

flétan *m.* halibut

flétrir *vt.* to fade, wither; tarnish, stain; se — to fade, wither

flétrissure *f.* fading; withering; tarnish; stigma

fleur *f.* flower; blossom; prime; à — de level with

fleuraison *f.* flowering, blooming

fleuret *m.* fencing foil

fleurette *f.* little flower

fleuri *a.* in bloom; flowery; florid

fleurir *vt.* to decorate with flowers; — *vi.* to flower, bloom; flourish

fleuriste *m. & f.* florist

fleuve *m.* river

flexibilité *f.* flexibility

flexible *a.* flexible; pliant, pliable

flexion *f.* bending, flexion; inflexion

flibuster *vt.* to rob; — *vi.* to steal; commit piracy

flibustier *m.* buccaneer, pirate

flirt *m.* flirting, flirtation

flirter *vi.* to flirt

flocon *m.* snowflake; tuft; fleece

floconner *ri.* to form flakes; become fleecy
floconneux *a.* fleecy, fluffy
floraison *f.* blossoming, flourishing
flore *f.* flora
florentin *a.* Florentine; à la —e served with spinach
florissant *a.* flourishing
flot *m.* wave; flood, tide; floating; raft; à — floating, afloat
flottabilité *f.* buoyancy
flottable *a.* buoyant
flottant *a.* floating; vacillating, undecided
flotte *f.* fleet; float
flottement *m.* vacillation, wavering; undulation; flapping, waving
flotter *vt.* to float; — *vi.* to float; vacillate, waver; wave
flotteur *m.* float; buoy
flottille *f.* flotilla
flou *a.* light and soft; blurred, hazy; fluffy
fluctuer *vi.* to fluctuate
fluer *vi.* to flow
fluet *a.* thin, slender
fluide *m. & a.* fluid; liquid
fluidifier *vt.* to liquefy
fluidité *f.* fluidity
fluor *m.* fluorine
fluorescent *a.* fluorescent
flûte *f.* flute; tube, shaft
flûter *vi.* to play the flute
flux *m.* flow; flux; ebb
fluxion *f.* fluxion; — de poitrine pneumonia
foc *m.* (naut.) jib
foetal *a.* foetal
foetus *m.* foetus
foi *f.* faith; fidelity; belief; trust, confidence; de bonne — sincere, honest; digne de — trustworthy, reliable
foie *m.* liver; — gras goose liver paste
foin *m.* hay
foire *f.* fair, market
fois *f.* time; à la — at once, simultaneously, at a time; une — que once; encore une — once again; une — pour toutes definitely
foison *f.* abundance
foisonnant *a.* plentiful, abundant
foisonner *vi.* to abound
folâtre *a.* frisky, playful
folâtrer *vi.* to play, frolic, romp
folie *f.* folly; insanity, madness
folié *a.* foliated
folio *m.* folio; page number
folklorique *a.* concerning folklore
follement *adv.* madly, foolishly
follet *a.* merry, gay
follicule *m.* follicle
fomentateur *m.* fomenter, agitator
fomenter *vt.* to foment
foncé *a.* dark, deep, somber (color)
foncer *vt.* to drive (in); deepen, darken — *vi.*, — sur to charge, rush
foncier *a.* pertaining to land or property; (fig.) fundamental; biens — *m. pl.* real property, real estate
foncièrement *adv.* fundamentally, basically
fonction *f.* function, duty, office
fonctionnaire *m. & f.* civil servant, petty official

fonctionnarisme *m.* bureaucracy
fonctionnel *a.* functional
fonctionnement *m.* functioning; order, condition
fonctionner *vi.* to function, work, run
fond *m.* bottom; foundation; back; end; à — thoroughly; au — basically; de — fundamental, main, most important; sans — bottomless
fondamental *a.* fundamental, (fig.) essential
fondant *a.* melting; — *m.* flux for soldering; candy, bonbon
fondateur *m.* founder
fondation *f.* founding; foundation
fondé *a.* founded; justified; — *m.* agent; manager
fondement *m.* foundation; basis, base
fonder *vt.* to found; lay the foundation of; establish
fonderie *f.* foundry; casting; smelting
fondre *vt.* to melt, dissolve; smelt (iron); cast; — *vi.* to melt
fondrière *f.* quagmire; mud hole
fonds *m.* land; landed property; capital; funds
fondu *a.* melted, molten; — *m.* fadeout (films)
fontaine *f.* fountain, spring, well, source
fonte *f.* melting; cast iron; casting; smelting; alloy; (print.) font, type of one style and size
footing *m.* walk, hike, walking
forage *m.* drilling, boring
forain *a.*, fête — *f.* fair
forban *m.* pirate
forçat *m.* galley slave; convict, one condemned to hard labor
force *f.* force, strength, power; à — de by means of, by dint of; -s *f. pl.* shears (for metal, hedges, etc.)
forcé *a.* forced
forcément *adv.* necessarily
forcement *m.* forcing
forcené *a.* frantic, mad
forcer *vt.* to force, compel; break into; break out of
forer *vt.* to drill, bore
forestier *a.* of the forest; — *m.* forest ranger
foret *m.* drill
forêt *f.* forest
foreuse *f.* drilling machine, drill, borer
forfaire *vt.* to forfeit; — à to be remiss in
forfait *m.* crime; forfeit; contract
forfaitaire *a.* contractual
forfanterie *f.* bragging, boasting
forgé *a.* forged; fer — *m.* wrought iron
forgeage *m.* forging
forger *vt.* to forge; (fig.) invent, imagine
forgeron *m.* blacksmith
forgeur *m.* forger, inventor
formaldéhyde *m.* formaldehyde
formaliser *v.*, se — to be offended
formaliste *a. & f.* formalist
formalité *f.* formality; form, ceremony
format *m.* size, format
formatif *a.* formative
formation *f.* formation; forming

forme f. form, shape; formality; politeness; **sous la — de** in the form of
formel a. formal; express; strict
formellement adv. formally; strictly
former vt. to form; formulate; model; bring up, train, educate
formidable a. formidable; tremendous
formique a. formic
formulaire m. set of rules or regulations
formule f. formula; form, blank
formuler vt. to formulate
forniquer vi. to fornicate
forsythia m. forsythia
fort a. strong, vigorous; high (wind); loud; heavy (sea); large, great; — adv. very, extremely; loudly; strongly; — m. strong point; strong man; fort
forteresse f. fortress
fortifiant a. fortifying; — m. tonic
fortification f. fortification
fortifier vt. to fortify, strengthen
fortuit a. chance, casual, fortuitous
fortune f. fortune; chance; destiny; **faire — to become rich
fortuné a. fortunate, happy; well-off
forum m. forum
fosse f. pit, hole; grave
fossé m. ditch; moat
fossette f. dimple
fossile a. & m. fossil
fossilisation f. fossilization
fossiliser vt. to fossilize
fossoyeur m. gravedigger
fou m. fool; madman; jester; bishop (chess)
fou, fol (folle) a. mad, foolish; in love
foucade f. impulse, whim
foudre f. thunderbolt; thunder; lightning; **coup de — m.** love at first sight
foudroyant a. crushing, overwhelming
foudroyer vt. to strike with lightning; strike down; blast; dumbfound
fouet m. whip
fouettement m. whipping
fouetter vt. to whip, flog; — vi. to whip, lash; flap
fougère f. fern
fougue f. spirit, fire, mettle
fougueux a. firery, impetuous, spirited
fouille f. digging, excavation
fouiller vt. to dig, excavate; search, look through; — vi. search
fouillis m. jumble, disorder
fouiner vi. to pry, ferret
fouir vt. to burrow, dig
foulard m. scarf, foulard cloth
foule f. crowd; pressing, milling
foulée f. tread; stride; track, spoor
fouler vt. to tread on; press; crush, trample; sprain; **se — la cheville** to sprain one's ankle
foulure f. sprain
four m. oven; kiln; **faire — to fail; **petit — cooky, pastry; **— soufflé** blast furnace
fourbe m. deceiver, cheat; — a. deceitful
fourberie f. deceit; cheating
fourbir vt. to furbish, polish
fourbissage m. polishing, furbishing
fourbu a. exhausted

fourche f. fork, pitchfork
fourcher vt. & vi. to fork
fourchetée f. forkful of food
fourchette f. fork
fourchon m. prong, tine
fourchu a. forked; cloven
fourgon m. wagon, van; baggage car; truck; poker
fourmi f. ant; **— blanche** termite
fourmilier m. anteater
fourmilière f. ant hill
fourmillement m. swarming; pricking sensation
fourmiller vi. to swarm, teem
fournaise f. furnace
fourneau m. cooking stove; furnace; **haut — blast furnace
fournée f. batch, ovenful
fourni a. bushy, thick
fournir vt. to furnish, provide, supply; produce
fournisseur m. contractor, supplier, caterer
fourniture f. furnishing; **—s** pl. supplies
fourrage m. fodder; foraging
fourrager vi. to forage; search; — vt. to ravage
fourreau m. scabbard, sheath; case
fourré a. fur-lined, furry; densely wooded; — m. thicket
fourrer vt. to put in; stuff, cram, poke
fourre-tout m. duffel bag
fourreur m. furrier
fourrière f. dog pound
fourrure f. fur; hair; skin; lining
fourvoyer vt. to lead astray
foyer m. hearth; home; center, source, seat; foyer, lobby; focus
frac m. dress coat
fracas m. bustle, noise
fracasser vt. to break in pieces, shatter
fraction f. fraction
fractionner vt. to split, divide
fracture f. fracture; breaking
fracturer vt. to fracture; break open
fragilité f. fragility; frailty
fragment m. fragment
fragmentaire a. fragmentary
fragmenter vt. to break into fragments
fraîchement adv. freshly; coolly; recently, lately
fraîcheur f. freshness; coolness; chill
fraîchir vi. to freshen; become cooler
frais (fraîche) a. fresh; cool; recent; — m. fresh air; cool(ness)
frais m. pl. expenses; cost
fraise f. strawberry
framboise f. raspberry
franc (franche) a. free; frank; open; sincere; — adv. frankly
franc (franque) a. Frankish, of the Franks
franc m. franc (currency)
français m. the French language; — a. French; **à la —e** in the French fashion
Français m. Frenchman
France f. France
franchement adv. frankly, sincerely
franchir vt. to leap over; clear; overcome; cross
franchise f. frankness, sincerity; im-

munity, exemption

franchissement *m.* crossing, act of crossing

francique *a.* Frankish

franciscain *a.* & *m.* Franciscan

franciser *vt.* to gallicize

francium *m.* francium

franc-maçon *m.* freemason

franc-maçonnerie *f.* freemasonry

franco *adv.* postpaid

franco-bord *m.* & *adv.* free on board (F.O.B.)

franc-parler *m.* frankness

franc-tireur *m.* sniper

frange *f.* fringe; —r *vt.* to fringe

frangible *a.* breakable, fragile

frappant *a.* striking, surprising

frappe *f.* minting, striking of coins

frappé *a.* cooled, chilled (wine)

frapper *vt.* to strike, hit; knock; mint stamp; ice

frasque *f.* escapade

fraternel *a.* fraternal; brotherly

fraternisation *f.* fraternizing

fraterniser *vi.* to fraternize

fraternité *f.* fraternity, brotherhood

fratricide *m.* & *f.* fratricide

fraude *f.* deceit, imposture; fraud; — fiscale tax evasion

frauder *vt.* to defraud, cheat

fraudeur *m.* cheat, defrauder

frauduleux *a.* fraudulent

frayer *vt.* to scrape; open, clear, trace; — *vi.* to associate with; spawn (fish)

frayeur *f.* fright, terror

fredaine *f.* frolic, prank

fredonner *vt.* & *vi.* to hum

frégate *f.* frigate

frein *m.* brake; bit; bridle; sans — unbridled, unchecked

freiner *vt.* to brake, apply the brakes; check

frelater *vt.* to adulterate

frêle *a.* frail, weak

frelon *m.* hornet

frémir *vi.* to shudder, tremble, quiver

frémissement *m.* shivering, shuddering, quivering

frêne *m.* (bot.) ash

frénésie *f.* frenzy

frénétique *a.* frantic; frenzied

fréquemment *adv.* frequently

fréquence *f.* frequency

fréquent *a.* frequent

fréquentation *f.* frequenting; association, company

fréquenter *vt.* to frequent, haunt; associate with

frère *m.* brother

fresque *f.* fresco

fret *m.* (naut.) freight, cargo; chartering; (naut.) charge for freight transportation by boat

fréter *vt.* (naut.) to load freight; charter

frétillant *a.* brisk, lively; frisky; wagging; wriggling

frétiller *vi.* to wriggle; fidget

fretin *m.* menu — small fish thrown back; small fry

frette *f.* hoop, iron ring; fret

freudien *a.* Freudian

freudisme *m.* Freudianism

friable *a.* friable, capable of being pulverized

friand *a.* dainty, nice; fond

friandise *f.* daintiness; —s *pl.* dainties, delicacies

fricassée *f.* fricassee

fricasser *vt.* to fricassee; squander

fricatif *a.* fricative (phonetics)

friche *f.* fallow land; en — fallow

friction *f.* rub, massage; friction

frictionner *vt.* to rub, massage

frigide *a.* frigid

frigidité *f.* frigidity

frigorification *f.* refrigeration

frigorifier *vt.* to refrigerate

frigorifique *a.* refrigerating

frimas *m.* rime, hoarfrost

fringale *f.* hunger pang

fringant *a.* frisky, lively; dapper

fringuer *vi.* to frisk, frolic

fripé *a.* rumpled, mussed

friper *vt.* to rumple, wrinkle

friperie *f.* secondhand clothes; rubbish

fripier *m.* secondhand clothier, ragman

fripon *m.* rogue

friponnerie *f.* roguery

frire *vi.* to fry

frise *f.* frieze

frisé *a.* curly, crisp

friser *vt.* & *vi.* to curl

frisoir *m.* hair curler

frisson *m.* shivering, shaking; thrill

frissonnement *m.* shiver; thrill

frissonner *vi.* to shiver, shudder; be thrilled

frisure *f.* curliness

frit *a.* fried; —es *f. pl.* French fried potatoes

friture *f.* frying; fritter; any fried food; fat for frying; radio static

frivole *a.* frivolous, trifling

frivolité *f.* frivolity

froc *m.* frock (of a monk)

froid *m.* coldness, chilliness; il fait — it is cold (weather); avoir — to be cold (person); — *a.* cold; cool

froideur *f.* coldness; coolness

froidure *f.* coldness; frostbite

froissant *a.* hurting, hurtful, injurious

froissement *m.* rumpling; rustling; clash, jostling

froisser *vt.* to bruise; rumple; jostle; hurt (feelings); se — to take offense

frôlement *m.* rustling sound

frôler *vt.* to touch lightly, brush

fromage *m.* cheese

froment *m.* wheat

fronce *f.* crease, fold, pucker

froncement *m.* frown, frowning; wrinkling

froncer *vt.* to pucker, wrinkle; — le sourcil to frown

frondaison *f.* foliage; foliation

fronde *f.* slingshot; (bot.) frond

fronder *vt.* to sling

front *m.* forehead, brow, face, head; front; boldness, impudence, nerve

frontal *a.* frontal

frontière *f.* frontier, border

frontispice *m.* frontispiece

fronton *m.* façade

frottement *m.* rubbing, friction; chafing

frotter *vt.* to rub, polish; — *vi.* to rub

frotteur *m.* polisher

frottoir *m.* polisher; brush; sandpaper on a matchbox

froufrou *m.* swish, rustling; pomp, show

fructifère *a.* fruit-bearing

fructification *f.* fruition

fructifier *vi.* to bear fruit

fructueux *a.* fruitful, profitable

frugal *a.* frugal

frugalité *f.* frugality

fruit *m.* fruit; profit; sans — fruitless(ly)

fruiterie *f.* fruit dealer's, fruit and vegetable store

fruitier *m.* fruit dealer

frumentaire *a.* pertaining to wheat

fruste *a.* rough; worn

frustration *f.* frustration; cheating

frustrer *vt.* to frustrate, disappoint; cheat

fugace *a.* fleeting

fugitif *a.* fugitive; transitory, fleeting; — *m.* fugitive

fugue *f.* fugue; flight

fuir *vi.* to flee; leak; — *vt.* to avoid

fuite *f.* flight; avoiding; leak

fulgurant *a.* flashing

fulgurer *vi.* to flash, shine

fuligineux *a.* sooty, smoky

fulminant *a.* fulminating

fulminer *vt. & vi.* to fulminate

fumage *m.* smoking (of meat)

fumage, fumaison *m.* manuring, fertilizing

fumant *a.* smoking, steaming

fume-cigarette *m.* cigarette holder

fumée *f.* smoke, steam; fumes

fumer *vt.* to smoke; fertilize, manure; — *vi.* to smoke, steam; fume

fumet *m.* bouquet (of wine); aroma; scent

fumeur *m.* smoker

fumeux *a.* smoky; heady

fumier *m.* dung, manure

fumigation *f.* production of smoke *or* steam; treatment using a vaporizer

fumiger *vt.* to fumigate

fumoir *m.* smoking room, smoker; smoke house

funambule *m. & f.* tightrope artist

funambulesque *a.* fantastic

funèbre *a.* funeral; dismal, funereal

funérailles *f. pl.* funeral ceremony

funéraire *a.* funereal, funeral urn

funeste *a.* fatal

funiculaire *a. & m.* (rail.) funicular

fur *m.*, au — et à mesure que as, in proportion to

furet *m.* ferret; (coll.) busybody

fureter *vi.* to ferret, pry about, search

fureur *f.* fury, rage, craze, passion

furibond *a.* furious

furie *f.* fury; rage

furieux *a.* furious, wild, raging

furoncle *m.* (med.) boil, furuncle

furtif *a.* furtive

furtivement *adv.* furtively, stealthily

fusain *m.* art charcoal; charcoal drawing

fuseau *m.* spindle; time zone

fusée *f.* rocket; fuse; axle; avion à — *m.* rocket plane

fuselage *m.* fuselage

fuselé *a.* tapered; streamlined

fuseler *vt.* to taper

fuser *vi.* to fuse, melt; run (color)

fusible *m.* (elec.) fuse; — *a.* fusible

fusil *m.* gun, rifle; whetstone; — à deux coups double-barreled gun; coup de — *m.* gunshot, report; pierre à — *f.* flint

fusillade *f.* rifle fire, fusillade, volley

fusiller *vt.* to shoot; execute by firing squad

fusion *f.* fusion, melting; (com.) merger

fusionner *vt. & vi.* to unite, blend; (com.) to merge

fustiger *vt.* to beat, whip, thrash

fût *m.* stock of a gun; bole of a-tree; cask, barrel; shaft of a column, stem

futaie *f.* forest of tall trees

futaille *f.* cask, barrel

futé *a.* smart, cunning, shrewd

futile *a.* futile

futilité *f.* futility

futur *a.* future; — *m.* (gram.) future; fiancé, husband-to-be

fuyant *a.* fleeing; fleeting

fuyard *m.* runaway, fugitive

G

gabare *f.* barge, lighter

gabarit *m.* mold; model; gauge

gabelle *f.* salt tax (history)

gâche *f.* catch; notch; clip; staple

gâcher *vt.* to spoil; bungle; squander

gâchette *f.* catch, pawl; trigger

gâcheur *a. & m.* spoiling, bungling; bungler

gâchis *m.* slush; mud; unhardened cement; (coll.) mess

gaélique *a. & m.* Gaelic

gaffe *f.* boat hook; blunder; faire une — to put one's foot in it

gaffer *vt.* to hook; — *vi.* to put one's foot in it

gage *m.* pawn, pledge; token; mettre en — to pawn; —s *pl.* wages; prêteur sur — pawnbroker

gagé *a.* salaried

gager *vt.* to hire, pay wages to; bet, wager

gageur *m.* bettor, wagerer

gageure *f.* bet, wager

gagiste *m.* pledger (law); (theat.) bit player, extra

gagnant *m.* winner

gagne-pain *m.* livelihood, living; breadwinner

gagner *vt.* to gain; win, earn; reach; — *vi.* gain, improve

gai *a.* gay, lively, cheerful

gaîté *f.* gaiety

gaillard *a.* hearty; fresh; strong; ribald; — *m.* (naut.) quarterdeck; fellow; strong, attractive man; quick-witted man

gaillardise *f.* cheerfulness; risqué remark

gain *m.* gain, earnings, profit

gaine *f.* sheath, casing; holster

gainer *vt.* to sheath, cover

gala *m.* gala, celebration, festivity

galamment *adv.* gallantly; politely

galant *a.* gallant; gay; elegant; — *m.* wooer, suitor, lover

galanterie *f.* politeness; gallant talk; escapade, love affair

galaxie *f.* galaxy; Milky Way

galbe *m.* curve; curving shape, outline

gale *f.* itch; scab; mange

galère *f.* (naut.) galley; (fig.) labor

galerie *f.* gallery; (theat.) balcony; arcade; cornice

galérien *m.* galley slave; convict

galet *m.* pebble; shingle; roller

galetas *m.* garret; hovel

galette *f.* flat thin cake; pancake

galeux *a.* mangy

galimatias *m.* nonsense, jumble

galion *m.* galleon

galle *f.* gall

Galles *f.* Wales

gallois *a.* Welsh; — *m.* Welshman; Welsh language

galoche *f.* clog; overshoe

galon *m.* braid, stripe, chevron

galonner *vt.* to braid, trim with braid

galop *m.* gallop; petit — canter

galopade *f.* gallop, galloping

galoper *vt. & vi.* to gallop

galopin *m.* rascal; (coll.) mischievous child

galuchat *m.* sharkskin

galvanique *a.* galvanic

galvaniser *vt.* to galvanize; electroplate

galvanomètre *m.* galvanometer

galvanoplastie *f.* electroplating

galvauder *vt.* (coll.) to smear; botch; — *vi.* roam

galvaudeux *m.* (coll.) tramp

gambade *f.* gambol, frolic, caper

gambader *vi.* to gambol, frolic, caper

gambit *m.* gambit

gamelle *f.* mess kit

gamin *m.* street urchin, rascal, youngster

gaminer *vi.* to play in the streets

gaminerie *f.* urchin's prank

gamme *f.* gamut; scale; range

ganglion *m.* ganglion

gangrène *f.* gangrene; (bot. *and* med.) canker

gangrener *vt.* to gangrene

ganse *f.* braid, piping, cord

gant *m.* glove

gantelet *m.* gauntlet

ganter *vt.* to glove; se — to put on one's gloves

ganterie *f.* glovemaking; glove department; glove shop

gantier *m.* glover

garage *m.* garage; parking place; boathouse; docking, dock; (rail.) siding

garagiste *m.* garageman; auto mechanic

garant *m.* guarantee; surety; security

garantie *f.* guarantee; warranty; deposit, security; underwriting

garantir *vt.* to guarantee, vouch for; insure, protect

garce *f.* trollop

garçon *m.* boy; fellow, young man; bachelor; waiter; — d'honneur best man

garçonnière *f.* tomboy; bachelor's apartment

garde *m.* guard, watchman; —*f.* keeping; guard; guarding; care, custody; watch; watching; fly-leaf; chien de — *m.* watchdog; prendre — (de) to be careful (not to)

garde-à-vous *m.* (mil.) attention

garde-barrière *m.* gatekeeper; crossing guard

garde-boue *m.* mudguard

garde-chasse *m.* gamekeeper

garde-corps *m.* railing, guardrail; parapet, barrier; (naut.) life line

garde-côte *m.* coast guardsman; coast guard cutter

garde-feu *m.* fire screen

garde-fou *m.* guardrail; parapet

garde-frein *m.* (rail.) brakeman

garde-magasin *m.* warehouseman

garde-malade *m. & f.* nurse

garde-manger *m.* pantry, larder

garde-meuble *m.* furniture warehouse

garde-nappe *m.* table mat, place mat

gardénia *m.* gardenia

garde-pêche *m.* fishing warden

garde-phare *m.* lighthouse keeper

garde-place(s) *m.* (rail.) reservations office

garder *vt.* to keep; guard; protect, watch over; preserve; — le lit to stay in bed, be confined to bed, be ill; se — de to beware of, take care not to

garderie *f.* nursery school

garde-robe *f.* wardrobe

gardeur *m.* keeper; herder

garde-vue *m.* eyeshade; lamp shade

gardien *m.* guardian, keeper; prison guard; policeman; goal tender

gare *f.* railway station; chef de — *m.* stationmaster

gare *interj.* watch out!, look out!

garer *vt.* to dock; shunt; put in the garage; se — to get out of the way

gargariser *v.*, se — to gargle

gargarisme *m.* gargle

gargote *f.* ordinary, cheap restaurant (in lower-class area)

gargouille *f.* spout of a gutter; drainpipe; (arch.) gargoyle

gargouiller *vi.* to gurgle; rumble

garnement *m.* scamp, rogue

garni *a.* garnished; served with parsley or watercress; plat — *m.* main dish with potatoes or vegetable; chambre —e *f.* furnished room; choucroute —e *f.* sauerkraut with frankfurters; — *m.* furnished room

garnir *vt.* to furnish; strengthen; trim; garnish; line; (mil.) garrison

garnison *f.* garrison

garniture *f.* garnish, ornaments, trimming; lining; complete set; — de lit bedding; — de feu, — de foyer set of fire irons; — de frein brake lining

garrot *m.* (med.) tourniquet; withers of a horse

garrotte *f.* garrote; garroting, strangling

garrotter *vt.* to garrote, strangle; secure, pinion

garrulité *f.* garrulity, garrulousness, loquacity

Gascogne f. Gascony; Golfe de — m. Bay of Biscay

gascon a. & m. Gascon

gasconner vi. (coll.) boast, brag

gasoil m. Diesel fuel

gaspiller vt. to waste, squander

gastrique a. gastric

gastrite f. gastritis

gastronome m. epicure, gourmet

gastronomie f. gastronomy

gastronomique a. gastronomical

gâté a. spoiled; pampered

gâteau m. cake; honeycomb

gâte-papier m. hack writer; scribbler

gâter vt. to spoil, harm, damage; pamper, overindulge

gâterie f. spoiling, overindulgence

gâtisme m. senility

gauche a. left; crooked; awkward; à — to the left; — m. left; left wing

gaucher a. left-handed; leftist, left-wing

gaucherie f. awkwardness; blunder; left-handedness

gauchir vt. to warp; — vi. to warp, buckle; flinch

gaufrage m. fluting; embossing; corrugating

gaufre f. honeycomb; waffle, wafer

gaufrer vt. to flute; emboss; corrugate

gaufrette f. wafer

gaufrier m. waffle iron

gaule f. pole, rod, stick

Gaule f. Gaul

gaulois a. Gallic

gauloiserie f. risqué joke or story

gausser vt. & vi., se — to scoff; jest, banter

gaver vt. to cram; forcefeed; se — to gorge with food

gaz m. gas; compteur à — gas meter

gaze f. gauze

gazéifier vt. to carbonate; ærate

gazelle f. gazelle

gazer vi. to gas; cover with gauze; gloss over

gazeux a. gaseous; fizzy, carbonated

gazon m. turf, lawn, sod

gazonner vt. to cover with sod

gazouillement m. warbling; babbling

gazouiller vi. to warble; babble

gazouillis m. warbling

geai m. jay

géant m. giant; — a. gigantic

geignard a. (coll.) whining; — m. habitual whiner

geignement m. whine, whining, whimpering

geindre vi. to whine, whimper

gel m. frost, freezing

gélatine f. gelatin

gélatineux a. gelatinous

gelé a. frozen; frostbitten

gelée f. frost; jelly

geler vt. & vi. to freeze; jelly

gélose f. agar-agar

gelure f. frostbite

géminé a. twin

gémir vi. to groan, moan

gémissement m. groan, moan; groaning, moaning

gemme f. gem, precious stone; resin; sel — m. rock salt

gemmer vi. to bud; — vt. to cut, tap for resin

gênant a. troublesome, embarrassing

gencive f. (anat.) gums

gendarme m. policeman

gendarmer vt. to arouse, stir up

gendarmerie f. police; police headquarters; gendarmes

gendre m. son-in-law

gêne f. discomfort, embarrassment; sans — unconstrained

gêné a. embarrassed, troubled; having difficulty; short of money

généalogie f. genealogy; pedigree

généalogique a. genealogical; arbre — m. family tree

gêner vt. to pinch; obstruct; hinder, inconvenience, embarrass

général a. general; en — generally, in general; — m. general; —e f. general alert, general quarters

généralement adv. generally, in general

généralisateur a. generalizing; — m. generalizer

généralisation f. generalization

généraliser vt. to generalize

généralissime m. generalissimo

généralité f. generality

générateur (génératrice) a. generating; n. generator

génératif a. generative

génération f. generation

générer vt. to generate

généreux a. generous, liberal

générique a. generic

générosité f. generosity, liberality

Gênes f. Genoa

genèse f. genesis, origin

genêt m. (bot.) broom plant

génétique f. genetics

genevois a. of Geneva

genévrier m. juniper

génial a. brilliant, ingenious

génie m. genius; spirit; genie; engineering; (mil.) engineers

genièvre m. (bot.) juniper; gin

génisse f. heifer

génital a. genital

géniteur m. sire, father

génitif m. (gram.) genitive

génocide m. genocide

génois a. of Genoa

genou m. knee; (mech.) joint; ball and socket

genouillère f. knee guard, knee pad, kneecap

genre m. genus; (gram.) gender; kind, type, manner; style; genre; — humain man, mankind

gens m. pl. people, men; servants; jeunes — young people; young men

gentil (gentille) a. nice; pretty; m. gentile

gentilhomme m. gentleman, nobleman

gentilité f. pagans

gentillesse f. graciousness, kindness

gentillet a. rather nice

gentiment adv. nicely; gracefully

génuflexion f. (eccl.) kneeling, genuflexion

géocentrique *a.* geocentric

géodésique *a.* geodetic

géographie *f.* geography

géographique *a.* geographic(al)

geôle *f.* jail

geôlier *m.* jailor

géologie *f.* geology

géologique *a.* geological

géologue *m.* geologist

géométrie *f.* geometry

géométrique *a.* geometric(al)

géophysique *a.* geophysical; — *f.* geophysics

gérance *f.* management; board of directors

géranium *m.* geranium

gérant *m.* manager; director; — d'une publication managing editor

gerbe *f.* sheaf; column, cone

gerbée *f.* straw (rye or corn)

gerber *vt.* to bind in sheaves; stack

gerce *f.* crack, split; chap; clothes moth

gercer *vt.* to crack, split; chap

gerçure *f.* crack, cracking; chap, chapping

gérer *vt.* to manage, operate, run

gériatrie *f.* geriatrics

germain *a.* german; cousin — *m.* first cousin

germain *a. & m.* German

germanique *a.* Germanic

germanium *m.* germanium

germe *m.* germ, seed; sprout, shoot

germer *vi.* to germinate, sprout

germicide *a. & m.* germicide

germination *f.* germination

gérondif *m.* (gram.) gerundive

gérontologie *f.* gerontology

gésier *m.* gizzard

gésir *vi.* to lie; lie dead

gesse *f.* (bot.) vetch; — odorante sweet pea

gestation *f.* gestation

geste *m.* gesture, movement, motion; wave, waving

geste *f.* heroic exploit; chanson de — *f.* medieval French epic

gesticuler *vi.* to gesticulate

gestion *f.* management, administration

gestionnaire *m. & f.* manager

geyser *m.* geyser

gibbeux *a.* hunchbacked; humped

gibecière *f.* game bag; satchel

gibelotte *f.* rabbit stew

giberne *f.* cartridge pouch; satchel

gibet *m.* gibbet; gallows

gibier *m.* game; gros — big game; — de potence jailbird

giboulée *f.* shower, squall of sleet or hail

gicelée *f.* spurt of liquid; squirt

giclement *m.* spurting

gicler *vi.* to squirt, spurt

gicleur *m.* jet, nozzle; sprayer; carburetor opening

gifle *f.* slap, smack; humiliation

gifler *vt.* to slap, smack; affront

gigantesque *a.* gigantic

gigone *a.*, table — *f.* stack-table (nested tables)

gigot *m.* leg of lamb

gigue *f.* jig

gilet *m.* vest, cardigan, waistcoat; — de force strait jacket; — de sauvetage life jacket

gingembre *m.* ginger

gingivite *f.* gingivitis

girafe *f.* giraffe

girandole *f.* cluster; centerpiece, candelabrum; earring

giration *f.* gyration

giratoire *a.* turning, gyratory

girofle *m.* clove

giron *m.* lap; — de l'Eglise bosom of the church

girouette *f.* weather vane

gisant *a.* lying; lying dead

git (*from* gésir), ci-git here lies

gitan *a.* Gypsy

gite *m.* lodging, resting place; refuge, lair; stratum, layer, (mining)

gite *f.* (naut.) list, heeling

giter *vt.* to shelter, lodge; — *vi.* to lie; perch; (naut.) list; run aground

givre *m.* hoarfrost

givrer *vt.* to frost

glabre *a.* smooth shaven, beardless; (fig.) smooth

glace *f.* ice; plate glass; mirror; windshield; glaze; icing; ice cream

glacé *a.* frozen; cold; iced; icy; chilled; glazed; glossy

glacer *vt.* to freeze; glaze; frost; ice

glacerie *f.* glass factory

glaciaire *a.* glacial

glacial *a.* icy, cold, freezing, frigid

glacier *m.* (geol.) glacier; ice-cream vendor

glacière *f.* icehouse; refrigerator, icebox

glacis *m.* slope; colorless glaze (art); tacking (sewing)

glaçon *m.* ice floe; icicle

glaçure *f.* ceramic glaze, glazing

gladiateur *m.* gladiator

glaïeul *m.* gladiolus

glaire *f.* white of egg; mucus

glaise *f.* clay; potter's earth

glaisière *f.* clay pit

glaive *m.* sword

gland *m.* acorn; tassel

glande *f.* gland

glandulaire, glanduleux *a.* glandular

glaner *vt.* to glean

glanure *f.* gleaning

glapir *vi.* to yelp; scream

glas *m.* knell

glaucome *m.* glaucoma

glauque *a.* blue-green

glèbe *f.* clod, sod; soil

glène *f.* (naut.) coil of rope; (anat.) socket

glissade *f.* slip, slide, sliding; glide

glissant *a.* slippery; sliding; unstable

glissement *m.* slipping, sliding; landslide

glisser *vt. & vi.* to slip, slide; skid; glide; se — to glide, steal, slip

glisseur *m.* glider; slider

glissière *f.* slide, groove; shoot; porte à —s *f.* sliding door

glissoir *m.* icy slide

glissoire *f.* sliding, slide on ice

global *a.* global; total; lump (sum)

globe *m.* globe, ball, sphere

globulaire *a.* globular
globuleux *a.* globular
globulin *m.* globulin
gloire *f.* glory; halo; pride; vanity
gloria *m.* coffee with brandy
gloriette *f.* arbor, summerhouse
glorieux *a.* glorious; proud; vain
glorification *f.* glorification
glorifier *vt.* to glorify; se — to boast
gloriole *f.* vainglory, vanity
glose *f.* gloss; commentary
gloser *vt.* to gloss, comment on; — *vi.* to find fault; criticize
glossaire *m.* glossary
glotte *f.* (anat.) glottis; coup de — *m.* glottal stop (phonetics)
glouglou *m.* gurgle, gurgling sound; coo, cooing; gobble
glouglouter *vi.* to gurgle; gobble; coo
glousser *vi.* to cluck; (coll.) chuckle
glouton *m.* glutton; — *a.* gluttonous
gloutonnerie *f.* gluttony
glu *f.* birdlime; glue; (fig.) trap, snare
gluant *a.* sticky, viscous; (fig.) tenacious
glucose *f.* glucose
glutineux *a.* glutinous
glycérine *f.* glycerin
glycine *f.* wistaria
go (tout de) *adv.* at once; easily; at one shot; suddenly
goal *m.* goal tender, goalie
gobelet *m.* goblet, cup, tumbler
gobe-mouches *m.* flycatcher (bird) (fig.) gullible person
gober *vt.* to swallow greedily, gulp down; (fig.) believe credulously se — to be conceited
gobeter *vt.* to plaster; fill in cracks
gobeur *a. & m.* easily fooled person
goder *vi.* to wrinkle, pucker
godet *m.* mug; bowl; basin; pan; scoop; flare of a skirt
godille *f.* oar, scull
godiller *vi.* to scull
goéland *m.* sea gull
goélette *f.* (naut.) schooner
goguenard *a.* jeering, mocking
goguenarder *vi.* to mock; banter
goitre *m.* goiter
golf *m.* golf; terrain de — golf course
golfe *m.* gulf
gomme *f.* gum; — élastique gum eraser; — laque shellac
gommelaquer *vt.* to shellac
gommer *vt.* to gum; erase; — *vi.* to stick, become stuck
gommeux *a.* gummy
gommier *m.* gum tree
gonade *f.* gonad
gond *m.* door hinge; sortir de ses —s to fly off the handle
gondole *f.* gondola
gondoler *vi.* to warp, buckle
gondolier *m.* gondolier
gonfalon *m.* gonfalon, pennant
gonflage *m.* inflating
gonflement *m.* inflating, inflation
gonfler *vt.* to inflate; fill with air; pump up; bulge; puff up; swell; — *vi.* to be inflated, become inflated

gonfleur *m.* (auto.) air pump
goret *m.* young pig; (coll.) dirty person
gorge *f.* throat; bosom; bust; gorge; avoir mal à la — to have a sore throat
gorgée *f.* mouthful, gulp
gorger *vt.* to gorge, stuff
gorille *m.* gorilla
gosier *m.* throat; gullet
gosse *m. & f.* (coll.) youngster; child
gothique *a. & m.* Gothic
gouape *f.* (coll.) good-for-nothing person; hoodlum
gouaper *vi.* to loaf, idle
goudron *m.* tar
goudronner *vt.* to tar
gouffre *m.* gulf, abyss; whirlpool
gouge *f.* gouge, chisel
gouger *vt.* to gouge
goujat *m.* lout, boor
goujon *m.* gudgeon; (fig.) bait
goulasch *m.* goulash
goule *f.* ghoul
goulet *m.* (naut.) channel, narrows
goulot *m.* neck of a bottle
goulu *a.* gluttonous; greedy
goupille *f.* peg, pin, bolt
goupillon *m.* brush; (eccl.) holy water sprinkler
gourd *a.* benumbed, numb
gourde *f.* gourd; metal flask
gourdin *m.* club, bludgeon
gourmand *m.* greedy person; glutton; — *a.* greedy, gluttonous
gourmander *vi.* to guzzle; — *vt.* rebuke
gourmandise *f.* greediness, gluttony; sweets
gourme *f.* rash; impetigo
gourmé *a.* formal, stiff; stuck up (U.S. coll.)
gourmet *m.* connoisseur of food and drink; epicure
gourmette *f.* curb (of a harness); watch chain
gousse *f.* pod, husk; — d'ail clove of garlic
gousset *m.* watch pocket, vest pocket
goût *m.* taste; flavor; aroma; liking; style
goûter *vt.* to taste, like, enjoy; — *m.* afternoon snack
goutte *f.* drop; speck, spot, bit; nothing, anything; (med.) gout
gouttelette *f.* droplet
goutteux *a.* gouty
gouttière *f.* gutter; rainspout; —s *pl.* eaves
gouvernail *m.* rudder; helm, steering wheel
gouvernante *f.* housekeeper; governess; governor's wife
gouverne *f.* guidance; —s *pl.* (avi.) controls
gouvernement *m.* government; management; control; steering
gouvernemental *a.* governmental
gouverner *vt.* to govern, manage; direct; control; (naut.) to steer
gouverneur *m.* governor
grabat *m.* pallet, litter; sickbed
grâce *f.* grace; gracefulness; favor; pardon; mercy; thanks; actions de — *f. pl.* thanksgiving; avec — gracefully; de —l please!, I beg of you!; de bonne — graciously, willingly; — à thanks to;

faire — to pardon, reprieve
graciable a. pardonable
gracier vt. to pardon, reprieve
gracieusement adv. graciously; gracefully; gratuitously
gracieuseté f. graciousness, kindness
gracieux a. gracious; graceful; à titre — free, gratis; as a favor
gracile a. slender, svelte
gracilité f. slenderness
gradation f. gradation
grade m. grade, rank, degree
gradé m. noncommissioned officer
gradient m. gradient, variation
gradin m. tier, row; tiered seating
gradué a. graduated, measured, graded
graduel a. gradual; (eccl.) verse between epistle and gospel
graduellement adv. gradually
graduer vt. to graduate, scale; grade
graillement m. hoarseness, huskiness
grailler vi. to speak in a hoarse manner; cough up phlegm
grain m. grain; berry, bean; bead; particle, iota, speck; (naut.) squall; — de beauté beauty mark
grain-d'orge m. (coll.) sty of the eye
graine f. seed
grainer vt. to grain; granulate
graissage m. greasing, lubrication
graisse f. grease, fat; — de rôti meat drippings
graisser vt. to grease, oil, lubricate
graisseux a. greasy, oily; fatty
grammaire f. grammar
grammairien m. grammarian
grammatical a. grammatical
gramme m. gram
grand a. great; large, tall, high; important, big; main, chief, principal; — m. great person; grownup; grandee
grand-chose m. something important; something significant
Grande-Bretagne f. Great Britain
grandelet a. rather big
grandeur f. greatness, tallness, largeness, magnitude; size; nobility; grandeur
grandiloquence f. grandiloquence
grandiose a. grandiose, impressive
grandir vi. to grow, grow up; — vt. to increase; magnify
grandissant a. growing
grandissement m. growth, growing; magnification
grand-livre m. ledger
grand'mère f. grandmother
grand-messe f. (eccl.) high mass
grand-oncle m. great-uncle
grand-père m. grandfather
grand'route f. main highway
grand'rue f. main street
grands-parents m. pl. grandparents
grand-tante f. great-aunt
grange f. barn; building for keeping straw or hay
granit m. granite
granulaire a. granular
granuler vt. to granulate
granuleux a. granular
graphique a. graphic; — m. graph

graphite m. graphite
graphologue m. graphologist
grappe f. bunch, cluster of fruit
grappillon m. little bunch or cluster
grappin m. grapnel, grappling hook
gras (grasse) a. fat, stout; fatty, greasy; thick; containing meat; caractères — m. pl. bold-faced type; jours — m. (eccl.) carnival days (pre-lenten) temps — m. foggy weather; — m. fat
gras-double m. tripe
grassement adv. comfortably; generously
grassouillet a. plump, chubby
gratification f. tip; bonus; reward
gratifier vt. to confer, bestow
gratin m. breading, crust; au — served or cooked with cheese and bread crumbs
gratiné a. au gratin; breaded
gratis adv. gratis, free
gratitude f. gratitude
gratte-ciel m. skyscraper
gratte-papier m. (coll.) hack writer; copyist
gratte-pieds m. doormat; scraper for shoes
gratter vt. to scrape, scratch; scratch out, erase
grattoir m. scraper; eraser
gratuit a. gratuitous; free; unmotivated à titre — free of charge
gratuité f. gratuitousness
grave a. grave, serious, important; (phy.) heavy; (mus.) flat; (gram.) accent grave
graveler vt. to gravel
graveleux a. gravelly, gritty
gravelle f. gravel
gravement adv. gravely, seriously
graver vt. to engrave; carve; — à l'eau forte etch
graveur m. engraver; etcher
gravier m. gravel; grit
gravir vt. to climb with effort
gravité f. gravity; graveness; seriousness; (mus.) lowness, flatness
graviter vi. to gravitate
gravure f. engraving, etching; print; carving
gré m. will, liking; de bon — willingly; bon — mal — willy-nilly; de son propre — freely, of one's own free will; savoir (bon) — de to be grateful for; — adv. de — à — amiably; de son pleine — voluntarily
grec (grecque) a. Greek, Grecian; — m. Greek
Grèce f. Greece
gredin m. scoundrel
gréement m. (naut.) rig, rigging
gréer vt. (naut.) to rig
greffe f. (med., bot.) graft, grafting
greffer vt. to graft
greffier m. recorder, clerk of the court
grégaire a. gregarious
grégorien a. Gregorian
grêle f. hail; hailstorm; — a. slender; shrill
grêlé a. pock-marked
grelin m. (naut.) hawser
grêlon m. large hailstone
grelot m. little bell

grelotter vi. to shiver, tremble; jingle
grenade f. pomegranate; grenade
grenadier m. grenadier; pomegranate tree
grenadine f. grenadine syrup
grenailler vt. to granulate
grenat a. & m. garnet
grené a. stippled (art); — m. stipple
grenier m. granary; hayloft; attic
grenouille f. frog
grenouillère f. swamp, marsh
grenu a. granular, grainy, rough-grained
grès m. sandstone; stoneware
grésil m. sleet
grésiller vi. to crackle; sizzle; patter
grève f. sandy shore, beach; strike (labor);
  faire — to strike, go out on strike
gréver vt. to entail legally, encumber
gréviste m. & f. worker on strike, striker
gribouillage m. scribble, scrawl
gribouiller vt. to scribble, scrawl
grief m. grievance; injury, wrong
grièvement adv. grievously, seriously,
  gravely
griffe f. claw, talon; clamp, clip; coup de
  — m. scratch; — à papiers paper clip;
  marteau à — claw hammer
griffer vt. to claw, scratch
griffonnage m. scribble, scribbling, scrawl
griffonner vt. to scrawl, scribble
grignoter vt. to pick at, nibble
gril m. grill, gridiron
grillade f. grilled meat
grillage m. grating, latticework; grilling,
  toasting
grille f. iron bars; gate, grate; grid
grille-pain m. toaster
griller vt. & vi. to grill; toast; broil; bar,
  grate
grillon m. cricket
grimacer vi. to grimace
grimacier a. grimacing; affected
grimer vt. (theat.) to apply makeup, make
  up
grimper vt. & vi. to climb up; scale
grimpeur a. climbing; — m. climber
grincement m. gnashing
grincer vi. to gnash; grind; scratch; — des
  dents grit one's teeth in anger
grincheux a. grumpy, crabby; — m. grumbler, crab
gringalet m. weakling, runt
grippe f. influenza; (fig.) dislike
grippé a. having influenza; stuck together
gripper vt. to grab, seize; — vi. to grab,
  stick, jam
grippe-sou m. miser, skinflint
gris a. gray; gray-haired; drunk, tipsy;
  cloudy, overcast (weather)
grisailler vt. to daub with gray; — vi. to
  turn gray (hair)
grisâtre a. grayish
griser vt. to intoxicate; se — to become
  intoxicated
griserie f. intoxication, drunkenness, tipsiness
grisonner vi. to become gray (hair)
grive f. thrush
grivelé a. speckled
grivois a. risqué, off-color
grizzly m. grizzly bear

Groenland m. Greenland
grog m. grog, toddy
grognard a. grumbling; — m. grumbler
grognement m. grumbling, growling;
  grunt, grunting
grogner vi. to grunt, grumble, growl
grognerie f. grumbling, growling
grognon a. grumbling; — m. grumbler.
grognonner vi. to grumble, complain,
  whine
groin m. snout of a pig
grommeler vi. to grumble, mutter
grondement m. rumbling, roaring; growling
gronder vt. to scold; — vi. to grumble
  growl; rumble
gronderie f. scolding
grondeur a. grumbling; scolding; — m.
  grumbler
grondeuse f. nag, shrew
gros (grosse) a. big, bulky, large; rich;
  heavy; thick; loud; coarse; vulgar;
  pregnant, swollen; — sel m. coarse salt;
  — jeu m. high stakes; — temps m. bad
  weather; — m. bulk, main part; —
  adv. en — in bulk, wholesale; rough,
  roughly
gros-bec m. grosbeak
groseille f. currant; gooseberry
grosse f. (com.) gross, twelve dozen
grossesse f. pregnancy
grosseur f. size; bulk; swelling; largeness
grossier a. coarse, rough; rude; vulgar
grossièreté f. grossness, coarseness, rudeness, vulgarity
grossir vt. & vi. to enlarge, increase
grossissant a. growing, increasing, swelling; verre — m. magnifying glass
grossissement m. increase, growth, swelling; enlargement; magnification
grossiste m. wholesaler
grotte f. grotto; cavern
grouiller vi. to swarm, teem, crawl
groupe m. group; unit; set, section
groupement m. group, grouping; coupling
grouper vt. to group; bring together;
  couple; se — to form a group
gruau m. groats, oatmeal; fine flour; small
  crane
grue f. crane
grumeler v., se — to curdle, clot
grumeleux a. curdled; gritty, grainy
gruyère m. variety of Swiss cheese; crème
  de — f. processed gruyère cheese
gué m. ford, crossing
guéable a. fordable
guéer vt. to ford; water
guelte f. (com.) commission, percentage,
  fee
guenille f. ragged garment, tatters
guenilleux a. ragged, in rags
guenipe f. whore, trollop
guenon f. monkey
guépard m. cheetah
guêpe f. wasp
guêpier m. wasps' nest; (fig.) hornets' nest
guère adv. not much; not long; but little;
  ne . . . — hardly
guéret m. (agr.) unsown land
guéridon m. small table

guérilla f. guerilla warfare; guerilla army

guérillero m. guerilla, guerilla fighter

guérir vt. to cure, heal; — vi. to recover, be cured, healed

guérison f. cure, recovery; healing

guérissable a. curable

guérisseur a. healing; — m. healer; quack

guérite f. turret, sentry box; shack, hut (for watchman); (rail.) signal box; — téléphonique call box

guerre f. war, warfare; struggle, strife; en — at war

guerrier a. warlike; — m. warrior

guerroyant a. warlike, bellicose

guerroyer vi. to make war

guerroyeur a. fighting; — m. fighter

guet m. watch, lookout; au — on the lookout

guet-apens m. ambush; (fig.) premeditation

guêtre f. gaiter; legging; (auto.) tire patch

guetter vt. to watch for; (coll.) lie in wait for

guetteur m. lookout

gueulard m. furnace mouth, gun muzzle; powerful loudspeaker

gueule f. mouth; muzzle; avoir la — de bois to have a hangover

gueule-de-loup f. snapdragon

gueuse f. beggar; hussy; fer en — m. pig iron

gueuser vi. to beg in the streets

gueuserie f. begging; wretchedness

gueux (gueuse) a. beggarly, wretched, poor; — m. beggar

gui m. mistletoe; (naut.) guy; boom

guichet m. grilled window; ticket window; box-office window

guide f. guide, guidebook; — f. rein

guide-âne m. manual, set of instructions; travel guide

guider vt. to guide, lead; steer; drive

guidon m. handlebar; gun sight or bead; (naut.) pennant

guigne f. white-heart cherry; (coll.) bad luck

guigner vt. to ogle; eye

guignol m. Punch and Judy show; puppet theater

guignolet m. cherry liqueur

guillemeter vt. to put in or between, quotation marks

guillemets m. pl. quotation marks

guiller vi. to ferment

guilleret a. gay, lively

guillotine f. guillotine; fenêtre à — sash window

guillotiner vt. to guillotine

guindé a. stiff, affected, stuck-up

guindeau m. windlass; hoist

guinder vt. to hoist; se — to act superior

Guinée f. Guinea

guingan m. gingham

guingois (de) adv. askew

guipage m. wrapping, covering, winding; tape, taping

guiper vt. to wrap, cover; wind; tape

guipure f. lace

guirlande f. garland, wreath

guirlander vt. to garland

guise f. manner, fashion, way; en — de by way of

guitare f. guitar

guppy m. guppy

gustation f. taste, tasting; eating

Guyane f. Guiana

gymnase m. gymnasium

gymnaste m. & f. gymnast

gymnastique a. gymnastic; — f. gymnastics

gynécologie f. gynecology

gynécologue; gynécologiste m. gynecologist

gypse m. gypsum; plaster of Paris

gyrocompas m. gyrocompass

gyroscope m. gyroscope

H

* Indicates a word which allows neither elision nor linking

habile a. clever, skilful; capable

habileté f. cleverness; skill, ability

habilité f. ability (law), title

habillé a. dressed

habillement m. clothing, clothes

habiller vt. to dress; clothe; put together; s' — to get dressed

habit m. suit, full-dress suit; evening clothes; (eccl.) habit; frock; —s pl. clothes; prendre l' — to become a nun or monk

habitabilité f. habitability

habitable a. habitable

habitacle m. cockpit; (naut.) binnacle

habitant m. inhabitant, dweller

habitat m. habitat

habitation f. habitation; housing; dwelling

habiter vt. & vi. to inhabit; live in

habitude f. habit, custom; avoir l' — de to be used to; be in the habit of; d' — usually; comme d' — as usual

habitué m. regular customer, frequenter

habituel a. habitual; usual, regular

habituer vt. to habituate, accustom; s' — à to get used to

*hâbler vi. to brag

*hâblerie f. bragging

*hâbleur m. braggart

*hache f. axe, hatchet

*haché a. chopped; choppy, jerky

*hacher vt. to hash, chop, mince; hack

*hachette f. hatchet

*hachis m. hash, minced meat

.hachisch m. hashish, hasheesh

*hachoir m. chopper; cleaver; chopping board

*hachurer vt. (art) to shade

*hagard a. haggard, drawn

*haie f. hedge; hurdle

*haillon m. rag, tatter

*haillonneux a. ragged, in rags

*haine f. hate, hatred

*haineux a. full of hate

*haïr vt. to hate; loathe; feel repugnance for

*haïssable a. hateful; odious

*halage m. towing

halcyon m. kingfisher

*hâle m. sunburn, tan; searing wind

*hâlé a. sunburned, tanned

haleine *f.* breath, wind

halenée *f.* whiff

*haler *vt.* to tow; (naut.) heave; — *vi.* to heave, haul

*hâler *vt.* to burn, tan; se — to be burned by the sun, become tanned

*haletant *a.* breathless, out of breath, panting

halètement *m.* breathlessness, panting

*haleter *vi.* to burn; pant; puff

*hall *m.* hall, hallway; lounge; shop in a factory

*halle *f.* covered market place

*hallier *m.* thicket

hallucination *f.* hallucination

halluciner *vt.* to hallucinate, delude

*halo *m.* halo (meteorology)

*halte *f.* halt, stop; faire — to halt, come to a halt; —! (mil.) halt! halt! stop!

haltère *m.* dumbbell (gymnastics)

*hamac *m.* hammock

*hameau *m.* hamlet

hameçon *m.* hook, fishhook; (fig.) bait

*hamman *m.* Turkish bath(s)

*hampe *f.* pole, shaft; stem

*hamster *m.* hamster

*hanche *f.* hip, haunch; (naut.) lee quarter

*hanché *a.* (mil.) at ease

*handicap *m.* handicap

*handicaper *vt.* to handicap (sports)

*hangar *m.* shed; boathouse; (avi.) hangar

*hanter *vt.* to haunt, frequent; obsess

*hantise *f.* obsession

*happe *f.* tongs; staple

*happer *vt.* to grab, snatch, seize; — *vi.* to stick

*harangue *f.* speech, harangue

*haranguer *vt.* to harangue

*harasser *vt.* to harass; exhaust

*harceler *vt.* to harass, harry; torment; nag, pester

*harde *f.* flock, herd; dog leash

*hardes *f. pl.* ordinary clothes

*hardi *a.* hardy, bold, daring

*hardiesse *f.* boldness, daring, audacity

*harem *m.* harem

*hareng *m.* herring; — saur smoked herring

*harenguet *m.* sprat

*hargne *f.* irritation, peevishness, ill temper

*hargneux *a.* surly, snapping; ill-tempered, cross; nagging

*haricot *m.* bean; — vert string bean; — de mouton mutton stew

*haricot-beurre *m.* butter bean

harmonie *f.* harmony; accord

harmonieux *a.* harmonious; melodious

harmonique *a. & m.* harmonic

harmonisation *f.* harmonizing, harmonization

harmoniser *vt.* to harmonize; s'— to harmonize; blend; agree

*harnachement *m.* harness, harnessing; saddlery

*harnacher *vt.* to harness; rig, deck out

*harnais *m.* harness, armor; gears

harpagon *m.* miser

*harpe *f.* harp

*harpie *f.* harpy

*harpin *m.* boat hook

*harpiste *m. & f.* harpist

*harpon *m.* harpoon

*harponner *vt.* to harpoon

*hasard *m.* hazard, chance, luck, accident; au — at random; coup de — *m.* stroke of luck; par — by chance, accidentally

*hasardé *a.* risky, hazardous; rash; indiscreet

*hasarder *vt.* to risk, hazard, venture

*hasardeux *a.* risky, hazardous

*hâte *f.* haste, speed; à la — hastily; avoir — de to be in a hurry to; be anxious to, be eager to

*hâter *vt.* to hasten, hurry, quicken; se — to hurry oneself

*hâtif (hâtive) *a.* hasty; early, premature

*hâtivement *ads.* hastily, hurriedly

*hauban *m.* (naut.) shroud; stay

*haubert *m.* coat of mail, hauberk

*hausse *f.* rise, increase; (mil.) elevation, range

*haussement *m.* raising; — d'épaules shrug

*hausser *vt.* to raise, lift, elevate; — *vi.* to rise; — les épaules shrug

*haussier *m.* bull stock

*haussière *f.* hawser

*haut *a.* high; tall; elevated; great; loud; upper, higher; —*ads.* high, up; loud(ly), aloud; back (in time); — *m.* height; top: au — de at the top of; de — en bas from top to bottom; condescendingly; en — above; upstairs

*hautain *a.* haughty, proud, arrogant

*hautbois *m.* oboe

*hautboïste *m. & f.* oboist

*haut-de-chausses *m.* breeches

*haut-de-forme *m.* top hat

*hautement *adv.* highly; nobly; loudly

*hauteur *f.* height, elevation; rise; hill; haughtiness, scorn; (mus.) pitch; à la — de level with

*haut-fond *m.* shallows, shoal

*haut-fourneau *m.* blast furnace

*haut-le-cœur *m.* nausea

*haut-le-corps *m.* start, jump

*haut-parleur *m.* speaker, loudspeaker

*havana *m.* Havana cigar

la Havane *f.* Havana

*hâve *a.* gaunt, sunken; pale and sickly

*havre *m.* haven, harbor

*havresac *m.* bag, kit; knapsack

hawaiien *a. & m.* Hawaiian

la Haye *f.* the Hague

hebdomadaire *a.* weekly; — *m.* weekly paper

héberger *vt.* to lodge, shelter

hébété *a.* dazed, bewildered

hébétement *m.* daze, bewilderment, stupor

hébéter *vt.* to dull, blunt; daze, stupefy

hébraïque *a.* Hebrew, Hebraic

hébreu *a.* Hebrew

hectare *m.* hectare (about 2½ acres)

hédonisme *m.* hedonism

hégémonie *f.* hegemony

*hein *interj.* what?; right?

*hélas *interj.* alas!

*héler *vt.* to hail, call

hélianthe *m.* sunflower

hélice *f.* (naut.) screw; helix, spiral; (avi.) propeller

hélicoptère *m.* helicopter.

hélio *f.* heliogravure

héliocentrique *a.* heliocentric

héliotherapie *f.* sun lamp, sun-lamp treatment

héliotrope *m.* heliotrope

héliport *m.* heliport

hélium *m.* helium

hélix *m.* helix

hellène *a.* Hellenic

hellénique *a.* Hellenic, Hellenistic

hellénisme *m.* Hellenism

hellénistique *a.* Hellenistic

helvétique *a.* Swiss

hématie *f.* red blood corpuscle

hémisphère *m.* hemisphere

hémisphérique *a.* hemispherical

hémistiche *m.* hemstitch

hémoglobine *f.* hemoglobin

hémophile *a.* & *n.* hemophiliac

hémophilie *f.* hemophilia

hémorragie *f.* hemorrhage

hémorroïdes *f.* *pl.* hemorrhoids·

hémostatique *a.* styptic

*henné *m.* henna

*hennir *vi.* to neigh, whinny

*hennissement *m.* neigh, whinny

hépatique *a.* hepatic

hépatite *f.* hepatitis

heptagone *a.* heptagonal; — *m.* heptagon

heptemètre *m.* heptameter

héraldique *a.* heraldic; — *f.* heraldry

*héraut *m.* herald; sign, harbinger

herbacé *a.* (bot.) herbaceous

herbage *m.* grass; pasture, meadow

herbe *f.* grass; herb; weed; en — budding; green (unripe); mauvaises —s *pl.* weeds; fines —s seasoning herbs

herbeux *a.* grassy

herbivore *a.* herbivorous

herbu *a.* grassy

herculéen *a.* Herculean

*hère *m.* wretch

héréditaire *a.* hereditary

hérédité *f.* inheritance; heredity

hérésie *f.* heresy

hérétique *a.* heretical; — *m.* & *f.* heretic

*hérissé *a.* bristling; brushy, shaggy

*hérisser *vt.* to bristle

*herisson *m.* hedgehog; series of bristles or spikes; bottle brush; pinwheel; — de mer sea urchin

héritable *a.* inheritable

héritage *m.* heritage, inheritance, legacy

hériter *vt.* & *vi.* to inherit

héritier *m.*, héritière *f.* heir, heiress

hermétique *a.* hermetic, tight; hermetically sealed

hermine *f.* ermine

herminette *f.* adze

hermite *m.* hermit, recluse

*herniaire *a.* hernial; bandage — *m.* truss

*hernie *f.* (med.) hernia, rupture

*hernieux *a.* ruptured

héroïne *f.* heroine; (chem.) heroin

héroïque *a.* heroic

héroïsme *m.* heroism

*héron *m.* heron

*héros *m.* hero

hésitant *a.* hesitant, hesitating

hésitation *f.* hesitation

hésiter *vi.* to hesitate; falter

hétéroclite *a.* unusual, odd; eccentric

hétérodoxe *a.* heterodox

hétérogène *a.* heterogeneous

*hêtre *m.* beech tree

heur *m.* luck, good luck

heure *f.* hour; time; moment; à l'— on time; de bonne — early; à la bonne —! well!, fine!; tout à l'— in a little while; a little while ago; à tout à l'— see you soon!, see you later!, so long!

heureusement *adv.* fortunately

heureux *a.* happy, fortunate, lucky, successful

*heurt *m.* blow, bump, shock; sans — without a hitch

*heurtement *m.* shock, clash

*heurter *vt.* & *vi.* to strike against, hit against, knock; bump into; conflict with

*heurtoir *m.* bumper, stop; knocker of a door

hexagone *a.* hexagonal; — *m.* hexagon

hiatus *m.* hiatus; gap, break

hibernant *a.* hibernating

hiberner *vi.* to hibernate

hibiscus *m.* hibiscus

*hibou *m.* owl

*hideur *f.* hideousness, ugliness

*hideux *a.* hideous, ugly

hiémal *a.* pertaining to winter

hier *adv.* yesterday; — soir last night

*hiérarchie *f.* hierarchy

*hiérarchique *a.* hierarchical

hiéroglyphe *m.* hieroglyph; —s *pl.* hieroglyphics

hilarant *a.* producing laughter; gaz — *m.* laughing gas

hilare *a.* hilarious

hilarité *f.* hilarity, laughter

hindou *a.* & *m.* Hindu

hippique *a.* equine; pertaining to horses

hippisme *m.* horse racing

hippocratique *a.* Hippocratic

hippodrome *m.* race track; hippodrome

hippopotame *m.* hippopotamus

hirondelle *f.* swallow

hirsute *a.* hirsute, hairy

hispanique *a.* Hispanic, Spanish

hispano-américain *a.* Spanish-American

*hisser *vt.* (naut.) to hoist; raise, pull up

histoire *f.* history; story

histologie *f.* histology

historien *m.* historian

historier *vt.* to illuminate a book; illustrate

historiette *f.* short story, anecdote

historique *a.* historic(al)

histrion *m.* histrion, actor

histrionique *a.* histrionic

hiver *m.* winter

hivernage *m.* winter quarters; winter season

hivernal *a.* of the winter

hiverner *vi.* to hibernate; winter

*hoche f. notch, cut, nick
*hochement m. head shaking, affirmative, nod
*hocher vt. to shake, nod; notch, nick
*hochet m. toy, teething ring
*holà interj. stop!; hello!
*holding m. (com.) holding company
*hollandais a. & m. Dutch
*Hollande f. Holland
holocauste m. holocaust
*homard m. lobster
homélie f. homily
homérique a. Homeric, epic
homicide m. homicide (person or the act); — involontaire manslaughter; — a. homicidal; murderous
hommage m. homage; present; testimony; tribute; —s pl. respects
homme m. man; — d'affaires businessman
homogène a. homogeneous
homologation f. probating
homologuer vt. confirm (law); probate
homonyme m. homonym
homosexuel a. & m. homosexual
*hongre m. gelding, castrated horse
*hongrer vt. to geld
*Hongrie f. Hungary
*hongrois a. & m. Hungarian
honnête a. honest, sincere; respectable; gentlemanly; proper, decent, mannerly; reasonable
honnêteté f. honesty, integrity; respectability; courtesy; decency
honneur m. honor; respect
honorabilité f. respectability
honorable a. honorable, respectable
honoraire a. honorary; — m. honorarium, fee; royalty
honorer vt. to honor, respect
honorifique a. honorary
*honte f. shame, dishonor, disgrace; avoir — to be ashamed
*honteux a. shameful; disgraceful; shame-faced
hôpital m. hospital
*hoquet m. hiccup; gasp
*hoqueter vi. to hiccup, have the hiccups
horaire m. timetable, schedule
horizon m. horizon
horizontal a. horizontal
horloge f. timeclock
horloger m. watchmaker, clockmaker
horlogerie f. clocks, watches; watch business; watch factory; watch and clock shop
*hormis prep. except, save, but
hormone f. hormone
horoscope m. horoscope
*horreur f. horror, terror; abhorrence; avoir — de to abhor; faire — à to horrify
horrible a. horrible; horrid
horrifier vt. to horrify
horrifique a. horrific
horripilant a. hair-raising
horripilation f. goose flesh
*hors prep. except, out of; — de out of, outside of; — de combat out of action; — de soi beside oneself
*hors-bord m. outboard motorboat

*hors-caste m. & f. untouchable, outcast
*hors-d'œuvre m. outwork; digression; first course, hors d'œuvres
*hors-jeu m. offside (sports)
*hors-la-loi m. outlaw
hortensia m. hydrangea
horticole a. horticultural
horticulture f. horticulture
hosanna m. hosanna, praise
hospice m. charitable institution; asylum, home; poorhouse
hospitalier a. hospitable; pertaining to charitable institutions
hospitalisation f. hospitalizing, hospitalization, hospital care
hostie f. (eccl.) host
hostile a. hostile, inimical; opposed
hostilité f. hostility
hôte m. host; landlord; guest; table d'— f. fixed menu
hôtel m. hotel; mansion; building; — de ville city hall; — meublé lodginghouse; maître d' — head waiter
hôtel-Dieu m. main hospital
hôtelier m. innkeeper
hôtellerie f. hostelry; inn
hôtesse f. hostess; guest; — de l'air airline stewardess
*hotte f. hod; basket; (chem.) hood
*houache f. (naut.) wash, wake
*houblon m. (bot.) hops
*houe f. hoe
*houer vt. to hoe
*houille f. coal; — blanche water power
*houillère f. coal mine
*houilleur m. coal miner
*houle f. surge; swell
*houlette f. crook, staff; trowel
*houleux a. stormy, surging
*houppe f. tuft; puff; powder puff; tassel; crest on an animal
*houppelande f. overcoat, greatcoat
*houppette f. powder puff
*houspiller vt. to jostle; abuse
*housse f. cover; slipcover; dust cover; (auto.) seat cover
*housser vt. to dust
*houssine f. furniture and rug beater; switch (for punishment)
*houssoir m. brush, whiskbroom
*houx m. (bot.) holly
*hoyau m. pickax; hoe used to flatten
*hublot m. porthole; verre de — m. bull's-eye
*huche f. bin; hopper; trough
*huer vt. & vi. to hoot, shout, boo
*huguenot a. & m. Huguenot
huile f. oil
huiler vt. to oil, grease
huileux a. oily; greasy
huilier m. oiler; oilcan; oil seller or maker
huis m. door
huisserie f. door frame
huissier m. usher; bailiff
*huit a. & m. eight; d'aujourd'hui en — a week from today; — jours a week
*huitaine f. about eight; week
*huitième a. & m. eighth
huître f. oyster
*huit-reflets m. top hat

huîtrière f. oyster bed

humain a. human; humane; — m. human being

humanisation f. humanization

humaniser vt. to humanize

humaniste m. humanist; classicist

humanitaire a. & n. humanitarian

humanité f. humanity; mankind; —s pl. humanities

humble a. humble

*humecter vt. to moisten

*humer vt. to suck in, breathe in

humérus m. (anat.) humerus

humeur f. humor; disposition, mood; temper

humide a. humid, moist, damp

humidifier vt. to humidify, moisten

*humidité f. humidity, moisture, dampness

humiliant a. humiliating

humiliation f. humiliation

humilier vt. to humiliate, humble

humilité f. humility

humoriste m. humorist; — a. humorous

humoristique a. humorous

humour m. comic irony, humor

humus m. humus

*hune f. (naut.) top; — de vigie crow's nest

*hunter m. hunting horse, jumper

*huppe f. crest of a bird

*huppé a. crested; well-dressed, decked out

*hurlement m. howl, howling, roar, yell

*hurler vi. to howl, roar, yell

*hurleur a. howling, yelling; — m. howler; powerful loudspeaker

hurluburlu m. silly person, scatterbrain

*hussard m. hussar

*hussarde f. Hungarian dance; à la — adv. roughly, unceremoniously

*hutte f. hut, cabin, shack

hyalin a. glassy

hybridation f. crossbreeding

hybride a. & m. hybrid

hybrider vt. to cross breeds or strains

hydratation f. hydration

hydrate m. hydrate; — de carbone carbohydrate; —r vt. to hydrate

hydraulique a. hydraulic; — f. hydraulics

hydravion m. seaplane

hydre f. hydra

hydrocarbure m. hydrocarbon

hydrodynamique a. hydrodynamic; — f. hydrodynamics

hydroélectrique a. hydroelectric

hydrofuge a. waterproof

hydrofuger vt. to make waterproof or watertight

hydrogène m. hydrogen

hydroglisseur m. speedboat

hydrologie f. hydrology

hydrolyse f. hydrolysis

hydrophile a. absorbent

hydrophobie f. hydrophobia, fear of the water

hydropisie f. dropsy

hydroplane m. seaplane

hydroscope m. dowser, divining rod

hydrosphère f. hydrosphere

hydrothérapie f. hydrotherapy, water cure

hydrure m. hydride

hyène f. hyena

hygiène f. hygiene, health; sanitation

hygiénique a. hygienic; sanitary

hygiéniste m. & f. hygienist

hymen, hyménée m. marriage

hymnaire m. hymnal

hymne m. hymn; song, anthem

hyperbole f. hyperbole; (math.) hyperbola

hypercritique a. hypercritical

hypersensibilité f. hypersensitivity

hypersensible a. hypersensitive

hypersonique a. hypersonic

hypertension f. hypertension

hypertrophie f. hypertrophy; (fig.) excessive development

hypnose f. hypnosis

hypnotique a. hypnotic

hypnotiser vt. to hypnotize

hypnotisme m. hypnotism

hypocondriaque a. & n. hypochondriac

hypocondrie f. hypochondria

hypocrisie f. hypocrisy

hypocrite m. hypocrite; — a. hypocritical

hypodermique a. hypodermic

hypotension f. low blood pressure

hypoténuse f. hypotenuse

hypothécable a. mortgageable

hypothécaire a. mortgage; — n. mortgagee

hypothèque f. mortgage

hypothéquer vt. to mortgage

hypothèse f. hypothesis

hypothétique a. hypothetical

hystérie f. (med.) hysterics

hystérique a. hysterical

I

iambique a. iambic

ibère, ibérique a. & n. Iberian

ibis m. ibis

ichtyologie f. ichthyology

ichtyologiste m. ichthyologist

ici adv. here; d'— from hence, hence; par — this way; d'— là between now and then; jusqu'— until now; this far

ici-bas adv. here on earth

icone f. icon, ikon

iconoclaste a. iconoclastic; — m. iconoclast

ictère m. (med.) jaundice

idéal m. & a. ideal; —iser vt. to idealize

idéalisme m. idealism

idéaliste m. & f. idealist; — a. idealistic

idéation f. ideation

idée f. idea, thought, opinion; changer d'— to change one's mind; — fixe obsession

identification f. identification

identifier vt. to identify

identique a. identical

identité f. identity; carte d'— f. identification card

idéologie f. ideology

idéologique a. ideological

idéologue m. ideologist

ides f. pl. ides

idiomatique a. idiomatic

idiome m. language, speech, idiom, dialect

idiosyncrasie f. idiosyncrasy
idiot a. idiot; idiotic; — m. idiot; fool
idiotie f. idiocy; stupidity
idiotisme m. (gram.) idiom, idiomatic expression
idolâtre a. idolatrous; — m. idolater
idolâtrer vt. to worship, idolize
idole f. idol, god
idylle f. idyl
idyllique a. idyllic
if m. (bot.) yew
igname f. Chinese yam
ignare a. ignorant; uninstructed
igné a. igneous
ignifuge a. fireproof
ignoble a. ignoble, base
ignominie f. ignominy, shame
ignominieux a. ignominious, shameful
ignorance f. ignorance
ignorant a. ignorant; unaware; — m. ignoramus, dunce
ignoré a. unknown
ignorer vt. to be ignorant of, not to know
iguane m. iguana
il pron. he, it; — y a there is, there are; ago; —s they
île f. island
iléon m. (anat.) ileum
ilex m. holm oak
iliaque a. iliac
illégal a. illegal; unlawful
illégalité f. illegality
illégitime a. illegitimate; unlawful
illégitimité f. illegitimacy; unlawfulness
illettré a. illiterate
illicite a. illicit, illegal
illimité a. unlimited
illisibilité f. illegibility
illisible a. illegible, unreadable
illogique a. illogical
illuminant a. illuminating
illuminateur m. illuminator
illumination f. illumination; light; lighting
illuminer vt. to illuminate, enlighten
illusion f. illusion, delusion; self-deception
illusionner vt. to delude; deceive
illusionnisme m. conjuring, conjurer's art
illusionniste m. & f. conjurer
illusoire a. illusive; fallacious
illustrateur m. illustrator
illustration f. illustriousness; glorification; glory; explanation; illustration
illustre a. illustrious
illustré m. tabloid; — a. illustrated
illustrer vt. to make illustrious; illustrate
îlot m. small island, islet; block of houses
ilote m. helot
image f. picture; image; metaphor
imagé a. metaphorical
imager vt. to embellish with metaphors, images
imagerie f. imagery
imaginable a. imaginable
imaginaire a. imaginary
imaginatif a. imaginative
imagination f. imagination, fancy
imaginer vt. to imagine, conceive, contrive; picture; s'— imagine, think
imbattable a. unbeatable

imbattu a. unbeaten
imbécile m. & f. imbecile; idiot, fool
imbécillité f. imbecility; stupidity
imberbe a. beardless; very young
imbiber vt. to imbue, soak, steep; imbibe, absorb
imbrifuge a. waterproof
imbrisable a. unbreakable
imbrûlable a. fireproof
imbu a. imbued, steeped, soaked
imbuvable a. undrinkable
imitateur m. imitator; — a. imitative
imitatif a. imitative
imitation f. imitation; copy; forgery, counterfeit
imiter vt. to imitate; copy; forge, counterfeit
immaculable a. stainless
immaculé a. immaculate; (fig.) untarnished; stainless
immanent a. immanent
immangeable a. uneatable, inedible
immanquable a. infallible, inevitable
immatériel a. immaterial
immatriculation f. registration; enrollment
immatricule f. registration number
immatriculer vt. to matriculate; register; enroll
immaturité f. immaturity
immédiat a. immediate; imminent; urgent
immédiatement adv. immediately, right away
immémorial a. immemorial
immense a. immense; vast
immensément adv. immensely
immensité f. immensity
immensurable a. immeasurable
immerger vt. to immerse; (naut.) submerge
immérité a. undeserved
immersion f. immersion; plunging; submersion
immesurable a. immeasurable
immeuble a. real (law); biens —s m. pl. real estate; — m. real estate; building, apartment house
immigrant a. & m. immigrant
immigré m. immigrant
immigrer vi. to immigrate
imminence f. imminence
imminent a. imminent, impending
immiscer vt. to involve; mix up; s'— to meddle; intrude
immixtion f. interference, meddling
immobile a. immovable, motionless
immobilier a. pertaining to real property; agent — m. realtor
immobiliser vt. to immobilize
immobilité f. immobility
immodéré a. immoderate
immodeste a. immodest
immodestie f. immodesty
immolation f. immolation, sacrifice
immoler vt. to immolate, sacrifice
immonde a. unclean, foul
immondices f. pl. rubbish, refuse, filth
immoral a. immoral
immoralité f. immorality

immortaliser *vt.* to immortalize
immortalité *f.* immortality
immortel *a.* immortal, everlasting
immotivé *a.* unmotivated
immuable *a.* immutable, unchangeable
immunisation *f.* immunization
immuniser *vt.* to immunize
immunité *f.* immunity
immutabilité *f.* immutability
impact *m.* impact
impair *a.* odd, uneven; — *m.* blunder
impalpabilité *f.* impalpability
impalpable *a.* impalpable
impardonnable *a.* unpardonable, unforgivable
imparfait *a.* imperfect; incomplete; — *m.* (gram.) imperfect
imparité *f.* inequality; (math.) oddness
impartial *a.* impartial; without prejudice
impartialité *f.* impartiality
impartir *vt.* (law), to grant accord
impassable *a.* impassable
impasse *f.* dead end; deadlock
impassibilité *f.* impassibility
impassible *a.* impassible; impassive; without emotion
impatiemment *adv.* impatiently, eagerly
impatience *f.* impatience, eagerness
impatient *a.* impatient, eager
impatienter *vt.* to make impatient; s'— to fret, grow impatient
impavide *a.* fearless
impayable *a.* invaluable, inestimable, priceless
impayé *a.* unpaid
impeccabilité *f.* impeccability
impeccable *a.* impeccable; flawless
impécunieux *a.* impecunious
impédance *f.* impedance
impénétrabilité *f.* impenetrability, inscrutability
impénétrable *a.* impenetrable; inscrutable
impénitent *a.* unrepentant
impensable *a.* unthinkable
impératif *a.* imperative; — *m.* (gram.) imperative
impératrice *f.* empress
imperceptible *a.* imperceptible
imperfection *f.* imperfection; incompleteness
impérial *a.* imperial
impériale *f.* style of beard; upper deck of a two-decker bus
impérialisme *m.* imperialism
impérialiste *m.* imperialist
impérieux *a.* imperious; imperative
impérissable *a.* imperishable
impéritie *f.* incapacity, lack of experience
imperméabiliser *vt.* to waterproof
imperméable *a.* impervious, waterproof; — *m.* raincoat
impersonnel *a.* impersonal
impertinemment *adv.* impertinently
impertinence *f.* impertinence, impropriety; irrelevance
impertinent *a.* impertinent; rude; irrelevant
imperturbable *a.* imperturbable
impétueux *a.* impetuous, impulsive
impétuosité *f.* impetuosity, impulsiveness

impie *a.* impious, irreligious
impiété *f.* impiety; blasphemy
impitoyable *a.* unmerciful, merciless; pitiless
implacabilité *f.* implacability
implacable *a.* implacable, unforgiving
implanter *vt.* to implant, insert; graft; s'— to take root
implication *f.* implication; suggestion of contradiction
implicite *a.* implicit
impliquer *vt.* to implicate; imply
imploration *f.* imploring, beseeching
implorer *vt.* to implore, beseech
imployable *a.* unyielding, unbending, inflexible
impoli *a.* impolite, rude, discourteous
impolitesse *f.* impoliteness, rudeness, discourtesy
impolitique *a.* ill-advised
impondérable *a.* imponderable
impopulaire *a.* unpopular
impopularité *f.* unpopularity
importable *a.* unbearable; importable
importance *f.* importance, consequence; seriousness; authority; social standing, self-conceit
important *a.* important; having authority; — *m.* essential point
importateur *m.* importer
importer *vt.* to import; — *v.* to be of importance; be of consequence, to concern; n'importe it does not matter; n'importe qui no matter who, anyone; n'importe quoi no matter what, anything; qu'importe? what does it matter?
importun *a.* importunate; annoying, bothersome
importuner *vt.* to importune; annoy, bother
imposable *a.* taxable
imposant *a.* imposing, impressive
imposé *m.* taxpayer
imposer *vt.* to impose; inspire, command; tax; — *vi.* to command respect; — à impose on; deceive; s'— command, inspire; assert oneself; force oneself on someone
imposition *f.* imposition; imposing; tax; assessment
impossibilité *f.* impossibility
impossible *a.* impossible
imposte *f.* transom; (arch.) impost
imposteur *m.* imposter
imposture *f.* imposture; swindle
impôt *m.* tax, duty; — sur le revenu income tax
impotence *f.* impotence, infirmity, helplessness
impotent *a.* impotent; infirm, crippled; — *m.* cripple
impraticable *a.* impracticable, impractical; impassable
impratiqué *a.* unused, out-of-the-way
imprécation *f.* curse, imprecation
imprécis *a.* not precise, indefinite
imprécision *f.* lack of precision
imprégner *vt.* to impregnate
imprenable *a.* impregnable

impréparation *f.* lack of preparation

imprésario *m.* impresario

impression *f.* impression; printing process; print; mark; edition; faute d'— *f.* typographical error, misprint

impressionnable *a.* impressionable; sensitive

impressionnant *a.* impressive

impressionner *vt.* to impress; make an impression upon; s'— to get excited; be moved

impressionniste *m.* impressionist

imprévisible *a.* unpredictable, unforeseeable

imprévision *f.* lack of foresight

imprévoyable *a.* unpredictable, unforeseeable

imprévoyance *f.* improvidence; lack of foresight

imprévoyant *a.* improvident

imprévu *a.* unforeseen, unexpected; — *m.* contingency

imprimé *m.* printed paper; -s *p.* printed matter

imprimer *vt.* to print, stamp; impart

imprimerie *f.* printing; print shop; typography

imprimeur *m.* printer

imprimeuse *f.* printing press

improbabilité *f.* improbability

improbable *a.* improbable, unlikely

improbatif *a.* disapproving

improbation *f.* lack of approval, disapproval

improbité *f.* lack of probity; dishonesty

improductif *a.* unproductive

improductivité *f.* unproductiveness

impromptu *m. & a.* impromptu; à l'— extemporaneously

imprononçable *a.* unpronounceable

impropre *a.* improper; incongruous; unfit

impropriété *f.* impropriety

improuvable *a.* unprovable

improvisateur *m.* improviser

improviser *vt. & vi.* to extemporize, improvise

improviste *adv.*, a l'— unawares, unexpectedly

improvoqué *a.* unprovoked

imprudemment *adv.* imprudently

imprudence *f.* imprudence, indiscretion

imprudent *a.* imprudent; indiscreet; unwise

impubliable *a.* unpublishable; not fit for publication

impudemment *adv.* impudently

impudence *f.* impudence

impudent *a.* impudent; immodest; shameless

impudeur *f.* shamelessness, immodesty; lewdness

impudicité *f.* lack of chastity; act of lust

impudique *a.* immodest, unchaste

impuissance *f.* impotence, inability; vainness

impuissant *a.* impotent, powerless; vain

impulsif *a.* impulsive, without deliberation

impulsion *f.* impulse, impetus, urge

impulsivité *f.* impulsiveness

impunément *adv.* with impunity

impuni *a.* unpunished

impunité *f.* impunity

impur *a.* impure, tainted; (fig.) unchaste

impureté *f.* impurity; (fig.) immorality

impurifié *a.* unpurified

imputable *a.* attributable, imputable; (com.) chargeable; creditable

imputation *f.* imputation, charge; (com.) deduction

imputer *vt.* to impute, attribute, charge; deduct; (com.) credit; debit

inabondance *f.* scarcity, short supply

inabordable *a.* inaccessible; too costly

inabrité *a.* unsheltered

inaccentué *a.* unaccented, unstressed

inacceptable *a.* unacceptable

inacceptation *f.* nonacceptance, refusal

inaccessible *a.* inaccessible; unattainable

inaccompagné *a.* unaccompanied

inaccompli *a.* unaccomplished, unfulfilled

inaccordable *a.* irreconcilable; untunable; inadmissible

inaccoutumé *a.* unaccustomed, unused; unusual

inachevé *a.* unfinished, not completed

inachèvement *m.* state of incompletion

inactif *a.* inactive; inert

inaction *f.* inaction; lack of business activity

inactivité *f.* inactivity; inertness

inadéquat *a.* inadequate

inadmissibilité *f.* inadmissibility

inadmissible *a.* inadmissible; nonqualifying

inadvertance *f.* oversight, inadvertance, carelessness

inadvertant *a.* inadvertent

inaliénable *a.* inalienable

inaliéné *a.* unalienated

inaltérabilité *f.* unchanging nature; permanence

inaltérable *a.* unchangeable; incorruptible; unalterable

inamical *a.* unfriendly, hostile; discourteous

inamovible *a.* irremovable; permanent

inanimé *a.* inanimate, lifeless; unconscious

inanité *f.* inanity; inane remark

inapaisable *a.* inappeasable, unquenchable

inapaisé *a.* unappeased, unquenched

inapercevable *a.* unperceivable

inaperçu *a.* unperceived, unnoticed, unseen

inapparent *a.* unapparent

inappétence *f.* lack of appetite

inapplication *f.* lack of application

inappliqué *a.* unapplied; lacking in application

inappréciable *a.* invaluable, inestimable; unperceivable; inappreciable

inapprécié *a.* unappreciated

inapprivoisable *a.* untamable

inapprivoisé *a.* untamed

inapte *a.* inapt, inept; unfit

inaptitude *f.* lack of aptitude

inarticulé *a.* inarticulate; inarticulated

inassociable *a.* incompatible, unmixable

inassouvi *a.* unsatisfied, unquenched

inassouvissable *a.* insatiable

inattaquable *a.* unquestionable; unassailable

inattendu *a.* unexpected; unforeseen

inattentif *a.* inattentive

inattention *f.* carelessness; lack of attention

inauguration *f.* inauguration; unveiling

inaugurer *vt.* to inaugurate; unveil a monument; (fig.) mark a beginning

inauthenticité *f.* lack of authenticity

inauthentique *a.* unauthentic

inautorisé *a.* unauthorized

inaverti *a.* uninformed; unwarned

inavouable *a.* shameful

inavoué *a.* unconfessed; unacknowledged

incalculable *a.* incalculable

incandescence *f.* incandescence

incandescent *a.* white-hot, incandescent

incapable *a.* incapable, unable, unfit

incapacité *f.* incapacity, incapability, inability, unfitness; disability

incarcération *f.* incarceration

incarcérer *vt.* to incarcerate

incarnadin *a.* pink, rosy

incarnat *m.* flesh color; — *a.* rosy, pink

incarné *a.* incarnate; ingrown

incarner *vt.* to incarnate; s'— to become incarnate; grow into, embody

incartade *f.* tirade; prank

incassable *a.* unbreakable

incendiaire *a. & m.* incendiary

incendie *m.* fire, arson, conflagration; pompe à — *f.* fire engine

incendié *m.* victim of a fire

incendier *vt.* to burn, set fire to

incertain *a.* uncertain; doubtful, undecided

incertitude *f.* uncertainty, doubt, indecision

incessamment *adv.* incessantly, continually; shortly, without delay

incessant *a.* incessant, unceasing

incessible *a.* inalienable

inceste *m.* incest

incestueux *a.* incestuous

inchangé *a.* unchanged

incidemment *adv.* incidently

incidence *f.* (phy.) incidence

incident *a.* incidental; parenthetical; — *m.* incident; difficulty

incinérateur *m.* incinerator

incinération *f.* incineration; cremation

incinérer *vt.* to incinerate; cremate

incirconcis *a.* uncircumcized

inciser *vt.* to cut, make an incision in

incisif *a.* incisive

incisive *f.* (dent.) incisor

incision *f.* incision, cut, cutting

incitant *a.* stimulating; — *m.* tonic, stimulant

incitation *f.* incitement, inciting

inciter *vt.* to incite; urge

incivil *a.* uncivil, rude

incivilisé *a.* uncivilized

incivilité *f.* incivility, rudeness

incivique *a.* uncivil

inclassable *a.* unclassifiable

inclémence *f.* inclemency

inclément *a.* inclement

inclinaison *f.* inclination; incline, slope; tilt, slant

inclination *f.* inclination; bowing, stooping; love; mariage d'— *m.* love match

incliné *a.* inclined; bowed

incliner *vt. & vi.* to incline, bow; tilt, slant; s'— bow, yield; slope, slant; (avi.) bank; (naut.) heel

inclure *vt.* to enclose; insert

inclus *a.* enclosed

inclusif *a.* inclusive

inclusion *f.* enclosing; inclusion; enclosure

inclusivement *adv.* inclusively

incohérence *f.* incoherence

incohérent *a.* incoherent, unconnected

incohésion *f.* lack of cohesion

incolore *a.* colorless

incomber *vi.* to be incumbent

incombustible *a.* fireproof

incomestible *a.* inedible

incommensurable *a.* incommensurate; immeasurable

incommodant *a.* disagreeable, annoying

incommode *a.* uncomfortable, inconvenient

incommodé *a.* indisposed

incommoder *vt.* to annoy, trouble, inconvenience; upset

incommodité *f.* inconvenience; discomfort

incommunicable *a.* incommunicable

incommutable *a.* nontransferable (at law)

incomparablement *adv.* incomparably

incompatibilité *f.* incompatibility

incompatible *a.* incompatible

incompétence *f.* incompetency, lack of authority

incompétent *a.* incompetent; unauthorized, unqualified

incomplaisant *a.* disobliging

incomplet *a.* unfinished, incomplete

incomplètement *adv.* incompletely

incompréhensibilité *f.* incomprehensibility

incompréhensible *a.* incomprehensible

incompréhension *f.* lack of understanding

incompris *a.* not understood; unappreciated

inconcevable *a.* inconceivable

inconciliable *a.* irreconcilable

inconditionnel *a.* unconditional

inconduite *f.* misconduct (law); misbehavior

inconfort *m.* lack of comfort

inconfortable *a.* uncomfortable

incongru *a.* incongruous; inappropriate

incongruité *f.* incongruity; impropriety

inconnu *a.* unknown; strange; — *m.* unknown; unknown person, stranger

inconsciemment *adv.* unconsciously, unknowingly

inconscience *f.* unconsciousness, unawareness

inconscient *a.* unconscious, unaware

inconséquence *f.* inconsequence

inconséquent *a.* inconsequent, inconsistent; inconsequential

inconsidération *f.* lack of consideration,

inconsidéré *a.* inconsiderate; thoughtless; ill-considered
inconsistance *f.* inconsistency; lack of solidity
inconsistant *a.* inconsistent; loose, soft
inconsolable *a.* inconsolable; disconsolate
inconstance *f.* inconstancy; fickleness; changeability
inconstant *a.* inconstant, changeable, fickle
inconstitutionnalité *f.* unconstitutionality
inconstitutionnel *a.* unconstitutional
incontestable *a.* incontestable, indisputable
incontesté *a.* uncontested, undisputed
incontinence *f.* incontinence
incontinent *a.* incontinent; — *adv.* at once, immediately
incontrôlable *a.* impossible to check *or* verify
incontrôlé *a.* unchecked, unverified
incontroversé *a.* uncontroverted, undisputed
inconvaincu *a.* unconvinced
inconvenance *f.* impropriety; indecency; lack of suitability
inconvenant *a.* unbecoming, improper; indecent
inconvénient *m.* inconvenience; disadvantage, objection
inconvertissable *a.* beyond conversion
inconvié *a.* uninvited
incoordination *f.* lack of co-ordination
incorporel *a.* incorporeal
incorporer *vt.* to incorporate
incorrect *a.* incorrect; wrong; unseemly, improper
incorrection *f.* incorrectness; mistake, error; inaccuracy
incorrigibilité *f.* incorrigibility
incorruptibilité *f.* incorruptibility
incrédibilité *f.* incredibility
incrédule *a.* incredulous; unbelieving; — *m. & f.* infidel, unbeliever
incrédulité *f.* incredulity; disbelief
incrément *m.* increment
increvable *a.* puncture-proof
incrimination *f.* incrimination; indictment; accusation
incriminer *vt.* to incriminate; indict; accuse
incrochetable *a.* burglarproof
incroyable *a.* incredible, unbelievable
incroyant *a.* unbelieving; — *m.* unbeliever
incrustation *f.* incrustation; inlaying; scale, crust
incruster *vt.* to incrust; inlay
incubateur *m.* incubator
incubation *f.* incubation; hatching
incuber *vt.* to incubate (eggs)
incuit *a.* uncooked
inculpabilité *f.* blamelessness, innocence; liability to indictment (law)
inculpable *a.* liable to indictment (law)
inculpation *f.* indictment, charge
inculpé *m.* defendant (law), accused
inculper *vt.* to accuse, charge; indict
inculquer *vt.* to inculcate
inculte *a.* uncultivated, untilled
incultivé *a.* uncultivated, untilled; uncultured; rude
incurable *a. & n.* incurable
incurie *f.* lack of concern; negligence, carelessness
incurieux *a.* not curious
incuriosité *f.* lack of curiosity
incursion *f.* inroad, incursion
incurvé *a.* incurvated, concave
Inde *f.* India; —s *pl.* Indies
inde *m.* indigo plant, indigo blue
indébrouillable *a.* tangled
indécemment *adv.* indecently; immodestly; improperly
indécence *f.* indecency
indécent *a.* indecent; unbecoming, immodest; improper
indéchiffrable *a.* undecipherable; illegible
indéchirable *a.* untearable
indécis *a.* undecided; vague; hesitating, doubtful
indécisif *a.* indecisive
indécision *f.* indecision; irresolution
indéclinable *a.* not refusable; indeclinable
indécousable *a.* rip-proof
indécouvrable *a.* undiscoverable, hidden
indécrottable *a.* uncleanable
indédoublable *a.* indecomposable
indéfendable *a.* indefensible
indéfini *a.* indefinite; undefined
indéfinissable *a.* indefinable
indéformable *a.* not capable of losing shape *or* form
indéfrisable *a.* permanent (curls); — *f.* permanent wave
indélébile *a.* indelible
indélébilité *f.* indelibility
indélibéré *a.* undeliberated, unpremeditated
indélicat *a.* indelicate; tactless; unscrupulous
indélicatesse *f.* indelicacy; tactlessness; unscrupulousness
indémaillable *a.* run-proof
indemne *a.* undamaged, unhurt; without loss
indemnisable *a.* entitled to damages *or* compensation
indemnisation *f.* indemnification
indemniser *vt.* to indemnify, compensate, pay damages to
indemnité *f.* indemnity, compensation, damages; grant, benefit; expenses
indémontrable *a.* undemonstrable
indéniable *a.* undeniable
indénouable *a.* secure, fast, tight; not able to be untied
indépendamment *adv.* independently
indépendance *f.* independence
indépendant *a.* independent
indéracinable *a.* firmly rooted; not able to be uprooted; impossible to eradicate
indéréglable *a.* foolproof; impossible to upset
Indes *f. pl.* Indies
indescriptible *a.* indescribable
indésirable *a. & n.* undesirable
indesserrable *a.* self-locking (nut); very tight
indestructible *a.* indestructible

indéterminable a. indeterminable

indétermination f. indetermination, lack of determination; indefiniteness

indéterminé a. indeterminate, undetermined; indefinite; undecided

indevinable a. unguessable; mysterious

indévot a. undevout, irreligious

indévotion f. irreligion

index m. table of contents, index; index finger; indicator, pointer

indicateur a. indicatory; telltale; doigt — m. index finger; poteau — m. signpost; — m. indicator; gauge; speedometer; timetable; spy, informer

indicatif a. indicative, indicating, indicatory; — m. (gram.) indicative; (rad.) program theme music

indication f. indication, sign; information; —s pl. directions, instructions

indice m. sign, mark; clue; index; indication; (com.) trace

indicible a. unspeakable, indescribable

indien a. & m. Indian

indienne f. print; calico; chintz; overarm swimming stroke

indiennerie f. printed cotton fabric

indifféremment adv. indifferently, indiscriminately

indifférence f. indifference

indifférent a. indifferent, unconcerned; immaterial

indigence f. indigence, poverty

indigène a. & m. native

indigent a. indigent, poor, needy; — m. pauper; — s pl. the poor, needy, destitute

indigeste a. indigestible; undigested

indigestion f. indigestion

indignation f. indignation

indigne a. unworthy, undeserving; odious

indigné a. indignant

indigner vt. to make indignant, shock; s'— to be indignant

indignité f. indignity; unworthiness

indigo m. indigo dye or color

indigotier m. (bot.) indigo plant

indiquer vt. to indicate, point out, show; appoint

indirect a. indirect; underhand(ed); circumstantial (law)

indirectement adv. indirectly

indiscernable a. indistinguishable

indisciplinable a. intractable

indiscipliné a. undisciplined, unmanageable

indiscret a. indiscreet, tactless; — m. indiscreet, tactless person

indiscrètement adv. indiscreetly

indiscrétion f. indiscretion; tactlessness

indiscutable a. indisputable

indisponibilité f. unavailability

indisponible a. unavailable; inalienable (law)

indisposé a. indisposed, unwell; unfriendly, angry

indisposer vt. to indispose; make unwell; turn against

indisposition f. indisposition, mild illness

indisputable a. indisputable, unquestionable

indissolubilité f. indissolubility; insolubility

indissoluble a. indissoluble; insoluble

indistinct a. indistinct; vague, hazy, faint, blurred

indistinguible a. indistinguishable

individu m. individual; person, fellow; character

individualiser vt. to individualize

individualiste a. individualistic; — m. & f. individualist

individualité f. individuality

individuel a. individual; private, personal

indivisibilité f. indivisibility

indivisible a. indivisible

indivulgué a. undivulged, unrevealed

Indo-Chine f. Indo-China

indochinois a. & m. Indochinese

indocile a. indocile, intractable

indocilité f. indocility, intractability

indo-européen a. & m. Indo-European

indolemment adv. indolently, lazily

indolence f. indolence, laziness

indolent a. indolent, lazy

indolore a. painless

indomptable a. untamable, unmanageable, unconquerable; indomitable

indompté a. untamed, unconquered

Indonésie f. Indonesia

indonésien a. & m. indonesian

indu a. undue; unowed; not due

indubitable a. indubitable, unquestionable

inductance f. (elec.) inductance; inductance coil

inducteur a. (elec.) inductive; — m. inductor

inductif a. inductive

induire vt. to induce; infer; lead

induit a. (elec.) induced; — m. armature

indulgence f. indulgence

indulgent a. indulgent

indûment adv. unduly

indurer vt. to harden

industrialisation f. industrialization

industrialiser vt. to industrialize

industrialisme m. industrialism

industrie f. industry; ingenuity, skill

industriel a. industrial; — m. industrialist

industrieux a. industrious; skillful

inébranlable a. firm; unshakable; resolute

inéchangeable a. unexchangeable

inéclairci a. unexplained, unelucidated

inéclairé a. unlighted, unlit; unenlightened

inédit a. unpublished; new, latest, original

ineffaçable a. ineffaceable, unforgettable; indelible

inefficace a. ineffectual, unavailing

inefficacité f. inefficacy, inefficiency

inégal a. unequal; uneven; irregular

inégalité f. inequality; unevenness; irregularity, disparity

inélégance f. inelegance

inélégant a. inelegant

inéligibilité f. ineligibility

inéligible a. ineligible

inéluctable a. ineluctable; unescapable, irrevocable

inéludable a. unescapable, inevitable

inemployé a. unemployed, unused

inentamé a. uncut; whole, intact

inepte a. inept, unfit; foolish

ineptie f. ineptness, ineptitude

inépuisable a. inexhaustible

inépuisé a. unexhausted, unused, remaining

inéquitable a. inequitable, unfair, unjust

inerte a. inert; passive; dull

inertie f. inertia; dullness

inespéré a. unhoped for, unexpected

inessayé a. untried, untested

inestimable a. inestimable, invaluable

inétudié a. unstudied, natural

inévitable a. inevitable; unavoidable

inexact a. inexact, inaccurate; wrong, incorrect; careless, remiss; unpunctual

inexactitude f. inexactitude, inaccuracy; incorrectness; error, mistake; carelessness, remissness; unpunctuality

inexécutable a. impracticable; impossible to do

inexecuté a. undone, unfulfilled, unperformed; not carried out

inexecution f. inexecution; nonfulfillment

inexercé a. unexercised; unpracticed, untrained

inexistant a. nonexistent

inexistence f. nonexistence

inexpérience f. inexperience, lack of experience

inexpérimenté a. inexperienced; untested, untried

inexpiable a. unatonable, inexpiable

inexpié a. unatoned

inexplicable a. inexplicable, unaccountable

inexpliqué a. unexplained

inexploitable a. unexploitable; unworkable

inexploité a. unexploited, undeveloped; unworked

inexploré a. unexplored

inexplosible a. nonexplosive

inexpressif a. expressionless; inexpressive

inexprimable a. inexpressable; ineffable, unspeakable

inexprimé a. unexpressed

inexpugnable a. impregnable

in-extenso (en entier) adv. fully, in detail

inextinguible a. inextinguishable; unquenchable; irrepressible

infaillibilité f. infallibility

infaillible a. infallible; unfailing; certain

infaisable a. impracticable, not feasable

infamant a. dishonorable, defamatory

infâme a. infamous; vile, fowl, base

infamie f. infamy; infamous action

infanterie f. infantry

infantilisme m. infantilism

infatigable a. indefatigable, tireless

infatuation f. infatuation, self-satisfaction

infatué a. self-satisfied

infécond a. sterile, barren

infécondité f. sterility

infect a. foul, filthy; smelly, noisome, stinking

infecter vt. to infect; taint, corrupt; pollute

infectieux a. infectious

infection f. infection; smell, stench

inférence f. inference

inférer vt. to infer

inférieur a. inferior, lower; of poor(er) quality; — m. subordinate, underling

infériorité f. inferiority

infertile a. sterile; infertile; unfruitful

infertilité f. sterility, infertility; unfruitfulness

infester vt. to infest

infidèle a. unfaithful; faithless; dishonest; inexact, incorrect; heathenish; — m. infidel, unbeliever

infidélité f. infidelity, unfaithfulness; faithlessness; dishonesty; inexactitude, inaccuracy; unbelief

infiltration f. infiltration; filtering; seepage

infiltrer vt., s' — to infiltrate; seep

infime a. lowest; smallest; infinitesimal, minute

infini a. infinite; endless; unlimited; — m. infinite; infinity; à l' — ad infinitum, to infinity; -té f. infinity

infiniment adv. infinitely

infinitésimal a. infinitesimal

infinitif a. & m. (gram.) infinitive

infinitude f. infiniteness

infirme a. infirm; frail, feeble; crippled — m. & f. cripple; invalid

infirmer vt. to weaken; invalidate; annul (law); set aside

infirmerie f. infirmary, sickroom

infirmier m. male nurse; hospital attendant

infirmière f. nurse

infirmité f. infirmity; disability

inflammabilité f. inflammability

inflammation f. inflammation; firing; igniting

inflammatoire a. inflammatory

inflation f. inflation

inflationniste a. inflationary; — m. inflationist

infléchir vt. to inflect, bend

infléchissable a. unbendable; unbending, inflexible

inflexibilité f. inflexibility

inflexible a. inflexible; unbending, unyielding

inflexion f. inflexion, inflection; modulation; bending

infliger vt. to inflict, impose

influençable a. able to be influenced

influence f. influence, sway; effect

influencer vt. to influence, sway

influent a. influential

influer (sur) vi. to influence

influx m. influx

informateur m. informant

informatif a. informative

information f. inquiry; information; news; legal investigation; proceedings; prendre des —s to make inquiries

informe a. shapeless, formless; unshapely; informal

informer vt. to inform, tell, apprise; — vi. to inform; investigate (law); s'— to make inquiries, ask

informulé a. unformulated

infortune f. misfortune

infortuné a. unfortunate, unhappy, unlucky

infraction f. infraction, violation; infringement

infranchissable a. impassable

infrangible a. unbreakable

infrarouge a. infrared

infrastructure f. substructure; undercarriage, underframe

infréquent a. infrequent, unusual, rare

infréquenté a. unfrequented

infructueux a. unfruitful, unprofitable; fruitless

infus a. infused, innate

infusé m. infusion

infuser vt. to infuse, steep; instill

infusion f. infusion, tea

ingambe a. active, alert, nimble

ingénier v., s'— to tax one's ingenuity

ingénieur m. engineer

ingénieusement adv. ingeniously

ingénieux a. ingenious

ingéniosité f. ingenuity

ingénu a. ingenuous; naïve, artless; —e f. naïve girl; (theat.) ingénue

ingénuité f. ingenuousness

ingérence f. interference, meddling

ingérer vt. to ingest; s'— de to interfere in, meddle in

inglorieux a. inglorious

ingouvernable a. ungovernable, unmanageable

ingrat a. ungrateful; thankless; unpleasant; unproductive

ingratitude f. ingratitude, ungratefulness; thanklessness

ingrédient m. ingredient, component

inguéable a. unfordable

inguérissable a. incurable; chronic

ingurgitation f. swallowing, gulping

ingurgiter vt. to swallow

inhabile a. unfitted, unskilled, inept; clumsy, awkward; legally incompetent

inhabileté f. clumsiness, awkwardness; lack of skill or knack; incapability

inhabilité f. legal incompetency, incapacity

inhabitable a. uninhabitable

inhabité a. uninhabited

inhabitude f. lack of familiarity or experience

inhabitué a. accustomed, not used to

inhabituel a. not habitual, unusual

inhalateur m. inhalator

inhalation f. inhalation

inhaler vt. to inhale

inharmonieux a. inharmonious, unmelodious; discordant

inhérent a. inherent

inhiber vt. to inhibit

inhibiteur, inhibitif a. inhibiting, inhibitive

inhibition f. inhibition

inhospitalier a. inhospitable

inhumain a. inhuman

inhumanité f. inhumanity

inhumation f. inhumation, burial

inhumer vt. to inter, bury, inhume

inimaginable a. unimaginable, inconceivable

inimitable a. inimitable

inimitié f. emnity, hatred, hostility

imprimé a. unprinted, unpublished

ininflammable a. fireproof; noninflammable

inintelligemment adv. unintelligently

inintelligence f. lack of intelligence

inintelligent a. unintelligent

inintelligibilité f. unintelligibility

inintelligible a. unintelligible

inintéressant a. uninteresting

ininterrompu a. uninterrupted, unbroken

inique a. unjust, iniquitous; sinful

iniquité f. iniquity

initial a. initial; — e f. first letter (name, word, person's name); —ement adv., originally

initiateur m. initiator

initiative f. initiative

initié m. initiate

initier vt. to initiate

injecté a. injected; bloodshot

injecter vt. to inject; s'— become bloodshot

injecteur m. injector

injection f. injection

injonction f. injunction, formal order

injouable a. unplayable

injudicieux a. injudicious, unwise

injure f. insult; wrong, injury; tort (law)

injurier vt. to insult, abuse

injurieux a. insulting, abusive, outrageous

injuste a. unjust, unfair

injustice f. injustice; wrong; unfairness

injustifiable a. unjustifiable

injustifié a. unjustified

inlassable a. untiring; tireless

innavigable a. unnavigable; unseaworthy

inné a. innate, inborn; —ité f. innateness

innocemment adv. innocently, foolishly

innocence f. innocence; simplicity

innocent a. innocent; harmless; simple; — m. simpleton

innocenter vt. to find innocent, clear; excuse

innocuité f. harmlessness, innocuousness

innombrable a. innumerable, numberless

innovateur m. innovator

innover vt. to innovate

inobservance f. nonobservance

inobservation f. nonobservance, disregard

inobservé a. unobserved; disregarded

inoccupation f. inoccupation, idleness, unemployment

inoccupé a. unoccupied; vacant; not busy, idle; not in use

inoculer vt. to inoculate; infect

inodore a. odorless

inoffensif a. inoffensive, harmless

inondation f. flood, inundation

inondé a. flooded; deluged; — m. flood victim

inonder vt. to flood, inundate

inopérable a. inoperable

inopérant a. inoperative

inopiné a. unexpected, unforeseen

inopportun a. inopportune; not appropriate

inopportunité f. inopportuneness

inopposable a. unanswerable

inorganique a. inorganic

inoubliable a. unforgettable; memorable

inoublié a. unforgotten

inouï a. unheard of; unbelievable; fantastic

inoxydable a. rustproof; stainless (steel)

inqualifiable a. unqualifiable; unspeakable

inquiet (inquiete) a. uneasy, anxious, disturbed, nervous, restless, upset, concerned

inquiétant a. disturbing, upsetting

inquiéter vt. to disturb, upset, make uneasy; s'— to be anxious, worry, be uneasy

inquiétude f. uneasiness, anxiety, nervousness, concern

inquisiteur m. inquisitor; — a. inquisitive

inquisition f. inquisition

inrouillable a. rustproof, stainless

insaisissable a. unseizable, difficult to grasp; fleeting, imperceptible

insalubre a. unhealthy, unwholesome

insalubrité f. unhealthiness, unwholesomeness

insanité f. insanity

insatiabilité f. insatiability

insatiable a. insatiable

insatisfaction f. lack of satisfaction

insatisfait a. unsatisfied

insciemment adv. unknowingly, unwittingly

inscripteur m. recorder, recording apparatus

inscriptible a. inscribable

inscription f. inscription; inscribing; registration, enrolling; recording

inscrire vt. to inscribe; register, enroll; s'— to register, sign up

inscrutable a. inscrutable

insécable a. indivisible

insecte m. insect

insécurité f. insecurity

insémination f. insemination

insensé a. insane, mad, senseless; — m. madman

insensiabilisation f. local anesthesia, removal of sense of feeling

insensibiliser vt. to anesthetize

insensibilité f. lack of sensitivity, lack of feeling(s); insensibility; coldness, indifference

insensible a. insensitive; unfeeling; insensible; cold, indifferent; imperceptible

inséparable a. inseparable

inséparablement adv. inseparably

insérer vt. to insert; wedge, sandwich in

insertion f. insertion

inserviable a. not obliging, disobliging

insidieusement adv. insidiously

insidieux a. insidious

insigne a. notorious; unusual; distinguished; — m. sign of membership, authority, dignity

insignes m. pl. insignia

insignifiance f. insignificance

insignifiant a. insignificant

insincère a. insincere

insincérité f. insincerity

insinuant a. insinuating

insinuation f. insinuation, implication; hint

insinuer vt. to insinuate; insert; s'— (dans) to steal (into); penetrate; insinuate oneself

insipide a. insipid; tasteless; uninteresting; flat

insipidité f. insipidity; lack of taste; flatness

insistance f. insistence

insistant a. insisting, insistent

insister vt. to insist; emphasize; persist

insobriété f. lack of sobriety, intemperance

insociabilité f. unsociableness

insociable a. unsociable

insolation f. sunstroke; insolation

insolemment adv. insolently

insolence f. insolence, impudence

insolent a. insolent, impudent; rude

insoler vt. to expose to the sun; s'— to sunbathe

insolite a. unusual

insolubilité f. insolubility

insoluble a. insoluble; unsolvable

insolvabilité f. insolvency

insolvable a. insolvent

insomnie a. insomnia

insondable a. unfathomable, mysterious; unsoundable

insonore a. soundproof

insonorisation f. soundproofing

insonoriser vt. to soundproof, insulate

insonorité f. lack of sonority

insouciance f. lack of care or concern, unconcern; carelessness, thoughtlessness

insouciant a. unconcerned; careless; thoughtless

insoucieux a. unmindful, heedless

insoumis a. unsubdued, unruly

insoumission f. unruliness, lack of submissiveness; insubordination

insoupçonnable a. above suspicion

insoupçonné a. unsuspected

insoutenable a. untenable, unmaintainable; unbearable

inspecter vt. to inspect; survey

inspecteur m. inspector; examiner; surveyor, supervisor

inspection f. inspection; examining

inspirant a. inspiring

inspirateur a. inspiring; — m. inspirer

inspiration f. inspiration; prompting; inhaling

inspiré a. inspired

inspirer vt. to inspire; motivate; inhale, breathe in; s'— de be inspired by

instabilité f. instability; uncertainty

instable a. unstable, unsteady; uncertain

installation f. installation; arranging; setting up; moving in; equipment; plant, shop; apparatus, set

installer vt. to install; arrange; settle; set up; equip; s'— to install oneself; settle; move in; make oneself comfortable

instamment a. urgently, insistently; immediately

instance f. instance, instancy; request; immediacy, urgency; legal proceedings, action

instant a. urgent; — m. instant, moment; **à l'**— immediately, at once; just now, a moment ago

instantané a. instantaneous; — m. snapshot

instar, à l'— de in the manner of

instaurateur m. founder of an institution

instauration f. founding, establishment

instaurer vt. to found, establish

instigateur m. instigator

instigation f. instigation; suggestion

instiller vt. to instill, pour by drops

instinct m. instinct; **d'**— instinctively

instinctif a. instinctive

instinctivement adv. instinctively

instituer vt. to institute, establish, found; appoint

institut m. institute

instituteur m., **institutrice** f. grade school teacher; tutor; founder

institution f. institution; establishment

institutionnel a. institutional

instructeur m. instructor

instructif a. instructive

instruction f. instruction; direction; training, education, schooling; lesson; legal investigation; **juge d'**— m. examining magistrate

instruire vt. to instruct, educate, teach, inform, train; investigate legally, examine

instruit a. educated; trained; learned; informed, aware

instrument m. instrument, tool

instrumentation f. instrumentation, orchestration

instrumenter vt. to score, orchestrate; — vi. to order proceedings (law)

instrumentiste m. instrumentalist

insu m., **à l'**— de unknown to, without the knowledge of

insubmersible a. unsinkable

insubordonné a. insubordinate

insuccès m. lack of success; failure

insuffisamment adv. insufficiently

insuffisance f. insufficiency, deficiency; inadequacy; incapacity; — **de pose** (phot.) underexposure

insuffisant a. insufficient, inadequate; incapable

insuffler vt. to inflate, blow up; breathe in; insufflate; (med.) spray

insulaire a. insular; — m. & f. islander

insularité f. insularity

insuline f. insulin

insultant a. insulting

insulte f. insult, affront

insulter vt. to insult

insupportable a. unbearable; intolerable; insufferable

insurgé a. & m. insurgent

insurger v., **s'**— to rebel

insurmontable a. insuperable, insurmountable

insurpassable a. unsurpassable; incomparable

insurrection f. insurrection, rebellion

intact a. intact, untouched; undamaged; whole

intangibilité f. intangibility

intarissable a. inexhaustible; endless

intégral a. integral; whole; full, in full, unexpurgated

intégrale f. (math.) integral

intégralement adv. wholly, fully, in full

intégralité f. wholeness, entireness

intégrant a. integral

intégration f. integration

intègre a. upright, honest; ethical; incorruptible

intégrer vt. to integrate

intégrité f. integrity, honesty; entirety, wholeness

intellect m. intellect

intellectualité f. intellectuality

intellectuel a. & m. intellectual

intellectuellement adv. intellectually

intelligemment adv. intelligently

intelligence f. understanding, intellect, intelligence, comprehension; **être d'**— to have an understanding together; **-s** pl. relations, connections, dealings

intelligent a. intelligent

intelligentsia f. intelligentsia, intellectuals

intelligibilité f. intelligibility

intelligible a. intelligible

intempérance f. intemperance

intempérant a. intemperate

intempéré a. immoderate, intemperate; inclement

intempérie f. inclement weather

intempestif a. untimely, inopportune

intemporel a. timeless, eternal

intenable a. untenable

intendance f. direction, management

intendant m. steward, manager; intendant

intense a. intense; intensive; severe; high; deep

intensément adv. intensely

intensif a. intensive

intensifier vt. to intensify

intensité f. intensity; strength; depth; force; severity

intensivement adv. intensively

intenter vt. to bring legal suit

intention f. intention; intent; purpose; wish; **à l'**— de for, for the sake of; designed for, destined for; in honor of; **avoir l'**— de to intend to

intentionné a. intentioned

intentionnel a. intentional, deliberate

intentionnellement adv. intentionally

interallié a. interallied, interrelated

interastral a. interstellar

interattraction f. mutual attraction

intercalaire a. interpolated

intercalation f. interpolation, intercalation

intercaler vt. to intercalate, interpolate

intercéder vi. to intercede

intercellulaire a. intercellular

intercepter vt. to intercept

intercepteur m. (avi.) interceptor

interception f. interception

intercesseur m. intercessor, mediator

intercession f. intercession

interchangeable a. interchangeable

intercontinental a. intercontinental

intercostal a. intercostal

interdépartemental a. interdepartmental

interdépendance f. interdependence

interdépendant a. interdependent

interdiction f. interdiction, prohibition

interdire vt. to forbid, ban, prohibit; bewilder

interdit a. speechless, taken aback; prohibited, forbidden; — m. (eccl.) interdict, prohibitory decree

intéressant a. interesting

intéressé a. interested; selfish; — m. interested party

intéresser vt. to interest; be interesting to; concern; s'— à to take an interest in

intérêt m. interest, concern, self-interest; share; advantage

intérieur a. interior; internal; inner; — m. interior, inside

intérieurement adv. internally; inwardly; inside

intérim m. interim

intérimaire a. temporary, provisional

interindividuel a. among individuals, group

injecter vt. to utter, ejaculate

interjection f. interjection

interjeter vt. to interject; — appel (law) lodge an appeal

interligne f. space between lines; (print.) leading

interligner vt. to interline; write between the lines

interlinéaire a. interlinear

interlocuteur m. interlocutor

interlocutoire a. interlocutory

interlope a. illegal; unauthorized; suspect

interloquer vt. to make speechless, confuse

intermède m. intermediary; (theat.) interlude

intermédiaire a. intermediate; — m. intermediary, agent, middleman

intermezzo m. (mus.) intermezzo

interminable a. interminable, endless

intermittence f. intermittency; par — intermittently

internat m. living-in, residing; internship; boarding school

international a. international

internationaliser vt. internationalize

internationaliste m. & f. internationalist

internationalité f. internationality

interne m. resident student; intern; boarder; — a. internal, interior, inner

internement m. internement

interner vt. to intern; confine

internissable a. untarnishable

interpellation f. interpellation; question, challenge

interpeller vt. to challenge, demand an accounting; interpellate

interplanétaire a. interplanetary

interpolation f. interpolation

interpoler vt. to interpolate

interposer vt. to interpose; s'— to intervene

interposition f. intervention; interposition

interprétable a. interpretable

interprétateur m. commentator, interpreter (of a work of art)

interprétation f. interpretation

interprète m. & f. interpreter

interpréter vt. to interpret; render, perform; read, make out, translate

interrègne m. interregnum

interrogateur a. questioning, interrogatory; — m. questioner, interrogator

interrogatif a. interrogative

interrogation f. interrogation, questioning, examination; point d'— m. question mark

interrogatoire m. questioning, examination, cross-examination

interroger vt. to interrogate, question, examine

interrompre vt. to interrupt; break; break off; stop

interrupteur m. interrupter; (elec.) switch, circuit-breaker

interruption f. interruption; break, breaking; disconnecting

inter-saison f. offseason (sports)

intersecté a. intersecting

intersection f. intersection

intersession f. intersession, break, recess

intersidéral, interstellaire a. interstellar

interstitiel a. interstitial

interurbain a. interurban

intervalle m. interval; period; space, distance

intervenir vi. to intervene, interfere; happen

intervention f. intervention; interference

interventionniste m. interventionist

interversion f. inversion

intervertir vt. to invert, reverse, transpose

interviewer vt. to interview

intestat a. intestate

intestin a. internal, intestine; civil; — m. intestine, bowel

intestinal a. intestinal

intimation f. notice, notification

intime a. intimate, close; inner; — n. close friend

intimement adv. intimately, closely

intimer vt. to notify; summon at law

intimidant a. intimidating

intimidateur a. intimidating; — m. intimidator

intimidation f. intimidation; threat, threatening

intimider vt. to intimidate; threaten, frighten; s'— to become nervous

intimité f. intimacy, closeness, privacy; inner being

intitulé m. title, heading

intituler vt. to entitle

intolérable a. intolerable, unbearable

intolérance f. intolerance

intolérant a. intolerant

intouchable a. & n. untouchable

intoxicant a. toxic, poisonous

intoxication f. poisoning

intoxiquer vt. to poison

intraduisible a. untranslatable

intraitable a. intractable, unmanageable

intra-muros a. intramural

intransférable a. untransferable

intransigeance f. intransigence

intransigeant a. intransigent, uncompromising, inflexible

intransitif a. intransitive

intraveineux a. intravenous

intrépide a. intrepid, fearless, undaunted

intrépidité f. intrepidity

intrigant a. intriguing, scheming; — m. intriguer, schemer

intrigailler vi. to scheme, plot

intrigue f. intrigue, plot

intriguer vt. to perplex; intrigue; — vi. to intrigue, scheme, plot

intrinsèque a. intrinsic

introducteur m. introducer, usher

introductif a. introductory

introduction f. introduction; insertion; induction

introduire vt. to bring in, show in; insert, introduce; s'— to enter, penetrate

intronisation f. enthronement; founding, establishment

introniser vt. to enthrone; found, establish

introspectif a. introspective

introspection f. introspection

introuvable a. which cannot be found, undiscoverable; incomparable

introverti a. introverted; — m. introvert

intrus a. intruding; trespassing; — m. intruder; trespasser

intrusion f. intrusion; trespassing

intuitif a. intuitive

intuition f. intuition

inusable a. that will never wear out; everlasting

inusité a. not in use; unusual; obsolete

inutile a. useless, needless, vain, unavailing

inutilisable a. unusable, unserviceable

inutilisé a. unused, unutilized

inutilité f. uselessness, inutility

invaincu a. unvanquished, unconquered

invalidation f. invalidating, invalidation

invalide a. invalid; disabled; void; — m. invalid, disabled veteran

invalider vt. to invalidate

invalidité f. disability; ill-health; invalidism; invalidity

invariabilité f. invariability

invariable a. invariable

invariablement adv. invariably

invasion f. invasion

invective f. invective

invectiver vi. to inveigh; — vt. to insult, abuse

invendable a. unsaleable

invendu a. unsold

inventaire m. inventory, stock

inventer vt. to invent; make up

inventeur m. inventor, discoverer

inventif a. inventive

invention f. invention, discovery; inventiveness; lie

inventorier vt. to inventory, take stock of

invérifiable a. unverifiable

invérifié a. unverified

inverse a. & m. inverse, opposite, reverse

inversement adv. inversely

inverser vt. to reverse

inversion f. inversion; reversing

invertébré a. invertebrate

invertir vt. to reverse, invert

investigateur a. investigating; — m. investigator

investigation f. investigation

investir vt. to invest

investissement m. investment, investing

investiture f. investiture

invétéré a. inveterate, confirmed

invétérer v., s'— to become inveterate

invincibilité f. invincibility

invincible a. invincible; insurmountable

inviolabilité f. inviolability

inviolable a. inviolable; sacred

invisibilité f. invisibility

invisible a. invisible

invitant a. inviting

invitation f. invitation

invite f. signal, cue (cards); discard conveying information to one's partner

invité m. guest

inviter vt. to invite

involontaire a. involuntary

involontairement adv. involuntarily

involuté a. involute(d)

involution f. involution

invoquer vt. to invoke

invraisemblable a. improbable, unlikely

invraisemblance f. unlikelihood, improbability

invulnérabilité f. invulnerability

invulnérable a. invulnerable

iode m. iodine

ioder vt. to iodize

iodure m. iodide

iodurer vt. to iodize

ion m. ion

ionien a. Ionian

ionique a. (arch.) Ionic; (phy.) ionic

ionisation f. ionization

ioniser vt. to ionize

ionosphère f. ionosphere

iota m. iota; bit, scrap, speck

iouler vi. to yodel

ipréau m. white poplar

Irak m. Iraq

irakien a. & m. Iraqi

Iran m. Iran

iranien a. & m. Iranian

irascibilité f. irascibility, irritability

irascible a. irascible, irritable

ire f. anger

iridescence f. iridescence

iridium m. iridium

iris m. iris; rainbow; halo; — m. or f. (bot.) iris

irisation f. iridescence

irisé a. iridescent; rainbow-colored

irlandais a. Irish; Erse

Irlande f. Ireland

ironie f. irony

ironique a. ironical

ironiser vi. to speak or write ironically

irraccommodable a. unrepairable, unmendable

irrachetable a. irredeemable

irradiation f. irradiation, radiation

irradier vi. to irradiate, radiate; spread, increase, advance

irraisonnable *a.* irrational
irrassasiable *a.* insatiable
irrationalisme *m.* irrationalism
irrationalité *f.* irrationality
irrationnel *a.* irrational
irréalisable *a.* unrealizable; impossible
irrecevable *a.* unacceptable, inadmissible
irréconciliable *a.* irreconcilable
irrécusable *a.* irrecusable, unimpeachable
irréductible *a.* irreducible; firm, unyielding, inflexible
irréel *a.* unreal
irréfléchi *a.* thoughtless, unthinking, hasty
irréflexion *f.* thoughtlessness, haste
irréfragable *a.* unimpeachable
irréfutable *a.* irrefutable
irréfuté *a.* unrefuted
irrégularité *f.* irregularity; unevenness; unpunctuality
irrégulier *a.* uneven; unpunctual; (gram.) irregular; — *m.* irregular, guerilla
irrégulièrement *adv.* irregularly
irréligieux *a.* irreligious
irréligion *f.* irreligion
irréligiosité *f.* irreligiousness
irrémédiable *a.* irremediable, incurable
irrémédiablement *adv.* irremediably, incurably
irremplaçable *a.* irreplaceable
irréparable *a.* irreparable
irrépréhensible *a.* not reprehensible, blameless
irrépressible *a.* irrepressible
irréprimable *a.* irrepressible
irréprochable *a.* irreprochable
irrésistible *a.* irresistible
irrésolu *a.* irresolute; uncertain; hesitant, undecided; unsteady; unsolved
irrésoluble *a.* irresolvable; unsolvable
irrésolution *f.* irresolution; hesitation; indecision
irrespect *m.* disrespect, lack of respect
irrespectueux *a.* disrespectful
irrespirable *a.* unbreathable
irresponsabilité *f.* irresponsibility
irresponsable *a.* irresponsible
irrévérence *f.* irreverence
irrévérencieusement *adv.* irreverently
irrévérencieux *a.* irreverent
irréversible *a.* irreversible
irrévocabilité *f.* irrevocability
irrévocable *a.* irrevocable
irrigateur *m.* watering hose
irrigation *f.* irrigation; watering; flooding; spraying
irriguer *vt.* to irrigate; water; flood; spray
irritabilité *f.* irritability; sensitivity
irritable *a.* easily irritable; sensitive
irritant *a.* irritating; — *m.* irritant
irriter *vt.* to irritate; s'— to become irritated; get angry
irruption *f.* irruption; inrush; inroad, invasion; bursting in; flooding
Islam *m.* Islam
islamique *a.* Islamic
islandais *a. & m.* Icelandic
Islande *f.* Iceland
isobare *f.* isobar
isocèle *a.* isosceles

isolant *a.* isolating; insulating; bouteille —e *f.* vacuum bottle, Thermos bottle
isolateur *a.* (elec.) insulating; — *m.* insulator
isolation *f.* insulating, insulation
isolationnisme *m.* isolationism
isolationniste *m. & f.* isolationist
isolé *a.* isolated; apart; lonely, desolate; insulated
isolement *m.* isolation, loneliness; (elec.) insulation
isolément *adv.* individually, singly, separately; solitarily
isoler *vt.* to isolate; segregate; (elec.) insulate
isoloir *m.* insulator; voting booth
isomère *m.* isomer
isomorphe *m.* isomorph
isotherme *m.* isotherm
isotope *m.* isotope
isotrope *m.* isotrope
Israël *m.* Israel
israélien *a. & m.* Israeli
issu *a.* descended, born; (fig.) resulting
issue *f.* outlet, exit; conclusion; issue; —s *pl.* by-products
isthme *m.* isthmus
Italie *f.* Italy
italien *a. & m.* Italian
italique *a.* Italic; — *m.* italics
itération *f.* iteration, repetition
itinéraire *m.* itinerary, route; — *a.* pertaining to roads
itinérant *a.* itinerant
ivoire *m.* ivory
ivoirin *a.* resembling ivory
ivre *a.* inebriated, intoxicated, drunk
ivresse *f.* intoxication, drunkenness; (fig.) ecstasy
ivrogne *a.* drunken; — *m.* drunkard
ivrognerie *f.* chronic drunkenness

J

jabot *m.* bird's crop; ruffle, neck frill
jabotage *m.* chatter, talk, gossip
jaboter *vi. & vt.* to jabber; chatter; talk unintelligibly
jacasse *f.* gossip, chatterbox; magpie
jacasser *vi.* to jabber, chatter; gossip
jacasserie *f.* chatter, gossip
jachère *f.* fallow land
jacinthe *f.* (bot.) hyacinth
jack *m.* (elec.) jack
jacobée *f.* (bot.) ragwort
jacobin *m.* Dominican friar; Jacobin
Jacques (*m.*) James
jacquet *m.* backgammon
jactance *f.* boasting, bragging
jade *m.* jade
jadis *adv.* of old, formerly
jaguar *m.* jaguar
jaillir *vi.* to spout out, spurt, gush, squirt; fly up; flash; (fig.) show liveliness
jaillissant *a.* gushing, spurting; flying
jaillissement *m.* spurt, spurting, gushing
jais *m.* jet; noir comme du — jet-black
jalon *m.* marker (post, stake, rod, staff); landmark
jalonner *vt.* to mark; stake (out); blaze
jalouser *vt.* to envy, be jealous of
jalousie *f.* jealousy; chagrin; Venetian

blind
jaloux *a.* jealous, envious; desirous
Jamaïque *f.* Jamaica
jamais *adv.* ever; ne . . . — never; à —, pour — for ever
jambage *m.* jamb of a door; side
jambe *f.* leg; shank; stem of a glass; brace, support; à toutes —s at full speed
jambière *f.* elastic stocking; —s *pl.* leggings; shin guards (sports)
jambon *m.* ham
jamboree *m.* jamboree, international scout meeting
janissaire *m.* janissary; 14th century Turkish soldier
jansénisme *m.* Jansenism
janséniste *a. & n* Jansenist
jante *f.* rim of wheel
janvier *m.* January
Japon *m.* Japan
japonais *a. & m.* Japanese
japonaiseries *f. pl.* Japanese art objects
jappement *m.* yelp, yelping
japper *vi.* to yelp, yap
jaquemart *m.* jack, figure which strikes the hours
jaquette *f.* jacket, coat
jardin *m.* garden; — d'enfants kindergarten; — des plantes botanical garden(s); — potager vegetable garden; truck farm
jardinage *m.* gardening; gardening products; produce
jardiner *vi.* to garden
jardinet *m.* small garden
jardinier *m.* gardener
jardinière *f.* gardener; flower stand; à la — served with various vegetables
jardiniste *m.* landscape gardener
jargon *m.* jargon
jargonner *vi.* to speak in jargon; use jargon
jarre *f.* large jar
jarret *m.* shin; hock; knuckle; part of leg back of the knee joint
jarretelle *f.* garter
jarretière *f.* garter; rope
jars *m.* (zool.) gander
jaser *vi.* to prattle, chatter, talk; gossip
jaserie *f.* chatter, gossip, talk
jaseur *a.* talkative, gossipy; — *m.* talker, chatterbox; gossip
jasmin *m.* jasmine
jaspe *m.* jasper
jasper *vt.* to marble
jatte *f.* bowl, basin
jattée *f.* bowlful
jauge *f.* gauge; (naut.) tonnage
jaugeage *m.* gauging, measuring
jauger *vt.* to gauge, measure
jaunâtre *a.* yellowish
jaune *a.* yellow; — *m.* yellow; (coll.) non-union worker; — d'œuf egg yolk; race — yellow race
jaunir *vt.* to make yellow; — *vi.* grow yellow
jaunisse *f.* (med.) jaundice
javanois *a. & m.* Javanese
javeline *f.* javelin
javellisation *f.* chlorination
javelliser *vt.* to chlorinate; add bleach to

javelot *m.* javelin, spear
je, (j') *pron.* I
Jean (*m.*) John
Jeanne (*f.*) Jane, Joan, Jean
jeannette *f.* small gold crucifix (pendant)
jérémiade *f.* lament, complaint, jeremiad
jersey *m.* jersey material
jésuite *m.* Jesuit
Jésus *m.* Jesus depicted as infant
jet *m.* throwing, casting; jet, spurt, spout, gush; blast, burst; jettisoning; (bot.) shoot; premier — rough draft, first attempt; — d'eau fountain
jetée *f.* pier, jetty
jeter *vt.* to throw, cast, fling, toss, hurl; utter
jeton *m.* counter, chip, token
jeu *m.* (*pl.* jeux) play, game, sport, performance; acting; gambling; slack, play, looseness; set; en — at stake; in action; — de cartes pack of cards; — d'esprit witticism; — de mots pun; — de paume tennis court; maison de — *f.* gambling house; table de — *f.* card table; gambling table
jeudi *m.* Thursday
jeun, *adv.* à — fasting; without having eaten
jeune *a.* young, youthful; green (not ripe)
jeûne *m.* fast, fasting
jeûner *vi.* to fast
jeunesse *f.* youth, young people; youthfulness
jeunet *a.* (coll.) very young
joaillerie *f.* jewelry
joaillier *m.* jeweller
jobard *a. & m.* (coll.) easy mark, fool, dupe
jocrisse *m.* fool, dupe
jodler *vi.* to yodel
joie *f.* joy, gladness; feu de — *m.* bonfire
joindre *vt.* to join, put together, connect; meet; adjoin; add; combine; weld; se — to join; meet; adjoin
joint *a.* joined, united — *m.* joint
jointif *a.* joined
jointure *f.* joint; juncture
joker *m.* joker (cards)
joli *a.* pretty
joliment *adv.* nicely; very
jonc *m.* rush, rattan, reed
joncher *vt.* to strew, scatter; litter, be spread over
jonction *f.* junction; joining
jongler *vi.* to juggle
jonglerie *f.* juggling
jongleur *m.* juggler; jongleur
jonque *f.* (naut.) junk
jonquille *f.* jonquil
jouable *a.* playable
joue *f.* cheek; flange; coucher en — to aim at, point a gun at
jouer *vt.* to play; perform; act; bet on; feign; trick; — *vi.* to play; gamble; act, work; come into play, operate; faire — to bring into play
jouet *m.* plaything, toy
joueur *m.* player, gambler; performer; mauvais — poor sport
joug *m.* yoke; slavery
jouir *vi.* to enjoy; possess

jouissance f. enjoyment; possession
joujou m. plaything, toy
jour m. day, daylight, light; opening; du
— au lendemain at any moment; soon;
faire — to grow light; grand — broad
daylight; mettre au — to bring to light;
give birth to; petit — early dawn; plein
— broad daylight; -s pl. days; life; de
nos -s today, nowadays
Jourdain m. Jordan
journal m. (pl. journaux) journal, diary;
log; newspaper
journalier a. daily, everyday; — m. day-
laborer
journalisme m. journalism
journaliste m. & f. journalist; reporter
journalistique a. journalistic
journée f. daytime; day's work; day's
pay; day's march; à la — by the day;
toute la — all day long
journellement adv. daily
joute f. joust, jousting; competition, contest
jouter vi. to joust, fight
jouvence f. youth
jovialité f. joviality
joyau m. jewel
joyeusement adv. joyfully
joyeuseté f. prank, joke
joyeux a. joyful; glad, merry
jubilation f. jubilation
jubilé m. jubilee; golden anniversary
jubiler vi. to jubilate, be jubilant, exult
jucher vi. & vt. to perch
juchoir m. perch, roost
judaïque a. Judaic, Jewish
judaïsme m. Judaism
judas m. traitor; peephole
judéo-allemand a. & m. Yiddish
judiciaire a. judicial, judiciary
judicieusement adv. judiciously
judicieux a. judicious
juge m. judge; — d'instruction examining
magistrate
jugement m. judgment, understanding;
trial; sentence, decision, verdict; opinion; sense
jugeotte f. (coll.) common sense
juger vt. to judge, try; pass sentence;
think; consider, deem
Jugoslave a. & n. Yugoslav(ian), Jugoslav
jugulaire a. jugular; — f. jugular vein;
chin strap
juguler vt. to strangle; cut the throat of
juif (juive) a. Jewish
juillet m. July
juin m. June
Jules (m.) Julius
julien a. Julian
julienne f. consommé Julienne (made with
herbs and vegetables)
jumeau (jumelle) a. & n. twin
jumelé a. paired, coupled; twin; dual
jumeler vt. to pair
jumelles f. pl. binoculars
jument f. mare
jumping m. steeplechase (racing)
jungle f. jungle
junior a. & m. junior
junte f. junta
jupe f. skirt

jupon m. petticoat
juré a. sworn; — m. juror; les -s pl. the
jury
jurement m. cursing, swearing
jurer vt. to swear, vow; — vi. curse; to
clash (color)
juridiction f. jurisdiction
juridictionnel a. jurisdictional
juridique a. judicial, juridical
jurisconsulte m. lawyer, law expert
jurisprudence f. jurisprudence
juriste m. jurist
juron m. oath, swear word
jury m. jury, board, panel
jus m. juice; gravy
jusant m. ebb tide
jusque, jusqu'à prep. until; as far as;
even; jusqu'ici, jusqu'à present till
now, hitherto; jusqu'à ce que conj. until
justaucorps m. doublet
juste a. just, equitable, right, fair; precise, exact; au — exactly, precisely;
— adv. right, very, exactly; — m. just
person; person in state of grace
juste-milieu m. moderation, golden mean
justesse f. exactness, accuracy; fairness
justice f. justice; law; faire — de to treat
as one deserves; se faire — to punish
oneself; avenge oneself
justiciable a., — de under the jurisdiction
of
justicier m. officer of justice, judge; — vt.
to punish
justifiable a. justifiable
justificateur a. justifying
justicatif a. justificative
justification f. justification
justifier vt. to justify, vindicate; — de to.
give proof of
juteux a. juicy
juvénile a. juvenile
juvénilité f. character of what is juvenile
juxtaposer vt. to juxtapose

K

kaki a. khaki-colored
kaléidoscope m. kaleidoscope
kangourou m. kangaroo
kaolin m. kaolin
kapok m. kapok
kayac m. kayak
keepsake m. album, scrapbook
képi m. military cap
kermesse f. village fair
kérosène m. kerosene
kitchenotte f. peasant's bonnet
kidnapper vt. to kidnap
kidnappeur m. kidnapper
kilo(gramme) m. kilogram
kilomètre m. kilometer
kilométrer vt. to mark off in kilometers
kilométrique a. kilometric
kilowatt m. kilowatt
kilt m. kilt
kimono m. kimono
kinescope m. kinescope
kiosque m. kiosk; newsstand; conning
tower
kirsch m. kirsch, cherry brandy
klaxon m. (auto.) horn
klaxonner vi. to blow the horn

kleptomanie (cleptomanie) *f.* kleptomania

knock-out *m.* boxing knockout

knockouter *vt.* to knock out

kodak *m.* camera

krach *m.* financial crash

krypton *m.* krypton

kyrie *m.* (eccl.) Kyrie eleison (invocation)

kyrielle *f.* (coll.) tirade, avalanche of words

kyste *m.* (med.) cyst

L

la *art. f.* the; — *pron.* her, it; — *m.* (mus.) French key of A; 6th note of a scale

là *adv.* there, that, that way; then

là-bas *adv.* over there; yonder

label *m.* guarantee; inspection mark

labeur *m.* labor, work

laborantine *f.* laboratory technician

laboratoire *m.* laboratory

laborieusement *adv.* laboriously

laborieux *a.* hard-working; painstaking, difficult

labour *m.* tillage, plowing

labourable *a.* arable

labourage *m.* plowing

labourer *vt.* to till, plow

laboureur *m.* plower; farm hand

labyrinthe *m.* labyrinth, maze

lac *m.* lake

laçage *m.* lacing

lacer *vt.* to lace; se — to tie one's shoelaces, lace one's shoes

lacération *f.* laceration

lacérer *vt.* to lacerate

lacet *m.* shoelace; hairpin turn; snare; route en –s winding road

lâche *a.* loose, lax; cowardly; — *m.* coward

lâcher *vt.* to release, loosen; let go, drop; — prise to let go

lâcheté *f.* cowardice; cowardly action

lâcheur *m.* (coll.) quitter

lacis *m.* network

laconique *a.* laconic

lacrymal *a.* teary

lacrymogène *a.*, gaz — *m.* tear gas

lacs *m.* knotted cord; trap, snare

lacté *a.* lacteal, milky; voie –e *f.* Milky Way

lactique *a.* lactic

lactose *m.* lactose, milk sugar

lacune *f.* gap, void, lacuna

lad *m.* stable boy

là-dessus *adv.* thereupon

ladre *a.* mean, stingy; leprous

lagon *m.* lagoon of an atoll

lagune *f.* lagoon

là-haut *adv.* up above, up there

lai *m.* lay, song; — *a.* lay; frère — *m.* lay brother

laïc *a.* lay, secular

laid *a.* ugly

laideron *f.* ugly young woman

laideur *f.* ugliness

lainage *m.* wool goods

laine *f.* wool

laineux *a.* woolly, fleecy

lainier *a.* wool; — *m.* wool merchant

laïque *a.* laic, lay; — *m.* layman

laisse *f.* leash

laissé-pour-compte *m.* unsold item; unwanted thing

laisser *vt.* to let, allow; leave behind, leave alone

laisser-aller *m.* unconstraint

laissez-passer *m.* pass, permit

lait *m.* milk; — écrémé skim milk; cochon de — *m.* suckling pig; dents de — *f. pl.* milk teeth, baby teeth; petit — whey

laitance *f.* milt

laiterie *f.* dairy, dairy store

laiteux *a.* milky

laitier *m.* milk seller, milkman; — *m.* vitrified slag

laitière *f.* milkmaid; dairy cow

laiton *m.* brass

laitue *f.* lettuce

laize *f.* cloth width

lamaserie *f.* lamasery

lambeau *m.* rag, tatter; shred

lambin *a.* slow; loitering

lambiner *vi.* to move slowly, dawdle

lambourde *f.* studding

lambrequin *m.* valence, hanging

lambris *m.* wainscoting, paneling, wall plaster

lame *f.* knife blade; slat; wave

lamentation *f.* lamentation

lamenter *v.*, se — to lament, complain

laminage *m.* laminating

laminer *vt.* to laminate

lampadaire *m.* lamppost; floor lamp

lampe *f.* lamp; light; bulb, (rad.) tube

lampion *m.* oil lamp

lampiste *m. & f.* lampmaker; lamp seller

lamproie *f.* lamprey

lampyre *m.* firefly

lance *f.* lance; lancer; nozzle

lance-flammes *m.* flame-thrower

lance-fusées *m.* rocket launcher

lance-grenades *m.* grenade launcher

lancement *m.* throw, throwing; start, send-off

lance-pierres *m.* slingshot

lancer *vt.* to fling, hurl, throw, start; launch

lance-torpille *m.* torpedo tube

lancette *f.* lancet

lancier *m.* lancer

lanciner *vi.* to shoot (pain)

lande *f.* heath, moor

langage *m.* language, speech

lange *m.* swaddling cloth

langer *vt.* to swaddle

langoureux *a.* languishing, languid

langouste *f.* spiny lobster

langoustine *f.* very small lobster

langue *f.* tongue; speech, language

languette *f.* tongue, tab; (mus.) instrument reed

langueur *f.* languor

languir *vi.* to languish, pine; — pour to long for

languissant *a.* languishing

lanière *f.* strap

lanoline *f.* lanolin

lanterne *f.* lantern, light; projector

lanterner *vi.* to loaf, idle, waste time

Laos *m.* Laos

lapement *m.* lapping

laper *vt. & vi.* to lap
lapereau *m.* young rabbit
lapidaire *m. & a.* lapidary
lapidation *f.* stoning, lapidation
lapider *vt.* to stone
lapin *m.* rabbit, (coll.) brave man, cunning man
lapis *m.* lapis lazuli
Laponie *f.* Lapland
lapsus *m.* error, slip of the tongue
laquais *m.* lackey; flunky
laque *f.* lac; — en feuilles shellac; — *m.* lacquer
laquelle *pron. f.* who, which, that
laquer *vt.* to lacquer
larcin *m.* larceny, theft
lard *m.* bacon; pork, fat
larder *vt.* to lard; interlard, sprinkle; pierce, riddle
lardon *m.* bit of fat
large *a.* wide, broad; liberal, generous; large; — *m.* room, space; width; open sea
largesse *f.* liberality, generosity
largeur *f.* breadth, width
largue *a.* slack; (naut.) on the quarter
larguer *vt.* to slacken
larme *f.* tear; drop
larmoiement *m.* weeping, tears
larmoyant *a.* weeping, tearful
larmoyer *vt.* to weep constantly
larron *m.* thief, robber
larvaire *a.* larval
larve *f.* larva
laryngite *f.* laryngitis
laryngologiste *m.* throat specialist
las *interj.* alas!
las (lasse) *a.* tired, weary
lascif *a.* lascivious
lasciveté *f.* lasciviousness
lassant *a.* tiring; tedious
lasser *vt.* to tire; se — to grow tired
lassitude *f.*. weariness, fatigue, lassitude
latent *a.* latent
latéral *a.* lateral; —ement *adv.* on the side
Latin *m. & a.* Latin
latiniser *vt.* to latinize
latiniste *m. & f.* latinist
latino-américain *a. & m.* Latin-American
latrines *f. pl.* latrines
lattage *m.* lathwork
latte *f.* lath, slat
latter *vt.* to lath
lattis *m.* lathwork; latticework
latvien *a. & m.* Latvian
laudatif *a.* laudatory
lauré *a.* crowned with laurel, laureate
lauréat *m.* laureate, winner
Laurent(*m.*) Lawrence
laurier *m.* laurel
lavable *a.* washable
lavabo *m.* wash basin, sink; lavatory; (eccl.) priest's prayer
lavage *m.* washing
lavallière *f.* necktie with large flat knot
lavande *f.* lavender
lavandière *f.* washerwoman
lave *f.* lava
lavé *a.* washed out; water-color wash (art)
lavement *m.* washing; enema

laver *vt.* to wash
lavette *f.* dishcloth
laveur *m.* washer; raton — raccoon
laveuse *f.* washing machine
lavis *m.* wash (art)
lavoir *m.* wash house, laundry
laxatif *a. & m.* laxative
lazaret *m.* quarantine station
lazzi *m. pl.* (theat.) tricks, jokes
le *art. m.* the; — *pron. m.* him, it
leader *m.* political leader; editorial
lèche *f.* thin slice (food)
lèchefrite *f.* dripping pan
lécher *vt.* to lick; polish; polish excessively
lècherie *f.* gluttony
leçon *f.* lesson, assignment; reading, version
lecteur *m.* reader
lecture *f.* reading
légal *a.* legal
légalement *adv.* legally
légalisation *f.* legalization
légaliser *vt.* to legalize; authenticate
légalité *f.* legality
légat *m.* papal legate
légataire *m. & f.* heir, legatee; — universel residual heir
légation *f.* legation
légendaire *a.* legendary
légende *f.* legend
léger *a.* light; slight; active; agile; frivolous
légèrement *adv.* lightly
légèreté *f.* lightness, levity, triviality
légion *f.* legion
légionnaire *m.* legionary; member of the Foreign Legion; member of the Legion of Honor
législateur *m.* legislator
législatif *a.* legislative
législation *f.* legislation
législature *f.* legislature
légiste *m.* jurist, legist
légitime *a.* legitimate; lawful
légitimer *vt.* to recognize, legitimatize
légitimité *f.* legitimacy, lawfulness
legs *m.* legacy
léguer *vt.* to leave, bequeathe
légume *m.* vegetable; — *f.* (coll.) very important person
légumeuse *f.* legume
légumier *m.* vegetable dish; — *a.* vegetable; vegetable garden
légumineux *a.* leguminous
lendemain *m.* next day, tomorrow
lénifier *vt.* to mitigate, attenuate
lénitif *a.* soothing
lent *a.* slow
lente *f.*. nit
lentement *adv.* slowly
lenteur *f.* slowness
lenticulaire *a.* lenticular
lentille *f.* lentil; lens; — s *pl.* freckles
léonin *a.* leonine; part —e *f.* lion's share
léopard *m.* leopard
léopardé *a.* spotted
lèpre *f.* leprosy
lépreux *a.* leprous; — *m.* leper
lequel *pron. m.* which, who, that
les *art.* (*pl. of* le, la); — *pron.* them

lès *prep.* near
lesbien *a.* Lesbian
lèse-humanité *f.* crime against humanity
lèse-majesté *f.* high treason
léser *vt.* to wrong, injure
lésine *f.* stinginess
lésiner *vi.* to be stingy, be niggardly
lésion *f.* wrong, damage, hurt; lesion
lessivage *m.* washing
lessive *f.* lye; laundry, washing powder
lessiver *vt.* to launder
lest *m.* (naut.) ballast
lestage *m.* ballasting
leste *a.* nimble, brisk, agile
lester *vt.* to ballast, weight
léthargie *f.* lethargy
léthargique *a.* lethargic
Lette *m. & f. & a.* Lett, Latvian
letton *a. & m.* Lett, Latvian
Lettonie *f.* Latvia
lettrage *m.* lettering
lettre *f.* letter; à la —, au pied de la — literally
lettré *a.* literate; learned
lettrine *f.* large initial capital letter; reference letter at head of dictionary column
leucémie *f.* leukemia
leucocyte *m.* leucocyte, white blood cell
leur *a.* their; — *pron.* to them, for them; le —, la — theirs
leurre *m.* lure, decoy
leurrer *vt.* to lure, trap, decoy
levain *m.* leaven, yeast; poudre — *f.* baking powder
levant *a.* rising; — *m.* east
Levantin *m. & a.* Levantine
levée *f.* raising, lifting; adjourning; harvesting; levying; mail collection; trick (at cards); removal; levee, dike
lever *m.* rising; — du soleil sunrise
lever *vt.* to lift, raise; collect; levy; remove; draw (a plan); — *vi.* to come up (plants); to rise (dough)
léviathan *m.* leviathan
levier *m.* lever; crowbar
lévitation *f.* levitation
levraut *m.* young hare
lèvre *f.* lip; rim
lévrette *f.*, lévrier *m.* greyhound
levure *f.* yeast; — chimique baking powder
lexicographe *m.* lexicographer
lexicologie *f.* lexicology
lexique *m.* lexicon; glossary; vocabulary
lézard *m.* lizard
lézarde *f.* crevice, crack
lézarder *vt.* to crack
liaison *f.* binding, joining, relation; intimacy, affair
liane *f.* liana, vine
liant *a.* good-natured, engaging; flexible; — *m.* flexibility, affability
liard *m.* ¼ sou; tiny sum, cent; un rouge — a red cent
liasse *f.* bundle, wad, file
Liban *m.* Lebanon
Libanais *m. & a.* Lebanese
libation *f.* libation
libelle *m.* lampoon, satire; libel
libellé *m.* composition, wording (judiciary *or* administrative)
libeller *vt.* to draw up, compose, word
libelliste *m.* satirist
libellule *f.* dragonfly
libéral *a. & m.* liberal
libéralement *adv.* liberally
libéralisation *f.* liberalization
libéraliser *vt.* to liberalize
libéralisme *m.* liberalism
libéralité *f.* liberality, generosity
libérateur *m.* liberator
libération *f.* liberation
libérer *vt.* to free, liberate, discharge
libertaire *m. & f.* anarchist
liberté *f.* liberty, freedom
libertin *a.* libertine, licentious; — *m.* libertine; freethinker (history)
libertinage *m.* licentiousness, debauchery; libertinage
libidineux *a.* libidinous, lascivious
libraire *m. & f.* bookseller
librairie *f.* bookstore; book trade; publishing house
libre *a.* free; unoccupied
libre-échange *m.* free trade
librement *adv.* freely
libre-service *m.* self-service; restaurants de — cafeteria
librettiste *m.* librettist
Libye *f.* Libya
lice *f.* lists, jousting field; bitch; entrer en — to undertake, enter upon
licence *f.* license; Master's degree
licencié *m.* holder of a Master's degree
licenciement *m.* dismissal, firing
licencier *vt.* to dismiss, fire
licencieux *a.* licentious
lichen *m.* lichen
licitation *f.* sale at auction
licite *a.* lawful
liciter *vt.* to sell at auction
licorne *f.* unicorn
licou, licol *m.* halter (of a harness)
licteur *m.* lictor
lie *f.* lees, (dregs) — de vin wine dregs; red-violet color
lié *a.* tied, united; intimate
liège *m.* cork, cork oak; à bout(s) de — cork-tipped
lien *m.* tie, bond
lier *vt.* to tie, bind, fasten; establish; bind, thicken (cooking); se — to become close friends, become intimate; thicken
lierre *m.* ivy
liesse *f.* joy, gaiety
lieu *m.* place; cause, reason; — x *pl.* premises; au — de instead of; avoir — to take place; avoir — de to have reason to; — commun commonplace, banality; tenir — de to replace
lieue *f.* league (2 ½ miles)
lieutenance *f.* lieutenancy
lieutenant-colonel *m.* lieutenant-colonel
lièvre *m.* hare
liftier *m.* elevator operator
ligament *m.* ligament
ligaturer *vt.* to ligature, bind
lignage *m.* lineage
ligne *f.* line
lignée *f.* issue, stock; chien de bonne — *m.* pedigreed dog

ligneux a. ligneous
lignite m. lignite
ligoter vt. to bind, tie up
ligue f. league
liguer vt. to bind together, unite
ligueur m. member of the League (historical)
ligurien a. & m. Ligurian
lilas m. lilac; lilac color, light purple
lilliputien a. Lilliputian, tiny
limace f. (zool.) slug
limaçon m. snail
limande f. straight edge (carpentry)
limbe m. border; — s pl. limbo
lime f. file
limer vt. to file; (fig.) to polish, rework
limier m. bloodhound; sleuth
liminaire a. prefatory, introductory
limitable a. limitable
limitatif a. limiting
limite f. boundary, limit
limiter vt. to limit
limitrophe a. surrounding, bordering
limon m. lime; mud, slime; silt; shaft; support of a stair step
limonade f. lemon soda, lemonade
limoneux a. slimy; full of mud; silted
Limousin m. inhabitant of Limoges region
limousine f. limousine
limpide a. limpid
limpidité f. limpidness, clearness
lin m. flax; linen; graine de — f. linseed
linceul m. shroud
linéaire a. linear
linéal a. lineal
linéament m. feature; stoke; line; element
linette f. linseed
linge m. linen; table linen; underclothing; soiled clothes
lingerie f. linen goods; underclothing; linen closet; vente de — f. white-goods sale
lingot m. ingot
linguiste m. linguist
linguistique a. linguistic; — f. linguistics
liniment m. liniment
links m. pl. golf course
linoléum m. linoleum
linon m. batiste
linotype f. linotype machine
linotypiste m. & f. linotypist
linteau m. lintel
lion m. lion; — ne f. lioness
lionceau m. lion cub
lippe f. protruding lower lip; faire la — to pout
liquéfaction f. liquefying, liquefaction
liquéfier vt. to liquefy
liqueur f. liqueur; liquor, liquid; (chem.) solution
liquidation f. settlement, liquidating of debts
liquide a. liquid; — m. liquid; — f. liquid consonant
liquider vt. to liquidate; settle
liquoriste m. dealer in liqueurs
lire vt. to read
lire f. lira
lis, lys m. (bot.) lily; (fig.) teint de — very white
Lisbonne f. Lisbon

lise f. quicksand
liséré m. piping; a sewed-on border
lisérer vt. to edge, border
liseur m. reader; bookmark
liseuse f. reader; protective cover of a book
lisibilité f. legibility
lisible a. legible, readable
lisière f. selvage; border, edge; support
lisse a. sleek, smooth, glossy
lisser vt. to smoothe, make glossy
lisseuse f. polishing machine
liste f. list
listel m. edging, frame
lit m. bed; layer; — de sangle folding bed
litanie f. litany
litée f. litter of young animals
literie f. bedding
lithium m. lithium
lithographe m. lithographer
lithographie f. lithograph; lithography
lithographier vt. to lithograph
litière f. litter
litige m. litigation
litigieux a. litigious; contentious (law)
litre m. liter
lit-sac m. sleeping bag
littéraire a. literary
littéral a. literal
littéralement adv. literally
littérateur m. literary man, man of letters
littérature f. literature
littoral m. & a. coast; littoral
Lituanie f. Lithuania
Lituanien m. & a. Lithuanian
liturgie f. liturgy
liturgique a. liturgical
livarot m. livarot cheese
livide a. livid
lividité f. lividness, lividity
Livourne f. L ghorn
livrable a. deliverable
livraison f. delivery; part, installment (of book)
livre f. pound (weight or Eng. money)
livre m. book, register; grand — ledger
livrée f. livery; colors
livrer vt. to deliver; hand over; betray; se — à to give oneself over to; devote oneself to; go in for, indulge in; surrender to
livresque a. relating to books
livret m. small book; passbook; libretto
livreur m. delivery man
livreuse f. delivery truck
lobaire a. lobar
lobe m. lobe
local m. premises; — a. local
localisation f. localization
localiser vt. to localize
localité f. locality
locataire m. & f. tenant
locatif m. (gram.) locative
location f. renting; bureau de — m. box office
loch f. (naut.) log; table de — f. log book
locomoteur a. locomotive
locomotion f. locomotion
locuste f. locust
locution f. locution; phrase
logarithme m. logarithm

logarithmique a. logarithmic

loge f. (theat.) box; dressing room; janitor's apartment; loggia

logement m. lodging, housing

loger vt. to lodge, house; — vi. to reside

logeur m. landlord

logicien m. logician

logique a. logical; — f. logic

logis m. home, dwelling

logistique f. logistics

loi f. law

loin adv. far, far off, at a distance

lointain a. far, remote, distant; — m. distance

loir m. dormouse

loisible a. permissible

loisir m. leisure; time-off

lombago m. lumbago

lombaire a. lumbar

lombes m. pl. lumbar region

lombric m. earthworm

londonien m. Londoner; — a. of London

Londres m. London

long (longue) a. long, lengthy; à la — ue in the long run; — m. length; de — en large up and down, back and forth; le — de prep. along

longanimité f. longanimity; forbearance

long-courrier m. ocean-going ship

longe f. tether; loin

longer vt. to go along, skirt

longeron m. crossbeam

longévité f. longevity

longitudinal a. longitudinal

longtemps adv. a long time

longue f. long vowel

longuement adv. for a long time, at length

longuet a. rather long; — m. long roll

longueur f. length

longue-vue f. telescope

looping m. (avi.) loop

lopin m. bit, piece

loquace a. loquacious

loquacité f. loquaciousness

loque f. rag, tatter

loquet m. latch

loqueteau m. small latch

loqueteux a. ragged, dressed in rags

loquette f. scrap, waste

lorgner vt. to ogle, stare at

lorgnette f. opera glasses

lorgnon m. lorgnette

loriot m. oriole

lorrain a. Lorraine

lors adv. at the time; dès — from that time; — de at the time of

lorsque conj. when

losange f. lozenge

lot m. lot, part, share; jack pot; prize (gambling)

loterie f. lottery

loti a. favored; divided

lotion f. lotion; hair tonic

lotionner vt. to lotion, bathe

lotir vt. to divide into lots; sort out; provide for

loto m. lotto

lotus m. lotus

louable a. praiseworthy

louage m. letting out; hiring

louange f. praise

louanger vt. to praise

louangeur a. praising, laudatory

louche f. soup ladle; — a. cross-eyed, squinting; shady, suspect, unwholesome

loucher vi. to squint; be cross-eyed

louchet m. spade

louer vt. to praise; hire, rent; se — de to be pleased with

loufoque m. crank

lougre m. (naut.) lugger

louis m. 20-franc gold piece

loulou m. Pomeranian dog

loup m. wolf; evil person; mask; defect

loupe f. magnifying glass; cyst, wen, tree gnarl

louper vt. to botch

loup-garou m. werewolf

lourd a. heavy, weighty, dull

lourdaud a. clumsy

lourdement adv. heavily

lourdeur f. heaviness; dullness; sultriness

loutre f. otter

louveteau m. wolf cub

louveterie f. wolf hunt; hunting gear

louvoyer vi. dodge, be evasive; (naut.) to tack

lover vt. to coil

loyaliste a. & n. loyalist

loyauté f. loyalty

loyer m. rent, rental

lubie f. whim, fancy

lubricité f. lewdness, inclination toward obscenity

lubrifiant m. lubricant; — a. lubricating

lubrificateur a. lubricating

lubrifier vt. to lubricate

lubrique a. lewd

Luc (m.) Luke

lucarne f. skylight, dormer window

lucide a. lucid

lucidité f. lucidity

luciole f. firefly

lucratif a. lucrative

lucre m. profit, love of profit

luette f. uvula

lueur f. gleam, glimmer

luge f. sled

lugubre a. lugubrious, gloomy

lui pron. he, him, to him, to her, to it

luire vi. to shine, gleam

luisance f. shininess, glossiness

luisant a. shining, gleaming; glossy

lumière f. light, illumination

lumignon m. small light; wick

luminaire m. luminary; lights, lighting

luminescent a. luminescent

lumineux a. luminous

luminosité f. luminosity

lunaire a. lunar

lunaison f. lunation, lunar month

lunatique a. fantastic; — m. & f. lunatic

luncher vi. to have lunch

lundi m. Monday

lune f. moon; clair de — m. moonlight; — de miel honeymoon

luné a. crescent-shaped

lunetier m. optician

lunette f. glass, telescope; hole; — de tir telescopic gunsight; — s pl. eyeglasses

lunetterie f. optician's trade

lustre *m.* luster, gloss; chandelier; 5-year period, lustrum
lustrer *vt.* to gloss; glaze
lustrine *f.* cotton satin
luth *m.* lute
Luthérien *m.* Lutheran
luthier *m.* maker of stringed instruments
lutin *m.* sprite, elf
lutiner *vt.* to tease, torment
lutrin *m.* lectern
lutte *f.* struggle, wrestling
lutter *vi.* to wrestle, struggle
lutteur *m.* wrestler
luxation *f.* dislocation
luxe *m.* luxury
luxer *vt.* to dislocate
luxmètre *m.* light meter
luxueux *a.* luxurious
luxure *f.* lewdness, lust
luxuriant *a.* luxuriant
luxurieux *a.* lustful, lewd
luzerne *f.* alfalfa
lycée *m.* secondary school, junior college
lycéen *m.* schoolboy, student, lycée student
lymphatique *a.* lymphatic
lymphe *f.* lymph
lynchage *m.* lynching
lyncher *vt.* to lynch
lynx *m.* lynx
lyonnais *a.* from Lyons
lyre *f.* lyre
lyrique *a.* lyrical

M

ma *a. f.* my
macabre *a.* macabre, deathly; danse — *f.* dance of death
macadamiser *vt.* to pave with macadam
macaron *m.* macaroon
macaronis *m. pl.* macaroni
macédoine *f.* mixed salad; mixed vegetables
Macédoine *f.* Macedonia
Macédonien *m. & a.* Macedonian
macération *f.* maceration
macérer *vt.* to macerate; se — to mortify the flesh
mâchefer *m.* clinker, dross, slag
mâchelier *a.* molar
mâcher *vt.* to chew
machette *f.* machete
machin *m.* thing, gadget
machinal *a.* mechanical; instinctive
machinalement *adv.* mechanically
machine *f.* machine, engine; — à coudre sewing machine; — à écrire typewriter
machiner *vt.* to machinate, put together, prepare; to handle scenery
machinerie *f.* machinery; machine works; engine room
machiniste *m.* bus driver; (theat.) stagehand
mâchoire *f.* jaw, jawbone
mâchonner *vt.* to munch, chew slowly; mutter, mumble
mâchure *f.* bruise; defect in cloth
mâchurer *vt.* to daub, blacken
macis *m.* mace (spice)
maçon *m.* mason, bricklayer
maçonnage *m.* masonry

maçonner *vt.* to construct with masonry
maçonnerie *f.* masonry; free-masonry
maçonnique *a.* masonic
macrocosme *m.* macrocosm, the Universe
maculation, maculature *f.* macule; spotted sheet; poorly printed sheet
macule *f.* spot, stain
maculer *vt.* to spot, stain
Madagascar *m.* Madagascar
madame *f.* madam, Mrs.
madécasse *a.* Malagasy
Madeleine (*f.*) Magdalen
madeleine *f.* small sponge cake
mademoiselle *f.* miss
Madère *f.* Madeira; — *m.* Madeira wine
madone *f.* madonna
madras *m.* madras
madré *a.* cunning, sly
madrier *m.* thick plank
madrigal *m.* madrigal
madrilène *a.* of Madrid, from Madrid
magasin *m.* store; warehouse; magazine of a rifle; grand — department store
magasinage *m.* warehousing
magasinier *m.* warehouse clerk; stock clerk; library stack boy
mage *m.* magus, wizard; les — s, les rois — s the Magi, the Wise Men
magicien *m.* magician
magie *f.* magic
magique *a.* magic
magister *m.* country teacher
magistère *m.* mastery; teaching
magistral *a.* imposing; authoritative; magisterial
magistrat *m.* magistrate
magistrature *f.* magistrate's position; the bench; magistrates
magnanarelle *f.* silkworm raiser; mulberry-leaf picker
magnanerie *f.* silkworm house
magnanime *a.* magnanimous
magnanimité *f.* magnanimity
magnat *m.* magnate
magnésie *f.* magnesia
magnésium *m.* magnesium
magnétique *a.* magnetic
magnétisation *f.* magnetization, magnetizing
magnétiser *vt.* to magnetize
magnétisme *m.* magnetism
magnéto *f.* magneto
magnétophone *m.* tape recorder; wire recorder
magnificat *m.* Magnificat
magnificence *f.* magnificence
magnifier *vt.* to glorify, magnify
magnifique *a.* magnificent
magnitude *f.* magnitude
magnolia *m.* magnolia
magnum *m.* magnum, two-liter bottle
magot *m.* ape, monkey; treasure; grotesque figurine
Mahométan *m. & a.* Mohammedan
mahométisme *m.* Mohammedanism
mai *m.* May
maie *f.* kneading trough
maigre *a.* thin, lean; meager; jour — *m.* fast day, meatless day
maigrelet *a.* somewhat thin

maigreur *f.* thinness; meagerness
maigrir *vi.* to make thin; — *vi.* to grow thin, lose weight
mail *m.* mall; public walk
maille *f.* stitch; mesh; link mail; avoir — à partir to have a disagreement, have a bone to pick (U.S. coll.)
maillechort *m.* German silver
maillet *m.* mallet
mailloche *f.* large mallet
maillon *m.* link of a small chain
maillot *m.* swaddling clothes; tights; swim suit; jersey
main *f.* hand; handwriting; coup de — *m.* aid, de longue — for a long time; battres des — s to applaud; en venir aux — s to come to blows
main-d'œuvre *f.* manual labor, manpower
main-forte *f.* help, assistance
mainmise *f.* legal seizure
mainmorte *f.* mortmain, perpetual possession
maint *a.* many, undetermined number; —es fois on many occasions, often
maintenant *adv.* now, at present
maintenir *vt.* to maintain, support
maintien *m.* maintenance, support
maire *m.* mayor; — sse *f.* mayor's wife
mairie *f.* town hall
mais *conj.* but
mais *m.* corn
maison *f.* house, home
maisonnée *f.* household, houseful
maisonnette *f.* small house
maître *m.* master, teacher; lawyer's title; — d'hôtel head waiter
maître-autel *m.* high altar
maîtresse *f.* mistress
maîtrise *f.* mastery; lectureship; choir school; choir boys; master's degree
maîtriser *vt.* to master, control
majesté *f.* majesty
majestueusement *adv.* majestically
majestueux *a.* majestic
majeur *a.* major; of age; *f.* force — e absolute necessity; — *m.* middle finger; — e *f.* major premise
major *m.* (mil.) executive officer of a regiment; medical officer
majoration *f.* increase in price
majordome *m.* majordomo, butler
majorer *vt.* to increase the price
majoritaire *a.* majority, of the majority
majorité *f.* majority
Majorque *f.* Majorca
majuscule *f.* capital letter
mal *m.* (*pl.* maux) evil, harm, wrong; pain, ailment; — de tête, — à la tête headache; — de mer seasickness; — du pays homesickness; — *adv.* ill, badly; pas — de (coll.) many, a great deal of
malade *a.* sick, ill
maladie *f.* sickness, illness
maladif *a.* sickly
maladresse *f.* awkwardness, clumsiness
maladroit *a.* awkward
malaga *m.* Malaga wine
malaire *a.* (anat.) of the cheek
Malais *m.* & *a.* Malay
malaise *m.* uneasiness; indisposition

malaisé *a.* difficult
Malaisie *f.* Malaya
malandrin *m.* vagabond
malappris *a.* ill-bred
malavisé *a.* ill-advised
malaxer *vt.* to mix, knead
malaxeur *m.* mixer; concrete mixer
malbâti *a.* ill-formed; ill-shaped
malchance *f.* bad luck, mishap
malchanceux *a.* unlucky
maldonne *f.* misdeal (at cards)
mâle *a.* male, manly; — *m.* male
malédiction *f.* curse
maléfice *m.* witchcraft
maléfique *a.* harmful, malignant
malemort *f.* violent death, tragic death
malencontre *f.* mishap
malencontreux *a.* unfortunate, unlucky
malendurant *a.* impatient
mal-en-point *adv.* in a bad way, badly off
malentendu *m.* misunderstanding
malfaçon *f.* defect
malfaire *vi.* to do evil
malfaisance *f.* evil-doing
malfaisant *a.* harmful; evil-minded
malfaiteur *m.* malefactor, evildoer, criminal
malfamé *a.* ill-famed, infamous, notorious
malgache *a.* from Madagascar
malgracieux *a.* ungraceful
malgré *prep.* in spite of, notwithstanding; — que *conj.* in spite of the fact that
malhabile *a.* awkward
malheur *m.* misfortune; ill luck, bad luck
malheureusement *adv.* unfortunately
malheureux *a.* unhappy, unfortunate, unlucky
malhonnête *a.* dishonest; rude; indecent
malhonnêteté *f.* dishonesty; rudeness
malicieusement *adv.* maliciously
malicieux *a.* malicious
malignité *f.* malignity
malin (maligne) *a.* malicious, malignant; shrewd, sharp; — *m.* devil
malingre *a.* sickly
malintentionné *a.* ill-disposed, evil-intentioned
mal-jugé *m.* miscarriage of justice
malle *f.* trunk; faire une — to pack a trunk
malléabilité *f.* malleability
malléable *a.* malleable
malle-poste *f.* mail coach
mallette *f.* small trunk
malmener *vt.* to mistreat, abuse
malodorant *a.* malodorous, foul-smelling
malotru *m.* uncouth individual
malpropre *a.* slovenly; dirty; improper
malpropreté *f.* dirtiness; impropriety; dishonesty
malsain *a.* unhealthy, unwholesome
malséance *f.* unseemliness; inopportuneness
malséant *a.* unbecoming, unseemly
maisonnant *a.* clashing; unseemly
malt *m.* malt
maltais *a.* & *m.* Maltese
Malte *f.* Malta
malthusianisme *m.* theory of birth control

maltose m. maltose

maltraiter vt. to mistreat

malveillamment adv. malevolently

malveillance f. ill will, malevolence

malveillant a. malevolent

malvenu a. uncalled for, unwarranted

malversation f. embezzlement of public funds

maman f. mama, mother

mamelle f. breast; udder

mamelon m. nipple; hillock

mammaire a. mammary

mammouth m. mammoth

manager m. trainer, athlete's manager

manant m. peasant; uncouth individual

manche f. sleeve; hose; air shaft: channel; (avi.) wind sock — m. handle; — à balai broomstick; (avi.) control stick

Manche, La f. English Channel

manchette f. cuff; marginal note; headline

manchon m. muff; casing, sleeve; mantle of gas light

manchot a. one-armed, one-handed — m. penguin

mandarine f. mandarin orange; tangerine

mandat m. mandate; warrant; power of attorney; proxy; order; — poste postal money order; — lettre money order with space for message

mandataire m. & f. representative, agent, proxy

Mandchourie f. Manchuria

mandement m. mandamus; bishop's charge

mander vt. to send for; send word

mandibule f. mandible

mandoline f. mandolin

manège m. horsemanship; riding school; mill, treadmill; merry-go-round, carousel; intrigue

mânes m. pl. manes, dead souls (Roman history)

manette f. handle, lever

manganèse m. manganese

mangeable a. eatable

mangeoire f. manger, crib

mangeotter vt. to pick at one's food

manger vt. & vi. to eat, eat up; — m. food

mange-tout m. bean, pea with which pods are eaten

mangeur m. eater; wastrel

mangouste f. mongoose

mangue f. mango

manguier m. mango tree

maniabilité f. maneuverability; suppleness

maniable a. tractable, pliable; supple; maneuverable

maniaque m. & f. maniac; — a. maniacal

manie f. mania; passion

maniement m. handling; maneuvering

manier vt. to handle; feel; manage; work, use, drive, activate

manière f. manner, way; de — que so that; de — à so as to

maniéré a. affected

maniérisme m. mannerism, affectedness

manieur m. handler, manager

manifestant m. demonstrator

manifestation f. manifestation

manifeste m. manifesto; — a. obvious, evident, manifest

manifester vt. to manifest, show; — vi. to make a demonstration

manifold m. notebook; sales book

manigance f. intrigue, plot, trick

manigancer vt. to plot, scheme, be up to something

Manille f. Manila

manille f. link; manilla (card game); — m. cigar originating in Manila; hat of manilla straw

manioc m. manioc, source of tapioca

manipulateur m. manipulator

manipule m. (eccl.) maniple

manipuler vt. to manipulate; wield

manivelle f. handle, crank; winch

manne f. manna; two-handled basket

mannequin m. model, mannequin; fashion model; — de couturière dressmaker's dummy

manœuvrabilité f. maneuverability

manœuvrable a. maneuverable

manœuvre f. working, handling (boat); maneuver; (mil.) drill, maneuvers; — m. common laborer

manœuvrer vt. to maneuver, work; — vt. to maneuver

manœuvrier m. tactician; able seaman

manoir m. manor

manomètre m. pressure gauge

manqué a. which has failed, who has failed; inadequate; defective; short of the mark

manquement m. failing; infraction

manquer vt. to miss, fail; — vi. want, lack; — à quelqu'un to be missed by someone

mansarde f. mansard roof; attic; dormer

mansardé a. with dormers, dormered

mansuétude f. mildness, gentleness, indulgence

mante f. mantle; mantis

manteau m. coat, overcoat, cloak; mantle

mantelet m. short coat

mantille f. mantilla

manucure f. manicurist

manuel a. manual, hand; — m. manual

manuellement adv. manually, by hand

manufacture f. factory; manufacture

manufacturer vt. to manufacture

manufacturier a. manufacturing; — m. factory owner

manumission f. manumission, freeing of slaves

manutention f. maintenance; handling; manipulation; administration; (mil.) bakery

manutentionner vt. to handle, manipulate

mappemonde f. world map (global projection)

maquereau m. mackerel; pimp

maquette f. sketch, design; model; d'après la — de designed by

maquignon m. horse dealer; (fig.) go-between

maquignonner vt. to deal underhandedly

maquillage m. make-up

maquiller vt. to put on make-up

maquilleur m. make-up man

maquis *m.* underbrush, scrub; (pol.) underground unit *or* movement

maquisard *m.* member of the underground

maraicher *m.* truck farmer; — *a.* of truck farming

marais *m.* marsh, bog, swamp; truck-garden land; — salants saltern, salt bed

marasme *m.* apathy; atrophy

marasque *f.* maraschino cherry

marasquin *m.* maraschino liqueur

marâtre *f.* stepmother; cruel mother

maraud *a.* rascal

maraude *f.* marauding; petty thievery from gardens; taxi en — cruising taxi

marauder *vi.* to maraud; prowl

maraudeur *m.* marauder

marbre *m.* marble

marbré *a.* marbled, veined

marbrer *vt.* to marble, vein

marbrière *f.* marble quarry

marc *m.* marc, residue; dregs (from wine making); — de café coffee grounds; eau-de-vie de — brandy made from marc

marcassin *m.* young boar

marchand *m.* merchant, shopkeeper, dealer

marchander *vt. & vi.* to bargain, haggle

marchandise *f.* merchandise

marche *f.* step; march; functioning, running (machine); (mus.) march (fig.) progress se mettre en — to start out; — arrière reverse motion

marché *m.* market, market place; bargain; deal; shopping, marketing; bon — cheapness: — noir black market bon — *a.* cheap, inexpensive, low-cost

marchepied *m.* stepladder; running board; step of a carriage; (fig.) stepping stone

marcher *vi.* to march, walk; move, function

marcheur *m.* walker

mardi *m.* Tuesday; — gras Shrove Tuesday

mare *f.* stagnant pond

marécage *m.* marsh, swamp

marécageux *a.* swampy

maréchal *m.* (mil.) marshal; — des logis master sergeant (cavalry, artillery)

maréchale *f.* marshal's wife

maréchal-ferrant *m.* blacksmith

maréchaussée *f.* constabulary, state police

marée *f.* tide; salt-water fish

marelle *f.* hopscotch

marémoteur *a.* tide-powered

mareyeur *m.* wholesale fishmonger

marge *f.* page margin; edge, rim; leeway

margelle *f.* stone rim around a well

marger *vt.* to feed into a press

Margot (*f.*) Marjorie

marguerite *f.* daisy

Marguerite (*f.*) Margaret

marguillier *m.* churchwarden, deacon

mari *m.* husband

mariable *a.* marriageable

mariage *m.* marriage, wedding

marial *a.* pertaining to the Virgin Mary

Marie (*f.*) Mary

marié *a.* married; — *m.* bridegroom; — e *f.*

bride; nouveaux — s *m. pl.* newlyweds

marier *vt.* to marry off; wed, unite; match; se — (avec) to get married (to), marry

marin *a.* marine, nautical; — *m.* sailor, seaman

marine *f.* navy

mariner *vt.* to marinate, pickle

marinier *a.* marine; — *m.* sailor, bargeman

marinière *f.* middy, blouse

marionnette *f.* marionette, puppet

maritime *a.* maritime; gare — *f.* boatside railway terminal

maritorne *f.* (coll.) slut, wench

marivaudage *m.* banter, witty patter

marjolaine *f.* marjoram

mark *m.* German mark

marmaille *f.* (coll.) brood of children

marmelade *f.* marmelade, preserves

marmite *f.* pot, pan; — norvégienne fireless cooker; petite — vegetable soup

marmitée *f.* potful

marmiton *m.* kitchen boy, apprentice cook

marmonner *vi.* to mutter, mumble

marmoréen *a.* marble, marblelike

marmot *m.* lad; youngster

marmotte *f.* marmot; babushka; sample case

marmottement *m.* mumbling

marne *f.* marl; chalk and clay mixture used as fertilizer

Maroc *m.* Morocco

marocain *a.* Moroccan

maroquinerie *f.* leather goods

maroquinier *m.* dealer in Morocco leather goods

marotte *f.* whim, hobby; fool's sceptre; dummy head

maroufle *m.* rascal

marquage *m.* marking process

marque *f.* mark; trademark, brand; score; — déposée registered trademark

marquer *vt.* to mark, stamp, brand

marqueter *vt.* to splatter; inlay

marqueterie *f.* marquetry, inlay work

marquisat *m.* marquisate, marquis' lands

marquise *f.* marchioness; marquee

marquoir *m.* sampler; marker

marraine *f.* godmother; sponsor

marri *a.* sorry, grieved

marron *m.* chestnut; — *a.* maroon, brown; — *a. & m.* runaway, fugitive

marronnier *m.* chestnut tree

mars *m.* March

marseillais *a. & m.* of Marseilles, from Marseilles

Marseillaise *f.* Marseillaise, French national anthem

marsouin *m.* porpoise

marteau *m.* hammer; — pneumatique air-pressure hammer

marteau-pilon *m.* pile driver

martelage *m.* hammering operation

martèlement *m.* hammering, result of hammering

marteler *vt.* to hammer, pound; (fig.) to torment

martien *a.* martian

martinet *m.* trip hammer; cat-o'-nine-tails, lash; swift

martingale *f.* martingale; jouer à la — to play double or nothing

martin-pêcheur *m.* kingfisher

martre *f.* marten

martyr *m.*, martyre *f.* martyr

martyre *m.* martyrdom

martyriser *vt.* to martyr, martyrize

marxisme *m.* Marxism

marxiste *m. & f.* Marxist

maryland *m.* Maryland tobacco

mas *m.* farmhouse, country house (southern France)

mascarade *f.* masquerade

mascotte *f.* charm, mascot

masculin *a.* masculine, male

masculinité *f.* masculinity

masochisme *m.* masochism

masochiste *m. & f.* masochist

masque *m.* mask; masked person

masquer *vt.* to mask, conceal

massacrant *a.* disagreeable

massacrer *vt.* to massacre

massage *m.* massage

masse *f.* mass, lump; sledge hammer; mace; group; fund; en — in a body, all at once

massepain *m.* marzipan

masser *vt.* to mass; massage

massette *f.* bullrush; sledge hammer

massier *m.* mace-bearer; seargeant-at-arms

massif *a.* massive, massy; solid; argent — *m.* solid (sterling) silver

massivement *adv.* massively

massivité *f.* massiveness

massue *f.* club

mastic *m.* putty

mastiquer *vt.* to masticate; putty

mastoc *m.* heavy metal

mastodonte *m.* mastodon

mastoïdien *a.* mastoid

mastoïdite *m.* mastoid infection

masure *f.* hut; house in ruins

mat *a.* unpolished, dull; — *m.* mate (chess); être — to be in check

mât *m.* (naut.) mast

matador *m.* matador

matamore *m.* braggart

match *m.* match, game

matelas *m.* mattress

matelasser *vt.* to pad, stuff

matelassure *f.* stuffing

matelot *m.* seaman, sailor

matelote *f.* fish stew using red wine

mater *vt.* to check (chess); (fig.) to check, overcome

matérialisation *f.* materialization, realisation

matérialiser *vt.* to materialize

matérialisme *m.* materialism

matérialiste *m.* materialist; — *a.* materialistic

matérialité *f.* materiality, reality

matériaux *m. pl.* materials

matériel *a.* material, corporeal; — *m.* materials; apparatus; equipment

matériellement *adv.* materially

maternel *a.* maternal; école —le *f.* kindergarten

maternellement *adv.* maternally

maternité *f.* maternity; lying-in hospital

mathématicien *m.* mathematician

mathématique *a.* mathematical; —s *f. pl.* mathematics

matière *f.* matter, materials, body, subject

matin *m.* morning; — *adv.* early

mâtin *m.* mastiff

matinal *a.* morning, early

mâtiné *a.* crossbred

matinée *f.* morning, forenoon; morning's occupation; afternoon performance; morning dress; faire la grasse — to sleep late

mâtiner *vt.* to crossbreed (dogs)

matines *f. pl.* Matins

matineux *a.* early-rising

matinière *a. f.* morning; étoile — morning star

matité *f.* dullness

matois *a.* sharp, cunning, foxy

matoiserie *f.* cunning

matou *m.* tomcat

matraque *f.* bludgeon

matraquer *vt.* to club, bludgeon

matriarcal *a.* matriarchal

matrice *f.* matrix; womb

matricide *m. & f.* matricide

matricule *f.* matriculation; — *m.* (auto.) license number; serial number

matriculer *vt.* to register, matriculate

matrimonial *a.* matrimonial

matrone *f.* matron

mâture *f.* (naut.) masts

maturité *f.* maturity, ripeness

matutinal *a.* morning, of the morning

maudire *vt.* to curse

maudit *a.* cursed; very bad

maugréer *vi.* to fume, be angered, grumble

Maure *m. & f.* Moor; — *a.* Moorish

mauresque *a.* Moorish

mausolée *m.* mausoleum

maussade *a.* sulky, sullen

maussaderie *f.* sullenness

mauvais *a.* bad, ill, evil; il fait — (temps) the weather is bad

mauve *f.* mallow; — *f. & a.* mauve

mauviette *f.* lark

maxillaire *a.* maxillary

maxima *a. & f.* maximum

maximal *a.* maximal

maxime *f.* maxim

maximum *m. & a.* maximum

Mayence *f.* Mains

mazout *m.* oil residue

me *pron.* me, to me

méandre *m.* meander; winding

mécanicien *m.* mechanic, machinist; (rail.) engineer

mécanique *f.* mechanics; — *a.* mechanical

mécaniquement *adv.* mechanically

mécanisation *f.* mechanization

mécaniser *vt.* to mechanize

mécanisme *m.* mechanism

mécène *m.* patron

méchamment *adv.* wickedly, maliciously

méchanceté *f.* wickedness, malice

méchant *a.* wicked, bad; poor, sad, worthless

mèche f. wick; fuse; bit, drill; cloth filter; plot; — de cheveux lock of hair

mécompte m. miscalculation, mistake

méconnaissable a. unrecognizable

méconnaissance f. lack of appreciation, lack of recognition, lack of awareness

méconnaître vt. not to know; disown; ignore

méconnu a. unappreciated, unrecognized

mécontent a. dissatisfied

mécontentement m. discontent

mécontenter vt. to discontent

Mecque f. Mecca

mécréant m. miscreant

médaille f. medal

médaillé a. decorated; — m. decorated soldier, decorated individual

médailler vt. to decorate

médaillier m. medal cabinet; medal collection

médaillon m. medallion

médecin m. physician, doctor

médecine f. medicine

médial a. median, middle

médian a. median; —e f. median

médianoche m. midnight supper; midnight supper following a meatless day

médiateur m. mediator

médiation f. mediation

médical a. medical

médicament m. medicine

médicamenter vt. to dose, administer medicine

médicamenteux a. medicinal

médicastre m. quack doctor, charlatan

médication f. medication

médicinal a. medicinal

médiéval a. medieval

médiévisme m. Medieval studies

médiéviste m. & f. medievalist

médiocre a. mediocre, moderate; indifferent

médiocrité f. mediocrity

médire vi. to slander

médisance f. slander, scandal

méditatif a. meditative

méditation f. meditation

méditer vt. & vi. to meditate

Méditerranée, Mer — f. Mediterranean Sea

méditerranéen a. Mediterranean

médium m. medium, spiritualist; (mus.) middle voice

médius m. middle finger

médoc m. Medoc (a Bordeaux wine)

médullaire a. medullar

médulle f. medulla

méduse f. jellyfish

meeting m. political meeting, sports meet

méfaire vi. to do wrong

méfait m. misdeed

méfiance f. mistrust, distrust

méfiant a. distrustful, suspicious

méfier v., se — (de) to mistrust, distrust

mégacycle m. megacycle

mégalithique a. megalithic

mégalomanie f. megalomania

mégaphone m. megaphone

mégarde f. inadvertency; par — inadvertently

mégère f. shrew, vixen

mégisserie f. leather dressing

mégissier m. leather dresser

mégot m. cigarette butt; cigar stump

méhari m. camel

méhariste m. camel-mounted soldier

meilleur a. better; le — best

méjuger vi. to misjudge, be mistaken

mélancolie f. melancholy

mélancolique a. melancholy

mélanésien a. & m. Melanesian

mélange m. mixture; —s pl. miscellany

mélanger vt. to mix

mélangeur m. mixer

mélasse f. molasses

mêlée f. conflict; scuffle

mêler vt. to mix, mingle; se — to mingle, blend; se — de to meddle in; pay attention to

méli-mélo m. (coll.) combination, jumble

mélinite f. melinite

mélisse f. balm

mellifiue a. mellifluous

mélodie f. melody

mélodieusement adv. melodiously

mélodieux a. melodious

mélodique a. melodic

mélodiste m. & f. melodist, composer of melodies

mélodramatique a. melodramatic

mélodrame m. melodrama

mélomane m. music lover

melon m. melon; — d'eau watermelon; chapeau — m. derby

melonnière f. melon patch

membrane f. membrane

membre m. member; limb

membru a. long-legged, long-armed; with large arms and legs

même pron. same, self, itself; — adv. same, like; very; even, also; de — in the same way; tout de — all the same; de — que as well as; à — de in a position to

mémento m. notebook, memorandum book; résumé, compendium; memento

mémoire f. memory, remembrance; — m. memorandum; memorial; bill, statement; report, monograph, dissertation; —s pl. proceedings, reports; memoirs

mémorable a. memorable

mémorandum m. memorandum, notebook

mémoratif a. memorative

mémorial m. report; memorabilia

mémorialiste m. author of memoirs

mémorisation f. memorization, memorizing

menacer vt. to menace, threaten

ménage m. household; housekeeping; married couple; family; femme de — f. cleaning woman/maid

ménagement m. care, prudence

ménager vt. to spare; handle, treat with tact; humor; arrange

ménager a. household; sparing, prudent; arts — s m. pl. home economics

ménagère f. housekeeper

ménagerie f. menagerie

mendiant m. beggar; — a. begging, mendicant

mendicité f. begging; beggars (collectively)

mendier *vt. & vi.* to beg

meneau *m.* (arch.) mullion

menée *f.* plot, intrigue

mener *vt.* to lead, conduct, govern; steer; manage (an enterprise); treat

ménestrel *m.* minstrel

ménétrier *m.* country fiddler

meneur *m.* leader; head, chief

méningite *f.* meningitis

ménopause *m.* menopause

menotter *vt.* to handcuff

menottes *f. pl.* handcuffs

mensonge *m.* lie, falsehood

mensonger *a.* lying, deceitful

menstruation *f.* menstruation

mensualité *f.* monthly payment

mensuel *a.* monthly

mensuellement *adv.* monthly, by the month

mensurabilité *f.* mensurability

mensurer *vt.* to measure

mental *a.* mental

mentalement *adv.* mentally

mentalité *f.* mentality; state of mind

menterie *f.* lie, lying

menteur *m.* liar; — *a.* deceitful, false

menthe *f.* mint

menthol *m.* menthol

mentholé *a.* mentholated

mentionner *vt.* to mention

mentir *vi.* to lie

menton *m.* chin

mentonnet *m.* catch of a lock

mentonnière *f.* chin strap

mentor *m.* mentor, guide

menu *m.* menu; table d'hote, fixed menu; — *a.* small, thin; — peuple *m.* lowest class; —s plaisirs *m. pl.* pocket money, mad money (U.S. coll.); — *adv.* fine, in small pieces

menuet *m.* minuet

menuiser *vi.* to do woodworking

menuiserie *f.* woodwork; carpentry

menuisier *m.* carpenter, cabinet maker

méplat *a.* thicker on one side

méprendre *v.*, se — to be mistaken

mépris *m.* contempt, scorn, disdain

méprisable *a.* despicable, contemptible

méprise *f.* mistake

mépriser *vt.* to despise, scorn, slight

mer *f.* sea; pleine —, haute — high seas; basse — low tide; d'outre — oversea; mal de — *m.* seasickness

mercanti *m.* dishonest businessman

mercantile *a.* mercantile, commercial

mercenaire *m. & a.* mercenary

mercerie *f.* notions, knick-knacks

merceriser *vt.* to mercerize

merci *m.* thanks; — *f.* mercy; —! thank you; no thank you; — bien! thank you very much!

mercier *m.* notions salesman

mercredi *m.* Wednesday; — des Cendres Ash Wednesday

mercure *m.* mercury

mercuriale *f.* grain market prices; reprimand, rebuke

mercuriel *a.* mercurial

mercurique *a.* mercuric

merde *f.* excrement

mère *f.* mother

méridien *a. & n.* meridian

méridional *a.* southern

mérinos *m.* merino sheep; merino wool

merisier *m.* wild cherry tree

méritant *a.* worthy, meritorious

mérite *m.* merit

mériter *vt.* to merit, deserve; — *vi.* to be deserving

méritoire *a.* meritorious

merlan *m.* whiting

merle *m.* blackbird

merlin *m.* cleaver; club

merluche *f.* dried cod

Mérovingien *m. & a.* Merovingian

merrain *m.* stave; clapboard

merveille *f.* marvel; à — wonderfully

merveilleusement *adv.* marvelously, wonderfully

merveilleux *a.* marvellous; wonderful

més *a. pl.* my

mésalliance *f.* misalliance

mésallier *v.*, se — to marry beneath one's station

mésange *f.* titmouse, tomtit

mésaventure *f.* misadventure

mesdames *f. pl.* ladies, women

mesdemoiselles *f. pl.* young ladies; misses

mésentente *f.* misunderstanding

mésestime *f.* poor opinion of someone, lack of consideration, scorn

mésestimer *vt.* to underrate, scorn

mésintelligence *f.* incompatibility, lack of understanding

mésinterpréter *vt.* to misinterpret

mesmérisme *m.* mesmerism

mésopotamien *a. & m.* Mesopotamian

mesquin *a.* stingy, shabby, low, mean

mesquinerie *f.* stinginess, meanness

messager *m.* messenger

messagerie *f.* steamship line; transport line; parcel delivery service

messe *f.* (eccl.) Mass

messianique *a.* Messianic

Messie *m.* Messiah

messieurs *m. pl.* gentlemen, sirs

messin *a.* of Metz, from Metz

mesurable *a.* measurable

mesurage *m.* measuring

mesure *f.* measure, proportion; restraint; mean(s); à — que *conj.* in proportion as; sur — made to order

mesuré *a.* measured, cautious

mesurer *vt.* to measure, consider, calculate; se — avec — to compete with; compare oneself with

métabolisme *m.* metabolism

métairie *f.* farm of a sharecropper

métal *m.* metal

métallifère *a.* metal-bearing

métallique *a.* metallic

métalliser *vt.* to plate, metallize

métallurgie *f.* metallurgy

métallurgique *a.* metallurgical

métallurgiste *m.* metallurgist

métamorphique *a.* metamorphic

métamorphisme *m.* metamorphism

métamorphose *f.* metamorphosis

métamorphoser *vt.* to transform, metamorphose

métaphore f. metaphor
métaphorique a. metaphorical
métaphysicien m. metaphysician
métaphysique f. metaphysics
métapsychique f. psychic research
métastase f. metastasis
métatarse m. metatarsus
métatarsien a. metatarsal
métathèse f. metathesis
métayage m. tenant farming, sharecropping
métayer m. tenant farmer, sharecropper
méteil m. mixture of wheat and rye
métempsycose f. metempsychosis, transmigration of souls
météore m. meteor
météorique a. meteoric
météoriser vt. to distend
météorisme m. gas, flatulence
météorite f. meteorite
météorologie f. meteorology
météorologique a. meteorological
météorologiste, météorologue m. meteorologist
métèque m. foreigner
méthane m. methane
méthode f. method, system
méthodique a. methodical
méthodisme m. methodism
méthodiste m. Methodist
méthodologie f. methodology
méthyle m. methyl
méthylène m. methylene; (com.) methyl or wood alcohol
méthylique a. methyl
méticuleusement adv. meticulously
méticuleux a. meticulous
méticulosité f. meticulousness
métier m. trade, profession; loom
métis a. & m. half-breed, half-caste
métissage m. crossbreeding
métisser vt. to cross, crossbreed
métrage m. measuring by the meter
mètre m. meter; yardstick
métrer vt. to measure out by the meter
métreur m. surveyor; measurer
métrique a. metrical; metric; tonne — metric ton (1000 kg.); — f. metrics, versification
Métro m. Paris subway
métromanie f. mania for writing verse
métronome m. metronome
métropole f. metropolis; continental France
métropolitain a. metropolitan; chemin de fer — m. Paris subway
métropolite m. (eccl.) metropolitan
mets m. dish; cooked or prepared food
mettable a. wearable
metteur m. one who places; — en pages (print.) make-up man; — en scène (theat.) director
mettre vt. to put, place; put on; suppose; se — à to begin to
meuble m. piece of furniture; -s pl. furniture
meubler vt. to furnish; stock
meuglement m. bellow
meugler vi. to bellow
meule f. millstone; haystack; round,

wheel of cheese
meulière f. flint
meunier m. miller
meunière f. miller's wife; à la — sautéed in butter
meurtre m. murder
meurtrier m. murderer; — a. murderous, dangerous
meurtrière f. gun slit
meurtrir vt. to bruise
meurtrissure f. bruise
meute f. pack, band
mévendre vt. to sell at a loss
mévente f. sale at a loss
Mexicain m. & a. Mexican
Mexico m. Mexico City
Mexique m. Mexico
mi m. (mus.) mi; — a. half, mid
miasme m. miasma, evil odor
miaulement m. mew, meow
miauler vi. to mew, meow
miche f. round loaf of bread
Michel (m.) Michael
micheline f. (rail.) diesel car or train
mi-chemin, à — adv. halfway, at the halfway point
mi-clos a. half-closed
micro m. microphone
microbiologie f. microbiology
microcosme m. microcosm
microfilm m. microfilm
microfilmer vt. to microfilm
micrographie f. micrography
micromètre m. micrometer
micron m. micron, 1-millionth meter
micro-organisme m. micro-organism
microphone m. microphone
microphotographie f. microphotography
microphysique f. microphysics
microscope m. microscope
microscopique a. microscopic
microsillon m. record microgroove; long-playing record
midi m. noon; south
midinette f. seamstress, shop girl
mie f. inside part of bread; pain de — m. sandwich bread, American-style bread; ma — (coll.) my dear, my darling; — adv. not at all
miel m. honey
mielleux a. honeyed, honey-like
mien pron., le —, la —ne mine
miette f. bread crumb, bit
mieux adv. better, rather; le — best; de — en — better and better; aimer — prefer
mièvre a. affected; roguish
mièvrerie f. affectedness; roguishness
mignard a. nice, delicate, sweet
mignarder vt. to indulge, coddle; be over-nice to
mignardise f. delicacy, daintiness
mignon a. delicate, cute, nice, slight; — m. favorite
mignonnerie f. niceness; cuteness; delicateness
migraine f. headache
migraineux a. migraine
migrateur a. migrating

migratoire *a.* migratory

mijaurée *f.* finicky woman; faire la — to be finicky

mijoter *vi.* to simmer

mil *a.* thousand; — *m.* millet

milady *f.* lady, wife of a lord; my lady (salutation)

milan *m.* kite (bird)

milanais *a.* of Milan, from Milan

milice *f.* militia

milicien *m.* militiaman

milieu *m.* middle; environment; area; au — de in the middle of; au beau — in the very middle

militaire *m.* soldier; — *a.* military

militariser *vt.* to militarize

militarisme *m.* militarism

militariste *m. & f.* militarist

militer *vi.* to militate, work, fight

mille *m.* mile; — *a.* thousand

mille-feuille *f.* napoleon (pastry); milfoil

millénaire *m.* 1000 years; 1000th anniversary; — *a.* 1000-year-old

millésime *m.* date

milliaire *a.,* pierre — *f.* milestone

milliard *m.* billion

milliardaire *m. & f. & a.* billionaire

millibar *m.* millibar

millième *m. & a.* thousandth

millier *m.* about a thousand; -s *pl.* thousands

milligramme *m.* milligram

millimètre *m.* millimeter

millionnaire *m. & f. & a.* millionaire

milord *m.* lord; my lord (salutation)

mime *m.* mime, pantomime

mimer *vt. & vi.* to mime, mimic

mimi *m.* kitty, pussycat (baby talk); darling

mimique *a.* mimetic; — *f.* mimicry; pantomime

mimodrame *m.* pantomime play

mimosa *m.* acacia

minable *a.* pitiful, shabby

minaret *m.* minaret

minauder *vi.* to mince, be or act affected, smirk

minauderie *f.* mincing manner; affectedness

minaudier *a.* mincing

mince *a.* thin, slender

minceur *f.* thinness, slenderness, scantiness

mine *f.* look, appearance; mine, excavation; mina (Greek coin); pencil lead; (mil.) mine; avoir bonne (mauvaise) — to look well (bad)

miner *vt.* to mine; wear away, undermine

mineral *m.* ore

minéral *a. & m.* mineral

minéralisation *f.* mineralization

minéraliser *vt.* to mineralize

minéralogie *f.* mineralogy

minéralogique *a.* mineralogical

minéralogiste *m.* mineralogist

minestrone *m.* minestrone soup

minet *m.,* minette *f.* (coll.) kitty, pussy

mineur *m.* minor; miner; — e *f.* minor premise

miniature *f.* miniature

miniaturer *vt.* to paint in miniature

minier *a.* mining

minimal *a.* minimal

minime *a.* insignificant, trifling

minimiser *vt.* to minimize

minimum *m.* minimum

ministère *m.* ministry, office; cabinet

ministériel *a.* of the ministry, of the cabinet, pro-government

ministre *m.* minister, secretary (government)

minium *m.* red lead

minoritaire *a.* minority, belonging to the minority

minorité *f.* minority

Minorque *f.* Minorca

minoterie *f.* flour milling

minotier *m.* miller

minuit *m.* midnight

minuscule *a.* tiny; — *f.* lower-case letter

minute *f.* minute, moment; rough draft; original copy

minuter *vt.* to take minutes; limit

minuterie *f.* (elec.) time-switch (which stays on for only a short time)

minutie *f.* minutia; minuteness

minutieusement *adv.* minutely

minutieux *a.* minute; detailed

mioche *m. & f.* (coll.) brat; young child

mi-parti *a.* half

mi-partition *f.* dividing in half

mirabelle *f.* small yellow plum; mirabelle liqueur

miracle *m.* miracle

miraculeusement *adv.* miraculously

miraculeux *a.* miraculous

mirador *m.* watchtower

mirage *m.* mirage

mire *f.* gun sight; aim

mirer *vt. & vi.* to aim at; se — to look at oneself

mirliton *m.* reed flute; vers de — doggerel

mirmillon *m.* gladiator

miroir *m.* mirror, looking glass

miroitant *a.* reflecting, sparkling

miroitement *m.* mirroring, reflection, sparkling

miroiter *vi.* to shine, glisten

miroitier *m.* dealer in mirrors

miroton *m.* onion stew

misaine *f.* (naut.) foremast

misanthrope *m. & f.* misanthrope

misanthropie *f.* misanthropy

miscellanées *f. pl.* miscellanea, miscellany

miscible *a.* miscible, which can be mixed

mise *f.* putting, placing; dress, clothing, appearance; game stake; investment; bid; — en plis finger wave; — en scène (theat.) direction

miser *vt.* to bet; bid

misérable *a.* miserable; wretched; wicked; poverty-stricken

misérablement *adv.* miserably, wretchedly

misère *f.* misery, poverty

miséreux *m.* pauper

miséricorde *f.* mercy, pardon

miséricordieux *a.* merciful

misogyne *m.* mysogynist

missel *m.* missal

missionnaire *m.* missionary
missive *f.* missive, letter
mistral *m.* cold north wind of Provence
mitaine *f.* mitten, mitt
mite *f.* clothes moth
mité *a.* moth-eaten
miteux *a.* pitiful
mitigation *f.* mitigation
mitiger *vt.* to mitigate, soften
mitonner *vi.* to simmer; — *vt.* to coddle
mitoyen *a.* intermediate, joint, dividing (line)
mitraille *f.* (mil.) grapeshot, canister shot
mitrailler *vt.* to machine gun
mitraillette *f.* tommy gun
mitrailleur *m.* machine gunner
mitrailleuse *f.* machine gun
mitre *m.* miter
mitré *a.* mitered
mitron *m.* baker's boy
mi-voix, à — *adv.* in a low voice
mixte *a.* mixed; école — *f.* coeducational school
mixtion *f.* mixture
mixtionner *vt.* to mix
mnémonique *a.* mnemonic
mnémotechnie *f.* memory training
mobile *m.* spring; motive; — *a.* movable; quick
mobilier *m.* furniture
mobilisation *f.* mobilization, mobilizing
mobiliser *vt.* to mobilize
mobilité *f.* mobility
mocassin *m.* moccasin
moche *f.* skein, hank
modal *a.* (gram.) modal
modalité *f.* modality
mode *m.* (gram.) mood; mode; — *f.* fashion, custom, way; -s *pl.* millinery; à la — in fashion; à la — de . . . in the . . . fashion
modelage *m.* modelling
modèle *m.* model
modeler *vt.* to model
modeleur *m.* modeller
modéliste *m. & f.* model designer
modérantisme *m.* (pol.) moderation in political matters
modérantiste *m. & f.* (pol.) moderate
modérateur *m.* moderator; governor
modération *f.* moderation
modéré *a.* moderate
modérer *vt.* to moderate, regulate, reduce
moderne *a.* modern
modernisation *f.* modernization
moderniser *vt.* to modernize
modernisme *m.*, modernité *f.* modernity
moderniste *m. & f.* modernist
modeste *a.* modest
modestement *adv.* modestly
modestie *f.* modesty
modicité *f.* smallness, lowness
modifiable *a.* modifiable
modification *f.* modification
modifier *vt.* to modify
modique *a.* moderate, small in importance, low in price
modiste *f.* milliner, modiste
module *m.* modulus; module; diameter of coins; thickness of bells

moduler *vt. & vi.* to modulate
moelle *f.* marrow; pith
moelleux *a.* pithy; soft, mellow
moellon *m.* small stone used in walls
mœurs *f. pl.* manners, morals, customs, mores
mofette *f.* poison gas
mogol *m.* mogul
moi *pron.* I, me; — *m.* self, ego
moignon *m.* stump, stub
moindre *a.* less, lesser; le — least, slightest
moine *m.* monk, friar; warming pan
moineau *m.* sparrow
moins *adv.* less; minus; au —, pour le —, du — at least; à — que *conj.* unless; — le — least; à — at a lower price; *prep.* minus, less
moins-perçu *m.* underpayment
moins-value *f.* depreciation, loss of value
moire *f.* watered silk, moire
moirer *vt.* to water silk
mois *m.* month; monthly salary, monthly payment
moïse *m.* cradle, baby basket
Moïse (*m.*) Moses
moise *f.* tie beam, brace
moisi *a.* moldy, musty; — *m.* mustiness
moisir *vt. & vi.* to mildew
moisissure *f.* mold, mildew
moisson *f.* harvest
moissonnage *m.* reaping, harvesting
moissonner *vt.* to reap, harvest
moissonneur *m.*, moissonneuse *f.* reaper; (person)
moissonneuse *f.* reaper, harvester (machine)
moite *a.* moist, clammy
moiteur *f.* moistness
moitié *f. & a.* half; à — prix *adv.* half-price
moitir *vt.* to moisten
moka *m.* mocha coffee; mocha cake
mol *a.* soft
molaire *a. & n.* molar
môle *m.* mole, pier
moléculaire *a.* molecular
molécule *f.* molecule
moleskine *f.* leatherette
molestation *f.* molesting, molestation
molester *vt.* to molest
molette *f.* roller; serrated roller; rowel; trimming tool; edging tool; clé à — *f.* adjustable wrench
mollesse *a.* apathetic, flabby
mollesse *f.* softness; flabbiness
mollet *m.* calf of the leg; — *a.* soft; œuf — *m.* soft-boiled egg
molletière *f.* legging
molleton *m.* flannel
mollification *f.* mollification, mollifying
mollir *vt. & vi.* to soften, grow soft; give way, slacken
mollusque *m.* mollusk
molosse *m.* mastiff, watchdog
molybdène *m.* molybdenum
momentané *a.* momentary
momentanément *adv.* momentarily
momie *f.* mummy
momification *f.* mummification
momifier *vt.* to mummify

mon a. m. my
monacal a. monkish
monarchie f. monarchy
monarchique a. monarchical
monarchisme m. monarchism
monarchiste m. & f. & a. monarchist
monarque m. monarch
monastère m. monastery; convent
monastique a. monastic
monceau m. heap, pile
mondain a. worldly; mundane; society; — m. society person
mondanité f. mundaneness, mundanity, worldliness; —s pl. social events (newspaper)
monde m. world; society; people; tout le — everybody
monder vt. to clean; husk
mondial a. worldwide
monégasque a. from Monaco
monétaire a. monetary
Mongol m. & a. Mongol; purée –e f. tomato and pea soup
Mongolie f. Mongolia
mongolien a. (med.) Mongolian
Mongoloïde a. Mongoloid
moniteur m. monitor
monnaie f. money, coin; mint; change; — légale legal tender
monnayage m. coinage, minting
monnayer vt. to coin, mint
monnayeur m. coiner, minter
monobloc a. in one piece
monochrome a. monochromatic
monoculture f. one-crop farming
monodie f. (mus.) unaccompanied solo singing
monogame a. monogamous
monogamie f. monogamy
monogramme m. monogram
monographie f. monograph
monologue m. monologue
monologuer vi. to talk to oneself; soliloquize
monomane, monomaniaque m. & f. monomaniac
monomanie f. monomania
monôme m. student parade, demonstration, snake dance; (math.) monomial
monophasé a. (elec.) single-phase
monoplace a. in one place; voiture — f. one-seater
monoplan m. monoplane
monopole m. monopoly
monopolisation f. monopolization
monopoliser vt. to monopolize
monosyllabe m. monosyllable
monosyllabique a. monosyllabic
monothéisme m. monotheism
monothéiste m. & f. monotheist; — a. monotheistic
monotone a. monotonous
monotonie f. monotony
monotype f. (print.) typesetting machine
monovalent a. univalent
monseigneur m. highness; monsignor; lock pick
monsieur m. sir, gentleman; Mister, Mr.
monstre m. monster
monstrueux a. monstrous

monstruosité f. monstruousness; monstrosity
mont m. mount, mountain
montage m. carrying up; layout; (elec.) wiring; editing (movie film)
montagnard m. mountaineer
montagne f. mountain
Montagnes Rocheuses f. pl. Rocky Mountains
montagneux a. mountainous
montant m. amount, sum; goal post; upright; side piece of a ladder; odor, taste; — a. rising, uphill; high-cut (dress)
mont-de-piété m. municipal pawn shop
monte-charge m. freight elevator
montée f. rise, ascent
monte-plats m. dumb waiter
monter vt. & vi. to go up, climb, rise; carry up, take up; mount, sit on a horse; to set up; arouse, excite
monteur m. mounter
montgolfière f. hot-air balloon
monticule m. hillock
montmorency f. variety of sour cherry
montoir m. stepping-stone for mounting a horse
montrable a. showable
montre f. watch; display, shop window
montre-bracelet m. wristwatch
montrer vt. to show, exhibit
montreur m. displayer; showman
montueux a. hilly
monture f. mount; setting; frame
monument m. monument; curiosity, sight; visiter les —s to sightsee
moquer v.; se — de to mock, laugh at; not to care
moquerie f. mockery, derision
moquette f. velvet carpet, carpeting
moqueur a. mocking; — m. mocker
moral a. moral, ethical; — m. state of mind; morale
morale f. morals, ethics; morale
moralement adv. morally
moralisateur a. moralizing
moraliser vi. & vt. to moralize; lecture
moraliste m. & f. moralist
moralité f. morality, morals; moral; morality play
morasse f. (print.) final proof
moratoire m. moratorium
morave a. & n. Moravian
morbide a. morbid
morbidesse f. morbidezza; suppleness, delicacy of skin (fine arts)
morbidité f. morbidness
morceau m. bit, piece
morceler vt. to break, divide into pieces
morcellement m. fragmentation, breaking-up
mordacité f. bitterness; corrosiveness
mordancer vt. to size, varnish
mordant a. biting; corrosive; — m. sizing, varnish; bitterness
mordicus adv. stoutly, tenaciously
mordiller vt. to nibble
mordorer vt. to give a russet color to
mordre vt. to bite, corrode; — vi. to engage, take hold
morfondre vt. to chill, freeze, benumb

morganatique *a.* morganatic
morgue *f.* haughtiness; morgue
moribond *a.* moribund
moricaud *a.* black, dark-skinned
morigéner *vt.* to reprimand
morille *f.* morel (edible mushroom)
morne *a.* gloomy, dull, dejected
morosité *f.* moroseness
morphine *f.* morphine
morphinomane *m. & f.* morphine addict
morphologie *f.* morphology
morphologique *a.* morphological
mors *m.* curb, bit
morse *m.* walrus
morsure *f.* bite
mort *f.* death; — *a. & m.* dead, deceased; dummy (at cards)
mortadelle *f.* large Italian sausage
mortaise *f.* dovetail
mortaiser *vt.* to dovetail
mortalité *f.* mortality; death rate
mort-aux-rats *f.* rat poison
mort-bois *m.* deadwood
mortel *a.* mortal, fatal
mortellement *adv.* mortally
morte-saison *f.* off-season
mortier *m.* mortar
mortifère *a.* death-dealing
mortifiant *a.* mortifying
mortification *f.* mortification
mortifier *vt.* to mortify
mort-né *a.* stillborn
mortuaire *a.* mortuary
morue *f.* codfish
morve *f.* nasal discharge; glanders
morveux *a.* one with a clogged or running nose; sick with glanders; — *m.* brat
mosaïque *f.* mosaic
mosaïquer *vt.* to decorate with mosaic tile
Moscou *m.* Moscow
Moscovite *m. & f. & a.* Muscovite
mosquée *f.* mosque
mot *m.* word; bon — witticism; en un — *a.* briefly
moteur *m.* motor, engine; moving force; (fig.) instigator; — *a.* motivating, moving, driving
motif *m.* motive, reason, motif, theme
motion *f.* parliamentary motion
motivation *f.* motivation
motiver *vt.* to motivate, justify
motoculture *f.* mechanized farming
motocycle *m.* motorbike
moto(cyclette) *f.* motorcycle
motocycliste *m. & f.* motorcyclist
motorisation *f.* motorization
motoriser *vt.* to motorize
mots-croisiste *m. & f.* crossword-puzzle fan
motte *f.* clod; mound; butter pat
motus! *interj.* quiet!
mou, (mol, molle) *a.* soft, mellow; weak; (fig.) effeminate; limp; muggy; — *m.* edible animal lungs
mouche *f.* fly; speck, stain; bull's-eye; beauty spot; vandyke beard; secret policeman; — à miel bee
moucher *vt.* to wipe the nose; se — to blow one's nose
moucheron *m.* fly

moucheter *vt.* to spot; polka dot
mouchette *f.* candle snuffer
moucheture *f.* spot; polka dot
mouchoir *m.* handkerchief
mouchure *f.* nasal mucus
moudre *vt.* to grind, mill
moue *f.* pout; faire la — to pout
mouette *f.* sea gull
mouffette *f.* skunk
moufle *f.* mitten; block and tackle; — *m.* kiln, furnace
mouflon *m.* wild sheep, moufflon
mouillage *m.* wetting; watering, adulterration with water; (naut.) anchor, anchorage
mouiller *vt.* to wet, soak; water, adulterate; (naut.) heave (anchor); lay (mine)
mouilleur *m.* moistener; — de mines minelayer
mouillure *f.* wetting; water spot; wet spot
moulage *m.* molding, casting; grinding
moule *m.* mold, cast; — *f.* mussel
moulé *a.* well-molded, well-made; tight-fitting; — *m.* printed letter, printing
mouler *vt.* to mold, cast
mouleur *m.* molder, caster
moulin *m.* mill; — à vent windmill; — à café coffee grinder
moulinet *m.* wheel; paddle wheel; reel; turnstile; winch
moulu *a.* ground, powdered
moulure *f.* molding
mourant *a.* dying; fading
mourir *vi.* to die; se — to be dying
mousquet *m.* musket
mousquetaire *m.* musketeer
mousqueton *m.* carbine
mousse *f.* (bot.) moss; foam, lather; whipped dessert; — *m.* cabin boy; — *a.* dull, calm
mousseline *f.* muslin; pommes — mashed potatoes
mousser *vi.* to foam, lather, whip; sparkle
mousseux *a.* mossy; foamy; — *m.* sparkling wine
moussoir *m.* beater, whipper, eggbeater
mousson *f.* monsoon
moussu *a.* mossy
moustache *f.* mustache
moustiquaire *f.* mosquito net
moustique *m.* mosquito
moût *m.* grape juice, unfermented fruit juice
moutarde *f.* mustard
moutardier *m.* mustard pot; mustard maker
mouton *m.* sheep; mutton; sheepskin; pile driver, rammer, —s *pl.* (naut.) white-caps
moutonné *a.* fleecy; frizzy
moutonner *vt.* to curl; — *vi.* to form white-caps
moutonneux *a.* fleecy; (naut.) white-capped
moutonnier *a.* sheeplike
mouture *f.* grinding, milling; mixture of wheat, rye, barley
mouvant *a.* moving; shifting; sable — *m.* quicksand

mouvement *m.* motion, movement

mouvementé *a.* agitated, animated; hilly, undulating

mouvoir *vt.* to move, propel

moyen *m.* means, way; au — de by means of; — *a.* middle, intermediate; average, mean; le — Âge Middle Ages

moyenâgeux *a.* medieval

moyennant *prep.* on condition that, in return for; by means of

moyenne *f.* average

moyennement *adv.* to an average degree

moyeu *m.* hub

muable *a.* mutable, changeable

mucilagineux *a.* mucilaginous

mucosité *f.* mucosity, mucus

mue *f.* moulting, moulting time; adolescent change of voice

muer *vi.* to moult; have an adolescent change of voice

muet *a.* mute, dumb, speechless; — *m.* mute

mufle *m.* snout; (fig.) cad, coarse individual

muflerie *f.* coarseness

muge *m.* mullet

mugir *vi.* to bellow, low (cattle); roar; howl (wind)

mugissant *a.* roaring

mugissement *m.* roaring, bellowing; of cattle; howling of wind

muguet *m.* lily of the valley

muid *m.* hogshead

mulâtre *a. & n.* mulatto

mule *f.* mule; backless slipper

mulet *m.* mule; mullet

muletier *m.* mule driver

mulot *m.* field mouse

mulsion *f.* milking

multicolore *a.* multicolored

multiforme *a.* multiform, many-formed

multimillionnaire *m. & f.* multimillionaire

multiplicande *m.* multiplicand

multiplicateur *m.* multiplier

multiplication *f.* multiplication

multiplicité *f.* multiplicity

multiplier *vt.* to multiply

multitude *f.* multitude

municipalité *f.* municipality

munificence *f.* munificence

munificent *a.* munificent

munir *vt.* to provide, furnish; se — de to procure, provide oneself with

munitionnaire *m.* commissary

munitions *f. pl.* munitions, stores, supplies

muqueuse *f.* mucous membrane

muqueux *a.* mucous

mur *m.* wall

mûr *a.* ripe, mature

murage *m.* walling, walling up

muraille *f.* outer wall

mural *a.* mural, wall

mûre *f.* blackberry

murène *f.* marine eel

murer *vt.* to wall in, wall up, block up

muret *m.*, murette *f.* small wall

muriatique *a.* muriatic

mûrier *m.* blackberry bush; mulberry tree

mûrir *vt. & vi.* to ripen, mature

murmurant *a.* murmuring

murmure *m.* murmur

murmurer *vi.* to murmur; grumble

musaraigne *f.* shrew mouse

musard *a.* dawdling; — *m.* dawdler

musarder *vt.* to dawdle

musc *m.* musk

muscade *f.* nutmeg; fleur de — *f.* mace

muscadier *m.* nutmeg tree

muscat *m.* muscatel wine, muscatel grape

muscle *m.* muscle

musclé *a.* muscled

muscler *vt.* to develop the muscles of

musculaire *a.* muscular

musculature *f.* musculature

musculeux *m.* muscular, brawny

muse *f.* muse

museau *m.* animal snout, muzzle

musée *m.* museum

museler *vt.* to muzzle

muselière *f.* muzzle

muser *vi.* to loiter, dawdle

musette *f.* bagpipe; bag, musette bag; bal — dance, small dance, country dance, dance to accordion

muséum *m.* museum, natural history museum

music-hall *m.* vaudeville theater

musicien *m.* musician

musique *f.* music; band

musqué *a.* musk-scented; rat — *m.* muskrat

Musulman *m. & a.* Moslem

mutabilité *f.* mutability

mutable *a.* mutable

mutation *f.* mutation

muter *vt.* to transfer; transform

mutilateur *m.* mutilator

mutilation *f.* mutilation

mutiler *vt.* to mutilate

mutin *a.* disobedient, unruly; mutinous

mutiner *v., se* — to mutiny; be disobedient

mutinerie *f.* mutiny

mutisme *m.* muteness

mutualité *f.* mutualness; mutuality; mutual-aid society

mutuel *a.* mutual

mutuellement *adv.* mutually

myope *a.* nearsighted

myopie *f.* myopia; near-sightedness

myosotis *m.* forget-me-not

myriade *f.* myriad

myriapode *m.* myriapod, millipede

myrrhe *f.* myrrh

myrte *m.* myrtle

myrtille *f.* blueberry

mystère *m.* mystery; mystery play

mystérieusement *adv.* mysteriously

mystérieux *a.* mysterious

mysticisme *m.* mysticism

mystificateur *a.* mystifying; — *m.* mystifier

mystification *f.* mystification, hoax

mystifier *vt.* to mystify, hoax

mystique *a. & n.* mystic

mythe *m.* myth

mythique *a.* mythical

mythologie *f.* mythology

mythologique *a.* mythological

N

nabab m. nabob

nabot m. small person

nacelle f. small boat; (avi.) cockpit

nacre f. mother-of-pearl

nacré a. pearl-colored, pearly

nævus m. birthmark

nage f. swimming; rowing; à la — by swimming; être tout en — to be soaking with perspiration

nageoire f. fin of a fish

nager vi. to swim, float; row

naguère adv. a short time ago

naïade f. naiad, water nymph

naïf a. artless, ingenuous, innocent, inexperienced

nain m. & a. dwarf

naissance f. birth, origin, beginning; acte de — m. birth certificate

naissant a. dawning; incipient

naitre vi. to be born; arise, come about

naïvement adv. naively

naïveté f. artlessness, ingenuousness

naja m. cobra

nanan m. goodies (baby talk); delight; something exquisite

nantir vt. to give as security, pledge; provide

nantissement m. pledge, security

naphte m. naphtha

napoléon m. gold 20-franc piece

napoléonien a. Napoleonic

napolitain a. & m. Neapolitan

nappe f. tablecloth, cloth, cover; sheet

napper vt. to cover with a cloth

napperon m. tea-table cloth; petit — doily

narcisse m. narcissus

narcose f. narcosis

narcotique a. & m. narcotic

narguer vt. to harrass; flout; jeer at

narguilé m. Turkish water pipe

narine f. nostril

narquois a. sly, cunning; mocking

narrateur m. narrator

narratif a. narrative

narration f. narration, narrative

narrer vt. to narrate, tell of

narthex m. narthex, vestibule

nasal a. nasal; -e f. nasal consonant

nasaliser vt. to nasalize

nasarde f. blow on the nose; affront

naseau m. animal nostril

nasillard a. nasal

nasiller vi. to speak through the nose

nasonnement m. nasal voice, nasal speech

nasse f. fish trap

natal a. native; jour — m. birthday; pays — m. native country

natalité f. birth rate

natation f. swimming

natatoire a. pertaining to swimming

natif a. native; natural

national a. national

nationaliser vt. to nationalize

nationaliste m. & f. nationalist; — a. nationalistic

nationalité f. nationality

nativement adv. natively, by nature

nativité f. nativity; (eccl.) celebration of saints' birthdays

Nativité f. feast of Christmas

natte f. mat; braid

natter vt. to weave, braid

naturalisation f. naturalization

naturaliser vt. to naturalize

naturaliste m. naturalist; naturalist author; — a. naturalistic

nature f. nature; character; kind; d'après — from nature, from life; contre — unnatural; — morte still life; — a. plain; boiled; café — m. black coffee

naturel m. nature, disposition; — a. natural; illegitimate; au — ungarnished, plain

naturellement adv. naturally

naufrage m. shipwreck

naufrager vi. to be wrecked, sink

nauséabond a. nauseating

nausée f. nausea

nauséeux a. nauseous

nautique a. nautical, aquatic

navarin m. mutton stew with turnips and potatoes

navet m. turnip

navette f. shuttle; faire la — to shuttle back and forth

navigabilité f. navigability

navigable a. navigable

navigateur m. navigator

navigation f. navigation

naviguer vi. & vt. to navigate, sail

navire m. ship, vessel

navrant a. heartrending

navrer vt. to grieve, break the heart of

ne adv. no, not; — . . . . pas not

né a. born

néanmoins conj. nevertheless, still, yet

néant m. nothingness, nothing

nébuleux a. nebulous, cloudy

nébulosité f. nebulousness, nebulosity

nécessaire a. necessary; — m. necessities of life; kit, set

nécessairement adv. necessarily

nécessité f. necessity

nécessiter vt. to necessitate

nécessiteux a. needy

nécrologie f. necrology, obituary

nécromancie f. necromancy

nécromancien m. necromancer

nécrose f. necrosis

nectar m. nectar

néerlandais a. Dutch

nef f. nave of a church

néfaste a. ill-fated, fatal, harmful

négatif a. negative; — m. (phot.) negative

négative f. negative side (debating)

négation f. negation

négativement adv. negatively

négligé a. neglected, careless, informal

négligeable a. negligeable

négligemment adv. negligently, indifferently

négligence f. negligence

négligent a. negligent; indifferent

négliger vt. to neglect

négoce m. negotiation

négociable a. negotiable

négociant m. merchant, dealer, trader

négociateur m. negotiator

négociation f. nogotiation

négocier vt. & vi. to negotiate; trade; deal

nègre, négresse n. & a. Negro; ghost writer; petit — m. pidgin French

négrier m. slave ship; slave dealer

négroïde a. negroid

neige f. snow; battre en — to beat stiff

neiger vt. to snow

neigeux a. snowy

ne-m'oubliez-pas m. forget-me-not

nénuphar m. water lily

Néo-caledonien m. & a. New Caledonian

néolithique a. neolithic

néon m. neon

neophyte m. & f. neophyte

Néo-zélandais m. New Zealander; — a. of New Zealand

néphrite f. nephritis

néo-platonicien a. neo-Platonic; — m. neo-Platonist

néo-platonisme m. neo-Platonism

népotisme m. nepotism

neptunien a. Neptunian

néréide f. Nereid

nerf m. nerve; sinew, (coll.) tendon; leaf vein

nerveusement adv. nervously

nerveux a. nervous, high-strung; sinewy, vigorous

nervosité f. nervousness

nervure f. leaf rib; nervure, cording of a book binding

net a. clean; clear, clear-cut; net; — adv. flatly, outright; s'arrêter — to stop dead; — m., mettre au — to put in final form

nettement adv. cleanly; clearly; flatly

netteté f. cleanness, clearness; neatness

nettoiement, nettoyage m. cleaning, cleansing; nettoyage au sec dry-cleaning

nettoyer vt. to clean, cleanse, scour

nettoyeur m. cleaner

neuf a. nine; new, fresh

neurasthénie f. neurasthenia

neurasthénique a. neurasthenic

neurologie f. neurology

neurologue, neurologiste m. neurologist

neurone m. neuron

neutralisation f. neutralization

neutraliser vt. to neutralize

neutraliste m. & f. neutralist

neutralité f. neutrality

neutre a. neuter; neutral

neutron m. neutron

neuvaine f. novena

neuvième a. ninth

neveu m. nephew

névralgie f. neuralgia

névrite f. neuritis

névropathie f. nervous disorders

névrose f. neurosis

névrosé a. neurotic

nez m. nose; cape of land; prow; — à — face to face; piquer du — to nose-dive

ni conj. neither, nor

niable a. deniable

niais a. silly; foolish

niaiserie f. silliness

niche f. prank, trick; niche; — à chien doghouse

nichée f. nestful

nicher vi. to nestle

nickel m. nickel

nickelage m. nickel-plating

nickeler vt. to nickel-plate

nicotine f. nicotine

nid m. nest

nidifier vi. to make a nest

nièce f. niece

nielle m. enamel inlay; cereal blight; cockleweed

nier vt. to deny

nigaud a. simple; — m. simpleton, idiot

nigauderie f. stupidity

nihilisme m. nihilism

nihiliste m. & f. nihilist; — a. nihilistic

Nil m. Nile

nimbe f. halo, nimbus

nimber vt. to halo

nimbus m. numbus cloud

nippes f. pl. things, old clothes, possessions

nippon a. Nipponese

nique f. gesture of scorn; faire la — à to make fun of, scorn

nirvanâ m. nirvana

nitouche f. apparently or falsely innocent person

nitrate m. nitrate

nitre m. saltpeter, niter

nitreux a. nitrous

nitrique a. nitric

nitrite m. nitrite

nitroglycérine f. nitroglycerin

niveau m. level; — de vie standard of living; passage à — m. level crossing

nivelage m. leveling

niveler vt. to level

nivellement m. leveling

nobiliaire a. of the nobility

noble a. & m. & f. noble

noblesse f. nobility

noce, noces f. wedding; faire la — (coll.) to be living it up, living riotously

nocif a. harmful

nocivité f. noxiousness, harmfulness

noctambule m. & f. sleepwalker; person active at night

nocturne a. nocturnal

nocuité f. noxiousness

nodal a. nodal

nodosité f. node; knot

nodule m. nodule

Noé (m.) Noah

Noël m. Christmas; veille de — f. Christmas Eve

nœud m. knot

noir a. black, dark

noirâtre a. blackish

noiraud a. black-haired, dark

noirceur f. blackness, darkness

noircir vt. & vi. to blacken, darken

noircissement m. blackening

noircissure f. black spot

noire f. (mus.) quarter note

noise f. quarrel

noisetier m. hazelnut tree

noisette f. hazelnut

noix *f.* nut, walnut; — de veau veal shoulder

noliser *vt.* to charter, rent

nom *m.* name; surname; (gram.) noun; au — de in the name of; petit — given name; nickname; — et prénoms full name

nomade *a.* nomadic, wandering; — *m. & f.* nomad

nombrable *a.* countable

nombre *m.* number

nombrer *vt.* to number, count

nombreux *a.* numerous, many

nombril *m.* navel

nomenclature *f.* nomenclature, list

nominal *a.* nominal

nominalement *adv.* nominally

nominatif *m. & a.* nominative

nomination *f.* nomination

nommer *vt.* to name; se — to be called

non *adv.* no, not

nonagénaire *m. & f.* nonagenarian

non-agression *f.* nonaggression

nonante *a.* ninety (in Belgium and Switzerland)

nonce *m.* nuncio, papal legate

nonchalamment *adv.* nonchalantly

nonchalance *f.* nonchalance

nonchalant *a.* negligent, unconcerned

non-combattant *a. & m.* noncombattant

non-conformisme *m.* non-conformity, non-conformism

non-conformiste *a. & n.* nonconformist

non-être *m.* (phil.) non-existence

non-intervention *f.* non-intervention

non-lieu *m.* no grounds for prosecution

nonne *f.* nun; pet de — *m.* apple turnover

nonnette *f.* round gingerbread

nonobstant *prep. & adv.* notwithstanding

non-paiement *m.* nonpayment

nonpareil *a.* peerless, without equal

non-réussite *f.* failure

non-sens *m.* nonsense

non-syndiqué *a.* nonunion

non-violence *f.* nonviolence

nord *m.* north

nord-africain *a.* North African

nord-américain *a.* North American

nord-est *m.* northeast

nordique *a.* Nordic

nord-ouest *m.* northwest

normal *a.* normal; école —e *f.* teachers' college

normalement *adv.* normally

normalien *m.* normal school student

normalisation *f.* normalization

normand *a.* Norman

Normandie *f.* Normandy

norme *f.* norm, standard

Norvège *f.* Norway

norvégien *a. & m.* Norwegian

nos *a. pl.* our

nostalgie *f.* homesickness; nostalgia

notabilité *f.* notability; notable

notable *a. & m. & f.* notable

notaire *m.* notary

notamment *adv.* especially

notarié *a.* notarized

notation *f.* notation

note *f.* note, memorandum; mark, grade; bill, invoice

noter *vt.* to note, mark; signify

notice *f.* account, review

notification *f.* notification

notifier *vt.* to notify

notion *f.* notion, acquaintance, slight knowledge

notoire *a.* notorious, well-known

notoriété *f.* notoriety

notre *a.* our

nôtre *pron.*, le (la) — ours

notule *f.* gloss, short note

nouer *vt.* to tie, knot; stiffen; se — to kink, twist; knit

noueux *a.* knotty, gnarled

nouilles *f. pl.* noodles

nourrice *f.* wet nurse

nourricier *a.* nutritive; père — *m.* foster father

nourrir *vt. & vi.* to nourish; nurse; feed; bring up; foster

nourrissant *a.* nourishing

nourrisseur *m.* cattle feeder

nourrisson *m.* infant at the breast

nourriture *f.* nourishment, food

nous *pron. pl.* we, us, to us

nouveau (nouvel, nouvelle) *a.* new, recent; novel, different; de — again, anew

nouveau-né *a. & m.* new-born child

nouveauté *f.* novelty, newness; something new

nouvelle *f.* news; short story

Nouvelle-Écosse *f.* Nova Scotia

nouvellement *adv.* lately, recently

nouvelliste *m.* short-story writer

novateur *m.* innovator

novembre *m.* November

novice *m. & f.* novice

noviciat *m.* noviciate

noyade *f.* drowning

noyau *m.* pit, core, stone; nucleus; (pol.) cell, unit

noyautage *m.* forming of political units

noyauter *vt.* to form political cells

noyer *vt.* to drown; inundate; — *m.* walnut tree

nu *a.* naked, bare, nude; mettre à — to expose; — *m.* nude; nudity

nuage *m.* cloud; — artificiel smoke screen

nuageux *a.* cloudy

nuance *f.* shade, tinge; suggestion

nuancer *vt.* to shade, blend, vary

nubile *a.* nubile, marriageable

nucléaire *a.* nuclear

nucléé *a.* having a nucleus

nucléon *m.* nucleon

nudisme *m.* nudism

nudiste *m. & f.* nudist

nudité *f.* nudity

nue *f.* cloud

nuée *f.* cloud; (fig.) swarm

nuer *vt.* to shade colors in embroidery

nuire *vi.* to injure, harm, wrong, prejudice

nuisible *a.* detrimental, injurious

nuit *f.* night; darkness; (fig.) — blanche sleepless night

nuitamment *adv.* by night, at night

nul *a.* null, void; no, not one; match —, partie —le *f.* tie game, draw

nullement *adv.* not at all, by no means

nullifier *vt.* to nullify

nullité *f.* nullity, nothing, negative quantity

nûment *adv.* openly, frankly

numéraire *m.* coin, coined money, cash

numéral *a.* numeral

numérateur *m.* numerator

numération *f.* numbering

numérique *a.* numerical

numéro *m.* number; issue of a periodical

numérotage *m.* numbering

numéroter *vt.* to number; (print.) page

numéroteur *m.* numbering stamp

numismate *m.* numismatist, coin collector

nuptualité *f.* marriage rate

nuque *f.* nape of the neck

nurse *f.* child's nurse

nutritif *a.* nutritive

nutrition *f.* nutrition

nymphe *f.* nymph

nymphéa *m.* water lily

O

oasis *m.* oasis

obéir(à) *vi.* to obey, comply

obéissance *f.* obedience; compliance

obéissant *a.* obedient

obélisque *m.* obelisk

obérer *vt.* to burden with debt

obèse *a.* obese

obésité *f.* obesity

obi *f.* Japanese sash

obit *m.* memorial service

obituaire *a. & m.* obituary

objecter *vt.* to object

objecteur *m.* objector; — de conscience conscientious objector

objectif *a.* objective; — *m.* lens; objective

objection *f.* objection

objectivement *adv.* objectively

objectiver *vt.* to make objective

objectivité *f.* objectivity

objet *m.* object; subject; (gram.) complement

objurgation *f.* objurgation

oblat *m.* oblate

oblataire *m. & f.* bondholder

obligation *f.* obligation; bond

obligatoire *a.* obligatory, compulsory

obligé *a.* obliged, compelled

obligeamment *adv.* obligingly

obligeance *f.* kindness

obligeant *a.* kind, obliging

obliger *vt.* to oblige, compel; bind

oblique *a.* oblique, slanting

obliquer *vi.* to strike at an angle; go off at an angle, swerve

oblitération *f.* obliteration; cancellation

oblitérer *vt.* to obliterate; cancel (stamp); obstruct

obole *f.* obole, bit; (fig.) penny, red cent

obscène *a.* obscene, smutty

obscénité *f.* obscenity

obscur *a.* obscure; abstruse; of humble birth

obscurcir *vt.* to obscure, darken; s'— to become dark, cloud over

obscurcissement *m.* obscuring, darkening

obscurément *adv.* obscurely, dimly

obscurité *f.* obscurity, darkness

obséder *vt.* to obsess

obsèques *f.* funeral, obsequies

obséquieusement *adv.* obsequiously

obséquieux *a.* obsequious

obséquiosité *f.* obsequiousness

observable *a.* observable

observance *f.* observance

observateur *m.* observer

observation *f.* observation

observatoire *m.* observatory; observation post

observer *vt.* to observe; s'— to be careful, watch one's step

obsession *f.* obsession

obsolète *a.* obsolete

obstacle *m.* obstacle

obstétrical *a.* obstetric(al)

obstétrique *f.* obstetrics

obstination *f.* obstinacy

obstiné *a.* obstinate

obstinément *adv.* obstinately

obstiner *v.*, s'— (à) to persist in

obstruction *f.* obstruction

obstructionnisme *m.* obstructionism

obstructionniste *m. & a.* obstructionist

obstruer *vt.* to obstruct

obtempérer *vi.* to obey, yield

obtenir *vt.* to obtain

obtention *f.* attainment, obtaining

obturateur *m.* (phot.) shutter

obturer *vt.* to close, stop

obtus *a.* obtuse

obus *m.* (mil.) shell

obusier *m.* howitzer

obvier *vi.*, — à to obviate

oc *m.,* langue d'— southern-French dialect, old Provençal

ocarina *m.* ocarina

occasion *f.* occasion, opportunity; bargain; d'— secondhand

occasionnel *a.* occasional; chance

occasionner *vt.* to occasion, cause, bring about, result in

occident *m.* Occident

occidental *a.* Western, Occidental

occipital *a.* occipital

occis *a.* killed

occlure *vt.* to occlude

occlusif *a.* occlusive

occlusion *f.* occlusion

occulte *a.* occult

occupant *m.* occupant; — *a.* occupying

occupé *a.* busy, occupied

occuper *vt.* to occupy; busy; s'— to keep busy; be interested in

occurrence *f.* occurrence; chance happening

océan *m.* ocean

océanide *f.* sea nymph

Océanie *f.* Oceania

océanien *a.* of Oceania, from Oceania

océanique *a.* oceanic

océanographie *f.* oceanography

ocelot *m.* ocelot

ocre *f.* ochre

ocré *a.* ochre-colored

octaèdre *m.* octahedron

octante *a.* eighty (in Belgium and Switzerland)

octave *f.* (mus., poet.) octave; week following a festival

Octave (*m.*) Octavius

octobre *m.* October

octogénaire *a.* octogenarian

octogonal *a.* octagonal

octogone *a.* octagonal; — *m.* octagon

octroi *m.* grant, granting; city tariff; city customs

octroyer *vt.* to grant, accord

oculaire *a.* ocular; — *m.* eye piece of microscope; témoin — *m.* eyewitness

oculiste *m. & f.* oculist, ophthalmologist

odalisque *f.* odalisk

ode *f.* ode

odelette *f.* short ode

ōdeur *f.* odor, smell, scent

odieux *a.* odious, hateful; heinous; — *m.* odiousness, hatefulness

odomètre *m.* odometer, mileage meter

odontalgie *f.* toothache

odorant *a.* odorous, fragrant

odorat *m.* sense of smell

odorer *vt.* to smell

odoriférant *a.* sweet-smelling

odyssée *f.* odyssey

œdème *m.* edema

œdipe *m.* œdipus

œil *m.* (*pl.* yeux) eye; sight; à vue d'— visibly; coup d'— *m.* glance, look

œil-de-boeuf *m.* (arch.) bull's-eye window; oxeye daisy

œillade *f.* ogling, ogle, glance

œillère *f.* eyecup; horse blinder

œillet *m.* carnation; eyelet

œsophage *m.* esophagus

œuf *m.* egg: — à la coque soft-boiled egg; — brouillé scrambled egg; — sur le plat fried egg

œuvre *m. & f.* work, working; literary production

œuvrer *vi.* to produce, turn out

offensant *a.* offensive

offense *f.* offense

offenser *vt.* to offend; s'— de to take offense at

offenseur *m.* offender

offensif *a.* offensive

offensivement *adv.* offensively

offertoire *m.* offertory

office *m.* office, function; church service; d'— officially; — *f.* pantry

officiant *m.* officiating priest

officiel *a.* official

officiellement *adv.* officially

officier *m.* officer; — *vt.* to officiate; — *vi.* to say a divine service

officieusement *adv.* officiously

officieux *a.* officious

offrande *f.* offering; (eccl.) offertory

offrant *adj. & m.*, au plus — to the highest bidder

offre *f.* offer

offrir *vt.* to offer

offset *m.* offset printing

offusquer *vt.* to cloud; dazzle; offend

ogival *a.* (arch.) Gothic

ogive *f.* Gothic arch; warhead

ogre *m.* ogre

ohé! *interj.* hey!

ohm *m.* ohm

oie *f.* goose

oignon *m.* onion; bunion

oïl *adv.*, langue d'— *f.* Northern French

oindre *vt.* to anoint; (eccl.) to consecrate sacramental oil

oint *a.* anointed; consecrated; — *m.* something that has been consecrated

oiseau *m.* bird; à vol d'— *a.* in a straight line, as the crow flies; vue à vol d'— *f.* bird's eye view

oiseau-mouche *m.* hummingbird

oiseleur *m.* bird trapper

oiselier *m.* bird seller

oisellerie *f.* bird store; bird farm

oiseux *a.* idle, useless

oisif *a.* lazy; idle, unemployed

oisillon *m.* little bird

oisiveté *f.* idleness

oison *m.* gosling

oléagineux *a.* oleaginous, oily

oléandre *m.* oleander

olfactif *a.* olfactory

oligarchie *f.* oligarchy

oligophrénie *f.* mental retardation

olivacé *a.* olive-colored

olivaie *f.* olive orchard

olivâtre *a.* olive-colored, greenish

olive *f.* olive

olivette *f.* olive orchard

olivier *m.* olive tree

Olivier Oliver

Olympe *m.* Olympus; — *f.* Olympia

olympiade *f.* Olympiad

olympique *a.* Olympic

ombilic *m.* navel

ombilical *a.* umbilical

omble *m.* fresh-water salmon

ombrage *m.* shade; umbrage, suspicion

ombrager *vt.* to shade

ombrageux *a.* skittish; umbrageous, suspicious

ombre *f.* shadow; shade; darkness; ghost; sienna

ombrelle *f.* parasol

ombrer *vt.* to shade

ombreux *a.* shaded, shadowed

omelette *f.* omelet

omettre *vt.* to omit; neglect

omission *f.* omission, oversight

omnibus *a.*, train — *m.* local train

omnipotence *f.* omnipotence

omniprésence *f.* omnipresence

omniprésent *a.* omnipresent

omniscience *f.* omniscience

omniscient *a.* omniscient

omnivore *a.* omnivorous

omoplate *f.* shoulder blade

on *pron.* one, we, they, people

onagre *m.* wild ass

onanisme *m.* onanism

once *f.* ounce

oncle *m.* uncle

onction *f.* unction, annointing

onctueusement *adv.* unctuously

onctueux *a.* unctuous; oily

onctuosité *f.* unctuousness

onde f. wave

ondé a. waved, wavy, with wavy lines

ondée f. shower, passing storm

ondoiement m. undulation; baptism

ondoyer vi. to undulate, billow

ondulant a. undulant, undulating

ondulation f. wave; undulation; — permanente permanent wave

ondulatoire a. undulating

onduler vt. & vi. to wave the hair; undulate

onéreux a. onerous, burdensome

ongle m. nail; claw; coup d'— m. scratch

onglé a. nailed

onglée f. numbness, frostbite of the fingers

onglet m. tab; boîte à -s miter box

onglier m. manicure set; -s pl. nail scissors

onguent m. ointment

ongulé a. having hoofs, nails

oniromancie f. dream interpretation

ontologie f. ontology

O.N.U. f. United Nations

onyx m. onyx

onze a. eleven

onzième a. eleventh

opacifier vt. to make opaque

opacité f. opaqueness

opale f. opal

opalescence f. opalescence

opalescent a. opalescent

opalin a. opaline

opaque a. opaque

opéra m. opera, grand opera; opera house

opéra-comique opera with alternate songs and spoken dialogue

opérable a. operable

opérateur m. operator

opération f. operation

opérationnel a. operational

opercule m. cover, lid

opérer vt. to operate, effect, perform; s'— to take place; se faire — to undergo an operation

opérette f. operetta, musical comedy

ophtalmie f. ophthalmy

ophtalmologue, ophtalmologiste m. ophthalmologist

opiacé a. containing opium

opiner vi. to be of the opinion; — de la tête to nod approval

opiniâtre a. obstinate, stubborn

opiniâtrer v., s'— to be obstinate

opinion f. opinion

opiomane m. & f. opium addict

opium m. opium

opossum m. opossum

oppidum m. fortified city

opportun a. opportune

opportunément adv. opportunely

opportunisme m. opportunism

opportuniste m. & f. opportunist

opportunité f. opportuneness

opposable a. opposable

opposant a. opposing; — m. opponent

opposé a. opposing, opposite; — m. opposite

opposer vt. to oppose; s'— to be against

opposite m. opposite

opposition f. opposition

oppresser vt. to oppress; weigh on

oppresseur m. oppressor

oppressif a. oppressive

oppression f. oppression

opprimer vt. to oppress

opprobre m. shame, disgrace

opter vi. to choose, make a choice

opticien m. optician

optimisme m. optimism

optimiste m. & f. optimist; — a. optimistic

optimum a. & m. optimum

option f. option

optique a. optical; — f. optics

optométrie f. optometry

opulence f. opulence

opulent a. opulent

opuscule m. short work; pamphlet, booklet

or m. gold; — conj. now

oracle m. oracle

orage m. electrical storm

orageux a. stormy, violent

oraison f. oration; prayer

oral a. oral

oralement adv. orally

orange f. orange; — pressée orangeade; — m. orange color

orangé a. orange-colored

orangeade f. orange drink

oranger m. orange tree

orangeraie f. orange grove

orangerie f. hothouse for orange trees

orang-outan m. orangutang

orateur m. orator

oratoire a. oratorical; — m. oratory, chapel

oratorio m. oratorio

orbe m. orb; sphere

orbital a. orbital

orbite f. orbit

orchestral a. orchestral

orchestration f. orchestration

orchestre m. orchestra

orchestrer vt. to orchestrate

orchidée f. orchid

ordalie f. ordeal, trial by ordeal

ordinaire a. ordinary, common, usual; — m. custom, practice; d'— adv. usually

ordinairement adv. ordinarily

ordinal a. ordinal

ordination f. ordination

ordonnance f. order; class; ordinance; prescription; (mil.) orderly

ordonner vt. to order, put in order; ordain

ordre m. order; numéro d'— m. serial number; de premier — first-class, first-rate; billet à — m. promissory note

ordure f. filth, dirt; excrement; garbage

ordurier a. filthy

orée f. border, edge

oreille f. ear; hearing

oreiller m. pillow

oreillette f. auricle

oreillons m. pl. mumps

ores adv., d'— et déjà from now on

orfèvre m. goldsmith, silversmith

orfèvrerie f. jewelry; goldsmith's shop; goldsmith's trade

orfraie f. osprey
organdi m. organdy
organe m. organ
organique a. organic
organisateur m. organizer
organisation f. organization
organiser vt. to organize
organisme m. organism
organiste m. & f. organist
orge f. barley; sucre d'— m. barley sugar
orgelet m. (med.) sty on the eye
orgie f. orgy
orgue m. (mus.) organ; — de barbarie barrel organ, hand organ
orgueil m. pride
orgueilleusement adv. proudly
orgueilleux a. proud
Orient m. Orient, East
oriental a. oriental, eastern
orientation f. orientation
orienter vt. to orient, direct; s'— to become oriented; get one's bearings
orifice m. orifice
origan m. marjoram
originaire a., — (de) native (to)
original a. original; eccentric
originalité f. originality; eccentricity
origine f. origin
originel a. original, inherited
orignal m. moose
orillon m. handle, ear, grip of a bowl
oripeau m. tinsel, false gold, false silver; trash
ormaie f. elm grove
orme m. elm
orne m. ash tree
ornement m. ornament
ornemental a. ornamental
ornementation f. ornamentation
ornementer vt. to ornament
orner vt. to adorn, ornament
ornière f. rut, groove
ornithologie f. ornithology
ornithologue m. ornithologist
orpailleur m. prospector who pans for gold
orphelin m. orphan
orphelinat m. orphanage
orteil m. toe; gros — big toe
orthodoxe a. orthodox
orthodoxie f. orthodoxy
orthographe f. spelling
orthographier vt. to spell
orthographique a. orthographic, spelling
orthopédie f. orthopedics
orthopédique a. orthopedic
orthopediste m. orthopedist
ortie f. nettle
os m. bone
oscillation f. oscillation
oscillatoire a. oscillating
osciller vi. to oscillate; hesitate
osé a. bold, daring
oseille f. sorrel
oser vt. & vi. to dare, venture
oseraie f. willow grove
oseur a. daring
osier m. (bot.) willow; wicker work
osmium m. osmium
osmose f. osmosis
ossature f. bones, bone structure; frame

osselet m. little bone, osselet; knucklebone
ossements m. pl. bones
osseux a. bony
ossification f. ossification
ossifier vt. to ossify
ossu a. bony
ossuaire m. ossuary: bone pile
ostensible a. ostensible
ostensoir m. monstrance
ostentateur a. ostentatious
ostentation f. ostentation
ostéomyélite f. osteomyelitis
ostracisme m. ostracism
ostréiculture f. oyster farming
otage m. hostage; guarantee
otalgie f. earache
otarie f. sea lion
ôter vt. to take away, take off; remove
otique a. pertaining to the ear
ottoman m. & a. ottoman
ou conj. or; ou . . . ou either . . . or
où adv. where, on which, when; d'— whence, from where; par — which way; — que wherever
ouaille f. member of a spiritual flock
ouate f. cotton batting
ouater vt. to stuff with cotton batting: pad
oubli m. oblivion, forgetfulness, neglect
oubliable a. forgettable
oublier vt. to forget
oubliette f. dungeon, cell
oublieux a. forgetful
ouest m. west
oui adv. yes
oui-dire m. hearsay
ouïe f. hearing
ouïr vt. to hear
ouragan m. hurricane
ourdir vt. to plot; weave (intrigue)
ourler vt. to hem; — à jour to hemstitch
ourlet m. hem
ours m. bear
Ourse, la Grande — Ursa Major; la Petite — Ursa Minor
oursin m. sea urchin
ourson m. bear club
out adv. out; out of bounds (sports)
outarde f. bustard
outil m. tool, implement
outillage m. tools, tool kit; apparatus
outiller vt. to furnish, supply
outrage m. outrage, abuse, insult
outrageant a. insulting, abusive
outrager vt. to outrage
outrageusement adv. insultingly; outrageously
outrageux a. outrageous; insulting
outrance f. excess
outrancier a. excessive
outre adv. further, beyond; en — moreover, besides; — prep. beyond; — f. goatskin waterbag
outré a. overdone, exaggerated
outrecuidance f. presumption, conceit
outrecuidant a. conceited, self-satisfied
outremer m. ultramarine; lapis lazuli
outre-mer adv. overseas
outrepasser vt. to overtake, go beyond
outrer vt. to overdo, exaggerate; anger

ouvert *a.* open; candid; sincere

ouvertement *adv.* openly, frankly

ouverture *f.* opening; beginning; overture

ouvrable *a.* workable, capable of being worked; working; jour — *m.* working day

ouvrage *m.* work, piece of work

ouvrager *vt.* to work on, work over

ouvre-boites *m.* can opener

ouvrer *vt.* to work

ouvreuse *f.* (theat.) usher

ouvrier *m.* laborer, worker

ouvrir *vt.* to open

ouvroir *m.* workroom

ovaire *m.* ovary

ovale *a.* & *m.* oval

ovarien *a.* ovarian

ovation *f.* ovation

ovationner *vt.* to applaud, give an ovation to

ove *m.* egg, egg-shaped ornament; ovum

ové *a.* egg-shaped

oviducte *m.* oviduct

ovin *a.* ovine

ovipare *a.* oviparous

ovoïde *a.* ovoid

ovulation *f.* ovulation

ovule *m.* ovule

oxalide *f.* oxalis

oxalique *a.* oxalic

oxhydrique *a.* oxyhydric

oxyacétylénique *a.* oxyacetylene

oxydant *a.* oxidizing; — *m.* oxidizer

oxygène *m.* oxygen

oxyure *f.* tapeworm

P

pacage *m.* pasture

pacager *vt.* to put to pasture

pachyderme *m.* pachyderme

pacificateur *m.* pacifier; — *a.* pacifying

pacification *f.* pacifying

pacifier *vt.* to pacify, appease

pacifique *a.* peaceful; mild

pacifisme *m.* pacifism

pacifiste *m.* pacifist; — *a.* pacifistic

pacotille *f.* cheap merchandise, trash

pacte *m.* pact

pactiser *vi.* to make a pact; compromise

pactole *m.* source of great wealth

padou *m.* narrow tape

Padoue *f.* Padua

pagaie *f.* paddle

pagaille, pagaye *f.* disorder, confusion

paganisme *m.* paganism

pagayer *vt.* & *vi.* to paddle

pagayeur *m.* paddler

page *f.* page; (fig.) epoch; à la — up to date; — *m.* page boy (court)

pagination *f.* pagination

paginer *vt.* to paginate

pagne *m.* loincloth

pagode *f.* pagoda

paie *f.* pay; paying off; salary

paiement *m.* payment, paying

païen *m.* & *a.* pagan, heathen

pairie *f.* paymaster's office

paillard *a.* lecherous

paillasse *f.* straw mattress; — *m.* pagliac-

cio, clown

paillasson *m.* straw mat

paille *f.* straw; flaw; — de fer steel wool; tirer à la courte — to draw straws

pailler *vt.* to cover with straw

pailleté *a.* spangled, sequined

pailleter *vt.* to spangle

paillette *f.* sequin, spangle; gold nugget; flake

paillon *m.* spangle; straw basket; straw wrapping (of a bottle); large gold nugget

pain *m.* bread, loaf; petit — roll

pair *m.* peer, equal; equality; au — at par; without salary, with board and lodging in exchange for services; — *a.* even, equal; nombre — even number; de — *adv.* on the same level

paire *f.* pair

pairesse *f.* peeress

paisible *a.* peaceable; peaceful, calm

paître *vi.* to browse; — *vt.* to put to pasture

paix *f.* peace, quiet

pal *m.* stake; pale

palabre *f.* talk, conference

paladin *m.* paladin, knight

palais *m.* palace; (anat.) palate; — de justice courthouse

palan *m.* block of a pulley; tackle

palanche *f.* yoke

palanque *f.* stockade

palanquin *m.* palanquin

palatalisation *f.* palatalization

pale *f.* post, stake, pale; (mech.) blade

pâle *a.* pale, wan, pallid

palefrenier *m.* horse's groom

palefroi *m.* palfrey; parade horse (Middle Ages)

paléographie *f.* paleography

paléolithique *a.* paleolithic

paleron *m.* part of an animal's shoulder; cut of meat

palestinien *a.* & *m.* Palestinian

palet *m.* quoit

paletot *m.* topcoat, overcoat

palette *f.* pallette; paddle; oar blade

palétuvier *m.* mangrove

pâleur *f.* paleness, pallor

palier *m.* landing of a staircase; (fig.) level; degree

palindrome *m.* palindrome

palinodie *f.* retraction

pâlir *vi.* to turn pale, wane; fade; — *vt.* make pale

palis *m.* picket; picket fence; pale, enclosure

palissade *f.* fence, fencing; palisade; stockade

palissader *vt.* to fence in, enclose; palisade

palliatif *a.* & *m.* palliative

pallier *vt.* to palliate, alleviate

palmarès *m.* list of honors and awards

palme *f.* palm; palm tree; —s *pl.* honors or insignia

palmé *a.* palmate; web-footed

palmeraie *f.* palm grove

palmette *f.* (arch.) palm-leaf design

palmier *m.* palm tree

palmiste *m.* palmetto
palombe *f.* wood pigeon
palourde *f.* clam
palpable *a.* palpable, obvious
palpe *f.* feeler, palp of an insect
palper *vt.* to feel with the hand
palpitation *f.* palpitation
palpiter *vi.* to palpitate; flutter; thrill
paludéen *a.* pertaining to marshes or swamps; fièvre —ne *f.* malaria
paludisme *m.* malaria
pâmer *v.*, se — to be overcome, faint; be excessively happy
pâmoison *f.* faint, fainting
pamphlet *m.* lampoon, satire
pamphlétaire *m.* lampooner, pamphleteer
pamplemousse *f.* grapefruit
pampre *m.* branch of a fruit vine
pan *m.* section, piece; flap; wall panel; — *interj.* bang!
panacée *f.* panacea
panache *m.* decorative plume, stripe; swagger
panaché *a.* plumed; streaky; varied
panacher *vt.* to plume; decorate with different colors
panais *m.* parsnip
Panama *m.* Panama; Panama hat
panaméricain *a.* Pan-american
pancarte *f.* placard, sign, folder
panchromatique *a.* panchromatic
pancréas *m.* pancreas
panda *m.* panda
pandémonium *m.* pandemonium
pandit *m.* pundit
pané *a.* breaded
panégyrique *m.* panegyric, eulogy
paner *vt.* to bread
panerée *f.* basketful
panier *m.* basket; hoop skirt
panique *f.* panic
panne *f.* breakdown, failure; lard; plush; être en — to be out of order, not to work
panneau *m.* wood panel; trap, snare; (naut.) hatch
panneton *m.* window catch
panoplie *f.* suit of armor; panoply
panoramique *a.* panoramic
panse *f.* paunch, (coll.) belly
pansement *m.* bandage, dressing
panser *vt.* to bandage, dress
pantalon *m.* pair of pants, trousers
panteler *vi.* to pant
panthéisme *m.* pantheism
panthéiste *m.* pantheist; — *a.* pantheistic
panthéon *m.* pantheon
panthère *f.* panther, leopard, jaguar
pantin *m.* puppet; jumping jack
pantographe *m.* pantograph
pantomime *f.* pantomime; — *m.* pantomimist
pantoufle *f.* house slipper
panure *f.* bread crumbs
paon *m.* peacock
paonner *vi.* to strut
papal *a.* papal
papauté *f.* papacy
pape *m.* pope
paperasse *f.* old paper

paperasserie *f.* red tape
papeterie *f.* paper mill; stationery; stationery store
papetier *m.* stationer; papermaker
papier *m.* paper; — à lettres stationery; — hygiénique toilet tissue; — peint wallpaper; — de soie tissue paper; — de verre sandpaper
papier-cuir *m.* imitation leather, leatherette
papille *f.* papilla
papillon *m.* butterfly; leaflet; amendment; — de nuit moth; nœud — *m.* bow tie
papillonner *vi.* to flit, flutter
papillote *f.* curlpaper
papillotement *m.* fluttering, flickering
papilloter *vi.* to flicker, twinkle; glitter
papoter *vi.* to talk, chatter, gossip
paprika *m.* paprika
papule *f.* papule, rash, blemish
papyrus *m.* papyrus
Pâque *f.* Passover
paquebot *m.* liner, ship, steamer, mail boat
Pâques *f. pl.* Easter
paquet *m.* bundle, parcel, pack
paquetage *m.* packaging
paqueter *vt.* to bale, package, tie up
par *prep.* by, through; by means of; per; in; on; finir — (faire quelque chose) to end up doing something, finally to do something; — ici this way; — là that way; — où? which way? — trop much too much
parabole *f.* parable; parabola
parachever *vt.* to complete to perfection
parachutage *m.* parachuting, air-drop
parachuter *vt.* to parachute
parachutiste *m.* parachutist, paratrooper
parade *f.* display, show, pomp; parade; parry
parader *vi.* to display, show off; parade
paradis *m.* paradise; (theat.) upper balcony, gallery
paradisier *m.* bird of paradise
paradoxe *m.* paradox
paradoxal *a.* paradoxical
parafe *m.* initials; flourish
parafer *vt.* to initial; sign
paraffine *f.* paraffin
paraffiner *vt.* to coat with paraffin
parage *m.* trimming, paring; lineage, birth —s *m. pl.* ocean localities, vicinity
paragraphe *m.* paragraph
paraître *vi.* to appear, seem; be apparent; be published; vient de — to be just published
parallèle *a. & m.* parallel
parallélogramme *m.* parallelogram
paralogisme *m.* fallacy
paralysant *a.* paralyzing
paralyser *vt.* to paralyze
paralytique *a. & n.* paralytic
paramécie *f.* (zool.) paramecium
paramètre *m.* parameter
parangon *m.* paragon, model, example
paranoïa *f.* paranoia
parapet *m.* parapet
paraphrase *f.* paraphrase
paraphraser *vt.* to paraphrase; stretch

paraplégique a. paraplegic
parapluie m. umbrella
parasite m. parasite; -s pl. (coll.) static;
— a. parasitic
parasitaire, parasitique a. parasitic
parasol m. parasol
paratonnerre m. lightning rod
paravent m. folding screen
parc m. park; grounds; parking space;
pen for livestock
parcage m. parking
parcelle f. piece; plot, parcel, lot; bit,
scrap
parceller vt. to divide into parcels
parce que conj. because
parchemin m. parchment
parcimonie f. parsimony
parcimonieux a. parsimonious; sparing;
stingy
parcourir vt. to travel over; (fig.) run
through, read over
parcours m. trip, distance; route, course
par-dessous adv. & prep. under, underneath
pardessus m. overcoat, topcoat
par-dessus adv. & prep. over, on top of
pardon m. pardon, forgiveness
pardonnable a. pardonnable, forgivable
pardonner vt. to pardon, forgive
paré a. dressed up; adorned
pare-boue m. mudguard
pare-brise m. windshield
pare-bruit m. (auto.) muffler
pare-chocs m. (auto.) bumper
pare-étincelles m. fire-screen
parégorique a. & m. paregoric
pareil (pareille) a. like, alike; equal, same;
similar; such; — m. equal, peer, like;
sans — without equal, peerless
pareillement adv. similarly; in the same
way; also
parement m. adornment, ornament; ornamentation; curb; facing of outer wall
parent m. relative, relation; -s pl. parents; family, relatives
parentage m. parentage, lineage; family,
relatives
parenté f. relationship; relatives
parenthèse f. parenthesis, parenthetical
phrase; en -s adv. parenthetically
parer vt. to adorn; trim; prepare; parry,
avoid; se — to adorn oneself; dress up
pare-soleil m. visor, shade
paresse f. laziness
paresseux a. lazy; sluggish, slow
parfaire vt. to perfect
parfait a. complete, perfect; absolute; —
m. (gram.) perfect tense
parfaitement a. completely, perfectly; absolutely, certainly
parfois adv. sometimes
parfum m. perfume, scent, fragrance
parfumer vt. to perfume, scent
pari m. wager, bet
paria m. pariah, outcast
parier vt. to bet, wager
parieur m. better
Paris m. Paris
parisien a. & m. Parisian
parité f. parity, equality

parjure a. perjured; — m. perjury; per-
jurer
parjurer vt., se — to perjure oneself, commit perjury
parking m. garage, parking place
parlant a. speaking; expressive
parlé a. spoken
parlement m. parliament; court
parlementaire a. parliamentary; drapeau
— m. flag of truce
parlementer vi. to confer, parley
parler vi. to speak, talk; entendre — de
to hear about; — m. speech, language
parleur m. speaker, talker
parloir m. parlor
Parme f. Parma
parmesan a. from Parma; — m. Parmesan
cheese
parmi prep. among
parnassien a. & m. Parnassian
parodie f. parody
parodier vt. to parody
paroi f. partition, wall; (anat.) lining
paroisse f. parish
paroissial a. parochial, parish
paroissien m. parishioner; prayer-book
parole f. word, spoken word, parole,
promise; speech, speaking; avoir la —
to be speaking, have the floor
paroxysme m. paroxysm
Parque f., les -s pl. the Fates
parquer vt. to pen up; park
parquet m. floor, flooring; court, bar of·
justice; pit, trading floor
parqueter vt. to parquet a floor
parqueterie f. parquet floor, inlaid floor
parrain m. godfather; sponsor
parricide m. & f. parricide
parsemer vt. to strew, scatter; intersperse
part f. portion, share; à — aside; peculiar;
autre — elsewhere; de — et d'autre on
both sides; nulle — nowhere; quelque
— somewhere; de ma — from me; for
me; de la — de on behalf of; d'une —
on one hand; d'autre — on the other
hand; faire — de to announce; inform,
notify
partage m. share, portion; sharing, dividing
partager vt. to share, divide
partance f. (naut.) leaving, departure,
sailing; en — pour bound for
partant conj. therefore; consequently
partenaire m. & f. partner
parterre m. flower bed; (theat.) orchestra,
rear of orchestra, audience
parti m. party, faction, cause; decision;
profit; match, prospective husband or
wife; du — de on the side of; prendre
son — to make up one's mind; — pris
prejudice; closed mind; prendre le —
de to take the side of; to decide to;
tirer — de to take advantage of
partialement adv. partially, in a prejudiced manner
partialité f. prejudice, partiality
participant m. participant
participation f. participation; sharing
participe m. participle
participer vi. to participate, share

participial a. participial

particulariser vt. to specify; go into detail about

particularité f. particularity; peculiarity; particular, detail

particule f. particle

particulier a. particular; special; peculiar; characteristic; private, personal; en — privately; — m. individual, private party

particulièrement adv. particularly, especially

partie f. part, portion; game, match; party (law); — civile plaintiff; en — in part, partly; en grande — for the most part, largely

partiel a. partial, part, incomplete

partiellement adv. partially, in part

partir vi. to depart, leave, go away; start, come, emanate; come off; go off (gun); à — d'aujourd'hui from this day on; — à l'anglaise to take French leave

partisan m. partisan; believer, follower

partitif a. partitive

partition f. division; (mus.) score

partout adv. everywhere; — ailleurs anywhere else

parure f. dress, ornament; decoration; necklace

parution f. appearance of a published work

parvenir vi. to arrive, reach; manage, succeed

parvenu m. upstart

parvis m. church square

pas m. step, footstep, pace; threshold; narrow passage; defile; (fig.) precedence; faux — stumble, slip, mistake; mauvais — scrape, difficulty; — de ce — immediately; à — de loup stealthily; — à — step by step, slowly

pas adv. no, not, none; — du tout not at all; — mal de many, quite a few

Pas de Calais m. Straits of Dover

pascal a. (eccl.) Paschal

passable a. passable, fair

passage m. passage; passing; voyage; crossing; droit de — m. right of way; — clouté crosswalk

passager a. transient, transitory, fleeting, momentary; migratory (bird); — m. passenger

passant m. passer-by

passavant m. (naut.) gangway; pass, permit

passe f. pass; passing; permit; fencing thrust; mauvaise — difficult situation

passé a. past, over, gone by; — m. past time; (gram.) past tense

passement m. braid, lace

passementerie f. braid or lace trimming

passe-partout m. skeleton key, master key

passe-passe m. sleight of hand, magic

passepoil m. braid, braiding

passeport m. passport

passer vi. to pass, go by; go over; go through; pass away; pass on; — vt. to pass; exceed, go beyond; strain; go over, pass over, cross; hand, give; put; put on; spend time; sign an agreement;

se — to happen, occur, go on; go by; pass away; se — de to do without

passereau m. sparrow

passerelle f. foot bridge

passe-temps m. pastime

passe-thé m. tea strainer

passeur m. ferryman

passible a. liable, subject

passif a. passive; — m. passive; (com.) liabilities, debt

passion f. passion

passionnant a. exciting, moving, thrilling

passionnel a. pertaining to passion(s); crime — m. crime committed in the heat of jealousy

passionner vt. to excite; impassion; thrill

passivité f. passivity

passoire f. strainer

pastel m. pastel color or drawing

pastèque f. watermelon

pasteur m. shepherd; pastor, minister

pasteuriser vt. to pasteurize

pastiche m. parody, pastiche, imitation

pasticher vt. to parody, imitate

pastille f. drop, candy; cough drop; rubber patch

pastoral a. pastoral

pat m. stalemate

patate f. sweet potato; (coll.) potato

pataud a. & m. clumsy person

pataugeage, pataugement m. floundering

patauger vi. to flounder; splash, wade

pâte f. paste, dough; pasta, spaghetti products; — dentifrice toothpaste

pâté m. pâté of meat; ink blot; clump; block of houses

pâtée f. mash for animals

patelinage m. glib talk, smooth talk

patenôtre f. Lord's prayer

patent a. patent, obvious, clear

patente f. license, permit, certification, authorization

patenter vt. to license, authorize

patère f. clothing peg; curtain hook

paterne a. benevolent, kindly

paternel a. paternal; fatherly

paternité f. paternity, fatherhood

pâteux a. pasty; thick

pathétique a. pathetic; — m. pathos

pathologie f. pathology

pathologiste m. pathologist

patiemment adv. patiently

patience f. patience; jeu de — m. jigsaw puzzle; solitaire (cards)

patient a. patient; — m. patient

patienter vi. to have patience, be patient

patin m. skate; runner; brake shoe; —s à roulettes roller skates

patine f. patina

patiner vi. to skate; slip

patinette f. child's scooter

patineur m. skater

patinoire f. skating rink

pâtir vi. to suffer

pâtis m. pasture

pâtisser vi. to make pastry

pâtisserie f. pastry; pastry shop

pâtissier m. pastry cook, baker of cake and pastry

patois m. dialect; jargon

patouiller *vi.* to flounder in mud
pâtre *m.* shepherd
Patrice (*m.*) Patrick
patricien *a. & m.* patrician
patrie *f.* native country
patrimoine *m.* patrimony
patrimonial *a.* patrimonial
patriote *a.* patriotic; — *n.* patriot
patriotique *a.* patriotic
patriotisme *m.* patriotism
patron *m.* patron; employer, boss, chief, proprietor; skipper; pattern; — à jour stencil
patronage *m.* patronage; church social group
patronal *a.* pertaining to employers; pertaining to a patron saint
patronne *f.* patroness; owner, proprietress
patronner *vt.* to patronize, support; pattern; stencil
patrouiller *vi.* to patrol
patrouilleur *m.* soldier on patrol; patrol boat
patte *f.* paw, foot; tab, strap; à quatre —s four-footed; on all fours
patte-d'oie *f.* wrinkle, crow's foot
pâturage *m.* pasture, grazing
pâture *f.* feed, fodder; pasture
pâturer *vi. & vt.* to graze, feed
paume *f.* palm of the hand; jeu de — *m.* tennis court (history)
paumer *vt.* to strike, slap with the palm
paupière *f.* eyelid
pause *f.* pause, stop, respite, interval; (mus.) rest
pauser *vi.* to pause
pauvre *a.* poor; wretched, unfortunate; — *n.* poor person
pauvresse *f.* poor woman, beggar
pauvreté *f.* poverty, poorness
pavage *m.* pavement; paving
pavaner *v... se — vi.* to strut, parade
pavé *m.* pavement; slab, block of paving stone; street; sidewalk
paver *vt.* to pave
pavillon *m.* pavillion; lodge; flag; — de golf golf clubhouse
pavoiser *vt.* to trim, adorn with bunting
pavot *m.* poppy
payable *a.* payable
payant *a.* paying; — *m.* payer
paye *f.* wages, pay
payement *m.* payment
payer *vt.* to pay, pay for, pay back; treat; se — to treat oneself to
payeur *m.* payer; bursar; bank teller; paymaster
pays *m.* country, land, region; avoir le mal du — to be homesick
paysage *m.* landscape; scenery; countryside
paysagiste *m. & f.* landscape painter
paysan *m.* peasant
paysannerie *f.* peasantry
Pays-Bas *m. pl.* Netherlands
péage *m.* toll; pont à — *m.* toll bridge
péan *m.* paean
peau *f.* skin, hide; pelt; peel; à fleur de — skin-deep
Peau-Rouge *m.* Indian, redskin

pécari *m.* peccary
pechblende *f.* pitchblende
pêche *f.* peach; fishing
pêcher *vi.* to fish, fish up, catch; — *m.* peach tree
pécher *vi.* to sin
pécheresse *f.* sinner; trespasser; — *a.* sinning
pêcherie *f.* fishery
pêcheur *m.* angler, fisherman; fishing boat
pécheur *m.* sinner
pectine *f.* pectin
pectoral *a. & m.* pectoral
péculat *m.* embezzlement
péculateur *m.* embezzler
pécule *m.* nest egg, savings
pécuniaire *a.* pecuniary
pédagogique *a.* pedagogic(al)
pédagogue *m.* pedagogue
pédale *f.* pedal; frein à — *m.* foot brake; — d'embrayage (auto.) clutch
pédaler *vi.* to pedal
pédaleur *m.* bicyclist
pédant *a.* pedantic; — *m.* pedant
pédanterie *f.*, pédantisme *m.* pedantry
pédantesque *a.* pedantic
pédestre *a.* pedestrian
pédiatre *m.* pediatrician
pédiatrie *f.* pediatrics
pédicure *m.* chiropodist
pedigree *m.* pedigree
peigne *m.* comb
peigné *a.* combed; bien — well-groomed; mal — unkempt
peigner *vt.* to comb, card wool; (coll.) beat, thrash; se — to comb one's hair
peignoir *m.* dressing gown, wrapper
peindre *vt.* to paint, portray, depict
peine *f.* pain, punishment, penalty; difficulty; trouble; à — hardly, scarcely; faire de la — à to trouble, disturb, distress; se donner (de) la — to take the trouble
peiner *vt.* to pain, trouble, distress; — *vi.* to work hard, struggle, labor
peintre *m.* painter; artist; — en bâtiments house painter
peinture *f.* painting; paint; picture
peinturer *vt.* to paint, coat with paint
péjoratif *a.* pejorative
péjorativement *adv.* pejoratively
pekinois *m.* Pekinese
pelage *m.* fur, coat of an animal; skinning
pelé *a.* hairless; skinless; peeled
pêle-mêle *adv.* pell-mell; hastily; in confusion; — *m.* jumble, disorder
peler *vt.* to peel, pare, skin; remove the hair from; — *vi.* to peel; se — peel; lose hair
pèlerin *m.* pilgrim
pèlerinage *m.* pilgrimage
pèlerine *f.* cape, tippet
pélican *m.* pelican
pelisse *f.* pelisse, cloak
pellagre *f.* pellagra
pelle *f.* shovel, scoop; blade of a paddle
pelletée *f.* shovelful
pelleter *vt.* to shovel
pelleterie *f.* furs, fur trade
pelletier *m.* furrier

pellicule *f.* skin, film; (phot.) film; —s *pl.* dandruff

pelote *f.* wad, ball; pincushion; pelota

peloter *vt.* to wind into a ball

peloton *m.* group; (mil.) platoon; wad, ball; cluster

pelotonner *v.*, se — to group together; huddle; roll up, curl up

pelouse *f.* lawn, grass, a green

peluche *f.* plush, shag

pelucher *vi.* to shed the nap (fabric), become nappy

pelucheux *a.* fluffy

pelure *f.* paring, peel; rind; papier — *m.* onionskin paper

pelvien *a.* pelvic

pénal *a.* penal

pénalisation *f.* sports penalty

pénaliser *vt.* to penalize

pénalité *f.* penalty

penaud *a.* sheepish, crestfallen

penchant *a.* sloping, inclined; — *m.* slope; inclination, leaning, bent

penché *a.* bent, leaning

pencher *vt. & vi.* to incline, tilt, lean over; se — bend, stoop; lean out

pendable *a.* deserving of hanging

pendaison *f.* hanging on the gallows

pendant *a.* hanging; pending; — *m.* pendant; match, one of a pair; — *prep.* during, for; — que *conj.* while

pendeloque *f.* earring; crystal of a chandelier

pendiller *vi.* to dangle, hang

pendre *vt. & vi.* to hang, hang up

pendule *f.* clock with pendulum; — *m.* pendulum

pêne *m.* bolt of a lock

pénétrabilité *f.* penetrability

pénétrable *a.* penetrable

pénétrant *a.* penetrating, sharp, keen, searching, deep, profound

pénétration *f.* penetration; insight

pénétrer *vt.* to penetrate, pierce; fill; — *vi.* penetrate, enter, get into

pénible *a.* painful; difficult, hard, rough

péniblement *adv.* painfully

péniche *f.* canalboat, barge

pénicilline *f.* penicillin

péninsulaire *a.* peninsular

péninsule *f.* peninsula

pénis *m.* penis

pénitence *f.* penitence, penance; repentance

pénitencier *m.* penitentiary

pénitent *a. & m.* penitent

pénitentiaire *a.* penitentiary

penne *f.* feather, plume

pennon *m.* pennant

pénombre *f.* semidarkness, half-light

pensant *a.* thinking

pensée *f.* thought, idea; (bot.) pansy

penser *vi.* to think; remember; — *vt.* to think, believe, conceive, imagine

penseur *m.* thinker

pensif *a.* pensive, thoughtful, thinking

pension *f.* pension; boardinghouse, boarding school; room and board; — alimentaire alimony

pensionnaire *m. & f.* boarder; pensioner; inmate

pensionnat *m.* boarding school

pensionner *vt.* to pension

pensivement *adv.* pensively

pensum *m.* task, chore (as punishment)

pentagone *m.* pentagon; — *a.* pentagonal

pentamètre *m.* pentameter

pentathlon *m.* pentathlon

pente *f.* slope, incline, grade

Pentecôte *f.* Pentecost

pénultième *a. & f.* penultimate, last but one

pénurie *f.* penury, poverty; scarcity

pépiement *m.* cheeping, chirping

pépin *m.* pip, seed

pépinière *f.* nursery garden

pépite *f.* nugget

pepsine *f.* pepsin

percale *f.* percale

perçant *a.* piercing; penetrating; biting, sharp; shrill

perce *f.* drill, punch; boring implement

perce-bois *m.* teredo, ship worm, borer

percée *f.* opening, break

percepteur *m.* tax collector; — *a.* discerning

perceptible *a.* perceptible

perception *f.* perception; revenue collection

percer *vt.* to pierce; go through, penetrate; bore, drill, sink; — *vi.* to pierce, come through

perceur *m.* driller, borer

perceuse *f.* drill, drilling machine

percevable *a.* perceivable; collectable

percevoir *vt.* to perceive; collect taxes

perche *f.* fresh-water perch; pole

percher *vi.* to perch, roost; se — to come to rest, alight

percheron *m.* percheron

perchoir *m.* perch, roost

perclus *a.* stiff-jointed, crippled

perçoir *m.* awl; punch; borer

percolateur *m.* percolator

percussion *f.* percussion

percutant *a.*, fusée —e *f.* percussion fuse

percuter *vt.* to percuss, tap

percuteur *m.* hammer of a gun

perdant *a.* losing; — *m.* loser

perdition *f.* perdition; (naut.) sinking

perdre *vt.* to lose; ruin, destroy; waste time; — *vi.* lose; lose value; fall; leak; se — be lost; get lost

perdrix *f.* partridge

perdu *a.* lost, ruined; wasted

père *m.* father

pérégrination *f.* peregrination

péremptoire *a.* peremptory

perfection *f.* perfection

perfectibilité *f.* perfectibility

perfectionnement *m.* improvement; perfecting

perfectionner *vt.* to perfect; improve

perfide *a.* perfidious, treacherous

perfidie *f.* perfidy, treachery

perforateur *m.* drill, punch

perforation *f.* perforation; drilling; puncture

perforer *vt.* to perforate; drill; puncture

pergola *f.* pergola

péri m. & f. genie, peri
péricarde m. pericardium
périclitant a. risky, shaky
péricliter vi. to be in danger
péril m. peril, risk, danger
périlleusement adv. perilously
périlleux a. perilous, dangerous
perimé a. overdue; expired; out of date
périmer vi. to lapse, expire
périmètre m. perimeter
période f. period; age, era; (med.) phase;
(elec.) cycle
périodicité f. periodicity
périodique a. & m. periodical
périodiquement adv. periodically
péripatétique a. peripatetic
péripétie f. sudden turn of fortune; —s pl.
vicissitudes, up and downs
périphérie f. periphery; circumference
périphérique a. peripheral
périr vi. to perish, die
périscope m. periscope
périscopique a. periscopic
périssable a. perishable
péristyle m. peristyle
péritoine m. peritoneum
péritonite f. peritonitis
perle f. pearl, bead
perlé a. pearled; pearly; beaded
perler vt. to husk; — vi. to bead
permanence f. permanence; en — permanent; without cessation; permanently
permanent a. permanent; lasting; open
continuously; open day and night;
spectacle — m. continuous performance
permanganate m. permanganate
perméable a. permeable; porous
permettre vt. to permit, allow
permis a. permitted; — m. permit,
license; — de conduire m. driver's
license
permission f. permission; (mil.) leave,
pass
permissionnaire m. soldier on leave
permutable a. interchangeable
permutation f. permutation; transfer, exchange of positions
permutatrice f. (elec.) rectifier, commutator
pernicieusement adv. perniciously
pernicieux a. pernicious, harmful, injurious
perniciosité f. perniciousness
péroné m. fibula
péroraison f. peroration
pérorer vi. to harangue
Pérou m. Peru
peroxyde m. peroxide
perpendiculaire a. perpendicular
perpétration f. perpetration
perpétrer vt. to perpetrate
perpétuel a. perpetual; endless; for life
perpétuellement adv. perpetually
perpétuer vt. to perpetuate
perpétuité f. perpetuity; à — for life,
forever
perplexe a. perplexed; perplexing
perplexité f. perplexity
perquisition f. search; mandat de — m.

search warrant
perquisitionner vi. to search, conduct a
search
perron m. flight of steps to a house
perroquet m. parrot
perruche f. parakeet
perruque f. wig
pers a. gray-green
persan a. & m. Persian
perse f. chints
Perse f, Persia; — n. & a. Persian
persécuter vt. to persecute; harass; annoy
persécuteur m. persecutor
persécution f. persecution
persévérance f. perseverance
persévérant a. persevering
persévérer vi. to persevere, persist
persienne f. outside shutter
persiflage m. persiflage, banter
persifler vt. to treat lightly, banter
persil m. parsley
persillé a. marbled, streaked
persique a. Persian
persistance f. persistence, persistency
persistant a. persistent
persister vi. to persist
personnage m. personage, important person; (theat.) character, role
personnalité f. personality; personage; individuality
personne f. person; en — in person, per-
sonified; — pron. nobody, no one; anybody, anyone
personnel a. personal; — m. personnel
personnellement adv. personally
personnifier vt. to personify; impersonate
perspective f. perspective; prospect; view
perspicacité f. perspicacity
persuadant a. persuasive, convincing
persuadé a. positive, convinced, sure
persuader vt. to persuade, convince
persuasif a. persuasive, convincing
persuasion f. persuasion, conviction
persuasivement adv. persuasively, con-
vincingly
perte f. loss, damage, ruin; leakage; falling off, drop; (med.) discharge; à — de
vue as far as the eye can see
pertinence f. pertinence, relevance
pertinent a. pertinent, relevant
pertuis m. channel, narrows; opening; narrow pass, passage; sluice
perturbateur a. disturbing; — m. dis-
turber
perturbation f. perturbation; disturbance
perturber vt. to perturb; disturb
péruvien a. & m. Peruvian
pervenche f. periwinkle
pervers a. perverse
perversement adv. perversely
perversion f. perversion
perversité f. perversity
pervertir vt. to pervert; se — to become
perverted
pesage m. weighing in
pesamment adv. heavily
pesant a. heavy, weighty; — m. weight
pesanteur f. weight; gravity; heaviness
pèse-alcool m. alcometer
pèse-bébé m. baby scale(s)

pesée f. weighing; leverage
pèse-lettres m. postal scale(s)
peser vt. to weigh, consider; measure; — vi. to weigh; press
pessimisme m. pessimism
pessimiste m. & f. pessimist; — a. pessimistic
peste f. plague, pestilence
pester vi. to rage, storm; curse
pestiféré a. stricken with the plague
pétale m. petal
pétarade f. backfire
pétard m. firecracker; detonator
pétarder vt. to blast; — vi. backfire
péter vi. to backfire, explode, pop
pétillant a. sparkling; crackling
pétillement m. crackling sound
pétiller vi. to sparkle; crackle; bubble
petit a. small, little; young; petty; minor, of humble origin, lesser; — à — little by little; — m. child; little boy; —e f. little girl; —s m. pl. children, little ones; en — adv. shortened
petit-cheval m. donkey engine
petit-cousin m. second cousin
petite-fille f. granddaughter
petitesse f. smallness, littleness; pettiness
petit-fils m. grandson
pétition f. petition
pétitionnaire m. & f. petitioner
pétitionner vi. to petition
petit-lait m. whey
petit-maître m. fop
petit-neveu m. grandnephew
petite-nièce f. grandniece
petits-enfants m. pl. grandchildren
petit-suisse m. cream cheese
pétoire f. popgun
pétoncle m. scallop
pétrel m. petrel
pétri a. kneaded, shaped; full of
pétrifier vt. to petrify
pétrin m. container for dough (bakery); (coll.) in trouble, difficulty
pétrir vt. to knead; shape
pétrole m. petroleum, oil
pétrolier m. (naut.) tanker
pétrolifère a. oil-yielding, oil-bearing
pétulance f. friskiness, vivacity
pétulant a. frisky, vivacious
pétunia m. petunia
peu adv. little; not very; — de few; — à — gradually; depuis — lately; quelque — somewhat; — m. small quantity; un — (de) a little
peuplade f. tribe, people
peuple m. people, nation; masses, lower class
peuplé a. populated
peupler vt. to people, populate, settle; stock with fish
peuplier m. poplar
peur f. fear, fright; avoir — to be afraid; de — de for fear of; de — que for fear that; faire — à to frighten; prendre — become afraid
peureux a. fearful; timid, shy
peut-être adv. perhaps, maybe
phalange f. phalanx
phalène f. moth

pharaon m. Pharaoh; faro
phare m. lighthouse, beacon; (auto.) headlight
pharisien m. pharisee
pharmacie f. pharmacy
pharmacien m. pharmacist, druggist
pharyngite f. pharyngitis
pharynx m. pharynx
phase f. phase, stage
Phénicie f. Phoenicia
phénicien a. & m. Phoenician
phénique a. carbolic
phénix m. phoenix
phénol m. phenol; carbolic acid
phénoménal a. phenomenal
phénomène m. phenomenon
philanthrope m. philanthropist
philanthropie f. philanthropy
philanthropique a. philanthropic
philatéliste m. & f. philatelist, stamp collector
philharmonique a. philharmonic
Philippe (m.) Philip
philistin a. & m. Philistine
philologie f. philology
philologue m. philologist
philosophe m. philosopher; — a. philosophical
philosopher vi. to philosophize
philosophie f. philosophy
philosophique a. philosophical
philtre m. philter, magic potion
phlébite f. phlebitis
phlogistique a. phlogiston
phlox m. phlox
phlyctène f. blister, vesicle
phobie f. phobia, dread
phonème m. phoneme
phonétique a. phonetic; — f. phonetics
phonique a. acoustic, phonic
phonographe m. phonograph
phonologie f. phonology
phoque m. (zool.) seal
phosphate m. phosphate
phosphore m. phosphorus
phosphorescence f. phosphorescence
phosphorescent a. phosphorescent
phosphure m. phosphide
photo f. photo, photograph
photocalque m. blueprint
photocopie f. photocopy
photo-électrique a. photoelectric
photogénique a. photogenic
photographe m. photographer
photographie f. photography; photograph
photographier vt. to photograph
photographique a. photographic
photogravure f. photoengraving
photostat m. photostat
photosynthèse f. photosynthesis
phrase f. sentence; phrase
phraséologie f. phraseology
phraser vi. to write or speak affectedly
phrénologie f. phrenology
phrénologiste m. phrenologist
phtisie f. pulmonary tuberculosis
phtisique a. tubercular, consumptive
physicien m. physicist
physico-chimie f. physical chemistry
physiologie f. physiology

physiologique a. physiological

physiologiste m. physiologist

physionomie f. face, features, character

physique a. physical; — f. physics; — m. physique

physiquement adv. physically

piaffer vi. to step, prance, paw the ground

piaillard a. bawling, crying; chirping

piailler vi. to bawl, squall, cry; chirp

piaillerie f. bawling, crying; whining; chirping

pianiste m. & f. pianist

piano m. piano: — à queue grand piano; — à demi-queue baby grand piano

piaulard a. crying, whining; chirping

piauler vi. to whine, cry; chirp

piaulis m. chirping

pic m. pickax; mountain peak; woodpecker; à — precipitous, sheer, abrupt

picard a. & m. native of Picardy

Picardie f. Picardy

picaresque a. picaresque

piccolo m. piccolo

pichet m. pitcher, jug

picorer vi. to peck, pick up food (birds)

picot m. splinter; picot

picotement m. pricking sensation, prickle; pins and needles (coll. U.S.)

picoter vt. to prick; pick at, peck at; — vi. sting, smart, burn

picrique a. picric

pictural a. pictorial

pie f. magpie; (coll.) chatterbox; — a. piebald

pièce f. piece; patch; room in a house; (theat.) play; coin; cask; part; — de rechange spare part

plécette f. one-act play; small coin

pied m. foot; footing; base; leg of a chair; support, stand; tripod; à — on foot; au — de la lettre literally; coup de — m. kick; en — full-length (portrait) mettre — à terre to dismount; step down from, get out of a vehicle; — de laitue head of lettuce; lâcher — to turn tail

pied-bot m. clubfooted person

pied-d'alouette m. larkspur, delphinium

pied-de-biche m. forceps; nail claw; bell pull

piédestal m. pedestal

piège m. snare, trap, pitfall

piéger vt. to trap

pie-grièche f. shrike

Piémont m. Piedmont

pierraille f. rubble, stones; ballast

pierre f. stone; flint; — à fusil flint; — d'achoppement stumbling block; — de touche touchstone

Pierre (m.) Peter

pierreries f. pl. precious stones, jewels

pierrette f. small stone

pierreux a. stony; gritty; gravelly

piété f. piety; devotion

piétinement m. trampling; treading

piétiner vt. to trample, tread on; — vi. to stamp

piéton m. pedestrian, person on foot

piètre a. poor, miserable, paltry

pieu m. stake, post, pile

pieusement adv. piously

pieuvre f. octopus

pieux a. pious, devoted, reverent

pige f. measuring stick

pigeon m. pigeon, dove; — voyageur homing pigeon

pigeonneau m. squab

pigeonnier m. dovecote, pigeon roost

piger vt. to measure, check; (coll.) nab, grab

pigmentation f. pigmentation

pigne f. pine cone

pignon m. house gable; chain-sprocket; pine seed

pilaf a. pilaf

pilastre m. pilaster, newel

pilau m. rice, pilaf

pile f. pile, heap; battery; — ou face heads or tails

piler vt. to pound, grind by pounding

pilet m. pintail duck

pileux a. hairy

pilier m. pillar, column

pillage m. pillage, plunder, sacking, looting; pilfering, stealing

pillard a. pillaging, looting; pilfering, stealing; — m. pillager, looter; pilferer, thief

piller vt. to pillage, plunder, sack, loot, steal from; plagiarize

pilleur a. pillaging; pilfering; — m. pillager

pilon m. hammer, rammer; pestle; crushing implement

pilonner vt. to ram, pound, crush

pilori m. pillory

pilot m. bridge pile

pilotage m. piloting; flying; pile driving

pilote m. pilot

piloter vt. to pilot, fly

pilotis m. piling

pilou m. cotton flannel

pilule f. pill

piment m. red pepper, allspice; — vert green pepper

pimenter vt. to spice, season with red pepper

pin m. pine tree; fir tree

pinacle m. pinnacle

pince f. pincers, tweezers, tongs; pliers; forceps; clip, clamp; lever, crowbar; claw of a lobster; hand grip; — à linge clothespin

pincé a. pinched; wry; — m. pizzicato

pinceau m. paint brush; beam of light

pincée f. pinch, small quantity

pincement m. pinching, pinch

pince-monseigneur m. jimmy

pince-nez m. pince-nez, nose glasses

pincer vt. to pinch; (mus.) pluck; clip; hold, grip; catch, nab

pincettes f. pl. pincers, tongs, tweezers

pingouin m. penguin; auk

pingre a. miserly, stingy; — m. miser

pinière f. pine forest

pinson m. finch

pintade f. guinea hen

pinte f. pint

pioche f. pickax

piocher vi. to dig; — vt. work hard

piocheur m. digger; (with a pick); plodder

hard worker

piolet *m.* ice axe; piolet

pion *m.* checker; pawn; monitor (coll.) school disciplinary officer

pionnier *m.* pioneer

pipe *f.* pipe

pipeau *m.* (mus.) pipe

pipée *f.* snaring birds with artifical bird calls

pipe-line *m.* pipeline

piper *vi.* to chirp, cheep, peep; — *vt.* to snare; lure birds; decoy

piquant *a.* sharp; spicy; witty; interesting; pricking, stinging; — *m.* sharpness; pointedness; best part, main point (of a story)

pique *f.* pike, lance; pique; — *m.* spade (at cards)

piqué *a.* piqued; stung, pricked, stuck; spotted, dotted; quilted; (mus.) staccato; (avi.) nose dive

pique-assiette *m.* parasite, sponger (person)

pique-nique *m.* picnic

pique-niquer *vi.* to picnic

piquer *vt.* to prick, sting; stick; inject; quilt; stimulate; irritate, pique; — *vi.* (avi.) to nose dive; se — prick oneself; be irritated, be offended; pride onself; become pitted

piquet *m.* picket, post, stake; piquet (at cards)

piqueter *vt.* to picket; stake out; spot, dot

piqueur *m.* machine sewer, stitcher; outrider; digger

piqûre *f.* puncture, sting; prick; vaccination; injection, shot (U.S.); quilting, stitching

pirater *vi.* to pirate

piraterie *f.* piracy

pire *a.* worse; le — the worst

pirogue *f.* pirogue, canoe

pirouette *f.* pirouette, whirling

pirouetter *vi.* to pirouette; whirl

pis *adv.* worse; le — the worst; de — en — worse and worse

pis *m.* udder

pis-aller *m.* worst alternative, last resort

pisan *a.* of Pisa, from Pisa

piscine *f.* pool, swimming pool

Pise *f.* Pisa

pissenlit *m.* dandelion

pisser *vi.* to urinate

pissoir *m.* urinal

pistache *f.* pistachio nut

piste *f.* path; track; scent, trail; — cavalière *f.* bridle path; — cyclable bicycle path

pister *vt.* to track, trail; follow, shadow

pisteur *m.* tracker, follower

pistolet *m.* pistol; (naut.) davit

piston *m.* piston; influence, pull; (mus.) cornet valve

pistonner *vt.* to use one's influence to help another; sponsor, back

pitance *f.* pittance, allowance, bare living

piteusement *adv.* piteously

piteux *a.* piteous, pitiable

pithécanthrope *m.* pithecanthropus

pitié *f.* pity, compassion, mercy

piton *m.* ring bolt; screw eye

pitoyable *a.* pitiful, pitiable

pitre *m.* clown

pittoresque *a.* picturesque

pituitaire *a.* pituitary

pivert *m.* woodpecker

pivoine *f.* peony

pivot *m.* pivot, fulcrum, axis; à — revolving, swivel

pivoter *vi.* to pivot, revolve, turn

placage *m.* veneering; plating

placard *m.* placard; poster; closet; cupboard; (print.) proof

placarder *vt.* to post a bill, placard

place *f.* square; seat; place, room, space; job, employment; faire — à to make room for; — d'armes parade ground

placement *m.* investment; placement; bureau de — employment agency

placer *vt.* to place; sell; invest

placeur *m.* placer; usher; seller

placide *a.* placid, calm

placidité *f.* placidity, calmness

placier *m.* traveling salesman; agent, canvasser

plafond *m.* ceiling; limit, maximum; top

plafonner *vt.* to equip with a ceiling

plage *f.* beach

plagiat *m.* plagiarism

plagier *vt.* to plagiarize

plaid *m.* plaid

plaider *vi. & vi.* to plead a case

plaideur *m.* party in a lawsuit, litigant

plaidoirie *f.* legal plea, pleading

plaidoyer *m.* legal plea, remarks by defense attorney

plaie *f.* wound

plaignant *m.* plaintiff at law

plain-chant *m.* (mus.) plainsong

plaindre *vt.* to pity; se — to complain

plaine *f.* plain, field

plain-pied *m.*, de — *adv.* on a level; even; smoothly, evenly

plainte *f.* complaint; moan

plaintif *a.* plaintive

plaintivement *adv.* plaintively

plaire *vi.* to please; s'il vous plaît please; plût à Dieu! would to God!; à Dieu ne plaise! God forbid!; se — enjoy oneself, take pleasure, be pleased

plaisamment *adv.* pleasantly, agreeably

plaisance *f.* pleasure; maison de — *f.* country home

plaisant *a.* amusing, funny; — *m.* joker; mauvais — practical joker

plaisanter *vi.* to joke, fool; — *vt.* to make fun of, tease

plaisanterie *f.* joke; trick

plaisir *m.* pleasure; enjoyment; faire — à to please

plan *m.* plane; plan; map, diagram; project; premier — foreground; gros — movie closeup; — *a.* flat, even, plane

planage *m.* planing; smoothing

planche *f.* plank, board; plate, illustration; faire la — to float on one's back; — à repasser ironing board; — de bord dashboard; —s *pl.* (theat.) stage

planchéier *vt.* lay a wooden floor

plancher *m.* floor; flooring; planking

planchette f. small plank

plancton m. plankton

plane m. plane tree

plané m. glide, gliding; rolled gold

planer vt. to plane, smooth; — vi. to glide soar; hover, hang

planétaire a. planetary; — m. planetarium

planète f. planet

planeur m. glider

planquer vt., se — to fall flat on the ground; take cover

plant m. sapling, seedling; grove, clump

plantage m. planting

plantain m. plantain

plantation f. plantation; planting

plante f. plant; sole of the foot

planter vt. to plant; place, put; stick

planteur m. planter

plantoir m. dibble

plantureux a. abundant, fertile; plump

planure f. wood shaving(s)

plaque f. plate; sheet of metal; chunk; badge; plaque; tag

plaqué a. plated

plaquemine f. persimmon

plaquer vt. to plate; veneer; cover; cake; plaster; tackle (sports); se — to lie flat, fall flat

plaquette f. small plate or sheet; brochure

plasticité f. plasticity

plastique a. plastic; matière — f. plastic

plastron m. breastplate, protective pad; front of a shirt, dickey; butt of a joke

plat a. flat; smooth; level; dull; à — flat; tired, run down; — m. flat surface, flat part; dish, course; plate

platane m. plane tree

plat-bord m. (naut.) gunwale

plateau m. tray; plateau; platform; plate; stage

plate-bande f. border, bed of flowers or grass

platée f. plateful, dishful

plate-forme f. platform

platine m. platinum; — f. gun lock; platen

platiner vt. to coat, plate with platinum

platitude f. platitude, dullness

Platon m. Plato

platonique a. platonic (love)

platonisme m. Platonism

plâtrage m. plastering

plâtras m. plaster rubbish

plâtre m. plaster; plaster cast

plâtrer vt. to plaster; cover over, smooth over

plâtrier m. plasterer

plausibilité f. plausibility

plausible a. plausible

plèbe f. common people, masses

plébéien a. & m. plebeian

plébiscite m. plebiscite

plein a. full, filled; complete; en — . . . in the middle of; en — air in the open air, out of doors; en — jour in broad daylight; — m. fullness, fill, plenum

pleinement adv. fully

plénière a. & f. plenary, full; complete

plénipotentiaire a. & m. plenipotentiary

plénitude f. plenitude, fullness

pléonasme m. pleonasm

pléthore f. plethora

pleur m. tear; —s pl. tears, crying

pleurard a. whimpering; — m. whimperer, whiner

pleurer vi. to cry, weep; run, water (eyes); drip, leak; — vt. to cry for, mourn

pleurésie f. pleurisy

pleureur m. whimperer, weeper; — a. whimpering, weeping

pleurnicher vi. to whine, whimper

pleuviner v. to drizzle

pleuvoir vi. to rain

plexus m. plexus

pli m. fold; wrinkle; crease; wave; tuck; pleat; cover, envelope; bend; sous ce — enclosed herewith

pliable a. pliable; folding

pliant a. pliant; tractable; folding; — m. folding chair

plier vt. to fold, bend; warp; discipline; — vi. to bend; yield, give in, submit; se — yield; obey

plinthe f. (arch.) plinth

plissement m. folding, pleating; creasing; wrinkling

plisser vt. to pleat; crease; wrinkle

ploiement m. folding, bending

plomb m. lead; plumb line; shot; (elec.) fuse; à — vertical, plumb

plombage m. leading; (dent.) filling

plombagine f. graphite, black lead

plombé a. leaden; lead-coated; livid

plomber vt. to lead, cover with lead; plumb; se — to become leaden

plomberie f. plumbing

plombier m. plumber; — a. leaden, about lead

plombières f. ice cream with glacé fruit

plongée f. plunge, dive; dip

plongement m. plunging

plongeoir m. diving board

plongeon m. dive, plunge

plonger vt. to plunge, immerse; — vi. to plunge, dive; dip; submerge

plongeur m. diver; washer of dishes; — a. diving

ploutocrate m. plutocrat

ployable a. pliable, tractable

pluie f. rain

plume f. feather; pen; quill

plumeau m. feather duster

plumer vt. to pluck; — vi. to feather oars

plumet m. plume

plumeux a. feathery

plupart f. most, majority; pour la — mostly

pluralité f. plurality, majority

pluriel a. & m. (gram.) plural

plus adv. more; plus; ne — no more, no longer; au — at most, maximum; — tôt sooner; le — the most; de — besides, moreover; more, additional; extra; de — en — more and more; non — either, neither; — m. more; most, best; greatest number; (math.) plus sign

plusieurs a. pl. several

plus-que-parfait m. (gram.) pluperfect

plutonium m. plutonium

plutôt adv. rather; better, preferably

pluvial a. rainy; pertaining to rain

pluvieux a. rainy
pluviosité f. precipitation, rainfall
pneu m. tire
pneumatique a. pneumatic; — m. tire; letter sent by pneumatic tube
pneumonie f. pneumonia
pochade f. work done hastily
pochard m. drunk, drunkard
poche f. pocket; pouch; sac; bag, sack; ladle
pochée f. pocketful, contents of a pocket
pocher vt. to bruise, blacken; poach; sketch; stencil
pochetée f. pocketful
pochette f. small pocket; pouch
podagre f. gout; — a. gouty
podium m. podium
podomètre m. pedometer
poêle f. frying pan, pan; — m. stove, cooker; pall
poêlée f. panful
poêlette f. small frying pan
poêlon m. saucepan
poème m. poem
poésie f. poetry; poem
poète m. poet
poétique a. poetical, poetic; — f. poetics
poids m. weight; load, burden; heaviness; consequence, importance
poignant a. poignant, gripping
poignard m. dagger
poignarder vt. to stab
poigne f. grip, hold, grasp
poignée f. handful; handle; grip, hold; hilt, haft; — de main handshake
poignet m. wrist; cuff
poil m. hair; bristle; nap; down; (coll.): à — a. naked; bareback; être de mauvais — bad humored
poilu a. hairy; — m. soldier of the First World War
poinçon m. punch; awl; die, stamp; hallmark
poinçonner vt. to stamp; punch
poinçonneuse f. punch, punching machine, hole punch
poindre vi. to appear, come into view; dawn; sprout
poing m. fist, hand; coup de — m. punch, blow; menacer du — to shake a fist at
point m. point; period, dot; mark; (med.) stitch; à — cooked to a turn, medium; à — apropos; au — ready, in shape; in tune; in focus; deux —s (gram.) colon; — d'appui fulcrum; basis; — d'interrogation question mark; — du jour dawn, daybreak; — et virgule semicolon; sur le — de about to, on the point of; — adv. no, not; — du tout not at all
pointage m. checking, checking off, ticking off; scoring; timing; aiming, pointing
pointe f. point; pointed tool; promontory; tip; diaper, kerchief; (fig.) sharpness
pointer vt. to sharpen; prick; check a list; aim, point; — vi. to appear; rise; sprout
pointeur m. checker, scorer; chien — m. pointer (dog)
pointiller vt. to stipple, dot; harass; — vi. quibble

pointillerie f. quibbling
pointilleux a. fastidious; finicky; touchy
pointu a. pointed; sharp
pointure f. size, fit
poire f. pear
poireau m. leek
poirier m. pear tree
pois m. pea; — chiche chick pea; petits — pl. green peas
poison m. poison
poissard a. common, vulgar speech
poisser vt. to cover with a sticky substance; make sticky; pitch, tar
poisseux a. sticky, gummy
poisson m. fish; — rouge goldfish
poissonnerie f. fish market
poissonneux a. full of fish
poissonnier m. fishmonger, operator of a fish market
Poitevin m. & a. native of Poitou
poitrail m. breast of a horse
poitrinaire a. & m. consumptive, tubercular person
poitrine f. chest; breast, bust, bosom; brisket
poivre m. pepper; grain de — m. peppercorn; — de Cayenne red pepper
poivré a. peppered; peppery, spicy
poivrer vt. to pepper, season, spice
poivrier m. pepperbox; pepper plant
poivrière f. pepper shaker
poivron m. green pepper; allspice
poix f. pitch, resin
polaire a. polar
polarisateur a. polarizing; — m. polarizer
polarisation f. polarization
polariser vt. to polarize
polarité f. polarity
pôle m. (elec., geog.) pole
polémique f. polemic; — a. polemical
poli a. polished; polite; — m. polish
police f. police; policy; — d'assurance insurance policy; agent de — m. policeman; bonnet de — m. overseas cap
policer vt. to regulate, organize, police
polichinelle m. Punch, buffoon; théâtre de — m. Punch and Judy show
policier a. police; roman — m. detective novel; — m. detective, policeman
poliment adv. politely
poliomyélite f. poliomyelitis, infantile paralysis
polir vt. to polish; refine
polisseur m. one who polishes, buffer
polisseuse f. polishing machine, buffing machine
polissoir m. polishing implement, buffer
polisson m. rascal; mischievous child
polissonnerie f. mischief, mischievousness; lewdness
politesse f. politeness, courtesy
politicien m. politician
politique a. political; politic; diplomatic; — f. policy; politics; — m. politician
polka f. polka
polker vi. to polka
pollinisation f. pollinization
polluer vt. to pollute
pollution f. pollution
Pologne f. Poland

polonais a. & m. Polish; — m. Pole

poltron m. coward; — a. cowardly

poltronnerie f. cowardice

polycopier vt. to duplicate, reproduce

polyèdre m. polyhedron; — a. polyhedral

polygame a. polygamous; — m. polygamist

polygamie f. polygamy

polyglotte a. polyglot

polygone m. polygon; — a. polygonal

polygraphe m. & f. versatile author, writer on varied subjects

polymorphe a. polymorphous

Polynésie f. Polynesia

Polynésien m. & a. Polynesian

polynôme m. polynomial

polype m. polyp

polyphasé a. multi-phase

polyphonique a. polyphonic

polysoc m. gangplow

polysyllabe a. polysyllabic

polytechnicien m. student at the École Polytechnique

polytechnique a. polytechnic

polythéiste m. & f. polytheist; — a. polytheist; — a. polytheistic

polyvalent a. polyvalent, multivalent

pommade f. pomade; salve, ointment

pommader vt. to pomade

pomme f. apple; knob; — d'arrosoir sprinkler; — de pin pine cone; — de terre potato; —s à l'huile potato salad; —s frites French fried potatoes; —s en purée, purée de —s mashed potatoes; —s vapeur boiled potatoes; —s rissolées roast potatoes

pommé a. round; consummate

pommeau m. knob; pummel of a sword

pommelé a. dappled, mottled

pommelle f. grating

pommeraie f. apple orchard

pommette f. cheekbone; knob

pommier m. apple tree

pompadour m. flowered cloth

pompe f. pump; pomp, splendor; —s funèbres pl. funeral

pomper vt. to pump

pompeux a. pompous

pompier m. fireman

pompon m. pompon; puff

pomponner vt. to ornament, adorn, deck out, festoon

ponant m. Occident

ponce f. pumice

ponceau m. culvert; corn poppy, red poppy

poncer vt. to sand, sandpaper; rub with pumice

poncho m. poncho

ponction f. (med.) opening, pricking; puncture

ponctualité f. punctuality

ponctuation f. punctuation

ponctué a. punctuated; having dotted line

ponctuel a. punctual

ponctuer vt. to punctuate; accentuate

pondaison f. egg laying

pondérable a. ponderable, weighable

pondérateur a. stabilizing

pondération f. ponderation; poise, balance

pondéré a. well-balanced; collected, cool

pondérer vt. to balance, stabilize

pondeuse f. laying hen

pondre vt. to lay (eggs)

poney m. pony

pongé m. pongee

pont m. bridge; deck of a ship; axle, shaft; platform; — aérien airlift; — élévateur (auto.) grease rack; tête de —f. bridgehead

ponte f. egg laying

ponté a. equipped with a deck

pontée f. deck cargo

ponter vt. to lay a deck (on a ship); — vt. play against the bank (at cards)

pontet m. trigger guard

pontife m. pontiff; pope

pontifical a. pontifical

pontificat m. pontificate

pontifier vi. to pontificate

pont-levis m. drawbridge

ponton m. pontoon; hulk

popeline f. poplin

populace f. populace, mob, rabble

populacier a. vulgar, common, low

populaire a. of the people; popular; chanson —f. folk song

populariser vt. to popularize

popularité f. popularity

population f. population

populeux a. populous

poquet m. hole for seeds

porc m. hog, pig; pork

porcelaine f. porcelain, china

porcelet m. piglet; wood louse

porc-épic m. porcupine

porche m. porch

porcher m. swineherd

poreux a. porous

pornographie f. pornography

pornographique a. pornographic

porosité f. porosity

porphyre m. porphyry

port m. port, harbor; postage; charge for transportation; carriage, deportment

portable a. portable; wearable

portage m. portage; transport, transporting; (mech.) bearing

portail m. portal, front gate

portant a. bearing; bien — in good health; mal — not well; — m. support; handle

portatif a. portable

porte f. door, gate; doorway; entrance; — cochère f. carriage entrance, gate at beginning of a driveway; — d'entrée front door

porté a. inclined; carried; worn; — à inclined to

porte-à-faux m. overhang; en — in a dangerous position

porte-affiches m. bulletin board; billboard

porte-aiguilles m. needle case

porte-allumettes m. matchbox

porte-amarre m. gun for shooting mooring lines

porte-avions m. aircraft carrier

porte-bagages m. baggage rack, luggage carrier

porteballe m. peddlar

porte-bannière m. & f. standard bearer

porte-bât m. pack animal

porte-billets m. billfold

porte-bonheur m. good luck charm

porte-cartes m. card case

porte-chapeaux m. hat rack

porte-cigarette m. cigarette holder

porte-clefs m. guard, turnkey

porte-copie m. copy stand

porte-couteau m. knife rest

porte-documents m. zippered portfolio

porte-drapeau m. flag bearer

portée f. brood, litter; scope, range, reach, extent; comprehension; implication, meaning; (mus.) staff

portefaix m. porter; stevedore

porte-fenêtre f. French door, French window

portefeuille m. portfolio; billfold, wallet

portemanteau m. coat rack; suitcase; saddlebag

porte-mine m. automatic pencil

porte-monnaie m. coin purse, change purse

porte-musique m. music case

porte-objet m. microscope slide

porte-parapluies m. umbrella stand

porte-parole m. spokesman

porte-pipes m. pipe rack

porte-plat m. trivet, hot pad; hot-pan holder

porte-plume m. penholder

porter vt. to carry, bear; raise, lift; indicate, mark; bring; take; wear; — vi. to bear, have an effect; se — bien to be well

porte-serviettes m. towel rack

porteur m. porter, carrier, bearer

porte-vent m. wind tunnel, air duct

porte-vêtement(s) m. clothes hanger

porte-voix m. megaphone; speaking tube

portier m. doorman; porter; janitor

portière f. door of a vehicle

portillon m. gate, barrier

portionner vt. to apportion

portique m. portico

portland m. Portland cement

Porto m. port wine

portrait m. portrait

portraitiste m. & f. portrait painter

portraiturer vt. to paint the portrait of

Portugais m. & a. Portuguese

Portugal m. Portugal

pose f. pose, posing, posture; (phot.) exposure; — instantanée snapshot

posé a. steady, even, sedate

posemètre m. (phot.) exposure meter

poser vt. to put, place; — vi. to pose; — une question to ask a question; se — (avi.) to land; se — en set oneself up as

poseur a. posing, putting on airs, affected; — m. affected person; — de mines (naut.) minelayer

positif a. positive

position f. position, location; standing, status; stance; post, job

positivisme m. positivism

possédé a. possessed; — m. person possessed by the devil

posséder vt. to possess, have, own

possesseur m. possessor

possessif a. & m. possessive

possession f. possession, ownership; property

possibilité f. possibility

possible a. possible; — m. everything possible, utmost

postage m. packing for mailing; mailing

postdater vt. to postdate

poste f. post, mail; post office; mettre (une lettre) à la poste to mail a letter; — recommandée f. registered mail; — restante general delivery; — m. post; station; job, position; entry in a ledger; — de TSF radio set

poster vt. to post, station

postérieur a. posterior; back, hind; later; — m. posterior

postérité f. posterity

posthume a. posthumous

postiche a. false, imitation

postier m. postal worker

postillon m. postilion

postopératoire a. post-operative

postscolaire a. postgraduate; after-school

post-scriptum m. postscript

postsynchronisation f. dubbing

postsynchroniser vt. to dub movies

postulant m. candidate, applicant

postulat m. postulate

postuler vt. to apply for

posture f. posture, position

pot m. pot; jug, jar; — d'échappement (auto.) muffler; — pourri stew; mixture

potable a. drinkable; eau — f. drinking water

potage m. soup

potager a. culinary; jardin — m. vegetable garden; truck farm

potasse f. potash

potassium m. potassium

pot-au-feu m. boiled or pot-roasted beef and vegetables

pot-de-vin m. tip; bribe

poteau m. post, stake, pole; — indicateur signpost

potée f. potful, jugful

potelé a. plump, chubby

potence f. gallows; bracket, support

potentat m. potentate

potentiel a. potential; — m. potential, potentialities

poter vt. & vi. to putt (in golf)

poterie f. pottery

poterne f. postern

potiche f. porcelain vase

potier m. potter

potin m. pewter; (coll.) talk, gossip; ado, fuss

potion f. potion

potiron m. pumpkin

pou m. louse, tick

pouah! interj. ugh!

poubelle f. garbage can, refuse can

pouce m. thumb; big toe; inch; (fig.) very small quantity

poucettes f. pl. thumbscrew

poudre f. powder; gunpowder; en — powdered, ground; — de riz face powder

poudrer *vt.* to powder
poudreux *a.* dusty, powdery
poudrière *f.* powder magazine; powder horn
poudrin *m.* spindrift, sea spray, fine spray
poudroyant *a.* dusty
poudrier *m.* powder box; compact
poudroyer *vt.* to cover with dust; — *vi.* to raise dust
pouf *m.* pouf, ottoman; — *interj.* phew! plop!
pouffer *vi.* to burst out laughing
pouillerie *f.* place infested with lice; hovel; poverty
pouilleux *a.* lousy, lice-ridden; wretched, filthy
poulailler *m.* henhouse; poulterer
poulain *m.* colt, foal
poulaine *f.* (naut.) latrine
poularde *f.* chicken
poule *f.* hen; gambling pool
poulet *m.* chicken
poulette *f.* pullet
pouliche *f.* filly
poulie *f.* pulley; block
pouliner *vi.* to foal
poulinière *f.* brood mare
pouliot *m.* windlass
poulpe *m.* octopus
pouls *m.* pulse
poumon *m.* lung
poupard *m.* baby; doll; — *a.* baby-like; chubby
poupe *f.* poop, stern
poupée *f.* doll; puppet
poupin *a.* baby-like, pink, rosy
pouponnière *f.* nursery school, day nursery
pour *prep.* for, in order to; for the sake of; because of; with regard to; — ainsi — dire so to speak; — que *conj.* in order that; — *m.* pros, advantages; le — et le contre pros and cons
pourboire *m.* gratuity, tip
pourceau *m.* hog, pig
pour-cent *m.* per cent; —age percentage
pourchasser *vt.* to pursue; harass
pourfendre *vt.* to attack, tilt with
pourlécher *v.*, se — to lick one's lips
pourparlers *m. pl.* parleys, conferences, negotiations
pourpier *m.* (bot.) purslane
pourpre *m.* dark red; — *f.* purple, symbol of royalty
pourpré *a.* dark red
pourquoi *adv.* why
pourri *a.* rotten; putrid
pourrir *vt. & vi.* to rot
pourriture *f.* rot, decay; rottenness
poursuite *f.* pursuit; —s *pl.* legal action
poursuivant *m.* plaintiff at law
poursuivre *vt.* to pursue, chase; prosecute; continue
pourtant *adv.* however, still, nevertheless
pourtour *m.* circumference, periphery
pourvoi *m.* appeal at law
pourvoir *vt.* to provide, supply, furnish
pourvoyeur *m.* provider; purveyor; caterer

pourvu que *conj.* provided
pousse *f.* shoot, sprout; growth
poussé *a.* deep; comprehensive; elaborate
poussée *f.* push, thrust, shove; growth, sprouting; buoyancy
pousse-pousse *m.* rickshaw
pousser *vt.* to push, urge, drive; utter — *vi.* push; grow; sprout
poussier *m.* coal dust
poussière *f.* dust; spray
poussiéreux *a.* dusty
poussin *m.* spring chicken; baby chick
poussinière *f.* incubator for chicks; chicken coop
poussoir *m.* push button
poutrage *m.* beams, rafters
poutre *f.* beam, girder
poutrelle *f.* small beam
pouvoir *vt.* to be able; be possible; — *m.* power, authority
pragmatique *a.* pragmatic
prairie *f.* meadow; grassland, prairie
pralin *m.* kind of fertilizer; burnt-sugar frosting
praline *f.* burnt almond candy, praline
praliner *vt.* to brown (in sugar)
praticabilité *f.* practicability, feasibility
practicable *a.* practicable, feasible; sociable, easy-going
praticien *m.* practitioner
pratiquant *a.* practicing, (eccl.) orthodox
pratique *f.* practice, exercise, use; application; custom; experience; — *a.* practical
pratiquer *vt.* to practice, use, exercise; effect; frequent
pré *m.* meadow
préalable *a.* previous; preliminary; au — previously, beforehand
préambule *m.* preamble
préau *m.* yard, playground, recreation area
préavis *m.* advance notice
préaviser *vt.* to give advance notice to
prébendier *m.* (eccl.) prebendary
précaire *a.* precarious
précaution *f.* precaution, caution, care
précautionner *vt.* to warn, caution; se — to take precautions
précautionneux *a.* cautious, careful
précédemment *a.* before, previously
précédence *f.* precedence, priority
précédent *a.* preceding, previous, having priority; — *m.* precedent
précéder *vt.* to precede; have precedence of
précellence *f.* superiority
précepte *m.* precept
précepteur *m.* tutor
préchauffage *m.* preheating
prêche *f.* sermon
prêcher *vt.* to preach
prêcheur *m.* (coll.) preacher; — *a.* preaching, sermonizing
précieux *a.* precious; affected
préciosité *f.* affectation; preciosity
précipice *m.* precipice
précipitamment *adv.* headlong, in haste, precipitately

précipitation *f.* precipitation, haste; rain, rainfall

précipité *a.* precipitate; precipitous, hasty; hurried, rushed; headlong; — *m.* (chem.) precipitate

précipiter *vt.* to precipitate, hurry; se — to rush upon, rush into

précis *a.* precise, exact; — *m.* brief summary

précisément *adv.* precisely, just, exactly

préciser *vt.* to specify

précision *f.* precision, preciseness, exactness; specification, detail

précité *a.* above, aforementioned

précoce *a.* precocious; maturing early

précocité *f.* precociousness, precocity

préconception *f.* preconception

préconcevoir *vt.* to preconceive

préconiser *vt.* to advocate

préconnaissance *f.* prior knowledge, foreknowledge

précurseur *m.* precursor, forerunner

prédateur *a.* predatory

prédécéder *vi.* to die first

prédécesseur *m.* predecessor

prédestination *f.* predestination

prédestiner *vt.* to predestine

prédéterminer *vt.* to predetermine

prédicat *m.* predicate

prédicateur *m.* preacher

prédicatif *a.* predicative

prédiction *f.* prediction, forecast

prédilection *f.* predilection; de — favorite

prédire *vt.* to predict, foretell

prédisposer *vt.* to predispose; prejudice

prédisposition *f.* predisposition; prejudice

prédominance *f.* predominance

prédominant *a.* predominant, prevailing

prédominer *a. & vi.* to predominate

prééminence *f.* pre-eminence

prééminent *a.* pre-eminent

préemptif *a.* pre-emptive

préemption *f.* pre-emption

préétabli *a.* pre-established

préétablir *vt.* to pre-establish

préexister *vi.* to pre-exist

préfabrication *f.* prefabrication

préfabriqué *a.* prefabricated

préface *f.* preface

préfacer *vt.* to preface

préfecture *f.* prefecture; police headquarters in Paris; administrative headquarters of a Department

préférable *a.* preferable, better

préféré *a.* preferred; — *m.* favorite

préférence *f.* preference; de — preferential; (com.) preferred; preferably

préférer *vt.* to prefer

préfet *m.* prefect; — de police chief of police

préfixe *m.* prefix

préfixer *vt.* to prefix; determine in advance

préhenseur *a.* prehensile

préhistorique *a.* prehistoric

préjudice *m.* prejudice, wrong, detriment

préjudiciable *a.* prejudicial, injurious

préjudicier *vi.* to be injurious, be prejudicial

préjugé *m.* prejudice, bias; presumption; legal precedent

préjuger *vt.* to prejudge

prélart *m.* tarpaulin

prélasser *v.*, se — to act important

prélat *m.* prelate

prélèvement *m.* deduction; sample

prélever *vt.* to deduct, take off

préliminaire *a.* preliminary

prélude *m.* prelude

prématuré *a.* premature, inopportune

préméditation *f.* premeditation

préméditer *vt.* to premeditate

prémices *f. pl.* first fruits; (fig.) beginnings

premier *a.* first; — ministre *m.* Prime Minister; premier; le — venu anyone

première *f.* first performance, opening night

premièrement *adv.* first, in the first place

premier-né *a. & m.* first-born

premier-paris *m.* lead article in newspaper

prémisse *f.* premise

prémonition *f.* premonition

prémunir *vt.* to forewarn; se — contre be prepared for

prenable *a.* pregnable, accessible

prenant *a.* attractive; adhesive; — *m.* taker

prénatal *a.* prenatal

prendre *vt.* to take; seize, grab; get; acquire; take on; catch; pick up, call for; take in; influence, gain, win; — *vi.* to take, set; be effective, work; succeed; freeze; — corps take form; — le change be mistaken; — le large flee; se — to catch, be caught; s'en — à to blame; s'y — to go about it, manage

preneur *m.* taker; purchaser; catcher

prénom *m.* first name

prénommé *a.* above-named

préoccupation *f.* preoccupation, care, concern; absent-mindedness

préoccupé *a.* preoccupied; absentminded

préoccuper *vt.* to preoccupy, concern; se — be preoccupied, be busy

préopiner *vi.* to speak or vote first

préordonné *a.* preordained

préparateur *m.* preparer; coach

préparation *f.* preparation

préparatoire *a.* preparatory

préparer *vt.* to prepare, get ready; se — to get ready; be in the process, be developing

prépondérance *f.* preponderance

prépondérant *a.* preponderant, major, key

préposé *m.* person in charge

préposer *vt.* to name, appoint

prépositif *a.* (gram.) prepositive, prepositional

préposition *f.* preposition

prérogative *f.* prerogative

près *adv.* near, close; à cela — except for that; à peu — almost, nearly; roughly, approximately; — de *prep.* near; nearly; ready to, about to

présage *m.* presage, omen, foreboding

présager *vt.* to forebode, presage, predict

pré-salé *m.* salt-marsh lamb

presbyte *a.* far-sighted

presbytère *m.* parsonage, rectory

prescience f. prescience
prescient a. prescient
prescription f. regulation(s); direction(s); prescription (at law)
prescrire vt. to prescribe, call for, ordain
préséance f. priority, precedence
présence f. presence; — d'esprit presence of mind
présent a. present; — m. present time; (gram.) present tense; à — at present, right now
présentable a. presentable
présentateur m. introducer, presenter
présentation f. presentation, introduction
présentement adv. at present, at the moment, right now
présenter vt. to present; introduce; se — to present oneself; appear; introduce oneself; arise, come about
préservateur a. preservative
préservatif a. & m. preservative; preventive
préservation f. preservation, conservation, saving
préserver vt. to preserve, save, protect
présidence f. presidency, chairmanship
président m. president, chairman, presiding officer
présidentiel a. presidential
présider vt. & vi. to preside over
présomptif a. presumptive
présomption f. presumption
présomptueux a. presumptuous
presque adv. almost, nearly
presqu'île f. peninsula
pressant a. pressing, urgent
presse f. press; crowd; haste; impressment (history)
pressé a. pressed; crowded; squeezed; in a hurry; citron — lemonade
presse-citron m. lemon squeezer
presse-fruits m. fruit press
pressentiment m. presentiment, feeling, foreboding
pressentir vt. to have a presentiment of, sense in advance
presse-papiers m. paperweight
presse-purée m. vegetable masher
presser vt. & vi. to press, squeeze; urge; hurry; se — to hurry; crowd
pressier m. pressman
pression f. pressure; (elec.) tension
pressoir m. wine press; push button
pressurer vt. to press, extract, squeeze
prestance f. bearing, carriage of a person
prestation f. prestation; oath; lending, loaning
preste a. quick, nimble, agile
prestesse f. nimbleness, quickness, agility
prestidigitateur m. prestidigitator, magician
prestige m. prestige, renown; wonder, marvel
prestigieux a. marvelous, amazing
présumer vt. to presume, assume; allege
présupposer vt. to presuppose
prêt a. ready, prepared; — m. loan
prétendant m. aspirant, candidate, applicant
prétendre vt. to claim, maintain; aspire

prétendu a. so-called, alleged; — n. (coll.) future spouse, intended
prête-nom m. figurehead, front
prétentieux a. pretentious
prétention f. pretension, claim
prêter vt. to lend; attribute; — attention to pay attention; — serment to take an oath; se — à to lend oneself to, agree to; indulge in
prétérit m. preterite
prétexte m. pretext, excuse; sous — de supposedly, presumably
prétexter vt. to offer as a pretext
prétoire m. courtroom
prêteur m. lender; — sur gages pawnbroker
prêtre m. priest; —sse f. priestess
prêtrise f. priesthood
preuve f. proof, evidence
preux a. valiant, courageous
prévaloir vi. to prevail; se — to avail oneself
prévaricateur a. dishonest public official
prévarication f. malfeasance, dishonesty
prévenance f. kind attention, consideration
prévenant a. considerate, attentive; engaging, prepossessing
prévenir vt. to anticipate; prevent; prejudice; warn, inform
préventif a. preventive; pre-emptive (cards)
prévention f. prejudice; custody
prévenu a. prejudiced, accused (at law)
prévision f. forecast, estimate
prévoir vt. to foresee; forecast; provide for, anticipate
prévôt m. provost
prévoyance f. foresight, precaution
prévoyant a. foreseeing, looking ahead, farsighted
prie-dieu m. prayer desk
prier vt. to pray; ask; invite; je vous (en) prie please, if you please
prière f. prayer; request
prieuré m. priory
primaire a. primary
primauté f. priority; primacy
prime f. premium; bonus, gift; (eccl.) prime; — a. first, earliest; de — abord first of all
primer vt. to surpass; give a prize to
primerose f. hollyhock
primesaut m. first impulse
prime-sautier a. impulsive; quick
primeur f. newness, earliness; early crop
primevère f. (bot.) primrose; cowslip
primitif a. primitive; primary; early; earliest; crude
primo adv. first of all, firstly
primogéniture f. primogeniture
primordial a. primordial, primeval
prince m. prince; ruler, monarch
princeps a., édition — f. first edition
princesse f. princess
princier a. princely, royal
principal a. principal, main, chief; — m. principal; main point, main thing
principauté f. principality
principe m. principle

printanier *a.* spring, springlike

printemps *m.* spring, springtime

priorité *f.* priority, precedence

pris *a.* taken, caught; busy, occupied; bien — having a good figure or shape

prise *f.* taking, capture; hold, grip; setting, hardening; engaging of gears; valve, intake; (naut.) prize; en venir aux —s to come to blows, come to grips; hors de — out of gear; lâcher — to let go; — de corps arrest; — de courant (elect.) plug, outlet; — de tabac pinch of snuff; — de vue viewfinder

prisée *f.* evaluation, appraisal

priser *vt.* to appraise, value, prize; to take snuff

priseur *m.* appraiser; auctioneer; user of snuff

prismatique *a.* prismatic

prisme *m.* prism

prisonnier *m.* prisoner

privation *f.* privation; deprivation; poverty; hardship

privautés *f. pl.* familiarity, liberties

privé *a.* private; privy; tame

priver *vt.* to deprive; se — to do without, stint

privilège *m.* privilege; authorization, license

privilégié *a.* privileged; authorized, licensed; preferred (stock)

privilégier *vt.* to privilege; authorize, license

prix *m.* price, value, cost; prize, award; à tout — at any price; au — de at the price of; compared with, in comparison with; hors de — prohibitive; — fixe set price

prix-courant *m.* price list, catalog

probable *a.* probable, likely

probabilité *f.* probability, likelihood

probe *a.* honest, upright, of integrity

problème *m.* problem

procéde *m.* proceeding, procedure; process

procéder *vi.* to proceed

procédure *f.* procedure; proceedings

procès *m.* lawsuit; trial; ceremony, formality, ado; process

processif *a.* pertaining to courtroom procedure

processionnel *a.* processional

processionner *vi.* to file by (as in a procession)

processus *m.* process; development

procès-verbal *m.* report, record, minutes

prochain *a.* next; neighboring, nearest; imminent; — *m.* neighbor, fellow man

prochainement *adv.* in the near future, shortly, soon

proche *a.* near, close; —es *m. pl.* relatives

proclamation *f.* proclamation

proclamer *vt.* to proclaim

proconsul *m.* proconsul

procréateur *a.* procreative; — *m.* procreator

procréation *f.* procreation

procréer *vt.* to procreate

procurable *a.* procurable, obtainable

procuration *f.* power of attorney; proxy

procurer *vt.* to procure, obtain

procureur *m.* attorney; prosecuting attorney, prosecutor

prodigalité *f.* prodigality; extravagance

prodige *m.* prodigy, marvel

prodigieux *a.* prodigious

prodigue *a. & m.* prodigal; spendthrift

prodiguer *vt.* to waste, squander; lavish

producer *m.* movie producer

producteur *a.* productive; — *m.* producer

productif *a.* productive

production *f.* production; producing; yield; product

productivité *f.* productivity

produire *vt.* to produce; yield, give, bear; se — to happen, take place, occur

produit *m.* product; proceeds

proéminence *f.* prominence; protuberance

proéminent *a.* prominent; protuberant

profanateur *m.* profaner

profanation *f.* profanation, desecration

profane *a.* profane; sacrilegious; secular, lay; — *m.* layman, uninitiated person; something profane

profaner *vt.* to profane, desecrate

proférer *vt.* to utter

professer *vt.* to profess; teach

professeur *m.* professor, teacher

profession *f.* profession; occupation, business

professionnel *a. & m.* professional

professoral *a.* professorial

professorat *m.* professorship

profil *m.* profile, side view; outline, shape, contour

profilé *a.* in sections, sectional; streamlined

profilée *f.* side view

profiler *vt.* to profile; shape; se — to be silhouetted, be outlined

profitable *a.* profitable, advantageous

profiter *vi.* to profit, be profitable; gain, by; grow, develop

profiteur *m.* profiteer

profond *a.* profound; deep; — *m.* deepest part, depth(s)

profondeur *f.* profundity, depth

profus *a.* profuse

profusion *f.* profusion, abundance

progéniture *f.* progeny, offspring

prognostique *a.* prognostic

programme *m.* program; plan; curriculum

progrès *m.* progress

progresser *vi.* to progress

progressif *a.* progressive

progressiste *a. & m. & f.* (pol.) progressive

progression *f.* progress, progression

prohiber *vt.* to prohibit, forbid

prohibitif *a.* prohibitive

proie *f.* prey; en — à prey to; subject to; affected by

projecteur *m.* projector; searchlight

projectile *a. & m.* projectile

projection *f.* projection; (phot.) slide; beam, shaft of light

projecture *f.* projection

projet *m.* project, plan

projeter *vt.* to project; plan; se — to project, stand out

prolétaire *a. & m.* proletarian
prolétariat *m.* proletariate
prolifération *f.* proliferation
prolifère *a.* proliferous
prolifique *a.* prolific
prolixe *a.* prolix, verbose
prolixité *f.* prolixity, verbosity
prolongateur *m.* extension cord
prolongation *f.* prolongation; extension of time
prolongé *a.* prolonged, long
prolongement *m.* prolongation; extension
prolonger *vt.* to prolong, extend, lengthen
promenade *f.* walking, walk, stroll; promenade; faire une — take a walk; — en auto auto ride; — en bateau boat ride
promener *vt.* to take for a walk; run one's hand, cast one's eyes; se — to take a walk
promeneur *m.* walker
promenoir *m.* promenade; (theat.) standing room
promesse *f.* promise
prometteur *a.* promising
promettre *vt. & vi.* to promise
promis *a.* promised; — *m.* fiancé; -e *f.* fiancée
promiscuité *f.* promiscuity
promontoire *m.* promontory, cape
promoteur *m.* promoter
promotion *f.* promotion
promouvoir *vt.* to promote
prompt *a.* prompt, ready, quick minded
promptitude *f.* promptitude; readiness, quickness
promu *a.* promoted
promulgation *f.* promulgation
promulguer *vt.* to promulgate, publish
pronation *f.* prone position
prône *m.* sermon
prôner *vt.* to praise; preach
pronom *m.* pronoun
pronominal *a.* pronominal; verbe — *m.* reflexive verb
prononçable *a.* pronounceable
prononcé *a.* pronounced, marked, decided, definite; — *m.* decision, verdict
prononcer *vt.* to pronounce; deliver; declare
prononciation *f.* pronunciation
pronostic *m.* prognostic, prognostication; (med.) prognosis
pronostiquer *vt.* to prognosticate, predict
propagande *f.* publicity, advertising, propaganda
propagandiste *m. & f.* propagandist
propagateur *a.* propagating; — *m.* propagator
propager *vt.* to propagate; se — to spread; be propagated
propédeutique *f.* first year of university studies
propension *f.* propensity
prophétie *f.* prophecy
prophétique *a.* prophetic
prophétiser *vt.* to prophesy; forecast
prophylactique *a.* prophylactic
prophylaxie *f.* prophylaxis
propice *a.* propitious, auspicious
propitiatoire *a.* propitiatory, conciliatory

proportionné *a.* proportioned; proportionate
proportionnel *a.* proportional, in proportion
proportionner *vt.* to proportion
propos *m.* discourse, talk, words; design; purpose; subject; à — suitable, appropriate; by the way; à — de on the subject of; hors de — inopportune, out of place
proposer *vt.* to propose, present, recommend, suggest
proposition *f.* proposition, proposal, motion; clause
propre *a.* one's own; clean; proper; fit, suitable
proprement *adv.* properly; cleanly; appropriately
propreté *f.* cleanliness, neatness
propriétaire *m. & f.* proprietor, owner; landlord
propriété *f.* property; ownership; propriety; quality, characteristic
propulser *vt.* to propel
propulseur *a.* propelling; — *m.* propeller; outboard motor
prorata *m.* share; au — pro rata
proroger *vt.* to extend, prolong; adjourn
prosaïque *a.* prosaic
prosateur *m.* prose writer
proscenium *m.* (theat.) proscenium
proscription *f.* proscription, proscribing
proscrire *vt.* to proscribe, outlaw; abolish, forbid
proscrit *a.* proscribed, outlawed; — *m.* proscript, outlaw
prosélyte *m. & f.* proselyte
prospecter *vt.* to prospect
prospecteur *m.* prospector
prospectus *m.* prospectus; leaflet, handbill
prospérer *vi.* to prosper, thrive
prospérité *f.* prosperity
prostate *f.* prostate
prosternation *f.* prone position; prostration; bowing
prosterné *a.* prone, prostrate
prosternement *m.* prone position, prostration; bowing
prosterner *vt.*, se — to prostrate oneself; bow down
prostituée *f.* prostitute
prostitution *f.* prostitution
prostration *f.* prostration, exhaustion, breakdown; prone position
prostré *a.* prostrate, exhausted
protagoniste *m.* protagonist
protane *m.* methane
protase *f.* (theat.) protasis, exposition
protecteur *m.* protector, guard; patron; — *a.* protective
protection *f.* protection, patronage
protectionisme *m.* protectionism
protectionniste *m. & f.* protectionist
protectorat *m.* protectorate
protéger *vt.* to protect, guard; patronize
protège-vue *m.* eyeshade
protéine *f.* protein
protestant *a. & m.* Protestant
protestantisme *m.* Protestantism
protestateur *m.* protestor

protestation f. protest; protestation
protester vt. & vi. to protest
protêt m. legal protest
prothèse f. prosthesis, artificial limb or part
protocolaire a. pertaining to protocol
protocole m. protocol, etiquette
proton m. proton
protoplasme m. protoplasm
prototype m. prototype
protozoaire m. protozoan
protubérance f. protuberance; bump; knob
protubérant a. protuberant
proue f. (naut.) prow, bow
prouesse f. prowess; feat
prouver vt. to prove, establish
provenance f. origin, source; production; en — de coming from
provençal a. Provençal, of Provence; m. Provençal
Provence f. Provence
provende f. fodder, provender
provenir vi. to proceed, arise, come, result, issue
proverbe m. proverb
providence f. providence
providentiel a. providential
province f. province; country; de — provincial
provincial a. & m. provincial
proviseur m. school principal
provision f. provision; supply; stock; deposit; reserve; funds
provisoire a. provisional, temporary, acting
provocant a. provocative
provocateur a. provocative; — m. provoker, instigator
provocatif a. provocative
provoquer vt. to provoke, instigate; arouse; challenge
proximité f. proximity, nearness
prude a. prudish; — f. prude
prudemment adv. prudently
prudence f. prudence, caution, discretion
prudent a. prudent, cautious, discreet
pruderie f. prudery, prudishness
prud'homme m. elected arbiter
prune f. plum
pruneau m. prune
prunelle f. pupil of the eye; sloe
prunier m. plum tree
prurit m. itching
Prusse f. Prussia
Prussien m. & a. Prussian
psalmiste m. psalmist
psalmodier vt. & vi. to intone
psaume m. psalm
psautier m. psalm book, Psalter
pseudonyme m. pseudonym
pseudopode n. pseudopod
psychanalyse f. psychoanalysis
psychanalyser vt. to psychoanalyze
psychanalyste m. & f. psychoanalyst
psyché f. movable mirror on a standard
psychiatre m. psychiatrist
psychiatrie f. psychiatry
psychique a. psychic
psychologie f. psychology

psychologique a. psychological
psychologue m. & f. psychologist
psychose f. psychosis
psychosomatique a. psychosomatic
psychothérapie f. psychotherapy
ptomaine f. ptomaine
P.T.T.: Postes Télégraphes Téléphones postal and telegraph service
puant a. smelly, stinking
puanteur f. stink, smell, stench
pubère a. in puberty, pubescent
puberté f. puberty
public (publique) a. public; open; — m. public, the people
publication f. publication, publishing
publiciste m. publicist, newspaperman
publicité f. advertising
publier vt. to publish
puce f. flea
pucelle f. maid, virgin
puceron m. aphid
pudeur f. decency, modesty
pudibond a. prudish, excessively modest
pudibonderie f. prudishness
pudique a. chaste
puer vi. to stink, smell
puériculture f. raising, rearing of children
puéril a. childish, puerile
puérilité f. puerility
puffisme m. publicity, boosting
puffiste m. booster
pugilat m. pugilism, boxing
pugiliste m. pugilist, boxer
puiné a. younger
puis adv. then, afterwards; moreover, besides
puisage m. pumping; droit de — m. water rights
puisard m. cesspool; sump
puisatier m. well digger
puisette f. scoop, ladle
puisoir m. large industrial scoop
puisque conj. since, as; but
puissamment adv. powerfully
puissance f. power, force, strength; authority, control
puissant a. powerful, strong, potent
puits m. well; shaft; hole
pullman m. luxury car; parlor car
pulluler vi. to multiply; swarm; pullulate
pulmonaire a. pulmonary
pulmonie f. lung disease
pulpe f. pulp
pulper vt. to pulp
pulpeux a. pulpy
pulsatif a. throbbing
pulsation f. pulsation, throbbing
pulvérisateur m. pulverizer; atomizer
pulvérisation f. pulverization
pulvériser vt. to pulverize, crush, grind; atomize
pulvériseur m. disc plow
puma m. puma
punaise f. bedbug; thumbtack
punch m. punch (beverage)
punir vt. to punish
punition f. punishment, punishing; penalty
pupe f. pupa, chrysalis
pupille m. & f. legal ward; — f. pupil of

the eye
pupitre m. desk; lectern; music stand
pur a. pure; simple; clear
purée f. thick soup; mashed vegetable
pureté f. purity, pureness
purgatif a. & m. purgative
purgation f. purgation, purging
purge f. purge; purgative; purging; draining; cleaning; redeeming, paying off
purger vt. to purge, cleanse; clear; redeem,
pay off; drain
purificateur a. purifying; — m. purifier
purification f. purification
purifier vt. to purify, refine; clean
puriste m. purist
purpurin m. crimson, dark red
pur-sang m. thoroughbred, race horse
purulent a. purulent
pus m. pus
pusillanime a. pusillanimous
pusillanimité f. pusillanimity
pustule f. pustule
putatif a. putative, supposed
putois m. skunk, polecat
putréfaction f. putrefaction
putréfier vt. to putrify
putride a. putrid, rotten
puzzle m. jigsaw puzzle
pygmée m. & f. pygmy
pyjama m. pajamas
pylône m. pylon, tower
pylore m. pyloris
pyorrhée f. pyorrhea
pyramidal a. pyramidal
pyramide f. pyramid
Pyrénées f. pl. Pyrenees
pyrite f. pyrite
pyrotechnie f. pyrotechnics
pyrotechnique a. pyrotechnic
python m. python

Q

Quadragésime f. old name of Lent;
dimanche de la — m. first Sunday in
Lent
quadrangulaire a. quadrangular
quadratique a. quadratic
quadrature f. squaring
quadriennal a. quadrennial
quadrilatéral a. quadrilateral
quadrilatère m. quadrilateral
quadrillage m. squaring, checkering,
cross-ruling
quadrillé a. squared, checked, cross-ruled
quadriller vt. to cross-rule
quadrimoteur a. four-engined
quadrupède m. quadruped
quadrupler vt. & vi. to quadruple
quai m. quay, wharf; embankment; (rail.)
platform
qualificatif a. qualifying
qualification f. qualification; qualifying;
character; naming, calling, designating
qualifier vt. to qualify; call, designate;
se — to qualify; call oneself
qualitatif a. qualitative
qualité f. quality, rank; characteristic,
property; qualification; occupation

quand adv. when; depuis — how long; —
conj. when; although, though, even if;
— même even though; in spite of all;
just the same
quant à prep. as to, as for
quant-à-moi, quant-à-soi m. reserve,
aloofness
quantième m. a day of the month
quantitatif a. quantitative; (gram.) quantity
quantité f. quantity, amount
quantum m. quantum; amount
quarantaine f. forty, around forty, two
score; quarantine
quarante a. forty
quarantième a. fortieth
quart m. quarter, fourth; (naut.) watch;
¼ liter; ¼ liter bottle; — d'heure quarter-hour, fifteen minutes
quarte f. quart; (mus.) fourth
quarteron a. & m. quadroon
quartier m. quarter, district; piece, part,
portion; barracks, camp; — général
headquarters
quarto adv. fourthly; in fourth place
quarts m. quarts
quasi adv. almost
quatorze a. fourteen; fourteenth
quatorzième a. fourteenth
quatrain m. quatrain
quatre a. four; fourth
quatre-saisons f. strawberry plant bearing
very small fruit; marchand des — m.
pushcart vendor of seasonal fruits and
vegetables
quatre-vingts a. eighty
quatrième a. fourth
quatuor m. quartet
que conj. that; if, when, as, than, till,
until, whether, than; afin — de sorts
— so that; ne . . . . — only; — pron.
that, whom, which; — interr. pron.
what; how; ce → that which, what; which;
(with exclamations)
quel (quelle) a. interr. which, what;
what (a) (in exclamations); — pron.
whatever
quelconque a. any, whatever, any at all;
mediocre
quelque a. some, any; a few; — chose
something, anything; — part somewhere; — adv. however; — pron. whatever
quelquefois adv. sometimes
quelqu'un, quelqu'une indefinite pron.
one; somebody, someone; quelques-
uns, quelques-unes pl. some
quémander vt. & vi. to beg for, solicit
quenelle f. meatball, fishball
quenouille f. distaff; bedpost; bulrush
querelle f. quarrel, row, feud
quereller vt. to quarrel with; se — to
quarrel; have a strong difference of
opinion; have a falling out
querelleur a. quarrelsome; — m. quarreler
quérir vt. to find, get, bring, fetch
qu'est-ce que interr. pron. what (as object
of verb)
qu'est-ce qui interr. pron. what (as sub-

ject of verb)

question f. question; matter; poser une —, faire une — to ask a question

questionnaire m. questionnaire; questions

questionner vt. to question, interrogate

questionneur a. inquisitive; — m. interrogator

quetsche f. purple plum

quête f. quest, search; (eccl.) collection

quêter vt. to collect; look for

queue f. tail; line; handle; stalk; train of a garment; piano à — m. grand piano; faire la — to line up

queue-d'aronde f. dovetail

queue-de-chat f. cat-o'-nine-tails; cirrus cloud

queue-de-rat f. round or rat-tail file

qui interr. pron. who, whom; à — whose, to whom; de — whose, of whom; — rel. pron. who, which, that; the one who, he who; ce — that which, what; which; — que whoever; — que ce soit anyone

quiconque pron. whoever; anyone

quidam m. unidentified person, someone; unknown party (law)

qui est-ce que interr. pron. whom

qui est-ce qui interr. pron. who

quiétude f. quietude

quignon m. hunk, chunk

quille f. ninepin, tenpin; (naut.) keel; jeu de —s m. bowling

quincaillerie f. hardware, hardware store

quincaillier m. hardware dealer

quinconce f., en — alternately; staggered, zigzag

quinine f. quinine

quinquennal a. quinquennial, five-year

quintal m. hundredweight, quintal

quinte f. (mus.) fifth; fit of coughing

quintette f. quintet

quinteux a. fitful, restive

quintuple a. quintuple

quintupler vt. & vi. to quintuple

quintuplés m. pl. quintuplets

quinzaine f. about fifteen; two-week period, fortnight

quinze a. fifteen; fifteenth; — jours two weeks

quinzième a. fifteenth

quiproquo m. mistake, mistaken identity

quittance f. receipt

quitte. a. free, clear; rid; quits, even; jouer à — ou double to play double or nothing

quitter vt. to leave; take off; abandon

qui-vive m. (mil.) challenge by a sentry, être sur le — to be on the watch, be alert

quoi interr. pron. what; — de nouveau what's new; un je ne sais — a certain something; — rel. pron. what; de — enough; wherewithal; reason, cause, justification; il n'y a pas de — you're welcome, don't mention it; — que whatever; — qu'il en soit be that as it may; sans — or else, otherwise

quoique conj. though, although

quolibet m. gibe, jeering remark

quote-part f. quota, share

quotidien a. daily; — m. daily newspaper

quotidiennement adv. every day, daily

quotient m. quotient; quota

R

rabâcher vi. to repeat, rehash

rabais m. reduction, discount, rebate

rabaisser vt. to lower, reduce, humiliate, deprecate

rabat m. flap

rabat-joie m. killjoy

rabattre vt. to turn down; lower; fold back; flatten; lower, reduce the price; — vi. to turn off; se — to fall back; fold

rabbin m. rabbi

râblé a. strong, strong-backed

rabonnir vt. & vi. to improve

rabot m. plane (tool)

raboter vt. to plane, smooth

raboteux a. rough, uneven; knotty

rabougrir vt. to stunt

rabouter vt. to place end to end

rabrouer vt. to snub; become very angry at, become surly toward

racaille f. rubbish, trash; social outcast

raccommodage m. mending, repairing; darning

raccommodement m. reconciliation

raccommoder vt. to mend, repair; darn; reconcile; se — to be reconciled, make up

raccord m. joint, coupling, connection; tieing together, joining

raccordement m. connecting, joining; junction

raccorder vt. to connect, join, tie together, link; se — to join, fit

raccourci a. abridged, shortened; — m. abridgment; short cut; book digest; en — briefly

raccourcir vt. to shorten; abridge; — vi. to become shorter

raccourcissement m. shortening; shrinking

raccoutrer vt. to repair, mend

raccroc m. stroke of luck, fluke, chance

raccrocher vt. to hook up; hang up (telephone); se — to grab hold; regain, recover

race f. race, family, breed; de — thoroughbred

racé a. thoroughbred

rachat m. buying back, repurchase; redemption

rachetable a. redeemable

racheter vt. to buy back, repurchase; redeem; ransom

rachitisme m. rickets

racine f. root

racketter m. racketeer

raclage m. scraping

racle f. scraper

racler vt. to scrape; rake

raclette f. scraper; hoe

racloir m. scraping implement

raclure f. scrapings

racoler vt. to recruit, enlist, enroll

racoleur m. recruiter

racontage m. recounting, telling; gossip,

talk

raconter *vt.* to relate, tell

raconteur *m.* storyteller

racornir *vt.* to harden, make horny

racquitter *v.*, se — to recoup

radar *m.* radar

radariste *m.* radar operator

rade *f.* (naut.) roadstead, basin, harbor

radeau *m.* raft, float

radiateur *m.* radiator; — *a.* radiating

radiation *f.* radiation; cancellation; erasure, crossing out; disbarment

radical *a. & m.* radical

radicelle *f.* (bot.) radicle

radier *m.* frame, foundation floor

radier *vi.* to radiate; — *vt.* to erase, cross out; strike off

radieux *a.* radiant, bright

radio *f.* radio; X ray; — *m.* radio operator, radio man

radio-actif *a.* radioactive

radio-activité *f.* radioactivity

radioballsage *m.* (avi.) radio beam

radiocommunication *f.* radio communication

radiodiffuser *vt.* to broadcast

radiodiffusion *f.* radio program; broadcasting

radio-émission *f.* broadcast; broadcasting

radiogramme *m.* X-ray picture; radiogram

radiographie *f.* X-ray photography, radiography

radiographier *vt.* to X ray

radiographique *a.* X-ray, radiographic

radiojournal *m.* radio newscast

radiologie *f.* radiology

radiologique *a.* radiological, X-ray

radiologue *m. & f.* radiologist, X-ray technician

radioreportage *m.* radio report, program

radioreporter *m.* radio commentator

radioscopie *f.* radioscopy

radiothérapie *f.* X-ray therapy

radium *m.* radium

radius *m.* (anat.) radius

radotage *m.* dotage; raving; nonsense

radoter *vi.* to be in one's dotage; talk nonsense

radoteur *m.* dotard

radoub *m.* (naut.) repair; bassin de — *m.* drydock

radouber *vt.* to repair; put in drydock

radoucir *vt.* to soften, appease; calm; se — to relent, soften; turn mild

rafale *f.* gust, flurry; burst, volley

raffermir *vt.* to strengthen, make firm(er), reinforce; harden; se — to become firmer, become stronger; harden

raffiné *a.* refined

raffinement *m.* refinement

raffiner *vt.* to refine; se — to become refined

raffinerie *f.* refinery; refining

raffoler (de) *vi.* to be wild about; be infatuated with; dote on

raffûter *vt.* to sharpen, resharpen

rafistoler *vt.* to patch up

rafle *f.* raid; loot; looting; police roundup

rafler *vt.* to loot, clean out (a house); round up (criminals)

rafraîchir *vt.* to refresh, cool; renovate; touch up; remind; trim hair; se — to refresh oneself; drink; become cooler (weather)

rafraîchissant *a.* cooling, refreshing

rafraîchissement *m.* refreshment, cooling; touching up; brushing up

rage *f.* rage, madness, passion, mania; rabies; à la — *adv.* excessively

rager *vi.* (coll.) to rage, fume

ragot *a.* stocky, squat; — *m.* (coll.) gossip, talk

ragoût *m.* stew, ragout; relish

ragoûter *vt.* to revive the appetite

rai *m.* radius; beam of light; spoke

raid *m.* raid; endurance contest; (avi.) long flight, trip

raide *a.* stiff; inflexible; steep; firm; — *adv.* quickly; on the spot

raideur *f.* stiffness; steepness

raidir *vt.* to stiffen; se — to get stiff, stiffen, become tight

raie *f.* line, stripe; part in the hair; furrow; ray, skate (fish)

raifort *m.* horseradish

rail *m.* rail

railler *vt.* to laugh at, make fun of; — *vi.* to joke

raillerie *f.* raillery, mockery, joking

railleur *f.* jeering, scoffing, joking; — *m.* scoffer, joker

rainer *vt.* to groove

rainette *f.* tree frog

rainure *f.* groove; channel

raiponce *f.* rampion

rais *m.* spoke

raisin *m.* grape, grapes; grappe de — *f.* bunch of grapes; — sec raisin; — de Corinthe currant

raison *f.* reason, cause, motive; justification; satisfaction, amends; (math.) ratio; à — de at the rate of; à plus forte — all the more; avoir — to be right; en — de by reason of, because of; — d'être rational explanation, justification

raisonnable *a.* reasonable, rational; just, fair

raisonné *a.* founded on reason, methodical

raisonnement *m.* reasoning; argument

raisonner *vi.* to reason; — *vt.* to think out, study

rajeunir *vt.* to make young again; rejuvenate; — *vi.* to grow young again; be rejuvenated

rajustement *m.* readjustment; setting in order

rajuster *vt.* to readjust, set in order again, straighten, fix

râle *m.* death rattle; rail

ralenti *a.* slow, slower, slowed down; — *m.* slow motion

ralentir *vt.* to slacken, lessen, slow down

ralentissement *m.* slackening, slowing down, abatement

râler *vi.* give the death rattle; grumble

ralliement *m.* rally, rallying

rallier *vt.* to rally; assemble, bring together

rallonge *f.* extension; table leaf

rallongement *m.* lengthening, extending

rallonger *vt.* to lengthen, extend; thin a sauce

rallumer *vt.* to light again, rekindle

ramage *m.* warbling of birds; prattle; flowering; floral pattern

ramas *m.* heap, accumulation, collection

ramassé *a.* stocky; compact

ramasse-miettes *m.* silent butler, crumb tray

ramasse-poussière *m.* dustpan

ramasser *vt.* to pick up, gather, collect; se — to gather together; pick oneself up; crouch

ramassis *m.* collection, accumulation

rambarde *f.* railing

rame *f.* oar; ream of paper; (rail.) train, string of cars; convoy; wooden support for plants

ramé *a.* supported by sticks

rameau *m.* bough, branch; dimanche des Rameaux *m.* Palm Sunday

ramée *f.* boughs, arbor

ramener *vt.* to bring back, lead back, take back; pull down one's hat; restore

ramequin *m.* casserole

ramer *vi.* to row; grow deer antlers

rameur *m.* rower, oarsman

rameux *a.* ramose, having many branches

ramification *f.* ramification; branch

ramifier *v.*, se — to ramify, branch out

ramille *f.* twig

ramoindrir *vt.* to lessen, diminish, reduce

ramollir *vt.* to soften; weaken; se — to become soft

ramollissement *m.* softening

ramonage *m.* chimney sweeping

ramoner *vt.* to sweep a chimney

ramoneur *m.* chimney sweep

rampant *a.* creeping, crawling; rampant (heraldry)

rampe *f.* flight of stairs; balustrade, banister, handrail; slope; ramp; footlights of a stage

ramper *vi.* to crawl, creep; grovel; toady

ramure *f.* branches; antlers

rance *a.* rancid

ranch *m.* ranch

rancidité *f.* rancidness

rancir *vi.* to become rancid

rancœur *f.* bitterness, rancor

rançon *f.* ransom

rançonner *vt.* to ransom

rancune *f.* grudge, ill-feeling, rancor, spite

rancunier *a.* rancorous, spiteful, vindictive

randonnée *f.* trip, outing, excursion

rang *m.* row, file, line; rank, standing

rangé *a.* ranged; steady, regular, orderly; pitched battle

rangée *f.* row, file, line

ranger *vt.* to range; rank, put in ranks; arrange, set in order; put away; se — to line up; pull up; take sides; settle down

ranimer *vt.* to restore, revive; rouse; se — to become animated again; enliven

Raoul (*m.*) Ralph

rapace *a.* rapacious; grasping; ravenous

rapacité *f.* rapacity

râpage *m.* grating, filing

rapatriement *m.* repatriation

rapatrier *vt.* to repatriate

râpe *f.* grater; file, rasp

râpé *a.* threadbare; grated

râper *vt.* to grate; file; wear out (clothing)

rapetasser *vt.* to patch up clothing; mend extensively

rapetisser *vt.* to make smaller, shorten; shrink; — *vi.* to become shorter, become smaller

raphia *m.* raffia

rapide *a.* rapid, swift, fast; — *m.* express train; —s *pl.* rapids in a river

rapidité *f.* rapidity, speed

rapiéçage *m.* patching, mending

rapiécer *vt.* to piece; patch, mend

rapière *f.* rapier

rapine *f.* pillage, pillaging

rapiner *vt. & vi.* to pillage

rappareiller *vt.* to match

rapparier *vt.* to pair, match

rappel *m.* recall; calling in; call to arms; (theat.) curtain call; reminder; revocation, repeal; back spacer of a typewriter

rappeler *vt.* to recall, call back; remind; se — to remember, recall

rapport *m.* report; return, profit; relation, connection; ratio; par — à, sous le — de with regard to, with respect to

rapportable *a.* attributable

rapporter *vt.* to bring back, carry back; return, produce, bring in; report, tell of; revoke; attribute; se — to refer, relate, have to do with; s'en — à to rely on

rapporteur *m.* reporter; tattletale; (math.) protractor; sponsor, introducer

rapprendre *vt.* to learn again; teach again

rapproché *a.* close, near; connected, related; close-set (eyes)

rapprochement *m.* reconciliation; bringing together; comparison, comparing; closeness

rapprocher *vt.* to draw near again, bring near; bring together; compare

rapsodie *f.* rhapsody

rapt *m.* abduction, kidnapping

râpure *f.* gratings, scrapings

raquette *f.* racket; snowshoe

rare *a.* rare; thin, sparse; unusual, uncommon

raréfaction *f.* rarefaction; scarcity

raréfier *vt.* to rarefy; make scarce

rareté *f.* rarity; scarcity; unusualness

rarissime *a.* very rare

ras *a.* short-haired, close-cut; smooth-shaven; bare; plain, smooth; open; flat; au — de on a level with; à — de level with; faire table —e start from scratch; make a clean sweep

rasant *a.* grazing, skimming, staying close to; boring, dull

rase-mottes *m.* (avi.) low-level flying, hedge-hopping

raser *vt.* to shave; raze; graze, skim; stay close to; bore; se — to shave; be bored

raseur *m.* shaver; bore

rasoir *m.* razor; — à lame straight razor; cuir à — *m.* razor strop; — de sûreté safety razor

rassasiant *a.* satisfying, filling

rassasiement *m.* satisfying, satiety

rassasier *vt.* to satiate, fill, satisfy; se — to fill up, eat one's fill

rassemblement *m.* assembling; assemblage

rassembler *vt.* to collect, assemble; unite; se — to meet; assemble

rasseoir *vt.* to seat again

rasséréner *vt.* to calm; se — to brighten, clear up

rassir *vi.* to harden (bread)

rassis *a.* calm, sedate; stale (bread)

rassortir *vt.* (com.) to restock

rassurer *vt.* to reassure; strengthen; se — be reassured

rat *m.* rat; — musqué muskrat

rataplan *m.* roll of a drum

ratatiner *vt.* to dry up; shrink, shrivel

'rate *f.* spleen

raté *a.* failed, missed; — *m.* failure; dud

râteau *m.* rake

râteler *vt.* to rake

rater *vi.* to miss; fail; misfire; — *vt.* miss, fail in

ratière *f.* rat trap

ratifier *vt.* to ratify

rationaliser *vt.* to rationalise

rationnel *a.* rational

rationner *vt.* to ration

ratisser *vt.* to scrape, rake

ratissoire *f.* rake; scraper

raton *m.* small rat; — laveur raccoon

rattacher *vt.* to tie again, attach, fasten; se — to be tied to, be connected with

ratteindre *vt.* to overtake; retake

rattraper *vt.* to catch again, retake; overtake, catch up with; get back, recover; se — to make up, recoup

rature *f.* erasure; scraping

raturer *vt.* to scratch out, erase

raucité *f.* hoarseness

rauque *a.* hoarse, harsh, raucous

ravager *vt.* to ravage, pillage, devastate; pit by smallpox

ravages *m. pl.* devastation; havoc

ravalement *m.* scraping, cleaning; resurfacing

ravaler *vt.* to reswallow; (fig.) hold back; take back, retract; se — to debase oneself

ravaudage *m.* mending, patching; bungling

ravauder *vt.* to mend, patch

ravi *a.* delighted

ravier *m.* hors-d'œuvres dish

ravigote *f.* sauce with shallots

ravilir *vt.* to vilify

ravin *m.* ravine

raviner *vt.* to furrow

ravir *vt.* to ravish, abduct, steal; delight

raviser *v.*, se — to change one's mind

ravissant *a.* delightful, ravishing

ravissement *m.* ravishing, abduction; delight, rapture

ravisseur *m.* ravisher, abductor, kidnapper

ravitaillement *m.* supplying, provisioning, revictualing; refueling

ravitailler *vt.* to supply, provision; se —

to take in fresh supplies

ravitailleur *m.* supply ship

raviver *vt.* to revive; renew, touch up; reopen a wound

ravoir *vt.* to have again; recover, get back

rayé *a.* striped; rifled; (fig.) suppressed; erased

rayer *vt.* to erase, cross out, strike out; rule, line; rifle a gun

rayon *m.* ray, beam; spoke; radius; furrow, row; shelf; department (in a store); chef de — floorwalker; — X X ray

rayonnant *a.* radiant, beaming; radiating

rayonne *f.* rayon

rayonnement *m.* radiation, radiancy

rayonner *vi.* to radiate, beam

rayure *f.* erasure, crossing out; scratch; stripe; groove, furrow; rifling

raz *m.* race, current; — de marée tidal wave

razzia *f.* raid

razzier *vt.* to raid

réabonnement *m.* renewal of a subscription

réabonner *vt.* to renew a subscription

réabsorber *vt.* to reabsorb

réaccoutumer *vt.* to reaccustom

réacteur *m.* reactor; — nucléaire nuclear reactor

réactif *m.* (chem.) reagent; — *a.* reactive

réaction *f.* reaction; avion à — *m.* jet plane; — en chaîne chain reaction; fusée à — *f.* jet-propelled missile; moteur à — *m.* jet engine

réactionnaire *m. & a.* reactionary

réadmettre *vt.* to readmit

réaffirmer *vt.* to reaffirm

réagir *vi.* to react

réalisable *a.* realisable; practicable, feasible

réalisation *f.* realisation, fulfilling, execution; — de produced by (movie credit)

réaliser *vt.* to realise, fulfil, execute; convert into money; se — to be realised; come true

réalisme *m.* realism

réaliste *m. & f.* realist; — *a.* realistic

réalité *f.* reality

réapparaître *vi.* to reappear

réapparition *f.* reappearance

réapprovisionner *vt.* to restock; revictual

réarmer *vt.* to rearm; refit; recock

réassurer *vt.* to reinsure

rébarbatif *a.* surly, grim

rebâtir *vt.* to rebuild

rebattre *vt.* to beat again; (fig.) repeat uselessly

rebattu *a.* repeated; trite; sentier — *m.* beaten track

rebelle *m. & f.* rebel; — *a.* rebellious

rebeller *v.*, se — to rebel, resist

rébellion *f.* rebellion, revolt

rebobiner *vt.* to rewind

reboire *vt.* to drink again

reboisement *m.* reforestation, tree conservation

reboiser *vt.* to reforest

rebond *m.* rebound, bounce

rebondi *a.* plump, chubby

rebondir *vt.* to rebound, bounce

rebord m. edge, border, rim; ledge

reboucher vt. to stop up again; recork

rebours m. wrong side; reverse; à —, au — against the grain; backwards; the wrong way

rebouter vt. to set (a broken bone)

reboutonner vt. to rebutton

rebrousse-poil (à) adv. — against the grain

rebrousser vt. to turn back; — chemin to retrace one's steps

rebuffade f. rebuff, snub

rébus m. rebus, puzzle

rebut m. outcast; reject; scrap, trash, rubbish

rebutant a. discouraging, tedious; repellent

rebuter vt. to reject, repulse, refuse, rebuff; dishearten

récalcitrance f. recalcitrance

récalcitrant a. recalcitrant

récapitulation f. recapitulation, summary

récapituler vt. to recapitulate, summarize

recel, recèlement m. concealment (law); receiving of stolen goods

recéler vt. to conceal stolen goods; harbor

recéleur m. receiver of stolen goods, fence

récemment adv. recently, lately

recensement m. census

recenser vt. to make a census; tally, count

recenseur m. census taker (counter)

récent a. recent, new, late

récépissé m. receipt, acknowledgment

réceptacle m. receptacle

récepteur m. receiver; — a. receiving

réception f. reception; receiving; receipt; accusé de — m. receipt, acknowledgment

réceptionnaire m. (com.) consignee; — a. receiving

recette f. receipt of money; receiving, collection; recipe; -s pl. receipts

recevable a. acceptable, allowable, admissible

receveur m. receiver; tax collector; postmaster

recevoir vt. to receive; accept; entertain

rechange m. spare, replacement; pièce de — spare part; pneu de — m. spare tire

rechaper vt. to recap, retread a tire

réchappé m. survivor of a disaster

réchapper vi. to escape, survive

recharger vt. to recharge, reload

réchaud m. chafing dish; heater; stove; — électrique hot plate

réchauffer vt. to warm up or over, rekindle; se — to get warm, warm oneself

rechausser vt. to put footwear on again

rêche a. harsh, rough; bitter

recherche f. search, inquiry, investigation; finery, care; à la — de in search of; -s pl. research

recherché a. choice, rare; much in demand; affected; studied

rechercher vt. to seek again; search for; court

rechigné a. sulky, crabby

rechigner vi. to look unhappy; balk

rechuter vi. to relapse; have a relapse

récidive f. recurrence, relapse; second offense

récidiver vi. to recur; relapse (crime)

récif m. reef, shelf of rocks

récipient m. receptacle, container

réciprocité f. reciprocity

récit m. recital, relation, narrative, story; (mus.) solo

récital m. recital

récitant m. (mus.) solo, solo part

récitatif m. (mus.) recitative

récitation f. recitation

réciter vt. to recite

réclamant m. legal claimant

réclamation f. claim; protest; complaint

réclame f. advertising; article de — feature article

réclamer vt. to claim, call for, demand; — vi. to protest, complain

reclasser vt. to reclassify, rearrange

reclus m. recluse

réclusion f. reclusion; solitary confinement (penal)

récognition f. recognition (of a nature or quality)

recoin m. corner, nook, cranny

récoler vt. to verify, audit, check

recoller vt. to paste together again, put together again; se — to mend, knit, or heal (a fracture); cling together

récolte f. crop; harvest

récolter vt. to reap, gather, harvest

recommandable a. commendable, praiseworthy

recommandation f. recommendation; registration of mail

recommandé a. registered (mail)

recommander vt. to recommend; register a letter

recommencer vt. & vi. to recommence, begin again

récompense f. reward, recompense

récompenser vt. to reward, recompense

réconciliable a. reconcilable

réconciliation f. reconciliation

réconcilier vt. to reconcile; se — to be reconciled

reconduire vt. to lead back, see someone home; drive home; show out, usher out

réconfort m. consolation, comfort; relief

réconfortant a. comforting, consoling; stimulating

réconforter vt. to comfort, cheer; strengthen, refresh

reconnaissable a. recognizable

reconnaissance f. recognition; gratitude, thankfulness; recompense, reward; acknowledgment; note, pawn ticket; (mil.) reconnaissance

reconnaissant a. thankful, grateful

reconnaître vt. to recognize, acknowledge; (mil.) to reconnoiter; se — to acknowledge; become oriented; (fig.) take one's bearings

reconquérir vt. to reconquer, regain

reconstituant m. tonic, stimulant, restorative

reconstituer vt. to reconstitute; restore

reconstruire vt. to rebuild

reconvention f. countersuit

recopier vt. to copy over, recopy

record *m.* sports record
recorder *vt.* to retie; restring
recordman *m.* record holder
recoucher *vt.*, se — to go back to bed, lie down again
recoudre *vt.* to sew in place again; sew up; (fig.) reunite
recoupement *m.* cross-check, verification
recouper *vt.* to cut again; mix, blend (wines)
recourber *vt.* to bend back
recourir *vi.* to run again; have recourse, resort to
recours *m.* recourse, resort
recouvrement *m.* recovery, getting back; recovering; cover
recouvrer *vt.* to recover, regain
recouvrir *vt.* to cover again, re-cover; cover
recracher *vt.* to spit out
récréatif *a.* recreational, entertaining
récréation *f.* recreation, amusement; recess
recréer *vt.* to create again, re-create
récréer *vt.* to entertain; please; se — to enjoy oneself, relax; be entertained
récrier *v.*, se — to exclaim; protest
récrimination *f.* recrimination
récriminer *vi.* to recriminate
récrire *vt.* to rewrite
recroqueviller *v.*, se — to retract; (fig.) to curl up, shrivel, wilt
recru *a.* worn out
recrû *m.* annual growth
recrue *f.* recruit, draftee
recruter *vt.* to recruit, enlist
rectal *a.* rectal
rectangle *m.* rectangle; — *a.* right-angled
rectangulaire *a.* rectangular
recteur *m.* rector; university president
rectificateur *m.* (elec.) rectifier
rectificatif *a.* rectifying; — *m.* correction
rectifier *vt.* to rectify, adjust, correct; straighten
rectifieuse *f.* rectifier
rectitude *f.* rectitude, uprightness; correctness; straightness
rectorat *m.* rectorate; university presidency
rectum *m.* rectum
reçu *m.* receipt; — *a.* received; usual; customary; être — to pass; graduate
recueil *m.* collection; anthology
recueillement *m.* contemplation, pious meditation
recueilli *a.* contemplative
recueillir *vt.* to gather, collect; shelter; se — to meditate
recuire *vt.* to recook, reheat; temper, anneal
recuit *a.* tempered, annealed
recul *m.* gun recoil; setback; backing up
reculade *f.* moving back; retreat
reculé *a.* remote, distant (in time); isolated
reculée *f.* space in which to move backward
reculement *m.* moving back, backing up; postponement
reculer *vi.* to move back; retreat; recoil;

— *vt.* to move back; postpone; hesitate
reculons, à — *adv.* backwards
récupérable *a.* recuperable
récupération *f.* recuperation, recovery
récupérer *vt.* to retrieve, recoup, recover; se — to recuperate, recover
récurage *m.* scouring, cleansing
récurer *vt.* to scour, cleanse
récurrence *f.* recurrence
récurrent *a.* recurrent, recurring
récusable *a.* exceptionable (at law)
récusation *f.* legal exception, objection
récuser *vt.* to object to, challenge; se — to disqualify oneself
rédacteur *m.* editor, compiler; writer; — en chef editor-in-chief
rédaction *f.* editorship, compiling; editorial staff; theme, composition
rédactionnel *a.* editorial
reddition *f.* surrender; rendering
redécouvrir *vt.* to rediscover
redemander *vt.* to ask again, ask return of something
rédempteur *m.* redeemer; — *a.* redeeming
rédemption *f.* redemption, redeeming
redescendre *vi.* to go down again; go back down; — *vt.* to bring down, take down
redevable *a.* indebted; bound by gratitude
redevance *f.* fee, tax; royalty
redevenir *vi.* to become again
rédiger *vt.* to phrase, draw up, write; edit
redingote *f.* frock coat
redire *vt.* to repeat, say again; trouver à — à to find fault with, criticize
redistribuer *vt.* to redistribute
redite *f.* repetition; redundancy
redondance *f.* redundancy
redondant *a.* redundant
redonner *vi.* to be redundant
redonner *vt.* to give again, give back
redorer *vt.* to re-gild
redoublé *a.* redoubled; pas — *m.* (marching) double-time, quick-step
redoublement *m.* doubling, redoubling
redoubler *vt.* to redouble; reline clothing; — *vi.* to redouble; increase
redoutable *a.* formidable, redoubtable; dreadful
redoute *f.* redoubt
redouter *vt.* to dread, fear; be afraid
redressé *a.* upright, erect
redressement *m.* making erect again, righting; straightening, rectifying; recovery
redresser *vt.* to make straight again; set upright; mend, correct; straighten, rectify; se — become upright again; sit up again
redresseur *m.* rectifier; righter
redû *m.* balance due
réducteur *m.* reducer; reducing agent; — *a.* reducing
réductible *a.* reducible
réduction *f.* reduction, reducing
réduire *vt.* to reduce, subdue, conquer
réduit *m.* redoubt; retreat; shack, hovel; — *a.* reduced, obliged
réduplication *f.* reduplication
réédifier *vt.* to rebuild

rééditer *vt.* to republish

réédition *f.* reprinting, republication

rééducatif *a.*, thérapie rééducative *f.* occupational therapy

rééducation *f.* rehabilitation

rééduquer *vt.* to re-educate; rehabilitate

réel *a.* real; — *m.* reality

réélection *f.* re-election

réélire *vt.* to re-elect

réellement *adv.* really, actually

réensemencer *vt.* to reseed

refaçonner *vt.* to refashion

réfaction *f.* (com.) allowance, rebate; repairs

refaire *vt.* to do again; remake; se — to recover, recuperate

réfection *f.* rebuilding; repairing, restoration

réfectoire *m.* refectory, dining room

refend *m.* (arch.) pierre de — *f.* cornerstone

refendre *vt.* to split

référence *f.* reference

référendum *m.* referendum

référer *vi.* to refer; — *vt.* to attribute; impute; se — à to refer to; s'en — to confide

refermer *vt.* to reclose, shut again

refiler *vt.* (coll.) to pass, pass off

réfléchi *a.* thoughtful; considered; premeditated; peu — hasty; verbe — *m.* reflexive verb

réfléchir *vt.* to reflect, reverberate; — *vi.* reflect, think; se — to be reflected

réfléchissement *m.* reflection, reflecting

réfléchissant *a.* reflecting

réflecteur *m.* reflector; — *a.* reflecting

reflet *m.* reflection

refléter *vt.* to reflect

refleurir *vi.* to flower again, flourish again

réflexe *a. & m.* reflex

réflexion *f.* reflection; thought; toute — faite all things considered

refluer *vi.* to ebb, flow back

reflux *m.* ebb, reflux, flowing back

refondre *vt.* to remelt, recast

refonte *f.* remelting, recasting

réformateur *m.* reformer

réformation *f.* reformation

réforme *f.* reform, reformation; (mil.) discharge

réformé *m.* Protestant; rejected serviceman, soldier discharged for wounds or unfitness

reformer *vt.* to re-form, form again

réformer *vt.* to reform; (mil.) discharge, retire

refoulement *m.* forcing back; repression; output

refouler *vt.* to force back; repress

réfractaire *a.* refractory, rebellious; fire resistant

réfracter *vt.* to refract

réfracteur *m.* refractor

réfraction *f.* refraction

refrain *m.* refrain; song; chorus

réfranger *vt.* to refract

refréner *vt.* to check, curb, bridle, restrain

réfrigérant *a.* refrigerating; cooling; — *m.* refrigerator; cooler

réfrigération *f.* refrigeration

réfrigérer *vt.* to refrigerate

refroidir *vt.* to cool, chill; — *vi.* to grow cool, grow cold

refroidissement *m.* cooling; chill

réfugié *m.* refugee

réfugier *v.*, se — to take refuge

refus *m.* refusal

refuser *vt.* to refuse, deny; reject; fail (a student); se — to object; refuse

réfutable *a.* refutable

réfutation *f.* refutation

réfuter *vt.* to refute

regagner *vt.* to regain, recover; reach again, return to

regain *m.* (agr.) aftergrowth; renewal

régal *m.* feast; treat

régalade *f.* regaling, feasting; treat

régalant *a.* entertaining, diverting

régale *a.*, eau — (chem.) aqua regia

régalement *m.* leveling

régaler *vt.* to treat, entertain; level, smooth out

régalien *a.* royal, regal

regard *m.* look, glance; eyes; aperture, opening; peephole; manhole

regardant *m.* onlooker; — *a.* particular, fussy; stingy

regarder *vt.* to look at; regard, concern; face

regarnir *vt.* to regarnish, restock, replenish

regate *f.* regatta, boat race

regel *m.* refreezing; new freeze

regeler *vt. & vi.* to refreeze, freeze again

régence *f.* regency

régénérateur *a.* regenerative; — *m.* hair restorer

régénération *f.* regeneration

régénérer *vt.* to regenerate

régent *m.* regent

régenter *vt.* to dominate

régicide *m.* regicide

régie *f.* administration, management; public corporation

regimbement *m.* recalcitrance

regimber *vi.* to balk, object

régime *m.* regime, administration; system; bunch of dates; diet; (gram.) object; être au — to be on a diet

régiment *m.* regiment

régimentaire *a.* regimental

région *f.* region, area

régional *a.* regional; local

régir *vt.* to govern, manage, supervise

régisseur *m.* administrator, manager; (theat.) stage manager

registre *m.* register, ledger, account book

réglable *a.* adjustable

réglage *m.* way of ruling paper; adjustment of machinery, tuning

règle *f.* rule, ruler; order; — à calcul slide rule; en — in order

réglé *a.* ruled, regular, orderly; vent — *m.* tradewind

règlement *m.* regulation; rule; adjustment, settlement; payment

réglementaire *a.* prescribed by law

réglementation *f.* regulating

réglementer *vt.* to regulate

régler vt. to rule; regulate; adjust, set; settle

réglet m. moulding

réglette f. small ruler; metal strip

régleur m. adjuster

réglisse f. licorice

réglure f. ruling of paper

règne m. reign; kingdom

régnant a. reigning; dominant

régner vi. to reign; prevail

regommer vt. to retread

regonfler vt. to pump up again, reinflate

regorgeant a. overflowing, brimming

regorger vt. to overflow, abound, be full, be packed; — vt. to regurgitate

regoûter vt. to taste again

regrat m. peddling used or retail articles

regrattage m. scraping

regratter vi. to peddle, hawk; — vt. rescrape, scrape clean

régressif a. regressive

régression f. regression, retrogression; recession

regret m. regret; à — regretfully, reluctantly

regretter vt. to regret, be sorry; miss

régularisation f. regularizing

régulariser vt. to regularize

régularité f. regularity; evenness

régulateur a. regulating; — m. regulator; governor

régulation f. regulating

régulier a. regular; even; steady; punctual

régurgitation f. regurgitation

régurgiter vt. to regurgitate

réhabilitation f. rehabilitation

réhabiliter vt. to rehabilitate; reinstate

réhabituer vt. to reaccustom

rehaussement m. raising; enhancing

rehausser vt. to raise; enhance, accentuate

réimperméabiliser vt. to waterproof again

réimposer vt. to reimpose

réimpression f. reprint, reprinting

réimprimer vt. to reprint

rein m. kidney; —s pl. lower part of back

réincarnation f. reincarnation

réincarner v., se — to be reincarnated

réincorporer vt. to reincorporate

reine f. queen

reine-claude f. greengage plum

réinscrire vt. to reinscribe; re-enter

réintégrer vt. to reinstate

réitération f. reiteration

réitérer vt. to reiterate

rejaillir vi. to spurt out; rebound; be reflected

rejet m. rejection; plant shoot, sprout; throwing out; enjambement

rejeter vt. to throw back; reject; se — move back, fall back

rejeton m. offspring, shoot

rejetonner vi. to throw off shoots (plants)

rejoindre vt. to rejoin; overtake; se — to meet again

rejouer vt. to play again, replay

réjoui a. jovial, joyful, happy

réjouir vt. to gladden; entertain; se — to rejoice, be happy

réjouissance f. rejoicing, merrymaking

réjouissant a. pleasing, entertaining, giving pleasure

relâchant a. (med.) laxative

relâche m. rest, respite; (theat.) no performance; interruption; (naut.) port of call

relâché a. loose, slack; relaxed

relâchement m. relaxation, loosening; abatement

relâcher vt. to relax; release, slacken; — vi. (naut.) to put into port; se — to become loose, slacken; diminish, abate; become milder

relais m. relay, shift

relancer vt. to throw again, throw back; start again; hunt

relater vt. to relate, tell of, give, state

relatif a. relative; pertinent, relating

relation f. relation, connection; report, statement, account

relationné a. having contacts or connections

relativité f. relativity

relaxation f. legal release; lessening, reduction

relaxer vt. to release, discharge at law

relayer vt. to relieve, relay; — vi. to relay; se — to take turns, work in shifts

relégation f. life sentence to penal colony

relégué m. convict serving life sentence

reléguer vt. to relegate; sentence for life, transport

relent m. musty smell, staleness

relevage m. lifting, raising; collecting of letters from a mail box

relevant a. pertaining; dependent

relevé a. raised, high; highly seasoned; — m. abstract, summary, statement; survey; meter reading

relève f. (mil.) relief, changing of the guard

relevée f. afternoon

relèvement m. raising, lifting; increase; restoration, recovery; (mil.) relieving; (naut.) bearing; (com.) statement

relever vt. to raise again, lift up, turn up; increase; enhance, heighten; season; point out; (mil.) relieve; (naut.) take the bearings of; (com.) bill; read a meter; — vi. be dependent, be responsible; recover from illness; se — get up again; revive, recover

relief m. relief, embossing, enhancement; —s pl. left-over food

relier vt. to tie again; bind, connect, join

relieur m. bookbinder

religieux a. religious; — m. monk

reliquaire m. (eccl.) shrine, reliquary

reliquat m. left-over portion, remainder; aftereffects; balance due

relique f. relic

relire vt. to read again; reread

reliure f. binding of a book; bookbinding trade

relouer vt. to sublet, relet

reluctance f. (elec.) reluctance

reluire vi. to shine, glitter, gleam

reluisant a. shining, glittering, gleaming; glossy

reluquer vt. to look at sideways, look at

from the corner of the eyes

remâcher vt. to chew again; mull over

remailler vt. to mend (knitted or meshed garments)

remaniement m. alteration; reshaping, rehandling

remanier vt. to handle again, alter; reshape

remarier vt., se — to marry again, remarry

remarquable a. remarkable; noteworthy

remarque f. remark; digne de — noteworthy

remarquer vt. to observe, notice, remark; mark again; se faire — to be noticed, attract attention

remballer vt. to repack

rembarquer vt. & vi. to re-embark

remblai m. fill for construction; earth; embankment

remblaver vt. to reseed

remblayer vt. to fill; embank

rembobinage m. rewinding

rembobiner vt. to rewind

remboîter vt. to repack, recase; reassemble; (med.) set a bone

rembourrer vt. to stuff, wad; pad, upholster

rembourrure f. stuffing material

remboursable a. refundable

remboursement m. reimbursement, redemption; refund; livraison contre — f. C.O.D.

rembourser vt. to reimburse, repay, refund

rembrunir vt. & vi. to darken; make gloomy; se — grow dark

remède m. remedy, cure

remédiable a. remediable, curable

remédier vt. to remedy, cure

remêler vt. to mix again, remix

remembrer vt. to assemble, consolidate

remémoratif a. commemorative

remémorer vt. to remind; se — to remember

remerciement m. thanks

remercier vt. to thank; discharge, dismiss

réméré m. (com.) repurchase

remettant m. sender, remitter

remetteur a. remitting; — m. remitter

remettre vt. to put back; put on again; restore; hand over, remit; postpone; se — recover one's health; se — à to start again; s'en — à rely on, depend on

remeubler vt. to refurnish

réminiscence f. reminiscence

remise f. putting back; remitting, remittance; remission; rebate, discount; shed, garage, or coachhouse; — en état repair, restoration; voiture de grande — f. rentable limousine

remiser vt. to house; put back in a garage, shed, or coachhouse; (coll.) to pension

rémissible a. remissible

rémission f. remission

remmener vt. to lead back, take back

rémois a. from Rheims

remontant a. & m. tonic, stimulant

remonte f. remounting; return, ascent of salmon

remontée f. going up again, ascent, climb

remonter vi. to go up again; remount; reascend; go back; — vt. go up again, climb again; take up again; pull up; wind up; remount, reassemble; (theat.) perform again, put on again, redo; se — recover one's strength or spirit

remontoir m. watch winder

remontrance f. remonstrance

remontrer vt. to show again; indicate, point out; en — à to remonstrate with

remords m. remorse, conscience

remorquage m. towing

remorque f. towing, tow; tow rope; (auto.) trailer; à la — in tow

remorquer vt. to tow, pull

remorqueur m. tugboat; tractor

remoudre vt. to grind again, regrind

rémoudre vt. to resharpen, regrind

rémouleur m. knife grinder

remous m. eddy, swirl, backwash

rempailler vt. to repair, recane, replace chair reeds

rempailleur m. repairer of chairs

rempart m. rampart

remplaçable a. replaceable

remplaçant m. replacement, substitute

remplacement m. replacing, substitution

remplacer vt. to replace, substitute for

rempli m. fold, tuck

remplier vt. to make a fold or tuck in

remplir vt. to refill, fill in; fill out; fill up; fulfill, do, carry out

remployer vt. to use again

remplumer v., se — to grow new feathers

rempoissonner vt. to stock with fish

remporter vt. to carry back, carry away; win, achieve, obtain

rempoter vt. to repot a plant

remuant a. moving; agitated

remue-ménage m. bustle, to-do, movement, agitation, stir, stirring

remuement m. movement, agitation, stir

remuer vt. to move, stir up; arouse, agitate; turn (earth); — vi. move, budge, stir

remugle m. musty odor, stale odor

rémunérateur a. remunerative, rewarding, profitable; — m. remunerator

rémunération f. remuneration

rémunérer vt. to remunerate, reward, pay for

renâcler vi. to snort; shirk; be hesitant, be reluctant

renaissance f. rebirth, revival

renaissant a. renascent

renaître vi. to be born again; revive; reappear

rénal a. renal, kidney

renard m. fox

renarde f. vixen

rencaisser vt. to recase, rebox; receive as a refund

renchaîner vt. to chain up again

renchéri a. fastidious

renchérir vi. to increase in price; —sur to outdo; outbid

renchérissement m. increase in price

renchérisseur m. one who outbids, highest bidder

rencogner vt. to drive into a corner; se — be pushed, retreat into a corner

rencontre f. meeting, encounter; occasion; aller à la — de to go to meet; de — chance, random, haphazard

rencontrer vt. to meet, come across, run into, encounter; se — meet, meet by chance; collide; come together, agree, check

rendement m. yield, profit, return; efficiency, output

rendez-vous m. appointment; meeting place, rendezvous

rendormir vt. to put back to sleep; se — to fall asleep again, go back to sleep

rendosser vt. to put on again

rendre vt. to give back; return; produce, yield; give up; vomit; render; make; se — to go, proceed; surrender

rendu a. tired out, exhausted, spent; — m. rendering; (com.) return of an article

rêne f. rein

renégat m. renegade

rêner vt. to rein in

renfaîter vt. to repair a roof

renfermé a. stuffy, close; uncommunicative

renfermer vt. to shut up, lock up, confine; contain, include, comprise; enclose; conceal

renflammer vt. to set fire to again, rekindle; se — catch fire again, be rekindled

renflement m. swelling, bulge

renfler vt. & vi. to swell

renflouer vt. to reinflate; refloat

renfoncé a. recessed; sunken

renfoncer vt. to drive in, hammer in; indent, recess

renforcé a. reinforced, strengthened, strong; absolute

renforcer vt. to reinforce, strengthen, brace; intensify; se — grow stronger

renfort m. reinforcement; backing, support

renfrogné a. frowning, scowling

renfrogner v., se — to frown, scowl

rengager vt. to engage again; pawn again; — vi. to re-enlist

rengaine f. refrain, old story

rengainer vt. to sheathe, put back (a sword)

rengorgement m. swagger, strutting

rengorger v., se — to strut, swagger

reniement m. denial, repudiation, disavowal

renier vt. to deny, disown, disavow, repudiate, abjure

reniflard m. air valve; sniffer, sniffler

reniflement m. sniffing, snorting, snort; sniffle, sniffling

renifler vi. to sniff, snivel, snuffle, snort; — vt. to sniff

reniveler vt. to level again

renne m. reindeer

renom m. renown, fame, repute

renommé a. renowned, famous, famed, celebrated, well-known

renommée f. fame, reputation, renown, repute

renommer vt. to renominate, rename

renonce f. renege, revoke (at cards)

renoncement m. renunciation; renouncing; self-denial

renoncer vi. to renounce, give up, waive; renege, revoke (at cards); — vt. to renounce

renonciation f. renunciation

renoncule f. buttercup

renouer vt. to tie again, knot again; renew

renouveau m. revival, renewal; springtime

renouvelable a. renewable

renouveler vt. to renew; revive; repeat; change, alter; se — be renewed; renew again; happen again

rénover vt. to renew, give a new form

renseignement m. piece of information; —s pl. information; (mil.) intelligence; prendre des —s sur to inquire about

renseigner vt. to inform; se — to inquire, ask

rente f. income, revenue; annuity, pension

renté a. endowed; of independent means, having a private income

renter vt. to endow, provide with an income

rentier m. person of independent means, stockholder, bondholder

rentrant m. recess in a wall; new participant, new player

rentré a. hollow, sunken; suppressed

rentrée f. return, homecoming; reopening of school; gathering, collecting, bringing in

rentrer vi. to re-enter, return, come home; reopen; bring in, take in

renverse f. (naut.) turn, change in weather; tomber à la — to fall backwards

renversement m. reversing, reversal, inversion; turn, turning, change; overturning, overthrowing

renverser vt. to reverse, invert; knock over, turn over, overturn, upset; overthrow; — vi. to overturn; (naut.) capsize; se — to fall down; turn over; lean back; capsize

renvoi m. sending back, returning; throwing back; reflection; discharge, dismissal; postponement; reference mark; caret; belch; (mus.) repetition

renvoyer vt. to send back, return, throw back; reflect; discharge, dismiss; postpone; refer

réoccupation f. reoccupation

réoccuper vt. to reoccupy

réordonner vt. to reorder

réorganisation f. reorganization

réorganiser vt. to reorganize

réorientation f. reorientation

réorienter vt. to reorient

réouverture f. reopening

repaire m. lair, den

repaître vt. to feed, se — de to eat one's fill of; delight in

répandre vt. to spread; spill, shed; give off; strew, scatter; se — to spread, spill, spill over

répandu a. widespread; fashionable

reparaitre vi. to reappear

réparation *f.* reparation; repairing; amends, satisfaction

réparer *vt.* to repair, fix, mend; make up for, make amends for

repartie *f.* repartee, reply, retort

repartir *vi.* to reply, retort; start out again, set out again

répartir *vt.* to divide, distribute; allocate, allot, apportion; assess

répartiteur *m.* distributor; assessor

répartition *f.* dividing, distribution; allocation, apportionment; assessment

repas *m.* meal

repassage *m.* ironing, pressing; sharpening

repasser *vi.* to pass by again; — *vt.* to pass again, pass over; go over; sharpen grind, strop; iron; planche à — *f.* ironing board

repasseur *m.* grinder, sharpener; finisher

repasseuse *f.* ironer

repavage *m.* repaving

repaver *vt.* to repave

repayer *vt.* to pay for again

repêcher *vt.* to fish out again, fish up; rescue

repeindre *vt.* to paint again, repaint

rependre *vt.* to hang up again

repenser *vt.* to think over again

repenti *a. & m.* repentant

repentir *v., se* — repent, be sorry about, rue; — *m.* repentance

repérable *a.* locatable, findable

repérage *m.* finding, locating

répercussion *f.* repercussion, reverberation; consequence, effect

répercuter *vt.* to reflect, reverberate; se — to have repercussions

reperdre *vt.* to lose again

repère *m.* reference mark; point de — point of reference, guidemark; landmark

repérer *vt.* to mark with points of reference (blaze a trail); fix, locate; se — to take one's bearings

répertoire *m.* index, list; directory; (theat.) stock, repertory

répertorier *vt.* to list; index; catalog

répéter *vt.* to repeat; rehearse; se — to repeat, be done again, recur

répétiteur *m.* tutor, helper, coach

répétition *f.* repetition; duplicate; rehearsal, practice; tutoring lesson

repeupler *vt.* to repopulate; restock

repiquer *vt.* to prick again; restitch; repair, mend; transplant

répit *m.* respite, delay

replacer *vt.* to put back, replace; reinvest

replanter *vt.* to replant

replâtrer *vt.* to replaster; patch up

replet *a.* plump, chubby

réplétion *f.* repletion; plumpness

repli *m.* fold; coil; bend; (mil.) retreat, falling back

replier *vt.* to fold again, fold up; tuck; coil cord; se — fold up; wind; (mil.) fall back, retreat

réplique *f.* answer, reply, retort, replica; (theat.) cue

répliquer *vi.* to reply, answer back, retort

replonger *vt.* to plunge again; — *vi.* dive again; sink again

repolir *vt.* to repolish

répondant *m.* guarantor, surety; (eccl.) server at mass

répondre *vt.* to answer, reply; — *vi.* to answer; respond; reciprocate; correspond

réponse *f.* answer, reply

report *m.* carry over, amount brought forward (bookkeeping)

reportage *m.* reporting, newspaper writing, commentary

reporter *vt.* to carry back, carry over; postpone; se — à refer to

repos *m.* rest, repose, tranquility; landing of a stairway; au — (mil.) at ease; en — resting, at rest

reposant *a.* restful

reposé *a.* rested; tranquil, calm; à tête -e *adv.* calmly, coolly, deliberately

reposer *vt.* to put back, replace; rest; — *vi.* to rest, lie; se — rest, repose; come to rest, alight; se — sur rely on

reposoir *m.* resting place; (eccl.) temporary parade altar; repository

repoussage *m.* stamping of sheet metal

repoussant *a.* repulsive; offensive, disgusting

repousse *f.* new growth

repoussé *a.* embossed; chased; — *m.* embossing; chasing

repoussement *m.* repulse, repulsing; rejecting, rejection; dislike; recoil

repousser *vt.* to repulse, repel, reject; deny; postpone; recoil; emboss; chase; — *vi.* produce new plant growths

repoussoir *m.* embossing punch; contrast, foil

répréhensible *a.* reprehensible

reprendre *vt.* to retake, take again, take back; resume; regain; reply; continue; reprove, criticise; — *vi.* return, come back; recover; se — take hold of oneself, regain composure; correct oneself

représailles *f. pl.* reprisals, retaliation

représentant *a. & m.* representative; — de commerce salesman

représentatif *a.* representative

représentation *f.* representation; agency; (theat.) performance; protest

représenter *vt.* to represent; reintroduce; present again; show, depict; perform; point out; se — present oneself again; represent oneself; recur, reappear

répressif *a.* repressive

répression *f.* repression

réprimable *a.* repressible

réprimandable *a.* censurable, worthy of censure

réprimande *f.* reprimand

réprimander *vt.* to reprimand, censure

réprimer *vt.* to repress; hold back, check

repris *m.,* — de justice habitual criminal

reprise *f.* retaking; recapture; renewal; recovery; repetition; mending, darning; (theatre) revival; (mus.) chorus, refrain; (auto.) trade-in; à plusieurs -s repeatedly

repriser *vt.* to darn, mend

réprobateur *a.* reproachful

réprobation *f.* reprobation, censure; rejection

reproche *m.* reproach, blame; **—s** *pl.* blame, criticism, censure

reprocher *vt.* to reproach, blame, find fault with; grudge, begrudge

reproducteur *a.* reproductive; **—** *m.* reproducer; stud, sire

reproductif *a.* reproductive

reproduire *vt.* to reproduce; **se —** to reproduce; recur, occur again

réprouvé *m.* reprobate

réprouver *vt.* to disapprove of; reject

reps *m.* repp

reptation *f.* crawling

reptile *m. & a.* reptile

repu *a.* sated, satiated, full

républicain *a. & m.* republican

républicanisme *m.* republicanism

republier *vt.* to republish

république *f.* republic

répudiation *f.* repudiation

répudier *vt.* to repudiate, renounce

repue *f.* franche **—** free dinner

répugnance *f.* repugnance, loathing, aversion, dislike; reluctance

répugnant *a.* repugnant, loathsome; loath, reluctant

répugner *vi.* to feel repugnance; be repugnant; be reluctant

répulsif *a.* repulsive

répulsion *f.* repulsion

réputation *f.* reputation, repute, name, renown

réputé *a.* of repute, well-known, famous

réputer *vt.* to repute, consider, think

requérable *a.* demandable

requérant *m.* legal petitioner, plaintiff

requérir *vt.* to demand, petition; ask

requête *f.* request, petition

requin *m.* shark; peau de **—** *f.* shagreen

requis *a.* requisite, required

réquisition *f.* requisition; requisitioning

réquisitionner *vt.* to requisition

réquisitoire *m.* legal indictment, charge

rescapé *a.* rescued, delivered; **—** *m.* rescued person, survivor

rescinder *vt.* to rescind

rescousse *f.* rescue

réseau *m.* network; net; (rad., rail.) system

réséda *m.* mignonette

réservation *f.* reservation

réserve *f.* reserve, reservation; à la **—** de except for; sans **—** unqualified, without exception; sous **—** de subject to

réservé *a.* reserved; shy; guarded

réserver *vt.* to reserve, save

réservoir *m.* reservoir; tank; well

résidence *f.* residence; dwelling

résider *vi.* to reside, dwell; consist

résidu *m.* residue; (com.) balance

résiduel *a.* residual

résignation *f.* resignation; submission, submissiveness

résigné *a.* resigned; submissive

résigner *vt.* to resign; submit; give up; se **—** to resign oneself, submit

résiliation *f.* cancellation, termination of

an agreement

résilience *f.* resilience

résilier *vt.* to cancel, terminate an agreement

résille *f.* hair net, snood; lattice

résine *f.* resin

résiner *vt.* to resin; tap for resin

résineux *a.* resinous

résistance *f.* resistance; stamina, strength; pièce de **—** *f.* main dish, main course; highlight, main feature

résistant *a.* resistant, strong; **—** *m.* member of the resistance

résister *vi.* to resist, withstand, endure

résolu *a.* resolute, determined

résoluble *a.* solvable; terminable

résolument *adv.* resolutely, determinedly

résolution *f.* resolution; resolve; solution; termination, cancellation

résonance *f.* resonance

résonnement *m.* resonance, reverberation

résonner *vi.* to resound, reverberate

résorber *vt.* to absorb again, reabsorb; imbibe

résoudre *vt.* to resolve; solve; dissolve; terminate, cancel; se **—** to make up one's mind

respect *m.* respect; rendre ses **—s** à to pay one's respects to

respectabilité *f.* respectability

respecter *vt.* to respect, have respect for; se **—** to act in a seemly fashion

respectif *a.* respective

respectueux *a.* respectful

respirateur *m.* respirator

respiration *f.* respiration, breathing

respiratoire *a.* respiratory

respirer *vt. & vi.* to breathe; inhale; (fig.) to pause for breath

resplendir *vi.* to shine, glow, be resplendent

responsabilité *f.* responsibility; liability

responsable *a.* responsible; liable

ressac *m.* surf; undertow

ressaigner *vi.* to open, start bleeding again

ressaisir *vt.* to seize again; retake, recapture; se **—** to recover, regain one's composure

ressasser *vt.* to repeat incessantly

ressaut *m.* projection; rise

ressauter *vi.* to rise; jump again

ressayer *vt.* to try again

resseller *vt.* to resaddle

ressemblance *f.* resemblance, likeness

ressembler *vi.* to resemble, look alike; be like; se **—** to be the same, be alike

ressemeler *vt.* to resole

ressentiment *m.* resentment

ressentir *vt.* to resent; feel, experience

resserre *f.* storing, storage; storeroom; shed

resserré *a.* tight, narrow, confined

resserrement *m.* tightening, contracting; oppression, heaviness; constipation

resserrer *vt.* to contract, constrict, tighten; confine; compress; lock up again; se **—** to become tighter; contract

resservir *vt. & vi.* to serve again

ressort *m.* spring; elasticity, resilience; motive; legal jurisdiction, competence;

resort; (fig.) function

ressortir vi. to go out again, emerge again; stand out, appear, be evident; — à belong to legally, be under the jurisdiction of; faire — make evident, bring out, stress, emphasize

ressouder vt. to solder or weld again; se — to heal, mend, or knit bone

ressource f. resource; expedient, resort; —s pl. resources, means; funds

ressouvenance f. remembrance, recollection

ressouvenir v. se — to remember, recollect; — m. memory, remembrance

ressuer vi. to sweat

ressusciter vt. to ressuscitate, revive, restore; — vi. to ressuscitate, come back to life, revive

ressuyer vt. to dry

restant a. remaining; poste -e f. general delivery; — m. remainder, balance, residue

restaurant m. restaurant; — a. & m. restorative

restaurateur m. restorer; restaurant proprietor

restauration f. restoration, restoring

restaurer vt. to restore; refresh; se — take refreshment; refresh oneself (fig.) to regain strength

reste m. remainder, rest, remains; au —, du — besides; de — left over; et le — and so forth

rester vi. to remain, be left; stay

restituer vt. to restore; give back; rehabilitate

restreindre vt. to restrict, limit; se — to limit oneself, retrench

restreint a. restricted, limited

restrictif a. restrictive

restringent a. & m. astringent

résultant a. resulting, resultant

résultat m. result

résulter vi. to result, follow

résumé m. summary, résumé, abstract; en — in short, in brief

résumer vt. to sum up, summarize

résurgence f. resurgence, reappearance

résurgin vi. to rise, reappear

résurrection f. resurrection

rétable m. retable, shelf or screen above an altar

rétablir vt. to re-establish, restore; recover, regain; se — to re-establish oneself; regain one's health

rétablissement m. re-establishment; restoration; recovery

retaille f. chip, portion removed

retailler vt. to cut again, recut; resharpen

retaillure f. cutting; sharpening

rétameur m. tinker

retaper vt. to fix, adjust, straighten; retype; se — to get well

retard m. delay; backwardness; slowness, lateness; en — late, behind, in arrears

retardataire a. late; backward; slow; in arrears; — m. & f. latecomer; person in arrears

retarder vt. to delay, retard; put back; defer; — vi. be late, be slow

reteindre vt. to dye again, redye

retendre vt. to stretch again; set (a trap) again

retenir vt. to retain, detain, keep back; hold back, withhold; restrain; se — to restrain oneself

rétenteur a. retaining

rétention f. retention, holding in

retentir vi. to resound, reverberate

retentissant a. resounding, loud

retentissement m. resounding, reverberation, effect, repercussion

retenu a. circumspect, prudent; reserved; booked; detained

retenue f. holding back; deduction; detention; reserve, modesty; restraint

réticence f. reticence

réticulaire a. reticular, netlike

réticule m. cross hairs in an eyepiece, reticle; reticule, bag, handbag

rétif a. restive, stubborn

rétiforme a. netlike, retiform

rétine f. retina

retirer vt. to withdraw, pull out; take off; take away; derive; reprint; se — to retire, withdraw; recede

rétivité f. stubbornness, obstinacy

retombant a. sagging, hanging, drooping

retomber vi. to fall again, sink again; hang down; droop

retordre vt. to twist again

rétorquer vt. to retort

retors a. wily, clever, crafty; twisted in weaving

retoucher vt. to retouch, touch up

retoucheur m. alterer; (phot.) retoucher

retour m. return; turn, twist; billet d'aller et — round-trip ticket; billet de — return ticket; être de — to be back

retournage m. turning, reversing

retourner vt. to turn, turn over; turn inside out; return; — vi. to return, go back; se — to turn around; s'en — return, be on the way back

retracer vt. to retrace

rétractation f. retraction, recantation

rétractable a. retráctable

rétracter vt. to retract; recant; se — to retract

retrait m. withdrawal; shrinkage; recess, indentation

retraite f. retreat; retirement; refuge, lair; (mil.) battre en — to beat a retreat; prendre sa — to retire

retraiter vt. to pension off, retire

retranché a. entrenched, fortified

retranchement m. entrenchment; cutting off

retrancher vt. to retrench, entrench, fortify; cut off, cut out

retransmettre vt. to retransmit; broadcast

retransmission f. rebroadcast

retravailler vt. to rework

retraverser vt. to cross again, recross, cross back

rétréci a. narrow, shrunken

rétrécir vt. to narrow, contract; shrink; take in; — vi. grow narrow

retremper vt. to soak again; retemper; se — to be invigorated

rétribuer vt. to remunerate, reward, pay

rétribution f. remuneration, reward, pay

rétroactif a. retroactive

rétroaction f. (elec.) feedback; retroactivity

rétrogradation f. retrogression; reduction in rank

rétrograde a. retrograde, reverse(d)

rétrograder vt. to reduce in rank; — vi. to retrogress; shift to a lower gear

rétrogressif a. retrogressive

rétrogression f. retrogression

rétrospectif a. retrospective

retroussé a. turned up; snub-nosed

retroussement m. curling

retrousser vt. to turn up, tuck up; roll up; se — tuck up a dress; lift out of the mud

retrouver vt. to find again, recover; meet, rejoin; se — to recover oneself, find oneself again, meet again

rétroviseur m. rear-view mirror; reflector

rets m. net, snare

réunion f. bringing together, meeting, gathering; reunion

réunir vt. to reunite, unite, assemble; bring together; se — to meet, gather

réussi a. successful, well-done

réussir vi. to succeed, have a happy outcome; — vt. to carry out, succeed in, bring off

réussite f. success; result, outcome, issue

revacciner vt. to revaccinate

revaloir vt. to pay back, get even with

revaloriser vt. to revalue

revanche f. revenge; return; return match; en — on the other hand; in return

rêvasser vi. to dream, daydream, be lost in thought

rêvasserie f. dreaming, daydreaming

rêve m. dream

revêche a. rough, harsh; crabby, ill-tempered

réveil m. waking, awakening; alarm clock; (mil.) reveille; (eccl.) revival

réveille-matin m. alarm clock

réveiller vt. to awaken, wake up; se — wake up, awake

réveillon m. midnight supper (Christmas Eve and New Year's Eve)

réveillonner vi. to celebrate Christmas or the New Year at a midnight supper

révélateur a. revealing; — m. revealer; (phot.) developer

révélation f. revelation

révéler vt. to reveal, show, display, disclose; (phot.) develop; se — to be revealed, appear

revenant a. pleasing; — m. ghost

revendeur m. secondhand dealer; retailer

revendication f. claim, demand, petition

revendiquer vt. to claim, demand

revendre vt. to sell again, resell

revenir vi. to come back, return, go back; recover, get over; s'en — to return, be coming back

revente f. resale

revenu m. revenue, income; profit, yield

rêver vt. & vi. to dream

réverbération f. reverberation

réverbère m. reflector; street light

réverbérer vt. & vi. to reverberate, reflect

revercher vt. to patch, solder

reverdir vi. to become green again; — vt. to make green again

révéremment adv. reverently

révérence f. reverence; bow, curtsey

révérenciel a. reverential

révérencieux a. ceremonious, overly formal

révérendissime a. very reverend, most reverend

révérer vt. to revere

rêverie f. musing, dreaming, reverie

revernir vt. to revarnish

revers m. reverse, back; lapel; coup de — m. backhand stroke; (fig.) setback

reverser vt. to pour again, pour back; shift, assign blame

réversible a. reversible

réversion f. reversion

reversoir m. irrigation dam

revêtement m. covering, casing, coating

revêtir vt. to clothe, reclothe, dress; se — put on again; put on; cover, case

rêveur a. pensive, musing, dreaming, dreamy; — m. dreamer

revient m., prix de — cost price

revigorer vt. to reinvigorate

revirement m. sudden change; reversal; (com.) assignment, transfer

réviser, reviser vt. to revise; audit; overhaul; re-examine

réviseur, reviseur m. reviser; auditor; proofreader

révision, revision f. revision; examination, inspection; proofreading; overhauling; conseil de — m. draft board

revisser vt. to screw tight, tighten

revivification f. revival

revivifier vt. to revive

revivre vi. to live again, come back to life

révocable a. revokable

révocation f. revocation, repeal; dismissal

revoir vt. to see again; revise, review; — m., au — good-bye

revoler vi. to fly again, fly back

révolte f. revolt, rebellion, uprising

révolté m. rebel

révolter vt. to cause to revolt; shock; se — to rebel, revolt

révolu a. completed, accomplished

révolution f. revolution; revulsion

révolutionnaire a. & n. revolutionary

révolutionner vt. to revolutionize

revolver m. revolver

revomir vt. to vomit, throw up

révoquer vt. to revoke, repeal; dismiss

revue f. review, inspection; revue

rez-de-chaussée m. ground floor, street floor, first floor

rhabiller vt. to dress again, reclothe; repair, fix, mend; se — to get dressed again, put on one's clothes again

rhabilleur m. repairer

rhabituer vt. to reaccustom

rhapsodie f. rhapsody

rhénan a. pertaining to the Rhine, Rhenish

rhénium m. rhenium

rhéostat m. rheostat

rhésus m. rhesus monkey; facteur — m. RH factor

rhétorique f. rhetoric

Rhin m. Rhine

rhinite f. rhinitis

rhinocéros m. rhinoceros

rhodanien a. pertaining to the Rhone

rhodium m. rhodium

rhododendron m. rhododendron

rhombe m. rhombus

rhomboïdal a. rhomboïd

rhomboïde m. rhomboid

rhubarbe f. rhubarb

rhum m. rum

rhumatisant a. & m. rheumatic person

rhumatisme m. rheumatism

rhume m. (med.) cold

riant a. laughing, smiling

ribaud a. ribald

riblons m. pl. scrap metal

ricanement m. sneering, snickering, scoffing

ricaner vi. to sneer, laugh derisively

ricaneur a. derisive, snickering; — m. derider

riche a. rich, wealthy

richesse f. riches, richness, wealth

ricin m. castor-oil plant; huile de — f castor oil

ricocher vi. to rebound; ricochet

ricochet m. rebound; ricochet

ride f. wrinkle; ripple; (naut.) lanyard

ridé a. wrinkled, lined; corrugated

rideau m. curtain; screen; (phot.) shutter — de fer iron curtain

ridelle f. side panel of a truck, or cart

rider vi. to wrinkle, line; ripple; corrugate; se — become wrinkled, become lined

ridicule a. ridiculous, absurd, laughable; — m. ridicule, ridiculousness; tourner en — to ridicule, make fun of

ridiculiser vt. to ridicule

rien pron. nothing, anything; de — you're welcome, don't mention it; — que only, merely; ne . . . — nothing, not anything; — m. nothing; bagatelle, trifle

rieur a. laughing; — m. laughter

riflard m. file; plastering trowel; jackplane; (coll.) very large umbrella

rifler vt. to file; plane; pare

rigide a. rigid, stiff; fixed, in place; tense

rigidité f. rigidity, stiffness; — cadavérique rigor mortis

rigole f. trench, gutter, drain

rigoleur a. fun-loving; laughing; — m. laugher; gay person

rigorisme m. absolute strictness

rigoriste a. very strict, rigorous; — m. & f. very strict person

rigoureux a. rigorous, strict, severe; hard, harsh

rigueur f. rigor, strictness, severity, harshness; à la — strictly; if necessary; de — required, obligatory

rillettes f. pl. minced pork

rillons m. pl. greaves, fryings

rimailler vi. to write verse, write second-

rate poetry

rimailleur m. rhymester, writer of verse

rime f. rhyme, verse

rimer vt. & vi. to rhyme

rimeur m. rhymer, writer of verse

rinçage m. rinsing

rince-bouteilles m. bottle-washer

rince-doigts m. finger bowl

rincer vt. to rinse, wash

rinçure f. dirty water, waste water, wash water

singard m. poker, fire iron

ripaille f. feast, celebration, party

ripailler vi. to feast, celebrate

ripe f. scraper

riper vt. & vi. to scrape, rub

ripolin m. enamel

ripoliner vt. to enamel

riposte f. retort; repartée; counter

riposter vi. to retort, counter, riposte

riquiqui m. little finger; tiny person

rire vi. to laugh; joke; — à smile at, smile upon; — de laugh at, laugh about; éclater de — burst out laughing; il n'y a pas de quoi — it's not at all funny; se — de laugh at, make fun of; — m. laugh, laughing, laughter

ris m. laugh; (naut.) reef in a sail; — de veau sweetbreads

risée f. mockery, laughing stock; (naut.) gust, squall

risette f. smile of a child, little smile

risible a. laughable, ludicrous

risque m. risk, peril, danger

risqué a. risqué, risky

risquer vt. to risk, chance, endanger; se — to dare, venture; take risks

risque-tout m. daredevil

rissoler vt. to brown

ristourne f. refund, rebate

ristourner vt. to refund, rebate

ritournelle f. (mus.) ritournelle, short instrumental passage; (coll.) same old story

ritualiste a. ritualistic; — m. & f. ritualist

rituel a. & m. ritual

rivage m. bank, shore

rivaliser (avec) vi. to rival, compete (with)

rivalité f. rivalry

rive f. bank, shore; edge, border, side

rivelaine f. pick (tool)

river vt. to rivet, clinch

riverain a. riparian; bordering on a waterway or road

riveraineté f. riparian rights

rivet m. rivet; clinch

rivetage m. riveting

riveter vt. to rivet

riveur m. riveter

riveuse f. riveting machine

rivière f. river, stream

rivoir m. riveting hammer

rivure f. riveting; riveted work

rixe f. scuffle, melee, brawl

riz m. rice; — au lait rice pudding; poudre de — face powder

rizière f. rice field

robe f. dress, gown, frock; robe; husk, animal coat; gens de — bar, legal pro-

fession
robinet *m.* spigot, faucet, tap
rob, robre *m.* rubber (at cards)
robuste *a.* robust, strong, sturdy
robustesse *f.* robustness, strength, sturdiness
roc *m.* rock
rocaille *f.* rocks; rubble; jardin de — *m.* rock garden
rocailleur *m.* ornamental stonemason
rocailleux *a.* rocky; rough, harsh
rocambolesque *a.* fantastic
roche *f.* rock, stone
rocher *m.* rock, crag; — *vi.* to froth
rochet *m.* ratchet
rocheux *a.* rocky
rochier *m.* rockfish
rococo *a. & m.* rococo, baroque
rodage *m.* grinding; polishing; wear, wearing away; breaking-in of an automobile motor
rodailler *vi.* to wander, loaf
roder *vt.* to grind, polish; break in (a motor)
rôder *vi.* to roam, prowl
rôdeur *a.* roaming, prowling, idling; — *m.* prowler, idler, loafer
rodoir *m.* grinder, grinding implement
rodomont *m.* boaster
rœntgenthérapie *f.* X-ray treatment
rogatons *m. pl.* scraps, bits of food
rogner *vt.* to pare, clip, trim
rognoir *m.* parer, paring implement
rognon *m.* edible animal kidney
rognures *f. pl.* cuttings, parings, trimmings; leftovers, scraps
rogue *a.* haughty
roi *m.* king
roide *a.* stiff; steep; firm
roideur *f.* stiffness
rôle *m.* roll, roster, list; (theat.) part, role; à tour de — in turn
Romain *m. & a.* Roman
romaine *f.* balance, scale; romaine lettuce
roman *m.* novel; romance; — *a.* Romance; (arch.) Romanesque
romance *f.* (mus.) ballad, song
romancier *m.* novelist
romand, *a.*, Suisse -e *f.* French-speaking Switzerland
romanesque *a.* romantic
roman-feuilleton *m.* serialized novel
romanichel *m.* gypsy, wanderer
romaniste *m.* specialist in Romance languages; (eccl.) Romanist
romantique *a.* romantic (literature, art); — *m.* romanticist
romantisme *m.* romanticism
romarin *m.* rosemary
rompre *vt.* to break, break off, break up; break in, train; disrupt, interrupt; — *vi.* break; se — to break off, break up; break oneself in, become accustomed
rompu *a.* broken; broken in, trained, experienced; fatigued, worn out
romsteck *m.* rump steak
ronce *f.* bramble; blackberry bush
ronce-framboise *f.* loganberry
ronceux *a.* thorny, brambly
ronchonner *vi.* to grumble, complain

rond *a.* round; plump; straightforward; — *m.* round, circle, ring; — de serviette napkin ring
rondache *f.* round shield
rond-de-cuir *m.* (coll.) bureaucrat, petty official
ronde *f.* (mus.) round; patrol
rondeau *m.* (mus.) rondo; rondeau (literature)
rondelet *a.* round, roundish; plump
rondelle *f.* ring, washer; disk; circular piece; round
rondement *adv.* roundly; promptly; in a straightforward manner
rondeur *f.* roundness; rotundity; frankness, straightforwardness
rondin *m.* log; stick; beam
rond-point *m.* circular intersection, circus
ronflant *a.* snoring; booming; rumbling; pretentious
ronflement *m.* snoring, snore; buzzing; booming cannon; rumbling
ronfler *vi.* to snore; roar; whirr; boom; rumble
ronfleur *m.* snorer
rongeant *a.* gnawing, eating away; corroding
ronger *vt.* to gnaw, nibble, eat away; erode; corrode; torment
rongeur *a.* gnawing; corroding; tormenting; — *m.* rodent
ronron *m.* hum, purr
ronronner *vi.* to hum, purr
roquer *vt.* to castle (chess)
roquet *m.* mongrel, cur, dog
rosaire *m.* (eccl.) rosary, beads
rosâtre *a.* pinkish
rosbif *m.* roast beef
rose *f.* rose; — *a.* pink; rosy
rosé *a.* light red
roseau *m.* (bot.) reed
rosée *f.* dew
roselet *m.* ermine fur
roséole *f.* (med.) roseola; German measles
roseraie *f.* rose garden
rosette *f.* rosette; ribbon, bow
rosier *m.* rose bush
rosir *vi.* to turn pink or rosy
rossard *m.* good-for-nothing
rossée *f.* beating, thrashing, licking
rosser *vt.* to thrash, whip, beat
rossignol *m.* nightingale
rossinante *f.* nag, old horse
rot *m.* belch
rôt *m.* roast
rotative *f.* rotary press
rotatoire *a.* rotary
roter *vi.* to belch, eructate
rôti *m.* roast
rôtie *f.* toast
rotin *m.* rattan
rôtir *vt. & vi.* to roast; toast
rôtissage *m.* roasting
rôtisserie *f.* roaster's shop
rôtissoire *f.* Dutch oven; roaster
rotonde *f.* rotunda
rotondité *f.* rotundity, roundness
rotor *m.* rotor
rotule *f.* kneecap; knee joint; (mech.) knuckle

roture *f.* low estate; commoners

roturier *m.* & *a.* plebeian, commoner

rouage *m.* wheels, gears, workings

rouan *a.* roan

roublard *a.* & *m.* shrewd, crafty person

roucouler *vi.* to coo

roue *f.* wheel

roué *m.* rake, profligate, roué; — *a.* clever, shrewd, crafty, sly

rouelle *f.* round piece, slice; filet of veal

rouennerie *f.* printed fabrics

rouer *vt.* to torture on a wheel; beat, thrash

rouerie *f.* cheating, trickery, sharping

rouet *m.* spinning wheel; pulley wheel

rouge *a.* red; — *m.* red; rouge; lipstick

rougeâtre *a.* reddish

rougeaud *a.* red-faced, ruddy

rouge-gorge *m.* robin

rougeole *f.* measles

rongeoyer *vi.* to turn red

rougeur *f.* redness; blush

rougir *vt.* to redden, turn red; heat, cause to glow; — *vi.* to grow red, turn red; blush

rouille *f.* rust; blight

rouillé *a.* rusty, rusted; blighted

rouiller *vt.* to rust, blight; se — to become rusty, rust

rouilleux *a.* rust-colored

rouillure *f.* rust, rustiness

roulade *f.* trill, roll

roulage *m.* rolling; hauling, transporting; traffic

roulant *a.* rolling; moving; smooth; fauteuil — wheel chair

rouleau *m.* roll; roller; coil; cylinder; rolling pin; — compresseur steam roller

roulement *m.* rolling; functioning, running; rotation, alternation; — à billes ballbearing

rouler *vt.* to roll; roll up; carry, haul; consider, turn over; — *vi.* roll; run; turn; move along; rove; rumble; rotate, alternate

roulette *f.* small wheel; roller; caster; roulette; patins à —s *m. pl.* roller skates

roulier *m.* hauler, trucker, carter

roulis *m.* (naut.) roll

roulotte *f.* caravan, house trailer

Roumain *m.* & *a.* Roumanian

Roumanie *f.* Roumania

roupie *f.* rupee

roussâtre *a.* reddish

rousselet *m.* russet pear

rousseur *f.* reddishness, redness; tache de — freckle

roussi *a.* burned; burning; browned

roussin *m.* draft horse, plow horse

roussir *vt.* & *vi.* to redden; turn brown; singe, burn

routage *m.* newspaper delivery *or* distribution

route *f.* route, road, way; grande — highway; en — on the way; go:on; let's go; se mettre en — to start out, set out

router *vt.* to deliver, distribute

routier *a.* of roads; — *m.* long-distance trucker; long-distance cyclist; -s *pl.* highwaymen; carte routière *f.* road map

routine *f.* routine, habit

routinier *a.* routine

rouvrir *vt.* to open again, reopen

roux (rousse) *a.* reddish, red-headed

royal *a.* royal; regal

royaliste *m.* & *f.* royalist

royaume *m.* kingdom, realm

royauté *f.* royalty

ru *m.* streamlet

ruade *f.* attack; kicking of an animal

ruban *m.* ribbon; tape; band, strip; — magnétique magnetic recording-tape

rubané *a.* striped

rubaner *vt.* to adorn with ribbons; cut into strips

rubéole *f.* German measles

rubicond *a.* rubicund

rubiette *f.* robin

rubigineux *a.* rusty; rust-colored

rubis *m.* ruby; watch jewel

rubrique *f.* rubric; red chalk; category, heading

ruche *f.* beehive; frill, ruche, ruffle

ruché *m.* ruche, frilling

ruchée *f.* bees of a hive

rucher *m.* apiary; — *vt.* to gather (sewing); trim with ruching

rude *a.* rough, rugged; hard, harsh; coarse; steep; brusque; primitive

rudement *adv.* roughly, harshly

rudesse *f.* roughness, ruggedness; harshness; coarseness; abruptness

rudiment *m.* rudiment

rudimentaire *a.* rudimentary, elementary

rudoyer *vt.* to treat roughly

rue *f.* street

ruée *f.* rush, stampede; attack, onslaught

ruelle *f.* narrow street, lane, alley

ruer *vi.* to kick; se — (sur) to rush upon, stampede

rufian *m.* ruffian

ruginer *vt.* to clean, scale teeth

rugir *vi.* to roar, bellow

rugissement *m.* roar, roaring, bellow, bellowing

rugosité *f.* roughness, ruggedness; wrinkle

rugueux *a.* rough, rugged; wrinkled, gnarled

ruine *f.* ruin; downfall; destruction

ruiner *vt.* to ruin, destroy; se — to be ruined; go to ruin; fall to ruins

ruineux *a.* ruinous; disastrous

ruisseau *m.* stream, brook; gutter

ruisseler *vi.* to stream, gush out, run; drip, trickle

ruisselet *m.* little brook *or* stream

rumba *f.* rhumba

rumen *m.* first stomach of a ruminant

rumeur *f.* noise, din, sound; rumor

ruminant *a.* & *m.* ruminant

rumination *f.* rumination

ruminer *vt.* & *vi.* to ruminate

rumsteck *m.* rump steak

runes *f. pl.* runes

runique *a.* Runic

rupteur *m.* (elec.) circuit breaker

rupture *f.* breaking, rupture; fracture; breaking up; breaking in two; breaking off; breach

ruse f. ruse, trick
rusé a. sly, cunning, crafty
ruser vi. to use trickery
Russe m. & a. Russian
Russie f. Russia
rustaud m. boor; hick, bumpkin; — a. boorish
rusticité f. rusticity
rustique a. rustic; strong, robust
rustre m. boor, lout; — a. boorish, loutish
ruthénium m. ruthenium
rutilant a. glowing, gleaming, red
rutiler vi. to glow, gleam, redden
rythme m. rhythm
rythmé, rythmique a. rhythmic, rhythmical

S

sa a. f. his, her, its; one's
Saba m. Sheba
sabbat m. Sabbath
sabbatique a. sabbatical
sabin a. & m. Sabine
sable m. sand; — mouvant quicksand
sablé a. sanded, covered with sand or gravel; — m. shortbread cookie
sabler vt. to sand, gravel, cover with sand or gravel; sand-blast; drink dry
sableux a. sandy
sablier m. hourglass
sablière f. sandbox; sand pit, gravel pit; — f. beam, plate, templet
sablon m. sand for cleaning or scouring
sablonner vt. to clean, scour with sand
sablonneux a. sandy
sabord m. port hole, gun port
saborder vt. to hit below the water line; se — to scuttle
sabot m. wooden shoe; hoof; (auto.) brake shoe; -s en caoutchouc rubbers
sabotage m. sabotage; manufacture of sabots
saboter vt. to sabotage
sabotier m. maker of sabots
sabre m. saber, sword
sabrer vt. to saber, cut down
sac m. sack, sac, bag, pouch; sackcloth; sacking (a place); — à main handbag, purse
saccade f. jerk, jolt
saccadé a. by jerks; abrupt; irregular, uneven
saccader vt. to jerk, jolt
saccager vt. to plunder, sack, pillage; ransack
saccageur m. plunderer
saccharine f. saccharine
sacerdotal a. priestly
sachée f. sackful, bagful
sachet m. sachet; small sack or bag
sacoche f. bag; handbag; satchel; saddle-bag; tool kit
sacre m. coronation; consecration
sacré a. sacred, holy; confounded; (anat.) sacral
sacrement m. sacrament
sacrer vt. to crown; consecrate
sacrificateur m. sacrificer
sacrificatoire a. sacrificial

sacrifice m. sacrifice; oblation
sacrifier vt. to sacrifice; devote
sacrilège m. sacrilege; — a. sacrilegious
sacristain m. sexton, sacristan
sacristie f. vestry
sacro-saint a. sacrosanct
sacrum m. (anat.) sacrum
sadique a. sadistic
sadisme m. sadism
sadiste m. & f. sadist
safran m. saffron, crocus
safrané a. saffron-colored
sagace a. sagacious
sagacité f. sagacity
sage a. wise; good, well-behaved; — m. sage, wise man
sage-femme f. midwife
sagesse f. wisdom; good behavior; discretion
sagittaire m. archer; (astrol., ast.) Saggitarius
sagittal a. arrow-shaped
sagou m. sago
Sahara m. Sahara
saharien a. of the Sahara
saie f. cape; hog-bristle brush
saignant a. bleeding, bloody; rare (meat)
saignée f. (med.) bleeding, bloodletting; drainage ditch; groove
saigner vt. & vi. to bleed
saigneux a. bloody
saillant a. projecting, prominent; salient; dents -es f. pl. buck teeth
saillie f. protrusion, projection; start; sally; spurt; gushing
saillir vi. to jut out, project; stand out, be prominent; spurt, gush; rush forth
sain a. sound, healthy; wholesome; sane; — et sauf safe and sound
sainfoin m. hay, forage
saindoux m. lard
saint a. saint; sacred, holy; saintly, godly; consecrated; — m. saint
saint-cyrien m. army cadet
Saint-Domingue m. Santo Domingo; Dominican Republic
Saint-Esprit m. (eccl.) Holy Ghost
sainte-nitouche f. hypocrite
sainteté f. sanctity, holiness
saint-frusquin m. possessions
Saint-Laurent m. St. Lawrence River
Saint-Marin m. San Marino
Saint-Père m. (eccl.) Pope, Holy Father
Saint-Siège m. (eccl.) Holy See
Saint-Sylvestre m. New Year's Eve
saisie f. seizure; attachment, foreclosure
saisie-arrêt f. legal garnishment, attachment
saisir vt. to seize, catch, grip, grasp; understand, apprehend; attach legally
saisissable a. perceptible
saisissant a. striking; startling; thrilling; gripping; keen, sharp
saisissement m. sudden shock, attack, seizure
saison f. season; de — in season; timely, opportune; hors de — out of season; untimely, inopportune
saisonnier a. seasonal
salacité f. salaciousness

salade f. salad
saladier m. salad bowl
salaire m. salary, wages, pay; fee; reward
salaison f. salting, curing; salted meat
salamandre f. salamander, newt
salanque f. salt marsh
salariat m. wage earners, salaried class
salarier vt. to pay, salary
sale a. dirty; foul; filthy; coarse
salé m. salt pork; petit — ham hock; — a. salted; risqué
saler vt. to salt; season; pickle, cure
saleté f. dirtiness, dirt, filth; obscenity
salicoque f. shrimp, prawn
salière f. salt cellar, salt shaker
salin a. saline, briny, salty
saline f. salt flats, salt mine
salinité f. salinity
salir vt. to soil, dirty; tarnish
salissure f. spot, stain, dirt mark
salivaire a. salivary
salive f. saliva
saliver vi. to salivate
salle f. hall, room; auditorium; audience; — à manager dining room; — d'attente waiting room; — de bain bathroom; — de conférences lecture hall
Salomon (m.) Solomon
salon m. living room, parlor; exhibition; — de thé tearoom; — de beauté beauty shop; — de coiffure barber shop
salopette f. dungarees, overalls
salpètre m. saltpeter
salsepareille f. sarsaparilla
salsifis m. salsify, oysterplant
saltimbanque m. quack, charlatan; mountebank; tumbler
salubre a. salubrious, wholesome, healthy
salubrité f. salubrity, wholesomeness, healthiness; health, hygiene
saluer vt. to salute, greet, bow
salure f. saltiness, salinity
salut m. bow, greeting, salutation, salvation; safety; welfare; —! interj. hello!
salutaire a. salutary, beneficial
salve f. salvo, salute
samaritain m. samaritan
samedi m. Saturday
samovar m. samovar, tea urn
sanctifier vt. to sanctify, hallow
sanction f. sanction; approval, consent; penalty, punitive action
sanctionner vt. to sanction, approve; penalize
sanctuaire m. sanctuary
sandale f. sandal
sandaraque f. sandarac
sang m. blood; lineage; coup de — (med.) stroke; pur — thoroughbred
sang-froid m. composure, self-control, calmness, coolness
sanglant a. bloody, covered with blood; cutting, keen
sangle f. strap; lit de — m. cot, camp bed
sangler vt. to strap; whip, lash
sanglier m. wild boar
sanglot m. sob
sangloter vi. to sob
sangsue f. leech

sanguin a. sanguine, blood-red; of blood
sanguinaire a. sanguinary; bloody; bloodthirsty
sanguine f. blood orange; bloodstone; red chalk
sanguinelle f. dogwood
sanitaire a. sanitary; medical
sans prep. without; were it not for; free of; — doute without a doubt; probably; perhaps
sanscrit, sanskrit a. & m. Sanskrit
sans-façon m. lack of formality, straightforwardness
sans-fil m. wireless, radio
sans-gêne m. excessive familiarity; lack of ceremony
sans-le-sou m. penniless person
sans-logis m. pl. homeless persons
sansonnet m. starling
sans-souci m. lack of concern; — m. & f. carefree person
sans-travail m. pl. unemployed persons
santal m. sandalwood
santé f. health
saoul a. (See soûl)
saouler vt. (See soûler)
sape f. (mil.) sap, sapping; undermining
saper vt. to sap, undermine
sapeur m. (mil.) sapper
sapeur-pompier m. fireman, fire fighter
saphir m. sapphire
sapide a. savory, flavorful
sapience f. wisdom
sapin m. fir tree; —ette f. spruce tree
sapine f. scaffolding; fir board; construction crane
sapinière f. fir forest
saponacé a. soapy
sarbacane f. blowpipe; pea shooter
sarcasme m. sarcasm
sarcastique a. sarcastic
sarcler vt. to weed; hoe
sarcleur m. weeder
sarcloir m. hoe
sarclure f. weeds
sarcome m. (med.) sarcoma
sarcophage m. sarcophagus
Sardaigne f. Sardinia
Sarde m. & a. Sardinian
sardinerie f. sardine cannery
sardinier m. sardine fishermen, cannery worker
sardoine f. sardonyx
sardonique a. sardonic
sargasse f. sargasso; mer des —s f. Sargasso Sea
S.A.R.L.: Société à Responsabilité Limitée incorporated
sarment m. shoot of a vine
sarracenique a. Saracen
sarrasin m. buckwheat
Sarrasin m. & a. Saracen
sarrasine f. portcullis
sarrau m. smock; overalls
Sarre f. Saar Basin
sariette f. savory
sas m. sifter, sieve, screen; lock of a dam
sasser vt. to sift, screen; (naut.) lock a vessel (in a canal)

Satan *m*. Satan, the Devil
satanique *a*. diabolical, devilish, satanic
satellite *m*. satellite
satiété *f*. satiety, repletion, fullness
satiné *a*. satin-like; glossy
satiner *vt*. to satin, gloss, glaze
satinette *f*. sateen
satire *f*. satire
satirique *a*. satirical; — *m*. satirist
satiriser *vt*. to satirize
satisfaction *f*. satisfaction; amends
satisfaire *vt*. to satisfy; please; make
amends to; — *vi*. to satisfy, carry out,
fulfil
satisfaisant *a*. satisfactory; satisfying
satisfait *a*. satisfied; pleased
satrape *m*. satrap
saturation *f*. saturation
saturer *vt*. to saturate
saturnin *a*. saturnine
saturnisme *m*. lead poisoning
satyre *m*. satyr
sauce *f*. sauce; gravy; dressing
saucer *vt*. to dip into sauce; soak, drench,
saucière *f*. gravy boat; sauce dish
saucisse *f*. sausage; — de Francfort frankfurter
saucisson *m*. sausage, salami
sauf *prep*. except, except for, but; barring;
— (sauve) *a*. safe
sauf-conduit *m*. safe conduct, pass, permit
sauge *f*. sage
saugrenu *a*. absurd, ridiculous
saule *m*. willow; — pleureur weeping willow
saumâtre *a*. brackish; salty; bitter
saumon *m*. salmon; ingot, bar; — de fonte
pig iron; — *a*. salmon, pink
saumoné *a*. pink-fleshed; truite -e *f*. salmon trout
saumurage *m*. curing in brine
saumure *f*. brine
saupiquet *m*. spicy sauce
saupoudrer *vt*. to sprinkle; powder; dust
with
saupoudroir *m*. shaker
saur *a*., hareng — *m*. smoked red herring
saure *a*. sorrel
saurer *vt*. to smoke, cure fish
saut *m*. jump, leap; waterfall; — à la
perche pole vault; — d'obstacles hur-
dles
saut-de-lit *m*. dressing gown; bedroom
scatter rug
saut-de-mouton *m*. overpass, underpass
saute *f*. jump, leap; rise, increase
sauté *a*. fried; — *m*. food fried rapidly
saute-mouton *m*. leapfrog
sauter *vt*. to leap, jump; skip, omit; — *vi*.
leap, jump; skip, explode, blow up;
fail; — au cou de throw one's arms
around; — aux veux to be very obvious;
faire — to blow up, explode; pop open
sauterelle *f*. grasshopper
sauterie *f*. leaping, jumping; hopping,
hop; dance, dancing
sauternes *m*. Sauterne wine
sauteur *a*. leaping, jumping; — *m*. leaper,
jumper
sautiller *vt*. to skip, leap, hop

sautoir *m*. X-shaped cross; frying pan;
sports hurdle; bar of a jump or vault;
en — crosswise
sauvage *a*. wild; savage; barbarous, uncivilized; shy, unsociable
sauvagerie *f*. wildness, savagery; shy-
ness, unsociability
sauvegarde *f*. safeguard, protection; bodyguard; safe-conduct; (naut.) lifeline
sauvegarder *vt*. to protect, safeguard
sauve-qui-peut *m*. wild flight, stampede
sauver *vt*. to save, preserve; rescue; se —
to escape; run away, flee
sauvetage *m*. salvage; saving, rescue;
canot de —, lifeboat; ceinture de — *f*.
life preserver
sauveteur *m*. saver, rescuer; salvager
sauvette; à la — *adv*. hastily
sauveur *m*. deliverer; saviour, redeemer
savamment *adv*. in a learned or scholarly
manner; knowingly
savane *f*. savanna
savant *a*. learned, scholarly, erudite;
knowing; — *m*. scholar; scientist
savarin *m*. rum cake
savate *f*. old shoe; foot boxing (French
style); (fig.) bungler
savetier *m*. cobbler, shoe repairer
saveur *f*. flavor, savor, taste
Savoie *f*. Savoy; gâteau de — *m*. sponge
cake
savoir *vt*. to know, know how, be able,
find out; à — namely, viz., to wit;
faire — to inform; reste à — it remains
to be seen; — *m*. knowledge, learning,
erudition
savoir-faire *m*. skill, ability, know-how;
tact
savoir-vivre *m*. manners, breeding, social
poise
savoisien *a*. of Savoy
savon *m*. soap; pain de — *m*. cake of
soap; pierre de — *f*. soapstone
savonnage *m*. soaping, washing
savonner *vt*. to soap; lather; wash
savonnette *f*. toilet soap
savonneux *a*. soapy
savourer *vt*. to relish, taste, savor, enjoy
savoureux *a*. savory, flavorful, tasty;
spicy
Saxe *f*. Saxony; porcelaine de — *f*.
Dresden china
saynète *f*. comic play, farce
Saxon *m*. & *a*. Saxon
saxophone *m*. saxophone
scabieux *a*. scabby
scabreux *a*. scabrous; risky, dangerous;
risqué
scalpe *m*. scalp
scalper *vt*. to scalp
scandale *m*. scandal, disgrace
scandaleux *a*. scandalous, disgraceful,
shocking
scandaliser *vt*. to scandalize
scander *vt*. to scan (poetry); stress, accentuate, measure
Scandinave *m*. & *a*. Scandinavian
Scandinavie *f*. Scandinavia
scansion *f*. scanning
scaphandre *m*. diving suit; aqualung

scaphandrier m. deep-sea diver

scapulaire m. (eccl.) scapular

scarabée m. beetle, scarab

scarlatine f. scarlet fever

scarole f. escarole

sceau m. seal; stamp, mark, imprint

scélérat a. villainous, wicked; sly, crafty; — m. villain, scoundrel

scélératesse f. villainy, wickedness

scellage m. sealing

scellé m. legal seal

scellement m. fixing in cement, plaster

sceller vt. to seal; fasten

scénario m. scenario, screenplay

scénariste m. & f. author of a screenplay

scène f. scene; stage; scenery; metteur en — m. director; mettre en — to direct, stage; mise en — f. direction, staging

scénique a. scenic; of the stage

scepticisme m. skepticism

sceptique a. skeptical; — m. & f. skeptic

sceptre m. scepter

schelem m. slam (in bridge)

schelling m. shilling

schéma m. plan, sketch, diagram

schématique a. schematic

schisme m. schism

schiste m. shale

schizophrène a. schizophrenic

schizophrénie f. schizophrenia

schnorkel m. snorkel

sciage m. sawing

sciatique a. sciatic; — f. sciatica

scie f. saw; — à chantourner jigsaw; — à métaux hack saw; — à refendre ripsaw; — à ruban band saw; — de mer sawfish

sciemment adv. knowingly; purposely

science f. science; knowledge, learning; homme de — m. scientist

scientifique a. scientific

scier vt. to saw; — vi. back water (rowing)

scierie f. sawmill

scinder vt. to split, divide

scintillant a. scintillating; twinkling

scintillation f. scintillation; twinkling; (phot.) flickering

scintiller vi. to scintillate; twinkle; flicker

scion m. scion, shoot, sprout

scission f. secession; division, split

sciure f. sawdust

sclérose f. sclerosis

scléroser vt. (med.) to harden

scolaire a. scholastic, academic, school

scolarisation f. teaching; school attendance

scolarité f. length of study; certificat de — m. attendance certificate

scolastique a. scholastic; — f. scholasticism

scolopendre f. centipede

scombre m. mackerel

scorbut m. scurvy

scorie f. slag, dross

scoutisme m. scouting, boy scout movement

scrofules f. pl. (med.) scrofula

scrupule m. scruple, qualm, doubt; sans —s unscrupulous

scrupuleux a. scrupulous

scruter vt. to scrutinize; examine at length

scrutin m. ballot, vote, voting

scrutiner vi. to vote, ballot

sculpter vt. to sculpt, sculpture, carve, chisel

sculpteur m. sculptor

scythe a. & n. Scythian

se pron. oneself, himself; herself, itself, themselves; each other, one another

séance f. sitting, session, meeting; showing, performance; lever la — to adjourn

séant a. sitting; in session; fitting, proper, becoming

seau m. pail, bucket

sébacé a. fatty

sébile f. wooden bowl

sec (sèche) a. dry, dried; lean; sharp, curt; barren; argent — m. hard cash; coup — m. snap; clean, hard blow; à — dry; aground; mettre à — to dry up, drain, pump out; — adv., boire — to drink straight; parler — to speak plainly, in a straightforward manner

sèche-cheveux m. hair dryer

sécheresse f. dryness; leanness; curtness; drought

sécher vt. to dry; (coll.) cut a class; fail a student; — vi. dry

sécheur m. drier

séchoir m. drier; towel rack

second a. second; en — lieu secondly, in the second place; sans — peerless, unequalled; — m. second in command; first mate

secondaire a. secondary

seconde f. second; second class

seconder vt. to second, assist, support, promote

secouer vt. to shake, shake off

secourable a. helpful; ready to help

secourir vt. to succor, help, assist, aid

secours m. succor, aid, assistance, help; crier au — to call for help; premiers — pl. first aid

secousse f. shake, shock, jolt

secret a. secret; concealed, hidden; — m. secret; secrecy

secrétaire m. & f. secretary

secrétariat m. secretariat; secretary's office

sécréter vt. to secrete

sécréteur a. secreting

sécrétion f. secretion

sectaire m. sectarian

sectateur m. member of a sect

secte f. sect, party, faction

secteur m. sector; area, district; segment

sectionner vt. to divide into sections

séculaire a. century-old, secular

sécularisation f. secularization

séculariser vt. to secularize

séculier a. secular, worldly; — m. layman

sécurité f. security; safety

sédatif a. & m. sedative

sédentaire a. sedentary

sédiment m. sediment

séditieux a. seditious

sédition f. sedition

séducteur *a.* enticing, seductive; — *m.* enticer; seducer

séduction *f.* seductiveness, charm; bribery; seduction

séduire *vt.* to charm, fascinate; bribe; seduce

séduisant *a.* charming; enticing, seductive

segment *m.* segment; — de piston piston ring

segmenter *vt.* to divide into segments

ségrégation *f.* segregation

seiche *f.* cuttlefish

seigle *m.* rye; pain de — *m.* rye bread

seigneur *m.* lord, nobleman

seigneurie *f.* lordship; domain

seille *f.* wooden bucket

seillon *m.* shallow tub

sein *m.* breast; bosom

seing *m.* signature; acte sous — privé simple contract

séisme *m.* earthquake

seize *a.* sixteen

seizième *a.* sixteenth

séjour *m.* sojourn, stay; abode, dwelling

séjourner *vi.* to stay, sojourn; reside

sel *m.* salt; (fig.) wit; — anglais *m.* Epsom salts; — blanc table salt; — gemme rock salt

sélecteur *a.* selective; — *m.* selector

sélection *f.* selection, choice, choosing

sélectivité *f.* selectivity

sélénium *m.* selenium

selle *f.* saddle; stool

seller *vt.* to saddle

sellette *f.* stool; saddle

selon *prep.* according to, by

seltz *m.*, eau de — *f.* seltzer, soda water

semailles *f. pl.* sowing, seeding

semaine *f.* week; week's pay; week's work; — anglaise five and one-half-day week

semaison *f.* seeding time

sémantique *a.* semantic; — *f.* semantics

sémaphore *m.* semaphore

semblable *a.* like, similar; such; — *n.* like, equal, fellow man

semblablement *adv.* likewise, similarly

semblant *m.* semblance, appearance; faire — (de) to pretend (to)

sembler *vi.* to seem, appear, look

semelle *f.* sole of a shoe; battre la — to be on the move, be roving

semence *f.* seed

semer *vt.* to sow; seed; spread, scatter

semestre *m.* semester, term; six-month period

semestriel *a.* six months long; taking place every six months, semi-annual

semeur *m.* sower; spreader

semi-circulaire *a.* semicircular

sémillant *a.* sprightly; light, gay

sémi-mensuel *a.* bimonthly

séminaire *m.* seminary

semis *m.* sowing, seeding; seed bed

sémitique *a.* Semitic

semi-voyelle *f.* semivowel

semoir *m.* mechanical sower, seeder

semonce *f.* summons; warning; lecture, talking-to

semoncer *vt.* to lecture, reprimand

semoule *f.* semolina

sempiternel *a.* eternal

sénat *m.* senate

sénateur *m.* senator

sénatorial *a.* senatorial

séné *m.* senna

senestrorsum *adv.* counterclockwise

sénévé *m.* mustard seed

sénile *a.* senile

sénilité *f.* senility

sens *m.* sense; judgment; meaning; direction; consciousness; bon — common sense; — interdit one-way street

sensation *f.* sensation; feeling; excitement

sensationnel *a.* sensational, exciting

sensé *a.* sensible, aware

sensibilisateur *a.* sensitizing; — *m.* sensitizer

sensibiliser *vt.* to sensitize

sensibilité *f.* sensitiveness, feeling; sensibility

sensible *a.* sensitive; sympathetic; tender, painful, sore; perceptible

sensiblement *a.* perceptibly, measurably

sensiblerie *f.* sentimentality

sensitif *a.* sensory; sensitive

sensualiste *a.* sensual; — *m.* sensualist

sensualité *f.* sensuality

sensuel *a.* sensuous, sensual

sentant *a.* sentient

sente *f.* path, footpath, trail

sentence *f.* maxim, saying; penal sentence; — de mort sentence of death

sentencieux *a.* sententious

senteur *f.* scent, perfume, fragrance; pois de — *m.* sweet pea

sentier *m.* path, track

sentiment *m.* septiment, feeling; sensation, sense

sentimentalité *f.* sentimentality

sentinelle *f.* sentinel; sentry

sentir *vt.* to feel; sense; smell; — *vi.* smell; smell of, reek of; se — feel

seoir *vi.* to suit, become; be located

sépale *m.* sepal

séparable *a.* separable

séparateur *m.* separator

séparatif *a.* separating, dividing

séparation *f.* separation; partition, division; parting

séparé *a.* separate; apart, separated

séparément *adv.* separately

séparer *vt.* to separate; divide; part; se — to separate, divide, part; break up; branch off

sépia *f.* sepia; cuttlefish

sept *a.* seven; seventh

septante *a.* seventy

septembre *m.* September

septicémie *f.* blood poisoning

septième *a.* seventh

septique *a.* septic; fosse — *f.* septic tank

sépulcral *a.* sepulchral

sépulcre *m.* sepulcher

sépulture *f.* burial; tomb; cemetery

séquence *f.* sequence

séquestration *f.* seclusion; sequestration (law)

séquestre *m.* sequestration (law); depository

séquestrer *vt.* to sequester; isolate, confine
sérail *m.* seraglio, harem
séraphin *m.* seraph
séraphique *a.* seraphic, angelic
Serbe *m. & f. & a.* Serb, Serbian
Serbo-Croate *m. & f. & a.* Serbo-Croatian
serein *a.* serene, calm, peaceful
sérénade *f.* serenade
sérénissime *a.* most serene
sérénité *f.* serenity, calm, calmness
sergent *m.* sergeant; — de ville policeman
sériculture *f.* silkworm raising
série *f.* series, succession, string, run; fin de — *f.* (com.) remainder, remnant
sérier *vt.* to arrange in series
sérieux *d.* serious, grave; genuine; — *m.* seriousness
sérigraphie *f.* (print.) silk screen process
serin *m.* canary
seringue *f.* syringe
seringuer *vt.* to syringe; squirt
serment *m.* oath; faux — perjury; prêter — to take an oath
sermonner *vi. & vt.* to sermonize, lecture
serpe *f.* billhook, pruning hook; rough work
serpente *f.* tissue paper
serpenter *vi.* to wind, meander, twist
serpentin *a.* serpentine; — *m.* coil
serpette *f.* billhook, pruning hook
serpillière *f.* sacking; apron
serpolet *m.* thyme
serrage *m.* tightening, clamping
serre *f.* grip; bird claw; squeezing; forceps; greenhouse; — chaude hothouse
serré *a.* tight, compact, dense, close
serre-frein *m.* brakeman
serre-livres *m.* book ends
serrement *m.* squeezing, gripping; — de cœur pang; — de main handshake
serre-papiers *m.* paper clip; paperweight; file, folder
serrer *vt.* to squeeze, tighten, clasp, grip; lock up; keep close to, hug; — la main (à) to shake hands (with); — les freins to put on the brakes; se — tighten; press, mill, be close together
serre-tête *m.* headband; kerchief; crash helmet
serrure *f.* lock
serrurerie *f.* locksmith's establishment; works, workings of a lock; iron work
serrurier *m.* locksmith; ironworker
sertir *vt.* to set; mount (jewel)
sertissure *f.* bezel; setting
sérum *m.* serum
servage *m.* bondage, slavery, serfdom
servant *m.* server (sports)
servante *f.* servant, serving woman; serving tray
serveur *m.* server; bartender; card dealer
serveuse *f.* server, waitress
serviabilité *f.* obligingness, usefulness
serviable *a.* obliging
service *m.* service; military service; chef de — *m.* department head; — compris service charge included; être de — be on duty

serviette *f.* napkin; towel; briefcase
servilité *f.* servility
servir *vi.* to serve, be useful; — de to serve as; — *vt.* serve, wait on; se — de to use, make use of
serviteur *m.* servant
servo-frein *m.* power brakes
ses *a. pl.* his, her, its
sésame *m.* sesame
session *f.* session, sitting; term
set *m.* tennis, movies; set of games (tennis); (theat.) scenery
sétacé *a.* bristly
séton *m.*, blessure en — *f.* flesh wound
seuil *m.* sill, threshold
seul *a.* sole, single; only; alone
seulement *adv.* only; even; merely
sève *f.* sap, juice; vitality
sévère *a.* severe, hard, harsh; strict
sévérité *f.* severity
sévices *m. pl.* maltreatment (law)
sévir *vi.* to be severe; rage
sevrer *vt.* to wean
sexe *m.* sex
sextuor *m.* (mus.) sextet
sexualité *f.* sexuality
sexuel *a.* sexual
seyant *a.* becoming, suitable
shake-hand *m.* handshake
shaker *m.* cocktail shaker
shampooing *m.* shampoo; liquid shampoo
shantung *m.* shantung
short *m.* movie short subject; clothing shorts
shunter *vt.* (elec.) to shunt
si *conj.* if; whether; suppose, how about, what if; — *adv.* so; yes; — . . . que however, no matter how
siamois *a. & m.* Siamese
Sibérie *f.* Siberia
sibilant *a.* sibilant
sicaire *m.* hired cutthroat
siccatif *a.* siccative, drying; — *m.* siccative, dryer
siccité *f.* dryness
Sicile *f.* Sicily
Sicilien *m. & a.* Sicilian
sidéral *a.* sidereal
sidération *f.* apoplectic stroke; sideration
sidéré *a.* struck, killed by lightning or apoplexy; thunderstruck
siècle *m.* century; age, time, period
siège *m.* seat; chair; (eccl.) see; center, focus; — social (com.) central office
siéger *vi.* to sit, be seated; (com.) have a central office
sien *pron.*, le —, la —ne his, hers, its; les —s *m. pl.* one's family, one's close friends
Sienne Sienna; terre de — *f.* burnt Sienna
sieste *f.* siesta, nap
sifflant *a.* whistling, hissing, sibilant
sifflante *f.* sibilant, consonant
sifflement *m.* whistling, hissing; sizzling; wheezing
siffler *vi.* to whistle, hiss; sizzle; wheeze; — *vt.* to whistle; hiss, hoot
sifflet *m.* whistle; hiss, hoot
siffleur *a.* whistling, hissing; — *m.* whist-

ler, hisser

siffloter *vi.* to whistle quietly, whistle to oneself

signalé *a.* conspicuous; notorious; signal; well-known

signalement *m.* description

signaler *vt.* to signal; signalize, point out, report; **se —** distinguish oneself

signaleur *m.* signalman

signalisateur *m.* traffic signal; burglar alarm

signataire *m. & f.* signer, subscriber

signe *m.* sign, mark, symbol, indication; omen; gesture; **faire — à** to signal to; motion to; **— de tête** nod; **— des yeux** wink

signer *vt.* to sign; mark; **se —** cross oneself

signet *m.* bookmark

significatif *a.* significant, meaningful

signification *f.* signification; meaning, sense; service of a legal writ

signifier *vt.* to signify, mean; declare, notify; serve a legal writ

silence *m.* silence; secrecy; (mus.) rest

silencieux *a.* silent, still, taciturn; **— *m.*** auto muffler

silex *m.* flint, silex

silhouette *f.* silhouette, outline

silhouetter *vt.* to silhouette, outline; **se —** be silhouetted, stand out

silicate *m.* silicate

silice *f.* silica

silicium *m.* silicon

sillage *m.* (naut.) wake, wash; headway, speed; (avi.) slipstream

sillon *m.* furrow, wrinkle, groove; wake, path

sillonner *vt.* to furrow, wrinkle; streak

simagrée *f.* affectation; **faire des —s** to make faces, fuss

simiesque *a.* simian, monkey-like

similaire *a.* similar, like

similarité *f.* similarity, likeness

similateur *m. & f.* pretender, malingerer

simili *m.* imitation

similicuir *m.* imitation leather

similigravure *f.* half-tone

similitude *f.* similitude; similarity, likeness; simile

similor *m.* imitation gold

simoun *m.* desert storm, sandstorm

simple *a.* simple; single; plain, ordinary; simple-minded; **corps — *m.*** (chem.) element

simplet *a.* ingenuous

simplicité *f.* simplicity; simpleness; ingenuousness

simplificateur *a.* simplifying; **— *m.*** simplifier

simplification *f.* simplification, simplifying

simpliste *a.* oversimple, simplistic

simulacre *m.* semblance, show; image

simulateur *m.* simulator, pretender; faker

simulation *f.* simulation, pretense

simulé *a.* simulated, pretended, feigned

simuler *vt.* to simulate, pretend, feign

simultané *a.* simultaneous

sinapisme *m.* mustard plaster

sincère *a.* sincere, genuine; frank

sincérité *f.* sincerity, genuineness; frankness

sinécure *f.* sinecure

singe *m.* monkey, ape; imitator

singer *vt.* to ape, imitate, mimic

singerie *f.* aping, imitation; monkey-like behavior; mimicry

singeur *a.* aping, imitating; **— *m.*** aper, imitator

singulariser *vt.* to singularize, make distinguished, make conspicuous; **se —** stand out, be conspicuous

singularité *f.* singularity; oddness, peculiarity

singulier *a.* singular; peculiar; odd; conspicuous

sinistre *a.* sinister, threatening; dismal; fatal; **— *m.*** disaster, catastrophe

sinistré *m.* victim of a disaster

sinon *conj.* if not, otherwise; except; **— que** except that

sinueux *a.* sinuous, winding

sinuosité *f.* sinuosity; bending, winding

sinus *m.* sinus; sine

sinusite *f.* sinus infection, sinusitis

siphonner *vt.* to siphon

sire *m.* lord, sire

sirène *f.* siren, mermaid; horn

siroc *m.* sirocco

sirop *m.* syrup

siroter *vt. & vi.* to sip

sirupeux *a.* syrupy

sisal *m.* sisal (hemp)

sismique *a.* seismic

sismographe *m.* seismograph

site *m.* site, location

sitôt *adv.* immediately; **de — soon; — que** *conj.* as soon as

situation *f.* situation; position, location; condition; circumstances

situé *a.* situated, located

situer *vt.* to situate, locate

six *a.* six

sixième *a.* sixth

sketch *m.* short theatrical sketch

ski *m.* ski, skiing; **faire du — to** ski

skier *vi.* to ski

skieur *m.* skier

Slave *m.* Slav; **— *a.*** Slavic, Slavonic

sleeping *m.* Pullman sleeper

slip *m.* shorts, briefs; **— (de bain)** bathing trunks, bathing suit

Slovaque *m. & f.* Slovak; **— *a.*** Slovakian

slovène *a. & m. & f.* Slovenian

smoking *m.* dinner jacket

snow-boot *m.* overshoe

sobre *a.* temperate; restrained, sober

sobriété *f.* sobriety, temperance, moderation, restraint

sobriquet *m.* nickname

soc *m.* plowshare

sociabilité *f.* sociability

sociable *a.* sociable, companiable

socialiser *vt.* to socialize

socialisme *m.* socialism

socialiste *m. & f.* socialist; **— *a.*** socialistic

sociétaire *m. & f.* member; stockholder

société f. society; company; association, club; partnership; — anonyme corporation

sociologie f. sociology

sociologique a. sociological

sociologue m. sociologist

socle m. base, pedestal; stand

socque m. clog; (fig.) (theat.) sock; comedy

socquettes f. pl. bobby socks, anklets

socratique a. socratic

soda m. soda water

sodium m. sodium

sœur f. sister; nun

soi pron. himself, herself, oneself, itself

soi-disant a. so-called, supposed, self-styled; — adv. supposedly

soie f. silk; papier de — m. tissue paper

soierie f. silk goods; silk factory

soif f. thirst; avoir — to be thirsty

soigné a. carefully done; well cared for; neat, well-groomed

soigner vi. to look after, take care of; attend, nurse

soigneux a. careful; neat, tidy

soi-même pron. oneself

soin m. care; attention; avec — carefully; premiers -s pl. first aid; aux bons -s de in care of

soir m. evening, late afternoon; hier — last night

soirée f. evening; evening out; evening performance; party

soit interj. all right, so be it; — conj., — (que) . . . — (que) either . . . or; tant — peu adv. very little

soixantaine f. about sixty

soixante a. sixty

soixante-dix a. seventy

soixantième a. sixtieth

soja m. soy bean

sol m. soil, ground, earth; (mus.) key of G; 5th note of a scale

solaire a. solar; cadran — m. sundial

soldat m. soldier

solde m. (com.) balance; surplus; (en) — at reduced prices; vente de -s f. clearance sale

solder vt. (com.) to settle, balance; sell, put on sale; (mil.) pay

sole f. sole; animal hoof

soleil m. sun; sunshine; coucher du — m. sunset; coup de — m. sunstroke; il fait du — it's sunny; lever du — m. sunrise; (coll.) piquer un — blush; prendre du — to sun oneself

solennel a. solemn; ceremonial, formal, official

solenniser vt. to solemnize; mark, celebrate

solennité f. solemnity; formality, ceremony

solidage f. goldenrod

solidaire a. responsible; integral; interlocked

solidariser vt. to make responsible; cause to interlock; se — join together in a common responsibility or cause

solidarité f. solidarity; joint responsibility

solide a. solid; strong; sound; reliable; — m. solid

solidification f. solidification, solidifying

solidifier vt. to solidify

solidité f. solidity; strength; soundness; reliability

soliloque m. soliloquy

soliloquer vi. to soliloquize

soliste m. & f. soloist

solitaire a. solitary, lonely; — m. solitaire; hermit

solitude f. solitude, loneliness

solive f. beam, joist, rafter, girder

soliveau m. small beam or joist

sollicitation f. solicitation, plea, request; pull of a magnet

solliciter vt. to solicit, canvass; request, beg, pull, attract

solliciteur m. canvasser; petitioner

sollicitude f. solicitude, concern, care

solubilité f. solubility; solvability

solution f. solution; solving; (med.) termination

solutionner vt. to solve

solvabilité f. solvency

solvable a. solvent

Somalie f. Somaliland

sombre a. dark, gloomy, somber; melancholy; overcast, cloudy; faire — to be dark

sombrer vi. to sink, go down

sommaire a. & m. summary

sommation f. legal summons, legal notice

somme m. sleep, nap; — f. sum, amount; en — in short; — toute all in all, on the whole; bête de — pack animal, beast of burden

sommeil m. sleep; avoir — to be sleepy

sommeiller vi. to slumber, doze, be dormant, lie dormant

sommer vt. to summon; sum up

sommet m. summit, top

sommier m. pack animal; transom; balance beam; mattress; register, file (law) — élastique spring mattress

sommité f. summit

somnambule m. somnambulist, sleepwalker

somnifère a. & m. soporific

somnolence f. somnolence, sleepiness

somnolent a. somnolent, sleepy

somnoler vi. to doze, drowse

somnose f. sleeping sickness; hypnotic sleep

somptuaire a. sumptuary

somptueux a. sumptuous

somptuosité f. sumptuousness

son m. sound; bran

son (sa) a. his, her, its

sonar m. sonar

sonate f. sonata

sondage m. (naut.) sounding; (med.) probing

sonde f. (naut.) lead; (med.) probe; (mining) boring apparatus

sonder vt. to probe; (naut.) sound; examine, explore

sondeur m. (naut.) sounder; prober; borer, driller

sondeuse f. drilling apparatus

songe m. dream

songe-creux *m.* dreamer, visionary

songer *vi.* to dream; think; imagine

songerie *f.* daydreaming

songeur *a.* dreamy, musing, pensive; — *m.* dreamer

sonique *a.* sonic; vitesse — *f.* speed of sound

sonnaille *f.* cow bell

sonnailler *m.* bellwether; — *vi.* to toll; ring incessantly

sonnant *a.* ringing, striking; hard (money); à . . . . heures —es at the stroke of . . .

sonné *a.* past; completed

sonner *vi. & vt.* to sound; ring; strike

sonnerie *f.* ringing; chimes; bell clapper

sonnette *f.* little bell; doorbell; coup de — *m.* ring, ringing; serpent à —s *m.* rattlesnake

sonneur *m.* sounder, ringer; bell-ringer; bugler

sonore *a.* sonorous, resonant; ringing; loud; voiced; film — *m.* sound film; onde — *f.* sound wave

sonoriser *vt.* to make resonant; add sound to

sonorité *f.* sonority, resonance

sophisterie *f.* sophistry

sophistication *f.* alteration, adulteration

sophistique *a.* sophistic; — *f.* sophistry

sophistiquer *vi.* to quibble; — *vt.* adulterate

soporatif *a. & m.* soporific

soporifique *a.* soporific, causing sleep

sopraniste *m.* male soprano, castrato

soprano *m. & f.* soprano

sorbet *m.* sherbet

sorbetière *f.* ice cream freezer

Sorbonne *f.* University of Paris

sorcellerie *f.* sorcery, witchcraft

sorcier *m.* sorcerer

sorcière *f.* sorceress, witch

sordide *a.* sordid; grubby; mean

sordidité *f.* sordidness

sornettes *f. pl.* foolishness, nonsense

sort *m.* fate, destiny, lot; spell, charm; coup du — *m.* stroke of fate; tirage au — *m.* drawing of a lottery; tirer au — to draw lots

sortable *a.* suitable

sortant *a.* outgoing, coming out, going out; numéro — *m.* winning number

sorte *f.* sort, kind; way, manner; de la — thus, in this manner; de — que so that; en quelque — in a certain way

sortie *f.* going out; exit; excursion; (com.) exporting; (mil.) sortie

sortilège *m.* spell, charm

sortir *vi.* to go out, come out, be out; leave; come from, issue; stand out; — *vt.* take out, bring out; pull out; put out; — *m.* coming out, going out, emerging

sosie *m.* double, image, twin

sot (sotte) *a.* stupid; silly, foolish; — *n.* fool

sottise *f.* foolishness, silliness; stupidity

sou *m.* sou, five-centime coin; cent, penny; cent —s five francs

soubresaut *m.* start, jolt; leap; gasp; -s

pl. trembling

soubresauter *vi.* to jolt, start, leap

soubrette *f.* maid, chambermaid

souche *f.* stump; stub; shaft of a chimney; lineage, ancestry; founder of a family; faire — to found a family

souci *m.* care, anxiety, worry; marigold; sans — carefree

soucier *vt.* to trouble; se — (de) to concern oneself (about), care (for)

soucieux *a.* uneasy, concerned, anxious, worried

soucoupe *f.* saucer

soudain *a.* sudden; — *adv.* suddenly

Soudan *m.* Sudan

Soudanais *m. & a.* Sudanese

soude *f.* soda; bicarbonate de — *m.* bicarbonate of soda, baking soda

souder *vt.* to solder; weld; lampe à — *f.* blowtorch; se — to be welded; fuse, join; mend, knit (bone)

soudoir *m.* soldering iron

soudoyer *vt.* to hire (for criminal purposes); bribe

soudure *f.* solder; soldering; welding

soue *f.* pigsty

soufflage *m.* blowing, blasting (of a furnace); glassblowing

souffle *m.* breath; breathing; blast, puff; à bout de — out of breath

soufflé *a.* puffed, puffy; unvoiced vowel; — *m.* soufflé

souffler *vi.* to blow; puff, pant, be short of breath; — *vt.* to blow, blow up, blow out; breathe; (theat.) prompt

soufflerie *f.* blower, bellows

soufflet *m.* bellows, blower; slap, box on ears; insult

souffleter *vt.* to slap; insult

souffleur *m.* blower; (theat.) prompter

souffliure *f.* air or gas blister, bubble

souffrance *f.* suffering, pain; abeyance

souffrant *a.* suffering, in pain; ailing, ill

souffre-douleur *m. & f.* butt, scapegoat

souffreteux *a.* suffering, poor, destitute; sickly

souffrir *vt.* to suffer, tolerate, endure, bear; allow; — *vi.* suffer, be in pain

soufre *m.* sulfur

souhait *m.* wish, desire; à — according to one's wish

souhaitable *a.* desirable

souhaiter *vt.* to wish, desire

souillarde *f.* laundry room

souiller *vt.* to dirty, stain; sully, taint

souillure *f.* stain, spot; blot, taint

soûl *a.* drunk; full, gorged, sated

soulagement *m.* relief, comfort, comforting

soulager *vt.* to ease, relieve, alleviate

soûler *vt.* to fill, gorge, stuff; make drunk; se — to get drunk; overeat, stuff oneself

soulèvement *m.* rising; uprising; — de cœur nausea

soulever *vt.* to lift, raise; stir up, arouse, excite; se — rise, swell; heave; revolt, rise up

soulier *m.* shoe, slipper

souligner *vt.* to underline, emphasize

soulte f. balance, balance due; settlement; difference between declared and actual value

soumettre vt. to submit; subdue

soumis a. submissive, compliant

soumission f. submission, obedience, compliance; tender, contract

soumissionner vt. to contract for, tender

soupape f. valve; plug; — de sûreté safety valve

soupçon m. suspicion; bit, tiny amount

soupçonner vt. to suspect; question

soupçonneux a. suspicious; suspecting

soupe f. soup; meal, mess

soupente f. attic, attic ceiling

souper m. supper; — vi. to eat supper

soupeser vt. to weigh, judge, heft

soupière f. soup tureen

soupir m. sigh; (mus.) quarter rest; dernier — last breath

soupirail m. vent; cellar window

soupirant m. suitor

soupirer vi. to sigh; — après to long for

souple a. supple

souplesse f. suppleness, flexibility

souquenille f. long smock

souquer vi. to strive, strain

source f. source, spring, fountain

sourcier m. dowser, user of a divining rod

sourcil m. eyebrow

sourciller vi. to knit the brow; frown

sourcilleux a. haughty, severe

sourd a. deaf; dull; dark; hollow; — m. deaf person

sourdine f. (mus.) mute; à la —, en — muted, soft; slyly

sourd-muet a. deaf and dumb; — m. deaf and dumb person

sourdre vi. to spring, well up, gush out (water)

souricier m. mouser, mouse catcher

souricière f. mousetrap; stake-out, police ambush; trap

sourire vi. to smile; be favorable

sourire, souris m. smile

souris f. mouse

sournois a. sly, cunning

sournoiserie f. cunning, slyness

sous prep. under, beneath, below; (in compound words) assistant, sub; — peu adv. shortly, soon, in a little while

sous-alimentation f. insufficient food supply

sous-bois m. underbrush

sous-chef m. assistant manager, second-in-command

souscripteur m. subscriber

souscription f. subscription; signature

souscrire vt. & vi. to subscribe

sous-cutané a. subcutaneous, under the skin

sous-développé a. underdeveloped

sous-diacre m. subdeacon

sous-directeur m. or f. assistant manager, assistant director

sous-entendre vt. to understand, leave unexpressed

sous-estimer vt. to undervalue

sous-évaluer vt. to undervalue

sous-garde m. trigger guard

sous-lieutenant m. second lieutenant

sous-locataire m. & f. subletter, subtenant

sous-location f. subletting, sublease

sous-louer vt. to sublet

sous-main m. desk blotter; en — adv. secretly

sous-marin a. & m. submarine

sous-marinier m. submarine crewman

sous-mentonnière f. chin strap

sous-nappe m. table pad

sous-officier m. noncommissioned officer

sous-préfecture f. subprefecture, second administrative capital of a department

sous-produit m. by-product

sous-secrétaire m. undersecretary, assistant secretary

sous-secrétariat m. work of a undersecretary

soussigné a. undersigned

sous-sol m. subsoil; basement

sous-titre m. subtitle

soustraction f. subtraction; abstraction

soustraire vt. to subtract, deduct; remove, protect

sous-ventrière f. cinch, strap

sous-verre m. bound slide, bound picture, picture covered with glass but unframed

sous-vêtements m. pl. underclothing

soutacher vt. to trim with braid

soutane f. cassock

soute f. magazine of a ship

soutenable a. supportable

soutenance f. oral exam covering a thesis, defense

soutènement m. retaining, support

souteneur m. upholder; white-slaver, procurer

soutenir vt. to support; bear

soutenu a. elevated, lofty; sustained

souterrain a. underground; — m. tunnel; underground passage, cave

soutien m. support

soutien-gorge m. brassière

soutirer vt. to draw off, obtain by deception

souvenance f. memory; remembrance

souvenir m. remembrance, memory; — v., se — (de) to remember

souvent adv. often

souverain m. & a. sovereign

souveraineté f. sovereignty

soviétique a. Soviet

soya m. soybean

soyeux a. silky

spacieux a. spacious

spahi m. North African trooper

sparadrap m. adhesive plaster, adhesive tape

Sparte f. Sparta

Spartiate m. & f. & a. Spartan

spasme m. spasm

spasmodique a. spasmodic

spatule f. spatula; spoonbill

speaker m. radio announcer

speakerine f. woman radio announcer

spécial a. special

spécialisation f. specialization

spécialiser vt. to specialize

spécialiste m. & f. specialist; — a. specialized, specializing
spécialité f. speciality
spécieux a. specious
spécification f. specification
spécifier vt. to specify
spécifique m. medication, remedy; — a. specific
spécimen m. specimen; sample
spectacle m. spectacle, show
spectaculaire a. spectacular
spectateur m. spectator
spectral a. spectral
spectre m. apparition, ghost; spectrum
spectroscope m. spectroscope
spéculateur m. speculator
spéculatif a. speculative
spéculation f. speculation
spéculer vi. to speculate
spéléologie f. cave exploration
sphère f. sphere
sphéricité f. sphericity, roundness
sphérique a. spherical
sphéroïde m. spheroid
spider m. (auto.) rumble seat
sphincter m. sphincter
sphinx m. sphinx
spinelle m. spinel
spiral a. spiral; — m. watch hairspring
spirale f. spiral
spire f. spiral line, helix
spirée f. spiraea
spirite m. & f. & a. spiritualist
spiritisme m. spiritualism
spiritualiser vt. to spiritualize
spiritualisme m. spiritualism
spiritualiste m. & f. & a. spiritualist
spiritualité f. spirituality
spirituel a. witty; religious; spiritual
spiritueux a. alcoholic, spiritous
spleen m. boredom, bitter melancholy
splendeur f. splendor
splendide a. splendid
spoliateur m. despoiler; — a. despoiling
spolier vt. to despoil
spongieux a. spongy
spontané a. spontaneous
spontanéité f. spontaneity
sporadique a. sporadic
sportif a. sportive, sporting; — m. sportsman
sportivité f. sportsmanship; loyalty
spot m. spotlight
spoutnik m. sputnik, satellite
sprinter vi. to sprint
spumeux a. foamy, frothy
squale m. shark
squame f. skin scale
squameux a. scaley
square m. small public square
squelette m. skeleton
stabilisateur m. stabilizer; — a. stabilizing
stabaliser vt. to stabilize
stabilité f. stability
stable a. stable
staccato adv. staccato
stade m. stadium
stage m. preparatory period, development stage; probationary period

stagiaire a. preparatory, probationary; — m. & f. probationer; apprentice
stagnant a. stagnant
stagnation f. stagnation
stagner vi. to stagnate
stalactite f. stalactite
stalagmite f. stalagmite
stalle f. choir stall; stall
stance f. stanza
stand m. display, stand; grandstand
standard m. standard; switchboard
standardisation f. standardization
standardiser vt. to standardize
standardiste m. & f. switchboard operator
standing m. standard of living; level of luxury
stase f. blood stagnation
station f. stop; station; resort; position
stationnaire a. stationary
stationnement m. parking; — interdit no parking
stationner vt. & vi. to park; stand
station-service f. service station
statique f. statics; — a. static
statisticien m. statistician
statistique f. statistics; — a. statistical
statuaire m. statuary (person); — f. statuary (art)
statuer vt. to decree; enact
statuette f. statuette
statu quo m. status quo
stature f. stature, height
statut m. statute, ordinance
statutaire a. statutory
stéatite f. soapstone
steeple m. steeplechase
stèle f. stele, monument, stone
stellaire a. stellar
sténo m. & f. stenographer; — dactylo stenographer-typist
sténographe m. & f. stenographer
sténographie f. stenography
sténographier vt. to take down in shorthand
sténographique a. stenographic
sténopé m. pinhole camera
sténotype f. stenotype machine
sténotypie f. stenotypy
stentor m. stentor; voix de — stentorian voice
stère m. cubic meter
stéreographique a. stereographic
stéréophonie f. stereophonic sound, stereophonic music
stéréophonique a. stereophonic
stéréoscope m. stereoscope; stereo camera
stéréoscopique a. stereoscopic
stéréotype a. stereotyped
stéréotyper vt. to stereotype
stéréotypie f. stereotyping
stérile a. sterile, barren
stérilisateur m. sterilizer
stérilisation f. sterilization
stériliser vt. to sterilize
stérilité f. sterility
sternum m. breastbone, sternum
stéthoscope m. stethoscope
stick m. hockey stick; walking stick
stigmate m. scar; stigma; stigmata
stigmatiser vt. to stigmatize, brand

stilligoutte *f.* medicine dropper
stimulant *a.* stimulating; — *m.* stimulant
stimulation *f.* stimulation
stimuler *vt.* to stimulate
stipendiaire *a.* hired
stipendier *vt.* to hire
stipulation *f.* stipulation
stipuler *vt.* to stipulate
stockage *m.* stocking up
stocker *vt.* to stock up, stockpile
stoïcien *a.* stoical
stoïcisme *m.* stoicism
stoïque *a.* stoic
stoppage *m.* repair
stopper *vi.* & *vt.* to stop; repair a stocking
store *m.* blind, shutter, venetian blind, curtain; windowshade, awning, metal curtain
strabisme *m.* crossed eyes
strangulation *f.* strangulation
strapontin *m.* folding seat
strass *m.* paste jewels
stratagème *m.* stratagem
stratège *m.* strategist
stratégie *f.* strategy
stratégique *a.* strategic
stratification *f.* stratification
stratifier *vt.* to stratify
stratosphère *f.* stratosphere
stratosphérique *a.* stratospheric
stratus *m.* stratus cloud
streptococcie *f.* streptococcus infection
streptocoque *m.* streptococcus
streptomycine *f.* streptomycin
strette *f.* (mus.) stretta, fugue passage
strict *a.* strict, severe; exact
strident *a.* shrill, strident, harsh
strié *a.* streaked, striate(d)
strier *vt.* to streak
strige *f.* vampire
strontium *m.* strontium
strophe *f.* stanza
structure *f.* structure
strychnine *f.* strychnine
stuc *m.* stucco
studieux *a.* studious
studio *m.* studio; studio apartment; one-room apartment
stupéfaction *f.* stupefaction
stupéfait *a.* stupefied, nonplussed
stupéfiant *a.* stupefying; — *m.* stupefactive
stupéfier *vt.* to stupify
stupeur *f.* stupor
stupide *a.* stupid; stupefied
stupidité *f.* stupidity
stuquer *vt.* to cover with stucco
stygien *a.* Stygian
style *m.* stylus; style
styler *vt.* to style
stylet *m.* stiletto
styliser *vt.* to stylize
styliste *m.* & *f.* stylist
stylo(graphe) *m.* fountain pen
suaire *m.* shroud
suave *a.* smooth, suave
suavité *f.* suavity, sweetness
subalterne *a.* & *m.* & *f.* subaltern
subconscience *f.* subconscious
subdiviser *vt.* to subdivide

subdivision *f.* subdivision, secondary division
subéreux *a.* corky
subir *vt.* to undergo, submit to
subit *a.* sudden
subjectif *a.* subjective
subjectivité *f.* subjectivity
subjonctif *m.* (gram.) subjunctive mood
subjuguer *vt.* to subjugate
sublimation *f.* sublimation
sublime *a.* sublime
sublimé *m.* sublimate
sublimer *vt.* to sublimate
subliminal *a.* subliminal
sublimité *f.* sublimity
submerger *vt.* to submerge
submersible *a.* submersible
submersion *f.* submersion
subodorer *vt.* to smell from afar
subordination *f.* subordination
subordonné *a.* & *m.* subordinate
subordonner *vt.* to subordinate
suborner *vt.* to suborn, bribe, tamper with
subreptice *a.* surreptitious, furtive
subrogé *a.* replacement, substitute
subroger *vt.* to replace
subséquent *a.* subsequent
subside *m.* subsidy
subsidiaire *a.* subsidiary
subsistance *f.* subsistence
subsister *vi.* to subsist, last
substantiel *a.* substantial
substantif *m.* noun
substantivement *adv.* as a noun
substituer *vt.* to substitute
substitut *m.* substitute
substrat(um) *m.* substratum
subterfuge *m.* subterfuge
subtil *a.* subtle, thin, sharp
subtiliser *vt.* to refine, make subtle; — *vi.* to be subtle
subtilité *f.* subtlety
subtropical *a.* subtropical
suburbain *a.* suburban
subvenir *vi.* to relieve, assist
subvention *f.* subsidy
subventionner *vt.* to subsidize
subversif *a.* subversive
subversion *f.* subversion
subvertir *vt.* to subvert, overthrow
suc *m.* juice, sap; cellular liquid
succéder *vi.* to follow
succès *m.* success, issue
successeur *m.* successor
successif *a.* successive
succession *f.* inheritance; estate; succession
succinct *a.* succinct
succion *f.* sucking
succomber *vi.* to succumb
succulence *f.* succulence
succulent *a.* succulent, juicy
succursale *f.* branch-office; regional office
sucer *vt.* to suck
sucette *f.* lollipop, sucker; child's pacifier
suçoir *m.* sucker
sucre *m.* sugar
sucré *a.* sugared; sweet
sucrer *vt.* to sugar, sweeten
sucrerie *f.* sugar factory; -s *pl.* candy

sucrier *m.* sugar bowl; sugar manufacturer; — *a.* sugary

sud *m.* south; — -est *m.* southeast; — -ouest *m.* southwest

Sud-Africain *m. & a.* South African

Sud-Américain *m. & a.* South American

sudiste *m.* southerner

Suède *f.* Sweden; — *m.* suede

Suédois *m. & a.* Swedish

suée *f.* sweating

suer *vt. & vi.* to perspire, sweat

sueur *f.* sweat, perspiration

suffire *vi.* to suffice, be sufficient

suffisamment *adv.* sufficiently

suffisance *f.* sufficiency

suffisant *a.* sufficient, conceited

suffixe *f.* suffix

suffocant *a.* suffocating

suffocation *f.* suffocation

suffoquer *vt. & vi.* to suffocate

suffrage *m.* suffrage, vote

suffragette *f.* suffragette

suggérer *vt.* to suggest

suggestif *a.* suggestive

suggestion *f.* suggestion

suicide *m.* act of suicide

suicidé *m.* person who commits suicide

suicider *v.*, **se** — to commit suicide

suie *f.* soot

suif *m.* tallow, suet

suint *m.* grease, lanolin

suintement *m.* oozing

suinter *vi.* to leak, ooze; trickle

Suisse *f.* Switzerland; — *m. & a.* Swiss; — *m.* beadle; porter; Swiss guard; petit — cream cheese

Suissesse *f.* Swiss woman

suite *f.* consequence; series; set; continuation; train, attendants; à la — de after, behind; de — without stopping; par — de as a result of; tout de — immediately

suivant *m.* follower; -e *f.* servant; — *a.* following, subsequent, next; — *prep.* according to

suivi *a.* connected, coherent; popular

suivre *vt. & vi.* to follow

sujet *m.* subject; reason; au — de about; — *a.* subject, exposed; — à apt to

sujétion *f.* subjection

sulfate *m.* sulfate

sulfure *m.* sulfide

sulfurer *vt.* to combine with sulfur

sulfureux *a.* sulfurous

sulfurique *a.* sulfuric

sultanat *m.* sultanate

sultane *f.* sultana

sunnite *m. & f.* orthodox Moslem

superbe *a.* superb; proud, haughty

supercarburant *m.* high-octane gas, ethyl

supercherie *f.* fraud, deceit

superfétation *f.* redundancy

superficie *f.* superficies, surface, area

superficiel *a.* superficial; shallow

superfin *a.* superfine

superflu *a.* superfluous

superfluité *f.* superfluity

supérieur *a.* superior, upper, higher; — *m.* superior

supériorité *f.* superiority

superlatif *a.* superlative

superposer *vt.* to place on top of one another

supersonique *a.* supersonic

superstitieux *a.* superstitious

superstition *f.* superstition

superstructure *f.* superstructure

superviser *vt.* to supervise

supin *a.* supine

supination *f.* supine position

supplanter *vt.* to supplant

suppléant *m.* substitute, assistant

suppléer *vt. & vi.* to supply, make up; substitute for; — à to remedy

supplément *m.* supplement, addition, supplemental charge; second helping

supplémentaire *a.* supplementary, additional

supplication *f.* supplication

supplice *m.* torture; punishment; death penalty

supplicier *vt.* to execute; torture; cause to suffer

supplier *vt.* to implore

supplique *f.* petition

support *m.* prop; assistance

supportable *a.* bearable

supporter *vt.* to bear, tolerate, support

supposé *a.* supposed, pretended; — que *conj.* supposing that

supposer *vt.* to suppose

supposition *f.* supposition

suppositoire *m.* suppository

suppôt *m.* supporter, upholder, partisan

suppression *f.* suppression, elimination, cancellation

supprimer *vt.* to suppress, cancel, eliminate; conceal

suppuration *f.* festering, suppuration

suppurer *vi.* to form pus

supputation *f.* calculation, evaluation

supputer *vt.* to calculate, evaluate

suprématie *f.* supremacy

suprême *a.* supreme; crowning; — *m.* chicken in cream sauce

sur *prep.* on, upon, over, in, by, near, about, towards

sur *a.* sharp tasting

sur- *prefix* super-, over-

sûr *a.* sure, certain

surabondance *f.* superabundance

surabondant *a.* superabundant

surabonder *vi.* to be superabundant

suractivité *f.* hyperactivity

surajouter *vt.* to add on

suralimenter *vt.* to overfeed, oversupply

suranné *a.* superannuated, old, obsolete

surcharge *f.* surcharge; excess load, overload; word written over another word

surcharger *vt.* to overload; surcharge; supercharge; write over another word

surchauffer *vt.* to overheat

surchoix *m.* first choice, first quality

surclasser *vt.* to outclass

surcontrer *vt.* to redouble (at bridge)

surcroît *m.* addition, increase, surplus; de — extra

surdi-mutité *f.* deafness and dumbness

surdité *f.* deafness

sureau *m.* elder tree

surélever *vt.* to raise, raise excessively

surenchère f. higher bid
surenchérir vt. to outbid
surestimer vt. to overvalue
suret a. sharp, somewhat sour
sûreté f. surety, security, safety
Sûreté f. security police
surévaluer vt. to overvalue
surexcitable a. overexcitable
surexcitation f. overexcitement
surexciter vt. to overexcite
surexposer vt. (phot.) overexpose
surexposition f. (phot.) overexposure
surface f. surface
surfaire vt. to overvalue, overcharge; overpraise
surfiler vt. to weave in and out
surfin a. superfine
surgeon m. offshoot
surgir vt. to arise, rise up; reach port
surhausser vt. to elevate; exaggerate
surhomme m. superman
surhumain a. superhuman
surimposer vt. to superimpose
surimposition f. superimposing; (phot.) double exposure
surintendance f. superintendence
surintendant m. superintendent; -e f. superintendent; morale officer
surir vi. to sour, become acid
surjeter vt. to overcast
sur-le-champ adv. immediately, instantly
surlendemain m. the second day after
surmenage m. overwork, overactivity
surmener vt. to overwork
sur-moi m. superego
surmonter vt. to surmount; overcome
surmulet m. red mullet
surnager vi. to float on the surface; survive, remain
surnaturel a. supernatural
surnom m. surname
surnombre m. excess
surnommer vt. to name, give a surname to
surnuméraire a. & m. & f. supernumerary
suroit m. southwest wind; sou'wester hat; jacket
surpaye f. extra pay
surpayer vt. to pay dearly for, overpay
surpasser vt. to surpass; exceed
surpeuplé a. overpopulated
surpeuplement m. overpopulation
surplis m. surplice
surplomb m. overhang; en — overhanging
surplomber vt. to overhang
surplus m. surplus; au — moreover
surprendre vt. to surprise
surpris a. surprised
surprise f. surprise
surproduction f. overproduction
surréalisme m. surrealism
surréaliste m. & f. surrealist; — a. surrealistic
sursaturer vt. to supersaturate
sursaut m. start; jump; en — adv. suddenly
sursauter vi. to somersault; jump, start
surseoir vt. to suspend
sursis m. suspension, delay; avec — with sentence suspended

surtaxe f. surtax
surtaxer vt. to overtax
surtension f. hypertension
surtout adv. especially; — m. overcoat; silver or gold centerpiece
surveillant m. inspector, overseer
surveille f. second day previous
surveiller vt. & vi. to oversee, superintend, watch over
survenir vi. to come unexpectedly; happen unexpectedly
survenue f. unexpected arrival
survie f. survival; afterlife
survivance f. survival
survivre vi. to survive
survoler vt. to fly over
survolté a., lampe -e f. photoflood lamp
sus prep. upon; en — besides, in addition
susceptibilité f. susceptibility
susceptible a. susceptible, likely
susciter vt. to create, cause
susdit a. aforementioned
susmentionné a. aforementioned
susnommé a. aforenamed
suspect a. suspected, suspicious
suspecter vt. to suspect
suspendre vt. to suspend, hang; put off
suspendu a. suspended, hanging; pont — suspension bridge
suspens a. suspended; en — in suspense
suspension f. suspension; hanging; ceiling fixture; points de — m. pl. elipsis
suspensoir m. suspensory
suspicion f. suspicion
sustentateur m. sustainer; — a. sustaining
sustenter vt. to sustain
susurrement m. murmur, buzz
susurrer vt. to murmer, buzz
suturer vt. to suture
suzerain a. paramount; — m. suzerain
svastike m. swastika
svelte a. svelte, slender
sveltesse f. slenderness, slimness
S.V.P.: s'il vous plait please
sycophante m. sycophant, deceiver
syllabaire m. spelling book
syllabe f. syllable
syllabique a. syllabic
syllogisme m. syllogism
sylvestre a. sylvan
sylviculture f. forestry
symbiotique a. (biol.) symbiotic
symbolique a. symbolic(al)
symbolisme m. symbolism
symboliste a. & m. symbolist
symétrie f. symmetry
symétrique a. symmetrical
sympathie f. sympathy, feeling; liking
sympathique a. sympathetic; likeable
sympathiser vi. to sympathize
symphonie f. symphony
symphonique a. symphonic
symposion m. symposium
symptomatique a. symptomatic
symptôme m. symptom
synchrone a. synchronized
synchronisation f. synchronization
synchroniser vt. to synchronize
syncope f. faint; syncope; syncopation;

tomber en — to faint

syncoper vt. to syncopate

syndic m. syndic, chief, mayor; receiver of a business in receivership

syndical a. union, trade union

syndicalisme m. trade unionism

syndicaliste a. & m. & f. unionist

syndicat m. syndicate; trade union

syndiquer vt. to syndicate; unionize; se — to join a union

synecdoque f. synecdoche

synode m. synod

synonyme a. synonymous; — m. synonym

synonymie f. synonymy

synoptique a. synoptic

syntaxe f. syntax

syntaxique a. syntactical

synthèse f. synthesis

synthétique a. synthetic; synthesizing

synthétiser vt. to synthesize

syntonisation f. (rad.) tuning

syphilitique a. & m. & f. syphilitic

Syrie f. Syria

Syrien m. & a. Syrian

systématique a. systematic

systématiser vt. to systematize

système m. system

systole f. systole

T

ta a. f. your

tabac m. tobacco

tabagie f. smoke-filled room

tabatière f. snuffbox

tabellion m. notary

tabernacle m. tabernacle

table f. table; board; list; — de jeu card table; mettre la — to set the table; — des matières table of contents; — volante end.table

tableau m. picture, painting; blackboard; — de bord (auto.) dashboard; (elec.) switchboard

tablée f. group at table

tablette f. tablet, notebook; shelf; slab; bar; — de cheminée mantel

tablier m. apron; dashboard; bridge roadway

tabou m. & a. taboo

tabouret m. stool; footstool

tabulaire a. tabular

tabulateur m. tabulator, tab key

tache f. spot, stain; blemish

tâche f. task; job

tacher vt. to spot, stain

tâcher vi. to endeavor, try

tâcheron m. pieceworker; taskmaster

tacheté a. spotted, speckled

tacheter vt. to speckle

tachymètre m. tachometer, speedometer

tacite a. tacit

tact m. touch; tact

tacticien m. tactician

tactique a. tactical; — f. tactics

taffetas m. taffeta

taie f., — d'oreiller pillowcase

taillable a. subject to head tax

taillade f. slash

taillader vt. to slash

taillandier m. maker of cutting tools

taillant m. cutting edge

taille f. cut, cutting, trimming; height; size; waist; figure; head tax; cutting edge; tenor; new growth

taille-crayons m. pencil sharpener

taille-douce f. engraving

taille-ongles m. nail clippers

tailler vt. to cut, trim; sharpen

taillerie f. gem cutting

tailleur m. tailor; cutter; lady's suit

tailleuse f. dressmaker, cutter

taillis m. copse

tailloir m. platter, meat-chopping block; (arch.) abacus

tain m. tinfoil; silver on a mirror; glace sans — f. plate glass

taire vt. to conceal, say nothing about, hush up; se — to stop talking, be silent; keep silent

talaire a. ankle-length (dress)

talc m. talc; talcum powder

talé a. bruised (of fruit)

talent m. talent, capacity

talentueux a. talented

talion m. retaliation

talisman m. talisman

talon m. heel; tub; pile, deck (at cards); keel; foot

talonner vt. to tread on with the heel; to follow close upon; — vi. to go aground

talonnette f. heel reinforcement; heel lift

talonnières f. pl. talaria, Mercury's heel wings

talquer vt. to spread with talcum

talus m. slope; embankment; en — at an angle

tamarin m. tamarind

tamarinier m. tamarind tree

tamaris m. tamarisk

tambour m. drum; drummer; cylinder; section of a column; spool; eardrum; embroidery hoop; — de basque tambourine; — de frein brake drum; sans — ni trompette quietly

tambourin m. tambourine; bongo drum, long narrow drum

tambourinaire m. drummer

tambouriner vi. to drum

tambour-major m. drum major

tamis m. sieve

tamisage m. sifting

Tamise f. Thames

tamiser vt. & vi. to sift; filter; sieve

tampon m. bung, stopper; stamp pad; surgical sponge; (rail.) buffer

tamponnement m. collision; (rail.) bump

tamponner vt. to plug; collide with; (rail.) to bump

tam-tam m. tom-tom; gong

tan m. bark used to tan leather

tancer vt. to reprimand

tandem m. tandem carriage, tandem bicycle

tandis que conj. whereas, while

tangage m. pitch of a boat

tangent a. tangeant; -e f. tangent

Tanger Tangiers

tango m. tango; — a. yellow-orange
tanguer vi. (naut.) to pitch
tanière f. den, lair
tannage m. tanning; dressing
tanné a. tan, tanned
tanner vt. to tan (leather)
tannerie f. tannery
tanneur m. tanner
tan(n)in m. tannin
tannique a. tannic
tan-sad m. extra saddle of a motorcycle
tant adv. so much, so many; — soit peu somewhat; — pis so much the worse; — mieux so much the better; — s'en faut far from it; — que as long as; en — que as
tantale m. tantalum; tantalus
tantaliser vt. to tantalize
tante f. aunt
tantinet m. small amount, mite
tantôt adv. soon, presently; just now; — . . . — sometimes . . . sometimes
taon m. horsefly, gadfly
tapage m. noise, din
tapageur a. noisy; showy; — m. noise-maker
tape f. slap, tap, pat
tapé a. dried (fruit)
tape-à-l'œil a. gaudy
tapecul m. jolting vehicle
taper vt. to tap, slap; typewrite
tapette f. tap, light tap; swatter
tapin m. drummer
tapinois, en — adv. secretly
tapioca m. tapioca
tapir m. tapir
tapir v., se — to squat, crouch, cower
tapis m. carpet; cloth; — roulant conveyor belt; sur le — under discussion; — vert gambling table
tapisser vt. to paper, hang
tapisserie f. tapestry; wallpaper; faire — be a wallflower
tapissier m. upholsterer; paper hanger; tapestry maker
taponner vt. to stopper
tapoter vt. to pat, rap; strum
taquet m. wedge, block
taquin a. teasing
taquiner vt. to tease; tantalize
taquinerie f. teasing
tarabiscoter vt. to overadorn, overornament
taraud m. threading tool
tarauder vt. to thread, make a thread
taraudeuse f. threading machine
tard adv. late
tarder vi. to delay; be long in; il me tarde (de) I am anxious (to)
tardif a. tardy, late; backward
tare f. defect, taint; (com.) depreciation
tarentelle f. tarentella
tarentule f. tarantula
tarer vt. to damage; tarnish
targette f. slide bolt
targuer v., se — (de) to pride oneself (on)
tarière f. auger; borer (of an insect)
tarif m. tariff; price list, rate; fare
tarifer vt. to set the price of
tarir vt. & vi. to dry up

tarissement m. drying up, exhausting
tarse m. instep
tarsier m. tarsus
tartane f. (naut.) tartan, small fishing boat
tarte f. tart
tartine f. slice of bread and butter, bread and jam
tartiner vt. to spread
tartre m. tartar
tartufe m. hypocrite
tas m. heap, pile
tasse f. cup
tasseau m. bracket, brace; lug; lathe
tasser vt. to compress, pack; se — to sink, settle; crowd together
tâter vt. to feel, handle
tâtonner vi. to grope; (fig.) to fumble
tâtonneur a. groping
tâtons, à — adv. gropingly
tatou m. armadillo
tatouage m. tattoo
tatouer vt. to tattoo
taudis m. hovel; — pl. slums
taupe f. mole
taupinière f. molehill
taure f. heifer
taureau m. bull
tauromachie f. bullfighting
taux m. rate, set price
tavelage m. fruit bruise, spot
taveler vt. to bruise, spot
taverne f. tavern
tavernier m. tavern keeper
taxatif a. taxable
taxe f. tax, duty, rate, charge; toll
taxer vt. to tax, regulate; — de to accuse; lettre taxée f. postage-due letter
taxi m. taxicab
taxidermie f. taxidermy
taximètre m. meter of a taxi
taxiphone m. telephone booth
Tchécoslovaque m. & f. & a. Czechoslovakian
Tchécoslovaquie f. Czechoslovakia
tchèque a. Czech
te pron. you, to you, yourself
té m. T-shape; T-square
technicien m. technician
technicité f. technical nature, technical complexity
technique a. technical; — f. technique
technologie f. technology
teck m. teakwood
teckel m. dachshund
teigne f. moth; dandruff, scaliness; (coll.) scurvy fellow
teigneux a. scurvy
teindre vt. to dye, stain
teint m. dye; complexion
teinte f. tint
teinter vt. to tint
teinture f. dye; dyeing; tinting; tincture; slight knowledge
teinturerie f. dye shop; dyeing
teinturier m. dyer
tel a. such, like; — que such as, like; — quel just as it is; — pron. such a one
télécommandé a. remote-controlled
télécommunication f. long-distance com-

munication
télégramme m. telegram; — sous-marin cablegram
télégraphe m. telegraph
télégraphie f. telegraphy; — sans fil wireless
télégraphier vt. & vi. to telegraph
télégraphique a. telegraphic
télégraphiste m. & f. telegrapher; telegram messenger
téléguidage m. radio control
téléguider vt. to control by radio
téléimprimeur m. teleprinter, teletype machine
télémécanique f. remote control
télémètre m. range finder
téléobjectif m. telephoto lens
télépathie f. telepathy
téléphérage m. aerial transport
téléphérique m. cable car
téléphone m. telephone; coup de — phone call
téléphoner vt. & vi. to telephone
téléphonique a. telephonic; cabine — f. phone booth
téléphoniste m. & f. telephonist, telephone operator
téléphotographie f. wire photo-transmission
télescopage m. telescoping, collision
télescope m. telescope
télescoper vt. to telescope, crash into
téléscripteur m. teletype machine
téléski m. ski lift
téléspectateur m. TV viewer
télétype m. teletype machine
télévisé a. televized
téléviser vt. to televize
téléviseur m. television set
télévision f. television; appareil de — television set
tellement adv. so, in such a manner
tellière m. foolscap paper
téméraire a. rash, bold
témérité f. rashness, boldness
témoignage m. testimony, evidence
témoigner vt. & vi. to testify; show
témoin m. witness
tempe f. (anat.) temple of the head
tempérament m. temperament
tempérant a. temperate
température f. temperature
tempéré a. temperate, moderate
tempérer vt. to temper, moderate
tempête f. tempest, storm
tempêter vi. to storm, fume
tempétueux a. stormy; tempestuous
temple m. protestant church; temple
temporaire a. temporary
temporal a. (anat.) relating to the temple of the head
temporel a. temporal; — m. temporals, church income; temporal power
temporisateur a. delaying, postponing
temporisation f. delay, postponement
temporiser vt. to delay, postpone
temps m. time; weather; tense; à — in time; avant le — prematurely; de en —, de — à autre from time to time; de tout — always; en même — together, at the same time; entre — meanwhile
tenable a. tenable
tenace a. tenacious; clinging; stubborn
ténacité f. tenacity
tenaille f. pincers
tenancier m. tenant operator or director of rented property
tenant a., séance -e forthwith; — m. defender, supporter; -s pl. details, particulars;. -s et aboutissants contiguous lands
tendance f. tendency
tendancieux a. tendentious; suggestive; prejudiced
tendeur m. spreader; shoe tree
tendoir m. clothesline
tendon m. tendon
tendre vt. & vi. to stretch out; hold out; hang; tend, lead; paper a room; — a. tender, soft; affectionate; — m. tenderness; love
tendresse f. tenderness, affection
tendreté f. tenderness of meat
tendron m. shoot; (coll.) very young girl; -s pl. cartilage
tendu a. stretched, strained, tight
ténèbres f. pl. darkness; (fig.) ignorance
ténébreux a. dark, gloomy
teneur f. tenor, literal text; — m. keeper
ténia m. tapeworm
tenir vt. & vi. to hold; have; keep; hold out, endure; — à to value, be anxious to, be determined, want; se — to remain, be, stand, stay; contain oneself
tennis m. tennis; tennis court
tenon m. bolt
ténor m. tenor
ténoriser vi. to sing tenor
tension f. tension, tenseness; pressure
tentacule m. tentacle
tentateur m. temptor; — a. tempting
tentation f. temptation
tentative f. attempt
tentatrice f. temptress
tente f. tent
tente-abri f. shelter tent
tenter vt. to tempt; try
tenture f. wallpaper; hanging(s)
tenu a. kept; obliged; firm
ténu a. tenuous, thin
tenue f. holding, keeping; behavior; dress, clothes, uniform
ténuité f. tenuousness
ter adv. thrice, three times; B, third entrance (house numbers)
térébenthine f. turpentine
térébrant a. boring, piercing
tergiversation f. hesitation, beating about the bush
tergiverser vi. to hesitate, beat about the bush
terme m. term, limit; end; rental period, quarter
terminaison f. ending
terminer vt. to terminate, end
terminologie f. terminology
terminus m. terminal point, end of the line, terminus
termite m. termite

termitière *f.* termite's nest

terne *a.* dull, leaden; colorless

ternir *vt.* to tarnish, dull

ternissure *f.* tarnished spot; tarnishing

terrain *m.* ground; playing field

terrasse *f.* terrace; sidewalk in front of a café

terrassement *m.* earth removal; ditch-digging

terrasser *vt.* to throw down; embank; dismay

terrassier *m.* ditchdigger, excavation worker

terre *f.* earth, ground, land; property; — à — earthy, common; ventre à — at full speed

terreau *m.* compost

terre neuve *m.* Newfoundland dog

Terre-Neuve *f.* Newfoundland

terre-neuvien *a.* of Newfoundland; — *m.* Grand Banks fishing boat; Grand Banks fisherman

terre-plein *m.* platform; terre-plein; terrace

terrer *vt.* to put dirt around a plant; se — to live in the ground; hide

Terre-Sainte *f.* Holy Land

terrestre *a.* terrestrial, earthly

terreur *f.* terror, dread

terreux *a.* earthen; earth-colored; earthy

terrien *a.* earth-inhabiting, ground-living; propriétaire — landed proprietor

terrier *m.* lair, burrow

terrifier *vt.* to terrify

terrine *f.* earthenware pot; casserole; potted meat

territoire *m.* territory

terroir *m.* soil, land

terroriser *vt.* to terrorize

terrorisme *m.* terrorism

terroriste *m.* terrorist

tertiaire *a.* tertiary

tertio *adv.* thirdly

tertre *m.* hillock, knoll

tes *a. pl.* your

tesson *m.* potsherd, pottery fragment

test *m.* testa; test

testacé *a.* testaceous; — *m.* testacean

testament *m.* will, testament

testamentaire *a.* testamentary

testateur *m.* maker of a will

tester *vi.* to make one's will; — *vt.* to test

testicule *m.* testicle

testimonial *a.* testimonial

tétanos *m.* tetanus, lockjaw

têtard *m.* polliwog, tadpole

tête *f.* head; mind; chief, leader; top; signe de — *m.* nod; avoir mal à la — to have a headache

tête-à-queue *m.* sharp full turn of a vehicle

tête-à-tête *m.* private conversation, intimate meeting; love seat

tête-bêche *adv.* upside-down

tétée *f.* act of suckling

téter *vt. & vi.* to suck, feed at the breast

tétin *m.* nipple

tétine *f.* udder; nipple of a nursing bottle

tétraèdre *m.* tetrahedron

tétralogie *f.* tetralogy

tette *f.* teat, dug

têtu *a.* stubborn, headstrong

Teuton *m.* Teuton; — *a.* teutonic

texte *m.* text

textile *a.* textile

textuel *a.* textual

texture *f.* texture

thaï *a.* Thai; — *n.* Thai language

Thaïlande *f.* Thailand

thé *m.* tea

théâtral *a.* theatrical

théâtre *m.* theater

thébaïde *f.* solitude

théier *m.* tea plant

théière *f.* teapot

thématique *a.* thematic

thème *m.* theme; translation into a foreign language

théocrate *m.* theocrat

théocratique *a.* theocratic

théologal *a.* theological

théologie *f.* theology

théologien *m.* theologian

théologique *a.* theological

théorème *m.* theorem

théoricien *m.* theorist

théorie *f.* theory

théorique *a.* theoretical

théosophie *f.* theosophy

thérapeute *m.* therapist

thérapeutique *a.* therapeutic

thermal *a.* thermal; station -e hot springs resort

thermes *m. pl.* hot springs resort; Roman baths

thermique *a.* thermic, thermal

thermite *f.* thermite

thermodynamique *f.* thermodynamics

thermo-électrique *a.* thermoelectric

thermogène *a.* warming, irritating

thermographe *m.* recording thermometer

thermomètre *m.* thermometer

thermométrique *a.* thermometric

thésauriser *vt.* to hoard

thésauriseur *m.* hoarder

thèse *f.* thesis; argument

thiamine *f.* thiamine

thomiste *m.* Thomist

thon *m.* tuna

thonier *m.* tuna boat

thoracique *a.* thoracic

thorax *m.* thorax

thorium *m.* thorium

thrombose *f.* thrombosis

thuriféraire *m.* incense bearer; (fig.) flatterer

thym *m.* thyme

thymus *m.* thymus

thyroïde *a.* thyroid

tiare *f.* tiara

Tibet *m.* Tibet

Tibétain *m. & a.* Tibetan

tic *m.* tic, twitch; mania

ticket *m.* ration ticket; ticket; — modérateur patient's share of payment for health insurance

tiède *a.* lukewarm, tepid

tiédeur *f.* lukewarmness

tiédir *vt. & vi.* to make tepid, grow tepid

tien *pron.*, le —, la -ne yours

tierce f. (eccl.) tierce (also, in fencing); triplet, three of a kind (at cards); (mus.) third

tiers m. third part; un — one third

tiers-point m. point of an arch; triangular file; triangular sail

tige f. tree trunk, stem; stalk; shaft

tignasse f. matted hair

tigre m. tiger; -sse f. tigress

tigré a. striped, tiger-striped

tillac m. (naut.) deck

tilleul m. lime tree, linden tree

timbale f. (mus.) kettledrum; mold, ring mold; food cooked in a ring mold; metal goblet; -s pl. timpani

timbalier m. tympanist

timbrage m. stamping

timbre m. stamp; bell; timbre; stamp bureau

timbré a. stamped; sonorous; (coll.) crazy; papier — paper with imprinted revenue stamp

timbre-poste m. postage stamp

timbre-quittance m. revenue stamp

timbrer vt. to stamp

timbreur m. stamper

timide a. timid

timidité f. timidity

timonerie f. steerage

timonier m. helmsman; wheel horse

timoré a. timorous

tin m. (naut.) block, support

tine f. water cask

tinette f. large bucket, cask

tintamarre m. noise, uproar

tinter vt. & vi. to ring, tinkle; tingle

tintinnabuler vi. to tinkle

tique f. (ent.) tick

tiqueté a. spotted

tir m. shooting, firing; rifle range; shooting gallery; — à la cible target shooting

tirage m. drawing, pulling; printing

tiraillement m. sniping, shooting; spasm; friction

tirailler vt. & vi. to snipe, shoot at intervals; pull in two directions

tirailleur m. sharpshooter

tirant m. (naut.) draft; bootstrap; drawstring

tire f. pull, tug; vol à la — pocket picking

tiré a. drawn; tired; — à quatre épingles dapper, neat; — par les cheveux far-fetched, unlikely

tire-botte m. bootjack

tire-bouchon m. corkscrew

tire-bouton m. buttonhook

tire-clou m. claw hammer

tire-d'aile, à — adv. rapidly, with rapid flapping of wings

tire-fond m. French railway spike; ceiling ring for light fixture

tirelire f. coin bank

tirer vt. & vi. to draw, pull; extract; derive; shoot; stick out; draw, trace; draw off, print; (phot.) print; (naut.) draw, have a draft of; deliver; se — d'affaire to get along, manage

tire-sou m. penny pincher, petty profiteer

tiret m. hyphen, dash

tirette f. drawstring, cord; table leaf

tireur m. drawer; shooter; fortune teller

tireuse f. (phot.) printing box

tiroir m. drawer

tisane f. infusion, tea

tison m. hot coal, ember

tisonner vi. to stir the fire

tisonnier m. poker

tissage m. weaving

tisser vt. to weave

tisserand m. weaver

tisseur m. weaver

tissu m. fabric

tissu-éponge m. terry cloth

tissure f. weave

titan m. titan

titane m. titanium

titanesque, titanique a. titanic

titillation f. titillation, tickling

titiller vt. & vi. to titillate, tickle

titrage m. quantitive analysis

titre m. title; quality, right; deed; headline; -s pl. degree, credentials; -s flamboyants banner headlines; à — de prep. as, in the capacity of; à juste — adv. deservedly, rightly

titrer vt. to title

tituber vi. to titubate, stagger

titulaire m. & f. & a. titular

toaster vi. to make a toast

toasteur m. toaster

toboggan m. toboggan; slide, chute

toc m. (coll.) imitation (of valuable objects); en — false, fake

toge f. toga; robe

tohu-bohu m. tumult, disorder

toi pron. you

toile f. cloth; curtain; painting, canvas; — cirée oilcloth; — d'araignée cobweb; — de fond backdrop

toilette f. toilet, dressing table; dress

toise f. toise (6½ feet, 2 meters); measuring scale

toisé m. measuring

toiser vt. to measure; evaluate; disdain

toison f. fleece; — d'or golden fleece

toit m. roof

toiture f. roofing

tokai m. Tokay wine

tôle f. sheet iron

tolérable a. tolerable

tolérance f. tolerance

tolérant a. tolerant

tolérantisme m. religious tolerance

tolérer vt. to tolerate

tôlerie f. sheet metal trade; sheet metal factory

tôlier m. sheet metal worker

tollé m. outcry

toluène m. toluene

tomaison f. volume number

tomate f. tomato

tombal a. tomb; pierre -e tombstone

tombe f. tomb

tombeau m. tomb, grave, gravestone

tombée f. fall

tomber vi. to fall, fall down; — vt. to fell

tombereau m. cart

tombola f. lottery

tome m. volume

ton a. your; — m. tune, note; tone; style

tonalité f. tonality; tone control
tondaison f. shearing
tondeur a. shearing
tondeuse f. shearing machine; lawn mower; hair clippers
tondre vt. to shear, clip; mow
tondu a. shorn, fleeced
tonicité f. tonicity, tone
tonifier vt. to tone; invigorate
tonique a. & m. tonic
tonitruant a. thundering
tonnage m. tonnage
tonnant a. thundering
tonne f. metric ton
tonneau m. cask
tonnelet m. small cask, keg
tonnelier m. cooper
tonnelle f. arbor; tunnel vault; hunting net
tonnellerie f. cooperage
tonner vi. to thunder; (fig.) to speak with fervor
tonnerre m. thunder
tonsure f. tonsure
tonsurer vt. to tonsure
tonte f. shearing
tonture f. clipping
tonus m. muscle tone
topaze f. topas
toper vi. to shake hands in agreement
topinambour m. Jerusalem artichoke
topique a. topic, topical; — m. topic
topographe m. topographer
topographie f. topography
topographique a. topographical
toponymie f. study of place names
toquade f. whim
toque f. cap, bonnet
toquer v., se — de to fall in love with
torche f. torch
torcher vt. to wipe
tochère f. torchere, torch holder, candelabrum
torchis m. mortar of adobe and straw
torchon m. cleaning cloth, rag
torchonner vt. to wipe
tordant a. very funny
tordeur m. twister
tordeuse f. twisting machine
tordre vt. to twist, wring
tore m. (arch) tore, torus, twisted column
toréador m. bullfighter
toréer vi. to fight bulls
toréro m. bullfighter
tornade f. tornado
toron m. cable strand
torpeur f. torpor
torpide a. torpid
torpillage m. torpedoing
torpille f. torpedo; bomb; mine
torpiller vt. to torpedo
torpilleur m. torpedo boat
torque f. coil; twist of tobacco
torréfacteur m. roaster
torréfaction f. roasting
torréfier vt. to roast; grill; scorch
torrentiel a. torrential
torrentueux a. torrentuous
torride a. torrid
tors a. twisted; crooked

torsade f. twisted braid
torse m. torso, trunk
torsion f. twisting
tort m. wrong, injury, harm; à — wrongly; à — et à travers helter skelter, indiscriminately; avoir — to be wrong; faire — à to harm
torticolis m. stiff neck
tortillage m. twisting
tortillard m. interurban train
tortillement m. twisting
tortiller vt. & vi. to twist
tortionnaire a. torturer; — a. torturing
tortu a. crooked, twisted
tortue f. turtle, tortoise
tortueux a. tortuous; winding
torturer vt. to torture
torve a. threatening
Toscan m. & a. Tuscan
Toscane f. Tuscany
tôt adv. soon
total a. & m. total; whole
totaliser vt. to total
totalitaire a. totalitarian
totalitairisme m. totalitarianism
totalité f. totality
toton m. top (toy)
touage m. towing
touchant a. touching, moving; — prep. relating to, concerning
touche f. (mus.) stop, key; touch, stroke; assay; touchstone; goad
touche-à-tout m. busybody
toucher vt. & vi. to touch, feel; play a musical instrument; cash, receive money; — m. touch, sense of touch
toucheur m. animal driver
toue f. tow, towing
touer vt. to tow
touffe f. tuft; cluster
touffeur f. stifling heat
touffu a. tufted, thick; full, luxuriant
touiller vt. to stir up
toujours adv. always; still
toundra f. tundra
toupet m. tuft of hair; toupee
toupie f. top (toy)
toupiller vi. to spin like a top
toupillon m. tuft
tour m. turn, turning; excursion, trip, circuit; lathe; trick; — f. tower; castle (chess)
tourbe f. peat, turf; crowd, throng
tourbière f. peat bog
tourbillon m. whirlwind
tourbillonnement m. whirling
tourbillonner vi. to whirl
tourelle f. turret
tourie f. demijohn
tourisme m. tourism; agence de — travel bureau
touriste m. tourist
touristique a. tourist, of tourist interest
tourment m. torment
tourmente f. tempest, storm
tourmenter vt. to torment, torture
tourmenteur m. tormentor; — a. tormenting
tournailler vi. to turn about
tournant m. turning, turning point, curve;

roundabout way; — *a.* turning

tourné *a.* turned; spoiled; bien — well-shaped

tourne-à-gauche *m.* wrench

tournebroche *m.* spit for roasting

tourne-disque *m.* record player, turntable

tournedos *m.* filet steak

tournée *f.* round, circuit; journey

tournemain, en un — *adv.* in a moment

tourner *vt. & vi.* to turn, turn over, turn out, go around; produce (movie), film; play a role

tournesol *m.* heliotrope

tourneur *m.* lathe man; — *a.* whirling, turning

tournevis *m.* screwdriver

tourniquet *m.* turnstile; turniquet; gambling wheel

tournoi *m.* tournament

tournoiement *m.* rotation, whirling

tournoyer *vi.* to turn, whirl

tournure *f.* turn; shape, figure; expression

tourte *f.* tart; pie

tourtière *f.* tart pan, pie pan

Toussaint *f.* All-Saints'-Day

tousser *vi.* to cough

toussoter *vi.* to cough intermittently

tout *m.* whole, all; du — not at all; — *a. & pron.* all, whole, any, every; — *adv.* all, any, wholly, quite; — à coup suddenly; — à fait entirely; — à l'heure in a little while; a little while ago; — de suite immediately

toute-épice *f.* allspice

toutefois *conj.* yet, however

toute-présence *f.* omnipresence

toute-puissance *f.* omnipotence

tout-puissant *a.* omnipotent

toux *f.* cough; coughing

toxicologie *f.* toxicology

toxicomanie *f.* drug addiction

toxine *f.* toxin

toxique *m. & a.* poison

trabe *f.* flagstaff

trac *m.* stage fright

traçage *m.* tracing

tracas *m.* bustle, fuss

tracasser *vt.* to trouble, worry

tracasserie *f.* annoyance, worry

trace *f.* trace, mark, footstep

tracé *m.* outline, draft

tracement *m.* tracing

tracer *vt.* to trace, outline

trachéal *a.* tracheal

trachée (artère) *f.* trachea

trachéen *a.* trachial

tract *m.* tract, pamphlet

tractation *f.* treatment, procedure

tracteur *m.* tractor

traction *f.* traction; — avant *f.* small front-wheel-drive auto

tradition *f.* tradition

traditionalisme *m.* traditionalism

traditionaliste *m. & f.* traditionalist; — *a.* traditionalistic

traditionnel *a.* traditional

traducteur *m.* translator; — juré official translator

traduction *f.* translation

traduire *vt.* to translate; transfer

traduisible *a.* translatable

trafic *m.* traffic, trade

trafiquant *m.* dealer

trafiquer *vi.* to traffic, trade, deal

trafiqueur *a.* trafficker

tragédie *f.* tragedy

tragédien *m.* tragedian, tragic actor

tragi-comédie *f.* tragi-comedy

tragique *a.* tragic

trahir *vt.* to betray, reveal

trahison *f.* treason, treachery

train *m.* (rail.) train; rate, pace; attendants; bustle, noise; rear, hind part; front, forepart; — d'atterrissage (avi.) landing gear; undercarriage; — avant (auto.) front assembly; — arrière rear assembly; — de marchandises freight train; — de voyageurs passenger train; — de plaisir excursion train; — express ordinary express; — omnibus local train; — poste mail train; — rapide fast express; — de maison housekeeping; — de vie way of life; — des équipages (army) transportation corps; en — (de) in spirits; in the act of; busy; — mixte combination freight and passenger train

trainage *m.* dragging

trainard *m.* straggler; slow poke (U.S. coll.)

trainasser *vi.* to loiter; — *vt.* to drag out

traine *f.* train of a dress; seine; dragging; à la — in tow

traineau *m.* sled; seine

trainée *f.* powder train; trail

trainer *vt. & vi.* to drag, drag out; loiter

traire *vt.* to milk

trait *m.* arrow, shaft, dart, bolt; line, leash; stroke; gulp; feature; trait; — d'union hyphen; — d'esprit witticism

traitable *a.* easy to deal with, tractable; treatable

traite *f.* trade, trading

traité *m.* treaty, agreement; treatise

traitement *m.* treatment; salary

traiter *vt. & vi.* to treat, negotiate; — de to call, style

traiteur *m.* caterer

traitre *m.* traitor; — (traitresse) *a.* traitorous, treacherous

traitrise *f.* treachery

trajectoire *f.* trajectory

trajet *m.* distance, journey; passage, crossing

tramer *vt.* to plot

tramontane *f.* north wind; perdre la — to lose one's bearings

tranchant *a.* sharp; decisive; — *m.* blade, cutting edge

tranche *f.* slice; fore edge of a book; series; rim, edge; doré sur — gilt-edged

tranchée *f.* trench; —s *pl.* colic; labor pains

tranchelard *m.* kitchen knife

tranche-montagne *m.* swaggerer

trancher *vt. & vi.* to slice; cut off; decide, determine

tranchoir *m.* chopping block

tranquille *a.* tranquil; quiet; still; calm

tranquilliser *vt.* to quiet, calm

tranquillité *f.* tranquility, quiet

transalpin *a.* transalpine
transat *m.* deck chair
Transat *f.* French Line
transatlantique *a.* transatlantic; — *m.* ocean liner; deck chair
transbordement *m.* transshipping
transborder *vt.* to transship
transbordeur *m.* transshipper; transporter; — *a.* transporting; pont — transporter bridge, bridge which carries passengers on a moving platform
transcendence *f.* transcendency
transcendant *a.* transcendent
transcendantal *a.* transcendental
transcontinental *a.* transcontinental
transcripteur *m.* transcriber
transcription *f.* transcription
transcrire *vt.* to copy; transcribe
transe *f.* apprehension; trance
transept *m.* transept
transfèrement *m.* transfer of a prisoner
transférer *vt.* to transfer
transfert *m.* transfer
transfiguration *f.* transfiguration
transfigurer *vt.* to transfigure
transformable *a.* transformable
transformateur *m.* transformer
transformation *f.* transformation; conversion
transformer *vt.* to transform
transfuge *m.* fugitive, deserter
transfuser *vt.* to transfuse; give a transfusion
transfusion *f.* transfusion
transgresser *vt.* to transgress against
transgresseur *m.* transgressor; trespasser
transgression *f.* transgression
transi *a.* numb, benumbed
transiger *vi.* to make concessions
transir *vt. & vi.* to chill, numb; be chilled
transistor *m.* transistor
transiter *vt. & vi.* to transit in bond
transitif *a.* (gram.) transitive
transition *f.* transition
transitoire *a.* transitory
translation *f.* removal; transfer
translucide *a.* translucid
transmetteur *m.* transmitter; — *a.* transmitting
transmettre *vt.* to transmit; forward
transmissible *a.* transmissible
transmission *f.* transmission; transmittal
transmu(t)able *a.* transmutable
transmuer *vt.* to transmute
transmutabilité *f.* transmutability
transocéanique *a.* transoceanic
transparaître *vi.* to be visible through, to be guessed
transparence *f.* transparency
transpercer *vt.* to pierce
transpiration *f.* perspiration
transpirer *vt.* to perspire
transplantation *f.* transplanting
transplanter *vt.* to transplant
transport *m.* transport; ecstasy, rapture
transportable *a.* transportable
transportation *f.* transfer of a prisoner
transporter *vt.* to transport, excite, upset
transporteur *a.* transporting; — *m.* transporter

transposer *vt.* to transpose
transposition *f.* transposition
transsonique *a.* of the speed of sound
transsuder *vt.* to transsude
transvasement *m.* decanting
transvaser *vt.* to decant
transversal *a.* transversal
transvider *vt.* to empty the contents from one vessel into another
trapèze *m.* trapezoid; trapeze; trapezium
trapézoïdal *a.* trapezoidal
trappe *f.* trap; trap door; pitfall
Trappe, la — *f.* Trappist order; Trappist monastery
trappeur *m.* trapper
trappiste *m.* trappist
trapu *a.* short and fat
traquenard *m.* snare, trap
traquer *vt.* to flush (game); pursue
traqueur *m.* tracker
traumatique *a.* traumatic
traumatisme *m.* traumatism
travail (*pl.* travaux) *m.* work; travaux forcés *m. pl.* penal servitude
travailler *vt. & vi.* to work, toil
travailleur *m.* laborer, workman
travailliste *m.* laborite
travée *f.* (arch.) bay of a vault
travers *m.* breadth; à —, au — across; en — across, sideways; de — crosswise
traverse *f.* traverse, crossarm; crossroad, short cut; (rail.) tie; obstacle
traversée *f.* voyage, crossing
traverser *vt.* to cross
traversier *a.* transverse; transversal
traversin *m.* bolster; cross bar
travesti *a.* costumed as the opposite sex; costumed
travestir *vt.* to disguise; travesty
travestissement *m.* disguise, travesty
trayon *m.* teat, dug
trébuchant *a.* stumbling; espèces sonnantes et –es *f. pl.* hard cash
trébucher *vi.* to stumble; trip; — *vt.* to weigh
trébuchet *m.* snare, trap; balance, scales
tréfilage *m.* drawing of wire
tréfiler *vt.* to draw wire
trèfle *m.* clover; cloverleaf; clubs (at cards)
tréfonds *m.* mineral rights; secret basis
treillage *m.* trellis
treille *f.* vine growing on a trellis
treillisser *vt.* to trellis, interweave
treize *a.* thirteen
treizième *a. & m.* thirteenth
tremble *m.* aspen
tremblement *m.* trembling, shaking; —de terre earthquake
trembler *vi.* to tremble
trembloter *vi.* to shiver
trémie *f.* loading device
trémousser *vt.* to stir up
trempe *f.* temper of iron; character; soaking
trempée *f.* tempering
tremper *vt. & vi.* to dip, soak; temper iron
tremplin *m.* trampoline; diving board; (fig.) stepping stone
trentaine *f.* about thirty

trente *a.* thirty
trentenaire *m.* thirtieth anniversary; — *a.* thirty-year old
trentième *m. & a.* thirtieth
trépaner *vt.* to trepan
trépas *m.* death
trépasser *vi.* to die
trépidant *a.* terror stricken
trépidation *f.* trepidation
trépied *m.* trivet; tripod
trépigner *vi.* to stamp on the ground
très *adv.* very
trésor *m.* treasure; treasury
trésorerie *f.* treasury
trésorier *m.* treasurer
tressaillement *m.* start, leap, shudder
tressaillir *vi.* to start; leap, thrill
tressauter *vi.* to jump, start
tresser *vt.* to braid, twist
tréteau *m.* platform; (theat.) the stage
treuil *m.* windlass
trève *f.* truce
tri *m.* sorting, choosing
triage *m.* choice; sorting
triangle *m.* triangle
triangulaire *a.* triangular
tribord *m.* (naut.) starboard
tribordais *m.* starboard watch
tribu *f.* tribe
tribulation *f.* tribulation
tribune *f.* tribune; gallery, stands; parliament; de la — parliamentary
tribut *m.* tribute; retribution
tributaire *m. & a.* tributary
tricher *vt. & vi.* to cheat
tricherie *f.* cheating
tricheur *m.* cheater
trichine *f.* trichina
trichinose *f.* trichinosis
trichromie *f.* (print.) three-color process
tricolore *a. & m.* tricolor
tricorne *m.* three-cornered hat
tricot *m.* knit fabric, tricot; knit ware
tricotage *m.* knitting, knitted work
tricoter *vt.* to knit
tricoteur *m.* knitter
trictrac *m.* backgammon
tricycle *m.* tricycle
tridimensionnel *a.* three-dimensional
trièdre *a.* three-sided
triennal *a.* triennial; three-year
trier *vt.* to pick, sort
trieur *m.* sorter
trigonométrie *f.* trigonometry
trigonométrique *a.* trigonometric
trilatéral *a.* three-sided
trille *f.* trill
triller *vi.* to trill
trilogie *f.* trilogy
trimestre *m.* quarter, three months
trimestriel *a.* quarterly
trimoteur *a.* trimotor
tringle *f.* rod; curtain rod
Trinité *f.* Trinity; Trinidad
trinquer *vi.* to toast, clink glasses
triomphal *a.* triumphal
triomphateur *a.* triumphant
triomphe *m.* triumph
triompher *vi.* to triumph
triparti(te) *a.* tripartite

tripatouiller *vt.* to tamper with a literary work; mishandle, butcher
triplace *a.* three-seater
triple *a.* triple; treble
triplex *m.* safety glass
triplicata *m.* second copy, second carbon
triporteur *m.* bicycle delivery truck
tripot *m.* gambling house, disorderly house
tripotage *m.* mess; intrigue; influence peddling; shady dealings
tripoter *vt.* to misuse, speculate with
triptyque *m.* triptych; international automobile documents
trisaïeul *m.* great-great-grandfather
trisannuel *a.* three-year; triannual
trisection *f.* trisection
trisme, trismus *m.* lockjaw
triste *a.* sad
tristesse *f.* sadness
triturer *vt.* to crush, grind
trivial *a.* trivial; vulgar
trivialité *f.* triviality; vulgar expression
troc *m.* barter
troène *m.* privet
troglodyte *m.* troglodyte, cave dweller
trognon *m.* fruit *or* vegetable core, stalk
trois *a.* three; –ième *a. & m.* third
trolleybus *m.* trolleybus, trackless trolley
trombe *f.* waterspout; arriver en — to arrive unexpectedly
tromblon *m.* blunderbuss
trombone *m.* trombone; trombone player; (coll.) paper clip
trompe *f.* hunting horn; elephant's trunk; — d'Eustache Eustachian tube
trompe-la-mort *m. & f.* unexpectedly recovered invalid
trompe-l'œil *m.* deceptively real painting; vain appearance, surface glitter
tromper *vt.* to deceive, delude; se — to be mistaken
tromperie *f.* deceit, cheat
trompeter *vt.* to trumpet, cry
trompette *f.* trumpet; — *m.* trumpet player
trompettiste *m.* trumpeter
trompeur *a.* deceitful
tronc *m.* trunk, stump, stem; poor box; — de cône truncated cone
troncature *f.* truncation
tronçon *m.* stump, piece, fragment
tronçonner *vt.* to cut to pieces
trône *m.* throne
trôner *vi.* to reign supreme
tronqué *a.* cut short, cut off, cut down, truncated
tronquer *vt.* to truncate, curtail
trop *adv.* too, too much, too many
trophée *m.* trophy
tropicalisé *a.* packed for the tropics
tropique *m.* tropic; — du Cancer Tropic of Cancer; — du Capricorne Tropic of Capricorn; — *a.* tropical
trop-perçu *m.* overcharge, overpayment
trop-plein *m.* overflow
troquer *vt.* to barter
troqueur *m.* barterer
trotte *f.* distance, way
trotte-menu *a.* short-stepping

trotter *vi.* to trot, trot along

trotteur *m.* trotter

trotteuse *f.* watch's second hand; fast walker

trottin *m.* errand boy

trottiner *vi.* to trot about

trottinette *f.* scooter

trottoir *m.* sidewalk, pavement

trou *m.* hole

troubadour *m.* troubadour

trouble *m.* confusion; uneasiness; — *a.* cloudy, dim; confused

trouble-fête *m.* kill-joy, wet blanket

troubler *vt.* to disturb, upset; confuse; se — to become overcast; become confused

trouée *f.* hole, opening

trouer *vt.* to make a hole, perforate

troupe *f.* troop, company

troupeau *m.* flock, herd

troupier *m.* soldier

troussage *m.* trussing of poultry

trousse *f.* bundle; case, kit; truss

troussé *a.* built, turned

trousseau *m.* bunch of keys; trousseau; layette

trousser *vt.* to tuck, turn up; finish off polish off

troussis *m.* tuck

trouvable *a.* findable

trouvaille *f.* find; godsend

trouver *vt.* to find; think; se — to be, be found; feel; happen

trouvère *m.* troubadour of Northern France

Troyen *m. & a.* Trojan

truand *m.* beggar, thief

truanderie *f.* beggars, vagrants; begging

truc *m.* trick; knack; thing, gadget

trucage *m.* faking; special effects (movies); camouflage; counterfeit

truchement *m.* go-between

truc(k) *m.* (rail.) flat-car

truculence *f.* truculence

truculent *a.* truculent

truelle *f.* trowel; fish server

truellée *f.* trowelful

truffe *f.* truffle; nose of a dog

truffer *vt.* to stuff with truffles

truffier *a.* of truffles, truffled; cochon — pig trained to hunt truffles

truffière *f.* truffle patch

truie *f.* female pig, sow

truisme *m.* truism

truite *f.* trout

trumeau *m.* pier glass; mirror surmounted by a picture; picture surmounting a mirror; panel between two windows

truquage *m.* falsifying; false aging; special effects (movies)

truquer *vt. & vi.* to fake

truqueur *m.* faker

trust *m.* trust, cartel

truster *vt.* to monopolize

tsar *m.* czar; -ine *f.* czarina

tsé-tsé *f.* tsetse fly

T.S.F. *f.* radio

tu *pron.* you

tuber *vt.* to tube

tubercule *m.* tuber, tubercle

tuberculeux *a.* tuberculous, tubercular

tuberculose *f.* tuberculosis

tubéreuse *f.* tuberose

tubereux *a.* tuberous

tubulaire *a.* tubular

tubulé *a.* tubular, tubulated

tudesque *a.* German

tue-mouches *a.*, papier — flypaper; tapette — fly swatter

tuer *vt.* to kill

tuerie *f.* massacre

tue-tête, à — *adv.* at the top of one's voice

tueur *m.* killer

tuffeau *m.* chalk

tuilerie *f.* tile factory

tuilier *m.* tilemaker

tularémie *f.* tularemia

tulipe *f.* tulip

tulipier *m.* tulip tree

tuméfaction *f.* swelling

tuméfier *vt.* to grow, swell

tumeur *f.* tumor, swelling

tumulaire *a.* tumular, pertaining to a grave

tumulte *m.* tumult

tumultueux *a.* tumultuous

tungstène *m.* tungsten

tunique *f.* tunic; envelope, covering

Tunisie *f.* Tunisia

Tunisien *m. & a.* Tunisian

tunnel *m.* tunnel

turbine *f.* turbine

turboréacteur *m.* turbojet

turbot *m.* turbot

turbulence *f.* turbulence

turbulent *a.* turbulent

turc (turque) *m. & f.* Turk; — *a.* Turkish

turf *m.* race track; racing

turfiste *m.* follower of horse races

turlupin *m.* punster, poor joker

turlupinade *f.* pun, poor joke

turlutaine *f.* mania

Turquie *f.* Turkey

turquoise *f.* turquoise

tutélaire *a.* tutelary, guardian

tutelle *f.* guardianship

tuteur *m.*, tutrice *f.* guardian; plant support, stake

tuteurer *vt.* to prop up, put on stakes

tutoiement *m.* use of familiar address

tutu *m.* ballet skirt

tuyau *m.* tube, pipe; hose; (coll.) tip, information

tuyautage *m.* pipes, pipe system; pleating

tuyauter *vt.* to pleat; (coll.) to inform

tuyauterie *f.* pipes, pipe system

tuyère *f.* furnace vent

tympan *m.* eardrum; panel between mouldings, tympanum

tympaniser *vt.* to decry; annoy; cry out, publish

type *m.* type; fellow, chap, individual

typhique *a.* typhous; typhoid; — *m. & f.* typhus victim; typhoid victim

typhoide *a.* typhoid

typhoidique *a.* typhoid

typhon *m.* typhoon

typhus *m.* typhus

typification *f.* standardization

typique *a.* typical

typographe *m.* typographer, printer

typographie f. typography
typographique a. typographical
tyran m. tyrant
tyrannie f. tyranny
tyrannique a. tyrannical
tyranniser vt. to tyrannize
Tyrol m. Tyrol
Tyrolien m. & a. Tyrolean
tzigane m. & f. & a. Gypsy

U

ubiquité f. ubiquity
ulcération f. ulceration
ulcère m. ulcer; sore
ulcérer vt. to ulcerate
ultérieur a. ulterior; later
ultimatum m. ultimatum
ultime a. final, last, ultimate
ultimo adv. lastly
ultra-sonore a. supersonic
ultra-violet a. ultraviolet
ululement m. hooting
ululer vi. to hoot
un (une) a. a, an; one
unanime a. unanimous
uni a. united; even; plain
unification f. unification
unifier vt. to unify
uniforme m. & a. uniform
uniformément a. uniformly
uniformiser vt. to standardize; make uniform
uniformité f. uniformity
unilatéral a. unilateral
unioniste m. unionist
unique a. only, sole; unique
unir vt. to unite, join, level; s'— à join forces with; marry
unisson m. unison; agreement
unitaire a. unitarian
unitarien m. Unitarian
unité f. unity; unit
univers m. universe
universalité f. universality
universel a. universal
universitaire a. university, academic; cité — university dormitories
université f. university
uranium m. uranium
urbain a. urban
urbanisme m. city planning
urbaniste m. city planner
urbanité f. urbaneness
urée f. urea
urémie f. uremia
urémique a. uremic
uretère m. ureter
urgence f. urgency; d'— immediately
urgent a. urgent; cas — m. emergency
urinaire a. urinary
urinal m. urinal
uriner vi. to urinate
urinoir m. urinal
urique a. uric
urne f. urn; ballot box
us m. pl. customs, usage
usage m. use; practice, custom
usagé a. used
usager m. user

usé a. worn, worn out, threadbare; frayed
user vt. & vi. to wear out; consume; use; s'— to wear out; be spent; decay; — de make use of
usine f. factory, works, mill
usiner vt. to tool, machine
usinier a. industrial; — m. industrialist
usité a. used, in use
ustensile m. utensil
usuel a. usual, ordinary
usure f. usury; erosion; wear and tear
usurier m. usurer, money-lender
usurpateur m. usurper; — a. encroaching; usurping
usurpation f. usurpation
usurper vt. to usurp
ut m. (mus.) C, do
utérin a. uterine; of the same mother by different fathers
utérus m. uterus
utile a. useful; profitable; convenient
utilisable a. usable, utilizable
utilisation f. use, utilization
utiliser vt. to utilize; make use of
utilitaire a. utilitarian, useful
utilité f. utility
utopie f. utopia
uval a. grape
uvulaire a. uvular
uvule f. uvula

V

va interj. go ahead; — pour cent francs a hundred francs is acceptable
vacance f. vacancy; -s pl. holidays, vacation; grandes —s summer vacation
vacant a. vacant; tenantless
vacarme m. uproar, din
vacation f. court hearing; -s pl. suspension of court
vaccin m. vaccine
vaccination f. vaccination
vacciner vt. to vaccinate, inoculate
vache f. cow; cowhide
vacher m. cowherd
vacherie f. cowbarn
vachette f. calfskin
vacillation f., vacillement m. vacillation
vaciller vi. to vacillate, reel, waver
vacuité f. emptiness
vade-mecum m. constant companion or accompaniment
va-et-vient m. seesaw; swinging motion; coming and going
vagabond m. & a. vagabond
vagabondage m. vagabonding, roving
vagabonder vi. to rove
vagir vi. to cry, wail
vagissement m. cry, wail of an infant
vague f. wave; — a. vague, indefinite
vaguemestre m. (mil.) regimental mail clerk
vaguer vi. to wander, rove
vaillamment adv. valiantly
vaillance f. valor, bravery
vaillant a. valiant, courageous; brave
vain a. vain; en — adv. uselessly
vaincre vt. to vanquish; conquer
vainqueur a. conquering, victorious; — m. conqueror, victor

vair *m.* fur, squirrel's fur

vairon *m.* minnow; — *a.* wall-eyed; having eyes unmatched in color

vaisseau *m.* vessel, ship; church nave

vaisselier *m.* china cupboard

vaisselle *f.* dishes, tableware

val *m.* valley, vale

valable *a.* valid

Valence *f.* Valencia

valence *f.* valence; Valencia orange

valenciennes *f.* Valenciennes lace

valériane *f.* valerian

valet *m.* valet; jack (at cards); clamp

valétudinaire *a.* sickly

valeur *f.* value, worth; valor; -s *pl.* securities, stocks

valeureux *a.* valorous

valgus *a.* bow-legged

valide *a.* valid; able-bodied

valider *vt.* to validate; authenticate

valise *f.* suitcase, valise; — diplomatique diplomatic pouch

vallée *f.* valley

vallon *m.* small valley

vallonné *a.* valleyed

valoir *vt. & vi.* to be worth, be of value; produce, yield; — mieux to be better; faire — to make the most of; à — on account

valorisation *f.* valuation

valse *f.* waltz

valser *vi.* to waltz

valve *f.* valve; scallop shell

valvulaire *a.* valvular

valvule *f.* valve, valvule

vampire *m.* vampire; vampire bat; (fig.) leech, bloodsucker

van *m.* winnowing basket; van

vanadium *m.* vanadium

vandale *m.* vandal

vandalisme *m.* vandalism

vanille *f.* vanilla

vanillé *a.* vanilla-flavored

vanilline *f.* vanillin, artificial vanilla

vanité *f.* vanity

vaniteux *a.* vain, conceited

vannage *m.* winnowing

vanne *f.* sluice

vanner *vt.* to winnow

vannerie *f.* basketry; basket making

vanneur *m.* winnower

vannier *m.* basketmaker; basket seller

vannure *f.* chaff

vantail *m.* leaf, panel

vantard *m.* boaster; — *a.* boasting, boastful

vantardise *f.* boasting

vanter *vt.* to praise, extol; se — to boast, brag

vanterie *f.* boasting

vapeur *f.* vapor, steam; gas, fumes; à toute — at full steam; full speed ahead; — *m.* (naut.) steamer

vaporeux *a.* vaporous, nebulous

vaporisateur *m.* vaporizer, atomizer, sprayer

vaporisation *f.* vaporizing, atomizing

vaporiser *vt.* to vaporize, atomize

vaquer *vi.* to be vacant; not to be in session; — à *vt.* to take care of, busy oneself with, pay attention to

varech *m.* seaweed

varenne *f.* game preserve, warren

vareuse *f.* blazer, jacket, middy blouse

variabilité *f.* variability

variable *a.* variable

variante *f.* variant

varice *f.* varicose vein

varicelle *f.* chicken pox

varier *vt. & vi.* to vary; variegate; fluctuate

variété *f.* variety

variole *f.* smallpox

variolé *a.* pockmarked

varioleux *a.* concerning smallpox; — *m.* smallpox victim

variqueux *a.* varicose

varlet *m.* squire; clamp

varlope *f.* jointing plane (tool)

varloper *vt.* to plane

Varsovie *f.* Warsaw

varus (vara) *a.* knock-kneed; pigeon-toed

vasculaire *a.* vascular

vase *m.* vase, receptacle; — *f.* slime, mud

vaseux *a.* muddy, slimy; (coll.) tired, lazy

vasistas *m.* transom

vaso-constricteur *a.* vaso-constrictor

vaso-dilateur *a.* vaso-dilator

vaso-moteur *a.* vasomotor

vasque *f.* basin of a fountain

vaste *a.* vast

Vatican *m.* Vatican; Cité du — Vatican City

vaticane *a.* Vatican

vaticiner *vi.* to prophesy, vaticinate

va-tout *m.* all or nothing (gambling)

vaudeville *f.* musical comedy; comedy

vaudevilliste *m.* musical comedy author

vaudou *m.* voodoo

vau-l'eau, à — *adv.* adrift, with the current

vaurien *m.* good-for-nothing

vautour *m.* vulture

vautrer *v.*, se — to wallow, sprawl

veau *m.* calf; veal; calfskin

vedette *f.* (theat.) star; speedboat; cavalry sentinel; (fig.) prominent position

végétal *a.* vegetable

végétarien *m. & a.* vegetarian

végétation *f.* vegetation; growth, tumor

végéter *vi.* to vegetate

véhémence *f.* vehemence

véhément *a.* vehement

véhicule *m.* vehicle

véhiculer *vt.* to transport, cart

veille *f.* staying up; watch, lookout; vigil; eve, day before; being awake, wakefulness

veillée *f.* watching, vigil, wake; social evening

veiller *vt. & vi.* to stay up, stay awake; watch, watch over

veilleur *a.* watchman

veilleuse *f.* night light; pilot light

veinard *m.* (coll.) lucky person; — *a.* lucky

veine *f.* vein, lode; luck

veiner *vt.* to vein; grain, streak, marble

veineux *a.* veined; veinous; veining; venal

veinule *f.* small vein

vêlage, vêlement *m.* calving

vêler *vi.* to calve

vélin *m.* vellum
velléitaire *a.* fanciful
velléité *f.* fancy, desire
véloce *a.* rapid, lively
vélocipède *m.* velocipede
vélodrome *m.* cycling arena
vélomoteur *m.* light motorcycle
velot *m.* sheepskin
velours *m.* velvet
velouté *a.* velvety; soft, downy; — *m.* creamed soup
velouter *vt.* to make like velvet
veloutine *f.* velveteen
velu *a.* hairy
vélum *m.* velum; awning; circus tent
venaison *f.* venison
vénal *a.* venal; bought, mercenary
vénalité *f.* venality
venant *a.* arriving; — *m.* comer; à tout — to the first comer
vendable *a.* sellable
vendange *f.* vintage, vine harvest
vendanger *vt.* to harvest (grapes)
vendangeur *m.* grape harvester; vintner
vendeur *m.* seller, salesperson
vendre *vt.* to sell; (fig.) betray; à — for sale
vendredi *m.* Friday; — saint Good Friday
vendu *a.* sold; in the pay of
venelle *f.* small street
vénéneux *a.* poisonous
vénérable *a.* venerable
vénération *f.* veneration
vénérer *vt.* to venerate
vénerie *f.* hunting; hunting with a pack of hounds
vénérien *a.* venerial
veneur *m.* master of the hunt; master of the hounds
vengeance *f.* vengeance, revenge
venger *vt.* to avenge; se — to be revenged, take vengeance
vengeur *m.* avenger; — *a.* avenging
véniel *a.* venial; slight
venimeux *a.* venimous
venin *m.* venom, poison
venir *vi.* to come; occur; reach; faire — to send for; — à (faire quelque chose) to happen to (do something); — de to have just
Venise *f.* Venice
Vénitien *m. & a.* Venetian
vent *m.* wind; coup de — *m.* gust of wind; faire du — to be windy; sous le — leeward; avoir — de get wind of
ventail *m.* visor of a helmet
vente *f.* sale; en — being sold
venteaux *m. pl.* vents
venter *vi.* to blow; be windy
venteux *a.* windy
ventilateur *m.* electric fan; ventilator
ventilation *f.* ventilation
ventiler *vt.* to ventilate
ventis *m. pl.* blown-down trees
ventosité *f.* gas in the stomach
ventouse *f.* suction cup; sucker; cup for bloodletting
ventouser *vt.* to cup, bleed
ventral *a.* ventral
ventre *m.* belly, stomach, womb; à plat — lying face down; bas — abdomen

ventriculaire *a.* ventricular
ventricule *m.* ventricle
ventrière *f.* bellyband
ventriloque *m.* ventriloquist
ventriloquie *f.* ventriloquism
ventru *a.* fat, pot-bellied, paunchy
venu *a.* received; successful; arrived; — *m.* comer; le premier — anyone; bien — welcome; mal — unwelcome
venue *f.* coming, arrival; advent
vénusté *f.* charm, beauty, elegance
vêpres *f. pl.* vespers
ver *m.* worm; maggot; — solitaire tapeworm
véracité *f.* veracity
véranda *f.* porch, veranda
verbalisation *f.* report, minutes
verbaliser *vi.* to prepare a detailed report
verbe *m.* verb; word
verbeux *a.* verbose, wordy
verbiage *m.* verbosity, wordiness
verdâtre *a.* greenish
verdeur *f.* greenness; tartness; vigor youth
verdict *m.* verdict
verdir *vt.* to make green; — *vi.* to become green
verdoyant *a.* verdant, green
verdoyer *vi.* to be verdant
verdunisation *f.* chlorination
verduniser *vt.* to chlorinate
verdure *f.* greenness; greens; verdure
véreux *a.* wormy; lowdown; no-good; false
verge *f.* rod, switch, whip; penis
vergé *a.* lined, corded with same material
verger *m.* orchard
vergeter *vt.* to whisk clean; stripe with strokes of a rod
vergette *f.* whisk; little rod
vergeture *f.* lash mark, whip mark
vergeure *f.* lines in the substance of cloth, paper
verglacé *a.* covered with freezing rain
verglas *m.* glazed frost; freezing rain
vergne *m.* alder tree
vergogne *f.* shame
vergue *f.* (naut.) yard
véridique *a.* veracious
vérifiable *a.* verifiable, checkable
vérificateur *m.* verifier
vérification *f.* verification, checking
vérifier *vt.* to verify; check
vérin *m.* jack, hoist
véritable *a.* true, genuine
vérité *f.* truth
verjus *m.* juice of green grapes, verjuice
vermeil *a.* vermilion-colored; ruby-colored; — *m.* gilt
vermiculaire *a.* vermiform; wormlike
vermiforme *a.* vermiform
vermifuge *m.* worm medicine
vermillon *m.* vermilion
vermine *f.* vermin
vermineux *a.* caused by intestinal worms; covered with vermin, buggy
vermisseau *m.* small worm
vermouler *v., se — to become worm-eaten
vermoulu *a.* worm-eaten
vermoulure *f.* worm hole
vermouth *m.* vermouth

vernaculaire m. & a. vernacular

vernier m. vernier, slide rule

verni a. varnished; cuir — m. patent leather

vernir vt. to varnish; polish

vernis m. varnish, polish, glaze

vernissage m. varnishing; premier, opening of an art show

vernisser vt. to glaze

vernisseur m. glazer

vérole f. syphilis; petite — smallpox

verrat m. boar, pig

verre m. glass; lens; crystal; — à vitre sheet glass; — de sûreté safety glass

verrerie f. glassware

verrière f. stained glass window; glass covering a picture

verroterie f. glass bibelots, glass figurines

verrou m. bolt

verrouiller vt. to bolt

verrue f. wart

verrugueux a. warty, covered with warts

vers m. verse: line; — pl. poetry, verses; –s blancs blank verse; –s libres lines of different lengths; –s libres modernes free verse

vers prep. toward(s); about

versage m. pouring; tilling of a fallow field

versant m. slope

versatile a. versatile; changeable, fickle

versatilité f. versatility; fickleness

verse f., il pleut à — it's pouring;

versé a. versed

versement m. payment, installment

verser vt. & vi. to pour; shed; pay; overturn

verseur m. pourer, server

verseuse f. straight-handled coffee pot

versicolore a. many-colored

versificateur m. versifier

versifier vt. & vi. to versify

version f. version; translation from a foreign language to one's own language

vert a. green; unripe; tart; fresh; lively, young, active; langue –e f. slang

vert-de-gris m. verdigris

ver-de-grisé a. covered with verdigris

vertébral a. vertebral

vertèbre f. vertebra

vertébré a. & m. vertebrate

vertical a. vertical; –e f. vertical line

verticalité f. verticalness

verticille m. whorl

verticillé a. in a whorl

vertige m. dizziness, giddiness

vertigineux a. dizzy, giddy

vertigo m. staggers (horses); whim, caprice

vertu f. virtue

vertueux a. virtuous

vertugadin m. farthingale

verve f. zest, life, spirit

verveine f. verbena

vervelle f. band, leg band on birds

verveux a. lively, spirited

vésanie f. insanity

vésical a. vesical

vésicant a. blistering, blister-forming

vésicatoire a. blistering, vesicatory

vésicule f. vesicle; bladder

vespasienne f. street urinal

vespéral a. evening

vesse-de-loup m. puffball mushroom

vessie f. bladder

vestale f. vestal virgin

veste f. jacket

vestaire m. checkroom

vestibule m. vestibule, entrance hall

vestimentaire a. clothing

veston m. suit coat; — intérieur smoking jacket

Vésuve m. Vesuvius

vêtement m. article of clothing

vétéran a. veteran

vétérinaire m. veterinarian; — a. veterinary

vétille f. trifle

vétilleux a. picayune, interested in trifles

vêtir vt. to clothe; se — to get dressed

vêture f. investiture, taking the habit, taking the veil

vétuste a. old, worn

vétusté f. oldness, age, deterioration

veuf m. widower

veule a. weak; awkward

veulerie f. weakness, lack of energy

veuvage m. widowhood

veuve f. widow

vexation f. vexation

vexatoire, vexatéure a. vexing

vexer vt. to vex

viabilité f. viability, ability to live; good condition

viable a. viable, durable

viaduc m. viaduct

viager a. lifelong; rente –ère life annuity

viande f. meat, flesh

vibrant a. vibrating; vibrant

vibration f. vibration

vibratoire a. vibratory

vibrer vi. to vibrate

vibreur m. vibrator

vibrion m. microbe

vicaire m. curate; vicar

vice m. vice; fault, imperfection

vice-amiral m. vice-admiral

vice-chancelier m. vice chancellor

vice-consul m. vice-consul

vice-consulat m. vice-consulate; vice-consulship

vicennal a. of 20 years' duration

vice-présidence f. vice-presidency

vice-président m. vice-president

vice-recteur m. university vice-president

vice-roi m. viceroy

vice-versa adv. vice versa

vichy m. Vichy water; toile de — cotton or cotton-rayon cloth

viciable a. corruptible; spoilable

viciateur a. corrupting

viciation f. spoiling; corruption; fouling

vicier vt. to vitiate, invalidate; corrupt; spoil

vicieux a. vicious; defective

vicinal a. local; parochial

vicinalité f. local character

vicissitude f. vicissitude

vicomte m. viscount; –sse f. vicountess

victime f. victim

victoire *f.* victory
victorien *a.* Victorian
victorieux *a.* victorious
victuailles *f. pl.* victuals
vidage *m.* emptying
vidange *m.* emptying; en — being emptied, opened
vidanger *vt.* to empty
vide *m.* void, vacuum, emptiness; — *a.* empty, void, vacant
vide-bouteille *m.* roadhouse
vide-cave *m.* cellar pump, sump pump
vide-citron *m.* fruit reamer
vide-gousset *m.* pickpocket
videlle *f.* darn; fruit pitter; pastry cutter
vide-ordures *m.* incinerator chute
vide-poches *m.* nightstand
vide-pomme *m.* apple corer
vider *vt.* to empty; leave; clean, dress; finish, settle; core; bore; gut; exhaust
vidimer *vt.* to certify as exact
vidoir *m.* dump
viduité *f.* widowhood
vie *f.* life, lifetime; à — for life
vieillard *m.* old man
vieille *f.* old woman
vieilleries *f. pl.* old things, old ideas
vieillesse *f.* old age
vieillir *vt. & vi.* to age; grow old
vieillot *a.* oldish, old-looking
vièle *f.* viol
vielle *f.* hurdy-gurdy
vieller *vi.* to play the hurdy-gurdy
Vienne *f.* Vienna
Viennois *m. & a.* Viennese; -e *f.* filled doughnut
vierge *f. & a.* virgin
vieux (vieil, vieille) *a.* old
vif *a.* live, alive, living; quick, lively
vif-argent *m.* quicksilver
vigie *f.* (naut.) lookout; watch tower
vigilamment *adv.* vigilant
vigilance *f.* vigilance
vigile *f.* vigil, eve; — *m.* night watchman
vigne *f.* vine, vineyard
vigneron *m.* vine grower, vintner
vignette *f.* engraving, cut; vignette; poster stamp, seal
vignoble *m.* vineyard, vines
vigoureux *a.* vigorous, sharp
vigogne *f.* vicuna
vigueur *f.* vigor, power
vil *a.* vile; mean; low, paltry
vilain *a.* villanous; ugly; base
vilebrequin *m.* brace, drill; cam shaft
vilenie *f.* vileness, low act, dastardly deed
vilipender *vt.* to vilify, decry, scorn
villa *f.* summer house, country house
village *m.* village
villageois *m.* villager
villanelle *f.* kind of pastoral poetry; kind of dance
ville *f.* town, city; en — downtown; diner en — to dine out
villégiateur *m.* vacationer
villégiature *f.* vacation
villégiaturer *vi.* to vacation
villeux *a.* hairy
villosité *f.* villosity; roughness; hairiness
vin *m.* wine

vinaigre *m.* vinegar
vinaigrer *vt.* to flavor with *or* add vinegar
vinaigrerie *f.* vinegar works
vinaigrette *f.* oil and vinegar sauce
vinaigrier *m.* vinegar cruet; vinegar manufacturer; vinegar seller
vinasse *f.* residue after distillation; poor wine
vindicatif *a.* vindicative
vindicte *f.* prosecution
viner *vt.* to fortify wine
vineux *a.* wine-producing; tasting of wine, winey; strong with alcohol
vingt *a.* twenty; -ième *m. & a.* twentieth
vingtaine *f.* score, about twenty
vinicole *a.* wine-growing
viniculture *f.* wine making; vine growing
vinification *f.* wine-making
vinylique *a.* vinyl
viol *m.* rape
violacé *a.* purplish
violateur *m.* violator
violation *f.* violation, breach
violâtre *a.* purplish
viole *f.* viol; viola
violemment *adv.* violently
violence *f.* violence
violenter *vt.* to force, do violence to
violer *vt.* to violate, rape
violet *a.* purple; — te *f.* violet (flower)
violine *f.* red violet, red purple; violine
violon *m.* violin, violinist; (coll.) jail
violoncelle *m.* cello; cellist
violoncelliste *m.* cellist
violoneux *m.* fiddler
violoniste *m. & f.* violinist
vipère *f.* viper
vipérin *a.* viperine
virage *m.* curve, turn; turning; (phot.) fixing; fixing-bath
virago *f.* virago, tomboy
viral *a.* virus
virement *m.* transfer; transfer payment
virer *vi.* to turn about; change; — de bord to tack, turn about; — *vt.* to transfer funds; (phot.) to fix
virevolte *f.* rapid movement back and forth
virevolter *vi.* to move back and forth
virginité *f.* virginity
virgule *f.* comma; point et — *m.* semicolon
viril *a.* virile
virilité *f.* virility
virole *f.* ferrule, ring
viroler *vt.* to attach a ferrule to
virtualité *f.* virtuality; potentiality
virtuel *a.* virtual; potential
virtuose *m. & f.* virtuoso
virtuosité *f.* virtuosity
virulence *f.* virulence
virulent *a.* virulent
vis *f.* screw; escalier à — circular staircase; pas de — thread of a screw
visa *m.* visa; certification, authentification
visage *m.* face
vis-à-vis *adv.* opposite; face to face
viscéral *a.* visceral
viscère *m.* viscera
viscose *f.* viscose
viscosité *f.* viscosity

visé *a.* certified

visée *f.* aim, end, design

viser *vt. & vi.* to aim, view; visa; certify; authenticate; — à to aim for

viseur *m.* aimer; viewer

visibilité *f.* visibility

visible *a.* visible, discernible, apparent, evident; at home, receiving visitors

visière *f.* visor

vision *f.* vision

visionnaire *a.* visionary

visionneuse *f.* slide viewer; film editor

visite *f.* visit; search; inspection; rendre — à to visit

visiter *vt.* to inspect; visit

vison *m.* mink

visqueux *a.* viscous

vissage *m.* screwing

visser *vt.* to screw

visserie *f.* nuts, bolts, and screws; manufacture of screws

visuel *a.* visual

vital *a.* vital

vitalisme *m.* vitalism

vitalité *f.* vitality

vitamine *f.* vitamin

vite *a. & adv.* quick(ly); fast

vitesse *f.* quickness, rapidity

viticole *a.* wine-producing, grape-growing

viticulteur *m.* grape grower

viticulture *f.* vine growing

vitrage *m.* glazing; windows

vitrail (*pl.* vitraux) *m.* stained glass window

vitre *f.* pane of glass, window

vitrer *vt.* to glaze; install windows in

vitrerie *f.* glazing, glass trade

vitreux *a.* vitrous, glassy, glasslike

vitrier *m.* glazier, glassworker

vitrifiable *a.* vitrifiable

vitrifier *vt.* to vitrify

vitrine *f.* store window

vitriol *m.* vitriol, sulphuric acid

vitrioler *vt.* to throw acid in the face of

vitupération *f.* vituperation

vitupérer *vt.* to vituperate

vivace *a.* long-lived, perennial

vivacité *f.* vivacity, vivaciousness; -s *pl.* outbursts

vivandier *m.* clerk, seller in an army canteen

vivant *a.* lively; alive; lifelike; langue -e modern language; — *m.* living person; — *pl.* the living

vivat *m.* cheer; —! *interj.* bravo!

vivement *adv.* bridly, vigorously, quickly

viveur *m.* playboy, rake

vivier *m.* fishpond

vivifiant *a.* animating

vivifier *vt.* to animate, recreate, make come alive

vivipare *a.* viviparous

vivisection *f.* vivisection

vivoter *vi.* to live from hand to mouth, eke out one's existence

vivre *m.* food; -s *pl.* provisions, food

vivre *vi.* to live

vlan! *interj.* bang!, slam!

vocable *m.* word, term

vocabulaire *m.* vocabulary; vocabulary list

vocalisation *f.* vocalization; vocalizing; vocal exercise

vocaliser *vi.* to do a vocal exercise

vocalisme *m.* vowel system

vocatif *m.* vocative case

vocation *f.* vocation

vocifération *f.* vociferation

vociférer *vi.* to vociferate

vœu *m.* vow, wish

vogue *f.* fashion, popularity

voguer *vi.* to sail, wander

voici *adv.* here is, here are

voie *f.* way, means, road; wheelbase; (anat.) canal; trail; -s de fait assault and battery; être en — de to be on the way to, be in the act of; — ferrée railroad

voilà *adv.* there is, there are

voile *m.* veil; — *f.* sail

voiler *vt.* to veil; se — to become bent, bow

voilette *f.* small veil on a hat

voilier *m.* sailing ship

voilure *f.* sails, canvas; (avi.) wings; warping

voir *vt. & vi.* to see

voire *adv.* indeed, verily, even

voirie *f.* highway department; dump, sewer

voisin *m.* neighbor; — *a.* neighboring

voisinage *m.* neighborhood, vicinity

voisiner *vi.* to visit with the neighbors

voiturage *m.* trucking, hauling

voiture *f.* carriage, coach; automobile

voiturer *vt.* to haul, cart

voiturier *m.* hauler

voix *f.* voice; vote; à haute — loudly; à — basse in a whisper

vol *m.* flight; robbery, theft; à — d'oiseau bird's-eye view

volage *a.* flighty, fickle

volaille *f.* poultry

volailler *m.* poultry store, poultry dealer; poultry yard

volant *a.* flying, winged; pont — *m.* movable bridge; table -e *f.* end table, light table; — *m.* steering wheel; balance wheel; flounce, ruffle; shuttlecock; badminton

volatil *a.* volatile

volatile *m.* bird; winged creature

volatilisation *f.* volatilization

volatiliser *vt.* to volatilize; se — (coll.) to disappear, get out

vol-au-vent *m.* filled patty shell (creamed meat or fish)

volcan *m.* volcano

volcanique *a.* volcanic

volcaniser *vt.* to vulcanize

vole *f.* grand slam; faire la — to take all the tricks (at cards)

volée *f.* flight of birds, flying; volley; class, rank; à la — in flight

voler *vi. & vi.* to rob, steal; fly

volerie *f.* petty theft

volet *m.* shutter

voleter *vi.* to fly about

voleur *m.* thief, robber

volière *f.* bird cage, aviary

volige f. scantling, board
volley-ball m. volley ball
volleyeur m. volley ball player
volontaire a. voluntary; — m. volunteer
volontariat m. (mil.) enlistment (as contrasted to the draft)
volonté f. will; willingness; payable à — payable at will
volontiers adv. willingly, gladly
voltaïque a. voltaic
voltaire m. high-backed chair
volte-face f. about face
voltiger vi. to fly about
voltigeur m. trapeze or equestrian performer
voltmètre m. voltmeter
volubile a. volubilate, spiraling
volubilité f. volubility, fluency
volumineux a. voluminous
volupté f. voluptuousness
voluptueux a. voluptuous
volute f. spiral, curl, scroll
vomir vt. & vi. to vomit
vomissement m. vomiting; vomit
vomitif a. vomitive; — m. emetic
vorace a. voracious, ravenous
voracité f. voraciousness
vos a. pl. your
votation f. voting
votif a. votive
votre a. your
vôtre pron., le —, la — yours
vouer vt. to devote; consecrate; pledge
vouloir vt. & vi. to wish; intend; — bien to be willing; — dire to mean; en — à to hold a grudge against; — m. will
voulu a. intentional; desired
vous pron. you
voussoir, vousseau m. stone of an arch, wedge-shaped stone
voussure f. curve of an arch, a vault
voûte f. vault, arched roof
voûté a. vaulted; crooked; round-shouldered
voûter vt. to vault, cover with vaulting; bend
voyage m. trip, journey, tour; — à forfait prepaid tour
voyager vi. to travel; migrate (birds)
voyageur m. traveller; passenger; commis — m. traveling salesman
voyant a. showy, gaudy; — m. sight, target; — m. seer
voyelle f. vowel
voyou m. scum, cad, hoodlum (U.S. coll.)
vrac, en — adv. in disorder; unpacked
vrai a. true, real
vraisemblable a. likely, probable
vraisemblance f. verisimilitude
vrille f. tendril of a vine; gimlet
vriller vt. to pierce with a gimlet; — vi. ascend in spiral; twist
vrombir vi. to rumble
vrombissement m. rumble
vu a. seen; — prep. in view of, considering; — que conj. seeing, considering that
vue f. sight; view
vulcanisation f. vulcanization
vulcaniser vt. to vulcanize

vulcanite f. vulcanite
vulgaire a. common
vulgarisateur a. popularizing; — m. popularizer
vulgarisation f. popularizing; ouvrage de — m. work for popular consumption
vulgariser vt. to popularize
vulgarité f. vulgarity
vulnérable a. vulnerable
vulnéraire a. vulnerary
vultueux a. flushed of face
vulve f. vulva

W

wagon m. railway car
wagon-bar m. club car
wagon-lit m. sleeping car
wagon-poste m. mail car
wagon-réservoir m. tank car
wagon-restaurant m. dining car
wagon-salon m. parlor car
wagonnet m. cart, handcart
warrant m. warrant, guarantee
warranter vt. to warrant
wattman m. motorman of a streetcar
whisky m. whiskey

X

xénophobie f. xenophobia
xérès m. sherry
xylographie f. wood engraving
xylophone m. xylophone

Y

y adv. there, here; il — a there is, there are; vous — êtes you are right, that's it; — pron. to it, to them
yachting m. yachting
yack m. yak
yaourt, yogourt m. yoghurt
yeuse f. ilex, holly oak
yeux m. pl. eyes
yole f. yawl
Yougoslave m. & f. & a. Yugoslavian
Yougoslavie f. Yugoslavia
youyou m. sampan, small boat

Z

zazou m. bobby-soxer, teen-ager
zèbre m. zebra
zébu m. zebu
zélateur a. zealous
zèle m. zeal, warmth; avec — zealously
zélé a. zealous
zénith m. zenith
zéro m. cipher, nought, zero
zeste m. citrous peel; -r vt. to peel
zézaiement m. lisp
zézayer vt. & vi. to lisp
zibeline f. sable; sable fur
zigzag m. zigzag; — m. & a. (coll.) drunk
zigzaguer vi. to zigzag
zinc m. zinc; (coll.) bar, counter
zinguer vt. to zinc-plate
zingueur m. zinc worker

zinnia *m.* zinnia
zinzolin *m.* red-violet
zircon *m.* sircon
zodiaque *m.* zodiac
zona *f.* (med.) shingles
zonier *a.* of the frontier
zoologie *f.* zoology
zoologique *a.* zoological; parc — zoo
zoologiste *m.* zoologist
zostère *f.* seaweed
zouave *m.* North African trooper
zut! *interj.* curses!

English-French

A

a, an *art.* un, une
Aachen *n.* Aix-la-Chapelle
aback, to be taken — être surpris
abandon *vt.* abandonner; to — oneself to s'abandonner à; –ed *a.* dissolu; –ment *n.* abandon *m.*
abase *vt.* avilir; –ment *n.* avilissement, abaissement *m.*
abate *vi.* diminuer, se calmer, s'apaiser; baisser; –ment *n.* diminution *f.*
abbess *n.* abbesse *f.*
abbey *n.* abbaye *f.*
abbot *n.* abbé *m.*
abbreviate *vt.* abréger
abbreviation *n.* abréviation *f.*
ABC *n.* abc *m.*; abécédaire *m.*
abdicate *vt. & vi.* abdiquer
abdication *n.* abdication, renonciation *f.*
abdomen *n.* abdomen, bas-ventre *m.*
abduct *vt.* enlever; –ion *n.* enlèvement *m.*; –or *n.* ravisseur *m.*
aberration *n.* égarement *m.*, aberration *f.*
abet *vt.* encourager; soutenir
abeyance *n.* attente *f.*; in — en suspens
abhor *vt.* abhorrer; –rence *n.* horreur *f.*; –rent *a.* répugnant
abide *vi.* demeurer, rester; — *vt.* supporter; — by respecter
abiding *a.* permanent, constant
ability *n.* habileté, capacité *f.*; to the best of one's — de son mieux
abject *a.* bas, abject, vil; –ion *n.* bassesse, abjection *f.*
abjuration *n.* abjuration *f.*
abjure *vt.* abjurer
ablative *n.* ablatif *m.*
ablaze *a.* en flammes
able *a.* capable; to be — pouvoir; savoir; être à même de
able-bodied *a.* propre au service; en bonne santé
ablution *n.* ablution *f.*
ably *adv.* bien, habilement
abnegate *vt.* renier, renoncer à
abnegation *n.* abnégation *f.*, renonce-

ment *m.*
abnormal *a.* anormal; –ity *n.* anormalité *f.*
aboard *adv.* à bord; to go — s'embarquer; to take — embarquer; all —! *interj.* à bord!; en voiture!
abode *a.* demeure, habitation *f.*; domicile *m.*
abolish *vt.* abolir
abolition *n.* abolissement *m.*, abolition *f.*; –ist *n.* abolitionniste, antiesclavagiste *m. & f.*
A-bomb *n.* bombe atomique *f.*
abominable *a.* abominable
abominate *vt.* avoir en abomination
abomination *n.* abomination *f.*
aboriginal *a.* aborigène
abort *vi.* avorter; –ion *n.* avortement *m.*; –ive *a.* avorté, manqué
abound *vi.* abonder; –ing *a.* abondant
about *adv.* çà et là; à peu près, environ; come — arriver; bring — causer; be — to être sur le point de; — *prep.* autour de, près de; parmi, par; vers; au sujet de; sur le point de
about-face *n.* volte-face *f.*
above *adv.* en haut, là-haut, plus haut; — *prep.* au-dessus de, plus haut que; — all surtout; over and — en outre
aboveboard *a.* franc, légitime
above-mentioned *a.* ledit, susdit
abrade *vt.* frotter, user en frottant
abrasion *n.* abrasion *f.*, frottement *m.*
abrasive *a.* abrasif, qui use en frottant; — *n.* émeri *m.*; abrasif *m.*
abreast *adv.* à côté l'un de l'autre; au courant; two — par deux
abridge *vt.* abréger
abridgment *n.* abrégé *m.*; résumé *m.*
abroad *adv.* à l'étranger; to get — se répandre
abrogate *vt.* abroger
abrogation *n.* abrogation, revocation *f.*
abrupt *a.* abrupte, précipité, brusque; –ness *n.* brusquerie *f.*; précipitation *f.*
abscess *n.* abcès *m.*

abscond *vi.* échapper, disparaître; –ing *n.* évasion, fuite *f.*

absence *n.* absence *f.*; leave of — congé *m.*

absent *a.* absent; — *vt.*, to — one's self s'absenter; –ee *n.* absent (de son poste) *m.*; –eeism *n.* absentéisme *m.*

absent-minded *a.* distrait; –ness *n.* distraction *f.*

absinth *n.* absinthe *f.*

absolute *a.* absolu; –ly *adv.* tout à fait; formellement; absolument

absolution *n.* absolution *f.*

absolve *vt.* absoudre; dégager

absorb *vt.* absorber; –ent *a. & n.* absorbant *m.*; –ent cotton coton hydrophile *m.*

abstain *vi.* s'abstenir; –er *n.* buveur d'eau *m.*

abstemious *a.* abstinent, sobre, modéré

abstention *n.* abstention, abstinence *f.*

abstinence *n.* abstinence, privation volontaire *f.*; day of — jour maigre *m.*

abstract *n.* résumé, sommaire *m.*; — *vt.* résumer, abréger; faire abstraction de; — *a.* abstrait; –ion *n.* abstraction *f.*

abstruse *a.* abstrus; –ness *n.* complexité *f.*

absurd *a.* absurde; –ity *n.* absurdité *f.*

abundance *n.* abondance *f.*

abundant *a.* abondant

abuse *n.* abus, outrage *m.*; — *vt.* abuser (de), tromper; injurier

abusive *a.* abusif, injurieux; –ness *n.* grossièreté *f.*; abus *m.*

abut *vi.* buter (contre); aboutir (à); –ment *n.* butée, culée *f.*

abysmal *a.* sans fond; profond

abyss *n.* abîme, gouffre *m.*

Abyssinia *n.* Abyssinie *f.*; –n *a. & n.* abyssinien *m.*

academic *a.* académique; universitaire

academy *n.* académie, école *f.*

accede *vt.* accéder

accelerate *vt.* accélérer; précipiter; — *vi.* s'accélérer

acceleration *n.* accélération *f.*

accelerator *n.* accélérateur *m.*

accent *vt.* accentuer, souligner, donner de l'emphase à; — *n.* accent, accent tonique *m.*; –uate *vt.* accentuer; –uation *n.* accentuation *f.*

accept *vt.* accepter; agréer; –able *a.* acceptable; –ance *n.* acceptation, réception *f.*; –ation *n.* acception, signification *f.*

access *n.* accès *m.*, entrée *f.*; –ible *a.* accessible, abordable; –ibility *n.* accessibilité *f.*; –ion *n.* avènement *m.*; addition *f.*; –ory *n. & a.* complice *m.*; accessoire *m.*

accident *n.* accident *m.*; by — par hasard; –al *a.* accidentel, fortuit; –ally *adv.* par hasard, fortuitement

acclaim *vt.* acclamer, applaudir; — *n.* acclamation, applaudissements *m. pl.*

acclamation *n.* acclamation *f.*

acclimate *vt.* acclimater

accommodate *vt.* accommoder, régler; pourvoir; loger; recevoir; obliger

accommodating *a.* accommodant, serviable, obligeant, complaisant

accommodation *n.* adaptation *f.*; accommodement *m.*; arrangement *m.*, convenance, commodité *f.*; logement *m.*

accompaniment *n.* accompagnement *m.*

accompany *vt.* accompagner

accomplice *n.* complice *m. & f.*

accomplish *vt.* accomplir, exécuter, achever; –ed *a.* accompli, habile, expert; –ment *n.* accomplissement, talent *m.*; — *pl.* connaissances *f. pl.*

accord *n.* accord *m.*, union *f.*; convention *f.*; consentement *m.*; of one's own — de son propre gré, de plein gré; with one accord d'un commun accord; — *vt.* accorder; –ance *n.* conformité *f.*; in –ance with selon; –ing *prep.*, –ing to d'après, selon; –ingly *adv.* conformément

accost *vt.* aborder, accoster

account *n.* compte, calcul *m.*; valeur, considération *f.*; importance *f.*; raison *f.*; rapport, récit *m.*; on — (com.) à valoir; on — of à cause de; on no — d'aucune façon; to take into — tenir compte de; to keep –s tenir des comptes; — book *n.* livre de comptes *m.*; — *vt.* compter, calculer; estimer; rendre compte de, rendre raison de, être responsable; –able *a.* responsable; –ant *n.* comptable *m.*; –ing *n.* comptabilité *f.*

accoutrement *n.* équipement *m.*; ornement *m.*

accredit *vt.* croire; accréditer; –ed *a.* approuvé, agréé

accrue *vi.* accroître; résulter

accumulate *vi.* s'accumuler; — *vt.* amasser

accumulation *n.* accumulation *f.*, entassement *m.*

accuracy *n.* exactitude, justesse *f.*

accurate *a.* exact, juste; –ly *adv.* exactement, avec justesse; –ness *n.* précision, justesse *f.*

accusation *n.* accusation *f.*

accusative *a.* accusatif *m.*

accuse *vt.* accuser; –d *n.* accusé *m.*; –r *n.* accusateur *m.*

accustom *vt.* accoutumer, habituer; to become –ed s'habituer, s'accoutumer; –ed *a.* accoutumé, habituel

ace *n.* as *m.*; expert *m.*; champion *m.*

acetate *n.* acétate *m.*

acetone *n.* acétone *f.*

acetylene *n.* acétylène *m.*

ache *n.* mal *m.*, douleur *f.*; — *vi.* faire mal, souffrir; my head –s j'ai mal à la tête

achievable *a.* réalisable

achieve *vt.* atteindre; achever, exécuter; –ment *n.* réalisation *f.*; fait, exploit *m.*

aching *n.* peine *f.*; — *a.* douloureux

acid *n. & a.* acide *m.*; — test épreuve déterminante *f.*; –ity *n.* acidité *f.*

acidulate *vt.* aciduler

acknowledge *vt.* reconnaître; avouer; — receipt accuser réception; –d *a.* reconnu

acknowledgment *n.* reconnaissance *f.*, aveu, *m.*; concession *f.*; accusé de réception m.

acme n. sommet m.; apogée f.; comble m.

acorn n. gland m.

acoustic a. acoustique; -s n. pl. acoustique f.

acquaint vt. informer, faire savoir; be -ed with connaître; become -ed with connaître, faire la connaissance de; -ance n. connaissance f.

acquiesce vi. acquiescer; -nce n. soumission f.; -nt a. soumis, consentant

acquire vt. acquérir, obtenir

acquisition n. acquisition f.

acquisitive a. capable d'acquérir; qui aime acquérir

acquit vt. acquitter, absoudre; -tal n. acquittement m.

acre n. acre f. (= 40.5 ares); arpent, demi-hectare m.

acreage n. superficie f., terrain, arpentage m.

acrid a. âcre; -ity, -ness n. âcreté f.

acrimonious a. acrimonieux

acrimony n. acrimonie f.

acrobat n. acrobate m.; -ic a. acrobatique; -ics n. acrobatie f.

across adv. de travers; — prep. à travers, au travers de; — the street de l'autre côté de la rue, en face; come — rencontrer; go — traverser, passer, franchir

act n. acte m., action f., fait, exploit m.; loi f.; be in the — of être en train de; put on an — faire semblant; Acts (eccl.) Actes des apôtres n. pl.; — vi. agir, opérer; faire; se comporter; — vt. jouer, représenter; — on suivre; agir d'après; -ing a. provisoire; intérimaire; -ing n. (theat.) jeu m.; -ing a. par intérim, gérant; -or n. acteur m.; -ress n. actrice f.

action n. action f., fait m.; bataille f.; procès m.; out of — hors de service; (mil.) hors de combat; take — agir

activate vt. activer; mettre en marche

active a. actif, agile; vif

activity n. activité, vivacité f.

actual a. réel, véritable, vrai; -ity n. réalité f.; -ly adv. réellement, véritablement

actuate vt. mettre en action; actionner; animer

acuity n. acuité f.

acumen n. finesse f.

acute a. aigu, pointu; subtil; fin; intense; -ness n. aiguité f.; acuité f.; finesse f.; perspicacité f.

A.D. (Anno Domini) de l'ère chrétienne

adage n. adage, proverbe m.

adamant a. inflexible

adapt vt. adapter, accommoder; -able a. adaptable, applicable; -ability n. qualité de pouvoir s'adapter f.; -ation n. adaptation f.

add vt. ajouter, joindre; to — up additionner; se résumer; -ing machine n. machine à calculer f.

adder n. vipère f.

addict vt. adonner, vouer; — n. personne adonnée à (un narcotique); -ion n. manie, disposition f., penchant m.

addition n. addition f., accroissement m.; in — en outre, en sus; -al a. additionnel, supplémentaire; de plus

addled a. fou; gâté

address n. adresse f.; allocution f., discours m.; plaidoyer m.; dextérité, habileté f.; — book carnet d'adresses m.; — vt. adresser; parler à; -ee n. destinataire m. & f.

addressograph n. machine à adresser (les lettres)

adenoids n. pl. adénoïdes m. pl.

adept a. habile; adepte; -ness n. habileté f.

adequacy n. suffisance f.

adequate a. suffisant; -ness n. suffisance f.

adhere vi. adhérer, s'attacher; -nce n. adhésion f.; -nt n. partisan m.

adhesion n. adhérence, adhésion f.

adhesive a. adhérent; collant; — n. colle f.; timbre-poste m.; — tape n. sparadrap m.; -ness n. adhésion f.

ad infinitum adv. à l'infini

adipose a. adipeux

adjacent a. adjacent, voisin, contigu

adjective n. & a. adjectif m.

adjoin vt. être contigu à, avoisiner; donner sur; -ing a. contigu

adjourn vt. ajourner, remettre; lever, clore (une séance); -ment n. ajournement m.; suspension f.

adjudicate vt. adjuger

adjudge vt. adjuger, condamner

adjunct n. accessoire m., appartenance f. adjoint m.

adjust vt. ajuster, arranger, régler; corriger; mettre à point; -able a. réglable; -ment n. règlement m.; réglage m.; adjustage m.; correction f.

adjutant n. adjudant major m.; — general général chef des archives militaires m.

ad-lib vi. & vt. improviser

administer, administrate vt. administrer, gouverner, gérer

administration n. administration f., gouvernement m.

administrative a. administratif

administrator n. administrateur m.

admiral n. amiral m.; rear — contre-amiral m.; -ty n. ministère de la marine m.

admire vt. admirer; -r n. admirateur m.

admiring a. admiratif

admission n. admission, réception f.; confession f., aveu m.; — charge entrée f., tarif m.

admit vt. admettre; permettre; avouer; reconnaître; laisser entrer; -tance entrée f.; no -tance entrée interdite; -ted a. avoué, reconnu; -tedly adv. reconnu comme; de son propre aveu

admonish vt. exhorter; admonester

admonition n. exhortation f.; admonestation f.

ado n. bruit m., cérémonies f. pl.; difficulté, peine f.

adobe n. terre cuite f.

adolescent a. & a. adolescent m. & a.

adopt vt. adopter; -ed a. adoptif, d'adoption; -ion n. adoption f.; -ive a.

adoptif, d'adoption

adorable *a.* adorable

adoration *n.* adoration *f.*

adore *vt.* adorer; —r *n.* adorateur *m.*; soupirant *m.*

adorn *vt.* orner, décorer; parer; embellir; —ment *n.* ornement *m.*; ornementation *f.*; parure *f.*

adrenalin *n.* adrénaline *f.*

Adriatic Sea *n.* Mer Adriatique *f.*

adrift *adv.* à la dérive

adroit *a.* adroit; habile; —ness *n.* adresse, dextérité *f.*

adulate *vt.* aduler

adulation *n.* adulation *f.*

adulatory *a.* adulateur

adult *n. & a.* adulte *m. & f.*

adulterate *vt.* adultérer; couper; falsifier, corrompre

adulteration *n.* falsification *f.*; adultération *f.*

adulterer, adulteress *n.* adultère *m. & f.*

adultery *n.* adultère *m.*

advance *n.* avance *f.*, avancement *m.*, approche *f.*; progrès *m.*; — guard avant-garde *f.*; in — d'avance, préalablement; — *vt.* avancer; faire avancer, pousser; approcher; — *vi.* s'avancer; —d *a.* avancé; —ment *n.* avancement *m.*

advantage *n.* avantage *m.*, supériorité *f.*; to take — of profiter de; abuser de; turn to one's — mettre à profit; —ous *a.* avantageux; profitable

advent *n.* venue *f.*, avènement *m.*; Avent *m.*

adventure *n.* aventure *f.*, accident, hasard *m.*; — *vt.* risquer; —r *n.* aventurier *m.*; —some *a.* aventureux

adventurous *a.* aventureux

adverb *n.* adverbe *m.*; —ial *a.* adverbial

adversary *n.* adversaire *m.*

adverse *a.* adverse, contraire; défavorable; —ly *adv.* au contraire; d'une façon défavorable

adversity *n.* adversité *f.*

advertise *vt.* annoncer; — *vi.* faire de la publicité; —ment *n.* annonce

advertising *n.* publicité *f.*; réclame *f.*; annonces *f. pl.*

advice *n.* conseil *m.*; avis *m.*; piece of — conseil *m.*; on the — of sur l'avis de; take someone's — suivre le conseil de quelqu'un

advisability *n.* convenance, opportunité *f.*

advisable *a.* prudent, judicieux; convenable; opportun

advise *vt. & vi.* conseiller; — against déconseiller; —r, advisor *n.* conseiller *m.*

advisory *a.* consultatif

advocacy *n.* appui *m.*; soutien *m.*

advocate *n.* défenseur *m.*; avocat *m.*; — *vt.* soutenir; défendre

Aegean Sea *n.* Mer Egée *f.*

aegis *n.* égide *f.*

aeon *n.* éternité *f.*; éon *m.*

aerate *vt.* aérer; gazéifier

aeration *n.* aération *f.*

aerial *a.* aérien; — *n.* antenne *f.*

aerodynamics *n. pl.* aérodynamique *f.*

aeronaut *n.* aéronaute *m.*; —ics *n. pl.*

aéronautique *f.*

aesthetic *a.* esthétique; —s *n.* esthétique *f.*

afar *adv.* loin; from — de loin

affability *n.* affabilité *f.*

affable *a.* affable, gracieux

affair *n.* affaire *f.*; love — liaison *f.*; foreign —s affaires étrangères *f. pl.*

affect *vt.* affecter; émouvoir, toucher; feindre; —ation *n.* affectation *f.*; —ed *a.* affecté; —ing *a.* touchant

affection *n.* affection *f.*; tendresse *f.*; —ate *a.* affectueux, tendre; affectionné

afferent *a.* afférent

affiance *vt.* fiancer

affidavit *n.* déclaration *f.*, affidavit *m.*

affiliate *vt.* affilier

affiliation *n.* affiliation *f.*; relation *f.*

affinity *n.* affinité *f.*; rapport *m.*

affirm *vt.* affirmer; —ation *n.* affirmation *f.*; —ative *n.* affirmative *f.*; —ative *a.* affirmatif

affix *vt.* fixer, apposer, attacher

afflict *vt.* affliger; —ion *n.* affliction *f.*

affluence *n.* affluence, opulence *f.*; abondance *f.*

affluent *a.* abondant, riche; — *n.* affluent *m.*

afford *vt.* pouvoir se payer, se permettre; fournir

affront *n.* affront *m.*, insulte *f.*; — *vt.* affronter; insulter

afghan *n.* couverture *f.* (tricotée *or* au crochet)

Afghanistan *n.* Afghanistan *m.*

afield *adv.* au champ; au loin; far —très loin

afire, aflame *adv.* en flammes, en feu

afloat *adv.* à flot, flottant

afoot *adv.* à pied, sur pied, en train

aforementioned, aforesaid *a.* précité, susdit

aforethought *a.* prémédité

afoul *adv.* contre; dans les mains

afraid *a.* effrayé; to be — avoir peur

Africa *n.* Afrique *f.*; —n *a. & n.* africain *m.*; North — *n.* Afrique du Nord *f.*; North —n *n. & a.* Nord-Africain *m.*

aft *adv.* à l'arrière

after *adv.* plus tard; derrière; — *prep.* après; derrière; à la suite de; d'après; à la poursuite de; — all après tout; enfin; be — chercher; day — tomorrow après-demain; take — tenir de; time — time bien des fois; — *conj.* après que; — *a.* arrière, d'arrière; futur, antérieur

afterbirth *n.* arrière-faix, délivre *m.*

aftereffect *n.* résultat *m.*; suite *f.*; répercussion *f.*; contre-coup *m.*

afterglow *n.* lueur (qui subsiste) *f.*

afterlife *n.* vie future *f.*

aftermath *n.* regain *m.*; conséquences, suites *f. pl.*

afternoon *n.* après-midi *m. & f.*

aftertaste *n.* arrière-goût *m.*

afterthought *n.* réflexion après coup *f.*

afterwards *adv.* après

again *adv.* encore, de nouveau; — and — sans cesse; now and — de temps en temps, de temps à autre; once —

encore une fois; then — d'autre part

against *prep.* contre; vers; sur; — the grain à contre-poil; — the will à contre-cœur; come up — se heurter contre; as — comparé à

agape *adv.* bouche bée

agar-agar n. gélase *f.*

agate n. agate *f.*; (print.) corps 5.5 m.

age n. âge m.; génération *f.*; vieillesse *f.*; under — a. mineur; of — majeur; over — a. trop vieux, périmé; to be ten years of — avoir dix ans; — *vi.* vieillir; -d a. âgé; middle —d a. d'un certain âge

agency n. agence *f.*; intermédiaire m. & *f.*; entremise *f.*; action *f.*

agenda n. ordre du jour, programme m.

agent n. agent m.

agglomeration n. agglomération *f.*

agglutination n. agglutination *f.*

aggrandizement n. agrandissement m.

aggravate *vt.* aggraver; agacer

aggravating a. aggravant; agaçant

aggravation n. aggravation *f.*; provocation *f.*, agacement m.

aggregate n. masse *f.*, rassemblement m.; in the — dans l'ensemble; — a. collectif

aggregation n. rassemblement m., réunion *f.*

aggression n. agression *f.*

aggressive a. agressif; entreprenant; -ness n. caractère agressif m.; entreprise *f.*

aggressor n. agresseur m.

aghast a. stupéfait

agile a. agile, leste

agility n. agilité, légèreté *f.*

agitate *vt.* agiter, remuer; troubler; — *vi.* faire de l'agitation

agitation n. agitation *f.*, trouble m.

agitator n. agitateur m.; (pol.) fauteur m.

aglow a. incandescent, luisant

agnostic n. & a. agnostique m. & *f.*; -ism n. agnosticisme m.

ago *adv.* il y a; passé; long — il y a long-temps

agog a. en train; en émoi

agonize *vi.* agoniser; — *vt.* torturer; -ed a. d'angoisse

agonizing a. angoissant; atroce

agony n. agonie *f.*; angoisse *f.*

agrarian a. agraire

agree *vi.* convenir; se mettre d'accord; tomber d'accord; être d'accord; s'accorder; -d a. convenu; d'accord; -able a. agréable; consentant; be -able vouloir bien; -ment n. accord m.; acte m.; contrat m.; entente *f.*; be in -ment être d'accord

agricultural a. agricole

agriculture n. agriculture *f.*

agriculturist n. agriculteur m.

agronomy n. agronomie *f.*

aground *adv.* à la côte; to run — s'échouer

ague n. fièvre (intermittente) *f.*

ahead *adv.* en avant; get — réussir; go — continuer, persévérer; aller en avant; straight — tout droit

aid n. aide, assistance *f.*, secours m.; aide m.; — *vt.* aider, assister, secourir

ail *vt.* chagriner, causer de la peine; what —s you? qu'avez-vous?; -ing a. souffrant; -ment n. maladie *f.*, mal m.

aileron n. aileron m.

aim n. visée *f.*; but m.; objet, dessein m.; -less a. sans but; — *vt.* viser, diriger; mettre en joue; (cannon) pointer

air n. air m.; chant m.; (of a person) mine *f.*; apparence *f.*, aspect m.; on the — (radio) en train d'être radio-diffusé; à la radio; give oneself -s, put on -s se donner des airs; in the open — en plein air. à la belle étoile; — base terrain d'aviation m.; — blast coup de vent m.; — brake frein à air comprimé m.; — chamber chambre à air *f.*; — corps aviation *f.*; — cushion matelas pneumatique m.; — force aviation *f.* — freight frêt aérien; m. — gun fusil à air comprimé m.; — hole évent, soupirial m.; — letter aérogramme m.; — passage route aérienne *f.*; passage aérien m.; — pocket trou d'air m.; — power forces aériennes *f.* pl.; — pressure pression atmosphérique *f.*; — pump pompe à air *f.*; — raid raid (aérien) m.; — shaft puits d'aérage m.; — valve soupape à air *f.*; — *vt.* aérer; exhiber, montrer; -ily *adv.* légèrement; -iness n. abondance d'air et d'espace dans une pièce *f.*; légèreté *f.*; -ing n. promenade *f.*; aération *f.*; aérage m.; ventilation *f.*; -y a. aéré; exposé à l'air; léger, chimérique

air-borne a. porté par les airs; — troops parachutistes m. pl.

airbrake n. aérofrein m.

airbrush n. pinceau pneumatique m.

air-condition *vt.* climatiser; -ing n. climatisation *f.*

air-cooled a. refroidi par air

aircraft n. avion m.; — carrier n. porte-avions m.

airfield n. terrain d'aviation m.; aérodrome m.

airlift n. pont aérien m.

airline n. ligne aérienne *f.*; -r n. avion pour passagers m.

airmail n. poste aérienne *f.*; — *adv.* & a. par avion

airman n. aviateur; soldat de l'air m.

airplane n. avion m.

airport n. aéroport, aérodrome m.

airship n. dirigeable m.

airstrip n. petit aérodrome m.; piste de roulement *f.*

air terminal n. aérogare *f.*

airtight a. étanche, hermétique

airway n. route aérienne *f.*; ligne aérienne *f.*

aisle n. passage m.

ajar a. entr'ouvert

akimbo *adv.* les mains sur les hanches

akin a. parent; allié

alabaster n. albâtre m.

alacrity n. vivacité, gaieté *f.*; empressement m.

à la mode a. (style) à la mode; (food) servi avec une glace

alarm n. alarme, épouvante f.; réveil m.;
alerte f.; — signal, avertisseur m.;
sound an — sonner l'alarme; — bell
n. tocsin m.; — clock n. réveille-matin,
réveil m.; — vt. alarmer; —ing a. inquiétant; —ist n. alarmiste m.

Albania n. Albanie f.

albatross n. albatros m.

albeit adv. quoique, bien que

albino n. albinos m.

album n. album m.

albumen n. (egg) albumine f.; (bot.)
albumen m.

alchemist n. alchimiste m.

alchemy n. alchimie f.

alcohol n. alcool m.; —ic n. & a. alcoolique
m. & f.; —ism n. alcoolisme m.

alcove n. alcôve f.; niche f.

alderman n. conseiller municipal m.

alert a. alerte, éveillé; vif; — n. alerte
f.; on the — en éveil; sur le qui-vive;
— vt. avertir, prévenir; alerter; —ness
n. état d'éveil m., vigilance f.; vivacité
f.

Aleutian Islands n. pl. Aléoutiennes f. pl.

Alexandria n. Alexandrie f.

alga (algae) n. (pl.) algue f.

algebra n. algèbre m.; —ic a. algébrique

Algeria n. Algérie f.; —n a. & n. algérien m.

alias n. faux nom m.; — adv. autrement
dit

alien n. & a. étranger m. & a.; —ate vt.
aliéner; —ist n. médecin aliéniste m.

alight vi. descendre, mettre pied à terre;
(birds) s'abattre; — a. allumé, illuminé

align vt. aligner; —ment n. alignement m.

alike a. semblable; pareil; — adv. également, de même

alimentary a. alimentaire

alimony n. pension alimentaire f.

alive a. vivant; gai; en vie; be — with
foisonner de, fourmiller de; grouiller de;
dead or — mort ou vif

alkali n. alcali m.; —ne a. alcalin; —ze vt.
alcaliser

alkaloid n. alcaloïde m.

all n. tout m.; — a. tout, tous m. pl.; —
adv. tout; entièrement; — aboard! en
voiture!; — along tout le temps; — but
presque; — clear (mil.) fin d'alerte; il
n'y a personne; — day toute la journée;
— in (coll.) fatigué, épuisé; — in
somme toute; — of a sudden tout à
coup; — of us nous tous; — over (adv.)
partout; (coll.) fini; — right (adv.)
bien, pas mal; eh bien; alors; honnête;
— set tout prêt; — the better tant
mieux; — the same tout de même;
— together tous ensemble; above —
surtout; at — hours à toute heure; by
— means certainement; mais oui; not
at — pas du tout, point du tout; on —
fours à quatre pattes; once and for —
une fois pour toutes; one — (sports)
un à un; one and — tout le monde

allay vt. apaiser, calmer; modérer, tempérer; dissiper

allegation n. allégation f.

allege vt. alléguer; citer; —d a. allégué;
présumé

allegiance n. obéissance f.; fidélité f.

allegoric(al) a. allégorique

allegory n. allégorie f.

allergic a. allergique

allergy n. allergie f.

alleviate vt. alléger; soulager; apaiser

alleviation n. soulagement m.

alley n. ruelle f.; blind — cul-de-sac m.

alliance n. alliance f.; parenté f.

allied a. allié; parent; voisin

alligator n. alligator m.; — pear poire
d'avocat f.

alliteration n. allitération f.

all-night a. ouverte tout la nuit; de toute
la nuit

allocate vt. attribuer, distribuer; allouer

allocation n. (com.) allocation f.; attribution f.

allot vt. accorder, attribuer; —ment n.
allocation f.; part, portion f.; (mil.)
délégation de solde f.

allow vt. permettre; laisser; autoriser;
allouer; avouer; — for avoir égard à;
— oneself se permettre; —able a.
permis; —ance n. argent de poche m.;
allocation f.; indulgence f.; part f.;
make —ances for faire la part de;
tenir compte de; —ing for vu, eu
égard à

alloy n. alliage m.; — vt. allier

all-powerful a. tout-puissant

all-purpose a. à tout faire; universel

all-round a. universel, varié, complet

All Saints' Day n. la Toussaint f.

allspice n. toute épice f.; piment m.

all-time a. de tous les temps

allude vi. faire allusion

allure vt. séduire, attirer

alluring a. attrayant, séduisant

allusion n. allusion f.

allusive a. figuré, fait par allusion

alluvial a. alluvien

ally n. allié m.; — vt. allier

almanac n. almanach m.

almighty a. tout-puissant

almond n. amande f.; — tree n. amandier
m.

almost adv. presque; à peu près

alms n. pl. aumône, charité f.

aloft adv. en haut, en l'air

alone a. seul; let me —! laissez-moi tranquille!; — adv. seulement

along adv. de compagnie; avec; en avant;
— prep. le long de; get — with s'ac-
comoder avec; s'entendre; go — suivre,
longer; go — with accompagner

alongside prep. le long de; — adv. bord à
bord; come — aborder

aloof a. à l'écart, distant; —ness réserve
f.; désintéressement m.

aloud adv. à haute voix

alpaca n. (zool.) alpaca m.; (material)
alpaga m.

alphabet n. alphabet m.; —ical a. alphabétique; —ize vt. alphabétiser

alpine a. alpin; alpestre

Alps n. Alpes f. pl.

already adv. déjà

Alsace n. Alsace f.

Alsatian a. & n. alsacien m.

also *adv.* aussi, également, encore

altar *n.* autel *m.*

alter *vt.* altérer; changer; modifier; — *vi.* s'altérer; changer; **-ation** *n.* changement *m.*; altération *f.*; modification *f.*

alternate *a.* alternatif, alternant, alterné; (rhyme) croisé; — *n.* suppléant, remplaçant *m.*; **-ly** *adv.* tour à tour, alternativement; — *vi.* alterner; — *vt.* faire alterner

alternating *a.* alternant; — current courant alternatif *m.*

alternation *n.* alternation *f.*; alternance *f.*

alternative *n.* alternative *f.*, choix *m.*; — *a.* alternatif

although *conj.* quoique, bien que; encore que

altimeter *n.* altimètre *m.*

altitude *n.* élévation, hauteur *f.*; altitude *f.*

altogether *adv.* entièrement, tout à fait

altruism *n.* altruisme *m.*

altruist *n.* altruiste; **-ic** *a.* altruiste

alum *n.* alun *m.*

aluminum *n.* aluminium *m.*

alumnus *n.* ancien élève *m.*

always *adv.* toujours

A.M. (ante meridiem) du matin

amalgam *n.* amalgame *m.*; **-ate** *vt.* amalgamer; **-ation** *n.* almagamation, fusion, union *f.*

amass *vt.* amasser

amateur *n.* nonprofessionnel, amateur *m.*; **-ish** *a.* gauche, inexpérimenté

amatory *a.* amoureux, d'amour, sentimental

amaze *vt.* étonner, émerveiller; **-ment** *n.* étonnement *m.*

amazing *a.* étonnant

amazon *n.* amazone *f.*

ambassador *n.* ambassadeur *m.*; **-ship** *n.* ambassade *f.*

amber *n.* ambre *m.*

ambidextrous *a.* ambidextre

ambiguity *n.* ambiguïté *f.*

ambiguous *a.* ambigu; confus; équivoque; **-ness** *n.* ambiguïté *f.*

ambition *n.* ambition *f.*

ambitious *a.* ambitieux

amble *vi.* aller doucement; (horses) ambler; — *n.* amble *m.*

ambling *a.* à l'amble

ambrosia *n.* ambroisie *f.*

ambulance *n.* ambulance *f.*

ambulatory *a.* ambulatoire; ambulant

ambush *n.* embuscade *f.*; guet-apens *m.*; in — en embuscade, embusqué; à l'affût; — *vt.* embusquer

ameliorate *vt.* améliorer; — *vi.* s'améliorer

amelioration *n.* amélioration *f.*

amen *interj.* amen; (prayer books) ainsi soit-il

amenable *a.* docile, traitable; responsable

amend *vt.* amender, corriger; — *vi.* s'amender; se corriger; **-ment** *n.* amendement *m.*

amends *n.* *pl.* compensation *f.*, dédommagement *m.*; to make — faire amende honorable

amenity *n.* aménité *f.*; amenities civilités

f. *pl.*; commodités *f.* *pl.*

America *n.* Amérique *f.*; North — Amérique du Nord *f.*; South — Amérique du Sud *f.*; Central — Amérique Centrale *f.*; **-n** *a.* & *n.* américain *m.*; — plan (hotels) prix qui comprend chambre et trois repas *m.*, pension complète *f.*

Americanize *vt.* américaniser

amiability *n.* amabilité *f.*

amiable *a.* aimable; **-ness** *n.* amabilité *f.*

amicability *n.* cordialité, amabilité *f.*

amicable *a.* amical, bienveillant

amidships *adv.* par le travers

amid(st) *prep.* au milieu de, parmi

amiss *adv.* mal, en mal, mal à propos; take — prendre en mauvaise part

amity *n.* amitié *f.*

ammeter *n.* ampère-mètre *m.*

ammonia *n.* ammoniaque *f.*; — gas *n.* ammoniaque *m.*

ammunition *n.* cartouches *f.* *pl.*; munitions *f.* *pl.*

amnesia *n.* amnésie *f.*

amnesty *n.* amnistie *f.*; — *vt.* amnistier

amoeba *n.* amibe *f.*

among(st) *prep.* parmi, entre

amoral *a.* amoral

amorous *a.* amoureux

amorphous *a.* amorphe

amortization *n.* amortissement *m.*

amortize *vt.* amortir

amount *n.* montant, total *m.*; somme, quantité *f.*; — *vi.*, to — to s'élever à; revenir à; valoir

amour *n.* amourette *f.*; intrigue *f.*

amperage *n.* ampérage *m.*

ampere *n.* ampère *m.*

ampersand *n.* symbole typographique pour *et* *m.*

amphibian *n.* amphibian, amphibie *a.* amphibie

amphitheater *n.* amphithéâtre *m.*

ample *a.* ample, large; **-ness** *n.* ampleur, étendue *f.*

amplification *n.* amplification *f.*

amplifier *n.* amplificateur *m.*

amplify *vt.* amplifier, augmenter

amplitude *n.* largeur *f.*; étendue *f.*; amplitude *f.*

amply *adv.* amplement

amputate *vt.* amputer

amputation *n.* amputation *f.*

amputee *n.* amputé *m.*

amuck *adv.* comme un furieux

amulet *n.* amulette *f.*

amuse *vt.* amuser, divertir; — oneself s'amuser; **-ment** *n.* amusement *m.*; divertissement *m.*; **-ment park** fête foraine *f.*

amusing *a.* amusant; divertissant

an *art.* un, une

anachronism *n.* anachronisme *m.*

anachronistic *a.* anachronique

anaconda *n.* boa (de l'Amérique du Sud) *m.*

anal *a.* anal

analgesic *a.* & *n.* analgésique *m.*

analogical *a.* analogique

analogous *a.* analogue

analogy *n.* analogie *f.*

analysis *n.* analyse *f.*

analyst n. analyste m.

analytic(al) a. analytique

analyze vt. analyser

anarchist n. anarchiste m. & f.

anarchy n. anarchie f.

anathema n. anathème m.; -tize vt. anathémiser

anatomical a. anatomique

anatomist n. anatomiste m.

anatomy n. anatomie f.

ancestor n. ancêtre, aïeul m.; -s pl. aïeux m. pl.

ancestral a. ancestral; héréditaire

ancestry n. lignée f.; aïeux m. pl.

anchor n. ancre f.; cast — jeter l'ancre; weigh — lever l'ancre; ride at — être à l'ancre; — vt. ancrer; — vi. jeter l'ancre; -age n. ancrage, mouillage m.

anchovy n. anchois m.

ancient a. antique; ancien; -ness n. ancienneté f.

and conj. et; (both) — . . . ., — et . . . . et; — so on et ainsi de suite

Andalusia n. Andalousie f.

Andes n. Andes f. pl.

andiron n. chenet m.

Andorra n. Andorre f.

anemia n. anémie f.

anemic a. anémique

anemometer n. anémomètre m.

aneroid a. anéroïde

anesthesia n. anesthésie f.

anesthetic n. anesthétique m.

anesthetist n. anesthésiste m.

anesthetize vt. anesthésier

anew adv. de nouveau; encore; à neuf

angel n. ange m.; -ic a. angélique

angelus n. (eccl.) angélus m.

anger n. colère f.; — vt. mettre en colère

angle n. angle m.; coin m.; (coll.) point de vue m.; — iron cornière f.; — vi. pêcher à la ligne; -r n. pêcheur (à la ligne) m.

angleworm n. ver de terre m.

Anglican a. anglican

Anglicism n. anglicisme m.

Anglicize vt. angliciser

angling n. pêche à la ligne f.

Anglo-Saxon a. & n. anglo-saxon m.

Angola n. Angola m.

angora n. angora m.

angry a. fâché, irrité; become — se mettre en colère; be — with être fâché contre

anguish n. angoisse f.

angular a. anguleux; -ity n. angularité f.

aniline n. aniline f.

animal n. & a. animal m.

animate vt. animer; encourager; —, -d a. animé

animation n. animation f.

animosity n. animosité f.

animus n. animosité f.

anise n. anis m.

ankle n. cheville f.; turn one's — se fouler la cheville

anklet n. chaussette courte f.; bracelet de cheville m.

annals n. pl. annales f. pl.

anneal vt. recuire, tempérer

annex n. annexe f.; — vt. annexer; -ation n. annexion f.

annihilate vt. annihiler, anéantir

annihilation n. anéantissement m.

anniversary n. anniversaire m.

annotate vt. annoter

annotation n. annotation f.

annotator n. annotateur m.

announce vt. annoncer; -ment n. annonce f.; faire-part m.; avis m.; -r n. speaker m.

annoy vt. ennuyer, troubler, gêner; -ance n. ennui m.; -ing a. ennuyeux

annual n. annuaire m.; plante annuelle f.; — a. annuel

annuity n. rente f.; life — rente viagère f.

annul vt. annuler, casser; -ment n. annulation f.; (marriage) dissolution f.

Annunciation n. Annonciation f.

anode n. anode f.

anodyne n. remède anodin m.

anoint vt. oindre; consacrer, sacrer; -ing n. onction f.

anomalous a. anomal, hétéroclite

anomaly n. anomalie f.

anon adv. bientôt, tout à l'heure

anonymity n. anonymat m.

anonymous a. anonyme

another a. un autre; encore un; one — l'un l'autre; les uns les autres — pron. autrui

answer n. réponse, réplique f.; raison f.; solution f.; — vt. répondre; réfuter; — for être responsable de; répondre de -able a. responsable

ant n. fourmi f.

antagonism n. antagonisme m.

antagonist n. antagoniste m.; -ic a. antagoniste; opposé

antagonize vt. contrarier, opposer

antarctic a. & n. antarctique m.

anteater n. fourmilier m.

antecedence n. antécédence f.; priorité f.

antecedent n. & a. antécédent m.

antechamber n. antichambre f.

antedate vt. précéder; antidater

antediluvian a. antédiluvien

antelope n. antilope f.

antenna n. antenne f.

anterior a. antérieur

anteroom n. vestibule m., salle d'attente f.

anthem n. antienne f.; hymne m.

anthill n. fourmilière f.

anthology n. anthologie, chrestomathie f.

anthracite n. anthracite m.

anthrax n. charbon m.

anthropological a. anthropologique

anthropologist n. anthropologiste m.

anthropology n. anthropologie f.

anthropomorphous a. anthropomorphe

antiaircraft n. antiavion m.

antibiotic n. & a. antibiotique m.

antibody n. anticorps m.

antic n. singerie, gambade f.

anticipate vt. anticiper; devancer, aller au-devant de; prévenir

anticipation n. anticipation f.; prévision f.

anticipatory a. par anticipation

anticlerical a. anticlérical

anticlimax n. dénouement décevant m., chute f.
antidote n. antidote m.
antifreeze n. antigel m.
antihistamine n. antihistamine f.
antimony n. antimoine m.
antipathy n. antipathie f.
antiphony n. contre-chant m.
anti-pope n. anti-pape m.
antiquarian, antiquary n. antiquaire m.
antiquated a. suranné, vieilli
antique n. antiquité f.; — a. ancien
antiquity n. antiquité f.
antiseptic n. & a. antiseptique m.
antisocial a. antisocial
antisubmarine a. anti-sousmarin
antitank a. antichar
antithesis n. antithèse f.
antithetical a. antithétique
antitoxin n. antitoxine f.
antitrust a. anticartel
antler n. andouiller m.
antonym n. antonyme m.
Antwerp n. Anvers m.
anus n. anus m.
anvil n. enclume f.
anxiety n. anxiété, inquiétude f.
anxious a. inquiet, soucieux; désireux; be — to tenir à; avoir hâte de
any adj. du, de la, des; quelque; (ne . . .) aucun; n'importe quel; tout; — pron. en; (ne . . .) aucun; n'importe lequel
anybody pron. (ne . . .) personne; quelqu'un; n'importe qui; le premier venu
anyhow adv. n'importe comment; en tout cas
anyone pron. (ne . . .) personne; quelqu'un; n'importe qui; le premier venu
anything pron. (ne . . .) rien; quelque chose; n'importe quoi, quoi que ce soit; not for — pour rien au monde
anyway adv. n'importe comment; en tout cas
anywhere adv. n'importe où, où que ce soit, partout; quelque part, (ne . . .) nulle part
aorta n. aorte f.
apart adv. à part, séparément; — from en dehors de; come — se défaire; take — démonter; tell — distinguer (entre)
apartment n. appartement m.; — building n. immeuble d'habitation f.
apathetic a. apathique
apathy n. apathie f.
ape n. singe m.; — vt. singer, imiter
aperture n. ouverture f.
apex n. sommet m., pointe f.
aphasia n. aphasie f.
aphorism n. aphorisme m.
aphoristic a. aphoristique
aphrodisiac a. aphrodisiaque
apiary n. rucher m.
apiece adv. par pièce, par tête, chacun
apish a. de singe; bouffon
aplomb n. aplomb m.
Apocalypse n. apocalypse f.
apocalyptic(al) a. apocalyptique
apocryphal a. apocryphe
apogee n. apogée m.
apologetic a. d'excuse; apologétique

apologist n. apologiste m.
apologize vi. s'excuser
apology n. excuses f. pl.; (defense) apologie f.
apoplectic a. apoplectique
apoplexy n. apoplexie f.
apostasy n. apostasie f.
apostate a. & n. apostat m.
apostle n. apôtre m.
apostolic a. apostolique
apostrophe n. apostrophe f.
apothecary n. pharmacien m.
appall vt. effrayer, consterner; —ing a. épouvantable
apparatus n. appareil m.
apparel n. vêtements, habits m. pl.
apparent a. apparent, visible; évident; (of heirs) présomptif; —ly adv. apparemment, évidemment
apparition n. apparition f.
appeal n. appel m.; charme, attrait m.; — vt. faire appel (à); se reporter (à); être séduisant; (law) interjeter appel; —ing a. séduisant, attrayant; sympathique
appear vi. apparaître, paraître; sembler; —ance n. apparition f.; aspect m.; air m.; apparence f.; — (book) parution f.; to all —ances apparemment
appease vt. apaiser, calmer; —ment n. apaisement m.
appellate a. d'appel; — court cour d'appel f.
append vt. apposer, ajouter; —age n. dépendance f.; accessoire m.
appendicitis n. appendicite f.
appendix n. appendice m.; (anat.) appendice m.
appertain vi. appartenir (à), concerner
appetite n. appétit m.
appetizer n. amuse-gueule, hors-d'œuvre m.; (drink) apéritif m.
appetizing a. appétissant
applaud vt. applaudir
applause n. applaudissements m. pl.
apple n. pomme f.; — brandy calvados m.; — core trognon de pomme m.; — dumpling n. chausson m.; — orchard n. pommeraie f.; — pie tarte aux pommes f.; — tree n. pommier m.; baked — pomme cuite f.
apple-pie order, in — impeccable; tout ce qu'il y a de mieux
applesauce n. compote de pommes f.
appliance n. appareil m.; application f.
applicability n. applicabilité f.
applicant n. pétitionneur, solliciteur m.; candidat, postulant m.
application n. application f.; demande f.; emploi, usage m.; attention f.; — blank n. formule f.
applied a. appliqué; — arts arts industriels m. pl.
apply vt. appliquer; employer; — for solliciter; — to s'adresser à
appoint vt. fixer, nommer, désigner; —ed a. désigné, dit, convenu; —ee n. fonctionnaire nommé m.; —ment n. rendez-vous m.; nomination f.; équipement m.
apportion vt. répartir, partager; —ment

n. répartition f., partage m.

apposite a. convenable, à propos

appraisal n. évaluation, estimation, expertise f.

appraise vt. priser, évaluer, estimer

appraiser n. estimateur, commissaire-priseur m.

appreciable a. appréciable; sensible

appreciably adv. sensiblement

appreciate vt. apprécier, évaluer; comprendre, se rendre compte de

appreciation n. appréciation f.; évaluation, estimation f.; augmentation de valeur f.

appreciative a. reconnaissant; sensible

apprehend vt. appréhender; saisir; redouter

apprehension n. appréhension, crainte f.

apprehensive a. craintif, inquiet; become — about redouter

apprentice n. apprenti m.; — vt. mettre en apprentissage; –ship n. apprentissage m.

apprise vt. apprendre; informer

approach n. approche f., accès, abord m.; — vt. approcher; s'approcher de; –able a. abordable

appropriate vt. approprier; — to oneself s'approprier; — a. approprié, convenable; à propos; –ness n. convenance, justesse f.

appropriation n. affectation f.; appropriation f.

approval n. approbation f.; on — (envoi) au choix, à condition

approve vt. approuver; –r n. approbateur m.

approving a. approbateur

approximate vt. approcher; s'approcher de; — a. approximatif

approximation n. approximation f.

appurtenance n. dépendance f., accessoire m.

apricot n. abricot m.; — tree n. abricotier

April n. avril m.; — Fool's Day premier avril m.; — fool's joke poisson d'avril

apron n. tablier m.; he is tied to his mother's — strings il est pendu aux jupes de sa mère

apropos a. à propos

apt a. apte; propre, enclin à; prompt, porté à; à propos; –ness n. aptitude, convenance f.

aptitude n. aptitude, disposition f.; talent m.

aquamarine n. aigue-marine f.

aquaplane n. aquaplane m.

aquarium n. aquarium m.

aquatic n. aquatique

aqueduct n. aqueduc m.

aqueous a. aqueux

aquiline a. aquilin

Arab n. Arabe m. & f.; –ia n. Arabie f.; Saudi –ia n. Arabie Soudite f.; –ian a. & n. arabe m.; –ic a. & n. arabe m.

arable a. labourable

arbiter n. arbitre m.

arbitrary a. arbitraire

arbitrate vt. arbitrer, déterminer, juger

arbitration n. arbitrage m.

arbitrator n. arbitre m.

arbor n. berceau m.; tonnelle, treille f.

arbutus n. aubépine f.

arc n. arc m.; — light arc voltaïque m.

arch n. arche f. voûte f.; arc m.; fallen –es pied bot m.; — vt. voûter; arrondir — a. espiègle; –ed a. cintré; voûté

archaeologist n. archéologue f.

archaeology n. archéologie f.

archaic a. archaïque

archaism n. archaïsme m.

archangel n. archange m.

archbishop n. archevêque m.

archduchess n. archiduchesse f.

archduke n. archiduc m.

archer n. archer m.; –y n. tir à l'arc m.

archetype n. archétype, prototype m.

archipelago n. archipel m.

architect n. architecte m.; –ural a. architectural; –ure n. architecture f.

archives n. pl. archives f. pl.

archivist n. archiviste m. & f.

archway n. voûte f.

arctic a. arctique

arc-weld vt. souder à l'arc

ardent a. ardent, violent; –ly adv. ardemment

ardor n. ardeur f.

arduous a. ardu; rude; difficile; –ness n. difficulté f.

area n. région f.; surface f.; superficie f.; aire f.; zone f.

arena n. arène f.; arènes f. pl.

Argentina n. Argentine f.

Argentine n. & a. Argentin m.

argon n. argon m.

argonaut n. argonaute m.

arguable a. discutable

argue vt. discuter; soutenir; démontrer; vi. discuter, disputer; argumenter

argument n. argument m.; discussion f.; –ation n. argumentation f.; –ative a. disposé à argumenter

aria n. air m.

arid a. aride; –ity n. aridité f.

arise vi. s'élever; provenir, résulter

aristocracy n. aristocratie f.

aristocrat n. aristocrate m.; –ic a. aristocratique

Aristotle n. Aristote m.

arithmetic n. arithmétique f.; –al a. arithmétique; –ian n. arithméticien m.

ark n. arche f.; — of the covenant arche d'alliance f.; Noah's — arche de Noé f.

arm n. bras m.; arme f.; — in — bras dessus, bras dessous; bear –s porter les armes; be up in –s être en rébellion; fold one's –s croiser les bras; small –s armes portatives f. pl.; — vt. armer; s'armer; –s n. pl. armoiries f. pl.

armada n. armada f.

armadillo n. tatou m.

armament n. armement m.

armature n. armature f.

armband n. brassard m.

armchair n. fauteuil m.

Armenia n. Arménie f.

armful n. brassée f.

armhole n. entournure f.

armistice n. armistice m., trève f.

armor n. armure f.; blindage m., cuirasse

f.; — plate plaque de blindage f.; — vt.
blinder, cuirasser; -ed a. blindé; -er n.
armurier m.; -ial a. armorial; d'armoiries; -y n. arsenal m.; fabrique d'armes

armor-plated a. blindé, cuirassé

armpit n. aisselle f.

arm-rest n. accoudoir m.

army n. armée f.

aroma n. arome m.; -tic a. aromatique

around prep. autour de; — adv. autour, à
la ronde; quelque part; (approximation) à peu près. environ°

arouse vt. soulever; éveiller; exciter

arraign vt. (law) accuser; -ment n.
accusation f.

arrange vt. arranger, mettre en ordre;
ranger; régler; disposer; -ment n.
arrangement m.; disposition f.; (mus.)
adaptation f.

array n. ordre de bataille m.; rang m.,
rangée f.; étalage m.; parure f.; — vt.
ranger

arrears n. pl. arriéré m.; be in — avoir
de l'arriéré

arrest n. arrestation f.; arrêt m.; place
under — mettre aux arrêts; — vt.
arrêter

arrival n. arrivée f.

arrive vi. arriver; parvenir; — at arriver
à; gagner, atteindre

arrow n. flèche f.

arrowhead n. pointe de flèche f.

arson n. crime d'incendie volontaire m.

art n. art m.; habileté f.; artifice m.; -s
and crafts arts et métiers m. pl.; the
fine -s les beaux-arts; -ful a. habile,
artificieux; fait avec art; -isan n.
artisan m.; -ist n. artiste m.; peintre
m.; -istic a. artistique; -istry n. art m.;
-less a. sans art, simple; -lessness n.
ingenuité, candeur, naïveté f.

arterial a. artériel

arteriosclerosis n. artériosclérose f.

artery n. artère f.

artesian a. artésien

arthritic a. arthritique

arthritis n. arthrite f.

artichoke n. artichaut m.

article n. article m.; condition, stipulation f.

articulate vt. articuler; énoncer; — a.
articulé

articulation n. articulation f.

artifice n. artifice m.

artificial a. artificiel; factice; -ity caractère
artificiel m.

artillery n. artillerie f.; -man n. artilleur

Aryan n. & a. Aryen m.

as conj. comme; aussi; que; selon que;
suivant, tandis que; puisque; — far —
jusqu'à; — far — I am concerned
quant à moi; — for quant à; — good
— aussi bon que; — is tel quel; — of
en date du; — well — aussi bien que;
comme; — if comme si; — it were pour
ainsi dire; — regards en ce qui concerne; — soon — aussitôt que; —
though comme si; — yet jusqu'ici; act
— servir de; agir en

asbestos n. asbeste, amiante m.

ascend vi. & vt. monter; — vt. s'élever;
-ancy, -ent n. ascendant m.

ascension n. ascension f.

ascent n. montée f.; ascension f.

ascertain vt. s'assurer de; prouver; constater, reconnaître; s'informer, vérifier;
-able a. vérifiable, reconnaissable

ascetic n. ascète m.; — a. ascétique; -ism
n. ascétisme m.

ascribable a. imputable

ascribe vt. attribuer, imputer

aseptic n. & a. aseptique m.

ash n. cendres f. pl.; (bot.) frêne m.; —
tray cendrier m.; Ash Wednesday
mercredi des cendres m.; -en a. couleur
de cendre

ashamed a. honteux; be — avoir honte

ash-blond a. blond cendré

ashore adv. à terre; go — débarquer

Asia n. Asie f.; — Minor Asie Mineure
f.; -n, -tic n. & a. Asiatique m.

aside adv. de côté, à part; à l'écart; —
from à part; lay, put, set — mettre de
côté; to turn — (se) détourner; —
n. aparté m.

asinine a. d'âne

ask vt. demander; réclamer; — a question
poser une question; — for demander;
demander à voir

askance adv. obliquement, de travers

askew adv. de biais

asleep adv. endormi; be — dormir, être
endormi; fall — s'endormir

asp n. aspic m.

asparagus n. asperges f. pl.

aspect n. aspect m., mine f., air m.

aspen n. tremble m.

asperity n. aspérité, âpreté f.

aspersion n. aspersion f.; diffamation f.

asphalt n. asphalte m.; bitume m.; — vt.
asphalter

asphyxia n. asphyxie f.; -te vt. asphyxier

aspic n. gelée f.

aspirant n. candidat, aspirant, m.

aspirate vt. aspirer; — a. aspiré

aspiration n. aspiration f., désir ardent m.

aspire vi. souhaiter ardemment; prétendre
(à); aspirer (à)

aspirin n. aspirine f.

aspiring a. qui aspire; ambitieux

ass n. âne m., ânesse f.

assail vt. assaillir, attaquer; -able a. attaquable; -ant n. assaillant m.

assassin n. assassin m.; -ate vt. assassiner;
-ation n. assassinat m.

assault n. assaut m.; attaque f.; atteinte
f.; viol m.; — and battery menaces et
voies de fait f. pl.; — vt. assaillir;
attaquer; violer

assay n. essai, examen m.; — vt. essayer,
éprouver; -er n. essayeur m.; -ing n.
essai m.

assemblage n. assemblage m.; réunion f.

assemble vt. assembler, rassembler; — vi.
s'assembler, se rassembler

assembly n. assemblée, réunion f.; assemblage, montage m.; — line production
fabrication en série f.

assemblyman n. député m.

assent n. consentement m.; assentiment

m.; — *vi.* consentir (à); — **to approuver**

assert *vt.* affirmer, maintenir, défendre; revendiquer; faire valoir; -ion *n.* affirmation *f.*; -ive *a.* assuré; -iveness *n.* assurance *f.*

assess *vt.* taxer, imposer, évaluer; -ment *n.* répartition *f.* (d'impôts): évaluation *f.*; cote *f.*; -or *n.* contrôleur-répartiteur *m.*

asset *n.* bien *m.*; -s *pl.* actif *m.*; avoir *m.*

assiduity *n.* assiduité *f.*

assiduous *a.* assidu; -ly *adv.* assidûment; -ness *n.* assiduité *f.*

assign *vt.* assigner, désigner; attribuer; -ment *n.* attribution, désignation *f.* (school) devoir *m.*

assimilate *vt.* assimiler; — *vi.* s'assimiler

assimilation *n.* assimilation *f.*

assist *vt.* aider, secourir; -ance *n.* aide *f.*, secours *m.*; -ant *n.* & *a.* assistant, adjoint *m.*

assizes *n. pl.* assises *f. pl.*

associate *n.* & *a.* associé, adjoint *m.*; *vt.* associer; — *vi.* s'associer; — **with** fréquenter

association *n.* association, alliance *f.*; union, société *f.*

assort *vt.* assortir; -ment *n.* assortiment *m.*

assuage *vt.* apaiser, soulager

assume *vt.* présumer, supposer; se charger de; prendre; -d *a.* d'emprunt; feint; supposé

assuming *a.* prétentieux; — (**that**) en supposant que

assumption *n.* présomption *f.*; (eccl.) Assomption *f.*

assurance *n.* assurance, confiance *f.*; promesse *f.*

assure *vt.* assurer, garantir; -dly *adv.* assurément

aster *n.* (bot.) aster *m.*

asterisk *n.* astérisque *m.*

astern *adv.* à l'arrière, en arrière

asteroid *n.* astéroïde *m.*

asthma *n.* asthme *m.*; -tic *a.* asthmatique

astigmatic *a.* astigmate

astigmatism *n.* astigmatisme *m.*

astonish *vt.* étonner; -ing *a.* étonnant; -ment *n.* étonnement *m.*

astound *vt.* étonner, ahurir, stupéfier

astraddle *adv.* à califourchon

astray *a.* & *adv.* égaré; go — s'égarer; lead — égarer

astride *adv.* à califourchon

astringency *n.* astringence *f.*

astringent *n.* & *a.* astringent *m.*

astrologer *n.* astrologue *m.*

astrological *a.* astrologique

astrology *n.* astrologie *f.*

astronomer *n.* astronome *m.*

astronomic(al) *a.* astronomique

astronomy *n.* astronomie *f.*

astute *a.* fin, rusé; -ness *n.* finesse, astuce *f.*

asunder *adv.* en deux

asylum *n.* asile, refuge *m.*; hospice *m.*; insane, lunatic — asile d'aliénés *f.*

asymmetric(al) *a.* asymétrique

at *prep.* à, dans; en; sur; après; contre;

— **all** du tout; — **all costs** à tout prix; — **all events** en tout cas; — **first** d'abord; — **home** à la maison; — **large** libre; — **last** enfin; — **least** au moins; — **length** in extenso; à la longue; — **once** tout de suite; — **peace** en paix; — **pleasure** à loisir; — **your house** chez vous; — **sea** en pleine mer; — **stake** en jeu; — **times** à moments; — **war** en guerre; — **will** à volonté; — **work** au travail; — **your service** à votre service

atavistic *a.* atavique

Athenian *a.* & *n.* athénien *m.*

Athens *n.* Athènes

atheism *n.* athéisme *m.*

atheist *n.* athée *m.*; -ic *a.* athée

athlete *n.* athlète *m.*; -'s foot favus (du pied) *m.*

athletic *a.* athlétique; -s *n. pl.* athlétisme *m.*

Atlantic Ocean *n.* Océan Atlantique *m.*

atmosphere *n.* atmosphère *f.*; ambiance *f.*

atmospheric *a.* atmosphérique

atom *n.* atome *m.*; -(ic) **bomb** bombe atomique *f.*; -ic *a.* atomique; -ic **pile** réacteur atomique *m.*

atomizer *n.* vaporisateur *m.*

atone *vi.* & *vt.*; — (**for**) expier; racheter; -ment *n.* expiation *f.*

atonic *a.* atone; (anat.) atonique

atop *adv.* en haut, au sommet

atrocious *a.* atroce

atrocity *n.* atrocité *f.*

atrophy *n.* atrophie *f.*; — *vi.* s'atrophier

attach *vt.* attacher, fixer; saisir; be -ed to se rattacher à; -ment *n.* attachement *m.*; accessoire *m.*

attaché *n.* attaché *m.*; — **case** mallette *f.*, porte-documents *m.*

attack *n.* attaque *f.*, assaut *m.*; crise *f.*, accès *m.*; — *vt.* attaquer, assaillir; -er *n.* attaquant *m.*

attain *vt.* atteindre, obtenir; — *vi.* parvenir (à); -able *a.* qu'on peut atteindre; -ment *n.* talent *m.*, connaissance *f.*; réalisation *f.*

attar *n.* essence (de rose) *f.*

attempt *n.* essai *m.*; tentative *f.*, effort *m.*; — *vt.* tenter, essayer; -ed *a.*, -ed **murder** tentative d'assassinat *f.*

attend *vt.* assister à; servir, soigner; — **to** s'occuper de; se charger de; -ance *n.* assistance *f.*; présence *f.*; -ant *n.* serviteur, aide *m.*; -ant *a.* attenant, qui accompagne

attention *n.* attention *f.*; (mil.) garde à vous *m.*; attract — se faire remarquer; pay — faire attention

attentive *a.* attentif; prévenant; -ness *n.* attention *f.*

attenuate *vt.* atténuer

attenuation *n.* atténuation *f.*

attest *vt.* attester, certifier; -ation *n.* attestation, certification *f.*

attic *n.* mansarde *f.*; comble *m.*

attire *n.* vêtement, habillement *m.*, parure *f.*; — *vt.* vêtir, parer

attitude *n.* attitude, posture *f.*

attorney *n.* avocat *m.*; avoué *m.*; **district**

— procureur *m.*; notaire *m.*; — general ministre de la justice *m.*; power of — procuration *f.*

attract *vt.* attirer; entraîner; séduire; -ion *n.* attraction *f.*, attrait *m.*; -ive *a.* séduisant; attrayant; attractif; -iveness *n.* attrait, charme *m.*

attributable *a.* attribuable, imputable

attribute *vt.* attribuer, imputer; — *n.* attribut *m.*

attribution *n.* attribution *f.*

attributive *a.,* — adjective adjectif qualificatif *m.*

attrition *n.* attrition *f.*; usure *f.*

attune *vt.* accorder

auburn *n. & a.* châtain clair *m.*

auction *n.* vente aux enchères *f.*; — *vt.* vendre aux enchères; -eer *n.* commissaire-priseur *m.*; crieur *m.*

audacious *a.* audacieux

audacity *n.* audace *f.*; hardiesse *f.*

audible *a.* distinct (à l'oreille)

audience *n.* auditoire *m.*, assistance *f.*; audience *f.*

audiometer *n.* audiomètre *m.*

audit *n.* vérification de comptes *f.*; — *vt.* vérifier; visiter (un cours universitaire); -or *n.* vérificateur *m.*; (school) visiteur *m.*

audio *a.* (coll.) qui se rapporte au son radiodiffusé d'une émission télévisée

audition *n.* audition *f.*; ouïe *f.*

auditorium *n.* salle *f.*

auditory *a.* auditif

auger *n.* tarière *f.*

augment *vt.* augmenter; — *vi.* s'accroître; -ation *n.* augmentation *f.*; -ative *a.* augmentatif

augur *vt.* augurer; — *n.* augure *m.*; -y *n.* augure *m.*

August *n.* août *m.*

august *a.* auguste

aunt *n.* tante *f.*

aura *n.* émanation *f.*; souffle *m.*

aural *a.* de l'oreille

aureomycin *n.* auréomycin *m.*

auricle *n.* auricule *f.*; (anat.) oreillette *f.*

auspices *n. pl.* auspices *m. pl.*

auspicious *a.* propice, favorable

austere *a.* austère, sévère

austerity *n.* austérité *f.*

Australia *n.* Australie *f.*; -n *n. & a.* Australien *m.*

Austria *n.* Autriche *f.*; -n *n. & a.* Autrichien *m.*

authentic *a.* authentique; vrai, véritable; conforme; -ate *vt.* vérifier, certifier, viser; -ity *n.* authenticité *f.*

author *n.* auteur *m.*; -ess *n.* femme auteur *f.*; -ship *n.* paternité (littéraire) *f.*

authoritarian *a. & n.* autoritaire *m.*

authoritative *a.* autoritaire; -ness *n.* autorité *f.*

authority *n.* autorité *f.*; mandat, pouvoir *m.*; on good — de bonne source

authorization *n.* autorisation *f.*

authorize *vt.* autoriser

autobiographer *n.* autobiographe *m.*

autobiographical *a.* autobiographique

autobiography *n.* autobiographie *f.*

autocracy *n.* autocratie *f.*

autocrat *n.* autocrate *m.*; -ic *a.* autocratique

autogiro *n.* hélicoptère *m.*

autograph *n.* autographe *m.*; — *vt.* signer; dédier

automatic *a.* automatique

automation *n.* automation *f.*

automaton *n.* automate *m.*

automobile *n.* automobile *f.*

automotive *a.* automobile

autonomous *a.* autonome

autumn *n.* automne *m.*; -al *a.* automnal

auxiliary *n. & a.* auxiliaire, assistant *m.*

avail *n.* utilité *f.*, secours *m.*; — *vt.* servir; — oneself of se servir de, profiter de; -able *a.* disponible; utilisable; -ibility *n.* disponibilité *f.*

avaricious *a.* avare

avenge *vt.* venger; -r *n.* vengeur *m.*

avenue *n.* avenue *f.*; boulevard *m.*

aver *vt.* affirmer

average *n.* moyenne *f.*; on the — en moyenne; — *vt.* calculer la moyenne; — *vi.* atteindre une moyenne de (vitesse, distance, consommation); — *a.* moyen

averse *a.* contraire, opposé

aversion *n.* aversion *f.*; répugnance *f.*

avert *vt.* détourner, écarter

aviator *n.* aviateur *m.*

avid *a.* avide; -ity *n.* avidité *f.*

avocado *n.* poire d'avocat *f.*

avocation *n.* occupation *f.*; distraction *f.*, délaissement *m.*

avoid *vt.* éviter; -able *a.* évitable; -ance *n.* action d'éviter *f.*

avow *vt.* avouer, confesser; -al *n.* aveu *m.*

await *vt.* attendre

awake *vi.* se réveiller; s'éveiller; — *a.* éveillé; -n *vt.* éveiller, réveiller; -ning *n.* réveil *m.*

award *n.* jugement *m.*; récompense *f.*, prix *m.*; — *vt.* décerner; adjuger

aware *a.* conscient, au courant; -ness *n.* conscience *f.*

awash *a.* à fleur d'eau; surnageant

away *a.* absent; loin; — *adv.* au loin, loin; go — s'en aller; take — enlever; send — renvoyer; right — tout de suite

awe *n.* crainte *f.*, respect *m.*; — *vt.* effrayer, impressionner

awe-inspiring, awesome *a.* impressionnant

awe-struck *a.* effrayé, impressionné

awful *a.* terrible; affreux; imposant

awhile *adv.* un peu, un moment

awkward *a.* gauche; maladroit; (situation) gênant; -ness *n.* maladresse *f.*

awl *n.* alène *f.*, poinçon *m.*

awning *n.* tente *f.*; abri *m.*; store *m.*

awry *adv.* de travers

ax, axe *n.* hache *f.*

axiom *n.* axiome *m.*; -atic *a.* axiomatique

axis *n.* axe *m.*

axle *n.* essieu *m.*; arbre *m.*

ay, aye *n. & adv.* oui *m.*; — *adv.* toujours

Azores *n.* Açores *f. pl.*

azure *n.* azur *m.*; — *a.* azuré, d'azur

B

B.A.: Bachelor of Arts n. bachelier ès lettres m.
babble n. babil m.; — vi. bavarder, parler avec incohérence; babiller, murmurer; -r n. babillard m.
babbling a. babillard; (brook) murmurant; — n. babil m.
babe n. bébé m.
babel n. tumulte m.; confusion f.
baboon n. babouin m.
babushka n. fichu (porté à la tête) m.
baby n. bébé m.; — a. de bébé; — carriage voiture d'enfant f.; — grand (piano) demi-queue f.; — hood première enfance f.; -ish a. enfantin; — vt. traiter d'enfant; amadouer
baccalaureate n. baccalauréat m.
bachelor n. célibataire, garçon m.; (educ.) bachelier m.; -hood n. célibat m.; -'s-button n. (bot.) bluet m.; -'s degree baccalauréat m.
bacillus n. bacille m.
back n. dos m., derrière f.; dossier m.; verso m.; fond f.; revers m.; — to — dos à dos; behind one's — à l'insu de; — talk (coll.) impertinence, réponse, impertinente f.; turn one's — tourner le dos; — a. de derrière; dorsal; — door porte de derrière f.; — number numéro ancien (d'un journal) m.; — payment arriéré m.; — seat siege de derrière m.; — stairs escalier de service m.; -street ruelle f.; — adv. en arrière, à l'arrière; de retour; en retour; — and forth de long en large; (in) — of derrière; bring — rapporter; come — revenir; give — rendre; go — retourner; go — on ne pas tenir (la parole donnée); — vt. soutenir, subventionner, seconder; parier pour; mettre un dos à; servir de dos (fond) à; — vi. reculer; faire reculer; aller (faire aller) en marche arrière; — down, — out se dédire; se soustraire (à); — up reculer; -er n. soutien m.; -ing n. appui m.; subvention f.
backbite vt. calomnier
backboard n. dossier m.
backbone n. épine dorsale f.
backbreaking a. dur; éreintant
backdrop n. toile de fond f.
backfire n. (engine) contre-allumage m.; (firefighting) contre-feu m.; — vi. pétarder; (fig.) retomber
backgammon n. trictrac m.
background n. fond m.
backhanded a. donné avec le revers de la main; (fig.) immoral
backlash n. contre-coup m.
backlog n. accumulation de travail f. (qui reste à faire)
backpedal vi. contre-pédaler; (fig.) reculer
backslide vi. retomber
backstage adv. dans les coulisses
backstroke n. brasse (sur le dos) f.
backtrack vi. rebrousser chemin
backward adv. en arrière, à la renverse; — a. arriéré; -ness n. retard m.

backwash n. remous m.
backwoodsman n. homme des forêts, homme des frontières m.
bacon n. lard m.; bacon m.
bacteria n. pl. bactéries f. pl.
bacteriologist n. bactériologiste m.
bacteriology n. bactériologie f.
bad a. mauvais, méchant; grave, sérieux; from — to worse de mal en pire; too — dommage; — debt mauvaise créance f.; -ly adv. mal; gravement; want -ly avoir grande envie de
badge n. plaque f.; insigne m.
badger n. blaireau m.; — vt. harceler
badminton n. badminton m.
baffle vt. confondre, déjouer
bag n. sac m.; sleeping — sac de couchage m.; be left holding the — être dupé; — vt. mettre en sac; (hunting) prendre; faire une poche; -gy a. qui font une poche
bagful n. sachée f.
baggage n. bagage m.; to be off bag and — plier bagage; — car fourgon m.; — check bulletin des bagages m.; excess — excédent de bagages m.
Bahamas n. Bahamas m. pl.
bagpipe n. cornemuse f.
bail n. caution f.; be out on — être libre sous caution; put up — se porter caution (pour); — vt. cautionner; — out (law) se porter caution pour; (avi.) sautor en parachute; (naut.) écoper
bailiff n. huissier m.; bailli m.
bailiwick n. bailliage m.; rayon m.
bait n. appât m., amorce f.; — vt. amorcer; appâter, leurrer; harceler
bake vt. & vi. cuire au four; faire le pain, boulanger; half -d prématuré, pas asses mûri; -r n. boulanger m.; -r's dozen treize; -ry n. boulangerie f.
baking n. cuisson au four f.; — powder levure chimique f.; — soda bicarbonate de soude m.
balance n. balance f.; équilibre m.; solde d'un compte m.; — sheet n. bilan m.; — vt. peser, balancer; équilibrer; — vi. hésiter; -d a. équilibré
balancing n. balancement m.; équilibre m.; (com.) solde m.
balcony n. balcon m.; galerie f.
bald a. chauve; nu; -ness n. calvitie f.
bale n. balle f. paquet m.; — vt. emballer
balearic a. baléare
baleful a. triste; fatal, funeste
balk vt. désappointer, frustrer; — vi. regimber; hésiter; reculer; -y a. rétif; hésitant, récalcitrant
Balkans n. Balkans m. pl.
ball n. balle, boule f., ballon m.; globe m.; bal m.; — bearing bille f.; roulement à billes m.; masked — bal masqué
ballad n. romance, chanson populaire f.
ballast n. lest m.; (rail.) ballast m.; — vt. lester; (rail.) empierrer
ballerina n. danseuse f.; prima — première danseuse f.
ballet n. ballet m.
ballistic a. ballistique; -s n. ballistique f.

balloon n. ballon m.; aérostat m.; –ist n. aérostier m.

ballot n. scrutin m.; bulletin de vote m.; — box urne f.; — vi. voter; –ing n. vote, scrutin m.

ballroom n. salle de danse f.

ballyhoo n. publicité extravagante f.

balm n. baume m.; (fig.) soulagement m.; –y a. balsamique; (coll.) loufoque

balsam n. baume m.

Baltic Sea n. Mer Baltique f.

bamboo n. bambou m.

ban vt. empêcher, interdire; — n. interdiction f.

banal a. banal; –ity n. banalité f.

banana n. banane f.; — tree bananier m.

band n. lien m.; ruban m.; bande f.; clique f.; musiciens m. pl.; musique, fanfare f.; (mus.) orchestre m.; military — musique militaire f.; — vt. entourer de bandes, bander; marquer de bandes; — together se grouper

bandbox n. carton de modiste m.

bandage n. pansement m.; — vt. panser

bandleader n. chef d'orchestre m.

bandstand n. kiosque m.

bandwagon n. char des victorieux m.; majorité victorieuse f.; climb, jump on the — suivre la majorité

bandy vt. discuter

bane n. poison m.; ruine f.; –ful a. funeste, nuisible

bang n. coup m., tape f.; — vt. rosser; fermer avec bruit; –! paf!

bangle n. bijou, bracelet m.

bangs n. pl. frange f. (de cheveux)

banish vt. bannir, exiler; –ment n. bannissement, exil m.

banister n. rampe f.

bank n. digue f.; bord, rivage m.; banc m.; banque f.; — vt. terrasser; déposer (de l'argent dans une banque); (avi.) virer; — on compter sur; –er n. banquier m.; –ing n. actions de banque f. pl.

bankbook n. carnet de banque m.

bank note n. billet de banque m.

bankrupt a. en faillite; — n. banqueroutier m.; go — faire banqueroute; — vt. réduire à la faillite; –cy n. banqueroute f.

banner n. bannière f.

banquet n. banquet, festin m.; — vi. banqueter

bantamweight n. poids bantam m.

banter n. raillerie, plaisanterie f.; — vt. railler, plaisanter

baptism n. baptême m.; –al a. de baptême, baptismal

baptistry n. baptistère m.

baptize vt. baptiser

bar n. barre, barrière f.; (mus.) mesure f.; barreau m.; (fig.) empêchement m.; obstacle m.; candy— n. tablette f.; bar m.; be-admitted to the — être reçu avocat; prisoner at the — prisonnier devant le banc des accusés m.; — vt. empêcher, interdire; barrer; excepter; –red a. barré, à barreaux; –ring prep. sauf

barb n. barbillon m.; –ed a. pointu; –ed wire fil de fer barbelé m.

Barbados n. Barbade f.

barbarian n. & a. barbare m.

barbaric a. barbare

barbarous a. barbare; –ness n. barabarie f.

barbecue vt. faire rôtir en entier; griller à la sauce piquante; — n. pique-nique m., grillade (faite en plein air) f.

barber n. coiffeur m.; — shop salon de coiffure m.

barbiturate n. & a. barbiturique m.

bard n. barde, poète m.

bare a. nu, découvert; simple; — vt. mettre à nu; –ly adv. à peine; juste

bareback adv. à nu

barefaced a. impudent, effronté

barefoot(ed) a. nu-pieds

bareheaded a. nu-tête

barelegged a. nu-jambes

bargain n. marché, contrat m.; bonne affaire f.; — counter rayon des marchandises soldées m.; — vt. & vi. marchander

barge n. chaland m.; péniche f.; — vi. entrer sans façons

baritone n. baryton m.

barium n. baryum m.

bark n. écorce f.; barque f., bateau m.; (dog) aboiement m.; — vi. aboyer; –er aboyeur m.; sideshow –er barnum m.

barley n. orge f.

barmaid n. fille de comptoir f.

barn n. grange f.; écurie, étable f.

barnacle n. barnacle f.

barnstorm vi. aller en tournée

barnyard n. cour, basse-cour f.

barometer n. baromètre m.

barometric a. barométrique

baron n. baron m.; –ess n. baronne f.; –et n. baronnet m.; –y n. baronnie f.

barracks n. caserne f.

barrage n. barrage m.

barrel n. baril m., barrique f.; tonneau m.; (gun) canon m.; — organ orgue de barbarie m.; — vt. mettre en tonneau

barren a. stérile; –ness n. stérilité f.

barricade n. barricade f.; — vt. barricader

barrier n. barrière f.

barroom n. cabaret m.

barrow n. brouette f.

bartender n. barman m.

barter vt. échanger; — n. échange m.

basal metabolism n. métabolisme basique m.

basalt n. basalte m.

base n. base f., piédestal m.; — a. bas, vil; — vt. baser; –ness n. bassesse f.

baseball n. baseball m.

basement n. cave f.

bash vt. (coll.) cogner, assommer

bashful a. timide; pudique; –ness n. timidité f.

basic a. fondamental; basique

basil n. (spice) basilic m.

basilica n. basilique f.

basin n. bassin m.; bol m.; cuvette f.

basis n. base f., fondement m.

bask vt. se chauffer (au soleil)

basket n. panier m., corbeille f.; waste-paper — n. panier m.

Basque n. & a. Basque m. & f.

bas-relief n. bas-relief m.

bass n. (fish) bar m.; (mus.) basse f.: — clef clef de fa f.; — drum grosse caisse f.; — horn basse f.; — viol contrebasse f.; — a. de basse; bas, grave

bassinette n. barcelonnette f.

bassoon n. basson m.

basswood n. tilleul (d'Amérique) m.

bastard n. & a. bâtard m.; -ize vt. abâtardir, avilir

baste vt. (cooking) arroser; (sewing) faufiler

basting n. (cooking) arrosage m.; (sewing) faufilure f.

bastion n. bastion m.

bat n. chauve-souris f.; bâton m.; (baseball) batte f.; be at — tenir la batte; go to — for (coll.) appuyer; — vt. tenir la batte; battre; without —ting an eye sans battre l'œil; (fig.) impassible; -ter n. joueur qui tient la batte

batch n. fournée f.; lot m.

bath n. bain m.; shower — douche f.

bathe vt. baigner; — vi. se baigner; -r n. baigneur m.

bathhouse n. établissement de bains m.

bathing n. bain m., baignade f.; — beach plage f.; — suit costume de bain m.; — trunks slip de bain, caleçon de bain m.

bath mat n. descente de bain f.

bathrobe n. peignoir m.

bathroom n. salle de bain f.

bathtub n. baignoire f.

baton n. bâton (de chef d'orchestre) m.

battalion n. bataillon m.

batter n. pâte f.; — vt. battre; renverser

battering-ram n. bélier m.

battery n. batterie f.; pile f.; (law) voies de fait f. pl.

battle n. bataille f., combat m.; — vi. livrer combat; lutter, se battre

battle-ax n. hache d'armes; (coll.) harpie f.

battlefield n. champ de bataille m.

battlement n. créneau m.

battleship n. cuirassé m.

bauble n. babiole, bagatelle f.

Bavaria n. Bavière f.; -n a. & n. bavarois m.

bawl vi. brailler, crier; — out réprimander

bay n. laurier m.; baie f. (sea) golfe m.; at — aux abois; — window n. fenêtre en saillie f.; (coll.) bedaine f.; — vi. aboyer; — a. bai

bayberry n. baie f.; (tree) laurier m.

bayonet n. baïonnette f.; — vt. blesser à coups de baïonnette

bayou n. anse f.

bazaar n. bazar m.; vente de charité f.

bazooka n. (mil.) fusil à fusées antichar m.

be vi. être, exister; devoir; so — it ainsi soit-il; —ing n. être m.; for the time —ing pour le moment

beach n. rivage m.; plage f.; grève f.; — vt. échouer

beachcomber n. vagabond des plages m.

beachhead n. débarquement m.; (mil.) tête de pont f.

beacon n. signal, phare m.

bead n. grain (de collier) m.; perle f.; -s n. pl. (eccl.) chapelet m.

beadle n. bedeau m.

beak n. bec m.; pic m.

beaker n. verre à expériences m.

beam n. (arch.) poutre f.; (naut.) bau m.; travers m.; (light) rayon m.; (rad.) signal m.; — vi. rayonner; sourire; -ing a. radieux; rayonnant

bean n. haricot m.; kidney — haricot de Soissons m.; lima — fève f.; navy — haricot m.; string — haricot vert m.

bean pole n. perche à fèves f.

bear n. ours m.; (stock market) baissier m.; -ish a. brutal, d'ours; (stocks) favorable à la baisse

bear vi. porter; supporter; — vt. porter; souffrir; — a grudge against en vouloir à; — down appuyer; — in mind tenir présent à l'esprit; — witness témoigner; -able a. supportable; -er n. porteur m.; -ing n. mine f.; (mech.) roulement m.; get one's -ings s'orienter; have —ing on avoir à faire avec; lose one's -ings se perdre

beard n. barbe f.; -ed a. barbu; -less a. imberbe; sans barbe

beast n. animal m.; bête f.; — of burden bête de somme f.; -liness n. bestialité, brutalité f.; -ly a. brutal, bestial

beat n. coup m.; battement m.; ronde f.; — vt. & vi. frapper, battre; vaincre; — a path frayer un chemin; — around the bush éviter la matière à traiter, esquiver; — back, — off repousser; — up battre sévèrement; that -s me je n'y comprends rien; -er n. pilon, battoir, batteur m.; -ing n. battement m.; raclée f.; défaite f.

beatify vt. béatifier

beatitude n. béatitude f.

beau n. beau, galant m.

beautician n. coiffeur m., coiffeuse f.

beautiful a. beau (belle)

beautify vt. embellir

beauty n. beauté f.; — salon, — shop salon de beauté m.; — spot tache de beauté f.

beaver n. castor m.

becalm vt. accalminer, déventer

because conj. parce que; — of prep. à cause de

beck n. signe de tête m.; be at one's — (and call) être aux ordres de quelqu'un

beckon vi. faire un signe

become vi. devenir; — vt. convenir à; what has — of him? qu'est-ce qu'il est devenu?

becoming a. convenable, joli

bed n. lit m.; to go to — se coucher; to put to — coucher; flower — plate-bande f.; folding — lit escamotable m.; four-poster — lit à quenouilles m.; mineral — gisement m.; oyster — parc d'huîtres m.; road — encaissement m.; — vt. coucher; — down

coucher; se coucher
bedbug *n.* punaise *f.*
bedding *n.* literie *f.*
bedeck *vt.* parer, orner
bedevil *vt.* ensorceler, harceler
bedfellow *n.* camarade de lit *m.*
bed hand *n.* chevet *m.*
bedjacket *n.* liseuse *f.*
bedlam *n.* tumulte *m.*
bedpan *n.* bassin de lit *m.*
bedpost *n.* pied de lit *m.*
bedraggled *a.* crotté; échevelé
bedridden *a.* alité
bedrock *n.* roche de fond *f.*
bedroom *n.* chambre à coucher *f.*
bedside *n.* bord du lit *m.*
bedspread *n.* dessus de lit *m.*
bedspring *n.* sommier *m.*
bedstead *n.* bois de lit *m.*
bedtime *n.* heure de coucher *f.*
bee *n.* abeille *f.;* spelling — concours
  d'orthographe *m.*
beef *n.* bœuf *f.;* — tea consommé *m.;*
  roast — rosbif, rôti de bœuf *m.*
beefsteak *n.* biftek, steak *m.*
beehive *n.* ruche *f.*
beekeeper *n.* apiculteur *m.*
beeline *n.* route la plus courte *f.*
beer *n.* bière *f.*
beeswax *n.* cire d'abeille *f.*
beet *n.* betterave *f.;* — sugar sucre de
  betterave *m.;* sugar — betterave à sucre
  f.
beetle *n.* scarabée *m.;* coléoptère *m.*
beetle-browed *a.* à sourcils épais
befall *vi.* arriver, survenir
befit *vi.* convenir à, être propre à; -ting
  a. convenable
befog *vt.* obscurcir
before *adv.* avant, auparavant; en avant;
  the day — la veille *f.;* the evening —
  la veille au soir *f.;* — *prep.* avant; devant; the day — yesterday l'avant-
  veille *f.;* — *conj.* avant que
beforehand *adv.* d'avance, préalablement
  auparavant
befoul *vt.* souiller, salir
befriend *vt.* venir en aide à; traiter en
  ami
beg *vt.* mendier; prier, supplier; — *vi.*
  mendier; I — of you! je vous en prie!,
  de grâce!; -gar *n.* mendiant, gueux
  m.; -ging *n.* mendicité *f.*
beget *vt.* engendrer
begin *vt. & vi.* commencer; débuter; se
  mettre à; to — with tout d'abord; -ner
  n. commençant, débutant *m.;* novice
  m. & f.; -ning *n.* commencement,
  début *m.,* origine *f.;* in the -ning au
  commencement
begrudge *vt.* envier; donner à contre-
  cœur
begrudgingly *adv.* à contre-cœur
beguile *vt.* tromper; charmer
behalf *n.* faveur, part *f.;* on — of au
  nom de, de la part de
behave *vi.* se conduire, se comporter;
  être sage
behavior *n.* conduite, tenue *f.,* comportement *m.*

behead *vt.* décapiter; -ing *n.* décapitation *f.*
behest *n.* ordre *m.;* demande *f.*
behind *adv.* derrière, par derrière; en
  retard; be — être en retard; fall —
  traîner en arrière; — *prep.* derrière;
  en arrière de
behold *vt.* voir, contempler
behoove *vt.* convenir
belabor *vt.* rosser, battre; trop insister sur
belated *a.* attardé; tardif
belch *vi.* éructer; — *n.* éructation *f.*
beleaguer *vt.* cerner; investir
belfry *n.* beffroi, clocher *m.*
Belgian *a. & n.* belge *m. & f.*
Belgian East Africa *n.* Ruanda-Urundi *m.*
Belgium *n.* Belgique *f.*
belie *vt.* démentir
belief *n.* croyance, foi *f.;* to the best of
  my — autant que je sache
believable *a.* croyable
believe *vt. & vi.* croire, penser; make —
  faire semblant; -r *n.* croyant *m.*
belittle *vt.* déprécier
bell *n.* cloche, clochette *f.;* (house) sonnette *f.;* — *vt.* attacher un grelot à
bellboy, bellhop *n.* chasseur *m.;* garçon
  d'hôtel *m.*
belle *n.* beauté *f.*
bell glass, bell jar *n.* cloche (de verre) *f.*
belligerent *a. & n.* belligérant *m.*
bellow *vi.* beugler, mugir; — *n.* beuglement, mugissement *m.*
bellows *n., pl.* soufflet *m.*
bellpull *n.* cordon de sonnette *m.*
bell tower *n.* campanile, clocher *m.*
bellwether *n.* sonnailler *m.*
belly *n.* ventre *m.;* -ful *n.* rassasiement,
  soûl *m.*
bellyband *n.* (horse) sous-ventrière;
  (baby) brassière *f.*
belong *vi.* appartenir (à), être (à); faire
  partie (de); -ings *n. pl.* biens, effets
  m. pl.
beloved *a.* bien-aimé, chéri
below *adv.* en bas, (au) dessous; ci-dessous, ci-après; — *prep.* au dessous de,
  sous
belt *n.* ceinture *f.;* zone *f.;* transmission
  — courroie *f.;* — *vt.* ceindre, entourer;
  -ed *a.* à ceinture; -ing *n.* ceinture *f.*
bemoan *vt.* déplorer
bench *n.* banc *m.,* banquette *f.;* (law)
  siège *m.;* magistrature *f.*
bend *n.* courbure *f.;* courbe *f.;* coude,
  tournant *m.;* — *vt. & vi.* courber; plier;
  fléchir; tourner; — down se courber, se
  baisser
bends *n. pl.* (coll.) mal des caissons *m.*
beneath *adv.* en bas, (au-) dessous; —
  prep. au-dessous de, sous
benedictine *n.* (monk) bénédictin *m.;*
  (liqueur) bénédictine *f.*
benediction *n.* bénédiction *f.*
benefaction *n.* bienfait *m.*
benefactor *n.* bienfaiteur *m.*
benefactress *n.* bienfaitrice *f.*
beneficence *n.* bienfaisance *f.*
beneficent *a.* bienfaisant
beneficial *a.* avantageux, profitable;

salutaire
beneficiary n. bénéficiaire m. & f.
benefit n. avantage, profit m.; bénéfice m.; — vt. être avantageux, profiter à; bénéficier
benevolence n. bienveillance f.; bienfait m.
benevolent a. bienveillant; charitable; bienfaisant; -ly adv. avec bienveillance
benign a. bénin, bénigne
benignant a. bienveillant; bénin
bent n. penchant m.; inclination f.; — a. courbé; fléchi; résolu, déterminé
benumb vt. engourdir
benzine n. benzine f.
bequeath vt. léguer
bequest n. legs m.
berate vt. gronder
bereave vt. priver; -d a. & n. affligé m.; -ment n. deuil m.
Bermuda n. Bermudes m. pl.
berry n. baie f.; raisin m.; grain m.
berserk a. forcené, affolé
berth n. couchette f.; emplacement m.
beseech vt. supplier; -ing a. suppliant
beset vt. assiéger, assaillir
beside prep. à côté de, auprès de; be — oneself être hors de soi; être transporté; -s adv. en outre, d'ailleurs, en plus, de plus, du reste
besiege vt. assiéger; -r n. assiégeant m.
besmear vt. barbouiller, enduire
besmirch vt. souiller, salir
best a. le meilleur, la meilleure; — man témoin m.; do one's — faire de son mieux; get the — of it l'emporter, avoir le dessus; make the — of s'ac-comoder de; — adv. le mieux; at — pour dire le mieux; — vt. l'emporter sur
bestial a. bestial, brutal; -ity n. bestialité f.
bestow vt. donner, accorder; conférer; -al n. don m.
best seller n. livre à gros tirage m.
bet n. pari m., gageure f.; — vt. parier; -ting n. paris m.; -tor n. parieur m.
betray vt. trahir; révéler; -al n. trahison f.; révélation f.; -er n. traître m.; traîtresse f.
betroth vt. fiancer; -al n. fiançailles f. pl.
better a. meilleur; supérieur; — adv. mieux; so much the — tant mieux; be — aller mieux; get — guérir; s'améliorer; get the — of l'emporter sur; it is — il vaut mieux; think — of se raviser; — vt. améliorer; — vi. s'améliorer; -ment n. amélioration f.
between prep. entre; — (us) entre nous
bevel adj. en biseau; — vt. couper en biseau, biaiser; -ed a. coupé en biseau
beverage n. breuvage m., boisson f.
bevy n. troupe, bande f.; (quail) volée f.
bewail vt. pleurer, regretter
beware vt. se garder de, se méfier de
bewilder vt. confondre, égarer; -ed a. con-fondu, abasourdi; -ment n. abasourdis-sement, trouble m.
bewitch vt. ensorceler, enchanter; -ing a. enchanteur; ravissant
beyond adv. au delà; — prep. au delà de;

be —, go — dépasser; it is — me je n'y comprends rien; — (a) doubt hors de doute; — n. au-delà m.
biannual a. semi-annuel
bias n. biais m.; penchant m.; prévention f., préjugé m.; on the — en biais, de biais; — vt. prévenir; -ed a. prédisposé, partial
bib n. bavette f.
Bible n. Bible f.
biblical a. biblique
bibliographer n. bibliographe m.
bibliography n. bibliographie f.
bicarbonate n. bicarbonate m.; — of soda bicarbonate de soude m.
biceps n. biceps m.
bicker vi. se quereller, disputer; -ing a. querelleur; -ing n. querelle(s) f. (pl.)
bicuspid n. prémolaire f.
bicycle n. bicyclette f.; vélo m.; — vi. faire de la bicyclette; aller à bicyclette
bicycling n. cyclisme m.
bicyclist n. cycliste m. & f.
bid n. enchère, offre f.; (cards) demande f.; — vt. commander, ordonner; dire; offrir; (cards) demander; — vi. faire une offre; -der n. offrant, enchérisseur m.; -ding n. commandement ordre m.; enchères f. pl.
bide vt. attendre
biennial a. bisannuel
bier n. cercueil m.
bifocal a. bifocal
big a. gros, grand; get -(ger) grossir; grandir; talk — faire l'important; -ness n. grosseur f.; grandeur f.; — wheel (coll.) gros bonnet m.
bigamist n. bigame m. & f.
bigamy n. bigamie f.
Big Dipper n. Grande Ourse f.
bigot n. sectaire m. & f.; fanatique m. & f.; bigot m., bigote f.; -ed a. fanatique; étroit; -ry n. fanatisme m.; étroitesse f.
bike n. bécane f., vélo m.
bilateral a. bilatéral
bilge n. sentine f.; — water eau de cale f.
bilingual a. bilingue
bilious a. bilieux
bilk vt. tromper, escroquer
bill n. (bird) bec m.; (com.) facture, note f.; (restaurant) addition f.; affiche f., placard m.; (law) projet de loi m.; — of fare carte f.; — of lading connaisse-ment m.; — of sale facture f., acte de vente m.; post no -s défense d'afficher; — vt. facturer
billboard n. panneau d'affichage m.; enseigne f.
billet n. billet, logement m.; — vt. loger, cantonner
billfold n. portefeuille m.
billiard ball n. bille f.
billiards n. pl. billard m.
billion n. milliard m.
billionaire n. milliardaire m.
billow n. vague f., flot m.; — vt. ondoyer; — a. onduleux, ondoyant
billy (stick) n. bâton d'agent de police m.
billy goat n. (coll.) bouc m.
bimonthly a. bimensuel

bin n. huche f.; coffre m.

binary a. binaire

binaural a. stéréophonique

bind vt. lier; relier; obliger; bander; attacher; -er lieur m.; relieur m.; -ery n. atelier de reliure m.; -ing a. obligatoire; (med.) astringent; -ing n. reliure f.

binoculars n. pl. jumelle(s) f. pl.

binomial a. & n. binôme m.

biochemistry n. biochimie f.

biographer n. biographe m.

biographical a. biographique

biography n. biographie f.

biological a. biologique; — warfare guerre bactériologique f.

biologist n. biologiste m.

biology n. biologie f.

bipartisan n. (pol.) dit d'une politique approuvée par les deux partis

biped n. bipède m.

birch n. bouleau m.; verge f.

bird n. oiseau m.; — cage n. cage f.

bird's-eye view n. vue à vol d'oiseau f.

birth n. naissance f.; give — to donner naissance à, donner le jour à, mettre au monde; — certificate acte de naissance m.; — control restriction de la natalité f.; — rate natalité f.

birthday n. anniversaire m.

birthmark n. tache, envie f.

birthplace n. lieu de naissance m.

birthright n. droit de naissance m.

biscuit n. biscuit m.; (genre de) petit pain m. (à la levure chimique)

bisect vt. couper en deux

bisexual a. bissexuel

bishop n. évêque m.; (chess) fou m.; -ric n. évêché m.

bit n. (bridle) mors m.; (drill) mèche f.; morceau, bout, brin m.; a — (of) un peu (de); — by — peu à peu, petit à petit

bitch n. chienne f.; (coll.) garce f.

bite n. bouchée f.; morsure, piqûre f.; (fishing) touche f.; — vt. mordre, piquer

biting a. mordant, piquant

bitter a. amer; aigre, âpre; acerbe; -ness n. amertume f.; acrimonie f., rancune f.

bittersweet a. aigre-doux

bituminous a. bitumineux; — coal houille f.

biweekly a. bihebdomadaire; — adv. deux fois par mois

blab vi. bavarder, jaser; — vt. laisser échapper

black a. noir; sombre; — eye œil poché m.; — and blue (tout) meurtri; — market marché noir m.; — sheep brebis galeuse f.; — n. noir m.; in — and white par écrit; in the — (com.) bénéficiaire; — vi. & vt. noircir; -en vt. noircir; obscurcir; calomnier; -ish a. noirâtre; -ness n. noirceur f.; obscurité f.

blackball vt. blackbouler

blackberry n. mûre f.; mûre de ronce f.; (bush) mûrier sauvage m., ronce f.

blackbird n. merle m.

blackboard n. tableau noir m.

blackguard n. goujat, vaurien m.

blackhead n. point noir m.

blackjack n. assommoir m.; (cards) vingt-et-un m.

black list n. index m., liste des personnes interdites f.; — vt. boycotter, interdire

blackmail n. chantage m.; — vt. faire chanter

blackout n. obscurcissement m.; blackout, camouflage des lumières m.

blacksmith n. forgeron m.

bladder n. vessie f.

blade n. lame f.; brin (d'herbe) m.; (mech.) aile, ailette, pale f.; (man) gaillard m.

blamable a. blâmable, coupable

blame n. blâme m.; reproches m. pl.; faute f.; — vt. blâmer, reprocher; s'en prendre (à); -less a. innocent, irréprochable; -worthy a. blâmable

blanch vt. blanchir; — vi. pâlir

bland a. doux; affable; narquois; -ness n. douceur f.

blandish vt. flatter; -ment n. flatterie f.

blank a. blanc (blanche); — n. blanc, vide m.; lacune f.; formule f.

blanket n. couverture f.; — a. général; — vt. envelopper, couvrir

blare vi. sonner; — n. sonnerie f.; bruit m.

blaspheme vt. & vi. blasphémer; -r n. blasphémateur m.

blasphemous a. blasphémateur; blasphématoire

blasphemy n. blasphème m.

blast n. bouffée f.; souffle m.; jet m.; charge f.; coup m.; full — (fig.) en pleine activité; — furnace haut fourneau m.; — vt. détruire; faire sauter; foudroyer; -ing n. abattage à la poudre m.

blatant a. vulgaire; criant

blaze n. flamme f., incendie m.; feu m.; — vi. flamber; flamboyer; — a trail tracer un chemin; frayer un chemin

blazer n. jacquette f., veston m.

blazing a. en feu, embrasé; flambant

bleach vt. blanchir; — n. blanchiment m.; eau de Javel f.

bleachers n. gradins m. pl.

bleak a. froid, désert, triste, morne; -ness n. tristesse f.; nudité f.

bleary a. chassieux; larmoyant

bleat vi. bêler; -ing n. bêlement m.

bleed vt. & vi. saigner; -ing a. saignant; -ing n. saignement m.; saignée f.

blemish n. tache f.; défaut m.; — vt. tacher; souiller

blench vi. pâlir

blend n. mélange m.; — vt. mêler, mélanger

bless vt. bénir; -ed a. saint; bienheureux; béni; -ing n. bénédiction f.

blight n. influence néfaste f.; (agr.) rouille f.; — vt. flétrir, frustrer, anéantir

blimp n. dirigeable m.

blind a. aveugle; — alley cul-de-sac m.; — person aveugle m. & f.; -ly adv. aveuglément; — vt. aveugler; éblouir; — n. store m.; jalousie, persienne f.; (fig.) feinte f., subterfuge m.; -ness n.

cécité f.; (fig.) aveuglement m.

blindfold n. bande f.; — vt. bander les yeux; -(ed) a. & adv. les yeux bandés

blink n. clignotement m.; — vi. cligner, clignoter, battre (des yeux); -er n. feu clignotant m.; (horses) œillère f.; -ing a. clignotant; -ing n. clignotement m.

bliss n. félicité f.; -ful a. heureux, bienheureux; -fullness n. béatitude, félicité f.

blister n. ampoule f.; cloque f.; boursouflure f.; — vi. se couvrir d'ampoules

blithe a. gai, heureux

blizzard n. tourmente de neige f.

bloat vt. & vi. enfler, bouffir; -ed a. enflé; congestionné

blob n. pâté (d'encre) m.; goutte f.; tache f.

block n. bloc m.; pâté de maisons m.; (com.) tranche f.; (toy) cube m.; — vt. bloquer, barrer; — up boucher; murer

blockade n. blocus m.; to run the — forcer le blocus; — vt. bloquer

blockbuster n. grosse bombe aérienne f.

blockhead n. sot, imbécile m.

blockhouse n. blockhaus m.

blood n. sang m.; parenté f.; race f.; — bank réserve de sang f.; — donor donneur de sang m.; — orange sanguine f.; — plasma plasma du sang m.; — poisoning septicémie f.; — pressure tension artérielle f.; high — pressure hypertension f.; — stream cours du sang m.; — vessel vaisseau sanguinaire m.; in cold — de sang-froid; -y a. sanglant; — hound n. limier m.

bloodshed n. effusion de sang f.; carnage m.

bloodshot a. injecté de sang; éraillé

bloodstain n. tache de sang f.; -ed a. taché de sang

bloodthirsty a. sanguinaire

bloom n. fleur f.; épanouissement m.; in — en fleur, épanoui; — vi. fleurir; -ing a. fleurissant, florissant; -ing n. fleuraison, floraison f.

bloomers n. pl. (sorte de) culotte de femme f.

blooper n. (coll.) gaffe, bévue f.

blossom n. fleur f.; — vi. fleurir

blot n. tache d'encre f.; pâté m.; — vt. tacher; sécher; — vi. boire; -ter n. buvard m.; -ting paper papier buvard m.

blotch n. pustule f.; tache f.; -y a. brouillé; tacheté

blouse n. blouse f.; corsage m.

blow n. coup m.; at a — d'un coup; come to —s en venir aux coups; — vi. souffler; — one's nose se moucher; — away emporter; — out (auto.) éclater; — over passer; — up éclater, sauter; (coll.) se mettre en colère; (phot.) agrandir; -er n. ventilateur m.

blowout n. (auto.) crevaison f.

blowpipe n. chalumeau m.

blowtorch n. lampe à braser f.

blubber n. graisse de baleine f.; — vi. pleurnicher

bludgeon n. assommer, rouer de coups; — n. assommoir m.; massue, matraque f.

blue a. bleu; (fig.) triste, mélancolique; — cheese espèce de fromage genre roquefort m.; — chips (stocks) premières valeurs f. pl.; -n. bleu m.; azur m.; light — bleu clair; navy — bleu marine; -s a. mélancolie f.; (mus.) blues m. pl.; — vt. & vi. bleuir

blueberry n. airelle myrtille f.

bluebird n. oiseau bleu m.

blue-eyed a. aux yeux bleus

blueprint n. négatif, bleu m.; plan m.

bluff a. escarpé; — n. falaise f.; à-pic m.; bluff m.; — vt. bluffer

bluing, blueing n. bleu m.

bluish a. bleuâtre

blunder n. bévue, gaffe f.; — vi. faire une bévue, gaffer; — into se heuter contre; -ing a. maladroit

blunt a. émoussé; brusque; — vt. émousser

blur n. tache f.; ternissure f.; — vt. barbouiller; brouiller; rendre indistinct

blurb n. annonce publicitaire f.

blurt vt., — out laisser échapper

blush n. rougeur f.; — vi. rougir

bluster vi. tempêter, tonner; — n. fracas, tapage m.; emportement m.

boar n. cochon mâle, verrat m.; wild — sanglier m.

board n. planche f.; table f.; tableau m.; (chess) tablier m.; commission f.; ironing — planche à repasser f.; room and — pension f.; — of directors conseil d'administration m.; on — à bord; — vi. être en pension, prendre la pension; — vt. s'embarquer; monter dans; — up boucher; -er n. pensionnaire m. & f.; (schools) interne m. & f.

boardinghouse n. pension f.

boardwalk n. promenade (faite de planches) au bord de la mer f.

boast n. vanterie f.; — vi. se vanter (de); -ful a. arrogant, vantard; -ing n. jactance f.

boat n. bateau m.; barque f.; canot m.; embarcation f.; -ing n. canotage m.; to go -ing faire du canotage, canoter

boat hook n. gaffe f.

boathouse n. hangar, garage m.

boatload n. batelée f.

boatman n. batelier m.

boat race n. régate f.

boatswain n. maître d'équipage m.

bob vi. s'agiter, danser; -bed a. coupé court

bobbin n. bobine f.

bobby pin n. épingle à cheveux f.

bobby-socks n. pl. chaussettes courtes f. pl.

bobby-soxer n. zazou m.

bobsled, bobsleigh n. bob m.

bode vt. & vi. présager

bodily a. corporel, physique; — adv. corporellement; en corps

body n. corps m.; cadavre m.; substance f.; (auto.) carrosserie f.

bodyguard n. garde du corps m.

bog n. marécage m.; fondrière f.; — vt. enliser; — (down) vi. s'enliser

bogus *a.* faux, fausse; simulé

Bohemia *n.* Bohême; **–n** *a. & n.* bohémien *m.*

boil *n.* ébullition *f.*; (med.) furoncle, clou *m.*; **—** *vi.* bouillir, bouillonner; **—** *vt.* faire bouillir; **–er** *n.* chaudière *f.*; **–ing** *a.* bouillant; **–ing** *n.* ébullition *f.*, bouillonnement *m.*; **–ing point** point d'ébullition *m.*

boilermaker *n.* chaudronnier *m.*

boisterous *a.* bruyant, débordant; **–ly** *adv.* bruyamment

bold *a.* audacieux, téméraire; hardi; effronté; **–ness** *n.* audace, témérité, hardiesse, effronterie *f.*

boldface (type) *n.* caractères gras *m. pl.*

bold-faced *a.* effronté

Bolivia *n.* Bolivie *f.*

boll weevil *n.* hélothis *m.*

Bolshevik *a. & n.* bolchevique *m. & f.*

bolster *n.* traversin *m.*; **—** *vt.* soutenir

bolt *n.* verrou, pêne *m.*; rouleau, coupon *m.*; coup de foudre *m.*; screw **—** boulon *m.* (à écrou); thunder **—** fuite *f.*; **—** *vt.* verrouiller; (food) gober; **—** *vi.* décamper

bomb *n.* bombe *f.*; **—** shelter abri (à l'épreuve des bombes) *m.*; **—** *vt.* bombarder; **–er** *n.* avion de bombardement, bomber *m.*; **–ing** *n.* bombardement *m.*

bombard *vt.* bombarder; **–ier** *n.* bombardier *m.*; **–ment** *n.* bombardement *m.*

bombast *n.* boursouflage *m.*; enflure *f.*; **–ic** *a.* boursouflé, enflé

bombproof *a.* à l'épreuve des bombes

bombshell *n.* (fig.) sensation *f.*

bombsight *n.* viseur *m.*

bonanza *n.* aubaine *f.*; trouvaille *f.*

bond *n.* lien *m.*; obligation *f.*; (com.) bon *m.*; titre *m.*; in **—** (com.) à l'entrepôt; **—** *vt.* (com.) entreposer, mettre à l'entrepôt; **–age** *n.* esclavage *m.*; servitude *f.*

bondholder *n.* obligataire *m. & f.*

bondsman *n.* (law) répondant *m.*

bone *n.* os *m.*; (fish) arête *f.*; have a **—** to pick avoir maille à partir; **—** *vt.* désosser; **–less** *a.* désossé, sans os, sans arêtes

bonfire *n.* feu de joie *m.*

bonnet *n.* bonnet, chapeau *m.*

bonus *n.* boni *m.*; prime *f.*; gratification *f.*

bony *a.* osseux; décharné

booby *n.* nigaud *m.*; **—** prize prix qu'on donne au plus mauvais joueur *m.*; **—** trap attrape-nigaud *m.*

book *n.* livre *m.*; bouquin *m.*; livret *m.*; carnet *m.*; telephone **—** annuaire *m.*; **—** ends serre-livres *m. pl.*; **—** review compte rendu *m.*; **—** *vt.* louer, réserver; **–ing** *n.* réservation *f.*; (theat.) location *f.*

bookbinder *n.* relieur *m.*

bookcase *n.* bibliothèque *f.*; étagère *f.*

bookkeeper *n.* comptable *m. & f.*

bookkeeping *n.* comptabilité *f.*

booklet *n.* livret *m.*; opuscule *m*; brochure *f.*

bookmark *n.* signet *m.*

bookmobile *n.* bibliobus *m.*

bookseller *n.* libraire *m. & f.*

bookshelf *n.* étagère. *f.*, rayon (de bibliothèque) *m.*

bookshop, bookstore *n.* librairie *f.*

bookworm *n.* ciron *m.*; (fig.) bibliomane, mangeur de livres *m.*

boom *n.* barrage *m.*; (naut.) bout-dehors, tangon, mât de charge *m.*; retentissement *m.*; (com.) boom *m.*; vogue *f.*; **—** *vi.* retentir, gronder; (com.) être en hausse, prospérer; **–ing** *a.* (com.) florissant; (voice) retentissant

boomerang *n.* boumerang *m.*; **—** *vi.* revenir vers soi; réagir sur soi

boon *n.* don *m.*, faveur *f.*

boor *n.* rustre *m.*; goujat *m.*; **–ish** *a.* grossier, rustre; **–ishness** *n.* grossièreté, rusticité *f.*

boost *n.* relèvement *m.* aide *f.*; **—** *vt.* soulever par derrière; faire du battage de la réclame pour; (elec.) survolter; **–er** *n.* réclamiste *m.*; (elec.) survolteur *m.*; **–er shot** (med.) rappel de vaccination *m.*; **–ing** *n.* battage *m.*, réclame *f.*

boot *n.* botte, bottine *f.*; to **—** *adv.* en sus; **—** *vt.* botter; **—** out chasser (à coups de pied); **–ee, –ie** *n.* chausson de bébé *m.*

bootblack *n.* cireur *m.*

booth *n.* tente *f.*; cabine *f.*

bootie *n.* chausson de bébé *m.*

bootleg *a.* de contrebande; **—** *vt.* faire la contrebande (de l'alcool); **–ger** *n.* contrebandier *m.*; **–ging** *n.* contrebande *f.*

booty *n.* butin *m.*

border *n.* bord *m.*, bordure *f.*; frontière *f.*; galon *m.*; **—** *vi.* border; **—** on toucher; approcher

borderline *n.* frontière *f.*; **—** *a.* limite

bore *n.* trou *m.*; calibre *m.*; (person) raseur *m.*; ennui *m.*; **—** *vt.* percer; sonder; ennuyer, raser; **–dom** *n.* ennui *m.*

boric *a.* borique

boring *a.* ennuyant, ennuyeux; (coll.) assommant

born, to be — naître; **—** *a.* né

boron *n.* bore *m.*

borough *n.* bourg *m.*

borrow *vt.* emprunter; **–er** *n.* emprunteur *m.*

bosom *n.* sein *m.*; poitrine *f.*; (fig.) giron *m.*

boss *n.* chef, patron *m.*; **—** *vt.* diriger, régenter; **–y** *a.* autoritaire

botanical *a.* botanique

botanist *n.* botaniste *m.*

botany *n.* botanique *f.*

botch *vt.* saboter; ravauder; mal faire

both *a.* les deux; **—** *pron.* tous les deux; **— . . .** and **et . . .** et

bother *n.* ennui *m.*; **—** *vt.* déranger, ennuyer, gêner; **–some** *a.* importun

bottle *n.* bouteille *f.*; bocal *m.*; **—** brush *n.* goupillon *m.*; nursing **—** biberon *m.*; **—** *vt.* mettre en bouteille; **—** up embouteiller

bottleneck *n.* goulot *m.*; embouteillage *m.*

bottling *n.* mise en bouteilles *f.*

bottom *n.* fond *m.*; bas *m.*; dessous *m.*;

at — au fond; — dollar dernier sou m.; —less a. sans fond

bough n. rameau m.

boulder n. bloc, rocher m.

bounce n. bond, rebond m.; — vi. rebondir; — vt. faire rebondir; (coll.) flanquer à la porte; -r n. (coll.) agent, souteneur m.

bound n. bornes, limites f. pl.; bond, saut m.; out of —s hors des limites; défendu; — vi. borner, limiter; sauter, bondir; — a. lié; engagé, obligé; — for en route pour; -less a. sans bornes; illimité

boundary n. borne, limite f; frontière f

bounteous, bountiful a. bienfaisant; généreux

bounty n. bonté, munificence f.; prime, subvention f.

bouquet n. bouquet m.

bout n. match m.; accès m.

bovine a. bovin

bow n. arc m.; (mus.) archet m.; (saddle) ,arçon m.; (ribbon) nœud m.; révérence f.; inclinaison f.; (naut.) avant m.; — tie nœud papillon m.; — vi. s'incliner; — vt. courber

bowels n. pl. entrailles f. pl.

bower n. tonnelle f., berceau m.

bowie-knife n. couteau-poignard m.

bowl n. bol m.; (spoon) cuilleron m.; (pipe) fourneau m.; (stadium) stade m.; — vt. jeter, lancer; — vi. jouer aux boules; (U.S.) jouer aux quilles; — over renverser; -er n. joueur (de boules, de quilles) m.; chapeau melon m.; -ing n. jeu de boules m.; -ing pin n. quille f.

bowlegged a. arqué, bancal; to be — avoir les jambes arquées

bowman n. archer m.

bowsprit n. beaupré m.

bowstring n. corde d'arc f.; cordon m.

box n. boîte f.; coffre, coffret m.; carton m.; caisse f.; cabine f.; (theat.) loge, baignoire f.; — on the ear claque f.; — camera détective m.; — office bureau de location m.; — vt. mettre en boîte; emboîter, encartonner; claquer; — vt. & vi. (sports) boxer; -er n. boxeur m.; -ing n. boxe f.

boxcar n. wagon de marchandises m.

boy n. garçon, enfant m.; gamin m.; — scout scout, éclaireur m.; -hood n. enfance f.; -ish a. d'enfant, de garçon; enfantin

boycott n. boycottage m.; — vt. boycotter

brace n. attache f., lien m.; écharpe f.; paire f.; vilebrequin m.; — vt. ancrer; fortifier

bracer n. tonique m.; brassard m.

bracing n. tonique

bracket n. console f.; (print.) crochet m.

brackish a. saumâtre

brad n. clou (sans tête) m.

brag n. vanterie f., jactance f.; — vi. se vanter; -gart n. vantard, fanfaron m.

braid n. tresse f.; galon m.; passementerie f.; — vt. tresser; galonner; passementer

brain n. cerveau m., cervelle f.; rack one's — se creuser la cervelle; -storm inspira-

tion f.; — vt. casser la tête à; -less a. stupide, sans intelligence; -y a. intelligent

brainwashing n. (coll.) indoctrination idéologique (imposée aux prisonniers politiques ou de guerre) f.

brake n. frein m.; — vt. freiner, serrer les freins

brakeman n. (rail.) serre-frein m.

bramble n. ronce f.

bran n. son m.

branch n. branche f.; succursale f.; embranchement m.; — v. — off s'embrancher, se bifurquer; — out se ramifier

brand n. brandon, tison m.; fer chaud m.; flétrissure f.; (com.) marque f.; — vt. marquer au fer chaud, flétrir; -ing iron n. fer (à flétrir)

brandish vt. brandir

brand-new a. tout neuf

brandy n. eau-de-vie f.

brash a. impertinent, insolent

brass n. cuivre jaune, laiton m.; airain m.; (mus.) cuivre m.

brassiere n. soutien-gorge m.

brat n. (coll.) gosse, marmot m.

bravado n. bravade f.

brave a. brave, courageux; — vt. braver; -ry n. bravoure f.

brawl n. bagarre f.; querelle f.; — vi. brailler; se quereller

brawn n. muscles m. pl.; -y a. musclé

bray n. braiment m.; — vi. braire

braze vt. braser; souder

brazen a. d'airain; impudent, effronté

brazier n. chaudronnier m.

Brazil n. Brésil m.; -ian a. & n. brésilien m.

breach n. brèche f.; rupture f.; infraction, violation f.; — of promise manque de parole m.; — of trust abus de confiance m.; — vt. ouvrir une brèche; battre en brèche

bread n. pain m.; — crumbs chapelure f.; — vt. paner, gratiner

breadbasket n. corbeille à pain f.; (coll.) estomac m.

breadboard n. planche à pain f.

breadth n. largeur f.

breadwinner n. gagne-pain m.; soutien de famille m.

break n. rupture, ouverture f.; cassure, fracture f.; lacune f.; interruption f.; répit, battement m.; — of day pointe du jour f.; aube f.; — vt. briser, casser, rompre; amortir; ruiner; — one's word manquer de parole; — in enfoncer; rompre; interrompre; — into entrer de force; cambrioler; — open forcer, enfoncer; — out éclater; s'échapper; — through percer; — up disperser; fragmenter; diviser; -able a. fragile; -age n. fracture f.; casse f.; -er n. (naut.) brisant m.

breakdown n. arrêt m.; épuisement m.; (auto) panne f.

breakfast n. petit déjeuner m.; — vi. déjeuner

breakneck a. casse-cou

breakwater n. brise-lames m.; digue f.

breast n. sein m.; mamelle f.; poitrine f.; — vt. affronter

breastbone n. sternum m.

breastplate n. cuirasse f.

breastwork n. parapet m.

breath n. haleine f., souffle m.; out of — essoufflé, à bout de souffle; -e vt. & vi. respirer, souffler; -ing n. respiration f., souffle m.; -ing space répit m.; -less a. essoufflé, haletant

breech n. (gun) culasse f.; -es n. pl. culotte f., pantalon m.

breed n. race f.; — vt. engendrer, produire; élever, faire de l'élevage; — vi. se reproduire; -ing n. éducation f.; élevage m.; -er n. éleveur m.; reproduction f.; manières f. pl.; savoir-vivre m.

breeze n. brise f.; vent m.

breezy a. venteux; jovial

brethren n. pl. frères m. pl.

brevity n. brièveté f.

brew n. breuvage m.; brassage m.; infusion f.; — vt. brasser; — vi. s'infuser; -er n. brasseur m.; -ery n. brasserie f.; -ing brassage m.

bribe n. pot-de-vin m.; — vt. corrompre, suborner; -ry n. corruption f.

brick n. brique f.; — vt. briqueter

brickbat n. briquaillon m.; hurl -s at (fig.) lapider

bricklayer n. maçon m.

brickyard n. briqueterie f.

bridal a. nuptial

bride n. épousée f.; future f.

bridegroom n. marié m.; futur m.

bridesmaid n. demoiselle d'honneur f.

bridge n. pont m.; (naut.) passerelle f.; (cards) bridge m.; — vt. construire un pont sur; — a gap combler une lacune

bridgehead n. (mil.) tête de pont f.

bridle n. bride f.; frein m.; — path piste f.; — vt. brider; maltriser

brief a. bref; court; to be — en résumé; — n. résumé, abrégé m.; dossier m.; — vt. mettre au courant; -ing n. mise au courant f.; -ness n. brièveté f.; -s n. pl. sous-vêtement court m.

brief case n. serviette f.

brig n. brick m.; prison navale f.

brigadier general n. général de brigade m.

brigantine n. brigantin m.

bright a. clair; brillant; lumineux; éclatant; vif; —en vt. faire briller; —en vi. s'éclaircir; -ness n. éclat m.; clarté f.; vivacité f.; intelligence f.

Bright's disease n. néphrite albumineuse f.

brilliance, brilliancy n. éclat m., splendeur f.

brilliant a. brillant, éclatant; -ly adv. brillamment

brilliantine n. brillantine f.

brim n. bord m.; — vi. déborder; -ful, -ming a. débordant

brimstone n. soufre m.

brine n. saumure f.

bring vt. apporter, amener; — about causer, opérer; — along amener; —

back ramener; rapporter; — down descendre; faire crouler; — in introduire; — out sortir; faire ressortir; — together réunir; — up éduquer, élever; monter; -ing n., -ing up éducation f.

brink n. bord m.

briny a. salé, amer, saumâtre

brisk a. actif; vif; rapide; vivifiant; -ness n. vivacité; activité f.

brisket n. poitrine f.

bristle n. soie f.; poil m.; — vi. se hérisser

bristling a. hérissé

Britain n., Great — Grande Bretagne f.

British a. britannique; anglais

Brittany n. Bretagne f.

brittle a. fragile, cassant; -ness n. fragilité f.

broad a. large; grand; général; — daylight plein jour m.; — jump saut (en longeur) m.; —en vt. élargir; —en vi. s'élargir; -ness n. largeur f.

broadcast n. radiodiffusion, émission f.; — vt. radiodiffuser, émettre; répandre; -ing n. radiodiffusion f.; -er n. (instrument) émetteur m.; (person) microphoniste m.

broadcloth n. popeline f.

broad-minded a. aux idées larges; tolérant

broadside n. bordée f.; côté m.; (print.) placard m.

brocade n. brocart m.; -d a. de brocart

broccoli n. brocoli m.

brochure n. brochure f.

brogue n. accent f. (irlandais) m.; patois m.; (shoe) brogue f.

broil vt. & vi. griller; -er gril m.

broke (coll.) fauché

broken a. brisé, cassé, rompu

broker n. agent m.; courtier m.; (stock) agent de change m.; -age n. courtage m.

bromide n. bromure m.

bromine n. brome m.

bronchi, bronchia n. pl. bronches f. pl.

bronchial a. bronchique

bronchitis n. bronchite f.

bronco n. cheval sauvage (américain) m.

brooch n. broche, épingle f.

brood n. couvée f.; — hen couveuse f.; — mare poulinière f.; — vi. couver; rêver (noir)

brook n. ruisseau m.; — vt. souffrir

broom n. balai m.

broomstick n. manche à balai m.

broth n. bouillon, consommé m.

brothel n. bordel m.

brother n. frère m.; -hood n. fraternité, confrérie f.; -ly a. fraternel; -ly adv. fraternellement

brother-in-law n. beau-frère m.

brow n. front m.; sourcil m.; to knit one's — froncer les sourcils

browbeat vt. intimider

brown a. brun; marron; châtain; bruni; — paper papier d'emballage m.; — sugar cassonade f.; — n. brun m.; — vt. dorer; brunir; rissoler; -ish a. brunâtre

browse vt. & vi. brouter; butiner (dans), feuilleter

bruise n. meurtrissure f.; bleu m.; — vt. meurtrir; —r n. costaud, fort, boxeur m.

brunette n. brune f.

brunt n. choc m.

brush n. brosse f.; (paint) pinceau m.; (elec.) balai m.; (bot.) brousse f.; — vt. brosser; — against frôler; — aside écarter; — up (on) repasser, rafraîchir

brushwood n. broussailles f. pl.; brindilles f. pl.

Brussels n. Bruxelles; — sprouts choux de Bruxelles m. pl.

brutal a. brutal; -ity n. brutalité f.; -ize vt. abrutir

brute n. brute f.; — a. brutal; sauvage

brutish a. brutal; -ness n. brutalité f.

bubble n. bulle f.; — gum gomme à bulles f., bubble-gum m.; — vi. bouillonner; — over déborder

buccaneer n. boucanier n.

buck n. daim, chevreuil m.; (coll.) dollar m.; — a., — private (mil.) simple soldat m.; — teeth dents saillantes f. pl.

bucket n. seau m.

buckle n. boucle, agrafe f.; — vt. boucler, agrafer; — vi. arquer, gauchir; — down s'appliquer

buckram n. bougran m.

buckshot n. gros plomb m.

buckskin n. peau de daim f.

buckwheat n. sarrasin m.; — cakes n. pl. crêpes de sarrasin f. pl.

bud n. bouton, bourgeon m.; — vi. boutonner; bourgeonner; -ding a. en bouton; en germe; en herbe

Buddhism n. bouddhisme m.

Buddhist n. bouddhiste m.

buddy n. copain m.

budge vi. bouger; reculer

budget n. budget m.; -ary a. budgétaire

buff a. & n. couleur chamois f.; — vt. polir, émeuler

buffalo n. buffle m.; bison m.

buffer n. (rail.) tampon m.; (polishing) brunissoir m.

buffet vt. frapper, jeter çà et là

buffoon n. bouffon m.; -ery n. bouffonnerie f.

bug n. insecte m.; (coll.) idée fixe f.

bugaboo, bugbear n. croque-mitaine f.

buggy n. buggy, boghei m.; baby — voiture d'enfant f.

bugle n. (mil.) cor de chasse; clairon m.; -r n. clairon m.

build vt. bâtir, construire m.; -er n. entrepreneur, constructeur m.; (fig.) fondateur m.; -ing n. bâtiment, édifice m.; maison f.; construction f.

bulb n. bulbe f., oignon m.; (elec.) ampoule f.; lampe f.; -ous a. bulbeux

Bulgaria n. Bulgarie f.; — a. & n. bulgare m. & f.

bulge n. bosse, protubérance f.; bombement, renflement m.; — vi. faire une bosse, bomber; -ing a. bombé; protubérant; bourré

bulk n. masse, quantité f.; volume m.; in — en volume, en bloc, en gros; en quantité; -y a. volumineux; gros

bulkhead n. cloison f.

bulldoze vt. intimider; -r n. bulldozer m.

bullet n. balle f.

bulletin n. bulletin m.; communiqué m.; — board tableau d'affichage m.

bulletproof a. à l'épreuve des balles

bullfight n. course de taureaux f.; -er n. toréador m.

bullfrog n. grosse grenouille f.

bullion n. or en lingot m.; argent en lingot m.

bullock n. bœuf m.

bull's-eye n. (target) noir, centre m.; (window) œil-de-bœuf m.

bully n. brutal, tyran m.; — vt. brutaliser, malmener

bulwark n. rempart m.

bumblebee n. bourdon m.

bump n. bosse f.; choc m.; cahot m.; — vt. cogner; — vi. se cogner; -er n. (auto.) pare-choc(s); (rail.) tampon m.; -er a., -er crop récolte magnifique f.; -y a. cahoteux

bumpkin n. rustre, lourdaud m.

bun n. petit pain m.; chignon m.

bunch n. botte f., bouquet m.; grappe f.; (keys) trousseau m.; bande f., groupe m.; — vt. grouper; — vi. se serrer

bunco n. mystification, escroquerie f.; tricherie f.

bundle n. paquet m.; liasse f.; ballot m.; — vt. empaqueter, mettre en paquet

bung n. bondon m.; — vt. bondonner

bungle vt. rater; gâcher; -r n. maladroit, gâcheur m.

bungling a. gauche, maladroit; — n. maladresse f.

bunion n. oignon (au pied) m.

bunk n. couchette f.; (coll.) balivernes f. pl.; — vi. se coucher

bunker n. soute f.; (golf) banquette f.

Bunsen burner n. bec Bunsen m.

bunting n. drapeaux m. pl.; étamine f.; (bird) bruant m.

buoy n. (naut.) bouée f.; — vt. faire flotter; soutenir; -ancy n. flottabilité f.; -ant a. flottable

burden n. fardeau m., charge f.; (mus.) refrain m.; beast of — bête de somme f.; — vt. charger; -some a. onéreux

bureau n. bureau m.; secrétaire m.; commode f.

bureaucracy n. bureaucratie f.

bureaucrat n. bureaucrate, rond-de-cuir m.; -ic a. bureaucratique

burgess, burgher n. bourgeois, citoyen m.

burglar n. cambrioleur m.; — alarm signalisateur antivol m.; -ize vt. cambrioler; -y n. cambriolage m.

Burgundy n. Bourgogne f.; — wine bourgogne m.; vin de bourgogne m.

burial n. enterrement m.

burlap n. toile d'emballage f.

burlesque a. burlesque; — n. burlesque m.; parodie f.; variété f.; — vt. parodier

burly a. solide, costaud

Burma n. Birmanie f.

burn n. brûlure f.; — vt. & vi. brûler; -er n. bec de gaz m.; brûleur m.; -ing *a.* brûlant; embrasé; en feu

burnish *vt.* brunir, polir

burro *n.* âne, baudet *m.*

burrow *n.* terrier *m.*; — *vt.* creuser; — *vi.* se terrer

bursar *n.* économe (d'une université) *m.*

burst *n.* explosion *f.*; éclat *m.*; jet *m.*; — *vi.* éclater, exploser; crever; — out laughing éclater de rire; — into tears se mettre à pleurer

bury *vt.* enterrer, inhumer

bus *n.* autobus, autocar, car *m.*

busboy *n.* garçon de restaurant (chargé d'enlever le couvert) *m.*

bush *n.* buisson *m.*; arbuste, arbrisseau *m.* -y *a.* buissonneux; touffu

bushel *n.* demi-boisseau *m.* (= 36 litres)

bushing *n.* garniture *f.*; fourrure *f.*; paroi intérieur *m.*

busily *adv.* . d'un air affairé; activement

business *n.* affaire(s) *f.* (*pl.*); it's none of your — cela ne vous regarde pas

businesslike *a.* capable, sérieux

businessman *n.* commerçant, homme d'affaires *m.*

bust *n.* (sculpture) buste *m.*; gorge, poitrine *f.*

bustle *n.* remue-ménage, affairement *m.*; .— *vi.* se remuer, s'affairer

bustling *a.* affairé

busy *a.* occupé, affairé; — *vt.*, — oneself with s'occuper à

busybody *n.* officieux *m.*

but *conj.* mais; toutefois; — *prep.* sauf, excepté; sinon

butcher *n.* boucher *m.*; — shop boucherie *f.*; — *vt.* massacrer, égorger; -y *n.* massacre *m.*, tuerie *f.*

butler *n.* maître d'hôtel *m.*

butt *n.* bout *m.*; (gun) crosse *f.*; (cigarette) mégot *m.*; (of a remark) plastron *m.*; (blow) coup de tête *m.*; — end gros bout *m.*; — *vt.* & *vi.* buter (contre); donner des coups de la tête (contre); — in intervenir sans façon

butter *n.* beurre *m.*; — dish beurrier *m.*; — *vt.* beurrer; — up (coll.) flatter; — fat gras de beurre *m.*

butterfingered *a.* maladroit

butterfly *n.* papillon *m.*

buttermilk *n.* petit lait *m.*; babeurre *m.*

buttock *n.* fesse *f.*

button *n.* bouton *m.*; — *vt.* boutonner

buttonhole *n.* boutonnière *f.*; — *vt.* interpeller, prendre à part, aborder

buttonhook *n.* tire-bouton *m.*

buttress *n.* arc-boutant *m.*; contrefort *m.*; — *vt.* arc-bouter

buxom *a.* plantureux

buy *vt.* acheter; -er *n.* acheteur

buzz *n.* bourdonnement *m.*; — saw scie circulaire *f.*; — *vi.* bourdonner; -er *n.* sonnerie *f.*

buzzard *n.* busard *m.*; vautour *m.*

by *prep.* par; près de; en; — *adv.* là; par là; close — tout près; — and — tout à l'heure; to stand — être là

bygone *a.* d'autrefois, passé

bylaws *n.* *pl.* ordonnances *f.* *pl.*; règlements *m.* *pl.*

by-line *n.* signature de journaliste *f.*

bypass *n.* contournement *m.*, déviation *f.*; — *vt.* contourner, dévier, éviter

byplay *n.* jeu muet *m.*

by-product *n.* dérivé, sous-produit *m.*

bystander *n.* assistant, spectateur *m.*

byway *n.* chemin obscur *m.*

byword *n.* proverbe *m.*

Byzantine *a.* byzantin; — Empire Bas-Empire *m.*

C

cab *n.* taxi *m.*; fiacre *m.*; cabine *f.*; — driver *n.* chauffeur de taxi *m.*

cabal *n.* cabale *f.*; — *vi.* cabaler; -istic *a.* cabalistique

cabaret *m.* boîte de nuit *f.*

cabbage *n.* chou *m.*

cabin *n.* case, cabane *f.*; (naut.) cabine *f.*; — boy mousse *m.*; — class deuxième classe *f.*

cabinet *n.* cabinet *m.*; conseil des ministres *m.*

cabinetmaker *n.* ébéniste *m.*

cable *n.* câble *m.*; chaîne *f.*; — *vt.* câbler

cable car *n.* funiculaire *m.*; téléférique *m.*

cablegram *n.* câblogramme *m.*

cable length *n.* encablure *f.*

caboose *n.* (train) fourgon de queue *m.*

cabstand *n.* taxiplace *f.*

cackle *n.* caquet *m.*; — *vi.* caqueter

cacophony *n.* cacophonie *f.*

cad *n.* mufle *m.*

cadaver *n.* cadavre *m.*

caddie, caddy *n.* (golf) caddie, cadet *m.*

cadence *n.* cadence *f.*, rythme *m.*

cadet *n.* cadet *m.*; élève-officier *m.*

Cadiz *n.* Cadix

cadmium *n.* cadmium *m.*

cæsarian *a.* césarienne

café *n.* café, restaurant *m.*; — curtains demi-rideaux *m.* *pl.*

cafeteria *n.* self-service, libre-service *m.*

caffein *n.* caféine *f.*

cage *n.* cage *f.*; — *vt.* mettre en cage; encager

cagey *a.* (coll.) malin, rusé, fin

Cairo *n.* Le Caire

caisson *n.* caisson *m.*

cajole *vt.* cajoler, enjôler

cajoling *a.* cajoleur

cake *n.* gâteau *m.*; pâtisserie *f.*; croûte *f.*; — of soap pain de savon *m.*; — *vi.* s'agglutiner, se prendre; faire croûte

calabash *n.* calebasse *f.*

calamitous *a.* calamiteux, désastreux

calamity *n.* calamité *f.*; malheur *m.*; désastre *m.*

calcify *vt.* calcifier; — *vi.* se calcifier

calcimine *n.* chaux *f.*

calcite *n.* calcaire *m.*

calcium *n.* calcium *m.*

calculate *vt.* calculer; compter

calculating *a.* calculateur

calculation *n.* calcul *m.*

calculator *n.* machine à calculer *f.*

calculus *n.* calcul, cacul infinitésimal *m.*

caldron *n.* chaudron *m.*

calendar n. calendrier m.
calf n. veau m.; (of the leg) mollet m.
calfskin n. veau m., peau de veau f.
caliber, calibre n. calibre m.
calibrate vt. calibrer; graduer
calico n. calicot m., indienne f.
calipers n. pl. compas à-calibrer m.
calisthenics n. pl. callisthénie f.
calk, caulk vt. calfater
call n. appel m.; cri m.; visite f.; curtain — rappel m.; telephone — coup de téléphone m.; — vt. appeler; crier; convoquer; — vi. faire une visite; (naut.) faire escale; — for venir chercher; demander; — off rompre; — up donner un coup de téléphone; (mil.) mobiliser; -ing n. vocation, profession f., métier m.; -ing card carte de visite f.
callous a. calleux; insensible, dur
callow a. jeune, inexpérimenté
callus n. callosité f.
calm vt. calmer; tranquilliser; — down vt. pacifier; — down vi. se calmer; — a. calme, tranquille; —, -ness n. calme m.; tranquillité f.
calorie, calory n. calorie f.
calumny n. calomnie, diffamation f.
caluminate vt. calomnier
calvary n. calvaire m.
calve vi. vêler
calyx n. calice m.
cam n. came f.; -shaft arbre de distribution m.
Cambodia n. Cambodge m.
cambric n. batiste f.
camel n. chameau m.
cameo n. camée m.
camera n. appareil (photographique) m.; movie — caméra m.
cameraman n. photographe m.
Cameroons n. pl. Cameroun m.
camouflage n. camouflage m.; — vt. camoufler
camp n. camp m.; — bed lit de sangle m.; — chair chaise pliante f.; — vi. camper, faire du camping
campaign n. campagne f.; — vi. faire une campagne; -r n. ancien combattant, vétéran m.
campfire n. feu m.
camphor n. camphre m.
campus n. parc d'une université m.
can n. boîte f.; bidon m.; — opener ouvre-boîtes m.; — vi. pouvoir; savoir; — vt. mettre en boîtes, conserver; -ned a. conservé; -ned goods conserves f. pl.; -ned music musique enregistrée f.; -nery conserverie f.
Canada n. Canada m.
Canadian n. & a. Canadien m.
canal n. canal m. (pl. canaux); -ize vt. canaliser
canary n. serin m.
cancel vt. annuler; rescinder; infirmer; rapporter; biffer; -lation n. annulation f.; oblitération f.
cancer n. cancer m.; -ous a. cancéreux
candelabrum n. candélabre m.
candid a. sincère; franc, franche
candidacy n. candidature f.

candidate n. candidat, aspirant m.
candied a. confit, glacé, candi
candle n. bougie f.; chandelle f.; (eccl.) cierge f.: — power bougie f.
candlelight n. lumière de bougie f.
candlestick n. chandelier, bougeoir m.
candor n. franchise, sincérité f.
candy n. confiserie f., sucreries f. pl.; — vt. glacer, faire candir
cane n. canne f.; jonc m.; bâton m., badine f.; — sugar sucre de canne m.; sugar — canne à sucre f.; — vt. battre, bâtonner; (chair) canner
canine a. canin, de chien; — tooth canine, œillère f.
canister n. boîte f.; (mil.) mitraille f.
canker n. chancre m.; (fig.) plaie f.; — vt. ronger, corrompre
cannibal n. cannibale, anthropophage m. & f.; -ism n. cannibalisme m., anthropophagie f.; -istic a. cannibale
cannon n. canon m.; — ball n. boulet de canon m.; — shot n. coup de canon m.
canoe n. canoë m.; pirogue f.; — vi. faire du canoë; pagayer; to go -ing faire du canoë; -ist n. canotier m.
canon n. canon m., règle f.; (person) chanoine m.; — law n. droit canon m.; -ize vt. canoniser
canopy n. dais, baldaquin m.; marquise f.
cant n. inclinaison f.; (arch.) pan coupé m.; argot, jargon m.; hypocrisie f.; — vt. incliner; -ing a. hypocrite
cantaloupe n. cantaloup m.
cantankerous a. revêche, acariâtre
cantata n. cantate f.
canteen n. cantine f.; bidon m.
canter n. petit galop m.; — vi. aller au petit galop
canto n. chant m.
canton n. canton m.
canvas n. toile f.; canevas m.; -back duck n. canard américain m.
canvass vt. solliciter; faire une tournée électorale; (com.) faire la place; -er n. solliciteur m.; placier m.; -ing n. sollicitation f.
canyon n. cañon m., gorge f.
cap n. bonnet m., casquette f.; toque f.; chapeau m.; capuchon m.; — and gown costume académique m.; — vt. coiffer; capsuler; couronner; (shell) amorcer
capability n. capacité f.; faculté f.
capable a. capable; habile; susceptible
capacious a. spacieux, vaste, ample
capacity n. capacité f.; intelligence, aptitude f.; contenance f.
capacitate vt. rendre capable
cape n. cap, promontoire m.; pèlerine, cape f.; manteau m.
Cape of Good Hope Cap de Bonne Espérance m.
caper n. cabriole f.; (bot.) câpre f.; — vi. faire des cabrioles
capillary a. capillaire
capital a. capital (pl. capitaux); — punishment peine capitale f.; — n. capital, fonds m.; (city) capitale f.; (letter) majuscule f.; (arch.) chapiteau m.; -ism n. capitalisme m.; -ist n. capitaliste m. &

f.; —ize *vt.* écrire avec une majuscule; capitaliser

Capitol *n.* Capitole *m.*; — *a.* capitolin

capitulate *vi.* capituler

capitulation *n.* capitulation *f.*

capon *n.* chapon *m.*

caprice *n.* caprice *m.*, lubie *f.*

capricious *a.* capricieux

capsize *vi.* chavirer; capoter; — *vt.* faire chavirer

capsizing *n.* chavirement, capotage *m.*

capstan *n.* cabestan *m.*

capsule *n.* capsule *f.*

captain *n.* capitaine *m.*; chef *m.*; (sports) chef d'équipe *m.*; — *vt.* commander, diriger, conduire; —cy *n.* grade de capitaine *m.*; direction *f.*, commandement *m.*

caption *n.* rubrique *f.*; sous-titre *m.*; (law) arrestation *f.*

captious *a.* captieux, pointilleux

captivate *vt.* captiver, fasciner, charmer

captivating *a.* captivant; séduisant, charmant

captive *a.* captif; — *n.* captif, prisonnier *m.*

captivity *n.* captivité *f.*

captor *n.* preneur, ravisseur *m.*

capture *n.* prise *f.*; capture *f.*; — *vt.* prendre; capturer

car *n.* auto, automobile, voiture *f.*; (rail.) wagon *m.*; — pool système coopératif de voyager entre la maison et le travail en employant des voitures particulières *m.* used — *n.* voiture d'occasion *f.*

carafe *n.* carafe *f.*

caramel *n.* caramel *f.*; caramel mou *m.*

caravan *n.* caravane *f.*; roulotte *f.*

caravansary *n.* caravansérail *m.*

caraway *n.* carvi, cumin *m.*; — seed graine de carvi *f.*

carbide *n.* carbure *m.*

carbine *n.* carabine *f.*

carbohydrate *n.* hydrate de carbone *m.*

carbolic *a.* phénique; — acid phénol *m.*

carbon *n.* carbone *m.*; — copy double *m.*, copie *f.*; — dioxide anhydride carbonique *m.*; — monoxide oxyde de carbone *m.*; — paper papier carbone *m.*

carborundum *n.* carborundum *m.*

carbuncle *n.* carboncle *m.*; (stone) escarboucle *f.*

carburetor *n.* carburateur *m.*

carcass *n.* cadavre, corps *m.*; carcasse *f.*

card *n.* carte *f.*; index — fiche *f.*; (coll.) original *m.*; (racing) programme *m.*; dance — carnet de bal *m.*; deck of —s jeu de cartes *m.*; — index fichier, classeur *m.*; — sharp *n.* tricheur *m.*; — table table de jeu *f.*; — *vt.* carder, peigner

cardboard *n.* carton *m.*

cardiac *a.* cardiaque

cardigan *n.* gilet *m.*

cardinal *a.* cardinal, fondamental; pourpre; — *n.* cardinal *m.*

cardiogram *n.* cardiogramme *m.*

cardiology *n.* cardiologie *f.*

care *n.* souci *m.*; attention *f.*; soins *m. pl.*; sollicitude *f.*; préoccupation *f.*; take —

not to se garder de, prendre garde de; take — of se charger de; arranger; soigner; — *vi.* se soucier; se préoccuper; I don't — cela m'est égal; — for soigner; aimer; —ful *a.* soigneux; attentif; prudent; —ful! faites attention!; —fully *adv.* soigneusement, avec soin; attentivement; —fulness *n.* soin *m.*, attention *f.*; —less *a.* négligent; insouciant; —lessly *adv.* négligemment; —lessness *n.* négligence *f.*; inattention *f.*; insouciance *f.*

careen *vi.* donner de la bande

career *n.* carrière *f.*

carefree *a.* sans souci; insouciant

caress *n.* caresse *f.*; — *vt.* caresser; —ing *a.* caressant

caret *n.* signe d'omission *m.*

caretaker *n.* concierge *m. & f.*; intendant *m.*; gardien *m.*; — government régime intérimaire *m.*

carfare *n.* prix d'un billet, tarif, billet de tramway *m.*

cargo *n.* cargaison *f.*; chargement *m.*; — ship cargo *m.*

Caribbean Sea *n.* mer des Caraïbes *f.*

caricature *n.* caricature *f.*; — *vt.* caricaturer

caricaturist *n.* caricaturiste *m.*

caries *n.* carie *f.*

carmine *n.* carmin *m.*; — *a.* carmin; carminé

carnage *n.* carnage *m.*

carnal *a.* charnel; sexuel; sensuel; — sin péché de la chair *m.*

carnation *n.* (bot.) œillet *m.*, — *a. & n.* (color) incarnat *m.*

carnival *n.* carnaval *m.*; fête foraine *f.*

carnivorous *a.* carnivore; carnassier

carol *n.* chant *m.*; Christmas — noël *m.*; — *vt. & vi.* chanter

carom *n.* carambolage *m.*; — *vi.* caramboler

carouse *vi.* faire la bombe

carp *n.* carpe *f.*; — *vi.* critiquer, trouver à redire, épiloguer; —ing *a.* pointilleux; —ing *n.* critique pointilleuse *f.*

carpenter *n.* charpentier *m.*; menuisier *m.*

carpentry *n.* charpenterie *f.*

carpet *n.* tapis *m.*; — sweeper balayeuse *f.*; lay a — poser un tapis; — *vt.* recouvrir d'un tapis; —ed *a.* (re)couvert d'un tapis; tapissé; —ing *n.* tapis *m.*

carport *n.* abri pour auto(s) *m.*

carriage *n.* voiture *f.*; port *m.*; maintien *m.*; allure *f.*; (gun) affût *m.*; (typewriter) chariot *m.*; baby — voiture d'enfant *f.*; — entrance porte cochère *f.*

carrier *n.* porteur *m.*; voiturier *m.*; — pigeon pigeon voyageur *m.*; aircraft — porte-avions *m.*; letter — facteur *m.*; luggage — porte-bagages *m.*

carrion *n.* charogne *f.*

carrot *n.* carotte *f.*

carry *vt.* porter; emporter; vendre, avoir; conduire; pousser; adopter; (math.) retenir; — away (emotion) entraîner, transporter; — forward avancer; reporter; — off enlever; emporter; réussir; — on continuer; soutenir; se comporter: — out exécuter; remplir; be carried être voté; be carried away (fig.) être entraîné; s'emporter; — n. portée f., trajet m.; -ing n. port, transport m.

carryall n. charrette, carriole f.

cart n. charrette f.; tombereau m.; — vt. charrier; -age n. charriage, transport m.; -er n. camionneur m.; charretier m.; voiturier m.

Cartesian a. cartésien

Carthusian a. & n. chartreux m.; chartreuse f.

cartilage n. cartilage m.

cartographer n. cartographe m

cartography n. cartographie f.

carton n. carton m.; boîte f.

cartoon n. caricature f.; (movies) dessin animé m.; -ist n. caricaturiste m.

cartridge n. cartouche f.; (record-player) cellule de lecture f.

cartwheel n. roue f.; do —s faire les roues

cartwright n. charron m.

carve vt. découper; graver, sculpter; tailler

carving n. découpage m.; gravure, sculpture f.; — knife n. couteau à découper m.; — set service à découper m.

cascade n. cascade, chute d'eau f.; — vi. cascader

case n. cas m.; (law) cause f.; caisse f.; colis m.; écrin m.; trousse f.; étui m.; boîte f.; (glass) vitrine f.; (med.) malade m. & f.; (typ.) casse f.; (watch) boîtier m.; in any — en tout cas; upper — haut de casse m.; — vt. encaisser; envelopper; (coll.) observer, épier

casehardened a. aciéré, cimenté; (person) endurci

casement window n. croisée f.

cash n. argent comptant n.; espèces f. pl.; — box n. caisse f.; cassette f.; — on delivery contre remboursement; — register caisse enregistreuse f.; — vt. toucher, escompter

cashew n. noix d'acajou f.

cashier n. caissier m., caissière f.; — vt. casser; -'s check chèque bancaire m.

cashmere n. cachemire m.

casing n. enveloppe f.; chemise f.

cask n. tonneau, fût m., barrique f.

casket n. cassette f.; cercueil m.

Caspian Sea n. Mer Caspienne f.

cassava n. cassave f.

cassock n. soutane f.

cast n. jet m.; coup m.; coulée f.; moulage m.; (theat.) distribution f.; — vt. lancer, jeter; fondre; mouler; couler; (theat.) distribuer; — lots tirer au sort; — aside mettre de côté; — off rejeter; (naut.) abattre; — out mettre à la porte; exorciser; —a. moulé; coulé; — iron fonte (de fer) f.; -ing n. fonte f., moulage m.; jet m.; pièce de fonte f.

castanet n. castagnette f.

castaway n. naufragé m.

caster n. roulette f.

castigate vt. châtier, corriger

castigation n. châtiment m., correction f.

Castile n. Castille f.; — soap savon blanc m.

castle n. château m.; château fort m.;

(chess) tour f.; — vt. (chess) roquer

castoff a. jeté, rejeté; vieux; — n. rejeté m.

castor oil n. huile de ricin f.

castrate vt. châtrer m.

castration n. castration f.

casual a. accidentel, fortuit; indifférent; désinvolte; insouciant; -ly adv. par hasard, fortuitement; négligemment

casualty n. blessé m.; mort m.; accidenté m.

cat n. chat m., chatte f.; let the — out of the bag vendre la mèche; -ty a. cancanier, méchant

cataclysm n. cataclysme m.; -ic a. cataclysmique

catacombs n. pl. catacombes f. pl.

catalepsy n. catalepsie f.

cataleptic a. cataleptique

catalog, catalogue n. catalogue m.; prix-courant m.; liste f.; — vt. cataloguer

Catalonia n. Catalogne f.

catalyst n. catalyseur m.

catalytic a. catalyseur, catalytique

catapult n. catapulte f.; lance-pierres m.; — vt. lancer

cataract n. cataracte f.

catastrophe n. catastrophe f.

catcall n. huée f.; sifflet m.

catch n. prise f.; (door) loquet m.; (clothing) agrafe f.; (buckle) ardillon m.; (fishing) pêche f.; attrape f.; — vt. attraper; saisir; prendre; surprendre; accrocher; — vi. prendre; s'engager; s'accrocher; — en réussir, prendre; comprendre; — up with rattraper; — cold s'enrhumer; — fire s'enflammer, prendre feu; -ing a. contagieux; communicatif; -y a. entraînant, facile à retenir

catchall n. sac ou panier pour recevoir tout m.; catégorie qui comporte un mélange de choses f.

catechism n. catéchisme m.

categorical a. catégorique

category n. catégorie f.

cater vi. pourvoir, approvisionner; -er n. approvisionneur, pourvoyeur m.; -ing n. approvisionnement m.

cater-cornered, catty-cornered, kitty-cornered a. diagonal

caterpillar n. chenille f.

catfish n. loup marin m.

catgut n. corde de boyau f.

cathartic a. cathartique, purgatif

cathedral n. cathédrale f.

catheter n. cathéter m.

cathode n. cathode m.

catholic a. universel; large; éclectique; — n. & a. (eccl.) catholique m. & f.; -ism n. catholicisme m.

catkin n. (bot.) chaton m.

catnap n. petit somme m.

catnip n. cataire f.

cat's-paw n. (fig.) dupe f.

catsup n. sauce tomaille f.

cattle n. bétail m.; bêtes f. pl.; bestiaux m. pl.

cattleman n. éleveur de bétail m.

catwalk n. coursive f.

caucus n. réunion f. (d'une clique politique)

cauliflower n. chou-fleur m.

cause n. cause f.; raison f.; sujet m.; procès m.; have —(to) avoir lieu (de); — vt. causer; faire; occasionner

causeway n. chaussée f.

caustic a. caustique; mordant

cauterize vt. cautériser

caution n. prudence, précaution f.; circonspection f.; avertissement m.; — interj. attention! — vt. avertir

cautious a. prudent; circonspect; -ly adv. prudemment; avec circonspection

cavalcade n. cavalcade f.

cavalier n. cavalier m.; — a. cavalier, désinvolte

cavalry n. cavalerie f.

cave n. grotte f., souterrain m.; caverne f., antre m.; — man troglodyte m.; — vi. — in s'effondrer

cavern n. caverne f.; -ous a. caverneux

cavil vi. ergoter, chicaner

cavity n. cavité f.; creux m.; trou m.; (tooth) carie f.

cavort vi. gambader, caracoler

caw n. croassement m.; —, -ing n. croassement m.

cease vt. & vi. cesser; (s')arrêter; — fire cesser le feu; — fire n. trêve f.; -less a. incessant, continuel; sans arrêt; -lessly adv. sans cesse

cedar n. cèdre m.

cede vt. & vi. céder

cedilla n. cédille f.

ceiling n. plafond m.; (avi.) ciel, plafond m.; — price prix maximum m.

celebrate vt. fêter; célébrer; commémorer; -ed a. célèbre, renommé

celebration n. fête f.; commémoration f.; célébration f.

celebrity n. célébrité f.; vedette f.

celery n. céleri en branches m.; — root céleri m.

celestial a. céleste

celibacy n. célibat m.

celibate a. & n. célibataire m. & f.

cell n. cellule f.; cachot m.; (pol.) noyau m.; (elec.) élément m.; pile f.

cellar n. cave f.; sous-sol m.

cello, 'cello n. violoncelle m.

cellophane n. cellophane f.

cellular a. cellulaire

celluloid n. celluloïd m.

cellulose a. celluleux; — n. cellulose f.

Celt n. Celte m. & f.; -ic a. celte; celtique; -ic n. celtique

cement n. ciment m.; cément m.; — vt. cimenter; cémenter; consolider

cemetery n. cimetière m.

cenotaph n. cénotaphe m.

censer n. (eccl.) encensoir m.

censor n. censeur m.; — vt. interdire; supprimer; -ing, -ship n. censure f.; contrôle m.

censurable a. blâmable, censurable

censure n. censure f.; blâme m.; — vt. censurer, blâmer

census n. recensement m.

cent n. cent m.; sou, liard m.; per — pour cent

centennial a. & n. centenaire m.

center n. centre m.; milieu m.; foyer m.; — vt. centrer; placer au centre; — vi. se concentrer

centerpiece n. surtout, milieu m.

centigrade a. centigrade

centigram n. centigramme m.

centimeter n. centimètre m.

centipede n. centipède m.; myriapode m.; mille-pattes m.

central a. central; -ization n. centralisation f.; -ize vt. centraliser

Central America n. Amérique Centrale f.

centrifugal a. centrifuge

centrifuge n. centrifugeuse f.

centripetal a. centripète

century n. siècle m.; — old a. séculaire

cereal a. & n. céréale f.

cerebellum n. cervelet m.

cerebral a. cérébral

cerebrum n. cerveau m.

ceremonial a. cérémonial, de cérémonie; — n. cérémonial m.

ceremonious a. cérémonieux

ceremony n. cérémonie f.; stand on — faire des façons; without — sans façon(s)

cerise a. & n. cerise m.

certain a. certain, sûr; make — s'assurer; -ly adv. certainement, assurément; parfaitement; certes; -ty n. certitude f.

certificate n. certificat m.; attestation f.; acte m.; titre m.; diplôme m.; birth — acte de naissance m.

certification n. certification, attestation f.

certified a. certifié; — check chèque visé m.; — public accountant expert-comptable diplômé m.

certify vt. certifier; attester; authentiquer, homologuer, légaliser; constater; diplômer

certitude n. certitude f.

cessation n. cessation f.

cesspool n. fosse d'aisance f.

Ceylon n. Ceylan m.

chafe vt. échauffer; frotter; frictionner; irriter; — vi. s'énerver, s'irriter

chaff n. paille menue f.; balle f.; (coll.) raillerie f.; — vt. railler, persifler

chafing n. écorchement, frottement m.; irritation f.; — dish réchaud de table m.

chagrin n. chagrin m.; mortification f.; dépit m. to be —ed être mortifié

chain n. chaîne f.; chaînette f.; enchaînement m.; — gang chaîne de forçats f.; — smoker fumeur à la file m.; — reaction réaction en chaîne f.; — stitch point de chaînette m.; — store succursale f.; — stores grand magasin à succursales m.; société coopérative f.; — vt. enchaîner; attacher

chair n. chaise f.; siège m.; fauteuil m.; (academic) chaire f.

chairman n. président m.; -ship n. présidence f.

chalice n. calice m.

chalk n. craie f.; (geol.) calcaire m. (billiards) blanc m.; French — n. talc m.; — vt., marquer à la craie; — up marquer; attribuer; -y a. crayeux challenge n. défi m.; (mil.) qui-vive m., interpellation f.; (sports) challenge m.; — vt. défier; interpeller; provoquer; disputer, mettre en doute

challenging a. de défi; provocateur; provocant; (coll.) très intéressant

chamber n. chambre f.; salle f., pièce f.; — music musique de chambre f.

chamberlain n. chambellan m.

chambermaid n. femme de chambre f.

chameleon n. caméléon m.

champ vt. & vi. mâcher, ronger

champagne n. (vin de) champagne m.

champion n. champion, recordman m.; — vt. défendre, soutenir; -ship n. championnat m.

chance n. hasard m., chance f.; sort m.; accident m.; occasion f.; risque m.; by — par hasard; off — chance moyenne; take a — encourir un risque; — vt. risquer; — vi. venir à; — a. fortuit; de rencontre

chancellor n. chancelier m.; ministre m.

chandelier n. lustre m.

change n. changement m.; monnaie f.; revirement m.; — of address changement de domicile m.; for a — comme distraction; — of clothes vêtements de rechange m. pl.; — vt. changer; échanger; donner la monnaie; transformer; modifier; — clothes changer de vêtements; — the subject changer de sujet; — color changer de visage; — vi. (se) changer; tourner; -ability n. mobilité f.; variabilité f.; -able a. mobile; variable; -less a. immuable; éternel

changing a. changeant; — n. changement m.; — of the guard relève f.

channel n. canal m.; lit m.; chenal m.; conduit m.; rigole f.; voie f.; — vt. canneler; creuser des rigoles

chant n. chant m.; (eccl.) psalmodie f.; — vt. chanter; (eccl.) psalmodier

chanty n. chanson (de bord) f.

chaos n. chaos m.

chaotic a. chaotique

chap n. type, individu m.

chap vt. crevasser, gercer; — n. crevasse, gerçure f.; -ped hands des crevasses aux mains

chapel n. chapelle f.; oratoire m.

chaplain n. aumônier m.

chapter n. chapitre m.; bureau régional ou local d'une société f.

char vt. carboniser; — vi. se carboniser

character n. caractère m.; marque f.; lettre f.; personnage m.; sujet m.; type m.; — actor acteur de genre m.; be in — s'accorder, s'harmoniser; -istic a. caractéristique; -istic n. trait m.; -istically adv. d'une manière caractéristique; -ization n. caractérisation f.; -ize vt. caractériser, dépeindre

charcoal n. charbon de bois m.; (art) fusain m.; — burner n. charbonnier m.

charge n. prix m.; charge f.; soin m.; accusation; devoir m.; fonction f.; (of a judge) résumé m.; free of — gratis; exempt de frais; take — of se charger de; — account compte courant m.; — vt.

charger; accuser; imputer; débiter; demander; porter; -able a. accusable; imputable; -r n. cheval de bataille m.; (elec.) chargeur m.

chariot n. char m.

charitable a. charitable

charity n. charité f.; aumônes f. pl.; bienfaisance f.

Charley horse n. crampe musculaire, raideur musculaire f. (comme résultat d'un exercice violent)

charm n. charme, sortilège m.; porte-bonheur m.; breloque f.; — vt. charmer, enchanter; ensorceler; -ing a. charmant

chart n. carte f.; diagramme m.; — vt. dresser la carte de; — n. carte f.; privilège m.; (naut.) affrètement m.; -er member membre fondateur m.; -er vt. accorder une charte à; (naut.) affréter; -ered a. à charte; privilégié; affrété

chase n. chasse, poursuite f.; — vt. chasser; poursuivre; (gold) ciseler; (metal) repousser; (gem) enchâsser; — away chasser; -r n. chasseur m.; pousse-café m.; boisson (d'ordinaire) non-alcoolique prise après un verre de whisky f.

chasm n. gouffre m.; chasme m.; abîme m.

chassis n. châssis m.

chaste a. chaste; pudique; pur; -n vt. châtier

chastise vt. châtier, corriger; -ment n. châtiment m.

chastity n. chasteté, pureté f.

chat n. causerie f.; — vi. causer, jaser; -ty a. causeur

chattel n. bien mobilier m.

chatter n. bavardage m.; caquetage m.; — vi. bavarder, caqueter, jaser; claquer; -ing n. (teeth) claquement m.; (people) bavardage m.; (birds) caquetage m.

chatterbox n. bavard, babillard m.

chauffeur n. chauffeur m.

chauvinism n. chauvinisme m.

cheap a. bon marché; (coll.) honteux; -en vt. baisser le prix de; -er a. meilleur marché; -ly adv. bon marché; -ness n. bon marché, bas prix m.; qualité inférieure f.; médiocrité f.

cheat n. tricheur, escroc m.; trompeur m.; — vt. tricher; tromper; frauder; -ing n. tricherie f.; tromperie f.

check n. chèque m.; billet, bulletin, ticket m.; contrôle m.; vérification f.; arrêt m.; frein m.; (chess) échec m.; carreau m.; — list liste de controle f.; — vt. vérifier; contrôler; arrêter; freiner; retenir, refouler; (chess) faire échec; (baggage) faire enregistrer; — vi. s'arrêter; hésiter; — off pointer; — in (hotel) s'inscrire dans le registre d'un hôtel; — out quitter l'hôtel; -ed a. (material) à carreaux; -er n. contrôleur m.; -ing n. contrôle m.; vérification f.; enregistrement m.; -ing account compte en banque m.

checkbook n. carnet de chèques m.

checkerboard n. damier m.

checkered a. à carreaux, quadrillé; — career vie mouvementée f.

checkers n. pl. dames f. pl.

checkmate n. échec et mat m.; — vt. faire

échec et mat à

checkroom n. vestiaire m.; consigne f.

checkup n. examen m.; vérification f.

cheddar n. cheddar m.

cheek n. joue f.; (coll.) impertinence f., toupet m.; –bone n. pommette f.

cheep vi. piauler; —, –ing n. piaulement m.

cheer n. humeur, disposition f.; encouragement m.; ban m.; acclamation f.; — vt. encourager; égayer; acclamer; — up se ragaillardir; — up! courage!; –ful a. de bonne humeur, gai, égayant; –fully adv. gaiement; volontiers, de bon cœur; –ing a. réjouissant; encourageant; –ing n. acclamation f.; –less a. triste, morne

cheerleader n. étudiant qui organise et dirige les bans aux événements sportifs m.

cheese n. fromage m.

cheesecake n. pâtisserie au fromage f.; (phot.) (coll.) cheesecake m.

cheesecloth n. gaze f.

chef n. chef de cuisine m.

chemical a. chimique; — n. produit chimique m.

chemist n. chimiste m.; –ry n. chimie f.

cherish vt. chérir; nourrir, caresser

cherry n. cerise f.; — orchard cerisaie f.; — tree cerisier m.; — a. cerise, vermeil; wild — merise f.

cherub n. chérubin m.; –ic a. chérubique

chess n. échecs m. pl.

chessboard n. échiquier m.

chessman, chesspiece n. pièce f.

chest n. poitrine f.; coffret m., caisse f.; — of drawers commode f.

chestnut n. châtaigne f.; marron m.; (tree) châtaignier, marronnier m.; — a. châtain, châtaigne

cheviot n. cheviote f.

chew vt. mâcher; (tobacco) chiquer; (fig.) méditer; — n. morceau m.; –ing n. mastication f.; –ing gum gomme à mâcher f.; chewing-gum m.

chicanery n. chicane, chicanerie f.

chicken n. poulet m.; spring — poussin m.; — pox n. varicelle f.

chick-pea n. pois chiche m.

chicory n. chicorée f.; endive f.

chide vt. reprocher; gronder

chief n. chef m.; patron m.; — of staff chef de l'état-major m.; — justice président du tribunal m.; — a. principal; en chef; –ly adv. surtout; principalement

chieftain n. chef m.

chiffon n. chiffon m., gaze f.

chilblain n. engelure f.

child n. enfant m. & f.; with — enceinte; –ish a. enfantin, d'enfant; puéril; –ishness n. puérilité f.

childbirth n. accouchement m.

childhood n. enfance f.

Chile n. Chili m.

chill n. froid m.; coup de froid m.; froidure f.; refroidissement m.; frisson m.; take the — off (faire) tiédir; — vt. glacer, refroidir; réfrigérer; faire frissonner; –ed a. glacé; –iness n. froideur f.; fraîcheur f.; –ing a. glacial; –y a. frais, froid; feel –y avoir froid; be –y (behavior) être

froid

chime n. carillon m.; — vt. & vi. carillonner; — in intervenir

chimerical a. chimérique

chiming n. carillonnement m.; sonnerie f.

chimney n. cheminée f.; — sweep n. ramoneur m.; — sweeping n. ramonage m.

chimpanzee n. chimpanzé m.

chin n. menton m.

China n. Chine f.

china n. porcelaine de Chine f.

chinchilla n. chinchilla m.

Chinese a. & n. chinois m.

chink n. fente, crevasse f.

chip n. copeau, éclat m.; brisure f.; fragment m.; (cards) jeton m.; — vt. ébrécher; enlever un copeau (un fragment) à; — vi. s'écailler; — in contribuer, cotiser

chipmunk n. tamias m.

chipper a. gai, heureux

chiropodist n. pédicure m.

chiropracter n. chiropracteur m.

chirp n. gazouillement m.; grésillement m.; chant m.; — vi. pépier, gazouiller; grésiller

chisel n. ciseau m.; — vt. ciseler

chitchat n. conversation f.; bavardage m.

chivalrous a. chevaleresque, de chevalerie

chivalry n. chevalerie f.

chive n. ciboulette f.

chloride n. chlorure m.

chlorinate vt. chlorurer

chlorination n. chloruration f.

chlorine n. chlore m.

chloroform n. chloroforme m.; — vt. chloroformer, chloroformiser

chlorophyll n. chlorophylle f.

chock-full a. bondé, comble; bourré

chocolate n. chocolat m.

choice n. choix m.; alternative f.; préférence f.; — a. de choix

choir n. chœur m.

choke n. (auto.) étrangleur m.; — vt. & vi. suffoquer, étouffer, étrangler; boucher; — back refouler; –r n. foulard m.; (necklace) collier court m.

choking n. étranglement, étouffement m.; suffocation f.

choleric a. colérique

choose vt. choisir; élire; préférer; opter; vouloir

choosing n. choix m.

choosy a. (coll.) difficile à plaire

chop n. côtelette f.; coup de hache m.; lick one's –s se lécher les babines; — vt. hacher; couper; — vi. clapoter; — down abattre; — off trancher, couper; –ped meat viande hachée f.; –per n. couperet, hachoir m.; –py a. clapoteux

chopsticks n. pl. baguettes f. pl., bâtonnets m. pl.

chord n. accord m.

chore n. devoir m.; corvée f.; –s n. pl. travaux de ménage m. pl.

choreography n. chorégraphie f.

chorister n. choriste m.; enfant de chœur m.

chortle vi. glousser

chorus n. chœur m.; refrain m.; — vt.

répéter en chœur

chosen *a.* choisi, élu

Christ *n.* Le Christ, Jésus-Christ *m.*

christen *vt.* baptiser; –ing *n.* baptême *m.*

Christendom *n.* chrétienté *f.*

Christian *n. & a.* chrétien *m.*; — name prénom *m.*, nom de baptême *m.*; –ity *n.* christianisme *m.*

Christmas *n.* Noël *m.*; Merry — joyeux Noël; — card carte de Noël *f.*; — carol chant de Noël *m.*; — Eve la veille de Noël *f.*; — presents cadeaux de Noël *m. pl.*

chromatic *a.* chromatique

chrome *n.* acier chromé *m.*; chromage *m.*

chromium *n.* chrome *m.*; chromium *m.*

chromosome *n.* chromosome *m.*

chronic *a.* chronique; continuel, constant

chronicle *n.* chronique *f.*; –r *n.* chroniqueur *m.*

chronological *a.* chronologique; in — order chronologiquement, par ordre des dates

chronometer *n.* chronomètre *m.*

chrysalis *n.* chrysalide *f.*

chrysanthemum *n.* chrysanthème *m.*

chubby *a.* rondelet; joufflu

chuck *vt.* jeter, lancer; flanquer; — *n.* petite tape sous le menton *f.*; — steak steak coupé à l'épaule du bœuf *m.*

chuckle *n.* petit rire *m.*; — *vi.* rire tout bas

chum *n.* copain *m.*; camarade *m.*; –my *a.* copain; intime, familier

chunk *n.* (gros) morceau *m.*

church *n.* église *f.*; (Protestant) temple *m.*; — service office *m.*

churchman *n.* ecclésiastique *m.*

churchyard *n.* cimetière *m.*

churlish *a.* grossier; mal élevé

churn *n.* baratte *f.*; — *vt.* battre, baratter

chute *n.* glissière *f.*; couloir, conduit *m.*; coulisse *f.*, coulisseau *m.*

cicada *n.* cigale *f.*

Cicero *n.* Cicéron *m.*

cider *n.* cidre *m.*

cigar *n.* cigare *m.*; — store bureau de tabac *m.*

cigarette *n.* cigarette *f.*; — butt mégot *m.*; — holder porte-cigarettes *m.*; — lighter *n.* allume-cigarette *m.*

cinch *n.* (saddle) sangle *f.*; (coll.) quelque chose de très facile

cincher *n.* ceinture-corselet *f.*

cinder *n.* cendre *f.*; — track piste cendrée *f.*

Cinderella *n.* Cendrillon *f.*

cinnamon *n.* cannelle *f.*

cipher *n.* chiffre *m.*; (math.) zéro *m.*; *vt.* chiffrer

circle *n.* cercle *m.*; milieu, monde *m.*; *vt.* entourer, ceindre; faire le tour de; — *vi.* tournoyer

circuit *n.* circuit *m.*; détour *m.*; tournée *f.*; short — court-circuit *m.*; — breaker *n.* coupe-circuit *m.*; –ous *a.* détourné

circular *a.* circulaire; — *n.* feuille publicitaire *f.*; –ize *vt.* prospecter

circulate *vi.* circuler; — *vt.* faire circuler

circulation *n.* circulation *f.*; (newspaper)

tirage *m.*

circumcise *vt.* circoncire; –d *a.* circoncis

circumcision *n.* circoncision *f.*

circumference *n.* circonférence *f.*; périphérie *f.*

circumflex *a. & n.* circonflexe *m.*

circumscribe *vt.* circonscrire; limiter

circumscription *n.* circonscription *f.*; restriction *f.*

circumspect *a.* circonspect, prudent; –ion *n.* circonspection, prudence *f.*

circumstance *n.* circonstance(s) *f.* (*pl.*); cas *m.*; incident *m.*; détail *m.*; situation *f.*; pompe, cérémonie *f.*

circumstantial *a.* circonstanciel; circonstancié, détaillé; accidentel; — evidence preuves indirectes *f. pl.*

circumvent *vt.* circonvenir

circus *n.* cirque *m.*

cirrus *n.* cirrus *m.*, (coll.) queue de vache *f.*

cistern *n.* citerne *f.*; réservoir *m.*

citadel *n.* citadelle *f.*

citation *n.* citation *f.*

cite *vt.* citer; assigner

citizen *n.* citoyen *m.*; citadin *m.*; fellow — concitoyen *m.*; –ry *n.* citoyens *m. pl.*; –ship *n.* nationalité *f.*; droit de cité *m.*

citric *a.* citrique

citron *n.* cédrat *m.*

citronella *n.* citronelle *f.*

citrus *n. & a.* citron *m.*

city *n.* ville *f.*; cité *f.*; — hall hôtel de ville *m.*

civet *n.* civette *f.*

civic *a.* civique; –s *n. pl.* instruction civique *f.*

civil *a.* civil; courtois, poli; — rights droits civiques *m. pl.*; — service administration publique *f.*; fonction de l'Etat *f.*; –ian *a. & n.* civil *m.*; –ian life civil *m.*; –ity *n.* civilité *f.*; politesse *f.*; –ization *n.* civilisation *f.*; –ize *vt.* civiliser

clad *a.* vêtu, habillé, couvert

claim *n.* prétention *f.*; titre *m.*; réclamation, revendication *f.*; (prospecting) concession *f.*; — *vt.* prétendre; réclamer, revendiquer; demander; faire valoir; soutenir; –ant *n.* prétendant *m.*; réclamant, revendicateur *m.*; demandeur *m.*

clairvoyant *a. & n.* voyant *m.*; clairvoyant *m.*

clam *n.* palourde *f.*

clamber *vi.* grimper; — over, — up escalader

clamminess *n.* moiteur froide *f.*

clammy *a.* humide, moite; collant

clamor *n.* clameur *f.*, bruit *m.*; — *vt.* vociférer; — for réclamer; –ous *a.* bruyant

clamp *n.* crampon *m.*; main de fer *f.*; agrafe *f.*; attache *f.*; — *vt.* fixer, attacher

clan *n.* clan *m.*; –nish *a.* de clan; –nishness *n.* étroitesse *f.*, esprit de corps étroit *m.*

clandestine *a.* clandestin

clang *n.* son métallique, résonnement *m.*;

–or son métallique, résonnement (des cloches) m.

clap n. battement m.; coup m.; applaudissements m. pl.; — vt. battre (des mains); taper, donner une tape à; — vi. applaudir; -per n. battant m.; applaudisseur m.; claqueur m.; -pers (theat.) claque f.; -ping n. applaudissements m. pl.

claret n. (vin de) bordeaux m.

clarify vt. éclaircir, clarifier

clarinet n. clarinette f.

clarion n. clairon m.

clarity n. clarté f.

clash n. choc m.; conflit m.; dispute f.; (color) disparate f.; — vi. se heurter, s'opposer; s'entre-choquer; faire disparate

clasp n. agrafe f.; fermoir m.; fermeture f.; étreinte f.; hand— serrement de mains m.; — knife couteau pliant m.; — vt. agrafer; étreindre, serrer; tenir

class n. classe f.; cours m.; genre m., sorte f.; catégorie f.; type m.; caste f.; lower — prolétariat m.; middle — bourgeoisie f.; — vt. classer; -ic a. & n. classique m.; -ical a. classique; -ics n. classiques m. pl. humanités f. pl.; -ification n. classement m.; classification f.; -ified a. classé; -ified advertisement petite annonce f.; -ified information document(s) déclaré(s) secret(s) par le gouvernement m. (pl.); -ify vt. classer, classifier; -y a. chic

classmate n. camarade de classe m.

classroom n. salle de classe f.

clatter n. bruit, cliquetis m.; — vi. faire du bruit

clause n. clause f.; article m.; (gram.) proposition f.

clavicle n. clavicule f.

claw n. griffe f., serre f.; pince f.; (hammer) panne fendue f.; — vt. griffer, déchirer

clay n. argile f.; glaise f.; — pipe pipe en terre f.; — pit argilière, glaisière f.; -ey a. argileux

clean a. propre; net; — adv. net; tout à fait; — vt. nettoyer; faire; récurer; (fish) vider; (streets) balayer; — out curer; ranger; (person) mettre à sec; — up nettoyer; se laver, se débarbouiller; -er n. nettoyeur m.; -ing n. nettoyage m.; dry -ing nettoyage à sec; -liness n. propreté f.; netteté f.

cleanse vt. nettoyer; purifier, écurer; assainir

cleansing n. nettoyage m.; curage m.

clear a. clair; net; dégagé; libre; certain; (property) franc d'hypothèque; all — (civil defense) fin d'alerte f.; keep — of éviter; — vt. éclaircir; clarifier; franchir; dégager; déblayer; liquider; faire un bénéfice; (com.) solder; (land) défricher; (customs) dédouaner; — away écarter, enlever; — oneself se disculper; — the table desservir; enlever le couvert; — up éclaircir; — vi. s'éclaircir; se dégager; — out filer; -ance n. jeu m.; espace m.; -ance sale

vente de soldes f.; -ing n. (forest) éclaircie f.; dégagement m.; (banking) compensation de chèques f.; -ing house comptoir de règlement m.; -ly adv. clairement, nettement; clair; évidemment; -ness n. clarté f.; netteté f.

clear-cut a. net

clearheaded a. lucide; perspicace

clear-sighted a. clairvoyant

cleat n. taquet m.

cleavage n. fendage m.; scission f.

cleave vt. fendre; — vi. se fendre; s'attacher, adhérer; -r n. couperet m.

cleft n. fente, crevasse f.; — a., — palate palais fendu m.

clemency n. clémence f.; (weather) douceur f.

clement a. clément; doux

clench vt. serrer, crisper

clergy n. clergé m.; -man n. ecclésiastique m.; pasteur m.

clerical a. clérical, de copiste; — error faute de copiste f.; — work travail de bureau m.

clerk n. commis m.; employé de bureau m.; (court) greffier m.; (eccl.) clerc m.

clever a. habile; adroit; fort; intelligent; -ness n. habileté f.; adresse f.; intelligence f.

cliché n. cliché m.

click n. clic, cliquet, cliquetis m.; clappement m.; — vt. & vi. cliqueter; claquer; — vi. (coll.) réussir; aller ensemble

cliff n. falaise f.; escarpement m.

climate n. climat m.

climatic a. climatique, climatérique

climax n. point culminant m.; comble m.

climb n. montée f.; ascension f.; — vt. & vi. monter, gravir; grimper; — down descendre; -er n. grimpeur m.; (bot.) plante grimpante f.; mountain -er alpiniste m. & f.; -ing a. grimpant; -ing n. montée f.; escalade f.; mountain -ing alpinisme m.

clinch n. crampon, rivet m.; (boxing) corps-à-corps m.; — vt. river; — vi. se prendre corps-à-corps; -er n. argument sans réplique m.

cling vi. adhérer; coller; s'attacher, s'accrocher alberge, pavie f.

clinic n. clinique f.; -al a. clinique

clink n. tintement (de verres) m.; — vi. tinter; — vt. trinquer; -er n. mâchefer m.

clip n. agrafe, griffe, attache, pince f.; attache-papiers m.; (rifle) chargeur m.; — vt. couper; tondre; découper; agrafer, pincer, attacher; -per n. (naut., avi.) clipper m.; -pers n. pl. tondeuse f.; -ping n. coupe f.; coupure f.; tondage m.

clique n. coterie f.

cloak n. manteau m.; (fig.) voile m.; — and dagger a. de cape et d'épée; — vt. (fig.) masquer

cloakroom n. vestiaire m.; (rail.) consigne f.

clock n. horloge, pendule f.; alarm —

réveil *m.*; one o'– une heure; two o'– deux heures; twelve o'– (noon) midi *m.*, (midnight) minuit *m.*; — *vt.* chronométrer

clockwise *a.* dextrorsum; à droite

clockwork *n.* mouvement, rouage *m.*; like — comme sur des roulettes

clod *n.* motte *f.*; (person) rustre *m.*

clog *n.* entrave *f.*; galoche *f.*; — *vt.* entraver; boucher; — *vi.* se boucher

cloister *n.* cloître *m.*; — *vt.* cloîtrer

close *a.* fin *f.*; bout *m.*; clôture *f.*; — *vt.* fermer; terminer; clore; serrer; — *vi.* se fermer; se terminer; — down fermer; — up boucher; se serrer; — *a.* renfermé; intime; proche; serré; étroit; at — quarters de près; have a — call l'échapper belle; — *adv.* (de) près; — by tout près; — *d a.* fermé; (theat.) relâche; — *d* shop usine où la main-d'œuvre est tout à fait syndiquée *f.*; -ly *adv.* étroitement; attentivement; -ness *n.* proximité *f.*; intimité; exactitude *f.*; réserve *f.*; (weather) lourdeur *f.*

close-cropped *a.* coupé ras

closefisted *a.* ladre, avare

close-fitting *a.* collant

closemouthed *a.* peu communicatif

closet *n.* placard *m.*; armoire *f.*; — *vt.*, be -ed être enfermé

close-up *n.* vue prise de près *f.*; — *n.* (movies) gros plan *m.*

closing *n.* fermeture *f.*; clôture *f.*; — *a.* final, dernier

closure *n.* clôture, fermeture *f.*

clot *n.* caillot *m.*; embolie *f.*; — *vi.* se coaguler; se cailler; se figer

cloth *n.* étoffe *f.*; drap *m.*; tissu *m.*; toile *f.*; -e *vt.* habiller, vêtir, revêtir; -es *n. pl.* vêtements, habits *m. pl.*; effets *m. pl.*; -ier *n.* drapier *m.*; -ing *n.* vêtements *m. pl.*

clothesbrush *n.* brosse à habits *f.*

clothes closet *n.* garde-robe *f.*

clothes hanger *n.* cintre *f.*

clothesline *n.* étendoir *f.*

clothespin *n.* pince *f.*; épingle à lingne *f.*

cloud *n.* nuage *m.*; nue, nuée *f.*; voile *m.*; — *vt.* voiler, obscurcir; troubler; — up se voiler, se couvrir; -less *a.* sans nuages; -y *a.* nuageux; couvert; trouble

cloudburst *n.* averse, trombe *f.*

clout *n.* linge *m.*; (coll.) claque *f.*

clove *n.* clou de girofle *m.*; — of garlic gousse d'ail *f.*

cloven *a.*, — hoof pied fourchu *m.*

clover *n.* trèfle *m.*

clown *n.* clown, pitre *m.*; fou *m.*; bouffon *m.*; — *vi.* faire le clown

cloy *vt.* rassasier

club *n.* club, cercle *m.*, société *f.*; cénacle *m.*; (weapon) massue *f.*; (cards) trèfle *m.*; — *vt.* assommer, frapper; — *vi.* se réunir, se cotiser

clubfoot *n.* pied bot *m.*

clubhouse *n.* pavillon *m.*

clubroom *n.* salle de réunion *f.*

club steak *n.* aloyau de bœuf *m.*

cluck *vi.* glousser; —, -ing *n.* gloussement *m.*

clue *n.* indice *m.*; piste *f.*; clef *f.*; indication *f.*

clump *n.* bouquet *m.*; massif *m.*; bloc *m.*; pas lourd *m.*; — *vi.* se grouper; marcher d'un pas lourd

clumsiness *n.* maladresse *f.*; gaucherie *f.*

clumsy *a.* maladroit, gauche

cluster *n.* bouquet *m.*; massif *m.*; groupe *m.*; (grapes) grappe *f.*; — *vt.* grouper; — *vi.* se grouper

clutch *n.* griffe, patte *f.*; (auto.) embrayage *m.*; let in the — embrayer; release the — débrayer; in the -es of sous la patte de; — *vt.* saisir; — at se raccrocher à

clutter *n.* désordre *m.*; encombrement *m.*; — *vt.*, — up mettre en désordre; encombrer

coach *n.* voiture *f.*; carrosse *m.*; (rail.) wagon *m.*; (sports) entraîneur *m.*; — *vt.* entraîner; (theat.) faire répéter

coachhouse *n.* remise *f.*

coachman *n.* cocher *m.*

coagulant *n.* coagulant *m.*

coagulate *vt. & vi.* (se) figer, (se) coaguler

coagulation *n.* coagulation *f.*

coal *n.* charbon *m.*; houille *f.*; — gas gaz d'éclairage *m.*; — mine mine de houille *f.*; houillère *f.*; — miner mineur *m.*; — mining exploitation de la houille *f.*

coalesce *vi.* s'unir, se combiner; fusionner; -nce *n.* coalescence, fusion *f.*

coalition *n.* ligue *f.*; coalition *f.*

coarse *a.* grossier; gros; rude; -ness *n.* grossièreté *f.*; rudesse *f.*; grosseur *f.*; gros grain *m.*

coarse-grained *a.* à gros grain; à gros fil

coast *n.* côte *f.*, rivage *m.*; littoral *m.*; — guard *n.* gardes-côte *m. pl.*; -guardsman garde-côte *m. s.*; — *vi.* descendre en roue libre; -ing *n.* descente en roue libre *f.*; (naut.) cabotage *m.*

coaster *n.* dessous *m.*

coat *n.* habit *m.*; veston *m.*; pardessus, manteau *m.*; (paint) couche *f.*; (animal) robe *f.*; — of arms armes, armoiries *f. pl.*; — of mail cotte de mailles *f.*; — hanger *n.* porte-vêtements *m.*; -room *n.* vestiaire *m.*; — *vt.* couvrir, enduire; -ed *a.* enduit, couvert, recouvert; -ed tongue langue chargée *f.*; -ing *n.* enduit *m.*; couche *f.*; (anat.) paroi *f.*; (com.) étoffe pour habits *f.*

coauthor *n.* coauteur, collaborateur *m.*

coax *vt.* câliner, cajoler, enjôler; -ing *a.* câlin, cajoleur; -ing *n.* cajolerie *f.*

cobalt *n.* cobalt *m.*

cobbler *n.* savetier, cordonnier *m.*

cobblestone *n.* caillou, galet *m.*

cobweb *n.* toile d'araignée *f.*

cocaine *n.* cocaïne *f.*

cock *n.* coq *m.*; robinet *m.*; (weapons) chien *m.*; crow of the — chant du coq *m.*; — *vt.* armer; dresser; (hat) retrousser; -iness *n.* suffisance *f.*; -y *a.* suffisant

cockade *n.* cocarde *f.*

cock-and-bull a., — story coq-à-l'âne m.

cockeyed a. de travers, de biais; insensé

cockfight n. combat de coqs m.

cockpit n. cockpit m.; carlingue f.

cockroach n. blatte f.., cafard m.

cocktail n. cocktail m.; apéritif m.

cocoa n. cacao m.

coconut n. noix de coco f.; — palm cocotier m.

cocoon n. cocon m.

cod n. morue f.

C.O.D. contre remboursement

coddle vt. gâter, dorloter, choyer

code n. code m.; chiffre m.; — vt. chiffrer

codfish n. morue f.

codicil n. codicille m.

codification n. codification f.

codify vt. codifier

cod-liver oil n. huile de foie de morue f.

coed n. étudiante d'école mixte f.

coeducational a. mixte

coefficient n. coefficient m.

coerce vt. contraindre, forcer

coercion n. contrainte f.; coercition f.

coercive a. coercitif

coeval a. contemporain

coexist vi. coexister; —ence n. coexistence f.

coffee n. café m.; black — café nature, café noir; — bean grain de café m.; — cup tasse à café f.; — grinder, — mill moulin à café m.; — grounds marc de café m.; — plantation n. caféière f.

coffeepot n. cafetière f.

coffer n. coffre f.

cofferdam n. bâtardeau m.

coffin n. cercueil m.

cog n. dent f.; — vt. denter

cogency n. force, puissance f.

cogent a. puissant

cogitate vi. réfléchir, méditer

cogitation n. réflexion, méditation f.

cognac n. cognac m.

cognizance n. connaissance f.

cognizant a. instruit

cogwheel n. roue dentée f.

cohabit vi. cohabiter

cohere vi. adhérer, se tenir; —nce n. cohérence f.; —nt a. cohérent; —ntly adv. avec cohérence

cohesion n. cohésion f.

cohesive a. cohésif

cohort n. cohorte f.

coif n. (headdress of a nun) cornette f.

coil n. pli m., repli, rouleau m.; anneau m.; (elec.) bobine f., enroulement m.; — vt. rouler, bobiner; enrouler; — vi. serpenter; s'enrouler, boucler

coin n. pièce f.; monnaie f.; espèces f. pl.; — collector numismate m.; — vi. battre (monnaie), frapper; inventer; —age n. monnayage m.; monnaie f.

coincide vi. coïncider; s'accorder; —nce n. coïncidence f.

coke n. coke m.

colander n. passoire f.

cold a. froid; indifférent, insensible; be — (person) avoir froid; (weather) faire froid; grow — se refroidir; — cream crème de beauté f.; — cuts charcuterie f.; assiette anglaise f.; — feet (coll.) trac m., peur f.; — storage entrepôt frigorifique m.; — n. froid; (med.) rhume m.; catch (a) — attraper un rhume, s'enrhumer; have a — être enrhumé; —ness n. froideur f.

cold-blooded a. (animal) à sang froid; insensible; prémédité

coleslaw n. salade de choux f.

colic n. colique f.

Coliseum n. Colisée m.

colitis n. colite f.

collaborate vi. collaborer

collaboration n. collaboration f.

collaborator n. collaborateur m.

collapse n. effondrement, écroulement m.; débâcle f.; chute f.; affaissement m., prostration f.; — vi. s'effondrer, s'écrouler; s'affaisser

collapsible a. pliant; démontable

collar n. col m.; collet m.; collier m.; (mech.) anneau m.; detachable — faux col m.; — vt. saisir; colleter

collarbone n. clavicule f.

collate vt. collationner

collateral a. collatéral; — n. garantie f.

colleague n. collègue m.; confrère m.

collect vt. rassembler; recueillir; collectionner; — oneself se reprendre; — vi. s'assembler, se rassembler; —ed a. recueilli; calme; —ion n. recueil m.; collection f.; (taxes) perception f.; (postal) levée f.; assemblage m.; —ive a. collectif, commun; —ivity n. collectivité f.; —or n. (tickets) contrôleur m.; (taxes) percepteur m.; collectionneur m.; receveur m.; encaisseur m.; collecteur m.

collective bargaining n. discussion entre les patrons et les ouvriers f.

college n. collège m. (établissement d'enseignement supérieur aux États-Unis)

collegiate a. collégial; de collège

collide vi. entrer en collision; se heurter

collie n. chien de berger écossais m.

collision n. collision f., choc m.; (naut.) abordage m.; (rail.) tamponnement m.

colloid n. colloïde m.

colloquial a. familier; vulgaire; —ism n. expression familière f.

collusion n. collusion f.; complicité f.

Colombia n. Colombie f.

colon n. (gram.) deux points m. pl.; (anat.) côlon m.

colonel n. colonel m.

colonial a. colonial

colonization n. colonisation f.

colonize vt. coloniser; —r n. colonisateur m.

colony n. colonie f.

color n. couleur f.; coloris m.; teint m.; —s n. pl. (mil., naut.) drapeau, pavillon m.; be off — être pâle; lose — devenir pâle; — vt. colorer; colorier; imager; — vi. se colorer; rougir; —ation n. coloration f.; —ed a. coloré, colorié; de couleur; en couleurs; —ing n. coloris m.; coloration f.; teint m.; —ful a. coloré; —less a. incolore; sans couleur

color-blind a. daltonien; —ness n. daltonisme m.

colossus n. colosse m.

colt n. poulain m.

column n. colonne f.; (newspaper) rubrique f.; -ist n. journaliste m.; chroniqueur m.

comatose a. comateux

comb n. peigne m.; carde f.; (cock) crête f.; — vt. peigner; — vi. se peigner; — one's hair se peigner les cheveux; — out démêler; éliminer

combat n. combat m.; — vt. combattre, lutter contre; -ant n. combattant m.; -ive a. combatif

combination n. combinaison f.; combiné, mélange m.

combine n. cartel m., combinaison f.; (agr.) machine qui bat et qui vanne le grain en même temps; fau cheuse-batteuse f.; — vt. combiner; joindre; — vi. se combiner, s'unir; -d a. réuni

combustible a. combustible, inflammable

combustion n. combustion f.; spontaneous — inflammation spontanée f.

come vi. venir, arriver; advenir; — about arriver, se passer; (naut.) virer de bord; — across tomber sur, rencontrer; — after suivre; succéder à; — again revenir; — along venir, arriver; accompagner; — apart se défaire; — back revenir; — before précéder; — between intervenir, s'interposer; — by passer; obtenir; — down descendre; tomber; baisser; se résumer; — for venir chercher; — forward s'avancer; — home rentrer, revenir; — in entrer; arriver; — off se détacher; avoir lieu; réussir; — out sortir; paraître, se découvrir; débuter; — through traverser, passer par; pénétrer; — to reprendre connaissance; — together se réunir, s'assembler; — up monter; — upon tomber sur, rencontrer; — now! allons!; — what may advienne que pourra; -r n. arrivant m.; all -rs tout le monde

comeback n. retour à la célébrité m.; riposte f.

comedian n. comique m.; comédien m.

comedy n. comédie f.

come on n. (coll.) leurre m., attrape f.

comet n. comète f.

comfort n. confort m.; consolation f., soulagement m.; — vt. consoler, soulager; bien-être m.; aise, aisance f.; be -able a. (things) confortable; (persons) être bien, être à l'aise; -er n. consolateur m.; couverture piquée f.; -ing a. réconfortant, de consolation

comic a. comique, — opera opéra bouffe, opéra comique m.; — n. comique; comédien m.; -al a. comique, drôle, risible

coming a. qui vient; prochain; futur; — n. venue, arrivée f.; avènement m.; — out n. début m.; sortie f.; parution f.; apparition f.

comma n. virgule f.

command n. commandement, ordre m.; gouvernement m.; disposition f.; maîtrise, connaissance f.; have at one's — avoir à sa disposition; be at someone's — être aux ordres de quelqu'un; — vt. commander, ordonner; inspirer; dominer; -ant n. commandant m.; -eer vt. réquisitionner; -er n. commandant m.; -ing a. imposant; d'autorité; -ing officer n. commandant m.; -ment n. commandement m.

commander-in-chief n. commandant en chef m.

commando n. commando m.

commemorate vt. commémorer, célébrer

commemoration n. commémoration f.; in — of en mémoire de

commence vt. & vi. commencer; -ment n. commencement m.; (school) distribution des prix f.; réception (d'un grade universitaire) f.

commend vt. louer; recommander, confier; -able a. louable; -ation n. louange f.

commensurate a. proportionné

comment n. commentaire m.; remarque f.; — vi. faire des observations; critiquer; commenter; -ary n. commentaire m.; reportage m.; -ator n. commentateur m.; speaker, reporter m.

commercial a. commercial, de commerce; — n. annonce publicitaire f.; -ize vt. commercialiser

commingle vt. mêler (ensemble); — vi. se mêler

commiserate vt. & vi.; — with avoir de la compassion pour

commiseration n. commisération, compassion f.

commissary n. (mil.) grand magasin à l'usage des militaires et de leurs familles m.

commission n. commission, charge f.; pourcentage, pot de vin m.; perpétration f.; — vt. commissioner; charger; (naut.) armer (un vaisseau); (painting) commander; -er n. commissaire m.; membre d'une commission m.; directeur m.; préfet m.

commit vt. commettre; confier; engager; — to prison envoyer en prison; — to memory apprendre par cœur; -ment n. engagement m.; -tal n. perpétration f.; mise en prison f.

committee n. comité m.; commission f., conseil m.

commodious a. spacieux, ample

commodity n. produit m.; denrée f.; marchandise f.

common a. commun; ordinaire; courant; vulgaire; — stock action(s) ordinaire(s) f. (pl.); — n. terrain commun m.; in — en commun; -er n. bourgeois m.; homme du peuple m.; -ness n. banalité f.; fréquence f.; House of C—s Chambre des Communes f.

commonplace a. banal; — n. lieu commun m.; banalité f.

commonwealth n. république f.; état m.

commotion n. commotion, agitation, confusion f.; bruit m.

communal a. communal

commune n. commune f.; — vi. s'entretenir

communicable a. communicable; contagieux

communicant n. (eccl.) communiant m.; informateur m.

communicate vt. & vi. communiquer; (eccl.) communier

communication n. communication f.

communicative a. communicatif

communion n. communion f.

communism n. communisme m.

communist n. communiste m. & f.; -ic a. communiste

community n. communauté f.; voisinage m.; société f.

commutation n. commutation f.; — ticket carte d'abonnement au chemin de fer f.

commutator n. (elec.) commutateur m.

commute vt. commuer; — vi. voyager régulièrement entre la maison dans la banlieue et le bureau en ville; -r n. habitant de banlieue qui travaille en ville m.

compact a. serré, compact; — n. pacte, accord m.; convention f.; (cosmetics) poudrier m.; -ness n. compacité f.; concision f.

companion n. compagnon m., compagne f.; -able a. sociable; -ship n. camaraderie f.; compagnie f.

company n. compagnie f.; assemblée f.; monde m.; (com.) société f.; (theat.) troupe f.; (naut.) équipage m.; keep someone — tenir compagnie à quelqu'un; part — (with) se séparer (de)

comparable a. comparable

comparative a. comparé; comparatif; relatif; -ly adv. relativement; par comparaison

compare vt. comparer; -d to en comparaison de; auprès de

comparison n. comparaison f.; in — with en comparaison de; auprès de

compartment n. compartiment m.; case f.

compass n. boussole f.; (mech.) compas m.; portée f.; — vt. entourer; comploter

compassion n. compassion f.; -ate a. compatissant

compatibility n. compatibilité, convenance f.

compel vt. contraindre, forcer; obliger; imposer, inspirer; -ling a. puissant, irrésistible; compulsif

compendium n. abrégé m.; manuel m.; recueil m.

compensate vt. compenser, dédommager; rémunérer; — for compenser; remplacer

compensation n. compensation f.; honoraires m. pl.; dédommagement m.

compensatory a. compensateur

compete vi. concourir; — with faire concurrence à

competence, competency n. compétence f.

competent a. compétent; capable

competition n. concurrence, compétition f.; concours m., rivalité f.

competitor n. concurrent m.

compilation n. compilation f.

compile vt. compiler; -r n. compilateur m.

complacence, complacency n. complaisance f.; suffisance f.

complacent a. complaisant; suffisant

complain vi. se plaindre; faire des réclamations; -ant n. plaignant m.

complaint n. complainte f.; réclamation f.; (med.) mal m.; cause for — n. grief m.

complaisant a. complaisant, obligeant

complement n. complément m.; (mil.) effectif m.; — vt. compléter; -ary a. complémentaire

complete vt. compléter; achever; remplir; — a. complet, entier; achevé, terminé; parfait, accompli

completion n. accomplissement, achèvement m.

complex a. complexe; — n. complexe m.; inferiority — complexe d'infériorité m.; -ity n. complexité f.

complexion n. complexion f.; teint m.; caractère, aspect m.

compliance n. complaisance f.; acquiescement m.; conformité f.; in — with conformément à

compliant a. complaisant, obligeant; soumis

complicate vt. compliquer, embrouiller; -d a. compliqué

complication n. complication f.

complicity n. complicité f.

compliment n. compliment m.; flatterie f.; to pay a — faire un compliment; — vt. complimenter; flatter; -ary a. complimenteur; gratuit

comply vi. se soumettre; se conformer; obéir, accéder

component n. partie constituante f.; composant m.; — a. composant; — parts éléments constitutifs m. pl.

compose vt. composer; arranger; calmer; — oneself se calmer; -d a. tranquille, calme; be -d of se composer de; -r n. compositeur m.

composite a. & n. composé m.

composition n. composition f.; rédaction f., thème m.; constitution f.; composé m.

compositor n. compositeur, typographe m.

compost n. engrais, compost m.

composure n. tranquillité f.; sang-froid m.

compound n. composé m.; (mil.) enceinte f.; — vt. composer, arranger; — a. composé; — interest intérêts composés m. pl.; — number n. nombre composé m.

comprehend vt. comprendre

comprehensible a. compréhensible

comprehension n. compréhension f.

comprehensive a. compréhensif; étendu; d'ensemble

compress n. compresse f.; — vt. comprimer; condenser; -ion n. compression f.

comprise vt. comprendre, contenir; comporter; renfermer; be -d of se composer de

compromise n. compromis m.; accomodement m.; — vi. faire un compromis; transiger; — vt. compromettre

compromising a. compromettant

comptometer n. machine à calculer f.

comptroller n. comptable m.; vérificateur m.

compulsion n. contrainte f.

compulsory a. forcé, obligatoire

compunction n. remords m., componction f.

computation n. calcul m.

compute vt. compter, calculer, computer

comrade n. camarade m.; -ship n. camaraderie f.

con n. contre m.; pros and -s le pour et le contre; — vt. étudier; (naut.) gouverner

concave a. concave, creux

conceal vt. cacher, dissimuler; masquer, voiler; dérober; recéler; -ment n. dissimulation f.; (law) recel m.

concede vt. concéder, accorder, admettre

conceit n. vanité f.; amour-propre m.; -ed a. vaniteux, vain

conceivable a. concevable, imaginable

conceive vt. & vi. concevoir; — of imaginer

concentrate vt. concentrer

concentration n. concentration f.; — camp camp de concentration m.

concentric a. concentrique

concept n. concept m.; -ion n. conception f.; idée f.

concern n. affaire, cause f.; intérêt, égard m.; inquiétude f., trouble m.; importance f.; compagnie, société anonyme f.; maison f.; — vt. regarder, concerner; inquiéter; toucher, intéresser; -ed a. inquiet; intéressé; as far as I am -ed quant à moi; -ing prep. touchant, au sujet de, concernant; in ce qui concerne

concert n. concert m.; in — de concert; (mus.) à l'unisson; — vt. concerter; -ed a. concerté

concertmaster n. premier violon m.; chef d'orchestre m.

concession n. concession f.; -naire n. concessionnaire m. & f.

concessive a. concessif

conciliate vt. concilier, réconcilier

conciliator n. conciliateur m.; -y a. conciliatoire, conciliant

concise a. concis, succinct; -ness n. concision f.

conclave n. conclave m., assemblée f.

conclude vt. conclure, terminer, achever; — vi. conclure, se terminer

concluding a. final, dernier

conclusion n. conclusion f.; fin f.; décision f.; in — pour conclure

conclusive a. concluant, décisif; -ly adv. d'une manière décisive

concoct vt. préparer, combiner; confectionner, composer; -ion n. breuvage m., boisson f.; mélange m.; confectionnement m.

concomitant a. concomitant

concord n. accord m., harmonie f.; concorde f.; -ance n. concordance f.; -ant a. concordant, d'accord

concourse n. concours m., foule f.; place publique f.

concrete a. concret; — n. béton m.;

reinforced — béton armé m.; — mixer malaxeur m., bétonnière f.; -ly adv. d'une manière concrète

concur vi. concourir; s'accorder, être d'accord; -rence n. accord m.; approbation f.; simultanéité f.; -rent a. concourant; simultané

concussion n. ébranlement m., secousse f.; brain — n. commotion cérébrale f.

condemn vt. condamner; censurer; -ation n. condamnation f.; censure f.

condense vt. condenser; abréger; — vi. se condenser; -r n. condenseur m.; condensateur m.

condescend vi. condescendre, daigner; -ing a. condescendant

condescension n. condescendance f.

condiment n. assaisonnement, condiment m.

condition n. condition f., état, rang m.; stipulation f.; on — that à condition que, pourvu que; — vt. conditionner; habituer, accoutumer; -al a. & n. conditionnel m.; -ed a. conditionné; habitué

condolence n. condoléance f.

condone vt. pardonner; permettre, approuver

conducive a. contribuant, contributif, favorable

conduct n. conduite f., comportement m.; — vt. conduire; mener, diriger; — oneself se comporter; -ion n. conduction f.; -ive a. conducteur; -ivity n. conductivité f.; -or n. conducteur m. (train, bus) controleur, receveur m.; (mus.) chef d'orchestre m.

conduit n. conduit, tuyau m.

cone n. cône m.; ice cream — glace en cornet f.; pine — pomme de pin f.

confection n. confiserie f.; — er n. confiseur m.; -ery n. confiserie f.

confederacy n. confédération f.

confederate n. & a. confédéré m.; complice m.; — vi. se confédérer

confer vt. conférer; — vi. consulter; -ence n. consultation f., conférence f.; (sport) groupement d'équipes) m.

confess vt. confesser, avouer; — vi. se confesser; -ion n. confession f.; aveu m.; (eccl.) confesse, confession f.; -ional n. confessionnal m.; -ional a. confessionnel; -or n. confesseur m.

confidant n. confident m.; confidente f.

confide vt. confier; — vi. se confier (à), se fier (à); -nt a. assuré, confiant; -nt n. confident m.; -ntial a. confidentiel; particulier

confidence n. confiance f.; have — in avoir confiance en

confiding a. confiant

configuration n. configuration f.

confine n. confins m. pl., frontière f.; — vt. enfermer, renfermer; — oneself to se borner à; -ment n. emprisonnement m.; accouchement m., couches f. pl.

confirm vt. confirmer, assurer; corroborer; -ation n. confirmation f.; -ed a. invétéré, endurci

confiscate vt. confisquer, saisir

conflagration n. incendie m., conflagration f.

conflict n. conflit m.; — vi. être en contradiction; se heurter; –ing a. contradictoire; opposé

confluence n. confluent m.

conform vt. rendre conforme; conformer; — vi. se conformer; obéir, se soumettre; –ation n. conformation f.; –ity n. conformité f.; in –ity with conformément à

confound vt. confondre; —! interj. diable!; –ed a. sacré

confraternity n. confraternité f.; confrérie f.

confront vt. confronter; faire face à, affronter; –ation n. confrontation f.

confuse vt. confondre, troubler; brouiller, embrouiller; –d a. confondu; confus; embrouillé; trouble; –dly adv. confusément

confusion n. confusion f.; désordre m.

congeal vt. geler, congeler; coaguler; figer; — vi. geler; se congeler; se figer

congenial a. sympathique, agréable

congenital a. congénital, inné; de naissance

congest vt. congestionner; encombrer; –ed a. congestionné; encombré; (traffic) embouteillé; –ion n. congestion f.; encombrement m.

conglomerate vt. conglomérer; — vi. se conglomérer; — a. conglomère

congratulate vt. féliciter

congratulation n. félicitation f.

congratulatory a. de félicitations

congregate vt. rassembler; — vi. s'assembler, se rassembler

congregation n. congrégation f.; assistance f.; rassemblement m.; –al a. de congrégation; (eccl.) indépendant; –alist a. & n. congrégationaliste m.

congress n. congrès m.; assemblée f.; réunion f.; –man n. député m.; –ional a. parlementaire

congruent a. congruent; conforme

congruity n. congruité f.; conformité f.

congruous a. conforme

conifer n. conifère m.

conjecture n. conjecture f.; — vt. & vi. conjecturer

conjugate vt. conjuguer; — a. conjugué

conjugation n. conjugaison f.

conjunction n. conjonction f.

conjunctive a. conjonctif

conjuncture n. conjoncture f.

conjure vt. conjurer; comploter; évoquer; — vi. conjurer, faire de la sorcellerie; –r n. sorcier m.

connect vt. joindre, lier; unir, réunir, rattacher, relier; — vi. se joindre, s'unir; se réunir, se lier; –ed a. suivi; connexe; –ing rod n. bielle f.; –ion n. connexion f.; liaison f., rapport m., correspondance f.; in –ion with à propos de, au sujet de

connive vi. conniver

connoisseur n. connaisseur m.

connotation n. connotation, signification f.

connote vt. signifier (en delà du sens littéral)

connubial a. conjugal

conquer vt. & vi. cohquérir, vaincre; –ing a. conquérant, triomphant, victorieux; –or n. vainqueur m.; conquérant m.

conquest n. conquête, victoire f.

consanguinity n. consanguinité f.; parenté f.

conscience n. conscience f.

conscience-stricken a. pris de remords

conscientious a. consciencieux; — objector n. réformé de guerre m. (pour cause de convictions religieuses); –ness n. conscience f.; assiduité f.

conscionable a. juste, raisonnable

conscious a. conscient; be — (awareness) avoir conscience; (physical state) avoir la connaissance; –ly adv. sciemment; –ness n. connaissance f.; conscience f.; sentiment m.; lose –ness perdre connaissance; regain –ness reprendre connaissance

conscript n. conscrit m., recrue f.; — a. conscrit; — vt. recruter, enrôler; –ion n. conscription f., enrôlement m.

consecrate vt. consacrer; bénir; –d a. consacré, béni, saint

consecration n. consécration f.; dévouement m.; sacre m.

consecutive a. consécutif, successif; de suite; –ly adv. de suite, consécutivement

consensus n. accord m.; orientation de l'opinion générale f.

consent n. consentement m.; accord m.; — vi. consentir (à)

consequence n. conséquence f.; importance f.; suite f.; by —, in — par conséquent

consequent a. conséquent; –ial a. important; consécutif, conséquent; –ly adv. conséquemment, par conséquent

conservation n. conservation, garde f.

conservative n. & a. conservateur m.

conservatory n. serre f.; (mus.) conservatoire m.

conserve vt. préserver, conserver; –s n. pl. conserves, confitures f. pl.

consider vt. considérer, regarder; estimer, penser; avoir égard à; — vi. réfléchir; –able a. considérable; –ate a. attentif, prévenant, soucieux; –ateness n. égards m. pl.; –ation n. considération f.; importance f.; égard m.; be under –ation être à l'étude; take into –ation tenir compte de; –ing prep. vu, étant donné

consign vt. consigner; livrer; –ee n. consignataire m.; –ment n. livraison f.; expédition f.; on –ment en consignation; –or n. consignateur m.

consist vi. consister; être composé (de); –ency n. consistance, substance f.; suite f.; –ent a. consistant; conséquent; d'accord; –ently adv. conséquemment

consistory n. consistoire m.

consolable a. consolable

console n. console f.; — vt. consoler; –r n. consolateur m.

consolidate vt. consolider; unifier; réunir; — vi. se consolider

consolidation n. consolidation f.; unification f.

consoling a. consolateur, consolant

consonance n. consonance f.; accord m.

consonant n. consonne f.; — a. consonant; conforme (à), d'accord

consort n. compagnon m.; époux m., épouse f.; — vi. s'associer; — with fréquenter

conspicuous a. apparent, frappant; become — se signaler, se faire remarquer

conspiracy n. conspiration f.

conspirator n. conspirateur m.

conspire vi. conspirer, comploter

constable n. constable m.; agent de police m.; connétable m.

constabulary n. police, gendarmerie f.

constancy n. constance f.; fidélité f.

constant a. constant, ferme; continuel; fidèle; — n. constante f.; -ly adv. constamment; continuellement

consternation n. consternation f.

constipate vt. constiper

constipation n. constipation f.

constituency n. circonscription (électorale) f.; électeurs m. pl.

constituent a. constituant; — n. constituant, composant m.; électeur m.

constitute vt. constituer

constitution n. constitution f.; tempérament m.; -al a. constitutionnel; -al n. promenade f.; -ality n. conformité (à la constitution)

constrain vt. contraindre, forcer; -ed a. contraint, forcé; -t n. contrainte, force f.; retenue f.

constrict vt. resserrer, contracter; gêner; -ion n. constriction f.; resserrement m.; -or n. constricteur m.; boa -or boa (constricteur) m.

construct vt. construire, bâtir; -ion n. construction f.; interprétation f.; under — en construction; -ive a. constructif; -or n. constructeur m.

construe vt. expliquer, interpréter

consul n. consul m.; -ar a. consulaire; -ate n. consulat m.

consult vt. consulter; — vi. délibérer, se consulter; demander conseil; -ant n. conseiller, consultant m.; -ation n. consultation f.; -ing a. consultant; conseil

consume vt. consumer; brûler; épuiser; dévorer; consommer; -r n. consommateur m.

consummate vt. consommer; terminer; — a. consommé, parfait, achevé

consummation n. consommation f., achèvement m.; couronnement, comble m.

consumption n. consommation f.; (med.) phthisie f.

consumptive a. & n. phthisique, poitrinaire m. & f.

contact n. contact m.; rapport m.; — lens verre de contact m.; — vt. se mettre en relations avec; entrer en communication avec; parler à; écrire à

contagious a. contagieux; communica-

tif; -ness n. contagiosité f.

contain vt. contenir; comporter, comprendre; retenir; -er n. contenant m.; boîte f.

contaminate vt. contaminer, corrompre

contamination n. contamination f.

contemplate vt. contempler; méditer; envisager; — vi. contempler; méditer

contemplation n. contemplation f.; méditation f.; recueillement m.

contemplative a. contemplatif

contemplator n. contemplateur m.

contemporaneous, contemporary a. & n. contemporain m.

contempt n. mépris, dédain m.; — of court n. contumace f.; hold in — mépriser; -ible a. méprisable; -ibly adv. d'une manière méprisable; -uous a. dédaigneux; -uously adv. avec mépris

contend vi. disputer, combattre; — vt. prétendre, soutenir

content n. contentement m.; contenu m.; -s n. pl. contenu m.; table of -s table des matières f.; to one's heart's — à volonté; — a. content, tranquille; — vt. contenter; be -(ed) with se contenter de; -ment n. contentement m.

contention n. contention, dispute f.; prétention f.; bone of — pomme de discorde f.

contentious a. litigieux, querelleur

contest n. disputer; contester; — n. concours m.; dispute f.; combat m.; -able a. contestable; -ant n. concurrent m.; -ation n. contestation f.

context n. contexte m.

contiguity n. contiguïté f.

contiguous a. contigu

continence n. continence f.

continent n. & a. continent m.; -al a. continental

contingency n. contingence f.; éventualité f.; cas imprévu m.

contingent a. contingent; éventuel, accidentel; imprévu; be — on dépendre de; — n. contingent

continual a. continuel; -ly adv. continuellement, sans cesse

continuance, continuation n. continuation f.; suite f.

continue vt. & vi. continuer; to be -d à suivre

continuity n. continuité, suite f.

continuous a. continu; — performance (movies) spectacle permanent m.

contort vt. tordre; -ed a. tordu, contorsionné; -ion n. contorsion f.; -ionist n. contorsionniste m. & f.

contour n. contour m.; profil m.

contraband n. contrebande f.

contract n. contrat, pacte m.; acte m.; entreprise f.; — vt. contracter; crisper; prendre, entreprendre; — vi. se contracter; faire un contrat; s'engager; entreprendre, mettre à l'entreprise; -ing n. entreprise f.; -ion n. contraction f.; -or n. entrepreneur m.; adjudicataire m.; -ual a. de contrat, contractuel

contradict vt. contredire; démentir; -ion n. contradiction f.; -ory a. contradictoire

contradistinction n. opposition f.
contraption n. machin, appareil m.
contrapuntal a. en contrepoint
contrariness n. contrariété f.
contrariwise adv. au contraire
contrary n. contraire, opposé; on the — au contraire; — a. contraire; — to contrairement à
contrast n. contraste m.; — vi. contraster; — vt. opposer, faire contraster; -ing a. opposé, en contraste
contravene vt. contrevenir à
contravention n. contravention f.
contribute vt. & vi. contribuer; collaborer
contribution n. contribution f.; apport m.
contributor n. collaborateur m.; contribuant m.; — a. contribuant, contributif
contrite a. contrit, pénitent
contrivance n. projet m.; appareil m.; invention f.
contrive vt. inventer, projeter, essayer; combiner; — vi. parvenir à; s'arranger
control n. contrôle m.; autorité, direction f.; empire m.; -s n. pl. commandes f. pl.; — vt. contrôler; diriger; commander; — oneself se maîtriser; se retenir; -lable a. gouvernable; maîtrisable; — stick n. (avi.) commande f.; manche à balai
controller n. comptable m.; contrôleur m.
controversial a. de controverse, discutable
controversy n. controverse m., polémique f.
controvert vt. disputer; controverser; -ible a. controversible
contumely n. outrage m., insulte m.; honte f.
contuse vt. contusionner
convalesce vi. guérir; se remettre; -nce n. convalescence f.; -nt a. convalescent
convection n. convection f.
convene vt. assembler, réunir, convoquer; — vi. s'assembler, se réunir
convenience n. aise, commodité f.; convenance f.; at your earliest — aussitôt que possible; at your own — quand il vous plaira; -s n. pl. confort m.
convenient a. commode, aisé
convent n. couvent m.
convention n. rassemblement, congrès m.; convention f.; bienséance f.; contrat m.; -al a. conventionnel; ordinaire, normal
converge vi. converger; -nce n. convergence f.; -nt a. convergent
converging a. convergent
conversant a. familier; versé (dans)
conversation n. conversation f., entretien m.; -al a. de conversation
converse a. & a. converse f.; réciproque f.; — vi. causer, s'entretenir; -ly adv. réciproquement
convert n. converti m.; — vt. convertir; changer, transformer; — vi. se convertir; -er n. convertisseur m.; -ibility n. convertibilité f.; -ible a. (auto) décapotable; convertible; convertissable
convex a. convexe
convey vt. transporter; communiquer;

transmettre; -ance n. voiture f.; moyen de transport m.; transmission f.; -er, -or n. transporteur m.; courroie f.; tapis roulant m.
convict n. condamné m.; forçat m.; — vt. convaincre, condamner; -ion n. condamnation f.; conviction f.
convince vt. convaincre, persuader
convincing a. convainquant
convivial a. sociable, joyeux
convocation n. convocation, assemblée f.
convoke vt. convoquer
convolution n. circonvolution f.
convoy n. convoi m., escorte f.; — vt. escorter, convoyer
convulse vt. convulsionner; ébranler; -d a. convulsé
convulsive a. convulsif
coo vi. roucouler; -ing n. roucoulement m.
cook n. cuisinier m.; cuisinière f.; chef m.; — vi. faire la cuisine; — up (coll.) comploter; -er n. réchaud m.; cuisinière f.; -ery n. cuisine; -ing n. cuisine f.; -ing utensils batterie de cuisine f.; -book n. livre de cuisine m.
cookie, cooky n. gâteau sec, biscuit, petit four m.
cool n. frais m., fraîcheur f.; — a. frais (fraîche); indifférent; tranquille; — vt. & vi. refroidir; — off se refroidir; — one's heels attendre; -er n. frigorifique m.; (coll.) prison f.; -ing a. rafraîchissant; -ing n. refroidissement m.; -ness n. frais m.; indifférence f.; froideur f.; clame; sang-froid m.
cooling-off period (com.) n, trève f., arrangée pour empêcher une grève
coop n. cage f., poulailler m.; fly the — s'évader; — up vi. enfermer
co-op n. (coll.) entreprise coopérative f.
cooper n. tonnelier m.; -age n. tonnellerie f.
co-operate vi. coopérer, collaborer
co-operation n. coopération f.
co-operative n. entreprise coopérative f.; — a. coopératif
co-ordinate vt. coordonner; — a. coordonné; — n. coordonné m.
co-ordination n. coordination f.
coot n. foulque f.
cope vi. combattre, lutter, se tirer d'affaire
copier n. copiste m. & f.; imitateur m.
coping n. faîte m.; — saw porte-scies m.
copious a. copieux, abondant; -ly adv. copieusement; -ness n. abondance f.
copilot n. copilote m.
copper n. cuivre m.; monnaie de cuivre f.; (coll.) flic m.; — a. de cuivre, en cuivre; — vt. cuivrer
copperhead n. (variété de) serpent vénéneux m.; partisan du sud m. (guerre de sécession, USA)
copperplate n. gravure sur cuivre f.; plaque de cuivre f.
coppersmith n. chaudronnier m.
copse n. taillis m.
copulate vi. s'accoupler
copulation n. copulation f.
copulative a. copulatif

copy n. copie, reproduction f.; exemplaire m.; numéro m.; —book n. cahier m.; —cat n. imitateur, singe m.; — writer (com.) rédacteur d'annonces publicitaires m.; rough — brouillon m.; — vt. copier; imiter; —ist n. copiste m.

copyright n. copyright, droit d'auteur m.; — vt. déposer; —ed a. dont tous les droits sont réservés

coquette n. coquette f.

coquettish a. coquet

cord n. corde f.; cordon m., ficelle f.; stère m., mesure f. (pour le bois: 128 pieds³); — vt. corder; ligoter; —age n. cordage m.; —ed a. à cordes; côtelé

cordial a. cordial; — n. liqueur f., digestif m.; —ity n. cordialité f.

Cordoba n. Cordoue f.

cordovan n. cuir de Cordoue m.

corduroy n. velours (rayé) m.

core n. cœur, intérieur m.; noyau m.; (apple) trognon m.; — vt. vider

corespondent n. coaccusé m.

cork n. liège, bouchon (de liège) m.; vt. boucher; —age n. débouchage m.

corkscrew n. tire-bouchon m.

cormorant n. cormoran m.

corn n. maïs m.; (foot) cor m.; — cob n. épi de maïs; —crib n. dépôt de maïs m.; — pone n. (sorte de) polenta f.; — popper appareil pour faire éclater le maïs m.; — vt. saler; —ed beef bœuf salé m.; —starch n. fécule de maïs m.; amidon m.

cornea n. cornée f.

corner n. coin, angle m.; extrémité f.; tournant, virage m.; — vt. attraper; acculer; (com.) accaparer

cornerstone n. pierre angulaire f.; pierre de refend f.

cornice n. corniche f.

Cornish a. cornouaillais

cornucopia n. corne d'abondance f.

Cornwall n. Cornouailles m.

corolla n. corolle f.

corollary n. corollaire m.

corona n. couronne f.

coronation n. couronnement, sacre m.

coronet n. petite couronne f.

corporal n. caporal m.; — a. corporel (eccl.) corporal

corporate a. incorporé

corporation n. société anonyme f.; (coll.) ventre m., bedaine f.

corporeal a. corporel, matériel

corps n. corps, corps d'armée m.

corpse n. cadavre m.; corps m.

corpsman n. (mil.) infirmier m.

corpulence n. corpulence f.

corpulent a. corpulent

corpuscle n. corpuscule, m.

corral n. enclos m.; — vt. mettre dans l'enclos

correct vt. corriger; châtier, punir; retoucher; — a. correct; exact; bienséant; —ion n. correction f.; —ive a. correctionnel; correctif; —ly adv. correctement, exactement; —ness n. correction f.; exactitude f.

correlate vi. correspondre; — vt. marquer la corrélation

correlation n. corrélation f.

correlative a. corrélatif, réciproque

correspond vi. correspondre; —ence n. correspondance f.; —ent n. correspondant m.; —ing a. correspondant; conforme

corridor n. couloir, corridor m.

corroborate vt. corroborer

corroboration n. corroboration f.

corroborator n. témoin m.

corrode vt. corroder, ronger; — vi. se corroder

corrosion n. corrosion f.

corrugate vt. rider, froncer, plisser; —ed iron tôle ondulée f.

corrupt vt. corrompre, gâter, séduire, suborner; — a. corrompu; —ible a. corruptible; —ion n. corruption f.

corsage n. fleur f., bouquet m. (porté au corsage)

Corsica n. Corse f.; —n a. & n. corse m. & f.

cortex n. substance corticale f.

cortisone n. cortisone m.

corundum n. corindon m.

cosmetic n. cosmétique m.; fard m.; — a. cosmétique

cosmic a. cosmique; — ray rayon cosmique m.

cosmopolitan n. & a. cosmopolite m.

Cossack n. Cosaque m.

cost n. prix m., frais m. pl., dépense f.; — price prix de revient m.; — of living coût de la vie m.; whatever the — coûte que coûte; — vi. coûter; —liness n. (haut) prix m.; cherté f.; —ly a. cher; coûteux

Costa Rica n. Costa Rica m.

costume n. costume m.; —r n. costumier m.

cot n. lit de sangle m.

cote n. pigeonnier, colombier m.

cottage n. cabane, chaumière f.; villa f.; — cheese lait caillé, fromage blanc m.

cotton n. coton m.; absorbent — coton hydrophile m.; — batting côton cardé m.; ouate f.; — flannel n. flanelle de coton f.; — goods cotonnades f. pl.; — mill filature de coton f.

couch n. lit m.; divan m.; canapé m.; — vt. coucher; — vi. se tapir

cougar n. couguar m.

cough n. toux f.; — drop pastille f.; — vi. tousser; —ing n. toux f.

council n. conseil m.; concile m.; city — conseil municipal m.; —or n. conseiller m.

counsel n. conseil, avis m.; consultation f.; avocat m.; — vt. & vi. conseiller; —or n. conseiller; avocat m.

count n. nombre, compte m.; (title) comte m.; — vi. compter; — on compter sur; —er n. compteur m.; jeton m.; contre m.; comptoir m.; Geiger —er n. compteur de Geiger m.; —er adv. contre; —es a. contraire; —less a. innombrable

count-down n. (coll.) longue vérification finale avant de lancer un projectile dans l'espace

countenance n. contenance f., visage m.; air, regard m.; — vt. soutenir, favoriser; approuver; encourager

counter vt. opposer, agir contre; riposter

counteract vt. contrebalancer

counterattack n. contre-attaque f.; — vt. contre-attaquer

counterbalance vt. contre-balancer; — n. contre-poids m.

countercharge n. contre-accusation f.

counterclockwise adv. au sens inverse des aiguilles d'une montre

counterfeit n. contrefaçon, fausse monnaie f.; — vt. contrefaire; -ing n. contrefait; -er n. contrefaiteur, faux-monnayeur m.

counterintelligence n. contre-espionnage m.

countermand vt. contremander; décommander

countermarch n. contremarche f.

counteroffensive n. contre-offensive f.

counterpane n. courtepointe f.

counterpart n. contre-partie f.; pendant m.

counterpoint n. contre-point m.

counterreformation n. contre-réforme f.

counterrevolution n. contre-révolution f.

countershaft n. contre-arbre m.

countersign n. contre-seing m.; (mil.) mot d'ordre m.; — vt. contresigner

countersink vt. fraiser; — n. fraise f.

countertenor n. haute-contre f.

counterweight n. contre-poids m.

countess n. comtesse f.

country n. pays m.; contrée, compagne f.; native — patrie f.; -man n. compatriote m.; compagnard m.

countryside n. paysage m.; région f.

county n. comté, département, canton m.; — seat chef-lieu m.

coupe n. coupé m.

couple n. couple m., paire f.; — vt. coupler; accoupler; embrayer; grouper; — vi. s'accoupler

coupling n. accouplement m.; couplage m.; attelage m.

coupon n. coupon m.; (com.) bon-prime m.

courage n. courage m.; -ous a. courageux

courier n. courrier m.

course n. course, carrière f.; cours m.; plat, service m.; chemin m., route f.; terrain m.; (naut.) cap m.; as a matter of — comme affaire routinière; in due — en temps voulu; in the — of time avec le temps; of — bien entendu; give a — faire un cours; take a — suivre un cours; — vi. courir

court n. cour f.; cour de justice f., tribunal m.; (sport) terrain m.; — vt. faire la cour (à), courtiser

courteous a. poli, courtois; -ness n. politesse f.

courtesan n. courtisane f.

courtesy n. courtoisie, politesse f.

courthouse n. palais de justice m.

courtier n. courtisan m.; homme de la cour m.

court-martial n. conseil de guerre m.; — vt. traduire en conseil de guerre

courtroom n. salle du tribunal f.

courtship n. cour f.

courtyard n. cour (de maison) f.

cousin n. cousin m., cousine f.; first — cousin germain m.

cove n. crique f.; abri m.; anse f.

covenant n. contrat, accord m.

cover n. couvert m., enveloppe f.; couverture f.; couvercle m.; abri m., protection f.; prétexte m.; — charge couvert m.; take — se mettre à l'abri; under separate — sous pli séparé; — vt. couvrir; recouvrir; cacher; parcourir; (newspaper) assurer un reportage; -age n. reportage m.; assurance f.; (insurance) n. couverture d'assurance f.; -ing n. couverture f.

coverlet n. (bed) couvre-lit m., (foot) couvre-pieds m.

covert a. couvert, caché

covet vt. & vi. convoiter; désirer ardemment; -ous a. cupide, désireux; avide; -ousness n. convoitise, cupidité f.

covey n. couvée, volée f.

cow n. vache f.; — vt. intimider

coward n. lâche m.; -ice n. lâcheté f.; -ly a. lâche

cowboy n. vacher, cow-boy m.

cower vi. s'accroupir, se tapir

cowhide n. vache, peau de vache f.

cowl n. capuchon m.; capot m.; -ing n. capuchonnement m.; capotage m.

cowlick n. épi de cheveux m.

co-worker n. collaborateur m.

cowslip n. primevère f.

coxcomb n. fat, petit-maître m.

coxwain n. patron de chaloupe m.; barreur m.

coy a. modeste; réservé; -ness n. modestie, timidité, réserve f.

coyote n. (genre de) loup m.

coziness n. confortable m.

C.P.A.: Certified Public Accountant comptable diplômé m.

crab n. crabe m.; tourteau m.; personne désagréable f.; — (apple) pomme sauvage f.; — vi. se plaindre, être désagréable; -by a. désagréable, grognon, revêche

crack n. fente f.; craquement, bruit m.; fêlure f.; — of dawn pointe du jour f.; — a. expert, de premier ordre; — vi. se fendre; — vt. fendre; — a joke faire une plaisanterie; -down (coll.) devenir très stricte; -ed a. fendu; (coll.) fou; -er n. biscuit m.; -ling n. friton m.; craquement m.

crackle vi. craqueter, pétiller; — n. craquement m.

crackpot n. (coll.) original, excentrique, tapé m.

crack-up n. collision f.; accident m.; écrasement m.; écroulement m.; accident d'avion m.

cradle n. berceau m.; — vt. bercer

craft n. métier m., profession f.; artifice m., fourberie f.; barque f., vaisseau m.; -iness n. ruse f.; -y a. rusé

craftsman n. artisan m.

crag n. rocher escarpé m.; -ged, -gy a. escarpé

cram vt. fourrer; farcir; — vi. (coll.)

étudier à la dernière heure; bûcher

cramp *n.* crampe *f.*; — *vt.* gêner, entraver; -ed *a.* serré; gêné

cranberry *n.* airelle *f.*; — sauce compote d'airelles *f.*

cranial *a.* cranien

cranium *n.* crâne *m.*

crank *n.* manivelle *f.*; (coll.) excentrique *m.*; — *vt.* tourner la manivelle (de); -iness *n.* irritabilité, mauvaise humeur *f.*; -y *a.* irritable, de mauvaise humeur

crankcase *n.* carter *m.*

crankshaft *n.* arme de manivelle, arbre-manivelle *m.*

cranny *n.* fente, crevasse *f.*; coin *m.*; niche *f.*

crape *n.* crêpe *m.*

crash *n.* craquement, fracas *m.*; écrasement *m.*; (com.) krach *m.*; — *vt.* briser, fracasser; — *vi.* retentir

crash-landing *n.* (avi.) atterrissage violent *m.* (exécuté par le pilote dans un cas urgent)

crass *a.* grossier

crate *n.* emballage à claire-voie *m.*; — *vt.* emballer

crater *n.* cratère *m.*

cravat *n.* foulard *m.*; cravate *f.*

crave *vt.* implorer, solliciter; désirer

craven *a.* lâche *m.*

craving *n.* désir ardent *m.*; soif *f.*

crawfish, crayfish *n.* écrevisse *f.*

crawl *vi.* ramper; se traîner; be -ing with fourmiller de; — *n.* rampement *m.*; (swimming) crawl *m.*

crayon *n.* couleur *f.*; crayon (de pastel) *m.*; — *vt.* crayonner

craze *n.* manie *f.*; vogue *f.*; — *vt.* rendre fou

craziness *n.* folie *f.*

crazy *a.* fou (folle); —, (funny), bone *n.* nerf du coude *m.*; — quilt courte-pointe multicolore *f.*

creak *vi.* crier, craquer; — *n.* cri *m.*; -y *a.* criard

cream *n.* crème *f.*; meilleur, élite *m.*; whipped — crème fouettée *f.*; — cheese fromage à la crème, fromage blanc *m.*; — puff chou à la crème *m.*; — *vt.* mélanger (beurre et sucre); -ery *n.* crèmerie, laiterie *f.*; -y *a.* crémeux

crease *n.* pli, faux pli *m.*; — *vt.* plisser, faire un faux pli; — *vi.* se plisser

create *vt.* créer, produire; inventer

creation *n.* création *f.*; invention *f.*

creative *a.* créateur, inventif

creator *n.* créateur *m.*

creature *n.* créature *f.*; être *m.*; (animal) bête *f.*

credence *n.* créance, foi *f.*

credentials *n. pl.* lettres de créance *f. pl.*, documents, papiers *m. pl.*

credibility *n.* crédibilité *f.*

credible *a.* croyable, digne de foi

credit *n.* crédit *m.*; foi, croyance *f.*; témoignage *m.*; influence *f.*; to be a — to faire honneur à; — *vt.* croire, ajouter foi à; donner à crédit; porter au crédit de; -able *a.* estimable; -or *n.* créditeur *m.*

credulity *n.* crédulité *f.*

credulous *a.* crédule; -ness *n.* crédulité *f.*

creed *n.* croyance *f.*; profession de foi *f.*

creek *n.* ruisseau *m.*; crique *f.*

creel *n.* panier de pêche *m.*

creep *vi.* ramper; se traîner; -er *n.* (bot.) plante rampante *f.*; -y *a.* (coll.) mystérieux

cremate *vt.* incinérer

cremation *n.* incinération *f.*

Creole *n.* Louisianais *m.* (d'origine française ou espagnole)

creosote *n.* créosote *f.*; — *vt.* créosoter

crepe *n.* crêpe *m.*; — paper papier crêpe *m.*

crepitation *n.* crépitation *f.*

crescent *a. & n.* croissant *m.*

cress *n.* cresson *m.*

crest *n.* crête *f.*; cimier *m.*; sommet *m.*; -ed *a.* huppé; à crête

crestfallen *a.* abattu, decouragé, penaud

Crete *n.* Crète *f.*

crevice *n.* crevasse, fente *f.*

crew *n.* troupe, bande *f.*; équipage *m.*; équipe *f.*

crib *n.* mangeoire, crèche, étable *f.*; petit lit *m.*; (grain) coffre *m.*; — *vt.* copier; -bing *n.* (coll.) emploi frauduleux d'un aide-mémoire pour réussir à un examen *m.*

cricket *n.* grillon *m.*; (sports) cricket *m.*

crier *n.* crieur *m.*

Crimea *n.* Crimée *f.*

criminal *n. & a.* criminel *m.*

criminologist *n.* criminaliste *m.*

criminology *n.* criminologie *f.*

crimp *vt.* friser; gaufrer; — *n.* (coll.) obstacle *m.*

crimson *n. & a.* cramoisi *m.*

cringe *vi.* ramper, s'abaisser

cringing *a.* craintif; servile; — *n.* crainte *f.*; servilité *f.*

crinkle *n.* pli *m.*; — *vt.* froisser, plisser

cripple *n.* estropié *m.*; — *vt.* estropier; paralyser

crisis *n.* crise *f.*

crisp *a.* croustillant; vif; brusque; frais; -ness *n.* qualité croustillante *f.*; netteté *f.*

crisscross *a.* en zigzag; en quinconce; — *vt. & vi.* aller en zigzag, (s')entrecroiser

criterion *n.* critérium, critère *m.*

critic *n.* critique *m.*; -al *a.* critique; -ism *n.* critique *f.*; -ize *vt.* critiquer; blâmer

croak *vi.* coasser; (coll.) crever; — *n.* coassement *m.*

Croatia *n.* Croatie *f.*

crochet *n.* ouvrage au crochet *m.*; — *vt.* faire su crochet; — *vi.* faire du crochet

crock *n.* pot de terre *m.*; -ery *n.* poterie *f.*

crocodile *n.* crocodile *m.*

crone *n.* vieille femme *f.*

crony *n.* copain *m.*

crook *n.* crochet *m.*; courbure *f.*; (eccl.) crosse *f.*; (coll.) escroc, malfaiteur, filou *m.*; — *vt.* courber; — *vi.* se courber; -ed *a.* courbé; tortueux; (coll.) malhonnête, filou; -edness *n.* nature tortueuse *f.*

croon *vi.* chantonner doucement; chanter

d'une maniere sentimentale; **-er** *n.* chanteur dont la voix est douce et sentimentale *m.*

crop *n.* récolte, moisson *f.*; (bird) jabot *m.*; (whip) manche *m.*; — *vt.* couper court; — up apparaître; **-per**, share **-er** *n.* métayer *m.*

cross *n.* croix *f.*; mélange, croisement *m.*; — *a.* fâché; contraire; — purpose opposition *f.*; — reference renvoi *m.*; — section coupe *f.*; — *vt. & vi.* traverser; croiser; — out rayer; **-ing** *n.* traversée *f.*; passage *m.*; level **-ing** (rail.) passage à niveau *m.*; pedestrian **-ing** passage clouté *m.*

crossbill *n.* bec-croisé *m.*

crossbow *n.* arbalète *f.*; **-man** *n.* arbalétrier *m.*

crossbreed *n.* personne de race croisée *f.*; — *vt.* croiser la race

cross-check *vt.* vérifier tous les éléments de

cross-country *a.* à travers campagne

crosscut *a.* qui coupe en travers

cross-examination *n.* contre-interrogatoire *m.*

cross-eyed *a.* louche

cross fire *n.* feu croisé *m.*

cross-legged *a.* les jambes croisées

cross-purposes *n. pl.* malentendu *m.*

crossroad *n.* carrefour *m.*; chemin de traverse *m.*

crosswise, crossways *a.* en travers

crossword puzzle *n.* mots croisés *m. pl.*

crotch *n.* entre-jambes *m.*

crotchety *a.* irritable, désagréable, revêche; capricieux

crouch *vi.* se baisser, s'accroupir; — *n.* accroupissement *m.*; (boxing) crouch *m.*

croup *n.* croupion *n.*; (med.) croup *m.*; croupe (d'un cheval) *f.*

crouton *n.* croûton *m.*

crow *n.* corneille *f.*; chant du coq *m.*; as the — flies à vol d'oiseau; — *vi.* chanter; se vanter

crowd *n.* foule, presse *f.*; (coll.) bande, côterie *f.*; — *vt.* encombrer; — *vi.* se presser, s'assembler en foule; **-ed** *a.* bondé

crown *n.* couronne *f.*; sommet *m.*; forme (d'un chapeau) *f.*; — prince prince héritier *m.*; — *vt.* couronner, sacrer; **-ing** *a.* suprême; **-ing** *n.* couronnement *m.*

crow's-foot *n.* patte-d'oie *f.*

crow's-nest *n.* (naut.) vigie *f.*

crucial *a.* crucial, décisif

crucible *n.* creuset *m.*

crucifix *n.* crucifix *m.*; **-ion** *n.* crucifixion *f.*

cruciform *a.* cruciforme, en forme de croix

crucify *vt.* crucifier

crude *a.* cru; rude; brut; fruste; grossier; — oil pétrole brut *m.*; **-ness** *n.* crudité *f.*; grossiereté; rudesse *f.*

crudity *n.* crudité *f.*

cruel *a.* cruel; **-ty** *n.* cruauté *f.*

cruet *n.* burette *f.*, huilier, vinaigrier *m.*

cruise *n.* croisière *f.*; — *vi.* faire une

croisière; **-r** *n.* croiseur *m.*

cruller *n.* beignet *m.*

crumb *n.* mie, miette *f.*; bread **-s** chapelure *f.*; — *vt.* paner; **-ed** *a.* pané

crumble *vt.* émietter; — *vi.* s'écrouler; crouler; s'émietter

crumbling *n.* écroulement *m.*

crumple *vt.* froisser

crunch *vt.* croquer; — *vi.* craquer

crupper *n.* croupe *f.*

crusade *n.* croisade *f.*; **-er** *n.* croisé *m.*

crush *n.* écrasement *m.*; choc *m.*; foule *f.*; (coll.) amourette *f.*; — *vt.* écraser; opprimer; **-ing** *a.* écrasant; accablant; **-ing** *n.* écrasement *m.*

crust *n.* croûte *f.*; incrustation *f.*; — *vt.* encroûter; **-y** *a.* couvert d'une croûte; vieux, maussade

crustacean *n.* crustacé *m.*

crutch *n.* béquille *f.*

crux *n.* crise *f.*; point central *m.*

cry *n.* cri *m.*; a far — from bien eloigné de; — *vt.* crier; — *vi.* pleurer; crier, s'écrier; **-ing** *n.* pleurs *f. pl.*; cri *m.*

crybaby *n.* pleurnicheur *m.*

crypt *n.* crypte *f.*; **-ic** *a.* secret; énigmatique

cryptography *n.* cryptographie *f.*

crystal *n.* cristal *m.*; (of a watch) verre *m.*; — *a.* de cristal; **-line** *a.* cristallin; **-lize** *vt.* cristaliser; **-lization** *n.* crystallisation *f.*

C.S.T.: Central Standard Time heure du centre (des USA)

cub *n.* petit d'un animal *m.*; (scout) louveteau *m.*; — reporter reporter débutant *m.*

cubbyhole *n.* case *f.*

cube *n.* cube *m.*; — *vt.* cuber

cubic *a.* cube; cubique

cubicle *n.* cabine *f.*

cuckoo *n.* coucou *m.*; — *a.* (coll.) fou

cucumber *n.* concombre *m.*

cud, to chew the — ruminer

cuddle *vt.* serrer, presser; — *vi.* se serrer

cudgel *n.* massue *f.*; — *vt.* rosser; — one's brains se casser la tête

cue *n.* (billiards) queue *f.*; (theat.) réplique *f.*; — *vt.* donner la réplique

cuff *n.* (blow) coup *m.*; (shirt) manchette *f.*; (trousers) revers *m.*; — links boutons de manchette *m. pl.*; — *vt.* battre, talocher

culinary *a.* de cuisine, culinaire

cull *vt.* cueillir; choisir; trier

culminate *vi.* culminer

culmination *n.* point culminant *m.*

culotte *n. pl.* pantalon court de femme *m.*

culpability *n.* culpabilité *f.*

culpable *a.* coupable

culprit *n.* coupable *m.*

cult *n.* culte *m.*

cultivate *vt.* cultiver

cultivation *n.* cultivation, culture *f.*

cultivator *n.* cultivateur *m.*

cultural *a.* culturel

culture *n.* culture *f.*; **-d** *a.* cultivé

culvert *n.* ponceau *m.*

cumbersome *a.* embarrassant, incommode

cumulative a. cumulatif
cumulus n. cumulus m.
cuneiform a. cunéiforme
cunning n. ruse f.; artifice m.; — a. adroit; rusé; (coll.) délicieux, charmant
cup n. tasse f.; coupe f.; (med.) ventouse f.
cupboard n. armoire f.; placard m.
cupcake n. petit gâteau m.
Cupid n. Cupidon m.
cupidity n. cupidité f.
cupola n. coupole f.
cur n. chien hargneux m.
curable a. guérissable
curate n. vicaire, curé m.
curative a. curatif
curator n. conservateur m.
curb n. frein m.; restreinte f.; bordure (de trottoir) f.; — vt. restreindre; brider
curbstone n. bordure (de trottoir) f.
curd n. lait caillé m.; -le vt. cailler; -le vi. se cailler
cure n. cure f.; guérison f., traitement m.; — vt. guérir; mariner, saler; préparer, travailler
cure-all n. panacée f.
curfew n. couvre-feu m.
curio n. bibelot m.
curiosity n. curiosité f.
curious a. curieux
curl n. boucle (de cheveux) f.; (fig.) ondulation f.; — vt. & vi. friser; — up enrouler; -y a. frisé, en boucles
curlicue n. parafe m.
currant n. groseille f.; black — cassis m.
currency n. circulation f., cours m., continuité f.; papier-monnaie m.
current n. courant m.; alternating — courant alternatif m.; direct — courant continu m.; — a. courant
curriculum n. cours d'études m.
curry n. cari m.; — powder cari m.; — vt. étriller; — favor (with) chercher à s'insinuer dans les bonnes grâces (de)
curse n. malédiction f.; — vt. maudire; — vi. jurer
cursing n. jurons m. pl.
cursory a. précipité; léger
curt a. court, brusque; -ness n. brusquerie f.
curtail vt. écourter; retrancher; -ment n. restriction f.
curtain n. rideau m.; — call rappel m.; — raiser lever de rideau m.; — rod monture f. (pour rideaux); — vt. garnir de rideaux
curtsy n. révérence f.; — vi. faire la révérence
curvature n. courbure f.
curve n. courbe f.; virage m.; — vt. courber; — vi. se courber; -d a. courbe, courbé
cushion n. coussin m.; — vt. rembourrer; amortir
custard n. flan m.; crème f.
custodian n. gardien m.
custody n. garde f.; emprisonnement m.
custom n. coutume, habitude f.; -s pl. douane f.; -ary a. habituel, ordinaire;

-er n. client m.; (coll.) type m.
custom-built, custom-made a. fait sur commande, fait sur mesure
customhouse n. douane f.
cut n. coupure f.; coupe f.; morceau m.; tranche f.; (print.) gravure f.; baisse f.; short — raccourci m.; — vt. couper, tailler; trancher; baisser; (prices) réduire; (records) enregistrer; (teeth) faire; — across traverser; — class sécher un cours; — down faucher, abattre; — out découper; (coll.) cesser; — short couper court (à); — up couper en petits morceaux; découper; (coll.) faire la noce; — a. coupé; taillé; tranché; baissé; — and dried décidé, fixé; — glass cristal taillé m.; -ting a. tranchant; mordant; cinglant; -ting n. coupe f.; découpage m.; coupon m.; coupure f.
cutaneous a. cutané
cutaway n. frac m.
cutback n. réduction de la force ouvrière d'une usine f.
cute a. joli, délicieux
cuticle n. pellicule f., épiderme m.
cutlass n. coutelas m.
cutlery n. coutellerie f.
cutlet n. (with bone) côtelette f.; (without bone) escalope f.
cutoff n. interrupteur m.; soupape f.; bifurcation f., chemin de traverse m.; raccourci m.
cutout n. (elec.) coupe-circuit m.; coupure f.
cut-rate a. à prix réduit
cutthroat n. coupe-gorge m.; — a. acharné
cwt.: hundredweight quintal m.
cyanide n. cyanure m.
cycle n. cycle m.; — vi. aller à bicyclette; pédaler
cyclist n. cycliste m. & f.
cyclotron n. cyclotron m.
cylinder n. cylindre m.
cylindrical a. cylindrique
cymbal n. cymbale f.
cynic n. cynique n.; -al a. cynique; -ism n. cynisme m.
cypress n. cyprès m.
Cyprus n. Chypre f.
cyst n. kyste m.; sac m.
Czar n. tsar m.; -ina n. tsarine f.
Czech a. & n. tchèque m. & f.
Czechoslovakia n. Tchécoslovakie f.

D

D.A.: District Attorney procureur m.
dab n. éclaboussure f.; tache f.; petit coup, petit morceau m.; — vt. éclabousser; tacher; tamponner
dabble vi. s'occuper en amateur
Dacron (trademark) n. dacron m.
dactyl n. dactyle m.; pied de trois syllabes dont la première accentuée m.
dad, daddy n. papa m.
daffodil n. asphodèle m.
daft a. idiot, fou
dagger n. poignard m.
daily n. quotidien m.; — a. journalier,

quotidien; — *adv.* tous les jours; quotidiennement;

daintiness *n.* délicatesse *f.*.

dainty *n.* friandise *f.*; — *a.* délicat

dairy *n.* laiterie *f.*; — farm vacherie *f.*; — industry industrie laitière *f.*

dairyman *n.* laitier, crémier *m.*

daisy *n.* marguerite *f.*

dale *n.* val *m.*

dalliance *n.* affaire *f.*; flirtage *m.*

dally *vi.* badiner, perdre son temps, s'amuser

Dalmatia *n.* Dalmatie *f.*

dam *n.* barrage *m.*; (zool.) mère *f.*; — *vt.* barrer

damage *n.* dommage *m.*; dégats *m. pl.*; avarie *f.*; — *vt.* endommager, avarier

damaging *a.* nuisible

damascene *vt.* damasquiner

Damascus *n.* Damas *m.*

damask *n.* damas *m.*

dame *n.* dame *f.*; (coll.) femme *f.*

damn *vt.* damner, condamner; —! *interj.* zut!; —able *a.* damnable; —ation *f.*; damnation *f.*; —ed *a.* damné; (coll.) sacré

damp *n.* humidité *f.*; — *a.* humide; —en *vt.* humidifier; humecter; étouffer; —er *n.* registre *m.*; étouffoir *m.*; —ness *n.* humidité *f.*

damsel *n.* demoiselle *f.*

damson *n.* prune de damas *f.*

dance *n.* danse *f.*; bal *m.*; dancing *m.*; — hall, salle de danse *f.*; dancing *m.*; — *vi.* danser; —er *n.* danseur *m.*, danseuse *f.*

dandelion *n.* pissenlit *m.*

dander *n.* colère *f.*

dandle *vt.* bercer, dorloter

dandruff *n.* pellicules *f. pl.*

dandy *n.* dandy *m.*; — *a.* (coll.) épatant

Dane, Danish *a. & n.* Danois *m.*

danger *n.* danger *m.*; —ous *a.* dangereux, périleux; —ously *adv.* dangereusement

dangle *vi.* être suspendu; pendre, pendiller; — *vt.* suspendre

dank *a.* humide, moite

dapper *a.* vif; élégant

dapple *a.* pommelé, bigarré; — *vt.* tacheter

dare *n.* défi *m.*; — *vt.* donner le défi (à); provoquer; oser; risquer; — *vi.* oser

daredevil *n.* casse-cou *m.*

daring *a.* hardi; audacieux; — *n.* audace *f.*

dark *a.* sombre, obscur; noir; (color) foncé; — horse candidat obscur *m.*; — *n.* obscurité, nuit *f.*; —en *vi.* faire nuit; —en *vt.* noircir; —ness *n.* nuit *f.*; obscurité *f.*

Dark Ages *n.* Moyen-Âge *m.*

darkroom *n.* chambre noire *f.*

darling *n.* favori *m.*, favorite *f.*, chéri *m.*, chérie *f.*; — *a.* chéri, favorite

darn *vt.* raccommoder; repriser; — *n.* raccommodage *m.*; reprise *f.*; —! *interj.* zut!; —ing *n.* raccommodage *m.*; —ing needle *n.* aiguille à repriser *f.*; demoiselle *f.*

dart *n.* dard, trait *m.*; — *vt.* darder, lancer; jeter; — *vi.* voler comme un trait

dash *n.* trait *m.*; petit brin, grain *m.*; course *f.*; ruée *f.*; (gram.) tiret *m.*; — *vt.* jeter; plonger; précipiter; éclabousser;

— *vi.* se briser, se heurter; se ruer; — off esquisser; —ing *a.* élégant

dastard *n.* lâche *m.*; —ly *a.* lâche

data *n.* données *f. pl.*

date *n.* date *f.*; époque *f.*; (bot.) datte *f.*; (coll.) rendez-vous *m.*; up to — à la page; — *vt. & vi.* dater; —d *a.* vétuste, démodé

dative *n.* datif *m.*

daub *vt.* barbouiller; enduire; peinturer; — *n.* barbouillage *m.*; enduit *m.*

daughter *n.* fille *f.*

daughter-in-law *n.* belle-fille *f.*

daunt *vt.* intimider, abattre; —less *a.* intrépide

davenport *n.* divan, canapé *m.*

davit *n.* (naut.) davier *m.*

dawdle *vi.* muser; flâner; —r *n.* traînard *m.*

dawdling *a.* musard, flâneur; — *n.* musarderie, flânerie *f.*

dawn *n.* aube, aurore *f.*, point du jour *m.*; — *vi.* paraître, naître; poindre

day *n.* jour *m.*; journée *f.*; a — par jour; by the — à la journée; carry the — vaincre; — after lendemain *m.*; — after — d'un jour à l'autre; — before yesterday avant-hier; — by — au jour le jour; jour par jour; every — tous les jours; every other — tous les deux jours; from — to — au jour le jour; on the following — le lendemain; — laborer manœuvrier *m.*; — nursery garderie d'enfants *f.*; — school externat *m.*; — shift équipe du jour *f.*

daybreak *n.* pointe du jour *f.*; aube *f.*

daydream *n.* rêverie *f.*; — *vi.* faire des châteaux en Espagne

daylight *n.* jour *m.*; — saving time *n.* heure d'été *f.*

daytime *n.* jour *m.*, journée *f.*

daze *vt.* éblouir; étourdir; — *n.* éblouissement *m.*, étourdissement *m.*

dazzle *vt.* éblouir

dazzling *a.* éblouissant

d.c.: direct current courant continu *m.*

deacon *n.* diacre *m.*

deactivate *vt.* déactiver

dead *a.* mort, sans vie; sourd; — body *n.* cadavre *m.*; — calm calme plat *m.*; — center point mort *m.*; — end impasse *f.*, cul-de-sac *m.*; — heat manche à manche; — letter rebut *m.*; — line *n.* experation d'un délai *f.*; — reckoning route estimée *f.*; — shot bon tireur *m.*; — silence silence total *m.*; — weight poids inerte *m.*; —wood *n.* bois mort *m.*; coulée d'un navire *f.*; the — *n.*; les morts *m. pl.*; — *adv.* tout à fait, entièrement; —en *vt.* assourdir; amortir; —ly *a.* mortel; vénéneux

dead line *n.* heure-limité *f.*

deadlock *n.* impasse *f.*

Dead Sea *n.* (la) Mer Morte *f.*

deaf *a.* sourd; insensible; stone — complètement sourd; — and dumb sourd-muet; —en *vt.* rendre sourd; —ening *a.* assourdissant; —ness *n.* surdité *f.*

deaf-mute *n.* sourd-muet *m.*

deal *n.* quantité, partie *f.*; (cards) donne *f.*; affaire *f.*: a great —, a good— beaucoup; — vt. (cards) donner, distribuer; — vi. avoir affaire, traiter; -er n. commerçant m.; (cards) donneur m.; -ings n. pl. affaires f. pl.

dean n. doyen m.

dear a. cher; coûteux; bien aimé; -ly adv. cher, chèrement; -ness n. cherté f.

dearth n. rareté f.; pénurie f.

death n. mort f., trépas m.; — rate mortalité f.; at — 's door à deux doigts de la mort; -blow n. coup de mort m.; — penalty n. peine capitale f.; — warrant ordre d'exécution m.; put to — exécuter, mettre à mort; -less a. immortel; -ly a. mortel

deathbed n. lit de mort m.

deathtrap n. coupe-gorge m.

debar vt. exclure, priver

debase vi. abaisser, avilir; falsifier; -ment n. avilissement m.

debatable a. contestable

debate n. débat m., dispute f.; — vt. & vi. débattre; disputer

debauch vt. débaucher; -ery n. débauche f.; libertinage m.

debenture n. reconnaissance, obligation f.

debilitate vt. débiliter, affaiblir

debility n. débilité f.

debit n. débit m.; — vt. débiter

debonair a. élégant, gai

debris n. débris m. pl.

debt n. dette f.; to run, get into — faire des dettes; -or n. débiteur m.

debunk vt. démentir

debut n. début m.; -ante n. débutante f.

decade n. décade f., dix ans m. pl.

decadence n. décadence f.

decamp vi. décamper, filer

decant vt. décanter; -er n. carafe f.

decapitate vt. décapiter

decay n. déclin m., décadence f.; (teeth) carie f.; — vi. tomber en ruine; pourrir

decease n. décès m.; — vi. décéder; -d a. décédé

deceit n. tromperie f.; -ful a. trompeur

deceive vt. tromper; -r n. trompeur m.

December n. décembre m.

decency n. décence, bienséance f.

decent a. décent, convenable, bienséant

decentralization n. décentralisation f.

decentralize vt. décentraliser

deception n. tromperie f.

deceptive a. trompeur

decibel n. décibel m.

decide vt. décider, résoudre; juger; — vi. se décider; -ed a. marqué; résolu; -edly adv. notablement; décidément

decimal a. décimal; — point virgule f.

decimate vt. décimer

decimation n. décimation f.

decipher vt. déchiffrer; -able a. déchiffrable

decision n. décision f.; résolution f.; jugement m.; parti m.; to come to a — prendre une décision

decisive a. décisif

deck n. tillac, pont, gaillard m.; (cards) jeu m.; — chair transat m.; — vt. parer, orner

declaim vt. & vi. déclamer; haranguer

declamation n. déclamation f.

declamatory a. déclamatoire

declaration n. déclaration f.; constatation f.

declare vt. déclarer; -d a. déclaré, avoué

declension n. déclinaison f.

decline n. déclin m., décadence f.; — vt. refuser; décliner; — vi. déchoir; baisser; pencher

declivity n. déclivité f.

decode vt. déchiffrer

decompose vt. décomposer; — vi. se décomposer, pourrir

decomposition n. décomposition f.

decompression n. décompression f.

deconsecrate vt. séculariser

deconsecration n. sécularisation f.

decontaminate vt. décontaminer

decontrol vt. libérer du contrôle

decorate vt. décorer, orner

decoration n. décoration f.; décor m.

decorative a. décoratif

decorator n. décorateur m.

decorous a. convenable, comme il faut

decorum n. décorum m., décence f.

decoy n. leurre m.; — vt. leurrer

decrease n. diminution f.; amoindrissement m.; — vt. & vi. diminuer; (s')amoindrir

decreasing a. diminuant; -ly adv. de moins en moins

decree n. décret, édit m.; arrêt, arrêté m.; jugement m.; — vt. & vi. décréter

decrepit a. décrépit; -ude n. décrepitude f.

decry vt. décrier

dedicate vt. dédier; dévouer; consacrer

dedication n. dédicace, dédication f.

dedicatory a. dédicatoire

deduce vt. déduire, inférer

deduct vt. déduire; -ion n. déduction; retranchement m., remise f.; -ive a. déductif

deed n. action f., acte, fait, exploit m.; (law) titre m.; — vt. transférer un titre

deem vt. & vi. juger, penser

deep a. profond; grave; (color) foncé; — n. mer f.; ciel m.; -en vt. approfondir; obscurcir; -en vi. s'approfondir; devenir plus foncé; -ness n. profondeur f.

Deepfreeze (trademark) n. frigorifique f.

deep-rooted, deep-seated a. enracinée

deep-sea a., — fishing grande pêche f.

deface vt. défigurer, détériorer, mutiler; -ment n. défiguration, mutilation f.

defalcate vi. détourner de l'argent

defalcation n. détournement d'argent m.

defamation n. diffamation f.

defamatory a. diffamatoire

defame vt. diffamer; -r n. diffamateur m.

default n. défaut m., faute f.; — vi. manquer; faire défaut

defeat n. défaite, déroute f.; — vt. vaincre, battre, défaire; -ist a. & n. défaitiste m. & f.

defect n. défaut m.; vice m.; — vt. faire défection; -ion n. défection f.; -ive a. défectueux; vicieux

defend vt. défendre, protéger; -ant n. accusé m.; -er n. défenseur m.

defense n. défense, protection f.; -less a.

sans défense
defensible a. défensible
defensive n. défensive f.; — a. défensif
defer vt. & vi. différer, remettre; déférer (à); -ence n. déférence f., respect m.; in-ence to par respect pour; -ential a. respectueux; -ment n. délai m.; (army) réformation temporaire f.
defiance n. défi m.; in — of au mépris de
defiant a. résistant, combattant; de défi
deficiency n. défaut m., insuffisance f.
deficient a. défectueux, imparfait; insuffisant
deficit n. déficit m.
defile n. défilé m.; — vt. souiller; — vi. défiler; -ment n. souillure, tache f.
definable a. définissable
define vt. définir; délimiter
definite a. défini, exact, précis; -ly adv. décidément, nettement; -ness n. netteté f.
definition n. définition f.
deflate vt. dégonfler
deflation n. dégonflement m.; (com.) déflation f.
deflect vt. détourner; défléchir; -ion n. déclinaison f.; déflexion f.
deforest vt. déboiser; -ation n. déboisement m.
deform vt. défigurer, déformer; -ation n. déformation f.; -ed a. difforme, déformé; -ity n. difformité f.
defraud vt. frauder, tromper; -er n. fraudeur m.
defray vt. défrayer, couvrir
defrost vt. dégivrer; -er n. dégivreuse f.
deft a. adroit, preste; -ness n. adresse, prestesse, dextérité f.
defunct a. défunt
defy vt. défier, braver
degeneracy n. dégénération f.
degenerate vi. dégénérer; — a. & n. dégénéré m.
degeneration n. dégénération f.
degradation n. dégradation f.
degrade vt. dégrader, avilir
degrading a. dégradant
degree n. degré m.; qualité, condition f., ordre, rang m.; (educ.) titre m.; in some — dans une certaine mesure; third — (coll.) cuisinage m.; by -s peu à peu, petit à petit
dehydrate vt. dessécher, déshydrater
deification n. déification f.
deify vt. déifier
deign vi. daigner
deist n. déiste m.
deity n. déité, divinité f.
deject vt. affliger, décourager; abattre; -ed a. découragé, abattu; -ion n. découragement n.; abattement m.
delay n. délai, retard m.; — vt. retarder; remettre, différer; — vi. retarder; tarder, s'attarder
delectable a. délectable
delegate n. délégué m.; — vt. déléguer
delegation n. délégation f.
delete vt. rayer, enlever, éliminer, supprimer, effacer
deletion n. rature f.; suppression f.

deliberate vt. délibérer; — a. délibéré; prémédité; voulu, calculé; réfléchi; -ly adv. avec préméditation; exprès; posément
deliberation n. délibération f.
delicacy n. délicatesse f.; friandise f.
delicate a. délicat; fin; friand; tendre; doux; faible
delicatessen n. charcuterie f.
delicious a. délicieux
delight n. délice m., délices f. pl., plaisir m.; joie f.; charme m.; — vt. réjouir, divertir; ravir; — vi. prendre plaisir (à); -ed a. ravi, enchanté; -ful a. charmant; ravissant; délicieux
delimit vt. délimiter
delineate vt. tracer, dessiner, décrire
delineation n. délinéation, esquisse f.
delinquency n. délit m.
delinquent n. délinquant m.
delirious a. en délire; be — délirer
delirium n. délire m.; — tremens delirium tremens m.
deliver vt. livrer; remettre, rendre; délivrer; (med.) accoucher; prononcer; s'acquitter de; distribuer; -ance n. délivrance f.; -er n. livreur m.; libérateur m.; -y n. livraison f.; (mail) distribution f.; (speech) débit m.; (med.) accouchement m.; (letter) general -y poste restante f.; special -y (letter) lettre exprès f.
Delphi n. Delphes f.; -c a. de Delphes
delude vt. tromper, abuser
deluge n. déluge m.; — vt. inonder
delusion n. tromperie, illusion f.
delusive a. trompeur
delve vt. creuser, fouir
demagogue n. démagogue m.
demand n. demande, requête f.; in great — très recherché; on — à présentation; — vt. réclamer, exiger
demarcate vt. délimiter
demarcation n. démarcation f.
demean vt., — oneself se comporter; se dégrader; -or n. conduite, tenue f.
demented a. aliéné
demerit n. démérite m.; mauvaise note f.
demigod n. demi-dieu m.
demilitarization n. démilitarisation f.
demilitarize vt. démilitariser
demise n. mort f., décès m.
demitasse n. café noir m.
demobilization n. démobilisation f.
demobilize vt. démobiliser
democracy n. démocratie f.
democrat n. démocrate m.; -ic a. démocratique
demolish vt. démolir, abattre
demolition n. démolition f.
demonstrability n. démontrabilité f.
demonstrable a. démontrable
demonstrate vt. démontrer; — vi. manifester
demonstration n. démonstration f.; (pol.) manifestation f.
demonstrative a. démonstratif
demonstrator n. démonstrateur m.; (pol.) manifestant m.
demoralization n. démoralisation f.

demoralize *vt.* démoraliser
demote *vt.* dégrader
demotion *n.* dégradation *f.*
demur *n.* hésitation *f* ; — *vi.* différer; hésiter
demure *a.* sobre; modeste
den *n.* caverne *f.,* repaire *m.;* étude *f.*
denaturalize *vt.* dénaturaliser
denature *vt.* dénaturer
deniable *a.* niable, reniable
denial *n.* dénégation *f.,* refus *m.*
denim *n.* étoffe croisée de coton *f.*
denizen *n.* habitant *m.*
Denmark *n.* Danemark *m.*
denominate *vt.* dénommer
denomination *n.* dénomination *f.;* culte *m.;* -al *a.* sectaire, confessionnel
denominator *n.* dénominateur *m.*
denote *vt.* dénoter, désigner
denouement *n.* dénouement *m.*
denounce *vt.* dénoncer, accuser
dense *a.* dense; épais; stupide
density *n.* densité *f.;* épaisseur *f.;* stupidité *f.*
dent *n.* renfoncement *m.;* coche *f.;* — *vt.* laisser une coche, bosseler
dental *a.* dentaire; dental
dentate *a.* denté
dentifrice *n.* dentifrice *m.*
dentist *n.* dentiste *m.*
denture *n.* dentier *m.,* fausses dents *f. pl.*
denude *vt.* dénuer, dépouiller; dénuder
denunciation *n.* dénonciation *f.*
denunciatory *a.* dénonciateur
deny *vt.* nier; dénier; désavouer, renoncer, refuser
deodorant *n.* désodorisant *m.*
deodorize *vt.* désodoriser; -r *n.* désodorisateur
depart *vi.* partir, s'en aller; -ed *a.* mort, défunt; -ure *n.* départ *m.*
department *n.* département *m.;* comptoir, rayon *m.;* — store grand magasin *m.;* -al *a.* départemental
depend *vi.* dépendre (de); résulter (de); se reposer, se fier; -able *a.* digne de confiance; -ence, -ency *n.* dépendance *f.;* -ent *a.* dépendant; -ent *n.* personne dépendante *f.;* be -ent on dépendre de
depict *vt.* dépeindre, décrire
depilation *n.* épilation *f.*
depilatory *a. & n.* dépilatoire *m.*
deplete *vt.* épuiser
depletion *n.* épuisement *m.*
deplorable *a.* déplorable, lamentable
deplore *vt.* déplorer, pleurer, plaindre
depopulate *vt.* dépeupler
deport *vt.* déporter; (se) comporter; -ation *n.* déportation *f.;* -ment *n.* comportement *m.*
depose *vt.* déposer; mettre bas; attester
deposit *n.* dépôt, gage *m.;* (geol.) gisement *m.;* (com.) arrhes *f. pl.;* — *vt.* déposer; -ion *n.* déposition *f.;* -or *n.* déposant *m.;* -ory *n.* dépôt *m.*
depot *n.* dépôt *m.;* (rail.) gare *f.*
deprave *vt.* dépraver, corrompre
depravity *n.* corruption *f.;* perversité *f.*
deprecate *vt.* s'opposer (à); désapprouver; déprécier

depreciate *vt.* déprécier; dénigrer; — *vi.* perdre sa valeur
depreciation *n.* dépréciation *f.*
depredation *n.* déprédation *f.,* pillage *m.*
depress *vt.* déprimer, abaisser; -ed *a.* abattu, déprimé; -ing *a.* attristant; -ion *n.* dépression *f.;* crise financière *f.;* abattement *m.*
deprivation *n.* privation *f.*
deprive *vt.* priver; destituer
depth *n.* profondeur *f.,* abîme *m.;* milieu, cœur, fort *m.;* hauteur, obscurité *f.;* get out of one's — perdre fond; — bomb, — charge bombe sous-marine *f.*
deputation *n.* députation *f.,* délégation *f.*
depute *vt.* déléguer, députer
deputize *vt.* députer
deputy *n.* délégué *m.;* adjoint *m.;* député *m.*
derail *vt.* faire dérailler; be -ed dérailler; -ment *n.* déraillement *m.*
derange *vt.* troubler, déranger; -ment *n.* dérèglement *m.;* dérangement *m.*
derby *n.* (racing) derby *m.;* (hat) chapeau melon *m.*
derelict *n.* vaisseau abandonné *m.;* personne abandonnée *f.;* clochard *m.;* — *a.* abandonné; -ion *n.* abandon *m.;* renoncement *m.*
deride *vt.* railler, se moquer de
derision *n.* dérision *f.;* risée *f.*
derisive *a.* dérisoire
derivation *n.* dérivation *f.;* source *f.*
derivative *n.* dérivé *m.*
derive *vt. & vi.* dériver; — *vi.* provenir, procéder
dermatitis *n.* dermite *f.*
dermatologist *n.* dermatologiste *m.*
derogate *vi.* déroger
derogatory *a.* dérogatoire
derrick *n.* grue *f.,* derrick *m.*
dervish *n.* derviche *m.*
descend *vi.* descendre; be -ed from descendre de; -ant, -ent *n.* descendant *m.*
descent *n.* descente *f.;* descendance *f.*
describable *a.* descriptible *a.*
describe *vt.* décrire, dépeindre
description *n.* description *f.*
descriptive *a.* descriptif
desecrate *vt.* profaner
desecration *n.* profanation *f.*
desensitize *vt.* rendre insensible; désensibiliser
desert *n.* désert *m.;* — *vt.* déserter; abandonner; -er *n.* déserteur *m.;* -ion *n.* désertion *f.*
deserts *n. pl.* dû *m.,* récompense *f.;* mérite *m.*
deserve *vt.* mériter
deserving *a.* méritoire, digne
desiccate *vt.* dessécher; — *vi.* se dessécher
desiccation *n.* dessiccation *f.;* dessèchement *m.*
desideratum *n.* desideratum *m.*
design *n.* dessein *m.;* intention *f.;* plan *m.;* (art) dessin *m.;* — *vt.* dessiner; destiner; -er *n.* dessinateur *m.;* -ing *a.* intrigant; -ing *n.* dessin *m.*
designate *vt.* désigner, indiquer, distinguer
desirability *n.* avantage *m.*

desirable a. désirable, souhaitable

desire n. désir m., envie f.; — vt. désirer; souhaiter

desirous a. désireux

desist vi. cesser; s'abstenir

desk n. bureau m.; pupitre m.; chaire f.

desolate vt. désoler, dépeupler; — a. désert, dépeuplé; désolé

desolation n. désolation f.

despair n. désespoir f.; — vi. désespérer (de); -ing a. désespéré

despatch n. expédition, diligence f.; dépêche f.; — vt. dépêcher, expédier

desperado n. risque-tout m.; hors-la-loi m.

desperate a. désespéré

desperation n. désespoir m.

despicable a. méprisable, bas

despise vt. dédaigner, détester, mépriser

despite prep. en dépit de, malgré

despoil vt. dépouiller

despondency n. abattement m.

despondent a. désolé; abattu; désespéré

despot n. despote, tyran m.; -ic a. despotique; -ism n. despotisme m.

dessert n. dessert, entremets m.

destine vt. destiner

destiny n. destinée f., destin m.

destitute a. abandonné, dans la misère; destitué

destitution n. dénûment m., misère f.; destitution f.

destroy vt. détruire; -er n. destructeur m.; (navy) destroyer m.

destruction n. destruction f.

destructive a. destructif; -ness n. caractère destructif m., nature destructive f.

desuetude n. désuétude f.

desultory a. décousu, sans suite

detach vt. détacher, séparer; -able a. détachable; -ed a. détaché; séparé; désintéressé; -ment n. détachement m.

detail n. détail m.; — vt. détailler

detain vt. détenir, retenir

detect vt. repérer, découvrir; distinguer; -ion n. découverte f.; -ive n. détective m.; -or n. détecteur, appareil récepteur m.

detention n. retard m., détention f.; arrêt m.; retenue f.; emprisonnement m.

deter vt. détourner, décourager; -rent n. empêchement m.

detergent n. & a. détersif, détergent m.

deteriorate vt. détériorer; — vi. se détériorer

deterioration n. détérioration f.

determinable a. déterminable

determinate a. déterminé, défini

determination n. détermination, décision f.

determinative a. déterminatif, déterminant

determine vt. & vi. déterminer, fixer, décider; -d a. résolu

detest vt. détester; -able a. détestable

dethrone vt. détrôner; -ment n. détrônement m.

detonate vi. détoner; — vt. faire détoner

detonation n. détonation f.

detonator n. détonateur m.

detour n. déviation f.; détour m.; — vt. dévier, se détourner

detract vt., — from diminuer; -or n. détracteur m.

detrain vi. débarquer, descendre (du train)

detriment n. détriment m., porte f.; -al a. nuisible, préjudiciable

devaluate vt. dévaluer

devaluation n. dévaluation f.

devalue vt. dévaluer

devastate vt. dévaster

devastating a. accablant; dévastateur

develop vt. développer; — vi. se développer; exploiter; contracter; -er n. développeur m.; révélateur m.; -ment n. développement m.; exploitation f.

deviate vi. dévier, s'égarer, dériver

deviation n. déviation f.; égarement m.

device n. appareil m.; moyen m.; ruse f.; devise f., emblème m.

devil n. diable m.; — vt. accommoder au poivre; -ish a. diabolique; espiègle; -try n. espièglerie f.

devil-may-care a. insouciant

devious a. détourné; dévié; -ness n. détours m. pl.

devise vt. inventer, imaginer

devoid a. vide, dénué

devolve vi. échoir; — vt. déléguer

devote vt. dévouer, dédier, consacrer; -ed a. dévoué

devotee n. amateur m.

devotion n. dévotion f.; dévouement m.; -al a. de dévotion

devour vt. dévorer

devout a. dévot; pieux; -ness n. dévotion, piété f.

dew n. rosée f.

dewlap n. fanon m.

dexterity n. dextérité, adresse f.

dexterous a. adroit; habile

dextrin n. dextrine f.

dextrose n. glucose m., dextrose m.

diabetes n. diabète m.

diabetic a. diabétique

diabolic(al) a. diabolique

diacritic(al) a.; — mark n. marque diacritique f.

diadem n. diadème m.

diaeresis n. tréma m.

diagnose vt. diagnostiquer

diagnosis n. diagnostic m.

diagnostic a. diagnostique

diagonal n. diagonale f.; — a. diagonal

diagram n. diagramme m.; figure f.; schéma m.; -matic a. schématique

dial n. cadran m.; — telephone téléphone automatique m.; — vt. composer (un numéro)

dialect n. dialecte m.

dialog(ue) n. dialogue m.

diameter n. diamètre m.

diametrical a. diamétral

diamond n. diamant m.; (cards) carreau m.; (sport) terrain de baseball m.; (print.) corps 4, 5 m.

diapason n. diapason m.

diaper n. couche f.

diaphanous a. diaphane

diaphragm n. diaphragme m.

diarrhea n. diarrhée f.

diary n. journal m.

diathermy n. diathermie f.

diatom n. diatomée m.

diatribe n. diatribe f.

dice n. pl. dés m. pl.; — vt. couper en cubes; — vi. jouer aux dés

dickey, dicky n. faux plastron de chemise m.

dictaphone n. dictaphone m.

dictate n. règle f., précepte m.; — vt. dicter, prescrire, déclarer

dictation n. dictée f.

dictator n. dictateur m.; -ial a. dictatorial; -ship n. dictature f.

diction n. diction f., style m.

dictionary n. dictionnaire m.

dictum n. dicton m.; (law) opinion f.

didactic a. didactique; -s n. pl. didactique f.

die n. dé m.; (coin) coin m.; (mech.) matrice f.

die vi. mourir; — away, — down, — out s'eteindre, se mourir

diesel engine n. diesel m.

diet n. nourriture f.; diète f., régime m.; — vi. être au régime; -etic a. diététique; -etics n. diététique f.

differ vi. différer; -ence n. différence f.; différend m.; -ent a. différent; autre; -ential n. différentiel; -entiate vt. différencier; -entiation n. différenciation f.

difficult a. difficile; -y n. difficulté f.; inconvénient m.; embarras m.

diffidence n. timidité, hésitation f.; défiance f.

diffident a. timide, hésitant

diffract vt. diffracter; -ion n. diffraction f.

diffuse vt. diffuser, répandre; — a. diffus; -r n. diffuseur m.

dig vt. creuser; — up déterrer; — n. (coll.) insulte f.; remarque sarcastique f.; -ging n. excavation f.; fouilles f. pl.

digest vt. & vi. digérer; résumer; — n. résumé, digest m.; -ible a. digestible; -ion n. digestion f.; -ive a. digestif

digit n. doigt m.; chiffre f.; -al a. digital; -al computer machine à calculer

digitalis n. digitale f.

dignified a. plein de dignité, digne

dignify vt. rendre digne, honorer

dignitary n. dignitaire m.

dignity n. dignité f.

digress vi. faire une digression; -ion n. digression f.

dike n. digue f.

dilapidate vt. dilapider; -d a. délabré

dilapidation n. délabrement m., dilapidation f.

dilate vt. dilater; — vi. se dilater

dilation n. dilation f.

dilatory a. dilatoire

dilemma n. dilemme m.

diligent a. diligent, assidu

dill n. aneth m.

dilute vt. délayer, diluer; -d a. dilué

dim vt. obscurcir; (lights) baisser; — a. obscur; pâle; sceptique; -mers n. pl. (headlights) feux de croisement m. pl.; -ness n. obscurité f.

dime n. pièce de dix cents f.; — novel roman populaire m.; — store (coll.) magasin à prix unique m.

dimension n. dimension, étendue f.

diminish vt. & vi. diminuer, amoindrir

diminution n. diminution, réduction f.

diminutive a. diminutif

dimple n. fossette f.

din n. bruit, tintamarre, vacarme m.; — vt. étourdir; to — something into someone étourdir quelqu'un à force de répéter quelquechose

dine vi. dîner; -r n. dîneur m.; (rail.) wagon-restaurant m.; -tte n. petite salle à manger f.

dinghy n. youyou, canot m.

dinginess a. couleur sombre f.; pauvreté f.

dingy a. terne, sale

dining a., — car n. wagon-restaurant m.; — room n. salle à manger f.

dinner n. dîner m.; — jacket smoking m.

dinosaur n. dinosaurien m.

dint n. coup m., force f.; by — of à force de

diorama n. diorama m.

dioxide n. bioxyde m.

dip vt. & vi. tremper, plonger; — n. plongeon m.; baisse f.; (road) cassis m.; (coll.) bain (de mer) m.; -per n. louche f., cuiller à pot f.; Big Dipper Grande Ourse f.

diphtheria n. diphthérie f.

diphthong n. diphtongue f.

diploma n. diplôme m.

diplomacy n. diplomatie f.

diplomat n. diplomate m.; -ic a. diplomatique; -ist n. diplomate m.

dire n. terrible, affreux; néfaste

direct a. direct; droit; exact; juste; — current courant continu m.; — adv. sans détours, sans s'arrêter; — vt. mener; conduire; régler; indiquer; -ion n. direction f.; sens m.; -ions n. pl. renseignements m. pl.; -ive n. ordre m.; avis m.; -or n. directeur m.; (theat.) metteur en scène m.; stage -or n. régisseur m.; board of -ors conseil d'administration m.; -ory n. annuaire m.; almanach m.

direction-finder n. radiogonomètre m.

dirge n. chant funèbre m.

dirk n. dague f., poignard m.

dirndl n. jupe paysanne f.

dirt n. saleté, crasse f.; -iness n. saleté f.; -y a. sale, crasseux; méchant, vilain; -y vt. salir, souiller

disability n. incapacité, impuissance f.

disable vt. rendre incapable, estropier; -d a. mutilé; frappé d'incapacité

disabuse vt. désabuser, détromper

disadvantage n. désavantage m.; inconvénient m.; -ous a. désavantageux, défavorable

disaffect vt. aliéner, déranger; -ion n. désaffection f.

disagree vi. différer; ne pas être d'accord; ne pas convenir; -able a. désagréable; facheux; -ment n. désaccord m.; différend m.; discordance f.

disallow vt. & vi. désapprouver, rejeter, interdire

disappear vi. disparaître; -ance n. disparition f.

disappoint vt. décevoir, désappointer; -ed a. déçu; -ment n. déception f.

disapprobation, disapproval n. désapprobation f.

disapprove vt. désapprouver

disarm vt. désarmer; -ament n. désarmement m.

disarrange vt. déranger; -ment n. dérangement, désordre m.

disarray n. désordre m., désarroi m.

disaster n. désastre, malheur m., catastrophe f.

disastrous a. désastreux

disavow vt. désavouer; -al n. désaveu m.

disband vt. licencier, congédier; — vi. se disperser

disbar vt. expulser (un avocat)

disbelief n. incrédulité f.

disbelieve vt. ne pas croire

disburse vt. débourser, dépenser; -ment n. déboursement m.

disc n. disque m.; — jockey n. joueur de disques (à la T.S.F.) m.

discard n. chose rejetée f.; carte écartée f.; — vt. écarter; jeter

discern vt. discerner, distinguer; apercevoir; -ible a. perceptible; -ing a. judicieux, pénétrant; -ment n. discernement m.

discharge n. décharge f.; déchargement m.; (med.) suppuration f.; (mil.) démobilisation f.; — vt. décharger; démobiliser; licencier, renvoyer (d'un poste); — vi. (med.) suppurer

disciplinarian n. homme fort sur la discipline m.

disciplinary a. disciplinaire

discipline n. discipline f.; — vt. discipliner

disclaim vt. désavouer, renier; -er n. désaveu public m.

disclose vt. découvrir, révéler

disclosure n. révélation f.

discolor vt. décolorer; — vi. se décolorer; -ation n. décoloration f.

discomfort n. malaise m.; gêne, incommodité f.; — vt. incommoder

disconcert vt. déconcerter, déranger

disconnect vt. désunir séparer, détacher

disconsolate a. insonsolable, désolé

discontent n. mécontentement m.; — vt. mécontenter —, -ed a. mécontent

discontinuation f. cessation, discontinuité f.

discontinue vt. discontinuer, interrompre

discord, discordance n. discorde, dissension f.; (mus.) dissonance f.

discordant a. dissonant; discordant

discount n. escompte, rabais m.; — vt. escompter, rabattre; -able a. escomptable

discountenance vt. désapprouver, décontenancer

discourage vt. décourager; -ment n. découragement m.

discouraging a. décourageant

discourse n. discours, entretien m.; — vi. discourir

discourteous a. impoli; -ness n. impolitesse f.; incivilité f.

discourtesy n. incivilité f.; impolitesse f.

discover vt. découvrir; divulguer; -er n. découvreur m.; -y n. découverte f.

discredit n. discrédit m.; — vt. discréditer

discreet a. discret; -ness n. discrétion f.

discrepancy a. différence f.; manque de conformité m.; désaccord m.

discretion n. discrétion f.; -ary a. discrétionnaire

discriminate vt. discerner, distinguer, séparer; — a. distinct; plein de discernement; -ly adv. avec discernement

discriminating a. éveillé, judicieux, fin

discrimination n. distinction f.; discernement m.

discursive a. décousu; discursif

discuss vt. discuter, examiner; -ion n. discussion f.; examen m.

disdain n. dédain, mépris m.; — vt. dédaigner, mépriser; -ful a. dédaigneux

disease n. maladie f., mal m.; -d a. malade

disembark vt. & vi. débarquer; -ation n. débarquement m.

disembody vt. désincorporer

disembowel vt. éventrer

disenchant vt. désenchanter; -ment n. désenchantement m.

disencumber vt. débarrasser, dégager

disengage vt. dégager, débarrasser; — vi. se dégager; -ment n. dégagement m.

disentangle vt. débrouiller, démêler; -ment n. dégagement m.

disentomb vt. exhumer

disfavor n. défaveur, disgrâce f.

disfiguration n. difformité f.

disfigure vt. défigurer, déformer; -ment n. difformité f.

disfranchise vt. empêcher de voter; ôter le suffrage à

disgrace n. disgrâce, défaveur; honte f.; — vt. disgracier; déshonorer; -ful a. honteux

disguise n. déguisement m.; dissimulation f.; — vt. déguiser

disgust n. dégoût m., aversion f.; — vt. dégoûter; -ing a. dégoûtant

dish n. assiette f.; (food) mets, plat m.; (coll.) goût m., préférence f.; — vt., — up servir; side —, n. entremets m.

dishcloth, dishrag n. lavette f., torchon de cuisine m.

dishearten vt. décourager

dishevel vt. écheveler

dishonest a. malhonnête; -y n. malhonnêteté f.

dishonor n. déshonneur m.; — vt. déshonorer; -able a. déshonorant

dishpan n. bassine à vaisselle f.

dishwasher n. (person) laveur de vaisselle, plongeur m.; (machine) laveuse de vaisselle f.

disillusion vt. désillusionner; désabuser; —, -ment n. désillusionnement m.

disincline vt. indisposer, éloigner

disinfect vt. désinfecter; -ant n. désinfectant m.; -ion n. désinfection f.

disinherit vt. déshériter

disintegrate vt. désagréger; — vi. se désagréger

disintegration n. désintégration, désagrégation f.

disinterested a. désintéressé

disjoint vt. disloquer, démembrer; -ed a. décousu; démembré

disk n. disque m.; — jockey joueur de disques à la T.S.F. m.

dislike n. aversion f., dégoût m., répugnance f.; — vt. ne pas aimer; désapprouver

dislocate vt. disloquer; déplacer

dislodge vt. déplacer; faire sortir

disloyal a. déloyal; perfide; -ty n. déloyauté, perfidie f.

dismal a. triste, sombre, sinistre, morne

dismantle vt. démonter, désassembler; dépouiller, dégarnir

dismay n. épouvante, frayeur f.; découragement m.; — vt. épouvanter; décourager

dismember vt. démembrer; -ment n. démembrement m.

dismiss vt. renvoyer, congédier; -al n. renvoi m.; (law) acquittement m.

dismount vi. descendre de cheval, mettre pied à terre

disobedience n. désobéissance f.

disobedient a. désobéissant

disobey vt. désobéir

disoblige vt. désobliger

disorder n. confusion f., désordre m.; indisposition f.; — vt. mettre en désordre, déranger; -ly a. déréglé; désordonné

disorganization n. désorganisation f.

disorganize vt. désorganiser

disown vt. désavouer, renoncer

disparage vt. déprécier, dénigrer; -ment n. dénigrement m.; blâme m.

disparity n. disparité, inégalité, différence f.

dispassionate a. sans passion, calme

dispatch n. dépêche f.; envoi m.; promptitude f.; — vt. dépêcher; expédier

dispel vt. disperser, dissiper

dispensary n. dispensaire m.; pharmacie f.

dispensation n. dispensation f.; dispense f.

dispense vt. dispenser, distribuer; — with se passer de; -r n. dispensateur m.; pharmacien m.

dispersal n. dispersion f.

disperse vt. disperser, dissiper; distribuer

dispirited a. abattu, découragé

displace vt. déplacer; -d person sinistré m.; -ment n. déplacement m.

display n. exposition f.; étalage m.; — vt. exposer; étaler; montrer, révéler

displease vt. & vi. déplaire

displeasing a. déplaisant

displeasure n. déplaisir m., mécontentement m.

disport vi. s'amuser, folâtrer

disposable a. qu'on peut jeter; disponible

disposal n. disposition f.; résolution f.; vente f.; cession f.; bomb — désobussage m.

dispose vt. disposer, diriger, arranger; — of se défaire de; jeter; -ed a. porté

disposition n. disposition f.; caractère m.

dispossess vt. déposséder; -ion n. dépossession f.; expropriation f.

disprove vt. réfuter

disputable a. disputable; contestable

dispute n. dispute; querelle f.; — vt. & vi. disputer

disqualification n. incapacité, non-admissibilité, inéligibilité f.

disqualify vt. rendre inéligible

disquiet n. inquiétude f.; — vt. inquiéter, troubler; agiter

disquisition n. dissertation, recherche f., examen m.

disregard n. indifférence f.; mépris m.; — vt. négliger; mépriser; -ful a. indifférent, négligent; dédaigneux

disreputable a. honteux, déshonorant; suspect

disrepute n. disgrâce f., déshonneur m.

disrespect n. manque de respect m., incivilité f.; -ful a. incivil, impoli; irrespectueux

disrobe vt. déshabiller; — vi. se déshabiller

disrupt vt. rompre; troubler; -ion n. rupture f.; dislocation f.

dissatisfaction n. mécontentement m.

dissatisfied a. mécontent

dissatisfy vt. mécontenter, déplaire (à)

dissect vt. disséquer; -ion n. dissection f.

dissemble vt. & vi. dissimuler

disseminate vt. semer, répandre

dissemination n. dissémination f.

disseminator n. propagateur m.

dissension n. dissension, discorde f.

dissent n. dissentiment m.; désaccord m.; — vi. différer; -er n. dissident m.

dissertation n. dissertation f.; thèse f.

disservice n. mauvais office, tort m.

dissidence n. dissidence, discorde f.

dissident a. dissident

dissimilar a. dissemblable; -ity n. dissemblance f.

dissimulation n. dissimulation f.

dissipate vt. dissiper; dépenser

dissipation n. gaspillage m., dissipation f.; dispersion f.; débauche f.

dissociate vt. dissocier

dissociation n. dissociation f.; séparation f.

dissolute a. dissolu; débauché; -ness n. débauche f.

dissolution n. dissolution f.

dissolve vt. dissoudre; fondre; — vi. se dissoudre

dissonance n. dissonance f.

dissonant a. dissonant

dissuade vt. dissuader, déconseiller, détourner

distance n. distance f., éloignement m.; respect m.; réserve f.; at a — à distance; in the — au loin; keep at a — se tenir à distance

distant a. éloigné; lointain; reculé; réservé; vague; distant; -ly adv. de loin

distaste n. dégoût, déplaisir m.; aversion f.; -ful a. désagréable

distemper n. maladie de chiens f.; (painting) détrempe f.

distend vt. dilater; distendre

distil(l) vt. distiller; -late n. produit de la distillation m.; -lation n. distillation f.; -lery n. distillerie f.

distinct a. distinct; différent; clair, net; –ion n. distinction f.; –ive a. distinctif; –ness n. séparation f.; netteté, clarté f.

distinguish vt. distinguer; –able a. visible, apparent; qui peut être distingué; –ed a. distingué

distort vt. tordre, contourner, défigurer; –ion n. contorsion f.; déformation f.

distract vt. distraire, détourner; troubler; –ed a. distrait; troublé; –ion n. distraction f.; folie f.

distraught a. distrait

distress n. détresse f.; misère f.; malheur m.; — vt. affliger, désoler

distribute vt. distribuer; répartir

distribution n. distribution f.; répartition f.

distributor n. distributeur, répartiteur m.; détaillant m.

district n. district m.; région f.; quartier m.; (pol.) circonscription f.; — attorney procureur m.

distrust n. méfiance, défiance f.; — vt. se méfier, se défier (de); –ful a. méfiant, défiant

disturb vt. déranger; troubler; inquiéter; agiter; –ance n. dérangement m.; trouble m.; émeute f.; bruit m.

disunite vt. désunir

disuse n. désuétude f.

ditch n. fossé m.; to the last — jusqu'au bout, jusqu'à la dernière extrémité

ditto n. ditto, idem m.

ditty n. chanson f., refrain m.

divagate vi. divaguer

dive n. plongeon m.; (naut.) plongée f.; (avi.) pique m.; (coll.) gargote f., bastringue m.; — vi. plonger; piquer; –r n. (sports) plongeur m.; (deep-sea) scaphandrier m.

dive bomber n. bombardier à piqué m.

dive-bombing n. bombardement à piqué m.

diverge vi. diverger; –nce n. divergence f.; –nt a. divergent

diverging a. divergent

diverse a. divers, différent, varié

diversification n. diversification f.

diversify vt. diversifier, varier

diversion n. diversion f.; divertissement m.; –ary a. de diversion

diversity n. diversité f.

divert vt. détourner; divertir, amuser

divest vt. dépouiller, dessaisir

divide vt. diviser; partager; séparer; désunir; — vi. se diviser; se partager; –r n. diviseur m.; –s n. pl. compas m.

dividend n. dividende m.

divination n. divination, prédiction f.

divine a. divin; — vt. deviner; –r n. prêtre, ecclésiastique m.; –r n. devin m.

diving board n. plongeoir, tremplin m.

diving suit n. scaphandre m.

divining rod n. baguette divinatoire f.

divinity n. divinité f.; dieu m.; théologie f.

division n. division f.; partage m.; répartition f.; désunion f.; –al a. divisionnaire; de division

divisor n. diviseur m.

divorce n. divorce m.; to get a — divorcer; — vt. divorcer; (fig.) séparer

divot m. (golf) motte f.

divulge vt. divulguer

dizziness n. vertige, étourdissement m.

dizzy a. vertigineux; feel — avoir le vertige; make — étourdir

do vt. faire; rendre, accomplir; servir, suffire; how — you — (je suis) enchanté de faire votre connaissance; have to — with avoir rapport à, avoir à voir à; — away with tuer; abolir; supprimer; — up emballer, ficeler; — without se passer de; –er n. faiseur m.; –ing n. fait m.; –ings n. pl. activités f.; remue-ménage m.; –ne a. fait; fini, terminé; cuit; well –ne (food) bien cuit

docility n. docilité f.

dock n. (law) banc des accusés m.; quai m.; bassin m.; dock m.; dry — bassin de radoub m.; — vt. entrer au bassin; arriver; — vt. supprimer; diminuer; (law) banc des accusés m.

dockyard n. chantier de construction maritime m.

doctor n. docteur m.; médecin m.; — vt. (coll.) falsifier, truquer; –al a. doctoral; –ate n. doctorat m.

document n. document m.; acte, titre m.; — vt. documenter; –ary a. & n. documentaire; –ation n. documentation f.

dodder vi. trembloter; –ing a. tremblotant; branlant

dodge n. esquive f.; mouvement de côte m.; (coll.) truc m.; ruse f.; — vt. & vi. esquiver, éviter

doff vt. ôter

dog n. chien m., chienne f.; — days canicule f.; — races courses de lévriers f. pl.; — show exposition canine f.; go to the –s se débaucher, se ruiner; — vt. filer; marcher sur les pas de; poursuivre; –ged a. tenace, obstiné

dogcart n. charrette (anglaise) f.

dog-eared a. corné

dogfight n. combat aérien m.

dog sled n. traineau à chiens m.

dog tag n. (mil.) plaque d'identité f.

dogtrot n. petit-trot m.

doily n. napperon m.

doldrums n. pl. cafard m.; (naut.) calmes m. pl.; be in the — avoir le cafard

dole n. aumône f.; chômage m.; — vt., — out distribuer; –ful a. triste; douloureux

doll n. poupée f.

dolorous a. douloureux

dolphin n. dauphin m.

dolt n. sot, benêt m.

domain n. domaine m.

dome n. dôme m.

domestic a. domestique; de ménage, de famille; intérieur; — n. servante f.; –ate vt. apprivoiser, domestiquer

domicile n. domicile m.

dominance n. prédominance f.

dominant a. dominant

dominate vt. dominer; commander

domination n. domination f

domineering a. tyrannique, autoritaire

Dominica n. Dominique f.

dominican a. & n. dominicain m.

Dominican Republic n. Dominicaine f.
dominion n. domination f.; dominion m.
domino n. domino m.
don vt. mettre, revêtir
donate vt. donner, faire un don de
donkey n. âne m., baudet m.; — engine petit-cheval m.
donor n. donneur m.
doom n. condamnation f.; destin; mort f.; — vt. condamner
doomsday n. dernier jugement m.
door n. porte f.; (vehicle) portière f.; out of —s en plein air, dehors; front — porte d'entrée; open the — to (fig.) rendre possible
doorbell n. sonnette f.
doorknob n. bouton de porte m.
doorman n. portier m.
doormat n. essuie-pieds m.
doorpost n. montant de porte m.
doorstep n. seuil, pas m.
doorway n. porte f.; encadrement de porte m.
dope n. enduit m.; laque f.; narcotique m.; (coll.) idiot, imbécile m.; (coll.) renseignements m. pl.; — fiend toxicomane m. & f.; — habit toxicomanie f.; — vt. enduire; doper; narcotiser; stupéfier
dormancy n. repos, sommeil m.
dormant a. endormi, assoupi
dormer window n. lucarne f.
dormitory n. dortoir m.
dormouse n. loir m.
dorsal a. dorsal
dose n. dose f.; — vt. doser; médicamenter
dot n. point m.; on the — à l'heure tapante; six o'clock on the — six heures précises; — vt. mettre un point sur; pointiller; -ted line ligne en pointillé f.
dotage n. radotage m.
dotard n. vieillard, radoteur m.
dote vi. radoter; — on aimer à la folie
doting a. radoteur; sénile; extravagant
double a. double; en deux; duplicata; — bass contrebasse f.; — bed grand lit, lit à deux personnes m.; — boiler bain-marie m.; — entry en partie double; — feature deux grands films (au même programme); — talk n. non-sens m.; — n. double; -s n. pl. (tennis) double m.; — vt. doubler, redoubler; — vi. doubler; — back faire un crochet; — up se plier; se tordre
double-barrelled a. à deux coups
double-breasted a. croisé
double-cross vt. tromper; trahir; — n. tromperie f.; trahison f.
double-dealing n. duplicité f.
double-edged a. à deux tranchants
double-faced a. hypocrite
double-header n. (sports) deux matchs au même programme m. pl.
double-jointed a. désarticulé
double-lock vt. fermer à double tour
doublet n. pourpoint m.
double time n. pas de gymnastique m.; salaire double m.; vitesse doublée f.
doubly adv. doublement
doubt n. doute m.; beyond a — à n'en pas douter; no — sans doute; without a —

sans (aucun) doute; — vt. douter (de); -er n. douteur m.; -ful a. douteux; indécis; suspect; -less a. sans doute
dough n. pâte f.; (coll.) frio m.
doughboy n. (coll.) poilu m.
doughnut n. beignet m.
doughty a. vaillant, preux
dour a. sévère, austère
douse vt. tremper; arroser; (lights) éteindre
dove n. colombe f.
Dover n. Douvres
dovetail vt. assembler en queue d'aronde; — vi. se raccorder; se réunir; — n. queue d'aronde f.
dowager n. douairière f.
dowdy a. gauche, mal mis
dowel n. cheville f.; goujon m.
down adv. en bas; à bas; descendu; (price) baissé; (sun) couché; — there là-bas; — under aux antipodes; — payment acompte m.; go — descendre; fall — tomber à terre; be — and out être décavé; être ruiné; ups and —s vicissitudes f. pl.; — with adv. à bas; — vt. descendre, abattre; battre; — n. duvet m.; -y a. duveteux; velouté
downbeat n. (mus.) accent principal m.; premier accent m.
downcast a. abattu
downfall n. chute f.; -en a. déchu, ruiné, tombé
downgrade n. descente f.; déclin m.; — vt. déclasser
downhearted a. abattu
downhill adv. en descendant; vers le bas, en pente
downpour n. déluge m.; averse f.
downright a. absolu, véritable; — adv. tout à fait
downstairs adv. en bas; go — descendre (l'escalier); — n. rez-de-chaussée m.
downstream adv. en aval
downtown adv. en ville; — n. centre de la ville m.
downtrodden a. opprimé
downturn n. (com.) baisse f.
downward(s) adv. en descendant; de haut en bas
dowry n. dot f.
doze n. somme m.; — vi. sommeiller, somnoler; — off s'assoupir
dozen n. douzaine f.; by the — à la douzaine
D.P.: Displaced Person n. sinistré m.
drab a. terne; gris; brun
draft, draught n. courant d'air m.; tirage m.; ébauche f.; conscription f.; (com.) mandat, effet m.; traite, lettre de change f.; (food & drink) coup, trait m., gorgée f.; — board (mil.) commission locale des conscriptions f.; — horse cheval de trait m.; beer on — bière au tonneau, bière à la pompe f.; rough — ébauche f.; sight — effet à vue m.; — vt. rédiger; lever, enrôler; -ee n. recrue f., conscrit m.; -ing n. dessin industriel m.
draftsman n. dessinateur m.
drag vt. & vi. traîner; entraîner; tirer; dra-

guer; — vi. traîner; — down entraîner; — out tirer; faire traîner

dragnet n. drague, seine f.; filet m.

drain n. tranchée f., canal m.; égout m.; tuyau d'écoulement m.; (med.) drain m.; — vt. faire couler; vider; drainer; épuiser; — vi. s'écouler, s'égoutter; -age n. écoulement m.; drainage m.

drainpipe n. tuyau d'écoulement m.

dram n. drachme f.; petit verre m.

drama n. drame m.; théâtre m.; -tic a. dramatique; -tics n. pl. art dramatique m.; -tist n. dramaturge, auteur dramatique m.; -tize vt. dramatiser

drape vt. draper, tendre; -r n. marchand de drap, drapier m.; -ery n. draperie f.; -s n. pl. rideaux m. pl.

drastic a. drastique

draw n. tirage m.; loterie f.; (sports) partie nulle f.; — vt. tirer; attirer; dessiner; (bow) bander, tendre; (water) puiser; (sports) faire partie nulle; — aside prendre à l'écart; — away s'éloigner; — back retirer; reculer; — blood faire saigner; — lots tirer au sort; — near approcher; s'approcher de; — off soutirer; — out faire parler; prolonger, traîner; — up relever; approcher; aligner; rédiger; (vehicle) s'arrêter; -er n. tireur m.; dessinateur m.; (furniture) tiroir m.; chest of -s commode f.; pair of -ers n. pl. caleçon m.; -ing n. tirage m.; dessin m.; mechanical -ing dessin industriel m.; -ing board planche à dessin f.; -ing card (coll.) attrait m., attraction f.; -ing room salon m.; -n a. tiré

drawback n. désavantage, inconvénient m.

drawbridge n. pont-levis m.

drawl n. voix traînante f.

dray n. haquet m.

dread n. terreur, crainte, peur f.; — vt. redouter, craindre; -ful a. redoutable, terrible; épouvantable

dreadnought n. bâtiment de ligne m.

dream n. rêve, songe m.; rêverie, songerie f.; — vt. & vi. rêver; songer; — up (coll.) imaginer, inventer; -er n. rêveur m., rêveuse f.; -y a. rêveur, songeur; (coll.) épatant

dreariness n. tristesse f.

dreary a. triste, morne

dredge n. drague f.; — vt. & vi. draguer; -r n. dragueur m.; (machine) drague f.

dregs n. pl. lie f.

drench vt. mouiller, tremper

Dresden n. Dresde f.; — china porcelaine de Saxe f.

dress n. robe f.; toilette f., costume m.; habillement m.; mise, tenue f.; evening — tenue de soirée f.; — circle premier balcon m.; — rehearsal répétition générale f.; — suit habit de cérémonie m.; — vt. habiller, vêtir; (med.) panser; (cooking) garnir; — vi. s'habiller; — hair coiffer; — windows faire l'étalage; get — ed s'habiller; — up parer; -er n. commode f.; -ing n. toilette f.; (med.) pansement m.; (cooking) assaisonnement m.; sauce f.; farce f.; -ing gown

peignoir m., robe de chambre f.; -ing room (theat.) loge f.; cabinet de toilette m.; -ing table toilette f.; -y a. élégant, chic

dressmaker n. couturier m., couturière f.

dribble n. bave f.; (sports) dribbling m.; — vi. dégoutter; baver; — vt. dribbler

dried a. séché, sec; en poudre

drift n. dérive f.; sens m., direction f.; (snow) amoncellement m.; — vi. dériver; se laisser aller; s'amonceler; -er n. (coll.) vagabond m.

driftwood n. bois flotté m.

drill n. mèche f., perforateur m.; vilebrequin m.; perceuse f.; (mil.) exercice m.; — vt. percer, perforer; forer; instruire; faire faire l'exercice à; (dent.) buriner; — vi. faire l'exercice; s'exercer

drillmaster n. maître de gymnastique m.

drink n. boisson f.; breuvage m.; boire m.; have a — prendre quelque chose (à boire); — vt. boire; prendre (quelque chose); — up boire; vider le verre; -able a. potable; -er n. buveur m.; alcoolique m. & f.; -ing n. boire m.; alcoolisme m.; -ing fountain n. robinet m.

drip n. goutte f.; dégouttement m.; — vi. dégoutter, s'égoutter; — vt. laisser tomber; -ping n. trempé; (faucet) qui pleure; -ping n. dégouttement m.; -pings n. pl. graisse f.

drip-coffee n. café-filtre m.

drip-dry a. qui n'a pas besoin d'être repassé

dripolator n. filtre à café m.

drive n. promenade f.; propulsion f.; énergie f.; initiative f.; transmission f.; (mil.) offensive f.; (fund-raising) campagne f.; (golf) crossée f.; go for a — faire une promenade (en auto); — vt. conduire; chasser; pousser, forcer; réduire; surmener; (nail) enfoncer; — a bargain conclure un marché; — (someone) crazy rendre fou; — along rouler; — away chasser; partir, démarrer; — back repousser; reconduire; — in enfoncer; entrer; — on continuer sa route; — out chasser; sortir; -r n. chauffeur m.; conducteur m.; -r's license permis de conduire m.

drivel vi. baver; radoter; — n. bave f.; bêtises f. pl.

driveway n. allée d'entrée pour autos f.

driving a. véhément; battant; qui pousse; — force force motrice f.; — n. conduite f.

drizzle n. pluie fine, bruine f.; — vi. bruiner

droll a. drôle

drone n. faux-bourdon m.; bourdonnement m.; (engine) vrombissement m.; (avi.) avion sans pilote m.

drool n. bave f.; — vi. baver

droop vi. languir, s'affaisser; se pencher; s'abaisser

drop n. goutte f.; pastille f.; baisse f.; perte f.; boîte aux lettres f.; — hammer marteau-pilon m.; — vt. laisser tomber; baisser; déposer; omettre; supprimer; abandonner; — vi. tomber, se laisser

tomber; baisser; — in entrer en passant;
— off tomber, se détacher; —per *n.*
compte-gouttes *m.*; — kick *n.* coup
tombé, drop-kick *m.*; — stitch *n.*
maille sautée *f.*

dropsy *n.* hydropisie *f.*

dross *n.* scorie, écume *f.*

drought *n.* sécheresse *f.*

drove *n.* troupeau *m.*; foule *f.*; —*r n.* bouvier *m.*

drown *vt.* noyer; — *vi.* se noyer; — out
couvrir; —ing *n.* asphyxie *f.*

drowse *vi.* somnoler, s'assoupir

drowsiness *n.* somnolence *f.*

drowsy *a.* assoupi, somnolent

drudge *n.* esclave *m. & f.*; souffre-douleur
m. & f.; — *vi.* piocher, travailler sans
cesse; —ry *n.* corvée *f.*; travail pénible *m.*

drug *n.* drogue *f.*; narcotique *m.*; — *vt.*
donner un narcotique à; —gist *n.* pharmacien *m.*

drugstore *n.* pharmacie *f.*

druid *n.* druide *m.*

drum *n.* tambour *m.*, caisse *f.*; tonneau *m.*;
gonne *f.*, bidon *m.*; — major tambour
major *m.*; play the — battre du tambour; — *vi.* battre du tambour; tambouriner; — into fourrer; — up faire du
recrutement; —mer *n.* tambour *m.*

drumstick *n.* baguette (de tambour) *f.*;
(coll.) cuisse *f.*; pilon *m.*

drunk *a.* ivre, soûl, gris; get — s'enivrer,
se soûler, se griser; — *n.* ivrogne *m.*;
—ard *n.* ivrogne *m.*; —en *a.* d'ivresse;
—enly *adv.* en ivrogne; —enness *n.* ivresse, ivrognerie *f.*

dry *a.* sec *m.*, sèche *f.*; tari; aride; simulé;
— cell *n.* pile sèche *f.*; — cleaner nettoyeur à sec *m.*; — cleaning nettoyage
à sec *m.*; — dock cale sèche *f.*; bassin de
radoub *m.*; — goods mercerie *f.*; articles de nouveauté *m. pl.*; — ice bioxide de carbone solidifié *m.*; glace sèche
f.; — land terre firme *f.*; — wash ruisseau desséché *m.*; — rot carie sèche *f.*; —
run répétition *f.*, exercice simulé *m.*; run
— se tarir; — *vt.* sécher, faire sécher, assorer; (dishes) essuyer; — *vi.* sécher, se
n. séchoir *m.*; essoreuse *f.*; —ness *n.* sécheresse *f.*; aridité *f.*

dual *a.* double; —ism *n.* dualisme *m.*; —ity
n. dualité *f.*

dub *vt.* donner l'accolade à; (films) postsynchroniser, doubler; enduire (de
graisse)

dubious *a.* douteux, incertain, de doute;
—ness *n.* doute *m.*, incertitude *f.*

duchess *n.* duchesse *f.*

duchy *n.* duché *m.*

duck *n.* cane *f.*, canard *m.*; (motion) esquive *f.*; (fabric) coutil *m.*; white —s
(pants) pantalon blanc *m.*; — *vi.* se
baisser, esquiver; plonger; — *vt.* plonger, baisser; —ing *n.* plongeon, bain *m.*;
—ling *n.* caneton *m.*, canette *f.*

duct *n.* conduit *m.*; canal *m.*; canalisation
f.; voie *f.*; —less *a.* (anat.) (glands) endocrines; à sécretion interne

due *a.* dû; échu, échéant, payable; juste;
(coll.) prêt; — to par suite de; fall —

venir à échéance; — *adv.* franc, droit,
— *n.* dû *m.*; give someone his — rendre
justice à quelqu'un; —s *n. pl.* cotisation
f.

duel *n.* duel *m.*; — *vi.* se battre en duel;
—ing *n.* duel *m.*; —ist *n.* duelliste *m.*

duenna *n.* duègne *f.*

duet *n.* duo *m.*

duffel bag *n.* sac, fourre-tout *m.*

duffer *n.* maladroit *m.*

dug *n.* mamelle *f.*

dugout *n.* pirogue *f.*, canot *m.*; abri *m.*

duke *n.* duc *m.*; —dom *n.* duché *m.*

dulcet *a.* doux (douce)

dull *a.* sourd; lent; lourd; ennuyeux; triste; (point) émoussé; (color) terne; —
vt. émousser; amortir; ternir; become
— s'émousser; (senses) s'engourdir;
—ness *n.* lenteur *f.*; émoussement *f.*;
ennui *m.*; tristesse *f.*; monotonie *f.*;
—ard *n.* lourdaud, sot *m.*

duly *adv.* dûment, justement

dumb *a.* muet, (muette); (coll.) stupide;
deaf and — sourd-muet; play — (coll.)
feindre l'innocence, faire l'innocent;
—ness *n.* mutisme *m.*; (coll.) stupidité *f.*

dumbbell *n.* haltère *m.*; (coll.) idiot *m.*

dumb-waiter *n.* monte-plats *m.*

dumfound *vt.* abasourdir, ébahir, confondre

dummy *n.* mannequin *m.*; prête-nom *m.*
(cards) mort *m.*; — *a.* faux (fausse)

dump *n.* décharge publique *f.*; — truck
camion à benne basculante *m.*; be in the
—s être mélancolique, avoir le cafard; —
vt. décharger; jeter à terre; —y *a.* trapu;
gros, lourd

dumpling *n.* dumpling *m.*, boulette *f.*; apple — chausson *m.*; potato — gnocchi *m.*

dun *vt.* poursuivre (un débiteur)

dunderhead *n.* imbécile, idiot *m.*

dung *n.* fumier *m.*; fiente, crotte *f.*

dungarees *n. pl.* treillis *m.*; bleus *m. pl.*;
pantalon de marin *m.*

dungeon *m.* cachot *m.*

Dunkirk *n.* Dunkerque *f.*

duodecimo *n.* (print.) in-douze *m.*

duplex *a.* duplex, double; — *n.* maison à
deux familles *f.*; appartement à deux
étages *m.*

duplicate *a.* double; — *n.* double, duplicata *m.*, copie *f.*; — *vt.* reproduire

duplication *n.* duplication, reproduction *f.*

duplicity *n.* duplicité *f.*

durability *n.* durabilité *f.*

duration *n.* durée *f.*

duress *n.* contrainte *f.*

during *prep.* pendant, durant

dusk *n.* crépuscule *m.*; —y *a.* sombre, obscur, noirâtre

dust *n.* poussière *f.*; poudre *f.*; — jacket
chemise *f.*, protège-livres *m.*; — *vt.*
épousseter; —er *n.* (feather) plumeau *m.*;
(cloth) chiffon *m.*; (garment) housse *f.*;
—ing *n.* époussetage *m.*; —y *a.* poussiéreux; (re)couvert de poussière

dustpan *n.* ramasse-poussière *m.*, pelle *f.*

Dutch *a. & n.* hollandais; néerlandais *m.*;
— oven rôtissoire *f.*; — treat (coll.) repas, pris ensemble, où chacun paye sa

part *m.*
dutiable *a.* taxable
dutiful *a.* respectueux
duty *n.* devoir *m.*; droit *m.*, taxe *f.*; fonctions *f. pl.*; (mil.) service *m.*, garde *f.*; be on — être de service; liable to — soumis aux droits de douane
duties (custom) *n.* droits de douane *m. pl.*
duty-free *a.* exempt de droits
dwarf *n.* nain *m.*; — *a.* nain; rabougri; — *vt.* rabougrir; rapetisser
dwell *vi.* demeurer, habiter; rester; — on appuyer sur; -er *n.* habitant *m.*; -ing *n.* demeure *f.*, habitation *f.*; maison *f.*; logis *m.*
dwindle *vi.* diminuer; s'affaiblir
dye *n.* teinture *f.*, teint *m.*; teinte *f.*; colorant *m.*; — *vt.* teindre; -ing *n.* teinture *f.*, teintage *m.*; -r *n.* teinturier *m.*
dyed-in-the-wool *a.* endurci, convaincu
dying *a.* mourant; moribond
dynamic *a.* dynamique; -s *n. pl.* dynamique *f.*
dynamite *n.* dynamite *f.*; — *vt.* dynamiter, faire sauter
dynastic *a.* dynastique
dynasty *n.* dynastie *f.*
dysentery *n.* dysenterie *f.*
dyspepsia *n.* dyspepsie *f.*

E

each *a.* chaque; — *pron.* chacun, *m.*, chacune *f.* — other l'un l'autre
eager *a.* ardent; empressé; impatient; avide; âpre; vif; -ness *n.* ardeur *f.*, empressement *m.*
eagle *n.* aigle *m.*; -t *n.* aiglon *m.*
eagle-eyed *a.* aux yeux d'aigle
ear *n.* oreille *f.*; (corn) épi *m.*; — specialist auriste *m.*; have a good — (for music) avoir de l'oreille; keep one's -s open se tenir aux écoutes
earache *n.* mal d'oreille(s) *m.*; have an — avoir mal à l'oreille
earl *n.* comte *m.*; -dom *n.* comté *m.*
early *a.* matinal; premier; précoce; prématuré; — *adv.* de bonne heure; tôt; d'avance; as — as dès
earmark *vt.* marquer (à l'oreille); — for destiner à; — *vt.* (fig) spécialiser des fonds
earmuff *n.* couvre-oreille *m.*
earn *vt.* gagner; mériter; -ings *n. pl.* salaire *m.*; gages *m. pl.*; profit *m.*
earnest *a.* sérieux; pressant; — *n.*, in — sérieusement; be in — être sérieux; — money arrhes *f. pl.*
earphone *n.* écouteur *m.*
earring *n.* boucle d'oreille *f.*
earshot *n.* portée de voix *f.*
ear-splitting *a.* à (vous) fendre les oreilles
earth *n.* terre *f.*; monde *m.*; sol *m.*; terrier *m.*; scorched — terre brûlée; where on — ...? où diable...?; -en *a.* de terre; -ly *a.* terrestre; moindre; -y *a.* terreux; grossier
earthenware *n.* poterie *f.*
earthquake *n.* tremblement de terre *m.*; séisme *m.*

ease *n.* aise *f.*; repos *m.*; tranquilité *f.*; facilité *f.*; loisir *m.*; at — tranquille; (mil.) au repos; at one's — à l'aise; — *vt.* calmer, tranquiliser; adoucir; modérer; soulager; — up ralentir
easel *n.* chevalet *m.*
easily *adv.* facilement; sans effort, sans difficulté; doucement
easiness *n.* facilité *f.*; insouciance *f.*; douceur *f.*
east *n.* est *m.*; orient, levant *m.*; — *a.* oriental, de l'est; — *adv.* à l'est; vers l'est; — of à l'est de; -erly *a.* d'est; -erly *adv.* vers l'est; -ern *a.* de l'est, oriental
Easter *n.* Pâques *m.*
eastward *adv.* vers l'orient
easy *a.* facile; aisé; tranquille; simple; — chair fauteuil *m.*; — mark (coll.) jobard *m.*; go — on ménager; take it — (coll.) se reposer; se calmer
easygoing *a.* insouciant; peu exigeant
eat *vt. & vi.* manger; — away ronger; — up consumer; — one's heart out se faire de la bile; -ing *n.* manger *m.*; cuisine *f.*
eaves *n. pl.* avant-toit *m.*
eavesdrop *vi.* écouter à la porte; -per *n.* écouteur *m.*
ebb *n.* reflux *m.*; baisse *f.*; déclin *m.*; — and flow flux et reflux; — tide marée descendante *f.*; — *vi.* refluer, baisser; décliner
ebullience *n.* ébullition *f.*; bouillonnement *m.*
ebullient *a.* bouillonnant; débordant
eccentric *a. & n.* excentrique *m.*; (person) original *m.*; -ity *n.* excentricité, originalité *f.*
ecclesiastic *a. & n.* ecclésiastique *m.*
echo *n.* écho *m.*; — *vt.* répéter; — *vi.* faire écho; retentir
eclipse *n.* éclipse *f.*; — *vt.* éclipser
eclogue *n.* églogue *f.*
economic *a.* économique; -al *a.* économique; (person) économe; -s *n. pl.* économie politique *f.*
economist *n.* économiste *m.*
economize *vt.* économiser, faire des économies
economy *n.* économie *f.*
ecstasy *n.* transport *m.*; ravissement *m.*; extase *f.*
ecstatic *a.* extatique
Ecuador *n.* Equateur *m.*
eczema *n.* eczéma *m.*
eddy *n.* tourbillon *m.*; — *vt.* tourbillonner
edge *n.* bord *m.*; fil, tranchant *m.*; lisière *f.*; on — nerveux, énervé; — *vt.* border; — away s'écarter peu à peu
edgewise *adv.* de côté; get a word in — glisser un mot
edging *n.* bord *m.*; bordure *f.*
edible *a.* comestible; bon à manger
edict *n.* édit *m.*
edification *n.* édification *f.*
edifice *n.* édifice
edify *vt.* édifier
Edinburgh *n.* Edimbourg *m.*
edit *vt.* éditer, rédiger; -ing *n.* rédaction *f.*; préparation *f.*; -ion *n.* édition *f.*; -or *n.*

éditeur *m.*; rédacteur *m.*; **-orial** *n.* article de tête, article de fond *m.*; **-orial** *a.* de la rédaction

educate *vt.* élever, instruire; **-d** *a.* cultivé; instruit

education *n.* enseignement *m.*; éducation, instruction *f.*; **-al** *a.* educatif; d'enseignement

educator *n.* éducateur *m.*

eel *n.* anguille *f.*

eerie *a.* étrange, mystérieux

effable *a.* qui peut être exprimé

efface *vt.* effacer; **-ment** *n.* effacement *m.*

effect *n.* effet *m.*; résultat *m.*; influence *f.*; go into — entrer en vigueur; have an — on affecter; in — en fait; effectivement; put into — mettre à exécution; take — prendre; faire effet; — *vt.* réaliser, effectuer; **-ive** *a.* efficace; en vigueur; **-iveness** *n.* efficacité *f.*; **-ual** *a.* efficace

effeminate *a.* efféminé

effervescent *a.* effervescent

effete *a.* stérile, épuisé

efficacious *a.* efficace

efficacy *n.* efficacité *f.*

efficiency *n.* efficacité *f.*; capacité *f.*; rendement *m.*

efficient *a.* efficace; effectif; capable

effigy *n.* effigie *f.*

effort *n.* effort *m.*; travail *m.*; initiative *f.*; **-less** *a.* sans effort; **-lessness** *n.* aise, simplicité *f.*

effrontery *n.* effronterie, impudence *f.*

effusion *n.* effusion *f.*, épanchement *m.*

effusive *a.* démonstratif; be — in se répandre en

egg *n.* œuf *m.*; fried — œuf sur le plat; hard-boiled — œuf dur; scrambled — œuf brouillé; soft-boiled — œuf à la coque; — cup coquetier *m.*; — white blanc d'œuf *m.*; — yolk jaune d'œuf *m.*; — *vt.*, — on encourager, pousser

egg beater *n.* fouet *m.*

eggplant *n.* aubergine *f.*

egg-shaped *a.* ovoïde; en forme d'œuf

eggshell *n.* coquille d'œuf *f.*

ego *n.* moi *m.*; **-ism** *n.* culte du moi *m.*; égoïsme *m.*; **-tism** *n.* égotisme *m.*; **-tist** *n.* égotiste *m. & f.*

egress *n.* sortie *f.*, issue *f.*

egret *n.* aigrette *f.*

Egypt *n.* Egypte *f.*; **-ian** *a.* égyptien

Egyptology *n.* Egyptologie *f.*

eiderdown *n.* édredon *m.*

eight *a. & n.* huit; — ball *n.* (billiards) huit *m.*; to be behind the — ball être dans une situation difficile; **-een** *a. & n.* dix-huit; **-eenth** *a.* dix-huitième; **-h** *a.* huitième; **-ieth** *a. & n.* quatre-vingtième; **-y** *a. & n.* quatre-vingts

either *a. & pron.* l'un ou l'autre, n'importe lequel; chaque, chacun; ni l'un ni l'autre; — *conj.* ou, soit; ou que, soit que; — *adv.* non plus

ejaculate *vt.* crier, s'écrier

eject *vt.* jeter; expulser; **-ion** *n.* expulsion *f.*

eke *vt.*, — out ménager

elaborate *a.* compliqué; orné, minutieux, travaillé; recherché; — *vt.* élaborer;

-ness *n.* élaboration *f.*

elaboration *n.* élaboration *f.*

elapse *vi.* s'écouler

elastic *a. & n.* élastique *m.*; **-ity** *n.* élasticité *f.*; souplesse *f.*

elate *vt.* transporter; ravir

elation *n.* fierté *f.*; transport *m.*; joie *f.*

elbow *n.* coude *m.*; rub -s with coudoyer; — *vt.* coudoyer; — one's way through se frayer un passage à travers

elder *a.* aîné, plus âgé; — *n.* aîné *m.*; ancien *m.*; (bot.) sureau *m.*; **-ly** *a.* d'un certain âge, d'âge, âgé

eldest *a.* aîné

elect *vt.* élire; choisir; — *n.* élus *m. pl.*; **-ion** *n.* élection *f.*; **-ioneering** *n.* propagande électorale *f.*; **-ive** *a.* électif; facultatif; **-or** *n.* électeur *m.*; **-oral** *a.* électoral; **-orate** *n.* corps électoral *m.*; votants *m. pl.*

electric *a.* électrique; — bulb *n.* lampe, ampoule *f.*; — eye cellule photo-électrique *f.*; — meter compteur de courant *m.*; — razor rasoir électrique *m.*; **-al** *a.* électrique; **-al engineer** *n.* ingénieur électricien *m.*; **-al engineering** *n.* technique électrique *f.*; **-ian** *n.* électricien *m.*; **-ity** *n.* électricité *f.*

electrify *vt.* électriser; électrifier

electrocute *vt.* électrocuter

electrocution *n.* électrocution *f.*

electrode *n.* électrode *f.*

electrodynamics *n.* électrodynamique *f.*

electrolysis *n.* électrolyse *f.*

electrolyte *n.* électrolyte *m.*

electromagnet *n.* électro-aimant *m.*

electron *n.* électron *m.*; — microscope microscope électronique *m.* **-ic** *a.* électronique

electroplate *vt.* plaquer à l'électricité

electroscope *n.* électroscope *m.*

elegance *n.* élégance *f.*

elegant *a.* élégant, gracieux

elegy *n.* élégie *f.*

element *n.* élément *m.*; facteur *m.*; **-s** *n. pl.* rudiments *m. pl.*; **-al** *a.* des éléments; élémentaire; **-ary** *a.* élémentaire; — school école primaire *f.*

elephant *n.* éléphant *m.*; **-ine** *a.* éléphantin

elevate *vt.* élever; **-d** *a.* élevé; haut; (railroad) aérien

elevation *n.* élévation *f.*; hauteur, altitude *f.*; hausse *f.*

elevator *n.* ascenseur *m.*; (grain) silo *m.*; (avi.) gouvernail *m.*; (freight) monte-charges *m.*

eleven *a. & n.* onze; **-th** *a. & n.* onzième

eleventh hour *a.* de dernière heure

elf *n.* lutin *m.*; **-in, -ish** *a.* des lutins

elicit *vt.* tirer, obtenir; découvrir

elide *vt.* élider

eligibility *n.* éligibilité, admissibilité *f.*

eligible *a.* éligible; acceptable; admissible

eliminate *vt.* éliminer, supprimer

elimination *n.* élimination *f.*

elision *n.* élision *f.*

elite *n.* élite *f.*; les élus *m. pl.*

elixir *n.* élixir *m.*

ellipsis *n.* ellipse *f.*; (punctuation) points de suspension *m. pl.*

elliptic(al) *a.* elliptique

elm *n.* orme *m.*

elocution *n.* élocution, diction *f.*; **-ist** *n.* déclamateur *m.*

elongate *vt.* allonger; — *vi.* s'allonger

elongation *n.* allongement, prolongement *m.*

elope *vi.* s'enfuir (avec un amant); **-ment** *n.* fuite *f.*

eloquence *n.* éloquence *f.*

eloquent *a.* éloquent; **-ly** *adv.* éloquemment

else *a.* autre, d'autre; anyone — tout autre; no one — personne d'autre; nothing — rien d'autre; nowhere — nulle partailleurs; someone — un autre; something — autre chose; somewhere — ailleurs, autre part; — *adv.* autrement; or — ou bien

elsewhere *adv.* ailleurs, autre part

elucidate *vt.* éclaircir, élucider

elude *vt.* échapper à, se soustraire à; esquiver

elusive *a.* évasif; insaisissable

Elysian *a.* élyséen; — Fields *n. pl.* Champs Elysées *m. pl.*

emaciated *a.* amaigri, décharné, émacié

emanate *vi.* émaner

emanation *n.* émanation *f.*

emancipate *vt.* émanciper; affranchir

emancipation *n.* émancipation *f.*, affranchissement *n.*

emasculate *vt.* émasculer, châtrer

embalm *vt.* embaumer; parfumer; **-er** *n.* embaumeur *m.*; **-ing** *n.* ombaumement *m.*

embank *vt.* remblayer; endiguer; **-ment** *n.* digue *f.*; levée *f.*; (road) remblai *m.*; (river) berge *f.*

embargo *n.* embargo *m.*; — *vt.* mettre un embargo sur

embark *vt.* embarquer; — *vi.* s'embarquer; **-ation** *n.* embarquement *m.*

embarrass *vt.* embarrasser, déconcerter; **-ed** *a.* embarrassé, gêné; **-ing** *a.* embarrassant, gênant; **-ment** *n.* confusion *f.*; embarras *m.*, gêne *f.*

embassy *n.* ambassade *f.*

embellish *vt.* embellir, orner; agrémenter; enjoliver; **-ment** *n.* embellissement *m.*, décoration *f.*

embers *n. pl.* braise *f.*

embezzle *vt.* s'approprier, détourner; **-ment** *n.* détournement *m.*; **-r** *n.* escroc, detourneur de fonds *m.*

embitter *vt.* aigrir; **-ed** *a.* aigri

emblazon *vt.* embellir

emblem *n.* emblème *m.*; insigne *m.*; devise *f.*; **-atic** *a.* éblématique

embodiment *n.* personnification *f.*; incarnation *f.*

embody *vt.* personnifier; incarner; incorporer

embolism *n.* embolisme *m.*

emboss *vt.* graver en relief; repousser

embrace *n.* étreinte *f.*; embrassement *f.*; — *vt.* étreindre; embrasser; comprendre, comporter

embroider *vt.* broder; **-y** *n.* broderie *f.*

embroil *vt.* brouiller, embrouiller

embryo *n.* embryon *m.*; **-logy** *n.* embryologie *f.*; **-nic** *a.* embryonnaire, en germe

emend *vt.* corriger; **-ation** *n.* correction *f.*

emerge *vi.* sortir; surgir; apparaître

emergency *n.* cas urgent, cas d'urgence *m.*; — brake frein de secours *m.*; — exit sortie de secours *f.*

emeritus *a.* honoraire; en retraite

emery *n.* émeri *m.*

emetic *n. & a.* émétique *m.*

emigrant *n.* émigrant *m.*; émigré *m.*

emigrate *vt.* émigrer

emigration *n.* émigration *f.*

eminence *n.* éminence *f.*; grandeur, distinction *f.*; élévation *f.*

eminent *a.* éminent; **-ly** *adv.* éminemment

emissary *n.* émissaire *m.*

emission *n.* émission *f.*

emit *vt.* émettre; répandre

emotion *n.* émotion *f.*; attendrissement *m.*; **-al** *a.* émotionnable; **-alism** *n.* émotivité *f.*

empanel *vt.* dresser (la liste des jurés)

emperor *n.* empereur *m.*

emphasis *n.* accentuation, force *f.*

emphasize *vt.* appuyer sur; accentuer; souligner

emphatic *a.* absolu, positif

empire *n.* empire *m.*

empiric(al) *a.* empirique

employ *n.* service, emploi *m.*; — *vt.* employer; occuper; **-ee** *n.* employé *m.*; **-er** *n.* patron *m.*; directeur *m.*; **-ment** *n.* emploi, travail *m.*; place, situation *f.*; occupation *f.*; **-ment agency** bureau de placement *m.*

emporium *n.* magasin, entrepôt, marché *m.*

empower *vt.* autoriser

empress *n.* impératrice *f.*

emptiness *n.* vide *m.*

empty *a.* vide; vain; creux; libre, inoccupé; — *vt.* vider; — *vi.* se vider; se déverser

empty-handed *a. & adv.* les mains vides

emulate *vt.* rivaliser, imiter

emulation *n.* émulation *f.*

emulator *n.* émule, émulateur *m.*

emulsify *vt.* émulsionner

emulsion *n.* émulsion *f.*

enable *vt.* rendre capable (de), mettre à même (de)

enact *vt.* décréter, arrêter; jouer, représenter; **-ment** *n.* décret *m.*; loi *f.*; établissement *m.*

enamel *n.* émail *m.* (*pl.* émaux); laque *f.*; vernis *m.*; — *vt.* émailler; vernir

enamored (with) *a.* amoureux, épris (de)

encamp *vt. & vi.* camper; **-ment** *n.* camp, campement *m.*

encase *vt.* encaisser, enfermer; recouvrir

enchant *vt.* enchanter, charmer; ensorceler; **-er** *n.* enchanteur *m.*; **-ing** *a.* charmant, ravissant; enchanteur; **-ment** *n.* enchantement *m.*; ensorcellement *m.*; **-ress** *n.* enchanteresse *f.*

encircle *vt.* encercler; entourer

enclose *vt.* entourer; joindre; envoyer

enclosure *n.* clos, enclos *m.*; enceinte,

clôture *f.*; action de clore *f.*; (letter) pièce jointe *f.*

encompass *vt.* envelopper; entourer; comporter

encore *n.* bis *m.*; répétition *f.*; — *adv.* bis

encounter *n.* rencontre *f.*; — *vt.* rencontrer; essuyer; affronter

encourage *vt.* encourager; —ment *n.* encouragement *m.*

encouraging *a.* encourageant

encroach *vi.* empiéter; abuser; —ment *n.* empiétement *m.*; usurpation *f.*

encumber *vt.* encombrer, embarrasser, gêner

encumbrance *n.* charge *f.*; embarras *m.*

encyclopedia *n.* encyclopédie *f.*

end *n.* bout *m.*, fin *f.*; conclusion *f.*; extrémité *f.*; terme *m.*; but *m.*; in the — à la longue; à la fin; on — de suite; sur bout, debout; put an — to mettre fin à; en finir avec; to no — en vain; — *vt.* finir, terminer, conclure, achever; — *vi.* finir, se terminer; — (up) by finir par; —ing *n.* fin *f.*; terminaison, conclusion *f.*; —less *a.* sans fin; éternel; infini; sans bornes; continuel; —lessly *adv.* sans cesse, sans fin

endanger *vt.* mettre en danger, risquer; compromettre

endear *vt.* faire aimer, rendre cher *à*; —ing *a.* tendre, affectueux; —ment *n.* tendresse *f.*, charme *m.*

endeavor *n.* effort *m.*, tentative *f.*; — *vi.* s'efforcer de, tâcher de

endive *n.* endive, chicorée *f.*

endorse *vt.* endosser; appuyer; souscrire à; —ment *n.* endos, endossement *m.*; approbation *f.*; appui *m.*; —r *n.* endosseur *m.*

endow *vt.* doter, fonder; —ment *n.* dotation, fondation *f.*; don *m.*

endurable *a.* supportable

endurance *n.* résistance, endurance *f.*; durée *f.*; — test épreuve d'endurance *f.*

endure *vt.* supporter, endurer; — *vi.* durer

enduring *a.* durable; endurant, patient

enema *n.* lavement *m.*

enemy *n. & a.* ennemi *m.*

energetic *a.* énergique

energize *vt.* activer, stimuler, donner de l'énergie à

energy *n.* énergie, force *f.*; atomic — énergie atomique *f.*

enervate *vt.* énerver

enfold *vt.* envelopper; embrasser

enforce *vt.* mettre en vigueur; appuyer; faire valoir; faire observer; appliquer; —ment *n.* mise en vigueur *f.*; application *f.*; exécution *f.*

engage *vt.* engager; occuper; retenir; fiancer; embaucher; — in conversation entrer en conversation avec; —d *a.* fiancé; become —d se fiancer; be —d in s'occuper de; faire; —ment *n.* fiançailles *f. pl.*; (mil.) combat *m.*; action *f.*; rendez-vous *m.*; promesse *f.*, engagement *m.*

engaging *a.* séduisant, charmant, engageant

engender *vt.* engendrer

engine *n.* machine *f.*; moteur *m.*; locomotive *f.*; fire — pompe *f.*; — room (naut.) chambre des machines *f.*

engineer *n.* ingénieur; (rail., naut.) mécanicien *m.*; (mil.) soldat du génie *m.*; chemical — ingénieur chimiste *m.*; electrical — ingénieur électricien *m.*; mechanical — ingénieur mécanicien *m.*; — *vt.* manigancer, diriger; machiner; —ing *n.* génie *m.*; electrical —ing technique électrique *f.*; mechanical —ing industrie mécanique *f.*; —s (mil.) génie *m.*

England *n.* Angleterre *f.*

English *a. & n.* anglais (print.) corps 14 *m.*; — Channel La Manche *f.*; (print.) Old — gothique

engrave *vt.* graver; —r *n.* graveur *m.*

engross *vt.* absorber, occuper

engulf *vt.* engouffrer; engloutir

enhance *vt.* rehausser; relever; augmenter

enigma *n.* énigme *f.*; —tic *a.* énigmatique

enjoin *vt.* enjoindre, ordonner, prescrire

enjoy *vt.* jouir de; prendre plaisir à, goûter; — oneself s'amuser, se divertir; —able *a.* agréable; excellent; —ment *n.* jouissance *f.*; plaisir *m.*

enlarge *vt.* agrandir; élargir; — *vi.* s'agrandir, s'élargir; —ment *n.* agrandissement *m.*; élargissement *n.* (med.) hypertrophie *f.*; —r *n.* agrandisseur, amplificateur *m.*

enlighten *vt.* éclairer; —ment *n.* éclaircissements *m. pl.*; (hist., lit.) lumière(s) *f. (pl.)*

enlist *vt.* enrôler; — *vi.* s'enrôler, s'engager; —ed *a.*, — man simple soldat *m.*; —ment *n.* enrôlement, engagement *m.*

enliven *vt.* animer, égayer

enmity *n.* inimitié *f.*

ennoble *vt.* anoblir

enormity *n.* énormité *f.*

enormous *a.* énorme; —ness *n.* énormité *f.*

enough *a. & adv.* assez (de); de quoi; be — suffire; that's — cela suffit

enrich *vt.* enrichir; —ment *n.* enrichissement *n.*

enrage *vt.* faire enrager; mettre en colère

enrapture *vt.* ravir, transporter

enroll *vt.* enrôler; inscrire; immatriculer; —ment *n.* enrôlement *m.*; inscription *f.*; immatriculation *f.*; — *vi.* s'inscrire

ensemble *n.* ensemble *m.*; série *f.*, jeu *m.*

enshrine *vt.* enchâsser

ensign *n.* enseigne *f.*, drapeau *m.*; pavillon *m.*; (naval officer) enseigne *m.*

enslave *vt.* asservir, rendre esclave; —ment *n.* asservissement, esclavage *m.*

ensnare *vt.* prendre au piège, attraper

ensue *vi.* s'ensuivre; résulter

ensuing *a.* suivant

entail *vt.* occasionner; entraîner; comporter

entangle *vt.* embrouiller; empêtrer; —ment *n.* embrouillement *m.*; embarras *m.*

enter *vt. & vi.* entrer (dans); pénétrer (dans); (vehicle) monter (dans); inscrire; porter; s'engager

enterprise *n.* entreprise *f.*

enterprising *a.* entreprenant

entertain *vt.* amuser, divertir; régaler; éprouver; nourrir, chérir; **-er** *n.* acteur, comédien, exécutant *m.*; **-ing** *a.* amusant, divertissant; **-ment** *n.* amusement, divertissement *m.*; spectacle *m.*

enthrall *vt.* captiver, ravir

enthrone *vt.* mettre sur le trône; **-ment** *n.* intronisation *f.*

enthusiasm *a.* enthousiasme *m.*

enthusiast *n.* (sports) enragé *m.*; enthousiaste *m. & f.*; **-ic** *a.* enragé, passionné; enthousiaste

entice *vt.* attirer, séduire; entraîner; **-ment** *n.* attrait, appât *m.*; tentation, séduction *f.*

enticing *a.* séduisant, attrayant

entire *a.* entier; tout; complet; **-ly** *adv.* entièrement; tout à fait; absolument; **-ty** *n.* totalité *f.*; in its — en entier; intégralement; totalement

entitle *vt.* intituler; donner le droit; be **-d** to avoir droit à; avoir le droit de

entity *n.* entité *f.*

entomb *vt.* enterrer; **-ment** *n.* sépulture *f.*; enterrement *m.*

entomologist *n.* entomologiste *n.*

entrain *vi.* prendre le train, entrer dans le train

entrance *n.* entrée *f.*

entrance *vt.* ensorceler; extasier, transporter

entrancing *a.* enchanteur

entrant *n.* inscrit *m.*

entreat *vt.* supplier, prier; **-ing** *a.* suppliant; **-y** *n.* prière, supplication *f.*

entrench *vt.* retrancher

entrust *vt.* confier; charger; remettre

entry *n.* entrée *f.*; début *m.*; inscription *f.*; article *m.*; — blank feuille d'inscription *f.*; single (double) — bookkeeping comptabilité en partie simple (double) *f.*

entwine *vt.* entrelacer, enlacer

enumerate *vt.* énumérer, dénombrer

enumeration *n.* énumération *f.*, dénombrement *m.*

enunciate *vt.* prononcer, articuler; énoncer

enunciation *n.* énonciation, articulation *f.*

envelop *vt.* envelopper; entourer; **-ment** *n.* enveloppement *m.*; action de cerner

envelope *n.* enveloppe *f.*; in an — sous enveloppe, sous pli; window — enveloppe à panneau transparent *f.*

enviable *a.* digne d'envie

envious *a.* envieux, d'envie

environment *m.* milieu *m.*, ambiance *f.*

environs *n. pl.* environs, alentours *m. pl.*

envoy *n.* envoyé *m.*

envy *n.* envie *f.*; green with — dévoré d'envie; — *vt.* porter envie à, envier

enzyme *n.* enzyme *f.*

eon *n.* éternité *f.*

epaulet *n.* épaulette *f.*

ephemeral *a.* éphémère, fugitif

epic *a.* épique; — *n.* épopée *f.*, poème épique *m.*

epicure *n.* gourmet, gastronome *m.*; **-an** *a. & n.* épicurien *m.*

epidemic *a.* épidémique; — *n.* épidémie *f.*

epidermis *n.* épiderme *m.*

epiglottis *n.* épiglotte *f.*

epigram *n.* épigramme *f.*; **-matic** *a.* épigrammatique

epigraph *n.* épigraphe *f.*

epileptic *a. & n.* épileptique *m. & f.*

epilogue *n.* épilogue *m.*

episcopal *a.* épiscopal; **-ian** *n. & a.* épiscopalien *m.*

episode *n.* épisode *m.*

epistle *n.* épître *f.*

epitaph *n.* épitaphe *f.*

epithet *n.* épithète *f.*

epitome *n.* abrégé *m.*; épitomé *m.*

epitomize *vt.* abréger

epoch *n.* époque *f.*

Epsom salts *n. pl.* sels anglais, sels d'Epsom *m. pl.*

equal *a.* égal (*pl.* égaux); be — to (doing) être à même de (faire); avoir la force de; — *n.* égal *m.*; pair *m.*; pareil *m.*; semblable *m.*; — *vt.* égaler; **-itarian** *a. & n.* égalitaire *m. & f.*; **-ity** *n.* égalité *f.*; **-ization** *n.* égalisation *f.*; **-ize** *vt.* égaliser, compenser

equanimity *n.* égalité d'âme, tranquillité d'esprit *f.*

equate *vt.* égaliser; mettre en équation

equation *n.* équation *f.*

equator *n.* équateur *m.*; **-ial** *a.* de l'équateur, équatorial

Equatorial Africa *n.* Afrique Équatoriale *f.*

equestrian *a.* équestre; — *n.* cavalier *m.*; écuyer *m.*

equidistant *a.* équidistant

equilateral *a.* équilatéral

equilibrium *n.* équilibre *m.*

equine *a.* de cheval

equinox *n.* équinoxe *m.*

equip *vt.* munir; équiper; monter; outiller; armer; **-ment** *n.* outillage *m.*; matériel *m.*; armement *m.*; équipement *m.*

equitable *a.* équitable, juste

equity *n.* équité, justice *f.*

equivalence *n.* équivalence *f.*

equivalent *a. & n.* équivalent *m.*

equivocate *vi.* équivoquer; tergiverser

equivocation *n.* équivocation *f.*

era *n.* ère, époque *f.*

eradicate *vt.* déraciner; extirper

eradication *n.* déracinement *m.*; extirpation *f.*

erase *vt.* effacer; raturer; **-r** *n.* grattoir *m.*; gomme à effacer *f.*; (blackboard) chiffon *m.*

erasure *n.* rature *f.*; grattage *m.*; suppression *f.*

ere *prep.* avant; — *conj.* avant que

erect *a.* droit; debout; — *vt.* ériger, édifier, construire; dresser; **-ile** *a.* érectile; **-ion** *n.* construction *f.*; dressage *m.*; érection *f.*; **-or** *n.* constructeur *m.*; **-or set** *n.* mécano *m.*

ermine *n.* hermine *f.*

erode *vt.* éroder

erosion *n.* érosion *f.*

erosive *a.* érosif; corrosif

erotic *a.* érotique

err *vi.* faire erreur, se tromper; s'égarer; errer; pécher; **-or** *n.* faute, erreur *f.*;

clerical —or faute de copiste *f.*; typographical —or faute d'impression *f.*

errand *n.* message *m.*, commission *f.*; course *f.*; — boy commissionnaire *m.*; — girl coursière *f.*

errant *a.* errant, vagabond; knight — chevalier errant *m.*

erratic *a.* irrégulier; désordonné; erratique; excentrique

erroneous *a.* erroné; -ly *adv.* par erreur

erstwhile *a.* d'autrefois; d'antan

erudite *a.* érudit, savant

erudition *n.* érudition *f.*

erupt *vi.* faire irruption; -ion *n.* irruption *f.*

escalator *n.* escalier roulant *m.*

escallop *vt.* cuire au four et à la crème

escapade *n.* escapade, aventure *f.*

escape *n.* évasion *f.*; fuite *f.*; échappement *m.*; have a narrow — l'échappée belle; make one's — se sauver, s'échapper; — *vt.* échapper à; éviter; — *vi.* se sauver, s'échapper, s'évader; -e *n.* évadé *m.*

eschew *vt.* éviter; s'abstenir de

escort *n.* escorte *f.*; compagnon *m.*; — *vt.* escorter; accompagner

Eskimo *a.* & *n.* Esquimau *m.*

esophagus *n.* œsophage *m.*

especially *adv.* particulièrement; surtout

espionage *n.* espionnage *m.*

espousal *n.* adoption; adhérence *f.*

essay *n.* essai *m.*; — *vt.* essayer; -ist *n.* essayiste *m.* & *f.*

essential *a.* essentiel, indispensable; — *n.* essentiel *m.*

EST: Eastern Standard Time heure de l'est *f.* (USA)

establish *vt.* établir, fonder; -ment *n.* établissement *m.*; fondation *f.*; maison *f.*

estate *n.* domaine *m.*; biens *m. pl.*; succession *f.*; terre, propriété *f.*; état *m.*, condition *f.*; real — biens immeubles, biens-fonds *m. pl.*; propriété (immobilière) *f.*; real —agency agence de location *f.*

esteem *n.* estime *f.*; — *vt.* estimer

esthetic *a.* esthétique; -s *n.* esthétique *f.*

estimable *a.* estimable

estimate *n.* évaluation, appréciation *f.*; calcul *m.*; (com.) devis *m.*; — *vt.* évaluer, apprécier; estimer

estimation *n.* avis, jugement *m.*

Estonia *n.* Estonie *f.*

estrange *vt.* aliéner; éloigner

etch *vt.* graver à l'eau-forte, — *er n.* aquafortiste *m.*; -ing *n.* eau-forte *f.*

eternal *a.* éternel

eternity *n.* éternité *f.*

ether *n.* éther *m.*; -eal *a.* éthéré, céleste, aérien

ethical *a.* moral

ethics *n. pl.* éthique, morale *f.*

Ethiopia *n.* Ethiopie *f.*

ethnological *a.* ethnologique

ethnology *n.* ethnologie *f.*

ethyl *n.* éthyle *m.*

etiquette *n.* étiquette *f.*, cérémonial *m.*

etymological *a.* étymologique

etymology *n.* étymologie *f.*

eucalyptus *n.* eucalyptus *m.*

Eucharist *n.* Eucharistie *f.*

eugenics *n. pl.* eugénisme *m.*, eugénique *f.*

eulogize *vt.* faire l'éloge de

eulogy *n.* panégyrique, éloge *m.*

eunuch *n.* eunuque *m.*

euphemism *n.* euphémisme *m.*

euphemistic *a.* euphémique

euphonious *a.* euphonique, mélodieux

euphony *n.* euphonie *f.*

Europe *n.* Europe; -an *a.* & *n.* européen (Européenne)

Eustachian tube *n.* trompe d'Eustache *f.*

euthanasia *n.* euthanasie *f.*

evacuate *vt.* évacuer

evacuation *n.* évacuation *f.*

evacuee *n.* évacué *m.*

evade *vt.* éviter; éluder; se soustraire à; tourner

evaluate *vt.* évaluer

evaluation *n.* évaluation *f.*

evangelic(al) *a.* évangélique; protestant

evangelist *n.* évangéliste *m.*

evangelize *vt.* évangéliser; prêcher

evaporate *vi.* s'évaporer; — *vt.* faire évaporer; -d milk lait condensé *m.* (non sucré)

evaporation *n.* évaporation *f.*

evasion *n.* évitement *m.*; échappatoire *f.*; détour *m.*

evasive *a.* évasif

eve *n.* veille *f.*; Christmas — la veille de Noël *f.*

even *a.* égal, *pl.* égaux; uni, uniforme; régulier; (number) pair; — bet pari égal *m.*; — temper humeur égale *f.*; get — with se venger de; — *adv.* même; encore; seulement; jusque; — now à l'instant même; même aujourd'hui; — so quand même; cependant; — then déjà; — though même, quand même; — *vt.* égaliser; aplanir; rendre égal; -ly *adv.* également; régulièrement; -ness *n.* égalité *f.*; régularité *f.*

evening *n.* soir *m.*, soirée *f.*; good — bonsoir, bonjour; in the — le soir; all — toute la soirée; every — tous les soirs; the — before la veille au soir *f.*; — clothes tenue de soirée *f.*

event *n.* événement *m.*; cas *m.*; in any —, at all —s in tout cas, dans tous les cas; quoi qu'il arrive; in the — that dans le cas où, -ful *a.* mémorable; mouvementé; -ual *a.* éventuel; final; -uality *n.* éventualité *f.*; -ually *adv.* par la suite, en fin de compte

ever *adv.* jamais; toujours; — since depuis (que)

evergreen *a.* toujours vert; — *n.* arbre vert *m.*

everlasting *a.* éternel; sempiternel; vivace; inusable

evermore *adv.* pour toujours

every *a.* chaque, tout; — day tous les jours; — other day tous les deux jours; — now and then de temps en temps; de temps à autre

everybody *pron.* tout le monde, chacun

everyday *a.* quotidien; de tous les jours; in — use d'usage courant everyone *pron.* tout le monde, chacun

everything *pron.* tout

everywhere *adv.* partout

evict *vt.* évincer, expulser; -ion *n.* éviction *f.*

evidence *n.* évidence *f.*; preuve *f.*; déposition *f.*, témoignage *m.*; signe *m.*, marque *f.*; give — déposer, témoigner; — *vt.* manifester, démontrer

evident *a.* évident; -ly *adv.* évidemment

evil *a.* mauvais; malin; méchant; néfaste; — *n.* mal (*pl.* maux); -ness *n.* méchanceté *f.*

evil-minded *a.* malveillant, malintentionné

evince *vt.* montrer, démontrer

eviscerate *vt.* éventrer, vider

evisceration *n.* éviscération *f.*

evocation *n.* évocation *f.*

evocative *a.* évocateur

evoke *vt.* évoquer

evolution *n.* évolution *f.*; développement *m.*; -ary *a.* évolutionnaire

evolve *vt.* développer; élaborer; — *vi.* évoluer, se développer; se dérouler

ewe *n.* brebis *f.*

ewer *n.* aiguière *f.*

exact *a.* exact; précis; juste; — *vt.* exiger; -ing *a.* exigeant; -ly *adv.* exactement; précisément; justement; au juste; -ness *n* exactitude *f.*

exaggerate *vt.* exagérer

exalt *vt.* élever; exalter; -ation *n.* exaltation *f.*

examination *n.* examen *m.*; inspection *f.*; (competitive) concours *m.*; fail an — échouer à un examen; pass an — réussir à un examen, être reçu à un examen; take an — passer un examen

examine *vt.* examiner; inspecter; vérifier; interroger; visiter; -r *n.* examinateur *m.*; inspecteur *m.*

example *n.* exemple *m.*; précédent *m.*; for — par exemple; set an — donner l'exemple

exasperate *vt.* exaspérer, irriter

exasperation *n.* exaspération, irritation *f.*

excavate *vt.* excaver, creuser; faire des fouilles

excavation *n.* excavation *f.*; fouille *f.*

excavator *n.* (hand labor) terrassier *m.*; (archaeology) personne qui fait des fouiles *f.*; (machine) excavateur *m.*

exceed *vt. & vi.* dépasser; -ingly *adv.* très, extrêmement

excel *vi.* exceller; — *vt.* surpasser; -lence *n.* excellence *f.*; -lency *n.* Excellence *f.*; -lent *a.* excellent; -lently *adv.* excellemment

excelsior *n.* copeaux d'emballage *m. pl.*

except *prep.* sauf, excepté; à l'exception de; à part; — *vt.* excepter; -ing *prep.* sauf; -ion *n.* exception *f.*; be an -ion faire exception; -ional *a.* exceptionnel

excerpt *n.* extrait *m.*; — *vt.* extraire

excess *n.* excès *m.*; excédent *m.*; to — trop loin; — weight surpoids *m.*; -ive *a.* excessif; immodéré; -ively *adv.* à l'excès, trop

exchange *n.* échange *m.*; change *m.*; in — for en échange de; rate of — taux du change, cours du change *m.*; stock — bourse *f.*; — *vt.* échanger; -able *a.* échangeable

excise *n.* contributions indirectes *f. pl.*; — *vt.* retrancher, exciser

excitable *a.* émotionnable

excite *vt.* exciter; stimuler; enflammer; surexciter; (curiosity) piquer; get -d s'agiter; -ment *n.* agitation, sensation *f.*; surexcitation *f.*

exciting *a.* émouvant, passionnant; excitant, stimulant; épatant

exclaim *vt.* s'écrier

exclamation *n.* exclamation *f.*

exclamatory *a.* exclamatif

exclude *vt.* exclure

excluding *prep.* à l'exclusion de; sans compter

exclusion *n.* exclusion *f.*

exclusive *a.* exclusif; fermé; de choix; — of sans; — rights exclusivité *f.*; -ness *n.* exclusivité *f.*, caractère exclusif *m.*

excommunicate *vt.* excommunier

excrete *vt.* excréter; sécréter

excruciating *a.* affreux

excursion *n.* excursion *f.*; voyage *m.*; randonnée *f.*; promenade *f.*; voyage à forfait, voyage en groupe *m.*

excusable *a.* excusable, pardonnable

excuse *n.* excuse *f.*; prétexte *m.*; — *vt.* excuser, pardonner; dispenser

execrate *vt.* exécrer

execration *n.* exécration *f.*

execute *vt.* exécuter; effectuer

execution *n.* exécution *f.*; -er *n.* bourreau *m.*

executive *a. & n.* exécutif *m.*; — *a.* de direction, de la direction

executor *n.* exécuteur testamentaire *m.*

exemplary *a.* exemplaire; modèle

exemplify *vt.* servir d'exemple à; donner un example de

exempt *a.* exempt, dispensé; — *vt.* exempter; dispenser; -ion *n.* exemption, dispense *f.*

exercise *n.* exercice *m.*; devoir *m.*; -s *pl.* cérémonies *f. pl.*; — *vt.* exercer; pratiquer; (animals) promener; — *vi.* s'entraîner

exert *vt.* exercer; to — oneself faire des efforts; -ion *n.* effort *m.*

exhalation *n.* exhalaison *f.*

exhale *vt.* exhaler; — *vi.* s'exhaler

exhaust *n.* échappement *m.*; — fan ventilateur aspirant *m.*; — pipe tuyau d'échappement *m.*; — *vt.* épuiser; éreinter; tarir; aspirer; -ed *a.* épuisé; -ible *a.* épuisable; -ing *a.* épuisant; -ion *n.* épuisement *m.*; -ive *a.* approfondi; -less *a.* inépuisable

exhibit *n.* exposition *f.*; envoi, objet *m.*; étalage *m.*; — *vt.* exhiber, exposer, montrer; -or *n.* exposant *m.*

exhibition *n.* exposition, démonstration *f.*; étalage *m.*; -ism (psychology) exhibitionnisme *m.*; -ist *n.* exhibitionniste *m. & f.*

exhilarate *vt.* vivifier

exhilarating *a.* vivifiant

exhilaration n. joie de vivre f.

exhort vt. exhorter; -ation n. exhortation f.

exhumation n. exhumation f.

exhume vt. exhumer

exigency n. exigence f.; nécessité f., besoin m.

exigent a. exigeant; urgent

exile n. exil m.; (person) exilé m.; — vt. exiler, bannir

exist vi. exister; subsister, vivre; être; -ence n. existence f.; vie f.; -ent a. existant, actuel; -ing a. actuel; présent; existant

existential a. existentiel; -ism n. existentialisme m.; -ist a. & n. existentialiste m. & f.

exit n. sortie f.; — vi. sortir

exodus n. exode m.; sortie f.

exonerate vt. disculper

exoneration n. disculpation f.

exorbitant a. exorbitant

exorcize vt. exorciser

exotic a. exotique

expand vt. élargir, développer; dilater; détendre; — vi. se développer, se dilater; se détendre

expanse n. étendue f.

expansion n. développement m.; dilation f.; expansion f.: — band, — bracelet bracelet extensible m.

expansive a. expansif; -ness n. expansivité f.; nature expansive f.

expatriate vt. expatrier; — n. expatrié m.

expatriation n. expatriation f.

expect vt. attendre; s'attendre à; compter (sur); espérer; what do you —? que voulez-vous?; -ancy n. attente f. -ant a. expectant, qui attend; -ation n. espérance f.; prévision f.; attente f.; probabilité f.

expectorate vi. expectorer, cracher

expediency n. opportunité f.

expedient a. opportun, convenable; — n. expédient m.

expedite vt. expédier, hâter, accélérer; -r n. expéditeur m.

expedition n. expédition f.; -ary a. expéditionnaire

expeditious a. expéditif

expel vt. expulser; chasser

expend vt. dépenser; consommer; employer; -able a. non-essentiel; qui peut être abandonné; -iture n. dépense f.

expense n. dépense f., frais m. pl.; dépens m.

expensive a. cher, coûteux; be — coûter cher; -ness n. cherté f.; prix (élevé) m.

experience n. expérience f.; épreuve f.; pratique f.; habitude f.; — vt. éprouver; -d a. expérimenté

experiment n. expérience f.; essai m.; vi. expérimenter; faire des expériences; -al a. expérimental; -er n. expérimentateur m.; -ing n. expérimentation f.

expert a. expert; — n. expert m.; spécialiste m.; connaisseur m.; -ness n. habileté f.; adresse f.

expiation n. expiation f.

expiration n. expiration f.; terme m.; déchéance f.; échéance f.

expire vt. exhaler, expirer; — vi. expirer, mourir; déchoir

explain vt. expliquer, éclaircir; -able a. explicable; justifiable

explanation n. explication f.

explanatory a. explicatif

expletive a. & n. explétif m.

explicable a. explicable

explicit a. explicite; clair, précis; -ly adv. explicitement

explode vt. faire éclater; discréditer; — vi. éclater, sauter; exploser

exploit n. exploit m.; — vt. exploiter; -ation exploitation f.

exploration n. exploration f.

explorative, exploratory a. exploratoire

explore vt. explorer; -r n. explorateur m.

explosion n. explosion f.

explosive a. explosible; — n. explosif m.; -ness n. explosibilité f.

exponent n. interprète m.; (math.) exposant m.

export n. exportation f.; — vt. exporter; -ation n. exportation f.; -er n. exportateur m.

expose vt. exposer; mettre à nu; étaler; dévoiler; -d a. exposé; à nu

exposition n. exposition f.; interprétation f.

expostulate vi. faire des remontrances

exposure n. exposé m.; froid m.; exposition f.; scandale m.; (phot.) pose f.; — meter cellule photo-électrique f.

express a. exprès, formel; — n. (rail.) express, rapide m.; exprès m.; — vt. exprimer; témoigner; envoyer par exprès; -ible a. exprimable; -ion n. expression f.; mot m.; phrase f.; -ionless a. impassible; -ive a. expressif; -ion n. expression f.; mot m.; phrase f.; -ionless a. impassible; -ive a. expressif; -iveness n. nature expressive f.; -ly adv. expressément, formellement

expressway n. autostrade f.

expropriate vt. exproprier

expropriation n. expropriation f.

expulsion n. expulsion f.

expurgate vt. expurger

expurgation n. expurgation f.

exquisite a. exquis

extemporaneous a. impromptu; improvisé; -ly adv. d'abondance; à l'impromptu

extemporize vt. improviser; — vi. parler d'abondance

extend vt. & vi. étendre, allonger; prolonger; tendre; proroger; — vi. s'étendre, s'allonger; se prolonger

extension n. extension f.; prolongation f.; délai m.; annexe f.; (table) allonge f.; (telephone) poste m.; — cord prolongateur m.; — ladder échelle à coulisse f.

extensive a. vaste; considérable; étendu; -ly a. beaucoup, très loin, très profondément

extent n. étendue f.; to a certain — dans une certaine mesure

extenuating a. atténuant

exterior a. & n. extérieur m.

exterminate vt. exterminer

F

extermination n. extermination f.

exterminator n. exterminateur m.

external a. extérieur; (med.) externe

extinct a. éteint; —ion n. extinction f.

extinguish vt. éteindre; fire —er extincteur m.

extol vt. exalter

extort vt. extorquer; arracher; —ion n. extorsion f.; —ionist n. extorqueur m.

extra a. supplémentaire; de plus; — charge(s) supplément m.; — pay surpayé f.; — adv. non compris, en plus; extra; — n. supplément m.; (newspaper) édition spéciale f.

extract n. extrait m.; morceau m.; — vt. extraire; (tooth) arracher; —ion n. extraction f.; arrachement m.; origine f.; —or n. extracteur, forceps m.

extracurricular a. en sus du programme d'études

extradite vt. extrader

extradition n. extradition f.

extraneous a. étranger

extraordinary a. extraordinaire, remarquable

extrasensory a. clairvoyant; — perception n. clairvoyance f.

extravagance n. extravagance f.; prodigalité f.

extravagant a. extravagant; dépensier; outré

extravaganza n. grand spectacle m.

extreme a. extrême; exceptionnel; — penalty dernier supplice m.; — n. extrême; go to —s pousser (les choses) à l'extrême

extremist n. extrémiste m. & f.

extremity n. extrémité f.; bout m.

extricate vt. dégager

extrovert n. extroverti m.

exuberance n. exubérance f.

exuberant a. exubérant

exude vt. & vi. exsuder

exult vi. exulter, triompher; se réjouir; —ant a. exultant, triomphant; —ation n. exultation f.; triomphe m.

eye n. œil m. (pl. yeux); (needle) chas m.; black — œil poché m.; catch the — of attirer l'attention de; electric — cellule photo-électrique f.; keep an — on surveiller; ne pas quitter des yeux; open someone's —s (fig.) désabuser; see — to — voir du même œil; shut one's —s to (fig.) être aveugle sur; — vt. mesurer (des yeux); toiser; regarder

eyebrow n. sourcil m.; knit one's —s froncer le sourcil

eyeful n. vue f.

eyeglasses n. pl. lunettes f. pl.

eyelash n. cil m.

eyelet n. œillet m.

eyelid n. paupière f.

eye opener n. révélation f.

eyeshade n. visière f.; abat-jour m.

eyesight n. vue f.; portée de vue f.

eyestrain n. fatigue des yeux f.; les yeux fatigués m. pl.

eyetooth n. canine, œillère f.

eyewash n. collyre m.; (coll.) la poudre aux yeux

fable n. fable f., apologue m.; légende f.; —d a. fabuleux, légendaire

fabric n. tissu m.; étoffe f.; fabrique f.; édifice m.; —ate vt. fabriquer, inventer; —ation n. fabrication, invention f.; —ator n. fabricateur m.; menteur m.

fabulous a. fabuleux

facade n. façade f.

face n. visage m., figure f.; face f.; mine f.; physionomie f.; aspect m.; surface f.; façade f.; (watch) cadran m.; — card figure f.; — cream crème de beauté f.; — lifting ridectomie f.; — powder poudre de riz f.; — towel serviette de toilette f.; — to — en présence; — value valeur nominale f.; fall on one's — tomber à plat ventre; in the — of en présence de; contre; lose — perdre l'honneur; make a — faire une grimace; on the — of it au premier aspect; save — sauver les apparences; — vt. faire face à; affronter; confronter; donner sur; revêtir, mettre un revers à; —d a. revêtu, à revers

facet n. aspect m.; (gem) facette f.; —ed a. à facettes

facetious a. facétieux; —ness n. facétie f.; plaisanterie f.

facial a. facial

facile a. facile, trop facile, simple

facilitate vt. faciliter

facility n. facilité f.; installation f.

facing n. revers, parement m.

fact n. fait m.; réalité f.; in — en fait; de fait; as a matter of — en effet; à vrai dire; the — is c'est que; —ual a. des faits

factor n. facteur m.; élément m.; (com.) agent m.; — safety — coefficient de sûreté m.

factory n. fabrique, usine f.

faculty n. faculté f.; membres de la faculté m. pl.; corps enseignant m.

fad n. marotte f.; mode f., cri m.

fade vi. se faner, se flétrir; se déteindre; — vt. décolorer; — away s'évanouir; s'effacer

fade-out n. fondu m.; (movies) disparition graduelle f.

fail vi. manquer, faire défaut; baisser; faiblir; échouer; rater; — vt. refuser; — n., without — sans remise, sans faute; —ing n. défaut, faible m.; faiblesse f.; —ing prep. à défaut de; —ure n. défaut m., manque m.; insuccès m.; échec m.; fiasco m.; (person) raté m.; (com.) faillite f.

faint a. faible; pâle; léger; vague, indistinct; — n. évanouissement m.; — vi. s'évanouir; —ness n. faiblesse f.; malaise m.

fainthearted a. timide

fair n. foire f.; exposition f.; — a. juste, équitable; passable; beau; blond; — ball n. vraie balle, bonne balle f.; — play franc jeu, jeu loyal m.; — weather beau temps m.; —ly adv. impartialement; loyalement; passablement; assez;

-ness n. impartialité, équité f.; blancheur f.; -ground n. parc des expositions m.

fair-minded a. impartial; -ness n. impartialité f.

fairway n. terrain de golf m.; (naut.) chenal m.

fairy n. fée f.; — a. de fée, féerique; -land n. royaume des fées m.; -like a. féerique; — tale n. conte de fées m.

faith n. foi f.; fidélité f.; confiance f.; good — bonne foi, loyauté f.; honneur m.; -ful a. fidèle, loyal; exact; -fulness n. fidélité, loyauté f.; exactitude f.; -less a. sans foi; déloyal; infidèle

fake a. (coll.) faux; — n. faux m.; truc m.; trucage m.; — vt. truquer; feindre; -r n. truqueur m.; simulateur m.

fall n. chute f.; baisse, descente f.; échec m.; déchéance f.; automne m. or f.; -s pl. chute d'eau f.; — vi. tomber; baisser; descendre; échoir; capituler; s'écrouler; — back tomber en arrière; reculer; — back on avoir recours à; — behind rester en arrière; se laisser distancer; — for (coll.) tomber amoureux de; se laisser prendre par; — in s'effondrer; (mil.) former les rangs; — into someone's hands tomber entre les mains de quelqu'un; — into a trap donner dans un piège; — off tomber de; baisser; diminuer; — out tomber; (mil.) quitter les rangs; se brouiller; — over tomber à la renverse; buter contre; — through échouer; — upon se jeter à; attaquer; -ing a. qui tombe, tombant

fallacious a. fallacieux; -ness fausseté f.

fallacy n. erreur f.; sophisme m.

fallibility n. faillibilité f.

fallible a. faillible

fall-out n. poussière radioactive f.

fallow a. en friche

false a. faux (fausse); postiche, artificiel; simulé; — alarm fausse alerte f.; — bottom double fond m.; — teeth fausses dents f. pl.; dentier m.; -ly adv. à faux, faussement; -hood n. mensonge m.; -ness n. fausseté f.

falsetto n. fausset m.; — a. de fausset

falsification n. falsification f.

falsify vt. falsifier; fausser

falsity n. fausseté f.

falter vi. hésiter; chanceler; défaillir; -ing a. hésitant; chancelant

fame n. renom m., renommée f.; -d a. renommé, célèbre

familiar a. familier; intime; be — with connaître; -ity n. familiarité f.; intimité f.; connaissance f.; -ize vt. familiariser; habituer

family n. famille f.; — man père de famille m.; — tree arbre généalogique m.

famished a. affamé

famous a. célèbre, fameux, renommé

fan n. éventail m.; ventilateur m.; amateur m.; enragé m.; — vt. éventer

fanatic a. & n. fanatique m.; -ism n. fanatisme m.

fancier n. amateur m.

fanciful a. imaginaire; capricieux; fantaisiste

fancy a. de fantaisie; — n. fantaisie, imagination f.; idée f.; caprice m.; — vt. s'imaginer, se figurer

fancy-free a. libre, gai

fanfare n. sonnerie, fanfare f.

fang n. croc m.; crochet m.

fantastic a. fantastique

fantasy n. fantaisie f.

far a. lointain, distant, éloigné; — adv. loin; beaucoup; — prep. loin de; — and wide partout; — from it tant s'en faut; as — as prep. jusqu'à; as — as conj. autant que; as — as I am concerned quant à moi; by — de beaucoup; so — jusqu'ici; thus — jusqu'ici

faraway a. éloigné, distant

farcical a. de farce, burlesque

fare n. prix, tarif m.; chère, alimentation f., manger m.; client m.; full — place entière f.; half — demi-place f.; — vi. aller

farewell n. adieu

farfetched a. tiré par les cheveux

far-flung a. étendu, dispersé; vaste

farm n. ferme f.; (sports) stage préparatoire m.; — vt. cultiver; -er n. fermier m.; -ing n. agriculture f.

farm hand n. ouvrier agricole m.

farmhouse n. ferme, maison de ferme f.

farmyard n. cour, basse-cour f.

far-off a. lointain, distant, éloigné

far-reaching a. important, sérieux, de conséquence

farseeing a. clairvoyant; perspicace

farsighted a. presbyte; clairvoyant

farther a. plus éloigné; — back antérieur; — adv. plus loin; — back plus en arrière

farthest a. le plus éloigné; — adv. le plus loin

fascinate vt. fasciner, séduire

fascinating a. séduisant

fascination n. fascination f.

fascism n. fascisme m.

fasciste a. & n. fasciste m. & f.

fashion n. mode, vogue f.; façon, manière f.; coutume, habitude f.; after a — tant bien que mal; in — à la mode, en vogue; out of — démodé; — vt. confectionner; faire; façonner; -able a. à la mode, en vogue; élégant

fashion plate (coll.) élégant m., élégante f.

fast n. jeûne m.; — day jour maigre m.; — vi. jeûner; — a. rapide; solide, ferme; fermé; (clock) en avance; — adv. vite, rapidement; solidement; ferme; bon

fasten vt. attacher; fixer; agrafer; — vi. s'attacher, se fixer; -er n. attache, agrafe f.; fermoir m.; bouton m.; -ing n. attache, fermeture

fastidious a. délicat; difficile; -ness n. goût difficile m., goût délicat m.

fat a. gras; gros; riche; — n. gras m.; graisse f.; -ness n. corpulence f.; embonpoint m.; -ten vt. engraisser; -tening a. engraissant; -ty a. graisseux; adipeux

fatal a. fatal; mortel; -ism n. fatalisme m.; -ist n. fataliste m. & f.; -ity n. fatalité f.; accident mortel m.

fate n. destin, sort m.; -d a. destiné, voué

-ful a. fatal

father n. père m.; -'s day fête des pères f.;
— vt. engendrer; -hood n. paternité f.;
-less a. sans père; -ly a. paternel

father-in-law n. beau-père m.

fatherland n. patrie f.

fathom n. brasse f.; — vt. sonder; pénétrer; -able a. compréhensible, pénétrable -less a. sans fond

fatigue n. fatigue f.; (mil.) corvée f.; -s pl. (mil.) bleus m. pl., tenue de corvée f.; — vt. fatiguer, lasser

fatuity n. stupidité, sottise f.

fatuous a. stupide, sot

faucet n. robinet m.

fault n. défaut m.; faute f.; travers m.; (geol.) faille f.; at — en défaut; find — trouver à redire; blâmer; to a — à l'excès; -iness n. imperfection f.; incorrection f.; -less a. irréprochable, sans défaut; -y a. défectueux; erroné

faultfinder n. épilogueur m.; mécontent m.

favor n. faveur f.; service m.; grâce f.; partialité f.; protection f.; be in — of tenir pour; be in — with jouir de la faveur de; in — of pour; en faveur de; show — favoriser; — vt. favoriser, préférer; être pour; avantager; ressembler (à); -able a. favorable; avantageux; propice; -ite a. & n. favori m. (favorite f.); -itism n. favoritisme m.

fawn n. faon m.; — a. fauve; — vi. — upon, — over flatter, cajoler, caresser, câliner

fear n. peur, crainte f.; for — of de peur de, de crainte de; — vt. craindre, avoir peur de, redouter; -ful a. peureux; terrible, effrayant; -less a. sans peur, intrépide; -some a. redoutable

feasibility n. practicabilité, possibilité f.

feasible a. faisable, practicable

feast n. banquet, festin m.; — day fête f.; — vt. régaler; — vi. se régaler

feat n. fait, exploit m.

feather n. plume f., -s pl. plumage m.; — duster n. plumeau m. — vt. emplumer; empenner; (oars) ramener à plat; -y a. plumeux

featherbed n. lit de plumes, édredon m.; -ding n. pratique des syndicats d'employer plus d'ouvriers qu'il ne faut f.

featherbrained a. sot, idiot

featherweight n. poids (de) plume m.

feature n. trait m.; caractéristique f.; spécialité f.; — film grand film m.; double — deux grands films m. pl.; — vt. distinguer, marquer, caractériser; -d a. à traits

February n. février m.

fecund a. fécond; -ity n. fécondité f.

federal a. fédéral

federate vt. fédérer; — vi. se fédérer

federation n. fédération f.

fedora n. chapeau mou m.

fee n. honoraires m. pl.; cachet m.; droit m.; frais m. pl.

feeble a. débile; faible; -ness n. faiblesse, débilité f.

feeble-minded a. d'esprit faible

feed n. pâture, nourriture f.; alimentation f.; — vt. nourrir, donner à manger; approvisionner; alimenter; — vi. manger; paître; -er n. appareil d'alimentation m.; -er (line) n. (bus, train) ligne secondaire (qui alimente les grandes lignes) f. -ing n. alimentation f.

feedback n. rétroaction f.

feel n. tact m.; touche f.; — vt. sentir; éprouver; toucher, tâter, palper; croire, penser; — for être plein de pitié pour; — like avoir envie de; -er n. antenne f.; put, send out a -er tâter le terrain; -ing n. sensation f.; sentiment m.; -ings n. pl. sensibilité f.

feign vt. feindre, simuler

feint n. feinte f.; — vi. feinter

felicitate vt. rendre heureux; féliciter

felicitation n. félicitation f.

felicity n. félicité f.

feline a. félin

fell vt. abattre; — a. cruel, féroce

fellow n. homme m.; gars m.; type m.; compagnon m.; boursier m.; membre m.; — citizen concitoyen m.; — countryman compatriote m.; — creature, — man semblable m.; — traveler compagnon de voyage m.; (pol.) communisant m.; — worker compagnon, confrère m.; -ship n. bourse f.; camaraderie f.

felon n. criminel m.; -ious a. criminel; -y n. crime m.

felt n. feutre m.

female a. femelle; féminin, de femme; — n. femelle f.; femme f.

feminine a. féminin

femininity n. féminité f.

femur n. fémur m.

fence n. clôture f.; barrière f.; (coll.) receleur m.; — vt. clôturer; — vi. faire de l'escrime; -r n. escrimeur m.

fencing n. clôture f.; (sport) escrime m.; — master maître d'armes m.; — match assaut d'armes m.; — school salle d'armes f.

fend vi. — off parer; — vi., — for oneself se défendre, se tirer d'affaire

fender n. (auto.) aile f.; garde-boue m.

fennel n. fenouil m.

ferment n. ferment m., fermentation f.; — vt. faire fermenter; cuver; — vi. fermenter, travailler; -ation n. fermentation f.

fern n. fougère f.

ferocious a. féroce; -ness n. férocité f.

ferocity n. férocité f.

ferret n. furet m.; — vi. fureter; — out dénicher

ferric a. ferrique

ferrous a. ferreux; de fer

ferry n. bac, passage m.; — vt. transborder, passer en bac; transporter

fertile a. fertile, fécond

fertility n. fertilité, fécondité f.

fertilization n. fertilisation f.; pollinisation f.

fertilize vt. fertiliser; amender; -r n. engrais m.

fervency n. ferveur f.

fervent a. fervent; -ly adv. ardemment

fervid a. ardent, chaud

fervor n. ferveur, ardeur f., zèle m.

fester vi. suppurer; **-ing** n. suppuration f.

festival n. fête f., festival m.

festive a. de fête

festivity n. fête f.; réjouissance f.

festoon vt. festonner; — n. feston m.

fetch vt. aller chercher, apporter; rapporter; **-ing** a. séduisant

fête vt. fêter

fetid a. fétide; **-ness** n. fétidité f.

fetish n. fétiche m.

fetter n. lien m.; **-s** n. pl. fers m. pl., chaînes f. pl.; — vt. enchaîner; entraver

fettle n. condition f.

feud n. querelle f.; vendetta f.

feudal a. féodal; **-ism** n. féodalité f.

fever n. fièvre f.; **-ish** a. fiévreux, fébrile; **-ishness** n. fièvre f.

few a. peu de; rares; peu nombreux; a — a. quelques; — pron. peu; quelques-uns; **-er** a. moins de; moins nombreux

fiat n. autorisation f.; décret m.

fib n. petit mensonge m.; — vi. mentir; **-ber** n. menteur m.

fiber n. fibre f.; nature f.

fibroid a. fibroïde; — n. fibrome m.

fibrous a. fibreux

fickle a. volage, inconstant; **-ness** n. inconstance f.

fiction n. fiction f.; ouvrage d'imagination m.; **-al** a. d'imagination, romanesque

fictitious a. fictif, imaginaire

fiddle n. violon m.; — vt. jouer du violon; bricoler, tripoter; **-r** n. (joueur de) violon m.

fidelity n. fidélité, loyauté f.; exactitude f.; high — haute fidélité f.

fidget vi. se trémousser; s'inquiéter; — vi. with tripoter; **-y** a. nerveux

field n. champ m.; terrain m.; théâtre m.; — artillery artillerie de campagne f.; — day fête f.; — glasses jumelles f. pl.; — gun pièce de campagne f.; — hospital ambulance f.; hôpital mobile m.; — marshal n. maréchal m.; — mouse mulot m.; **-er** n. (sports) chasseur m.

fiend n. démon, monstre m.; **-ish** a. diabolique, infernal; **-ishness** n. caractère diabolique m.

fierce a. féroce; acharné; **-ness** n. férocité f.; acharnement m.

fieriness n. ardeur f.

fiery a. ardent, enflammé; fougueux

fifteen a. quinze; **-th** a. quinzième

fifth a. cinquième

fiftieth a. cinquantième

fifty a. cinquante

fifty-fifty a. & adv. moitié-moitié

fig n. figue f.; — leaf (art) feuille de vigne f.; — tree figuier m.

fight n. bataille f., combat m.; lutte f.; dispute f.; match de boxe m.; — vi. se battre, combattre; lutter; boxer; — vt. se battre avec, combattre; — off résister, repousser; **-er** n. combattant m.; boxeur m.; **-ing** n. combat m.; boxe f.

figment n. fiction, invention f.

figurative a. figuratif; figuré

figure n. taille f.; forme, figure f.; personnage m.; chiffre m.; — of speech métaphore f.; figure de rhétorique; — vt. figurer, représenter; estimer, calculer; — on compter sur; se trouver; — out calculer; déchiffrer; **-d** a. à dessein, décoré

figurehead n. prête-nom m.; (naut.) figure de proue f.

Fiji n. Fiji m.

filament n. filament m.; fil m.

filch vt. voler, chiper

file n. classeur m.; dossier m.; fichier m.; (tool) lime f.; — card n. fiche f.; — clerk n. archiviste m. & f.; in single — à la file indienne; — vt. classer, ranger; limer; — by défiler (devant)

filial a. filial

filibuster n. obstruction f.; (hist.) flibustier m.

filigree n. filigrane f.

filing n. classement m.; limage m.; — cabinet classeur m.; — clerk archiviste m. & f.; **-s** n. pl. limaille f.

fill n. suffisance f.; — vt. remplir, emplir; charger; combler; occuper; (order) exécuter; — vi. se remplir, s'emplir; (sail) s'enfler; — in remplir; remblayer; insérer; — out remplir; **-er** n. remplissage m.; remplisseur m.; papier (pour un cahier) m.; **-ing** a. rassasiant; **-ing** n. remplissage m.; (dent.) plombage m.; **-ing** station poste d'essence m., station-service f.

fillet n. filet m.; — vt. lever les filets

filly n. pouliche f.

film n. pellicule f.; film m.; couche f.; **-strip** film (à projection) fixe m.; — vt. filmer; **-y** a. voilé; transparent

filter n. filtre m.; (phot.) écran m.; — vt. & vi. filtrer; **-able** a. filtrant; — tip n. bout filtrant m.

filth n. saleté f.; corruption f.; ordure f.; obscénité f.; **-y** a. sale; immonde

filtrate n. filtrat m.

filtration n. filtration f.

fin n. nageoire f.

final a. final, dernier; définitif; **-e** n. finale m.; **-ist** n. finaliste m. & f.; **-ity** n. finalité f.; irrévocabilité f.; **-ly** adv. finalement; enfin

finance n. finance f.; — vt. financer

financial a. financier

financier n. financier m.

financing n. financement m.

find n. trouvaille f.; découverte f.; — vt. trouver, découvrir; retrouver; apprendre; (law) déclarer; — out apprendre; savoir, découvrir; se renseigner; **-er** n. trouveur m.; détecteur m.; (law) inventeur m.; **-ings** n. conclusions f. pl.

fine n. amende f.; — a. fin; raffiné; beau; excellent; menu; affilé; — arts beaux-arts m. pl.; **-ly** adv. finement; menu; bien; **-ness** n. excellence f.; élégance f.; — vt. frapper d'une amende; condamner à une amende

finery n. parure f.

finesse n. finesse f.; — vt. faire une impasse

finger n. doigt m.; — bowl rince-doigts

m.; ring — annulaire m.; — vt. manier;
-ing n. maniement m.; touche f.
fingernail n. ongle m.
fingerprint n. empreinte digitale f.; — vt.
prendre les empreintes digitales de
finicky a. méticuleux; difficile
finis n. fin f.
finish n. fin f.; achevé m.; finesse f.; — vt.
finir, terminer, achever; — vi. finir, se
terminer; —ed a. fini; accompli, achevé;
-er n. polisseur m.; -ing n. achèvement
m.; photo -ing développement et tirage
m.; -ing a. dernier, final
finite a. fini, limité
Finland n. Finlande f.
Finn n. Finlandais m.; -ish a. & n. finlandais, Finnois
finnan haddie n. merluche f.
fire n. feu m.; incendie m.; catch — prendre feu; — alarm avertisseur m.; — department pompiers, sapeurs-pompiers
m. pl.; — drill exercices de sauvetage
(en cas d'incendie) m. pl.; — engine
pompe à incendie; — escape échelle de
sauvetage f.; — extinguisher extincteur m.; — insurance assurance contre
l'incendie f.; light a — faire du feu; on
— en feu, en flammes; set — to mettre
le feu à; — vt. mettre le feu à; enflammer; (ceramics) cuire; (weapon) tirer,
faire feu; décharger; (employment)
congédier, licencier; mettre à la porte
firearms n. pl. armes à feu f. pl.
fireboat n. bateau-pompe m.
firebox n. poste avertisseur d'incendie m.
firebrand n. brandon, tison m.; rebelle m.
fire chief n. commissaire de pompiers m.
firecracker n. pétard m.
firefighter n. pompier m.
fireless cooker n. marmite norvégienne f.
fireplace n. cheminée f.; feu m.; foyer m.
fireplug n. bouche d'incendie f.
fireproof a. à l'épreuve du feu, ignifuge
fireside n. coin du feu m.
firetrap n. bâtiment inhabitable, bâtiment qui invite l'incendie m.
firewood n. bois de chauffage m.
fireworks n. pl. feux d'artifice m. pl.
firing n. (furnace) chauffage m.; (ceramics) cuite f.; (mil.) feu, tir m.; (employment) renvoi m.; — line traine de
combat f.; — pin aiguille f.
firm n. maison f., établissement m.; — a.
ferme; fixe; solide; résolu; — adv.
stand — tenir bon; -ness n. fermeté f.
first a. premier; — aid premiers soins m.
pl.; — aid kit trousse de pansement f.;
— aid station poste de secours m.; —
night (theat.) première f.; in the —
place en premier lieu; d'abord; — adv.
premièrement, d'abord; plûtot
first-class a. de choix, de première qualité; (travel) de première classe
firsthand a. de première main
first-rate a. excellent, supérieur; de première qualité
fish n. poisson m.; — vt. & vi. pêcher;
-erman n. pêcheur m.; -ery n. pêcherie
f.; -ing n. pêche f.; -ing reel n. moulinet
m.; -ing rod canne à pêche f.; -ing

tackle appareil de pêche m.; -y a. de
poisson; véreux; louche
fishbone n. arête f.
fishbowl n. aquarium m.
fishhook n. hameçon m.
fishmonger n. marchand de poisson m.
fishpond n. vivier m.
fission n. scission f.; fission f.
fissure n. fente f.
fist n. poing m.; shake a — at menacer du
poing; -ful n. poignée f.
fisticuffs n. pl. boxe f.; lutte f.; combat m.;
bagarre f.
fistula n. fistule f.
fit a. bon, propre; capable; digne; — to
drink potable; — to be seen présentable; see — trouver bon; — n. attaque
f., accès m.; crise f.; convulsion f.;
coughing — quinte de toux f.; — vt.
aller (à); ajuster; préparer; munir; —
vi. aller; — in (with) s'accorder, être
en harmonie (avec); — out équiper;
-ful a. irrégulier; -ness n. aptitude f.;
bonne santé f.; -ter n. essayeur m.;
-ting a. convenable, bienséant; à propos; -ting n. garniture f.; montage,
ajustage m.; essayage m.; -ting n. pl.
garniture f.; armement m.
five a. cinq
fix n. (coll.) mauvais pas, embarras m.; —
vt. fixer; préparer; arrêter; réparer; —
up arranger; -ed a. fixe; -edness, -ity
n. fixité f.; -ings n. pl. (coll.) accessoires
m. pl.; garniture f.; -ture n. meuble à
demeure m.
fizz vi. pétiller; — n. pétillement m.
fizzle vi. avorter, ne pas aboutir; — n.
(coll.) avortement, insuccès m.
flabbiness n. mollesse, flaccidité f.
flabby a. mou (molle), flasque
flaccid a. flasque
flag n. drapeau m.; pavillon m.; — vt.
traîner, se ralentir; — stop n. arrêt sur
demande m.; -pole n. hampe de
drapeau f.
flagellate vt. flageller
flagellation n. flagellation f.
flagging n. dallage m.; — a. traînant,
languissant
flagon n. flacon m.
flagrancy n. énormité f.
flagrant a. flagrant
flagship n. amiral, vaisseau amiral m.
flagstone n. dalle f.; dallage m.
flail n. fléau m.
flair n. flair m.
flake n. flocon m.; éclat m., paillette f.;
— vi. tomber en flocons; — off se feuilleter, s'écailler
flaky a. floconneux; feuilleté
flame n. flamme f.; feu m.; ardeur, passion f.; — thrower lance-flammes m.;
— vi. flamber; s'enflammer
flange n. rebord, boudin m., saillie f.
flank n. flanc, côté m.; — vt. flanquer;
(mil.) prendre en flanc
flannel n. flanelle f.; -ette n. flanelle de
coton f.
flap n. pan m.; patte f.; battement m.;
(avi.) volet m.; — vt. & vi. battre

flare n. flamme f., feu m.; fusée éclairante f.; (skirt) évasement m.; — vi. flamboyer; s'évaser; — up s'enflammer

flash n. éclair m.; (coll.) ostentation f., faste m.; — adapter (phot.) prise de flash f.; — attachment (phot.) flash m.; in a — en un clin d'œil; — in the pan feu de paille m.; — vi. jeter des éclairs, éclater; — vt. projeter; faire étinceler; faire parade de; -ing a. clignotant; -ing n. clignotement m.; -y a. fastueux, vaniteux

flash back n. rappel m.

flash bulb n. ampoule flash f.

flash gun n. flash m.

flashlight n. torche, lampe f.

flask n. flacon m.; gourde f.; fiole f.

flat a. plat, uni; aplati; net; fade, insipide; (mus.) bémol; — broke a. complètement fauché; — refusal refus net m.; — tire crevaison f.; fall — manquer (son effet); — on one's face (tomber) à plat ventre; — n. plat m.; appartement m.; (mus.) bémol m.; (theat.) châssis m.; -ten vt. aplatir

flat-bottomed a. à fond plat

flatcar n. wagon en plate-forme m.

flat-footed a. aux pieds plats

flatiron n. fer à repasser m.

flatter vt. flatter; -er n. flatteur m.; -ing a. flatteur; -y n. flatterie f.

flattop n. (coll.) porte-avions m.; cheveux taillés en brosse m. pl.

flatware n. couvert (fourchettes, couteaux, cuillers) m.

flaunt vt. étaler, faire étalage de

flavor n. goût m., saveur f.; parfum m.; — vt. assaisonner, parfumer; -ing n. assaisonnement m.; -less a. insipide

flaw n. défaut m.; imperfection f.; tache f.; -less a. sans défaut; sans tache

flax n. lin m.; -en a. de lin; blond

flay vt. écorcher, fouetter

flea n. puce f.

fleck n. particule; tache f.; — vt. tacheter

fledgling n. oisillon m.; novice m. & f.

flee vt. & vi. fuir; s'enfuir (de)

fleece n. toison f.; — vt. (coll.) plumer, tondre

fleecy a. moutonneux, moutonné; floconneux; laineux

fleet a. flotte f.; — a. au pied léger; rapide; — vi. s'enfuir; -ing a. passager; fugitif; -ness n. vitesse f.

fleet-footed a. au pied léger

Flemish a. & n. flamand m.

flesh n. chair f.; corps m.; — color carnation f.; couleur de chair f.; — wound blessure légère f.; -y a. charnu

flex vt. fléchir

flexibility n. flexibilité f.; souplesse f.

flexible a. flexible, pliant, souple

flick n. chiquenaude f.; tour de main m.; — vt. taper

flicker n. petite lueur f.; tremblotement m.; battement m.; — vi. vaciller, trembloter; scintiller

flier n. prospectus m.; (train) rapide m.; (stocks) spéculation au hasard f.

flight n. fuite f.; vol m.; volée f.; — of stairs escalier m.; put to — mettre en fuite; -iness n. légèreté, inconstance f.; -y a. volage, frivole

filmsiness n. légèreté. pauvreté f.

flimsy a. léger, peu solide; pauvre

flinch vi. reculer; broncher

fling n. jet m.; essai m., tentative f.; (coll.) noce, débauche f.; — vt. jeter, lancer; — vi. se précipiter

flint n. silex m.; pierre à briquet f.

flintlock n. fusil à pierre m.

flip vt. tourner, renverser; — n. renversement m.; — a. léger, cavalier

flippancy n. légèreté f.; désinvolture f.

flippant a. léger; désinvolte

flipper n. nageoire f.

flirt n. coquette f.; — vi. flirter; -ation f. flirt, flirtage m.

flit vi. voltiger

float n. flot, radeau m.; (parade) char bas de cortège m.; — vi. flotter; nager; faire la planche; — vt. flotter; — a loan émettre un emprunt; -ing a. flottant; libre; -ing n. flottement m.; (swimming) planche f.; émission f.

flock n. troupeau m.; troupe f.; bande, foule f.; — vi. s'assembler, s'attrouper; faire foule

floe n. glaçon flottant m., banquise f.

flog vt. fouetter, flageller; -ging n. coups de fouet m. pl.; flagellation f.

flood n. inondation f., déluge m.; flux m.; flot m.; — tide marée montante f.; — vt. inonder; irriguer, noyer; — vi. déborder; (auto) se noyer

floodgate n. vanne f.; porte d'écluse f.

floodlight n. projecteur, phare m.

floor n. plancher, parquet m.; étage m.; fond m.; ground — rez-de-chaussée m.; tiled — carrelage m.; have the — avoir la parole; — vt. parqueter; terrasser; -ing n. plancher, parquetage m.

floorwalker n. chef de rayon (d'un grand magasin) m.

flop n. échec, fiasco m.; — vi. échouer; s'affaler, s'effondrer

floral a. florale, pl. floraux

florid a. fleuri; flamboyant; rubicond

florist n. fleuriste m. & f.

floss n. duvet m.; (metal) floss m.; -y a. duveteux

flotilla n. flottille f.

flounce n. volant m.; — vt. garnir de volant

flounder n. carrelet m.; — vi. se débattre; patauger

flour n. farine f.; — vt. fariner; -y a. farineux

flourish n. fioriture f.; parafe m.; fanfare f.; brandissement m.; — vi. fleurir, prospérer; — vt. brandir; -ing a. florissant; prospère

flout vi. se moquer de; -ing n. moquerie f.

flow n. flux, courant m.; écoulement m.; affluence f.; cours m.; — vi. couler, s'écouler; circuler; se répandre; abonder; — into déboucher dans, se verser dans; -ing a. coulant; flottant; fleuri; gracieux; fluide

flower n. fleur f.; élite f.; — shop boutique

de fleuriste f.; — vi. fleurir; -ed a. à fleurs; -ing a. fleuri, en fleur; -ing n. fleuraison f.; -y a. fleuri

flowerbed n. platebande f.

flu n. grippe f.

fluctuate vi. fluctuer; varier; osciller; flotter

fluctuating a. variable

fluctuation n. fluctuation f.

flue n. tuyau m.

fluency n. facilité f.

fluent a. coulant, facile; -ly adv. couramment

fluff n. duvet m.; peluches f. pl.; — vt. lainer; (coll.) louper; -y a. pelucheux

fluid a. fluide; — n. fluide, liquide m.; -ity n. fluidité f.

flunkey n. laquais m.

fluorescence n. fluorescence f.

fluorescent a. fluorescent

fluoride n. fluorure m.

fluorine n. fluor m.

fluoroscope n. fluoroscope m.

flurry n. risée f.; agitation f.; snow — rafale de neige f.

flush n. chasse d'eau f.; élan m.; éclat m.; rougeur f.; (cards) flush m.; — vi. rougir; — vt. donner une chasse; (hunting) faire lever; — a. à fleur; de niveau; (coll.) en fonds -ed a. qui rougit: empourpré; ivre

fluster vt. agiter; — vi. s'agiter

flute n. flûte f.; (arch.) cannelure f.; -d a. flûté; cannelé

fluting n. striure f.; cannelure f.

flutist n. flûtiste m. & f.

flutter n. voltigement m.; flottement m.; (wings) battement m.; (heart) palpitation f.; — vt. agiter; battre; — vi. flotter, s'agiter; battre; palpiter

flux n. flux m.; fondant m.

fly n. mouche f.; vol m.; (trousers) braguette f.; — fishing pêche à la mouche f.; on the — en vol; — vi. voler; aller en avion; aller à toute vitesse; fuir; — vt. faire voler; piloter; — into a rage s'emporter; — off the handle sortir de ses gonds; — away s'envoler; -er, flier n. aviateur m.; pilote m.; -ing a. volant; -ing boat hydravion m.; -ing buttress arc-boutant m.; -ing saucer soucoupe volante f.; -ing n. aviation f., vol m.

flyleaf n. garde f.

flypaper n. papier attrape-mouches m.

flyweight n. poids mouche m.

flywheel n. volant m.

F.M.: Frequency Modulation n. modulation de fréquence f.

foal n. poulain m.; — vi. mettre bas

foam n. écume f.; mousse f.; — rubber n. mousse de caoutchouc f.; — vi. écumer; mousser; -y a. écumeux; mousseux

F.O.B.: free on board rendu à bord

fob n. régence f.; ornement (sur une chaîne de montre) m.; (pocket) gousset m.

focus n. foyer m.; in — au point; — vt. concentrer; mettre au point; — vi. converger; -ing n. mise au point f.

fodder n. fourrage m.

foe n. ennemi, adversaire m.

foetus n. foetus m.

fog n. brouillard m., brume f.; — vt. embrumer; embrouiller; voiler; -gy a. brumeux; brouillé; it's -gy il fait du brouillard

foghorn n. sirène (de brume) f.

foible n. faible m.

foil n. feuille, lame f.; tain m.; (fencing) fleuret m.; — vt. déjouer; faire manquer

foist vt. imposer; insérer

fold n. pli, repli m.; (sheep) parc m.; — vt. plier, replier; — one's arms se croiser les bras; — vi. se plier; (coll.) échouer, sombrer; -er n. chemise f.; dossier m.; prospectus m.; -ing a. pliant; -ing bed lit pliant, lit escamotable m.; -ing chair chaise pliante f.; -ing door porte brisée f.

foliage n. feuillage m.

folio n. folio m.; feuille f.; in-folio m.

folk n. gens m. pl.; peuple m.; — music musique populaire f.; — song chanson populaire f.; -s (coll.) famille f., parents m. pl.

follicle n. follicule m.

follow vt. suivre; poursuivre; succéder à; se conformer; comprendre; — vi. suivre; s'ensuivre; — up suivre, poursuivre; -er n. disciple m.; partisan m.; -ing a. qui suit; suivant; -ing n. (pol.) parti m.; partisans m. pl.; -ing the leader adv. à la queue leu leu

folly n. folie f.; sottise f.

foment vt. fomenter

fond a. tendre, affectueux; friand; be — of aimer (bien); être amateur de; -ness n. affection f.; goût m.

fondle vt. caresser

font n. fontaine f.; (eccl.) fonts baptismaux m. pl.; (printing) fonte f.

food n. nourriture f.; aliment m.; manger m.; vivres m. pl.; cuisine f.

fool n. sot m.; fou (folle) m.; niais m.; imbécile m. & f.; dupe f.; — vt. duper; berner; -ery n. bouffonnerie f.; -ing n. duperie f.; dissipation f.; no -ing sans blague -ish a. fou (folle); insensé; bête; ridicule; -ishness n. folie f.; sottise f.

foolhardiness n. témérité f.

foolhardy a. téméraire; imprudent

foolproof a. indétraquable

foolscap n. papier ministre m.

foot n. pied m.; patte f.; base f.; bas m.; — locker petite malle f.; — soldier soldat d'infanterie m.; on — à pied; set — on mettre pied sur; -ing n. équilibre m.; lose one's -ing perdre pied

foot-and-mouth disease n. fièvre aphteuse f.

footbridge n. passerelle f.

footfall n. pas m.

foothills n. pl. contreforts m. pl.

foothold n., get a — prendre pied

footlights n. pl. rampe f.

foot-loose a. libre; sans entraves

footman n. valet de pied, laquais m.

footnote n. note f., renvoi m.

footpath n. sentier m.

footprint n. trace f.; empreinte (de pas) f., pas m.

foot race n. course à pied f.

footsore a. aux pieds meurtris

footstep n. pas m.

footstool n. tabouret m.

foot warmer n. chaufferette f.

footwear n. chaussures f. pl.

footwork n. jeu de pieds m.

fop n. petit-maître m.

for conj. car; — prep. pour; comme; contre; à; de; pendant; depuis; — example par exemple; — sale à vendre; as — quant à; what — pour quoi faire; pourquoi

forage vi. fourrager; — n. fourrage m.

foray n. incursion f.

forbear vt. & vi. s'abstenir; -ance n. abstention f.

forbid vt. défendre, interdire; God —! à Dieu ne plaise!; -den a. défendu; -ding a. sinistre, sombre

force n. force f.; contrainte f.; énergie f.; effort m.; puissance f.; in — en vigueur; police — la police f.; — vt. forcer; obliger; contraindre; arracher; enfoncer; — one's way into pénétrer de force dans; — back repousser; -d a. forcé; obligé; -ful a. énergique; puissant

forceps n. pl. pince f.

forcibly adv. de force, par force

ford n. gué m.; — vt. traverser à gué

fore n. (naut.) avant m.; to the — en vue; — ! interj. (golf) gare devant!

forearm n. avant-bras m.; — vt. prémunir, avertir

forebode vt. présager; pressentir

forecast n. prévision f.; weather — prévisions météorologiques f. pl.; — vt. prédire, prévoir

forecastle n. gaillard d'avant m.

foreclose vt. saisir

foreclosure n. saisie f.

forefather n. aïeul m.

forefinger n. index m.

forefront n. premier rang m.

forego vt. renoncer à; -ing a. précédent, antérieur; -ne a. décidé, déterminé; -ne conclusion n. parti pris m.

foreground n. premier plan m.

forehead n. front m.

foreign a. étranger; — trade commerce extérieur m.; -er n.; étranger m., étrangère f.

foreleg n. jambe de devant f.

foreman n. contremaître m.; chef d'équipe m.; (jury) chef m.

foremast n. mât de misaine m.

foremost a. premier; — adv., first and — tout d'abord

forenoon n. matinée f.

forerunner n. précurseur m.

foresee vt. prévoir; entrevoir

foreshadow n. présager; -ing n. présage, pressentiment m.

foreshorten vt. raccourcir

foresight n. prévoyance f.; prévision f.

forest n. forêt f.; — ranger (garde) forestier m.; -ry n. sylviculture f.

forestall vt. anticiper, devancer

foretell vt. prédire

forethought n. prévoyance f.; préméditation f.

forever adv. pour toujours, à jamais

forewarn vt. avertir, prévenir

foreword n. avant-propos m.; préface f., avis au lecteur m.

forfeit n. amende f.; gage m.; forfait m.; — vt. être déchu de; perdre; -ure n. confiscation, forfaiture f.

forge n. forge f.; atelier de forge m.; — vt. forger; contrefaire, falsifier; -r n. forgeron m.; faussaire m. & f.; -ry n. contrefaçon, falsification f.; faux m.

forget vt. oublier; -ful a. oublieux; -fulness n. manque de mémoire m.; oubli m.

forget-me-not n. myosotis m.

forgivable a. pardonnable

forgive vt. pardonner; -ness n. pardon m.

forgiving a. indulgent, généreux

fork n. fourchette f.; fourche f.; bifurcation f.; tuning — diapason m.; — vi. fourcher; se bifurquer; — over, — out (coll.) payer, donner de l'argent -ed a. fourchu

forlorn a. abandonné, délaissé; désespéré

form n. forme f.; figure f.; formalité f.; ton m.; formule f.; bulletin m.; classe f.; — letter lettre circulaire f.; good — bon ton m.; matter of — formalité f.; — vt. former; faire; façonner; organiser; — vi. se former; -ation n. formation f.; organisation f.; -less a. informe; amorphe

formal a. formel; cérémonieux; -ity n. formalité f.; cérémonie f.

formaldehyde n. aldéhyde formique f.

former a. ancien; précédent; premier; — pron., the — celui-là, celle-là; -ly adv. autrefois, jadis; anciennement

formidable a. formidable

formula n. formule f.

formulate vt. formuler

forsake vt. abandonner

forswear vt. abjurer, répudier

fort n. forteresse f.; fort m.

forte n. fort m.

forth adv. en avant; and so — et ainsi de suite

forthcoming a. à venir, à paraître

forthright a. direct

forthwith adv. sur-le-champ

fortieth a. quarantième

fortification n. fortification f.

fortify vt. fortifier; renforcer

fortitude n. force d'âme f.

fortnight n. quinze jours m. pl.; quinzaine f.; -ly a. tous les quinze jours

fortress n. forteresse f.

fortuitous a. fortuit; -ly adv. par hasard; -ness n. fortuité f.

fortunate a. fortuné, heureux; -ly adv. heureusement

fortune n. fortune f.; hasard m.; sort m.; — hunter coureur de dots m.; aventurier m.; -teller diseur (diseuse) de bonne aventure m. & f.; tireur (tireuse) de cartes m. & f.; -telling bonne aventure f.; cartomancie f.

forty a. quarante

forward a. en avant; de devant; avancé;

effronté; –(s) *adv.* en avant; à l'avant; **–pass** *n.* (football) passe en avant *f.*; **—** *vt.* faire suivre; envoyer, expédier; avancer; **–ness** *n.* présomption *f.*, empressement *m.*

fossil *n. & a.* fossile *m.*; **–ize** *vi.* se fossiliser

foster *vt.* nourrir, élever; encourager, développer; **— brother** frère adoptif *m.*; **—** frère de lait *m.*; **— child** enfant adopté *m.*; nourrisson *m.*; **— mother** mère adoptive *f.*; mère nourricière *f.*

foul *a.* immonde; infect; vicié; gros; sale; (sport) hors jeu; **—** balle hors jeu *f.*; **— play** jeu déloyal *m.*; malveillance *f.*; **—** *n.* faute *f.*; coup déloyal *m.*; **—** *vt.* embarasser; engager; salir, crasser; **–mouthed** *a.* grossier

found *vt.* fonder, établir; **–ation** *n.* fondation *f.*, établissement *m.*; fondement *m.*; base *f.*; assise *f.*; **–er** *n.* fondateur *m.*

founder *vi.* sombrer

foundling *n.* enfant trouvé *m.*

foundry *n.* fonderie *f.*

fount(ain) *n.* fontaine *f.*; jet d'eau *m.*; source *f.*; **— pen** stylo *m.*

fountainhead *n.* source, origine *f.*

four *a.* quatre; on all **–s** à quatre pattes; **–teen** *a.* quatorze; **–teenth** *f.* quatorzième; **–th** *a.* quatrième; (fraction) quart *m.*

four-engined *a.* quadrimoteur

four-footed *a.* quadrupède

four-poster *n.* lit à colonnes *m.*

foursome *n.* (golf) partie double *f.*

fowl *n.* volaille *f.*

fox *n.* renard *m.*; **— terrier** *n.* fox *m.*; **–y** *a.* rusé

foxhole (mil.) *n.* trou *m.*, tranchée individuelle *f.*

foyer *n.* foyer, vestibule *m.*

fracas *n.* dispute, bagarre *f.*

fraction *n.* fraction *f.*; **–al** *a.* fractionnaire; fractionné

fracture *n.* fracture *f.*; set a **—** réduire une fracture; **—** *vt.* fracturer; casser

fragility *n.* fragilité *f.*

fragment *n.* fragment, morceau *m.*; éclat *m.*; **–ary** *a.* fragmentaire

fragrance *n.* parfum *m.*

fragrant *a.* parfumé

frail *a.* frêle, fragile; faible, délicat; **–ty** *n.* faiblesse *f.*; fragilité *f.*

frame *n.* cadre *m.*; taille *f.*; châssis *m.*; armature *f.*; (film) image *f.*; **— of mind** disposition *f.*; **—** *vt.* encadrer; former; projeter; (coll.) monter une accusation contre; **–r** *n.* encadreur *m.*; (fig.) créateur *m.*

framework *n.* charpente *f.*; organisation *f.*; systeme *m.*

framing *n.* encadrement *m.*

France *n.* France *f.*

franchise *n.* franchise *f.*; privilège *m.*; droit de vote *m.*; **–ment** *n.* exclusivité *f.*

Franciscan *n.* franciscain *m.*

frank *a.* franc (franche); **–ly** *adv.* franchement; **–ness** *n.* franchise *f.*

Frank *n.* Franc *m.*; **–ish** *a.* franc

frankfurter *n.* saucisse de Francfort *f.*

frantic *a.* frénétique; effréné

fraternal *a.* fraternel

fraternity *n.* fraternité *f.*; société de collégiens *f.*

fraternize *vt.* fraterniser

fraternizing *n.* fraternisation *f.*

fraud *n.* fraude *f.*; tromperie *f.*; imposteur *m.*; **–ulent** *a.* frauduleux

fraught *a.* plein, riche

fray *n.* combat *m.*; bagarre *f.*; **—** *vi.* s'érailler

freak *n.* monstre *m.*; curiosité *f.*; **— of chance** jeu du hasard *m.*; **–ish** *a.* monstrueux, bizarre

freckle *n.* tache de rousseur *f.*; **–d** *a.* taché de rousseur

free *a.* libre; gratuit; franco; libéral; franc; exempt; dégagé; **— and easy** désinvolte, dégagé; **— for all** lutte pour tous *f.*; **— hand** carte blanche *f.*; **— speech** libre parole *f.*; **—** ticket billet de faveur *m.*; **— trade** libre échange *m.*; **— will** (phil.) libre arbitre *m.*; of one's own **— will** de son propre gré; **—** *vt.* libérer; affranchir; élargir; dégager; **–dom** *n.* liberté *f.*; franchise *f.*; **–dom of speech** franc-parler *m.*

free-for-all *n.* bagarre *f.*; mêlée *f.*

freehand *a.* (art) à main levée

freemason *n.* franc-maçon *m.*; **–ry** *n.* franc-maçonnerie *f.*

freethinker *n.* libre penseur *m.*

freeway *n.* autostrade *f.*

freeze *vt.* geler, congeler, glacer; **—** *vi.* prendre; se figer; **–r** *n.* frigorifique *m.*

freezing *n.* congelation *f.*; **—** *a.* très froid; it's **—** il gèle

freight *n.* cargaison *f.*, fret *m.*; **— train** train de marchandises *m.*; **—** *vt.* fréter; **–er** *n.* cargo *m.*

French *a. & n.* français *m.*; **— fried potatoes** pommes (de terre) frites *f. pl.*; **–door** *n.* porte vitrée à petits carreaux *f.*; **— dressing** *n.* sauce à l'huile (pour la salade) *f.*; **— horn** cor (d'harmonie) *m.*; **— toast** tranche de pain frite *f.*, pain perdu *m.*; **— window** porte-fenêtre *f.*; **—** *n.* français *m.*, langue française *f.*; **–man** *n.* Français *m.*; **–woman** *n.* Française *f.*

frenzy *n.* frénésie, fureur *f.*

frequency *n.* fréquence *f.*; **— modulation** *n.* modulation de fréquence *f.*

frequent *a.* fréquent; **–ly** *adv.* fréquemment; **—** *vt.* fréquenter; **–er** *n.* habitué *m.*

fresco *n.* fresque *f.*

fresh *a.* frais (fraîche); pur; vert; nouveau; impudent, effronté; **— air** grand air, plein air *m.*; **— water** eau douce *f.*; **–en** *vt.* rafraîchir; rafraîchir; **–ness** *n.* fraîcheur *f.*; effronterie *f.*

freshman *n.* étudiant de première année *m.*

fresh-water *a.* d'eau douce

fret *n.* (mus.) touche, touchette *f.*; agitation *f.*; **—** *vi.* se faire du mauvais sang; **–ful** *a.* agité; irritable

friar *n.* moine *m.*

fricassee *n.* fricassée *f.*

friction *n.* friction *f.*, frottement *m.*;

désaccord m.

Friday n. vendredi m.; Good — a. vendredi saint m.

fried a. frit; — eggs œufs sur le plat m. pl.

friend n. ami m.; amie f.; intime m. & f.; make -s se lier d'amitié; -less a. sans amis; -liness n. amitié, amabilité f.; -ly a. amical; d'amitié; sympathique; -ship n. amitié f.

frieze n. frise f.

frigate n. frégate f.

fright n. peur f.; épouvante f.; -en vt. effrayer, épouvanter, faire peur à; -ened a. apeuré; be -ened avoir peur; -ening a. effrayant; -ful a. épouvantable, effroyable; affreux, terrible

frigid a. froid; glacial; -ity n. frigidité f.

frill n. ornement m.; jabot m.; dentelle f.

fringe n. frange f.; bord m., bordure f.; marge f.; — benefit avantage en dehors du salaire offert aux employés par la direction m. — vt. franger

frisk vi. sauter, bondir; — vt. (coll.) fouiller; -y a. vif

fritter n. beignet m.; friture f.; — vt., — away gaspiller

frivolity n. frivolité f.

frivolous a. frivole

fro adv. en arrière; go to and — aller et venir

frock n. robe f.; — coat n. redingote f.

frog n. grenouille f.; -man n. homme-grenouille m.

frolic n. gaieté f.; fantaisie, folie f.; — vi. folâtrer; -some a. folâtre

from prep. de, par, dès, depuis, d'après

front n. façade f.; devant m.; (coll.) prête-nom m.; in — of devant; — a. de devant; premier; — vi. donner, faire face; -al a. frontal; -age n. façade f.; largeur (du côté de la rue, de la mer) f.

frontier n. frontière, limite f.

frontispiece n. frontispice m.

frost n. givre m.; — vt. glacer, couvrir de fondant; -ed a. givré; (cake) glacé; -ed glass verre dépoli m.; -ing n. fondant; -y a. couvert de givre

frostbite n. engelure f.

frostbitten a. gelé

froth n. écume, mousse f.; — vi. écumer, mousser; -y a. mousseux

frown n. froncement des sourcils m.; — vi. froncer les sourcils; — on désapprouver

frozen a. gelé, glacé, congelé

frugal a. frugal; -ity n. frugalité f.

fruit n. fruit m.; produit m.; — seller fruitier m.; — stand fruiterie f.; — a. fruitier; -ful a. fécond; -less a. stérile; vain

fruition n. maturation f.; jouissance f.

frustrate vt. frustrer, annuler; refouler

frustration n. refoulement m.

fry n. (fish) frai m.; friture f.; — vt. frire, faire frire; -ing n. friture f.; -ing pan n. poêle à frire f.

fuel n. carburant m.; aliment m.; — gauge indicateur d'essence m.; — oil gas-oil m.; — tank réservoir à essence

fugitive n. & a. fugitif m.

fulcrum n. point fixe m.; point d'appui m.

fulfil vt. accomplir, remplir; acquitter; réaliser; -ment n. accomplissement m.; réalisation f.

full a. plein; rempli; complet, comble; entier; at — speed à toute vitesse; — dress grande tenue f.; — blast en pleine activité; — moon pleine lune f.; in — en entier; in — swing en activité, en train; -ness n. plénitude f.; ampleur f.; abondance f.; -y adv. tout à fait, entièrement

fullback n. arrière m.

full-blooded a. de race pur; robuste

full-blown a. en pleine fleur

full-fledged a. qui a tous ses titres

full-grown a. mûr

full-length a. en pied

fulminate vi. fulminer

fumble n. action maladroite f.; — vi. agir maladroitement; — vt. laisser tomber

fumbling a. maladroit

fume n. fumée, vapeur f.; — vt. & vi. fumer; être en colère

fumigate vi. faire des fumigations

fumigation n. fumigation f.

fuming a. fulminant

fun n. amusement m., gaieté f.; for — pour le sport; have — s'amuser; make — of se moquer de; -ny a. drôle; rigolo; amusant, comique; bizarre

function n. fonction f.; faculté f.; — vi. fonctionner, aller, marcher; — as servir de; -al a. fonctionnel; -ary n. fonctionnaire m.

fund n. fond, bien m.; réserve f.; -s pl. fonds m. pl.; argent m.

fundamental a. fondamental; de fond; -s n. pl. principes m. pl.

funeral n. funérailles, obsèques f. pl.; — director entrepreneur de pompes funèbres m.; — home — parlor entreprise de pompes funèbres f.

funereal a. funèbre, lugubre, triste

fungicide a. & n. fongicide m.

fungus n. fongus m.

funicular a. & n. funiculaire m.

funnel n. entonnoir m.

fur n. fourrure f.; pelleterie f.; — coat manteau de fourrure m.; -red a. à fourrure; -rier n. fourreur, pelletier m.; -ry a. à fourrure, fourré

furbish vt. fourbir, polir

furious a. furieux; -ly adv. furieusement

furl vt. ployer; (naut.) ferler, serrer

fur-lined a. doublé de fourrure

furlong n. furlong m.

furlough n. congé m., permission f.; on — en permission; — vt. donner un congé (à)

furnace n. fourneau m.; (fig.) fournaise f.

furnish vt. fournir; meubler, garnir; -ed a. meublé, garni; -ings n. pl. mobilier m.; ameublement m.

furnisher n. fournisseur m.

furniture n. mobilier m.; meubles m. pl.; piece of — meuble m.

furor n. fureur f.; tumulte m.

furrow n. sillon m.; ride f.; guéret m.; — vt. sillonner; rider

further vt. avancer, aider; — adv. de plus, en outre; plus avant, au delà, plus loin; — a. supplémentaire, additionnel; without — ado sans plus de cérémonie; -ance n. avancement m.

furthermore adv. d'ailleurs, de plus

furthest a. le plus éloigné; — adv. le plus loin

furtive a. furtif; -ly adv. à la dérobée

fury n. furie, frénésie, rage, fureur f.

fuse vt. fondre; fusionner; — vi. fondre; se fusionner; — n. mèche f.; (elec.) fusible m.

fuselage n. fuselage m. .

fusillade n. fusillade f.

fusion n. fusion, fonte f.

fuss n. fracas, embarras, bruit m.; — vi. se plaindre; causer de l'embarras; se donner de la peine; -y a. difficile, délicat; regardant

futile a. futile, frivole, vain

futility n. futilité, frivolité f.

future n. avenir m.; (gram.) futur m.; in the — à l'avenir, -s n. pl. (stocks) valeurs négociées à terme f. pl.; — a. futur

futurity n. futur, avenir m.

fuzz n. duvet, poil m.; -y a. duveté, couvert de poil; vague

G

gab n. langue f.; bavardage m.; have the gift of — avoir la langue bien pendue; — vi. bavarder; -by a. bavard

gable n. pignon, gable m.

gad vi., — about courir ça et là

gadget n. machin, outil m.; truc m.

Gaelic a. & n. gaélique m.

gaff n. harpon, crochet m.

gag n. bâillon m.; (coll.) blague f.; — vt. bâillonner; — vi. avoir envie de vomir

gaiety n. gaieté, joie f.

gaily adv. gaiement

gain vt. gagner; prendre; — weight prendre du poids; — n. gain, profit m.; -ful a. profitable

gainsay vt. contredire; nier

gait n. démarche, allure f.

gaiter n. guêtre f.

gala n. gala m.; — a. de gala

galaxy n. galaxie f.

gale n. gros vent m.

gall n. bile f.; rancune, malice f.; (coll.) toupet m.; — bladder vésicule biliaire f.; -stones calculs biliaires m. pl.; — vt. vexer, irriter

gallant a. & a. vaillant, brave m.; élégant, galant a.; -ry n. vaillance f.; galanterie f.

galleon n. galion m.

gallery n. galerie f.; corridor m.

galley n. galère f.; (print.) épreuve f., placard m.; (naut.) cuisine f.; — slave n. galérien, forçat m.

Gallic a. gaulois; -ism n. gallicisme m.

gallivant vi. vagabonder, aller et venir, courir

gallop n. galop m. — vi. galoper; aller au galop

gallows n. gibet m., potence f.

galore adv. en abondance, à profusion

galoshes n. pl. galoches f. pl.

galvanization n. galvanisation f.; zingage m.

galvanize vt. galvaniser

gamble vi. jouer; — vt., — away perdre en jouant; — n. aventure f.; entreprise hasardeuse f.; -r n. joueur m.

gambling n. jeu m.; — house maison de jeu f.; tripot m.

gambol n. gambade f.; — vi. gambader

game n. divertissement, jeu m.; (sports) partie f., match m.; (hunting) gibier m.; — warden garde champêtre m.; — a. brave, intrépide; blessé; estropié

gamecock n. coq de combat m.

gamekeeper n. garde-chasse m.

gamma n. gamma m.; — globulin globule gamma m.; — ray rayon gamma m.

gang n. troupe, bande f.; — vi. se grouper; — up on attaquer en masse

ganglion n. ganglion m.

gangplank n. passerelle f.

gangrene n. gangrène f.; — vi. se gangrener

gangrenous a. gangreneux

gangway n. passage m.; (naut.) passe-avant m.

gantlet, gauntlet n. gantelet m.; (mil.) baguettes f. pl.; run the — courir les baguettes

gap n. ouverture, fente, brèche f.; lacune f.; trou m.

gape vi. bâiller; rester bouche bée

gaping a. béant

garage n. garage m.; — vt. garer; — man n. garagiste m.

garb n. vêtement m.; costume m.; — vt. vêtir, habiller

garbage n. ordures f. pl.; — can, — pail boîte à ordures, poubelle f.

garble vt. transformer, mutiler

garden n. jardin m.; — vi. jardiner; -er n. jardinier m.; -ing n. jardinage m.

gardenia n. camélia m.

gargle vt. gargarisme m.; — vt. se gargariser

gargoyle n. gargouille f.

garish a. voyant, criard

garland n. guirlande f.; — vt. guirlander

garlic n. ail m.; clove of — gousse d'ail f.

garment n. vêtement m.

garner vt. amasser

garnish n. garniture f., ornement m.; — vt. garnir, parer, orner

garnishee vt. saisir (par saisie-arrêt)

garotte n. garotte f.; — vt. garotter

garret n. mansarde f.; grenier m.

garrison n. garnison f.; — vt. mettre en garnison

garrulous a. babillard, bavard, loquace

garter n. jarretière, jarretelle f.; support-chaussettes m.; — snake n. couleuvre à collier f.

gas n. gaz n.; essence f.; — heater réchaud à gaz m.; — jet bec de gaz m.; — main conduit à gaz m.; — mask masque à gaz m.; — meter compteur à gaz m.; —

station poste d'essence m., station-service f.; — stove cuisinière à gas f.; — tank réservoir à essence m.; — vt. gazer; —eous a. gazeux; —ify vt. gazéifier; —y a. gaseux

Gascony n. Gascogne f.

gash n. coupure f.; entaille f.; — vt. couper; entailler

gasket n. garniture f.; obturateur de joint m.; (naut.) garcette f.

gaslight n. éclairage au gas m.; bec de gas m.

gasoline n. essence f.; — tank réservoir à essence; — station poste d'essence m.

gasp n. halètement m.; souffle m.; (hiccup) hoquet m.; last — dernière extrémité f.; — vi. haleter; —ing a. haletant; —ing n. halètement m.

gastric a. gastrique

gastritis n. gastrite f.

gastronomy n. gastronomie f.

gasworks n. usine à gas f.

gate n. porte f., portail m., grille, barrière f.

gatehouse n. loge de garde f.

gatekeeper n. portier m.

gateway n. portail m.; (fig.) entrée f.

gather vt. cueillir; ramasser; assembler, réunir; froncer; conclure; — vi. s'assembler; s'accumuler; — n. froncis m., fronce f.; —er n. ramasseur m.; —ing n. rassemblement m., réunion f.; cueillette, récolte f.

gaudy a. voyant, criard

gauge n. jauge f.; calibre m.; indicateur m.; largeur f.; — vt. jauger; mesurer; calibrer

Gaul n. (person) Gaulois m.; (country) Gaule f.

gaunt a. maigre, décharné

gauntlet n. gantelet m.; run the — courir les baguettes

gauze n. gaze f.

gavel n. marteau m.

gawk vi. regarder fixement; —y a. gauche

gay a. gai, joyeux

gaze n. yeux m. pl. regard, regard fixe m.; — vi. at contempler, regarder fixement

gazetteer n. dictionnaire géographique m.

gear n. accoutrement, appareil, habillement m.; (mech.) engrenage m.; (auto) vitesse f.; shift —s changer de vitesse; throw out of — disloquer; débrayer; — vt. embrayer; gréer; — vi. (coll.) se préparer

gearshift n. changement de vitesse m.

gelatin n. gélatine f.

geld vt. châtrer; —ing n. cheval hongre m.

gem n. pierre précieuse f., bijou m.

gender n. genre m.

gene n. gène m.

genealogy n. généalogie f.

general n. général m.; — staff état-major m.; brigadier — général de brigade m.; major — général de division m.; lieutenant — général de corps d'armée m.; — of the armies maréchal m.; in — en général, généralement; — a. général; — delivery poste restante f.; —ity n. gé-

néralité f.; —ization n. généralisation f.; —ize vt. généraliser; —ly adv. en général, généralement; —ship n. tactique f.

generate vt. engendrer, produire; générer

generator n. générateur m., génératrice f.

generic a. générique

generosity n. générosité f.; libéralité f.

generous a. généreux; libéral

genesis n. genèse f.

genetics n. eugénique f.

Geneva n. Genève

genial a. agréable, affable, aimable; —ity n. amabilité, affabilité f.

genie n. génie m.

genitals n. pl. parties génitales f. pl.

genitive n. génitif m.

genius n. génie m.

Genoa n. Gênes f.

genteel a. honnête, poli; civil; élégant

gentile n. gentil m.

gentility n. politesse f.; élégance f.

gentle a. doux, paisible; —ness n. douceur f.

gentleman n. gentilhomme m.; homme honorable m.; monsieur m.; —'s agreement contrat verbal m.; —ly a. comme il faut, convenable

gently adv. doucement, avec soin

gentry n. haute bourgeoisie f.; petite noblesse f.

genuflection n. génuflexion f.

genuine a. véritable, réel; authentique; —ness n. réalité, authenticité f.

genus n. genre m.

geographic(al) a. géographique

geography n. géographie f.

geological a. géologique

geologist n. géologue m.

geology n. géologie f.

geometric(al) n. géométrique

geometry n. géométrie f.; plane — géométrie plane f.; solid — géométrie dans l'espace f.

geophysics n. géophysique f.

geopolitics n. géopolitique f.

Georgia n. Géorgie f.

germ n. germe m.; microbe m.

German a. allemand; — measles rubéole f.

germane a. à propos

Germanic a. germanique; allemand

Germany n. Allemagne f.

germicide n. microbicide m.

germinate vi. germer, pousser

gerrymander vt. (pol.) truquer (une élection); — n. truquage (électoral) m.

gerund n. gérondif m.

gestation n. gestation f.

gesticulate vi. gesticuler

gesticulation n. gesticulation f.

gesture n. geste, signe m.; — vi. faire un signe; faire des gestes

get vt. devenir, se faire; aller, se mettre; — vt. obtenir, avoir, gagner, acquérir, s'emparer de, recevoir; atteindre; chercher, aller chercher; attraper; (coll.) comprendre; — about sortir; se répandre; — a kick out of (coll.) prendre plaisir à; — along circuler; procéder; se tirer d'affaire; — a move on (coll.) se dépêcher; — around contourner; aller partout; sortir; — at atteindre; vouloir dire; — away s'en aller; s'échapper; s'évader; se sauver; — away with s'en aller avec; échapper (sans être puni) —; down descendre; (coll.) décourager; — even with se venger sur; — in, — into entrer dans; — in someone's hair ennuyer, irriter; — it over with (coll.) en finir; — off descendre (de); enlever; se tirer d'affaire, s'échapper; — on monter (sur); mettre; continuer; vieillir; — on with continuer; — out sortir; enlever, éliminer; — over passer; se remettre (de); faire comprendre; — rid of se défaire de; — the better of triompher de; — through traverser, passer par; finir; — to arriver à; avoir l'occasion de; — together rassembler; se réunir; — up monter; se lever; arranger, dresser; — well se remettre, guérir

getaway n. démarrage m.; fuite f.
get-together n. réunion f.; soirée f.
geyser n. geyser m.
Ghana n. Ghana m.
ghastliness n. horreur f.
ghastly a. horrible, terrible, pâle, affreux
Ghent n. Gand m.
gherkin n. cornichon m.
ghost n. esprit, fantôme m.; ombre f.; — town ville abandonnée f.; — writer rédacteur secret m.; -ly a. de fantôme
ghoul n. goule f.
G.I. n. soldat; — a. fourni par l'armée
giant a. & n. géant m.
gibberish n. jargon m.
gibbet n. gibet m., potence f.
gibe n. raillerie, moquerie f.; — vt. & vi. railler, se moquer de
giblets n. pl. abattis m.
giddiness n. vertige, étourdissement m.; légèreté f.
giddy a. étourdi; frivole, léger
gift n. cadeau m.; don m.; talent m.; -ed a. doué
gig n. cabriolet m.; (naut.) canot m.
gigantic a. gigantesque
giggle vi. pousser des petits rires; — n. petit rire m.
giggling n. petits rires m. pl.
gigolo n. gigolo m.
gild vt. dorer; -ed a. doré; -ing n. dorure f.
gills n. pl. ouïes, branchies f. pl.
gilt n. dorure f.; — a. doré
gilt-edged a. doré sur tranche; d'excellente qualité; très sûr
gimlet n. perçoir m., vrille f.
ginger n. gingembre m.; — ale, — beer soda au gingembre m.; -ly adv. doucement, avec soin
gingerbread n. (genre de) pain d'épices m.
gingersnap n. gâteau sec au gingembre m.
gingham n. guingan m.
gird vt. ceindre, attacher; -er n. poutre f.
girdle n. gaine f., (garment) gaine f.; ceinture f.; — vt. ceindre, ceinturer
girl n. jeune fille f.; fille f.; — scout éclaireuse f.; -hood n. jeunesse f. (de jeune fille); -ish a. de jeune fille

girth n. sangle f.; circonférence f.; tour de la taille m.
gist n. fond m., substance f.
give vt. donner, présenter; — vi. donner; — account rendre compte; — away donner; révéler; — evidence témoigner; — in se rendre; — off émettre; — out distribuer; se rendre, s'épuiser; — over remettre; — up se rendre; — way faire place, reculer; — n. élasticité f.; — and take compromis m., concession mutuelle f.; -n a. donné, fixé; vu, étant donné; -n name prénom m.; -r n. donneur, donateur m.
give-and-take n. donnant donnant, libre échange m.
giving n. don m., donation f.
gizzard n. gésier m.
glacial a. glacial
glacier n. glacier m.
glad a. content; heureux; bien aise; joyeux; -den vt. réjouir; contenter; -ly adv. volontiers, avec plaisir; -ness n. contentement m.; joie f.
glade n. clairière f.
gladiator n. gladiateur m.
gladiolus n. glaïeul m.
glamor n. éclat, charme m.; -ous a. éclatant, ravissant
glance n. coup d'œil m.; at a — d'un coup d'œil; — vi. jeter un coup d'œil; — off ricocher
glancing a. oblique
gland n. glande f.; -ular a. glandulaire, glanduleux
glare n. lumière éblouissante f.; regard féroce m.; — vi. éblouir, briller; regarder d'un œil terrible
glaring a. éblouissant; évident; menaçant
glass n. verre m.; glace f., miroir m.; vitre f.; télescope m.; lorgnon m.; baromètre m.; cut — cristal taillé m.; magnifying — loupe f.; pane of — carreau m.; vitre f.; stained — verre de couleur m.; — blowing soufflage (du verre) m.; -es n. pl. lunettes f. pl.; -y a. vitreux, de verre; -ful n. verre m.
glassware n. verrerie f.
glaucoma n. glaucome m.
glaze n. vernis m.; dorure f.; fondant m.; glace f.; — vt. glacer; vernir; (glass) vitrer
glazier n. vitrier m.
gleam n. rayon m., clarté f.; lueur f.; reflet m.; — vi. rayonner, briller; (re)luire; -ing a. luisant; rayonnant
glean vt. glaner; recueillir
glee n. joie, allégresse f.; chanson (à plus de deux voix) f.; — club chœur m.; -ful joyeux
glib a. coulant, glissant; délié
glide vi. couler, glisser, planer; — n. glissement m.; -r n. planeur m.
glimmer n. lueur (faible) f.; — vi. jeter une faible lueur, reluire
glimpse vi. apercevoir; entrevoir; — n. aperçu m.
glint n. étincellement m.; lueur f.; reflet m.; — vi. étinceler
glisten vi. briller, reluire, étinceler

glitter vi. étinceler, reluire; — n. éclat, lustre m.

gloaming n. crépuscule m., brune f.

gloat vi., triompher de; — over se réjouir de

global a. global

globe n. globe m.; sphère f.

globetrotter n. grand voyageur m.

globular a. globuleux

globule n. globule m.

gloom n. obscurité f.; tristesse f.; —y a. lugubre, triste, morne

glorify vt. glorifier

glorious a. glorieux, illustre

glory n. gloire f.; — (in) vi. se glorifier, s'enorgueillir (de)

gloss n. lustre, éclat m.; vernis m.; glose f.; — vt. gloser; rendre éclatant; — over mettre en ordre; fausser; —iness n. poli, lustre, brillant m.; —y a. poli, éclatant; brillant

glossary n. glossaire m.

glottal a., — stop coup de glotte m.

glottis n. glotte f.

glove n. gant m.; — store, — shop ganterie f.; — vt. ganter

glow n. lueur f.; — vi. luire, briller; —ing a. rayonnant; luisant; rouge; chaleureux

glower vi. froncer le sourcil, regarder en menaçant

glowworm n. ver luisant m.

glucose n. glucose m.

glue n. colle f.; — vt. coller

glum a. sombre, mélancolique; —ness n. tristesse, mélancolie f.

glut n. abondance f.; satiété f.; — vt. rassasier; (com.) inonder

glutton n. glouton, gourmand m.; —ous a. glouton; —y n. gourmandise f.

glycerine n. glycérine f.

gnarled a. noueux

gnash vt. grincer (des dents)

gnat n. moucheron m.

gnaw vt. ronger; —ing a. rongeur; —ing n. rongement m.

go n. énergie f.; essai m.; succès m.; have a — at essayer; make a — of réussir à; no — échec m.; on the — actif; — vi. aller; s'en aller; marcher, fonctionner; — against s'opposer à; — ahead aller au-devant, prévenir; continuer; — astray s'égarer; — at attaquer, approcher; — away s'en aller; — back on ne pas tenir (la parole donnée); — by agir selon; passer; croiser; — down descendre; tomber; — for aller chercher; (coll.) aimer; — in for participer à; faire; — into entrer dans; — off partir; s'en aller; — on continuer; se passer; — out sortir; — over se convertir; franchir; examiner; — through traverser; — to it! allez-y; — under succomber; submerger; — with accompagner; — without se passer de; let — of lâcher; —ing a. actif; courant; —ing n. départ m.; allée f.

goad n. aiguillon m.; — vt. aiguillonner, piquer, exciter

go-ahead a., — signal signal d'aller en avant m.; permission d'agir f.

goal n. but m.

goalie, goalkeeper n. but m.

goat n. chèvre f.; bouc m.

goatee n. barbiche f.

gobble vi. gober; — up avaler; —r n. dinde f.; dindon m.

go-between n. entremetteur m.; intermédiaire m. & f.

goblet n. coupe f.

goblin n. lutin m.

God, god n. Dieu, dieu m.; — forbid! à Dieu ne plaise!; — willing plût à Dieu; thank — grâce à Dieu; —less a. impie; —like a. de dieu; —liness n. piété, dévotion f.; —ly a. pieux; de dieu

goddaughter n. filleule f.

goddess n. déesse f.

godfather n. parrain m.

God-fearing a. élevé dans la crainte de Dieu; craignant Dieu

Godforsaken a. perdu

godmother n. marraine f.

godsend n. aubaine f.

godson n. filleul m.

Godspeed n. succès m.

goggles n. pl. lunettes (d'aviateur) f. pl.

goiter n. goitre m.

gold n. or m.; — brick n. lingot d'or m.; — dust poussière d'or f.; — leaf or en feuille m.; — rush ruée vers l'or f.; — standard étalon d'or m.; —en a. d'or; —en mean juste milieu m.

goldfish n. poisson rouge m.

gold-plated a. plaqué d'or

goldsmith n. orfèvre m.

golf n. golf m.; — course, — links golf m.; — club club m.; — vi. jouer au golf; —er n. golfeur m.

gondola n. gondole f.

gondolier n. gondolier m.

gonorrhoea n. gonorrhée f.

good a. bon; valable; sage; for — pour toujours; have a — time s'amuser; in — time bien à temps; it's no — ça ne vaut pas la peine; ça ne vaut rien; make — réussir; indemnifier; that's very — of you c'est bien aimable à vous; — morning bonjour; — afternoon bonjour; — evening bonsoir; bonjour; — night bonsoir; (before retiring) bonne nuit; — turn service m.; bonne action f.; — will bonne volonté f.; (com.) clientèle f.; — n. bien m.; —s pl. biens m. pl.; possessions f. pl.; produits m. pl.; tissu m.; —! for you! interj. très bien!; bravo!; à la bonne heure!; —ly a. considérable; —ness n. bonté f.; for —ness' sake pour l'amour de Dieu; my —ness mon Dieu

good-by(e) n. adieu m.; — interj. adieu; au revoir

good-for-nothing n. vaurien m.

Good Friday n. vendredi saint m.

goodhearted a. charitable

good-humored a. de bonne humeur

goodies n. pl. (coll.) friandises f. pl.

good-looking a. beau (belle), joli

good-natured a. aimable, paisible; accomodant, obligeant

goon n. (coll.) terroriste professionnel m.

goose n. oie f.; — flesh, — pimples chair de poule f.; — step pas d'école m., pas de l'oie m.

gooseberry n. groseille verte f.

gopher n. (genre de) rongeur m.

gore n. sang m.; pointe f.; piqûre f.; — vt. percer, piquer

gorge n. gorge f.; — vi. se gorger

gorgeous a. splendide; fastueux

gory a. ensanglanté, sanglant

gosling n. oison m.

gospel n. évangile m.

gossamer n. toile d'araignée f.; gaze f.; — a. ténu

gossip n. commère, causeuse f.; commérage m.; — vi. bavarder; faire des commérages

Gothic a. gothique; (arch.) ogival

gouge n. gouge f.; — vt. arracher; gouger

goulash n. ragoût m.

gourd n. calebasse f.; gourde f.

gourmet n. gourmet m.

gout n. goutte f.

govern vt. & vi. gouverner; diriger, régler; —ess n. institutrice f.; gouvernante f.; —ment n. gouvernement m.; —mental a. gouvernemental; —or n. gouverneur, préfet m.; —orship n. poste de gouverneur m.

gown n. robe f.; —ed a. en robe

grab vt. saisir, se saisir de; — n., — bag sac à surprises m.

grace n. grâce, faveur f., bienfait m.; (before meals) bénédicité m.; — vt. orner, honorer; —ful a. gracieux; —fulness n. grâce f. —less a. sans grâce

grace note (mus.) note d'agrément f.

gracious a. gracieux; favorable; — interj. mon Dieu; —ness n. grâce f.; bienveillance f.

grade n. grade, rang m.; pente f.; montée f.; (educ., mark) note f.; (educ., class) classe f.; — crossing passage à niveau m.; — school école primaire f.; — vt. niveler; évaluer; noter; graduer

gradient a. & n. montée, descente f.

gradual a. graduel

graduate vt. graduer; décerner un diplôme; — vi. recevoir un diplôme; — n. verre gradué m.; (educ.) étudiant diplômé m.; ancien élève m.

graduation n. graduation f.; décernement d'un diplôme m.; réception d'un diplome f.

graft vt. greffer; — n. greffe f.; (pol.) pot-de-vin m.; corruption f.

graham wheat n. blé entier m.; — bread n. pain bis m.

grain n. grain, blé m.; (wood) grain m.; — alcohol n. alcool ordinaire n.; — elevator n. élévateur à grain m.; against the — à rebrousse-poil; — vt. grainer, veiner

gram n. gramme m.

grammar n. grammaire f.; — school école primaire f.; —ian n. grammairien m.

grammatical a. grammatical

Granada n. Grenade f.

granary n. grenier m.

grand a. grand; sublime; illustre; — jury jury d'accusation m.; — larceny grand larcin m.; — opera opéra m.; — piano piano à queue m.; — slam (cards) grand chelem m.

grandchild n. petit-enfant m.

granddaughter n. petite-fille f.

grandee n. grand m.

grandeur n. grandeur f.

grandfather n. grand-père, aïeul m.

grandiose a. grandiose

grandiloquent a. pompeux, emphatique

grandmother n. grand'mère f.

grandnephew n. petit-neveu

grandniece n. petite-nièce f.

grandparents n. grands-parents m. pl.

grandson n. petit-fils m.

grandstand n. gradins m. pl., tribune f.

grange n. ferme, métairie f.; grange f.

granite n. granit m.

grant n. concession f.; (educ.) bourse f.; subvention f.; — vt. accorder; décerner; octroyer; reconnaître; take for —ed supposer, présumer

granular a. granulaire

granulate vt. granuler; —ed sugar sucre en poudre m.

grape n. raisin m.; —shot (mil.) mitraille f.; bunch of —s n. grappe de raisin(s) f.

grapefruit n. grappefruit m., pamplemousse m.

graph n. courbe f.; —ology n. graphologie f.; — vt. représenter en courbe; —ic a. graphique; vivant

graphite n. graphite m.; mine de plomb f.

grapple vi. lutter; — with (fig.) s'attaquer à

grasp vt. prise f.; connaissance f.; (with)in one's — entre ses mains; à sa portée; — vt. prendre, saisir; comprendre; —ing a. avide

grass n. herbe f., gazon m.; blade of — brin d'herbe m.; —y a. couvert d'herbe

grasshopper n. sauterelle, cigale f.

grass roots a. populaire, du peuple

grate n. grille f., treillis m.; foyer m.; gril m.; — vt. râper; (sound) grincer; — vi. choquer, ennuyer; —r n. râpe f.

grateful a. reconnaissant; —ness n. reconnaissance f.

gratification n. gratification, récompense f.; satisfaction f.

gratified a. content, satisfait

gratify vt. gratifier, récompenser; satisfaire; —ing a. agréable

grating n. grille f.; (sound) grincement m.; — a. ennuyant, choquant

gratis adv. gratuitement, gratis

gratitude n. reconnaissance f.

gratuitous a. gratuit

gratuity n. gratification f.; pourboire m.

grave n. fosse f., tombeau m.; — a. grave; sérieux; — vt. graver; —ness n. gravité f.

gravedigger n. fossoyeur m.

gravel n. gravier m.; (med.) gravelle f.

gravestone n. pierre tombale f.

graveyard n. cimetière m.

gravitate vi. graviter

gravitation n. gravitation f.

gravity n. gravité f.

gravy n. sauce f.; — boat saucière f.

gray a. gris; **-ish** a. grisâtre; **turn —** (hair) grisonner

gray-haired a. aux cheveux gris

graze vt. faire paître; effleurer, raser; — vi. paître

grazing, grazing ground n. pâturage m.

grease n. graisse f.; — vt. graisser; — **cup** n. godet graisseur m.

grease gun n. graisseur m.

grease paint n. fard m.; crayon gras m.

greasy a. graisseux; gras

great a. grand; gros; éminent; **a — deal, a — many** beaucoup; **to a —** extent en grande partie; **-ly** adv. grandement, fort, beaucoup; **-ness** n. grandeur f.; pouvoir m.; force f.

greatcoat n. capote f.

great-grandchild n. arrière-petit-fils m., arrière-petite-fille f.

great-grandfather n. arrière-grand-père m.

great-grandmother n. arrière-grand'mère f.

Grecian a. grec (grecque)

Greece n. Grèce f.

greed n. avidité, cupidité f.; **-iness** n. cupidité f.; **-y** a. avide, cupide

Greek n. & a. Grec (Grecque)

green a. vert; frais, récent; jeune; novice; **— light** (coll.) voie libre f.; **— thumb** (coll.) capacité de cultiver un jardin avec succès; — n. vert m.; verdure f.; (golf) pelouse d'arrivée f.; **-s** n. pl. légumes verts m. pl.; **-ery** n. verdure f.; **-ish** a. verdâtre; **-ness** n. vert m.; verdeur f.; verdure f.

green-eyed a. aux yeux verts; (coll.) jaloux

greengage n. reine-claude f.

greenhouse n. serre f.

Greenland n. Groënland m.; **Greenland** m.

greet vt. & vi. saluer; **-ing** n. salut m.

gregarious a. grégaire, qui vit en troupe

Gregorian a. grégorien

grenade n. grenade f.

grenadine n. grenadine f.

grid n. gril m.; grillage m.; **— line** ligne de quadrillage f.

griddle n. poêle plate sans bords f.

gridiron n. gril m.; terrain de football m.

grief n. chagrin, regret m., affliction, douleur f.

grief-stricken a. accablé, affligé (de douleur)

grievance n. grief, tort m.; abus m.

grieve vt. chagriner, affliger; — vi. se chagriner, s'affliger, se désoler

grievous a. grave, affligeant; horrible

grill n. gril m.; mixed **—** grillade f.; — vt. cuire sur le gril; faire griller; (coll.) cuisiner

grim a. renfrogné, hideux, effrayant; sérieux; lugubre

grimace n. grimace f.; — vi. grimacer

grime n. crasse f.; saleté; poussière de charbon f.

grimy a. noirci, sale; (face) barbouillé

grin n. sourire m.; — vi. sourire

grind vt. moudre; broyer; aiguiser; — n. (coll.) tâche désagréable f.; broiement m.; **-er** n. broyeur m.; organ **-er** joueur d'orgue de Barbarie m.; **-ing** n. meulage m.; (sound) grincement m.

grindstone n. pierre à aiguiser f.; meule f.

grip n. empoignement m.; griffe f.; prise f.; levier m.; pouvoir m.; valise f.; — vt. saisir; serrer; fasciner; **-ping** a. fascinant; passionnant

gripe n. plainte, réclamation f.; — vi. se plaindre, faire des réclamations

grisly a. horrible, hideux

grist n. blé à moudre m.; profit m.

gristle n. cartilage m.

gristly a. cartilagineux

grit vt. se grincer (les dents); — n. grès m.; sable m., poussière sablonneuse f.; (coll.) courage m.; **-s** n. pl. (food) gruau m.; **-ty** a. sablonneux

grizzled a. grisonnant

grizzly a. grisonnant; **— bear** ours gris m.

groan n. gémissement m.; — vi. gémir, soupirer; **-ing** n. gémissement m.

grocer n. épicier m.; marchand de comestibles m.; **-y** n. épicerie f.; magasin d'alimentation m.; **-ies** n. pl. épicerie f.; alimentation f.; provisions f. pl.

grog n. grog m.; **-gy** a. étourdi, ébloui; ivre, gris

groin n. aine f.; (arch.) arête f.

groom n. palefrenier m.; marié m.; — vt. soigner; (horse) panser

groove n. rainure f.; sillon m.; — vt. rainer, rainurer

grope vi. tâtonner, aller à tâtons

groping a. tâtonnant; — n. tâtonnement m.; **-ly** adv. à tâtons

gross n. grosse f.; — a. gros, épais; grossier; rude, brut; **-ness** n. grossièreté f.; **-ly** adv. grossièrement, fortement

grotesque a. grotesque

grotto n. grotte f.

grouch n. personne maussade f.; — vi. se plaindre; **-y** a. maussade

ground n. terrain, champ m.; terre f.; pays m.; lieu m.; raison f.; (elec.); **-s** n. pl. lie f.; raison, cause f.; prise de terre f.; **— floor** rez-de-chaussée m.; — vt. mettre à terre; garder à terre; établir une prise de terre; fonder; **-ing** n. (elec.) mise à terre f.; (avi.) période dans laquelle on refuse la permission de voler f.; **-less** a. sans fondement; **— breaking** premiers coups de pioche faits au début d'une entreprise de construction m. pl.

groundwork n. fondement m.; travail préliminaire m.

group n. groupe m.; cercle m.; — vt. grouper; — vi. se grouper; **-ing** n. groupement m.

grouse n. coq de bruyère m.; — vi. grogner, ronchonner

grove n. bocage m., bosquet m.

grovel vi. ramper; se vautrer

grow vt. cultiver; faire pousser; — vi. croître, pousser; grandir; augmenter; s'élargir, se développer; devenir, se faire; **— from** prendre racine dans; prendre naissance dans; **— old** vieillir; **— up** grandir, mûrir; **-er** n. cultivateur m.; -ing a. croissant; grandissant; -ing n. croissance f.; culture f.; développement m.; -th n. croissance f., poussée f.; développement m.; (med.) excroissance f.; tumeur f.

growl n. grondement m.; — vi. gronder

grub n. larve f.; ver m.; (coll.) soupe, nourriture f.; — vi. piocher; bêcher, creuser; -by a. sale

grudge n. rancune f.; envie f.; bear a — against, have a — against en vouloir à; — vt. refuser; envier

grudgingly adv. à contre-cœur

gruel n. gruau m., bouillie f.

grueling a. écrasant, épuisant

gruesome a. lugubre, terrifiant

gruff a. refrogné, brusque; -ness n. brusquerie f.

grumble vi. grogner, grommeler

grumbling a. grognon; — n. grognonnement m.

grumpy a. maussade

grunt n. grognement m.; — vi. grogner

Guadeloupe n. Guadeloupe f.

guarantee n. garant f.; garantie, caution f.; — vt. garantir; -d a. (com.) avec garantie

guarantor n. garant f.

guard n. (person) garde m.; garde, protection f.; advance — avant-garde f.; on — en garde, prévenu; (mil.) en faction, de faction; — vt. garder, protéger; — against se protéger contre; -ed a. voilé, circonspect; -ian n. tuteur m., tutrice f.; -ian a. gardien; -ianship n. tutelle f.; -rail n. garde-fou, parapet m.

guardhouse n. corps-de-garde m.; guérite f.; prison militaire f.

Guatemala n. Guatémala m.

guava n. goyave f.

gubernatorial a. de gouverneur

guerilla n. partisan m.; — warfare guerre de guerillas, guerre de partisans f.

guess n. conjecture f.; — vt. & vi. deviner, conjecturer; — vt. croire, penser, estimer

guesswork n. conjecture f.

guest n. hôte, convive, invité m.

guffaw n. gros rire m.

Guiana n. Guyane f.

guidance n. conseils m. pl.; gouverne f.; orientation f.

guide n. guide, conducteur m.; exemple m.; — vt. guider, conduire, mener; -d a., -d missile engin téléguidé m.

guidebook n. guide m.

guidepost n. poteau indicateur m., borne f.

guiding a. directeur

guild n. société, compagnie f.

guile n. fourberie, tromperie, ruse f.; artifice m.; -ful a. rusé; -less a. simple, sans artifice

guillotine n. guillotine f.; — vt. guillotiner

guilt n. crime m., culpabilité, faute f.; -less a. innocent; -y a. coupable

guinea n. guinée f.; — hen n. poule de Guinée f.; — pig cochon d'Inde m.; sujet d'une expérience m.

Guinea n. Guinée f.

guise n. manière, f.; extérieur m.; in the — of sous la forme de; sous l'apparence de

guitar n. guitare f.

gulch n. ravin m.

gulf n. golfe m.; gouffre m.

Gulf Stream n. Gulf-Stream m.

gull n. mouette f.

gullet n. gosier m., gorge f.

gullibility n. crédulité f.

gullible a. facile à duper, crédule

gully n. ravin m.

gulp n. gorgée f.; trait m.; — vt. avaler (avec avidité)

gum n. gomme f.; (anat.) gencive f.; chewing — chewing gum m.; — tree gommier m.; — vt. gommer; -med a. gommé; -my a. gommeux

gumdrop n. pâte de fruits f.; loukoum m.

gumption n. esprit m., cervelle, initiative f.

gun n. fusil m.; arme à feu f.; canon m.; pistolet m.; revolver m.; -ner n. canonnier m.; -nery n. tir m.; — barrel canon m.

gunboat n. canonnière f.

gunfire n. fusillade, canonnade f.; coups de feu m. pl.

gunman n. gangster m.; bandit m.

gunny sack n. sac de serpillière m.

gunpowder n. poudre à canon f.

gunshot n. coup de fusil, coup de canon m.; portée de fusil, portée de canon f.

gunsmith n. armurier m.

gunwale n. plat-bord m.

gurgle vi. glousser; glou-glouter; murmurer; — n. gloussement m.; glou-glou m.; murmure m.

gush n. écoulement, flux m.; jaillissement m.; — vi. jaillir; ruisseler; -er n. puits à pétrole m. (dont le pétrole jaillit à flots); -ing a. jaillissant; chaleureux

gust n. bouffée de vent f.; -y a. orageux

gusto n. goût m.; entrain m.

gut n. boyau, intestin m.; -s pl. (coll.) toupet m.; courage m.; — vt. vider, étriper; détruire, laisser en ruines

gutter n. gouttière f., ruisseau m.; (coll.) rue f.

guttersnipe n. gamin m.

guttural a. guttural

guzzle vt. & vi. boire avidement

gym, gymnasium n. gymnase m.

gymnastic a. gymnastique; -s n. pl. gymnastique f.

gynecologist n. gynécologue m.

gynecology n. gynécologie f.

gypsum n. gypse m.

gypsy n. Bohémien m., (fig.) bohême m. & f.; — a. bohémien, de bohême

gyrate vi. tourner

gyration n. gyration, giration f.

gyrocompass n. gyro-compas m.

gyroscope n. gyroscope m.

H

haberdasher n. marchand de vêtements pour hommes m.; -y n. vêtements d'homme m. pl.

habit n. habitude, coutume f.; disposition f.; habit, habillement, vêtement m.; **break oneself of the —** of se déshabituer de; **get into the —of** s'habituer à; -ual a. habituel; -ually adv. d'habitude, d'ordinaire; -uate vt. habituer, accoutumer

habitation n. demeure, habitation f.

hack n. (blow) entaille f.; (cab) fiacre m.; (writer) écrivassier m.; — vt. & vi. hacher, donner des coups de hache

hackneyed a. banal, trivial

haddock n. merluche f.

hag n. sorcière f.; furie f.

haggard a. hagard, farouche

haggle vi. marchander

Hague n., **The — La Haye** f.

hail n. grêle f.; — vt. saluer; héler; — vi. (weather) grêler; — **from** être originaire de; — interj. salut!

hailstone n. grêlon m.

hailstorm n. tempête de grêle f.

hair n. cheveu m., cheveux m. pl.; poil m.; fil m.; **split** — **s** couper les cheveux en quatre; -less a. chauve, sans cheveux; sans poil; -y a. poilu; velu; chevelu

hairbrush n. brosse à cheveux f.

haircut n. coupe (des cheveux) f.

hairdo n. coiffure f.

hairdresser n. coiffeur m., coiffeuse f.; -'s salon de coiffure m.

hairpin n. épingle à cheveux f.; — **turn** lacet m.

hair-raising a. terrifiant

hairsplitting n. ergoterie f.

Haiti n. Haïti f.

hale a. sain, vigoureux

half n. moitié f.; demi m.; — a. demi; — **a dozen** une demi-douzaine f.; — **an hour** une demi-heure f.; — **fare** demi-place f.; — adv. à demi, à moitié

half-breed n. métis m.

halfhearted a. (fait) sans enthousiasme

half-hour n. demi-heure f.

half-light n. pénombre f.

half-mast n., **at —** en berne

half-moon n. demi-lune f.

half note (mus.) blanche f.

half-turn n. demi-révolution f.

halfway adv. à mi-chemin

half-wit n. idiot m.; niais m.; -ted a. faible d'esprit; idiot; niais

halibut n. flétan m.

halitosis n. mauvaise haleine f.

hall n. vestibule m.; corridor m.; couloir m.; salle f.

hallmark n. marque, estampille f.

hallow vt. consacrer, bénir; **All Hallows** n. la Toussaint f.

Halloween n. veille de la Toussaint f.

hallucinate vt. halluciner

hallway n. corridor m.; couloir m.

halo n. halo m., auréole f.

halt n. halte f.; arrêt m.; — vi. halter, faire halte; s'arrêter; —! halte!; -ing a. hésitant; -ingly adv. en hésitant

halter n. corde f.; licou m.

halve vt. diviser en deux (parties)

ham n. jambon m.; (coll.) cabotin m.;

radio amateur m.; — **and eggs** œufs au jambon m. pl.

Hamburg n. Hambourg

hamburger n. viande hâchée f.; sandwich à la viande hâchée m.

hamlet n. hameau m.

hammer n. marteau m.; (gun) chien m.; — vt. marteler; forger; travailler

hammock n. hamac m.

hamper n. panier m.; — vt. embarrasser, gêner

hamstring n. tendon du jarret m.; — vt. couper le jarret à; rendre inactif, rendre incapable d'action

hand n. main f.; (watch) aiguille f.; (worker) ouvrier m.; (help) coup de main m.; (applause) applaudissements m. pl.; (writing) écriture f.; (measure) palme f.; (cards) jeu m., partie f.; (naut.) matelot m.; **at —** sous la main; **at first —** de première main; **be on —** être présent; (com.) être en caisse; **by —** à la main; **change —s** changer de possesseur; **from — to —** de main en main; **get out of —** échapper au contrôle; **—s down** sans peine; **—s off!** interj. n'y touches pas!; **—s up!** interj. haut les mains!; **in —** en main; **lend a (helping) —** donner un coup de main; **— of God** doigt de Dieu m.; **on —** disponible; **old —** vétéran m.; **on the one —** d'un côté; **on the other —** de l'autre côté, d'autre part; **shake —s (with)** serrer le main (à); **upper —** dessus m.; — vt. donner; livrer; présenter; **— down** prononcer (un jugement); **— in** remettre; **— out** distribuer; **— over** céder; **— up** passer en haut; -iness n. habileté f.; -y a. habile, utile

handbag n. sac à main m.

handball n. pelote f.

handbill n. affiche f., prospectus m.

handbook n. manuel m.

handclasp n. poignée de main f.

handcuff vt. mettre les menottes à; (fig.) lier les mains à, empêcher d'agir; -s n. pl. menottes f. pl.

handful n. poignée f.

handicap n. handicap m.; incapacité f.; — vt. handicaper; incapaciter

handicraft n. métier m.; artisanat m.

handiwork n. travail à la main m.; ouvrage m.

handkerchief n. mouchoir m.

handle n. manche m., anse f.; queue (d'une poêle) f.; poignée f.; — vt. manier, traiter; diriger

handle bar n. guidon m.

handling n. maniement m.; manutention f.; traitement m.; direction f.

handmade a. fait à la main

handout n. aumône f.

hand-picked a. soigneusement choisi

handrail n. rampe f.

handshake n. poignée de main f.

handsome a. beau, élégant; généreux; -ness n. beauté f.; générosité f.

hand-to-hand adv. corps à corps

hand-to-mouth a. au jour le jour

handwriting n. écriture f.
handwritten a. manuscrit
handyman n. bricoleur, homme à tout faire m.
hang vt. pendre; suspendre; tapisser; — vi. être pendu; être suspendu; être en suspens; balancer; dépendre; — around fréquenter; flâner; — on se cramponner; subsister; — out (coll.) se rassembler; demeurer; — up pendre; (telephone) raccrocher; — get the — of comprendre; s'habituer à, se faire à; -er n. portemanteau m.; -ing n. tenture f.; (human beings) pendaison f.
hangar n. hangar m.
hangdog a. honteux, contrit
hangman n. bourreau m.
hangnail n. envie f.
hangout n. repaire, lieu fréquenté m.; rendez-vous m.
hang-over n. gueule de bois f.
hank n. botte f.; écheveau m.
hanker vi. soupirer (après); -ing n. désir, souhait m., envie f.
hansom n. cabriolet de place m.
haphazard n. chance f.; — a. fortuit, accidentel
hapless a. malheureux, infortuné
happen vi. arriver, avoir lieu, se passer; -ing n. événement m.
happiness n. bonheur m., félicité f.
happy a. heureux; content; propice
happy-go-lucky a. sans souci
harangue vt. haranguer; — vi. faire un discours; — n. discours m., harangue f.
harass vt. tourmenter; harceler; -ment n. harcèlement m.
harbinger n. avant-coureur m.
harbor n. port m.; — vt. héberger; entretenir; — master n. capitaine de port m.
hard a. dur; difficile; drive a — bargain conclure un marché très avantageux; — and fast établi, inébranlable; — cash espèces sonnantes et trébuchantes f. pl.; — cider cidre fermenté m.; — coal anthracite m.; — labor travaux forcés m. pl.; — liquor n. alcool m.; whisky m.; — luck guigne f.; be — of hearing avoir l'oreille dure; — to please exigeant; regardant; — up pauvre; — adv. fort; dur; ferme; fixement; try — bien essayer; -en vt. durcir; -en vi. se durcir; -ly adv. à peine; ne . . . . guère; presque; -ness n. dureté f.; difficulté f.; -ship n. difficulté, pénurie f.
hard-earned a. bien gagné
hardhearted a. dur, sans compassion
hardihood n. hardiesse, audace f.
hardiness n. hardiesse f.
hardly adv. à peine; — ever presque jamais
hardtack n. biscuit de mer m.
hardware n. quincaillerie f.; — store quincaillerie f.
hardwood n. bois dur m.
hard-working a. industrieux, assidu
hardy a. hardi, brave, courageux; robuste
harebrained a. écervelé

harelip n. bec de lièvre m.
harem n. harem, sérail m.
hark vt. & vi. écouter; —! interj. écoutez!
harlequin n. arlequin m.
harlot n. prostituée f.
harm n. tort, mal m.; dommage m.; malheur m.; — vt. faire du mal à; -ful a. dangereux; nuisible; -less a. innocent; sans danger
harmonica n. harmonica m.
harmonious a. harmonieux
harmonize vt. rendre harmonieux; accorder; — vi. être d'accord, s'accorder
harmony n. harmonie f.
harness n. harnais m.; — vt. (en)harnacher; (fig.) maîtriser
harp n. harpe f.; — on revenir sur, rabâcher; -ist n. joueur de harpe m., harpiste m. & f.
harpoon n. harpon m.; — vt. harponner
harpsichord n. clavecin m.
harpy n. harpie f.
harrow n. herse f.; — vt. herser; torturer; -ing a. terrifiant
harry vt. harceler
harsh a. rude; âpre; sévère; dur; -ness n. sévérité f.; rudesse f.
harum-scarum a. écervelé
harvest n. moisson, récolte f.; — vt. moissonner; -er n. moissonneur m.; (machine) moissonneuse f.
has-been n. (coll.) personne qui n'est plus en vue f.; vedette qui n'est plus à la mode f.
hash n. hachis m.; (fig.) gâchis m.; — vt. hacher
hasp n. loquet m.; morailion m.
hassock n. pouf m.
haste n. hâte, diligence f.; in — à la hâte; -n vi. se dépêcher; -n vt. dépêcher, hâter
hastily adv. à la hâte; précipitamment; trop vite; sans trop y penser
hastiness n. hâte, précipitation f.
hasty a. hâtif; prompt, précipité
hat n. chapeau m.; opera — chapeau claque m.; top — chapeau haut de forme m.; -less sans chapeau; (woman) en cheveux; -ter n. chapelier m.
hatband n. ruban (de chapeau) m.
hatbox n. carton de modiste m.; (luggage) étui à chapeau m.
hatch n. couvée f.; guichet m.; (naut.) panneau m.; — vt. & vi. couver; tramer
hatchet n. hachette f.
hate n. haine f.; — vt. haïr, détester; -ful a. haïssable
hatpin n. épingle à chapeau f.
hat rack n. porte-chapeaux m.
hatred n. haine, détestation f.
haughtiness n. hauteur f., orgueil m.
haughty a. hautain, orgueilleux
haul n. action de tirer f.; trait m.; (coll.) coup m.; — vt. tirer, traîner, haler
haunch n. hanche f.
haunt n. lieu fréquenté m.; retraite f.; — vt. hanter, fréquenter, visiter; -ed a. fréquenté par des revenants; -ing a. obsédant
Havana n. La Havane f.

have vt. avoir, posséder; contenir; — on porter, être vêtu de; — something done faire faire quelque chose; — to devoir; avoir à

haven n. port, havre m.

haversack n. havresac m.

havoc n. ravage, dégât m.

Hawaii n. Hawaï m.

hawk n. faucon m.; épervier m.; — vi. chasser au faucon; — vt. colporter; -er n. colporteur m.

hawk-eyed a. aux yeux d'épervier, qui a la vue bonne

hawser n. haussière f., grelin m.

hay n. foin m.; — fever fièvre des foins f.

hayloft n. grange à foin f.

haymaker n. faneur m.; (coll.) coup très fort m.

haystack n. tas de foin m., meule de foin f.

hazard n. hasard, risque m.; chance f.; — vt. hasarder, risquer; -ous a. hasardeux, dangereux

haze n. brouillard m., brume f.; — vt. (coll.) berner

hazy a. nébuleux, sombre; vague; (weather) brumeux

he pron. il, lui; celui; ce

head n. tête f.; chef m.; sommet m.; source f.; (beer) mousse f.; titre m.; at the — en tête; by a — à une tête de distance; come to a — mûrir; suppurer; atteindre le point culminant; from — to foot des pieds à la tête; go to one's — monter à la tête de quelqu'un; — first tête première; — of hair chevelure f.; — over heels pêle-mêle; — or tail pile ou face; I can't make — or tail of it je n'y comprends goutte; keep one's — rester tranquille; lose one's — perdre la tête; out of one's — fou; put -s together prendre conseil; take it into one's — avoir l'idée de; — a. premier; en chef; de tête; — vt. diriger, commander; — off prévenir; détourner; -ing n. titre m.; -less a. sans tête

headache n. mal de tête m.; (coll.) souci m.

headband n. bandeau m.

headdress n. coiffure f.

headland n. cap, promontoire m.

headlight n. phare, feu de route m.

headline n. titre, en-tête m.

headlong adv. précipitamment; — a. précipité

headmaster n. proviseur m.; principal m.

head-on adv. face à face; de front

headphone n. écouteur m.

headpiece n. coiffure f.

headquarters n. quartier général m., état-major m.; police — commissariat m.

headrest n. appui-tête m.

headsman n. bourreau m.

headstone n. pierre tombale f.

headstrong a. têtu, obstiné

headwaiter n. maître d'hôtel m.

headwater(s) n. (pl.) source(s) d'un fleuve f. (pl.)

headway n. progrès m.; make — progresser

head wind n. vent contraire m.

heal vt. guérir; — vi. guérir, se guérir, se remettre; -ing n. guérison f.

health n. santé f.; -ful a. sain; salubre; -y a. sain, salutaire; salubre

heap n. tas, amas m.; foule f.; — vt. entasser; amasser; combler

hear vt. entendre; ouïr; entendre dire; apprendre, savoir; — of, — about entendre parler de; -ing n. audience f.; audition f.; (sense) ouïe f.; oreille f.; hard of -ing dur d'oreille

hearken vi. écouter

hearsay n. ouï-dire, bruit m.

hearse n. corbillard m.

heart n. cœur m.; centre m.; milieu m.; fond m.; courage m.; at — au fond; broken — chagrin m.; by — par cœur; have the — avoir le courage; sick at — chagrin, désolé; to one's -'s content à volonté; — and soul corps et âme; — attack (med.) crise cardiaque f.; — trouble maladie de cœur f.; -en vt. encourager; réjouir; -ily adv. sincèrement; ardemment; -iness n. sincérité f.; cordialité f.; -less a. sans cœur; cruel; -y a. sincère; généreux; cordial; chaleureux; copieux; en bonne santé

heartache n. souffrance f.; chagrin m.

heartbeat n. pouls, battement de cœur m.

heartbreaking a. navrant

heartbroken a. désolé, navré, chagrin

heartburn n. dyspepsie f.

heartfelt a. qui vient du cœur

hearth n. foyer, âtre m.

heart-rending a. désolant, navrant, affligeant

heartsick a. désolé, chagrin

heart-to-heart a. intime; sérieux; — adv. à cœur ouvert

heat n. chaleur f.; chaud m.; ardeur f.; animosité f.; (sports) course f., manche f.; dead — partie nulle f.; in — en chaleur; prickly — démangeaison, éruption (due à la chaleur) f.; — wave période de chaleur f.; — vt. chauffer; échauffer; — vi. chauffer; s'échauffer; — up chauffer, réchauffer; -ed a. chauffé; chaud; -er n. réchaud m.; radiateur m.; water -er chauffe-eau m.; -ing n. chauffage m.; -ing pad chauffe-corps m.

heath n. bruyère f.

heathen n. & a. païen m.

heat-resistant a. à l'épreuve de la chaleur, calorifuge; isolant

heatstroke n. insolation f.

heave n. soulèvement m.; soupir m.; secousse f.; — vt. lever, soulever, pousser; lancer, jeter; — vi. se soulever; s'enfler; palpiter

heaven n. ciel m.; -s! interj. ciel!; -ly a. céleste, divin

heavily adv. lourdement; fortement; avec difficulté

heaviness n. pesanteur f.; poids m.; langueur f., ennui m.

heavy a. pesant, lourd; gros; (phy.) grave

heavyweight n. poids-lourd m.

Hebrew a. & n. hébreu m.

heckle *vt.* taquiner, se moquer (de); interrompre; ennuyer; *-r n.* critique moqueur *m.*

hectic *a.* agité

hectograph *n.* appareil à polycopier *m.*; — *vt.* polycopier

hedge *n.* haie *f.*; — *vt.* entourer d'une haie; — *vi.* reculer, hésiter

hedgerow *n.* haie *f.*

hedging *n.* indécision *f.*; hésitation *f.*

hedonist *n.* hédoniste *m. & f.*

heed *n.* soin *m.*, attention *f.*; — *vt.* prendre garde, observer, écouter; *-ful a.* attentif; *-less a.* inattentif; négligent

heel *n.* talon *m.*; (coll.) goujat *m.*; take to one's *-s* prendre la fuite; — *vt.* mettre des talons (à); — *vi.* (naut.) pencher

hefty *a.* robuste, fort

heifer *n.* génisse *f.*

height *n.* hauteur, élévation *f.*; altitude *f.*; sommet *m.*; grandeur *f.*; *-en vt.* rehausser; perfectionner, embellir; accentuer

heinous *a.* odieux; atroce

heir *n.* héritier *m.*; — apparent héritier présomptif *m.*; *-ess n.* héritière *f.*

heirloom *n.* bijou de famille, meuble de famille *m.*

helicopter *n.* hélicoptère *m.*

heliport *n.* aéroport pour hélicoptères *m.*

helium *n.* hélium *m.*

hell *n.* enfer *m.*; *-ish a.* infernal, diabolique

Hellenic *a.* hellène; hellénique

hello *interj.* bonjour; (telephone) âllô

helm *n.* casque *m.*; (naut.) gouvernail *m.*; timon *m.*; *-sman n.* timonier *m.*

helmet *n.* casque *m.*

help *n.* aide *f.*, secours *m.*; employés *m. pl.*; *-l interj.* au secours!; — *vt.* aider, secourir; — oneself se défendre; (food) se servir; — out donner un coup de main; I cannot — it ce n'est pas de ma faute; *-er n.* aide *m.*; *-ful a.* utile, secourable; *-ing n.* portion *f.*; *-ing a.* utile; *-less a.* sans secours; impuissant

helpmate *n.* aide *m. & f.*; épouse *f.*

helter-skelter *adv.* en désordre, pêle-mêle

hem *n.* ourlet, bord *m.*; — *vt. & vi.* ourler, border; — in *n.* cerner, entourer

hemisphere *n.* hémisphère *f.*

hemoglobin *n.* hémoglobine *f.*

hemophilia *n.* hémophilie *f.*

hemorrhage *n.* hémorrhagie *f.*

hemorrhoids *n. pl.* hémorrhoïdes *f. pl.*

hemp *n.* chanvre *m.*; *-en a.* de chanvre

hemstitch *vt.* ourler à jour

hen *n.* poule *f.*

hence *adv.* d'ici; donc, pour cette raison, par conséquent

henceforth *adv.* désormais, dorénavant

henchman *n.* bras droit, partisan *m.*

hencoop *n.* cage à poules *f.*

henhouse *n.* poulailler *m.*

henna *n.* henné *m.*

henpeck *vt.* maltriser; harceler; *-ed a.*, *-ed husband* mari docile, mari harcelé sans cesse par sa femme *m.*

heptagonal *a.* heptagone; heptagonal

her *a.* son, sa, ses; — *pron.* elle; la; lui; *-s pron.* le sien, la sienne; à elle

herald *n.* héraut *m.*; avant-coureur *m.*; — *vt.* annoncer; *-ic a.* héraldique; *-ry n.* blason *m.*

herb *n.* herbe *f.*; *-age n.* herbage *m.*

herbaceous *a.* herbacé

herbivorous *a.* herbivore

herd *n.* troupeau *m.*, troupe *f.*; foule *f.*; — *vi.* vivre en troupeau; — *vt.* grouper, mener; élever (des animaux); *-er n.* berger *m.*; *-sman n.* berger *m.*

here *adv.* ici; — below ici-bas; — comes voici; — is voici; — lies ci-gît; *-'s* to you à votre santé; that's neither — nor there ça n'a rien à faire

hereabouts *adv.* aux environs, près d'ici

hereafter *adv.* à l'avenir, désormais; ci-dessous; — *n.* avenir *m.*, vie future *f.*

hereby *adv.* par ce moyen

hereditary *a.* héréditaire

heredity *n.* hérédité *f.*

herein *adv.* ci-inclus; ici

heresy *n.* hérésie *f.*

heretic *n.* hérétique *m. & f.*; *-al a.* hérétique

heretofore *adv.* jusqu'ici

herewith *adv.* ci-joint

heritage *n.* héritage *m.*

hermetic *a.* hermétique; *-ally adv.* hermétiquement

hermit *n.* hermite *m.*; *-age n.* hermitage *m.*

hernia *n.* hernie *f.*

hero *n.* héros *m.*; *-ic a.* héroïque; *-ics n. pl.* héroïsme ostentatoire *m.*; *-ine n.* héroïne *f.*; *-ism n.* héroïsme *m.*

heroin *n.* héroïne *f.*

herring *n.* hareng *m.*; smoked — hareng saur *m.*

herringbone *n.* point de chausson *m.*

herself *pron.* elle-même; soi

hesitancy *n.* hésitation *f.*

hesitant *a.* hésitant

hesitate *vi.* hésiter

hesitation *n.* hésitation *f.*

heterodox *a.* hétérodoxe

heterogeneous *a.* hétérogène

hew *vt.* couper, tailler

hexagon *n.* hexagone *m.*; *-al a.* hexagonal

hexameter *n.* hexamètre *m.*

heydey *n.* meilleure période *f.*; fleur *f.*

hiatus *n.* hiatus *m.*; lacune *f.*

hibernate *vi.* hiberner

hibernation *n.* hibernation *f.*

hiccup, hiccough *n.* hoquet *m.*; — *vi.* avoir le hoquet

hide *n.* peau *f.*; cuir *m.*

hide *vt.* cacher; — *vi.* se cacher; de dérober

hide-and-seek *n.* cache-cache *m.*

hidebound *a.* étroit; conservateur

hideous *a.* hideux; effroyable; horrible; atroce; *-ness n.* horreur *f.*; laideur *f.*; atrocité *f.*

hide-out *n.* retraite *f.*, abri *m.*; cachette *f.*

hiding *n.*, in — caché; — place cachette *f.*

hierarchy *n.* hiérarchie *f.*

hieroglyph *n.* hiéroglyphe *m.*; *-ics n. pl.* hiéroglyphes *m. pl.*

hi-fi *a.* (coll.) de haute fidélité; — radio-phonographe de haute fidélité *m.*

high *a.* haut, élevé; sublime; grand; fort; gros; (meat) avancé; (wind) violent; (coll.) saoul, gris; — and dry échoué; abandonné; leave — and dry abandonner; — and low partout; — and mighty hautain; act — and mighty le prendre de haut; — jump saut en hauteur *m.*; — noon plein midi *m.*; — priest grand prêtre *m.*; — school école secondaire *f.*; — seas haute mer *f.*; — sign signal *m.*; — stakes gros jeu *m.*; — voltage haute tension *f.*; — water marée haute *f.*; in — spirits joyeux, gai; it is — time il est bien temps; — *adv.* haut, en haut; — record *m.*; —er *a.* plus haut, plus élevé; supérieur; —ly *adv.* très, fort; think very —ly of avoir une très bonne opinion de; estimer beaucoup; —ness *n.* hauteur *f.*; élévation *f.*; (title) Altesse *f.*

high-and-low *adv.* de tous côtés

highball *n.* whisky à l'eau, cognac à l'eau *m.*, fine à l'eau *f.*

highborn *a.* de haute naissance

highboy *n.* chiffonnier *m.*

highbrow *a.* (coll.) intellectuel, de l'élite; hautain

high-class, high-grade *a.* de (première) qualité, supérieur

high-flown *a.* ampoulé

high-frequency *a.* à haute fréquence

highhanded *a.* arbitraire

highland *m.* pays montagneux *m.*; montagnes *f. pl.*; —er *n.* montagnard *m.*

highlight *n.* chose principale *f.*; événement le plus important *m.*

high-minded *a.* magnanime

high-pitched *a.* aigu

high-powered *a.* de haute puissance; fort, puissant

high-pressure *a.* à haute pression; insistant

high-priced *a.* cher, coûteux

high-sounding *a.* beau, impressionnant (mais vide)

high-spirited *a.* joyeux, gai; fougueux

high-strung *a.* nerveux

high-test *a.* (gasoline) très raffinné

highway *n.* route *f.*; grand'route *f.*; grand chemin *m.*

highwayman *n.* voleur des grands chemins *m.*

hijack *vt.* (coll.) arrêter (un camion) sur la route et en voler les marchandises; —ing *n.* vol à main armée (d'un camion) sur la route *m.*

hike *n.* longue promenade à pied *f.*; — *vi.* faire de longues promenades à pied; — *vt.* (coll.) hausser, augmenter

hiking *n.* longue(s) promenade(s) à pied *f. (pl.)*

hilarious *a.* gai, joyeux

hilarity *n.* gaieté *f.*

hill *n.* colline, côte *f.*, coteau *m.*; pente *f.*; montée *f.*; descente *f.*; —y *a.* montagneux

hillbilly *n.* (coll.) montagnard du Sud des Etats-Unis *m.*

hillock *n.* petite colline *f.*; butte *f.*

hillside *n.* (flanc de) coteau *m.*

hilt *n.* poignée, garde *f.*, manche *m.*

him *pron.* lui; le

himself *pron.* lui-même; se

hind *n.* biche *f.*

hind *a.* postérieur, de derrière; — legs pattes de derrière *f. pl.*; —quarters *n.* arrière-train *m.*

hinder *vt.* empêcher; embarrasser; troubler

hindmost *a.* dernier

hindrance *n.* empêchement, obstacle *m.*

hindsight *n.* expérience acquise après l'événement *f.*, conscience de qu'on aurait dû faire *f.*

Hindu *a. & n.* hindou *m.*

hinge *n.* gond *m.*; pivot *m.*; charnière *f.*; — *vi.* tourner; dépendre

hint *n.* suggestion, insinuation *f.*; avis *m.*; demi-mot *m.*; soupçon *m.*; give a —, drop a — donner un bienveillant avis; take a — accepter un conseil; know how to take a — entendre à demi-mot; — *vt.* suggérer, donner à entendre

hinterland *n.* arrière-pays *m.*

hip *n.* hanche *f.*

hire *n.* louage *m.*; location *f.*; for — à louer; — *vt.* louer; employer

hireling *n.* mercénaire *m.*; laquais *m.*

hirsute *a.* velu, poilu

his *a.* son, sa, ses; — *pron.* le sien, la sienne; à lui

Hispanic *a.* hispanique

hiss *vt. & vi.* siffler; — *n.* sifflement *m.*; —ing *n.* sifflement(s) *m. (pl.)*

histology *n.* histologie *f.*

historian *n.* historien *m.*

historic(al) *a.* historique

history *n.* histoire *f.*

histrionic *a.* de comédien, de la scène; —s *n. pl.* art du théâtre *m.*

hit *n.* coup *m.*; atteinte *f.*; succès *m.*, réussite *f.*; be a —, make a — réussir; — *vt.* frapper, atteindre; se heurter contre; — it off s'entendre, se trouver d'accord; — the ceiling (coll.) se mettre en colère; — the jackpot (coll.) gagner le prix; faire fortune d'un seul coup; — the spot plaire, satisfaire; rafraîchir

hitch *n.* saccade *f.*; entrave *f.*, obstacle *m.*, condition *f.*; (naut.) nœud *m.*, (coll.) période de service militaire *f.*; — *vt.* atteler, attacher

hitchhike *vi.* faire de l'autostop

hither *adv.* ici; — *a.* qui est de ce côté

hitherto *adv.* jusqu'ici

hit-or-miss *a. & adv.* à tout hasard

hive *n.* ruche *f.*

hives *n. pl.* (med.) éruption allergique *f.*

hoarfrost *n.* gelée blanche *f.*

hoarse *a.* enroué, rauque; —ness *n.* enrouement *m.*

hoary *a.* blanc; blanchi; gris

hoax *n.* mystification *f.*; — *vt.* mystifier

hobble *vi.* clocher, boiter; — *vt.* lier, attacher (par les pieds)

hobby *n.* distraction, marotte *f.*

hobbyhorse *n.* cheval d'enfant, cheval de bois *m.*

hobgoblin *n.* lutin *m.*

hobnail *n.* caboche *f.*

hobnob vi. — with frequenter, s'associer avec

hobo n. chemineau, vagabond m.

hock n. jarret m.; vin du Rhin m.; **in** — (coll.) en gage; — **shop** (coll.) mont de piété m.; — vt. mettre en gage

hockey n. hockey m.

hocus-pocus n. jonglerie f., tour de passe-passe m.

hod n. hotte, auge f.; — **carrier** aide-maçon m.

hodgepodge n. salmigondis m.; mélange m.

hoe n. houe, binette f.; — vt. houer, sarcler

hog n. cochon, porc, pourceau m.

hogshead n. barrique f.

hoist vt. lever, guinder; — n. poulie, grue f.

hold n. prise f.; appui m.; pouvoir m.; (naut.) cale f.; **get** — **of, take** — **of** prendre, saisir, se saisir de; — vt. tenir; prendre; avoir; retenir; détenir; maintenir, soutenir; arrêter; estimer, penser, croire; — vi. tenir; — **back** retenir; — **forth** discourir; — **good** être valable; — **no water** être défectueux; — **off** hésiter, attendre; — **on** tenir; subsister; — **one's own** tenir ferme; se défendre; — **one's tongue** se taire; — **out against** résister à; — **over** continuer, remettre; — **together** tenir; — **true** être vrai; — **up** retarder; voler (à main armée); — **with** être du même avis que; approuver; souffrir, supporter; — **er** n. propriétaire m. & f.; détenteur m.; (cigarettes) porte-cigarette m.; — **ing** n. possession f.; tenue f.

holdup n. vol à main armée m.

hole n. trou m.; orifice m.; (coll.) mauvais pas m.; — vt. trouer, percer

holiday n. jour de fête m., fête f.; jour férié m.

holiness n. sainteté f.

Holland n. Hollande f.

hollow n. creux, trou m.; cavité f.; — a. creux; enfoncé; peu sincère; (sound) sourd; — vt. creuser; évider

hollow-cheeked a. aux joues creuses

holly n. houx m.

hollyhock n. rose trémière f.

holster n. fourreau de pistolet m.; gaine f.

holocaust n. holocauste m.

holy a. saint; béni, sacré; — **water** eau bénite f.

Holy Week n. semaine sainte f.

homage n. hommage m.

home n. maison f.; logis m., demeure f.; foyer m.; intérieur m.; patrie f.; **at** — chez soi; à la maison; **make oneself at** — se mettre à l'aise, faire comme chez soi; — a. de (la) famille; familial; — **rule** autonomie f.; **-stretch** dernière étape f.; — **team** locaux m. pl.; — **town** ville natale f.; — adv. à la maison, chez soi; **strike** — frapper juste

homeland n. patrie f.; pays m.

homelike a. familial, comme à la maison

homeliness n. laideur f.

homely a. laid

homemade a. fait à la maison

homemaker n. femme d'intérieur f.; épouse f.

homesick a. qui a le mal du pays; **-ness** n. mal du pays m.

homespun n. filé à la maison; grossier

homestead n. maison, propriété f.

homeward(s) adv. à la maison, vers la maison

homework n. devoirs à faire à la maison m. pl.

homicidal a. homicide, meurtrier

homicide n. homicide m.

homily n. homélie f.

homing pigeon n. pigeon voyageur m.

hominy n. gruau de maïs m.

homogeneous a. homogène

homogenize vt. homogénéiser

homologous a. homologue

homonym n. homonyme m.

homosexual a. homosexuel

Honduras n. pl. Honduras m. pl.

hone vt. affiler; (razor) repasser

honest a. honnête; sincère; loyal; **-y** n. honnêteté, probité f.; sincérité f.

honey n. miel m.; douceur f.; (coll.) chérie f.; **-ed** a. emmielé, couvert de miel; mielleux, onctueux; **-bee** abeille, mouche à miel f.

honeycomb n. rayon de miel n.; — vt. veiner

honeydew melon n. melon espagnol m.

honeymoon n. lune de miel f.

honk n. bruit de klaxon m.; cornement m.; — vi. klaxonner, corner

honor n. honneur m.; dignité f.; **word of** — parole d'honneur f.; — vt. honorer; **-able** a. honorable; **-able mention** m. accessit; **-ary** a. honoraire; **-ary degree** grade honoris causa m.; **-ed** a. honoré; honorable

hood n. chaperon m.; capuchon m.; (auto) capote f.; (coll.) gangster m.; **-ed** a. à capuchon

hoodwink vt. tromper; mystifier

hoof n. sabot m.

hoofbeat n. pas de cheval m.

hook n. crochet m.; crampon m.; hameçon m.; — **and eye** agrafes f. pl.; —, **line and sinker** tout à fait; **by** — **or by crook** n'importe comment; — vt. accrocher; prendre; — vi. s'accrocher; — **up** accrocher; **-ed** a. crochu; fait au crochet; pris

hookup n. chaîne f.

hooky n., **play** — faire l'école buissonnière

hoop n. cercle m.; cerceau m.; — **skirt** jupe à panier f.

hoot n. huée f.; **owl's** — ululement m.; — vi. huer; ululer

hop n. saut, bond m.; (bot.) houblon m.; (avi.) escale, étape f.; — vi. sauter, sautiller

hope n. espérance f., espoir m.; — vi. espérer; **-ful** a. qui a de l'espoir; prometteur; **-less** a. sans espoir, désespéré; (person) incorrigible

hopper n. trémie f.

hopscotch n. marelle f.

horde n. horde, troupe f.

horizon n. horizon m.; –tal a. horizontal

hormone n. hormone f.

horn n. corne f.; cor m.; (auto) klaxon m.; draw in one's –s (fig.) rentrer les cors; –ed a. cornu, à cornes; –ed owl duc m.; –y a. de corne

hornpipe n. cornemuse f.; danse des matelots f.

horn-rimmed a. en corne

horoscope n. horoscope m.

horrible a. horrible, terrible

horrid a. horrible; affreux

horrify vt. horrifier

horror n. horreur f.

horror-stricken a. épouvanté

hors d'œuvre n. hors-d'œuvre m.

horse n. cheval m.; cavalerie f.; — chestnut marron d'Inde m.; — race course de chevaux f.; — racing courses de chevaux f. pl.; — sense (coll.) bon sens m.; get on one's high — monter sur ses grands chevaux; ride a — monter (à cheval)

horsefly n. taon m.

horsehair n. crin m.

horseman n. cavalier; –ship équitation f.

horsepower n. cheval-vapeur m.

horse-radish n. raifort m.

horseshoe n. fer (à cheval) m.

horsewhip n. cravache f.; — vt. fouetter

horsewoman n. cavalière, amazone f.

horticultural a. horticulture f.; jardinage m.

horticulturist n. horticulteur m.

hose n. bas m. pl.; tuyau m.; (garden) tuyau d'arrosage m.; — vt. arroser

hosiery n. bonneterie f.; bas m. pl.

hospitable a. hospitalier

hospital n. hôpital m.; –ization insurance assurance médicale f.

hospitality n. hospitalité f.

host n. hôte m.; armée f.; (eccl.) hostie f.; –ess n. hôtesse f.

hostage n. otage m.

hostel n. hôtel m., auberge f.; youth — auberge de la jeunesse f.

hostility n. hostilité f.

hot a. chaud; ardent, violent; échauffé; be — être chaud; (person) avoir chaud; (weather) faire chaud; — air bavardage m.; — dog saucisse de Francfort f.; — water (coll.) situation difficile f.

hotbed n. couche f.; (fig.) centre, foyer m.

hot-blooded a. fougueux

hotel n. hôtel m.

hothouse n. serre chaude f.

hot plate n. réchaud, chauffe-assiette m.

hot rod n. (coll.) vieille auto dont la puissance a été fortement augmentée f.

hot-tempered a. colérique

hot-water bottle n. bouillotte f.

hot-water heater n. chauffe-eau m.

hound n. chien de chasse m.; — vt. persécuter, poursuivre, harceler

hour n. heure f.; by the — à l'heure; half an — demi-heure f.; per — à l'heure; for –s pendant des heures; –hand petite aiguille f.; –ly adv. toutes les heures

hourglass n. sablier m.

house n. maison, habitation f.; ménage f.; logis m.; (legislature) chambre f.; private — maison particulière f.; keep — tenir maison, tenir le ménage; — vt. loger, abriter

houseboat n. bateau-maison m.

housebreaker n. cambrioleur m.

housebreaking n. cambriolage m., effraction f.

housebroken a. (animals) dressé

housecoat n. peignoir m.

housefly n. mouche (commune) f.

houseful n. pleine maison f.

household n. famille f., ménage m.; — a. de ménage, de la maison, de famille

housekeeper n. femme de menage f.

housekeeping n. ménage f.

housemaid n. bonne f.

house physician n. médecin interne m.

housetop n. toit m.

housewarming n. pendaison de la crémaillère f.

housewife n. mère de famille, ménagère f.

housework n. travail de ménage m.

housing n. logement m.; boîte f.; enchâssure f.; (machinery) housse, monture f.

hovel n. taudis m.

hover vi. voltiger; rôder; hésiter

how adv. comment; comme; (in exclamations) que, comme; — about (doing) si nous faisions . . . .; — are you? comment-allez-vous?; comment ça va?; — do you do enchanté; — much, many combien de; — often? combien de fois?; — old are you? quel âge avez-vous?

however adv. cependant, pourtant, toutefois; quelque . . . . que

howitzer n. obusier m.

howl vi. hurler; — n. hurlement m.

hub n. moyeu m.; (fig.) centre m.

hubbub n. tumulte m., remue-ménage m.

hubcap n. couvre-moyeu m.

huckleberry n. airelle f.

huckster n. revendeur m.; agent de publicité m.

huddle n. groupe, tas m.; — vi. se grouper, se réunir; –d a. blotti; entassé

hue n. couleur, teinte f.; cri m.; — and cry cri de haro m.

huff n. accès de colère, emportement m.; –y a. brusque; irrité, arrogant

hug n. étreinte f.; — vt. étreindre; embrasser, serrer; rester près de; longer, raser

huge a. vaste; énorme, immense; –ness n. énormité, immensité f.

Huguenot n. Huguenot m.

hulk n. (person) pataud m.; (ship) carcasse f.; –ing a. gros, lourd

hull n. (bot.) cosse, coque f.; (ship) coque f.; — vt. écosser

hullabaloo n. tumulte, brouhaha m.

hum n. bourdonnement m.; ronflement m.; — vi. bourdonner; ronfler; (song) chantonner

human n. & a. humain m.; –e a. humain; humanitaire; –ism n. humanisme m.; –ist n. humaniste m.; –itarian a. & n.

humanitaire *m.*; –ity *n.* humanité *f.*;
–ize *vt.* rendre humain; –kind *n.* genre
humain *m.*

humble *vt.* humilier, abattre; — *a.* humble, modeste; –ness *n.* humilité *f.*

humbly *adv.* modestement; avec humilité

humbug *n.* charlatan *m.*; blague, duperie
f.

humdrum *a.* banal; ennuyeux

humerus (anat.) humérus *m.*

humid *a.* humide, moite; –ifier *n.* humidificateur *m.*; –ify *vt.* humidifier; –ity *n.*
humidité *f.*; –or *n.* boîte à tabac *f.*

humiliate *vt.* humilier

humiliation *n.* humiliation *f.*

humility *n.* humilité *f.*

hummock *n.* tertre *m.*

humor *n.* humeur *f.*, disposition du
caractère *f.*; humour, comique, esprit
m.; bad — mauvaise humeur *f.*; — *vt.*
ménager, accéder (aux lubies d'une
personne); –ist *n.* humoriste *m.*; –ous
a. comique, spirituel; humoristique

hump *n.* bosse *f.*

hunch *n.* bosse *f.*; (coll.) pressentiment
m.; — *vi.* s'accroupir

hunchback *n.* bossu *m.*; –ed *a.* bossu

hundred *n.* cent *m.*, centaine *f.*; — *a.* cent;
–fold *adv.* au centuple; –th *a.* centième

hundredweight *n.* quintal *m.* (50 kilogrammes)

Hungarian *a. & n.* hongrois *m.*

Hungary *n.* Hongrie *f.*

hunger *n.* faim *f.*; — *vi.* avoir faim

hungrily *adv.* avidement

hungry *a.* affamé; be — avoir faim

hunk *n.* (coll.) gros morceau *m.*

hunt *n.* chasse *f.*; poursuite *f.*; recherches
f. pl.; — *vi.* chasser; — for chasser;
chercher; –er *n.* chasseur *m.*; chercheur
m.; –ing *n.* chasse *f.*; –ress *n.* chasseresse *f.*; –sman *n.* chasseur *m.*

hurdle *n.* claie *f.*; haie *f.*; barrière *f.*; –s
pl. (sports) course d'obstacle *f.*; — *vi.*
faire une course à la haie

hurdy-gurdy *n.* vielle *f.*; orgue de Barbarie
f.

hurl *vt.* lancer, jeter; précipiter; — back
repousser, refouler

hurly-burly *n.* tohu-bohu, tintamarre *m.*

hurrah *interj. & n.* hourra *m.*

hurricane *n.* ouragan *m.*

hurried *a.* pressé, rapide

hurry *n.* hâte, précipitation *f.*; to be in a
— être pressé; there is no — cela ne
presse pas; — *vt.* presser, hâter; —
vi. se dépêcher, se hâter; — away s'en
aller vite; — back revenir vite; retourner vite; — on se presser, continuer
rapidement; — over venir vite; aller
vite; — up se dépêcher

hurt *n.* mal *m.*, blessure *f.*; tort, dommage
m.; — *vt.* faire tort à; faire mal à;
blesser; — *a.* blessé; –ful *a.* nuisible

hurtle *vi.* se précipiter

husband *n.* mari, époux *m.*; — *vt.*
ménager; cultiver; –ry *n.* agriculture
f.; élevage *m.*

hush *n.* silence *m.*; — *vt.* faire taire; —
vi. se taire; — *interj.* chut!

husk *n.* cosse, gousse, peau *f.*; — *vt.*
écosser

husky *n.* chien arctique, chien esquimau
m.; — *a.* gros, costaud; fort; (voice)
enroué

hussar *n.* hussard *m.*

hussy *n.* gueuse, coquine *f.*; effrontée *f.*

hustle *n.* (coll.) énergie, activité *f.*;
ambition *f.*; — *vt.* presser, pousser; —
vi. se presser; –r *n.* (coll.) débrouillard
m.

hut *n.* hutte, cabane *f.*

hutch *n.* huche *f.*

hybrid *a. & n.* hybride *m.*

hydrant *n.* bouche à eau, bouche d'incendie *f.*

hydraulic *a.* hydraulique; –s *n.* hydraulique *f.*

hydrocarbon *n.* hydrocarbone *m.*

hydrochloric *a.* chlorhydrique

hydrodynamic *a.* hydrodynamique; –s *n.*
hydrodynamique *f.*

hydroelectric *a.* hydroélectrique

hydrogen *n.* hydrogène *f.*; — bomb bombe
à hydrogène *f.*; — peroxide *n.* eau
oxygénée *f.*

hydrolysis *n.* hydrolyse *f.*

hydrophobia *n.* hydrophobie *f.*

hydroplane *n.* hydravion *m.*

hydroponics *n. pl.* culture de légumes
dans une solution aqueuse *f.*

hydrostatics *n. pl.* hydrostatique *f.*

hydrotherapy *n.* hydrothérapie *f.*

hygiene *n.* hygiène *f.*

hygienic *a.* hygiénique

hymn *n.* hymne *m.*; –al *n.* livre d'hymnes
m.

hyperbola *n.* (math.) hyperbole *f.*

hypercritical *a.* critique à l'excès

hypersensitive *a.* excessivement sensible

hypertension *n.* hypertension *f.*

hypertrophy *n.* hypertrophie *f.*

hyphen *n.* trait d'union *m.*; –ate *vt.*
écrire avec un trait d'union

hypnosis *n.* hypnose *f.*

hypnotic *a.* hypnotique

hypnotism *n.* hypnotisme *m.*

hypnotize *vt.* hypnotiser

hypo *n.* (coll.) fixateur *m.*, hyposulfite de
soude *m.*

hypochondria *n.* hypocondrie *f.*; –c *n.*
hypocondriaque *m.*

hypocrisy *n.* hypocrisie *f.*

hypocrite *n.* hypocrite *m.*

hypocritical *a.* hypocrite

hypodermic *a.* hypodermique; — syringe
n. seringue à injections *f.*

hypotenuse *n.* hypoténuse *f.*

hypothesis *n.* hypothèse *f.*

hypothetic *a.* hypothétique

hysteria *n.* hystérie *f.*

hysterical *a.* hystérique

hysterics *n. pl.* hystérie *f.*; crise de nerfs *f.*

I

I *pron.* je; moi

ice *n.* glace *f.*; — cream glace(s) *f.* (*pl.*);
— water eau glacée; — age *n.* période glaciaire *f.*; — *vt.* glacer; refroidir; frapper;

—d a. glacé

ice bag n. sac à glace m.

icebound a. pris dans la glace

icebox n. glacière

icebreaker n. brise-glace m.

ice-cream cone n. glace en cornet f.

Iceland n. Islande f.; -ic a. & n. islandais m.

iceman n. glacier m.

ichthyology n. ichtyologie f.

icicle n. glaçon m.

iciness n. froideur f.

icing n. fondant m.

icon n. icone f.

iconoclasm n. iconoclasme m.

iconoclast n. iconoclaste m.; -ic a. iconoclaste

icy a. glacé; glissant

idea n. idée f.; notion f.

ideal n. & a. idéal m.; -ism n. idéalisme m.; -ist n. idéaliste m. & f.; -istic a. idéaliste; -ize v. idéaliser

identical a. identique

identification n. identification f.; — card, — papers carte d'identité f.

identify v. identifier

identity n. identité f.

ideological a. idéologique

ideology n. idéologie f.

idiocy n. idiotisme m., idiotie f.

idiom n. idiome m.; idiotisme m. -atic a. idiomatique

idiosyncrasy n. idiosyncrasie f.

idiot n. idiot, benêt m.; -ic a. idiot

idle vi. être oisif, fainéanter; (engine) tourner au ralenti; — away perdre; — a. inoccupé; au repos; paresseux, oisif; vain; perdu; -ness n. oisiveté f.; -r n. flâneur m.; paresseux m.

idol n. idole f.; -ater n. idolâtre m.; -atrous a. idolâtre; -atry n. idolatrie f.; -ize vt. idolâtrer, adorer

idyl(l) n. idylle f.; -lic a. idyllique

i.e.: it est c'est-à-dire

if conj. si; — not sinon; — so dans ce cas

igneous a. ignée

ignite vt. allumer, incendier; — vi. prendre feu

ignition n. allumage m.; — switch contacteur du démarreur m.

ignominious a. ignominieux

ignominy n. ignominie f.

ignoramus n. ignorant m.

ignorance n. ignorance f.

ignorant a. ignorant; be — of ignorer

ignore vt. dédaigner, ne pas faire attention à; ne pas tenir compte de

ilium n. (anat.) ilion m.

ilk n. espèce f., genre m.

ill n. mal, malheur m.; — a. malade, souffrant; mauvais; mal; become — tomber malade; — at ease mal à l'aise; — health mauvaise santé; — adv. mal; -ness n. maladie f.

ill-advised a. mal conseillé

ill-bred a. mal élevé

ill-considered a. (fait) sans réflexion

ill-disposed a. mal disposé

illegal a. illégal; illicite; -ity n. illégalité f.

illegible a. illisible

illegitimate a. illégitime

ill-fated a. malheureux

ill feeling n. rancune f.

ill-founded a. mal fondé

ill-gotten a. mal acquis

ill-humored a. maussade; de mauvaise humeur

illicit a. illicite, défendu

illiteracy n. analphabétisme m.

illiterate a. illettré

ill-mannered a. impoli

ill-natured a. maussade

illogical a. illogique

ill-starred a. malheureux; de mauvais augure

ill-timed a. inopportun, déplacé

illuminate vt. illuminer, éclairer

illumination n. illumination f.; éclairage m.

illumine vt. illuminer

illusion n. illusion f.

illustrate vt. illustrer; expliquer, éclaircir

illustration n. illustration f.; gravure f.; explication f., éclaircissement m.

illustrative a. explicatif

illustrator n. dessinateur m.; illustrateur m.

illustrious a. illustre, célèbre

ill will n. mauvaise volonté f.

image n. image f.; portrait m.; -ry n. images f. pl.

imaginable a. imaginable, concevable

imaginary a. imaginaire, idéal

imagination n. imagination f.

imaginative a. imaginatif

imagine vt. imaginer; s'imaginer; inventer; se figurer

imbecile n. & a. imbécile, idiot m.

imbecility n. imbécillité f.

imbibe vt. absorber; boire, imbiber

imbue vt. imprégner, pénétrer

imitate vt. imiter

imitation n. imitation f.; (comm.) contrefaçon f.; — a. simili-; imitatif; factice

imitative a. imitatif

imitator n. imitateur m.

immaculate a. immaculé; impeccable

immanent a. immanent

immaterial a. immatériel; qui n'a rien à faire, qui n'a aucun rapport

immature a. vert, pas mûr

immaturity n. immaturité f.

immeasurable a. immesurable; incommensurable

immediate a. immédiat; urgent; -ly adv. tout de suite; aussitôt; immédiatement

immemorial a. immémorial, très-ancien

immense a. immense, vaste; -ly adv. énormément

immensity n. immensité f.

immerse vt. immerger; plonger

immersion n. immersion f.

immigrant n. immigrant m.

immigrate vi. immigrer

immigration n. immigration f.

imminence n. imminence f.

imminent a. imminent

immobility n. immobilité f.

immobilize vt. immobiliser

immoderate a. immodéré

immodest a. immodeste, impudique; -y n. immodestie f.

immolate vt. immoler

immolation n. immolation f.

immoral a. immoral; -ity n. immoralité f.

immortal a. immortel; -ity n. immortalité f.; -ize vt. immortaliser

immovable a. immobile; inébranlable; (fig.) insensible

immune a. immunisé

immunity n. immunité f.; exemption f.

immunization n. immunisation f.

immunize vt. immuniser

immutability n. immutabilité f.

immutable a. immuable, invariable

imp n. diablotin m.; petit drôle m.; -ish a. espiègle

impact n. impact m., collision f.; choc m.

impair vt. détériorer, affaiblir, diminuer; endommager

impale vt. empaler

impalpable a. impalpable

impart vt. donner, communiquer

impartial a. impartial; -ity n. impartialité f.

impassable a. impraticable; insurmontable

impassibility n. insensibilité f.

impassioned a. passionné

impassive a. insensible; impassible; -ness n. insensibilité f.; impassibilité f.

impatience n. impatience f.

impatient a. impatient; -ly adv. impatiemment

impeach vt. accuser; -able a. susceptible d'être accusé; attaquable; douteux; -ment n. accusation f.

impecunious a. indigent

impeccable a. impeccable

impedance n. impédance f.

impede vt. empêcher, arrêter, entraver

impediment n. empêchement, obstacle m.

impel vt. pousser, forcer

impend vi. menacer, être imminent; -ing a. imminent

impenetrability n. impénétrabilité f.

impenetrable a. impénétrable

imperative a. impératif; — n. impératif m.

imperceptible a. imperceptible, insensible

imperfect a. imparfait; -ion n. imperfection f.

imperial a. impérial; -ism n. impérialisme m.; -ist n. impérialiste m.; -istic a. impérialiste

imperil vt. mettre en danger

imperious a. impérieux, exigeant

impermeable a. imperméable

impersonal a. impersonnel

impersonate vt. personnifier; contrefaire, se déguiser en

impersonation n. personnification f.; rôle m.; représentation f.

impertinence n. impertinence f.

impertinent a. impertinent, insolent; sans aucun rapport

imperturbable a. imperturbable

impervious a. impénétrable, inaccessible; étanche

impetuosity n. impétuosité f.

impetuous a. impétueux

impetus n. impulsion, force motrice f.

impiety n. impiété f.

impinge vt. heurter; — on enfreindre

impious a. impie

implacability n. implacabilité f.

implant vt. implanter; imprimer; — n. implantation f.; (med.) greffe f.

implement n. outil, ustensile m.; — vt. exécuter, réaliser; complémenter; rendre effectif

implicate vt. impliquer

implication n. implication f.

implicit a. implicite; absolu

implied a. implicite

implore vt. implorer, supplier

imploring a. suppléant

imply vt. impliquer

impolite a. impoli; -ness n. impolitesse f.

imponderable a. impondérable

import n. importation f.; importance f.; sens m., valeur f.; — duty douane f.; — vi. importer; -ation n. importation f.; -er n. importateur m.; -ing n. importation f.

importance n. importance f.; be of — importer

important a. important; be — importer

importunate a. importun

importune vt. importuner

impose vt. imposer; — upon gêner, abuser de, en imposer à

imposing a. imposant; splendide, magnifique

imposition a. imposition f.; tromperie f.; impôt m.

impossibility n. impossibilité f.

impossible a. impossible

impostor n. imposteur m.

imposture n. imposture f.; tromperie f.

impotence n. impuissance f.; impotence f.

impotent a. (med.) impotent; impuissant; faible

impound vt. confisquer; mettre en fourrière (un animal)

impoverish vt. appauvrir

impracticability n. impossibilité f.

impracticable a. impraticable

impractical a. peu pratique

imprecate vt. maudire

imprecation n. malédiction f.

impregnable a. imprenable

impregnate vt. imprégner; féconder

impresario n. imprésario m.

impress n. empreinte, impression f.; — vt. imprimer, empreindre, graver; impressionner; enrôler par force; -ion n. impression f.; -ionable a. impressionnable; -ive a. impressionnant

impressionism n. impressionnisme m.

impressionist n. impressionniste m.; -ic a. impressioniste

imprint vt. empreindre, imprimer, graver; — n. empreinte f.

imprison vt. emprisonner; -ment n. emprisonnement m.; prison f.

improbability n. improbabilité f., invraisemblance f.

improbable a. improbable; invraisemblable

impromptu a. & n. impromptu m.

improper a. impropre; inconvenant

impropriety n. impropriété f.; inconvenance f.

improve vt. améliorer, perfectionner; — vi. s'améliorer, faire des progrès; –ment n. amélioration f.; perfectionnement m.

improvidence n. imprévoyance f.

improvident a. imprévoyant

improvisation n. improvisation f.

improvise vt. & vi. improviser

imprudence n. imprudence f.

imprudent a. imprudent

impudence n. impudence f.; effronterie, insolence f.

impudent a. impudent; effronté, insolent

impugn vt. attaquer; contester

impulse n. impulsion, incitation f.; mouvement m.

impulsive a. impulsif; –ly adv. par impulsion; d'un mouvement naturel

impunity n. impunité f.

impure a. impur; souillé

impurity n. impureté f.

impute vt. imputer, attribuer

in prep. en, dans; à; sous; sur; — adv. dedans; (pol.) au pouvoir; be — (at home) être chez soi, être la; — n. (coll.) entrée f.

inability n. incapacité f.

inaccessibility n. inaccessibilité f.

inaccessible a. inaccessible

inaccuracy n. inexactitude f.

inaccurate a. inexact

inaction n. inaction f.

inactive a. inactif

inactivity n. inactivité f.

inadequacy n. insuffisance f.

inadequate a. insuffisant

inadmissible a. inadmissible

inadvertence n. inadvertance f.

inadvertent a. négligeant; fait par mégarde; –ly adv. par mégarde

inadvisability n. inopportunité f.

inalienable a. inaliénable

inane a. idiot, stupide

inanimate a. inanimé

inapplicable a. inapplicable

inappropriate a. inopportun; pas convenable; impropre

inarticulate a. inarticulé

inasmuch as conj. vu que, attendu que

inattention n. inattention, négligence f.

inattentive a. inattentif

inaudible a. imperceptible

inaugurate vt. inaugurer

inauguration n. inauguration f.

inauspicious a. peu propice

inborn, inbred a. inné

incalculable a. incalculable

incandescence n. incandescence f.

incandescent a. incandescent

incantation n. incantation f.

incapability n. incapacité, impuissance f.

incapable a. incapable

incapacitate vt. rendre incapable

incapacity n. incapacité f.

incarcerate vt. incarcérer

incarceration a. emprisonnement m.

incarnation n. incarnation f.

incase vt. encaisser, enfermer

incautious a. négligent, imprudent

incendiary n. & a. incendiaire m.

incense n. encens m.; — vt. encenser; exaspérer; –d a. irrité

incentive n. motif m.; encouragement m.; ambition f.

inception n. début, commencement m.

incessant a. incessant, continuel; –ly adv. sans cesse

incidence n. incidence f.

incident n. incident m.; — a. accidentel, casuel; –al a. accidentel, fortuit; accessoire; –ally adv. par hasard; accessoirement; incidamment; à propos

incinerate vt. incinérer

incinerator n. four (à brûler les ordures) m.; incinérateur m.

incipient a. naissant, commençant

incise vt. inciser

incision n. incision f.

incisive a. incisif; pénétrant

incisor n. incisive f.

incite vt. inciter, exciter; –ment incitation, excitation f.

incivility n. incivilité f.

inclemency n. inclémence, intempérie f.

inclement a. inclément, rigoureux, dur

inclination n. inclination f., penchant m., inclinaison f.

incline n. pente f.; rampe f.; — vt. & vi. incliner, pencher; s'incliner; être porté à

include vt. renfermer, comprendre

including prep. y compris

inclusive a. inclus; y compris

incognito n. & adv. incognito m.

incoherence n. incohérence f.

incoherent a. incohérent

incombustible a. incombustible

income n. revenu m., rentes f. pl.; — tax n. impôt sur le revenu m.

incoming a. rentrant; nouveau

incommensurable a. incommensurable

incommode vt. incommoder

incommunicable a. incommunicable

incommunicado a. sans communication

incommutable a. incommuable

incomparable a. incomparable

incompatibility n. incompatibilité f.

incompatible a. incompatible

incompetence n. incompétence f.; incapacité f.

incompetent a. incompétent; incapable

incomplete a. incomplet, inachevé

incomprehensible a. incompréhensible

inconceivable a. inconcevable

inconclusive a. inconcluant, peu concluant

incongruity n. incongruité f.

incongruous a. incongru

inconsequent a. inconséquent; –ial a. inconséquent

inconsiderable a. insignifiant

inconsiderate a. inconsidéré

inconsistency n. incompatibilité, inconsistance, incongruité f.

inconsistent a. inconsistant, incompatible

inconsolable a. inconsolable

inconspicuous a. peu remarquable, peu en vue

inconstancy n. inconstance f.

incontestable a. incontestable

incontinence n. incontinence f.

incontinent a. incontinent

incontrovertible a. indisputable; incontestable

inconvenience n. incommodité f.; dérangement m.; — vt. troubler, déranger

inconvenient a. inopportun; incommode

incorporate vt. incorporer; — vi. s'incorporer; -d a. incorporé; (com.) anonyme

incorporation n. incorporation f.

incorrect a. incorrect; inexact

incorrigible a. incorrigible

incorruptible a. incorruptible

increase n. accroissement m.; augmentation f.; — vt. augmenter; accroître; redoubler; — vi. (s')augmenter; s'accroître

increasing a. augmentant, croissant; -ly adv. de plus en plus

incredible a. incroyable

incredulity n. incrédulité f.

incredulous a. incrédule

increment n. augmentation f.; accroissement, surcroît m.

incriminate vt. inculper, incriminer

incrust vt. incruster

incubate vt. & vi. couver

incubation n. incubation f.

incubator n. couveuse f.

incubus n. cauchemar, incube m.

inculcate vt. inculquer

inculpate vt. inculper

incumbent n. bénéficier m.; titulaire m.; — a. obligatoire; be — on incomber à

incur vt. encourir, s'attirer

incurable a. incurable

incursion n. irruption f.

indebted a. endetté; redevable; obligé; reconnaissant; -ness n. obligation f.

indecency n. indécence f.

indecent a. indécent

indecision n. indécision f.

indecisive a. indécis

indeed adv. en vérité, vraiment, réellement; en effet

indefatigable a. infatigable

indefensible a. indéfendable, insoutenable

indefinable a. vague; indéfinissable

indefinite a. indéfini

indelible a. indélébile, ineffaçable

indelicate a. indélicat, grossier

indemnify vt. indemniser, dédommager

indemnity n. indemnité f., dédommagement m.

indent vt. denteler; renfoncer; faire un alinéa; -ation n. denteleure f.; renforcement m.; alinéa m.

indenture n. contrat d'apprentissage m.; — vt. mettre en apprentissage

independence n. indépendance f.

independent a. indépendant

indescribable a. indescriptible

indestructible a. indestructible

indeterminable a. indéterminable

indeterminate a. indéterminé, indécis

index n. table des matières f.; index m.; — finger index m.; — vt. cataloguer, classer; faire l'index de

India n. Inden f., Indes f. pl.

Indian n. & a. Indien m.; — giver (coll.) homme qui veut qu'on lui rende le cadeau qu'il a fait m.; — Summer période de beau temps; qui suit la première gelée f.

indicate vt. indiquer

indication n. indication f., indice m.

indicative n. & a. indicatif m.

indicator n. indicateur m.; aiguille f.

indict vt. accuser; -ment n. acte d'accusation m.

Indies n. pl. Indes f. pl.; East — Indes orientales· West — Antilles f. pl.

indifference n. indifférence f.

indifferent a. indifférent

indigence n. indigence f.

indigenous a. indigène

indigent a. indigent

indigestible a. indigeste

indignant a. indigné

indignity n. indignité, injure f., affront m.

indigo n. indigo m.

indiscernible a. imperceptible

indiscreet a. indiscret

indiscretion n. indiscrétion f.; imprudence f.

indiscriminate a. sans discernement, sans distinction; indistinct, confus

indispensable a. indispensable

indispose vt. indisposer; rendre malade

indisposition n. indisposition, maladie f.

indisputable a. indisputable, incontestable

indistinct a. indistinct; vague

indistinguishable a. indistinct; imperceptible

individual n. individu m.; — a. individuel; -ism n. individualisme m.; -ity n. individualité f.

indivisible a. indivisible, inséparable

Indo-China n. Indochine f.

indoctrinate vt. indoctriner

Indo-European a. & n. indo-européen, aryen m.

indolent a. indolent

indomitable a. indomptable

Indonesia n. Indonésie f.

indoor a. d'intérieur; -s adv. à l'intérieur

indorse vt. endosser; -ment n. endos, endossement m.; (fig.) approbation f.; -r n. endosseur m.

induce vt. induire, persuader, engager, causer; -ment n. encouragement, motif m.

induct vt. installer; mobiliser; -ion n. induction f.; mobilisation f.; -ive a. (elec.) inducteur; inductif

indulge vt. avoir de l'indulgence pour; tolérer; — vi. s'abandonner (à); se laisser aller; — in se livrer à; se permettre; -nce n. indulgence f.; -nt a. indulgent

industrial a. industriel; -ism n. industrialisme m.; -ist n. industriel m.; -ization n. industrialisation f.; -ize vt. industrialiser; -ize vi. s'industrialiser

industrious a. industrieux, assidu

industry n. industrie f.

inebriate n. ivrogne m.; — vt. saouler, enivrer; -d a. ivre, saoul

ineffable a. ineffable, inexprimable

ineffective, ineffectual a. inefficace, inutile; -ness n. inefficacité f.

inefficacious a. inefficace

inefficacy n. inefficacité f.

inefficiency n. inefficacité f.

inefficient a. inefficace

ineligible a. inéligible

inept a. inepte; incapable; -itude, -ness n. ineptie f.; inaptitude f.

inequality n. inégalité f.

inequitable a. inéquitable

inert a. inerte, inactif; -ia n. inertie f.

inescapable a. inévitable

inestimable a. inestimable

inevitable a. inévitable

inexact a. inexact

inexcusable a. inexcusable

inexhaustible a. inépuisable

inexpensive a. bon marché, pas cher; -ness n. bon marché m.

inexperienced a. inexpérimenté

inexplicable a. inexplicable

inexpressible a. inexprimable

inextricable a. inextricable

infallibility n. infaillibilité f.

infallible a. infaillible

infamous a. infâme, honteux

infamy n. infamie f.

infancy n. première enfance f.

infant n. bebé m.; -icide n. infanticide m.; -ile a. enfantin; -ile paralysis n. poliomiélite m.; paralysie infantile f.

infantry n. infanterie f.; -man n. soldat d'infanterie m.

infatuate vt. infatuer; become -d s'engouer

infatuation n. engouement m.

infect vt. infecter; contagionner; -ion n. infection f.; contagion f.; -ious a. contagieux; infectieux

infer vt. inférer; -ence n. déduction, conclusion f.

inferior n. inférieur m.; — a. inférieur; subalterne, subordonné; -ity n. infériorité f.; — complex complexe d'infériorité m.

infernal a. infernal, d'enfer

inferno n. enfer m.

infest vt. infester

infidel n. infidèle m.; -ity n. infidélité f.

infiltrate vi. s'infiltrer (dans)

infinite a. infini

infinitesimal a. infinitésimal

infinitive n. infinitif m.

infinity n. infinité f.; infini m.

infirm a. infirme; irrésolu; -ary n. infirmerie f.; -ity n. infirmité f.

inflame vt. enflammer; irriter; — vi. s'enflammer

inflammable a. inflammable

inflammation n. inflammation f.

inflammatory a. inflammatoire; (fig.) incendiaire

inflate vt. gonfler; enfler; hausser

inflation n. gonflement m.; (finance) inflation f.

inflect vt. fléchir; (gram.) décliner, conjuguer; -ion n. inflexion f.

inflexibility n. inflexibilité f.

inflexible a. inflexible

inflict vt. infliger, imposer; -ion n. infliction f.

influence n. influence f.; (coll.) piston, bras long m.; — vt. influencer

influential a. influent

influenza n. grippe f.

influx n. flux m., affluence f.

inform vt. faire savoir; faire part à; avertir; renseigner; informer, instruire; — against dénoncer; -ant n. accusateur, dénonciateur; informateur m.; source f. (d'un renseignement); -ation n. renseignements m. pl.; piece of -ation renseignement m.; -ed a. instruit; -er n. dénonciateur m.

informal a. sans cérémonie; non-officiel; -ity n. manque de cérémonie m.

infraction n. violation, infraction f.

infrared a. infra-rouge

infrequent a. rare

infringe vt. enfreindre, violer; -ment n. infraction f.

infuriate vt. rendre furieux

infuse vt. infuser; inspirer

infusion n. infusion f.; inspiration f.

ingenious a. ingénieux, inventif

ingenuity n. génie m.; ingéniosité f.

ingenuous a. ingénu, naïf, candide; -ness n. ingénuité f.; naïveté, candeur f.

inglorious a. inglorieux; honteux

ingrained a. inné; enraciné

ingrate n. ingrat m.

ingratiate vt. mettre en faveur; — oneself se mettre en faveur; s'insinuer

ingratitude n. ingratitude f.

ingredient n. ingrédient m.

ingress n. entrée f.

ingrown a. retourné; tourné en dedans; — toenail ongle incarné m.

inhabit vt. habiter; -able a. habitable; -ant n. habitant m.

inhale vt. inspirer, aspirer

inharmonious a. inharmonieux

inherent a. inhérent

inherit vt. hériter; -ance n. héritage m.; -ance tax n. impôt de succesion m.

inhibit vt. prohiber; refouler; -ion n. prohibition f.; refoulement m.

inhospitable a. inhospitalier

inhuman a. inhumain; -ity n. inhumanité f.

inhume vt. inhumer, enterrer

inimical a. ennemi, hostile

inimitable a. inimitable

iniquitous a. inique, injuste f.

iniquity n. iniquité, injustice f.

initial n. initiale f.; — a. initial; — vt. parapher

initiate vt. initier; commencer

initiation n. initiation f.; commencement m.

initiative n. initiative f.; énergie f.

initiator n. initiateur m.

inject vt. injecter; piquer; -ion n. injection f.; piqûre f.

injudicious a. injudicieux

injunction n. injonction f.

injure vt. faire tort à; injurier; nuire; blesser

injurious a. injurieux; nuisible

injury *n.* injustice *f.*; tort *m.*; mal *m.*; blessure *f.*

injustice *n.* injustice, iniquité *f.*

ink *n.* encre *f.*; — blot pâté d'encre *m.*; India — encre de Chine *f.*; — *vt.* couvrir d'encre; —y *a.* couvert d'encre; très obscur, noir foncé

inkling *n.* pressentiment, soupçon *m.*

ink pad *n.* tampon à impression *m.*

inkwell *n.* encrier *m.*

inlaid *a.* marqueté, parqueté

inland *n. & a.* intérieur *m.*; — *adv.* vers l'intérieur

in-laws *n. pl.* parents par alliance *m. pl.*; beaux-parents *m. pl.*

inlay *vt.* marqueter; incruster; — *n.* marqueterie, incrustation *f.*

inlet *n.* anse *f.*; débouché *m.*; admission *f.*

inmate *n.* pensionnaire *m.*; prisonnier *m.*

inmost, innermost *a.* le plus intérieur; le plus intime

inn *n.* auberge *f.*

innate *a.* inné

inner *a.* intérieur; — tube chambre à air *f.*; —most *a.* le plus intime

inning *n.* (baseball) période *f.*

innkeeper *n.* aubergiste *m.*

innocence *n.* innocence *f.*

innocent *a. & n.* innocent *m.*

innocuous *a.* innocent, inoffensif

innovate *vi.* innover

innovation *n.* innovation *f.*

innuendo *n.* allusion, insinuation *f.*

innumerable *a.* innombrable

inoculate *vt.* inoculer; vacciner

inoffensive *a.* inoffensif

inoperative *a.* inefficace

inopportune *a.* mal à propos, inopportun

inordinate *a.* déréglé; irrégulier; démesuré

inorganic *a.* inorganique

inquest *n.* enquête judiciaire *f.*

inquire *vi.* s'enquérir, s'informer; demander (un avis); s'adresser

inquiry *n.* enquête, recherche *f.*, examen *m.*

inquisitive *a.* curieux; —ness *n.* curiosité *f.*

inquisitor *n.* inquisiteur *m.*

inroad *n.* incursion, invasion *f.*

insane *a.* insensé, fou; aliéné; — asylum asile des aliénés *m.*; maison de fous *f.*

insanity *n.* folie, démence *f.*

insatiability *n.* insatiabilité *f.*

insatiable *a.* insatiable

inscribe *vt.* inscrire; dédier

inscription *n.* inscription *f.*; (book) dédicace *f.*

insect *a.* insecte *m.*; —icide *n. & a.* insecticide *m.*

insecure *a.* mal assuré, peu sûr

insecurity *n.* insécurité, incertitude *f.*, danger *m.*

insensible *a.* insensible

insensitive *a.* insensible

inseparable *a.* inséparable

insert *vt.* insérer, introduire; — *n.* insertion *f.*; —ion *n.* insertion; introduction *f.*

inset *vt.* insérer (un cliché, un texte, dans un autre cliché, un autre texte); — *n.* objet inséré *m.*; hors-texte *m.*

inside *n.* intérieur *m.*; dedans *m.*; — out

à l'envers; —s *pl.* entrailles *f. pl.*; — *a.* intérieur; — of (time) en moins de; — track (coll.) avantage *m.*; — *adv.* à l'intérieur, vers l'intérieur; — *prep.* dans, à l'intérieur de; —r *n.* personne de la maison *f.*; initié *m.*

insidious *a.* insidieux

insight *n.* intuition *f.*; goût, jugement *m.*; aperçu *m.*

insignia *n. pl.* insignes *m. pl.*

insignificance *n.* insignifiance *f.*

insignificant *a.* insignifiant; peu important, sans importance

insincere *a.* peu sincère; faux, trompeur

insincerity *n.* manque de sincérité *m.*

insinuate *vt.* insinuer, suggérer, laisser entendre, donner à entendre

insinuating *a.* insinuant

insinuation *n.* insinuation *f.*

insipid *a.* insipide; fade; —ity *n.* insipidité *f.*; fadeur *f.*

insist *vi.* insister, persister; — on persister à; tenir à; — that insister pour que; —ence *n.* insistence *f.*; —ent *a.* insistant

insole *n.* semelle intérieure *f.*

insolence *n.* insolence *f.*

insolubility *n.* insolubilité *f.*

insoluble *a.* insoluble; irrésoluble

insolvency *n.* insolvabilité *f.*

insolvent *a.* insolvable

insomnia *n.* insomnie *f.*

insomuch as *conj.* dans la mesure que; à un tel pointe que

inspect *vt.* inspecter, surveiller, examiner; visiter; —ion *n.* inspection *f.*; visite *f.*; —or *n.* inspecteur *m.*

inspiration *n.* inspiration *f.*; respiration *f.*

inspire *vt.* inspirer, respirer

instability *n.* instabilité *f.*

install *vt.* installer; —ation *n.* installation *f.*

installment *n.* mensualité *f.*, versement, paiement, acompte *m.*

instance *n.* sollicitation *f.*; circonstance *f.*; for — par exemple

instant *n.* moment, instant *m.*; — *a.* immédiat, instantané; (dates) courant; —ly *a.* immédiatement; tout de suite; à l'instant; —aneous *a.* instantané

instead *adv.* à sa place; — of *prep.* au lieu de

instep *n.* cou-de-pied *m.*

instigate *vt.* instiguer, exciter, provoquer

instigator *n.* instigateur *m.*

instill *vt.* instiller; inculquer

instinct *n.* instinct *m.*; —ive *a.* instinctif

institute *n.* institut *m.*; — *vt.* instituer, établir, fonder

institution *n.* institution *f.*

instruct *vt.* instruire, enseigner; —ion *n.* enseignement *m.*; —ions *n. pl.* instructions *f. pl.*; ordres *m. pl.*; —ive *a.* instructif; —or *n.* professeur, chargé de cours *m.*

instrument *n.* instrument *m.*; outil *m.*; (law) acte *m.*; —al *a.* instrumental; be —al in contribuer à, jouer un rôle dans; —alist *n.* instrumentiste *m.*; —ation *n.* instrumentation *f.*

insubordinate *n.* insubordonné

insubordination *n.* insubordination *f.*

insufferable *a.* intolérable, insupportable
insufficiency *n.* insuffisance *f.*
insufficient *a.* insuffisant
insular *a.* insulaire
insulate *vt.* isoler
insulator *n.* isolateur *m.*
insulin *n.* insuline *f.*
insult *n.* insulte *f.*; — *vt.* insulter
insuperable *a.* insurmontable
insupportable *a.* insupportable
insurable *a.* assurable
insurance *n.* assurance *f.*; life — assurance sur la vie; fire — assurance contre l'incendie; — policy police d'assurance *f.*
insure *vt.* assurer
insurgent *n. & a.* insurgé, révolté *m.*
insurmountable *a.* insurmontable
insurrection *n.* insurrection *f.*
intake *n.* adduction *f.*; robinet d'adduction *m.*; prise, entrée, admission *f.*
intangibility *n.* intangibilité *f.*
integer *n.* nombre entier *m.*
integral *n.* (math.) intégrale *f.*; — *a.* intégral, entier
integrate *vt.* intégrer
integration *n.* intégration *f.*
integrity *n.* intégrité, probité *f.*
intellect *n.* intellect *m.*; -ual *a. & n.* intellectuel *m.*
intelligence *n.* intelligence *f.*; nouvelle *f.*, avis, rapport *m.*
intelligent *a.* intelligent
intelligible *a.* intelligible, clair
intemperance *n.* intempérance *f.*
intemperate *a.* immodéré
intend *vi.* se proposer, compter, penser; avoir l'intention de; — *vt.* destiner; -ed *a.* projeté; voulu; -ed *a. & n.* fiancé *m.*, fiancée *f.*
intense *a.* intense, véhément; fort; -ness *n.* intensité *f.*
intensify *vt.* renforcer; intensifier
intensity *n.* intensité *f.*
intensive *a.* intensif
intent *a.* absorbé; appliqué, attentif; déterminé; with — to dans l'intention de; — *n.* intention *f.*; -ion *n.* intention *f.*; -ional *a.* intentionnel; voulu; -ionally *adv.* exprès, à dessein; -ness *n.* attention *f.*
inter *vt.* enterrer, ensevelir; -ment *n.* enterrement *m.*
interact *vi.* réagir réciproquement
interbreed *vt.* croiser deux espèces
intercede *vi.* intercéder
intercept *vt.* intercepter; capter; -ion *n.* interception *f.*; captation *f.*
interchange *n.* échange *m.*; communication *f.*; alternance *f.*; — *vt.* échanger; -able *a.* interchangeable
interdepartmental *a.* interdépartemental
interdict *n.* (eccl.) interdit *m.*; — *vt.* interdire; -ion *n.* interdiction *f.*
interest *n.* intérêt *m.*; profit *m.*; participation *f.*; compound — intérêts composés *m. pl.*; rate of — taux de l'intérêt *m.*; take an — in s'intéresser à; — *vt.* intéresser; -ed *a.* intéressé, d'intérêt; be -ed in s'intéresser à

interfere *vi.* intervenir; se mêler; s'interposer; — with gêner; -nce *n.* intervention *f.*; (rad.) brouillage *m.*
interim *a.* intérimaire; — *adv.* entre temps; en attendant; — *n.* intérim *m.*
interior *n. & a.* intérieur *m.*
interjection *n.* interjection *f.*
interlace *vt.* entrelacer
interlinear *a.* interlinéaire
interlining *n.* doublure intermédiaire *f.*
interlock *vi.* s'entrecroiser, s'entrelacer; -ing *a.* qui s'entrecroisent; — *vt.* (rail.) enclencher
interloper *n.* intrus *m.*
interlude *n.* intermède *m.*
intermarriage *n.* intermariage *m.*
intermarry *vi.* se marier les uns avec les autres
intermediary *a. & n.* intermédiaire *m.*
intermediate *a.* intermédiaire; moyen
interminable *a.* interminable
interminably *adv.* sans fin
intermingle *vt.* entremêler; — *vi.* se mêler, s'entremêler
intermission *n.* entr'acte *m.*
intermittent *a.* intermittent; -ly *adv.* par intervalles
intern *vt.* interner; — *n.* interne des hôpitaux *m.*; -ment *n.* internement *m.*; -ship *n.* internat *m.*
internal *a.* interne, intérieur; intestin
international *a.* international
interplanetary *a.* interplanétaire
interpolate *vt.* interpoler, intercaler
interpolation *n.* interpolation *f.*
interpret *vt.* interpréter; expliquer; -ation *n.* interprétation *f.*; -er *n.* interprète *m. & f.*
interrelated *a.* en relation mutuelle
interrelation *n.* corrélation *f.*
interrogate *vt.* interroger, questionner
interrogation *n.* interrogation *f.*; interrogatoire *m.*; — point point d'interrogation *m.*
interrogative *a.* interrogatif
interrupt *vt.* interrompre; -er *n.* (elec.) interrupteur *m.*; coupe-circuit *m.*; -ion *n.* interruption *f.*
interscholastic *a.* interscolaire
intersect *vt.* entrecouper, intersecter; — *vi.* se couper, se croiser, s'intersecter; -ion *n.* intersection *f.*; (roads) carrefour *m.*; croisement *m.*; coin *m.*
intersperse *vt.* entremêler
interstate *a.* entre les états; — commerce commerce dans lequel les marchandises sont transportées au delà des frontières de l'état *m.*
interurban *a.* interurbain
interval *n.* intervalle *m.*; at -s par intervalles
intervene *vi.* intervenir; arriver; (time) s'écouler
interview *n.* entrevue *f.*; interview *m.*; entretien *m.*; — *vt.* interviewer
interwoven *a.* entrelacé, entremêlé
intestate *a.* intestat
intestine *n.* intestin *m.*
intimacy *n.* intimité *f.*
intimate *a.* intime; étroit; — *n.* intime *m.*,

& f.; — vt. donner à entendre; suggérer
intimation n. suggestion f.
intimidate vt. intimider
intimidation n. intimidation f.
into prep. dans, en; entre
intolerable a. intolérable; insupportable
intolerance n. intolérance f.
intolerant a. intolérant
intonation n. ton m., intonation f.
intone vt. entonner
intoxicate vt. enivrer; griser; —d a. ivre; gris
intoxicating a. enivrant
intoxication n. ivresse f.; enivrement m.
intractable a. intraitable
intransitive a. intransitif
intravenous a. dans les veines, intraveineux
intrepid a. intrépide; -ity n. intrépidité, hardiesse f.
intricacy n. complexité f.
intricate a. compliqué
intrigue n. intrigue f.; — vt. & vi. intriguer; -r n. intrigant m.
intriguing a. intrigant; très intéressant; qui intrigue; — n. intrigues f. pl.
intrinsic a. intrinsèque
introduce vt. présenter; introduire
introduction n. présentation f.; introduction f.; (book) avant-propos m.
introductory a. préliminaire; d'introduction
introspection n. introspection f.
introspective a. introspectif
introvert n. introverti m.; -ed a. introverti, recueilli
intrude vi. s'ingérer; s'infiltrer; — on déranger; -er n. intrus m.
intrusion n. intrusion f.; importunité f.
intrust vt. confier
intuition n. intuition f.
intuitive a. intuitif; -ly adv. par intuition
inundate vt. inonder
inundation n. inondation f.
inure vt. accoutumer, habituer; endurcir
invade vt. envahir; -r n. envahisseur m.
invalid n. & a. (health) malade; infirme; valétudinaire m. & f.; -ate vt. invalider; vicier; infirmer
invalid a. invalide; -idate vt. invalider, déclarer de nul effet
invaluable a. inestimable
invariable a. invariable
invariably adv. invariablement
invasion n. invasion f., envahissement m.; violation f.
invective n. invective f.
inveigh vi. invectiver
inveigle vt. séduire, entraîner, enjôler
invent vt. inventer; -ion n. invention f.; -ive a. inventif; -iveness n. don d'invention m.; imagination f.; -or n. inventeur m.
inventory n. inventaire m.; — vt. faire l'inventaire de
inverse a. inverse; — n. inverse, contraire m.
inversion n. (gram.) inversion f.; renversement m.
invert vt. renverser; invertir

invertebrate n. & a. invertébré m.
invest vt. (money) placer, mettre; (mil.) investir; -ment n. placement, investissement m.; -or n. actionnaire m. & f.; rentier m.
investigate vt. faire une enquête sur; examiner, étudier
investigation n. enquête, investigation f.; étude f.
investigator n. investigateur m.; agent m.
inveterate a. invétéré, acharné; implacable
invigorate vt. fortifier; vivifier
invigorating a. fortifiant, vivifiant
invincibility n. invincibilité f.
invincible a. invincible
inviolable a. inviolable
invisibility n. invisibilité f.
invisible a. invisible
invite vt. inviter; provoquer
inviting a. attrayant, invitant; séduisant
invocation n. invocation f.
invoice n. facture f.; — vt. facturer
invoke vt. invoquer; évoquer
involuntarily adv. involontairement
involuntary a. involontaire
involve vt. envelopper; compliquer; engager; impliquer; entraîner; nécessiter; -ed a. compliqué; embrouillé; engagé; impliqué
invulnerable a. invulnérable
inward a. interne, intérieur; vers l'intérieur; -ly adv. en dedans; à l'intérieur; -s adv. vers l'intérieur
iodide n. iodure m.
iodine n. iode m.; tincture of — teinture d'iode f.
ion n. ion m.; -ization n. ionisation f.; -ize vt. ioniser
I.O.U. n. reconnaissance de dette f.
Iran n. Iran m.; -ian a. & n. iranien m.
Iraq n. Irak m.; -i a. & n. irakien m.
irascible a. irascible
irate a. en colère
ire n. colère f.; courroux m.
Ireland n. Irlande f.
iridescence n. iridescence f.
iridescent a. iridescent, irisé
Irish a. & n. Irlandais m.; -man n. Irlandais; -woman n. Irlandaise f.
irk vt. ennuyer; -some a. ennuyeux
iron n. fer m.; (laundry) fer à repasser m.; cast — fer de fonte m.; curling — fer à friser m.; — curtain rideau de fer m.; — lung poumon de fer m.; — ore minerai de fer m.; pig — fonte en saumon f.; scrap — ferraille f.; wrought — fer forgé m.; -s n. pl. fers m. pl., chaînes f. pl.; — a. de fer; — vt. repasser, donner un coup de fer à; — out faire disparaître; aplanir; -ing n. repassage m.
ironclad a. cuirassé; (fig.) parfait, qui ne peut être démenti
ironic(al) a. ironique
irony n. ironie f.
irradiate vt. rayonner, illuminer, éclairer
irrational a. déraisonnable; irrationnel
irreconcilable a. implacable; irréconciliable; inconciliable

irrecoverable *a.* irréparable

irreducible *a.* irréductible

irrefutable *a.* incontestable, irréfutable, irrécusable

irregular *a.* irrégulier; -ity *n.* irrégularité *f.*

irrelevance *n.* inapplicabilité *f.*

irrelevant *a.* inapplicable, hors de propos, non pertinent

irreligious *a.* irréligieux

irremediable *a.* irrémédiable

irremovable *a.* inamovible

irreparable *a.* irréparable

irreplaceable *a.* qui ne peut être remplacé

irrepressible *a.* irréprimable

irreproachable *a.* irréprochable

irresistible *a.* irrésistible

irresolute *a.* irrésolu

irrespective *a.* indépendent; — *adv.,* — of sans égard à; sans tenir compte de

irresponsibility *n.* irresponsabilité *f.*

irresponsible *a.* irréfléchi, étourdi

irretrievable *a.* irrémédiable

irreverence *n.* irrévérance *f.*

irreverent *a.* irrévérent; irrévérencieux

irreversible *a.* irrévocable

irrevocable *a.* irrévocable

irrigate *vt.* irriguer; arroser

irrigation *n.* irrigation *f.*

irritability *n.* irritabilité *f.*

irritable *a.* irritable

irritant *n.* irritant *m.*

irritate *vt.* irriter, agacer

irritating *a.* irritant, agaçant

irritation *n.* irritation *f.*

isinglass *n.* colle de poisson *f.*

island *n.* île *f.*; îlot *m.*; -er *n.* insulaire *m. & f.*

isle *n.* île *f.*

isolate *vt.* isoler; -ed *a.* isolé, écarté

isolation *n.* isolement *m.*; solitude *f.*; -ism (pol.) politique d'isolement *f.*; -ist adhérent de la politique d'isolement *m.*

isosceles *a.* isocèle

isotope *n.* isotope *m.*

Israel *n.* Israël *m.*; -i *a. & n.* israélien *m.*; -ite *a. & n.* israélite *m. & f.*

issue *n.* question *f.*; publication *f.*; émission *f.*; délivrance *f.*; numéro *m.*; issue, sortie *f.*; résultat *m.*; fin *f.*; enfants *m., pl.*; — *vt.* publier; émettre; lancer; donner; délivrer; — *vi.* sortir, provenir

Istanbul *n.* Istamboul *m.*

isthmus *n.* isthme *m.*

it *pron.* il, elle; ce, cela; le, la

Italian *a. & n.* italien *m.*

italicize *vt.* mettre en italique

italics *n., pl.* italique *m.*

itch *n.* démangeaison *f.*; — *vi.* démanger

item *n.* article, détail *m.*; question *f.*; news — fait divers *m.*; -ize faire la liste de

iterate *vt.* réitérer

itinerant *a.* ambulant

itinerary *n.* itinéraire *m.*

its *a.* son, sa, ses

itself *pron.* se; lui-même, elle-même, soi-même

ivory *n.* ivoire *m.*; — *a.* d'ivoire; — tower tour d'ivoire *f.*

J

jab *n.* coup de pointe *m.*; (boxing) coup sec *m.*; — *vt.* piquer

jabber *vi.* bavardage *m.*; jacasserie *f.*; jacasser; —; -ing *n.* baragouinage *m.*

jack *n.* cric, lève-roue *m.*; (cards) valet *m.*; — *vt.,* — (up) soulever; augmenter; — rabbit *n.* lapin de plaine *m.*

jackass *n.* âne, baudet *m.*

jacket *n.* veston *m.*; veste *f.*; jaquette *f.*; (book) chemise, couverture *f.*

jack-in-the-box *n.* diable *m.,* boîte à surprise *f.*

jackknife *n.* couteau de poche *m.*

jack-o'-lantern *n.* feu follet *m.*

jack pot *n.* gros lot; hit the — (coll.) gagner le prix; faire fortune d'un seul coup

jade *n.* jade *m.*; (person) coquine *f.*; -d *a.* fatigué, éreinté

jag *vt.* ébrécher; — *n.* dent de scie *f.*

jagged *a.* dentelé, ébréché; -ness *n.* dentelure *f.*

jail *n.* prison *f.*; — *vt.* mettre en prison; -er *n.* gardien *m.*

jam *n.* confiture *f.*; presse *f.*; (traffic) embouteillage *m.*; — *vt.* presser, serrer; fourrer, enfoncer; coincer; (radio) brouiller; — *vi.* se coincer; (gun) s'enrayer

jamboree *n.* (coll.) grande réunion *f.*

jangle *vi.* cliqueter, s'entre-choquer; — *vt.* faire entre-choquer; -d *a.* agacé

janitor *n.* concierge, portier *m.*

January *n.* janvier *m.*

Japan *n.* Japon *m.*; -ese *a. & n.* japonais *m.*

jar *n.* bocal *m.,* pot *m.*; choc *m.,* secousse *f.*; — *vt.* choquer; agacer; — *vi.* être en désaccord; — on choquer, crisper

jaundice *n.* jaunisse *f.*

jaunt *n.* excursion, sortie *f.*; -y *a.* désinvolte; vif

Java *n.* Java *m.*; -nese *n. & a.* Javanais *m.*

javelin *n.* javeline *f.*, javelot *m.*

jaw *n.* jawbone *n.* mâchoire *f.*

jaywalker (coll.) *n.* piéton imprudent *m.* (qui traverse la rue en dehors du passage clouté)

jealous *a.* jaloux; -y *n.* jalousie *f.*

jeans *n.* pantalon de coutil *m.*

jeep *n.* jeep *f.*

jeer *vi.* se moquer; — at railler; siffler; se moquer de; -ing *a.* railleur; -ing *n.* raillerie *f.*

jellied *a.* en gelée

jelly *n.* gelée *f.*; — *vt.* faire prendre en gelée; — *vi.* se prendre en gelée

jeopardize *vt.* compromettre; mettre en péril

jeopardy *n.* péril, danger *m.*

jerk *n.* saccade, secousse *f.*; — *vt.* tirer (d'un coup sec); — *vi.* se mouvoir par saccades; -ed beef bœuf séché *m.*; -y *a.* coupé, saccadé

jersey *n.* tricot *m.*; (sports) maillot *m.*

jest *n.* plaisanterie *f.*; — *vi.* plaisanter; -er *n.* bouffon *m.*

Jesus Christ *n.* Jésus-Christ *m.*

jet n. jet m.; brûleur bec m.; (motor) réacteur m.; (mineral) jais m.; — plane avion à reaction m.

jet-black a. noir comme du jais

jet-propelled a. à réaction

jettison vt. jeter

jetty n. jetée f.

Jew n. Juif m.; -ish a. juif m., juive f.

jewel n. bijou, joyau m.; (watch) rubis m.; -er n. bijoutier, joaillier m.; -ry n. bijouterie, joaillerie f.

jib n. (naut.) foc m.

jibe vi. s'accorder; être d'accord

jig n. gigue f.; — vi. danser une gigue

jigger n. chique f.; (drink measure) deux doigts m. pl.

jigsaw n. scie à chantourner f.; — puzzle jeu de patience f.

jilt vt. abandonner

jingle n. tintement m.; — vi. tinter; — vt. faire tinter

jitterbug n. jitterbug m.

jitters n. pl. (coll.) nervosité f.; crise de nerfs f.

jive n. jive m.

job n. emploi m.; poste m., situation f.; travail m.; métier m.; — lot lot de soldes; — work travail à la pièce m.; -ber n. revendeur m.; -less a. sans travail, désœuvré; -less n. chômeurs m. pl.

jockey n. jockey m.; -vt. & vi. manœuvrer

jocose a. plaisant, badin

jocular a. rieur, facétieux

jocund a. enjoué, jovial

jodhpurs n. pl. pantalon d'équitation m.

jog n. secousse f.; petit trot m.; — vi. aller au petit trot

join vt. & vi. joindre, unir, réunir; ajouter; relier; (club) entrer dans; — vi. se joindre, s'unir; — in prendre part; — up s'engager; -er n. (carpentry) menuisier m.

joint n. joint m., jointure f.; articulation f.; out of — disloqué; — a. commun; collectif, combiné; — account compte conjoint, compte en participation m.; — heir cohéritier m.; -ly adv. en commun; ensemble; conjointement

joist n. solive f.

joke n. blague, plaisanterie f.; practical — mystification f.; play a — on mystifier; jouer un tour a; — vi. plaisanter; -r n. plaisant, farceur m.; (cards) joker m.; practical -r mauvais plaisant m.

joking a. moqueur; -ly adv. en plaisantant; — n. plaisanterie f.

jolly a. gai, enjoué

jolt n. cahot m., secousse f.; — vt. cahoter, secouer

Jordan n. (river) Jourdain m.; (country) Jordanie f.

jostle vt. bousculer, coudoyer, serrer

jot n. iota m.; — vt.; — down prendre note de, noter; -tings n. pl. notes f. pl.

jounce vt. secouer

journal n. journal m.; -ese n. (coll.) jargon des journaux m.; -ism n.

journalisme m.; yellow -ism n. journalisme sensationnel m.; -ist n. journaliste m. & f.; -istic a. journalistique

journey n. voyage m.; — vi. voyager; -man n. ouvrier, compagnon m.

joust vi. jouter; — n. joute f.

jovial a. jovial; -ity n. jovialité, joie f.

jowl n. joue, bajoue f.

joy n. joie f.; -ful a. joyeux; -fully adv. joueusement; -less a. triste; -ous a. joyeux

jubilant a. joyeux, réjoui; triomphant

jubilate vt. jubiler

jubilee n. jubilé m.

Judaism n. judaïsme m.

judge n. juge m.; arbitre m.; connaisseur m.; be a good — of s'y connaître en; — vt. juger; estimer, mesurer

judgment n. jugement m.; arrêt m., sentence f.; avis m., opinion f.; — day jugement dernier m.

judicial a. judiciaire; juridique

judiciary a. judiciaire; — n. magistrature f.

judicious a. judicieux

jug n. cruche f., pot, broc m.; — vt. mettre en pot; -ged hare n. civet de lièvre m.

juggle vi. jongler; -r n. jongleur, bateleur m.

jugular a. jugulaire

juice n. jus, suc m.

juiciness n. succulence f.

juicy a. juteux, succulent; fondant

jukebox n. grand tourne-disque à sous, jukebox m.

julep n. julep m.; mint — boisson au whisky et à la menthe f.

July n. juillet m.

jumble n. confusion f.; — vt. brouiller

jumbo a. énorme

jump n. saut, bond m.; saute f.; (racing) obstacle m.; broad — saut en longueur m.; high — saut en hauteur m.; — vi. sauter, bondir; — vt. sauter, faire sauter; attaquer; — at saisir; — the gun devancer; commencer prématurément; — the track dérailler; -er n. sauteur m.; (clothes) casaquin m.; (elec.) connexion volante f.; -iness n. agitation, nervosité f.; -ing a. sautant, sautillant; actif; -ing jack pantin m.; -ing n. saut m.; -y a. nerveux, irritable

jump rope n. corde à sauter f.

junction n. jonction f.; bifurcation f.; carrefour m.; — point connexion f.

juncture n. jointure f.; moment m.

June n. juin m.

jungle n. jungle f.

junior a. plus jeune, cadet; (in names) fils; (mil.) subalterne; — college établissement qui ne fait que les deux premières années des études universitaires m.; — high school établissement qui ne fait que les deux premières années des études secondaires m.

juniper n. genièvre m.

junk n. débris, rejets m. pl.; (naut.) jonque f.; — vt. mettre au rancart

junket n. voyage fait aux frais de l'Etat m.

junta n. junte f.
juridical a. juridique
jurisdiction n. juridiction f.; -al a. juridictionnel
jurisprudence n. jurisprudence f.
jurist n. juriste m.
juror n. juré, membre du jury m.
jury n. jury m., jurés m. pl.; — box banc des jurés m.
just a. juste; équitable; — adv. justement, juste; au juste; précisément; tout simplement; — as au moment où; — now tout à l'heure; actuellement, pour le moment; -ly adv. justement; avec justice
justice n. justice f.; (person) juge, magistrat m.
justifiable a. justifiable, légitime
justification n. justification f.
justify vt. justifier; motiver
jut vi. — (out) faire saillie; — out over surplomber
juvenile a. juvénile; puéril; — delinquent accusé mineur m.; — n. jeune m. & f.
juxtaposition n. juxtaposition f.; in — juxtaposé

K

kale n. chou frisé m.
kaleidoscope n. kaléidoscope m.
Kashmir n. Cachemire m.
kayak n. kayac m.
keel n. quille f.
keen a. vif; ardent; aigu; fin; —ness n. finesse f.; ardeur f.; acuité f.
keep n. (castle-) donjon m.; board and — nourriture f.; for —s pour de bon; — vt. garder; tenir; entretenir, maintenir; retenir; empêcher; conserver, préserver; — vi. se tenir, rester; continuer; se conserver; — an eye on ne pas perdre de vue; — from s'abstenir de; empêcher de; s'empêcher de; — in retenir; rester dedans; rester à la maison; — off ne pas toucher (à); éloigner; — on garder; avancer; continuer; — out empêcher d'entrer; ne pas se mêler; rester dehors; — quiet rester tranquille; ne pas parler; se taire; — up maintenir, entretenir; faire veiller; — waiting faire attendre; -er n. garde, gardien m.; -ing n. garde f.; in -ing with en accord avec
keepsake n. souvenir m.
keg n. tonnelet, barillet m.
kelp n. soude de varech f.
ken n. savoir m., compréhension f.
kennel n. niche f.; chenil m.
kerchief n. fichu m.
kernel n. grain m.
kerosene n. kérosène m.
kettle n. bouilloire, marmite f.
kettledrum n. timbale f.
key n. clé, clef f.; (piano) touche f.; — industry n. industrie-clef f.; — ring porte-clefs m.; sending — manipulateur m.; — word mot-clé m.; master — passe-partout m.
keyboard n. clavier m.
keyhole n. trou de serrure m.
keynote n. (mus.) tonique f.; (fig.) point principal m.

keystone n. clef de voûte f.
khaki n. khaki m.
kick n. coup de pied m.; (coll.) frisson m.; (gun) recul m.; — vt. donner un coup de pied à; (sports) botter; — vi. donner un coup de pied; regimber; reculer; — out mettre à la porte; chasser à coups de pied
kickoff n. coup d'envoi m.
kid n. chevreau m., chevrette f.; (coll.) gosse m. & f.; — gloves gants de chevreau m. pl.; handle with — gloves ménager; — vt. (coll.) plaisanter, faire marcher; no —ding! (coll.) sans blague!
kidnap vt. enlever, voler; -per n. kidnapper, ravisseur m.; -ping n. kidnapping, enlèvement, vol m.; rapt m.
kidney n. rein m.; (food) rognon m.; — bean haricot de Soissons m.
kidney-shaped a. réniforme
kidskin n. peau de chevreau f.
kill vt. tuer; (animal) abattre; (fig.) supprimer; -er n. assassin, meurtrier m.; tueur m.; -ing n. meurtre m.; tuerie f., massacre m.; (coll.) coup m.
kill-joy n. rabat-joie m.
kiln n. four m.
kilocycle n. kilocycle m.
kilogram n. kilo, kilogramme m.
kilometer n. kilomètre m.
kilometric a. kilométrique
kilowatt n. kilowatt m.
kilowatt-hour n. kilowatt-heure m.
kilt n. kilt m.
kilter n. bon ordre m.; out of — détraqué, déréglé
kin n. parents m. pl.; famille f.; next of — le plus proche parent m.; -ship n. parenté f.
kind n. genre m., espèce f., sorte f.; nothing of the — rien de la sorte; payment in — paiement en nature m.; — a. bon; aimable; bienveillant; -liness n. bonté, bienveillance f.; -ly a. bon, bienveillant; -ness n. bonté, bienveillance f.; prévenance f.; service m.
kindergarten n. jardin d'enfants m.; école maternelle f.
kindhearted a. bon, bienveillant
kindle vt. allumer, enflammer; susciter; — vi. s'allumer, s'enflammer
kindling (wood) n. petit bois m.
kindred a. de la même famille; de la même nature; — souls âmes sœurs f. pl.
kinescope n. tube à rayons cathodiques m.
kinetic a. cinétique; -s n. pl. cinétique f.
king n. roi m.; (checkers) dame f.; -dom n. royaume m.; règne m.; -ly a. de roi royal
king-size a. grand, (plus) long
kink n. nœud m.; coque f.; faux pli m.; — vi. se nouer; -y a. crépu
kinsfolk n. parents m. pl., famille f.
kinsman n. parent m.
kinswoman n. parente f.
kiosk n. kiosque m.

kiss n. baiser m.; — vt. embrasser; (hand) baiser

kit n. trousseau m., trousse f.; nécessaire m.

kitchen n. cuisine f.; -ette n. petite cuisine f.; — police (K.P.) n. (mil.) corvée de cuisine f.; — range n. cuisinière f.; — utensils batterie de cuisine f.

kite n. cerf-volant m.; fly a — lancer un cerf-volant

kith n. parents, amis m. pl.

kitten n. chaton, petit chat m.; -ish a. enjoué, folâtre

kleptomania n. kleptomanie f.; -c n. kleptomane m. & f.

knack n. don m., habileté f.; coup m.; flair m.

knapsack n. sac m.

knave n. coquin, fripon m.; -ry n. friponnerie f.

knead vt. pétrir, travailler

knee n. genou m.; on one's -s à genoux, agenouillé

kneecap n. rotule f.

knee-deep a. jusqu'aux genoux

knee-high a. à la hauteur du genou

kneel vi. s'agenouiller, se mettre à genoux; -ing a. à genoux, agenouillé

knell n. glas m.; death — glas funèbre m.

knickers, knickerbockers n. (pl.) culotte f.; knickerbockers m. pl.

knicknack n. bibelot, colifichet m.

knife n. couteau m.; — grinder rémouleur m.; — vt. poignarder

knight n. chevalier m.; (chess) cavalier m.; — vt. armer chevalier, faire chevalier; -hood n. chevalerie f.; -ly a. chevaleresque

knight-errant n. chevalier errant m.; -ry n. chevalerie errante f.

knit vt. tricoter; lier, joindre; — one's brows froncer les sourcils; -ted a. tricoté, en tricot; -ing n. tricot m.; tricotage m.; union f.; -ing needle aiguille à tricoter f.

knob n. bouton m.; bosse f.

knock n. coup m.; (engine) cognement m.; — out knock-out m.; — vt. frapper, cogner; heurter; (coll.) trouver à redire; — vi. (engine) cogner; -down renverser; abattre; — off (coll.) finir; cesser de travailler; — out knockouter; supprimer; -er n. (door) marteau m.; -ing n. coups m. pl.

knock-kneed a. cagneux

knoll n. monticule, tertre, mamelon m.

knot n. nœud m.; groupe m.; overhand — nœud simple m.; reef — (naut.) nœud marin m.; slip- nœud coulant m.; tie a — faire un nœud; — vt. nouer; — vi. se nouer; -ted a. à nœuds; -ty a. noueux, -ty question question épineuse f.

knothole n. trou de nœud m.

know vt. savoir; connaître; apprendre; as far as I — autant que je sache; -ing a. fin; (look) entendu; -ingly adv. sciemment; -n a. connu

know-how n. connaissances techniques f. pl.; savoir-faire m.

knowledge n. science f.; savoir m.; connaissance(s) f. (pl.); not to my — pas que je sache; without my — à mon insu; -able a. intelligent

knuckle n. articulation du doigt f.; (animal) manche m.

Koran n. Coran m.

Korea n. Corée f.

kosher a. cawoher, kascher, cacher

kowtow vi. se prosterner; — vt. & vi. saluer à la chinoise

L

label n. étiquette f.; — vt. étiqueter

labial a. labial; — n. labiale f.

labor n. travail m.; labeur m.; ouvriers m. pl.; main-d'œuvre f.; (med.) couches f. pl.; hard — travail disciplinaire m.; — union syndicat ouvrier m.; — vi. travailler; élaborer; -er n. travailleur, ouvrier m.; manœuvre m.; -ious a. laborieux, pénible

laboratory n. laboratoire m.

laborsaving a. qui économise le travail

lace n. dentelle f.; (shoe) lacet, cordon m.; — vt. lacer; entrelacer

lacerate vt. lacérer; déchirer

laceration n. lacération f.; déchirure f.

lack n. manque, défaut m., absence f.; for — of faute de; — vt. & vi. manquer (de); -ing a. qui manque; dépourvu de; insuffisant

lackadaisical a. apathique; languissant

lackey n. laquais m.

laconic a. laconique

lacquer n. lacque, vernis m.; — vt. laquer

lacrimose a. larmoyant

lactate vi. sécréter du lait

lactation n. lactation f.

lactic a. lactique

lactose n. lactose f.

lad n. garçon, jeune homme m.

ladder n. échelle f.

lading n. chargement m.; bill of — connaissement m.

ladle n. louche f.; puisoir m.; — vt., — out servir

lady n. dame f.; ladies and gentlemen mesdames et messieurs, (coll.) messieurs-dames; young — jeune fille, demoiselle f.

ladylike a. de dame; comme il faut

lag n. retard, décalage m.; — vi. traîner, rester en arrière

lager n. bière blonde f.

laggard n. traînard m.; — a. tardif

lagoon n. lagune f.; (atoll) lagon m.

laid a. posé, laissé; (paper) couché

laid up a. malade; en panne

lair n. repaire m., tanière f.

laity n. laïques m. pl.

lake n. lac m.

lamb n. agneau m.; — chop côtelette d'agneau f.; — vi. agneler

lame a. boiteux, estropié; (excuse) faible, pauvre; — vt. rendre boiteux; estropier; -ness n. boitement m.; faiblesse f.

lament n. lamentation, complainte f.; — vt. pleurer; -able a. déplorable, lamentable; –ation n. lamentation f.; –ed a. regretté

laminate vt. laminer

lamp n. lampe f.

lampoon n. libelle m., satire f.; — vt. lancer des satires contre; –er n. libelliste, satiriste m.

lamppost n. réverbère m.

lamp shade n. abat-jour m.

lance n. lance f.; — vt. inciser, percer; –r n. lancier m.; –t n. lancette f., bistouri m.

land n. terre f.; terrain m.; pays m.; — vt. débarquer; (plane) atterrir; (fish) amener à terre; (coll.) gagner, remporter; — vi. débarquer; atterrir; on one's feet retomber sur ses pieds; –ed a. foncier; qui possède des terres; –ing n. débarquement m.; atterrissage m.; (stair) palier m.; –ing barge, –ing craft n. péniche de débarquement f.; –ing field n. terrain d'atterrissage m.; –ing strip n. piste d'atterrissage f.

landfall n. atterrage m.; aubaine f.

landlady n. propriétaire f.; aubergiste f.

landlord n. propriétaire m.; aubergiste m.

landlubber n. marin d'eau douce m.

landmark n. repère m.; point coté m.; monument m.

land office n. bureau du cadastre m.; do a — business faire des affaires inouies, avoir un chiffre d'affaires énorme

landowner n. propriétaire foncier m.

landscape n. paysage m.; — garden n. jardin à l'anglaise m.; — gardener n. jardiniste m.; — painter n. paysagiste m.

landslide n. glissement de terre m.; (pol.) victoire écrasante f.

landward adv. vers la terre

lane n. ruelle f., passage m.; route f.

language n. langue f.; langage m.

languid a. languissant, langoureux; –ness n. langueur f.

languish vi. languir; –ing a. languissant, langoureux

languor n. langueur f.; –ous a. langoureux

lanky a. grand et maigre

lanolin n. lanoline f.

lantern n. lanterne f.; fanal m.; Chinese — lanterne vénitienne f.; — slide n. diapositive de projection f.

lantern-jawed a. aux joues creuses

lanyard n. garant m.

Laos n. Laos m.

lap n. genoux m. pl.; (sports) circuit, tour m., étape f.; — vt. boucler; dépasser; — vi. (waves) clapoter; — up laper; gober

lapel n. revers m.

lapidary a. & n. lapidaire m.

Lapland n. Laponie f.

lapse n. laps m.; délai m.; intervalle m.; lapsus m., faute f.; — vi. manquer; périmer; tomber; –d a. périmé; déchu; caduc

larboard n. bâbord m.

larceny n. larcin, vol m.

lard n. saindoux, lard m.; — vt. larder

larder n. garde-manger m.

large a. grand, gros; fort; nombreux; grow –(r) grandir, grossir; –ly adv. en grande partie; — n., at — libre, en liberté; –ness n. grandeur f.; grosseur f.; étendue f.

large-scale a. à grande échelle, de grande échelle; de grande envergure

lariat n. lasso m.

larva n. larve f.

laryngitis n. laryngite f.

larynx n. larynx m.

lascivious a. lascif; –ness n. lascivité f.

lash n. coup de fouet m.; — vt. fouetter; cingler; attacher, lier; –ing n. coups de fouet m. pl., flagellation f.; (rope) ligne d'amarrage f.

lass n. jeune fille f.

lassitude n. lassitude f.

last a. dernier; — night hier soir; cette nuit; — week la semaine passée, la semaine dernière; next to — l'avant-dernier; — n. dernier; bout m., fin f.; at — enfin; — vi. durer; –ing a. durable; –ly adv. en dernier lieu

latch n. loquet m.; — vt. fermer à demi-tour; — on to (coll.) saisir

latchkey n. clef f., passe-partout m.

late a. en retard; tard; tardif; récent; (deceased) feu; of — depuis peu; — adv. en retard; tard; –ly adv. récemment, depuis peu; –ness n. heure avancée f.; arrivée tardive f.; –r a. plus récent; ultérieur; –r adv. plus tard; après; –st a. le plus récent, le plus nouveau, dernier

latent a. latent, caché

lateral a. latéral

lath n. latte f.

lathe n. tour m.

lather n. mousse de savon f.; — vt. savonner; — vi. mousser

Latin a. & n. latin m.; — America Amérique latine f.

latitude n. latitude f.; (fig.) liberté f.

latrine n. latrines f. pl.

latter a. dernier; the — celui-ci; celle-ci

latter-day a. moderne

lattice n. treillis, treillage m.

Latvia n. Lettonie, Latvie f.; –n a. & n. letton m.; (language) lette m.

laud vt. louer; –able a. louable; –atory a. élogieux

laugh n. rire m.; — vi. rire; — at rire de; — to oneself rire tout bas; — off se moquer de, traiter à la légère; –able a. ridicule, risible; –ing a. riant; rieur; it is no –ing matter il n'y a pas de quoi rire; –ing gas n. gaz hilarant m.; –ingstock n. risée f.; –ter n. rires m. pl.

launch n. chaloupe f.; — vt. lancer; –ing n. lancement m.; mise à l'eau f.

launching pad n. plate-forme de lancement f.

launder vt. blanchir

laundress n. blanchisseuse f.

laundry n. blanchisserie f.; linge à blanchir m.; –man n. blanchisseur m.

lava n. lave f.

lavatory n.; lavabo; lavoir; cabinet de toilette m.

lavender a. & n. lavande f.

lavish a. prodigue; somptueux; — st. prodiguer; -ness n. prodigalité f.; somptuosité f.

law n. loi f.; droit m.; civil — droit civil m.; lay down the — to faire la loi a; —ful a. légal, permis; légitime; valide; -less a. sans loi; désordonné; -lessness n. désordre m.; anarchie f.

law-abiding a. respectueux des lois

lawbreaker n. transgresseur de la loi m.

lawmaker n. législateur m.

lawn n. pelouse f.; gazon m.

lawn mower n. tondeuse f.

lawsuit n. procès m.

lawyer n. avocat, avoué m.

lax a. relâché; négligent, inexact; -ity n. relâchement m.; inexactitude f.

laxative n. & a. laxatif m.

lay n. lai m., chanson f.; (land) configuration f.; — a. lai, laïque; — vt. placer, mettre, coucher, poser; (egg) pondre; (bet) parier; — aside, — away mettre de côté; — before présenter à, soumettre à; — by mettre de côté; — down déposer; imposer; décréter; — in se faire une provision de; — off (labor) congédier; (coll.) laisser tranquille; — on appliquer; — out disposer, étaler; (money) débourser; — siege to assiéger; — up mettre hors de service; tenir au lit, tenir enfermé; -er n. couche f.; (hen) pondeuse f.

layman n. laïque m.

layoff n. renvoi d'ouvriers en masse m.

layout n. disposition f.; dessin, schéma de montage m.; plan m.

layover n. arrêt en cours de route m. (pour attendre une correspondance)

laziness n. paresse f.

lazy a. paresseux; fainéant

lead n. (mineral) plomb m.; (pencil) mine de plomb f.; (naut.) sonde f.; — pencil crayon à mine de plomb; — poisoning saturnisme m.; -en a. de plomb; pesant

lead n. exemple m., direction f.; (theat.) premier rôle m.; (elec.) câble de canalisation m.; (journalism) article de fond m.; take the — prendre le pas; — vt. conduire, mener; guider; commander, diriger; porter, entraîner; — vi. conduire; aboutir; — away emmener; entraîner; — off commencer, être le premier; emmener; — on encourager; — up to amener à; -er n. conducteur, chef m.; (pol.) leader m.; (film) amorce f.; -erless a. sans chef; -ership n. direction f., commandement m.; -ing a. principal; important; premier; -ing man, -ing lady premier rôle m.; vedette f.; -ing question question tendancieuse f.

leaf n. feuille f.; (book) feuillet m.; (door) battant m.; (table) rallonge f.; turn over a new — faire peau neuve; — vt., — through feuilleter; -age n. feuillage m.; -let n. feuille f.; annonce f.; -y a. touffu, couvert de feuilles

league n. ligue f.; (measurement) lieue f.; (sports) groupement m., association f.; in — with d'intelligence avec; — vi.,

— together se liguer

leak n. fuite, perte f.; écoulement m.; (naut.) voie d'eau f.; — vi. fuir, couler; (naut.) faire eau; — out (rumor) s'ébruiter; -age n. fuite, perte f.; -y a. qui fuit, qui coule

leakproof a. étanche

lean vi. s'appuyer; (se) pencher; s'adosser; incliner; — vt. appuyer; adosser; — back se pencher en arrière, se renverser; — out se pencher à; -ing a. penchant, penché; -ing n. inclination, tendance f., penchant m.

lean a. maigre; décharné; — n. maigre m.; -ness maigreur f.

lean-to n. abat-vent m.; remise f.

leap n. saut m.; — year année bissextile f.; — vt. & vi. sauter

leapfrog n. saute-mouton m.

learn vt. apprendre; savoir; -ed a. instruit, savant; -ing n. science, érudition f.; savoir m.

lease n. bail f.; — vt. louer; donner à bail; prendre à bail

leash n. laisse, attache f.

least a. moindre; plus petit; — n. le moins m.; at — au moins; du moins; not in the — pas du tout; — adv. le moins

leather n. cuir m.; — a. en cuir, de cuir; — goods maroquinerie f.; -ette n. simili-cuir m.; -y a. (food) coriace; comme de cuir

leave n. congé m.; permission f.; — of absence congé m.; — vt. laisser; quitter; partir de; — vi. partir; s'en aller; — behind laisser; oublier; — out omettre

leaven n. levain m.; — vt. faire lever

leave-taking n. adieux m. pl.

leaving n. départ m.; -s n. pl. restes m. pl.; reliefs m. pl.

Lebanon n. Liban m.

lecherous a. lascif, débauché; -ness n. lasciveté f.

lecture n. conférence f.; — vi. faire une conférence; — vt. (coll.) sermonner; -er n. conférencier m.

ledge n. rebord m.; corniche f.

ledger n. registre, grand livre m.

lee, leeward a. sous le vent; — n. côté sous le vent m.

leek n. poireau m.

leer n. œillade f.; — vi., — at lancer des œillades à

lees n. pl. lie f.

leeway n. (naut.) dérive; (coll.) liberté f.; (plus de) temps m.; (plus de) place f.

left a. & n. gauche f.; — adv. à gauche; on the —, to the — à gauche; -ist n. partisan de la gauche m.

left-handed a. gaucher

leg n. jambe f.; patte f.; (fowl) cuisse f.; (lamb) gigot m.; (object) pied m.; pull someone's — faire marcher quelqu'un; -ged a. à jambes

legacy n. legs m.

legal a. légal; juridique; -ity n. légalité f.; -ize vt. légaliser, authentiquer

legatee n. légataire m. & f.

legation n. légation f.

legend n. légende f.; -ary a. légendaire
legerdemain n. tour d'adresse m.
leggings n. pl. jambières f. pl.
Leghorn n. Livourne f.
leghorn n. paille d'Italie f.; poule blanche f.
legibility n. lisibilité f.
legible a. lisible
legion n. légion f.; -ary n. légionnaire m.
legislate vi. faire des lois
legislation n. législation f.
legislator n. législateur m.
legislature n. législature f.
legitimacy n. légitimité f.
legitimize vt. légitimiser
legume n. légume m.
leisure n. loisir m.; at — à loisir, à tête reposée; -ly a. posé, mesuré; in a -ly manner sans se presser
lemon n. citron m.; — (tree) citronnier m.; -ade n. citron pressé m.; (lemon drink) citronnade f.; (carbonated) limonade f.; — squeezer n. presse-citron m.
lend vt. prêter; -er n. prêteur m.; -ing n. prêt m.; (com.) prestation f.
lend-lease n. prêt-bail m.
length n. longueur f.; bout, morceau m.; (fabric) coupon m.; (pipe) tronçon m.; at — longuement; en détail; enfin; -en vt. allonger, rallonger, prolonger; — vi. s'allonger; augmenter; -y a. long, prolixe
lengthwise adv. en long, en longueur
leniency n. clémence f.; indulgence f.
lenient a. clément; indulgent
lens n. lentille f., verre m.; (phot.) objectif m.; — speed n. ouverture relative f.
Lent n. Carême m.; -en a. de Carême
lentil n. lentille f.
leprosy n. lèpre f.
leprous a. lépreux
lesion n. lésion f.
less a. moindre; moins (de); — adv. moins (de); -en vt. amoindrir; diminuer; — vi. diminuer; -er a. moindre; petit
lessee n. locataire m. & f.
lesson n. leçon f.; exemple m.
lessor n. bailleur m.
lest conj. de peur que, de crainte que
let vt. & vi. laisser; permettre; louer; — go de lâcher; — in laisser entrer; — off laisser partir, tirer, décharger; — out laisser sortir; faire sortir; — up laisser monter; ralentir, devenir moins sévère
lethargic a. léthargique
lethargy n. léthargie f.
letter n. lettre f.; caractère m.; capital — majuscule f.; — box boîte aux lettres; — carrier facteur m.; — of credit n. lettre de crédit f.; — opener ouvre-lettres m.; — vt. marquer avec des lettres; -ing n. lettrage m.; inscription f.
letterhead n. en-tête (de papier à écrire) m.
letter-perfect a. impeccable, parfait dans tous les détails
letterpress n. (print.) typographie f.

lettuce n. laitue f.
letup n. relâche f.
Levantine n. & a. Levantin m.
levee n. levée f.; (reception) lever m., réception f.
level n. niveau m.; palier m.; on a — with de niveau avec; à la hauteur de; égal à; — a. égal; à niveau; — with à ras de, à fleur de; — vt. niveler; égaliser
levelheaded a. pondéré, sensé
lever n. levier m.; -age n. force de levier f., bras de levier m.
levity n. légèreté f.
levy n. levée f.; impôt m.; — vt. lever, imposer
lewd a. lascif, impudique; débauché; -ness n. lasciveté, luxure f.
lexicography n. lexicographie f.
lexicon n. lexique m.
liability n. responsabilité f.; liabilities pl. passif m.; dettes, obligations f. pl.
liable a. responsable; passible (de); sujet (à)
liar n. menteur m.
libel n. diffamation f.; libelle m.; — vt. diffamer; -ous a. diffamatoire
liberal a. libéral; généreux; large; ample; — n. libéral; -ism n. libéralisme m.; -ity n. générosité f.; -ly ada. libéralement; généreusement
liberal-minded a. large d'esprit
liberate vt. libérer
liberation n. libération f.
liberator n. libérateur m.
Liberia n. Libéria m.
libertine n. libertin m.
liberty n. liberté f.; at — libre; en liberté; take the — of se permettre de
librarian n. bibliothécaire m. & f.
library n. bibliothèque f.; circulating — cabinet de lecture m.
Libya n. Libye f.
license n. permis m., permission f.; patente f.; autorisation f.; licence f.; driver's — permis de conduire m.; — number n. (auto) immatriculation f.; numéro matricule m.; — plate n. plaque d'immatriculation f.; — vt. accorder un permis à
licentious a. licencieux; -ness n. licence f., dérèglement m.
licit a. licite
lick n. coup de langue m.; — vt. lécher; (coll.) battre, rosser; — one's chops se lécher les babines
licorice n. réglisse f.
lid n. couvercle m.; (eye) paupière f.
lie n. mensonge m.; (of land) disposition, configuration f.; — vi. mentir; (position) être couché; se trouver, être; — down se coucher; — still rester tranquille; here — s ci-gît
lie detector n. polygraphe m.
lien n. hypothèque f.
lieu n., in — of au lieu de
lieutenant n. lieutenant m.; — commander lieutenant de vaisseau m.; — general lieutenant de division m.; second — sous-lieutenant m.
life n. vie f.; existence f.; vivant m.;

biographie *f.*; animation *f.*; come to —
s'animer; for — à la vie, à perpétuité; it's
a matter of — and death il y va de la
vie; — annuity rente viagère *f.*; —
insurance assurance sur la vie, assu-
rance-vie *f.*; -less *a.* sans vie; still —
nature morte

life belt *n.* ceinture de sauvetage *f.*

lifeblood *n.* sang *m.*; (fig.) vie, âme *f.*

lifeboat *n.* canot de sauvetage *m.*

lifeguard *n.* surveillant de plage *m.*

life jacket *n.* ceinture de sauvetage *f.*

lifelong *a.* de toute la vie

life preserver *n.* appareil de sauvetage
m.; bouée *f.*; brassière de sauvetage *f.*

lifesaving *n.* sauvetage *m.*

life-size *a.* en grand; de grandeur normale

lifetime *n.* vie *f.*; vivant *m.*; espace d'une
vie *m.*

lift *n.* haussement *m.*, levée *f.*; (elevator)
ascenseur *m.*; (shoe) talon *m.*; give a —
to conduire, faire monter (dans une
auto); encourager; rafraîchir; animer;
ski — télésiège *m.*; — *vt.* lever; soulever; élever; (coll.) plagier; — *vi.*
s'élever

ligament *n.* ligament *m.*

light *n.* lumière *f.*; lueur *f.*; jour *m.*; lampe
f.; feu *m.*; phare *m.*; electric — bulb
ampoule *f.*; — wave onde lumineuse
f.; by the — of à la lumière de, au
clair de; bring to — mettre au jour;
come to — se révéler; throw — on
éclairer; — *vt.* allumer; éclairer, illuminer; — *vi.* s'allumer; s'éclairer;
— *a.* clair; blond; (weight) léger; —
vt. alléger; soulager; hausser; -er *n.*
briquet *m.*; (naut.) péniche *f.*; -ing
n. éclairage *m.*; allumage *m.*; -ly *adv.*
légèrement; à la légère; -ness *n.*
légèreté *f.*

light-fingered *a.* fripon, voleur

light-footed *a.* agile

lightheaded *a.* étourdi

lighthearted *a.* au cœur léger; gai

lighthouse *n.* phare (marin) *m.*

light meter *n.* (phot.) luxmètre, photo-
mètre, posemètre *m.*

lightning *n.* foudre *f.*; éclair *m.*; flash of
— éclair *m.*; — rod paratonnerre *m.*;
forked — foudre en zigzag *f.*

lightship *n.* bateau-phare *m.*

lightweight *n.* poids léger; — *a.* leger

light-year (ast.) année-lumière *f.*

likable, likeable *a.* sympathique, aimable,
agréable

like *a.* pareil, semblable; tel; — *prep.*
comme; what is he —? comment est-
il?; what is the weather —? quel temps
fait-il?; — *n.* semblable *m.* & *f.*; goût
m.; — *vt.* aimer; trouver; vouloir;
-lihood *n.* probabilité, vraisemblance
f.; chance *f.*; -ly *a.* probable, vraisemblable; -ly *adv.* probablement; -n *vt.*
comparer; -ness *n.* ressemblance *f.*;
image *f.*; portrait *m.*

likewise *adv.* de même, autant; aussi

liking *n.* goût *m.*; gré *m.*; penchant *m.*

limb *n.* membre *m.*; branche *f.*; (math.)
limbe *m.*

limber *a.* souple, flexible

limelight *n.* projecteur *m.*; in the —
(très) en vue

limestone *n.* calcaire *m.*; pierre à chaux
f.

limit *n.* limite, borne *f.*; — *vt.* limiter,
borner; restreindre; -ation *n.* limita-
tion *f.*; -ed *a.* borné, limité; restreint;
-less *a.* sans bornes

limp *n.* boitement, clochement *m.*; — *vi.*
boiter, clocher; — *a.* mou; souple; -ing
a. boiteux; -ly *adv.* mollement; sans
énergie; -ness *n.* mollesse *f.*

limpid *a.* limpide, clair; -ity *n.* limpidité,
clarté *f.*

linden *n.* tilleul *m.*

line *n.* ligne *f.*; trait *m.*; forme *f.*; rangée,
queue, file *f.*; (of a poem) vers *m.*;
métier *m.*; compagnie *f.*; stand in —
faire la queue; — *vt.* ligner, régler;
border; (clothes) doubler; (brakes)
rapetasser; — up aligner; faire la
queue; -age *n.* lignée *f.*; -al *a.* linéal,
en ligne directe; -ar *a.* linéaire; -d *a.*
doublé

lineman *n.* poseur de lignes *m.*; (football)
arbitre de touche *m.*; (tennis) arbitre
de lignes *m.*; (railroad) garde-ligne *m.*

linen *n.* toile de lin *f.*; linge *m.*, lingerie
f.; — closet lingerie *f.*

liner *n.* (ship) paquebot *m.*; garniture,
bande de remplissage *f.*

line-up *n.* queue, file *f.*; disposition *f.*

linger *vi.* s'attarder; traîner; -ing *a.*
lent; prolongé

lingual *a.* lingual

lingerie *n.* linge *m.*

linguist *n.* linguiste *m.* & *f.*; -ic *a.* linguistique; -ics *n. pl.* linguistique *f.*

liniment *n.* liniment *m.*

lining *n.* doublure *f.*; (brake) garniture
f.; (hat) coiffe *f.*

link *n.* chaînon *m.*; anneau *m.*; lien *m.*;
— *vt.* enchaîner; lier, relier

linoleum *n.* linoléum *m.*

linotype *n.* linotype *f.*

linseed *n.* graine de lin *f.*; — oil *n.* huile
de lin *f.*

lint *n.* charpie *f.*

lintel *n.* linteau *m.*

lip *n.* lèvre *f.*; bord *m.*; — reading lecture
sur les lèvres *f.*

lipstick *n.* rouge à lèvres *m.*

liquefaction *n.* liquéfaction *f.*

liquefy *vt.* liquéfier; — *vi.* se liquéfier

liqueur *n.* liqueur *f.*

liquid *n.* liquide *m.*; — *a.* liquide;
assets valeurs disponibles *f. pl.*; -ate
vt. liquider; -ation *n.* liquidation *f.*

liquor *n.* boisson alcoolique *f.*; alcool *m.*

Lisbon *n.* Lisbonne *f.*

lisle *n.* fil d'Écosse *m.*

lisp *n.* zézayement *m.*; — *vt.* & *vi.* zézayer;
zozoter

list *n.* liste *f.*; état *m.*; (naut.) bande,
gîte *f.*; (fabric selvage) lisière *f.*; —
price *n.* prix marqué *m.*; — *vt.* faire
une liste de; cataloguer; — *vi.* (naut.)
donner de la bande

listen *vt.* écouter, prêter l'oreille, faire

attention; –er n. auditeur m.; –ing n.
écoute f.

listless a. apathique, insouciant

litany n. litanies f. pl.

liter n. litre m.

literacy n. capacité de lire et d'écrire f.

literal a. littéral; sans imagination; –ly
à la lettre, au pied de la lettre; littéralement

literary a. littéraire

literate a. qui sait lire et écrire

literature n. littérature f.; (com.) prospectus m. pl.

lithe a. agile, souple

lithograph n. lithographie f.; – vt. lithographier; –er n.; –ic a. lithographique;
lithographe m.; –y n. lithographie f.

Lithuania n. Lithuanie f.

litigate vt. & vi. plaider

litigation n. litige, procès m.

litmus n. tournesol m.; – paper n. papier
de tournesol m.

litter n. civière, litière f.; encombrement
m.; détritus, débris m. pl.; (of an animal) portée f.; – vt. mettre en désordre;
joncher; –ed a. encombré

little a. petit; peu de; a — un peu de;
— adv. peu; –a. peu m.; — by —
peu à peu, petit à petit; –ness n.
petitesse f.

liturgy n. liturgie f.

live a. vivant, en vie; (coal) ardent; (wire)
en charge; (television) en direct; —
pickup, — show (television) prise de
vues en direct f.; –lihood n. vie f.;
gagne-pain m.; –liness n. vivacité f.;
vie f.; animation f.; –ly a. vif (vive);
animé; –n vt., –n up animer

live vi. vivre, exister; demeurer, habiter;
durer

liver n. foie m.

livery n. livrée f.; — stable n. écurie de
chevaux de louage f.

livestock n. bétail m., bestiaux m. pl.

livid a. livide; plombé

living a. vivant, en vie; vif; — room salon
m.; — wage salaire vital m.; — n. vie
f.; make a — gagner de quoi vivre,
gagner sa vie; standard of — niveau
de vie m.

load n. fardeau m.; charge f.; poids m.;
— vt. charger; accabler; — vt. prendre
charge; –ing n. chargement n.

loaf n. pain m.; — vi. fainéanter; flâner;
–er n. fainéant m.; flâneur m.; –ing n.
fainéantise f.

loam n. terre grasse f.

loan n. prêt m.; emprunt m.; — shark n.
usurier m.; — vt. prêter

loath a. fâché, peu enclin

loathe vt. détester, abhorrer

loathing n. dégoût m.

loathsome a. dégoûtant, repoussant

lobby n. vestibule m.; — vi. chercher à
faire valoir l'influence (sur la législature); –ist n. agent, représentant (d'un
groupe cherchant à faire valoir son
influence) m.

lobster n. homard m.; spiny — langouste
f.

local a. local; régional; –e n. scène f.;

lieu m.; –ity n. localité f.; région f.;
voisinage m.; –ize vt. localiser; –ly
adv. localement; dans la région; dans
le voisinage

locate vt. trouver, découvrir, localiser;
situer; be –d se trouver, être situé

location n. situation f.; lieu, endroit m.

lock n. serrure f.; (rifle) platine f.; (dam)
écluse f.; air — sas m.; écluse pneumatique f.; pick a — crocheter une
serrure; under — and key sous clef; —
vt. fermer à clef; enfermer; — vi.
s'enrayer; s'enclencher; –er n. armoire
f.; compartiment m.

locket n. médaillon m.

lockjaw n. trisme m.

lock nut n. contre-écrou m.

lockout n. lock-out m.

locksmith n. serrurier m.

lockup n. prison f.

locomotion n. locomotion f.

locomotive a. locomotif; — n. locomotive
f.

locus n. (math.) lieu m.

lode n. filon m., veine f.

lodge n. cabane f.; pavillon m.; loge f.;
— vt. loger; — a complaint porter
plainte; — vt. se loger; –r n. pensionnaire m. & f.

lodging n. logement m.

loft n. grenier m.; soupente f.; atelier m.

loftiness n. élévation, hauteur f.

lofty a. élevé, haut; sublime

log n. bûche f.; (naut.) livre de loch m.,
journal de navigation m.; — cabin
cabane de bois f.; — vt. & vi. exploiter
(une forêt); –ger n. bûcheron m.

loganberry n. ronce-framboise f.

logarithm n. logarithme m.

loggerhead n., be at –s être aux prises

logic n. logique f.; –al a. logique

logistics n. pl. approvisionnement, ravitaillement m.

loin n. (beef) aloyau m.; (veal) longe f.;
–s pl. reins m. pl.

loiter vi. flâner; rôder; –er n. flâneur m.;
rôdeur m.; –ing n. flânerie f.; vagabondage m.

loll vi. flâner, s'étaler; pendre

London n. Londres

lone a. seul, solitaire; –liness n. solitude
f.; –ly a. solitaire; isolé; –some a.
seul, solitaire

long a. long (longue); –shot (coll.) concurrent qui a peu de chance de gagner;
a — time longtemps; in the — run à la
longue; — adv. longtemps; as — as
tant que; be — in tarder à; how long?
(depuis) combien de temps; depuis
quand; — vi., — for avoir envie de;
soupirer après; brûler de; –ing n. désir
m., envie f.

long-distance a. à longue distance; —
call communication interurbaine f.;
— operator inter m.

longevity n. longévité f.

long-faced a. triste, à triste mine

longhand n. écriture ordinaire f.; — a.
non-dactylographié, écrit à main

longitude n. longitude f.

longitudinal a. longitudinal

long-legged *a.* aux jambes longues
long-lived *a.* à longue vie; à longue durée
long-lost *a.* perdu depuis longtemps
long-playing *a.* microsillon, à longue durée; — record disque microsillon *m.*
longshoreman *n.* docker, débardeur *m.*
long-standing *a.* de longue date
long-suffering *a.* endurant, patient
long-winded *a.* de longue haleine; intarissable, interminable
look *n.* regard *m.*; coup d'œil *m.*; air, aspect *m.*, apparence *f.*; — *vt.* regarder, avoir l'air, paraître; — like ressembler à; — after s'occuper de; soigner; veiller sur; — at regarder; — away détourner les yeux; — for chercher; — into étudier, examiner; — out prendre garde; — over parcourir; — up lever les yeux; se ranimer; consulter; (person) rechercher; -ing *a.*, -ing glass miroir *m.*, glace *f.*
lookout *n.* (person) guetteur *m.*, (naut.) vigie *f.*; be on the — guetter; être sur le qui-vive
loom *n.* métier à tisser *m.*; — *vi.* paraître; surgir
loop *n.* boucle *f.*; œil *m.*; attache *f.*; — *vt.* & *vi.* boucler
loophole *n.* meurtrière *f.*; (fig.) échappatoire *f.*
loose *a.* détaché; défait; branlant; dégagé; lâche; relâché; dissolu; be at — ends être sans occupation; come — se détacher, se dégager, se défaire; — *vt.* lâcher, libérer; -n *vt.* relâcher; dénouer; dégager; — *vi.* se défaire, se relâcher, se dégager; -ness *n.* relâchement *m.*; jeu *m.*
loose-leaf *a.* à feuilles mobiles
loot *n.* butin *m.*; — *vt.* piller; -ing *n.* pillage, sac *m.*
lop *vt.* élaguer, couper
lope *n.* galop lent *m.*; pas lent *m.*; — *vi.* aller doucement
lopsided *a.* déversé, déséquilibré
loquacious *a.* loquace
lord *n.* seigneur *m.*; châtelain *m.*; lord *m.*; — *vt.*, — it faire l'important; -ly *a.* noble; hautain; -ship *n.* seigneurie *f.*
Lord *n.* Seigneur; Dieu *m.*; in the year of Our — en l'an de grâce; —'s Prayer *n.* patenôtre *f.*; oraison dominicale *f.*
lore *n.* science *f.*, savoir *m.*
lose *vt.* perdre, égarer; — oneself s'absorber dans; — one's temper s'emporter; — one's way se perdre, s'égarer; — sight of perdre de vue; -r *n.* battu, perdant *m.*; bad -r mauvais joueur *m.*
loss *n.* perte *f.*; privation *f.*; be at a — to avoir de la peine à; ne pas savoir
lot *n.* sort *m.*, fortune *f.*; (portion) lot *m.*, quantité *f.*; (land) terrain *m.*; a — (of) beaucoup (de); draw —s tirer au sort
lottery *n.* loterie *f.*
loud *a.* fort, haut; bruyant; (color) criard; — *adv.* à haute voix; -ness *n.* bruit *m.*; force *f.*
loud-speaker *n.* haut-parleur *m.*
lounge *n.* hall, salon *m.*; foyer *m.*; chaise — chaise longue *f.*; — *vi.* flâner; s'étendre
louver *n.* bande, grille *f.*, cloison *m.*; -ed *a.* à bandes, cloisonné
lovable *a.* aimable
love *n.* amour *m.*; tendresse, affection *f.*; (person) ami *m.*, amie *f.*; amour *m.* & *f.*; (tennis) rien, zéro *m.*; be in — (with) être amoureux (de), être épris (de); fall in — (with) tomber amoureux (de), s'éprendre (de); — affair liaison *f.*; — letter billet doux *m.*; — song romance, chanson d'amour *f.*; — *vt.* aimer; adorer; -less *a.* sans amour; -liness *n.* beauté *f.*; -ly *a.* beau (belle); charmant, ravissant; -r *n.* amant *m.*; amoureux *m.*; amateur *m.*
love-making *n.* cour *f.*
lovesick *a.* féru d'amour
loving *a.* aimant, affectueux; — cup trophée *f.*
low *a.* bas; vil; peu élevé; (dress) décolletée; (spirits) abattu; (sound) grave; — *adv.* bas; — *n.* niveau le plus bas *m.*; -er *a.* inférieur; plus bas; -er *vt.* baisser; abaisser; rabaisser; descendre; -liness *n.* humilité *f.*; -ly *a.* petit, humble, modeste; -ness *n.* petitesse *f.*; faiblesse *f.*; (action) bassesse *f.*; (spirits) abattement *m.*
low *n.* (cow) meuglement; — *vi.* meugler
lowboy *n.* commode basse *f.*
low-cut *a.* décolleté
lowland *n.* plaine basse *f.*; -s *pl.* terres basses *f. pl.*
low-pitched *a.* grave
low-pressure *a.* à basse pression
low-priced *a.* pas cher, bon marché
low-spirited *a.* triste, abattu
low-water mark *n.* niveau des basses eaux.
loyal *a.* fidèle; loyal; -ist *n.* loyaliste *m.* & *f.*; -ty *n.* fidélité *f.*
lozenge *n.* pastille *f.*; lozenge *f.*
lubricant *n.* lubrifiant *m.*
lubricate *vt.* lubrifier, graisser
lubrication *n.* lubrification *f.*, graissage *m.*
lucid *a.* lucide; -ity *n.* lucidité *f.*
luck *n.* chance *f.*; hasard *m.*; bad — malheur *m.*; malchance *f.*; good — bonheur *m.*; bonne chance *f.*; stroke of — coup de veine *m.*; -ily *adv.* heureusement, par bonheur; -less *a.* infortuné, malheureux; -y *a.* fortuné; be -y avoir de la chance; (object) porter bonheur
lucrative *a.* lucratif
ludicrous *a.* risible; ridicule; absurde; -ness *n.* ridicule *m.*
lug *vt.* traîner; — *n.* saillie, oreille, cosse, lamelle, patte *f.*
luggage *n.* bagages *m. pl.*
lugubrious *a.* lugubre
lukewarm *a.* tiède; -ness *n.* tiédeur *f.*
lull *n.* moment de calme *m.*; accalmie *f.*; — *vt.* bercer, endormir; — *vi.* se calmer
lullaby *n.* berceuse *f.*
lumber *n.* bois de charpente *m.*; — *vi.* se traîner; -ing *a.* lourd, lent
lumberjack *n.* bûcheron *m.*
lumberjacket *n.* gros blouson *m.*, canadienne *f.*

lumberyard n. dépôt de bois de charpente, chantier de bois m.

luminary n. luminaire m.

luminescence n. luminescence f.

luminous a. lumineux

lump n. morceau m.; bloc m.; motton m.; (throat) serrement m.; — sum somme grosse f.; prix à forfait m.; — vt. mettre en bloc; — together réunir ensemble; –y a. grumeleux

lunacy n. folie f.; aliénation, démence f.

lunar a. lunaire

lunatic a. fou; de fou; — n. aliéné, fou, dément m.

lunch n. déjeuner, lunch m.; — vi. déjeuner; –eon n. déjeuner, lunch m.

lunchtime n. heure du déjeuner f.

lung n. poumon m.; iron — poumon d'acier m.

lunge n. mouvement en avant m.; — vi. se jeter en avant

lurch n. embarras m.; embardée f., cahot m.; titubation f.; — vi. embarder; marcher en titubant

lure n. leurre n., piège m.; (fig.) attrait, appel m.; — vt. leurrer; attirer, séduire; — away détourner

lurid · a. sensationnel, éblouissant, choquant

lurk vi. se cacher; rôder; –ing a. caché

luscious a. succulent

lush a. surabondant; plein de sève n.

lust n. convoitise f.; concupiscence f.; désir m.; luxure f.; soif f.; — vi. désirer ardemment; — after convoiter; –ful a. luxurieux; –y a. robuste, vigoureux

luster, lustre n. éclat, lustre, brillant m.

lustrous a. éclatant, lustré

lute n. luth m.

Luxemburg n. Luxembourg m.

luxuriant a. luxuriant

luxuriate vi. croître avec abondance; s'abandonner, vivre dans l'abondance

luxurious a. luxueux; somptueux; –ness n. luxe m.

luxury n. luxe m.

lye n. lessive f.

lying a. menteur; (position) couché, étendu; — n: mensonge m.

lying-in hospital n. (hospice de la) maternité f.

lymph n. lymphe f.; –atic a. lymphatique

lynch vt. lyncher; –ing n. lynchage m.

Lyons n. Lyon

lyre n. lyre f.

lyric(al) a. lyrique

M

M.A.: Master of Arts licencié ès lettres m.

macadam n. macadam m.

macaroni n. macaronis m. pl.

macaroon n. macaron m.

mace n. masse f.; (bot.) macis m., fleur de muscade f.

macerate vt. macérer

machination n. machination f., complot m., intrigue f.

machine n. machine f.; (pol.) organisation f.; — gun mitrailleuse f.; — tool machine-outil f.; — vt. usiner; –ry n. machines f. pl.; mécanisme m.

machine-gun vt. mitrailler

machine shop n. atelier de construction de machines m.

machinist n. machiniste, mécanicien m.

mackerel n. maquereau m.

mad a. fou, aliéné; insensé; furieux; enragé; go — devenir fou; –den vt. rendre fou; exaspérer; –ly adv. follement; furieusement; love –ly aimer éperdument; –ness n. folie f.; démence f.; rage f.

Madagascar n. Madagascar m.

madam n. madame f.

madcap n. & a. fou, insensé m.

made a. fait; confectionné; fabriqué

Madeira n. Madère f.

made-to-order, made to measure a. fait sur mesure, fait sur commande

made-up a. maquillé; inventé; fait; factice

madhouse n. maison de fous f.

madman n. fou, aliéné m.

madonna n. madone f.

madras n. madras m.

madrigal n. madrigal m.

maestro n. maître m.

magazine n. revue f., périodique m.; (mil.) magasin, dépôt m.; (camera) chargeur m.; powder — poudrière f.

maggot n. asticot m.

magic n. magie f.; —, –al a. magique; –ian n. magicien m.

magistrate n. magistrat m.; juge m.

magnanimity n. magnanimité f.

magnanimous a. magnanime

magnate n. magnat m.

magnesia n. magnésie f.

magnesium n. magnésium m.

magnet n. aimant m.; –ic a. magnétique, d'aimant, aimanté; –ic (recording) tape n. ruban magnétique m.; –ic speaker n. haut-parleur électro-magnétique m.; –ism n. magnétisme m.; –ize vt. magnétiser

magneto n. magnéto m.

magnification n. amplification f., grossissement m.

magnificence n. magnificence f.

magnificent a. magnifique

magnifier n. loupe f.

magnify vt. grossir, amplifier, agrandir

magnifying glass n. verre grossissant m., loupe f.

magnitude n. grandeur f.; magnitude f.

maid n. servante, bonne f.; fille f.; old — vieille fille f.; –en n. jeune fille f.; vierge f.; –en a. de jeune fille, de demoiselle; –en speech discours de début m.; — voyage n. voyage d'inauguration m.

mail n. courrier m.; poste f.; (armor) maille f.; — vt. mettre (une lettre) à la poste; expédier; — order n. commande par la poste f.

mailbox n. boîte aux lettres f.

mailman n. facteur m.

mail-order house n. établissement de vente par correspondance m.

mailplane n. avion postal m.

maim vt. estropier, mutiler

main n. (water) canalisation maîtresse f.; océan m., mer f.; in the — en général; — a. principal, essentiel; grand; le plus important; — office (com.) siège social m.; — thing essentiel m.; -ly adv. principalement

mainland n. continent m.; terre firme f.

mainspring n. grand ressort, ressort principal m.

mainstay n. point d'appui m.; appui principal m.

maintain vt. maintenir, soutenir; entretenir; garder; défendre; prétendre; subvenir aux besoins de; -ance n. entretien; maintien m.; pension alimentaire f.

majestic a. majestueux; -ally adv. majestueusement

majesty n. majesté f.

major n. commandant m.; (age) majeur m.; — general général de division m.; — a. majeur, plus grand; — vi. (school) se spécialiser; -ity n. majorité f.; la plus grande partie f.

Majorca n. Majorque f.

make n. marque f.; fabrication f.; — vt. faire; fabriquer; façonner; créer; construire; confectionner; (with adjective) rendre; causer; nommer; (cards) battre; (money) gagner; — a living gagner son pain; — for se diriger vers; (naut.) mettre le cap sur; favoriser; — fun of se moquer de; — good réussir; — it (coll.) réussir, y arriver; — off filer, décamper; — over céder, transmettre; — out faire; (list) dresser; (check) écrire, tirer; comprendre; déchiffrer; — up regagner; préparer; inventer; se maquiller; se réconcilier; -r n. fabricant m.; faiseur m.

Maker n. Créateur m.

make-believe n. semblant m.; land of — pays des chimères m.; — vt. faire semblant

makeshift n. improvisé; de fortune

make-up n. maquillage, fard m.; composition f.

making n. fabrication f.; confection f.; construction f.; composition f.; création f.; have the -s avoir tout ce qu'il faut; in the — en train de se faire; — up préparation, composition f.; compensation f.; réconciliation f.

maladjusted a. mal adapté, inadapté

maladjustment n. ajustement défectueux m.

malady n. maladie f.

Malay a. & n. malais m.; -an n. Malaisie f.

malcontent a. & n. mécontent m.

male a. & n. mâle m.

malefactor n. malfaiteur m.

malevolence n. malveillance f.

malevolent a. malveillant

malfeasance n. malfaisance f.

malformation n. malformation f.

malformed a. malformé

malice n. méchanceté f.; malice f.; with — aforethought avec préméditation

malicious a. méchant; malveillant; rancunier; -ness n. malice, malveillance f.

malign a. pernicieux; — vt. diffamer, calomnier; -ancy n. malignité f.; -ant a. malin (maligne)

mall n. mail m.

malleability n. malléabilité f.

malleable a. malléable, forgeable

mallet n. maillet m.

malnutrition n. sous-alimentation f.

malodorous a. malodorant

malpractice n. malversation f.

malt n. malt m.; -ed milk n. boisson composée de lait et de crème glacée, parfumée au malt f.

Malta n. Malte f.

Maltese a. & n. maltais m.

maltreat vt. maltraiter; -ment n. mauvais traitement m.

mama, mamma n. maman f.

mammal n. mammifère m.; -ian a. des mammifères

mammary a. mammaire

mammoth n. mammouth m.; — a. géant

man n. homme m.; mari m.; ouvrier m.; domestique m.; (chess) pièce f.; (sports) joueur m.; dead — mort m.; old — vieillard m.; to a —, to the last — jusqu'au dernier; — vt. armer, équiper, garnir; -hood n. âge d'homme m.; -kind n. humanité f., homme, genre humain m.; -liness m. virilité f.; -ly a. d'homme; viril

manacles n. pl. menottes f. pl.

manage vt. diriger, conduire; gérer, arranger; faire; savoir; arriver à; -able a. maniable, traitable; -ment n. direction, conduite f.; gérance f.; administration f.; -r n. directeur, gérant, administrateur m.; chef m.

managing a. directeur, gérant

Manchukuo n. Mandchoukouo m.

Manchuria n. Mandchourie f.

mandate n. mandat m.; commandement m.

mandatory a. obligatoire, mandatif

mandible n. mandibule f.

mandolin n. mandoline f.

mane n. crinière f.

man-eater n. mangeur d'hommes m.

maneuver n. manœuvre f.; — vt. manœuvrer

manganese n. manganèse m.

mange n. gale (de chien) f.

manger n. mangeoire, crèche f.

mangle n. calandre f.; — vt. mutiler, déchirer; (laundry) calandrer

mangy a. galeux

manhandle vt. malmener; manutentionner

manhole n. trou de visite m., bouche d'égout f.

mania n. manie f.; -c n. fou m., folle f.; -cal a. maniaque

manicure n. manucure m.; — vt. soigner les ongles (mains), se faire les ongles (mains)

manicurist n. manucure f.

manifest a. manifeste, évident; — n. manifeste m.; — vt. manifester; montrer, témoigner; -ation n. manifestation f.; -o n. manifeste m.

manifold a. varié, divers, multiple, nom-

breux; (engine) tubulure *f.*
manikin *n.* mannequin *m.*
Manila *n.* Manille *f.*
manila *n.* manille *f.*; — paper papier
bulle *m.*
manipulate *vt.* manipuler; tripoter
manipulation *n.* manipulation *f.*; tripotage *m.*
manipulator *n.* manipulateur *m.*
manna *n.* manne *f.*
manner *n.* manière *f.*; façon *f.*; sorte *f.*, genre *m.*; air, maintien *m.*; in a
— of speaking pour ainsi dire; in such a
— that de manière que, de sorte que; in
this — de cette façon, de cette manière;
-s *pl.* manières *f. pl.*; politesse *f.*; mœurs
f. pl.; -ism *n.* affectation *f.*, maniérisme *m.*; -ly *a.* poli; bien élevé
man-of-war *n.* vaisseau de guerre *m.*
manor *n.* château seigneurial *m.*; seigneurie *f.*
man power *n.* main-d'œuvre *f.*; (mil.) ef-
fectifs *m. pl.*
mansard *n.* toit en mansarde *m.*
mansion *n.* hôtel (particulier) *m.*; château
m.
manslaughter *n.* homicide involontaire *m.*
mantel *n.* manteau de cheminée *m.*; dessus de cheminée *m.*
mantle *n.* manteau *m.*, pèlerine *f.*; (fig.)
voile *m.*; (heraldry) lambrequin *m.*; —
vt. voiler, couvrir
manual *a.* manuel, de manœuvre; à bras,
à main; — training *n.* apprentissage
manuel *m.*; — *n.* manuel *m.*
manufacture *n.* fabrication *f.*; — *vt.* fabriquer, manufacturer; -r *n.* fabricant,
manufacturier, industriel *m.*
manufacturing *n.* fabrication *n.*; — *a.* industriel
manure *n.* fumier *m.*; engrais *m.*; — *vt.* fumer, engraisser
manuscript *n.* manuscrit *m.*
Manx *n. & a.* Mannois *m.*
many *a. & n.* beaucoup (de); bien des; un
grand nombre (de); maint; pas mal
(de); as — autant (de); how — combien
(de); so — tant (de); too — trop (de)
many-sided *a.* à plusieurs côtés; à de mul-
tiples reflets; polygone
map *n.* carte *f.*; plan *m.*; — maker cartographe *m.*; — making cartographie *f.*;
road — carte routière *f.*; — *vt.* tracer
une carte de; — out arranger, projeter,
préparer; -ping *n.* cartographie *f.*; action de tracer une carte *f.*
mar *vt.* gâter, troubler
maraschino *n.* marasquin *m.*
marauder *n.* maraudeur *m.*; malandrin *m.*
marble *n.* marbre *m.*; bille *f.*; — a en marbre; — *vt.* marbrer; -d *a.* marbré
march *n.* marche *f.*; pas *m.*; — *vi.* marcher;
— in entrer; — by défiler; — *vt.* faire
marcher; -ing *n.* marche *f.*; -ing *a.* en
marche
March *n.* mars *m.*
marchioness *n.* marquise *f.*
mare *n.* jument *f.*
margin *n.* marge *f.*; bord *m.*; (stock)
acompte *m.*; -al *a.* marginal

margin release *n.* (typewriter) déclanche-
marge *m.*
marimba *n.* xylophone *m.*
marine *a.* marin; maritime; — *n.* marine
f.; soldat d'infanterie marine *m.*; merchant — marine marchande *f.*; -r *n.*
marin *m.*
marital *a.* marital; matrimonial
maritime *a.* maritime
marjoram *n.* marjolaine *f.*
mark *n.* marque *f.*; signe *m.*; preuve *f.*; témoignage *m.*; trace *f.*; tache *f.*; but *m.*;
(school) note *f.*; question — point d'interrogation *m.*; — *vt.* marquer; indiquer; (cards) maquiller, piper; (school)
noter, coter; — down (com.) démarquer; solder; noter; — off mesurer; —
time marquer le pas; — up défigurer,
couvrir de taches; hausser le prix de;
-ed *a.* marqué; sensible
marked-down *a.* soldé
market *n.* marché *m.*; halle *f.*; — place
place du marché *f.*; — price prix courant *m.*; on the — en vente; — *vt.* lancer
sur le marché; — *vi.* faire son marché;
-able *a.* vendable; -ing *n.* marché
marksman *n.* bon tireur *m.*; -ship *n.*
adresse au tir *f.*
markup *n.* bénéfice, profit *m.*
marmalade *n.* marmelade *f.*
marmoset *n.* marmouset *m.*
marmot *n.* marmotte *f.*
maroon *a. & n.* marron *m.*; — *vt.* abandonner (dans une île); isoler
marquee *n.* marquise *f.*
marquetry *n.* marqueterie *f.*
marquis *n.* marquis *m.*
marriage *n.* mariage *m.*; by — par alliance; give (away) in — donner en mariage; — certificate acte de mariage *m.*;
-able *a.* en d'âge à (se) marier, nubile
married *a.* marié; conjugal; get — se marier; — couple ménage *m.*
marrow *n.* mœlle *f.*
marry *vt.* se marier (avec), épouser; — into s'allier à; — off marier
Marseilles *n.* Marseille
marsh *n.* marais, marécage *m.*; -y *a.* marécageux
marshal *n.* maréchal *m.*; maître es cérémonies *m.*; — *vt.* ranger; rassembler
marshmallow *n.* guimauve *f.*
marsupial *a.* marsupial *m.*
mart *n.* marché *m.*; entrepôt *m.*
martinet *n.* homme fort sur la discipline
m.
Martinique *n.* Martinique *f.*
martyr *n.* martyr *m.*; -dom *n.* martyre *m.*
marvel *n.* merveille *f.*; — *vi.* s'étonner,
s'émerveiller; -ous *a.* merveilleux;
-ously à merveille, merveilleusement
Marxist *a. & n.* marxiste
marzipan *n.* massepain *m.*
mascara *n.* rimmel *m.*
mascot *n.* mascotte *f.*
masculine *a.* masculin; mâle; viril; — *n.*
masculin *m.*
masculinity *n.* masculinité *f.*
mash *n.* mâche *f.*; pâtée *f.*; purée *f.*; — *vt.*
brasser, broyer; mettre en purée; -ed *a.*

en purée; **-ed potatoes** purée de pommes de terre *f.*

mask *n.* masque *m.*; — *vt.* masquer; cacher

mason *n.* maçon *m.*; **franc-maçon** *m.*; **-ic** *a.* maçonnique; **-ry** *n.* maçonnerie *f.*; franc-maçonnerie *f.*

masquerade *n.* mascarade *f.*; bal masqué *m.*

Mass *n.* (eccl.) Messe *f.*; **High —** grand, messe; **Requiem —** Messe des morts *f.*; — *vt.* masser; **(to) hear —** *vt.* assister à la messe; **— book** *n.* missel *m.*; — *vi.* se masser; **-ive** *a.* massif; **en masse**

mass *n.* masse *f.*; multitude, foule *f.*; (eccl.) **High — grand'messe** *f.*; **— meeting** réunion en masse *f.*; **— production** fabrication en série *f.*; construction en série *f.*

massacre *n.* massacre *m.*; — *vt.* massacrer

massage *n.* massage *m.*; (head) friction *f.*; — *vt.* masser; malaxer

masses *pl.* foule *f.*; peuple *m.*

mast *n.* mât *m.*; pylône *m.*

master *n.* maître *m.*; chef, patron *m.*; (duplicator) cliché *n.*; **— key** passe-partout *m.*; **— of arts** licencié ès lettres *m.*; **— stroke** coup de maître *m.*; — *vt.* maîtriser, dompter; apprendre à fond; **-ful** *a.* autoritaire; **-ly** *a.* de maître; **-y** *n.* maîtrise *f.*; connaissance *f.*

mastermind *n.* chef, organisateur, cerveau *m.*; — *vt.* diriger, organiser

masterpiece *n.* chef d'œuvre *m.*

masticate *vt.* mâcher, mastiquer

mastiff *n.* mâtin *m.*

mastoid *a.* mastoïde

mat *n.* natte *f.*, paillasson *m.*; **picture —** passe-partout *m.*; **place — dessous** *m.*; — *vt.* natter; — *vi.* s'emmêler; **-ted** *a.* emmêlé

match *n.* allumette *f.*; mariage *m.*; (colors) assortiment *m.*; (sports) match *m.*; partie *f.*; égal, pareil *m.*; — *vt.* égaler; assortir; — *vi.* s'assortir; **-ing, to — a.** assorti; **-less** *a.* sans pareil, sans égal; incomparable

matchbox *n.* boîte à allumettes *f.*

matchmaker *n.* marieur *m.*, marieuse *f.*

mate *n.* époux *m.*, épouse *f.*; compagnon *m.*, compagne *f.*; mâle *m.*, femelle *f.*; (chess) échec et mat *m.*; (naut.) officier *m.*; **first — second** *m.*; — *vt.* accoupler; (chess) faire échec et mat; — *vi.* s'accoupler

material *a.* matériel; pertinent, important; — *n.* matière *f.*, matériaux *m. pl.*; étoffe *f.*, tissu *m.*; sujet *m.*; **-ism** *n.* matérialisme *m.*; **-istic** *a.* matérialiste; matériel; **-ize** *vi.* se matérialiser; se réaliser; **-ly** *adv.* matériellement; sensiblement

maternal *a.* maternel

maternity *n.* maternité *f.*; **— hospital** *n.* (hospice de la) maternité *f.*

mathematical *a.* mathématique

mathematician *n.* mathématicien *m.*

mathematics *n. pl.* mathématiques *f. pl.*

matriarch *n.* femme chef d'une famille *f.*

matriculate *vt.* immatriculer

matriculation *n.* immatriculation *f.*

matrimonial *a.* matrimonial; conjugal

matrimony *n.* mariage *m.*; vie conjugale *f.*

matrix *n.* matrice *f.*; moule *f.*

matron *n.* matrone *f.*; intendante *f.*; **-ly** *a.* domestique, en femme mariée, d'un certain âge

matter *n.* matière *f.*; sujet *m.*; chose, affaire *f.*; question *f.*; **as a — of fact** à vrai dire; en effet; **— of course** chose qui va de soi *f.*; **— of form** formalité *f.*; **— in hand** chose dont il s'agit *f.*; **what is the —? qu'y a-t-il?**, qu'avez-vous?; **what is the — with him?** qu'a-t-il?; — *vi.* importer; **it does not —** n'importe

matter-of-course *a.* qui va sans dire

matter-of-fact *a.* positif, pratique, calme

matting *n.* natte *f.*; ouate *f.*

mattress *n.* matelas *m.*; (spring) sommier *m.*

mature *a.* mûr, d'âge mûr; (bond) échu; — *vt.* mûrir; — *vi.* mûrir; arriver à, échéance

maturity *n.* maturité *f.*; échéance *f.*

maudlin *a.* excessivement sentimental

maul *vt.* meurtrir, malmener

Mauritania *n.* Mauritanie *f.*

Mauritius *n.* (île) Maurice *f.*

mausoleum *n.* mausolée *m.*

maverick *n.* bœuf non marqué au fer *m.*; solitaire, sauvage *m.*

maxim *n.* maxime *f.*, dicton *m.*

maximum *a. & n.* maximum *m.*

may *vi.* pouvoir; **it — be** il se peut

May *n.* mai *m.*; **— Day** le premier mai *m.*

mayhem *n.* mutilation *f.*; (fig.) ravage, dégât *m.*

maybe *adv.* peut-être

mayor *n.* maire *m.*; président du conseil municipal *m.*

maypole *n.* arbre du premier mai *m.*

maze *n.* labyrinthe *m.*

M.C.: Master of Ceremonies maître des cérémonies *m.*

me *pron.* me, moi

meadow *n.* pré *m.*; prairie *f.*; **— lark** *n.* étourneau *m.*

meager, meagre *a.* maigre; pauvre; peu nombreux

meal *n.* repas *m.*; farine *f.*; **-y** *a.* farineux

mealtime *n.* heure du repas *f.*

mean *a.* bas, vil, méprisable; sale, vilain; mesquin; misérable; (math.) moyen; **— n.** milieu; (math.) moyenne *f.*; **-s** *pl.* moyen *m.* (*pl.*); ressources *f. pl.*; **by all -s** (mais) certainement; **by no -s** pas du tout; en aucune façon; **by -s of** au moyen de; **-ness** *n.* vilenie, mesquinerie *f.*; bassesse *f.*, petitesse *f.*; médiocrité *f.*

mean *vt.* vouloir dire, signifier; avoir l'intention de; **-ing** *n.* sens *m.*, signification *f.*; **-ingful** *a.* significatif; **-ingless** *a.* dépourvu de sens

meander *vi.* serpenter; — *n.* méandre *m.*

meantime *adv. & n.*; **in the —** sur ces entrefaites; dans l'intervalle

meanwhile *adv.* sur ces entrefaites

measles *n. pl.* rougeole *f.*

measurable *a.* mesurable

measurably *adv.* sensiblement; modérément

measure n. mesure f.; démarche f.; in some — en partie; — vt. mesurer; métrer; avoir; —d a. compté; modéré; —less a. vaste, sans bornes; —ment n. mesure f.; mesurage m.

meat n. viande f.; nourriture f.; (fig.) moelle f.; —ball n. boulette de viande f.; —less a. (eccl.) maigre; —y a. charnu

meat market n. boucherie f.

Mecca n. Mecque f.

mechanic n. mécanicien m.; (auto) garagiste m.; —al a. mécanique; automatique; —al engineer a. ingénieur mécanicien m.; —al engineering n. mécanique f.; —s n. pl. mécanique f.

mechanism n. mécanisme m.; appareil m.

mechanize vt. mécaniser

medal n. médaille f.; —lion n. médaillon m.

meddle vi. se mêler (de), s'occuper (de); —some a. qui se mêle de tout

medial a. moyen, médial

median a. médian

mediate vi. s'interposer; servir de médiateur

mediation n. médiation f.

mediator n. médiateur m.; arbitre m.

medical a. médical; — school école de médecine f.

medicate vt. médicamenter

medicine n. médecine f.; médicament m.

medicine chest n. pharmacie f.

medicine dropper n. compte-gouttes m.

medicine man n. médecin indien, sorcier indien m.

medieval a. médiéval; du moyen-âge

mediocre a. médiocre

mediocrity n. médiocrité f.

meditate vt. & vi. méditer

meditation n. méditation f.

meditative a. méditatif

Mediterranean n. Méditerranée f.

medium n. moyen m.; milieu m.; intermédiare m.; organe m.; (spiritualist) médium m.; — a. moyen; (cooking) à point

medium-sized a. de grandeur moyenne, de taille moyenne

medley n. mélange m.; (color) bigarrure f.; (mus.) pot pourri m.

medulla n. moelle f.

Medusa n. Méduse f.

meek a. humble, doux; timide; —ness n. humilité, douceur f.

meerschaum n. écume de mer f.

meet vt. rencontrer; retrouver; croiser; faire la connaissance de; — vi. se rencontrer; se joindre; se réunir; go to — aller au-devant de, aller à la rencontre de; make both ends — joindre les deux bouts; until we — again au revoir; — with éprouver, essuyer; —ing n. réunion f., meeting m.; rencontre f.; —ing place rendez-vous m.

megaphone n. mégaphone m.

melancholia n. mélancolie f.

melancholy a. mélancolique; — n. mélancolie f.

meld n. (cards) combinaison f.; — vi. annoncer

mellow a. doux (douce); mûr; moelleux; — vt. adoucir; mûrir; — vi. s'adoucir; mûrir; —ness n. moelleux m.; maturité f.; mollesse f.

melodious a. mélodieux; —ness n. mélodie f.

melodrama n. mélodrame m.; —tic a. mélodramatique

melody n. air m.; mélodie f.

melon n. melon m.

melt vt. fondre; — vi. (se) fondre; —ing a. fondant; —ing n. fonte, fusion f.; —ing point point de fusion m.; —ing pot creuset m.

member n. membre m.; partie f.; (pol.) représentant, député m.; —ship n. nombre des membres m.; qualité de membre f.; membres m. pl.

membrane n. membrane f.; tunique f.

memento n. souvenir, mémento m.

memo n. mémo, mémorandum m.

memoir n. mémoire m.; —s pl. mémoires m. pl.

memorable a. mémorable

memorandum n. mémorandum, mémo m.; — pad bloc-notes m.

memorial a. commémoratif; — n. monument commémoratif m.; —ist n. auteur de mémoires m.

memorize vt. apprendre par cœur

memory n. mémoire f.; souvenir m.; commit to — apprendre par cœur

menace n. menace f.; — vt. menacer

menagerie n. ménagerie f.

mend n. raccommodage m., reprise f.; on the — en voie de guérison; — vt. raccommoder; réparer; — vi. se remettre; —able a. réparable; —ing n. raccommodage m.

mendicant a. & n. mendiant m.

menial a. bas, servile; — n. domestique, laquais m.

meningitis n. méningite f.

menopause n. ménopause f.

menstruation n. menstruation f.

mental a. mental; de tête; de l'esprit; — hospital maison de santé f.; asile d'aliénés m.; —ity n. mentalité f.

mention n. mention f.; — vt. mentionner; faire mention de; citer; don't — it il n'y a pas de quoi; de rien; not to — sans parler de

mentor n. mentor, guide m.

menu n. carte f., menu m.

mercantile a. mercantile, commercial

mercenary a. & n. mercenaire m.

mercerize vt. merceriser

merchandise n. marchandise f.

merchant n. marchand m.; commerçant, négociant m.; — marine marine marchande f.

merchantman n. vaisseau marchand m.

merciful a. miséricordieux; clément

merciless a. impitoyable

mercurial a. mercuriel, ardent, vif

mercurochrome n. mercurochrome m.

mercury n. mercure m.

Mercury-switch n. interrupteur à mercure m.

mercury-vapor lamp n. lampe à vapeur de mercure f.

mercy n. miséricorde f.; clémence, grâce, merci f.; pitié f.; be at someone's —. être à la merci de; have — on avoir pitié de

mere a. seul; simple, pur; -ly adv. seulement, (tout) simplement

merge vt. fondre, fusionner; — vi. se fondre; fusionner; s'amalgamer

meridian n. méridien m.; -al a. méridional

merit n. mérite m.; -s pl. le pour et le contre; — vt. mériter; -orious a. méritoire

mermaid n. sirène f.

merrily adv. joyeusement

merriment n. gaieté, réjouissance f.

merry a. joyeux, gai

merry-go-round n. manège (de chevaux de bois) m.

mesa n. plateau élevé m.

mesh n. maille f.; engrenage m., prise f.; — vt. engrener, endenter; — vi. être en prise, engrener

mesmerism n. mesmérisme m.

mesmerize vt. hypnotiser

mesotron n. électron lourd, méson m.

mess n. désordre m.; saleté f.; gâchis m.; (mil.) soupe f., mess m.; -y a. sale; en désordre

message n. message m.; mot m.; communication f.

messenger n. messager m.; commissionnaire m.; courrier m.

Messiah n. Messie m.

mess hall n. (mil.) salle de mess f., réfectoire m.; (navy) carré des officiers m.

mess kit n. gamelle f.

Messrs. MM. n. pl. messieurs m. pl.

metabolism n. métabolisme m.

metal n. métal m.; -lic a. métallique; -lurgy n. métallurgie f.

metamorphosis n. métamorphose f.

metaphor n. métaphore f.; -ical a. métaphorique

metaphysical a. métaphysique

metaphysics n. pl. métaphysique f.

metatarsal a. métatarsien

mete vt. distribuer

meteor n. météore m.; -ic a. météorique; rapide; -ite n. aérolithe m.; -ological a. météorologique; -ologist n. météorologiste, météo m.; -ology n. météorologie f.

meter n. mètre m.; compteur m.

methane n. méthane m.

method n. méthode f.; procédé m.; -ical a. méthodique

methyl n. méthyle m.; -ate vt. méthyler

meticulous a. méticuleux

metric a. métrique; -al a. métrique; en vers, mesuré

metronome n. métronome m.

metropolis n. métropole f.

metropolitan a. métropolitain

mettle n. courage, coeur m.

mew vi. miauler

Mexican a. & n. mexicain m.

Mexico n. Mexique m.

mezzanine n. entresol m.

microbe n. microbe m.

microbiology n. microbiologie f.

microcosm n. microcosme m.

microfilm n. microfilm m.; — vt. microfilmer

microgroove n. microsillon m.

micrometer n. micromètre m.

micron n. micron m.

microörganism n. micro-organisme m.

microphone n. microphone m.

microscope n. microscope m.; electron — microscope électronique m.

microscopic a. microscopique

mid a. du milieu, moyen

midday n. midi m.

middle n. milieu m.; centre m.; in the — of au milieu de; en train de; — a. moyen, central; du milieu; — class bourgeoisie f.

Middle Ages n. pl. Moyen-Âge m.

middle-aged a. d'un certain âge

middle-class a. bourgeois

middleman n. intermédiaire m.; revendeur m.; entremetteur m.

middleweight n. poids moyen m.

middling a. moyen; médiocre

middy blouse n. blouse de matelot f.

midget n. nain m., naine f.

midland a. intérieur, de l'intérieur

midnight n. minuit m.

midriff n. diaphragme m.; tour de ceinture m.

midshipman n. aspirant de marine, midship m.

midst n., in the — of au milieu de; parmi; en train de

midsummer n. milieu de l'été m.

midway adv. à mi-chemin, à mi-distance; — n. allée centrale f.; fête foraine f.

midwife n. sage-femme f.

mien n. mine f., air m.

might n. puissance, force f.; -y a. puissant, fort; grand; -y adv. (coll.) très, fort

migraine n. migraine f.

migrant n. nomade m.

migrate vi. émigrer

migration n. migration f.

migratory a. migrateur, de passage

milch a. laitière

mild a. doux (douce); léger; (climate) tempéré; -ness n. douceur f.

mildew n. moisissure f.; chancissure f.; rouille f.; — vt. moisir; chancir; rouiller

mile n. mille m.; -age n. milles m. pl.; distance en milles f.; kilométrage m.

milestone n. borne f.

militarism n. militarisme m.

military a. militaire; — n. militaires m. pl.

militate vi. militer

militia n. milice f.; garde nationale f.; -man n. milicien m.

milk n. lait m.; bottle of — carafe de lait f.; — of magnesia magnésie f.; — sugar n. sucre de lait m.; lactine f.; — tooth dent de lait f.; — vt. traire; exploiter; -y a. laiteux

milkmaid n. laitière f.

milkman n. laitier m.

milkweed n. laiteron m.

Milky Way n. voie lactée f.

mill n. moulin m.; fabrique, usine f.; — vt.

moudre; fraiser; laminer; meuler; usiner; canneler; — *vi.* se presser; fourmiller; —er *n.* meunier *m.*

millennium *n.* millénaire *m.*; (eccl.) millénium *n.*

milligram *n.* milligramme *m.*

millimeter *n.* millimètre *m.*

milliner *n.* modiste *f.*; —y *n.* modes *f. pl.*; —y shop magasin de modes *m.*

million *n.* million *m.*; —aire *n.* millionnaire *m. & f.*; —th *a.* millionième

millrace *n.* canal de moulin *m.*

millstone *n.* meule *f.*

milt *n.* laite, laitance *f.*

mime *n.* mime *m.*; — *vi.* mimer

mimeograph *n.* machine à polycopier *f.*; — *vt.* polycopier

mimic *n.* imitateur *m.*; — *vt.* imiter, mimer; —ry *n.* imitation; mimique *f.*

minaret *n.* minaret *m.*

mince *vt.* hacher; not to — one's words parler sans phrases; —d *a.* haché; —d meat hachis *m.*

mincemeat *n.* mincemeat *m.*

mind *n.* esprit *m.*; âme *f.*; intelligence *f.*; mémoire *f.*; — reader personne qui lit dans la pensée des autres *f.*; bear in — ne pas oublier; be of one — être d'accord; bring to — rappeler; change one's — changer d'avis; have a — to avoir envie de; have in — avoir en vue; make up one's — se décider, prendre le parti (de); peace of — tranquillité d'esprit *f.*; state of — état d'âme *m.*; — *vt.* garder, surveiller; faire attention à; s'occuper de; ne pas vouloir; I don't — cela m'est égal; je veux bien; never — n'importe; ne vous inquiétez pas; —ful *a.* attentif

mine *n.* mine *f.*; — field champ de mines *m.*; — *pron.* le mien *m.*; — *a.* à moi; — layer *n.* poseur de mines *m.*; — shaft puits *m.*; — sweeper *n.* dragueur de mines, balayeur de mines *m.*; — *vt.* fouiller; (coal) exploiter; (mil.) miner; —r *n.* mineur *m.*

mineral *a. & n.* minéral *m.*; — water eau minérale *f.*; boisson gazeuse *f.*; —ogist *n.* minéralogiste *m.*; —ogy minéralogie *f.*

mingle *vi.* se mêler, se mélanger

miniature *n.* miniature *f.*; — *a.* en miniature

minim *n.* goutte *f.* (music) blanche *f.*; (measure) minim *m.*

minimize *vt.* réduire au minimum

minimum *a. & n.* minimum *m.*

mining *n.* exploitation des mines, industrie minière *f.*; (naut.) pose des mines *f.*

minion *n.* mignon *m.*; (print.) corps 7 *m.*

minister *n.* ministre *m.*; pasteur *m.*; — *vi.*, — to someone's needs subvenir aux besoins de

ministry *n.* (administration) ministère *m.*; (eccl.) le saint ministère; (pol.) gouvernement *m.*

mink *n.* vison *m.*

minnow *n.* vairon *m.*

minor *a.* petit, mineur, peu important; — *n.* mineur *m.*; —ity *n.* minorité *f.*

minstrel *n.* ménestrel *m.*; chanteur, musicien *m.*

mint *n.* monnaie *f.*; (bot.) menthe *f.*; — *vt.* frapper, battre

minuet *n.* menuet *m.*

minus *prep.* moins; (coll.) sans; — *n.* moins *m.*; — *a.* négatif

minute *n.* minute *f.*; instant, moment *m.*; note *f.*; any — à tout moment; — hand grande aiguille *f.*; —s *pl.* notes *f. pl.*, procès-verbal *m.*; — *a.* menu, minuscule; moindre; minutieux

minx *n.* coquine *f.*

miracle *n.* miracle *m.*; — play *n.* miracle *m.*; — worker thaumaturge, faiseur de miracles *m.*

miraculous *a.* miraculeux

mirage *n.* mirage *m.*

mire *n.* boue, fange *f.*; — *vi.* s'enfoncer dans la boue; s'embourber

mirror *n.* miroir *m.*, glace *f.*; rear-view — rétroviseur *m.*

mirth *n.* gaieté, joie *f.*

misadventure *n.* mésaventure *f.*

misalliance *n.* mésalliance *f.*

misanthrope *n.* misanthrope *m.*

misanthropic *a.* misanthrope

misapprehension *n.* méprise *f.*, malentendu *m.*

misappropriation *n.* détournement *m.*

misbehave *vi.* se comporter mal, se conduire mal

misbehavior *n.* mauvaise conduite *f.*

miscalculate *vt.* mal calculer; — *vi.* se tromper

miscalculation *n.* mécompte *m.*, erreur de calcul *f.*

miscarriage *n.* (med.) fausse couche *f.*; avortement, insuccès *m.*; — of justice erreur judiciaire *f.*

miscarry *vi.* (med.) faire une fausse couche; avorter, manquer, échouer

miscellaneous *a.* divers, varié

miscellany *n.* mélanges *m. pl.*

mischief *n.* espièglerie *f.*; mauvais tour *m.*; mal *m.*; malice *f.*

mischievous *a.* espiègle, malicieux; méchant

misconception *n.* idée fausse *f.*

misconduct *n.* mauvaise conduite *f.*; mauvaise administration *f.*

misconstrue *vt.* mésinterpréter; mal prendre

miscount *n.* erreur d'addition *f.*

miscreant *n.* mécréant *m.*

misdeal *n.* (cards) maldonne *f.*; — *vt.* faire maldonne

misdeed *n.* méfait *m.*

misdemeanor *n.* délit *m.*

misdirect *vt.* mal diriger; mal renseigner

miser *n.* avare *m.*; —ly *a.* avare

miserable *a.* misérable; malheureux

misery *n.* misère *f.*; souffrance *f.*

misfire *vi.* rater

misfit *n.* vêtement manqué *m.*; (person) raté *m.*; déchu *m.*

misfortune *n.* malheur *m.*, infortune *f.*

misgiving *n.* appréhension, hésitation *f.*; doute *m.*

misguide *vt.* mal guider, égarer

mishap *n.* contretemps *m.*, mésaventure *f.*; accident *m.*

misinform *vt.* mal renseigner

misinterpret *vt.* mal interpréter; -ation *n.* fausse interprétation *f.*

misjudge *vt.* mal juger; méconnaître

mislay *vt.* égarer

mislead *vt.* *tr.* égarer, tromper; -ing *a.* trompeur

mismanage *vt.* mal conduire, mal administrer; -ment *n.* mauvaise administration *f.*

mismatch *vt.* mal assortir

misnomer *n.* faux nom *m.*; nom mal approprié *m.*

misplace *vt.* mal placer; déplacer; perdre

misprint *n.* faute d'impression *f.*

mispronounce *vt.* mal prononcer

misquote *vt.* citer à faux

misrepresent *vt.* mal représenter; travestir; -ation *n.* faux rapport *m.*, fausse déclaration *f.*

misrule *n.* désordre *m.*; mauvaise administration *f.*

miss *n.* mademoiselle *f.*; jeune fille, demoiselle *f.*

miss *n.* coup manqué, coup raté *m.*; -- *vt.* manquer, rater; ne pas trouver; ne pas avoir; ne pas saisir; regretter; -ing *a.* absent; disparu; qui manque

misshapen *a.* difforme; déformé

missile *n.* projectile *m.*; (rocket) engin *m.*; guided -- engin téléguidé *m.*; intercontinental -- engin intercontinental *m.*

mission *n.* mission *f.*; -ary *a.* & *n.* missionnaire *m.*

misspell *vt.* mal épeler; -ing *n.* faute d'orthographe *f.*

misstate *n.* mal énoncer; annoncer à faux; -ment rapport inexact *m.*

misstep *n.* faux pas *m.*

mist *n.* brume *f.*; buée *f.*; voile *m.*; -y *a.* brumeux; vague

mistake *n.* faute, erreur *f.*; méprise *f.*; by -- par erreur; make a -- faire une faute; se tromper; -- *vt.* se tromper; mal comprendre; -n *a.* erroné; dans l'erreur

mister *n.* Mr. *m.* monsieur *m.*

mistranslation *n.* erreur de traduction *f.*; contre-sens *m.*

mistress *n.* maîtresse *f.*

mistrust *n.* méfiance, défiance *f.*; -- *vt.* se méfier de; -ful *a.* méfiant

misunderstand *vt.* mal comprendre; mal interpréter; se méprendre; méconnaître; -ing *n.* malentendu; quiproquo *m.*

misuse *n.* abus *m.*; mauvais usage *m.*; -- *vt.* faire mauvais usage

mite *n.* mite *f.*; brin *m.*, miette *f.*

mitigate *vt.* atténuer, mitiger; adoucir

mitigating *a.* atténuant

mitre *n.* onglet *m.*; (eccl.) mitre *f.*; -- *vt.* tailler à onglet

mitten *n.* mitaine *f.*

mix *vt.* mêler, mélanger; confondre; composer; malaxer; -- *vi.* se mêler, se mélanger; aller (bien) ensemble; -ed *a.* mêlé; mixte; assorti; -er *n.* agitateur *m.*; malaxeur, mixer *m.*; -ture *n.* mélange *m.*; mixture *f.*, (med.) potion *f.*

moan *n.* gémissement *m.*; -- *vi.* gémir; -- *vt.* dire en gémissant

moat *n.* fossé *m.*

mob *n.* foule, cohue *f.*; populace *m.*; canaille *f.*; -- *vt.* faire foule autour de; -- *vi.* s'ameuter; s'attrouper

mobile *a.* mobile; changeant; -- unit *n.* groupe mobile *m.*

mobility *n.* mobilité *f.*

mobilization *n.* mobilisation *f.*

mobilize *vt.* mobiliser

moccasin *n.* mocassin *m.*

mocha *n.* moka *m.*

mock *a.* faux; factice; feint; d'imitation; (as prefix); simili-; -- tortoise-shell *n.* écaille imitation *f.*; -- trial *n.* simulacre de procès *m.*; -- *vt.* se moquer de, railler; imiter; -ery *n.* moquerie, raillerie *f.*; -ing *a.* moqueur, railleur

modal *a.* modal

mode *n.* mode *m.*; manière *f.*; (fashion) mode *f.*

model *n.* modèle *m.*; patron *m.*; maquette *f.*; (person) modèle *n.* & *f.*; -- *a.* modèle; -- *vt.* modeler; (clothes) exposer, montrer; -ing *n.* modelage *m.*

moderate *vt.* modérer; tempérer; -- *vi.* se modérer; -- *a.* modéré; raisonnable, mesuré; modique

moderation *n.* modération *f.*; mesure *f.*

moderator *n.* président, arbitre *m.*

modern *a.* moderne; -- languages languages vivantes *f. pl.*; -istic *a.* moderne; -ize *vt.* moderniser

modest *a.* modeste; pudique; -y *n.* modestie *f.*; pudeur *f.*

modicum *n.* petite quantité *f.*; un peu *m.*

modification *n.* modification *f.*

modify *vt.* modifier

modulate *vt.* & *vi.* moduler

modulation *n.* modulation *f.*

mohair *n.* mohair *m.*

Mohammedan *a.* & *n.* mahométan *m.*; -ism *n.* mahométisme *m.*

moist *a.* humide, moite; mouillé; -en *vt.* mouiller, humecter, moitir; -ness *n.* humidité *f.*; moiteur *f.*; -ure *n.* humidité *f.*

molar *a.* & *n.* molaire *f.*

molasses *n.* mélasse *f.*

mold *n.* moule *m.*, matrice *f.*; moisissure *f.*, moisi *m.*; -- *vt.* mouler; pétrir; -- *vi.* moisir; -er *vi.* tomber en poussière; -iness *n.* moisissure *f.*; -ing *n.* moulage *m.*; moulure *f.*; -y *a.* moisi

mole *n.* grain de beauté *m.*

molecular *a.* moléculaire

molecule *n.* molécule *f.*

molehill *n.* taupinière *f.*; make a mountain out of a -- exagérer

moleskin *n.* moleesquine *f.*

molest *vt.* molester

mollify *vt.* apaiser

mollusk *n.* mollusque *m.*

molt *vi.* muer; -ing *a.* en mue; -ing *n.* mue *f.*

molten *a.* fondu

molybdenum *n.* molybdène *m.*

moment *n.* moment, instant *m.*; importance *f.*; (fig.) heure *f.*; at the -- en ce moment, pour le moment; of -- important; -ary *a.* momentané; -ous *a.* très important

momentum n. force vive f., moment m.; vitesse f.

Monacan a. & n. monégasque m.

Monaco n. Monaco m.

monarch n. monarque m.; -ic a. monarchique; -ist n. monarchiste m.; -y n. monarchie f.

monastery n. monastère m.

monastic a. monastique

Monday n. lundi m.

monetary a. monétaire

money n. argent m.; monnaie f.; espèces f. pl.; counterfeit — fausse monnaie f.; — belt ceinture à porte-monnaie f.; — box caisse f.; — order mandat-poste m.; -ed a. riche, opulent

Mongol n. Mongol m.; -ia n. Mongolie f.; -ian a. mongol, mongolique

mongrel n. bâtard m.; métis m.

monitor vt. contrôler, écouter; — n. moniteur m.; (school) pion m.; détecteur m.; contrôleur m.; -ing n. écoute f.; contrôle f.

monk n. moine, religieux m.

monkey n. singe m.; guenon f.; — wrench clé anglaise f.; — vi., — around (with) (coll.) tripoter

monochromatic a. monochrome

monogamous a. monogame

monogamy n. monogamie f.

monogram n. chiffre, monogramme m.

monograph n. monographie f.

monologue n. monologue m.

monomania n. monomanie f.; -c n. monomane m. & f.

monoplane n. monoplan m.

monopolistic a. de monopole, monopoleur

monopolize vt. monopoliser; accaparer

monopoly n. monopole m.

monorail n. monorail m.

monosyllabic a. monosyllabique

monotonous a. monotone

monotony n. monotonie f.

monoxide n. protoxyde m.; carbon — sous-oxyde de carbone m.

monsoon n. mousson f.

monster n. monstre m.

monstrance n. (eccl.) ostensoir m.

monstrosity n. monstruosité f.; monstre m.; enormité f.

monstrous a. monstrueux; -ness n. monstruosité f.

month n. mois m.; by the — au mois; -'s pay mois m.; once a — une fois par mois, mensuellement; -ly a. mensuel; -ly payment mensualité f.; -ly adv. une fois par mois, mensuellement

monument n. monument m.; -al a. monumental

moo vi. meugler, beugler

mood n. disposition, humeur f.; (gram.) mode m.; -iness n. humeur changeante f.; -y a. d'humeur changeante; maussade

moon n. lune f.; — vi. musarder

moonbeam n. rayon de lune m.

moonlight n. clair de lune m.

moon-struck, moon-stricken a. lunatique

moor n. bruyère, lande f.; — vt. amarrer; — vi. s'amarrer; -ing n. amarrage m.; (rope) amarre f.

Moor n. Maure m., Mauresque f.; -ish a. mauresque, maure, des Maures

moors n. pl. landes f. pl., bruyère f.

moot a. discutable; — court n. procès simulé m.

mop n. guipon m.; — of hair tignasse f.; — vt. nettoyer avec un guipon; essuyer, éponger

mope vi. rêver; s'ennuyer

moral a. moral; — n. morale, moralité f.; -s pl. moralité f.; -ist n. moraliste m. & f.; -ity n. moralité f.; bonnes mœurs f. pl.; -ize vi. moraliser; -ly adv. moralement

morass n. marais m.

morbid a. morbide; maladif

more a. plus de; encore de, encore un; d'autres; — n. davantage; — adv. plus; davantage; all the — d'autant plus; — and — de plus en plus; once — encore une fois; no — ne . . . plus (de)

moreover adv. d'ailleurs, du reste

mores n. pl. mœurs f. pl.

moribund a. moribond

Mormon n. Mormon m.

morning n. matin m.; matinée f.; good — bonjour; in the — le matin; (clock time) du matin; the next — le lendemain matin m.

Moroccan a. & n. marocain m.

Morocco n. Maroc m.; — leather maroquin m.; — leather goods maroquinerie f.

moron n. idiot m.

morose a. morose; -ness n. morosité f.

morphology n. morphologie f.

Morse code n. alphabet Morse m.

morsel n. morceau m.

mortal a. mortel; fatal; à mort; — n. mortel m.; -ity n. mortalité f.; -ly adv. mortellement; à mort

mortar n. mortier m.; enduit m.

mortgage n. hypothèque f.; — vt. hypothéquer

mortician n. entrepreneur de pompes funèbres m.

mortification n. mortification f.; gangrène f.

mortify vt. mortifier; humilier; — vi. se mortifier; se gangrener

mortuary a. mortuaire; — n. morgue f.

mosaic n. mosaïque f.; — a. en mosaïque

Moscow n. Moscou m.

Moslem a. & n. mahométan, musulman m.

mosque n. mosquée f.

mosquito n. moustique m.; —net n. moustiquaire f.

moss n. mousse f.; -y a. moussu

most a. la plupart de; le plus de; — n. le plus m.; la plupart; — adv. le plus; très; -ly adv. pour la plupart

moth n. mite f.; papillon de nuit m.; phalène f.; -y a. mité

mothball n. boule de naphtaline f.

moth-eaten a. mité

mother n. mère f.; maman f.; — tongue langue maternelle f.; — vt. dorloter; -hood n. maternité f.; -less a. sans mère; —ly a. maternel

mother-in-law n. belle-mère f.

mother-of-pearl n. nacre f.

motion n. mouvement m.; signe m.; (debate) motion, proposition f.; — picture film m.; — pictures n. pl. cinéma m.; set in — mettre en marche, mettre en mouvement; — vt. & vi. faire signe; —less a. immobile

motion-picture a. cinématographique; du cinéma; — camera n. caméra m.

motivate vt. motiver

motive a. moteur (motrice); — n. motif, mobile m.

motley a. bigarré, bariolé

motor a. moteur (motrice); automobile; — n. moteur m.; — launch n. chaloupe à moteur m.; — truck n. camion automobile m.; — vi. aller en auto; —ist n. automobiliste m. & f.; —ize vt. motoriser

motorbike n. vélomoteur m.

motorboat n. canot automobile m., vedette f.

motorcade n. défilé (d'autos) m.

motorcycle n. moto, motocyclette f.

motorman n. wattman m.

mottle vt. marbrer; tacheter; —d a. marbré

motto n. devise f.

mound n. monticule m., tertre m.; tas m.

mount n. mont m., montagne f.; — montage m.; armement m.; (horse) monture, monte f.; — vt. monter (sur); gravir; armer; — vi. monter; monter à cheval; — up croître; —ed a. à cheval; monté; —ing n. montage m.; garniture f.

mountain n. montagne f.; — a. des montagnes; montagneux; (person) montagnard; — range chaîne de montagnes; — climber n. alpiniste m. & f.; — climbing n. alpinisme m.; —eer n. alpiniste m. & f.; —ous a. montagneux

mountebank n. charlatan m.

mourn vt. & vi. pleurer, déplorer; —er n. affligé m.; personne qui est en deuil f.; —ful a. funèbre, lugubre; —ing a. en deuil; —ing n. deuil m., affliction f.

mouse n. souris f.; — trap n. souricière f.

moustache, mustache n. moustache f.

mouth n. bouche f.; gueule f.; ouverture f.; (river) embouchure f.; — organ harmonica m.; — wash dentifrice m.; — vt. & vi. déclamer; —ful n. bouchée f.; mouthpiece n. embouchure f.; bec, bocal m.

movable a. mobile; mobilier

move n. mouvement m.; (household) déménagement m.; (chess) coup m.; — vt. bouger, remuer, pousser; mouvoir; émouvoir, toucher; attendrir; déménager; (debate) proposer; (chess) jouer; — vi. bouger; se mouvoir, se déplacer; jouer; — off s'éloigner; — on continuer son chemin; — out déménager; —ment n. mouvement m.; transport m.; déplacement m.; —r n. moteur m.; déménageur m.

moving a. en marche, en mouvement; moteur, motrice; attendrissant; émouvant; — n. déménagement m.

mow vt. faucher; (lawn) tondre; —er n.

faucheuse f.; (lawn) tondeuse f., (person) faucheur m.

Mrs.: Mistress, Mme. n. madame f.

much a. beaucoup (de); bien (de); — adv. beaucoup; bien; as — autant (de), how — combien de; so — tant (de); too — trop (de); very — beaucoup

mucilage n. mucilage m., colle f.

muck n. fange f.; crotte f.

mucous a. muqueux

mucus n. mucus m.

mud n. boue f.; fange f.; vase f.; —dy a. boueux, fangeux, vaseux; (liquid) trouble

muddle n. confusion f.; — vt. brouiller, embrouiller

mudguard n. garde-boue m.

muff n. manchon m.; — vt. rater, louper, gâcher

muffin n. galette f.; (sorte de) brioche f.

muffle vt. envelopper; emmitoufler; étouffer; —r n. cache-nez m ; (auto) pot d'échappement m.

mufti n. tenue de ville f.; in — en civil

mug n. pot m., chope f.

muggy a. chaud et humide; lourd

mulatto n. mulâtre m., mulâtresse f.

mule n. mulet m., mule f.; —teer n. muletier m.

mulish a. obstiné, entêté

mull vt. (wine) chauffer avec des épices; — (coll.) méditer, ruminer; —ed wine vin chaud, vin chauffé m.

mullet n. (fish) mulet m.; red — rouget m.

multicolored a. multicolore

multigraph n. multigraphe m., machine à imprimer f.

multimillionaire n. multimillionaire, milliardaire m. & f.

multiple a. & n. multiple m.

multiplication n. multiplication f.

multiplicity n. multiplicité f.

multiply vt. multiplier; — vi. se multiplier

multitude n. multitude f.; foule f.

mumble vt. & vi. marmotter; marmonner

mummify vt. momifier

mummy n. momie f.

mumps n. oreillons m. pl.

munch vt. mâcher, mâchonner, croquer

mundane a. du monde, mondain

municipal a. municipal; —ity n. municipalité f.

munificence n. munificence f.

munificent a. munificent, généreux

munitions n. pl. munitions f. pl.

murder n. meurtre m.; assassinat m.; — vt. assassiner; —er n. meurtrier, assassin m.; —ous a. meurtrier, assassin

murky a. brouillé; ténébreux

murmur n. murmure m.; — vt. & vi. murmurer, parler à voix basse

Murphy-bed n. (trademark) lit escamotable m.

muscatel n. muscat m.

muscle n. muscle m.

muscle-bound a. aux muscles raides

muscular a. musculaire; musculeux, musclé; —ity n. constitution musculaire f.

muse n. muse f.; — vi. méditer, rêver

museum n. musée m.; (natural-history)

muséum m.

mush n. polenta f.; —y a. mollet, mou; (fig.) sentimental

mushroom n. champignon m.; — vi. faire champignon

music n. musique f.; — box boîte à musique f.; —al a. de musique; musical; mélodieux; —al comedy n. opérette f.; —ale n. soirée musicale f.; —ian n. musicien m., musicienne f.

musing n. méditation, rêverie f.

musket n. mousquet m.; —eer n. mousquetaire m.

muskmelon n. cantaloup m.

muskrat n. rat musqué m.

muslin n. mousseline f.

muss n. désordre m.; — vt. mettre en désordre; froisser

mussel n. moule f.

must n. nécessité f.; — vt. devoir; falloir; I — je dois; il me faut, il faut que je . . . .

must n. moisi m.; —iness n. relent m.; odeur de moisi f.; —y a. de moisi, de relent; qui sent le renfermé

mustard n. moutarde f.; — gas n. gas moutarde m.; — pot n. moutardier m.; — plaster n. cataplasme m.; sinapisme m.

muster n. revue f.; assemblée f.; rassemblement m.; — vt. rassembler; (mil.) passer en revue

mustiness n. moisi m.; renfermé m.

mutability n. mutabilité f.

mutable a. changeant, instable

mutant n. mutante f.

mutation n. changement m.

mute a. muet (muette); — n. muet m., (mus.) sourdine f.; — vt. amortir, assourdir; —d a. en sourdine; —ness n. mutisme m.

mutilate vt. mutiler, estropier

mutilation n. mutilation f.

mutineer n. mutin n., révolté m.

mutinous a. mutin; séditieux

mutiny n. mutinerie f.; — vi. se mutiner

mutter vt. & vi. marmotter, marmonner, murmurer

mutton n. mouton m.

mutual a. réciproque, mutuel; commun; — aid n. entr'aide f.

muzzle n. museau m.; muselière; (gun) bouche f.; — vt. museler

my pron. mon, ma, mes; —! interj. tiens!; —self pron. me; moi; moi-même

myopia n. myopie f.

myopic a. myope

myriad n. myriade f.

mysterious a. mystérieux; —ness n. mystère m.

mystery n. mystère m.

mystic a. mystique; occulte; — n. mystique m. & f.; —al a. mystique; —ism n. mysticisme m.

mystify vt. mystifier

myth n. mythe m.; —ical a. mythique; —ological a. mythologique; —ology n. mythologie f.

N

nab vt. arrêter, saisir, pincer

nag n. bidet m.; — vt. & vi. gronder, quereller; —ging a. grondeur, querelleur; agaçant

nail n. clou m.; (finger) ongle m.; — file lime à ongles f.; — vt. clouer; clouter

naive a. naïf

naked a. nu; découvert; —ness n. nudité f.

name n. nom m.; réputation f., renom m.; by — de nom; Christian —, first — prénom, nom de baptême m.; family — nom, nom de famille m.; maiden — nom de demoiselle f.; nick — sobriquet n.; my — is je m'appelle; — vt. nommer; citer; be —d s'appeler, se nommer; —less a. sans nom; anonyme; —ly adv. c'est-à-dire; à savoir

name plate n. plaque; étiquette, marque f.

namesake n. homonyme m.

nap n. somme m.; (cloth) poil, duvet m.; — vi. sommeiller

nape n. nuque f.

naphtha n. naphte m.

napkin n. serviette f.; — ring n. rond de serviette m.

narcotic a. & n. narcotique, stupéfiant m.

narrate vt. raconter, narrer

narration n. narration f.

narrator n. narrateur m.

narrow a. étroit; borné; faible; have a — escape l'échapper belle; — vt. borner, rétrécir; — vi. devenir plus étroit; se rétrécir; —ness n. étroitesse f.

narrow-minded a. borné, à l'esprit étroit; —ness n. étroitesse d'esprit f.

narrows n. détroit m.

nasal a. nasal; nasillard; —ize vt. nasaliser

nasty a. désagréable; vilain, sale; mauvais; méchant

natal a. natal, de naissance

nation n. nation f.; pays m.; —al a. national; de la nation; —alism n. nationalisme m.; —alist n. nationaliste m. & f.; —ality n. nationalité f.; —alization n. nationalisation f.; —alize vt. nationaliser

nationwide a. national, de toute la nation, à travers toute la nation, à travers le pays

native n. natif m., native f.; indigène m. & f.; originaire m. & f.; — a. natal; de naissance; indigène, originaire; inné, naturel; — land patrie f.; pays natal m.; — language langue maternelle f.

nativity n. nativité f.

natural a. naturel; inné; de la nature; — n. (mus.) bécarre m.; —ism n. naturalisme m.; —ist n. naturaliste m. & f.; —ization n. naturalisation f.; —ize vt. naturaliser; —ly adv. naturellement; de nature; —ness n. naturel m.

nature n. nature f.; naturel m.; tempérament m.; genre m., sorte, espèce f.; by — de nature; par tempérament; from — (art) d'après nature; — study n. histoire naturelle f.

naughty a. méchant, mauvais; espiègle

nausea n. nausée f.; mal au cœur m.; —te vt. écœurer; —ting a. écœurant, nauséabond

nauseous a. nauséabond

nautical a. nautique, marin

naval a. naval; de marine
nave n. nef f.
navel n. nombril m.
navigable a. navigable
navigate vi. naviguer; — vt. naviguer, gouverner
navigation n. navigation f.
navigator n. navigateur m.
navy n. marine f.; flotte f.; — bean n. haricot m.; — blue a. bleu foncé, bleu marine m.; — yard arsenal maritime m.
Nazi a. & n. nazi m.; -sm n. nazisme m.
near a. proche; — adv. près; proche; — prep. près de; auprès de; — vt. s'approcher de; -ly adv. à peu près; presque; près de; -ness n. proximité f.
nearby adv. tout près
nearsighted a. myope
neat a. soigné; rangé; net (nette); sec; -ness n. (bon) ordre m.; netteté f.
nebula n. nébuleuse f.
nebulous a. nébuleux
necessary a. nécessaire; indispensable; if — au besoin, s'il le faut; it is — il faut
necessitate vt. nécessiter
necessity n. nécessité f.; besoin m.
neck n. cou m.; (bottle) goulot m.; (dress) encolure f.; (land) langue f.
neckband n. collet de chemise m.
necklace n. collier m.; parure f.
necktie n. cravate f.
neckwear n. cravates f. pl.; foulards m. pl.
necromancy n. nécromancie f.
nectar n. nectar m.; -ine n. brugnon m.
need n. besoin m.; nécessité f.; indigence f.; — vt. avoir besoin de; falloir, manquer; -less a. inutile; -iness n. indigence f.; -y a. nécessiteux; indigent
needle n. aiguille f.
needlework n. ouvrage à l'aiguille m.
nefarious a. infâme
negation n. négation f.
negative a. négatif; — n. négative f.; (phot.) négatif m.; (gram.) négation f.
neglect n. négligence f.; inattention f.; — vt. négliger; omettre; -ed a. négligé; à l'abandon; -ful a. négligent
negligee n. négligé m.
negligence n. négligence f.
negligent a. négligent
negligible a. négligeable
negotiable a. négociable
negotiate vt. négocier; conclure; surmonter
negotiation n. négociation f.; in — with en pourparlers avec
negotiator n. négociateur m.
Negress n. négresse f.
Negro a. & n. nègre m.
neigh n. hennissement m.; — vi. hennir
neighbor n. voisin m.; (fig.) autrui m.; prochain m.; -hood n. voisinage m.; quartier m.; environs, alentours m. pl.; -ing a. voisin, proche; -ly a. amical
neither conj. ni; — adv. ni; non plus; — pron. ni; — . . . . nor ni . . . . ni
neon n. néon m.; — a. au néon; — sign n. enseigne au néon f.
neophyte n. néophyte m.
nephew n. neveu m.

nepotism n. népotisme m.
nerve n. nerf m.; sang-froid m.; (coll.) toupet m.; — cell n. cellule nerveuse f.; — center n. centre nerveux m.; — fibre n. fibre nerveuse f.
nerve-racking a. énervant
nervous a. nerveux; irrité; énervé; inquiet; -ness n. nervosité f.; inquiétude f.; — system n. système nerveux m.
nest n. nid m.; nichée f.; — egg nichet m.; bas de laine m.; — vi. (se) nicher; -le vi. se nicher; se serrer
net n. filet m.; réseau m., tulle m.; — vt. prendre au filet; (com.) rapporter net; — a. net
Netherlands n. pl. Hollande f.; Pays-Bas
nettle n. ortie f.; — vt. piquer, irriter
network n. réseau m.; système m.
neuralgia n. névralgie f.
neuritis n. névrite f.
neurologist n. nevrologue m.
neurology n. névrologie f.
neurosis n. névrose f.
neurotic a. & n. névrotique, névrosé m.
neuter a. neutre
neutral a. & n. neutre; — n. (auto.) point mort m.; -ity n. neutralité f.; -ize vt. neutraliser
neutron n. neutron m.
never adv. jamais, ne . . . jamais; — mind n'importe
never ending a. perpétuel, éternel, sans fin
nevertheless conj. néanmoins, cependant, pourtant, toutefois; quand même
new a. nouveau (nouvelle); neuf (neuve); -ly adv. récemment, fraîchement; -ness n. nouveauté f.; inexpérience f.; -s pl. nouvelles f. pl.; piece of -s nouvelle f.
newborn a. nouveau-né
New Caledonia n. Nouvelle Calédonie f.
newcomer n. nouveau venu m.
Newfoundland n. Terre-Neuve f.
New Hebrides n. Nouvelles Hébrides f. pl.
newlywed n. nouveau marié m., nouvelle mariée f.; -s nouveaux mariés m. pl.
New Orleans n. La Nouvelle Orléans f.
newsboy n. crieur de journaux m.
newscast n. bulletin d'informations, journal parlé m.; -er n. rédacteur de journal parlé m.
newspaper n. journal m.
newsprint n. papier de journal m.
newsreel n. actualités f. pl.
newsstand n. kiosque m.
newsworthy a. d'actualité
New Year n. nouvel an m.; -'s Day jour de l'an m.
New Zealand n. Nouvelle Zélande f.; — a. néo-zélandais
New Zealander n. Néo-Zélandais m.
next a. prochain; voisin; d'à côté; suivant; — day le lendemain m.; — door à côté; dans la maison voisine; — morning lendemain matin m.; — adv. après; ensuite; puis; — n. suivant m.; — prep. auprès de, à côté de
nibble vt. & vi. grignoter; mordre; — n. grignotement, petit morceau m.
Nicaragua n. Nicaragua m.
nice a. gentil (gentille); aimable; agré-

able; sympathique; bon; **-ly** *adv.* gentiment; agréablement; bien; **-ty** *n.* finesse *f.*; minutie *f.*

nick *n.* coche, encoche, entaille *f.*; in the — of time à pic; juste à point; — *vt.* encocher, entailler

nickel *n.* nickel *m.*; pièce de cinq cents *f.*

nickel-plated *a.* nickelé

nickname *n.* sobriquet *m.*

niece *n.* nièce *f.*

Nigeria *n.* Nigérie *f.*

niggardly *a.* mesquin, chiche

nigh *a.* proche, près; well — à peu près; — *adv.* presque; de près

night *n.* nuit *f.*; soir *m.*; at — la nuit *f.*; by — de nuit; good — bonsoir; (before retiring) bonne nuit; last — hier soir; cette nuit; the — before la veille au soir; — club *n.* boîte de nuit *f.*, cabaret *m.*; — letter télégramme de nuit (sans priorité) *m.*; — light veilleuse *f.*; — watchman veilleur de nuit *m.*; **-ly** *a.* & *adv.* tous les soirs

nightblindness *n.* nyctalopie *f.*

nightcap *n.* bonnet de nuit *m.*; (coll.) boisson alcoolique prise avant de se coucher *f.*

nightfall *n.* tombée de la nuit *f.*; at — à la nuit tombante

nightgown *n.* chemise de nuit *f.*

nightmare *n.* cauchemar *m.*

nightshirt *n.* chemise de nuit *f.*

nighttime *n.* nuit *f.*

nihilist *n.* nihiliste *m.*

nil *n.* nul, zéro *m.*

Nile *n.* Nil *m.*

nimble *a.* leste, agile

nimbus *n.* nimbe *m.*; (cloud) nimbus *m.*

nincompoop *n.* sot, niais *m.*

nine *a.* neuf; **-teen** *a.* dix-neuf; **-teenth** *a.* dix-neuvième; **-tieth** *a.* quatre-vingt-dixième; **-ty** *a.* quatre-vingt-dix

ninth *a.* neuvième

nip *n.* pincement *m.*; morsure *f.*; goutte *f.*; — *vt.* pincer; piquer; mordre; — in the bud étouffer dans le germe; **-per** *n.* pince *f.*

nipple *n.* mamelon *m.*; (bottle) tétine *f.*

niter, nitre *n.* nitre, salpêtre *m.*

nitrate *n.* nitrate, azotate *m.*

nitric *a.* nitrique, azotique

nitrocellulose *n.* nitrocellulose *f.*

nitrogen *n.* azote *m.*

nitroglycerin *n.* nitroglycérine *f.*

nitrous *a.* nitreux, azoteux

no *adv.* non; — *a.* pas de; aucun, nul; ne . . . . pas; peu; by — means pas du tout; in no aucune façon; in — way en aucune façon; — one personne; —, smoking défense de fumer; — *n.* non *m.*; voix contre *f.*

nobility *n.* noblesse *f.*

noble *a.* noble; grand; — *n.* noble *m.*; **-ness** *n.* noblesse *f.*; grandeur *f.*

nobleman *n.* noble *m.*

noblewoman *n.* femme noble *f.*

nobly *adv.* noblement; superbement

nobody *pron.* personne; — *n.* nullité *f.*

nocturnal *a.* nocturne

nod *n.* signe de tête *m.*; inclination de tête

f.; — *vt.* faire un signe de tête; incliner la tête

node *n.* nœud *m.*

nodule *n.* nodule *m.*

noise *n.* bruit *m.*; fracas, vacarme *m.*; son *m.*; make — faire du bruit; **-less** *a.* sans bruit; **-lessly** *adv.* sans bruit; silencieusement

noisily *adv.* bruyamment

noisiness *n.* grand bruit, tumulte *m.*

noisome *n.* infect, dégoûtant

noisy *a.* bruyant

nomad *n.* nomade *m.* & *f.*; **-ic** *a.* nomade

nomenclature *n.* nomenclature *f.*

nominal *a.* nominal; de nom

nominate *vt.* nommer, désigner; proposer

nomination *n.* nomination *f.*

nominative *a.* & *n.* nominatif *m.*

nominee *n.* candidat *m.*

nonacceptance *n.* refus *m.*, non-acceptation *f.*

nonaggression *n.* non-agression *f.*

nonattendance *n.* absence *f.*

nonchalant *a.* nonchalant

noncompliance *n.* refus d'acquiescer *m.*

noncombatant *n.* non-combattant *m.*

noncommissioned *a.* sans brevet; — officer gradé, sous-officier *m.*

noncommittal *a.* qui n'engage à rien

nonconductor *n.* non-conducteur *m.*

nonconformist *a.* & *n.* dissident *m.*

nondescript *a.* hétéroclite; inclassable

none *pron.* aucun, nul; personne; rien; — too soon juste à temps, juste à point

nonentity *n.* nullité *f.*

nonessential *a.* non-essentiel, peu essentiel

nonexistent *a.* non-existent, fictif

nonintervention *n.* non-intervention *f.*

nonobservance *n.* inobservance *f.*

nonpareil *a.* sans pareil

nonpayment *n.* non-payement *m.*

nonplussed *a.* confus, étourdi

nonresistance *n.* obéissance passive *f.*

nonsectarian *a.* sans esprit sectaire; sans prévention religieuse

nonsense *n.* non-sens *m.*, absurdité *f.*

nonsensical *a.* absurde

nonstop *a.* & *adv.* sans arrêt; (avi.) sans escale

nonsupport *n.* non-support *m.*

nonunion *a.* non-syndiqué

noodle *n.* nouille *f.*

nook *n.* coin, recoin, enfoncement *m.*

noon *n.* midi *m.*; **-day** *a.* de midi

noose *n.* corde *f.*; (trap) lacs, nœud coulant *m.*

nor *conj.* ni; neither . . . . — ni . . . . ni

Nordic *a.* nordique

norm *n.* norme *f.*; **-al** *a.* normal; ordinaire; **-al** school *n.* école normale *f.*; **-alcy** *n.* normalité *f.*; **-ally** *adv.* normalement; d'ordinaire

Norman *a.* & *n.* normand *m.*; **-dy** *n.* Normandie *f.*

Norse *a.* norvégien *m.*; **-man** *n.* Norvégien *m.*

north *n.* nord *m.*; — *a.* nord, du nord; septentrional; — *adv.* au nord, vers le nord;

—erly a. au nord, vers le nord; —ern a. du nord; septentrional

North America n. Amérique du Nord f.

northeast a. & n. nord-est m.; — adv. vers le nord-est

North Pole n. pôle du nord m.

northward a. au nord, du nord; —s adv. vers le nord

northwest a. & n. nord-ouest m.; — adv. vers le nord-ouest

Norway n. Norvège f.

Norwegian a. & n. norvégien m.

nose n. nez m.; (animals) museau m.; (ballistics) cône m.; blow one's — se moucher; hold one's — se boucher le nez; lead by the — mener par le bout du nez

nosebleed n. saignement du nez m.

nose dive vi. piquer du nez; — n. piquage du nez m.; piqué m.

nostalgia n. nostalgie f.

nostril n. narine f.; (horse) naseau m.

nostrum n. panacée f.

not adv. pas; point; ne . . . . pas; — at all pas du tout; — including sans compter; — that ce n'est pas que

notability n. notabilité f.

notable a. notable; remarquable; considérable; éminent; — n. notable m.

notably adv. notamment

notary n. notaire m.

notation n. notation f.

notch n. encoche, entaille f.; — vt. encocher, entailler

note n. note f.; annotation f.; remarque m.; billet, mot m., lettre f.; renom m.; son m.; (mus.) caractère m.; (piano) touche f.; make a — of prendre note de; take —s prendre des notes; — vt. noter, constater, remarquer; —d a. éminent, distingué; remarquable;

notebook n. cahier, carnet m.; loose-leaf — n. cahier à feuilles mobiles m.; —filler n. feuilles mobiles f. pl.

noteworthy a. digne d'attention

nothing n. rien m.; ne . . . . rien; rien de; zéro m.; — but rien que; — else rien d'autre; —ness n. néant m.

notice n. avis, avertissement m.; délai m.; affiche f.; annonce f.; attention f.; revue f.; at short — du jour au lendemain; à court délai; à l'instant; give — (to employee) donner son congé à; (to employer) donner sa démission; take — of faire attention à; tenir compte de; until further — jusqu'à nouvel avis; — vt. observer, remarquer, tenir compte de; —able a. qui se voit; perceptible, sensible

notification n. notification, faire-part m.

notify vt. notifier, faire savoir

notion n. notion, pensée, opinion f.; —s pl. mercerie f.

notoriety n. notoriété, évidence f.

notorious a. notoire; fameux; —ness n. notoriété f.

notwithstanding prep. & adv. nonobstant; — conj. bien que

nougat n. nougat m.

nought n. rien, néant m.; zéro m.

noun n. nom, substantif m.

nourish vt. nourrir; —ment n. nourriture f.; —ing a. nutritif

novel n. roman m.; — a. nouveau, neuf; —ist n. romancier m.; —ty n. nouveauté f.

November n. novembre m.

novena n. neuvaine f.

novice n. novice m.

novitiate n. noviciat m.

novocaine n. novocaïne f.

now adv. à présent, maintenant; by — à l'heure qu'il est; just — pour le moment; — and then, — and again de temps; until — jusqu'ici; — interj. or; eh bien; tiens

nowadays adv. de nos jours

nowhere adv. nulle part

noxious a. nuisible; pernicieux

nozzle n. lance f., bec m.

nuance n. nuance f.

nuclear a. nucléaire

nucleus n. noyau m.

nude a. nu

nudge n. coup de coude m.; — vt. pousser légèrement (du coude)

nudism n. nudisme m.

nudist n. nudiste m. & f.

nudity n. nudité f.

nugget n. pépite f.

nuisance n. incommodité f.; ennui m.

null a. nul, non valide; —ification n. annulation f.; —ify vt. annuler; —ity n. nullité f.

numb vt. engourdir; — a. engourdi; —ness n. engourdissement m.

number n. nombre m., quantité f.; numéro m.; chiffre m.; — vt. numéroter; —ing n. numérotage, calcul m.; —ing a. au nombre de; —ing machine n. numéroteur m.; —less a. innombrable

numeral n. chiffre m.; — a. numéral

numerator n. numérateur m.

numerical a. numérique

numerous a. nombreux

numskull, numbskull n. sot, lourdaud m.

nun n. nonne, religieuse f.; —nery n. couvent (de femmes) m.

nuncio n. (eccl.) nonce m.

nuptial a. nuptial; —s n. pl. noces f. pl.

nurse n. infirmière f.; garde-malade f.; male — infirmier m.; wet — nourrice f.; — vt. nourrir (au sein); soigner; — vi. téter; —ry n. chambre d'enfants f.; (bot.) pépinière f.; —ry school jardin d'enfants m., école maternelle f.

nursemaid n. nourrice f.

nursing n. profession d'infirmière f.; tétée f.; — bottle biberon m.

nursling n. nourrisson m.

nurture vt. nourrir, élever

nut n. noix f.; (mech.) écrou m.; a hard — to crack un problème épineux; —s, —ty a. (coll.) fou

nutcracker n. casse-noisettes m.

nutmeg n. muscade f.

nutrient n. aliment m.; —a nutritif

nutriment n. nourriture f., aliment m.

nutrition f. nutrition f.; nourriture f., aliment m.

nutritious a. nourrissant

nutshell n. coquille de noix f.; in a — en

un mot
nymph n. nymphe f.

O

oaf n. sot, benêt m.
oar n. rame f., aviron m.; –sman n. rameur m.
oasis n. oasis f.
oat(s) n. avoine f.; sow one's wild — jeter sa gourme
oath n. serment, jurement m.
oatmeal n. bouillie d'avoine f.
obdurate a. endurci; obstiné
obedience n. obéissance f.
obedient a. obéissant
obeisance n. salut m., révérence f.
obelisk n. obélisque m.
obese a. obèse
obesity n. obésité f.
obey vt. obéir à; — vi. obéir
obituary n. notice nécrologique f.
object n. objet m., matière f., sujet m.; (gram.) complément d'objet m.
object vt. objecter; –ion n. objection f.; –ionable a. désagréable; –ive n. objectif m.; — a. objectif; –ivity n. objectivité f.; –or n. objecteur m.; conscientious –or objecteur de conscience m.
obligation n. obligation f.
obligatory a. obligatoire
oblige vt. obliger; contraindre; — someone to do something obliger quelqu'un à faire quelque chose; be –d to do something être obligé de faire quelque chose
obliging a. obligeant
oblique a. oblique
obliterate vt. oblitérer, effacer
obliteration n. rature f.; oblitération f.
oblivion n. oubli m.
oblivious a. oublieux
oblong a. oblong
obnoxious a. nuisible, coupable, désagréable, dégoûtant
obscene a. obscène
obscenity n. obscénité f.
obscure vt. obscurcir; — a. obscur
obscurity n. obscurité f.
obsequious a. obséquieux
observable a. remarquable, appréciable
observance n. observation f.; observance f.; pratique f.
observant a. observateur, attentif; respectueux
observation n. observation f.
observatory n. observatoire m.
observe vt. observer; remarquer; fêter; –r n. observateur m.
observing a. observateur
obsess vt. obséder; –ion n. obsession f.
obsolescence n. désuétude f.
obsolescent a. qui tombe en désuétude
obsolete a. désuet, inusité, vieilli; become — tomber en désuétude
obstacle n. obstacle m.
obstetrician n. accoucheur m.
obstetrics n. pl. obstétrique f.
obstinacy n. opiniâtreté f.
obstinate a. obstiné
obstreperous a. déréglé, insoumis, bruyant, turbulent

obstruct vt. encombrer, obstruer; mettre obstacle à; –ion n. obstacle, empêchement m., opposition f.; –ive a. embarrassant, obstructif
obtain vt. obtenir; –able a. trouvable, disponible
obtrusive a. importun
obtuse a. obtus
obviate vt. obvier à
obvious a. clair, évident; –ly adv. évidemment; –ness n. évidence f.
occasion n. occasion f., incident m.; besoin m.; motif m., cause f.; — vt. occasionner, causer; –al a. occasionnel, casuel; intermittent; –ally adv. de temps en temps
occident n. occident m.; –al a. occidental
occult a. occulte; –ism n. occultisme m.
occupancy n. prise de possession f.; habitation f.
occupant n. occupant, possesseur, habitant m.
occupation n. occupation f., emploi m.; possession f.; –al a. du métier; –al therapy n. thérapie rééducative f.
occupier n. occupant m.
occupy vt. occuper, employer; habiter; prendre possession de; be occupied with s'occuper de
occur vi. arriver; avoir lieu; venir (à l'esprit); –ence n. événement m.
ocean n. océan m.; –ic a. océanique
Oceana n. Océanie f.
o'clock adv., it is one — il est une heure; it is two — il est deux heures
octagon n. octogone m.; –al a. octogonal
octane n. & n. (gasoline) octane m.
octet n. octuor m.
October n. octobre m.
ocular a. oculaire
oculist n. oculiste m.
odd a. singulier, étrange; (numbers) impair; –ity n. singularité, bizarrerie f.; –s n. pl. inégalité f.; avantage m.; chances f. pl.; –s and ends restes m. pl., pièces diverses f. pl.; be at –s être brouillé
ode n. ode f.
odious a. odieux
odium n. haine f.
odor n. odeur f.; bouquet m.
odorous a. parfumé
of prep. de
off a. éloigné; loin, loin de; distant; — adv. au loin; à distance; — and on de temps en temps; be — partir, démarrer; come — tomber, se détacher; réussir; go — s'en aller; se passer; put — remettre; right —, straight — (coll.) tout de suite; set — mettre en valeur; take — enlever; (avi.) décoller; take — on satiriser; turn — (lights) éteindre; (road) bifurquer — prep. de, de dessus, éloigné de; à une petite distance de; (naut.) au large; — limits défendu; défense d'entrer; — the record non-officiel
offal n. rebuts m. pl.; ordures f. pl.
off-color a. salé, risqué
offend vt. & vi. offenser, irriter; –er n. offenseur m.; –ing a. offensant, fautif

offense n. offense f.; faute f.; crime m.

offensive a. offensant, injurieux; — n. offensive f.

offer vt. & vi. offrir, présenter; — n. offre f.; -ing n. offrande f.; -tory n. offertoire m.; quête f.

offhand a. cavalier, improvisé; — adv. cavalièrement, sans préparation

office n. bureau m.; office m.; fonction, charge f.; -r n. officier m.; (police) agent m.; — seeker n. candidat à un poste, intrigant m.

official n. employé m.; fonctionnaire m.; officier m.; -ese n. jargon officiel m.

officiate vi. administrer; officier

officious a. officieux

offing n. large m.; in the — en vue

offset n. compensation f.; (print.) offset m.; — vt. contrebalancer

offshoot n. rejeton m.

offshore adv. vers la haute mer, en s'éloignant de la côte; — adj. éloigné de la côte

off side adv. hors des limites; de l'autre côté; hors jeu

offspring n. descendants m. pl.; lignée f.; rejeton m.

off stage adv. dans les coulisses

often adv. souvent; how — combien de fois

ogle vt. lorgner, regarder fixement

ogre n. ogre m.; -ss n. ogresse f.

oh! interj. oh!; ah!; hélas!; ouf!; aïe!

ohm n. ohm m.

oil n. huile f.; pétrole m.; crude — pétrole brut m.; mineral — huile minérale f.; — paint, — painting n. peinture à l'huile f.; — well n. puits à pétrole m.; — slick n. couche d'huile f.; — vt. huiler; -y a. huileux; — can n. broc à huile m.

oilcloth n. toile cirée f.

ointment n. onguent, baume m.

okra n. quingombo m.

old a. vieux, ancien; become —, grow — vieillir; how — are you? quel âge avezvous?; I am ten years — j'ai dix ans; — hand vétéran m.; — maid vieille fille f.; -ish a. plutôt vieux; -ness n. âge m.; vieillesse f.; ancienneté f.

old-fashioned a. démodé

old-line a. de vieille famille; qui remonte très loin

old-time a. du bon vieux temps

oleomargarine n. margarine f.

olfactory a. olfactif

oligarchy n. oligarchie f.

olive n. olive f.; (tree) olivier m.; — oil huile d'olive f.; — a. de couleur olive

Olympiad n. olympiade f.

Olympian a. olympien

Olympic a. olympique; -s n. pl. jeux olympiques m. pl.

omelet n. omelette f.

omen n. présage, augure m.

ominous a. de mauvais augure

omission n. omission f.

omit vt. omettre; négliger; oublier

omnibus n. omnibus m.; anthologie f.

omnipotence n. toute-puissance f.

omnipotent a. tout-puissant

omnipresence n. ubiquité f.; présence universelle f.

omnipresent a. présent en tous lieux

omniscient a. omniscient

omnivorous a. omnivore

on prep. sur; à; dans; — adv. en avant; and so — et ainsi de suite

once adv. une fois; autrefois; at — tout de suite; — and for all une fois pour toutes; — upon a time (il était) une fois

oncoming a. à venir, qui vient; approchant; hardi

one a. un, une; — pron. on; — another l'un l'autre, les uns les autres; — by — un à un; —'s son, sa, ses

one-eyed a. borgne

one-horse a. à un cheval; (fig.) provincial, insignifiant

onerous a. onéreux

oneself pron. soi, soi-même; se

one-sided a. à un seul côté; partial; -ness n. partialité f.

onetime a. ancien, d'autrefois

one-track a. à une voie; (fig.) borné

one-way a. à sens unique; — ticket billet simple, aller m.

onion n. oignon m.

onionskin (paper) n. papier pelure m.

onlooker n. spectateur m.

only a. seul; unique; — adv. ne . . . que; seulement

onomatopoeia n. onomatopée f.

onrush n. ruée f.; attaque f.

onset n. assaut, m., attaque f.; début, commencement m.

onslaught n. attaque f., assaut m.

on-the-job a. (coll.) à sur place

onto prep. sur; à; dans

onus n. fardeau, poids m., charge f.

onward adv. en avant

ooze n. vase, bourbe f.; — vi. filtrer; suinter; s'écouler

opalescent a. opalescent

opaque a. opaque; -ness n. opacité f.

open vt. ouvrir; commencer; découvrir; — vi. s'ouvrir; — a. ouvert; franc, sincère; — house réception f.; — shop entreprise qui emploie des ouvriers syndiqués et non syndiqués; -er n., can -er ouvre-boîtes m.; -ing n. ouverture f.; (theat.) première f.; débouché m.; -ness n. franchise f.

open-air a. en plein air; à la belle étoile

open-eyed a. les yeux écarquillés

openhanded a. généreux

openhearted a. franc

open-minded a. large d'esprit

openmouthed a. étourdi, abasourdi; bouche bée

openwork n. ouvrage à jour

opera n. opéra m.; — glasses jumelles de théâtre f. pl.; — hat chapeau claque; — house n. opéra m.; -atic a. d'opéra

operate vi. opérer, agir; — vt. faire marcher

operating room n. amphithéâtre m.

operation n. opération f.; have an — être opéré; -al a. en état de marche

operator n. opérateur m.

opiate n. opiat m.

opine vt. opiner

opinion n. opinion f., sentiment m.; avis

m.; in my — à mon avis; -ated a. opiniâtre

opium n. opium m.

opossum n. opossum m.

opponent n. antagoniste, adversaire m.

opportune a. opportun; à propos; -ness n. opportunité f.

opportunism n. opportunisme m.

opportunist n. opportuniste m.

opportunity n. occasion f.

oppose vt. & (vi.) (s')opposer

opposite a. & n. opposé m.

opposition n. opposition, résistance f.

oppress vt. opprimer; -ion n. oppression f.; -ive a. oppressif; -or n. oppresseur m.

opprobrium n. opprobre m.

optic a. optique, visuel; -al a. optique; -ian n. opticien m.; -s n. optique f.

optimism n. optimisme m.

optimist n. optimiste m. & f.; -ic a. optimiste

optimum a. le meilleur

option n. option f., choix m.; -al a. facultatif

optometry n. optométrie f.

opulence n. opulence f.

opulent a. opulent

opus n. composition musicale f.

or conj. ou; either . . . . — ou . . . . ou; soit (que) . . . . soit (que); — else ou bien

oral a. oral; par la bouche; -ly adv. oralement; par la bouche

orange n. orange f.; (tree) oranger m.; — a. orangé, couleur orange

orangeade n. orange pressée f.

orangutang m. orang-outan m.

orate vi. pérorer

oration n. discours m., harangue f.; (funeral) oraison f.

orator n. orateur m.; -ical a. oratoire

orb n. orbe m., sphère f.; globe m.

orbit n. orbite f.

orchard n. verger m.

orchestra n. orchestre m.; — seat fauteuil d'orchestre m.; -al a. orchestral; -te vt. orchestrer; -tion n. orchestration f.

orchid n. orchidée f.

ordain vt. ordonner; établir; sacrer

ordeal n. épreuve f.

order n. ordre, rang m.; commande f.; précepte, commandement m.; billet m.; mandat m.; décoration f.; (com.) demande f.; money — mandat-poste m.; call to — rappeler à l'ordre; in — to pour; in — en règle; par rang; in — that pour que, afin que; in alphabetical — par ordre alphabétique; in chronological — par ordre de date; make to — faire sur commande; on — commandé; out of — détraqué, déréglé; déplacé; — vt. ordonner; commander; régler, disposer; -liness n. bon ordre m.; -ly a. ordonnance f.; -ly a. bien réglé, régulier; ordonné; rangé

ordinance n. ordonnance f.; règlement municipal m.

ordinal a. ordinal

ordinarily adv. d'ordinaire, d'habitude

ordinary a. ordinaire; — n. ordinaire m.; out of the — peu ordinaire; extraordinaire

ordnance n. service des munitions m.

ore n. minerai m.

organ n. organe m.; (mus.) orgue m.; — loft n. tribune d'orgue f.; — pipe n. tuyau d'orgue m.; — stop n. jeu d'orgue m.; -ic a organique; -ism n. organisme m.; -ist n. organiste m.

organdy n. organdi m.

organ-grinder n. joueur d'orgue de barbarie m.

organization n. organisation f.

organize vt. organiser; — vi. s'organiser; -r n. organisateur m.

orgy n. orgie f.

orient n. orient m.; — vt. orienter; -al a. oriental; -ate vt. orienter; -ation n. orientation f.

orifice n. orifice m., ouverture f.

origin n. origine, source f.; commencement m.; -al a. original; originaire; (eccl.) originel -al n.; original m.; -ality n. originalité f.; -ally adv. originalement; -ate vt. produire, faire naître; -ate vi. provenir, naître; -ator n. initiateur, auteur m.

ornament n. ornement m.; décoration f.; — vt. orner, parer; ornementer; -al a. ornemental; -ation n. ornementation f.

ornate a. orné; fleuri

ornithology n. ornithologie f.

orphan n. orphelin m., orpheline f.; — a. orphelin; -age, — asylum n. orphelinat m.

orthodox a. orthodoxe; -y n. orthodoxie f.

orthography n. orthographe f.

orthopedic a. orthopédique

orthopedist n. orthopédiste m.

oscillate vi. osciller

oscillation n. oscillation f.

osmosis n. osmose f.

ossification n. ossification f.

ossify vt. ossifier; — vi. s'ossifier

ostensible a. ostensible, visible; soi-disant, prétendu

ostentation n. ostentation f.; parade f.

ostentatious a. fastueux

osteopathy n. malaxion médicale, osteopathie f.

ostracism n. ostracisme m.

ostracize vt. ostraciser

other pron. autre; each — l'un l'autre; — a. autre; every — day tous les deux jours; — adv. autrement; -s pron. d'autres; autrui

otherwise adv. autrement

ottoman n. pouf m.

ought vt. devoir; — vi. falloir; — n. zéro m.; — pron. rien, quoi que ce soit

ounce n. once f. (30 grammes)

our a. notre, (pl. nos); -s pron. le nôtre, la nôtre, les nôtres

ourselves pron. nous-mêmes, nous

oust vt. déloger; évincer

out adv. dehors, au dehors; sorti; (book) paru; (flower) épanoui, en fleur; (tide) bas; (sports) hors jeu; — a. de dehors, extérieur; détaché; — of prep. hors de; en dehors de; dans; de; sur; -er a. extérieur; -s n. pl., ins and -s coins et recoins m. pl.; at -s, on the -s brouillé(s) out-and-out *a.* entier, complet; achevé

outbid *vt.* enchérir sur

outboard *n.* hors-bord *m.*

outbreak *n.* éruption *f.*

outbuilding *n.* annexe, dépendance *f.*

outburst *n.* explosion *f.*; accès *m.*

outcast *n.* exilé *m.*; rebut *m.*

outclass *vt.* surpasser; surclasser

outcome *n.* résultat *m.*; issue *f.*

outcry *n.* cri *m.*, clameur *f.*

outdated *a.* périmé; suranné

outdistance *vt.* dépasser, surpasser

outdo *vt.* l'emporter sur

outdoor *a.* du dehors; –s *adv.* au dehors, en plein air

outfit *n.* équipement *m.*; nécessaire *m.*; garde-robe *m.*; costume et accessoires *m. pl.*; — *vt.* équiper

outflank *vt.* déborder

outflow *n.* écoulement *m.*

outgoing *a.* sortant, partant; sociable, cordial, communicatif; sympathique

outgrow *vt.* surpasser en croissance; devenir trop grand pour; –th *n.* excroissance *f.*; résultat *m.*

outguess *vt.* deviner mieux que; l'emporter sur

outhouse *n.* dépendance *f.*

outing *n.* excursion *f.*; piquenique *m.*

outlandish *a.* bizarre

outlast *vt.* surpasser en durée; survivre à

outlaw *n.* proscrit *m.*; hors-la-loi *m.*; — *vt.* proscrire

outlay *n.* dépense *f.*; déboursés *m. pl.*

outlet *n.* sortie *f.*; issue *f.*; (com.) débouché *m.*

outline *n.* contour *m.*; silhouette *f.*; esquisse *f.*; plan *m.*; — *vt.* dessiner les contours de; silhouetter; esquisser; dresser un plan de

outlive *vt.* survivre à

outlook *n.* perspective *f.*, point de vue *m.*

outlying *a.* éloigné, écarté

outmaneuver *vt.* tourner (l'ennemi); manœuvrer plus habilement que

outmoded *a.* démodé

outnumber *vt.* surpasser en nombre

out-of-date *a.* périmé, démodé

out-of-doors *adv.* au dehors

out-of-print *a.* épuisé

out-of-the-way *a.* caché, obscur

outpatient *n.* malade ambulant *m.* (traité à l'hôpital sans être hospitalisé)

outpoint *vt.* battre aux points

outpost *n.* avant-poste *m.*

outpouring *n.* effusion *f.*, épanchement *m.*

output *n.* production, chiffre de production *f.*; puissance *f.*

outrage *n.* outrage *m.*; — *vt.* outrager; –ous *a.* scandaleux; outrageux

outrank *vt.* surpasser de rang

outrider *n.* piqueur *m.*

outright *adv.* sur-le-champ, tout de suite; (com.) à forfait; parfaitement; franchement; — *a.* parfait, complet

outrun *vt.* dépasser à la course, distancer

outset *n.* commencement, début *m.*

outshine *vt.* surpasser en éclat; dépasser

outside *n.* dehors *m.*, surface *f.*, extérieur *m.*; — *adv.* au dehors; dehors; en dehors, à l'extérieur; — *a.* du dehors, extérieur; — *of prep.* sauf; en dehors de; hors de; –r *n.* étranger *m.*

outskirts *n.* banlieue *f.*; environs *m. pl.*

outspoken *a.* franc

outspread *a.* étendu

outstanding *a.* éminent, remarquable; (com.) non-payé

outstare *vt.* décontenancer

outstay *vt.* rester plus longtemps que; — one's welcome rester plus longtemps qu'on ne le veut

outstretch *vt.* étendre

outstrip *vt.* dépasser, surpasser

outward *a.* extérieur; — *adv.* au dehors; — bound en destination pour l'étranger; –ly *adv.* à l'extérieur; –s *adv.* en dehors; vers l'extérieur

outwear *vt.* user; ne plus avoir besoin (d'un vêtement)

outweigh *vt.* peser plus que; l'emporter sur

outwit *vt.* surpasser en finesse; tromper, duper

oval *a. & n.* ovale *m.*

ovary *n.* ovaire *m.*

ovate *a.* ové

oven *n.* four *m.*; (fig.) fournaise *f.*; Dutch — cuisinière *f.*

over *prep.* sur, au-dessus de; par-dessus; plus de; pendant; — *adv.* au-delà; de l'autre côté; fini, passé; de nouveau; — again une fois de plus; all — partout; — and above par dessus; — and — (again) sans s'arrêter; — there là-bas; –ly *adv.* trop, à l'excès

overabundant *a.* surabondant

overage *a.* trop vieux

over-all *a.* complet

overalls *n.* cotte à bretelles *f.*; bleus *m. pl.*

overawe *vt.* impressionner, épouvanter

overbalance *vt.* l'emporter sur; renverser; peser plus que

overbearing *a.* arrogant, impérieux

overboard *adv.* à la mer

overburden *vt.* surcharger

overcast *vt.* obscurcir; surjeter; couvrir; — *a.* couvert (de nuages), sombre

overcharge *n.* prix exorbitant *m.*; surtaxe *f.*; — *vt.* surcharger, accabler; faire payer trop cher

overcoat *n.* pardessus *m.*

overcome *vt.* dompter, vaincre, maîtriser; — *a.* accablé

overconfidence *n.* suffisance *f.*

overconfident *a.* confiant à l'excès

overcooked *a.* trop cuit

overcrowd *vt.* encombrer, bonder

overdeveloped *a.* trop développé; (phot.) trop poussé

overdo *vt.* trop faire, outrer; — *vi.* se surmener; –ne *a.* trop cuit

overdose *n.* dose trop forte *f.*

overdraw *vt.* excéder son crédit, tirer à découvert

overdrive *vt.* surmener; — *n.* (auto) quatrième vitesse qui économise l'essence *f.*

overdue *a.* en retard; échu

overeat *vi.* trop manger

overestimate *vt.* surestimer

overexcite *vt.* surexciter

overexertion n. surmenage m.

overexposure n. excès d'exposition m.; (photo.) excès de pose m.

overfeed vt. surnourrir, suralimenter

overflow n. inondation f.; trop-plein m.; débordement ; — vi. déborder; surabonder; —ing a. débordant

overgrown a. excessivement accru, énorme; (with weeds) couvert

overgrowth n. couverture f.

overhang vt. surplomber; menacer

overhaul vt. réparer; réfectionner; — n. réparation f.; revision f.

overhead adv. au-dessus de la tête, en haut; — n. frais généraux m. pl.

overhear vt. entendre; surprendre

overheat vt. surchauffer

overindulge vt. & vi. gâter; —nce n. excès d'indulgence m.; abus m.

overjoyed a. ravi; transporté de joie, au comble de la jolie

overland a. & adv. par voie de terre

overlap vt. & vi. recouvrir, chevaucher; — n. recouvrement, chevauchement

overload vt. surcharger; surmener; — n. surcharge f.

overlook vt. passer sous silence, négliger, mépriser; donner sur

overlord n. suzerain m.

overnight adv. toute la nuit; pour (tóute) la nuit; jusqu'au lendemain; — a. de nuit

overpass vt. passer au-delà, franchir; — n. passage supérieur m.; pont-route m.

overpayment n. paiement en trop m.

overpopulate vt. surpeupler

overpower vt. dominer, opprimer, accabler; —ing a. accablant; irrésistible

overproduction n. surproduction f.

overrate vt. évaluer trop haut; surestimer

overreach vt. dépasser; — oneself aller trop loin, se duper

override vt. fouler; l'emporter sur

overripe a. trop mûr

overrule vt. casser, annuler

overrun vt. envahir, ravager

oversea a. d'outre-mer; —s adv. outre-mer

oversee vt. surveiller; —r n. inspecteur, surveillant, intendant m.

overshadow vt. ombrager; éclipser

overshoe n. galoche f.

overshoot vt. dépasser

oversight n. méprise, erreur, inadvertance f.

oversleep vi. dormir trop longtemps

overstate vt. exagérer; —ment n. exagération f.

overstep vt. dépasser

oversupply n. excédent m., abondance f.

overt a. manifeste; ouvert

overtake vt. dépasser, surpasser; rattraper; arriver à

overtax vt. surtaxer; surmener

overthrow n. renversement m.; défaite f.; — vt. renverser; détruire, défaire

overtime n. heures de travail supplémentaires f. pl.

overtone n. note harmonique f.

overtrick n. (cards) levée en plus f.

overtrump vt. surcouper

overture n. ouverture f.

overturn vt. renverser; — vi. se renverser

overvalue vt. trop estimer, surestimer

overview n. vue, perspective f.

overweight n. excédant (de poids) m.; surpoids m.; — a. obèse; (baggage) en excédent; qui pèse trop

overwhelm vt. accabler, écraser; combler; —ing a. irrésistible; accablant

overwork vi. se surmener; — vt. surmener; trop employer; — n. excès de travail m.; surménage m.

overwrought a. surmené; excédé

overzealous a. trop zélé

oviparous a. ovipare

ovum n. œuf m.

owe vt. devoir

owing a. dû; — to prep. à cause de, en raison de, par suite de

own vt. posséder; reconnaître, avouer; -er n. possesseur, propriétaire m.; -ership n. possession, propriété f.

own a. propre; my — à moi; le mien

ox n. bœuf m.

oxalic a. oxalique

oxide n. oxyde m.

oxidize vt. oxyder; — vi. s'oxyder

oxygen n. oxygène m.; — tent tente à oxygène f.

oyster n. huître f.; — bed banc d'huîtres m.; — plant salsifis m.

ozone n. ozone

P

pace n. pas m.; allure f.; (horse) amble m.; keep — rester aux côtés (de quelqu'un); rester à la page; — vi. aller au pas, faire les cent pas; — off mesurer (au pas); —r n. cheval qui va à l'amble m.

pacemaker n. entraîneur m.

pacific a. pacifique; —ation n. pacification f., apaisement m.

Pacific Ocean n. Océan Pacifique m.

pacifist n. pacifiste m. & f.

pacify vt. pacifier, apaiser

pack n. paquet, ballot m.; fardeau m.; (cards) jeu m.; bande, meute f.; — animal n. bête de somme f.; — horse n. cheval de bât m.; — vt. & vi. emballer, empaqueter; fourrer; (earth) tasser; faire (une valise); — off envoyer; — up faire ses valises; -age n. colis, emballage m.; -er n. emballeur m.; -ing n. emballage m.; action de faire les valises f.; (mech.) garniture f.; -ing case caisse d'emballage f.; -ing house abattoir m.

packet n. paquet m.

packsaddle n. bât m.

pact n. pacte, contrat m.

pad n. (paper) bloc m.; tampon m.; — vt. rembourrer, ouater; gonfler; — vi. aller doucement, aller à pas sourds; —ding n. remplissage m., ouate f.

paddle n. rame f.; pagaie f.; — wheel roue à aubes f.; — vt. & vi. pagayer, ramer; (coll.) fesser

paddock n. paddock m.; paddock m.

padlock n. cadenas m.; — vt. cadenasser

pagan n. & a. païen m.; -ism n. paganisme m.

page n. page f.; (court) page m.; (messenger) chasseur m.; (book) (left) verso (right) recto m.; — vt. chercher; crier (le nom d'une personne), faire appeler (par un chasseur); (print.) paginer
pageant n. spectacle, défilé m., parade f.; -ry n. faste m., pompe, parade f.
pagination, paging n. (print.) pagination f.
pail n. seau m.
pain n. peine, douleur f.; mal m.; be in — souffrir; take great -s to se donner de la peine pour; — vt. peiner, donner de la peine à; faire mal à; -ful a. pénible; douloureux; -less a. sans douleur
painstaking a. soigné; laborieux; assidu
paint n. couleur f.; peinture f.; — vt. peindre; dépeindre; -er n. peintre m.; (naut.) amarre f.; house -er peintre en bâtiments m.; -ing n. peinture f.; tableau m.
paintbrush n. pinceau m.
pair n. paire f.; couple m.; — vt. apparier; assortir; — off s'apparier
paisley n. châle écossais m.
pajamas n. pyjama m.
Pakistan n. Pakistan m.
palace n. palais m.
palatable a. agréable au goût
palate n. palais m.
palatial a. semblable à un palais; somptueux, magnifique
palatinate n. palatinat m.
Palatine n. Palatin m.
palaver n. verbiage m.; palabre f.
pale n. pieu m.; enceinte f.; beyond the — inaccessible; — a. pâle, blême; — vi. pâlir, blêmir; -ness n. pâleur f.
paleography n. paléographie f.
paleolithic a. paléolithique
Palestine n. Palestine f.
palette n. palette f.
palfrey n. palefroi m.
palisade n. palissade f.
pall n. poêle m.; — vi. affaiblir; devenir insipide
pallbearer n. porteur d'un cercueil m.
pallet n. petit lit, grabat m.
palliate vt. pallier
palliative a. & n. palliatif m.
pallid a. pâle, blême
pallor n. pâleur f.
palm n. (tree) palmier m.; (leaf) palme f.; (hand) paume f.; — vt. empaumer, escamoter; — off faire accepter (une chose pour ce qu'elle n'est pas)
Palm Sunday n. Dimanche des Rameaux m.
palmist n. chiromancier m.; -ry n. chiromancie f.
palpitate vi. palpiter
palpitation n. palpitation f.
palsied a. paralysé
palsy n. paralysie f.
paltry a. méprisable, bas, pauvre, mesquin
pamper vt. dorloter, choyer
pamphlet n. pamphlet m.; brochure f., dépliant m.; -eer n. pamphlétaire m.
pan n. poêle, casserole f.; cuvette f.; — vt. (gold) laver; (coll.) critiquer; — out

(coll.) arriver; réussir
panacea n. panacée f.
Panama n. Panama m.
Pan-American a. pan-américain
pancake n. crêpe f.; — landing atterrissage à plat m.
panchromatic a. panchromatique
pancreas n. pancréas m.
pandemonium n. pandémonium m.
pander n. maquereau m.; — vi. faire le maquereau
pane n. carreau (de vitre), panneau m.
panegyric a. panégyrique
panel n. panneau m.; jury m.; — vt. diviser en panneaux; lambrisser; -ing n. lambris m.; boiserie f.; -ist n. membre du jury m.
pang n. angoisse f.
panhandle n. queue de poêle f.; — vt. (coll.) mendier; -r n. (coll.) mendiant m.
panic n. panique f.; — vt. terrifier, affoler; -ky a. (coll.) affolé; inquiet
panic-stricken a. pris de panique; terrifié
panoply n. panoplie f.
panorama n. panorama m.
panoramic a. panoramique
pant n. halètement m.; — vi. palpiter; haleter; -ing n. halètement m.
pantaloons n. pl. pantalon m.
pantheism n. panthéisme m.
pantheist n. panthéiste m.
pantheon n. panthéon m.
panther n. panthère f.
pantomimist n. (actor) pantomime, mime m.
pantry n. office f.; garde-manger m.
pants n. pl. pantalon m.
pap n. mamelle f.; bouillie f.; pulpe f.
papacy n. papauté f.
papal a. papal
paper n. papier m.; journal m.; écrit m.; article m.; communication f.; blotting — papier buvard m.; carbon — papier carbone m.; toilet — papier hygiénique; — bag sac m.; — boy crieur, vendeur de journaux m.; — clip attache f.; — cutter, — knife coupe-papier m.; — money papier-monnaie m.; — vt. tapisser (de papier peint)
paperback n. livre broché, livre bon marché m.
paperhanger n. colleur m.
paperweight n. presse-papiers m.
papier-mâché carton-pâte m.; papier-mâché m.
papist n. papiste m.
paprika n. paprika; piment hongrois m.
Papua n. Papouasie f.
papyrus n. papyrus m.
par n. valeur égale f.; pair m.; niveau m.
parable n. parabole f.; — vt. représenter par un parabole
parabola n. parabole f.
parachute n. parachute m.; — vt. & vi. parachuter
parachutist n. parachutiste m.
parade n. défilé m.; — vi. défiler; faire la parade; — vt. faire parade de

paradise n. paradis m.
paradox n. paradoxe m.; –ical a. paradoxal
paraffin n. paraffine f.; — oil pétrole m.
paragraph n. paragraphe, alinéa m.
Paraguay n. Paraguay m.
parallel n. parallèle f.; ressemblance f.; — vt. mettre en parallèle, comparer; — a. parallèle; –ism n. parallélisme m.
parallelogram n. parallélogramme m.
paralysis n. paralysie f.
paralytic a. paralytique
paralyze vt. paralyser
paramount a. supérieur, éminent
paramour n. amant, m., amante f.
paranoia n. paranoïa f.
parapet n. parapet m.
paraphernalia n. attirail m.; équipement m.; outillage m.; effets, bagages m. pl.
paraphrase vt. paraphraser; — n. paraphrase f.
paraplegia n. paraplégie f.
parasite n. parasite m.; pique-assiette m.
parasitic a. parasite
parasol n. parasol m., ombrelle f.
paratroops n. pl. paras m. pl.
parboil vt. bouillir (avant de rôtir)
parcel n. paquet, colis m.; parcelle, quantité f.; — post n. colis postal m.; — vt. morceler, parceller
parch vt. brûler légèrement, griller; dessécher
parchment n. parchemin m.
pardon n. pardon m., grâce f.; — vt. pardonner; gracier; –able a. pardonnable; –er n. vendeur d'indulgences m.
pare vt. peler; rogner
paregoric a. & n. parégorique m.
parent n. père m., mère f.; –s pl. parents m. pl.; –age n. parenté, parentage m.; naissance f.; –al a. paternel, maternel; –hood n. parenté f.
parenthesis n. parenthèse f.
parenthetical a. entre parenthèses
parfait n. glace mêlée de sirop de fruits f.
pariah n. paria m.
paring n. rognure, pelure, écorce f.; — knife éplucheuse f.
Paris n. Paris m.; –ian a. & n. parisien m.
parish n. paroisse f.; — a. paroissial; –ioner n. paroissien m.
parity n. parité f.
park n. parc m.; — vt. & vi. stationner; –ing n. stationnement m.; no –ing stationnement interdit; –ing light feu de position, feu de stationnement m.
parkway n. boulevard m.; autostrade f.
parlance n. langage m.
parley n. pourparler m.; — vi. discuter; (mil.) parlementer
parliament n. parlement m.; –ary a. parlementaire
parlor n. petit salon m.; (convents, schools) parloir m.; funeral — établissement de pompes funèbres m.; — car voiture-salon f.
Parnassian a. & n. parnassien m.
parochial a. (eccl.) paroissial; communal
parody n. parodie f.; — vt. parodier
parole n. parole f.; liberté provisoire f.;

— vt. libérer provisoirement
paroxysm n. paroxysme m.
parquet n. parquet m.; (theat.) orchestre m.
parry vt. parer, éviter; — n. parade f.
parse vt. (gram.) expliquer (une phrase), faire l'analyse (d'une phrase)
parsimonious a. parcimonieux
parsimony n. parcimonie f.
parsley n. persil m.
parsnip n. panais m.
parson n. curé m.; prêtre m.; –age n. presbytère m.; cure f.; maison du curé f.
part n. partie, part, portion f.; parti, rôle m.; (hair) raie f.; for my — pour ma part; quant à moi; in — en partie, partiellement; in great — en grande partie; the greater — la plupart; be — of faire partie de; play a — jouer un rôle; take — in prendre part à; take someone's — prendre le parti de; spare — pièce détachée f.; pièce de rechange f.; — adv. en partie; moitié; — vt. diviser; séparer; — vi. se séparer; se diviser; se quitter; –ing n. départ m.; séparation f: –ly adv. en partie, partiellement
partake vi. avoir part, participer, prendre part
partial a. (prejudiced) partial; (part) partiel; –ity n. partialité f.
participant n. participant m.
participate vi. participer
participation n. participation f.
participial a. (gram.) participial
participle n. (gram.) participe m.
particle n. (gram.) particule f.; parcelle f., brin, atome m.
particular n. particularité f., détail m.; particulier m.; — a. particulier; singulier; exigeant, regardant, pointilleux; in — notamment, en particulier; –ity n. particularité f.; –ize vt. particulariser, spécifier; –ly adv. en particulier, particulièrement
partisan n. partisan m.; — a. de parti
partition n. partition, division f.; cloison f.; (pol.) partage m.; — vt. diviser (par une cloison), cloisonner
partitive a. partitif
partner n. associé m.; compagnon m.; partenaire m. (& f.); silent — associé commandataire m.; –ship n. association f.; go into — with s'associer avec
part owner n. copropriétaire m. & f.
part-time a.; — work emploi partiel m.
party n. parti m.; partie f.; intérêt m.; individu m.; soirée f., divertissement m., fête f.; be (a) — to prendre part à, participer à; être complice de; give someone a — fêter quelqu'un; — line ligne téléphonique utilisée par plusieurs abonnés f.; doctrine (d'un parti politique) f.
pass n. passage étroit, défilé m.; situation f., état m.; billet gratuit m.; laissez-passer m.; passe f.; come to — se passer, arriver; — vt. passer; dépasser, doubler; croiser; voter; — vi.

passer; se passer; (education) être reçu (à un examen), réussir (à); — away décéder; — by passer (par); — judgment prononcer un jugement; — off faire passer; — on procéder; décéder; — out se pâmer; perdre connaissance; — over laisser passer, négliger; -able a. passable; praticable; -ing n. passage m.; mort f.; -ing a. passager; passant; by- n. bec-allumeur m.; route d'évitement f.

passage n. passage m.; couloir m.

passageway n. corridor, passage m.

passbook n. livret de banque m.

passenger n. passager m.; voyageur m.

passer-by n. passant m.

passion n. passion f.; -ate a. passionné

passive a. & n. passif m.; -ness n. passivité f.

passkey n. passe-partout m.

Passover n. Pâque f.

passport n. passeport m.

password n. mot d'ordre m.

past n. & a. passé m.; — prep. plus loin que; devant; hors de; au delà de; — adv., go — passer

paste n. colle f.; pâte f.; (jewels) strass m.; — vt. coller

pasteboard n. carton m.

pasteurization n. pasteurisation f.

pasteurize vt. pasteuriser; -d a. pasteurisé

pastiche n. pastiche m.; — vt. pasticher

pastime n. passe-temps m.

pastor n. pasteur m.; -al n. pastorale f.; — a. pastoral

pastry n. pâtisserie f.; -cook n. pâtissier m.; -shop pâtisserie f.

pasturage n. pâturage m.

pasture n. pâture f.; pré m.; pâturage m.; — vi. paître; — vt. faire paître

pasty a. blême; pâteux

pat n. petit coup m., tape f.; rondelle f.; petit morceau (de beurre) m.; — vt. frapper légèrement, taper; — a. convenable, propre, tout prêt

patch n. pièce f., morceau m.; (eye) tampon m.; (face) mouche f.; terrain, plant m., plantation f.; — vt. rapiécer, raccommoder

patchwork n. rapiéçage m.; travail à la pièce m.

pate n. tête f.

patella n. (anat.) rotule f.

patent n. brevet m.; — a. breveté; évident, patent; — leather n. cuir verni; — vt. faire breveter

paternal a. paternel

paternity n. paternité f.

path n. sentier, chemin m.; route f.

pathetic a. pathétique

pathfinder n. explorateur m.

pathological a. pathologique

pathology n. pathologie f.

pathos n. pathétique m.; pathos m.

pathway n. sentier m.

patience n. patience f.

patient n. malade m.; — a. patient; endurant; be — patienter

patina n. patine f.

patriarch n. patriarche m.

patrician a. & n. patricien m.

patrimony n. patrimoine m.

patriot n. patriote m.; -ic a. patriotique; -ism n. patriotisme m.

patrol n. patrouille f.; — vi. faire la ronde; — vt. surveiller

patrolman n. agent de police (qui fait la ronde) m.

patron n. patron, protecteur m.; — saint patron m., patronne f.; -age n. patronage m.; clientèle f.; -ize vt. patronner; donner sa clientèle à; traiter avec condescendance

patter vi. bavarder; piétiner; faire du bruit; — n. bavardage m.; bruit m.

pattern n. patron, modèle m.

paucity n. manque m., disette f.

paunch n. panse f.; bedaine f.

pauper n. pauvre m., pauvresse f.

pause n. pause f.; — vi. faire une pause; s'arrêter; hésiter

pave vt. paver; frayer; (fig.) préparer; -ment n. pavé m.; pavage m.

pavilion n. pavillon m.

paving n. pavage m.; pavé m.

paw n. patte f.; — vt. & vi. frapper du pied; griffer; caresser avec la patte

pawl n. cliquet m.

pawn n. (chess) pion m.; gage m.; -broker n. prêteur sur gages m.; -shop n. mont-de-piété m.; — ticket n. reconnaissance de mont-de-piété f.; — vt. engager, mettre en gage

pay n. solde f.; salaire m.; — vt. payer; acquitter; — attention prêter attention; — a visit rendre visite, faire visite; — back rembourser; — for payer; — off payer; réussir; — up solder; -able a. payable; -ment n. paiement m.; versement, acompte m.

payday n. jour de paie m.

paymaster n. trésorier, payeur m.

payroll n. feuille de paie, liste de paie f.

pea n. pois m.; — shooter sarbacane f.; — soup potage Saint-Germain m.; purée de pois; — soup fog (coll.) brouillard épais

peace n. paix f.; justice of the — juge de paix m.; -ful a. paisible, tranquille; -fulness n. paix, tranquillité f.; — offering n. sacrifice expiatoire, cadeau de réconciliation m.

peace-loving a. pacifique

peacemaker n. conciliateur m.

peach n. pêche f.; (tree) pêcher m.

peak n. pic, sommet m., cime f.; pointe f.; — a. meilleur; premier; -ed a. en pointe; (hat) à visière

peal n. carillon m.; bruit m.; coup m.; — vt. faire retentir; — vi. retentir; gronder

peanut n. arachide, cacahuète f.; — brittle caramel aux arachides m.; — butter crème d'arachides f.

pear n. poire f.; (tree) poirier m.

peasant n. paysan m.; -ry n. paysans m. pl.

peat n. tourbe f.

pebble n. caillou m.

pebbly a. caillouteux

pecan n. pacane f.; (tree) pacanier m.

peccadillo n. peccadille f.

peck n. coup de bec m.; (measure) peck m. (= 9 litres); — vt. & vi. becqueter, picoter

pectoral a. & n. pectoral m.

peculiar a. particulier, singulier, unique; -ity n. singularité f.

pecuniary a. pécuniaire

pedagogical a. pédagogique

pedagogue n. pédagogue m.

pedagogy n. pédagogie f.

pedal n. pédale f.; — vi. pédaler

pedant n. pédant m.; -ic a. pedant; -ry n. pédanterie f.

peddle vt. colporter; -r n. colporteur m.

pedestal n. piédestal m.

pedestrian n. piéton m.

pediatrician n. pédiatre m.

pedigree n. généalogie f.; lignage m.; pedigree m.; -d a. de race, pur-sang

pediment n. fronton m.

pedlar n. colporteur m.

pedometer n. podomètre m.

peek n. aperçu m.; coup d'œil m.; — vi. regarder furtivement

peekaboo n. cache-cache m.

peel n. pelure f.; peau f.; écorce f.; — vt. peler, éplucher

peep n. regard furtif m.; cri (d'un poussin) m.; pépiement m.; — vi. regarder furtivement; crier, pépier

peephole n. judas m.

peer n. pair m.; — vi. regarder longuement; -age n. pairie f.; -less a. incomparable, sans pareil

peevish a. bourru, maussade; -ness n. mauvaise humeur f.

peg n. cheville f.; (tent) piquet m.; — vt. cheviller

pegleg n. jambe de bois f.

pejorative a. péjoratif

pellagra n. pellagre f.

pellet n. boulette f.; grain de plomb m., balle f.

pell-mell adv. pêle-mêle

pelt n. peau, fourrure f.; — vt. assaillir; battre

pelvic a. pelvien

pelvis n. bassin m.

pen n. plume f.; stylographe, stylo m.; (cattle) enclos m.; (poultry) poulailler; ballpoint — stylo à bille m.; name nom de plume m.; — vt. écrire; — in, — up enfermer

penal a. pénal; -ize vt. punir; (sport) pénaliser

penalty n. pénalité, peine, punition, amende f.

penance n. pénitence f.

pencil n. crayon m.; — sharpener taille-crayons m.; — vt. dessiner au crayon

pendant n. pendant m., pendeloque f.

pending a. pendant, indécis; — prep. en attendant

pendulum n. pendule m.

penetrate vt. & vi. pénétrer

penetrating a. pénétrant

penetration n. pénétration f.; sagacité f.

penholder n. porte-plume m.

penicillin n. pénicilline f.

peninsula n. péninsule f.; -r a. péninsulaire

penis n. pénis m.

penitence n. pénitence f.

penitent a. & n. pénitent m.

penitentiary n. prison f.

penknife n. canif m.

penmanship n. écriture f.

pennant n. banderole, flamme f.

penniless a. sans le sou

penny n. sou m.

pension n. pension f.; retraite f.; allocation f.; — vt., — off mettre à la retraite; -er n. pensionnaire, retraité m.

pensive a. pensif

pentagon n. pentagone m.; -al a. pentagonal

pentameter n. pentamètre m.

penthouse n. appartement (aménagé au sommet d'un grand bâtiment) m.

pent-up a. (emotion) refoulé; enfermé

penumbra n. pénombre f.

penurious a. parcimonieux; pauvre

penury n. indigence, pénurie f.

people n. peuple m.; gens m. pl.; parents m. pl.; public m.; — vt. peupler

pepper n. poivre m.; poivron, piment m.; — vt. poivrer; (fig.) saupoudrer; -y a. poivré

peppercorn n. grain de poivre m.

peppermint n. menthe poivrée f.

pepsin n. pepsine f.

peptic a. digestif, gastrique

per prep. par, pour; — cent pour cent

perambulator n. voiture d'enfant f.

perceivable a. perceptible

perceive vt. apercevoir, sentir, voir

per cent n. pour cent m.

percentage n. pourcentage m.

perceptibility n. perceptibilité f.

perceptible a. perceptible

perception n. perception f.

perceptive a. perceptif

perch n. (fish) perche f.; perchoir m.; — vt. & (vi.) (se) percher

perchance adv. par hasard

percolate vt. & vi. filtrer

percolator n. cafetière (à l'américaine) f.

percussion n. percussion f., coup m.; — cap n. capsule f.

perdition n. perdition f.; ruine f.

peremptory a. péremptoire, absolu

perennial a. perpétuel; (bot.) vivace; -ly adv. éternellement; tout le temps

perfect vt. perfectionner, achever, compléter; — a. parfait; complet; -ion n. perfection f.

perfidious a. perfide

perfidy n. perfidie f.

perforate vt. perforer, percer

perforation n. perforation f.

perforce adv. forcément

perform vt. & vi. exécuter, accomplir, faire; réussir; -ance n. accomplissement m., exécution f.; ouvrage m.; exploit, fait m., action f.; représentation f.; -er n. exécutant, artiste, acteur m.

perfume n. parfum m.; — vt. parfumer;

—r n. parfumeur m.

perfunctory a. superficiel, négligent

perhaps adv. peut-être

pericardium n. péricarde m.

peril n. péril m., danger; —ous a. périlleux, dangereux

perimeter n. périmètre m.

period n. période f.; époque f.; âge m.; terme m.; (punctuation) point m.; —ic(al) a. périodique; —ical n. périodique f.

peripatetic a. péripatétique; ambulant

peripheral a. périmétrique

periphery n. périphérie f.

periphrasis n. périphrase f.

periscope n. périscope m.

perish vi. périr; —able a. périssable

peristalsis n. mouvement péristaltique

peritoneum n. péritoine m.

peritonitis n. péritonite f.

perjure vt. parjurer; —d a. parjure; —er n. parjure m.

perjury n. parjure m.

perk vi. se rengorger; — up se ranimer; —y a. animé, vif

permanent a. permanent; — wave n. ondulation permanente, indéfrisable f.; —ly adv. d'une manière permanente

permanganate n. permanganate m.

permeable a. perméable

permeate vt. passer à travers, pénétrer, saturer

permeation n. pénétration f.

permissible a. admissible, tolérable

permissive a. qui permet; indulgent

permit n. permis m.; — vt. permettre; laisser

permutation n. permutation f.

pernicious a. pernicieux

peroration n. péroraison f.

peroxide n. peroxyde m.; peroxyde d'hydrogène m.

perpendicular a. & n. perpendiculaire m.

perpetrate vt. commettre, faire

perpetration n. perpétration f.

perpetrator n. auteur m.

perpetual a. perpétuel; sans cesse, sans fin

perpetuate vt. perpétuer

perpetuation n. perpétuation f.

perplex vt. embarrasser; confondre; embrouiller; —ity n. perplexité f., embarras m.

perquisite n. casuel, émolument m.

persecute vt. persécuter

persecution n. persécution f.

persecutor n. persécuteur m.

perseverance n. persévérance f.

persevere vi. persévérer

persevering a. persévérant

Persia n. Perse f.; —n a. & n. persan m.; —n Gulf Golfe Persique m.

persimmon n. plaqueminier m.

persist vi. persister; —ence, —ency n. persistance f.; —ent a. persistant

person n. personne f.; individu m.; personnalité f.; —able a. bien fait; aimable, sociable; —age n. personnage m.; personne f.; —al a. personnel;

particulier; —ality n. personnalité f.; —ification n. personnification f.; —ify vt. personnifier

perspective n. perspective f.; — a. perspectif

perspicacity n. perspicacité f.

perspiration n. transpiration, sueur f.

perspire vi. transpirer, suer

persuade vt. persuader, convaincre

persuasion n. persuasion, conviction f.

persuasive a. persuasif

pert a. vif, pétulant, impertinent

pertain vi. appartenir, concerner

pertinence n. convenance, propriété f.; justesse f.

pertinent a. pertinent, convenable; juste, à propos

perturb vt. troubler, perturber; —ation n. perturbation f., trouble m.

Peru n. Pérou m.

perusal n. lecture f., examen m.

peruse vt. lire, parcourir

pervade vt. pénétrer

pervasive a. pénétrant

perverse a. pervers; têtu

perversion n. perversion f.

perversity n. perversité f.; méchanceté f.

pervert vt. pervertir, dépraver; — n. perverti m.

pervious a. perméable

pessimism n. pessimisme m.

pessimist n. pessimiste m.; —ic a. pessimiste

pest n. fléau m.; personne gênante f.; —er vt. gêner, ennuyer

pestilence n. peste f.

pestilent a. pestilentiel

pestle n. pilon m.

pet n. favori m.; animal favori m.; — name petit nom m.; — vt. caresser

petal n. pétale m.

petition n. pétition, supplication f.; demande f.; requête f.; — vt. pétitionner, supplier; demander à; réclamer à; —er n. demandeur m.; pétitionnaire m. & f.

petrel n. pétrel m.

petrify vt. & (vi.) (se) pétrifier

petroleum n. pétrole m.

petticoat n. jupon m.

pettiness n. petitesse f.

petty a. petit, inférieur; chétif; — cash petite caisse f.; — officer (navy) sous-officier m.

petulance n. pétulance f.

petulant a. pétulant

pew n. banc d'église m.

pewter n. étain m.

phalanx n. phalange f.

phantom n. fantôme m.

Pharaoh n. Pharaon m.

Pharisee n. Pharisien m.

pharmaceutic(al) a. pharmaceutique

pharmacist n. pharmacien m.

pharmacy n. pharmacie f.

pharynx n. pharynx m.

phase n. phase f.

phenol n. phénol m.

phenomenal a. phénoménal

phenomenon n. phénomène m.

Philadelphia n. Philadelphie f.
philander vi. courir; -er n. coureur m.
philanthropic a. philanthropique
philanthropist n. philanthrope m.
philatelic a. philatélique
philatelist n. philatéliste m.
philharmonic a. philharmonique
Philippines n. Philippines f. pl.
Philistine n. Philistin m.
philologist n. philologue m.
philology n. philologie f.
philosopher n. philosophe m.
philosophic(al) a. philosophique
philosophize vi. philosopher
philosophy n. philosophie f.
phlegm n. flegme m.; -atic a. flegmatique
phobia n. phobie f.
Phoenicia n. Phénicie f.; -n a. & n.
  phénicien m.
phone n. téléphone m.; — vi. téléphoner
phonetic a. phonétique; -s n. phonétique
  f.
phonic a. phonique
phosphate n. (chem.) phosphate m.;
  (beverage) soda m.
phosphide n. phosphure m.
phosphorescence n. phosphorescence f.
phosphoric a. phosphorique
phosphorus n. phosphore m.
photoelectric a. photo-électrique
photoengraving n. photogravure f.
photograph n. photographie f.; — vt.
  photographier; -er n. photographe m.;
  -ic a. photographique; -y n. photographie f.
photostat n. photocopie f.
photosynthesis n. photosynthèse f.
phrase n. phrase, expression f.; locution
  f.; — vt. exprimer, rédiger
phraseology n. phraséologie f.
phrenetic a. frénétique
phrenology n. phrénologie f.
physic n. médicament m.; purgatif m.;
  médecine f.; -s n. physique f.; -al a.
  physique; matériel
physician n. médecin m.
physicist n. physicien m.
physiognomy n. physionomie f.
physiological a. physiologique
physiologist n. physiologiste m.
physiology n. physiologie f.
physiotherapy n. physicothérapie f.
physique n. physique m.
pianist n. pianiste m. & f.
piano n. piano m.; baby grand — piano
  à demi-queue m.; grand — piano à
  queue; upright — piano droit m.
Picardy n. Picardie f.
picayune a. mesquin
piccolo n. piccolo, octavin m.
pick n. pioche f.; — vi. piquer, becqueter;
  — vt. cueillir, glaner, ramasser; éplucher, trier; choisir; — out choisir; — up
  ramasser; acheter à bon marché; retrouver; relever; apprendre; -ings n. pl.
  épluchures f. pl., petits morceaux m. pl.;
  profit m.
pickaback adv. sur le dos
pickax(e) n. pioche f.
pickerel n. brocheton m.

picket n. piquet m.; pieu m.; (striker)
  piquet de grève, débaucheur m.; —
  fence palis m.; — vt. entourer de
  débaucheurs
pickle n. cornichon m.; (coll.) difficulté
  f.; mauvais pas m.; — vt. conserver au
  vinaigre
picklock n. crochet m.
pickpocket n. pickpocket m.
pickup n. (radio, television, or phonograph) pick-up m.; (coll.) fille, personne
  rencontrée dans la rue f.; (auto) accélération f.
picnic n. pique-nique m.; — vi. piqueniquer
picot n. picot m.; — vt. picoter
pictorial a. pittoresque, illustré
picture n. tableau m.; peinture f.; image
  f.; film m.; — vt. peindre; représenter
picturesque a. pittoresque; -ness n. pittoresque m.
piddling a. insignifiant, mesquin
pidgin a., — English jargon anglo-oriental m.
pie n. tarte f.
piebald a. pie
piece n. pièce f., morceau m.; bout m.;
  partie f.; — vt. raccommoder, rapiécer;
  — together joindre, unir, réunir
piecemeal a. séparé, divisé; — adv. par
  petits morceaux
piecework n. travail à la pièce m.
pied a. pie, bigarré
pier n. môle m.; pilier, pied-droit m.; pile
  f.
pierce vt. & vi. percer, pénétrer
piercing a. pénétrant; aigu
piety n. piété, dévotion f.
pig n. cochon m.; porc m.; buy a — in a
  poke acheter chat en poche; — iron fer
  en fonte m.; -gish a. semblable à un
  cochon; glouton
pigeon n. pigeon m.; clay — pigeon
  artificiel m.; homing — pigeon voyageur m.
pigeon-breasted a. (qui a) la poitrine en
  saillie
pigeonhole n. case f.
pigheaded a. têtu, entêté; -ness n. entêtement m., obstination f.
pigment n. pigment m.; couleur f.; -ation
  n. pigmentation f.
pigmy n. pygmée m.
pigpen, pigsty n. étable à cochons f.
pigskin n. peau de porc f.; (coll.) ballon
  de football m.
pigtail n. tresse f.
pike n. pique f.; pointe f.; (fish) brochet
  m.; (coll.) autostrade f.
pilaster n. pilastre m.
pilchard n. sardine f.
pile n. pieu, pilotis m.; monceau, tas m.;
  bûcher m.; édifice m.; duvet m.; (coll.)
  fortune f.; — vt. entasser; amonceler;
  amasser; — vi., — up s'entasser
piles n. pl. hémorroïdes f. pl.
pilfer vt. voler, chiper; -age, -ing n.
  petits vols m. pl.
pilgrim n. pèlerin m.; -age n. pèlerinage
  m.

pill n. pilule f.

pillar n. pilier m.

pillbox n. boîte à pilules f.; (mil.) réduit en béton armé m.

pillory n. pilori m.; — vt. mettre au pilori

pillow n. oreiller m.; — vt. reposer, coucher

pillowcase n. taie d'oreiller f.

pilot n. pilote m.; — vt. piloter; — light n. veilleuse f.

pimento n. piment m.

pimple n. bouton m., pustule f.

pimply a. boutonneux

pin n. épingle f.; (bowling) quille f.; — money argent de poche m.; safety — épingle de sûreté f.; — vt. épingler; fixer, attacher

pinafore n. bavette f.; sarrau m.

pincers n. pl. pinces, tenailles f. pl.

pinch n. pince f.; prise f.; difficulté f., embarras m.; — vt. & vi. pincer; serrer; —ed a. tiré; à l'étroit

pinch-hit vi. (coll.); — for remplacer, suppléer (provisoirement)

pincushion n. pelote à épingles f.

pine n. pin m.; — vi. languir, soupirer

pineapple n. ananas m.

pinhole n. trou d'épingle m.; (phot.) sténopé m.

pinion n. pignon m.; — vt. lier

pink n. (bot.) œillet m.; rose (couleur) f.; — of condition en parfaite santé f.; — a. rose; — vt. denteler, découper

pinnacle n. pinacle, sommet m.; couronnement m.

pinpoint vt. localiser, mettre au net

pint n. demi-litre m.; pinte f.

pinwheel n. roue à fuseaux f.

pioneer n. pionnier m.

pious a. pieux

pip n. (bot.) pépin m.; signal m.

pipe n. tuyau m.; pipe f.; — vt. jouer; faire passer par un tuyau; —r n. joueur de flûte m.; —line n. pipe-line m.

pipecleaner n. cure-pipe m.

piping n. passe-poil m.; tuyauterie f.; — a. maladif; — hot tout chaud

piquancy n. piquant m.

piquant a. piquant

pique n. pique f.; — vt. piquer, irriter

piracy n. piraterie f.; (literature) plagiat m.

pirate n. pirate m.; — vi. commettre un plagiat; pirater

pirouette n. pirouette f.; — vi. pirouetter

pistachio n. pistache f.

pistol n. pistolet m.

piston n. piston m.; — rod n. tige du piston f.

pit n. fosse f.; trou m.; carrière f., tombeau m.; (theat.) parterre, creux m.; — vt. opposer; grêler, marquer de trous

pitch n. poix f.; degré, point m.; hauteur f.; portée f.; (mus.) ton m.; — vt. poisser; fixer, planter, ranger; jeter, lancer; paver; obscurcir; — vi. tomber; (naut.) tanguer; — (in) se mettre au travail; —er n. cruche f.; (sport) joueur qui lance la balle m.

pitchblende n. pechblende f.

pitchfork n. fourche f.

pitch pipe n. diapason m.

piteous a. piteux, pitoyable

pitfall n. piège m.

pith n. moelle f.; —y a. plein de moelle

pitiable a. digne de pitié

pitiful a. déplorable, pitoyable; méprisable

pitiless a. impitoyable

pittance n. pitance, portion f.

pitter-patter n. bruit de la pluie sur un toit m.

pituitary a. pituitaire

pity n. pitié, compassion f.; it is a — c'est dommage; to take — on prendre en pitié; — vt. plaindre, avoir pitié de

pivot n. pivot m.; — vi. pivoter

pixie n. lutin m., fée f.

placard n. placard m., affiche f.; — vt. afficher

placate vt. apaiser

place n. place f.; lieu m.; endroit m.; rang m.; emploi m.; demeure f.; position f.; in — of au lieu de; out of — déplacé; take — avoir lieu; — vt. placer, mettre; —ment n. mise f.; position f.; — kick n. (football) coup placé, coup d'envoie m.

placer n. (mining) placer m.; placeur m.

placid a. paisible, calme, placide; —ity n. placidité f., calme m.

plagiarism n. plagiat m.

plagiarize vt. plagier

plague n. peste, contagion f.; tourment m.; — vt. tourmenter

plaid n. tartan, plaid, tissu écossais m.

plain n. plaine f.; — a. plat, uni, simple, sincère, franc; clair; laid; —ness n. simplicité, franchise f.; laideur f.

plainsman n. homme des plaines m.

plaintiff n. demandeur m.

plaintive a. plaintif

plait n. pli m., tresse f.; — vt. plisser; tresser

plan n. plan, dessin m.; projet m.; — vt. projeter; dresser le plan de; compter; avoir l'intention de

plane n. plan m.; (tool) rabot m.; (avi.) avion m.; — vt. raboter; — a. plan, plat; — tree n. platane m.

planet n. planète f.; —ary a. planétaire; —arium n. planétaire m.

plank n. planche f.; — vt. planchéier; —ing n. planchéiage m., planches f. pl.

plant n. plante f.; plant m.; (industry) usine f.; — vt. planter; établir; — louse n. puceron m.; —er n. planteur m.

plantain n. plantain m.

plantation n. plantation f.

plaque n. plaque f.

plasma n. plasma m.

plaster n. plâtre m.; emplâtre m.; — vt. plâtrer; adhesive — emplâtre resineux; sparadrap m.; mustard — sinapisme m.; —board n. panneau de plâtre et de papier m.; — of Paris n. gypse m.; plâtre fin m.; —er n. plâtrier m.; —ing n. plâtrage m.

plastic a. plastique; — n. matière plastique f.; -ity n. plasticité f.

plat n. plan m., carte f.

plate n. (metal) plaque f.; (dish) assiette f.; (flatware) argenterie f.; (food) plat m.; (teeth) dentier m.; (engraving) gravure f.; — vt. plaquer, laminer; étamer; argenter; — **glass** glâce (sans tain) f.

plateau n. plateau, massif m.

plateful n. assiettée f.

platform n. plate-forme f.; (rail.) quai m.; (politics) programme politique m.

platinum n. platine m.

platitude n. platitude f.

platonic a. platonique

platoon n. peloton m.

platter n. plat m.

plaudit n. applaudissement m.

plausibility n. plausibilité f.

plausible a. plausible

play n. jeu m.; (theat.) pièce f.; — **on words** calembour m.; — vi. jouer; — vt. jouer; faire; — **a trick on** jouer un tour à; — **on** abuser de; — **tennis** jouer au tennis; — **the piano** jouer du piano; — **up to** courtiser; flatter; -er n. joueur m.; (theat.) acteur, comédien m.; -er **piano** piano à rouleau m.; -ful a. badin, espiègle; -ing n. jeu m.; -ing **cards** cartes à jouer f. pl.; -ing **field** terrain m.

playboy n. luron, libertin m.; homme riche qui fréquente les boîtes de nuit m.

playgoer n. habitué du théâtre m.

playground n. terrain de jeu m., cour de récréation f.

playhouse n. théâtre m.

playmate n. camarade de jeu m.

plaything n. jouet m.

playwright n. auteur dramatique m.

plea n. défense f.; excuse f.; prières f. pl.

plead vi. plaider; — vt. défendre; alléguer, prétexter; -ing n. prières f. pl.; (law) plaidoirie f.

pleasant a. agréable; -ness n. agrément, charme m.; -ry n. pl. plaisanterie f.

please vt. & vi. plaire à, être agréable, contenter; — interj. s'il vous plaît; **as you** — comme il vous plaira; **if you** — s'il vous plaît; — **be seated** veuillez vous asseoir; -d a. content, heureux; -d **to meet you** enchanté de faire votre connaissance

pleasing a. agréable, charmant

pleasurable a. agréable

pleasure n. plaisir, gré m.; **with** — avec plaisir, volontiers

pleat n. pli, pli creux m.; — vt. plisser, mettre en plis

plebeian a. & n. plébéien m.

plebiscite n. plébiscite m.

pledge n. gage m.; caution f.; toast m.; vœu m., promesse f.; — vt. engager; promettre

plenary a. plein, complet, parfait

plenipotentiary n. & a. plénipotentiaire m.

plentiful a. abondant

plenty n. abondance f.; **have** — **of** ne pas manquer de, avoir beaucoup de

plethora n. pléthore f.

pleurisy n. pleurésie f.

plexus n. plexus m.

pliability n. souplesse, flexibilité f.

pliable, pliant a. flexible, pliable; docile

pliers n. pl. pince f.

plight n. condition f., état m.; — vt. engager

plod vi. piocher; marcher avec peine; -der n. piocheur m.

plop n. & interj. pouf, plouf m.; — vi. faire plouf

plot n. morceau de terre m.; plan, complot m.; intrigue f.; — vt. & vi. comploter, conspirer, machiner; inventer; -ter n. conspirateur m.; -ting n. machinations f. pl.

plow, plough n. charrue f.; bouvet m.; **gang** — charrue polysoc f.; — vt. labourer; sillonner; -ing n. labourage m.; -man n. laboureur m.

plowshare n. soc de charrue m.

pluck n. action intrépide f.; courage m.; fressure (d'un animal) f.; — vt. arracher; (feathers) plumer; cueillir; -y a. courageux

plug n. tampon m., cheville f.; piston m ; bouchon m.; prise (de courant) f.; fiche f.; **spark** — bougie f.; — vt. boucher; cheviller; tamponner; — **away** vi. (coll.) persévérer; — **in** mettre la fiche dans (la prise)

plum n. prune f.; (tree) prunier m.

plumb n. plomb m.; sonde f.; — **line** n. niveau m.; fil à plomb m.; — vt. mettre à plomb; — adv. à plomb; -er n. plombier m.; -ing n. installation sanitaire f.

plume n. plume f., panache m.; plumet m.; — vt. orner d'une plume; lisser

plummet n. plomb m., sonde f.; — vi. tomber

plump vi. s'enfler; tomber lourdement; soutenir (une candidature); — a. dodu, potelé, plantureux; -ness n. embonpoint m.

plunder n. pillage, butin m.; — vt. piller, spolier

plunge vt. plonger; — vi. se plonger; (se) jeter; -r n. plongeon m.; piston m.; (person) risque-tout m.

pluperfect n. plus-que-parfait m.

plural n. & a. pluriel m.; -ity n. pluralité f.

plus prep. plus

plush n. peluche f.; — a. (coll.) somptueux, élégant

plutocracy n. plutocratie f.

plutocrat n. ploutocrate m.

plutonium n. plutonium m.

ply n. épaisseur f.; — vt. se servir de; accabler, offrir

plywood n. bois contreplaqué m.

P.M. de l'après-midi, du soir

pneumatic a. pneumatique

pneumonia n. pneumonie f.; fluxion de poitrine f.

poach vt. pocher; — vi. piller; braconner; -er n. braconnier m.

pocket n. poche f.; (billiards) blouse f.; — **book** livre de poche m.; -knife couteau de poche *m.*; — *vt.* empocher; blouser; avaler (un affront)

pocketbook *n.* (ladies) sac *m.*

pock-marked *a.* grêlé

pod *n.* cosse, écale *f.*

poem *n.* poème *m*

poet *n.* poète *m.*; –ic(al) *a.* poétique; –ics *n.* art poétique *m.*; –ry *n.* poésie *f.*

poignancy *n.* piquant *m.*

poignant *a.* piquant; douloureux, aigu

point *n.* pointe *f.*; cap *m.*; point, moment *m.*; degré *m.*; lieu *m.*; but *m.*; sujet *m.*, idée *f.*; (math.) virgule *f.*; — blank directement, de but en blanc; — of departure point de départ *m.*; — of view point de vue *m.*; in — of fact en fait; make a — of faire un devoir de; to the — à propos; to the — of jusqu'à; — *vt.* pointer; aiguiser, affiler; — out montrer, signaler; — up (coll.) souligner; –ed *a.* pointu; piquant, mordant; marqué; –er *n.* (dog) chien d'arrêt *m.*; aiguille *f.*; baguette *f.*; –less *a.* sans pointe; sans but, sans raison

poise *vt.* tenir suspendu; tenir prêt; — *vi.* se tenir suspendu, se tenir prêt; — *n.* sang-froid, savoir-faire *m.*; équilibre *m.*; –d *a.* bien équilibré, suave, imperturbable

poison *n.* poison *m.*; — *vt.* empoisonner; –ing *n.* empoisonnement *m.*, –ous *a.* empoisonné; venimeux; (plants) vénéneux

poke *n.* coup de poing *m.*; (coll.) sac *m.*; — *vi.* fouiller; — *vt.* donner un coup de poing à; taper; (head) passer; (fire) tisonner; –r *n.* tisonnier *m.*; (game) poker *m.*

Poland *n.* Pologne *f.*

polar *a.* polaire; –ity *n.* polarité *f.*; –ize *vt.* polariser

pole *n.* pôle *m.*; perche *f.*; timon *m.*; poteau *m.*; — vault saut à la perche *m.*

Pole *n.* Polonais *m.*

polecat *n.* putois *m.*

polemic *n.* polémique *f.*

police *n.* police *f.*; — chief, chief of — *n.* commissaire de police *m.*; — court *n.* tribunal de police *m.*; — dog berger allemand *m.*; — headquarters, — station commissariat de police *m.*; — *vt.* surveiller, policer

policeman *n.* agent de police *m.*

policewoman *n.* femme-agent de police *f.*

policy *n.* politique *f.*; ruse *f.*; police *f.*; plan *m.*; insurance — police d'assurance *f.*

polio(myelitis) *n.* poliomyélite *f.*

polish *n.* poli *m.*; élégance *f.*; — *vt.* polir; vernir; cirer

Polish *a. & n.* polonais *m.*

polite *a.* poli; courtois; –ness *n.* politesse *f.*; courtoisie *f.*

politic *a.* politique; prudent, judicieux; –al *a.* politique; –s *n.* politique *f.*

politician *n.* politicien *m.*

polka *n.* polka *f.*; — dot *n.* rond de couleur *m.*; pois *m.*

polka-dot, dotted *a.* à pois

poll *n.* liste électorale *f.*; enquête *f.*; voix

f., vote *m.*; –s *n. pl.* urnes *f. pl.*; — tax *n.* capitation *f.*; — *vt.* consulter; voter

pollen *n.* pollen *m.*

pollinate *vt.* féconder, effectuer la pollinisation de

polling booth *n.* isoloir; bureau de scrutin *m.*

pollute *vt.* polluer; souiller

pollution *n.* pollution *f.*; souillure *f.*

polo *n.* polo *m.*; — shirt maillot *m.*

poltroon *n.* poltron, lâche *m.*

polygamous *a.* polygame

polygamy *n.* polygamie *f.*

polyglot *n. & a.* polyglotte *m.*

polygon *n.* polygone *m.*; –al *a.* polygone

Polynesia *n.* Polynésie *f.*; –n *a. & n.* polynésien *m.*

polyp *n.* polype *m.*

polyphonic *a.* polyphonique

polyphony *n.* polyphonie *f.*

polysyllabic *a.* polysyllabe

polysyllable *n.* polysyllabe *m.*

polytechnic *a.* polytechnique

pomade *n.* pommade *f.*

pomegranate *n.* grenade *f.*; (tree) grenadier *m.*

pommel *n.* pommeau *m.*; — *vt.* rosser

pomp *n.* pompe *f.*, éclat *m.*, faste *m.*; –ous *a.* pompeux; ampoulé; suffisant; –ousness *n.* suffisance *f.*; emphase *f.*

pompadour *n.* coiffure à la Pompadour *f.*

pompom *n.* (mil.) canon-mitrailleuse *m.*

pond *n.* étang *m.*; vivier *m.*; mare *f.*

ponder *vt. & vi.* peser; méditer; –able *a.* pondérable; –ous *a.* pesant

pontiff *n.* pontife *m.*

pontifical *a.* pontifical

pontificate *n.* pontificat *m.*; — *vi.* parler ex-cathedra; pontifier

pontoon *n.* ponton *m.*

pony *n.* poney *m.*; (educ.) traduction *f.* (utilisée par un élève pour éviter de traduire lui-même)

pony tail *n.* (hair) queue de cheval *f.*

poodle *n.* caniche *f.*

pool *n.* étang *m.*; mare *f.*; (swimming) piscine *f.*; (game) billard (à blouses) *m.*; (betting) poule *f.*; exploitation en commun *f.*; dépôt *m.*; — *vt.* mettre en commun, exploiter en commun; — room *n.* salle de billard *f.*

poop *n.* poupe *f.*; (coll.) potins *m. pl.*

poor *a.* pauvre; indigent; mauvais; inférieur; — *n.* pauvres *m. pl.*; –ness *n.* pauvreté *f.*; infériorité *f.*

poorhouse *n.* maison de charité *f.*, refuge *m.*

pop *n.* petit coup *m.*; (coll.) père *m.*; (beverage) soda *m.*, boisson gazeuse; — *vi.* éclater; — *vt.* faire éclater; — in (coll.) entrer en passant; — up arriver; apparaître; — *interj.* crac!

popcorn *n.* maïs éclaté *m.*

Pope *n.* pape *m.*; (Greek Church) pope *m.*

popgun *n.* canonnière *f.*

poplar *n.* peuplier *m.*

poplin *n.* popeline *f.*

populace *n.* populace *f.*

popular *a.* populaire; à la mode; –ity *n.* popularité *f.*; –ize *vt.* populariser populate *vt.* peupler

population *n.* population *f.*

populous *a.* populeux

porcelain *n.* porcelaine *f.*

porch *n.* porche, portique *m.*, véranda *f.*

porcine *a.* de porc

porcupine *n.* porc-épic *m.*

pore *n.* pore *m.*; — *vi.* avoir les yeux fixés; — over dévorer; méditer; être absorbé dans

pork *n.* porc *m.*; — chop côtelette de porc *f.*; -er *n.* porc, cochon *m.*

pornographic *a.* pornographique

pornography *n.* pornographie *f.*

porosity *n.* porosité *f.*

porous *a.* poreux

porphyry *n.* porphyre *m.*

porpoise *n.* marsouin *m.*

porridge *n.* bouillie *f.*

port *n.* port *m.*; (gun opening) sabord *m.*; (wine) porto *m.*; (side) bâbord *m.*; (hole) hublot *m.*; — *vt.* (arms) porter; (naut.) mettre à bâbord

portable *a.* portatif

portage *n.* portage *m.*

portal *n.* portail *m.*, porte *f.*

portcullis *n.* herse *f.*

portend *vt.* présager

portent *n.* présage *m.*; -ous *a.* de mauvais augure

porter *n.* portier *m.*; porteur, portefaix *m.*

porterhouse *n.* châteaubriant *m.*

portfolio *n.* portefeuille *m.*; carton *m.*

portico *n.* portique *m.*

portion *n.* portion, part, partie *f.*; dot *m.*; — *vt.* partager; doter

portliness *n.* embonpoint *m.*

portly *a.* corpulent

portrait *n.* portrait *m.*; — painter portraitiste *m.*

portray *vt.* peindre, dépeindre, décrire; -al *n.* portrait *m.*; peinture *f.*; description *f.*

Portugal *n.* Portugal *m.*

Portuguese *a. & n.* portugais *m.*

pose *n.* pose, attitude *f.*; — *vt.* poser; proposer; — as se faire passer pour; confondre (avec)

position *n.* position, situation *f.*; attitude, posture *f.*; thèse *f.*; in a — to à même de; in — en place; — *vt.* situer

positive *n.* positif *m.*; — *a.* positif; certain, sûr, assuré; affirmatif; vrai; -ly *adv.* positivement; certainement

positivism *n.* positivisme *m.*

positron *n.* positron *m.*

posse *n.* force publique d'un comté; milice *f.*

possess *vt.* posséder; jouir de; avoir; disposer de; be — ed of posséder; -ion *n.* possession *f.*; -ive *a.* possessif; -or *n.* possesseur *m.*

possibility *n.* possibilité *f.*; moyen *m.*; éventualité *f.*

possible *a.* possible; éventuel; if — si (c'est) possible

possibly *adv.* peut-être

post *n.* poste *f.*; courrier *m.*; poste, emploi *m.*; poteau *m.*; pilier *m.*; pieu (x) *m.*

(*m. pl.*) (*mil.*) (lieu de) garnison *f.*; — office bureau de poste *m.*; — *vt.* afficher; mettre à la poste; — no bills défense d'afficher; -al *a.* postal; -er *n.* affiche *f.*

postage *n.* affranchissement *m.*; — due letter lettre taxée *f.*; — stamp timbreposte *m.*

post card *n.* carte postale *f.*

postdate *vt.* postdater

posterior *a.* postérieur; — *n.* postérieur, derrière *m.*

posterity *n.* postérité *f.*

postgraduate *n.* étudiant *m.* (qui poursuit des études au-delà du baccalauréat)

posthaste *adv.* promptement, en grande diligence; en grand hâte

posthumous *a.* posthume

postilion *n.* postillon *m.*

postman *n.* facteur *m.*

postmark *n.* oblitération *f.*

postmaster *n.* receveur des postes *m.*

post-mortem *n.* (med.) autopsie *f.*; — *a. & adv.* après décès

postpaid *a.* port payé; — *adv.* franco

postpone *vt.* remettre, différer; -ment *n.* ajournement *m.*

postscript, P.S. *n.* post-scriptum *m.*

postulate *n.* postulat *m.*; — *vt.* poser, postuler

posture *n.* posture, attitude; pose *f.*

postwar *a.* d'après-guerre

pot *n.* pot *m.*; -herb herbe potagère *f.*; — roast estouffade *f.*; take -luck courir la fortune du pot; — *vt.* mettre en pot

potable *a.* potable

potash *n.* potasse *f.*

potato *n.* pomme de terre *f.*; baked — pomme au four *f.*; boiled — pomme à l'anglaise *f.*; fried -es (pommes) frites *f.*; mashed -es purée de pommes *f.*; sweet — patate *f.*; — masher presse-purée *m.*

potbellied *a.* ventru

potency *n.* puissance, force *f.*

potent *a.* puissant, fort; -ate *n.* potentat *m.*; -ial *a.* virtuel, potentiel, latent; -iality *n.* potentialité *f.*

potholder *n.* poignée pour les pots chauds *f.*

potion *n.* breuvage *m.*; philtre *m.*

potshot *n.* coup tiré sans viser *m.*

potter *n.* potier; -y *n.* poterie *f.*

pouch *n.* poche, pochette *f.*; bourse *f.*

poultice *a.* cataplasme *m.*

poultry *n.* volaille *f.*; — yard *n.* basse-cour *f.*

pounce *vi.* fondre, se précipiter

pound *n.* livre *f.*; livre sterling *f.*; (animal) fourrière *f.*; — *vt.* piler, broyer; -age *n.* (taux de) poids *m.*

pour *vt.* verser, épancher; — *vi.* pleuvoir à verse; couler rapidement; se précipiter avec violence; — off décanter; — out verser; épancher; sortir en foule

pout *vi.* bouder, faire la moue; — *n.* moue *f.*

poverty *n.* pauvreté, indigence *f.*; misère *f.*

poverty-stricken *a.* dans la misère

powder *n.* poudre *f.*; — puff houppe *f.*; — *vt.* pulvériser; poudrer, saupoudrer; -y *a.* poudreux

power *n.* pouvoir *m.*, puissance, faculté, force *f.*; autorité *f.*; -ful *a.* puissant; fort; -less *a.* impuissant; -lessness impuissance *f.*

powwow *n.* réunion, conférence *f.*; — *vi.* se réunir

practicability *n.* praticabilité *f.*

practicable *a.* praticable, faisable

practical *a.* pratique; — joke canular *m.*, farce *f.*; — nurse infirmière non-diplômée *f.*; -ly *adv.* en pratique; presque

practice *n.* pratique *f.*, habileté *f.*; expérience *f.*; coutume *f.*; habitude *f.*; méthode *f.*; clientèle *f.*; — *vt.* pratiquer; exercer; répéter; — *vi.* s'exercer; -d *a.* expérimenté; habile

practitioner *n.* praticien *m.*; general — médecin non-spécialisé *m.*

pragmatic *a.* pragmatique

prairie *n.* prairie *f.*; — dog *n.* marmotte des prairies *f.*

praise *n.* louange *f.*; éloge *m.*; — *vt.* louer; célébrer; -worthy *a.* louable, méritoire

praline *n.* pratique *f.*, bonbon au praliné *m.*

prance *vi.* piaffer; se pavaner; se cabrer

prancing *a.* fringant; — *n.* action de se cabrer *f.*

prank *n.* folie *f.*; farce *f.*, tour *m.*

prate *vi.* caqueter, jaser

prattle *n.* babil *m.*; — *vi.* babiller, jaser

pray *vt.* & *vi.* prier; -er *n.* prière *f.*; Lord's -er *n.* patenôtre, oraison dominicale *f.*

preach *vt.* & *vi.* prêcher; -er *n.* prédicateur *m.*; prêcheur *m.*; ministre *m.*; -ing *n.* prédication *f.*

preamble *n.* préambule *m.*

prearrange *vt.* arranger au préalable

precarious *a.* précaire

precaution *n.* précaution *f.*; -ary *a.* préventif

precede *vt.* précéder, devancer; préfacer; -nce *n.* préséance *f.*; priorité *f.*; -nt *n.* précédent *m.*

preceding *a.* précédent

precept *n.* précepte *m.*; -or *n.* précepteur *m.*

precinct *n.* borne, limite *f.*; circonscription électorale *f.*

precious *a.* précieux; -ness *n.* valeur *f.*

precipice *n.* précipice *m.*

precipitate *n.* précipité *m.*; — *vt.* précipiter; hâter; — *vi.* (se) precipiter; — *a.* précipité

precipitation *n.* précipitation *f.*

precipitous *a.* précipité, rapide; escarpé

precise *a.* précis, exact; scrupuleux; -ly *adv.* précisément; avec précision; -ness *n.* précision *f.*

precision *n.* précision *f.*

preclude *vt.* exclure; empêcher

precocious *a.* précoce; -ness *n.* précocité *f.*

precocity *n.* précocité *f.*

preconceive *vt.* concevoir d'avance; -d *a.* préconçu

preconception *n.* préconception *f.*

precursor *n.* précurseur *m.*; avant-coureur *m.*

predatory *a.* rapace; de rapine

predecessor *n.* prédécesseur, devancier *m.*

predestination *n.* prédestination *f.*

predestine *vt.* prédestiner

predetermine *vt.* prédéterminer, déterminer d'avance

predicament *n.* mauvais pas *m.*; situation difficile *f.*

predicate *n.* prédicat *m.*; attribut *m.*; — *vt.* affirmer

predict *vt.* prédire; -ion *n.* prédiction *f.*

predilection *n.* prédilection, partialité *f.*

predispose *vt.* prédisposer

predisposition *n.* prédisposition *f.*

predominance *n.* ascendant *m.*; prédomination *f.*

predominant *a.* prédominant

predominate *vi.* prédominer

pre-eminence *n.* prééminence *f.*

pre-eminent *a.* prééminent

pre-emption *n.* préemption *f.*

preen *vt.* lisser, ajuster; — oneself faire des grâces

pre-established *a.* pré-établi

pre-existent *a.* pré-existant

prefabricate *vt.* préfabriquer

preface *n.* préface *f.*; — *vt.* préfacer

prefatory *a.* préliminaire

prefect *n.* préfet *m.*; -ure *n.* préfecture *f.*

prefer *vt.* préférer; présenter, apporter; -able *a.* préférable; -ence *n.* préférence *f.*; -ential *a.* privilégié; -red *a.* préféré; -red stock action de priorité *f.*

prefix *n.* préfixe *m.*; — *vt.* mettre devant

pregnant *a.* enceinte

preheat *vt.* faire chauffer au préalable

prehensile *a.* préhensile

prehistoric *a.* préhistorique

prejudge *vt.* préjuger

prejudice *n.* préjugé *m.*; prévention *f.*; — *vt.* être préjudiciable pour; prévenir; be -d *a* avoir des préjugés

prejudicial *a.* préjudiciable

preliminary *a.* & *n.* préliminaire *m.*

prelude *n.* prélude *m.*; — *vt.* préluder

premature *a.* prématuré

premedical *a.* qui prépare la médecine; qui précède les cours de médecine

premeditate *vt.* préméditer; -d *a.* prémédité, réfléchi

premeditation *n.* préméditation *f.*

premier *n.* premier ministre *m.*; (France) président du conseil *m.*

première *n.* première, générale *f.*

premise *n.* prémisse *f.*; -s *pl.* locaux *m. pl.*; — *vt.* poser

premium *n.* prime *f.*; récompense *f.*; at a — à prime; en prime

premonition *n.* prémonition *f.*

prenatal *a.* prénatal

preoccupation *n.* préoccupation *f.*

preoccupy *vt.* préoccuper

preordain *vt.* préordonner, ordonner d'avance

prepaid *a.* payé d'avance; franc de port; — *adv.* franco

preparation *n.* préparation *f.*; -s *pl.* préparatifs *m. pl.*

preparatory a. préparatoire, préliminaire;
— school lycée m., école secondaire f.
prepare vt. préparer; apprêter; — vi. se
préparer, s'apprêter; — for préparer
prepay vt. payer d'avance; envoyer
franco; —ment n. paiement d'avance
m.; affranchissement m.
preponderance n. prépondérance f.
preponderant a. prépondérant
preposition n. préposition f.; -al a. prépositif, prépositionnel
prepossess vt. pénétrer, préoccuper; —ed
a. pénétré, imprégné; —ing a. prévenant, engageant
preposterous a. absurde; déraisonnable;
-ness n. absurdité f.
prerequisite n. nécessité préalable f.; condition nécessaire f.; cours obligatoire m.
prerogative n. prérogative f.
presage n. présage m.; — vt. présager;
augurer
prescience n. prescience f.
prescribe vt. prescrire; (med.) ordonner;
— vi. (med.) faire une ordonnance;
faire la loi
prescription n. (law) prescription f.;
(med.) ordonnance f.
presence n. présence f.; — of mind sang-
froid m., présence d'esprit f.; in the —
of en présence de
present n. (time) présent m.; (gift) cadeau
m.; at — à present, actuellement, en ce
moment; —s pl. (law) présentes f. pl.;
— vt. présenter, offrir; — a. présent; actuel, courant; -able a. présentable;
-ation n. présentation f.; -ly adv. tout
à l'heure; à présent
present-day a. d'aujourd'hui
presentiment n. pressentiment m.
preservation n. préservation f.; conservation f.
preservative a. & n. préservatif m.
preserve n. conserve f.; refuge (pour animaux) m.; réserve f.; — vt. préserver;
conserver; mettre en conserve
preside vi. présider
presidency n. présidence f.
president n. président m.; -ial a. présidentiel
press n. presse f.; force f.; (clothing)
armoire f.; imprimerie f.; in — sous
presse; — vt. presser, (se) serrer; appuyer; exprimer; harceler; insister;
(iron) repasser; —ing a. pressant; —ing
n. repassage m.
pressure n. pression f.; presse f.; urgence
f.; blood — tension artérielle f.; high
blood — hypertension f.; — cooker
marmite f. norvégienne f.; autoclave m.;
— group groupe organisé pour influencer les autres; un bloc de politique
pressurize vt. maintenir la pression atmosphérique (dans)
prestige n. prestige m.
presumable a. présumable
presumably adv. à ce qu'il paraît, vrai-
semblablement
presume vt. présumer, supposer
presuming a. présomptueux
presumption n. présomption f.

presumptive a. présomptif
presumptuous a. présomptueux; -ness n.
présomption f.
presuppose vt. présupposer
pretend vi. faire semblant (de); — vt.
feindre, simuler; -er n. prétendant m
pretense n. prétention f.; prétexte m.
pretension n. prétention f.
pretentious a. prétentieux; -ness n. pré-
tension f.
preterit n. (gram.) prétérit, passé m.
preternatural a. surnaturel
pretext n. prétexte m.; on the — of sous
prétexte de
prettiness n. gentillesse, élégance f.;
beauté f.
pretty a. joli; gentil; — adv. assez
pretzel n. bretzel m.
prevail vi. prévaloir; régner; -ing a.
régnant, courant; commun, ordinaire
prevalence n. étendue, généralité f.
prevalent a. dominant, répandu, général
prevaricate vi. prévariquer; tergiverser
prevaricator n. prévaricateur m.
prevent vt. prévenir; empêcher (de); -able
a. évitable; -ion n. prévention f.; empêchement m.; -ive a. & n. préventif m.
preview n. examen préliminaire m.; (film)
avant-première f.; — vt. examiner
d'avance
previous a. préalable; précédant; antérieur; -ly adv. auparavant
prewar a. d'avant-guerre
prey n. proie f.; fall — to être en proie
à; — vi. piller, ronger; — on tourmenter; attaquer, piller
price n. prix m., valeur f.; at any — à
tout prix; cost — prix de revient m.;
sale — prix de vente m.; prix de réclame
m.; — list prix courant m.; — vt.
évaluer, mettre le prix à; demander le
prix de; -less sans prix
prick n. piqûre f.; — vt. piquer, percer;
éperonner; tourmenter; to — up one's
ears dresser les oreilles; -ly a. piquant;
-ly heat lichen m.; -ly pear fruit de
cactus m.
pride n. orgueil m.; fierté f.; — vt.; —
oneself on s'enorgueillir de, se vanter
de
priest n. prêtre m.; -hood n. prêtrise f.;
sacerdoce m.; -ly a. de prêtre; sacerdotal
prig n. fat m.; prude m.; -gish a. pédant,
fat
prim a. réservé; soigné; guindé
primacy n. primauté f.
primarily adv. surtout, principalement
primary a. primaire, primitif; principal
prime n. perfection f.; élite f.; fleur,
force f., printemps m.; (math.) nombre
premier m.; — vt. amorcer; préparer; —
a. premier; de meilleure qualité; principal; — minister premier ministre m.
primer n. premier livre, abécédaire m.;
amorce f.; great -er (print.) corps 18
m.; long -er (print.) corps 10 m.
primeval a. primitif, vierge
priming n. amorce f.; préparation f.
primitive a. primitif; -ness n. rudesse f.

primordial a. primordial

primp vi. se parer

prince n. prince m.; **-ly** a. princier

princess n. princesse f.

principal n. chef m.; directeur m.; proviseur m.; — a. principal, premier

principality n. principauté f.

principle n. principe m.

print n. empreinte, impression; caractères d'imprimerie m. pl.; (phot.) épreuve f.; out of — épuisé; — vt. imprimer; (phot.) tirer (des épreuves); écrire en caractères d'imprimerie; **-ed** matter imprimés m. pl.; **-er** n. imprimeur m: **-er's** devil apprenti imprimeur m: **-er's** ink encre d'imprimerie f.; **-ing** n. impression; (phot.) tirage m.; **-ing press** presse (à imprimer) f.; — **shop** n. imprimerie f.

prior a. antérieur; — **to** avant; **-ity** n. priorité f.; — n. (eccl.) prieur m.; **-y** n. prieuré m.

prism n. prisme m.; **-atic** a. prismatique

prison n. prison f.; **-er** n. prisonnier m.

pristine a. primitif, ancien

privacy n. secret, isolement m., retraite, solitude f.; intimité f.

private n. simple soldat m.; — a. privé, particulier; secret, retiré; — **house** maison particulière f.

privateer n. corsaire m.; **-ing** n. course f.

privilege n. privilège m.; prérogative f.; — vt. privilégier

privy a. privé, particulier; secret; — n. cabinets m. pl.

prize n. prix m.; récompense f.; prise f.; lot m.; — **fight** n. partie de boxe f.; — vt. évaluer, faire cas de; — **fighter** n. boxeur m.

pro prep. & adv. pour; et con pour et contre; — n. professionnel m.

probability n. probabilité f.; vraisemblance f.

probable a. probable; vraisemblable

probate n. (law) vérification, homologation f.; — vt. valider (un testament)

probation n. épreuve f.; noviciat m.; sursis (avec surveillance) m.; **-ary** a. d'épreuve

probe n. sonde f.; — vt. sonder

problem n. problème m.; **-atical** a. problématique

procedure n. procédé m.; procédure f.

proceed vi. procéder; provenir, poursuivre; continuer; **-ings** n. pl. procédure f.; délibérations f. pl.; **-s** n. pl. produit, revenu m.

process n. progrès, cours m.; procédé m.; procès m.; — vt. traiter; développer; **-ion** n. procession f.; cortège m.

proclaim vt. proclamer, déclarer

proclamation n. proclamation f., édit m.

proclivity n. inclination f., penchant m.

procrastinate vi. temporiser, s'attarder, hésiter

procrastinator n. temporisateur m.

procreate vt. procréer

procreation n. procréation f.

proctor n. avoué m.; censeur m: surveillant m.; pion m.

procurable a. qui peut se procurer

procure vt. procurer; **-ment** n. aquisition f.; ravitaillement m.; **-r** n. entremetteur m.

prod n. aiguillon m.; — vt. piquer; aiguillonner; pousser

prodigal a. & n. prodigue m.; **-ity** n. prodigalité f.

prodigious a. prodigieux

prodigy n. prodige m.

produce n. produit m.; denrées f. pl.; — vt. produire; faire, fabriquer; exhiber; (theat.) monter; **-r** n. producteur m.; (theat.) directeur m.

product n. produit m.; **-ion** n. production f.; fabrication f.; produit m.; **-ive** a. productif; **-ivity** n. productivité f.

profane vt. profaner; — a. profane; blasphématoire

profanity n. juron m.; emploi de jurons m.; impiété f.

profess vt. professer, faire profession de; **-ed** a. déclaré; (eccl.) profès; **-edly** adv. ouvertement; **-ion** n. profession f.; metier m.; **-ional** n. professionnel m.; **-ional** a. professionnel; de carrière, de métier; **-or** n. professeur m.; **-orial** a. professoral; **-orship** n. professorat m.; chaire de professeur f.

proffer n. offre, proposition f.; — vt. proposer, offrir

proficiency n. capacité f.; connaissance f.; niveau m.

proficient a. habile; capable; ayant atteint un niveau déterminé

profile n. profil m.; — vt. profiler

profit n. profit, gain, avantage m.; produit, revenu m.; bénéfice m.; — vt. & vi. profiter; être utile, — **by** profiter de; **-able** a. profitable, avantageux; **-eer** vi. gagner des bénéfices démesurés; **-eer** n. profiteur m.; **-eering** n. mercantilisme m.; **-less** a. sans profit; — **sharing** n. participation aux bénéfices f.

profligate n. & a. débauché m.

profound a. profond; **-ly** adv. profondément

profundity n. profondeur f.

profuse a. prodigue; abondant; **-ness** n. profusion f.; **-ly** adv. excessivement

profusion n. profusion f.; abondance f.; prodigalité f.

progenitor n. ancêtre m.

progeny n. progéniture f.; lignée f.

prognosis n. (med.) prognose f., pronostic m.

prognostic n. pronostic m.; **-ate** vt. prognostiquer; **-ation** n. prognostication f., pronostic m.

program n. programme m.; — vt. établir un programme pour

progress n. progrès m.; **in** — en cours, en voie; — vi. faire des progrès; **-ion** n. progression f.; **-ive** a. progressif; (pol.) progressiste

prohibit vt. prohiber; défendre; interdire; **-ion** n. prohibition, défense f.; **-ive** a. prohibitif

project n. projet, dessein m.; — vt. projeter; — vi. saillir; **-ile** n. projectile m.;

-ion *n.* projection *f.*; saillie *f.*; -or *n.* projecteur *m.*

proletarian *a.* prolétaire, prolétarien: — *n.* prolétaire *m. & f.*

proletariat *n.* prolétariat *m.*

prolific *a.* prolifique, fertile

prologue *n.* prologue *m.*

prolong *vt.* prolonger; -ation *n.* prolongation *f.*, prolongement *m.*

promenade *n.* promenade *f.*; bal *m.*; — *vi.* se promener

prominence *n.* proéminence *f.*; éminence *f.*

prominent *a.* proéminent; éminent; prononcé; (qui est) très en vue; -ly *adv.* très en vue

promiscuous *a.* mêlé; confus; au hasard; libre, sans contrainte

promise *n.* promesse *f.*; espérances *f. pl.*; avenir *m.*; break a — manquer de parole; — *vt. & vi.* promettre

promissory *a.* qui contient une promesse; — note *n.* billet à ordre *m.*

promontory *n.* promontoire *n.*

promote *vt.* promouvoir, avancer; élever; encourager; -r *n.* homme d'affaires *m.*, animateur *m.*; auteur *m.*; promoteur *m.*

promotion *n.* promotion *f.*; avancement *m.*; publicité, réclame *f.*

prompt *vt.* souffler; suggérer; — *a.* prompt; immédiat; -er *n.* souffleur *m.*; -ly *adv.* promptement; ponctuellement; immédiatement, sur-le-champ; à l'heure; -ness *n.* promptitude *f.*

promulgate *vt.* promulguer, publier

promulgation *n.* promulgation *f.*

prone *a.* couché le visage contre terre; — to enclin à, susceptible de

prong *n.* fourchon *m.*; dent *f.*; -ed *a.* à fourchons, à dents

pronominal *a.* pronominal

pronoun *n.* pronom *m.*

pronounce *vt.* prononcer; articuler; -able *a.* prononçable; -d *a.* prononcé, marqué; -ment *n.* déclaration *f.*

pronunciation *n.* prononciation *f.*

proof *n.* preuve *f.*; épreuve *f.*; épreuves *f. pl.*; essai *m.*; — *a.* à l'épreuve (de); impénétrable

proofread *vt.* corriger les epreuves de; -er *n.* correcteur *m.*; -ing *n.* correction *f.*

prop *n.* appui, soutien *m.*; étai *m.*; (theat.) accessoire *m.*; — *vt.* appuyer, soutenir; étayer

propaganda *n.* propagande *f.*

propagandist *n.* propagandiste *m.*

propagate *vt.* propager; répandre; — *vi.* se propager, se reproduire

propagation *n.* propagation *f.*; dissémination *f.*

propel *vt.* pousser en avant; -ler *n.* hélice *f.*

propensity *n.* penchant *m.*, inclination *f.*

proper *a.* propre; bon; convenable; comme il faut; exact; -ly *adv.* proprement; correctement; comme il faut

property *n.* propriété, qualité *f.*; possession *f.*; (theat.) accessoire *m.*

prophecy *n.* prophétie *f.*

prophesy *vt. & vi.* prophétiser

prophet *n.* prophète *m.*; -ic *a.* prophétique

prophylactic *a.* prophylactique

prophylaxis *n.* prophylaxie *f.*

propinquity *n.* proximité *f.*

propitiate *vt.* rendre propice; apaiser

propitious *a.* propice, favorable

proponent *n.* partisan *m.*

proportion *n.* proportion *f.*; mesure *f.*; in — as à mesure que; in — to en proportion de, proportionné à; — *vt.* proportionner; -al *a.* proportionnel; -ate *a.* proportionné; -ed *a.* proportionné

proposal *n.* proposition, offre *f.*; plan, projet *m.*; demande (en mariage) *f.*

propose *vt.* proposer; avoir l'intention de; — *vi.* se déclarer, faire une déclaration, faire une demande en mariage

proposition *n.* proposition *f.*; offre *f.*

propound *vt.* proposer, offrir; poser

proprietary *a.* de propriété, de propriétaire

proprietor *n.* propriétaire *m. & f.*

propriety *n.* convenance *f.*, décorum *m.*; à-propos *m.*, opportunité *f.*

propulsion *n.* propulsion *f.*

prorate *vt.* répartir

prosaic *a.* prosaïque

proscenium *n.* (theat.) avant-scène *f.*

proscribe *vt.* proscrire, interdire

proscription *n.* proscription *f.*; interdiction *f.*

prose *n.* prose *f.*

prosecute *vt.* poursuivre

prosecution *n.* poursuite *f.*

prosecutor *n.* procureur *m.*; plaignant *m.*

proselyte *n.* prosélyte *m. & f.*

prospect *n.* perspective *f.*; vue *f.*, aspect *m.*; — *vi.* prospecter; (min.) faire des recherches; -ive *a.* à venir; -or *n.* prospecteur *m.*

prospectus *n.* prospectus *m.*

prosper *vi.* prospérer, réussir; -ity *n.* prospérité *f.*; -ous *a.* prospère

prostitute *n.* prostituée *f.*; — *vt.* prostituer

prostrate *vt.* renverser, abattre; prosterner; accabler; — *a.* prosterné; (med.) prostré; -d *a.* abattu

prostration *n.* prosternation *f.*; abattement *m.*; (med.) prostration *f.*

protagonist *n.* protagoniste *m.*

protect *vt.* protéger, défendre; sauvegarder; patronner; -ion *n.* protection, défense *f.*; sauvegarde *f.*; abri *m.*; patronage *m.*; -ive *a.* protecteur; préservatif; -or *n.* protecteur *m.*; protectrice *f.*; -orate *n.* protectorat *m.*

protein *n.* protéine *f.*

protest *n.* protestation *f.*; représentation *f.*; under — sous réserve; — *vt. & vi.* protester; -ation *n.* protestation *f.*

protocol *n.* protocole *m.*

proton *n.* proton *m.*

protoplasm *n.* protoplasme *m.*

prototype *n.* prototype, archétype *m.*

protozoa *n. pl.* protozoaires *n. pl.*

protract *vt.* prolonger; traîner; -ion *n.* prolongation *f.*; relevé *m.*; -or *n.* (math.) rapporteur *m.*

protrude *vi.* s'avancer, faire saillie; — *vt.* pousser dehors

protruding *a.* saillant; en saillie; débordant

protrusion *n.* protubérance, saillie *f.*

protuberance *n.* protubérance *f.*

proud *a.* orgueilleux, fier; superbe

provable *a.* démontrable

prove *vt.* prouver; éprouver; démontrer; vérifier; — *vi.* se trouver; se montrer

provender *n.* provende *f.*; fourrage *m.*; nourriture *f.*

proverb *n.* proverbe *m.*; –ial *a.* proverbial

provide *vt.* pourvoir, fournir, munir; — *vi.* (se) pourvoir; –d *a.* muni, pourvu; –d that *conj.* pourvu que; –r *n.* pourvoyeur, fournisseur *m.*

provident *a.* prévoyant; –ial *a.* providentiel

provincial *a.* provincial; de province; — *n.* provincial *m.*

provision *n.* clause *f.*, article *m.*; disposition *f.*; –s *pl.* comestibles, vivres *m. pl.*; — *vt.* approvisionner, ravitailler; –al *a.* provisoire

proviso *n.* condition *f.*

provisory *a.* provisoire

provocation *n.* provocation *f.*; défi *m.*

provocative *a.* provocateur; provocant

provoke *vt.* provoquer; exciter; inciter; irriter; contrarier; défier

provoking *a.* contrariant, irritant

provost *n.* prévôt *m.*

prow *n.* proue *f.*

prowess *n.* prouesse *f.*; vaillance *f.*

prowl *vi.* rôder; –er *n.* rôdeur *m.*; (inside) cambrioleur *m.*

proximity *n.* proximité *f.*

proxy *n.* procuration *f.*; mandat, mandataire *m.*; délégué *m.*

prude *n.* prude *f.*; –ry *n.* pruderie *f.*

prudence *n.* prudence *f.*

prudent *a.* prudent, judicieux

prudish *a.* prude; –ness *n.* pruderie *f.*

prune *n.* pruneau *m.*; — *vt.* tailler; élaguer

pruning *n.* taille *f.*; élagage *m.*; — hook ébranchoir *m.*; — knife serpette *f.*; — shears sécateur *m.*

Prussia *n.* Prusse *f.*; –n *a. & n.* prussien *m.*

pry *vt.* soulever; forcer; — *vi.* fouiller (dans); fureter; — *n.* levier *m.*; –ing *a.* curieux

Psalm *n.* psaume *m.*

Psalter *n.* psautier *m.*

pseudonym *n.* pseudonyme *m.*

psychiatric *a.* psychiatrique

psychiatrist *n.* psychiatre *m.*

psychic *a.* psychique

psychoanalist *n.* psychanalyste *m.*

psychological *a.* psychologique

psychologist *n.* psychologue *m.*

psychology *n.* psychologie *f.*

psychopathic *a.* psychopathique

ptomaine *n.* ptomaïne *f.*; — poisoning intoxication alimentaire *f.*

puberty *n.* puberté *f.*

public *n.* public, peuple *m.*; in — en public, publiquement; — *a.* public,

publique; make — publier, rendre public; — holiday fête légale; — library bibliothèque municipale *f.*; — official fonctionnaire *m.*; — school école municipale *f.*; — spirit civisme *m.*; — works travaux publics; –ation *n.* publication *f.*

publicity *n.* publicité *f.*; réclame *f.*

publicize *vt.* publier; faire de la réclame pour

publish *vt.* publier; just –ed vient de paraître; –er *n.* éditeur *m.*; –ing *n.* publication *f.*; –ing house maison d'édition *f.*

puck *n.* (sport) palet; lutin *m.*

pucker *n.* pli *m.*; ride *f.*; fronce *f.*; — *vt.* plisser; rider; — *vi.* (se) froncer

puddle *n.* flaque d'eau *f.*; — *vt.* corroyer

pudgy *a.* rondelet; replet

puerile *a.* puéril

Puerto Rico *n.* Porto-Rico *m.*

puff *n.* bouffée *f.*; souffle *m.*; (clothes) bouffant; powder — houppe *f.*; — pastry pâte feuilletée *f.*; — *vt.* gonfler; fumer; — *vi.* souffler; haleter; –iness *n.* boursouflure *f.*; bouffissure *f.*; –y *a.* bouffi; boursouflé

pug *n.* (dog) carlin *m.*; — nose *n.* nez épaté *m.*

pugilism *n.* pugilat *m.*, boxe *f.*

pugilist *n.* pugiliste, boxeur *m.*

pugnacious *a.* batailleur

pull *n.* traction *f.*; attraction *f.*; appel *m.*; poignée *f.*; (coll.) influence *f.*, piston, bras long *m.*; — *vt.* tirer; traîner; — apart déchirer; séparer; — off enlever; remporter; — out tirer, sortir; — through guérir; se tirer d'affaire; — (oneself) together se reprendre; — up remonter; hisser; hausser; s'arrêter; se ranger

pullet *n.* poulette, poularde *f.*

pulley *n.* poulie *f.*; — block *n.* moufle *f.*

Pullman *n.* (rail.), — car voiture Pullman *f.*; wagon-lit, wagon-salon *m.*

pulmonary *a.* pulmonaire

pulp *n.* pulpe *f.*; pâte *f.*; chair *f.*; –y *a.* charnu; pulpeux

pulpit *n.* chaire *f.*

pulsate *vi.* palpiter, vibrer, (se) battre

pulsation *n.* pulsation *f.*, battement *m.*

pulse *n.* pouls *m.*; battement *m.*, pulsation *f.*

pulverization *n.* pulvérisation *f.*

pulverize *vt.* pulvériser; atomiser

pumice *n.* ponce *f.*

pummel *vt.* battre (de coups de poing)

pump *n.* pompe *f.*; (shoe) escarpin *m.*; air — pompe à air; — room chambre des pompes; buvette *f.*; — *vt.* pomper; — up gonfler; faire monter

pumpkin *n.* citrouille *f.*, potiron *m.*

pun *n.* calembour *m.*

punch *n.* poinçon *m.*; perçoir *m.*; emporte-pièce *m.*; coup de poing *m.*; (drink) punch *m.*; — *vt.* poinçonner; percer; donner un coup de poing à; –ing bag punching *m.*

Punch and Judy show *n.* guignol *m.*

punctilious *a.* pointilleux

punctual a. exact, ponctuel; -ity n. ponctualité, exactitude f.
punctuate vt. ponctuer
punctuation n. ponctuation f.
puncture n. piqûre, perforation f.; (tire) crevaison f.; (med.) ponction f.; — vt. perforer, crever; ponctionner
puncture-proof a. increvable
pungency n. odeur forte f.; saveur f.
pungent a. piquant, âcre; mordant
puniness n. chétiveté f.
punish vt. punir, châtier; corriger; -able a. punissable; -ment n. punition f.; châtiment m.; peine f.; capital — peine capitale f.
punitive a. punissant; pénal
punt n. (sports) coup de volée m.; (boating) bateau plat m., plate f.
puny a. chétif; faible
pup, puppy n. petit chien, jeune chien m.
pupa n. chrysalide f.
pupil n. (anat.) pupille f.; élève m. & f.
puppet n. marionnette f.; pantin m.; — show théâtre de marionnettes m.
purchase n. achat m., acquisition f., emplette f.; prise f., point d'appui m.; — vt. acheter; -r n. acheteur m.
purchasing agent n. acheteur m.
pure a. pur; -ly adv. purement; absolument; tout à fait
purgation n. purgation f.
purgative a. & n. purgatif m.
purgatory n. purgatoire m.
purge n. purgatif m.; purgation f.; — vt. purger; purifier; épurer
purging n. purgation f.
purification n. purification f.; épuration f.
purifier n. épurateur m.
purify vt. purifier; épurer
purist n. puriste m. & f.
puritan a. & n. puritain; -ical a. de puritain
purity n. pureté f.
purloin vt. voler
purple a. & n. violet m.; (fig.) pourpre f.; royal —, imperial — pourpre f.
purport n. sens m.; portée f.; — vt. avoir la prétention de
purpose n. but, objet, dessein m.; intention f.; fin f.; détermination f.; for the — of dans le but de; on — exprès; to no — en vain; -ful a. avisé; réfléchi; -ly adv. exprès; à dessein
purr vi. ronronner; -ing n. ronron m.
purse n. bourse f.; porte-monnaie m.; sac à main m.; — vt. pincer (les lèvres); -r n. commissaire m.
pursuant adv. conformément
pursue vt. poursuivre; suivre; -r n. poursuivant m.
pursuit n. poursuite f.; recherche f.; profession f.; occupation f.; in — of à la poursuite de; (fig.) à la recherche de
purvey vt. fournir; -or n. fournisseur, pourvoyeur m.
push n. poussée, impulsion f.; effort m.; — button poussoir, pressoir m.; — vt. pousser; bousculer; — back repousser; -ing a. entreprenant, ambitieux

pushcart n. charrette à bras f.
pushover n. quelque chose de tres facile m.; adversaire facile à vaincre m.
pusillanimous a. pusillanime
puss(y) n. minette f.
pustule n. pustule f.
put vt. mettre, poser, placer; — to bed coucher; — away ranger; serrer; (money) mettre de côté; — back remettre; retarder; — down déposer, poser; supprimer; noter; — in faire; (naut.) entrer; — in order ranger; — off remettre; ajourner; différer; — on mettre; enfiler; (shoes) chausser; — on the light(s) allumer; — on weight prendre du poids; — out tendre; mettre à la porte; (light) éteindre; contrarier; publier; — oneself out se déranger; — together assembler; — up construire, bâtir; poser; proposer; loger, descendre; — up with souffrir de; se résigner à
putrefaction n. putréfaction f.
putrefy vi. se putréfier, pourrir
putrid a. putride
putty n. mastic m.; — knife spatule f.; — vt. mastiquer
puzzle n. énigme f.; casse-tête m.; crossword — mots croisés m. pl.; jigsaw — patience f.; — vt. confondre; embarrasser; — vi. se casser la tête
pylon n. pylône m.
pygmy n. pygmée m.
pyorrhea n. pyorrhée f.
pyramid n. pyramide f.
pyre n. bûcher m.
Pyrenees n. pl. Pyrénées f. pl.
pyrotechnic a. pyrotechnique; -s n. pl. pyrotechnie f.

Q

quack n. charlatan m.; (sound) couincouin m.; — vi. faire couin-couin; -ery n. charlatanisme m.
quadrangle n. cour carrée f.; (math.) quadrilatère m.
quadrangular a. quadrangulaire
quadrant n. quart, quadrant, secteur m.
quadratic a., — equation équation du second degré f.
quadrilateral a. quadrilatéral, quadrilatère; — n. quadrilatère m.
quadruped a. & n. quadrupède m.
quadruple a. quadruple; -ts n. pl. quatre enfants nés de la même couche m. pl.
quaff vt. boire (d'un seul trait)
quagmire n. fondrière f.
quail n. caille f.; — vi. fléchir
quaint a. pittoresque; suranné; -ness n. pittoresque m.
quake vi. trembler
qualification n. qualité f., titre m.; capacité f.; réserve, condition f.
qualified a. capable; breveté; diplômé; conditionnel
qualify vt. qualifier; modifier; — vi. être reçu; se qualifier; -ing a. qualificatif; (sports) éliminatoire
qualitative a. qualitatif
quality n. qualité f.; — a. de qualité, de

première qualité

qualm n. scrupule, remords; soulèvement de cœur m.; **—ish** a. qui a mal au cœur; **—ishness** n. nausée f.

quandary n. incertitude f.; impasse f.

quantitative a. quantitatif

quantity n. quantité f.

quarantine n. quarantaine f.; — vt. mettre en quarantaine

quarrel n. querelle, dispute f.; — vi. se disputer, se quereller; se brouiller; **—some** a. querelleur

quarry n. carrière f.; proie f.; — vt. exploiter une carrière

quart n. litre m. 1 qt. (dry) = 0.95 litre (sec); 1 qt. (liquid) = 1.06 litres (liquides)

quarter n. (fraction) quart m.; quartier m.; trimestre m.; côté m.; (money) vingt-cinq cents m. pl.; a — after, a — past et quarrel; a — to moins le quart, moins un quart; — of an hour quart d'heure m.; **—s** pl. quartiers m. pl., appartement, logement m.; (naut.) poste m.; — vt. diviser en quatre; écarteler; loger, cantonner; **—ly** a. trimestriel; **—ly** adv. par trimestre

quarter-deck n. gaillard arrière m.

quartermaster n. (mil.) intendant général m.

quartet n. quatuor m.

quash vt. étouffer; casser

quaver vi. trembloter; — n. tremblement m.; (mus.) trémolo m.; croche f.

quay n. quai m.

queen n. reine f.; (cards) dame f.; — vt. faire la reine; (chess) damer; **—ly** a. de reine; royale

queer a. bizarre; étrange; drôle; original; **—ness** n. bizarrerie, étrangeté f.; — vt. gâter, gâcher

quell vt. étouffer, réprimer

quench vt. éteindre; étouffer; étancher; — one's thirst se désaltérer

query n. question f.; — vt. s'informer

quest n. recherche f.; quête f.; in — of à la recherche de

question n. question f.; demande f.; doute m.; — mark point d'interrogation m.; ask a — poser une question, faire une question; in — en question; it is a — of il s'agit de; out of the — impossible; without — sans aucun doute; — vt. interroger, questionner; mettre en doute; **—able** a. douteux; contestable; problématique; **—er** n. interrogateur m.; **—ing** a. interrogateur; **—ing** n. interrogation f.; interrogatoire m.

quibble n. chicane f.; argutie f.; — vi. chicaner; ergoter

quibbling n. chicane f.

quick n. vif m.; — a. rapide; vif, vive; prompt; agile; be **—!** dépêchez-vous!; **—ly** adv. vite, rapidement; vivement; **—en** vt. accélérer, presser, hâter; animer, vivifier; **—en** vi. s'accélérer; s'animer; **—ness** n. rapidité, vitesse f.; vivacité f.; promptitude f.

quick-acting a. à action rapide

quick-freeze vt. congeler

quicklime n. chaux vive f.

quicksand n. sable mouvant m.

quicksilver n. vif-argent, mercure m.

quick-tempered a. emporté; qui s'emporte facilement

quick-witted a. éveillé, vif; à l'esprit prompt

quiescence n. quiétude f.

quiescent a. en repos

quiet n. tranquillité f., calme m.; silence m.; repos m.; — a. tranquille, calme; silencieux; intime; simple; be —, keep — se taire; — vt. calmer, apaiser; faire taire; — (down) se calmer, s'apaiser; **—ly** adv. tranquillement; silencieusement, sans bruit; doucement; **—ness** n. tranquillité f., calme m.; repos m.; paix f.; **—ude** n. quiétude f.

quill n. plume f.; tuyau m.

quilt n. couverture piquée f.; courtepointe f.; édredon m.; — vt. contrepointer, piquer; **—ed** a. piqué, contrepointé

quintessence n. quintessence f.

quintuple a. quintuple; **—ts** n. pl. cinq enfants nés de la même couche

quip n. repartie f.

quire n. main de papier f.

quirk n. habitude particulière f.; idiosyncrasie f.

quisling n. quisling, traître m.

quit vt. quitter, démissionner; — vi. cesser, s'arrêter; **—s** a. quitte; **—ter** n. lâcheur m.

quite adv. tout à fait; complètement, entièrement

quiver n. frémissement, tremblement m.; (archery) carquois m.; — vi. frémir, trembler; trembloter

quixotic a. visionnaire

quiz n. petit examen m.; — vt. examiner, interroger

quorum n. quorum m.

quota n. quote-part f.; contingentement m.

quotation n. citation f.; (com.) cote f., cours m.; — marks guillemets m. pl.

quote vt. citer; faire un prix; coter

quotient n. quotient m.

R

rabbi n. rabbin m.

rabbit n. lapin m.

rabble n. canaille, populace f.

rabid a. enragé; furieux

rabies n. rage, hydrophobie f.

race n. course f.; (breed) race f., sang m.; human — race humaine f.; humanité f.; foot — course à pied f.; horse — course de chevaux f.; boat — régate f.; — horse cheval de course m.; — track n. champ de courses m.; piste f.; — vi. faire une course; courir; lutter de vitesse; — vt. lutter de vitesse avec; faire courir; (engine) emballer; **—r** n. coureur m.; auto de course f.

racial a. de race

racing n. courses f. pl.

rack n. (luggage) porte-bagages m.; filet m.; (coat) porte-manteau m.; (torture) chevalet *m.*; — *vt.* torturer, tourmenter; — one's brains se creuser l'esprit; -ing *a.* atroce, terrible

racket *n.* raquette *f.*; bruit, vacarme, tapage *m.*; (slang) métier, genre d'affaires *m.*, affaire louche *f.*; -eer *n.* gangster *m.*

racy *a.* savoureux

radar *n.* radar *m.*

radial *a.* radial

radiance *n.* rayonnement *m.*; éclat *m.*

radiant *a.* rayonnant; radieux

radiate *vi.* rayonner; — *vt.* émettre

radiation *n.* (phy.) radiation *f.*; rayonnement *m.*

radiator *n.* radiateur *m.*

radical *a. & n.* radical *m.*; -ism *n.* radicalisme *m.*

radicle *n.* (bot.) radicelle *f.*; radicule *f.*

radio *n.* radio *f.*; T.S.F. (télégraphie sans fil) *f.*; — *vt.* envoyer (un message) par radio; — operator radio *m.*; — set poste de T.S.F. *m.*; — station poste émetteur *m.*

radio broadcast *n.* radio diffusion *f.*; — *vt.* radiodiffuser, transmettre; -er *n.* appareil émetteur *m.*; (person) microphoniste *m.*; -ing *n.* radio-émission, radiophonie *f.*

radioactive *a.* radio-actif

radio-frequency *n.* radio-fréquence *f.*

radiogram *n.* radiogramme *m.*

radiology *n.* radiologie *f.*

radiosensitive *a.* radiosensible

radiotherapy *n.* radiothérapie *f.*

radish *n.* radis *m.*

radium *n.* radium *m.*

radius *n.* rayon *m.*; within a — of dans un rayon de

raffle *n.* tombola *f.*; — *vt.* mettre en tombola

raft *n.* radeau *m.*; (coll.) grand nombre *m.*

rafter *n.* chevron *m.*

rag *n.* chiffon *m.*; lambeau *m.*; — doll poupée de chiffons *f.*; -s *pl.* guenilles *f.* pl., haillons *m.* pl.; -ged *a.* en haillons; inégal; désordonné

ragamuffin *n.* gamin *m.*; va-nu-pieds *m.*

rage *n.* fureur *f.*; rage *f.*; manie *f.*; fly into a — s'emporter; — *vi.* être furieux; faire rage

raging *a.* furieux

ragout *n.* ragoût *m.*

ragpicker *n.* chiffonnier *m.*

ragweed *n.* jacobée *f.*

raid *n.* raid *m.*; incursion *f.*; razzia *f.*; (police) descente *f.*; — *vt.* faire un raid à; razzier; faire une descente dans; -er *n.* maraudeur *m.*; attaquant *m.*

rail *n.* rail *m.*; rampe *f.*; balustrade *f.*; garde-fou *m.*; barreau *m.*; grille *f.*; by — par chemin de fer *m.*; third — rail de contact *m.*; -ing *n.* barrière *f.*; balustrade *f.*; garde-fou *m.*

rail *vi.*, — at s'en prendre à; crier contre

raillery *n.* raillerie *f.*

railroad, railway *n.* chemin de fer; — track voie *f.*; — station gare *f.*

rain *n.* pluie *f.*; — *vi.* pleuvoir; it's -ing il pleut; -y *a.* pluvieux; des pluies

rainbow *n.* arc-en-ciel *m.*

raincoat *n.* imperméable *m.*

rainfall *n.* pluie, précipitation *f.*

rainproof *a.* imperméable

rain water *n.* eau de pluie *f.*

raise *vt.* lever, soulever; hausser; relever; élever; cultiver; (salary) augmenter; — a cry pousser un cri; — an objection soulever une objection

rake *n.* râteau *m.*; râtissoire *f.*; (person) roué *m.*; — *vt.* râteler, ratisser; — off prélever

rally *n.* ralliement *m.*; réunion *f.*; (sports) reprise *f.*; retour *m.*; — *vt.* rallier; — *vi.* se rallier; (mil.) se reformer; (med.) se remettre; (sports) se reprendre

ram *n.* (animal) bélier *m.*; pilon *m.*; — *vt.* heurter; enfoncer; (naut.) éperonner

ramble *n.* balade, promenade *f.*; — *vi.* errer, rôder; battre la compagne; parler sans suite

rambling *a.* vagabond; sans suite; — *n.* vagabondage *m.*; radotage *m.*

ramification *n.* ramification *f.*

ramify *vi.* se ramifier

ramp *n.* rampe *f.*; pont *m.*

rampage *n.* furie, folie *f.*; — *vi.* déclamer, divaguer

rampant *a.* rampant; be — s'étaler; se répandre

rampart *n.* rempart *m.*

ramshackle *a.* délabré

ranch *n.* grosse ferme d'élevage *f.*; ranch *m.*; -er *n.* fermier *m.*; propriétaire de ranch *m.*

rancid *a.* rance; -ness *n.* rancidité *f.*

rancor *n.* rancune *f.*

random *n.* at — au hasard; à tort et à travers; — *a.* fait au hasard

range *n.* portée *f.*; étendue *f.*; champ *m.*; gamme *f.*; distance *f.*; (mountains) chaîne *f.*; (kitchen) cuisinière *f.*; — finder télémètre *m.*; in — à portée; out of — hors de portée; — *vt.* ranger; — *vi.* s'étendre; errer; s'échelonner; —*r* *n.* (garde) forestier *m.*

rank *n.* rang *m.*; classe *f.*; (mil.) grade *m.*; — and file la troupe *f.*; — *vi.* se ranger; être classé; — *a.* fétide; luxuriant; criant; parfait; -ing *a.* premier; en chef

ransack *vt.* piller, saccager; fouiller

ransom *n.* rançon *f.*; — *vt.* rançonner; racheter

rant *vi.* extravaguer

rap *n.* coup *m.*; (coll.) sou *m.*; — *vt.* frapper; donner sur

rapacious *a.* rapace; -ly *adv.* avec rapacité; -ness *n.* rapacité *f.*

rape *n.* viol *m.*; — *vt.* violer

rapid *a.* rapide; -ly *adv.* rapidement, vite; -ity *n.* rapidité *f.*; -s *n.* pl. rapides *m.* pl.

rapid-fire *a.* à tir rapide

rapier *n.* rapière *f.*

rapt *a.* absorbé; ravi; -ure *n.* transport *m.*; ravissement *m.*; extase *m.*; -urous *a.* d'extase

rare *a.* rare; (meat) saignant -ness *n.* rareté *f.*

rarefaction *n.* raréfaction *f.*

rarefied a. raréfié

rarefy vt. raréfier

rarity n. rareté; chose rare f.; objet rare m.

rascal n. coquin, fripon m.; -ity n. coquinerie f.

rash n. éruption f.; — a. irréfléchi; téméraire; -ness n. témérité f.

rasp n. (tool) râpe f.; grincement m.; — vt. râper; racler; — vi. grincer; -ing a. grinçant; âpre

raspberry n. framboise f.

rat n. rat m.; — poison mort aux rats f.; -trap ratière f.; smell a — se douter de quelque chose

ratchet n. cliquet, rochet m.

rate n. taux m.; cours m.; tarif m.; prime f.; vitesse f.; allure f.; at any — en tout cas, dans tous les cas; at the — of au taux de; à la vitesse de; sur le pied de; birth — natalité f.; death — mortalité f.; — of exchange cours du change m.; — of interest taux de l'intérêt m.; — vt. classer; considérer; estimer, évaluer; — vi. être classé; se ranger

rather adv. plutôt; assez; I would — j'aimerais mieux . . . , je préférerais . . .

ratification n. ratification f.

ratify vt. ratifier

rating n. classement m., classification f.; estimation f.

ratio n. proportion f.; rapport m.

ration n. ration f.; — vt. rationner; -ing n. rationnement m.

rational a. raisonnable; raisonné; (math.) rationnel; -ize vt. rationaliser

rattle n. cliquetis m.; tapotis m.; (child's) hochet m., hochette f.; (snake) sonnette f.; (med.) râle m.; — vi. cliqueter; trembler; (med.) râler; — vt. faire cliqueter; agiter; — off dire rapidement; — on continuer à parler; -r n. serpent à sonnettes m.

rattlesnake n. serpent à sonnettes m.

raucous a. rauque

ravage n. ravage m.; — vt. ravager

ravaging a. ravageur

rave vi. extravaguer; délirer; s'extasier

ravel vt. emmêler

ravenous a. vorace

ravine n. ravin m.; défilé m.

ravish vt. ravir; violer; -ing a. ravissant

raw a. cru; vert; inexpérimenté; -ness n. crudité f.; inexpérience f.

rawhide n. cuir vert m.

ray n. rayon m.; (fish) raie f.

rayon n. rayonne f.

raze vt. raser

razor n. rasoir m.; — blade lame de rasoir; f.; safety — rasoir de sûreté m.

re n., in — au sujet de

reach n. étendue f.; allonge f.; portée f.; out of — hors de portée; within — à la portée de; — vt. arriver à, atteindre; parvenir; — vi. s'étendre; — out tendre la main

react vi. réagir; -ion n. réaction f.; -ionary a. & n. réactionnaire m. & f.

read vt. lire; étudier; parcourir; (meter) relever; -able a. lisible; -er n. lecteur

m., lectrice f.; livre de lecture m.; (child's) livre de lectures, abécédaire m.; -ing n. lecture f.; interprétation f.; observation f.; façon de lire f.; (meter) relevé m.; -ing room salle de lecture f.

readily adv. volontiers; facilement

readiness n. promptitude f.; bonne volonté f.; facilité f.; in — prêt

readjust vt. rajuster; -ment n. rajustement m.

ready a. prêt; prompt, facile; get — se préparer, se disposer, s'apprêter

ready-made a. tout fait; de confection

reaffirm vt. réaffirmer

reagent n. réactif m.

real a. réel; vrai, véritable; naturel; — estate propriété immobilière f.; biens immeubles m. pl.; -ism n. réalisme m.; -ist n. réaliste m. & f.; -istic a. réaliste; -ity n. réalité f.; réel m.; -ization n. connaissance, conception f.; réalisation f.; -ize vt. se rendre compte de; réaliser; -ly adv. vraiment; réellement; sans blague

realm n. royaume m.

realtor n. agent immobilier m.

ream n. rame f.; — vt. aléser

reanimate vt. ranimer

reap vt. moissonner; cueillir, recueillir; -er n. (person) moissonneur m.; (machine) moissonneuse f.; -ing n. moisson f.

reappear vi. reparaître; -ance n. réapparition f.

rear n. arrière m.; derrière m.; — a. postérieur; d'arrière; — admiral contre-amiral m.; — guard arrière-garde f.; — vt. élever; — vi. se cabrer

rearm vt. réarmer; -ament n. réarmement m.

rearrange vt. rarranger, arranger; -ment n. nouvel arrangement m.

rearview a., — mirror rétroviseur m.

reason n. raison f.; argument m.; sujet, lieu m.; cause f.; have — to avoir lieu de; avoir sujet à; it stands to — c'est évident; listen to — entendre raison; — (why) pourquoi m.; — vi. raisonner; vt. arguer, discuter; -able a. raisonnable; modéré; -ing n. raisonnement m.

reassemble vt. rassembler; remonter; — vi. se rassembler

reassurance n. promesse f.; encouragement m.

reassure vt. rassurer

reawaken vt. & (vi.) (se) réveiller

rebate n. rabais m.; escompte m.; ristourne f.; — vt. diminuer

rebel n. rebelle, révolté, insurgé m.; — vt. & (vi.) (se) révolter, (s')insurger, (se) soulever; -lion n. révolte f.; -lious a. rebelle

rebind vt. relier de nouveau

rebirth n. renaissance f.

rebound n. ricochet m.; rebondissement m.; — vi. rebondir

rebroadcast vt. (radio) diffuser de nouveau

rebuff n. refus m.; — vt. repousser; refuser

rebuild vt. rebâtir, reconstruire

rebuke n. réprimande f.; — vt. réprimander, blâmer

recalcitrance n. récalcitrance f.

recalcitrant a. récalcitrant; réfractaire

recall n. révocation f.; rappel m.; — vt. rappeler; se souvenir de

recant vt. rétracter; — vi. se rétracter; chanter la palinodie

recap vt. rechaper

recapitulation n. récapitulation f.

recapture vt. reprendre; — n. reprise f.

recede vi. reculer; s'éloigner; (forehead) fuir

receipt n. reçu m.; recette f.; réception f.; récépissé m., quittance f., accusé de réception m.; acknowledge — accuser réception; — vi. acquitter

receivable a. recevable; bills — effets à recevoir m. pl.

receive vt. recevoir; accueillir; —r n. destinataire m. & f.; (law) administrateur m.; (stolen goods) receleur m.; (phone) récepteur m.

receiving n. réception f.; — station poste récepteur m.

recent a. récent, nouveau; —ly adv. récemment

receptacle n. réceptacle m.

reception n. réception f.; accueil m.; —ist n. employé de bureau chargé de recevoir les clients m.

receptive a. réceptif

recess n. (school) récréation f.; (court) vacances f. pl.; enfoncement m.; recoin m.; embrasure f.; —ion n. recul m.; régression f.; crise financière f.; —ional n. hymne de sortie m.; —ive a. régressif, récessif; — vt. encastrer, enfoncer

recipe n. recette f.

recipient n. bénéficiaire m. & f.; destinataire m. & f.

reciprocal a. réciproque; mutuel; inverse

reciprocate vt. payer de retour; — vi. retourner un compliment, rendre la pareille

reciprocity n. réciprocité f.

recital n. récitation f.; récit m.; (mus.) recital m.

recitation n. récitation f.

recite vt. réciter, déclamer; (school) répondre (à une question)

reckless a. insouciant; imprudent

reckon vt. compter; calculer; juger; — vi. compter; calculer; — with compter avec; —ing n. calcul, compte m.; estime f.

reclaim vt. réformer; (land) défricher; mettre en valeur

reclamation n. réforme f.; défrichement m.; mise en valeur f.; réclamation f.

recline vt. appuyer, coucher; — vi. être couché; être étendu

recognition n. reconnaissance f.

recognizable a. reconnaissable

recognizance n. (law) caution personnelle f.

recognize vt. reconnaître; donner la parole à

recoil n. recul m.; contre-coup m.; détente f.; — vi. reculer; se détendre

recollect vt. se rappeler; se souvenir de; —ion n. souvenir m.

recommence vt. & vi. recommencer

recommend vt. recommander; —ation n. recommandation f.

recompense n. récompense f.; dédommagement m.; — vt. récompenser; dédommager

reconcilable a. conciliable

reconcile vt. réconcilier, raccommoder; concilier; mettre d'accord; — oneself to se résigner à

reconciliation n. réconciliation f.; conciliation f.

recondition vt. rénover; mettre à neuf

reconnaissance n. reconnaissance f.

reconnoiter vt. reconnaître; — vi. faire une reconnaissance

reconquer vt. reconquérir

reconsider vt. reviser; considérer de nouveau; revenir sur

reconstitute vt. reconstituer

reconstruct vt. rebâtir, reconstruire; —ion n. reconstruction f.

record n. registre m.; note f.; procès-verbal m.; document m.; dossier m.; (sports) record m.; (phonograph) disque m.; — off the — non-officiel; —s pl. archives f. pl.; — vt. enregistrer; rapporter; graver; faire une note de; —er n. enregistreur m.; archiviste m.; machine à enregistrer f.; tape —er magnétophone m.; —ing n. enregistrement m.

record-breaking a. qui bat le record; surpassant le record

recount vt. raconter

re-count vt. recompter

recoup vt. & (vi.) (se) dédommager; (se) rattraper (sur); rembourser, dédommager (de)

recourse n. recours m.

recover vt. retrouver, regagner; (loss) réparer, reprendre; recouvrer; (oneself) revenir à soi; — vi. guérir, se remettre (de); —y n. guérison f.; recouvrement m.; reprise f.

re-cover vt. recouvrir

recreation n. récréation f.; divertissement m.

recrimination n. récrimination f.

recrudescence n. recrudescence f.

recruit n. recrue f.; — vt. (mil.) recruter; racoler; réparer; —ing n. recrutement m.

rectal a. rectal

rectangular a. rectangulaire

rectification n. rectification f.

rectifier n. (elec.) redresseur, rectificateur m.

rectify vt. rectifier; réparer, corriger; (elec.) redresser

rectilinear a. rectiligne

rectitude n. rectitude, droiture f.

rector n. recteur m.; curé m.; —y n. presbytère m.

recumbent a. couché

recuperate vi. se remettre, se rétablir; guérir

recuperation n. rétablissement m.; guérison f.

recur vi. se reproduire; revenir; —rence n. retour m.; (med.) récidive f.; —rent a. recurrent; qui revient; —ring a. recurrent; périodique

red n. rouge m.; in the — en déficit; — a. rouge; (hair) roux (rousse); pourpre; — tape paperasserie f.; see — voir rouge; turn — rougir; —den vi. rougir; (sky) rougeoyer; —dish a. rougeâtre; —ness n. rougeur f.; (hair) rousseur f.

red-blooded a. robuste, vigoureux

redcap n. porteur (de gare) m.

redecorate vt. repeindre; refaire

redeem vt. racheter; amortir; dégager; -able a. rachetable; -er n. rédempteur m.

redemption n. rachat m.; amortissement m.; (eccl.) rédemption f.

red-eyed a. aux yeux éraillés

red-haired a. roux (rousse), aux cheveux roux

red-handed a. en flagrant délit

redhead n. personne aux cheveux roux f.; -ed a. roux (rousse), aux cheveux roux

red-hot a. (chauffé au) rouge

rediscover vt. retrouver

redistribute vt. redistribuer

red-letter a., — day jour mémorable m.

redolence n. odeur f., parfum m.

redolent a. parfumé, odorant; — of qui sent

redouble vt. & vi. redoubler; (cards) surcontrer

redoubtable a. redoutable

redound vi. contribuer

redress n. réparation f.; — vt. réparer

redskin n. peau-rouge m.

reduce vt. réduire; diminuer; abaisser; — vi. maigrir

reducible a. réductible

reduction n. réduction f.; diminution f.; baisse f.

redundancy n. redondance f.

redundant a. redondant

reduplicate vt. redoubler

re-echo vi. résonner, retentir

reed n. roseau m.; (mus.) anche f.

reef n. récif, écueil m.; (naut.) ris m.; — vt. prendre un ris dans

reek n. odeur f.; relent m.; — vi. sentir; suer; —ing a. qui sent

reel n. bobine f., dévidoir m.; (fishing) moulinet m.; — vt. bobiner, dévider; — vi. chanceler, tournoyer; tituber; — off réciter, énumérer rapidement

re-elect vt. réélire; -ion n. réélection f.

re-enact vt. reproduire

re-enlist vi. se rengager

re-enter vt. rentrer (dans)

re-entry n. rentrée f.

re-establish vt. rétablir; -ment n. rétablissement m.

re-examination n. nouvel examen m.

re-examine vt. examiner de nouveau

refashion vt. refaire, refaçonner

refasten vt. rattacher

refectory n. réfectoire m.

refer vt. soumettre; renvoyer; — vi. se rapporter; se reporter; faire allusion; parler; -ence n. référence f.; renvoi m.; appel m.; rapport m.; -ence work ouvrage à consulter m.

referee n. arbitre m.; — vt. arbitrer

refill n. rechange m.; pièce de rechange f.; — vt. remplir

refine vt. raffiner; purifier; -d a. raffiné; cultivé, distingué; -ment n. raffinage m.; raffinement m.; -ry n. raffinerie f.

refit vt. remonter; (naut.) réarmer

reflect vt. refléter; réfléchir; — vi. réfléchir; méditer; se dire; faire du tort; -ion n. réflexion f., réfléchissement m.; reflet m.; image f.; -or n. réflecteur m.

reflex a. & n. réflexe m.; -ive a. (gram.) réfléchi

reforestation n. reboisement m.

reform n. réforme f.; — vt. réformer, corriger; — vi. se réformer, se corriger; -ation n. réforme f.; réformation f.; -atory n. maison de correction f.; -er n. réformateur m.

re-form vt. reformer; — vi. se reformer

refract vt. réfracter; -ion n. réfraction f.; -ory a. réfractaire; insoumis

refrain n v. (mus.) refrain m.; — vi. s'abstenir, se retenir

refresh vt. rafraîchir; -ing a. rafraîchissant; -ment n. rafraîchissement m.; boisson f.; quelque chose à boire (ou à manger) m.

refrigerate vt. réfrigérer, refroidir; frigorifier

refrigeration n. réfrigération f.; frigorification f.

refrigerator n. glacière f., frigidaire m.

refuel vi. faire le plein d'essence

refuge n. refuge m.; abri m.; take — se réfugier; -e n. réfugié, sinistré m.

refulgence n. éclat m.

refund n. remboursement m.; — vt. rembourser; -able a. remboursable

refurnish vt. remonter

refusal n. refus m.; first — première offre f.

refuse n. rebut m.; — vt. refuser; ne pas vouloir

refutation n. réfutation f.

refute vt. réfuter

regain vt. regagner; reprendre; — consciousness reprendre connaissance

regal a. royal; -ia n. insignes m. pl.

regale vt. régaler

regard n. attention f., égard m.; estime f.; in — to en ce qui concerne; out of — for par égard pour; with — to quant à; have no — for ne pas estimer; faire peu de cas de; show — témoigner de l'estime; -s pl. amitiés f. pl.; give my -s to faites mes amitiés à; — vt. regarder, considérer; -ing prep. en ce qui concerne; quant à; à l'égard de; -less a. sans regarder; sans se soucier; -less adv. en tout cas; quand même

regatta n. régate f.

regency n. régence f.

regeneration n. régénération f.

regenerate vt. régénérer; — vi. se régénérer; — a. régénéré

regenerator n. régénérateur m.

regent n. régent m.

regime, regimen n. régime m.

regiment n. régiment m.; -al a. du régiment; -ation n. régimentation f.; — vt.

réglementer

region n. région f.; -al a. régional

register n. registre m.; compteur m.; cash — caisse enregistreuse f.; — vt. enregistrer; inscrire; immatriculer; (letter) recommander; (trademark) déposer; — vi. s'inscrire; s'immatriculer

registrar n. archiviste, secrétaire; teneur de registres m.

registration n. enregistrement m.; inscription f.; (school, auto) immatriculation f.

registry n. secrétariat m.; bureau d'enregistrement m.

regress vi. régresser; -ion n. régression f.

regret n. regret m.; — vt. regretter; être désolé; -ful a. plein de regrets; -fully adv. avec regret; -table a. regrettable; à regretter

regroup vt. regrouper

regular a. régulier; ordinaire; habituel; (officer) de carrière; (coll.) vrai; -ity n. régularité f.; -ize vt. régulariser; -ly adv. régulièrement; d'ordinaire, d'habitude

regulate vt. régler

regulation n. règlement m.; ordonnance f.

regulator n. régulateur m.

regurgitate vt. régurgiter; — vi. regorger

regurgitation n. régurgitation f.

rehabilitate vt. réhabiliter

rehabilitation n. réhabilitation f.

rehearsal n. répétition f.

rehearse vt. répéter

reheat vt. réchauffer

reign n. règne m.; — vi. régner; -ing a. régnant

reimburse vt. rembourser; -ment n. remboursement n.

rein n. bride, rêne, guide f.; — vt. brider

reincarnation n. réincarnation f.

reincorporate vt. réincorporer

reinforce vt. renforcer; appuyer; -d a. renforcé; -d concrete béton armé m.; -ment n. renforcement m.; -ments n. pl. renfort m.

reinstate vt. réintégrer, rétablir; -ment n. réintégration f.

reinsurance n. réassurance, contre-assurance f.

reinsure vt. réassurer

reissue vt. émettre de nouveau; publier de nouveau

reiterate vt. réitérer

reiteration n. réitération f.

reject n. pièce de rebut f.; — vt. rejeter; refuser; -ion n. rejet m.; refus m.

rejoice vt. réjouir; — vi. se réjouir (de)

rejoin vt. rejoindre; retrouver; — vi. répondre, répliquer; -der n. réplique f.

rejuvenate vt. & vi. rajeunir

rekindle vt. rallumer; ranimer

relapse n. rechute f.; — vi. rechuter, avoir une rechute; retomber (dans)

relate vt. raconter; relater; rapporter; — vi. avoir rapport (à), se rapporter; -d a. apparenté; parent; allié

relation n. (narrative) récit m.; rapport m.; relation f.; (relative) parent m.; -ship n. rapport m.; relation f.; parenté f.; in — to à l'égard de

relative a. relatif; n. parent m. — to au sujet de

relativity n. relativité f.

relax vt. détendre, relâcher; — vi. se détendre, se relâcher; -ation n. détente f.; repos m.; relâchement m.

relay n. relais m.; relève f.; — race course à relais f.; — vt. relayer

re-lay vt. reposer, poser de nouveau

release n. libération f.; élargissement m. déclencheur m.; (document) quittance f., acquit m.; — vt. libérer; élargir; lâcher; déclencher; acquitter

relegate vt. reléguer; remettre

relent vi. revenir sur; s'adoucir; -less a. impitoyable, implacable; -lessness n. implacabilité f.

relevance n. à propos m.

relevant a. à propos, pertinent; qui se rapporte à

reliability n. régularité f.; honnêteté f.

reliable a. sûr; digne de confiance

reliance n. confiance f.

reliant a., be — on dépendre de; avoir confiance en

relic n. relique f.; -s pl. restes m. pl.

relief n. soulagement m.; aide f.; secours m.; assistance publique f.; relief m.; — map carte en relief

relieve vt. soulager; aider, secourir; relever; dégager

relight vt. rallumer

religion n. religion f.; culte m.

religious a. religieux; dévot; pieux; -ly adv. religieusement; scrupuleusement

reline vt. redoubler; (brakes) regarnir

relinquish vt. renoncer; délaisser; abandonner

relish n. goût m.; assaisonnement, condiment m.; entremets m.; — vt. goûter, savourer

reload vt. recharger

relocate vt. reloger, changer de place

relocation n. relogement m.

reluctance n. regret m.; répugnance f.; hésitation f.; (elec.) reluctance f.

reluctant a. hésitant; peu disposé; -ly adv. à regret; à contre-cœur

rely vi., — on compter sur

remain vi. rester; demeurer; se tenir; -s n. pl. restes m. pl.; vestiges m. pl. -der n. reste m.; (book) solde d'édition m.

remake vt. refaire

remand n. renvoi m.; — vt. renvoyer

remark n. remarque f., observation f.; attention f.; — vt. remarquer, observer, constater; — vi. faire une remarque; -able a. remarquable

remarry vi. se remarier

remediable a. remédiable

remedial a. réparateur; curatif

remedy n. remède m.; recours m.; — vt. remédier

remember vt. se souvenir de; se rappeler

remembrance n. souvenir m.; mémoire f.

remind vt. rappeler; faire penser; faire souvenir; -er n. rappel m.; souvenir m.; mémento m.

reminiscence n. réminiscence f.; souvenir m.

reminiscent a. qui rappelle

remiss a. négligent; -ion n. rémission f.; remise f.; -ness n. négligence f.

remit vt. remettre, envoyer; pardonner; -tance n. remise f.; envoi m.; -ter n. remettant m.

remnant n. reste m.; coupon m.

remodel vt. remodeler

remonstrance n. remontrance f.

remonstrate vi. faire des remontrances; — vi. protester

remorse n. remords m.; -ful a. plein de remords; -less a. sans remords; sans pitié

remote a. lointain, éloigné; reculé; peu probable; -ly adv. loin; de loin; -ness n. éloignement m.

removable a. amovible; détachable

removal n. enlèvement m.; déplacement m.; transport m.; révocation f.

remove vt. enlever, écarter; déplacer, transporter; -d a. éloigné; loin

remunerate vt. rémunérer

remuneration n. rémunération f.

remunerative a. rémunérateur

renaissance n. renaissance f.

renal a. rénal

rename vt. renommer, rebaptiser

renascence n. renaissance

renascent a. renaissant

rend vt. déchirer; fendre; faire retentir

render vt. rendre; traduire; interpréter; (cooking) fondre; -ing, rendition n. rendu m.; traduction f.; interprétation f.

rendezvous n. rendez-vous m.

renegade n. renégat m.

renew vt. renouveler; (subscription) réabonner; — vi. renouer -able a. renouvelable; interchangeable; -al n. renouvellement m.; réabonnement m.

renounce vt. renoncer à; abandonner; répudier

renovate vt. renouveler; rénover; mettre à neuf

renovation n. rénovation f.

renown n. renom m., renommée f.; -ed a. renommé, célèbre, illustre

rent n. (property) loyer m.; (clothing) déchirure f.; fente, fissure f.; (income) n. pl. rentes f.; revenu m. — vt. louer, affermer; — vi. se louer; -al n. loyer m.; -er n. locataire m. & f.

renunciation n. renonciation f., renoncement m.; répudiation f.

reoccupy vt. réoccuper

reopen vt. rouvrir; — vi. (se) rouvrir; (school) rentrer; -ing n. réouverture f.; rentrée f.

reorder vt. commander de nouveau; — vi. renouveler une commande

reorganization n. réorganisation f.

reorganize vt. & vi. réorganiser

repair n. réparation f.; état m.; — shop n. atelier de réparation m.; — vt. réparer; raccommoder; — vi. aller, se rendre; -ing n. réparation f.; (clothes) raccommodage m.; (mech.) dépannage m.

repairman n. réparateur m.; dépanneur m.

reparable a. réparable

reparation n. réparation; satisfaction f.

repartee n. repartie f.; réplique f.

repast n. repas, festin m.

repatriate vt. rapatrier

repave vt. repaver

repay vt. rembourser; récompenser; rendre; -able a. payable, à rembourser; -ment n. remboursement m.

repeal n. révocation, abrogation f.; — vt. révoquer, (law) abroger

repeat n. répétition f.; (mus.) reprise f.; — vt. répéter; réitérer; — vi. se répéter; -ed a. répété; réitéré; -edly adv. à plusieurs reprises; -ing a. qui répète

repel vt. repousser; répugner à; -lent a. répulsif; repoussant; insect -lent n. chasse-insectes m.; -ling a. répulsif

repent vt. & vi. se repentir (de); -ance n. repentir m.; -ant a. repenti; repentant

repercussion n. répercussion f.; contrecoup m.

repertoire, repertory n. répertoire m.

repetition n. répétition f.; (mus.) reprise f.

rephrase vt. rédiger de nouveau, dire d'une autre façon

replace vt. remplacer; replacer; remettre; -able a. remplaçable; interchangeable; -ment n. remplacement m.; pièce de rechange f.; remise f.; -ment a. de remplacement, de rechange

replate vt. replaquer

replenish vt. remplir; se réapprovisionner (de); -ing, -ment n. recharge f.

replete a. rempli, plein

replica n. réplique f.; copie f.

reply n. réponse f.; réplique f.; — vt. & vi. répondre, répliquer

report n. rapport m.; compte-rendu m.; procès-verbal m.; bruit m., rumeur f.; (firearms) détonation f.; weather — bulletin météorologique m.; — vt. rapporter; rendre compte de; signaler; dire; -er n. reporter, journaliste m.; -ing n. reportage m.

repose n. repos m.; calme m., tranquillité f.; — vi. (se) reposer

repository n. dépôt m.

repossess vt. reprendre (possession); -ion n. rentrée en possession f.

reprehensible a. blâmable, répréhensible

represent vt. représenter; symboliser; jouer; -ation n. représentation f.; -ative a. représentatif; -ative n. représentant m.; député m.; House of Representatives Chambre des Représentants

repress vt. réprimer; refouler; -ed a. réprimé; refoulé; -ion n. répression f.

reprieve n. commutation f.; sursis, répit m.; — vt. accorder une commutation à

reprimand n. réprimande f.; — vt. réprimander

reprint n. réimpression f.; tirage à part; tiré à part; m.; — vt. réimprimer; tirer à part

reprisal n. représaille f.

reproach n. reproche m.; beyond — irréprochable; — vt. faire des reproches à; -ful a. plein de reproches

reprobate n. vaurien m.; roué m.; — vt. réprouver

reproduce vt. reproduire; multiplier; — vi. se reproduire; se multiplier

reproduction n. reproduction f.; copie f.

reproof n. reproche m., réprimande f.

reprove vt. réprimander, reprendre, réprouver

reproving a. de reproche; réprobateur

republic n. république f.; **-an** a. & n. républicain

republish vt. rééditer; republier

repudiate vt. répudier, désavouer, renier

repudiation n. répudiation f., désaveu m., reniement m.

repugnant a. répugnant

repulse vt. repousser, refouler

repulsion n. répugnance f.; répulsion f.

repulsive a. repoussant, dégoûtant, répulsif

repurchase n. rachat m.; — vt. racheter

reputable a. honorable, estimable

reputation n. réputation f., renom m.

repute n. réputation f.; renom m., renommée f.; estime f.; **-d** a. réputé; attribué; supposé, censé

request n. demande f.; requête f.; sollicitation f.; on — sur demande; — vt. demander; solliciter; prier

require vt. exiger; demander; falloir; **-d** a. exigé, demandé; requis, nécessaire, prescrit; voulu; **-ment** n. exigence f.; besoin m.; nécessité f.

requisite a. requis, nécessaire; — n. nécessaire m., chose nécessaire f.

requisition n. réquisition, demande f.; — vt. réquisitionner

reroute vt. transmettre par une autre route; envoyer par une autre route; faire dévier

rerouting n. (telephone) transmission déroutée f.

resaddle vt. reseller

resale n. revente f.

rescind vt. rescinder; abroger

rescue n. délivrance f.; sauvetage m.; — vt. délivrer, sauver; **-r** n., libérateur, sauveur m.

research n. recherche f.; enquête f.; investigation f.; travaux de recherche m. pl.

resemblance n. ressemblance f.

resemble vt. ressembler (à)

resent vt. ressentir; s'offenser de; **-ful** a. plein de ressentiment; **-ment** n. ressentiment m.

reservation n. réserve f.; place louée; chambre retenue f.; restriction f.; terres réservées f. pl.

reserve n. réserve f.; — power n. réserve de puissance f.; — vt. réserver; louer; retenir; **-d** a. réservé; loué; retenu; (person) renfermé

reservoir n. réservoir m.

reset vt. remettre; remonter; recomposer

resettle vt. réinstaller; — vi. se réinstaller

reside vi. résider, demeurer; **-nce** n. résidence f.; demeure f.; domicile m.; séjour m.; habitation f.; maison f.; hôtel m.; **-nt** n. habitant m.; résident m.; interne m.; **-ntial** a. d'habitation

residue n. résidu m.

resign vt. résigner; démissionner; — oneself se résigner; **-ation** n. démission f.; résignation f.; **-ed** a. résigné

resilience n. résilience f.; élasticité f.; rebondissement m.

resiliency n. élasticité, résilience f.

resilient a. élastique

resin n. résine f.; **-ous** a. résineux

resist vt. résister; **-ance** n. résistance f.; (elec.) impédance f.; — coil n. bobine de résistance f.; **-ant** a. résistant; **-ible** a. résistible; **-or** n. (elec.) résistance f.

resole vt. ressemeler

resolute a. résolu, ferme, déterminé; **-ness** n. résolution f.

resolution n. résolution f.; décision f.; détermination f.

resolve n. résolution f.; — vt. résoudre; décider; — vi. se résoudre; se décider; **-d** a. résolu; décidé

resonance n. résonance f., retentissement m.

resonant a. résonnant; sonore; accordé

resonator n. résonateur m.

resort n. recours m., ressource f.; (place) station f.; summer — station balnéaire f.; — vi. avoir recours, recourir

resound vi. résonner; retentir; **-ing** a. résonnant; retentissant

re-sound vt. répéter

resource n. ressource f.; **-ful** a. débrouillard; **-fulness** n. ressource f.

respect n. respect m., estime, considération f.; égard m.; rapport m.; in this — à cet égard; with — to en ce qui concerne; **-s** pl. hommages, respects m. pl.; — vt. respecter; estimer, honorer; **-ability** n. respectabilité f.; **-able** a. respectable; honorable; convenable, comme il faut; **-ful** a. respectueux; **-fully** adv. respectueusement; **-ive** a. respectif; **-ively** adv. respectivement

respirator n. respirateur m.; **-y** a. respiratoire

respite n. répit, relâche m.; délai m.

resplendent a. resplendissant

respond vi. répondre

response n. réponse, réplique f.; réaction f.; accueil m.; fonction f., rendement m.

responsibility n. responsabilité f.; charge f.; devoir m.

responsible a. responsable; compétent

responsive a. sensible; sympathique; **-ness** n. sensibilité f.

rest n. repos m.; reste m.; (support) appui m.; (mus.) pause f., whole — pause f., half — demi-pause f., quarter — soupir m.; come to — s'arrêter; take a — se reposer; — room lavabo m.; — vt. reposer; appuyer; — vi. se reposer; s'appuyer; peser; **-ful** a. reposant; tranquille; **-ive** a. inquiet; rétif; **-less** a. sans repos; troublé, agité; inquiet; impatient

restate vt. énoncer de nouveau; énoncer en d'autres termes

restive a. rétif; opiniâtre

restoration n. restitution, restauration f.

restore vt. restituer, restaurer; rendre; remettre; rétablir

restrain vt. retenir; contraindre; empêcher; **-t** n. contrainte f.; réserve f.

restrict vt. restreindre; **-ed** a. restreint; limité; **-ion** n. restriction f.; **-ive** a. restrictif

result n. résultat m.; as a — par conséquent; as a — of par suite de; — vi. résulter; s'ensuivre; -ant a. résultant

resume vt. reprendre; se remettre à

resumé n. résumé m.

resumption n. reprise f.

resurface vt. donner une nouvelle surface
à; (road) refaire le revêtement de

resurgent a. renaissant

resurrect vt. ressusciter; -ion n. résurrection f.

resuscitate vt. ressusciter

resuscitation n. retour à la vie m.; renaissance f.

retail n. vente au détail f.; détail m.; —
price prix de détail m.; — vt. vendre au
détail, détailler; -er n. marchand au
détail; détaillant m.

retain vt. retenir; garder, conserver; -er
n. avance f.; honoraires payés d'avance
m. pl.; serviteur m.; -ing a., -ing fee n.
honoraires payés d'avance m. pl.; —
wall n. mur de soutènement m.

retaliate vi. user de représailles

retaliation n. représailles f. pl.; talion m.

retaliatory a. de représailles

retard vt. retarder; -d a. attardé

retch vi. vomir

retell vt. redire, répéter

retention n. conservation f.

retentive a. tenace; qui retient; -ness n.
ténacité f.

reticence n. réticence f.

reticent a. taciturne

retina n. rétine f.

retinue n. suite f.

retire vi. se retirer; prendre la retraite; se
coucher; se replier; — vt. mettre à la
retraite; -d a. retiré; retraité; en retraite; -ment n. retraite f.

retiring a. réservé; qui prend la retraite;
sortant

retort n. réplique f.; (chem.) cornue f.;
— vt. & vi. répliquer, riposter; renvoyer

retouch vt. retoucher

retrace vt. retracer; revenir sur

retract vt. rétracter; escamoter; se dédire;
-able a. escamotable; -ion n. rétraction
f.; désaveu m.

retread n. pneu rechapé m.; — vt. rechaper

retreat n. retraite f.; asile m.; — vi. battre
en retraite; se retirer; -ing a. qui bat la
retraite; (forehead) fuyant

retrench vt. restreindre; -ment n. réduction f.

retribution n. récompense f.; jugement m.

retrieve vt. rapporter; retrouver; -r n.
chien rapporteur m.

retroactive a. rétroactif; réactif, de réaction

retrograde a. rétrograde; — vi. rétrograder

retrospect, retrospection n. coup d'œil rétrospectif, examen rétrospectif m.

return n. retour m.; profit, revenu m.; restitution f.; in — en retour; in — for en
retour de; en échange de; moyennant;
by — mail par retour du courrier; —
address adresse de l'expéditeur f.; —
match match retour m.; — ticket billet,
de retour m.; — trip voyage de retour

m.; — vi. revenir; retourner; être de re;
tour; rentrer; — vt. rendre, restituer-
remettre; répondre; rapporter

reunite vt. réunir; réconcilier; — vi. se
réunir; se réconcilier

revamp vt. refaçonner, refaire, réorganiser

reveal vt. révéler, découvrir; laisser voir;
dévoiler; mettre à jour; -ing a. révélateur

reveille n. (mil.) diane f.

revel n. divertissement m.; orgie f.; — vi.
se divertir; faire bombance; -ry n. di-
vertissements m. pl.; bombance f.; orgie
f.

revelation n. révélation f.

revenge n. vengeance f.; take — se venger
(de); — vt. venger; -ful a. vengeur, vindicatif

revenue n. revenu m.; rente f.

reverberate vi. retentir; réverbérer

reverberation n. réverbération, répercussion f.

revere vt. révérer, honorer, vénérer; -nce
n. révérence, vénération f.; -nd a. & n.
révérend m.; -nt a. respectueux

reverie n. rêverie f.

reversal n. revirement m.; inversion f.;
renversement m.; (law) réforme f.

reverse a. opposé, contraire; inverse; —
side dos m.; envers m.; revers m.; verso
m. — n. opposé, contraire, inverse, verso m.; revers m.; verso m.; (auto.) marche arrière f.; — vt. renverser; invertir;
retourner; faire marche arrière; (law)
réformer, révoquer

revert vi. retourner, revenir

review n. revue f.; révision f.; examen m.
compte rendu m.; — vt. reviser; passer
en revue; faire le compte rendu de; -er
n. critique m.

revile vt. injurier, insulter

revisal n. revision f.; (print.) seconde f.,
(2nd) troisième épreuve d'auteur

revise vt. revoir, reviser; corriger

reviser n. réviseur m.

revision n. révision f.

revisit vt. visiter de nouveau, revisiter

revival n. retour à la vie m.; renaissance
f.; reprise f.; réveil m.; renouveau m.;
-ist n. revivaliste m. & f.

revive vt. faire revivre, ressusciter; réveiller; renouveler; ranimer; — vi. reprendre connaissance; ressusciter se ranimer; renaître; reprendre

revocable a. révocable

revocation n. révocation f.

revoke vt. révoquer

revolt n. révolte f.; — vi. se révolter,
se rebeller, s'insurger, se soulever; -ing
a. en révolte; repoussant, révoltant

revolution n. révolution f.; tour m.; -ary
a. & n. révolutionnaire m. & f.; -ist n.
révolutionnaire m. & f.; -ize vt. révolutionner

revolve vt. faire tourner, retourner; — vi.
tourner; -r n. révolver m.

revolving a. tournant; pivotant

revulsion n. revirement m.

reward n. récompense f.; — vt. récompenser

rewind vt. rembobiner, réenrouler

reword vt. redire en d'autres termes; rédiger de nouveau

rewrite vt. récrire; refaire, remanier

rhapsody n. rapsodie f.

Rheims n. Reims

Rhenish a. rhénan, du Rhin

rhetoric n. rhétorique f.; –al a. de rhétoriqué; –ian n. rhétoricien, rhéteur m.

rheumatic a. rhumatismal; — fever n. rhumatisme articulaire m.; — n. rhumatisant m.

rheumatism n. rhumatisme m.

Rhine n. Rhin m.

rhinestone n. faux diamant m.

rhubarb n. rhubarbe f.

rhyme n. rime f.; vers m.; — vi. rimer; vt. faire rimer; neither — nor reason ni rime ni raison

rhythm n. rythme m.; –mically adv. avec rythme; –mical a. rythmique, rythmé

rib n. côte f.; nervure f.; support m.; — vt. garnir de nervures; (coll.) faire marcher; taquiner; –bed a. à nervures, à cotes

ribald a. libertin, obscène; –ry n. libertinage m.; langage licencieux m.

ribbon n. ruban m.; bande f.; tear to –s déchiqueter; mettre en lambeaux

rice n. ris m.; — field, — paddy n. rizière — paper n. papier de ris m.; — pudding n. ris au lait m.

rich a. riche; fertile; gras; somptueux; — n. riches m. pl.; –es n. pl. richesse f.; –ness n. richesse f.; fertilité f.; somptuosité f.

rickets n. pl. rachitisme m.

rickety a. délabré, boiteux, bancal; (med.) rachitique

rickrack n. passement en zigzag m., bordure f.

ricochet vt. ricocher

rid vt. débarrasser; purger; délivrer; get — of se débarrasser de, se défaire de; –dance n. débarras m.

riddle n. devinette f.; énigme f.; — vt. cribler

ride n. voyage m., promenade f.; trajet m.; go for a — (aller) faire une promenade (en auto); — vi. aller, voyager, se promener; aller à cheval, monter à cheval; — vt. monter; (coll.) ennuyer; harasser; taquiner; –r n. personne qui va en auto passager m. & f.; cavalier m.; jockey m.; (law) clause additionnelle f., annexe, allonge f.

ridge n. arête f.; crête f.; ride f.

ridicule n. ridicule m.; risée f.; raillerie, moquerie f.; — vt. se moquer de

ridiculous a. ridicule; –ness n. ridicule m.

riding n. équitation f.; — boots n. pl. bottes f. pl.; — breeches n. pl. culotte de cheval f.; — habit n. amazone f.; — master maître d'équitation m.

RH factor n. facteur RH m.

Rhodesia n. Rhodésie f.

rife a., to be — sévir

riffraff n. canaille f.

rifle n. fusil m.; carabine f.; — range champ de tir m.; — shot coup de fusil m.; within — shot à portée de fusil; — vt. (guns) rayer; piller; fouiller

rifleman n. chasseur, tirailleur, fusilier m.

rifling n. pillage m.; (rifle bore) rayage m.

rift n. fente, fissure f.; (persons) brouille f.

rig n. (naut.) gréement m.; équipement m.; voiture f.; attelage m.; — vt. gréer, équiper; installer, monter; (coll.) truquer; –ging n. gréage m.; équipage m.; agrès m. pl.

right a. droit; juste; bon; correct; exact; (watch) à l'heure; all — bon; bien; entendu; — angle n. angle droit m.; be — avoir raison; that's — c'est cela; — side endroit, bon côté m.; — side up à l'endroit; — adv. droit; tout; do — faire bien; go — réussir; aller à droite; — and left de tous les côtés; — away tout de suite, sur-le-champ; — n. droit m.; bien m.; titre m.; droite f.; — and wrong le bien et le mal; on the —, to the — à droite; keep to the — tenir la droite; serrer à droite; –s n. pl. droit(s) m. pl.; within one's –s dans son droit; vt. redresser, réparer; rectifier; –eous a. droit, juste; –eousness n. droiture f.; –ful a. légitime; –ist n. partisan de la droite m.; –fully adv. à juste titre; –ness n. justesse f.

rightabout face n. demi-tour à droite m.; (fig.) revirement m.

right-hand a. de droite; de la main droite; — man bras droit m.; –ed a. droitier

right-of-way n. priorité f.; (rail.) voie f.

right-wing a. de droite; –er n. partisan de la droite m.

rigid a. rigide; raide; sévère; –ity n. rigidité f.; raideur f.; sévérité f.

rigmarole n. procédure compliquée f.; galimatias m.

rigor n. rigueur f.; sévérité f.; — mortis rigidité cadavérique f.; –ous a. rigoureux; sévère; –ousness n. rigueur f.

rile vt. troubler; faire enrager

rim n. bord m.; (eyeglasses) monture f.; — vt. border; –less a. sans monture

rind n. peau f.; pelure f.; écorce f.; croûte f.

ring n. anneau m., bague f.; cercle m.; alliance f.; rond m.; groupe m.; bande f.; arène f.; (boxing) ring m.; (circuit) enceinte f.; sonnerie f.; coup de téléphone m.; — finger annulaire m.; — wedding alliance f.; — vt. entourer; sonner; — vi. sonner; résonner, retentir; tinter; –ing n. son m.; tintement m.; –er n. (bell) sonnette f.; (person) sonneur m.; dead –er (coll.) jumeau, double m.

ringleader n. chef, meneur m.

ringworm n. teigne (tonsurante) f.

rink n. patinoire f.

rinse vt. rincer; — n. (hair) rinçage m.

riot n. émeute f.; — vi. s'ameuter; –ing n. émeute f. pl.; –ous a. tumultueux; déréglé, dissipé

rip n. déchirure f.; –cord n. corde d'ouverture f.; — vt. découdre, déchirer; — vi. se déchirer; — open ouvrir en déchirant

ripe a. mûr; prêt; –n vt. (faire) mûrir; –n vi. mûrir; –ness n. maturité f.

ripple n. ride f.; gazouillement m.; ondulation *f.*; murmure *m.*; — *vt.* rider; — *vi.* se rider; onduler; murmurer; parler

rippling *n.* murmure *m.*; clapotage *m.*; — *a.* murmurant

rise *n.* lever *m.*; hausse *f.*; élévation *f.*; (ground) éminence *f.*; (tide) montée *f.*; — *vi.* se lever; s'élever; monter; se soulever; se dresser; —*r n.* contremarche *f.*

rising *a.* levant; montant; en hausse; — *n.* lever *m.*; hausse *f.*

risk *n.* risque, péril *m.*; run a — courir un risque; — *vt.* risquer; hasarder; —*y a.* hasardeux; (story) risqué

rite *n.* rite *m.*; cérémonie *f.*

ritual *a.* rituel; — *n.* rituel *m.*; rites *m. pl.*; –istic *a.* rituel

rival *a. & n.* rival *m.*; émule *m. & f.*; — *vt.* rivaliser avec; —ry *n.* rivalité *f.*; émulation *f.*

river *n.* fleuve *m.*; rivière *f.*; down — en aval; up — en amont

riverside *n.* bord de la rivière *m.*; — *a.* qui s'étend au bord de l'eau; riverain

rivet *n.* rivet *m.*; clou (à river) *m.*; — *vt.* river, riveter; –er *n.* (machine) riveteuse; *f.*; –ing *n.* rivetage *m.*

Riviera *n.* Côte d'Azur *f.*

rivulet *n.* ruisseau *m.*

road *n.* chemin *m.*; route *f.*; voie *f.*; — map carte routière *f.*; on the — en voyage; en province

roadbed *n.* empierrement *m.*

roadblock *n.* barricade *f.*

roadhouse *n.* cabaret au bord de la route *m.*; auberge *f.*

roadside *n.* bord de la route *m.*; — *a.* qui se trouve au bord de la route

roadster *n.* coupé *m.*

roadway *n.* voie *f.*; chaussée *f.*

roam *vi.* errer, rôder (dans); — *vt.* parcourir, errer çà et là (par); —ing *a.* errant; –er *n.* vagabond *m.*

roar *n.* rugissement *m.*; mugissement *m.*; grondement *m.*; éclat *m.*; — *vi.* rugir; mugir; gronder; éclater; –ing *a.* mugissant, pétillant

roast *a. & n.* rôti *m.*; — beef rosbif *m.*; — *vt.* rôtir; griller; (coffee) torréfier; –er *n.* rôtissoire *f.*; (coffee) brûloir *m.*; –ing *n.* cuisson *f.*; (coffee) torréfaction *f.*

rob *vt.* voler; –ber *n.* voleur *m.*; –bery *n.* vol *m.*

robe *n.* robe *f.*; couverture *f.*; — *vt.* vêtir; — *vi.* se vêtir

robot *n.* automate *m.*

robust *a.* robuste, vigoureux; –ness *n.* vigueur, force *f.*

rock *n.* roc, rocher *m.*, roche *f.*, pierre *f.*; — candy *n.* sucre candi *m.*; — crystal cristal de roche *m.*; — garden jardin de rocaille *m.*; — salt sel gemme *m.*; — *vt.* balancer, bercer; — *vi.* balancer; –er *n.* bascule *f.*; (chair) chaise à bascule *f.*, fauteuil à bascule *m.*; –ing *a.* à bascule; –ing *n.* bercement, balancement *m.*; tremblement *m.*; –y *a.* rocheux; rocailleux

rock-bottom *a.* dernier, le plus bas

rocket *n.* fusée *f.*; — *a.* à fusée(s)

rocket launcher *n.* lance-fusées *m.*

rocking chair *n.* chaise à bascule *f.*

Rocky Mountains *n. pl.* Montagnes Rocheuses *f. pl.*

rococo *a.* rococo

rod *n.* baguette, verge *f.*; tige *f.*; (measurement) perche *f.*; connecting — bielle motrice *f.*; curtain — tringle *f.*; fishing — canne à pêche *f.*

rodent *a. & n.* rongeur *m.*

rodeo *n.* concours d'équitation des cowboys *m.*

Roentgen *n.* röntgen *m.*; — rays *n. pl.* rayons X *m. pl.*; — tube *n.* tube à rayons X *m.*

rogue *n.* fripon, coquin *m.*

roguish *a.* fripon, malin; –ness *n.* friponnerie, malice *f.*

roil *vt.* troubler

role *n.* rôle *m.*

roll *n.* rouleau *m.*; petit pain *m.*; liste *f.*; roulement *m.*; (naut.) roulis *m.*; call the — faire l'appel; — call appel *m.*; — *vt.* rouler; (metal) laminer; — *vi.* rouler; — over (se) retourner; — up enrouler; (sleeve) retrousser; –er *n.* rouleau *m.*; (metal) cylindre; –er bearings *n. pl.* roulement à rouleaux *m.*; –er coaster *n.* montagnes russes *f. pl.*; –er skates patins à roulettes *m. pl.*; –ing *a.* roulant; ondulé; –ing *n.* roulement *m.*; roulis *m.*; –ing mill usine de laminage *f.*; –ing pin rouleau *m.*, bille *f.*

roly-poly *a.* dodu, potelé

romaine *n.* romaine *f.*

Roman *a. & n.* romain *m.*; — numerals chiffres romains *m. pl.*; — type caractères romains *m. pl.*; –ic *a.* roman

romance *n.* roman *m.*; aventure sentimentale *f.*; histoire romanesque *f.*; (mus.) romance *f.*; — *vt.* romancer

Romance languages *n.* langues romanes *f. pl.*

Romanesque *a. & n.* roman *m.*

Romania *n.* Roumanie *f.*; –n *a. & n.* rouman *m.*

romantic *a.* romanesque; sentimental; (lit.) romantique; –ism *n.* romantisme *m.*

Romany *n.* les gitanes *m. pl.*; langue des gitanes *f.*

romp *vi.* jouer, folâtrer, badiner; — *n.* gamine *f.*; (play) tapage; –ers *m. pl.* barboteuse *f.*

rood *n.* quart d'arpent *m.*; crucifix *m.*; — screen *n.* jubé *m.*

roof *n.* toit *m.*; toiture *f.*; — of the mouth dôme du palais *m.*; — *vt.* couvrir; –ing *n.* toiture *f.*; –less *a.* sans toit, sans abri

rook *n.* (chess) tour *f.*; — *vt.* escroquer, (se) rouler, filouter

room *n.* place *f.*; espace *m.*; pièce *f.*; salle *f.*; chambre *f.*; at — temperature chambré; make — for faire place à; — *vi.* vivre en pension, vivre en garni; habiter; –er *n.* pensionnaire *m. & f.*; souslocataire *m. & f.*; –y *a.* ample; spacieux

roomette *n.* (rail.) cabine de wagon-lits *f.*

roommate *n.* compagnon de chambre *m.*

roost *n.* perchoir, juchoir *m.*; — *vi.* se percher, se jucher; –er *n.* coq *m.*

root *n.* racine *f.*; fond *m.*; source *f.*; —

beer (sorte de) boisson gazeuse *f.*; square — racine carrée *f.*; take — prendre racine; — *st.* enraciner; — for (sports) être partisan de; — out déraciner; extirper; –ed *a.* cloué, figé

rope *n.* corde *f.*; cordage *m.*; cordon *m.*; — *vt.* lier; corder

ropemaker *n.* cordier *m.*

rosary *n.* rosaire *m.*; (eccl.) chapelet *m.*

rose *n.* rose *f.*; (color) rose *m.*; — window (arch.) rosace *f.*; wild — églantine *f.*

rosebud *n.* bouton de rose *m.*

rosebush *n.* rosier *m.*

rose-colored *a.* couleur de rose, rosé; look through — glasses voir la vie en rose

rosemary *n.* romarin *m.*

rosin *n.* résine, colophane *f.*

roster *n.* tableau *m.*, liste *f.*

rostrum *n.* tribune *f.*

rosy *a.* couleur de rose; rose, rosé; vermeil

rot *n.* pourriture *f.*; mildiou *m.*; (fig., coll.) blague; sottise *f.* — *vi.* pourrir, se putréfier; se décomposer; (teeth) se carier; –ten *a.* pourri; (eggs) gâté; sale; (coll.) de chien; (teeth) carié

rotary *a.* de rotation; rotatif; — press *n.* rotative *f*

rotate *vi.* tourner tournoyer; pivoter; — *vt.* faire tourner; alterner; (crops) varier

rotation *n.* rotation *f.*; (agr.) assolement *m.*; in — à tour de rôle

rote *n.* routine *f.*; by — par routine; par cœur

rotogravure *n.* rotogravure *f.*

rotund *a.* rond, arrondi; –ity *n.* rondeur, rotondité *f.*

rotunda *n.* rotonde *f.*

rouge *n.* fard, rouge *m.*; — *vt.* mettre du rouge

rough *a.* rude; inégal; grossier; brutal; approximatif; — draft, — sketch ébauche *f.* croquis *m.*; premier jet *m.*; — weather gros temps *m.*; —, –en *vt.* rendre rude; —, –en *vi.* devenir rude; grossir; –ly *adv.* rudement, brutalement; à peu près, approximativement; treat –ly brutaliser, malmener; –ness *n.* rudesse *f.*; inégalité *f.*; –shod, ride –shod over fouler aux pieds; traiter brutalement

roughage *n.* matières cellulosique *f. pl.*

round *a.* rond, circulaire; (tone) plein; — numbers chiffres ronds *m. pl.*; — table table ronde *f.*; — trip *a.* & *n.* aller et retour *m.*; — *n.* rond, cercle *m.*; tour *m.* tournée *f.*; (mil.) ronde *f.*; salve *f.*; (mus.) canon *m.*; (boxing) round *m.*; — *vt.* arrondir; — up *vt.* rassembler; — *adv.* autour de; à la ronde; — *prep.* par, autour de; –ed *a.* arrondi; rebondi; –ness *n.* rondeur *f.*; — steak *n.* bifteck pris dans le jarret *m.*

roundabout *a.* indirect, détourné

roundhouse *n.* (rail.) remise pour locomotives *n.*

round-shouldered *a.* voûté

round-the-clock *a.* jour et nuit

roundup *n.* rassemblement *m.*

rouse *vt.* réveiller, éveiller; remuer; mettre en colère; — *vi.* se réveiller

rousing *a.* entraînant; bon, grand

rout *n.* déroute *f.*; — *vt.* mettre en déroute

route *n.* route *f.*; itinéraire *m.*; direction *f.*

routine *n.* routine *f.*; — *a.* courant

rove *vi.* rôder, errer, vagabonder; — *vt.* parcourir, errer par; –r *n.* vagabond *n.*

roving *a.* vagabond, errant

row *n.* rang *m.*, rangée, file, ligne *f.*; (agr.) rayon *m.*; — *vi.* ramer; nager, canoter; — *vt.* conduire à l'aviron; –er *n.* rameur *m.*; canotier *m.*; –ing *n.* canotage *m.*

rowboat *n.* bateau à rames *m.*

royal *a.* royal (*pl.* royaux); du roi; princier; –ist *n.* royaliste *m.* & *f.*; –ly *adv.* royalement; –ty *n.* royauté *f.*; redevance *f.*, droits d'auteur *m. pl.*

r.p.m.: revolutions per minute *n.* tours par minute *m. pl.*

rub *n.* frottement *m.*; friction *f.*; difficulté *f.*; — *vt.* frotter; frictionner; — *vi.* (se) frotter; — down frictionner; — out effacer

rubber *n.* caoutchouc *m.*; gomme *f.*; (cards) robre *m.*; (person) masseur *m.*, masseuse *f.*; — band élastique, bracelet de caoutchouc, ruban de caoutchouc *m.*; — stamp timbre en caoutchouc, tampon *m.*; –ize *vt.* caoutchouter

rubberneck *n.* & *a.* badaud *m.*; (coll.) touriste *m.* & *f.*; — *vi.* badauder

rubbish *n.* décombres *m. pl.*, ordures *f. pl.*; rebuts *m. pl.*; débris *m. pl.*; blague, bêtise *f.*; fatras *m.*

rubble *n.* rocaille *f.*; blocaille *f.*

rubric *n.* rubrique *f.*

rudder *n.* gouvernail *m.*

ruddy *a.* rouge, rougeâtre; coloré

rude *a.* impoli, mal élevé; grossier; rude; violent; –ness *n.* impolitesse *f.*; grossièreté *f.*; rudesse *f.*

rudiment *n.* rudiment *m.*; –s *pl.* éléments, rudiments *m. pl.*; –ary *a.* rudimentaire

rue *vt.* regretter, se repentir de; — *n.* rue *f.*; –ful *a.* triste; déplorable

ruff *n.* fraise *f.*

ruffian *n.* brute *f.*; bandit, brigand *m.*

ruffle *n.* volant *m.*, ruche *f.*; (fig.) trouble *m.*; (drum) roulement *m.*; — *vt.* troubler; froisser; plisser; rucher

rug *n.* tapis *m.*; bedside — descente de lit *f.*

rugged *a.* rude; raboteux; solide; –ness *n.* rudesse *f.*; aspérité *f.*

ruin *n.* ruine *f.*; go to — tomber en ruine; — *vt.* ruiner; perdre; abîmer; –ation *n.* ruine, perte *f.*; –ed *a.* abîmé; ruiné; en ruines

ruinous *a.* ruineux

rule *n.* règle *f.*; règlement *m.*; autorité *f.*; ordonnance *f.*; décision *f.*; as a — en général; en principe; slide — règle à calcul *f.*; — *vt.* régler (sur), régir; décider; tracer à la règle; — *vi.* régner; — out éliminer, écarter; –r *n.* souverain *m.*; roi *m.*; (measuring) règle *f.*, mètre *m.*

rule of thumb *n.* approximation *f.*

ruling *a.* dirigeant; dominant; — *n.* décision, ordonnance *f.*

rum *n.* rhum *m.*; –runner *n.* contrebandier d'alcool *m.*

Rumania *n.* Roumanie *f.*; –n *a.* & *n.* Roumain

rumble n. grondement m.; grouillement m.; (coll.) bagarre f.; — seat n. banquette arrière f.; — vi. gronder; grouiller

ruminate vi. ruminer; méditer

rummage n. choses usagées f. pl., objets usagés m. pl.; — sale vente d'objets usagés f.; — vt. fouiller

rumor n. bruit m., rumeur f.; — vt., it is —ed that le bruit court que

rump n. croupe f.; — steak n. romsteck m.

rumple vt. froisser, chiffonner

rumpus n. chahut, chamaillis, fracas m.

run n. course f.; cours m., marche f.; suite f.; parcours, trajet m.; libre accès m.; durée f.; (fish) remonte f.; (luck) veine f.; (stocking) point m.; (sports) point m.; libre accès m.; maille partie f.; first — a. (movies) en exclusivité; in the long — à la longue; on the — à courir; qui court; qui s'enfuit; — vi. courir; fuir, s'enfuir. se sauver; couler; marcher, fonctionner; (eyes) pleurer; (fish) remonter; (material) déteindre; durer; (pol.) être candidat, poser sa candidature; — vt. faire courir; diriger; tenir; — across rencontrer, tomber sur; — along longer; filer, s'en aller; — an errand faire une course; — a red light brûler un feu rouge; — a temperature avoir de la fièvre; — away se sauver, s'échapper, s'enfuir; — away with enlever; — down descendre en courant; couler; délabrer; — for it se sauver; — into rencontrer; heurter; — on continuer; — out expirer; s'épuiser; cesser; prendre fin; — over écraser; déborder; — through parcourir; transpercer; (money) manger, gaspiller; — up monter en courant; laisser accumuler; — up against se heurter contre, se briser contre; avoir à lutter avec; —ner n. coureur m.; courrier m.; galet m.; —ning a. courant; continu, soutenu; de suite; —ning n. course f.; marche f., fonctionnement m.; direction f.; —ning board marchepied m.

run-down a. épuisé; déchargé; délabré; — n. (coll.) résumé m., explication f.

rung n. traverse f., barreau, échelon m.

runner-up n. deuxième, accessit m.

run of the mill a. ordinaire, commun

runt n. avorton, nain m.

runway n. piste f.

rupture n. rupture f.; hernie f.; — vt. rompre; — vi. se rompre; —d a. rompu; hernié

rural a. rural; de la campagne; agreste; champêtre

rush n. ruée f.; bond m.; hâte f.; (bot.) jonc m.; — hours heures d'affluence f. pl.; — order commande urgente f.; — vi. se précipiter, s'élancer; se dépêcher; — vt. dépêcher; faire (quelque chose) d'urgence

rusk n. biscotte f.

russet a. roussâtre; rustique

Russia n. Russie f.; U.R.S.S. f.; —n a. & n. russe; Soviétique

rust n. rouille f.; — vi. & vt. (se) rouiller; —y a. rouillé; rouilleux; —proof a. antirouille; inoxydable

rustic a. agreste, rustique; — n. compagnard, paysan m.; -ate vi. vivre à la campagne, se faire campagnard

rustle n. froissement m.; — vi. bruire; — vt. froisser; faire bruire

rut n. ornière f.; routine f.

rutabaga n. rutabaga m.

ruthless a. impitoyable; brutal; -ly adv. sans pitié; -ness n. dureté, cruauté, inhumanité f.

rye n. seigle m.; (drink) whisky de seigle, whisky irlandais m.; — bread pain de seigle m.

S

Saar n. Sarre f.; -lander n. Sarrois m.

Sabbath n. sabbat m.; dimanche m.

saber, sabre n. sabre m.

sable n. zibeline f.; (heraldry) sable m.

sabotage n. sabotage m.; — vt. saboter

saccharin n. saccharine f.

sack n. sac m.; pillage m.; — vt. mettre en sac; saccager, piller

sackcloth n. toile à sacs f.; toile d'emballage f.; sac m.

sacrament n. sacrement m.; -al a. sacramental

sacred a. sacré; saint; consacré

sacrifice n. sacrifice m., immolation f.; offrande f.; (com.) vente à perte; — vt. sacrifier, immoler; renoncer à; (com.) vendre à perte

sacrificial a. sacrificatoire

sacrilege n. sacrilège m.

sacrilegious a. sacrilège

sacristan n. sacristan m.

sacristy n. sacristie f.

sacrosanct a. sacro-saint

sad a. triste; morne; —den vt. attrister; -ly adv. tristement; très, fort; -ness n. tristesse f.

saddle n. selle f.; -bag n. sacoche, musette f.; -cloth n. housse de cheval f.; — horse n. cheval de selle m.; — vt. seller; charger; be —d with avoir sur le dos

safe n. coffre-fort m.; — a. sauf; sûr; à l'abri; sans danger; — and sound sain et sauf; -ly adv. sans danger; sans accident; à coup sûr; -ness n. sûreté; sécurité f.; -ty n. sûreté, sécurité f.; -ty catch cran de sûreté; — pin épingle de sûreté f.; -ty valve soupape de sûreté f.

safe-conduct n. sauf-conduit m.

safe-deposit box n. (bank) coffre-fort m.

safeguard n. sauvegarde f.; — vt. sauvegarder

safekeeping n. bonne garde f.

safety island n. refuge; refuge pour piétons m.

safety match n. allumette de sûreté f.

safety razor n. rasoir de sûreté m.

saffron n. safran m.

sag n. fléchissement m.; flèche f.; — vi. fléchir, s'affaisser; pendre; -ging a. fléchissant; (com.) creux

sagacious a. sage, intelligent, sagace

sagacity n. sagacité f.

sage a. sage, prudent; — n. sage m.; philosophe m.; (bot.) sauge f.

said a. ledit, susdit

sail n. voile f.; toile f.; voyage m.; promenade à la voile f.; — vt. naviguer; conduire; — vi. aller à la voile; naviguer; voguer; planer; -ing a., -ing ship voilier m.; -ing n. navigation f.; marche f.; départ m.; -or n. marin, matelot m.

sailboat n. bateau à voiles m.; canot à voiles m.

sailcloth n. toile à voile f.

saint n. saint m., sainte f.; -ed a. saint; canonisé; -ly a. saint

Saint Helena n. Sainte-Hélène f.

sake n., for the — of pour; pour l'amour de; à cause de; dans l'intérêt de

salaam n. salamalec m.; — vi. faire des salamalecs

salable a. qui peut se vendre, qui se vend bien

salacious a. lubrique, lascif; -ness n. lubricité, lascivité f.

salad n. salade f.; fruit — macédoine de fruits f.; — bowl saladier m.; — dressing sauce f.; huile f. et vinaigre m.; assaisonnement pour salade m.

salaried a. aux appointements, salarié

salary n. salaire; traitement m., appointements m. pl.

sale n. vente f.; vente de soldes f.; solde(s) m. (pl.); auction — vente aux enchères; for — à vendre; on — en vente; solde(s); -s slip n. reçu m.

salesclerk n. vendeur m., vendeuse f.

salesman n. vendeur m.; représentant m.; (commis) voyageur m.; -ship n. art de vendre m.

salesroom n. salle des ventes f.

sales tax n. impôt sur la vente m.

saleswoman n. vendeuse f.

salicylic a. salicylique

salient a. & n. saillant

saline a. salin

saliva n. salive f.; -ry a. salivaire

sallow a. jaunâtre, olivâtre

salmon n. saumon m.; — trout n. truite saumonée f.

saloon n. buvette f.; café m.; bar m.

salsify n. salsifis m.

salt n. sel m.; coarse — gros sel m.; rock — sel gemme m.; table — sel blanc m.; -ed a. salé; — water n. eau de mer f.; — vt. saler; -y a. salé; de sel

saltceller, salt shaker n. salière f.

saltine n. biscuit très salé m.

saltpetre n. salpêtre m.

salt-water a. salé, d'eau de mer

salubrious a. salubre

salutary a. salutaire

salutation n. salutation f.; salut m.

salute n. salut m.; salve f.; — vt. (guns) salver; (person) saluer

salvage n. sauvetage m.; récupération f.; relevage m.; — vt. sauver; récupérer; relever

salvation n. salut m.

salve n. onguent, baume m.; — vt. adoucir, calmer

salvo n. salve f.

samaritan n. samaritain m.

same a. même; identique; all the — tout de même; quand même; it's all the —

to me cela m'est égal; at the — time en même temps; à la fois; the — to you à vous de même; -ness n. identité f.; monotonie f.

sample n. échantillon m.; exemple m.; — vt. goûter, déguster; essayer; échantillonner; -r n. (person) échantillonneur m.; modèle m.

sampling n. choix m.

sanctify vt. consacrer; sanctifier

sanctimonious a. confit; béat

sanction n. sanction f.; consentement m.; — vt. sanctionner

sanctity n. sainteté f.

sanctuary n. sanctuaire m.; asile, refuge m.

sand n. sable m.; — vt. sablonner; sabler; poncer; passer au papier de verre; -y a. sablonneux, sableux, sablé; (hair) blond roux

sandal n. sandale f.

sandbag n. sac à terre m.; — vt. protéger par des sacs à terre

sand bar n. banc de sable m.

sandblast n. jet de sable m.; — vt. décaper

sand box n. boîte à sable f.

sandpaper n. papier de verre m.; — vt. poncer, doucir, passer au papier de verre

sand pit n. sablière f.

sandstone n. grès m.

sandstorm n. tempête de sable f., simoun m.

sandwich n. sandwich m.; — man homme-affiches m.; — vt. intercaler; serrer

sane a. sain (d'esprit); raisonnable; sensé

sanforize vt. rendre irrétrécissable

sanguinary a. sanguinaire

sanitarium n. sanatorium m.

sanitary a. sanitaire; hygiénique

sanitation n. système sanitaire m.; hygiène f.

sanity n. santé (d'esprit) f.

San Marino n. Saint-Marin m.

Sanscrit a. & n. sanscrit m.

sap n. sève f.; (mil.) sape f.; — vt. saper, miner; -per n. sapeur m.

sapling n. jeune arbre m.

Saracen n. & a. Sarrasin m.

sarcasm n. sarcasme m.; ironie f.

sarcastic a. sarcastique

sarcophagus n. sarcophage m.

Sardinia n. Sardaigne f.

sash n. ceinture f.; écharpe f.; cadre, (window) châssis m.

Satan n. Satan m.

satanic a. satanique

satchel n. sacoche f.; valise f.

sateen n. satinette f.

satellite n. satellite m.

satiate vt. rassasier (de); — a. rassasié

satiation, satiety n. satiété f.

satin n. satin m.; — a. satiné; de satin; -y a. satiné

satirical a. satirique

satirist n. auteur satirique m.

satirize vt. & vi. satiriser

satisfaction n. satisfaction f.; contentement m.; réparation f.; dédommagement m.

satisfactory a. satisfaisant; acceptable

satisfy vt. & vi. satisfaire, contenter; remplir; faire réparation; suffire à; convaincre

saturate vt. saturer; tremper; become —d a'imprégner

saturation n. saturation f.; imprégnation f.

Saturday n. samedi m.

saucedish n. saucière f.

saucepan n. casserole f.

saucer n. soucoupe f.; flying — soucoupe volante f.

saucy a. impertinent; insolent; effronté

Saudi Arabia n. Arabie Soudite f.

sauerkraut n. choucroute f.

saunter vi. flâner, aller lentement

sausage n. saucisse f.; saucisson m.; — meat n. chair à saucisse f.

savage a. sauvage; brutal; féroce; — n. sauvage m. & f.; -ry n. sauvagerie f.; brutalité f.; férocité f.

save vt. sauver; préserver; protéger; réserver, retenir; économiser, mettre de côté; éviter; épargner; — prep. sauf, excepté, à l'exception de; hormis; -r n. sauveur m.; sauveteur m.; personne économe f.

saving a. qui sauve; économe; — n. sauvetage m.; salut m.; épargne, économie f.; —s bank n. caisse d'épargne f.; —s bond n. bon d'épargne m.

Saviour n. Le Sauveur m.

savor n. saveur f.; goût m.; —vt. savourer; -y a. savoureux; piquant

saw n. scie f.; — vt. scier

sawdust n. sciure (de bois) f.

sawhorse n. chevalet m.

sawmill n. scierie f.

saw-toothed a. en dents de scie

Saxon n. & a. Saxon m.

say n. voix f.; mot m., parole f.; have one's — dire son mot; — vt. dire; parler; faire; réciter; to — nothing of sans parler de; that is to — c'est-à-dire; -ing n. proverbe, adage, dicton m.; it goes without —ing cela va de soi

scab n. croûte f.; gale f.; jaune m.; — vi. former une croûte

scabbard n. gaine f., fourreau m.

scads n. pl. (coll.) des tas m. pl.; — of beaucoup de

scaffold n. échafaud m.; -ing n. échafaudage m.

scalawag n. fripon m.

scald n. échaudure f.; — vt. échauder; blanchir; -ing n. échaudage m.; -a. bouillant, tout bouillant

scale n. écaille f.; tartre m., incrustation f.; (weight) balance f.; plat de balance m.; (measurement) échelle, graduation, série f.; cadran m.; règle m.; étendue f.; (mus.) gamme f.; on a large — en grand; — a. à l'échelle; — vt. écailler; escalader; dessiner à l'échelle; établir à l'échelle; — vi. s'écailler; peser

scaling n. escalade f.; graduation f.

scallion n. ciboule f.

scallop n. coquille (Saint-Jacques) f.; pétoncle m.; (sewing) dentelure f.; feston m.; — vt. faire cuire en coquille;

(sewing) découper, festonner

scalp n. épicrâne m.; scalpe m.; -er n. trafiqueur m.; — vt. scalper; (coll.) vendre des billets à des prix exorbitants

scalpel n. scalpel m.

scaly a. écailleux

scamp n. vaurien, garnement m.

scamper vi. courir vite; se sauver

scan vt. scruter; parcourir; (verse) scander; -ner n. analyseur m., (radar) antenne tournante f.; -ning a. analyseur, explorateur

scandal n. scandale m.; médisance f.; -ize vt. scandaliser; -ous a. scandaleux; diffamatoire

scandalmonger n. médisant m.

Scandinavia n. Scandinavie f.; -n a. & n. scandinave m. & f.

scant a. à peine rempli; modique

scantily adv. à peine; insuffisamment

scanty a. insuffisant; étroit; sommaire

scapegoat n. bouc émissaire m.

scapular n. scapulaire m.

scar n. cicatrice f.; — vi. se cicatriser

scarce a. rare; -ly adv. à peine; ne . . . guère; presque (pas)

scarcity n. manque m.; rareté f.; disette f.

scare vt. épouvanter, effrayer, faire peur à, effarer

scarecrow n. épouvantail m.

scarf n. écharpe f., fichu m.; cache-nez m.; foulard m.

scarlet a. & n. écarlate f.; — fever scarlatine f.

scathing a. mordant, acerbe, cinglant

scatter vt. disperser; éparpiller, diffuser; — vi. se disperser; s'éparpiller; -ed a. dispersé; épars; -ing n. petit nombre m.

scatterbrained a. évaporé, écervelé

scavenger n. balayeur m.

scenario n. scénario m.

scene n. scène f.; lieu m.; décor m.; paysage m.; -ry n. paysage m.; (theat.) décor m.

scenic a. scénique

scent n. odeur f.; parfum m., senteur f.; piste, trace f.; — vt. parfumer; flairer; -ed a. parfumé

scepter n. sceptre m.

sceptic n. sceptique m. & f.; -al a. sceptique; -ism n. scepticisme m.

schedule n. horaire m.; liste f.; tarif m.; programme, plan m.; -d a. dans le programme; be -d devoir

scheme n. schéma m.; combinaison f.; projet, plan m.; intrigue, machination f.; — vt. projeter; intriguer; comploter; -r n. intrigant m.

scheming n. machinations f. pl.; — a. intrigant

schism n. schisme m.

schizophrenia n. schizophrénie f.

scholar n. érudit, lettré, savant m.; boursier m.; -ly a. érudit, savant; -ship n. bourse f.; érudition, science f.; savoir m.

scholastic a. scolaire; (phil.) scolastique; -ism n. scolastique f.

school n. école f.; académie f.; faculté;

classe *f.*; (fish) troupe de poissons *f.*; elementary — école primaire *f.*; high — école secondaire (supérieure) *f.*; private — école libre *f.*; — *vt.* instruire, former; enseigner; –ing *n.* instruction, éducation, enseignement *m.*; formation *f.*; — *a.* scolaire, classique

schoolbook *n.* livre de classe, livre classique *m.*

schoolboy *n.* écolier, élève *m.*

schoolgirl *n.* écolière, élève *f.*

schoolhouse *n.* école *f.*

schoolroom *n.* salle de classe *f.*

schoolteacher *n.* instituteur *m.*, institutrice *f.*

schooner *n.* goélette *f.*, schooner *m.*; (glass) chopine *f.*

sciatica *n.* sciatique *f.*

scientific *a.* scientifique; de science

scientist *n.* homme de science, savant *m.*

scimitar *n.* cimeterre *m.*

scintillate *vi.* étinceler, scintiller

scissors *n. pl.* ciseaux *m. pl.*

sclerosis *n.* sclérose *f.*

scoff *vi.* se moquer; — *vt.* tourner en dérision; –ing *n.* moquerie, raillerie *f.*

scold *vt. & vi.* gronder; — *n.* grondeuse *f.*; –ing *a.* grondeur; –ing *n.* gronderie *f.*; –ingly *adv.* en grondant

scoop *n.* cuiller *f.*; pelle *f.*; main *f.*; (journalism) primeur *f.*; nouvelle(s) *f.* (pl.); — *vt.* excaver; ramasser; écoper

scoot *vi.* filer; –er *n.* patinette, trottinette *f.*; motor –er scooter *m.*

scope *n.* portée, étendue *f.*; champ *m.*

scorch *vt.* roussir, brûler; dessécher; — *vi.* roussir; –er *n.* journée d'une chaleur accablante *f.*; –ed *a.* brûlé; –ing *a.* brûlant; torride

score *n.* entaille *f.*; compte *m.*; sujet *m.*; score *m.*, points *m. pl.*, marque *f.*; (mus.) partition *f.*; (number) vingtaine *f.*; — *vt.* entailler, encocher; compter; marquer; blâmer; faire; (mus.) orchestrer

scorn *n.* dédain, mépris *m.*; — *vt. & vi.* dédaigner, mépriser; –ful *a.* dédaigneux

Scot *n.* Écossais *m.*

scotch *n.* scotch, whisky écossais *m.*; — *vt.* faire manquer, faire avorter; mettre fin à

Scotch *a. & n.* écossais *m.*; — terrier terrier griffon *m.*

scot-free *a.* indemne; sans frais

Scotland *n.* Écosse *f.*

Scotsman *n.* Écossais *m.*

Scottish *a. & n.* écossais *m.*

scoundrel *n.* gredin, scélérat *m.*

scour *vt.* récurer; frotter; nettoyer; parcourir; chercher, fouiller; — the country battre la campagne; –ing *n.* recurage *m.*; nettoyage *m.*

scourge *n.* fléau *m.*; — *vt.* fouetter, châtier

scout *n.* éclaireur *m.*; boy — boy scout, éclaireur *m.*; girl — éclaireuse *f.*; — *vi.* aller en reconnaissance; — *vt.* éclairer, reconnaître

scoutmaster *n.* chef de troupe *m.*

scow *n.* chaland *m.*

scowl *n.* froncement de sourcils *m.*; air menaçant *m.*; — *vi.* froncer les sourcils, se refrogner

scraggy *a.* rocailleux; abrupt, escarpé; maigre

scramble *n.* mêlée *f.*; — *vi.* se bousculer, se battre; — *vt.* brouiller; –d eggs œufs brouillés *m. pl.*

scrap *n.* fragment, petit morceau, bout *m.*; parcelle *f.*; (talk) bribes *f. pl.*; dispute, querelle *f.*; –s *pl.* restes *m. pl.*; — heap tas de ferraille *m.*; rebut *m.*; — iron ferraille *f.*; — *vt.* mettre au rebut; supprimer, desaffecter; — *vi.* se battre

scrapbook *n.* album *m.*

scrape *n.* difficulté *f.*, mauvais pas *m.*; — *vt.* gratter, racler; érafler; frotter; — *vi.* gratter, grincer; –r *n.* grattoir, racloir *m.*

scratch *n.* égratignure *f.*; coup d'ongle *m.*; rayure *f.*; grattement, grincement *m.*; (sports) scratch *m.*; (coll.) argent, fric *m.*; — paper *n.* papier à brouillon *m.*; start from — partir de zéro; — *vt.* égratigner; érafler; rayer; gratter; — *vi.* gratter, grincer

scratch-pad *n.* bloc-notes *m.*

scrawl *n.* griffonnage *m.*; — *vt.* griffonner

scrawny *a.* maigre, décharné

scream *n.* cri aigu, cri perçant *m.*; — *vi.* crier, pousser un cri (perçant), hurler; –ing *a.* perçant, qui crie

screech *n.* cri perçant *m.*; — *vi.* pousser des cris perçants; — owl *n.* chat-huant *m.*

screen *n.* écran *m.*; paravent *m.*; — *vt.* cacher, masquer; (films) mettre à l'écran; (sift) passer

screw *n.* vis *f.*; (naut.) hélice *f.*; — *vt.* visser; serrer; — *vi.* tourner; — up pincer, grimacer; tortiller

screw driver *n.* tournevis *m.*

screw thread *n.* filet *m.*

scribble *n.* griffonnage *m.*; — *vt.* griffonner

scribe *n.* copiste *m.*; scribe *m.*; — *vt.* pointer, tracer; –r *n.* pointe à tracer *f.*

scrimmage *n.* mêlée *f.*

scrip *n.* coupons, tickets, bons *m. pl.*

script *n.* écriture *f.*; scénario *m.*

script-writer *n.* scénariste *m.*

scriptural *a.* biblique, scriptural; de l'Écriture Sainte

Scripture *n.* Écriture Sainte *f.*

scrofula *n.* scrofules *f. pl.*

scroll *n.* rouleau *m.*; (arch.) volute *f.*

scrounge *vt.* récupérer, glaner

scrub *n.* nettoyage, récurage *m.*; (bot.) brousse *f.*; — *vt.* nettoyer, récurer; laver; –by *a.* rabougri

scuff *n.* nuque *f.*

scruple *n.* scrupule *m.*; hésitation *f.*

scrupulous *a.* scrupuleux; méticuleux, minutieux

scrutinize *vt.* scruter, examiner

scrutiny *n.* examen rigoureux *m.*

scuff *vt.* frotter, user

scuffle *n.* mêlée, bagarre *f.*; — *vi.* se battre, se bousculer scullery n. laverie f.; — maid souillon f.

sculptor n. sculpteur m.

sculpture n. sculpture f.; — vt. sculpter

scum n. écume f.; rebut m.

scurry vi. se hâter, courir

scurvy n. scorbut m.

scuttle vt. (naut.) saborder; — vi., — away filer; — n. seau, panier m.

scythe n. faux f.; — vt. faucher

sea n. mer f.; océan m.; at — en mer; désorienté; by the — au bord de la mer; heavy — grosse mer f.; high —s le large m.; on the high —s au grand large; — a. de mer, de la mer; — breeze brise du large f.; — captain capitaine de vaisseau m.; — legs pied marin m.; — level niveau de la mer; — lion otarie f., phoque m.; — urchin oursin m.; — wall digue f.

seaboard n. côte f.; bord de la mer

seacoast n. côte f., littoral m.

seafarer n. marin, matelot m.

seafaring a. marin, de la mer

seafood n. poisson de mer m.; coquillages m.; — pl., fruits de la mer m. pl.

sea-going a. maritime; de haute mer

seal n. sceau m.; cachet m.; (zool.) phoque m.; — vt. sceller; cacheter; fermer; -ing a. — wax cire à cacheter f.

sealskin a. & n. peau de phoque f.

seam n. couture f.; joint m.; couche, veine f.; — vt. couturer; -less a. sans couture

seaman n. marin, matelot m.; -ship n. art de naviguer m.

seamstress n. couturière f.

seaplane n. hydravion m.

seaport n. port de mer m.

sea power n. puissance maritime f.

scar vt. dessécher, flétrir; — a. fané, séché f.

search n. recherche f.; visite f.; — warrant mandat de perquisition m.; in — of à la recherche de; — vt. chercher (dans); fouiller; (customs) visiter; perquisitionner; sonder; — vi. chercher, rechercher; -ing a. pénétrant, minutieux

searchlight n. projecteur, phare m.

sea shell n. coquillage m., coquille f.

seasick a. qui a le mal de mer; -ness n. mal de mer m.

seaside n. bord de la mer m.

season n. saison f.; temps m.; in — de saison; off — morte-saison f.; out of — hors de saison, mal à propos; — ticket carte d'abonnement f.; — vt. assaisonner; mûrir; conditionner; tempérer; — vi. mûrir; sécher; -able a. de saison; à propos; -al a. saisonnier, des saisons; -ed a. assaisonné; mûr; sec; expérimenté; -ing n. assaisonnement m.; condiment m.

seat n. siège m.; place f.; banquette f.; fond m.; derrière m.; centre, foyer m.; — cover n. housse f.; — vt. asseoir; be -ed s'asseoir; être assis; -ing n. places f. pl.; disposition des places f.; -ing capacity nombre de places m.

seaward(s) adv. vers la mer

seaweed n. varech m.

seaworthy a. en état de tenir la mer

secede vi. faire scission, faire sécession

secession n. sécession f.

seclude vt. éloigner, tenir éloigné, tenir retiré; — oneself se retirer; -d a. retiré

seclusion n. retraite, solitude f.

second n. seconde f.; instant m.; second m.; (com.) article de deuxième qualité, deuxième choix m.; — a. second, deuxième; autre, nouveau; — floor premier étage m.; — hand (watch, clock) trotteuse f.; — lieutenant sous-lieutenant m.; — nature seconde nature f.; — sight clairvoyance f.; — vt. seconder; (debate) appuyer; -ary a. secondaire; -ly adv. en second lieu, deuxièmement

second-class a. (rail.) de seconde (classe); de second ordre; de deuxième qualité

secondhand a. de seconde main; usagé; d'occasion; — dealer brocanteur m.

second-rate a. de qualité inférieure; de second ordre; médiocre

secrecy n. mystère, secret m.; discrétion f.

secret a. secret; caché; — n. secret m.; keep a — garder un secret; in —, -ly adv. en secret, secrètement; -ive a. réservé

secretary n. secrétaire m. & f.; private — secrétaire particulier m.

secrete vt. sécréter; cacher

secretion n. sécrétion f.

sect n. secte f.; -arian a. & n. sectaire m.; -arianism n. esprit sectaire m.

section n. section f.; coupe, tranche f.; profil m.; division, partie f.; (city) quartier m.; (store) rayon m.; — vt. sectionner, diviser en sections; -al a. en sections; (drawing) en coupe

sector n. secteur m.

secular a. séculier, laïque, profane, temporel; -ize vt. séculariser

secure a. assuré, en sûreté; hors de danger; à l'abri (de); ferme, fixe, solide; — vt. obtenir; se procurer; retenir; mettre en sûreté; fixer, assujettir

security n. sécurité, sûreté f.; (com.) gage, nantissement m., caution f.

securities n. pl. fonds, titres m. pl., valeurs f. pl.; actions f. pl.

sedan n. voiture à 6 places f.; (voiture à) conduite intérieure f.; — chair n. chaise à porteurs f.

sedate a. posé, composé; -ness n. calme m., tranquillité f.

sedative a. & n. sédatif m.

sedentary a. sédentaire

sediment n. sédiment m.; lie f.; -ary a. sédimentaire; -ation n. sédimentation f.

sedition n. sédition f.

seditious a. séditieux

seduce vt. séduire, dépraver

seduction n. séduction f.; charme m.

seductive a. séduisant; -ness n. séduction f.; charmes m. pl.

see n. (eccl.) siège épiscopale m.; — vt. voir; apercevoir; observer; regarder; comprendre; envisager; trouver; visiter; as far as I can — à ce que je vois; — fit trouver bon; — to it faire; — to the door accompagner à la porte; éconduire; — about s'occuper de; — off dire adieu; — through pénétrer; persévérer; -ing *a.* voyant; -ing that vu que, attendu que; -ing *n.* vue, vision *f.*; -ing is believing voir c'est croire

seed *n.* graine *f.*; semence *f.*; pépin *m.*; (fig.) germe *m.*; — *vt.* semer, ensemencer; -ling *n.* jeune plante *f.*; plante semée *f.*; -y *a.* d'aspect minable

seek *vt.* chercher, rechercher; demander; essayer, tâcher; — out rechercher

seem *vi.* sembler, paraître; avoir l'air; -ing *a.* apparent; -ingly *adv.* apparemment, en apparence; -ly *a.* convenable, bienséant

seep *vi.* suinter; fuir; s'infiltrer; -age *n.* suintement *m.*; fuite *f.*; infiltration *f.*

seer *n.* prophète *m.*; visionnaire *m.*

seesaw *n.* bascule *f.*; balançoire *f.*; — *vi.* basculer

seethe *vi.* bouillir, bouillonner; grouiller

segregate *vt.* séparer; mettre à part; — *vi.* se grouper à part

segregation *n.* ségrégation, séparation *f.*

Seine *n.* la Seine *f.*

seismograph *n.* sismographe *m.*

seize *vt.* saisir; s'emparer de; empoigner; prendre

seizure *n.* saisie, prise *f.*; accès *m.*; attaque *f.*

seldom *adv.* rarement

select *vt.* choisir; — *a.* choisi; de choix; d'élite; -ion *n.* choix *m.*; sélection *f.*; recueil *m.*; -ive *a.* sélectif; -ivity *n.* sélectivité *f.*

selectman *n.* conseiller municipal *m.*

selenium *n.* sélénium *f.*

self *a.* même; — *n.* moi *m.*

self-acting *a.* automatique

self-addressed *a.* adressé par le destinataire

self-apparent *a.* évident; qui va de soi

self-assurance *n.* confiance en soi

self-assured *a.* posé; maître de soi

self-centered *a.* égocentrique

self-confidence *n.* confiance en soi

self-confident *a.* sûr de soi

self-conscious *a.* embarrassé, gêné; -ness *n.* embarras *m.*; gêne *f.*

self-contained *a.* réservé, circonspect; (technical) incorporé

self-control *n.* maîtrise de soi *f.*; sangfroid *m.*; -led *a.* réservé, maître de soi; (technical) auto-entretenu

self-defense *n.* (law) légitime défense *f.*

self-denial *n.* renoncement *m.*; abnégation *f.*

self-discipline *n.* discipline *f.*

self-educated *a.* autodidacte

self-esteem *n.* amour-propre *m.*

self-evident *a.* évident; qui saute aux yeux

self-explanatory *a.* qui s'explique de soi-même, clair, concis

self-expression *n.* expression de l'individu *f.*

self-governed *a.* autonome

self-government *n.* autonomie *f.*

self-help *n.* efforts personnels *m. pl.*

self-induced *a.* inspiré par l'individu

self-indulgence *n.* indulgence de soi *f.*

self-indulgent *a.* qui ne se refuse rien

selfish *a.* égoïste, intéressé; -ness *n.* égoïsme, intérêt *m.*

self-liquidating *a.* qui s'amortit; se liquidant soi-même

self-made *a.* parvenu par ses propres moyens

self-possessed *a.* maître de soi

self-possession *n.* maîtrise de soi *f.*; sangfroid, aplomb *m.*

self-preservation *n.* conservation de soi-même *f.*

self-propelled *a.* autopropulsé

self-propelling *a.* automoteur

self-protection *n.* protection de soi *f.*

self-regulating *a.* à autorégulation

self-reliance *n.* indépendance *f.*

self-reliant *a.* indépendant

self-respect *n.* respect de soi *m.*; amour-propre *m.*

self-restraint *n.* retenue *f.*

self-righteous *a.* qui se croit juste, content de soi

self-sacrifice *n.* abnégation *f.*

selfsame *a.* identique

self-satisfied *a.* suffisant; content de soi

self-service *n.* & *a.* libre-service *m.*

self-styled *a.* soi-disant

self-sufficient *a.* suffisant en soi

self-supporting *a.* indépendant, qui gagne sa propre vie

self-taught *a.* autodidacte

sell *vt.* vendre; -out vendre tout; épuiser; -er *n.* vendeur *m.*, vendeuse *f.*; -ing *n.* vente *f.*

seltzer *n.* eau de selts *f.*

selvage *n.* lisière *f.*

semantic *a.* sémantique; -s *n. pl.* sémantique *f.*

semaphore *n.* sémaphore *m.*

semblance *n.* apparence, semblant *m.*

semester *n.* semestre *m.*

semiannual *a.* semi-annuel; -ly *adv.* tous les six mois

semiautomatic *a.* semi-automatique

semicircle *n.* demi-cercle *m.*

semicolon *n.* point et virgule *m.*

semifinal *n.* demi-finale *f.*

semimonthly *a.* bimensuel

seminar *n.* séminaire, groupe d'études *m.*

seminary *n.* séminaire *m.*

semiofficial *a.* demi-official

Semitic *a.* sémitique

semitransparent *a.* demi-transparent

semitropical *a.* subtropical

senate *n.* sénat *m.*

senator *n.* sénateur *m.*; -ial *a.* sénatorial

send *vt.* envoyer; expédier; — away, — back renvoyer; — for envoyer chercher; faire venir; — in faire entrer; remettre; — out lancer; émettre; jeter; -er *n.* expéditeur, envoyeur *m.*; -ing *n.* expédition *f.*; envoi *m.*

Senegal *n.* Sénégal *m.*

senile *a.* sénile

senility *n.* sénilité *f.*

senior *a.* aîné; père; supérieur; ancien;

— n. aîne m.; ancien m.; (Amer. college) étudiant de quatrième année m.; -ity n. ancienneté f.

sensation n. sensation f.; impression f.; sentiment m.; -al a. sensationnel;

sense n. sens m.; sensation f.; sentiment m.; raison f.; common — sens commun m.; make — (out) of comprendre; talk — parler raison; — of smell odorat m.; -s pl. sens m. pl.; raison, tête f.; — vt. sentir, pressentir; -less a. insensé, déraisonnable; (unconscious) sans connaissance

sensibility n. sensibilité f.

sensible a. raisonnable, sensé; pratique; perceptible, sensible

sensitive a. sensible; -ness n. sensibilité f.

sensitivity n. sensibilité f.

sensitize vt. sensibiliser; -ed a. sensible

sensory a. sensoriel

sensual a. sensuel; voluptueux; -ity n. sensualité f.

sensuous a. voluptueux

sentence n. phrase f.; (law) sentence f., arrêt m.; peine f.; prison — peine de prison; — vt. condamner

sentiment n. sentiment m.; opinion f.; -al a. sentimental; -ality n. sentimentalité f.

sentinel n. sentinelle f.; factionnaire m.

sentry n. factionnaire m.; sentinelle f.

separable a. séparable

separate a. séparé; distinct; détaché; particulier, individuel; — vt. séparer; détacher, dégager; — vi. se séparer; se détacher; se quitter

separation n. séparation f.

sepia n. sépia f.

September n. septembre m.

septic a. septique; — tank fosse septique f.

septicemia n. (med.) septicémie f.

sepulchral a. sépulcral

sepulchre n. sépulcre m.

sequel n. suite f.; conséquence f.

sequence n. suite, série, succession f.

sequin n. séquin m.; (decoration) paillette f.

Serbia n. Serbie f.

serenade n. sérénade f.; — vt. donner une sérénade à

serene a. serein; calme, tranquille

serenity n. sérénité f.; calme m.; tranquillité f.

serf n. serf m.; -dom n. servage m.

sergeant n. sergent m.; — at arms huissier m.; first — sergent chef, adjudant m.; master — adjudant chef m.

serial a. de série; — number numéro de série; — n. roman-feuilleton m.

series n. série, suite f.; (mus.) gamme f.; in — en série

serious a. sérieux; grave; -ly adv. sérieusement, gravement; grièvement; take -ly prendre au sérieux; -ness n. gravité f.; sérieux m.

sermon n. sermon m.; -ize vt. & vi. sermonner

serpent n. serpent m.; -ine a. serpentin, serpentant, sinueux

serrate a. en dents de scie

serried a. serré, compact

serum n. sérum m.

servant n. domestique m. & f.; servant m., servante f.; serviteur m.; civil — fonctionnaire m. & f.

serve vt. servir; desservir; suffire; (time) faire des années de prison; — vi. servir; — as servir de; -r n. serveur (serveuse)

service n. service m.; emploi m.; administration f.; utilité f.; (auto.) entretien m.; dépannage m.; (eccl.) office m.; (law) délivrance f.; at your — à votre disposition; be of — être utile; servir; — station n. station-service f., poste d'essence m.; — vt. entretenir; -able a. utilisable

serviceman n. soldat m.

servicing n. entretien m.; dépannage m.

servile a. servile; bas

servility n. servilité f.; bassesse f.

serving n. service m.

servitor n. serviteur m.

servitude n. servitude f., esclavage m.; prison f.

sesame n. sésame m.

session n. séance f.; session f.; be in — siéger

set n. jeu m.; série f.; ensemble m.; collection f.; coterie f.; (dishes) service m.; (hair) mise f.; (radio) poste m.; (theat.) décor m.; scène f.; — vt. poser, placer, mettre, asseoir; donner; ajuster; régler; (bone) remettre, réduire; (date) fixer; (gem) enchâsser; (type) composer; — vi. se coucher; prendre; se figer; — aside écarter, mettre à part; — back remettre; retarder; — forth avancer, exposer; partir, se mettre en route; — out se mettre en route; — the table mettre le couvert; — up établir; monter; — upon attaquer; — a. fixe; figé; réglé; imposé; déterminé; prêt; -ting a. couchant; -ting n. coucher m.; mise f.; réglage m.; montage m.; prise f.; (bone) réduction f.; (gem) monture f.; (theat.) décor m.; (type) composition f.; -ting up n. établissement m.; installation f.

setback n. revers m.; recul m.

setscrew n. vis de serrage f.

settee n. canapé m.

setter n. setter, chien d'arrêt m.

settle vt. arranger; résoudre, décider, déterminer; terminer; établir; coloniser; calmer; — vi. s'établir; s'installer; se calmer; déposer; se précipiter; — down se ranger; se caser; se calmer; -ment n. colonie f.; paiement m.; règlement m.; accord m.; -r n. colon m.

setup n. organisation f.; arrangement m.; montage m.

seven a. & n. sept; -teen a. & n. dix-sept; -teenth a. & n. dix-septième; -th a. & n. septième; -ty a. & n. soixante-dix

seventy-one soixante et onze

seventy-two soixante-douze

sever vt. rompre; couper; -ance n. séparation f.

several a. plusieurs; divers; différent; séparé

severance n. séparation f.

severe a. sévère; rigoureux; austère

severity n. sévérité f.; rigueur f.; austérité f.

sew vt. coudre; -ing n. couture f.; ouvrage m.; -ing machine machine à coudre f.

sewage n. eaux d'égout f. pl.

sewer n. égout m.

sex n. sexe m.; -ual a. sexuel; -uality n. sexualité f.

sextant n. sextant m.

sextet n. sextuor m.

sexton n. sacristain m.

shabby a. usé, râpé; minable; mesquin

shack n. case, cabane, hutte f.

shackle vt. enchaîner, entraver; -s n. pl. fers m. pl.

shad n. alose f.

shade n. ombre f.; nuance f.; (lamp) abatjour m.; (window) store m.; — vt. ombrager; nuancer; ombrer; -d a. ombragé; ombré

shadiness n. ombre f.; ombrage m.

shadow n. ombre f.; — vt. ombrager; (person) filer; -y a. vague; mystérieux

shady a. ombreux; ombragé; (coll.) louche

shaft n. puits m.; (elevator) cage f.; arbre m.; souche f.; manche m.; flèche f., trait m.; (arch.) tige f.; (light) rayon m.

shaggy a. poilu; touffu; à longs poils

shake n. secousse f.; — of the head hochement de tête m.; — vt. secouer; agiter; hocher; ébranler; — vi. trembler, trembloter; chanceler; — a fist at menacer du poing; — hands with serrer la main à; — down faire tomber; extorquer; — off secouer; se défaire de; -n a. bouleversé, confus; -r n. (salt) salière f.; (cocktail) frappe-cocktail m.

shake-up n. bouleversement m.; renversement m.; remaniement m.

shaking a. tremblant; (voice) ému; — n. tremblement m.; secouement m.

shaky a. tremblant; chancelant; faible

shallot n. échalote f.

shallow a. peu profond; superficiel; plat; — water hauts-fonds m. pl.; -ness n. manque de profondeur m.

sham a. feint, simulé, faux; — n. feinte f.; imposture f.; — vt. feindre, simuler

shambles n. pl. carnage m.; désordre m.

shame n. honte f.; what a —! quel dommage!; — vt. humilier, faire honte à; -ful a. honteux; -less a. effronté; honteux; scandaleux

shamefaced a. penaud; honteux

shampoo n. shampooing m.; — vt. (se) laver les cheveux, donner un shampooing à

shamrock n. trèfle m.

shank n. (meat) manche f.; tibia m.

shanty n. hutte, cabane, case f.

shape n. forme f.; façon f.; out of — déformé; — vt. façonner, former; tailler; -less a. informe; -liness n. jolie taille f.; belle forme f.; symétrie f.; -ly a. bien fait, bien tourné

share n. part, portion f.; (com.) action f., titre m., (plow) soc m.; — vt. partager; avoir part à; — vi. participer

sharecropper n. métayer m.

shareholder n. actionnaire m. & f.

shark n. requin m.

sharp a. aigu, tranchant, pointu; net, marqué; vif; fin; rusé, malin; piquant; — turn tournant brusque m.; — adv., two o'clock — deux heures précises; — n. (mus.) dièse m.; -en vt. tailler; aiguiser, affiler; aviver; -ener n. aiguisoir m.; (pencil) taille-crayons m.; -(er) n. (cards) tricheur f.; -ly adv. sévèrement; vivement; nettement; brusquement; -ness n. acuité, finesse f.; sévérité f.; netteté f.; piquant m.

sharp-edged a. affilé, tranchant

sharpshooter n. tireur d'élite m.

sharp-witted a. spirituel

shatter vt. fracasser, briser; — vi. se fracasser, se briser

shatterproof a. incassable; de sécurité

shave n. action de raser f.; have a — se raser; se faire raser; have a close — (fig.) l'échapper belle; — vt. raser, faire la barbe à; planer; -r n. barbier m.; electric -r rasoir électrique m.

shaving n. action de (se) raser f.; (wood) copeau m.; — brush blaireau m.; — cream savon à barbe m.

shawl n. châle, fichu m.

she pron. elle

sheaf n. gerbe f.; (papers) liasse f.

shear vt. tondre; couper; -s n. pl. ciseaux m. pl.; cisailles f. pl.; -ing n. tondaison f.; -ing machine n. tondeuse f.

sheath n. gaine f.; fourreau m.; enveloppe f.; -e vt. rengainer; revêtir

shed n. hangar m.; baraque f.; — vt. (tears) verser; (skin) jeter; — light on éclairer; -ding n. mue f.; perte f.

sheen n. luisant, lustre m.

sheep n. mouton m., brebis f.; black — brebis galeuse f.; -ish a. penaud

sheepskin n. peau de mouton f., parchemin m.; (coll.) diplôme m.

sheer a. pur, véritable; à pic

sheet n. drap m.; (paper) feuille f.; (glass) verre à vitres m.; (metal) tôle f.; (naut.) écoute f.; (mus.) feuille de musique f.; -ing n. drap m., toile pour draps f.; tôlerie f.

shelf n. étagère, tablette f., rayon m.

shell n. (peas, nuts) écaille, cosse f.; (egg) coque f.; (empty egg) coquille f.; (earth) écorce f.; (shellfish) coquillage m.; (cannon) obus m.; (gun) cartouche f.; tortoise —, turtle — écaille f.; — vt. (nuts) écaler; (peas) écosser; (oysters) ouvrir; (mil.) bombarder

shellac n. laque, gomme-laque f.; — vt. laquer

shellfire n. tir à obus m.

shellfish n. crustacé m.

shelter n. abri m.; asile m.; — vt. abriter, protéger

shelve vt. mettre sur les rayons; classer

shelving n. bois à faire des étagères m.; toile (papier) à recouvrir les étagères f. (m.)

shepherd n. berger, pâtre m.; pasteur m.; -ess n. bergère f.; — vt. garder; mener

sherbet n. sorbet m.

sheriff n. sheriff, chef de gendarmerie m.

sherry n. vin de Xérès m.

shield n. bouclier m.; (heraldry) écu m.; (fig.) protection f.; (mech.) armature, gaine f.; blindage, capot, carter, écran m.; — vt. protéger; blinder

shift n. déplacement m.; changement m.; (industry) équipe (d'ouvriers) f.; (auto.) levier de changement de vitesse m.; (typewriter) touche à majuscules f.; — vt. déplacer; — vi. se déplacer; changer; (auto.) changer de vitesse; — for oneself se tirer d'affaire; -less a. faible; incapable; paresseux; -y a. peu digne de confiance; (eyes) fuyant

shilly-shally vi. être indécis; temporiser

shimmer vi. scintiller, reluire; — n. faible clarté f.

shimmy n. dandinement des roues avant m.; — vi. dandiner

shin n. tibia, devant de la jambe m.; -ay (up) vi. (coll.) grimper

shine n. brillant, poli m.; take a — to s'éprendre de; — vt. polir; (shoes) cirer; — vi. luire, reluire, briller; -r n. (coll.) œil poché m.

shingle n. bardeau m.; (coll.) enseigne (d'un médecin) f.

shining a. luisant; brillant, éclatant; — n. éclat m.; splendeur f.

ship n. vaisseau, navire m.; paquebot m.; — vt. envoyer, expédier; embarquer. (oars) rentrer; -ment n. cargaison f., chargement m.; envoi m., expédition f.; -per n. expéditeur m.; -ping n. envoi m., expédition f.; commerce maritime m.; -ping room n. salle d'expédition f.

ship-to shore a. — telephone liaison radio maritime f.

shipwreck n. naufrage m.; -ed a. naufragé; — vi. faire naufrage

shipyard n. chantier de construction m.

shirk vt. manquer à, éviter

shirr vt. froncer

shirt n. chemise f.; -ing n. toile à chemises f.

shirtmaker n. chemisier m.

shiver n. frisson m.; — vi. frissonner; -ing a. qui frissonne; à faire frissonner

shoal n. banc de sable m.; endroit peu profond m.; banc de poissons m.

shock n. choc m.; coup m.; secousse f.; — absorber amortisseur m.; — treatment électronarcose m.; — vt. choquer; offenser; -ing a. choquant; -proof a. à l'épreuve des secousses (persons) inébranlable

shoddy a. de mauvaise qualité, inférieur

shoe n. chaussure f.; soulier m.; (wooden) sabot m.; (horse) fer m.; — polish cirage m.; — store cordonnerie f.; (magasin de) chaussures m.; — vt. chausser; (horse) ferrer

shoehorn n. chausse-pied m.

shoelace n. lacet m.

shoemaker n. cordonnier m.

shoestring n. lacet m.; on a — (coll.) avec très peu d'argent; — potatoes pommes-allumettes f. pl.

shoe tree n. forme à chaussures f.

shoot n. rejeton, scion m.; pousse f.; partie de chasse f.; — vt. tirer, lancer; fusiller; — vi. s'élancer; se précipiter; bourgeonner, pousser; -ing n. tir m.; action de tirer f.; -ing a., -ing star étoile filante f.

shop n. boutique f., magasin m.; (industry) atelier m.; — window vitrine, devanture f.; talk — parler affaires; — vi. faire des emplettes; — for chercher à acheter; -per n. acheteur, client m.; -ping n. action de faire les emplettes; go -ping faire des emplettes; faire des courses; -ping bag filet (à provisions) m.

shopkeeper n. marchand m.; boutiquier m.

shoplifter n. voleur à l'étalage m.

shopworn a. défraîchi

shore n. rivage m., côte f.; — leave permission (d'aller à terre) f.; — vt. étayer

shore line n. ligne de côte f., littoral m.

short a. court; bref; concis; serré; — subject n. court métrage m.; be — of être à court de; manquer de; cut — couper court (à); fall — of rester au-dessous de; — circuit n. (elec.) court-circuit m.; -age n. insuffisance f.; -en vt. raccourcir; -ening n. matière grasse f.; -ly adv. bientôt; -s n. pl. short m.; caleçon court m.

shortcake n. gateau recouvert de fruits frais m.

shortchange vt. rendre la monnaie insuffisante

short-circuit vt. court-circuiter

shortcoming n. faiblesse, insuffisance f.

shorthand n. sténographie f.

shorthanded a. & adv. avec une insuffisance de personnel

short-lived a. de courte durée

shortsighted a. myope; peu prévoyant

short-tempered a. qui s'emporte facilement

short-term a. à courte échéance

shortwave a. à ondes courtes

shot n. coup (de feu) m.; portée f.; plomb m.; (med.) piqûre f.; (coll.) verre d'alcool m.

shotgun n. fusil de chasse m.; — shell cartouche chargée à plomb f.

shoulder n. épaule f.; — strap bretelle f.; — vt. mettre sur les épaules; se charger de

shoulder blade n. omoplate f.

shout n. cri m.; — vt. & vi. crier

shove n. coup m., poussée f.; — vt. pousser; bousculer; — off partir; démarrer; (naut.) pousser au large

shovel n. pelle f.; — vt. pelleter

show n. spectacle m.; étalage m.; parade f.; — window vitrine f.; — vt. montrer, faire voir; démontrer; — off étaler, faire parade de; faire valoir; se faire voir; — up révéler, démasquer; (coll.) arriver; paraître; -y a. fastueux, voyant

showcase n. vitrine f.

showdown n. explication armée f.; moment décisif m.

shower n. douche f.; pluie, averse f.; vt. accabler, combler

showman n. impresario m.; acteur m.;

–ship n. art de présenter m.

showroom n. salle de vision, salle d'exposition f.

shred n. morceau m., rognure f.; — vt. couper en petits morceaux

shrew n. mégère f.; (zool.) musaraigne f.; –ish a. acariâtre

shrewd a. fin; rusé; –ness n. finesse, ruse f.

shriek n. cri perçant m.; — vi. pousser des cris perçants

shrill a. perçant, aigu

shrimp n. crevette f.

shrine n. chapelle f.; reliquaire m., châsse f.

shrink vi. se resserrer, se rétrécir, se raccourcir; reculer; –age n. rétrécissement m.

shrivel vi. (se) rider

shroud n. linceul, drap mortuaire m.; (naut.) hauban m.; — vt. défendre, protéger; couvrir d'un drap mortuaire

Shrove Tuesday n. mardi gras m.

shrub n. arbrisseau, arbuste m.; –bery n. verdure f.; arbrisseaux m. pl.

shrug n. haussement d'épaules m.; — vt. lever, hausser

shuck vt. écosser; éplucher; — n. cosse f.

shudder n. frissonnement m.; — vi. frissonner, frémir; trembler

shuffle n. mélange m.; mouvement traînant m.; — vt. mélanger, mêler; battre; — vi. traîner les pieds

shuffleboard n. jeu de palets m.

shuffling a. évasif; (gait) qui traîne les pieds; — n. battement de cartes m.; marche traînante f.

shun vt. éviter

shunt vt. changer de voie; dévier

shut vt. fermer, renfermer; — vi. se fermer; — down faire cesser; fermer; — in renfermer, garder à l'intérieur; — off fermer, interrompre; — out garder à l'extérieur; — up renfermer; se taire; –ter n. volet m.; store m.; (phot.) obturateur m.

shutdown n. cessation f.; fermeture f.

shut-in n. malade m. & f. (qui ne peut pas quitter la maison)

shuttle n. navette f.; — vi. faire la navette

shuttlecock n. volant m.

shy vi. faire un écart; se jeter de côté; — a. réservé; timide; farouche; –ness n. réserve, timidité f.; to be — of manque de; –ly adv. timidement

shyster n. avocat malhonnête m.

Siam n. Siam m.; –ese a. & n. siamois m.

Siberia n. Sibérie f.; –n n. & a. Sibérien m.

Sicilian a. & n. sicilien m.

Sicily n. Sicile f.

sick a. malade; indisposé; dégoûté; get — tomber malade; –en vt. rendre malade, dégoûter; –en vi. tomber malade; –ly a. maladif; –ness n. mal m.; maladie f.

sickbed n. lit de malade m.

sickle n. faucille f.

sick leave n. congé de convalescence m.

sickroom n. chambre de malade f.

side n. côté m.; flanc m.; bord m.; parti m.; — by — côte à côte; on all –s de tous côtés; on one — d'un côté; — a. de côté; oblique; auxiliaire, supplémentaire; — dish entremets m.; — vi., — with appuyer, prendre le parti de

sideboard n. buffet m., desserte f.

side light n. détail révélateur, détail intéressant m.

side line n. distraction f.; intérêt secondaire m.

sidelong a. oblique

side show n. exhibition de fête foraine f.

side-step vt. esquiver, éviter; — vi. faire un écart

sideswipe vt. prendre en écharpe

sidetrack vt. écarter, dévier

sidewalk n. trottoir, pavé m.

sidewards, sideways, sidewise adv. de côté, latéralement

siding n. (rail.) voie de garage f.

sidle vi. approcher latéralement

siege n. siège m.; lay — to assiéger; raise a — lever un siège

siesta n. sieste f.

sieve n. tamis m.; — vt. tamiser; trier

sift vt. tamiser, passer au tamis; trier; examiner, juger; –er n. tamis m.

sigh n. soupir m.; — vi. soupirer; pousser un soupir

sight n. vue f.; vision f.; aspect m.; spectacle m.; (gun) mire f.; — draft n. (com.) effet à vue m.; at — à première vue; by — (com.) de vue; in — en vue; lose — of perdre de vue; on — à vue; out of — hors de vue; — unseen sans examiner d'avance; — vt. apercevoir, remarquer; –less a. aveugle

sight-see vi. visiter les curiosités; –ing n. tourisme m.; voyage m.; visites f. pl.; –r n. touriste, visiteur m.

sign n. signe m., marque f., symbole m.; enseigne f., pancarte f.; — vt. signer; — off cesser d'émettre; — off n. (radio) fin de message f.; — up enrôler, inscrire; — language n. langage par signe m.; –post n. poteau indicateur m., borne f.; –er n. signataire m. & f.

signal n. signal, signe m.; — corps n. transmissions f. pl.; — light n. (nav.) fanal m.; — lights n. pl. feux de route m. pl.; — vt. signaler; — a. signalé, insigne; –ize vt. signaler

signature n. signature f.; (end) fin de message f.

signet n. cachet m.

significance n. signification f.; importance f.

significant n. significatif, signifiant

signify vt. signifier

silage n. fourrage ensilé m.

silence n. silence m.; — vt. faire taire; –r n. amortisseur m.

silent a. silencieux; (movies) muet; — partner n. commandataire m.

silica n. silice f.; –te n. silicate m.

siliceous a. siliceux

silicone n. silicone m.

silk n. soie f.; — a. de soie; –en, –y a. soyeux

silkworm n. ver à soie m.

sill n. seuil, appui m.

silliness n. sottise f.

silly a. sot; niais, simple

silver n. argent m.; — plate argenterie f.; — a. d'argent, en argent; argenté; — vt. argenter

silver-plated a. plaqué d'argent

silversmith n. orfèvre m.

silverware n. argenterie f.

similar a. semblable; —ity n. similarité, ressemblance f.; —ly adv. de la même façon

simile n. comparaison f.

similitude n. similitude f.

simmer vi. mijoter; — vt. faire mijoter

simper n. minauderie f.; — vi. sourire niaisement

simple a. simple, naïf; pur; —ness n. simplicité f.

simple-minded a. simple, idiot

simpleton n. niais, sot m.

simplicity n. simplicité f.

simplification n. simplification f.

simplify vt. simplifier

simulate vt. feindre, simuler

simultaneous a. simultané; —ness n. simultanéité f.

sin n. péché m.; mortal — péché capital m.; original — péché originel; — vi. pécher; —ful a. pécheur; —ner n. pécheur m.

since conj. puisque; depuis que; comme; — prep. depuis; — adv. depuis

sincere n. sincère

sincerity n. sincérité f.

sine n. (math.) sinus m.

sinecure n. sinécure f.

sinew n. nerf m.; tendon m.; —y a. nerveux; vigoureux

sing vt. & vi. chanter; —er n. chanteur m.; cantatrice f.; —ing n. chant m.

singe n. roussi m.; — vt. brûler légèrement, flamber, roussir

single a. seul, particulier, singulier, simple; célibataire; — file adv. à la file indienne; —ness n. nature simple f.; sincérité f.

single-breasted a. droit, non croisé

singlehanded a. sans aide, seul

single-minded a. sincère; qui n'a qu'un seul but

singly adv. un à un

singsong n. chant monotone m.; (fig.) psalmodie f.; — a. monotone, traînant

singular n. & a. singulier m.; —ity n. singularité f.

sinister a. sinistre

sink n. évier m.; — vi. couler; s'enfoncer; s'abaisser, succomber; — vt. enfoncer; creuser; abaisser; perdre; plonger, précipiter; —er n. (fishline) poids, plomb m.; (coll.) beignet m.

sinking fund n. caisse d'amortissement f.

sinuosity n. sinuosité f.

sinuous a. sinueux

sip n. petit coup m.; gorgée f.; — vt. déguster, siroter

sir n. monsieur m.; (title) Sir, chevalier

sire n. père m.; Sire m.

siren n. sirène f.

sirloin n. aloyau m.

sirup, syrup n. sirop m.

sister n. sœur f.; (eccl.) religieuse f.; —ly a. de sœur, comme une sœur

sister-in-law n. belle-sœur f.

sit vi. s'asseoir; demeurer; siéger; être situé; — down s'asseoir; — up se dresser sur son séant; —ter n. celui qui est assis m.; garde des enfants f.; —ting n. séance f.; -ting room salon m.

sit-down strike n. grève sur le tas f.

site n. site, emplacement m.

situate vt. localiser; —d a. situé; sis; be —d se trouver

six a. & n. six m.; —teen n. & a. seize m.; —teenth n. & a. seizième m.; —th a. & n. sixième m.; —tieth n. & a. soixantième m.; —ty a. & n. soixante m.

sizable a. de grandeur appréciable, assez grand

size n. grandeur, taille f.; grosseur f.; mesure f.; pointure f.; colle f.; — vt. encoller; — up évaluer; —d a. de taille, de grandeur

sizing n. colle f., collage, encollage m.

sizzle vi. griller en crépitant

sizzling a. crépitant; excessivement chaud

skate n. patin m.; (fish) raie f.; roller — patin à roulettes m.; — vi. patiner; —r n. patineur m.

skating n. patinage m.; — rink n. patinoire f.

skein n. écheveau m.

skeleton n. squelette m.; — key n. passepartout m.

skeptic n. sceptique m.; —al a. sceptique; —ism n. scepticisme m.

sketch n. esquisse f.; — vt. esquisser, ébaucher; —y a. esquissé, ébauché

sketchbook n. album m.

skewer n. brochette f.; — vt. embrocher

ski n. ski m.; — vi. faire du ski; — jump n. saut à ski m.; — lift n. remonte-pente, télésiège m.

skid n. dérapage m.; — vi. déraper

skiff n. esquif m.

skilful a. adroit; habile

skill n. habileté f.; —ed a. adroit, habile; —ed worker n. spécialiste m. & f.

skillet n. poêle épaisse f.

skim vt. & vi. écumer, effleurer; (milk) écrémer; — milk n. lait écrémé m.; —mer n. écumoire f.; écrémeur m.

skimp vi. être frugal, économiser; — on lésiner sur; —y a. frugal, chiche

skin n. peau f.; pelure f.; écorce f.; — vt. écorcher; dépouiller; dénuder

skin-deep a. superficiel

skin dive vi. plonger, explorer (au scaphandre)

skinflint n. avare m.

skinny a. décharné, maigre

skintight a. collant

skip n. saut m.; — vt. sauter

skipper n. sauteur m.; capitaine m.

skipping rope n. corde à sauter f.

skirmish n. escarmouche f.; — vi. escarmoucher

skirt n. (dress) jupe f.; (forest) bord m.; — vt. contourner

skit n. saynète f.; scénario m.

skittish a. ombrageux; capricieux, volage

skulk vi. se cacher, rôder

skull n. crâne m.; -cap n. calotte f.

skunk n. putois m.

sky n. ciel m.; -ward adv. vers le ciel

skylight n. lucarne f.

sky line n. silhouette (des bâtiments d'une ville) f.; horizon m.

skyrocket n. fusée f.; — vi. (coll.) monter rapidement

skyscraper n. gratte-ciel m.; maison démesurement haute f.

skywriting n. publicité aérienne f.

slab n. plaque, dalle f.; tranche f.

slack n. mou m.; -s pl. pantalon m.; — a. mou; inactif, mort; — vt. relâcher; -en vt. relâcher, détendre; -en vi. se détendre; -er n. lâche, paresseux m.; embusqué m.

slag n. crasses f. pl.

slain n. pl. morts m. pl.

slake vt. (lime) éteindre; (thirst) apaiser

slam vt. fermer avec bruit; — n. claquement m.; insulte f.; (cards) schlem m.; grand — grand schlem; small — petit schlem m.; make a — faire schlem

slander n. médisance f.; — vt. colomnier, diffamer; -er n. calomniateur m.; -ous a. calomnieux, médisant

slang n. jargon, argot m.

slant n. pente f.; (coll.) interprétation f.; point de vue m.; — vt. interpréter, préparer, destiner; — vi. être en pente; -ing a. en pente; oblique; de travers; -wise adv. en biais

slap n. claque, tape f.; soufflet m.; — in the face gifle f.; — vt. taper, claquer; — in the face gifler

slapstick n. bouffonnerie f.; burlesque f.

slash n. taillade f.; baisse, réduction f.; — vt. balafrer, taillader; réduire

slat n. latte f.; lamelle f.

slate n. ardoise f.; liste f.; (pol.) liste des candidats f.; — vt. couvrir d'ardoise; destiner

slaughter n. carnage, massacre m.; abattage m.; — vt. abattre; massacrer

slaughterhouse n. abattoir m.

Slav n. Slave m. & f.; -ic a. slave; -onic a. slave

slave n. esclave m. & f.; — driver n. (fig.) maître sévère et cruel m.; — vi. travailler comme un esclave; -r n. négrier m.; -ry n. esclavage m.; white -ry prostitution f.

slavish a. servile; d'esclave

slaw n. salade de choux f.

slay vt. tuer; -er n. tueur, meurtrier m.; -ing n. meurtre, assassinat m.

sled n. traîneau m.

sledge hammer n. marteau à frapper m.

sleek vt. lisser, polir; — a. lisse, poli

sleep n. sommeil m.; — vi. dormir; go to — s'endormir; put to — endormir; -er n. dormeur m.; voiture-lits f., wagon-lits m.; -iness n. somnolence f.; -ing bag n. sac de couchage m.; -ing car n. wagon-lits, sleeping (-car) m.; -ing room n. chambre à coucher f.; -ing sickness n. maladie du sommeil f.; -less a. sans

sommeil, blanc; -y a. endormi; be -y avoir sommeil

sleepwalking n. somnambulisme m.

sleet n. grésil m.; — vi. grésiller

sleeve n. manche f.; -less a. sans manche

sleigh n. traîneau m.; — bell n. clochette f., grelot m.

sleight n. tour d'adresse m.; ruse f.; — of hand paresseux m. tour de passe-passe

slender a. mince, svelte; chétif

sleuth n. détective m.

slice n. tranche f.; — vt. trancher

slick a. lisse, glissant; — vt. lisser; — n. (oil) couche d'huile f.; — adv. d'emblée; -er n. imperméable m.

slide n. glissade, glissoire f.; coulisse f.; (microscope) fiche f.; (projection) diapositif m.; — rule règle à calcul f.; — vt. & vi. glisser, faire glisser

sliding scale n. échelle mobile f.

slight n. dédain m.; — vt. dédaigner; manquer à; — a. mince, insignifiant; léger

slim a. mince, svelte; -ness n. minceur f.

slime n. limon m., bourbe f.; bave f.

sliminess n. viscosité f.

slimy a. visqueux, vaseux; gluant

sling n. écharpe f.; lancement m.; (gun) bretelle f.; — vt. lancer, jeter

slingshot n. lance-pierres m.; fronde f.

slink vi. s'en aller furtivement

slip n. glissade f.; erreur f.; barde f.; écoulement m.; (bot.) scion m.; (undergarment) chemise f.; combinaison f.; (paper) bout m.; — cover n. housse f.; — vt. glisser; faire une erreur; — vi. glisser; se tromper; faire un faux-pas

slipper n. pantoufle f.; mule f.

slippery a. glissant

slipshod a. négligé

slit n. fente f.; — vt. fendre

sliver n. éclat; — vi. éclater

slobber n. bave f.; — vi. baver

sloe n. prunelle f.; — gin n. prunelline f.

slogan n. slogan m.

sloop n. chaloupe f.

slop n. rinçure f.; eau de vaisselle f.; lavasse f.; — vt. répandre; -py a. négligé; désordonné; peu soigné; sale

slope n. pente, déclivité f.; talus m.; — vi. s'incliner

slot n. fente, ouverture f.; — machine n. machine à sous f.

sloth n. paresse f.; (zool.) paresseux m.; -ful a. paresseux

slouch vt. & vi. abaisser la tête; rabaisser le chapeau; se dandiner lourdement; — n. attitude affaissée f.; — hat n. chapeau mou m.

slough n. bourbier m.; dépouille f.; — vt. se dépouiller de

Slovakia n. Slovaquie f.

slovenly a. malpropre; sale

slow a. lent; tardif; — vt. ralentir; — down ralentir; -ly adv. lentement; -ness n. lenteur f.; (clocks) retard

slow-motion a. (films) film tourné au ralenti

sludge n. cambouis m.; calamine f.; dépôt carboné m.; boues f. pl.

slug n. (zool.) limace f.; (print., bar) lingot m. (token) jeton m.; — vt. (coll.) assomer

sluggish a. indolent; lent; —ness n. indolence f.; lenteur f.

sluice n. écluse f.; —gate n. porte éclusière f.; — vt. vanner

slum n. quartier misérable m.; go —ming visiter les quartiers misérables

slumber n. sommeil m.; — vi. sommeiller

slump n. chute, baisse f.; affaissement m.; — vi. baisser; s'affaisser; s'enfoncer

slur n. tache f.; blâme m.; (mus.) coulé m.; — vt. salir; passer légèrement; (mus.) lier les notes

slush n. neige à moitié fondue f.

sly a. fin; rusé; on the — en cachette; furtivement

smack n. goût m.; claque f.; (fishing) bâteau de pêche m.; — vt. claquer; — vi. avoir le goût; rappeler

small n. partie la plus mince f.; — of the back reins m.; — a. petit; léger; menu; — change n. menue monnaie f.; — fry enfants m. pl.; — hours heures matinales f. pl.; — intestine n. intestin grêle m.; — talk bavardage m.; —ish a. assez petit; —ness n. petitesse f.

smallpox n. petite vérole f.

small-town a. provincial

smart n. douleur aiguë f.; — vt. sentir une cuisante douleur; faire sentir une cuisante douleur; — a. intelligent, vif; élégant; —ness n. intelligence f.; élégance f.

smash vt. briser, écraser; — n. fracas m. collision f.; grande réussite f.

smashup n. collision f., accident m.

smattering n. connaissance superficielle f.; notions f. pl.

smear n. tache f.; avilissement m.; — vt. tacher, barbouiller; avilir; (coll.) calomnier, diffamer

smell n. odeur f.; — vt. & vi. sentir

smelt n. éperlan m.

smelt vt. fondre; —er n. fonderie f.

smile n. sourire m.; — vi. sourire

smirk vi. sourire, minauder

smite vt. frapper; enflammer

smith n. forgeron m.; —y n. forge f.

smithereens n. pl. atomes m. pl.; break to — atomiser

smock n. tablier m., blouse f.

smoke n. fumée f.; vapeur f.; — vt. & vi. fumer; — house n. fumoir m.; —less a. sans fumée; —r n. fumeur m.

smoke screen n. rideau de fumée m.

smokestack n. cheminée f.

smoking n. action de fumer f.; — car n. wagon des fumeurs m.; no —défense de fumer

smoking jacket n. veston d'intérieur m.

smoky a. fumeux; enfumé

smolder vi. brûler sans flamme

smooth vt. unir; lisser; apaiser; flatter; dérider; — a. uni; poli, lisse, doux; —ness n. douceur f.; poli, calme m.

smooth-spoken, smooth-tongued a. à langue dorée

smother vt. étouffer, suffoquer; couvrir

smudge n. barbouillage m.; dépôt de suie m.; tache; — vt. barbouiller

smug a. content de soi

smuggle vt. faire la contrebande; —r n. contrebandier m.

smuggling n. contrebande f.

smut n. tache de suie f.; obscénités f. pl.; — vt. noircir; —ty a. taché de suie; grossier

snack n. casse-croûte m.; goûter m.; collation f.

snag n. bosse f., nœud m.; entrave, difficulté f.; — vt. accrocher

snail n. limaçon, escargot m.; at a —'s pace à pas de tortue

snake n. serpent m.; — vt. onduler

snap n. claquement m.; bruit sec m.; fermoir m.; (coll.) quelque chose de facile m.; — vi. claquer; se briser; — at prendre dans les dents; parler sur un ton hargneux; — vt. casser, briser; —per n. fermoir m., fermeture f.

snapshot n. instantané m.

snare n. piège m.; — vt. prendre au piège

snarl vi. grogner, gronder; emmêler; — n. grognement m.; (coll.) embouteillage m.

snatch n. prise f.; accès m.; morceau m.; — vt. saisir, arracher violemment

sneak n. lâche m.; — vt. voler; — vi. se glisser; — thief n. voleur m.

sneer n. ricanement m., raillerie f.; — vi. ricaner

sneeze vi. éternuer; — n. éternuement m.

snicker n. ricanement m.; — vi. ricaner

sniff vt. renifler; — n. reniflement m.; respirée f.

sniffle vi. reniflement m.; — vt. renifler; pleurnicher; —s n. pl. reniflement m.; rhume de cerveau m.

snip n. coupure f.; petit morceau m.; — vt. couper; rogner

snipe n. bécassine f.; — vi. tirer; canarder; —r n. franc-tireur m.

snivel vi. pleurnicher

snob n. snob; parvenu m.; —bish a. snob; vulgaire; —bishness n. snobisme m.; suffisance f.

snoop n. curieux m.; espion m.; — vi. épier

snooze n. petit somme m.; — vi. somnoler

snore n. ronflement m.; — vi. ronfler

snoring a. qui ronfle; — n. ronflement m.

snort n. ébrouement m.; — vi. s'ébrouer

snout n. museau m.; groin m.

snow n. neige f.; — vi. neiger; —y a. neigeux

snowball n. boule de neige f.

snowbound a. bloqué par la neige

snow-capped a. couronné de neige

snowdrift n. amas de neige m.

snowfall n. chute de neige f.

snowflake n. flocon de neige m.

snow line n. limite des neiges f.

snowplow n. chasse-neige m.

snow slide n. avalanche de neige f.

snow storm n. tempête de neige f.

snub n. affront m.; — nose nez camus m.; — vt. tourner le dos à

snuff n. tabac à priser m.; — box tabatière f.; — vt. éteindre; moucher

snuffle vi. renifler; —s n. pl. reniflement m.; rhume de cerveau m.

snug a. serré; commode, confortable; bien

snuggle vi. se serrer

so adv. ainsi; si; tellement; tant; aussi; comme cela; de même; alors; and — on et ainsi de suite; — as to pour; — much tant; — that pour que, afin que; de sorte que; — long! su revoir, à bientôt

soak vt. & vi. tremper; -ing a., -ing wet trempé, mouillé (jusqu'aux os); -ing n. action de tremper f.; arrosage m.

soap n. savon m.; — bubble bulle de savon f.; -suds mousse de savon f.; toilet — savonnette f.; — vt. savonner; -y a. savonneux

soapbox n. caisse à savon f.; plate-forme improvisé m.

soapstone n. stéatite f.

soar vi. prendre l'essor; s'élever

sob n. sanglot m.; — vi. sangloter

sober a. sobre; pas ivre; — vt. calmer; ramener à la raison

sobriety n. sobriété f.; modération f.

so-called a. soi-disant; ainsi nommé

sociability n. sociabilité f.

sociable a. sociable; amical

social a. social; sociable; — security assurances sociales f. pl.; — service, — work travail d'amélioration sociale m.; -ism n. socialisme m., -ist n. socialiste m. & f.; -ite n. mondain m., mondaine f.; -ize vt. socialiser

society n. société f.; monde m.

sociological a. sociologique

sociology n. sociologie f.

sock n. chaussette f.; coup de poing m.; — vt. donner un coup de poing à, frapper du poing

socket n. douille f.; soc. m.; (elec.) prise f.; (eye) orbite f.; (tooth) alvéole m.; socle m.; — wrench clé à tube f.

sod n. motte de terre f.; gazon m.

soda n. soude f.; soda m.; baking —, bicarbonate of — bicarbonate de soude m.; — water soda m.; eau de Seltz f.

sodium n. sodium m.; — chloride n. chlorure de soude m.

sofa n. sofa, canapé m.; — bed n. canapé qui se transforme en lit, lit-divan m.

soft a. mou, doux; tendre, faible, facile, délicat; efféminé; (water) non-calcaire; — coal charbon m.; — drink boisson rafraîchissante f., boisson non-alcoolisée f.; —en vt. amollir, adoucir, attendrir; -ness n. douceur f.; mollesse f.

softball n. baseball (jouée avec une balle molle) m.

softhearted a. sensible; sentimental; compatissant

soft-pedal vt. étouffer, adoucir; minimiser

soft-spoken a. doux

soggy a. humide

soil n. souillure f.; terre f.; sol, terrain m.; — vt. souiller, salir

sojourn n. séjour m.; — vi. séjourner

sol n. (mus.) sol m.

solace n. consolation f.; — vt. consoler

solar a. solaire; du soleil; — plexus n. plexus solaire f.; -ium n. solarium m.

sold a., — out épuisé; complet; tout vendu

solder n. soudure f.; — vt. souder; -ing n. soudure f.; -ing iron n. fer à souder m.

soldier n. soldat m.

sole n. (foot) plante du pied f.; (shoe) semelle f.; (fish) sole f.; — vt. ressemeler; — a. unique, seul

solemn a. solennel; -ity n. solennité f.; -ize vt. solenniser

solicit vt. solliciter; inviter; -ation n. sollicitation f.; -or n. solliciteur m.; (law) avoué m.; -ous a. plein de sollicitude; -ude n. sollicitude f.

solid a. solide; massif; réel; grave, profond; (color) uni; — n. corps solide m.; -arity n. solidarité f.; -ify vt. solidifier; -ify vi. se solidifier; -ity n. solidité f.; — geometry n. géométrie dans l'espace f.

soliloquy n. monologue m.

solitaire n. solitaire m.; (game) patience f.

solitary a. solitaire; retiré

solitude n. solitude f.

solo n. solo m.; -ist n. soliste m. & f.; — a. & adv. seul

solstice n. solstice m.

soluble a. dissoluble

solution n. solution f.

solve vt. résoudre

solvency n. solvabilité f.

solvent n. dissolvant m.; — a. (com.) solvable

Somalia n. Somalie f.

somber a. sombre

some a. quelque, un peu de; du, de la; — pron. un peu; certains; quelques-uns; les uns; les autres

somebody, someone pron. quelqu'un

somehow adv. de façon ou d'autre

somersault n. culbute f.; — vi. culbuter

something pron. quelque chose

sometime adv. un jour, un de ces jours; — a. ancien, ci-devant, honoraire

sometimes adv. quelquefois, de temps en temps; tantôt

somewhat adv. un peu; assez

somewhere adv. quelque part; — else ailleurs; quelque part

somnambulist n. somnambule m. & f.

somnolent a. somnolent

son n. fils m.

sonata n. sonate f.

song n. chanson f.; chant m.; -ster n. chanteur m.; -stress n. chanteuse f.

Song of Songs Cantique des Cantiques f.

sonic a. sonique; — barrier barrière du son f.

son-in-law n. gendre m.

sonorous a. sonore

soon adv. bientôt, tôt, de bonne heure; as — as aussitôt que; how —? dans combien de temps?

soot n. suie f.; -y a. couvert de suie; fuligineux

soothe vt. flatter; apaiser

soothsayer n. devin m.

sop n. morceau trempé m.; (fig.) os à ronger; cadeau, présent m.; — vt. tremper; -ping a. trempé

sophisticated a. sophistiqué, blasé

sophistication n. sophistication f.

sophomore n. étudiant universitaire de deuxième année m.

sophomoric a. jeune, inexpérimenté

soporific n. & a. soporifique m.

sorcerer n. sorcier m.

sorceress n. sorcière f.

sorcery n. sorcellerie f., sortilège m.

sordid a. sordide

sore n. ulcère m., plaie f.; — a. douloureux; écorché; violent; —ness n. mal m.; douleur f.; sensibilité f.

sorority n. société d'étudiantes universitaires f.

sorrow n. chagrin m., affliction, tristesse f.; — vi. être affligé; être en deuil; —ful a. triste, affligé; affligeant; —fulness n. chagrin m., tristesse f.

sorry a. affligé; triste; fâché; désolé; be — regretter

sort n. sorte, espèce, classe, mantière f., genve m.; — vt. séparer, classer, trier, assortir

so-so a. comme ci comme ça

sot n. sot, imbécile m.; ivrogne m.; —tish a. sot; abruti

soul n. âme f., esprit m.; être m.; —ful a. plein d'émotion; plein d'âme

sound n. son, bruit m.; (med.) sonde f.; (geog.) goulet, détroit m.; — a. sain, bien portant, vigoureux; — effect effet sonore m.; — track piste sonore f.; — truck camion d'enregistrement m.; — wave onde sonore f.; — vt. & vi. sonner; (med.) sonder; —ing n. sondage m.; —ing a., —ing board table d'harmonie f.; —ing line ligne de sonde f.; —ness n. solidité f.

soundproof a. insonore; — vt. insonoriser; —ing n. insonorisation f.

soup n. soupe f., potage m.; — plate assiette creuse; — tureen n. soupière f.

sour a. aigre; acide; — vt. rendre acide; aigrir; — vi. tourner; s'aigrir; —ness n. aigreur f.

south n. sud, midi m.; —east n. sud-est m.; —ern a. méridional, du sud; —erner n. méridional; —land n. midi m.; —ward adv. vers le sud; —west n. sud-ouest m.

southpaw a. gaucher

sovereign a. souverain; —ty n. souveraineté f.

Soviet n. Soviet m.; — a. soviétique

sow n. truie f.; — vt. semer, ensemencer; —er n. semeur m.

soybean n. soya m.

spa n. ville d'eau f.

space n. espace m.; distance f., intervalle m.; — vt. espacer; —r n. (typewriter) barre d'espacement f.

spacious a. spacieux, vaste; —ness n. grandeur, immensité f.

spade n. bêche f.; (cards) pique m.; — vt. & vi. bêcher

Spain n. Espagne f.

span n. empan m.; portée, travée f.; durée f.; — vt. couvrir, traverser

spangle n. paillette f.; — vt. orner de paillettes

Spaniard n. Espagnol m.

Spanish a. & n. espagnol m.

spank vt. fesser; —ing n. fessée f.

spar n. espar m.; (geol.) spath m.; — vi. boxer

spare vt. & vi. épargner, ménager, traiter avec indulgence; — a. maigre; de rechange; disponible; — parts pièces de rechange f. pl.; — time loisir m.; — tire pneu de rechange m.

sparerib n. plat de côte m.

sparing a. rare; frugal; chiche

spark n. étincelle f.; — plug bougie f.

sparkle vi. & vt. étinceler

sparkling a. étincelant; (drink) mousseux

sparse a. épars

Sparta n. Sparte f.; —n a. & n. spartiate m. & f.

spasm n. spasme m.; —odic a. spasmodique

spastic a. spasmodique, spastique

spat n. guêtre f.; (coll.) dispute f.; — vi. se disputer

spatial a. de l'espace

spatter n. éclaboussure f.; — vt. éclabousser

spatula n. spatule f.

spawn n. frai m.; — vt. & vi. frayer; engendrer

spay vt. châtrer

speak vt. & vi. parler, discourir; prononcer; — out lever la voix; — up parler plus haut; —er n. parleur, conférencier m.; (organization) président m.; (radio) haut-parleur m.

spear n. lance f.; harpon m.; épieu m.; — vt. percer à coups de lance; harponner

spearhead n. fer de lance m.; pointe f.; (mil.) point d'attaque m.

special a. spécial; particulier; — delivery par exprès; — delivery letter n. lettre exprès f.; —ist n. spécialiste m. & f.; —ize vt. spécialiser; —ize vi. se spécialiser; —ty n. spécialité f.

species n. espèce, sorte f.

specific n. & a. spécifique m.; — gravity n. poids spécifique m.; —ation n. spécification f.

specify vt. spécifier

specimen n. spécimen, modèle m.

specious a. spécieux

speck n. tache f., point m.; — vt. tacher

speckle n. petite tache, bigarrure f.; — vt. tacheter, moucheter

spectacle n. spectacle m.; —s pl. lunettes f. pl.

spectacular a. à spectacle, grandiose

spectator n. spectateur m.

specter n. spectre m., apparition f.

spectral a. spectral

spectroscope n. spectroscope m.

spectrum n. spectre m.

speculate vi. spéculer; jouer

speculation n. spéculation, méditation f.

speculator n. spéculateur m.

speech n. discours m.; langage m., harangue f.; plaidoyer m.; figure of — n. figure de rhétorique f.; —less a. interdit; muet

speed n. vitesse f.; — limit vitesse maxima f.; — vi. se dépêcher; aller très vite; aller trop vite; — vt. dépêcher, hâter; — up intensifier; presser; aller plus vite; —y a. rapide; hâtif

speedboat n. canot automobile m.; vedette f.; hors-bord m.

speedometer n. indicateur de vitesse m.; tachymètre m.

speed-up n. accélération f.

speedway n. piste d'autos f.

spell n. charme m.; sortilège m.; moment m.; attaque f., accès m., crise f.; — vt.

épeler, orthographièr; remplacer; **-er** *n.* livre d'orthographe *m.*; **-ing** *n.* orthographe *f.*;**-ing** bee concours d'orthographe *m.*

spellbound *a.* charmé, fasciné

spend *vt.* dépenser, employer; consommer; dissiper; épuiser; **-er** *n.* dépensier, dissipateur *m.*

spendthrift *n.* prodigue *m.*

spent *a.* épuisé; dépensé

sperm *n.* sperme *m.*

sperm whale *n.* cachalot *m.*

spew *vt.* vomir

sphere *n.* sphère *f.*

spherical *a.* sphérique

spermatazoa *n. pl.* spermatozoïdes *m. pl.*

spheroid *n.* sphéroïde *m.*

sphinx *n.* sphinx *m.*

spice *n.* épice *f.*; **—** *vt.* épicer

spick-and-span *a.* impeccable

spicy *a.* aromatique, épicé

spider *n.* araignée *f.*

spigot *n.* fausset *m.*; robinet *m.*

spike *n.* épi de blé *m.*; pointe *f.*; long clou *m.*, cheville *f.*; **—** *vt.* clouer

spill *vt.* répandre, renverser

spillway *n.* déversoir *m.*

spin *vt.* & *vi.* filer; faire tournoyer; **—** *n.* promenade en auto *f.*; **-ning** *n.* filature *f.*; **-ning** jenny jenny *f.*; **-ning** mill filature *f.*; **-ning** wheel rouet *m.*

spinach *n.* épinards *m. pl.*

spinal *a.* spinal; **—column** *n.* colonne vertébrale *f.*; **—cord** *n.* moelle épinière *f.*

spindle *n.* fuseau *m.*, broche *f.*; pivot *m.*

spine *n.* épine dorsale *f.*; (book) dos *m.*

spinet *n.* épinette *f.*

spinnaker *n.* foc de yacht *m.*

spinster *n.* vieille fille *f.*

spiny *a.* épineux

spiral *a.* spiral; en spirale; **—** *n.* spirale *f.*

spire *n.* aiguille, flèche (de clocher) *f.*

spirit *n.* esprit *m.*, âme *f.*; courage, feu *m.*; génie *m.*; fantôme *m.*; liqueur spiritueuse *f.*; in high **—s** joie *f.*, abandon *m.*; low **—** abattement *m.*; raise one's **—s** remonter le courage de quelqu'un; **— lamp** *n.* réchaud à alcool *m.*; **— level** *n.* niveau à bulle d'air *m.*; **—** *vt.* animer, encourager; **— away** enlever; **-ed** *a.* animé, vigoureux; **-less** *a.* inanimé; **-ual** *a.* spirituel; **-ual** *n.* (mus.) chant religieux populaire *m.*; **-ualism** *n.* spiritisme *m.*; **-ualist** *n.* spiritualiste *m.*

spit *n.* (rod) broche *f.*; salive *f.*; **—** *vt.* embrocher; cracher; **-tle** *n.* crachat *m.*; **-toon** *n.* crachoir *m.*

spite *n.* dépit *m.*, rancune *f.*; in **—** of en dépit de, malgré; **—** *vt.* contrarier; **-ful** *a.* malicieux, rancunier

spitfire *n.* mégère *f.*; (avi.) spitfire *m.*

splash *n.* éclaboussure *f.*; **—** *vt.* éclabousser

spleen *n.* rate *f.*; (fig.) spleen *m.*

splendid *a.* splendide; magnifique, brillant

splendor *n.* splendeur *f.*; éclat *m.*

splice *n.* jointure, soudure *f.*; (film) collure *f.*; **—** *vt.* joindre à onglet; (naut.) épisser

splint *n.* éclisse *f.*

splinter *n.* éclat (de bois) *m.*; **—** *vt.* briser,

fendre; **—** *vi.* voler en éclats

split *n.* fente *f.*; querelle *f.*; division *f.*; (dance) grand écart *m.*; demi-bouteille *f.*; **—** *vt.* fendre, briser; **—** *vi.* se fendre; crever; **-ting** *n.* fendage *m.*; (atom) fissure *f.*; **-ting** *a.* écrasant

splotch *n.* tache *f.*; **—** *vt.* tacher

splurge *n.* faste, parade *f.*; **—** *vi.* faire parade; se payer une fête

splutter *vi.* bredouiller

spoil *n.* pillage *m.*; butin *m.*; dépouille *f.*; **—** *vt.* gâter, abîmer; **—** *vi.* se gâter; **— for** désirer; **-er** *n.* spoliateur *m.*; **-age** *n.* dégâts *m. pl.*; choses gatées *f. pl.*

spoilsport *n.* trouble-fête *m.*

spoke *n.* rais, rayon *m.*

spokesman *n.* porte-parole *m.*

sponge *n.* éponge *f.*; **— bath** *n.* bain anglais *m.*; **— cake** (genre de) gâteau de Savoie *m.*; **—** *vi.* éponger; **—** *vi.* (coll.) vivre en parasite; **-r** *n* ue-assiette *m.*

spongy *a.* spongieux

sponsor *n.* garant *m.*; parrain *m.*; marraine *f.*; (rad.) annonceur *m.*, commanditaire, patron; **—** *vt.* présenter; payer les frais; **-ship** *n.* parrainage *m.*; patronage *m.*

spontaneity *n.* spontanéité *f.*

spontaneous *a.* spontané; **-ly** *adv.* spontanément; **-ness** *n.* spontanéité *f.*

spool *n.* rouleau *m.*; bobine *f.*; **—** *vt.* embobiner

spoon *n.* cuiller, cuillère *f.*; **table— cuiller** à bouche *f.*; **tea—** cuiller à café *f.*; **—** *vt.* prendre dans une cuiller; **-ful** *n.* cuillerée *f.*

sporadic *a.* sporadique

sport *n.* sport *m.*; divertissement, amusement, jeu *m.*; **—** *vt.* & *vi.* faire parade de; se divertir, badiner; **-ing** *a.* juste, équitable; **-ing** goods articles de sport *m. pl.*; **-ive** *a.* sportif; gai; **— shirt** *n.* chemise de sport *f.*

sportsman *n.* sportif *m.*; **-ship** *n.* attitude du sportif *f.*

spot *n.* tache *f.*; lieu *m.*, place *f.*; (ground) coin *m.*; (coll.) pétrin, mauvais pas *m.*; **—** *vt.* tacher; tacheter; (coll.) marquer; **-less** *a.* sans tache; **-ted** *a.* tacheté; **-ty** *a.* taché, inégal

spotlight *n.* projecteur intensif, spot *m.*

spot welding *n.* soudage par points *m.*

spouse *n.* époux *m.*, épouse *f.*

spout *n.* tuyau de décharge *m.*; jet *m.*; **—** *vi.* jaillir; **—** *vt.* faire jaillir; énoncer, dire, prononcer

sprain *n.* foulure, entorse *f.*; **—** *vt.* se fouler; se donner une entorse à

sprawl *vi.* s'étaler

spray *n.* écume *f.*; vapeur *f.*; rameau *m.*; **—** *vt.* & *vi.* vaporiser; couvrir d'écume; **-er** *n.* vaporisateur *m.*

spread *n.* étendue *f.*; rayonnement *m.*; (bed) dessus de lit, couvre-lit *m.*; collation *f.*; **—** *vt.* répandre, faire rayonner, vulgariser; **—** *vi.* se répandre, rayonner

sprig *n.* brin *m.*, brindille *f.*

sprightliness *n.* vivacité, gaieté *f.*, feu *m.*

sprightly *a.* vif, gai

spring *a.* & *n.* (season) printemps *m.*;

(water) source *f.*; (mech.) ressort *m.*; (movement) élan, saut *m.*; — *vi.* s'élancer, bondir; — from naître de; —y *a.* élastique

springboard *n.* tremplin *m.*

springlike *a.* printanier

springtime *n.* printemps *m.*

sprinkle *vt. & vi.* asperger, arroser; (fig.) parsemer; — *n.* légère pluie *f.*; —r *n.* arroseur *m.*; arroseur automatique *m.*; pomme d'arrosage *f.*

sprinkling *n.* arrosage *m.*; petite quantité *f.*; connaissance superficielle *f.*, notions *f. pl.*

sprint *n.* course *f.*; sprint *m.*; — *vi.* courir à toute vitesse; —er *n.* coureur rapide *m.*

sprite *n.* esprit, fantôme *m.*

sprocket *n.* (mech.) dent *f.*; galet *m.*; — wheel roue dentée *f.*; pignon *m.*

sprout *n.* jet, rejeton *m.*; pousse *f.*; Brussels —s choux de Bruxelles *m. pl.*; — *vi.* germer, pousser

spruce *vi.*, — up se faire beau; — *a.* pimpant; bien mis; — *n.* sapin *m.*

sprung *a.* déformé

spry *a.* vif, animé, actif; —ness *n.* activité, vivacité *f.*

spume *n.* écume *f.*; — *vi.* écumer, mousser

spun *a.* filé, en fil

spur *n.* éperon *m.*; aiguillon *m.*; ergot *m.*; stimulant *m.*; hâte *f.*; on the — of the moment à l'impromptu; — *vt.* éperonner, instiguer, inspirer

spurious *a.* faux, falsifié

spurn *vt.* mépriser, dédaigner

spurt *n.* jet, jaillissement; — *vi.* jaillir

sputter *n.* bredouillement *m.*; — *vi.* bredouiller, balbutier

sputum *n.* expectorations *f. pl.*

spy *n.* espion *m.*, espionne *f.*; — *vt.* épier, espionner; —glass *n.* longue-vue *f.*

squab *n.* jeune pigeon *m.*

squabble *n.* querelle *f.*; bagarre *f.*; — *vi.* se chamailler

squad *n.* escouade *f.*; équipe *f.*; rescue — équipe de secours *f.*

squadron *n.* escadron *m.*; escadre *f.*

squalid *a.* sale, malpropre

squall *n.* cri alarmant *m.*; (weather) rafale *f.*, coup de vent, grain *m.*; — *vi.* crier, brailler

squalor *n.* misère, saleté *f.*

squander *vt.* dissiper, gaspiller

square *n.* carré *m.*; équerre *f.*; place *f.*; — *vt. & vi.* carrer; régler, ajuster; — *a.* carré; convenable; conforme; balancé; juste, honnête; équitable; — dance quadrille américain *m.*; — root racine carrée *f.*

squash *n.* courge, gourde *f.*; foule, presse *f.*; écrasement *m.*; (sport) jeu de paume *m.*; — *vt.* écraser

squat *vi.* s'accroupir, se tapir; — *a.* accroupi, blotti; —ter *n.* colon, squatter *m.*

squawk *n.* cri rauque *m.*; — *vi.* crier

squeak *n.* cri perçant *m.*; — *vi.* jeter des cris perçants; grincer; —y *a.* criard; (mech.) glapissant

squeal *n.* cri (du cochon) *m.*; — *vi.* (like a

pig) crier; (coll.) manger le morceau, chanter

squeamish *a.* délicat; dégoûté; —ness *n.* délicatesse exagérée *f.*

squeegee *n.* essuie-glace *m.*; rouleau en caoutchouc *m.*

squeeze *n.* compression *f.*; serrement *m.*; — *vt.* presser, serrer; — out exprimer; éliminer; —r *n.* presse *f.*; lemon —r presse-citrons *m.*

squelch *n.* réplique écrasante *f.*; — *vt.* écraser

squib *n.* (fig.) satire *f.*; bon mot *m.*

squint *n.* regard louche *m.*; — *vi.* loucher; cligner les yeux

squint-eyed *a.* louche

squire *n.* écuyer *m.*; propriétaire *m.*; cavalier *m.*; — *vt.* accompagner

squirm *vi.* se tortiller

squirt *n.* jet *m.*; — *vt.* jeter; — *vi.* jaillir

squirt gun *n.* seringue *f.*

stab *n.* coup de poignard *m.*; make a — at tenter, essayer; — *vt.* poignarder

stability *n.* stabilité, constance *f.*

stabilize *vt.* stabiliser; — *vi.* devenir stable; —r *n.* stabiliseur *m.*

stable *n.* étable, écurie *f.*; — *vt.* établer; — *a.* stable, fixe; constant, ferme

stack *n.* (hay) meule *f.*; (wood) pile *f.*; tas *m.*; — *vt.* entasser; mettre en meule

stadium *n.* stade *m.*

staff *n.* bâton *m.*; état-major *m.*; soutien *m.*; personnel *m.*; (mus.) portée *f.*

stag *n.* cerf *m.*; — party soirée pour hommes *f.*; go — aller sans compagne

stage *n.* échafaudage *m.*, estrade *f.*; théâtre *m.*, scène *f.*; degré, état *m.*; relais *m.*; journée *f.*; voiture publique *f.*; — box *n.* avant-scène *f.*; —coach *n.* diligence *f.*; — effect *n.* effet scénique *m.*; — fright *n.* trac *m.*; —hand *n.* machiniste *m.*; — manager *n.* régisseur *m.*; — whisper *n.* aparté *m.*; — *vt.* monter; mettre en scène

stagger *vi.* chanceler; hésiter, vaciller; — *vt.* ébranler, étonner; échelonner; —ed *a.* échelonné

staging *n.* mise en scène *f.*; échafaud *m.*; — area *n.* camp temporaire (avant l'embarquement) *m.*

stagnant *a.* stagnant; inactif

stagnate *vi.* être stagnant

stagy *a.* théâtral, artificiel

staid *a.* grave, posé; —ness *n.* gravité *f.*

stain *n.* tache, souillure *f.*; bonté *f.*; couleur *f.*; — *vt.* tacher; teindre; teinter; souiller; —less *a.* sans tache; qui ne se tache pas; —less steel *n.* acier inoxydible *m.*

stair *n.* marche d'un escalier *f.*; —s *n. pl.* escalier *m.*

staircase *n.* escalier *m.*

stairway *n.* cage d'escalier *f.*

stake *n.* poteau *m.*; enjeu *m.*; — *vt.* garnir de pieux; mettre en jeu; subventionner

stalactite *n.* stalactite *f.*

stalagmite *n.* stalagmite *f.*

stale *a.* vieux, usé, gâté; rassis; éventé; —ness *n.* vieillesse *f.*

stalk *n.* tige, queue *f.*; démarche fière *f.*;

— *vi.* marcher fièrement; — *vt.* suivre à la piste

stallion *n.* étalon *m.*

stalwart *a.* vaillant, vigoureux

stamen *n.* étamine *f.*

stamina *n.* force, vigueur *f.*

stammer *vi.* bégayer, balbutier; **-er** *n.* bègue *m. & f.*

stamp *n.* poinçon, coin *m.*; empreinte, impression *f.*; cachet *m.*, estampe *f.*; trempe *f.*; postage — timbre (-poste) *m.*; — **pad** *n.* tampon *m.*; revenue — timbre fiscal *m.*; rubber — timbre en caoutchouc *m.*; — *vt.* frapper du pied; broyer; imprimer; timbrer; (mail) affranchir; — **out** éliminer

stampede *n.* ruée *f.*; (cattle) fuite (de bœufs) *f.*; sauve-qui-peut *m.*; — *vi.* fuir, se ruer; — *vt.* provoquer une fuite, effaroucher

stance *n.* attitude *f.*

stanch, staunch *vt.* étancher; — *a.* solide; ferme; sûr

stand *n.* station *f.*; place *f.*; délai *m.*; pause, halte *f.*; résistance *f.*; embarras *m.*; guéridon *m.*, console *f.*, étalage *m.*; stand *m.*; **-s** *pl.* tribune *f.*; — *vi.* se lever; se mettre debout; rester debout; être debout; résister; supporter; — **aside** se tenir à l'écart; — **back** reculer; — **by** se tenir à l'écart; soutenir; se tenir prêt; attendre; — **for** signifier; tolérer; supporter; — **in for** remplacer; **off** se tenir à l'écart; repousser; — **on** insister sur; — **out** se détacher; — **still** se tenir tranquille; ne pas bouger; — **to** courir le risque de; avoir des chances de; — **up** se lever, se mettre debout; — **up against** opposer; combattre; — **up for** défendre, soutenir, appuyer; **-ing** *n.* position *f.*; durée *f.*; — **-ing** *a.* debout; permanent; **-ing room** place debout *f.*; promenoir *m.*

standard *n.* étendard *m.*; pavillon *m.*; étalon *m.*; titre *m.*; modèle *m.*; type *m.*; mesure *f.*; gold — étalon d'or *m.*; — **of living** niveau de la vie *m.*; — *a.* normal, ordinaire; classique; — time heure normale *f.*; — **works** classiques *m. pl.*; **-ization** *n.* standardisation *f.*; **-ize** *vt.* standardiser

standard-bearer *n.* porte-drapeau, enseigne *m.*; porte-étendard *m.*

stand-by *n.* service de secours *m.*; suppléant *m.*; adjoint *m.*

stand-in *n.* (movies) remplaçant *m.*

standpoint *n.* point d'arrêt *m.*

standstill *n.* point mort *m.*; affaire nulle *f.*

stanza *n.* strophe *f.*

staple *n.* denrée *f.*; matière première *f.*; crampon *m.*; — *a.* établi; principal; — *vt.* fixer (avec des crampons); **-r** *n.* brocheuse *f.*

star *n.* étoile *f.*; astre *m.*; (type) astérisque *m.*; (theat.) vedette *f.*; shooting — étoile filante *f.*; — *vt.* étoiler; parsemer; présenter comme vedette; — *vi.* apparaître comme vedette; **-less** *a.* sans étoiles; **-let** *n.* (movies) starlette, star-**-ry** étoilé; brillant

starboard *n.* tribord *m.*

starch *n.* empois *m.*; amidon *m.*; — *vt.* empeser

star-chamber *a.* clandestin

stare *n.* regard fixe *m.*; — *vi.* regarder fixement

stark *a. & adv.* fort; vrai; pur; tout-à-fait

starlight *n.* lumière des étoiles *f.*

starlit *a.* étoilé

star-spangled *a.* étoilé, parsemé d'étoiles

start *n.* tressaillement *m.*; saut *m.*; élan *m.*; premier pas *m.*; commencement *m.*; début *m.*; — *vi.* tressaillir; — *vt.* commencer, débuter; se mettre à; se mettre en route; — **out** se mettre en route; **-er** *n.* (auto) démarreur *m.*; **-ing point** *n.* point de départ *m.*

starting gate, starting post *n.* barrière *f.*

startle *vt.* effrayer; faire tressaillir, étonner

startling *a.* étonnant

starvation *n.* inanition *f.*; faim *f.*

starve *vt.* faire mourir de faim, affamer; — *vi.* mourir de faim

state *n.* état *m.*, condition *f.*; rang *m.*, dignité, pompe *f.*; — *vt.* établir, régler; constater, détailler; déclarer; — **house** *n.* parlement *m.*; **-liness** *n.* grandeur *f.*; **-ment** *n.* déclaration *f.*; procès-verbal *m.*; (com.) relevé de compte *m.*

statecraft *n.* politique *f.*

stateroom *n.* cabine *f.*

statesman *n.* homme d'état *m.*; **-ship** *n.* politique *f.*, art de gouverner *m.*

static *n.* (rad.) parasites *m. pl.*; **-s** *n.* statique *f.*; — *a.* statique

station *n.* situation, position, condition *f.*; poste *m.*, place *f.*, emploi *m.*; état, rang *m.*; (rail.) gare *f.*; — **house**, police — commissariat de police *m.*; — *vt.* poster, placer

station agent *n.* chef de gare *m.*

stationary *a.* stationnaire, fixe

stationer *n.* papetier, marchand de papier *m.*; libraire *m.*; **-'s** *n.* papeterie, librairie *f.*; **-y** *n.* papeterie *f.*

Stations of the Cross *n.* calvaire *m.*

statistic *n.* statistique *f.*; **-s** *pl.* statistique *f.*; **-al** *a.* statistique; **-ian** *n.* statisticien *m.*

statuary *n.* (sculptor) statuaire *m.*; (statues) statuaire *f.*

statue *n.* statue *f.*

statuesque *a.* de statue; comme une statue

statuette *n.* statuette *f.*

stature *n.* stature, taille *f.*

status *n.* condition *f.*; rang *m.*; — **quo** *n.* statu quo *m.*

statute *n.* statut *m.*, loi *f.*

statutory *a.* conforme à la loi; défini par la loi

staunch, stanch *a.* loyal, sûr; **-ness** *n.* loyauté, fidélité, force *f.*

stave *n.* douve *f.*; (mus.) portée *f.*; — *vi.*, — **in** défoncer; — **off** écarter, différer

stay *n.* séjour *m.*; soutien *m.*; **-s** *n. pl.* corset *m. pl.*; — *vt.* arrêter, empêcher; main — (fig.) principal soutien *m.*; — *vi.* rester, demeurer, s'arrêter; attendre; rester immobile; — **up** rester en haut; veiller

stay-at-home n. casanier m.

stead n. place f., lieu m.

steadfast a. stable, fixe; constant; -ness n. fermeté, constance f.

steadily adv. fermement; régulièrement

steadiness n. fermeté f.; régularité f.

steady vt. affermir, assurer; — a. ferme, solide

steak n. bifteck, steak m.

steal n. vol m.; — vt. voler; — vi. s'échapper; aller doucement, se glisser, aller à la dérobée

stealth n. action clandestine f.; by — à la dérobée; -ily adv. clandestinement; -y a. furtif

steam n. vapeur f.; — engine n. machine à vapeur f., locomotive f.; — (pressure) cooker n. marmite à vapeur f.; — vi. fumer; naviguer à la vapeur; — vt. (cooking) cuire à la vapeur

steamboat n. vapeur, paquebot m.

steampipe n. tuyau à vapeur m.

steam roller n. rouleau à vapeur m.

steamship n. vapeur, paquebot m.

steam shovel n. excavateur à vapeur m.

steed n. coursier, cheval m.

steel n. acier m.; — a. d'acier; — mill n. aciérie f.; — wool n. paille de fer, paille d'acier f.; — vt. endurcir; -works n. aciérie f.; -y a. d'acier

steep vt. tremper, infuser; — a. escarpé; raide; -ness n. raideur, pente f., escarpement m.

steeple n. clocher m.

steeple jack n. ouvrier qui monte sur les clochers m.

steer vt. gouverner, diriger; conduire; — n. bœuf m.; -age n. (boat) dernière classe f.; -ing a. do direction; -ing wheel n. volant m.

steersman n. timonier m.

stein n. chope f.

stellar a. stellaire

stem n. tronc m.; tige, queue f.; pédoncule m.; race f.; — vt. opposer, arrêter

stench n. puanteur f.

stencil n. pochoir m.; (duplicating machine) stencil m.; — vt. marquer au pochoir

stenographer n. sténographe m. & f.

stenotype n. stenotyping n. sténotypie f.

stentorian a. de stentor

step n. pas m., marche f.; échelon m.; marche pied m.; — vi. faire un pas, marcher; — se mettre à l'écart; — in entrer; — out sortir; — up s'approcher; monter; augmenter

stepbrother n. beau-frère m.

stepchild n. beau-fils m., belle-fille f.

stepdaughter n. belle-fille f.

stepfather n. beau-père m.

stepladder n. échelle double f.; marchepied m.

stepmother n. belle-mère f.

steppe n. steppe f.

steppingstone n. marchepied m.; moyen de parvenir m.

stepsister n. belle-sœur f.

stepson n. beau-fils m.

stereophonic a. stéréophonique

stereoscope n. stéréoscope m.

stereotype n. cliché m.; — vt. stéréotyper; — a. stéréotype m.

sterile a. stérile

sterility n. stérilité f.

sterilization n. stérilisation f.

sterilize vt. stériliser; -r n. stérilisateur m.

sterling a. sterling; vrai, véritable; honnête

stern n. poupe f.; — a. sévère; austère; rude; -ness n. sévérité f.

sternum n. sternum m.

stethoscope n. stéthoscope m.

stevedore n. arrimeur m.

stew n. étuvée, estouffade f., ragoût m.; compote f.; — vt. cuire à l'étuvée

steward n. intendant, économe, maître d'hôtel m.; -ess n. (boat) femme de chambre de bord f.; (avi.) hôtesse f.

stick n. bâton m.; canne f.; — vt. coller, fixer; percer; — vi. être collé, s'attacher; — out faire saillie; — to persévérer dans; — up (coll.) voler à main armée; — up for défendre; -er n. vignette (à coller) f.; -y a. collant

stickler n. personne méticuleuse f.; colle f., problème difficile m.

stickpin n. épingle à cravate f.

stiff a. raide; obstiné, gêné, affecté; empesé; — neck n. torticolis m.; -en vt. raidir; -en vi. se raidir; -ness n. raideur f.

stifle vt. étouffer

stifling a. étouffant

stigma n. stigmate m.; flétrissure f.; -tize vt. stigmatiser

stiletto n. poinçon m.; stylet m.

still n. silence m.; alambic m.; (movies) photographie vue fixe f.; — a. tranquille, calme; — life nature morte f.; — adv. encore, toujours; — vt. calmer, apaiser; distiller

stillborn a. mort-né

stilts n. échasses f. pl.; -ed a. ampoulé; gauche

stimulant n. & a. stimulant m.

stimulate vt. stimuler, piquer

stimulation n. stimulation f.

stimulus n. stimulant m.; aiguillon m.

sting n. piqûre f.; remords m.; aiguillon m.; — ray raie, torpile f.; — vt. piquer; mordre; -er n. (insects) aiguillon, dard m.; -ing a piquant, mordant

stinginess n. mesquinerie f.

stingy a. chiche, avare, mesquin

stink n. puanteur f.; — vi. puer; -er n. (coll.) cochon, chameau m.

stint n. limite, restreinte f.; tache f., travail du jour m.; — vt. & vi. restreindre, être parcimonieux

stipend n. salaire m., appointements m. pl.

stipple vt. pointiller

stipulate vi. stipuler

stipulation n. stipulation f.

stir n. tumulte m., agitation f.; — vt. remuer, agiter; inciter, animer; faire naître, provoquer; — vi. se remuer, se révolter; apparaître; — up fomenter; -ring a. émouvant

stirrup n. étrier m.

stitch n. point m.; maille f.; (med.) agrafe f.; — vt. piquer; coudre; brocher; — up recoudre, faire un point à

stock n. tronc m.; bloc m.; famille, race f.; assortiment m.; (cattle) bétail m.; (com.) actions f. pl.; (bot.) matthiole f.; (punishment) pilori m.; (inventory) stock, matériel, inventaire m.; (theat.) répertoire m.; laughing — risée f.; — exchange bourse f.; — a. classique, banal, d'usage; — vt. emmagasiner, garder, tenir; — up on s'approvisionner de; -y a. trapu

stockade n. palissade f.

stockbroker n. agent de change m.

stockholder n. actionnaire m. & f.

stocking n. bas m.; chaussette f.

stockpile n. dépôt m.; provision f.; réserve f.; — vt. emmagasiner

stockyard n. parc à bestiaux m.; abattoir m.

stodgy a. fade; lourd; trapu

stoic n. & a. stoïcien m.; -al a. stoïque; -ism n. stoïcisme m.

stoke vt. garnir, alimenter; chauffer; -er n. chauffeur m.

stole n. étole f.

stolid a. lourd; flegmatique; -ness n. flegme m.

stomach n. estomac m.; cœur m.; envie f.; turn the — donner mal au cœur; — vt. supporter

stone n. pierre f.; caillou m.; (seed) pépin, noyau m.; — a. de pierre; — adv.; — dead raide-mort; — deaf complètement sourd; — vt. lapider; ôter les pépins (de)

stonecutter n. tailleur de pierre(s) m.

stonemason n. maçon m.; -ry n. maçonnerie f.

stoneware n. grès m.

stonework n. ouvrage en pierre m.; maçonnerie f.

stony a. pierreux

stool n. tabouret m.; (med.) selle f.; — pigeon n. (coll.) mouchard m.

stoop n. inclination f.; abaissement m.; (arch.) perron m.; — vi. s'incliner, se baisser

stop n. pause f.; arrêt m., halte f.; obstacle m.; (organ) jeu m.; (phot.) ouverture du diaphragme f.; — signal (street) feu rouge m.; (auto.) feu stop, signal de freinage m.; — vt. arrêter, faire cesser; boucher; — vi. s'arrêter, cesser; — in venir voir, faire visite; — off, — over interrompre son voyage; -page n. cessation f.; panne f.; -per n. bouchon m.; -per vt. boucher; -ping n. arrêt m.

stopgap n. temporaire, provisoire

stop light n. feu rouge m.; (auto.) feu stop, signal de freinage m.

stopover n. halte f., séjour m.

stop watch n. chronographe, compte-secondes m.

storage n. entreposage, emmagasinage m.; frais d'entrepôt m. pl.; — battery n. accumulateur m.

store n. magasin, dépôt m.; quantité f.; provisions f. pl.; department — grand

magasin m.; in —, à venir; en réserve; set — by faire grand cas de; — vt. emmagasiner, mettre en dépôt

storehouse n. dépôt, magasin m.

storekeeper n. commerçant, boutiquier m.

storeroom n. magasin m., réserve f.

storied a. historié

storm n. orage m., tempête f.; assaut m.; — coat n. pardessus d'hiver avec col de fourrure m.; — troops troupes d'assaut f. pl.; — window contre-fenêtre f.; fenêtre extérieure utilisée en hiver f.; — vi. tempêter; — vt. assaillir; -iness n. assaut m.; -y a. orageux, violent

story n. histoire f.; récit m.; conte m.; fable f.; mensonge m.; (arch.) étage m.; short — nouvelle f., conte m.

storyteller n. conteur, raconteur m.

stout a. fort; résolu; gros; corpulent; — n. stout m., bière noire anglaise f.; -ness n. embonpoint m.

stouthearted a. brave, résolu

stove n. poêle m.; (range) cuisinière f.

stovepipe n. tuyau de poêle m.

stow vt. serrer, entasser; (naut.) arrimer; — away serrer; s'embarquer en cachette

stowaway n. passager clandestin m.

straddle vi. écarter les jambes; marcher les jambes écartées; être à califourchon; — vt. être à califourchon (sur); ne pas prendre parti (sur)

straggle vi. rester en arrière; -r n. traînard m.

straight a. droit; direct; franc; honnête, sincère; (beverage) sec; — adv. directement; droit; -way adv. tout de suite; -en vt. redresser; ranger; -en up ranger; se tenir droit; -ness droiture f.; rectitude f.; franchise f.

straightforward a. franc, honnête, sincère; loyal

straightway adv. tout de suite, sur-le-champ

strain n. effort m.; tension f.; (med.) entorse f.; manière f.; style m.; trace f.; (music) mélodie f.; — vt. tendre; filtrer; serrer, forcer; se fouler; — vi. s'efforcer, -er n. passoire f.

strait n. détroit m.; défilé m.; gorge f.; embarras m.; — a. étroit; sévère, pénible; -en vt. resserrer

strait-laced a. sévère; prude

strait jacket n. camisole de force f.

strand n. côte f., rivage m.; grève f.; fil m., fibre f.; brin m.; — vt. & vi. échouer

strange a. singulier; étrange; étranger; inconnu; -ness n. étrangeté, singularité f.; -r n. étranger m.; inconnu m.

strangle vt. étrangler

strangle hold n. prise de cou f.; prise inébranlable f.

strangulate vt. étrangler

strangulation n. étranglement m.

strap n. sangle, courroie, bretelle f.; — vt. attacher, lier, boucler; -ping a. solide, bien découplé

stratagem n. stratagème, artifice m.

strategic a. stratégique

strategist n. stratégiste m.

strategy n. stratégie f.

stratify *vt.* stratifier

stratosphere *n.* stratosphère *f.*

stratum *n.* couche *f.*; strate *f.*

straw *n.* paille *f.*; last — comble *m.*; — vote vote non-officiel qui s'informe de l'opinion publique *m.*

strawberry *n.* fraise *f.*; — bed *n.* fraisière *f.*

stray *n.* bête épave *f.*; bête égarée *f.*; — *a.* égaré; — *vi.* s'égarer

streak *n.* raie, bande *f.*; filet *m.*; — *vt.* rayer, bigarrer; -y *a.* rayé, bariolé

stream *n.* courant, torrent *m.*; ruisseau *m.*; rivière *f.*; flot *m.*; jet *m.*; — *vi.* couler, ruisseler; briller; -er *n.* banderole *f.*; serpentin *m.*

streamline *vt.* donner un profil aérodynamique à; caréner; moderniser; -d *a.* à profil aérodynamique; moderne

street *n.* rue *f.*; — floor rez-de-chaussée *m.*

streetcar *n.* tramway *m.*

street sweeper *n.* balayeur *m.*; (machine) balayeuse *f.*

streetwalker *n.* fille publique *f.*

strength *n.* force *f.*; résistance *f.*; forces *f. pl.*; solidité *f.*; at full — au complet; -en *vt.* fortifier; — *vi.* se fortifier

strenuous *a.* ardu; énergique; -ness *n.* ardeur *f.*

streptococcus *n.* streptocoque *m.*

streptomycin *n.* streptomycine *f.*

stress *n.* importance *f.*; violence *f.*; effort *m.*; accent tonique *m.*; — *vt.* souligner; accentuer; appuyer sur

stretch *n.* étendue *f.*; tension *f.*; at a — d'arrache-pied; — *vt.* étendre, élargir, allonger; exagérer; — *vi.* s'étendre, s'élargir, se déployer; -er *n.* (med.) brancard *m.*; -ing *n.* tension *f.*; allongement *m.* forcer

strew *vt.* parsemer, répandre çà et là; joncher

striated *a.* strié

stricken *a.* atteint; rayé

strict *a.* strict; exact; formel; sévère, rigoureux; -ly *adv.* rigoureusement, strictement; formellement; absolument; -ness *n.* sévérité, rigueur *f.*; exactitude *f.*; -ture *n.* contraction *f.*

stride *n.* enjambée *f.*; pas *m.*; — *vi.* marcher à grands pas

stridency *n.* stridence *f.*

strident *a.* strident

strife *n.* lutte *f.*; contestation *f.*; différend *m.*

strike *n.* grève *f.*; (geol.) découverte (d'un gisement) *f.*; — *vt.* frapper, heurter, battre; rencontrer, tomber sur; affliger; étonner, épouvanter; lancer; jeter, pousser; choquer, imprimer, graver; marquer; faire; — a bargain conclure un marché; — a match frotter une allumette; — *vi.* se mettre en grève, (labor) faire la grève, être en grève; — out partir, se lancer; — up se faire; commencer; -r *n.* gréviste *m.* & *f.*

strikebreaker *n.* (labor) briseur de grève *m.*

striking *a.* frappant

string *n.* corde *f.*, cordon *m.*, ficelle, attache *f.*, fil *m.*; fibre *f.*, tendon, filament *m.*; suite *f.*; — bean haricot vert *m.*; —

vt. mettre des cordes à; corder; bander; enfiler; — along (coll.) ménager; accepter (l'avis d'un autre); — up pendre; -ed *a.* à cordes; -y *a.* fibreux

stringency *n.* sévérité, rigueur *f.*

stringent *a.* fort, rigoureux

strip *n.* bande *f.*, ruban *m.*; — *vt.* dépouiller; déshabiller; dégarnir

stripe *n.* raie *f.*; barre *f.*; type *m.*, trempe, sorte *f.*; (mil.) chevron, galon *m.*; — *vt.* rayer; -d *a.* rayé, à raies

stripling *n.* jeune homme *m.*; débutant *m.*

strive *vi.* s'efforcer (de), tâcher (de); combattre; lutter

striving *n.* effort *m.*; lutte *f.*

stroke *n.* coup *m.*; trait de plume *m.*; (med.) attaque d'apoplexie *f.*; (swimming) brassée *f.*; — of luck coup de veine *m.*; on the — of à l'heure sonnante; — *vt.* caresser

stroll *n.* promenade *f.*; — *vi.* se promener; -er *n.* promeneur *m.*; voiture d'enfant *f.*; -ing *a.* ambulant

strong *a.* fort; vigoureux, robuste; puissant, énergique; solide, ferme; impétueux

strongbox *n.* coffre-fort *m.*

stronghold *n.* place forte *f.*

strontium *n.* strontium *m.*

strop *n.* cuir à repasser *m.*; — *vt.* repasser sur le cuir

structural *a.* de structure, structural

structure *n.* construction *f.*; édifice *m.*; structure *f.*

struggle *n.* combat *m.*, lutte *f.*; — *vi.* s'efforcer (de), se débattre, lutter (contre)

struggling *a.* pauvre; débutant

strum *vt.* gratter

strut *n.* démarche fière *f.*; (arch.) entretoise *f.*; — *vi.* se pavaner; — *vt.* entretoiser

strychnine *n.* strychnine *f.*

stub *n.* tronc, tronçon, chicot *m.*; (cigarette) mégot *m.*; (ticket) volet *m.* souche *f.* — *vt.* cogner; -by *a.* trapu, court

stubble *n.* chaume *f.*; poils de la barbe *m. pl.*

stubbly *a.* couvert de chaume; non-rasé

stubborn *a.* obstiné; entêté, têtu; tenace; -ness *n.* obstination *f.*, entêtement *m.*

stucco *n.* stuc *m.*

stuck *a.* coincé, collé

stud *n.* clou *m.*; bouton de plastron *m.*; (arch.) montant *m.*; — farm haras *m.*; — horse étalon *m.*; — *vt.* clouter, couvrir de clous; couvrir; -ded *a.* parsemé, constellé; -ding *n.* lattis *m.*

student *n.* étudiant *m.*

studied *a.* étudié, savant; recherché, voulu

studio *n.* atelier, studio *m.*

studious *a.* studieux; diligent

study *n.* étude *f.*; attention *f.*; méditation *f.*; cabinet *m.*; — *vt.* étudier; faire des études de

stuff *n.* matière, étoffe *f.*; (coll.) choses *f. pl.*, machins, ettrucs, rebuts *m. pl.*, — *vt.* fourrer; empailler; (cram) bourrer; (crowd) encombrer; (cooking) farcir; -ing *n.* empaillage *m.*; (cooking) farce *f.*; -y *a.* moisi, mal aéré; lourd; fastidieux, affecté

stultify vt. rendre ridicule; rendre inutile

stumble n. faux pas m.; — vi. trébucher, faire un faux pas; — on trouver par accident

stumbling block n. pierre d'achoppement f.

stump n. tronc, tronçon, bout, chicot m.; moignon m.; (coll.) estrade f.; — vi. marcher lourdement; faire une tournée de conférences en faveur de quelque chose; — vt. laisser sans réponse, maîtriser, triompher de

stun vt. étourdir, abasourdir; -ning a. ravissant; accablant

stunt n. tour m., acrobatie f.; — vt. empêcher de croître; rabougrir; — vi. faire des acrobaties

stupefaction n. stupéfaction f.; stupeur f.

stupefy vt. hébéter, stupéfier

stupendous a. prodigieux, étonnant

stupid a. stupide; bête; -ity n. stupidité f.; bêtise, niaiserie f.

stupor n. stupeur f.

sturdiness n. force, vigueur, hardiesse f.

sturdy a. vigoureux, fort, robuste

stutter n. & vt. bégayer, bredouiller; — n. bégaiement m.; -er n. bègue m. & f.; -ing n. bégaiement m.

sty n. étable à cochons f.; (med.) orgelet m.

style n. style m.; goût, genre m.; manière, façon f.; modèle m.; chic m., élégance f.; — vt. appeler; donner le titre de; dessiner

stylish a. de bon ton; élégant; -ness n. chic, ton m., élégance f.

stylist n. styliste m.; -ic n. stylistique f.

stylize vt. styliser

stylus n. style m.

styptic a. hémostitique

suave a. suave

suavity n. suavité, douceur f.

subcommittee n. sous-commission f., sous-comité m.

subconscious a. & n. subconscient m.

subcontract vt. sous-traiter; — n. sous-traite m.; -or n. sous-entrepreneur m.

subcutaneous a. sous-cutané

subdivide vt. subdiviser

subdivision n. subdivision f.

subdue vt. subjuguer; vaincre; dompter; amortir; atténuer

subheading n. subheading n. sous-titre m.

subject n. sujet m.; — vt. soumettre, subjuguer, exposer; — a. sujet, soumis à; -ion n. sujétion f.; soumission f.; -ive a. subjectif

subjugate vt. subjuguer, assujettir

subjugation n. subjugation f., assujettissement m.

subjunctive a. & n. subjonctif m.

sublease, sublet vt. sous-louer

sublimate n. & a. sublimé m.; — vt. sublimer

sublimity n. sublimité f.

submarine n. & a. sous-marin m.

submerge vt. submerger; plonger

submersion n. submersion f.; plongée f.

submission n. soumission f.; résignation f.

submissive a. soumis (à); -ness n. soumission f.

submit vt. soumettre; — vi. se soumettre

subnormal a. inférieur à la normale

subordinate vt. subordonner, soumettre; — n. & a. subordonné m.

subpoena n. assignation, citation f.; — vt. citer (à comparaître en justice)

subscribe vt. souscrire, s'abonner; consentir; -r n. abonné m.

subscription n. souscription f.; abonnement m.; cotisation f.

subsequent a. subséquent, suivant, qui suit; ultérieur

subservience n. utilité f.; subordination f.; dépendance f.; servilité f.

subservient a. subordonné; utile

subside vi. baisser; se calmer, s'apaiser

subsidiary n. & a. auxiliaire m.; subsidiaire m.; filiale f.

subsidize vt. subventionner

subsidy n. subvention f.

subsist vi. subsister, exister; -ence n. subsistence, existence f.; allocation f.

subsoil n. sous-sol m.

substance n. substance, matière f.; essentiel, m. corps m.; réalité f.; fortune f.

substantial a. substantiel; essentiel; réel; matériel, fort; solide

substantiate vt. établir; prouver par des faits

substantive n. substantif m.

substation n. sous-station f.

substitute vt. substituer; remplacer, suppléer, — vi. être substitué — n. remplaçant, suppléant m.; factice m.

substitution n. substitution f.; remplacement m.

substratum n. couche inférieure f.; sous-sol m.

substructure n. substructure f.

subterfuge n. subterfuge, faux-fuyant m.

subterranean a. souterrain

subtitle n. sous-titre m.

subtle a. subtil; fin; -ty n. subtilité f.; finesse f.

subtly adv. subtilement; avec finesse

subtract vt. soustraire; -ion n. soustraction f.

suburb n. ville de la banlieue f.; -an a. de la banlieue; -anite n. habitant de la banlieue m.; -ia n. (coll.) banlieue f.

subvention n. subvention f.; — vt. subventionner

subversion n. subversion f., renversement m.

subversive a. subversif

subvert vt. subvertir

subway n. passage souterrain m.; (rail.) métro m.

succeed vt. succéder; suivre; — vi. réussir, parvenir, arriver

success n. succès m.; réussite f.; -ful a. prospère, heureux, qui a du succès; -ion n. succession f.; héritage m.; suite, série f.; in -ion de suite; consécutif, successif -ive a. successif; -or n. successeur m.

succinct a. concis; succinct

succor n. secours m., aide f.; — vt. secourir, aider, assister, seconder

succumb vi. succomber

such a. tel; pareil, semblable; de la sorte;
— pron. ceux; tel; — as prep. tel que

suck n. action de sucer f.; — vt. & vi.
sucer; téter; —er n. (candy) sucette f.;
(fish) rémora m.; (animal) suçoir; (octopus) ventouse f.; (bot.) drageon m.;
(coll.) nigaud, innocent m.

suckle vt. allaiter

suckling n. nourrisson m.; — pig cochon
de lait m.

sucrose n. saccharose m.

suction n. aspiration f.; — pump pompe
aspirante f.

Sudan n. Soudan m.

sudden a. brusque; soudain, subit; all of
a — tout à coup; brusquement; —ly adv.
soudainement, soudain; tout à coup;
brusquement; —ness n. brusquerie f.;
rapidité f.

suds n. mousse de savon f.

sue vt. poursuivre en justice; supplier, implorer; demander

suede n. suède m.

suet n. suif m.

Suez n. — Canal Canal de Suez m.

suffer vt. souffrir; essuyer, subir; supporter; permettre; — vi. souffrir; —ance n.
tolérance f.; —ing a. souffrant; —ing n.
souffrance f.

suffice vi. suffire; — vt. suffire à

sufficiency n. suffisance f.

sufficient a. suffisant; —ly adv. suffisamment, assez

suffix n. suffixe m.

suffocate vt. & vi. suffoquer, étouffer

suffocation n. étouffement m.

suffuse vt. répandre, remplir

suffusion n. suffusion f.; épanchement m.

sugar n. sucre m.; beet — sucre de betterave m.; brown — sucre brut m.; cane
— sucre de canne m.; granulated —
sucre en poudre m.; lump — sucre en
morceaux m.; powdered — sucre de
confiseur m.; — beet betterave à sucre
f.; — bowl sucrier m.; — cane canne à
sucre f.; — mill moulin à cannes m.;
— vt. sucrer; saupoudrer de sucre; —y a.
sucré

suggest vt. suggérer, insinuer, inspirer;
—ion n. suggestion f.; —ive a. suggestif;
évocateur

suicide n. suicide m.; commit — se suicider

suit n. (men's) complet m.; (women's)
tailleur m.; costume m.; (request) requête f.; (law) procès m.; (cards) couleur f.; — vt. convenir à; aller à; —ability
n. convenance f.; conformité f.; —able a.
à propos; bon; sortable; convenable;
—or n. prétendant m.; soupirant m.

suitcase n. valise f.

suite n. suite f.; train m.; (furniture) mobilier m.

sulfide n. sulfure m.

sulfite n. sulfite m.

sulfur n. soufre m.; —ic a. sulfurique; —ous
a. sulfureux

sulk n. bouderie f.; — vi. bouder; —y a.
boudeur; maussade; —iness n. maussaderie f.

sulky n. voiture légère à deux roues (utili-

sée aux courses attelées) f.

sullen a. maussade; chagrin; sombre

sully vt. souiller, tacher

sultan n. sultan m.; —a n. sultane f.

sultry a. d'une chaleur étouffante; suffocant

sum n. somme f., tout, total m.; in — total
en somme, somme toute; — vt. additioner; —up résumer; —ming n., —ing up
résumé m.

summarize vt. résumer

summary n. sommaire, résumé m.; — a.
sommaire

summer n. été m.; — resort station estivale f.; — sausage saucisson m.

summerhouse n. pavillon m.; villa f.

summertime n. été m., saison d'été f.

summit n. sommet m.; cime f.; comble m.;
— conference conférence au sommet f.

summon vt. sommer; citer, assigner; ordonner, commander; appeler; convoquer; —s n. citation, assignation f.; appel m.

sump n. puisard m., fosse f.

sumptuous a. somptueux; —ness n. somptuosité f.; luxe m., richesse f.

sun n. soleil m.; — parlor, — porch solarium m.; — visor abat-jour m.; — vt. exposer au soleil; —oneself prendre le soleil; —ny a. ensoleillé; it is —ny il fait du
soleil

sun-bathe vi. prendre le soleil

sunbeam n. rayon de soleil m.

sunbonnet n. capeline f.

sunburn n. hâle m.; coup de soleil m.; —ed
a. hâlé; brûlé (par le soleil); — vt. bruler, hâler

sundae n. coupe (glace, sirop et fruit) f.

Sunday n. dimanche m.

sunder vt. séparer, partager

sundial n. cadran solaire m.

sundown n. coucher du soleil m.

sundries n. pl. diverses choses f. pl. (com.)
divers m. pl.

sundry a. divers

sunfast, sunproof a. inaltérable au soleil

sunglasses n. pl. lunettes contre le soleil
f. pl.

sunken a. creux; enfoncé

sunlight n. soleil m.; lumière du soleil f.;
jour m.

sun parlor n. (house) solarium m.

sunrise n. lever du soleil m.

sunset n. coucher du soleil m.

sunshine n. soleil m.

sunspot n. tache solaire f.

sunstroke n. insolation f.

sun tan n. hâle m.

sup vi. souper

superable a. surmontable

superabundance n. surabondance f.

superabundant a. surabondant

superannuated a. suranné; retraité

superb a. superbe

supercargo n. subrécargue m.

supercharge vt. supercompresser; —er n.
supercompresseur m.

supercilious n. hautain, arrogant; —ness n.
hauteur f.

superficial a. superficiel

superfine a. surfin
superfluous a. superflu; inutile
superhighway n. autostrade f.
superhuman a. surhumain
superimpose vt. superposer, surimposer
superintend vt. surveiller; —ent n. surintendant m.; inspecteur m.
superior a. & n. supérieur m.; —ity n. supériorité f.
superlative n. superlatif m.; — a. superlatif, suprême
superman n. surhomme m.
supermarket n. supermarket, grand magasin d'alimentation m.
supernatural a. surnaturel
supernumerary n. & a. surnuméraire m.
supersaturate vt. sursaturer
supersede vt. remplacer; faire supprimer; (law) surseoir à
supersensitive a. hypersensible
supersonic a. supersonique, ultrasonore
superstition n. superstition f.
superstructure n. édifice m.; superstructure f.
supervene vi. survenir
supervise vt. surveiller, diriger
supervision n. surveillance f.; direction f.
supervisor n. surveillant; inspecteur m.; directeur m.
supine a. couché sur le dos; — n. (gram.) supin m.
supper n. souper m.; have — souper
Supper, The Last la Sainte Cène f.
suppertime n. heure du souper f.
supplant vt. supplanter, remplacer
supple a. souple, flexible; —ness n. souplesse, flexibilité f.
supplement n. supplément m.; — vt. suppléer à; ajouter à, augmenter; —al, —ary a. supplémentaire
suppliant n. & a. suppliant m.
supplicant n. suppliant
supplicate vt. supplier
supplication n. supplication f.
supplier n. fournisseur m.; pourvoyeur, approvisionneur m.
supply n. fourniture f.; provision f.; approvisionnement m.; (mil.) ravitaillement m.; — and demand l'offre et la demande; — vt. approvisionner; fournir, pourvoir; munir
support n. soutien, appui, support m.; — vt. soutenir; entretenir; appuyer; assister; souffrir; supporter; faire subsister; — oneself gagner sa vie; —able a. supportable; —er n. soutien, partisan m.; (sport) slip (pour sportif) m.; (med.) suspensoire m.
suppose vt. supposer, imaginer; penser, croire; s'imaginer; —d a. censé; supposé; présumé; soi-disant; prétendu
suppress vt. supprimer; empêcher; étouffer, cacher; refouler, réprimer; —ion n. répression f.; refoulement m.
suppurate vi. suppurer
supremacy n. suprématie, supériorité f.
supreme a. suprême
Supreme Court n. Cour Suprême f.; grand tribunal m.
surcease n. arrêt m., interruption f.
surcharge n. surcharge f.; surtaxe f.; — vt.

surcharger
surd n. (sound) sourd m.; (math.) irrationnel m.
sure a. sûr, certain; assuré, ferme; to be —! assurément! certainement!; be — to — ne pas manquer de; make — s'assurer; —l interj. mais oui, bien sûr; entendu; —ly adv. sûrement; assurément
sure-footed a. au pied sûr
surety n. sûreté f.; caution f.
surf n. brisant, ressac m.
surface n. surface f.; on the — (fig.) en apparence; — vt. mettre une nouvelle surface à; — vi. revenir à la surface
surfacing n. apprêtage; (road) revêtement m.
surfboard n. aquaplane m.
surfeit n. satiété f.; surabondance f.; — vt. soûler, rassasier; — vi. se soûler; se gorger
surge n. vague f., flot m., houle f.; — vi. s'élever, s'enfler; se soulever
surgeon n. chirurgien m.
surgery n. chirurgie f.
surgical a. chirurgical
surging a. houleux
surly a. hargneux, maussade, bourru
surmise n. conjecture f.; — vi. conjecturer; — vi. se douter de
surmount vt. surmonter
surname n. surnom, nom de famille m.; — vt. surnommer
surpass vt. surpasser, dépasser; —ing a. supérieur
surplice n. surplis m.
surplus n. surplus m.; excédent m.
surprise n. surprise f.; étonnement m.; — vt. surprendre; étonner; be —d s'étonner
surprising a. surprenant; étonnant
surrealist n. surréaliste m.
surrender n. reddition f.; cession f.; — vi. se rendre; — vt. rendre; céder; renoncer à
surreptitious a. subreptice, clandestine
surrogate n. délégué m.; — court cour qui s'occupe des testaments f. — vt. subroger
surround vt. environner, entourer; —ings n. pl. environs m. pl.; milieu m.
surtax n. surtaxe f.; — vt. surtaxer
surveillance n. surveillance f.
survey n. coup d'œil m.; examen m.; inspection f.; référendum m.; arpentage m.; — vt. surveiller, examiner, observer; consulter; arpenter; —ing n. arpentage m.; —or n. arpenteur m.
survival n. survivance f.
survive vi. survivre; — vt. survivre à
survivor n. survivant m.
susceptibility n. susceptibilité f.
susceptible a. susceptible f.
suspect n. personne suspecte f.; — vt. soupçonner, se douter de
suspend vt. suspendre; —ers n. pl. bretelles f. pl.
suspense n. suspens, doute m., incertitude f.; cessation f.; in — en suspens
suspension n. suspension f.; — bridge n. pont suspendu m.
suspicion n. soupçon m.; doute m.; méfiance, défiance f.
suspicious a. soupçonneux; suspect; mé-

fiant; —ness n. méfiance f.; doute n.

sustain vt. soutenir, maintenir, entretenir; subir, essuyer, éprouver; —ed a. soutenu

sustenance n. subsistance f.; entretien m.

suture n. suture f.; — vt. suturer

swab n. faubert m.; (cotton) tampon d'ouate m.; — vt. fauberter; laver, nettoyer

swaddle vt. emmailloter

swaddling clothes n. pl. maillot m.

swagger vi. faire le fanfaron, fanfaronner; se pavaner; — stick (mil.) bâton d'officier m.; —er n. fanfaron m.; —ing a. important

swallow n. (bird) hirondelle f.; gorgée f.; avalement m.; coup m.; — vt. avaler, engloutir; gober; — up engloutir

swamp n. marécage, marais m.; — vt. embourber; engloutir; submerger; inonder; —y a. marécageux

swan n. cygne m.; — dive saut d'ange, plongeon en nage m.

sward n. gazon m., pelouse f.

swarm n. essaim m.; fourmillière f.; — vi. essaimer; fourmiller; grouiller

swarthy a. basané; noir, sombre

swashbuckler n. fanfaron m.

swatch n. échantillon m.

swath n. andain m., fauchée f.

swathe n. maillot m., langes m. pl.; — vt. emmailloter

sway n. pouvoir m., domination f.; prépondérance f.; — vt. influencer; balancer; détourner; — vi. vaciller; se balancer; s'incliner

sway-backed a. ensellé

swear vi. jurer; blasphémer; — vt. jurer; — to certifier, attester; — in faire prêter serment à; —ing n. jurons m. pl.; —ing in n. assermentation f.

sweat n. sueur, transpiration f.; — vi. suer, transpirer; bûcher, travailler dur; (wall) suinter; —shop n. entreprise dont les ouvriers sont surmenés f.; —ing n. transpiration f.; (wall) suintement m.

sweater n. chandail; pull-over; maillot m.; tricot m.

Swede n. Suédois m.

Sweden n. Suède f.

Swedish a. suédois

sweep n. balayage, coup de balai m.; (chimney) ramoneur m.; (naut.) aviron m.; at a —, at one — d'un seul coup; make a clean — faire table rase; — vt. balayer; couvrir; (chimney) ramoner; — away, — off balayer; emporter; — out, — up balayer; nettoyer; —er n. balayeur m.; carpet —er n. balayeuse f.; balai méchanique m.; —ing n. action de balayer f.; —ings n. pl. balayures f. pl.; —ing a. général; complet

sweepstake(s) n. (pl.) sweepstake(s) m.; poule(s) f.

sweet a. doux (douce); savoureux, odorant; sucré; mélodieux; gracieux; tendre; aimable, agréable; gentil; frais; — potato patate f.; — n. bonbon m., confiserie f.; sucrerie f.; —en vt. sucrer, —ening n. sucrage m.; sucre m.; —ness n. douceur f.

sweetbread n. ris de veau m.

sweetheart n. amoureux m., amoureuse f.; ami m., amie f.

sweetmeats n. pl. confiserie f.; sucreries f. pl.

swell n. élévation f.; (sea) houle f.; élégant m.; — vt. enfler, gonfler; augmenter; — vi. s'enfler; se gonfler; s'augmenter; accroître; — a. (coll.) formidable; épatant; excellent; élégant; —ing n. enflure f.; enflement m.; gonflement m.

swelter vi. étouffer de chaleur; —ing a. étouffant de chaleur

swerve vi. dévier; fléchir; se dérober; — n. crochet m., embardée f.

swift n. martinet m.; — a. prompt; rapide; léger; —ly adv. vite, rapidement; —ness n. vitesse, rapidité f.

swift-footed a. au pied léger

swill n. eaux grasses f. pl.

swim n. bain de mer m.; — vi. nager; — vt. traverser à la nage; —mer n. nageur m.; —ming a. (fig.) tournant; noyé; —ming n. natation f.; —ming pool piscine f.; —suit costume de bain m.

swindle n. escroquerie f.; — vt. & vi. escroquer; filouter; —r n. escroc m.; filou m.

swine n. cochon m.; porc m.

swineherd n. porcher m.

swing n. oscillation f.; dandinement m.; branle m.; escarpolette f.; balançoire f.; (mus.) swing m.; in full — en plein travail; en activité; — vt. balancer; tourner; basculer; brandir; — vi. se balancer; tourner; —ing a. balançant; rythmé; battant; —ing door porte battante f.

swipe n. coup m.; — vt. frapper; (coll.) chiper; voler

swirl n. tourbillon m.; — vi. tourbillonner

swish n. sifflement m.; froissement m.; — vt. faire siffler; — vi. bruire

Swiss a. & n. suisse m.

switch n. baguette f.; (rail.) aiguille f.; (elec.) interrupteur, bouton m.; (coll.) changement m., substitution f.; — vt. (whip) cingler; agiter; échanger; (rail.) aiguiller; — off couper, éteindre; — on allumer

switchboard n. (phone) standard (téléphonique) m.; — operator standardiste m. & f.

switchman n. (rail.) aiguilleur m.

Switzerland n. Suisse f.

swivel n. pivot m.; — chair fauteuil tournant m.; — vi. pivoter

swollen a. enflé, gonflé; (river) en crue

swoon n. évanouissement m.; — vi. s'évanouir

swoop n. descente f.; attaque f.; ruée f.; coup m.; — vi. fondre, s'abattre

sword n. épée f.; sabre m.

swordsman n. épéiste m.; duelliste m.

syllabification n. division en syllabes f.

syllable n. syllabe f.

syllabus n. sommaire, programme m.; syllabus m.

sylph n. sylphe m.; sylphide f.

sylvan a. sylvestre

symbol n. symbole m.; —ic(al) a. symbolique; —ism n. symbolisme m.; —ize vt. symboliser

symmetrical a. symétrique
symmetry n. symétrie f.
sympathetic a. sympathique; compatissant
sympathize vi. sympathiser; — with avoir de la compassion pour; être partisan de; comprendre, se rendre compte de; -r n. partisan m.
sympathy n. sympathie f.; compassion f.; condoléances f. pl.
symphonic a. symphonique
symphony n. symphonie f.; — orchestra orchestre symphonique m.
symposium n. réunion f.; discussion f.; banquet m.
sympton n. symptôme, indice m.; -atic a. symptomatique
synagogue n. synagogue f.
synchronize vt. synchroniser
syncopate vt. syncoper
syndicate n. syndicat m.; — vt. faire publier (un écrit) dans plusieurs journaux
synod n. synode m.
synonym n. synonyme m.; -ous a. synonyme
synopsis n. résumé m., analyse f.
syntax n. syntaxe f.
synthesis n. synthèse f.
synthesize vt. synthétiser; produire synthétiquement
synthetic a. synthétique
syphilis n. syphilis f.
syphilitic a. syphilitique
Syria n. Syrie f.; -c n. syriaque m.; -n a. & n. syrien m.
syringe n. seringue f.; — vt. seringuer
syrup n. sirop m.; -y a. siroupeux
system n. système, régime m., méthode f.; réseau m.; -atic a. systématique; méthodique; -atize vt. systématiser

T

tab n. oreille, oreillette f.; touche f.; patte f.; (coll.) addition f.; keep — on surveiller, contrôler
table n. table f.; tableau m.; bureau m.; liste f.; tablette f.; tablier m.; set the — mettre la table; — of contents table f.; turn the -s on faire tourner les chances contre; — vt. (a proposition) ajourner; classer
tablecloth n. nappe f.
tableland n. plateau m.
tablespoon n. cuiller à bouche, cuiller à soupe f.; -ful n. cuillerée à bouche f.
tablet n. tablette f.; plaque f.; comprimé m.; (paper) bloc m.
tableware n. service de table m.
tabloid n. journal de petit format m.; journal sensationnel m.
taboo, tabu n. & a. tabou m.; — vt. interdire
tabular a. en forme de table; tabulaire
tabulate vt. disposer en forme de table; classer, cataloguer
tachometer n. tachymètre m.

tacit a. tacite
taciturn a. taciturne
tack n. petit clou m., broquette f.; (naut.)

amure f.; — vt. accrocher, attacher; (naut.) louvoyer; thumb— n. punaise f.
tackle n. attirail m.; appareil m.; articles m. pl.; (sport) action de saisir, de renverser f.; block and — moufle m.; — vt. saisir, renverser; plaquer; chercher à résoudre, aborder
tacky a. collant; pas encore sec
tact n. tact m.; savoir-faire m.; -ful a. (plein) de tact; -less a. sans tact
tactical a. tactique
tactics n. pl. tactique f.
taffeta n. taffetas m.
tag n. étiquette f.; — vt. attacher une étiquette à; — along vi. (coll.) accompagner (sans être invité)
Tahiti n. Taïti m.
tail n. queue f.; culée f.; (coin) pile f.; (shirt) pan m.; turn — tourner les talons, se sauver, s'échapper; -light n. (auto.) feu rouge arrière m.; -s n. pl. habit à queue m.
tailor n. tailleur m.; — vi. exercer l'état de tailleur; — vt. confectionner, façonner, faire
tailor-made a. (fait) sur mesure
tail spin n. chute en vrille f.
taint n. souillure, tache f.; infection f.; — vt. gâter; souiller, infecter, corrompre
take n. prise f.; (coll.) profit m.; butin m.; — vt. prendre; saisir, s'emparer de; tenir; mener, conduire; amener; emporter; louer; accepter, recevoir, admettre; tolérer, souffrir, supporter; penser, croire, supposer; — vi. prendre; avoir effet; réussir; — after ressembler à, tenir de; — along emporter; amener; — apart démonter; — away enlever, emporter; emmener; — back reprendre; remporter, rapporter; — down descendre; — in duper, rouler, tromper; rentrer; recevoir; comprendre, comporter; — off enlever; ôter; partir, filer; (avi.) décoller; — on prendre; se charger de, s'occuper de; assumer; (industry) embaucher; — out enlever; sortir; accompagner dehors; — over prendre possession de; prendre la direction de; — to s'habituer à, s'accoutumer à, se faire à; s'adonner à; — up monter; prendre; rétrécir; occuper; étudier; absorber; — an examination passer un examen; — a walk faire une promenade; se promener; — care of se charger de, s'occuper de; prendre soin de; soigner; garder, surveiller; — charge of se charger de; prendre la direction de; — effect entrer en vigueur; produire son effet; — it easy se ménager; — place avoir lieu; — prisoner faire prisonnier; -n a. pris; saisi; occupé; be -n ill tomber malade
takeoff n. (avi.) décollage m.; imitation, satire f.

taking n. prise f.
talcum n. talc m.
tale n. conte m., histoire f.
talent n. talent m.; génie m.; flair m.; -ed a. de talent; doué
talk n. conversation f.; discours m.; cause-

rie f.; propos m. pl.; paroles f. pl.; — vi.
parler, causer, jaser; raisonner; — vt.
parler; — over discuter; -ative a. bavard; loquace; -ativeness n. loquacité
f.;-er n. bavard, causeur m.;-ing a. parlant; parlé; -ing n. conversation f.

tall a. grand; haut; (coll.) incroyable;
-ness n. hauteur f.; grande taille f.

tallow n. suif m.

tally n. compte m.; taille f.; entaille, coche
f.; — vi. correspondre; — vt. pointer,
contrôler

talon n. serre, griffe f.

tambourine n. tambourin m.

tame vt. apprivoiser; dompter; — a. apprivoisé, dompté, doux, domestique; abattu, humilié; -ness n. docilité f., caractère doux m.;-r n. apprivoiseur, dompteur m.

tamp vt. pilonner; bourrer

tamper vt. expérimenter (avec); — with se
mêler de; altérer; fausser, falsifier

tan n. tan m.; (sun) hâle m.; (color) brunjaune m.; — vt. tanner; hâler; (coll.)
fesser; -ner n. tanneur m.; -nery n. tannerie f.; -ing n. tan m.

tang n. goût âpre m.; saveur f.

tangent n. tangente f.; — a. tangent, tangentiel

tangerine n. mandarine f.

tangible a. tangible, tactile; sensible; matériel

Tangiers n. Tanger m.

tangle vt. embarrasser, embrouiller; emmêler; — n. embrouillement m.; embarras m.

tank n. citerne f.; réservoir m.; (mil.)
tank, char m.; gas — réservoir à essence
m.; — car wagon-citerne m.; -er n. bateau-citerne m.

tankard n. chope f.

tannic a. tannique

tannin n. tanin m.

tantalize vt. tourmenter, tantaliser, taquiner

tantalizing a. qui tantalise; (fig.) ravissant; délicieux; séduisant; provocant

tantalum n. tantale m.

tantamount a. équivalent

tantrum n. accès de colère m.

tap n. tape f., coup léger m.; cannelle f.,
robinet m.; — dance danse à claquettes
f.; — water eau du robinet f.; on — en
vidange; — vt. percer; taper; frapper

tap-dance vi. danser à la claque

tape n. ruban m.; bande f.; adhesive —
sparadrap m.; recording — ruban magnétique m.; red — paperasseries f. pl.;
— measure, — line mètre en ruban m.;
— recorder n. magnétophone m.; — vt.
entourer d'un ruban; entourer de sparadrap; enregistrer sur ruban

taper n. bougie f.; — vi. se terminer en
pointe; — vt. tailler en cône, côner; diminuer; -ed, -ing a. conique; en pointe;
effilé

tapestry n. tapisserie f.

tapeworm n. ver solitaire m.

taproot n. racine principale f.

taps n. (mil.) signal d'éteindre les lumières
dans les casernes m.

tar n. goudron m.; matelot m.; — vt. goudronner; -ry a. goudronneux

tarentella n. tarentelle f.

tardiness n. lenteur f.; manque de ponctualité m.

tardy a. tardif, lent; en retard

tare n. ivraie f.; (com.) tare f.

target n. cible f.; but m.

tariff n. tarif m.

tarnish n. ternissure f.; — vi. se ternir

tarpaulin n. bâche f.; prélart m.

tarragon n. estragon m.

tarry vi. tarder, attendre; demeurer

tart n. tarte f.; — a. aigre; acide; mordant,
piquant; -ness n. aigreur, acidité f.

tartar n. tartre m.

Tartar a. & n. tartare m.

tartar n. (chem.) tartre m.; cream of —
crème de tartre f.

task n. tâche, besogne f.; travail m.;
(school punishment) pensum m.; take
to — réprimander; — force (mil.)
groupe chargé d'une mission spéciale m.

taskmaster n. surveillant tyrannique m.

Tasmania n. Tasmanie f.

tassel n. gland m., houppe f.

taste n. goût m.; saveur, odeur f.; petit
morceau, petit peu m.; penchant m.; —
vt. goûter; déguster; sentir; — vi. avoir
le goût; sentir; -ful a. de bon goût; -less
a. sans goût; fade, insipide; -r n. dégustateur m.

tastiness n. saveur f., goût m.

tasty a. délicieux; savoureux

tat vt. confectionner de la dentelle; faire
de la frivolité; -ting n. frivolité; tit for
— à bon chat bon rat

tatter n. guenille f., lambeau m.; -ed a.
en lambeaux

tattle vi. cancaner; commérer; bavarder

tattletale n. rapporteur m.

tattoo n. tatouage m. (mil.) retraite f.; —
vt. tatouer; -ing n. tatouage m.

taunt n. insulte f.; raillerie f.; — vt. insulter; tourner en ridicule

taupe n. gris-jaune m.

taut a. raide, tendu; -ness n. raideur f.

tautology n. tautologie f.

tavern n. cabaret m., auberge f.; taverne
f.; — keeper aubergiste m.

tawdry a. clinquant; de mauvais goût,
vulgaire

tawny a. tanné; basané

tax n. taxe f., impôt m.; contributions
f. pl.; — collector percepteur m.; receveur m.; — vt. taxer; mettre à l'épreuve;
-able a. imposable, sujet à la taxe;
-ation n. taxation f.; impôts m. pl.

taxpayer n. contribuable m. & f.

taxi(cab) n. taxi m.; — vi. (avi.) rouler

taxidermist n. empailleur m.

taxidermy n. empaillage m., taxidermie f.

taximeter n. taximètre m.

tea n. thé m.; to come to — venir prendre
le thé; — bag n. sachet de thé m.; —
ball boule à thé f.

teach vt. enseigner, apprendre; professer;
-er n. professeur m.; instituteur m., institutrice f.; maître d'école m.; mai-

tresse d'école f.; -er's college école normale f.; -ing n. enseignement m.; -ing staff n. corps enseignant m.

teacup n. tasse à thé f.

teakettle n. bouilloire f.

team n. équipe f.; (horses) attelage m.; — vt. atteler; — vi., — (up) with collaborer avec; se joindre à

teamwork n. travail d'équipe m., collaboration f.

teapot n. théière f.

tear n. larme f.; -s pl. larmes f. pl., pleurs m. pl.; — gas gas lacrymogène m.; -ful en pleurs; larmoyant; -fully adv. en pleurant

tear n. déchirure f.; — vt. déchirer; arracher; — vi. se déchirer; aller à toute vitesse; — down démolir; — up déchirer

tearoom n. salon de thé m.; pâtisserie f.

tease a. taquiner, tourmenter; — n. taquin m.; -r n. question difficile f.

teasing a. taquin; raillant; — n. taquinerie f.; raillerie f.

teaspoon n. cuiller à café f.; -ful n. cuillerée à café f.

teat n. tétin m.; mamelon m.; tette f.

technical a. technique; -ity n. technicité f.; détail (technique) m.

technician n. technicien m.

technique n. technique f.

technological a. technologique

technology n. technologie f.

tedious a. ennuyeux, fatigant; -ness n. ennui m.

tedium n. ennui m.

tee, T n. té m.; golf — m. dé; pointe de départ m.; — vi., — off commencer

teem vi. fourmiller, foisonner, abonder, grouiller; pleuvoir à verse; -ing a. fécond, fertile

teen-age a. adolescent; âgé de 13 à 19 ans; -r n. adolescent m.

teens n. pl. numéros de 13 à 19 m. pl.; adolescence f.

teeth n. dents f. pl.; -e n vi. faire les dents; -ing n. dentition f.

teeter vi. vaciller; se balancer; faillir tomber

teeter-totter n. balançoire f.

teetotaler n. buveur d'eau m.

telecast n. émission de télévision f.

telegram n. télégramme m.

telegraph n. télégraphe m.; — vt. télégraphier; -ic a. télégraphique; -y n. télégraphie f.

telelens n. téléobjectif m.

telemeter n. télémètre m.

teleological a. téléologique

teleology n. téléologie f.

telepathic a. télépathique

telepathy n. télépathie f.

telephone n. téléphone m.; dial — téléphone automatique m.; — booth n. cabine téléphonique f.; — directory n. annuaire m.; — exchange n. central téléphonique m.; — operator n. standardiste m. & f.; — receiver n. recepteur m.; — a. téléphonique; — vt. & vi. téléphoner (à)

telephonic a. téléphonique

telephony n. téléphonie f.

teleprinter n. télétype, téléscripteur m.

teletypewriter n. télétype m.

telescope n. télescope m.; longue-vue f.; — vt. télescoper; — vi. (se) télescoper

telescopic a. télescopique

televise vt. téléviser

television n. télévision f.; — set téléviseur m.

tell vt. dire; raconter, conter; apprendre; marquer, indiquer; ordonner; distinguer; savoir; — vi. porter; -er n. conteur, raconteur m.; (bank) caissier, payeur m.; fortune — n. diseuse de bonne aventure f.; -ing a. efficace; frappant; -ing n. récit m., narration f.

telltale a. révélateur

tellurium n. tellure m.

temerity n. témérité, audace f.

temper n. caractère m.; naturel m.; humeur f.; irritation f.; colère f.; (metal) trempe f.; lose one's — se mettre en colère, s'emporter; — vt. tempérer, modérer; adoucir; broyer; tremper; -ed a. trempé, recuit

tempera n. détrempe f.

temperament n. tempérament m.; humeur f., caractère m.; -al a. d'humeur inégale, capricieux

temperance n. tempérance, modération f.

temperate a. tempéré, modéré; -ness n. modération f.; douceur f.

temperature n. température f.; fièvre f.

tempest n. tempête f., orage m.; -uous a. orageux

temple n. temple m.; (anat.) tempe f.

temporal a. temporel; (anat.) temporal

temporary a. temporaire, provisoire, intérimaire; passager

temporize vi. temporiser; transiger (avec)

tempt vt. tenter; -ation n. tentation f.; -er n. tenteur m.; -ress n. tentatrice f.

ten n. & a. dix m.; about — disaine f.; -th n. & a. dixième m.

tenable a. tenable

tenacious a. tenace

tenacity n. ténacité f.; entêtement m.

tenancy n. (law) usufruit m.; location f.

tenant n. tenancier, fermier m.; locataire m. & f.; — vt. tenir à bail; habiter; -less a. sans habitant

tend vt. garder, surveiller; avoir soin de; soigner; — vi. tendre; contribuer; -er n. offre f.; (rail.) tender m.; legal -er monnaie légale f.; -er vt. offrir

tendency n. tendance f.; disposition f.; penchant m., inclination f.

tendentious a. tandancieux

tender a. tendre; affectueux; délicat; sensible; -ness n. tendresse f.; délicatesse f.; sensibilité f.

tenderfoot n. bleu, débutant m.

tenderhearted a. sensible

tenderloin n. filet m.

tendril n. vrille f.

tenement n. immeuble d'habitation dans un quartier misérable m.

tenet n. dogme, principe m.

tenor n. caractère m.; teneur f.; (mus.) ténor m.

tense n. temps m.; — a. tendu, raide; nerveux; -ness n. tension f.

tensile a. de traction; extensible

tension n. tension f.; traction f.; raideur f.; voltage m.

tent n. tente f.; — vt. camper

tentacle n. tentacule m.

tentative a. d'essai; experimental

tenuous a. ténu, insaisissable, mince; —ness n. ténuité f.

tenure n. possession, occupation, tenure f.

tepid a. tiède

term n. terme m.; limite f.; période f.; (com.) échéance f.; condition, stipulation f.; expression f.; inscription f.; school — semestre m.; trimestre m.; be on good —s with être bien avec; come to —s with s'arranger avec; — vt. appeler, nommer

terminal a. final, terminal; — n. terminus m.; gare f.; (elec.) borne f.

terminate vt. terminer, mettre fin à; — vi. se terminer, finir

termination n. fin, limite f., terminaison f.

terminology n. terminologie f.

terminus n. terminus m.; (railroad) gare f.

termite n. termite m.

tern n. sterne m.

terrace n. terrasse f.; — vt. terrasser, disposer en terrasse

terra cotta n. terre cuite f.

terrestrial a. terrestre

terrible a. terrible, épouvantable; atroce

terrific a. terrible; (coll.) formidable; épatant; excellent; —ally adv. terriblement

terrify vt. effrayer, épouvanter, terrifier

territorial a. territorial

territory n. territoire m.

terror n. terreur f.; épouvante f.; effroi m.; —ism n. terrorisme m.; —ist n. terroriste m.; —ize vt. terroriser

terror-stricken a. épouvanté

terrycloth n. étoffe bouclée f.; tissu-éponge m.

terse a. net; concis; —ness n. netteté, concision f.

tertiary a. tertiaire

test n. épreuve f.; essai m.; examen m.; test m.; — tube n. éprouvette f.; — vt. éprouver; mettre à l'épreuve; essayer; examiner; vérifier, contrôler; —er n. essayeur m.; vérificateur m.

testament n. testament m.; —ary a. testamentaire

testator n. testateur m.

testicle n. testicule m.

testify vt. témoigner; — vi. déposer

testimonial n. certificat m., attestation f.; témoignage m.

testimony n. témoignage m., preuve f.; déposition f.

testiness n. irritabilité f.

testy a. maussade, bourru; irritable

tetanus n. tétanos m.

tether n. attache (des chevaux) f.; — vt. attacher

tetragonal a. tétragone, quadrilatère

tetrahedron n. tétraèdre m.

tetrameter n. tétramètre m.

text n. texte m.; —ual a. textuel, de texte

textbook n. texte m.; livre classique m.; manuel m.

Thailand n. Thaïland m.

Thames n. Tamise f.

than adv. que, (before numbers) de

thank vt. remercier; —s n. pl. grâces f. pl.; remerciments m. pl.; —s! merci, merci bien, merci beaucoup; je vous remercie; —fulness n. reconnaissance f.; —less a. ingrat

thanksgiving n. action de grâces f.

that a. ce, cet, cette; — conj. que, qui; afin que, pour que, de manière que; — pron. cela, ça, ce; — one celui-là, celle-là

thatch n. chaume m.; — vt. couvrir de chaume; —ed a. de chaume

thaw n. dégel m.; — vt. & vi. dégeler

the art. le, la, les

theater n. théâtre m.

theatrical a. théâtral, scénique; — n. spectacle m.

thee pron. toi, te

theft n. vol, larcin m.

their a. leur, leurs; —s pron. le leur; la leur; les leurs; à eux, à elles

theist n. & a. théiste m.

them pron. eux, elles; les; —selves pron. eux-mêmes, elles-mêmes, se

theme n. thème m.

then adv. alors; après, puis, ensuite; donc, par conséquent; till — jusque là, d'ici là; now and — de temps en temps, de temps à autre

thence adv. de là

thenceforth adv. dès lors

theocratic(al) a. théocratique

theologian n. théologien m.

theologic(al) a. théologique

theology n. théologie f.

theorem n. théorème m.

theoretic(al) a. théorique; —ally adv. en principe

theorist n. théoricien m.

theorize vi. & vt. théoriser

theory n. théorie f.

theosophy n. théosophie f.

therapeutic a. thérapeutique; —s n. thérapeutique f.

therapy n. traitement m.

there adv. là; y; here and — çà et là; — is, — are il y a; voilà

thereabouts adv. environ

thereafter adv. après, ensuite; dès lors

thereby adv. par là, ainsi

therefore adv. ainsi, donc; aussi

therefrom adv. de là, de cela

therein adv. là-dedans

thereon adv. là-dessus

thereupon adv. là-dessus; sur quoi

therm n. microthermie f.

thermic a. thermique

thermodynamics n. thermodynamique f.

thermometer n. thermomètre m.

thermos (bottle) n. thermos m., bouteille isolante f.

thermostat n. calorifère f.; thermostat m.

these pron. pl. ceux-ci, celles-ci; — a. ces

thesis n. thèse f.

they pron. ils, elles; eux; on

thick n. épaisseur f.; fort m.; — a. épais, gros, grand; touffu; trouble; grossier; fréquent; —en vt. & vi. épaissir; —ness n. épaisseur f.; grosseur f.

thicket n. taillis, fourré m.

thickheaded a. à la tête dure; bête; idiot
thickset a. trapu
thick-skinned a. insensible
thick-witted a. bête, stupide
thief n. voleur m.
thieve vt. & vi. voler; -ry n. vol, larcin m.
thievish a. voleur
thigh n. cuisse f.
thimble n. dé à coudre; -ful n. dé, doigt m.
thin a. mince, maigre; léger; ténu; (hair) rare; (voice) grêle; — vt. amincir, délayer; — vi. maigrir; s'amincir; -ly adv. à peine; -ness n. maigreur, minceur f.; légèreté f.; rareté f.
thine pron. à toi; le tien, la tienne
thing n. chose f.; objet m.; article m.; affaire f.; effet m.; créature f., être m.; latest — dernier cri m.
think vt. & vi. penser; croire; trouver; juger; réfléchir; songer; s'imaginer; I — so je pense que oui; — of penser à; — out peser, méditer; — over réfléchir; -able a. concevable, imaginable; -er n. penseur m.; -ing a. qui pense; -ing n. pensées f. pl.
thin-skinned a. susceptible, sensible
third a. troisième; — n. (fraction) tiers m.
thirst n. soif f.; altération f.; — vi. avoir soif; -y a. altéré; avide; be -y avoir soif
thirteen a. treize; -th a. treizième; treize
thirtieth a. trentième
thirty a. trente
this a. ce, cet, cette; — pron. ceci; cela; celui(-ci), celle(-ci)
thong n. courroie f.; lanière f.
thoracic a. thoracique
thorax n. thorax m.
thorium n. thorium m.
thorn n. épine f.; -y a. épineux
thorough a. complet; profondi; approfondi; -ly adv. complètement, tout à fait; parfaitement; à fond; -ness n. profondeur f.; assiduité f.
thoroughbred a. (horse) de race, pur sang; — n. (horse) cheval de race m.
thoroughfare n. voie, rue f.
thoroughgoing a. assidu, consciencieux
those a. ces; — pron. ceux(-là), celles(-là)
thou pron. tu; toi
though conj. bien que, quoique, encore que; — adv. cependant, pourtant
thought n. pensée f.; réflexion f.; idée f.; méditation f.; intention f.; -ful a. pensif; prévenant; -fulness n. prévenance f.; réflexion f.; -less a. irréfléchi; sans prévenance
thousand a. mille; — n. (un) millier m.; -th a. & n. millième n.
thrash vt. battre, rosser; -ing n. raclée, rossée f.
thread n. fil m.; (screw) filet, filetage m.; — vt. enfiler; fileter
threadbare a. râpé; usé
threat n. menace f.; — vt. menacer; intimider; -ening a. menaçant
three a. trois
three-act a. en trois actes
three-cornered a. triangulaire; (hat) tricorne
threefold a. triple

three-legged a. à trois pieds
three-ply a. à trois épaisseurs
threesome n. partie de trois f.
three-speed a. à trois vitesses
three-wheeled a. à trois roues
thresh vt. battre; -er n. (person) batteur m.; (machine) batteuse f.; -ing n. battage m.; -ing machine n. batteuse f.
threshold n. seuil, pas m.; limite f.
thrice adv. trois fois
thrift n. économie, frugalité f.; -iness n. économie f.; -y a. économe, frugal
thrill n. frémissement, tressaillement m.; émotion f.; — vt. émouvoir, émotionner; faire frémir; — vi. frémir, tressaillir; -er n. (coll.) écrit mélodramatique m.; -ing a. émouvant, passionnant
thrive vi. réussir; bien marcher; prospérer
thriving a. florissant; prospère
throat n. gorge f.; gosier m.; clear one's — s'éclaircir la voix; have a sore — avoir mal à la gorge; cut- a. concurrence ruineuse
throb vi. palpiter, battre; — n. battement m., pulsation f.; -bing n. pulsation f., battement m.
throes n. pl. agonie f.; douleurs f. pl.
thrombosis n. thrombose f.
throne n. trône m.
throng n. foule f.; — vi. affluer, se presser; — vt. encombrer
throttle n. étrangleur m.; — vt. étrangler
through prep. à travers; par; go — traverser, parcourir; fouiller; — adv. à travers; jusqu'au bout; — a. direct; (coll.) fini
throughout prep. partout (dans)
throw n. jet m.; coup m.; lancée f.; lancement m.; — vt. jeter, lancer; projeter; (horse) démonter; (wrestling) terrasser; — away jeter, rejeter; — back renvoyer; — off jeter; se défaire de; enlever; dépister; — out jeter, rejeter; expulser; metter à la porte; (clutch) débrayer; — up rejeter, vomir; (hands) lever; abandonner, renoncer à
throwback n. retour m.
thrust n. poussée f.; coup, trait m.; — vt. pousser; enfoncer; fourrer; — vi. porter un coup
thruway n. autostrade f.
thud n. bruit sourd m.; — vi. tomber avec un bruit sourd
thug n. bandit, gangster m.
thumb n. pouce m.; — index encoches f. pl.; — vt. manier; — a ride (coll.) faire de l'auto-stop; — through parcourir, jeter un coup d'œil à
thumbnail n. ongle du pouce m.; — a. petit, miniscule
thumbtack n. punaise f.
thump n. coup (de poing) m.; coup sourd m.; — vt. taper, bourrer, battre
thunder n. tonnerre m.; foudre f.; clap of — coup de foudre m.; — vt. & vi. tonner; -ing a. tonnant
thunderbolt n. coup de foudre m.
thundercloud, thunderhead n. cumulus à bords blancs m.
thunderstorm n. orage m.

thunderstruck a. abasourdi

Thursday n. jeudi m.

thus adv. ainsi; donc; aussi; de cette manière, de cette façon; — far jusqu'ici

thwart n. (naut.) banc de nage m.; — vt. faire avorter, contrecarrer

thy a. ton, ta, tes

thyme n. thym m.

thyroid a. thyroïde

tiara n. tiare f.

Tibet n. Thibet m.

tick n. tic-tac m.; trait m., marque f.; (zool.) tique f.; — vi. faire tic-tac; marcher, fonctionner; —er n. télégraphe imprimeur m.; (coll.) cœur m.; —ing n. tic-tac m.; coutil à matelas m.

ticket n. billet m.; ticket m.; bulletin m.; complimentary — billet de faveur m.; one-way — billet simple m.; round-trip — billet d'aller et retour m.; season — carte d'abonnement f.; — collector contrôleur m.; — window guichet m.

tickle vt. chatouiller; amuser; — vi. avoir des chatouillements; —r n. question difficile f.

tickling n. chatouillement m.

ticklish a. chatouilleux; délicat; difficile

tidal a. de la marée; — wave vague de fond f.

tidbit n. friandise, bouchée f.

tiddlywinks n. pl. jeu de puce m.

tide n. marée f.; (fig.) fortune f.; flood — marée montante f.; high — marée haute f.; low — marée basse f.

tidewater n. eau de marée f.

tidily adv. avec soin; avec ordre

tidiness n. bon ordre m.; propreté f.

tidings n. pl. nouvelles f. pl.

tidy a. en bon ordre; ordonné; propre; bien tenu; considérable, assez grand; — vt. ranger, arranger; mettre de l'ordre dans

tie n. cravate f.; nœud m.; lien m.; liaison f.; nombre égal m.; égalité f.; (rail.) traverse f.; — game match à égalité m.; — clip pince à cravate f.; — vt. lier, attacher, nouer; — vi. être à égalité; — a knot faire un nœud; — up ficeler, attacher; panser; immobiliser

tier n. rangée f.; gradin, étage m.

tie-up n. suspension des affaires f.; arrêt de la circulation m.

tiff n. querelle f.

tight a. serré; collant; tendu; imperméable; étanche; ivre, gris, soûl; avare; — adv. fermement; (sl.) —s n. pl. maillot m.; —en vt. serrer, resserrer; raidir; —ly adv. étroitement; fortement; bien; —ness n. tension f.; étroitesse f.

tightfisted a. avare, ladre

tight-fitting a. collant

tight-lipped a. aux lèvres serrées; silencieux; impassible

tightrope n. corde f.; — artist funambule m. & f.; danseur de corde m.

tile n. tuile f.; carreau m.; — vt. carreler; —d a. en tuiles; carrelé

tiling n. carrelage m.

till n. tiroir-caisse m.; — prep. jusqu'à; à; — conj. jusqu'à ce que; — vt. labourer, cultiver; —able a. arable, labourable; —age n. labour, labourage m.; —er n. laboureur, cultivateur m.; (naut.) barre f.; —ing n. labour m.

tilt n. pente, inclinaison f.; joute f.; at full — à toute vitesse; — vt. & vi. pencher, incliner

timber n. bois (de construction) m.; poutre f.; (coll.) étoffe f., calibre m.; trempe f.; — vt. boiser, blinder

timberland n. pays boisé m.

timbre n. timbre m.

time n. temps m.; heure f.; époque f.; moment m.; saison f.; âge m.; fois f.; (mus.) mesure f.; a short — after peu après; at all —s toujours; at no — jamais; at the same — en même temps; à la fois; d'autre part; at —s parfois; for the — being pour le moment; from — to — de temps en temps, de temps à autre; in — à temps; avec le temps; keep — suivre la mesure; on — à l'heure; spare — loisir m.; temps disponible m.; what — is it? quelle heure est-il?; — exposure pose f.; — lag retard m.; — limit délai m.; limite de temps f.; — signal signal horaire m.; — vt. régler, mesurer, calculer; chronométrer; —less a. éternel; —liness n. à propos m.; opportunité f.; —ly a. opportun, à-propos

time-honored a. consacré; vénérable

timekeeper n. chronométreur m.; controlleur

timepiece n. montre f.; pendule f.

timesaver n. économiseur de temps m.

timetable n. horaire, indicateur m.

timeworn a. vénérable; usé par le temps

timid a. timide; peureux; —ity n. timidité f.

timing n. réglage m.; chronométrage m.; calcul m.

timpani n. timbales f. pl.

tin n. étain m.; fer-blanc m.; (baking) plat m.; — can boîte f.; — plate ferblanterie f.; — vt. étamer; —ny a. d'étain; grêle

tincture n. teinture f.; — vt. tainter, teindre

tinder n. mèche de briquet f.

tine n. fourchon m., dent f.

tin foil n. feuille d'étain f.; papier d'étain m.

tinge n. teinte f.; — vt. teindre

tingle vi. tinter; picoter; — n. tintement m.; fourmillement m.

tingling n. tintement m.; fourmillement, picotement m.

tinker n. chaudronnier m.; — vi. bricoler; — (with) vt. rafistoler

tinkle vi. tinter; — n. tintement m.

tinsel n. clinquant m.; faux brillant m.

tinsmith n. ferblantier m.

tinware n. ferblanterie f.

tint n. teinte f.; — vt. teinter, colorer

tiny a. tout petit; minuscule

tip n. bout m., pointe, extrémité f.; pourboire m., gratification f.; (coll.) tuyau, conseil m.; — vt. donner un pourboire à; embouter; — over renverser; —ping n. pourboires m. pl.

tipple vi. boire à l'excès; —r n. ivrogne m.

tipsiness n. ivresse f.

tipsy a. ivre, gris

tiptoe n. pointe des pieds f.; on — sur la

pointe des pieds; — vi. marcher sur la pointe des pieds

tirade n. tirade, diatribe f.

tire n. pneu m.; flat — pneu à plat m.; crevaison f.; spare — pneu de rechange; — vt. fatiguer, lasser; — vi. se fatiguer, se lasser; —d a. fatigué; las (lasse); grow —d of se lasser de; —dness n. fatigue, lassitude f.; —less a. infatigable, inlassable; —some a. fatigant; ennuyeux

tissue n. tissu m.; — paper papier de soie m.

titanic a. titanique

tit for tat, à bon chat bon rat

tithe n. dîme f.

titillate vi. & vt. chatouiller, titiller

title n. titre m.; droit m.; — vt. intituler; —d a. titré; — n. (law) titre de propriété; acte m.; — rôle n. premier rôle m.

titlist n. champion m.

titrate vt. & vi. titrer

titter n. petit rire m.; — vi. pousser de petits rires

titular a. titulaire

to prep à; vers; en; chez; jusqu'à; de; pour; — adv., come — reprendre connaissance; go — and fro aller et venir

toadstool n. champignon vénéneux m.

toast n. pain grillé, toast m.; — vt. griller; boire à la santé de; —er n. grille-pain m.

toastmaster n. celui qui annonce les toasts m., celui qui préside à un banquet m.

tobacco n. tabac m., — pouch n. blague à tabac f.

toboggan n. toboggan m.; — vi. faire du toboggan

today adv. aujourd'hui; a week from — d'aujourd'hui en huit

toddle vi. marcher à petits pas; —r n. enfant qui commence à marcher m.

toddy n. grog m.

to-do n. remue-ménage m.; bruit, tapage m.

toe n. orteil, doigt du pied m.; (shoe) bout m., pointe f.; — vt., — the line se conformer, s'aligner

toenail n. ongle d'orteil m.

toffee n. (candy) caramel au beurre m.

together adv. ensemble; avec; à la fois; de concert; bring — rassembler, réunir

toggle n. barrette f.; cabillot m.

toil n. travail, labeur m.; — vi. travailler, peiner; —er n. travailleur m.; —some a. pénible

toilet n. cabinets m. pl., toilette f.; — paper papier hygiénique m.; — water eau de Cologne f.

token n. jeton m.; témoignage, signe m., marque f.; by the same — de plus; — of love gage d'amour m.

tolerance n. tolérance f.

tolerant a. tolérant

tolerate vt. supporter, tolérer

toleration n. tolérance f.

toll n. taxe f.; droit de passage m.; (bell) son m., son de cloches; death — mortalité f.; — bridge pont à péage m.; — call communication interurbaine f.; —gate barrière f.; — house péage m.; — vt. & vi. sonner

tomato n. tomate f.

tomb n. tombe f.; tombeau m.

tomboy n. garçon manqué m.

tombstone n. pierre tombale f.

tomfoolery n. niaiserie f.

tomorrow adv. demain; day after — après-demain m.; — morning demain matin; week from — de demain en huit

ton n. tonne f.; —nage n. tonnage m., jauge f.

tone n. ton, accent, son m.; voix f.; nuance f.; — vt., — down atténuer, adoucir; —less a. atone; sans éclat

tongs n. pl. pinces, tenailles, pincettes f. pl.

tongue n. langue f.; (buckle) ardillon m.; (shoe) languette f.; native — langue maternelle f.

tongue-tied a. interdit

tonic a. tonique; — n. tonique, fortifiant m.

tonight adv. ce soir; cette nuit

tonsil n. amygdale, tonsile f.; —litis n. amygdalite f.; —lectomy n. amygdalotomie f.

tonsure n. tonsure f.; — vt. tonsurer

too adv. trop; aussi; de plus, d'ailleurs; — much trop, trop de

tool n. outil, instrument, ustensile m.; —box coffre à outils m.; — vt. travailler, usiner; équiper; dorer; —ing n. usinage m.; dorure f.

toot n. cornement, coup de klaxon m.; (naut.) coup de sirène m.; — vt. corner, donner un coup de klaxon; sonner; — vi. corner; sonner

tooth n. dent f.; — powder poudre dentifrice f.; —ed a. denté; dentelé; —less a. édenté, sans dents

toothache n. mal de dents m.; have a — avoir mal aux dents

toothbrush n. brosse à dents f.

tooth paste n. pâte dentifrice f.

toothpick n. cure-dents m.

top n. sommet, haut m., cime f.; dessus m.; tête f.; (toy) toupie f.; — a. (le) plus haut; supérieur; (floor) dernier; (quality) premier; — hat chapeau haut de forme m.; — vt. surmonter; coiffer; surpasser, dépasser; être à la tête de

topcoat n. pardessus m.

topflight a. excellent, supérieur, premier

top-heavy a. trop lourd du haut

topic n. sujet m., matière f.; —al a. actuel, d'actualité; topique

topknot n. chignon m.; (bird) huppe f.

topmost n. le plus haut, le plus élevé

topographer n. topographe m.

topography n. topographie f.

topple vt. faire tomber; — vi. tomber; branler

top-secret a. extrêmement secret

topsoil n. terre végétale f.

topsy-turvy a. & adv. sens dessus dessous

tor n. pic m.

torch n. torche f., flambeau m.

torchlight n. lumière de flambeau f.; — procession retraite aux flambeaux f.

toreador n. toréador m.

torment n. tourment m.; torture f., supplice m.; — vt. tourmenter, torturer; —or

n. tourmenteur m.; bourreau m.
torn a. déchiré
tornado n. ouragan m., tornade f.
torpedo n. torpille f.; — boat torpilleur m.; — tube lance-torpille m.; — vt. torpiller
torpid a. engourdi
torpor n. torpeur f.
torque n. couple de torsion m.
torrent n. torrent m.; in —s (rain) par torrents, à verse; —ial a. torrentiel
torrid a. torride, brûlant
torso n. torse m.
tort n. (law) dommage m.
tortoise-shell n. écaille f.; — a. d'écaille
tortuous a. tortueux, sinueux
torture n. torture f.; supplice, tourment m.; — vt. torturer, mettre au supplice; —r n. bourreau m.
toss n. jet, lancement m.; coup m.; — vt. jeter, lancer; choisir (à pile ou face); hocher; secouer, agiter; (of horse) démonter; — vi. (s')agiter, (se) tourner; — off faire rapidement; expédier; (drink) lamper; —ing n. lancement m.; agitation f.
tossup n. chance égale f.
tot n. petit enfant m.
total a. total; global; complet; — n. total, montant m.; — vt. & vi. totaliser; —ity n. totalité f.; —ize vt. totaliser
totalitarian a. totalitaire
totter vi. chanceler; tituber; —ing a. chancelant; titubant
touch n. toucher, tact m.; coup m.; touche f.; contact, rapport m.; communication f.; soupçon m., pointe f.; in — with en rapport avec, en communication avec; — vt. toucher; effleurer; émouvoir, attendrir; — vi. se toucher; — off déclencher; — up faire des retouches; —iness n. susceptibilité f.; —ing a. touchant, émouvant, attendrissant; —y a. qui se pique facilement; susceptible; difficile
touchdown n. touché m.
touchstone n. pierre de touche f.
tough a. dur, difficile; fort; tenace; —en vt. durcir, endurcir; —ness n. dureté f., difficulté f.; force f.; ténacité f.
tour n. voyage m., excursion f.; tour m., tournée f.; — vi. voyager; — vt. visiter; —ist n. touriste m. & f.
tournament n. tournoi m.; concours m.
tousle vt. ébouriffer
tout vt. (coll.) donner des tuyaux; — n. pisteur m.
tow n. remorque f.; filasse f.; — vt. remorquer; —ing n. remorque f.
toward(s) prep. vers; envers; pour
towel n. serviette f.; essuie-mains m.; — rack porte-serviettes m.; — vt. essuyer; frotter; —ling n. tissu-éponge m.
tower n. tour f.; pylône m.; (church) clocher m.; — vi. dominer; —ing a. très haut; énorme
town n. ville f.; — hall hôtel de ville m.
township n. commune f.
townsman n. habitant de la ville m.
townspeople n. habitants de la ville, citoyens m. pl.
toxic a. toxique

toxicology n. toxicologie f.
toxin n. toxine f.
toy n. jouet m.; joujou m.; — dog chien de salon m.; — vi., — with s'amuser avec
trace n. trace f.; vestige m.; trait m.; — vt. tracer; calquer; —able a. qu'on peut suivre; attribuable; —r n. (mil.) traceuse f.
trachea n. trachée f.
tracheotomy n. trachéotomie f.
tracing n. tracé m.; calque m.; — paper papier à calquer m.
track n. piste, trace f.; chemin m., voie f.; (rail.) voie ferrée f.; rail(s) m. (pl.); (sports) courses à pied f. pl.; (tractor) chenille f.; keep — of ne pas perdre de vue; surveiller; suivre; on the right — sur la bonne voie; throw off the — dépister; — vt. suivre, traquer; — down vt. suivre, traquer
tract n. étendue f.; brochure f.; (anat.) appareil m.
tractable a. traitable, docile
traction n. traction f.
tractor n. tracteur m.
trade n. commerce m.; métier m.; — wind vent alizé m.; — vi. faire du commerce; — vt. échanger; —r n. commerçant, marchand m.
trade-in n. reprise en compte f.
trademark n. marque (de fabrique) f.
tradesman n. marchand, fournisseur m.
tradespeople n. marchands, fournisseurs m. pl.
trade-union n. syndicat (ouvrier) m.; —ism n. syndicalisme m.
trading n. commerce m.; — a. commerçant, marchand; commercial
traffic n. circulation f.; trafic, commerce m.; mouvement m.; — jam embouteillage m.; — light feu m.; — manager chef de mouvement m.; — sign indicateur m.; — ticket procès-verbal m., contravention f.; — vi. trafiquer
tragedian n. tragédien m.
tragedy n. tragédie f.
tragic a. tragique
tragicomedy n. tragicomédie f.
trail n. trace, piste f.; traînée f.; sentier m.; — vt. traquer, suivre à la piste; — vi. traîner; ramper; —er (auto.) baladeuse f.; caravane f.; roulotte f.; (film) film-annonce m.; —ing a. rampant; qui (se) traîne
train n. train m.; suite f.; série f.; (dress) queue f.; — vt. exercer; former, élever; préparer; (animal) dresser; (sports) entraîner; (cannon) pointer, orienter; — vi. s'exercer; s'entraîner; —ed a. exercé; dressé; —er n. entraîneur m.; dresseur m.; —ing n. formation, éducation f.; entraînement m.; dressage m.; physical —ing éducation physique f.
trait n. trait m.
traitor n. traître m.; —ous a. traître, perfide
trajectory n. trajectoire f.
trammel n. tramail m.; — vt. entraver
tramp n. pas lourd m.; vagabond, chemineau m.; — steamer cargo, chemineau m.; — vi. marcher à pas lourds
trample vt. fouler (aux pieds); piétiner;

écraser

trance n. transe, hypnose f.; extase f.

tranquil a. tranquille, calme; paisible; -ize vt. tranquilliser, calmer; apaiser; -izer n. calmant m.; -lity n, tranquillité f., calme m.

transact vt. faire; -ion n. affaire f.; conduite f.; opération f.

transatlantic a. transatlantique

transcend vt. aller au delà de; surpasser, dépasser; -ence, -ency n. transcendance f.; -ent a. transcendant; -ental a. transcendantal

transcribe vt. transcrire; -r n. transcripteur m.

transcript n. copie, transcription f.; enregistrement m.; -ion n. transcription f.; enregistrement m.

transfer n. transfert m.; transport m.; correspondance f.; bulletin de correspondance m.; — vt. transférer; transmettre; virer; calquer; — vi. faire une correspondance; -able a. transmissible; mobilier; -ence n. transfert m.

transfigure vt. transfigurer

transfix vt. transpercer

transform vt. transformer; convertir; métamorphoser; -ation n. transformation f.; conversion f.; métamorphose f.; -er n. transformateur m.

transfuse vt. transfuser

transgress vt. transgresser; — vi. pécher; -ion n. violation, transgression f.; péché m., faute f.; -or n. transgresseur m.; pécheur m., pécheresse f.

transient a. transitoire, passager, de passage; momentané

transit n. transport m.; transit m.; passage; -ion n. transition f.; passage m.; -ive a. transitif; -ory a. transitoire, de passage

translate vt. traduire

translation n. traduction f.; version f.

translator n. traducteur m.

translucence n. translucidité f.

translucent a. translucide

transmigration n. transmigration f.

transmission n. transmission f.; transport m.; émission f.

transmit vt. transmettre; transporter; (radio) émettre; -ter n. émetteur m.; transmetteur m.

transmute vt. transmuer, transformer

transoceanic a. transocéanien

transom n. vasistas m., imposte f.

transparency n. transparence f.; transparent m.; (phot.) diapositive f.

transparent a. transparent; clair

transpiration n. transpiration f.

transpire vt. & vi. transpirer

transplant vt. transplanter; -ation n. transplantation f.

transport n. transport m.; — vt. transporter; -ation n. transport m.

transpose vt. transposer

transposition n. transposition f.

transverse a. transversal; en travers

trap n. piège m.; trappe f.; (sink) collecteur m.; set a — tendre un piège, dresser un piège; — door trappe f.; -shooting tir aux pigeons m.; — vt. prendre au piège; — vt. trapper; -ped a. pris (au piège); -per n. trappeur m.; -pings n. pl. apparat m., atours m. pl.

trapeze n. trapèze m.

trapezoid n. quadrilatère irrégulier m.

trash n. débris m. pl.; camelote f.; -y a. de camelote

traumatic a. traumatique

travel n. voyage(s) m. (pl.); — vi. voyager, faire un voyage; parcourir; aller, circuler, marcher; -er n. voyageur m.; -ing n. voyages m. pl.; -ing a. de voyage; -ing salesman commis voyageur m.

traveler's check n. chèque de voyage m.

travelogue n. conférence avec projections décrivant un voyage f.

traverse n. traverse f.; — vt. traverser, passer à travers de

travesty n. travestissement m.; parodie f.; — vt. travestir; parodier

trawl n. chalut m.; — vi. & vt. pêcher au chalut; -er n. chalutier m.

tray n. plateau m.; cuvette f.

treacherous a. traître, perfide

treachery n. trahison, perfidie f.

treacle n. mélasse f.

tread n. pas m.; (stair) giron m.; (tire) chape f., roulement m.; — vi. marcher; — vt. fouler; — water nager debout

treadle n. pédale f.

treadmill n. moulin de discipline m.

treason n. trahison f.; -able a. traître, perfide; de trahison

treasure n. trésor m.; — vt. priser, aimer beaucoup; -r n. trésorier m.

treasury n. trésorerie f.; trésor m.

treat n. régal m.; plaisir m.; — vt. régaler; payer; traiter; soigner; — oneself to se payer, s'offrir

treatise n. traité m.

treaty n. traité m., convention f., accord m.

treble a. triple; — clef clef de sol f.; — vt. tripler

tree n. arbre m.; family — arbre généalogique m.

trek n. voyage m.; — vi. voyager

trellis n. treillis m., treillage m.

tremble n. frisson m., vibration f.; — vi. trembler, vibrer

trembling a. tremblant; — n. tremblement m.; vibration f.

tremendous a. énorme; terrible

tremolo n. trémolo m.

tremor n. tremblement, choc m., secousse f.; frémissement m.

tremulous a. tremblotant

trench n. tranchée f., fossé m.; — coat imperméable m.

trenchant a. tranchant

trencherman n. gros mangeur m.

trend n. tendance f.; — vi. tendre

trepidation n. trépidation f.

trespass n. (eccl.) péché m., offense f.; (law) violation f.; — vi. pécher; — on violer; empiéter; pénétrer sans autorisation dans une propriété; -er n. (eccl.) transgresseur, pécheur m.; personne qui commet une violation de propriété f.

tress n. tresse, boucle f.

trestle n. tréteau, chevalet m.; (rail.) pont (sur chevalets) m.

trey n. (cards) trois m.

triad n. triade f.

trial n. procès m., cause f., jugement m.; essai m., épreuve f.; — a. d'essai, d'épreuve; experimental — balance n. balance de vérification f.

triangular a. triangulaire

triangulation n. triangulation f.

tribal a. de tribu

tribe n. tribu f.

tribesman n. membre d'une tribu m.

tribulation n. tribulation f.

tribunal n. tribunal m.; cour (de justice) f.

tribune n. (person) tribune f., tribun m.

tributary a. tributaire; — n. affluent, tributaire m.

tribute n. tribut, hommage m.

trice n., in a — en un clin d'œil; tout de suite

trick n. tour m., ruse f.; truc m.; habitude, manie f.; (cards) levée f.; card — tour de cartes m.; play a — on jouer un tour à; — vt. jouer un tour à; tromper, duper; -ery n. tricherie f.; tromperie f.; -iness n. nature compliquée f.; -y a. compliqué, difficile; rusé

trickle vi. ruisseler, dégoutter, couler; — n. filet m.; petit peu m.

trickling a. dégouttant

tricolor n. drapeau français, drapeau tricolore m.

tricycle n. tricycle; (com.) triporteur m.

triennial a. triennal; trisannuel

trifle n. bagatelle, vétille f.; rien m.; — vi. jouer; vétiller; s'occuper à des choses peu importantes

trifling a. peu important, insignifiant

trigger n. gâchette, détente f.

trigonometry n. trigonométrie f.

trill n. (mus.) trille m.; — vt. triller; rouler; — vi. faire des trilles

trillion n. trillion m.

trilogy n. trilogie f.

trim n. ornement m., ornementation f.; bon état, bon ordre m.; équilibrage m.; (hair) coupe f.; in — en forme; — a. soigné; élégant; propre; — vt. orner, ornementer, parer; garnir; équilibrer; tailler, couper; (hair) rafraîchir; -ming n. ornement m., ornementation f.; garniture f., garnissage m.; parure f.; (sewing) passementerie f.; taille f.; -mings n. pl. garniture f., accompagnements m. pl.; -ness n. élégance f.; belle taille f.

Trinidad n. Trinité f.

trinity n. groupe de trois m.; (eccl.) Trinité f.

trinket n. babiole f.; bibelot m.

trip n. voyage m., excursion f.; trébuchement, faux pas m.; take a — faire un voyage; — vt. faire trébucher; donner un croc-en-jambe à; — vi. trébucher, faire un faux pas

tripe n. tripes f. pl.; gras-double m.; bêtises f. pl.; camelote f.

triphammer n. marteau à bascule m.

triple a. triple; — vt. & vi. tripler

triplet n. trijumeau m., trijumelle f.;

(mus.) triolet m.; -s n. pl. trois jumeaux

triplicate n. triple, triplicata m.; in — en triple (exemplaire)

tripod n. trépied m.; pied (à trois branches) m.

triptyque n. (auto.) triptyque m.

trite a. banal; -ness n. banalité f.

triumph n. triomphe m.; victoire f.; succès m.; — vi. triompher; — over triompher de; l'emporter, sur; -al a. de triomphe; triomphal; -ant a. triomphant; de triomphe

triumvirate n. triumvirat m.

trivet n. trépied m., chevrette f.

trivial a. trivial; sans importance, insignifiant; léger; -ity n. insignifiance f.

trochaic a. trochaïque

troche n. (med.) tablette f.

Trojan a. & n. Troyen m.

troll n. (fishing) moulinet m.; — vi. pêcher à la cuiller; -ing n. pêche à la cuiller f.

trolley n. trolley m., poulie f.; (car) tramway m.; chariot m.; — bus trolley-autobus m.

trollop n. souillon f.

troop n. troupe, bande f.; — vi. aller en troupe; s'attrouper; — in entrer en troupe; -er n. soldat, troupier m.

troopship n. transport militaire m.

trophy n. trophée n.

tropic n. tropique m.; -al a. tropical

trot n. trot m.; — vi. trotter, aller au trot; -ter n. cheval de trot m.

troubadour n. troubadour, trouvère m.

trouble n. difficulté f.; peine f.; ennui m.; trouble m.; be in — avoir des ennuis, avoir des difficultés; be worth the — to valoir la peine de; take the — to prendre la peine de; — vt. préoccuper, tourmenter, affliger, inquiéter; déranger, ennuyer, incommoder; donner de la peine à; troubler; — vi. s'inquiéter; se déranger; -d a. inquiet; trouble; -some a. difficile; ennuyeux, incommode

troublemaker n. fomentateur, fauteur m.

trough n. auge f.; baquet m.; abreuvoir m.; (wave) creux m.

trounce vt. écraser; rosser

troupe n. troupe f.; -r n. (theater) membre d'une troupe m.

trousers n. pl. pantalon m.

trousseau n. trousseau m.

trout n. truite f.

trowel n. truelle f.; déplantoir m.

troy (weight) n. poids troy m.

Troy n. Troie f.

truant n. élève absent sans permission m. & f.

truce n. trêve f.; flag of — drapeau parlementaire m.

truck n. camion m., camionnette f.; wagon m.; chariot m.; affaire f.; rapports m. pl.; — driver camionneur m.; — farm jardin maraîcher m.; — vt. porter en camion; camionner; -er n. camionneur m. -ing n. camionnage m.

truculent a. truculent; féroce

trudge vi. marcher lourdement

true a. vrai, véritable; fidèle; juste; réel; — adv. vrai; juste; come — se réaliser; hold — en être de même; — n., out of —

hors d'aplomb; décentré; faussé; gauchi; — *vt.* ajuster; défausser, dégauchir
truism *n.* axiome, truisme *m.*
truly *adv.* vraiment, véritablement; en vérité; fidèlement
trump *n.* atout *m.*; no — sans-atout; — *vt.* couper; — up forger, inventer
trumpet *n.* trompette *f.*; — *vi.* sonner de la trompette; (elephant) barrir; — *vt.* & *vi.* proclamer; **-er** *n.* trompette *m.*; trompettiste *m.*
truncate *vt.* tronquer
truncheon *n.* gros bâton *m.*
trundle *n.* roulette *f.*; — *vt.* faire rouler; pousser
trunk *n.* (tree) tronc *m.*; (luggage) malle *f.*; (elephant) trompe *f.*; — line (rail.) ligne principale *f.*; (telephone) ligne interurbaine *f.*; -s *pl.* caleçon; caleçon de bain; cache-sexe *m.*
truss *n.* cintre *m.*; armature *f.*; bandage (herniaire) *m.*; — *vt.* armer, renforcer; lier, ligoter
trust *n.* confiance *f.*; crédit *m.*; charge *f.*; garde *f.*; syndicat, trust *m.*; in — en dépôt; on — à crédit; — *vt.* se fier à; confier; espérer; faire crédit à; — *vi.* se fier; se confier; **-ed** *a.* de confiance; fidèle; **-ful** *a.* confiant; **-ing** *a.* plein de confiance
trustee *n.* dépositaire *m.*; administrateur *m.*; curateur *m.*; **-ship** *n.* administration *f.*
trustworthiness *n.* fidélité, loyauté *f.*
trustworthy *a.* digne de foi, digne de confiance, fidèle
trusty *a.* fidèle, loyal, sûr
truth *n.* vérité *f.*; vrai *m.*; in —, to tell the — à vrai dire; — *vt.* à vrai; véridique; **-fulness** *n.* véracité; véridicité *f.*
try *n.* essai *m.*; — *vt.* essayer, tenter, tâcher; expérimenter; éprouver; mettre à l'épreuve; faire l'essai de; goûter; (law) juger; — *vi.* essayer, tâcher; — on s'essayer; — out essayer, mettre à l'épreuve; **-ing** *a.* pénible, dur, difficile; fatigant
tryout *n.* essai *m.*, épreuve *f.*
tryst *n.* rendez-vous *m.*, assignation *f.*
tub *n.* baquet *m.*, cuve *f.*, cuvier *m.*; (bath) baignoire *f.*; bain *m.*; **-by** *a.* boulot; gros
tube *n.* tube, tuyau *m.*; canal, conduit *m.*; (radio) lampe, ampoule *f.*; inner — chambre à air *f.*; test — éprouvette *f.*; — *vt.* tuber
tuber *n.* tubercule *m.*; tuberacée *f.*
tubercular *a.* tuberculeux
tuberculosis *n.* tuberculose *f.*
tuberous *a.* tubéreux
tubing *n.* tube, tuyau *m.*; tuyautage *m.*
tubular *a.* tubulaire; à tubes
tuck *n.* pli, rempli *m.*; troussis *m.*; — *vt.* plisser; remplier; raccourcir; rentrer; — in (bedding) rentrer; border
Tuesday *n.* mardi *m.*; Shrove — mardi gras *m.*
tuft *n.* (hair) touffe *f.*; (bird) houppe *f.*; mèche *f.*; pompon *m.*; flocon *m.*; huppe *f.*; aigrette *f.*; — *vt.* former en touffes

-ed *a.* en touffe, en houppe, huppé
tug *n.* traction *f.*; serrement *m.*; (naut.) remorqueur *m.*; — of war lutte (de traction) à la corde *f.*; — *vt.* & *vi.* tirer; tirailler
tugboat *n.* remorqueur *m.*
tuition *n.* (frais d') instruction *f.*, enseignement *m.*
tumble *n.* chute, culbute *f.*; — *vi.* faire une chute, tomber; faire des culbutes; s'agiter; — into se jeter dans; — out of sauter de; **-r** *n.* acrobate *m.* & *f.*; verre *m.*; (elec.) culbuteur *m.*; (lock) gorge *f.*
tumble-down *a.* délabré; qui tombe en ruines
tumor *n.* tumeur *f.*
tumult *n.* tumulte, trouble *m.*; **-uous** *a.* tumultueux; turbulent
tun *n.* fût *m.*; tonne *f.*; (naut.) tonneau *m.*
tuna, tunny *n.* thon *m.*
tundra *n.* toundra *f.*
tune *n.* air *m.*; accord *m.*; in — (piano) d'accord, (engine) au point; out of — désaccordé; — *vt.* accorder, mettre d'accord; (radio) syntoniser — in accrocher; accorder; — up s'accorder; (engine) mettre au point, régler; **-ful** *a.* harmonieux, mélodieux; **-r** *n.* accordeur *m.*
tungsten *n.* tungstène *m.*
tunic *n.* tunique *f.*
tuning *n.* accordage *m.*; mise au point *f.*, réglage *m.*; — fork diapason *m.*
Tunis *n.* Tunis *m.*
Tunisia *n.* Tunisie *f.*
tunnel *n.* tunnel, souterrain *m.*; — *vt.* & *vi.* percer (un tunnel)
turbid *a.* trouble; **-ity** *n.* turbidité *f.*
turbo-motor *n.* turbomoteur *m.*
turbulence *n.* turbulence, agitation *f.*; trouble *m.*
turbulent *a.* turbulent, tumultueux
tureen *n.* soupière *f.*
turf *n.* gazon *m.*; turf *m.*
turgid *a.* turgide, enflé, ampoulé; **-ity** *n.* enflure, emphase *f.*
Turk *n.* Turc *m.*, Turque *f.*; **-ey** *n.* Turquie *f.*; **-ish** *a.* turc, turque; **-ish bath(s)** hammam(s) *m.* (*pl.*); **-ish towel** serviette éponge *f.*
turkey *n.* dindon *m.*, dinde *f.*
turmoil *n.* trouble *m.*, agitation *f.*
turn *n.* tour *m.*; tournure *f.*; tournant *m.*; virage *m.*; service *m.*; (done) to a — (cuit) au point; in — tour à tour, à tour de rôle; out of — avant son tour; — of mind tour d'esprit *m.*; — *vt.* tourner, retourner; passer; — *vi.* tourner; se tourner, se retourner; changer, se changer; dépendre; devenir; — around tourner; se retourner; — away détourner; — back rebrousser chemin, retourner sur ses pas; repousser; — down retourner; refuser; repousser; baisser; (collar) rabattre; — in aller se coucher; — off fermer, éteindre, couper; tourner; — on ouvrir, allumer; se jeter sur; — out mettre dehors; retourner; produire, confectionner, fabriquer; éteindre, fermer, couper; tourner; arriver; paraître; se réunir, se rassembler; — over tourner, re-

tourner; donner; capoter; — up relever; retrousser; retourner; trouver; arriver, se présenter; –ing a. tournant; –ing n. rotation f.; changement m.; virage m.; –ing point tournant m.; moment critique m.

turncoat n. renégat m.

turnip n. navet m.

turnout n. foule, assemblée f.

turnover n. changement m.; écoulement m.; apple — chausson aux pommes m.

turnpike n. grande route à péage f.

turnstile n. tourniquet m.

turntable n. plaque tournante f.; tourne-disques m.

turpentine n. térébenthine f.

turpitude n. turpitude f.

turret n. tourelle f.

turtle n. tortue f.

Tuscany n. Toscane f.

tusk n. défense, grosse dent f.

tussle n. lutte f.; mêlée f.; corps-à-corps m.; — vi. lutter

tutelage n. tutelle f.

tutor n. précepteur m.; — vt. instruire; donner des leçons particulières à; –ial a. individuel; particulier

tuxedo n. smoking m.

TV (television) n. télévision f.

twaddle n. balivernes f. pl.

twang n. son aigu m.; ton nasillard m.; speak with a — parler du nez; — vt. gratter, pincer; faire résonner; — vi. résonner, vibrer

tweak vt. pincer; tirer

tweed n. tweed m., cheviote f.

tweet n. pépiement m.; — vi. pépier

tweezers n. pl. pinces f. pl.; (hair) pinces à épiler f. pl.

twelfth a. douzième

twelve a. douze; une douzaine de; — o'clock (noon) midi; (midnight) minuit

twentieth a. vingtième

twenty a. vingt

twenty-one a. vingt et un

twice adv. deux fois

twiddle vt. (thumbs) tourner

twig n. brindille f.

twilight n. crépuscule m.

twill n. croisé m.

twin n. jumeau m., jumelle f.; — beds lits jumeaux m. pl.

twine n. ficelle f.; — vt. tordre; entrelacer; — vi. se tordre; s'enlacer

twin-engine (d) a. bimoteur

twinge n. élancement m.; — vi. élancer

twinkle n. scintillement m.; pétillement m.; lueur f.; — vi. scintiller; pétiller

twinkling n. scintillement m.; — of an eye clin d'œil m.

twirl vt. tortiller; (faire) tourner; faire des moulinets avec; — vi. tournoyer

twist n. torsion f.; tour m.; coude m.; cordon m.; tortillon m.; (tobacco) rouleau m.; — of the wrist tour de poignet m.; — vt. tordre; tortiller; — vi. se tordre; se tortiller; tourner; serpenter; — one's ankle se donner une entorse; –ed a. tordu; –er n. (coll.) tornade f.; –ing a. tortueux

twit vt. railler; taquiner

twitch n. tic m.; crispation f.; (pain) élancement m.; — vt. crisper, contracter; — vi. se crisper, se contracter; avoir un tic

twitter n. gazouillement m.; émotion f.; — vi. gazouiller

two a. deux

two-edged a. à deux tranchants

two-faced a. hypocrite; à deux visages

two-fisted a. (coll.) fort, vigoureux

twofold a. double

two-handed a. à deux mains

two-legged a. bipède

two-piece a. en deux pièces

two-seater n. voiture à deux places f.

two-step n. pas de deux m.

two-way a. (street) à deux sens

tycoon n. magnat industriel m.

type n. type m.; genre m.; (print.) caractère m.; set — composer; — vt. écrire à la machine, dactylographier, taper

typesetter n. compositeur m.

typesetting n. composition f.

typewriter n. machine à écrire f.

typhoid a. typhoïde; — fever fièvre typhoïde f.

typhoon n. typhon m.

typhus n. typhus m.

typical a. typique, caractéristique; –ly adv. d'une manière typique

typify vt. être caractéristique de; représenter, symboliser

typist n. dactylographe, dactylo m. & f.

typographer n. typographe m.

typographic(al) a. typographique

typography n. typographie f.

tyrannical a. tyrannique

tyrannize vt. tyranniser; — vi. faire le tyran

tyranny n. tyrannie f.

tyrant n. tyran m.

U

ubiquitous a. qui se trouve partout

udder n. mamelle f.; pis m.

ugliness n. laideur f.

ugly a. laid

ulcer n. ulcère m.; –ate vt. ulcérer; –ation n. ulcération f.; –ous a. ulcéreux

ulna n. cubitus m.

ulterior a. ultérieur; — motive arrière-pensée f., motif caché m.

ultimate a. final; dernier; décisif; –ly adv. en fin de compte

ultimatum n. ultimatum m.

ultra a. extrême

umbilical a. ombilical

umbrage n. ombrage m.; take — s'offenser

umbrella n. parapluie m.; — stand porte-parapluies m.

umpire n. arbitre m.; — vt. arbitrer

umpiring n. arbitrage m.

unabashed a. sans être décontenancé

unabated a. non-diminué

unabating a. soutenu

unable a. incapable; impuissant; be — ne pas pouvoir

unabridged a. intégral, non abrégé

unaccented a. sans accent; atone

unacceptable a. inacceptable

unaccommodating a. peu accommodant;

désobligeant

unaccompanied *a.* seul, inaccompagné; (mus.) sans accompagnement

unaccomplished *a.* inaccompli, inachevé; qui manque de talent

unaccountable *a.* inexplicable

unaccounted *a.*, — for inexpliqué; disparu, perdu; qui manque

unaccredited *a.* non-accrédité

unaccustomed *a.* peu habitué; inaccoutumé

unacknowledged *a.* non-reconnu; (letter) sans réponse

unacquainted *a.*, be — with ignorer; ne pas connaître

unaddressed *a.* sans adresse

unadorned *a.* sans parure, sans ornement; pur, simple

unadulterated *a.* naturel, pur, san mélange

unadvisable *a.* peu sage; imprudent

unaffected *a.* sans affectation, sans pose; sans recherche; sincère; réfractaire; qui n'est pas changé

unaffiliated *a.* non-affilié

unaided *a.* sans aide

unalloyed *a.* sans alliage, pur

unalterable *a.* immuable

unaltered *a.* sans changement

unambitious *a.* sans ambition

unanimous *a.* unanime; —ly *adv.* unanimement; à l'unanimité

unannounced *a.* sans se faire annoncer

unanswerable *a.* sans réponse, sans réplique

unanticipated *a.* imprévu

unappeased *a.* inapaisé

unappetizing *a.* peu appétissant

unappreciated *a.* inapprécié; méconnu

unappreciative *a.* insensible; qui manque de discernement

unapproachable *a.* inabordable, inaccessible

unarmed *a.* sans armes

unashamed *a.* sans honte; éhonté

unasked *a.* non-demandé; sans être invité

unassailable *a.* inattaquable

unassisted *a.* sans aide

unassimilated *a.* inassimilé

unassuming *a.* sans prétention, modeste

unattached *a.* indépendant; libre; qui n'est pas attaché

unattainable *a.* impossible à atteindre; inaccessible

unattended *a.* seul, sans être accompagné

unattractive *a.* peu attrayant; peu sympathique; laid

unauthorized *a.* sans autorisation, inautorisé

unavailing *a.* inutile

unavoidable *a.* inévitable

unavoidably *adv.* inévitablement

unavowed *a.* inavoué

unaware *adv.* ignorant; be — of ignorer; —s *adv.* à l'improviste; par inadvertance

unbalance *vt.* déséquilibrer –d *a.* instable, non balancé

unbearable *a.* insupportable; intolérable

unbeatable *a.* invincible

unbeaten *a.* non-battu

unbecoming *a.* peu convenable; déplacé;

qui ne va pas bien

unbeknown *a.* inconnu; — *adv.* à l'insu (de)

unbelievable *a.* incroyable

unbeliever *n.* incrédule *m. & f.*

unbelieving *a.* incrédule

unbend *vt.* détendre; redresser; — *vi.* se détendre; se déraidir; –ing *a.* ferme, inflexible

unbiased *a.* impartial; sans prévention, sans parti pris

unbidden *a.* sans être invité

unblemished *a.* sans tache; sans défaut

unblock *vt.* désencombrer

unbolt *vt.* déverrouiller

unborn *a.* pas encore né; à venir

unbound *a.* délié; (hair) dénoué; (books) non-relié; —ed *a.* illimité, sans bornes; démesuré

unbreakable *a.* incassable; inébranlable

unbridled *a.* débridé; effréné

unbroken *a.* non-cassé, non-brisé; intact; indompté; non-rompu; continu

unbuckle *vt.* déboucler

unburden *vt.* soulager, alléger

unburied *a.* non-enterré; déterré

unbusinesslike *a.* irrégulier; peu organisé

unbutton *vt.* déboutonner

uncalled *a.* non-appelé; — for déplacé, mal à propos; immérité

uncanny *a.* mystérieux, étrange; inquiétant

uncared-for *a.* délaissé; à l'abandon

unceasing *a.* continu, incessant; soutenu; —ly *adv.* sans cesse

uncensored *a.* non-expurgé

unceremonious *a.* sans façon

uncertain *a.* incertain; douteux; indéterminé; mal assuré; —ty *n.* incertitude *f.*

uncertified *a.* non-diplômé

unchain *vt.* déchaîner

unchallenged *a.* indisputé; sans être contredit

unchangeable *a.* immuable, invariable

unchanged *a.* toujours le même; inchangé

unchanging *a.* immuable, invariable

uncharitable *a.* peu charitable

uncharted *a.* qui ne se trouve pas sur la carte

unchecked *a.* sans frein; non vérifié

unchivalrous *a.* peu courtois

unchristened *a.* non baptisé

unchristian *a.* peu chrétien; infidèle

uncivil *a.* incivil, impoli; –ized *a.* incivilisé; barbare

unclaimed *a.* non-réclamé; — letter lettre de rebut *f.*

unclasp *vt.* défaire, dégrafer; desserrer

uncle *n.* oncle *m.*

unclean *a.* malpropre; impur; –liness *n.* saleté, malpropreté *f.*

unclench *vt.* desserrer

unclothed *a.* déshabillé, nu, sans vêtements

uncock *vt.* désarmer

uncoil *vt.* dérouler

uncolored *a.* non-coloré; incolore

uncombed *a.* non-peigné, mal peigné

uncomfortable *a.* mal à l'aise, inquiet; incommode; peu confortable; gênant, désagréable

uncommon a. peu commun; peu ordinaire; rare

uncommunicative n. peu communicatif

uncomplimentary a. peu flatteur

uncompromising a. intransigeant; absolu

unconcern n. indifférence, insouciance f.; —ed a. indifférent, insouciant, dégagé

unconditional a. sans condition(s); catégorique; inconditionnel

unconfirmed a. non-confirmé

uncongenial a. peu sympathique

unconnected a. sans rapport; sans suite

unconquerable a. invincible; insurmontable

unconquered a. non-vaincu; indompté

unconscionable a. sans conscience

unconscious a. sans connaissance; inconscient; be — être sans connaissance; be — of ignorer; —ly adv. inconsciemment; —ness n. inconscience f.; évanouissement m.

unconsidered a. inconsidéré

unconstitutional a. inconstitutionnel

unconstrained a. spontané; désinvolte

uncontested a. incontesté

uncontrollable a. irrésistible, ingouvernable

uncontrolled a. sans frein; indépendant

unconventional a. original

unconvinced a. non-convaincu; sceptique

unconvincing a. peu convaincant

uncooked a. non-cuit; cru

uncork vt. déboucher; —ed a. sans bouchon; débouché

uncouple vt. découpler; débrayer

uncouth a. grossier, rude; malappris; —ness n. rudesse f.; grossièreté f.

uncover vt. découvrir

uncrowned a. sans couronne, non-couronné

unction n. onction f.; extreme — extrême-onction f.

unctuous a. onctueux; grasseux; —ness n. onctuosité f.

uncultivated a. inculte; peu cultivé

uncultured a. incultivé

uncurbed a. sans frein, débridé; libre

uncured a. non-guéri

uncut a. non-coupé, non-taillé

undamaged a. non-endommagé; indemne

undated a. sans date, non-daté

undaunted a. intrépide

undeceive vt. détromper, désabuser, non-trompé

undecided a. indécis; hésitant

undecipherable a. indéchiffrable

undefeated a. invaincu

undefended a. sans défense

undefinable a. indéfinissable

undefined a. indeterminé, indéfini; vague

undelivered a. non-délivré; non livré

undemonstrative a. réservé, peu démonstratif

undeniable a. incontestable, indéniable

undeniably adv. incontestablement

under prep. sous, au-dessous de; — lock and key sous clef; — repair en réparation; — the circumstances dans les circonstances; — a. inférieur; de dessous; — adv. dessous, au-dessous

underage a. mineur

underbid vt. offrir moins que, demander moins cher que; (cards) demander au-dessous des valeurs

underbrush n. broussailles f. pl.

undercarriage n. dessous, châssis m.

undercharge vt. accepter trop peu d'argent, ne pas faire payer assez

underclothes, underclothing n. vêtements de dessous m. pl., linge m., lingerie f.

undercover a. secret, clandestin

undercurrent n. courant (de fond) m.

undercut vt. vendre moins cher que; couper

underdeveloped a. insuffisamment développé

underdog n. opprimé m.; concurrent dont les chances sont peu favorables m.; perdant probable m.

underdone a. pas assez cuit

underestimate vt. sous-estimer, faire trop peu de cas de

underexposed a. (phot.) qui manque de pose

underexposure n. (phot.) manque de pose m.

underfed a. mal nourri, sous-alimenté

undergarment n. sous-vêtement m.

undergo vt. subir; essuyer, éprouver

undergraduate n. (America) étudiant de collège n.

underground a. souterrain; — adv. sous terre, sous le sol; — n. (rail.) métro m., chemin de fer souterrain m.; (war) résistance f.; maquis m.

undergrowth n. sous-bois m.; broussailles f. pl.

underhand(ed) a. clandestin, secret; sournois; (sports) par en dessous; — adv. en secret; sous main, sournoisement; par en dessous

underlie vt. être au fond de, être à la base de

underline vt. souligner

underling n. subalterne, subordonné m.

underlying a. fondamental

undermanned a. à court de personnel; à court d'équipage

undermentioned a. sous-mentionné

undermost a. le plus bas

undermine vt. miner, saper; (fig.) détruire

underneath prep. sous, au-dessous de; — a. inférieur; de dessous; — adv. dessous, au-dessous

undernourished a. sous-alimenté, mal nourri

underpaid a. mal payé, mal rétribué

underpass n. passage souterrain m.

underpin vt. étayer, étançonner; —ning n. étayage, étançonnement m.

underprivileged a. nécessiteux, indigent; déshérité

underrate vt. sous-estimer, faire trop peu de cas de; mal juger

undersea a. sous-marin

undersecretary n. sous-secrétaire m.

undersell vt. vendre moins cher que, vendre à meilleur marché que

undershirt n. gilet, tricot m.

undersigned a. soussigné

undersized a. petit, trop petit; moins

grand que les autres

underskirt n. jupon m.

understand vt. comprendre; se rendre compte de; savoir; connaître; s'entendre; –able a. compréhensible; that is –able cela se comprend; –ing a. qui comprend; sympathique; –ing n. compréhension, appréhension f.; entendement m.; intelligence f., jugement m.; accord m., entente f.; have an –ing with être d'intelligence avec; on the –ing that à condition que

understate vt. amoindrir; –ment n. amoindrissement m.

understood a. compris; entendu, convenu, qui va sans dire

understudy n. doublure f.; — vt. doubler

undertake vt. entreprendre; se charger de; –r n. entrepreneur de pompes funèbres m.

undertaking n. entreprise f.; affaire f.

undertone n. ton bas m.; in an — à demi-voix

undertow n. contre-marée f., ressac m.

undervalue vt. sous-évaluer, sous-estimer; déprécier

underwear n. sous-vêtements m. pl., linge m., lingerie f.

underweight a. qui manque de poids; trop maigre

underworld n. bas-fonds m. pl., enfers m. pl.

underwrite vt. souscrire, garantir; –r n. assureur m.; –rs n. pl. syndicat de garantie m.

undeserved a. immérité; injuste; –ly adv. à tort, injustement

undeserving a. indigne; peu méritant, sans mérite

undesirable a. peu désirable, indésirable

undetected a. inaperçu

undetermined a. indécis, indéterminé

undeterred a. non-découragé

undeveloped a. a. inexploité; non-développé

undeviating a. constant, fidèle; droit

undigested a. mal digéré; indigeste

undignified a. peu digne, qui manque de dignité

undiluted a. pur; concentré; non dilué

undiminished a. non diminué

undiplomatic a. peu diplomatique; indiscret

undiscernible a. imperceptible

undiscerning a. peu pénétrant; sans discernement

undisciplined a. indiscipliné

undiscovered a. inconnu; caché; non-découvert

undiscriminating a. sans goût, sans discernement

undisguised a. non-déguisé; ouvert; –ly adv. ouvertement, franchement

undismayed a. non-découragé; sans perdre de courage; sans peur

undisputed a. incontesté, indisputé

undistinguished a. obscur; médiocre

undistinguishable a. indistinguible

undisturbed a. tranquille, paisible, calme; non dérangé

undivided a. indivisé, entier; non-partagé;

unanime

undo vt. défaire; dénouer; réparer; –ing n. ruine, perte f.

undone a. défait; ruiné; perdu; inaccompli, inachevé

undoubtedly adv. sans (aucun) doute; indubitablement

undraped a. nu

undress n. déshabillé m.; — vt. déshabiller, dévêtir; — vi. se déshabiller, se dévêtir; –ed a. déshabillé, dévêtu; (manufacturing) brut, non-préparé; (cooking) au naturel

undrinkable a. impotable, inbuvable

undue a. indû; peu justifié; illégitime

undulate vi. ondoyer, onduler

unduly adv. indûment; trop; à l'excès

undutiful a. peu fidèle à ses devoirs

undying a. immortel

unearned a. non gagné; immérité

unearth vt. déterrer; –ly a. sinistre, surnaturel

uneasiness n. inquiétude f.; malaise m.

uneasy a. inquiet; agité; mal à l'aise

uneducated a. qui manque d'instruction

unemotional a. impassible, peu émotionnable

unemployed a. sans travail; désœuvré; –person chômeur m.

unemployment n. chômage m.

unencumbered a. non-encombré, non-embarrassé, débarrassé

unending a. interminable, sans fin

unendurable a. insupportable

unenterprising a. peu entreprenant

unenviable a. peu enviable

unequal a. inégal; irrégulier; au-dessous de; –led a. sans égal; inégalé

unequivocal a. sans équivoque; clair

unerring a. infaillible

unessential a. non-essentiel

uneven a. inégal; irrégulier; (number) impair; (terrain) accidenté; –ness n. inégalité f.

uneventful a. calme, sans incident(s); monotone

unexcelled a. que l'on n'a pas surpassé

unexciting a. ennuyeux; monotone; peu passionnant

unexpected a. inattendu; imprévu; inopiné; inespéré

unexpired a. non-périmé

unexplained a. inexpliqué

unexploded a. non-éclaté

unexplored a. inexploré

unexposed a. (phot.) vierge

unexpurgated a. intégral, non expurgé

unfading a. impérissable

unfailing a. infaillible, certain, sûr

unfair a. injuste; inéquitable; –ness n. injustice f.

unfaithful a. infidèle; déloyal; inexact; –ness n. infidélité f.; inexactitude f.

unfaltering a. assuré, ferme

unfamiliar a. peu familier; inconnu; be — with ne pas connaître; ignorer; –ity n. manque de connaissance f.; ignorance f.

unfashionable a. qui n'est pas à la mode; démodé

unfasten vt. détacher; défaire

unfathomable a. insondable; impénétrable

unfavorable a. peu favorable; défavorable; désavantageux; (wind) impropice

unfeasible a. impraticable

unfeeling a. insensible

unfeigned a. non-simulé; franc, sincère

unfettered a. libre, sans entraves

unfilled a. non-rempli, vide

unfinished a. inachevé

unfit a. incapable; inapte; impropre; indigne; -ness n. incapacité f.; inaptitude; -ting a. peu convenable; mal à propos; déplacé

unflagging a. infatigable

unflattering a. peu flatteur

unflinching a. qui ne bronche pas

unfold vt. déplier; dérouler; exposer; — vi. se dérouler

unforseen a. imprévu, inattendu

unforgettable a. inoubliable

unforgivable a. impardonnable

unforgiving a. implacable

unfortified a. sans fortifications, non-fortifié, ouvert

unfortunate a. infortuné, malheureux; regrettable; -ly adv. malheureusement, par malheur

unfounded a. sans fondement

unfrequented a. peu fréquenté; écarté

unfriendliness n. manque d'amitié m.; hostilité f.

unfriendly a. peu amical; hostile; mal disposé

unfrock vt. défroquer

unfruitful a. peu fructueux; inutile

unfulfilled a. non-satisfait; inaccompli

unfurl vt. déployer; (naut.) déferler

unfurnished a. non-meublé

ungainly a. & adv. maladroit, gauche

ungenerous a. peu généreux

ungentlemanly a. mal élevé; peu comme il faut

unglazed a. non-glacé; non-verni; mat

ungodliness n. impiété f.

ungraceful a. sans grâce, disgracieux; gauche

ungracious a. de mauvaise grâce, malgracieux, mal vu; -ness n. mauvaise grâce f.

ungrammatical a. peu grammatical

ungrateful a. ingrat, peu reconnaissant; -ness n. ingratitude f., manque de reconnaissance m.

ungratified a. non-satisfait; inassouvi

ungrounded a. sans fondement

ungrudging a. libéral, généreux

unguarded a. sans défense; non-gardé; inattentif; indiscret

unguent n. onguent m.

unhallowed a. profane; non-béni

unhampered a. libre, qui n'est pas gêné

unhand vt. lâcher; -y a. maladroit, gauche

unhappily adv. tristement; malheureusement

unhappiness n. chagrin m., tristesse f.; malheur m.

unhappy a. triste; malheureux, infortuné; peu content, mécontent

unharmed a. sain et sauf; intact

unhealthiness n. insalubrité f.

unhealthy a. malsain, insalubre; maladif

unheard-of a. inouï; inconnu

unheeded a. inaperçu; négligé

unheeding a. inattentif; insouciant

unhesitating a. résolu, qui n'hésite pas; -ly adv. sans hésitation, sans hésiter

unhindered a. sans obstacle, sans empêchement

unhook vt. décrocher; dégrafer

unhoped a., — for inespéré

unhorse vt. démonter

unhurt a. sain et sauf; sans mal; intact

unidentified a. non-identifié; inconnu

unification n. unification f.

uniform a. uniforme, régulier; — n. uniforme m.; costume m.; tenue f.; -ity n. uniformité, régularité f.; unité f.; -ly adv. uniformément

unify vt. unifier

unilateral a. unilatéral

unimaginable a. inimaginable

unimaginative a. qui manque d'imagination

unimpaired a. non-altéré, non affaibli, non-diminué; intact

unimpeachable a. inattaquable, sûr

unimpeded a. sans empêchement

unimportant a. peu important, sans importance

unimpressed a. impassible, froid; peu impressionné

unimpressive a. peu imposant, peu impressionnant; ordinaire, médiocre

uninformed a. ignorant; be — ignorer; ne pas connaître

uninhabitable a. inhabitable

uninhabited a. inhabité

uninitiated a. non-initié

uninjured a. non-blessé; sain et sauf; sans mal; intact

uninspired a. sans inspiration

uninsured a. non-assuré

unintelligible a. inintelligible

unintentional a. involontaire; fait par inadvertance

uninterested a. non-intéressé; qui ne s'intéresse pas

uninteresting a. peu intéressant, sans intérêt

uninterrupted a. ininterrompu; suivi

uninvited a. sans être invité; inconvivié

uninviting a. peu engageant; peu appétissant

union n. union f.; (labor) syndicat m.; -ism n. syndicalisme m.; -ist n. syndicaliste m. & f., syndiqué m.; -ize vt. syndicaliser

Union of South Africa n. Union de l'Afrique du Sud f.

unison n. unisson m.; in — à l'unisson; de concert

unit n. unité f.; élément m.

Unitarian a. & n. unitarien m.

unite vt. unir; unifier; joindre; — vi. s'unir, se joindre; se confédérer; se combiner; -d a. uni; unique; réuni

United Arab Republic n. République Arabe Unie f.

United Nations n. Nations Unies f. pl.

United States n. Etats-Unis m. pl.

unity n. unité f.; concorde f., accord m.

univalent a. monovalent, univalent

universal a. universel

universe n. univers m.

university n. université f.; — a. universitaire

unjust a. injuste

unjustifiable a. injustifiable

unjustified a. non justifié

unkempt a. mal peigné; dépeigné; mal tenu

unkind a. peu aimable; cruel; méchant; –ly a. peu aimable; peu favorable; –ly adv. cruellement, méchamment; –ness n. manque de bienveillance m.; méchanceté f.

unknowing a. ignorant; –ly adv. sans le savoir

unknown a. inconnu; ignoré; obscur; — to à l'insu de; — n. inconnu m.; (math.) inconnue f.

unknot vt. dénouer, défaire

unlace vt. délacer, défaire

unlawful a. illégal, illicite

unleash vt. lâcher

unleavened a. sans levain; azyme; — bread azyme n.

unless conj. à moins que; si

unlettered a. illettré, peu lettré

unlicensed a. non-autorisé; sans patente

unlike a. différent; peu ressemblant; dissemblable; –lihood n. improbabilité, invraisemblance f.; –ly a. peu probable, invraisemblable

unlimited a. illimité; sans bornes

unload vt. décharger; –ed a. déchargé; non chargé; –ing n. déchargement m.

unlock vt. ouvrir

unlooked a., — for inattendu

unlucky a. malheureux, infortuné; de mauvais augure

unmanageable a. intraitable; indocile

unmanly a. indigne d'un homme; peu viril

unmannerly a. mal élevé, impoli, grossier

unmarked a. non-marqué; sans marque; sans blessure

unmarketable a. invendable

unmarried a. non-marié, célibataire

unmask vt. démasquer; dévoiler

unmatched a. sans égal, incomparable, sans pareil

unmentionable a. dont on ne doit pas parler

unmerciful a. impitoyable

unmerited a. non-mérité, immérité

unmindful a. négligent, oublieux

unmistakable a. clair, évident

unmistakably adv. clairement, évidemment

unmixed a. sans mélange; sans alliage; pur

unmolested a. sans être molesté, sans obstacle

unmoved a. impassible; inflexible

unnamed a. anonyme; sans nom

unnatural a. contre nature; non-naturel; (laugh) forcé

unnavigable a. innavigable

unnecessarily adv. sans nécessité, inutilement

unnecessary a. inutile, superflu, peu nécessaire

unneeded a. dont on n'a pas besoin; peu nécessaire

unneighborly a. de mauvais voisin

unnerve vt. démonter

unnoticed a. inaperçu, inobservé

unobservant a. inattentif, peu observateur

unobserved a. inobservé, inaperçu

unobstructed a. non-encombré, libre

unobtainable a. qui est impossible à obtenir

unobtrusive a. effacé; discret

unoccupied a. libre, disponible; inoccupé; inhabité

unofficial a. non-officiel; non confirmé

unopened a. (letter) non-décacheté

unopposed a. sans opposition

unorthodox a. peu orthodoxe; original

unostentatious a. sans faste; simple

unpack vt. défaire; dépaqueter

unpaid a. non-payé; sans traitement; non-acquitté

unpalatable a. désagréable, dégoûtant

unparalleled a. sans pareil; sans précédent

unpardonable a. impardonnable

unpatriotic a. peu patriotique; (person) peu patriote

unpaved a. non-pavé

unperceivable a. imperceptible

unperceived a. inaperçu

unperturbed a. peu ému; froid; impassible

unpin vt. défaire

unpitying a. impitoyable

unplaced a. sans place, non-placé

unplayable a. injouable

unpleasant a. désagréable; déplaisant; peu aimable; –ness n. chose désagréable f.; nature désagréable f.

unpleasing a. désagréable, peu agréable

unpolished a. non-poli; rude, grossier

unpolluted a. non-pollué; pur; sain

unpopular a. impopulaire; –ity n. impopularité f.

unpracticed a. inexpérimenté

unprecedented a. sans précédent, sans exemple; inouï

unprejudiced a. sans préjugés, sans prévention, impartial

unpremeditated a. non-prémédité

unprepared a. non-préparé; improvisé; sans préparation

unprepossessing a. peu engageant

unpresuming a. sans présomption

unpretentious a. modeste, sans prétention(s)

unprincipled a. sans principes; sans mœurs

unprocurable a. impossible à obtenir

unproductive a. improductif; stérile

unprofitable a. inutile; peu profitable, improfitable; peu lucratif

unpromising a. qui ne promet rien; qui s'annonce mal

unprompted a. spontané

unpropitious a. défavorable, impropice

unprotected a. sans protection, non-protégé, sans défense; exposé

unproved a. non-prouvé, improuvé; inéprouvé

unprovided a. dépourvu; — for a. sans ressources

unprovoked a. non-provoqué, improvoqué

unpublished a. non-publié; inédit

unpunished a. impuni

unqualified a. incapable; incompétent; sans réserve, catégorique

unquenchable a. inassouvissable

unquestionable a. incontestable, indubitable, indiscutable

unquestioned a. incontesté, indisputé

unquestioning a. sans question

unravel vt. effiler; débrouiller; — vi. s'effiler; se débrouiller

unread a. non-lu; illettré

unreadable a. illisible

unreal a. irréel; imaginaire

unreasonable a. déraisonnable, peu raisonnable

unrecognizable a. méconnaissable

unrecognized a. non-reconnu; méconnu

unreconcilable a. irréconciliable

unreconciled a. irréconcilié

unrecorded a. non-enregistré; qui n'est pas mentionné

unredeemed a. non-racheté; non dégagé

unrefined a. non-raffiné; grossier, peu raffiné

unregistered a. non-enregistré; non-inscrit

unrehearsed a. spontané; sans répétition(s)

unrelated a. sans rapport; non-apparenté

unrelenting a. implacable, inflexible

unreliability n. inexactitude f.; manque de fidélité m.

unreliable a. peu fidèle; sur lequel on ne peut pas compter

unremitting a. soutenu, ininterrompu

unremunerative a. peu lucratif, peu rémunérateur

unrepentant a. impénitent

unrequited a. non-partagé; non récompensé

unreserved a. sans réserve, franc; non réservé; complet

unresponsive a. peu sensible; impassible; froid

unrest n. agitation f.; inquiétude f.

unrestrained a. libre; non-restreint

unrestricted a. sans restriction; absolu

unrevenged a. non-vengé, invengé

unrewarded a. sans récompense

unripe a. vert, qui n'est pas mûr

unrivaled a. sans rival; sans pareil

unroll vt. dérouler; — vi. se dérouler

unromantic a. peu sentimental; peu romanesque

unruffled a. calme; imperturbable

unruly a. intraitable, insoumis

unsaddle vt. desseller; désarçonner

unsafe a. peu sûr; dangereux

unsanitary a. non-hygiénique

unsatisfactory a. peu satisfaisant

unsatisfied a. peu satisfait, mécontent

unsatisfying a. peu satisfaisant

unscathed a. sans blessure; sain et sauf; intact

unscientific a. peu scientifique

unscrew vt. dévisser

unscrupulous a. peu scrupuleux; sans scrupule

unseal vt. desceller; décacheter

unseasonable a. hors de saison; mal à propos

unseasoned a. non-assaisonné; inexpérimenté; (wood) vert

unseat vt. (horseman) démonter, désarçonner; (pol.) invalider

unsecured a. mal assujetti; non-garanti

unseeing a. aveugle

unseemliness n. inconvenance f.

unseemly a. peu convenable; malséant

unseen a. invisible; inaperçu

unselfish a. désintéressé; altruiste; -ness n. désintéressement m.

unserviceable a. inutilisable

unsettle vt. troubler; déranger; -d a. troublé, inquiet; dérangé; indécis; non colonisé; (bill) non-réglé, impayé

unshakeable a. inébranlable, ferme

unshaken a. inébranlé, ferme

unshapely a. difforme; informe; mal fait

unshaven a. non-rasé

unsheathe vt. dégainer

unsheltered a. sans abri; exposé

unsightly a. désagréable à la vue; laid; sale

unsigned a. non-signé

unsinkable a. insubmersible

unskilful a. malhabile, inhabile; maladroit

unskilled a. inexpert; inexpérimenté; — labor main-d'œuvre f.

unsociable a. insociable; peu aimable, peu amical

unsoiled a. sans tache

unsold a. invendu

unsolicited a. non-sollicité; spontané

unsolved a. non-expliqué; non-résolu

unsophisticated a. simple, ingénu; naïf

unsound a. malsain, non-sain, maladif; peu solide; mauvais, faible, peu convaincant; -ness n. manque de solidité m.; faiblesse f.

unsparing a. prodigue; impitoyable; infatigable

unspeakable a. inexprimable, indicible

unspecified a. non-spécifié

unspoiled a. non-gâté

unspoken a. non-prononcé; tacite

unsportsmanlike a. peu loyal, antisportif

unstable a. instable; inconstant

unstained a. sans tache; non-teint

unstamped a. non-affranchi, sans timbre

unsteadiness n. instabilité f.; irrésolution f.; irrégularité f.

unsteady a. peu solide, instable; irrésolu; irrégulier; (step) chancelant; (voice) mal assuré

unstrap vt. déboucler

unstressed a. sans accent; inaccentué

unstring vt. (fig.) détraquer

unsubdued a. insoumis; indompté

unsubsidized a. sans subvention

unsuccessful a. manqué, raté; sans succès; non réussi; refusé; be — échouer; -ly adv. sans succès

unsuitable a. qui ne convient pas; peu convenable; inopportun; peu fait, inapte; -ness n. inaptitude f.; inopportunité f.

unsuited a. peu fait, inapte; mal adapté

unsullied a. sans tache, sans souillure

unsupported a. sans soutien, sans appui

unsurpassed a. sans égal, sans pareil

unsuspected *a.* non-suspect; insoupçonné

unsuspecting, unsuspicious *a.* sans défiance, sans soupçons; qui ne se doute pas

unsweetened *a.* non-sucré

unswerving *a.* ferme, constant; qui ne s'écarte pas

unsymmetrical *a.* sans symétrie; asymétrique

unsympathetic *a.* peu compatissant; indifférent; peu sympathique

unsystematic *a.* sans méthode; sans système

untainted *a.* non-gâté; non-corrompu

untalented *a.* sans talent(s)

untamed *a.* non-apprivoisé; indompté

untapped *a.* (fig.) inutilisé

untarnished *a.* non-terni; (fig.) sans tache

untenable *a.* insoutenable; intenable

untenanted *a.* inhabité, inoccupé

untested *a.* pas encore mis à l'épreuve; inéprouvé, inessayé

unthinkable *a.* inconcevable, inimaginable

unthinking *a.* irréfléchi

untidiness *n.* désordre *m.*; malpropreté *f.*

untidy *a.* en désordre; négligé; malpropre

untie *vt.* délier, détacher, défaire, dénouer, déficeler

until *prep.* jusqu'à; — *conj.* jusqu'à ce que; wait — attendre que

untilled *a.* non-labouré; inculte, incultivé

untimely *a.* inopportun, mal à propos; hors de saison; indu; prématuré

untiring *a.* infatigable, inlassable

unto *prep.* à; vers; jusqu'à

untold *a.* non-compté; énorme; incalculable; inouï

untouchable *n.* hors-caste *m.*

untouched *a.* intact; sain et sauf; indifférent; non-discuté

untoward *a.* incommode; malheureux, fâcheux; malséant

untraceable *a.* introuvable

untrained *a.* inexpert, inexpérimenté, inexercé; (animal) non-dressé

untranslatable *a.* intraduisible

untraveled *a.* qui n'a pas beaucoup voyagé; inexploré

untried *a.* non-essayé, inessayé; pas encore mis à l'épreuve

untrimmed *a.* sans ornement, sans garniture; simple

untrodden *a.* non-frayé; inexploré

untroubled *a.* calme, tranquille

untrue *a.* faux (fausse); inexact; infidèle

untrustworthy *a.* qui n'est pas digne de confiance; infidèle; douteux

untruth *n.* mensonge *m.*; -ful *a.* menteur; mensonger; faux; -fulness *n.* fausseté *f.*

unturned *a.*, leave no stone — faire tout son possible

untutored *a.* illettré, sans instruction

unusable *a.* inutilisable

unused *a.* non-employé; inutilisé; peu habitué

unusual *a.* exceptionnel, rare; peu commun; peu usité; -ness *n.* rareté *f.*

unvanquished *a.* invaincu

unvaried *a.* sans variété; monotone; uniforme

unvarnished *a.* non-verni; (fig.) simple.

sans fard

unvarying *a.* invariable; uniforme

unveil *vt.* dévoiler; inaugurer; -ing *n.* inauguration *f.*

unverified *a.* invérifié; non-corroboré

unversed *a.* peu versé

unvoiced *a.* sourd

unwanted *a.* non-voulu, non-désiré

unwarrantable *a.* injustifiable

unwarranted *a.* peu justifié; déplacé; sans garantie

unwary *a.* imprudent, imprévoyant

unwavering *a.* ferme, résolu, constant

unwearying *a.* infatigable

unwelcome *a.* importun, mal venu; désagréable

unwell *a.* indisposé; souffrant, malade

unwholesome *a.* malsain; insalubre

unwieldy *a.* peu maniable

unwilling *a.* inserviable; qui ne veut pas; be — ne pas vouloir, être peu disposé; -ly *adv.* à contre-cœur; -ness *n.* mauvaise volonté *f.*

unwind *vt.* dérouler; débobiner

unwise *a.* peu sage, imprudent

unwitting *a.* inconscient; -ly *adv.* inconsciemment; sans le savoir

unwonted *a.* inaccoutumé

unworkable *a.* impraticable

unworked *a.* non-travaillé; inexploité

unworldly *a.* d'un autre monde; peu mondain; peu naturel

unworthiness *n.* manque de mérite, peu de mérite *m.*

unworthy *a.* indigne; peu méritoire

unwounded *a.* sans blessure

unwrap *vt.* défaire

unwrinkled *a.* sans rides; uni; lisse

unwritten *a.* non-écrit; oral

unyielding *a.* ferme, inflexible, qui ne cède pas

up *adv.* haut; en haut; debout; relevé; (sun) levé; be — against se heurter à; get — se lever; go — monter; it's — to you (to) c'est à vous (de); speak — parler plus haut; — there là-haut; — to jusqu'à; walk — and down se promener de long en large; -s *n. pl.*, -s and downs vicissitudes *f. pl.*

upbraid *vt.* reprocher

upbringing *n.* éducation *f.*

upgrade *n.* montée *f.*; be on the — monter; reprendre

upheaval *n.* soulèvement *m.*; bouleversement *m.*

uphill *a.* montant; — *adv.* en montant; go — monter

uphold *vt.* soutenir, maintenir; confirmer

upholster *vt.* tapisser, couvrir; garnir; -er *n.* tapisseur *m.*; -ing, -y *n.* tapisserie *f.*; garniture *f.*

upkeep *n.* entretien *m.*

upland *n.* haut pays *m.*

uplift *n.* élévation *f.*; — *vt.* soulever, élever

upon *prep.* sur; à; vers; sous; de; en

upper *a.* supérieur; de dessus; (plus) haut, plus élevé; — classes hautes classes *f. pl.*; — hand dessus *m.*; — part dessus *m.*

upper-class *a.* de la haute classe

uppermost *a.* le plus haut, le plus élevé; le plus important; — *adv.* en dessus

upright *a.* droit; vertical, perpendiculaire; debout; honnête, intègre; — *n.* montant *m.*; –ness *n.* droiture, intégrité *f.*

uprising *n.* soulèvement *m.*, insurrection *f.*

uproar *n.* chahut, tumulte, vacarme, grand bruit *m.*; –ious *a.* tumultueux

uproot *vt.* déraciner; arracher, extirper

upset *n.* désordre *m.*; renversement *m.*; bouleversement *m.*; — *vt.* renverser; bouleverser; troubler, inquiéter, agiter; déranger; démonter; émouvoir; indisposer; — *vi.* se renverser; — *a.* renversé; trouble; ému; bouleversé; dérangé

upshot *n.* issue *f.*, résultat *m.*

upside-down *adv.* sens dessus dessous; renversé; bouleversé

upstairs *adv.* en haut; — *n.* étage supérieur *m.*; go — monter (l'escalier) — *a.* d'en haut

upstanding *a.* honnête

upstart *n.* parvenu *m.*

upstream *adv.* en amont

up-to-date *a.* moderne

uptown *adv.* dans un quartier commercial, vers un quartier commercial (qui ne se trouve pas au centre)

upturn *n.* reprise *f.*; –ed *a.* relevé

upward *a.* montant, ascendant; –(s) *adv.* en montant; vers le haut; vers le ciel; en haut; en dessus; au-dessus

uranium *n.* uranium *m.*

urban *a.* urbain; –ity *n.* urbanité *f.*; –ization *n.* urbanisation *f.*; –ize *vt.* urbaniser

urbane *a.* poli

urchin *n.* marmot *m.*; gamin *m.*

urea *n.* urée *f.*

uremia *n.* urémie *f.*

ureter, urethra *n.* uretère *m.*

urge *n.* impulsion, poussée *f.*; désir *m.*, envie *f.*; — *vt.* pousser, exhorter; encourager; recommander; insister; –ncy *n.* urgence *f.*; importance *f.*; nécessité *f.*; –nt *a.* urgent, pressant

urinal *n.* urinoir *m.*

urinalysis *n.* analyse de l'urine *f.*

urinate *vi.* uriner

urine *n.* urine *f.*

urn *n.* urne *f.*; (coffee) grosse cafetière *f.*

Uruguay *n.* Uruguay *m.*

us *pron.* nous

usable *a.* utilisable

usage *n.* usage *m.*; traitement *m.*; coutume *f.*; emploi *m.*

use *n.* emploi *m.*; usage *m.*; service *m.*; utilisation *f.* utilité; be of — servir, être utile; for the — of à l'usage de; make — of se servir de; profiter de; what's the — of? à quoi bon?; –d *a.* usagé; — *vt.* employer, se servir de, utiliser, user de; — up user, épuiser; be –d to être habitué à; être accoutumé à; avoir l'habitude de; get –d to s'habituer à, s'accoutumer à, se faire à; –d car automobile d'occasion; –ful *a.* utile; –fulness *n.* utilité *f.* –less *a.* inutile; vain; –lessness *n.* inutilité *f.*; –r *n.* usager *m.*; consommateur *m.*; abonné *m.*

usher *n.* huissier *m.*; (theat.) ouvreuse *f.*;

(wedding) garçon d'honneur *m.*; — *vt.*, — in introduire, faire entrer; (fig.) inaugurer

U.S.S.R.: Union of Soviet Socialist Republics *n.* U.R.S.S.: Union des Républiques Soviétiques Socialistes *f.*

usual *a.* ordinaire, habituel; usuel; d'usage; accoutumé; as — comme d'ordinaire, comme d'habitude; –ly *adv.* d'ordinaire, d'habitude

usurp *vt.* usurper; –ation *n.* usurpation *f.*; –er *n.* usurpateur *m.*

usury *n.* usure *f.*

utensil *n.* ustensile *m.*; kitchen –s batterie de cuisine *f.*

uterus *n.* matrice *f.*

utilitarian *a.* utilitaire; –ism *n.* utilitarisme *m.*

utility *n.* utilité *f.*; public — (entreprise de) service public *m.*

utilization *n.* mise en valeur *f.*; utilisation *f.*

utilize *vt.* utiliser, se servir de; mettre en valeur

utmost *a.* dernier, extrême; le plus grand; — *n.* le plus possible *m.*; dernier degré *m.*; do one's — faire tout son possible

Utopia *n.* Utopie *f.*; –n *a.* utopique

utter *a.* absolu, complet; — *vt.* pousser; prononcer; débiter; dire; –ance *n.* parole(s) *f.* pl.; expression *f.*; –ly *adv.* complètement, tout à fait

uvula *n.* uvule *f.*; –r *a.* uvulaire

V

vacancy *n.* vide *m.*; vacance *f.*; poste vacant *m.*

vacant *a.* vide; libre, inoccupé; vague

vacate *vt.* quitter; vider; évacuer

vacation *n.* vacances *f.* pl.

vaccinate *vt.* vacciner

vaccination *n.* vaccination *f.*

vaccine *n.* vaccin *m.*

vacillate *vi.* vaciller

vacillation *n.* vacillation *f.*

vacuous *a.* vide; niais

vacuum *n.* vide *m.*; — bottle bouteille isolante, bouteille thermos *f.*; — cleaner *n.* aspirateur *m.*; — seal *n.* joint hermétique *m.*; — tube *n.* lampe à vide *f.*; tube à vide *m.*; — *vt.* nettoyer à l'aspirateur

vagabond *a.* vagabond, errant; — *n.* vagabond *m.*

vagary *n.* caprice *m.*

vagina *n.* vagin *m.*; –l *a.* vaginal

vagrancy *n.* vagabondage *m.*

vagrant *n.* vagabond *m.*

vague *a.* vague; imprécis; –ness *n.* vague *m.*; imprécision *f.*

vain *a.* vain; inutile, futile; vaniteux; in — en vain; inutilement; –ness *n.* vanité *f.*

vainglorious *a.* vaniteux, orgueilleux

valance *n.* draperie, garniture *f.*

vale *n.* vallée *f.*, val, vallon *m.*

valedictorian *n.* élève reçu premier pendant sa dernière année de high-school *m.* & *f.*

valedictory *n.* discours d'adieu *m.*; — *a.*

d'adieu

valentine n. carte qu'on envoie le jour de la Saint-Valentin f.; personne chérie f. (à qui on envoie une carte)

valiant a. vaillant, brave; **-ly** adv. vaillamment

valid a. valide, valable, bon; **-ate** vt. valider; **-ation** n. validation f.; **-ity** n. validité f.; justesse f.

valley n. vallée f.; val, vallon m.

valor n. valeur, vaillance f.; **-ous** a. valeureux, vaillant

valuable a. de valeur, de prix, précieux; **-s** n. pl. objets de valeur m. pl.

valuation n. évaluation, estimation f.

value n. valeur f., prix m.; face — valeur nominale, valeur faciale f.; of no — sans valeur; — vt. estimer, évaluer; tenir à; **-d** a. précieux, estimé; **-less** a. sans valeur

valve n. soupape f., clapet m.; vanne f.; valve f.; (anat.) valvule f.; safety — soupape de sûreté f.

vamp n. empeigne f.; avant-pied m.; (coll.) femme fatale f.; (mus.) accompagnement improvisé m.; — vt. raccommoder; séduire; improviser

van n. avant-garde f.; (vehicle) camion m.; camionnette f.; (rail.) fourgon m.

vanadium n. vanadium m.

vandal n. vandale m.; **-ism** n. vandalisme m.

vandyke n. barbe en pointe f.

vane n. girouette f.; bras m.; ailette f.

vanguard n. avant-garde f.

vanilla n. vanille f.; — bean n. gousse de vanille f.

vanish vi. disparaître; s'évanouir

vanity n. vanité f.; orgueil m.; (furniture) coiffeuse f.; table de toilette f.; — case n. poudrière f.

vanquish vt. vaincre; **-er** n. vainqueur m.

vantage n. avantage m.; — point n. terrain favorable m.

vapid a. insipide, fade; **-ity**, **-ness** n. insipidité, fadeur f.

vapor n. vapeur f.; — lamp n. tube à décharge m.; **-ize** vt. vaporiser, gazéifier; **-izer** n. vaporisateur, atomiseur m.; **-ous** a. vaporeux

variability n. variabilité f.

variable a. variable, inconstant, changeant; — n. variable f.

variance n. désaccord m.; at — en désaccord

variant n. variante f.

variation n. variation f.; changement m.; différence f.

varicose a. variqueux; — vein varice f.

varied a. varié; divers

variety n. variété f.; diversité f.; assortiment m.; — store n. prisunic m.

various a. divers; varié; différent; plusieurs

varnish n. vernis m.; vernissure f.; — vt. vernir; farder; glisser sur; **-ing** n. vernissage m.

varsity n. (university) classes supérieures f. pl.; — team n. première équipe, équipe des classes supérieures

vary vt. varier, diversifier; — vi. varier, changer; différer; **-ing** a. variable, changeant

vascular a. vasculaire

vasomotor a. vasomoteur

vassal n. vassal m.; **-age** n. vassalage m., vassalité f.

vast a. vaste, immense; **-ly** adv. énormément, immensément; **-ness** n. immensité f.

vat n. cuve f.; cuveau m.

Vatican n. Vatican m.; — City n. Cité du Vatican f.

vaudeville n. attractions sur scène f. pl.

vault n. (arch.) voûte f.; (bank) chambre forte f.; (cellar) cave f.; (cemetery) caveau m.; (motion) saut m.; — vt. voûter; — vi. sauter

vaunt vt. vanter, se vanter de

veal n. veau m.; — chop n. côtelette de veau f.; — cutlet n. escalope de veau f.; côtelette de veau f.

vector n. vecteur m.; — a. vectoriel

veer vi. tourner, virer; (naut.) changer de bord

vegetable a. végétal; — n. légume m.; végétal m.; — garden n. jardin potager m.

vegetal a. végétal

vegetarian a. & n. végétarien m.

vegetate vi. végéter

vegetation n. végétation f.

vehemence n. véhémence, force f.

vehement a. véhément; **-ly** adv. avec véhémence

vehicle n. voiture f.; véhicule m.; moyen m.

vehicular a. véhiculaire

veil n. voile m.; voilette f.; — vt. voiler; cacher; **-ed** a. voilé; caché

vein n. veine f.; nervure f.; disposition, humeur f.; **-ed** a. veiné; nervuré; marbré; **-ing** n. marbrure f.

vellum n. vélin m.; papier vélin m.

velocipede n. vélocipède m.

velocity n. vitesse f.

velvet n. velours m.; — a. de velours; velouté; **-een** n. velours de coton m.; **-y** a. velouté

venal a. vénal; **-ity** n. vénalité, corruption f.

vend vt. & vi. vendre; **-or** n. vendeur m.; machine à sous f.

veneer n. placage m.; bois de placage m.; contreplaqué m.; (fig.) vernis m.; — vt. plaquer

venerable a. vénérable

venerate vt. vénérer

veneration n. vénération f.

venereal a. vénérien

Venetian a. & n. vénitien m.; — blind jalousie f.

Venezuela n. Vénézuéla m.

vengeance n. vengeance f.; take — se venger

vengeful a. vindicatif

venial a. véniel, pardonnable

Venice n. Venise f.

venison n. venaison f.

venom n. venin m.; **-ous** a. venimeux; vénéneux

vent n. passage, trou m.; soupirail m.; lumière f.; give — to donner libre cours à; — vt. décharger

ventilate vt. ventiler, aérer

ventilation n. ventilation, aération f., aérage m.

ventilator n. ventilateur m.

ventricle n. ventricule m.

ventriloquist n. ventriloque m. & f.

venture n. enterprise f.; — vt. hasarder, risquer; oser; -some a. aventureux, risqué, aventuré

venue n. (law) voisinage m., juridiction f.

veracious a. véridique

veracity n. véracité, véridicité f.

veranda(h) n. véranda f.

verb n. verbe m.; -al a. verbal; oral; littéral; -ally adv. verbalement; -ose a. verbeux, prolixe; -osity n. verbosité, prolixité f.

verbatim adv. mot pour mot

verdant a. verdoyant, vert

verdict n. verdict m.; jugement m.

verdigris n. vert-de-gris m.

verge n. bord m.; bordure f.; verge f.; on the — of sur le point de; à la veille de; — vi., — on friser, toucher à

verger n. bedeau, sacristain m.

verifiable a. vérifiable, contrôlable

verification n. vérification f.

verify vt. vérifier; contrôler; confirmer

veritable a. véritable

verity n. vérité f.

vermiform a. vermiforme; — appendix n. appendice du cæcum m.

vermilion n. vermillon m.; — a. vermeil, vermillon

vermin n. vermine f.

vernacular a. vernaculaire; vulgaire

versatile a. varié; souple; versatile

versatility n. souplesse f.; versatilité f.

verse n. vers m.; strophe f.; couplet m.; poésie f.; (eccl.) verset m.; -d a. versé; expérimenté

versify vt. versifier, mettre en vers

version n. version f.; interprétation f.

versus prep. contre

vertebra n. vertèbre f.; -l a. vertébral; -te n. & a. vertébré m.

vertex n. sommet m.

vertical a. vertical; -ness n. verticalité f.

vertiginous a. vertigineux

vertigo n. vertige m.

very adv. très; bien, fort; at the — latest au plus tard; at the — most tout au plus; not — peu; — much beaucoup; — a. même; propre; seul; justement

vesicle n. vésicule f.

Vespers n. vêpres f. pl.

vessel n. vaisseau m.; vase m.; navire m.; instrument m.

vest n. gilet m.; — vt. revêtir, investir; -ed a. dévolu; -ed interests droits acquis m. pl.

vestal a. virginal; — virgin n. vestale f.

vestige n. vestige m., trace f.

vestigial a. qui tient des vestiges

vestment n. vêtement m.

vest-pocket a. de poche; petit

vestry n. sacristie f.

veteran n. vétéran m.; ancien combattant m.; — a. expérimenté; de vétéran

veterinarian, veterinary n. vétérinaire m.

veto n. veto m.; — vt. mettre le veto à; interdire

vex vt. vexer, fâcher; -ation n. vexation f.; dépit m., contrariété f., ennui m.; -atious a. contrariant, fâcheux, ennuyeux; -ed a. vexé, fâché, contrarié

via prep. via; par; — air mail par avion

viability n. viabilité f.

viaduct n. viaduc m.

vial n. fiole f.

viand n. mets m.; viande f.

vibrate vi. vibrer; osciller; — vt. faire vibrer

vibration n. vibration f.; oscillation f.

vibrator n. vibrateur m.; oscillateur m.; (elec.) vibreur m.

vicar n. vicaire m.; curé m.; -age n. cure f., presbytère m.; — general n. grand vicaire m.

vicarious a. substitutif; -ly adv. par substitution; à la place d'un autre

vice n. vice m.; défaut

vice-admiral n. vice-amiral m.

vice-chairman n. vice-président m.

vice-consul n. vice-consul m.

vice-president n. vice-président m.

viceroy n. vice-roi m.

vicinity n. voisinage m.; environs, alentours m. pl.

vicious a. vicieux; hargneux; — circle cercle vicieux m.

vicissitude n. vicissitude f.; péripétie f.

victim n. victime f.; -ize vt. tromper; abuser

victor n. vainqueur m.; -ious a. victorieux; -y n. victoire f.

Victorian a. victorien

victual vt. aprovisionner; -s n. pl. (coll.) provisions f. pl., vivres m. pl.

video n. télévision f.; — a. vidéo, visuel; — signal n. signal d'image m.

vie vi. rivaliser; disputer

Vienna n. Vienne f.

Viennese a. & n. viennois

Viet Nam n. Viet-Nam m.

view n. vue f.; regard m.; perspective f.; aperçu m.; opinion f., avis m.; idée f.; bird's-eye — vue à vol d'oiseau f.; in — en vue; in — of vu; in consideration of; point of — point de vue m.; — vt. regarder; voir; envisager; -er n. spectateur m.

viewfinder n. viseur m.

viewpoint n. point de vue m.

vigil n. veille f.; (eccl.) vigile f.; keep a — veiller; -ance n. vigilance f.; -ant a. éveillé, alerte, vigilant; -antly adv. avec vigilance

vigilante n. membre d'un comité de surveillance m.

vigor n. vigueur f.; énergie f.; -ous a. vigoureux; robuste; fort

vile a. vil, bas; abominable; sale; -ness n. bassesse f.

vilification n. dénigrement m.

vilify vt. diffamer, dénigrer

villa n. villa f.; maison de campagne f.

village n. village m.; -r n. villageois m.

villain n. scélérat m.; (theat.) traître m.;

-ous *a.* vil; scélérat; infâme; -y *n.* scélératesse, infamie *f.*

vim *n.* vigueur, énergie *f.*

vindicate *vt.* justifier; défendre, soutenir; revendiquer

vindication *n.* justification, défense *f.*; revendication *f.*

vindictive *a.* vindicatif; vengeur; -ness *n.* esprit de vengeance *m.*

vindicator *n.* défenseur *m.*

vine *n.* vigne *f.*; — grower vigneron, viticulteur *m.*

vinegar *n.* vinaigre *m.*; — cruet *n.* vinaigrier *m.*

vineyard *n.* vigne *f.*, vignoble *m.*

vintage *n.* vendange *f.*; crû *f.*; année *f.*; — wine *n.* vin de crû, grand vin, vin de marque *m.*

vintner *n.* marchand en vins *m.*

vinyl *n.* vinyl *m.*; — *a.* vinylique

viola *n.* (mus.) alto *m.*

violate *vt.* violer

violation *n.* violation *f.*; infraction, contravention *f.*

violator *n.* violateur; contrevenant *m.*

violent *a.* violent; fort; -ly *adv.* violemment, avec violence

violin *n.* violon *m.*; -ist *n.* violoniste *m.* & *f.*; violon *m.*

violincello *n.* violoncelle *m.*

viper *n.* vipère *f.*

virago *n.* mégère *f.*

virgin *a.* vierge; virginal; — *n.* vierge *f.*; -al *a.* virginal; -ity *n.* virginité *f.*

Virgin Islands *n. pl.* Iles Vierges *f. pl.*

virile *a.* viril; mâle

virility *n.* virilité *f.*

virtual *a.* vrai; de fait; virtuel; -ly *adv.* de fait, virtuellement; presque

virtue *n.* vertu *f.*; qualité *f.*; by — of en vertu de, en raison de .

virtuosity *n.* virtuosité *f.*

virtuoso *n.* virtuose *m.* & *f.*

virtuous *a.* vertueux

virulence *n.* virulence *f.*

virulent *a.* virulent

virus *n.* virus *m.*

visage *n.* visage *m.*, figure *f.*

viscid *a.* visqueux

viscosity *n.* viscosité *f.*

viscount *n.* vicomte *m.*; -ess *n.* vicomtesse *f.*

viscous *a.* visqueux

vise *n.* étau *m.*

visibility *n.* visibilité *f.*; vue *f.*

visible *a.* visible; visuel

vision *n.* vision *f.*; vue *f.*; apparition *f.*; imagination *f.*; -ary *a.* & *n.* visionnaire *m.* & *f.*

visit *n.* visite *f.*; — *vt.* rendre visite à; (place) visiter; -ation *n.* visite *f.*; apparition *f.*; -ing *n.* en visite; de visite; -or *n.* visiteur *m.*

visor *n.* visière *f.*; paresoleil *m.*; protège-vue *m.*

vista *n.* vue, perspective, échappée *f.*

visual *a.* visuel; optique; -ize *vt.* se représenter

vital *a.* vital, essentiel; — statistics état civil *m.*; -ity *n.* vitalité *f.*; vie, vigueur *f.*; -ly *adv.* d'une manière vitale; (coll.)

très, fort, extrêmement; -s *n. pl.* parties vitales *f. pl.*

vitamin *n.* vitamine *f.*

vitiate *vt.* vicier, corrompre

vitreous *a.* vitreux

vitrify *vt.* vitrifier; — *vi.* se vitrifier

vitriol *n.* vitriol *m.*; acide sulfurique *m.*; -ic *a.* acide; mordant

vituperation *n.* injures, insultes *f. pl.*

vituperative *a.* injurieux

vivacious *a.* vif; enjoué; gai; animé; -ness *n.* vivacité *f.*

vivacity *n.* vivacité *f.*; animation *f.*

vivid *a.* vif; vivant; -ly *a.* d'une manière vivante; -ness *n.* vivacité *f.*; vigueur *f.*; imagination *f.*

vivify *vt.* vivifier, animer

vixen *n.* (zool.) renarde *f.*; femme querelleuse *f.*

viz: videlicet à savoir, c'est-à-dire

vocabulary *n.* vocabulaire *m.*

vocal *a.* vocal; bruyant; — cords cordes vocales *f. pl.*; -ist *n.* chanteur *m.*, chanteuse *f.*; -ization *n.* vocalisation *f.*; -ize *vt.* vocaliser

vocation *n.* vocation *f.*; profession *f.*; métier *m.*; -al de(s) métiers; professionnel; -al school école des arts et des métiers *f.*

vociferate *vi.* vociférer

vociferation *n.* vocifération *f.*

vociferous *a.* vociférant; criard; -ly *adv.* bruyamment

vodka *n.* vodka *m.*

vogue *n.* vogue, mode *f.* in — en vogue, à la mode

voice *n.* voix *f.*; in a low — à voix basse, à mi-voix; — *vt.* exprimer; voiser; -d *a.* exprimé; voisé; sonore; -less *a.* sans voix; non voisé; sourd

void *a.* vide; nul; null and — nul et caduc; — of dénué de; — *vt.* vider, évacuer, annuler; — *n.* vide *m.*

volatile *a.* volatil; (fig.) vif, léger; volage

volatility *n.* volatilité *f.*

volcanic *a.* volcanique

volcano *n.* volcan *m.*

volition *n.* volonté, volition *f.*; gré *m.*

volley *n.* volée, décharge, salve *f.*; (sports) volée *f.*

volleyball *n.* volleyball *m.*

volt *n.* volt *m.*; -age *n.* voltage *m.*, tension *f.*; high -age haute tension *f.*; -aic *a.* voltaïque

voltmeter *n.* voltmètre *m.*

volubility *n.* volubilité *f.*

voluble *a.* facile; qui parle avec volubilité

volume *n.* volume *m.*; livre, tome *m.*

volume control *n.* réglage de puissance *m.*

voluminous *a.* volumineux; -ness *n.* grosseur, étendue *f.*

voluntarily *adv.* volontairement

voluntary *a.* volontaire; spontané

volunteer *n.* volontaire *m.*; — *vt.* offrir volontairement, donner volontairement; — *vi.* s'offrir; — *a.* de volontaire

voluptuous *a.* voluptueux; -ly *adv.* voluptueusement; -ness *n.* sensualité *f.*; volupté *f.*

vomit *n.* vomissement *m.*; — *vt.* & *vi.* vomir; -ing *n.* vomissement *m.*

voracious *a.* vorace; dévorant; **-ly** *adv.* avec voracité; **-ness** *n.* voracité *f.*

voracity *n.* voracité *f.*

vortex *n.* tourbillon *m.*

votary *n.* adorateur, dévoué *m.*; sectateur *m.*; partisan *m.*

vote *n.* voix *f.*; vote, scrutin *m.*; suffrage *m.*; résolution *f.*; put to a — mettre aux voix; — *vt. & vi.* voter, donner sa voix; **-r** *n.* votant, électeur *m.*

voting *n.* vote, scrutin *m.*

votive *a.* votif

vouch *vt. & vi.* affirmer, garantir; — for répondre de; **-er** bon *m.*; fiche *f.*, reçu *m.*; passavant *m.*

vow *n.* vœu *m.*; serment *m.*; — *vt. & vi.* vouer; faire vœu; jurer

vowel *n.* voyelle *f.*

voyage *n.* voyage *m.*; — *vi.* voyager; **-r** *n.* voyageur *m.*

vulcanite *n.* caoutchouc vulcanisé *m.*

vulcanize *vt.* vulcaniser

vulgar *a.* vulgaire; commun; grossier, de mauvais goût; **-ism** *n.* expression vulgaire *f.*; **-ity** *n.* vulgarité *f.*; grossièreté *f.*; **-ization** vulgarisation *f.*; **-ize** *vt.* vulgariser

Vulgate *n.* Vulgate *f.*

vulnerability *n.* vulnérabilité *f.*

vulnerable *a.* vulnérable

W

wad *n.* liasse *f.*; bourre *f.*; paquet *m.*; — *vt.* (garment) ouater; **-ding** *n.* ouate *f.*; bourre *f.*

waddle *n.* dandinement *m.*; — *vi.* se dandiner

wade *vi.* marcher dans l'eau; patauger; — across passer à gué

wafer *n.* gaufrette *f.*; (eccl.) hostie *f.*

waffle *n.* gaufre *f.*; — iron *n.* gaufrier *m.*

waft *vt.* transporter; — *vi.* flotter

wag *n.* mouvement de la queue *m.*; (person) farceur *m.*; — *vt.* remuer, agiter

wage *vt.*, — war faire la guerre; **-(s)** *n. & n. pl.* salaire *m.*; gages *m. pl.*; paye *f.*; récompense *f.*

wage earner *n.* salarié, gagne-pain *m.*

wager *n.* pari *m.*, gageure *f.*; — *vt.* parier, gager

wagon *n.* charrette *f.*; chariot *m.*; fourgon *m.*

waif *n.* enfant abandonné, enfant sans domicile *m.*

wail *n.* gémissement *m.*, plainte *f.*; — *vi.* gémir; se lamenter

wainscoting *n.* lambrissage *m.*; boiserie *f.*

waist *n.* taille, ceinture *f.*; (naut.) embelle *f.*

waistband *n.* ceinture *f.*

waistcoat *n.* gilet *m.*

waistline *n.* taille, ceinture *f.*

wait *n.* attente *f.*; in — en embuscade, à l'affût; — *vt. & vi.* attendre; — for attendre; — on servir; — up ne pas se coucher; attendre l'arrivée de quelqu'un (la nuit); — *er n.* garçon *m.*; head **-er** maître d'hôtel *m.*; **-ing** *n.* attente *f.*; service *m.*; **-ing game** **-ing tactics** tactique attentiste *f.*; lady in **-ing** dame d'honneur *f.*; **-ing list** *n.* liste supplémentaire *f.*; **-ing room** salle d'attente *f.*; antichambre *f.*

waitress *n.* serveuse *f.*

waive *vt.* renoncer à; ne pas exiger; ne pas insister sur; **-r** *n.* abandon *n.*; désistement *m.*

wake *n.* veillée (mortuaire) *f.*; (naut.) sillage *m.*; (fig.) traces *f. pl.*, suite *f.*; — *vi.* se réveiller; — *vt.* réveiller; éveiller; **-ful** *a.* éveillé, vigilant; **-fulness** *n.* vigilance *f.*, état de veille *m.*; — *n vt.* réveiller; éveiller; — *n vi.* se réveiller; s'éveiller

waking *n.* veille *f.*; réveil *m.*; — *a.* de veille

Wales *n.* (Pays de) Galles *m.*

walk *n.* promenade *f.*; marche *f.*; démarche *f.*; avenue, allée *f.*; promenoir *m.*; métier *m.*, profession *f.*; go for a —, take a — faire une promenade, (aller) se promener; — *vi.* marcher; aller à pied; se promener; (horse) aller au pas; — *vt.* faire marcher; promener; (streets) courir; **-er** *n.* marcheur *m.*; piéton *m.*; promeneur *m.*; **-ing** *n.* marche *f.*; promenade(s) *f.* (*pl.*)

walkie-talkie *n.* radio-téléphone portatif *m.*

walkout *n.* grève *f.*

walk-up *n.* appartement sans ascenseur *m.*

wall *n.* mur *m.*, muraille *f.*; paroi *f.*; — bracket *n.* console murale *f.*; — plug, — socket *n.* prise de courant murale *f.*; — *vt.* murer; in —, up murer; **-ed** *a.* muré

wallet *n.* portefeuille *m.*

walleyed *a.* qui a l'œil vairon

wallflower *n.* (fig.) tapisserie *f.*

wallop *n.* (gros) coup *m.*; — *vt.* rosser, frapper; tanner la peau à

wallow *vi.* se vautrer; se baigner

wallboard *n.* panneau de fibres de bois *m.*

wallpaper *n.* papier peint *m.*

walnut *n.* noix *f.*; (wood, tree) noyer *m.*

waltz *n.* valse *f.*; — *vi.* valser

wan *a.* pâle, blafard, blême; triste; **-ness** *n.* pâleur *f.*

wand *n.* baguette *f.*

wander *vi.* errer, vaguer; s'écarter; divaguer; **-er** *n.* voyageur, vagabond *m.*; **-ing** *a.* errant, vagabond; nomade; incohérent; **-ing** *n.* vagabondage *m.*; voyages *m. pl.*; divagation *f.*

wanderlust *n.* désir de voyager *m.*

wane *n.* décroissance *f.*, déclin *m.*; — *vi.* décroître; décliner

wangle *vt.* resquiller, carotter

waning *n.* déclin *m.*

want *n.* désir *m.*; besoin *m.*; défaut, manque *m.*; indigence *f.*; for — of faute de; — *vi.* manquer; — *a.* vouloir, désirer; manquer; falloir; avoir besoin de; exiger; demander; **-ed** *a.* voulu, demandé; recherché par la police; **-ing** *a.* qui manque, manquant

wanton *a.* impudique; gratuit; — *n.* femme impudique *f.*; **-ness** *n.* libertinage *m.*; étourderie *f.*

war *n.* guerre *f.*; cold — guerre froide *f.*; — of nerves guerre des nerfs *f.*; total — guerre totale *f.*; — *vi.* faire la guerre; lutter; **-ring** *a.* en guerre

warble *n.* gazouillement *m.*; — *vi.* gazouiller; chanter en gazouillant; -r n. fauvette f.; oiseau chanteur m.

ward n. pupille m.; quartier, arrondissement m.; (hospital) salle (d'hôpital) f.; — vt., — off prévenir; parer

warden n. directeur de prison m.; gardien m.; air raid — chef d'îlot m.

wardrobe n. garde-robe f.; vêtements m. pl.; armoire f.

wardroom n. carré des officiers m.

ware n. articles m. pl.; marchandise f.; -s pl. marchandise(s) f. (pl.)

warehouse n. magasin m.; entrepôt, dépôt m.; garde-meuble m.

warfare n. guerre f.

warehouseman n. magasinier m.; garde-magasin m.

warhead n. partie explosible f.

war horse n. cheval de bataille m.; vétéran m.

warily adv. prudemment

wariness n. prudence f.; défiance f.

warlike a. belliqueux; guerrier, martial

warm a. chaud; chaleureux; cordial; généreux; be — (person) avoir chaud; (weather) faire chaud; — vt. chauffer, réchauffer; — vi. se chauffer, se réchauffer; -ing n. chauffage m.; -th n. chaleur f.; cordialité f.

warm-blooded a. à sang chaud

warmhearted a. généreux

warmonger n. belliqueux m.

warmup n. temps de chauffage m.; répétition f.

warn vt. avertir, prévenir; -ing n. avertissement m.

warp n. chaîne f.; (wood) courbure, voilure f.; — vt. ourdir; (wood) faire voiler, déjeter; (naut.) touer; (fig.) pervertir, fausser; — vi. se déjeter; se déformer; se voiler; -ed a. déjeté, voilé; perverti, faussé

warrant n. mandat, ordre m.; warrant m.; garantie f.; — of arrest mandat d'arrêt m.; — officer n. adjudant m.; — vt. garantir; certifier; justifier; -ed a. garanti; justifié; -y n. garantie f.

warren n. garenne f.

warrior n. guerrier, soldat m.

Warsaw n. Varsovie f.

warship n. navire de guerre m.

wart n. verrue f.

wartime n. temps de guerre m.

wary a. prudent; attentif

wash n. lavage m.; blanchissage m.; lessive f.; (art) lavis m.; (naut.) sillage m.; — vt. laver; blanchir; lotionner; — one's hands se laver les mains; — vi. se laver; — away enlever; emporter; — down laver; (food) arroser; — out laver; rincer; enlever; -able a. lavable; -ed a. lavé; -ed out délavé; raté; -er n. laveur m.; plongeur m.; -ing n. lavage m.; blanchissage m.; linge m.; -ing machine laveuse méchanique f.; -ing soda soude m.

washbowl n. cuvette de lavabo f.

washcloth n. gant-éponge m., lavette f.

washroom n. lavabos m. pl.; cabinets m. pl.

washstand n. lavabo m.

washtub n. cuvier m.

waste n. gaspillage m.; déchets m. pl., rebut m.; désert m.; — of time perte de temps f.; -paper papiers m. pl., papiers de rebut m. pl.; — pipe tuyau d'écoulement m.; — a. de rebut; — vt. gaspiller; (time) perdre; user, consumer; — vi. s'user; se perdre; maigrir; -d a. gaspillé; perdu; dévasté; -ful a. gaspilleur; prodigue; -fulness n. gaspillage m.; prodigalité f.

wastebasket n. corbeille (à papiers) f.

wastepaper a., — basket corbeille (à papiers) f.

watch n. surveillance f.; garde f.; (naut.) quart m.; bordée f.; (timepiece) montre f.; on the — sur ses gardes, en observation; be on the — for guetter; — pocket gousset de montre m.; — vt. observer; regarder; veiller (sur); surveiller; assister à; — vi. veiller; — out être sur ses gardes; faire attention, prendre garde; — out! attention!, prenez garde!; — over garder; surveiller; -er n. observateur m.; -ful a. attentif; alerte, vigilant; -fulness n. vigilance f.

watchdog n. chien de garde m.

watch fire n. feu (de bivouac) m.

watchmaker n. horloger m.

watchman n. veilleur de nuit m.; garde, gardien m.

watchtower n. tour d'observation f.

watchword n. mot d'ordre m.

water n. eau f.; by — en bateau; cold — eau fraîche f.; drinking — eau potable f.; fresh — eau douce f.; running — eau courante f.; turn on the — ouvrir l'eau; under — submergé; inondé; — closet m.; cabinets m. pl.; — color aquarelle f.; — cure hydrothérapie f.; — faucet robinet m.; — front quartier de la ville qui fait face à l'eau m.; — gauge hydromètre m.; — glass verre m.; (chem.) silicate de soude m.; — level niveau d'eau m.; — line niveau d'eau m.; (naut.) flottaison f.; — lily n. lis d'eau m.; — main conduite principale f.; — polo waterpolo m.; — power force hydraulique f.; — softener adoucisseur d'eau m.; — system canalisation d'eau f.; — tower château d'eau m.; — wheel roue hydraulique f.; — vt. arroser; diluer; couper; abreuver; — vi. larmoyer, pleurer; — down atténuer; -ing n. irrigation f.; arrosage m.; dilution f.; abreuvage m.; (eyes) larmoiement m.; -ing can arrosoir m.; -y a. aqueux; larmoyant; (color) déteint

watercress n. cresson m.

waterfall n. chute d'eau, cascade f.

waterlog vt. imprégner d'eau; -ged a. plein d'eau

watermark n. (paper) filigrane m.; -ed a. à filigrane

watermelon n. pastèque f.

waterproof a. imperméable; — vt. rendre étanche

waterspout n. gouttière f.; tuyau m.; trombe f.

watertight a. étanche

waterway n. voie d'eau (navigable) f.

waterworks n. pl. service des eaux m.

watt n. watt m.; **-age** n. wattage m.; consommation en watts f.

wave n. (gesture) geste, salut m.; vague, onde f.; (hair) ondulation f.; permanent — indéfrisable f.; tidal — raz de marée m.; — vi. ondoyer; flotter, se balancer; tournoyer; faire un geste, saluer; — vt. agiter; (hair) onduler; **-d** a. ondulé

wave length n. longueur d'onde f.

waver vi. vaciller, chanceler; **-ing** n. vacillation, irrésolution f.; **-ing** a. irrésolu, vacillant; **—** n. hésitation, indécision f.

wavy a. ondoyant; ondulé, onduleux

wax n. cire f.; **—** paper papier ciré m.; — vt. cirer; — vi. croître, s'accroître; se faire; **-en** a. de cire; **-y** a. de cire, comme de la cire

way n. voie f.; chemin m., route f.; passage m.; moyen, expédient m.; manière, façon f.; all the — jusqu'au bout; by the — à propos; by — of par; get out of the — laisser passer; se ranger; give — céder le pas; se ranger; se rompre; (floor) se casser look the other — ne pas regarder; détourner les yeux; lose one's — se perdre, s'égarer; make — faire place (à); on the — en route; out of the — isolé; start on one's — se mettre en route; the right — la bonne voie, la bonne route f.; the wrong — la mauvaise voie, la mauvaise route f.; go the wrong — se tromper de chemin; prendre la mauvaise route; under — en route; en train; — in entrée f.; — out sortie f.

wayfarer n. voyageur m.

waylay vt. guetter au passage

wayside n. bord de la route m.; leave by the — abandonner; laisser en arrière

wayward a. vagabond; rebelle

we pron. nous; on

weak a. faible; débile; mou (molle); pauvre; sans vigueur; **-en** vi. s'affaiblir; — vt. affaiblir; **-ening** n. affaiblissement m.; **-ling** n. faible m.; **-ness** n. faiblesse f.; faible m.

weakhearted a. & adv. qui manque de courage; sans courage

weak-kneed a. irrésolu; aux genoux faibles

weakling n. personne faible f., homme faible m.; homme qui manque de force m.

weak-minded a. peu intelligent; à l'esprit faible

wealth n. bien m., richesses f. pl.; **-y** a. riche, opulent

wean vt. sevrer; priver de

weapon n. arme f.

wear n. usure f.; usage m.; — vt. porter; user; — vi. faire de l'usage; s'user; — away vt. user; ronger; effacer; — away vi. s'user; — out user; fatiguer, épuiser; **-able** a. propre à porter; **-ing** a. fatigant

weariness n. lassitude, fatigue f.; ennui m.

wearisome a. ennuyeux

weary vt. fatiguer; ennuyer; — a. las, fatigué, ennuyé

weather n. temps m.; — bureau bureau météorologique m.; — forecast prévisions météorologiques f. pl.; **-man** météorologue m.; — report bulletin météorologique m.; the — is nice il fait beau; the — is bad il fait mauvais; — vt. résister à; user, décolorer

weather-beaten a. battu par le vent

weatherproof a. à l'épreuve du temps; imperméable

weave n. texture f.; — vt. tisser; entrelacer; mêler, entremêler; **-r** n. tisserand m.

weaving n. tissage m.

web n. tissu m.; (spider) toile d'araignée f.; membrane f.; **-bed** a. palmé

web-footed a. aux pieds palmés

wed vt. épouser, se marier avec; — vi. se marier; **-ding** n. mariage m., noces f. pl.; **-ding** cake gâteau de noces m.; **-ding** ring alliance f.

wedge n. coin m.; — vt. fendre; serrer, forcer; coincer; caler; **-d** a. en forme de coin; cunéiforme

wedlock n. mariage m.

Wednesday n. mercredi m.; Ash — mercredi des cendres m.

wee a. tout petit

weed n. mauvaise herbe f.; **-s** pl. habits de deuil m. pl.; — vt. sarcler; — out sarcler; éliminer; **-er** n. sarcleur m.; (tool) sarcloir m.; **-ing** n. sarclage m.; **-y** a. plein de mauvaises herbes

week n. semaine f.; huit jours m.; two **-s** quinze jours m. pl.; deux semaines f. pl.; a — from today d'aujourd'hui en huit; **-ly** a. hebdomadaire

weekday n. jour de la semaine m.; jour ouvrable m.; **-s** a. des jours ouvrables

weekend n. fin de semaine f.; week-end m.

weep vi. pleurer; **-er** n. pleureur m.; **-ing** n. pleurs m. pl., larmes f. pl.; **-ing** willow saule pleureur m.; **-y** a. larmoyant

weigh vt. peser; soupeser; examiner, considérer; — vi. peser; — anchor lever l'ancre; — down surcharger; — in se faire peser; **-ing** n. pesée f.

weight n. poids m., pesanteur f.; fardeau m.; importance f.; force f.; gain — prendre du poids; lose — perdre du poids; maigrir; — vt. charger; plomber; **-iness** n. pesanteur f.; importance f.; **-y** a. pesant, important

weird a. mystérieux, surnaturel

welcome n. bon accueil m.; bienvenue f.; — interj. soyez le bienvenu; — a. bienvenu; agréable; you're — de rien; ce n'est rien; il n'y a pas de quoi; à votre service; — vt. accueillir, faire bon accueil à

weld n. soudure f.; — vt. souder (à chaud); **-er** n. soudeur m.; **-ing** n. soudage m.

welfare n. bien-être m.; — state état socialiste m.; — work bonnes œuvres f. pl.; assistance sociale f.

well n. puits m.; — vi. sourdre; jaillir — adv. bien; alors; — as — aussi; as — as aussi bien que; comme; very — très bien; — a. bien; bon; be — aller bien; se porter bien; — interj. eh bien

well-advised a. prudent, sage

well-behaved a. sage; bien élevé
well-being n. bien-être m.
wellborn a. de haute naissance
well-bred a. bien élevé; bien éduqué
well-chosen a. bien choisi
well-earned a. bien mérité
well-educated a. instruit
well-informed a. au courant; bien renseigné; instruit
well-kept a. bien tenu; (secret) bien gardé
well-known a. connu; célèbre; fameux
well-mannered a. bien élevé
well-meaning a. bien intentionné
well off a. aisé; qui a du bien
well-read a. instruit; savant
well-shaped a. bien formé
well-spent a. bien utilisé
well-suited a. to be — to être fait pour
well-to-do a. prospère, riche, aisé
Welsh a. gallois; -man n. Gallois m.
welt n. zébrure f.
welter n. désordre m., confusion f.
welterweight n. poids mi-moyen m.
wen n. loupe f., goître m.
wench n. fille f.; donzelle f.; gaillarde f.
wend vi. aller, poursuivre; —vt. se diriger, poursuivre son chemin
west n. ouest, occident m.; — adv. vers l'ouest; —a. de l'ouest; -erly a. de l'ouest; -ern a. occidental, de l'ouest; -ward vers l'ouest
wet n. humidité f.; — vt. mouiller, humecter, arroser; —a. mouillé, humide, get — se mouiller; soaking — mouillé jusqu'aux os; — blanket trouble-fête, rabat-joie m.; — nurse nourrice f.; -ness n. humidité f.
whack n. coup m.; — vt. battre, rosser
whale n. baleine f.; -r n. baleinier m.; — vi. faire la pêche à la baleine
wharf n. quai m.; embarcadère m.; apponotement m.; — vi. amarrer; -age n. quayage m.
what pron. que, qu'est-ce que, qu'est-ce qui; ce qui, ce que; quoi; —a. quel; — is the matter? qu'y a-t-il?; — is the matter with him? qu'a-t-il?; -'s the use? à quoi bon? — time is it? quelle heure est-il?; — interj. quoi; comment
whatever pron. tout ce qui, tout ce que; n'importe quoi; quoi que ce soit; — a. quelconque; quel . . . . que; aucun
whatsoever pron. quoi que ce soit; quelconque
wheat n. froment, blé m.; -en a. de blé
wheedle vt. enjôler, flatter
wheel n. roue f.; spinning — rouet m.; steering — volant m.; —vt. & vi. rouler, faire tourner -ed a. à roues
wheelbarrow n. brouet m.
wheel base n. distance entre les essieux f.
wheel chair n. fauteuil roulant m., voiture de malade f.
wheelwright n. charron m.
wheeze vi. respirer avec bruit; siffler
wheezing n. respiration sifflante f.
wheezy a. sifflant; asthmatique
whelp n. petit chien m.; — vi. mettre bas
when adv. quand; lorsque; tandis que; où; since — depuis quand
whenever adv. quand; n'importe quand;

toutes les fois que
where adv. où
whereabouts n. situation f.; où l'on se trouve
whereas conj. puisque, comme; vu que; tandis que
whereby adv. par quoi; par lequel
wherefore adv. pourquoi; — n. les pourquoi m. pl.
wherein adv. en quoi; où; dans lequel
whereof adv. de quoi
whereupon adv. sur quoi; là-dessus
wherever adv. n'importe où; où que; partout où
wherewithal n. de quoi; ce qu'il faut
whet vt. aiguiser; exciter
whether conj. soit que; que; si
whetstone n. pierre à aiguiser f.
which pron. lequel, laquelle; qui, que; — a. quel; quoi; — one lequel; — way par où; of — dont; duquel
whichever a. quel (que); — conj. quoi que; — pron. n'importe lequel
whiff n. souffle m., bouffée f.
while n. temps, espace de temps m.; a little — ago tout à l'heure; in a little — tout à l'heure; be worth — valoir la peine; — vt. to — away tuer (le temps); — conj. pendant que, tandis que; tant que; à mesure que; bien que, quoique
whim n. caprice m., fantaisie f.
whimper vi. pleurnicher; — n. pleurnichement m.; -er n. pleurnicheur m.; -ing n. pleurnichement m.
whimsical a. capricieux; bizarre
whine n. plainte f.; gémissement m.; — vi. se plaindre, geindre, gémir, se lamenter
whining a. plaintif, pleurnicheur; — n. plaintes f. pl., pleurnichement m.; sifflement m.
whinny n. hennissement m.; — vi. hennir
whip n. fouet m.; riding — cravache f.; — hand avantage, dessus m.; — vt. fouetter; battre, vaincre; -ped cream crème fouettée f.; -ping n. fouettée f.; fouettement m.; coups de fouet m. pl.
whirl n. tourbillon m.; tournoiement m.; — vt. faire tourner avec vitesse; — vi. tournoyer, pirouetter
whirlpool n. tourbillon m.
whirlwind n. tourbillon m.
whirr, whir n. ronflement m.; — vi. ronfler
whisk n. mouvement brusque m.; époussette f.; — broom petit balai m.; — vt. agiter; — away enlever, chasser; enlever; — vi. passer rapidement
whisker n. poil (de la barbe) m.; -s pl. barbe f.; side -s favoris m. pl.
whisper n. chuchotement m.; — vt. & vi. chuchoter
whistle n. sifflet m.; sifflement m.; — vt. & vi. siffler
whit n. point, iota m.
white a. blanc (blanche); pâle; pur; turn — blanchir; pâlir; — elephant n. (fig.) fardeau m.; chose encombrante f.; — heat n. incandescence f.; — n. blanc m.; -ness n. blancheur f.
whitecap n. mouton m.
white-collar — worker a. & n. employé (dans un bureau)
whitefish n. merlan m.

white-hot *a.* chauffé à blanc, incandescent

whiten *vt.* blanchir

whitewash *n.* blanc de chaux, lait de chaux *m.*; — *vt.* passer au chaux, blanchir à la chaux; (fig.) justifier, donner des apparences légitimes à

whither *adv.* où

whitish *a.* blanchâtre

whittle *vt.* couper, tailler; amenuiser

whiz *n.* sifflement *n.*; (coll.) expert, génie *m.*; — *vi.* siffler; passer très vite

who *pron.* qui, qui est-ce qui; quel

whoever *pron.* qui que; quiconque, celui qui; qui que ce soit

whole *n.* total, tout *m.*; totalité *f.*; entier *m.*; — number *n.* nombre entier *m.*; — note *n.* (mus.) ronde *f.*; on the — pour la plupart; dans l'ensemble; à tout prendre, en somme — *a.* tout, entier, complet; sain

wholehearted *a.* sincère, de tout cœur

wholesale *n.* gros *m.*; — *a. & adv.* en gros; — *vt.* vendre en gros; — *n.* marchand en gros *m.*

wholesome *a.* sain, salutaire

whole-wheat *a.* de blé entier

wholly *adv.* entièrement, complètement, tout cà fait

whom *pron.* que; qui; lequel; of — dont, duquel

whomever *pron.* quiconque, celui que

whoop *n.* huée *f.*; houp *m.*; — *vi.* huer, crier; -ing cough *n.* coqueluche *f.*

whore *n.* prostituée *f.*

whorl *n.* volute *f.*

whose *pron.* dont, de qui, à qui

why *adv.* pourquoi; — *interj.* mais

wick *n.* mèche *f.*

wicked *a.* méchant, scélérat; mauvais; -ness *n.* méchanceté *f.*

wicker *n.* osier *m.*; — *a.* en osier

wicket *n.* guichet *m.*

wide *a.* large; vaste, ample; — *adv.* largement; au loin; far and — partout; — awake *a.* tout à fait éveillé; ouvert; -ly *adv.* largement; très; beaucoup; — *vt.* élargir; — *vi.* s'élargir

wide-eyed *a.* abasourdi

wide-felt *a.* ressenti partout

wide-open *a.* ouvert

widespread *a.* répandu

widow *n.* veuve *f.*; — *vt.* rendre veuve; priver; -ed *a.* veuf; -er *n.* veuf *m.*; -hood *n.* veuvage *m.*

width *n.* largeur *f.*

wield *vt.* manier, tenir, porter

wife *n.* femme, épouse *f.*; -ly *a.* de femme, d'épouse

wig *n.* perruque *f.*

wiggle *vt.* manier, tortiller; — *vi.* se tortiller

wigwag *vt.* agiter; signaler par l'emploi de drapeaux

wild *a.* sauvage, farouche; agreste, inculte; irrégulier, dissolu; -s *n. pl.* désert *m.*; -ness *n.* férocité *f.*; état sauvage *m.*; fureur *f.*; extravagance *f.*

wildcat *n.* lynx *m.*; — *a.* spéculatif, risqué; — strike grève non autorisée *f.*

wilderness *n.* désert *m.*

wildfire *n.* feu grégeois *m.*; like — extrê-

mement vite

wild-goose chase *n.* entreprise infructueuse *f.*; démarches inutiles *f. pl.*

wile *n.* fourberie, ruse *f.*

wilful *a.* entêté; prémédité; -ly *adv.* à dessein, exprès; avec entêtement; -ness *n.* entêtement *m.*, obstination *f.*

wiliness *n.* astuce *f.*

will *n.* volonté *f.*; disposition *f.*; (law) testament *m.*; at — à volonté; of one's own free — de son plein gré; — *vt.* vouloir; laisser par testament; léguer; -ing *a.* disposé, consentant; be -ing vouloir bien; -ingness *n.* consentement *m.*; bonne volonté *f.*

willow *n.* saule *m.*; weeping — saule pleureur *m.*; -y *a.* svelte, souple

will power *n.* volonté *f.*

willy-nilly *adv.* bon gré mal gré

wilt *vi.* se faner, se flétrir

wily *a.* rusé, fin; malin

wimple *n.* guimpe *f.*

win *vt. & vi.* gagner; acquérir; — a prize remporter un prix; — over gagner; -ner *n.* gagnant *m.*; -ning *a.* gagnant; engageant

wince *vi.* broncher; faire une grimace

winch *n.* treuil *m.*

wind *n.* vent *m.*; haleine *f.*; get one's second — reprendre haleine; — instrument instrument à vent *m.*; — *vt.* essouffler; -ed *a.* essoufflé, hors d'haleine; -y *a.* venteux; it is -y il fait du vent

wind *n.* tour *m.*; tournant *m.*; — *vt.* tourner, tordre; envelopper, entourer; enrouler; — *vi.* tourner, se tordre, serpenter; — up remonter; terminer; -ing *m.* détour, tournant *m.*; enroulement *m.*; bandage *m.*; -ing *a.* sinueux, en lacet; -ing sheet *n.* linceul *m.*

windfall *n.* aubaine *f.*

windjammer *n.* voilier *m.*

windlass *n.* treuil, guindeau *m.*

windmill *n.* moulin à vent *m.*

window *n.* fenêtre; croisée *f.*; (ticket) guichet *m.*; (store) vitrine, devanture *f.*; French — porte-fenêtre *f.*; stained-glass — vitrail *m.*; — envelope enveloppe à fenêtre *f.*

window dresser, window trimmer *n.* étalagiste *m.*

window dressing *n.* art de l'étalage *m.*; (coll.) trompe-l'œil *m.*

windowpane *n.* carreau *m.*

window-shopping *n.* lèche-vitrines *m.*

window sill *n.* appui, rebord (de fenêtre) *m.*

windpipe *n.* trachée-artère *f.*; gosier *m.*

windshield *n.* pare-brise *m.*; — wiper essuie-glace *m.*

wind-swept *a.* venteux

wind tunnel *n.* tunnel aérodynamique *m.*

windward *a. & adv.* vers le vent, sous le vent

wine *n.* vin *m.*; — grower vigneron *m.*

winecellar *n.* cave au vin *f.*

wineglass *n.* verre à vin *m.*

wing *n.* aile *f.*; -s *pl.* (theat.) coulisses *f. pl.*; -ed *vi.* voler, s'envoler; -ed *a.* ailé

wingspan, wingspread *n.* envergure *f.*

wink *n.* clin d'œil *m.*; clignement d'œil

m.; — vi. clignoter; cligner de l'œil; fermer les yeux

winnow vt. vanner; éplucher

winsome a. séduisant

winter n. hiver m.; — vi. hiverner; passer l'hiver; -ize vt. équiper pour l'hiver

wintergreen n. wintergreen m., pyrole f.; gaulthérie (du Canada) f.; palommier m.

wintertime n. hiver m., saison d'hiver f.

wintry a. d'hiver; froid, glacial

wipe n. action d'essuyer; — vt. essuyer; — one's nose se moucher; — out détruire, exterminer; effacer

wire n. fil (de métal) m.; télégramme m.; pull -s (coll.) arranger les choses, user de l'influence; — vt. munir de fils; faire une installation électrique; — vi. (coll.) télégraphier; -less a. san fil; -less n. radio

wire cutter n. coupe-fil m.

wire-haired a. à poil dur

wire tapping n. captation f.

wiring n. canalisation, pose de fils f.

wiry a. de fil, de en fil (de metal); (hair) raide; (person) sec

wisdom n. sagesse f.; — tooth dent de sagesse f.

wise n. manière, façon f.; in no — d'aucune façon; — a. sage; prudent

wish n. souhait m.; désir m.; vœu m.; — vt. & vi. désirer, vouloir; souhaiter; -ful a. désireux

wishbone n. lunette f.

wishy-washy a. fade, indifférent

wisp n. touffe, poignée f.

wistful a. pensif; plein de regret

wit n. esprit m.; bel esprit m.; — vt. savoir; to — à savoir, c'est-à-dire; -less a. sans esprit; -tingly adv. à dessein; -ty a. spirituel

witch n. sorcière f.

witchcraft, witchery n. sorcellerie f.; sortilège m.

with prep. avec; de; par; parmi; à; malgré

withdraw vt. retirer; rappeler; — vi. se retirer, s'éloigner; -al n. retrait, rappel m.; retraite f.

wither vt. flétrir, faner, dessécher; — vi. se faner, se dessécher

withhold vt. retenir, détenir; empêcher; -ing a., -ing tax impôt retenu à la source m.

within prep. dedans, à l'interieur; — prep. à l'intérieur de; dans; à portée de; à moins de; avant

without prep. sans; hors de; do — se passer de; — adv. dehors; au dehors, en dehors; — conj. sans que

withstand vt. résister, s'opposer à

witness n. témoin, témoignage m.; to bear — to témoigner de; — vt. attester, être temoin de, assister à

witticism n. bon mot m.

wizard n. magicien, sorcier m.

wizened a. desséchée

wobble vi. chanceler, vaciller, tituber; branler

wobbly a. vacillant, branlant

woe n. douleur f.; malheur m.; -ful a. triste, malheureux

woman n. femme f.; -ly a. féminin; de femme

womb n. matrice f.; sein, ventre m.

wonder n. étonnement m., admiration f.; miracle m.; — vi. s'étonner; se demander; -ful a. merveilleux; -ment n. étonnement m., admiration f.

wonderland n. pays des merveilles m.

wondrous a. merveilleux

wont n. coutume, habitude f.; -ed a. accoutumé, habituel

woo vt. courtiser; faire la cour à

wood n. bois m.; forêt f.; -ed a. boisé; -en a. de bois, en bois; -en (fig.) gauche -y a. ligneux; fibreux; — alcohol n. alcool méthylique m.

wood carving n. sculpture sur bois f.

woodcut n. gravure sur bois f., bois m., xylographie f.

woodcutter n. bûcheron m.

woodland n. bois m.

woodshed n. bûcher m.

woodsman n. homme des bois m.

wood wind n. bois m.

woodwork n. boiseries f. pl.; charpenterie f.; menuiserie f.

woof n. trame f.

woofer n. haut-parleur (pour les sons graves) m.

wool n. laine f.; steel — laine d'acier f.; -en a. de laine; -ens n. pl. étoffes de laine f. pl.; -y a. laineux; touffu

word n. mot m.; parole f.; nouvelle f., renseignement m.; recommandation f.; in 2 — en un mot, bref; send — to faire savoir, avertir, prevenir; -s pl. dispute f.; have -s with se disputer avec; s'expliquer; — vt. exprimer, rédiger; -iness n. verbosité f.; -ing n. termes m. pl.; -y a. verbeux, prolixe

work n. travail m.; occupation f.; ouvrage m.; opération f.; œuvre f.; besogne, tâche f.; at — au travail; en jeu; -s pl. usine f.; — vi. travailler; (function) marcher, aller; fonctionner; agir; — vt. faire travailler; travailler; opérer; accomplir; exploiter; développer; élaborer; — out résoudre, trouver; s'arranger; — up susciter, causer; -able a. pratique; réalisable; -er n. ouvrier, travailleur m.; -ing a. qui travaille; ouvrier; -ing class classe ouvrière f.; ouvriers m. pl.; -ing n. travail m.; marche f. fonctionnement m.

workbench n. établi m.

workbook n. manuel m.

workday n. jour ouvrable m.

workhouse n. hôpital m.; maison de travail f.; prison municipale f.

workman n. ouvrier m.; -like a. bien travaillé; -ship n. fini m., construction f.; exécution f.

workout n. exercice m.; essai m.

workroom, workshop n. atelier m.

world n. monde, univers m., terre f.; milieu m.; a — of pas mal de; — war guerre mondiale f.; -liness n. mondanité f.; -ly a. du monde; mondain

world-famous a. très connu, célèbre

world-wide a. universel

worm n. ver m.; — vt. (coll.) tirer; -y a. vermoulu

worm-eaten a. vermoulu

worn a. usé

worry n. ennui, souci m.; inquiétude f.; tracasserie f.; chagrin, dépit m., contrariété f.; — vt. harasser, tourmenter, tracasser; inquiéter; — vi. s'inquiéter; se tracasser; don't — ne vous inquiétez pas; soyez tranquille

worse a. pire, plus mauvais; — adv. plus mal, pis; so much the — tant pis; -n vt. aggraver, empirer; -n vi. s'aggraver, empirer

worship n. adoration f., culte m.; — vt. adorer

worst n. pire, pis; at the — au pis; — vt. vaincre, défaire; l'emporter sur; — a. le pire, le plus mauvais; — adv. le pis, le plus mal

worsted a. laine filée, laine peignée f.

worth n. valeur f., prix m.; mérite m.; — a. qui vaut; digne de; be — valoir; be — the trouble, be — while valoir la peine; -iness n. mérite m.; -less a. sans valeur; -y a. digne; be -y of mériter, être digne de

worthwhile a. qui vaut la peine

would-be a. soi-disant

wound n. blessure f.; plaie f.; — vt. blesser; froisser

wraith n. apparition f.

wrangle n. querelle f.; — vi. se quereller; -er n. querelleur m.; vacher m.

wrap n. (garment) manteau m.; emballage m.; — vt. emballer; envelopper, entourer; -per n. emballage m.; couverture f.; chemise f.; robe de chambre f.; -ping n. emballage m., couverture f.; -ping paper papier d'emballage m.

wrath n. colère f., courroux m.; -ful a. courroucé

wreak vt. exécuter, infliger

wreath n. guirlande, couronne f.; -e vt. couronner, enguirlander

wreck n. naufrage m.; ruine f.; accident m.; — vt. causer un naufrage; causer la destruction de; ruiner; détruire; saboter; -age n. débris m. pl.; décombres m. pl.; -ed a. détruit; naufragé; -er n. (auto.) voiture de dépannage f.; (house) démolisseur m.; -ing n. ruine, destruction f.

wrench n. torsion f.; (tool) clé f.; monkey — clé anglaise f.; — vt. arracher, tordre; se fouler

wrestle vi. lutter; — with lutter avec, lutter contre; s'attaquer à; -r n. lutteur m.

wrestling n. lutte f., catch m.

wretch n. misérable m.; malheureux m.; -ed a. misérable; malheureux, méprisable; pitoyable; -edness n. misère f.; malheur m.

wriggle vi. se tortiller; frétiller; — vt. tortiller

wring vt. tordre, tortiller; arracher; -er n. essoreuse f.; -ing a., -ing wet mouillé jusqu'aux os

wrinkle n. ride f.; faux pli m.; (fig.) nouveau tour m.; — vt. rider; froncer;

vi. se rider; -d a. ridé

wrist n. poignet m.

wrist watch n. montre-bracelet m.

writ n. assignation f.; mandat m.

write vt. écrire; — vi. écrire; être écrivain; — down noter; inscrire; — off rayer, (com.) amortir; — out rédiger; — up rédiger, faire le procès-verbal de; -r n. écrivain m., auteur m.

writhe vi. se tordre

writing n. écrit, ouvrage m.; écriture f.; in — par écrit; — paper n. papier à écrire m.

wrong n. tort m.; dommage, détriment m., injustice f.; be in the — avoir tort; — vt. faire tort à; — a. faux; injuste; impropre; mauvais; mal; be — avoir tort; what's — qu'y a-t-il; what's — with you qu'avez-vous; — adv. mal; à tort; do — faire mal; to go — s'égarer; se détraquer, se déranger; -ful a. injuste; -ly adv. à tort; rightly or -ly à tort ou à raison

wrongdoer n. malfaiteur m.

wrongdoing n. mal, crime m.

wrought a. travaillé, ouvragé; — iron fer forgé m.

wry a. tors, tordu, difforme; — face n. grimace f.

X

xenon n. xénon m.

X ray n. rayon X m.; — picture n. radiogramme m.; — specialist n. spécialiste de radiologie m. & f.

xylography n. xylographie f.

xylophone n. xylophone m.

Y

yacht n. yacht m.; -ing n. yachting m.

yachtsman n. yachtman m.

yam n. patate f.

yank n. secousse f.; — vt. tirer brusquement

Yankee n. (coll.) Américain m.; habitant du Nord des Etats-Unis m.; habitant de la Nouvelle-Angleterre m.

yap n. aboiement m.; jappement m.; — vi. aboyer; japper

yard n. cour f.; chantier m.; (naut.) vergue f.; (rail.) dépôt m.; (measure) yard m, (= 91 cm.); — master n. maître de chantier m.

yardstick n. mètre en bois m.

yarn n. fil (pour tissage) m.; (coll.) histoire f.

yawl n. yole f.

yawn n. bâillement m.; — vi. bâiller; -ing a. qui bâille; (fig.) béant

ye pron. vous

yea adv. oui; vraiment

year n. an m., année f.; leap — année bissextile f.; last — l'année passée; school — année scolaire f.; -ly a. annuel; -ly adv. annuellement

yearbook n. annuaire m.

yearling n. animal d'un an m.

yearn *vi.*, — for soupirer après; —ing *n.* désir ardent *m.*, aspiration *f.*

yeast *n.* levure *f.*, levain *m.* levain en cubes *m.*

yell *n.* hurlement *m.*; cri *m.*; — *vi.* hurler; pousser un cri

yellow *n.* jaune *m.*; — *a.* jaune; lâche; infame; turn — jaunir; — fever fièvre jaune *f.*; — *vt. & vi.* jaunir; —ish *a.* jaunâtre

yelp *vi.* glapir, japper; — *n.* jappement *m.*

Yemen *n.* Yemen *m.*

yen *n.* désir *m.*

yeoman *n.* yeoman *m.*; hallebardier *m.*

yes *adv.* oui; (after negation) si; — man *n.* giroutte *f.*

yesterday *adv.* hier; **day before** — avanthier

yet *adv.* encore; cependant, toutefois; déjà; malgré tout; as — jusqu'ici

yield *n.* produit, rendement *m.*; — *vt.* céder; produire, rendre, donner; accorder; procurer; — *vi.* céder; succomber; consentir; —ing *a.* complaisant; souple; mou (molle)

yodel *n.* tyrolienne *f.*; — *vi.* chanter une tyrolienne; iouler

yoke *n.* joug, attelage *m.*; couple *m.*; (dress) empiècement *m.*; — *vt.* mettre au joug; subjuguer; accoupler

yokel *n.* provincial, rustique *m.*

yolk *n.* jaune d'œuf *m.*

yon, yonder *a.* qui est là; — *adv.* là-bas

yore *adv.* jadis, autrefois; **in days of** — au temps jadis

you *pron.* vous; tu; toi; on

young *a.* jeune; nouveau; tendre; —er *a.* cadet

youngster *n.* jeune personne *f.*, jeune homme *m.*; enfant *m.*

your *a.* votre, vos; ton, ta, tes; —s *pron.* le vôtre, la vôtre, les vôtres; à vous; le tien, la tienne; à toi; —self *pron.* vousmême, vous; toi-même, toi

youth *n.* jeunesse *f.*; jeune homme *m.*; —ful *a.* jeune; de jeunesse; —fulness *n.* jeunesse *f.*

yowl *n.* hurlement, jappement *m.*; — *vi.* hurler, japper

Yule *n.* Noël *m.*; — log bûche de Noël *f.*

Yuletide *n.* fêtes de Noël *f. pl.*

Z

zany *n.* bouffon *m.*; — *a.* (coll.) niais; fou; capricieux

zeal *n.* zèle *m.*; ardeur *f.*; —ous *a.* zélé

zealot *n.* fanatique *m. & f.*

zenith *n.* zénith *m.*; comble *m.*

zephyr *n.* zéphyr *m.*

zero *n.* zéro *m.*; (fig.) rien; — hour *n.* (mil.) heure de l'attaque, heure H *f.*

zest *n.* goût *m.*; appétit *m.*; enthousiasme *m.*

zigzag *n.* zigzag *m.*; — *a.* en zigzag; — *vi.* faire des zigzags

zinc *n.* zinc *m.*; — *vt.* zinguer

Zion *n.* Sion *m.*

zipper *n.* fermeture éclair *f.*

zircon *n.* zircon *m.*

zither *n.* cithare *f.*

zodiac *n.* zodiaque *m.*

zone *n.* zone *f.*; — *vt.* repartir en zones

zoo *n.* jardin *n.* jardin zoologique, zoo *m.*

zoologist *n.* zoologiste *m.*

zoology *n.* zoologie *f.*

zoom *n.* bourdonnement *m.*; — *vi.* monter verticalement; bourdonner

zouave *n.* zouave *m.*

Zulu *a. & n.* zoulou *m.*

Zuyder Zee *n.* Zuyderzée *m.*

TRAVELER'S CONVERSATION GUIDE
Guide de Conversation pour le Voyage

TRAVELER'S CONVERSATION GUIDE
Guide de Conversation pour le Voyage

STATION (OR AIRPORT)
LA GARE (OU L'AEROPORT)

Where do I go through customs?	Où se trouve la douane?
I have nothing to declare.	Je n'ai rien à déclarer.
All I have are my personal things and a few packages of cigarettes.	Je n'ai que des effets personnels et quelques paquets de cigarettes.
I need a porter.	J'ai besoin d'un porteur.
Where is my baggage?	Où sont mes bagages?
This is not my suitcase. Please look for mine.	Cette valise n'est pas à moi. Allez chercher la mienne, s'il vous plaît.
This is my baggage.	Voici mes bagages.
I checked two trunks.	J'ai fait enregister deux malles.
I'll carry this suitcase.	Cette valise, je vais la porter.
Are meals included on that flight?	Est-ce que le prix du billet comprend les repas?
Are the cars air-conditioned?	Est-ce que les wagons sont climatisés?

TAXI
LE TAXI

Will you get a taxi for me, please?	Voulez-vous bien me chercher un taxi?
Take me to the Hotel ———	L'Hôtel ———, s'il vous plaît.
How much is the fare?	Le tarif, c'est combien?
Is it very far?	Est-ce que très loin?
I am in a great hurry	Je suis très pressé.
Drive carefully, please.	Conduisez avec soin, s'il vous plaît.
Stop at the next corner.	Arrêtez (-vous) à la prochaine rue.
Faster, please.	Plus vite, s'il vous plaît.
Not so fast.	Pas si vite.
Slower.	Plus lentement.
Stop!	Arrêtez-vous!
Go on.	Continuez.
Go straight ahead.	Allez tout droit.
Turn to your left. (right)	Tournez à gauche. (droite)
This is for you.	Voici pour vous.

HOTEL

L'HÔTEL

Where is the office?
Où est le bureau?

I have a reservation.
J'ai fait réserver une chambre.

I want a single room with bath.
Je voudrais une chambre à un lit avec bain.

Have you a two-bed room?
Avez-vous une chambre à deux lits?

Is it a front room?
Est-ce que la chambre donne sur la rue?

I'm going to stay two weeks. (a week)
Je vais rester quinze jours. (huit jours)

Can I pay by the week or by the month?
Est-ce qu'on peut payer par semaine ou par mois?

Do you have anything less expensive?
Avez-vous quelque chose de moins cher?

Are meals included in the price?
Est-ce le prix de la chambre comprend les repas? Combien de repas?

How many?
What are your meal hours?
A quelle heure sert-on les repas?

Is there a bank near here?
Est-ce qu'il y a une banque près d'ici?

Is there a post office near here?
Est-ce qu'il y a un bureau de poste près d'ici?

Are there towels in the room?
Y a-t-il des serviettes dans la chambre?

Bring me some ice, please.
Apportez-moi de la glace, s'il vous plaît.

Is the water here drinkable?
L'eau ici est potable, n'est pas?

Don't you have any pillows?
N'avez-vous pas d'oreillers?

Please call me at eight o'clock.
Je voudrais qu'on m'appelle à huit heures.

Is there laundry service?
Puis-je faire blanchir mon linge ici?

I want this suit pressed.
Pouvez-vous donner un coup de fer à ce complet.

I want this dress cleaned.
Pouvez-vous nettoyer cette robe.

I would like an extra blanket.
Je voudrais une couverture supplémentaire.

Do you have a map of ———?
Avez-vous une carte de ———?

Do you have any stamps?
Avez-vous des timbres?

May I have the bill, please?
La note, s'il vous plaît.

Are taxes and service included?
Taxes et service compris, n'est pas?

Do you accept travelers' checks?
Acceptez-vous les chèques de voyageur?

Will you have my bags taken down, please?
Voulez-vous bien faire descendre mes bagages?

RESTAURANT

LE RESTAURANT

Do you have a table for two?
Avez-vous une table pour deux?

I would like to sit near a window. (outside) (inside)
Je préférerais une table près d'une fenêtre. (sur la terrase) (à l'intérieur)

I'll have the table d'hote dinner.
Le menu (à prix fixe), s'il vous plaît.

May I have a menu?
La carte, s'il vous plaît?

May I keep this as a souvenir?
Est-ce que je peux garder cela comme souvenir?

I have no napkin.
Je n'ai pas de serviette.

Bring me some butter, please.
Du beurre, s'il vous plaît.

How do you prefer the steak?
Comment préférez-vous le bifteck?

I prefer it very rare. (medium rare) (medium) (well-done)
Je le préfère saignant. (juste à point) (bien cuit) (très bien cuit)

What do you have for dessert?
Qu'avez-vous comme dessert?

Bring me some more bread please.
Apportez-moi encore du pain, s'il vous plaît.

Coffee with cream, please. (milk)
Un café à la crême, s'il vous plaît. (au lait)

Tea with lemon. (milk)
Un thé au citron. (au lait)

Waiter, the check, please.
Garçon, l'addition, s'il vous plaît.

Where is the washroom?
Où se trouvent les cabinets?

They have fish. (meat, fowl)
Il y a du poisson. (de la viande, de la volaille)

Do you want pork? (beef, veal, lamb, chicken, turkey, duck)
Voulez-vous du porc? (du bœuf, du veau, de l'agneau, du poulet, du dindon, du canard)

I want my eggs fried. (poached, scrambled, soft-boiled, with ham, with bacon)
Je préfère les œufs sur le plat. (pochés, brouillés, à la coque, au jambon, au lard)

A glass of milk, please.
Un verre de lait, s'il vous plaît.

Orange juice and black coffee.
Un jus d'orange et un café noir.

Rolls and butter.
Des petits pains avec du beurre.

Crescent rolls and coffee with milk.
Des croissants et un café au lait.

Continental breakfast. (coffee, rolls, butter and jam)
Un café (déjeuner) complet.

Toast and jam.
Du pain grillé avec de la confiture.

Waiter, I need a glass. (fork, spoon, knife)
Garçon, je n'ai pas de verre. (de fourchette, de cuillère, de couteau)

MONEY

L'ARGENT

Where can I cash a check?	Où puis-je toucher un chèque?
What is the rate of exchange?	Quel est le cours du change?
Here is my passport.	Voici mon passeport.

POST OFFICE

LE BUREAU DE POSTE

I want to send this letter by airmail.	Je veux expédier cette lettre par avion.
How much postage is needed for foreign mail?	Quel est l'affranchissement pour l'étranger?
When will this letter reach the United States by regular mail?	Quand est-ce que cette lettre arrivera au États-Unis, si je l'expédie par courrier ordinaire?
How much is it by regular mail?	Combien est-ce par courrier ordinaire?
I'd like to register this letter.	Je voudrais faire recommander cette lettre.
Are there any letters for me?	Y a-t-il des lettres pour moi?
Is the post office open on Saturday?	Le bureau de poste est-il ouvert le samedi?

AUTOMOBILE

L'AUTOMOBILE

Forty liters of gas, please.	Quarante litres d'essence, s'il vous plaît.
Will you please check the oil and water?	Voulez-vous bien vérifier l'huile et l'eau?
Fill the tank.	Faites le plein.
I've run out of gas.	J'ai une panne d'essence.
I have a flat tire.	J'ai un pneu dégonflé.
Can you fix this puncture?	Pouvez-vous réparer cette crevaison?
Check the tires, including the spare.	Vérifiez les pneus, y compris le pneu de rechange.
Add some air if necessary.	Gonflez-les un peu s'il le faut.
Where is the next gas station?	Où se trouve le prochain poste d'essence?
I want to leave the car here overnight.	Je veux laisser l'auto ici jusqu'à demain matin.
Wash it and change the oil.	Lavez-la et vidangez l'huile.
What do you charge for greasing?	Combien pour le graissage?
Is the road in good condition?	Le chemin est en bon état?

RAILROAD

LE CHEMIN DE FER

Where is the ticket window?
Où se trouvent les guichets?

Two first-class (second) tickets to ————.
Deux billets de première (seconde) class pour ————.

One way.
Aller seulement.

No, round trip.
Non, aller et retour.

Is this the train to ————?
Ce train va à ————?

Does it have Pullman cars?
Y a-t-il des wagons-lits?

I want an upper (lower) berth.
Je veux une couchette supérieure. (inférieure)

I want a one-berth compartment. (two-berth)
Je veux un compartiment individuel. (double)

When do we reach ————?
A quelle heure arrivons-nous à ————?

Are we on time?
Sommes-nous à l'heure?

How late are we?
De combien sommes-nous en retard?

Is there a dining car?
Y a-t-il un wagon-restaurant?

How late do they serve breakfast?
Jusqu'a quelle heure sert-on le petit déjeuner?

When do they start serving lunch?
A quelle heure commence-t-on à servir le déjeuner?

The first service is at noon.
Le premier service est à midi.

The second service is at one-thirty.
Le deuxième service est à une heure et demie.

I'm going to bed.
Je vais me coucher.

Is the berth made up?
Le lit est fait?

Please take down that suitcase.
Voulez-vous bien descendre cette valise?

I feel a draft.
Je sens un courant d'air.

May we turn off the fan?
Si l'on fermait le ventilateur?

May I open the window? (door)
Puis-je ouvrir la fenêtre? (porte)

Have you seen the conductor?
Avez-vous vu le contrôleur?

WEATHER

LE TEMPS

What is the weather like?
Quel temps fait-il?

It is fine weather. (bad, sunny, cold, cool, hot, windy)
Il fait beau. (mauvais, du soleil, froid, frais, chaud, du vent)

It is raining.
Il pleut.

It is snowing.
Il neige.

It is cloudy.
Il y a des nuages.

PHOTOGRAPHY

LA PHOTOGRAPHIE

Is picture taking permitted?
Est-ce qu'on peut photographier?

May I take my camera into the church? (museum)
Puis-je garder mon appareil photographique dans l'église? (le musée)

What is the fee for taking pictures?
Quelle est la taxe pour photographier?

I need some 620 films. (120, color)
J'ai besoin de quelques pellicules six-neuf, petite bobine. (six-neuf, grosse bobine, en couleur)

Where can I buy camera supplies?
Où puis-je acheter du matériel photographique?

My camera doesn't work. Can you fix it?
Mon appareil ne marche pas. Pouvez-vous le réparer?

Can you have this film developed?
Pouvez-vous faire développer cette pellicule?

I want three prints of each.
Je veux trois épreuves de chaque.

Do you have movie film?
Avez-vous des films cinématographiques?

Do you have flashbulbs?
Avez-vous des lampes flash?

May I have these enlarged?
Puis-je faire agrandir ces clichés?

When will it be ready?
Quand est-ce que ce sera prêt?

Does the price include developing?
Est-ce que le prix comprend le développement?

Will you put in the film?
Voudriez-vous mettre la pellicule?

SHOPPING

LES EMPLETTES

I'm going shopping.
Je vais faire des emplettes. (courses)

Is there a department store near here?
Est-ce qu'il y a un grand magasin près d'ici?

How much is this?
C'est combien?

It's too expensive.
C'est trop cher.

May I see something better?
Puis-je voir quelque chose de meilleure qualité?

May I see some shirts? (gloves, ties, handkerchiefs, socks, stockings)
Je voudrais voir des chemises? (gants, cravates, mouchoirs, chaussettes, bas)

Do you have it in white?
L'avez-vous en blanc?

I prefer solid colors.
Je préfère les couleurs unies.

I'd like to try on this dress.
Je voudrais essayer cette robe.

This suit doesn't look very well on me.
Ce tailleur ne me va pas très bien. (f.) Ce complet ne me va pas très bien. (m.)

What size?
Quelle taille?

Can you have them sent to the hotel?
Pourrez-vous les faire envoyer à l'hôtel?

I'll take these postal cards.
Je voudrais ces cartes postales.

KINDS OF STORES

LES MAGASINS

Bookstore	Librairie
Department store	Grand magasin
Drugstore (prescriptions, patent medicines only)	Pharmacie
Florist	Fleuriste
General Hardware, (paint, wallpaper)	Marchand de couleurs, Quincaillerie
Jewelry	Bijouterie
Leather goods	Maroquinerie
Perfumery	Parfumerie
Stationery	Papeterie
Tobacco, matches, stamps, bicycle licenses	Bureau de tabac
Watchmaker, watch repairs	Horlogerie
Variety, ten-cent stores	Prisunic, monoprix, uniprix
Bakery (bread, hard rolls)	Boulangerie
Butcher shop (beef, veal)	Boucherie
Dairy products (milk, cream, cheese, butter, margarine)	Laiterie
Delicatessen, pork (some canned goods)	Charcuterie
Fowl, rabbits	Marchand de volaille
General grocery	Grand magasin d'alimentation
Horsemeat	Boucherie chevaline
Pastries (fancy bread and rolls)	Pâtisserie
Pushcarts (usually only one item of fresh produce)	Marchand des quatre saisons
Spices, staples (sometimes fresh vegetables, fruits, and wine)	Épicerie
Vegetables	Marchand de légumes
Wines & Liqueurs (bottled, bulk)	Marchand de vin
Dressmaker, women's clothes	Couturière
Men's ready-made clothes	Vêtements de confection
Shoes	Chaussures
Tailor, men's made-to-order clothes	Tailleur
Women's hats	Modiste
Barber shop	Coiffeur pour hommes
Beauty shop	Coiffeur pour dames

GENERAL EXPRESSIONS

LES EXPRESSIONS ORDINAIRES

Good morning.	Bonjour
I don't speak French. (English)	Je ne parle pas français. (anglais)
I understand it a good deal, but I don't speak it.	Je comprends assez bien, mais je ne parle pas.
Where are you going?	Où alez-vous?
Come here, please.	Venez ici, s'il vous plaît.
I want to show you something.	Je veux vous montrer quelquechose.
Speak slowly, please.	Parlez lentement, s'il vous plaît.
Wait here.	Attendez ici.
I have no time today.	Je n'ai pas le temps aujourd'hui.
What can I do for you?	Qu'y a-t-il pour votre service?
Can you tell me. . . . ?	Pouvez-vous me dire. . . . ?
I think so. (not)	Je crois que oui. (non)
Is there a doctor near here?	Y a-t-il un médecin près ici?
What do you think?	Qu'en pensez-vous?
You know what I mean?	Vous savez ce que je veux dire?
How do you say that in French?	Comment dit-on cela en français?
What is that for?	A quoi est-ce que cela sert?
Do you understand me?	Me comprenez-vous?
I understand you when you speak slowly.	Je vous comprends quand vous parlez lentement.
Sorry, but I don't understand you.	Je regrette, je ne vous comprends pas.
Please repeat that question.	Veuillez répéter la question?
Now I understand.	Maintenant je comprends.
You are too kind.	Vous êtes trop aimable.
Thank you very much.	Merci beaucoup.
You are welcome.	De rien.
How are you?	Comment allez-vous?
Fine, thank you, and you?	Bien, merci, et vous?
Of course	Bien entendu
Right and left	À droite et à gauche
After all	Après tout
Willingly	Volontiers
By force	De force
From time to time	De temps en temps

DIVISIONS OF TIME

TELLING TIME
L'HEURE

What time is it?	Quelle heure est-il?
It is one o'clock. (two)	Il est une heure. (deux heures)
It is 10:15.	Il est dix heures et quart.
It is 10:30.	Il est dix heures et demie.
It is a quarter to eleven.	Il est onze heures moins le quart.
It is 11:20.	Il est onze heures vingt.
It is twenty minutes to eleven.	Il est onze heures moins vingt.
It is noon. (midnight)	Il est midi. (minuit)
It is 2 A.M.	Il est deux heures du matin.
It is 2 P.M.	Il est deux heures de l'après midi.
The train leaves at 2 P.M.	Le train part à quatorze heures.
It is 6 P.M.	Il est six heures du soir.

DAYS OF THE WEEK
JOURS DE LA SEMAINE

Monday	lundi
Tuesday	mardi
Wednesday	mercredi
Thursday	jeudi
Friday	vendredi
Saturday	samedi
Sunday	dimanche

MONTHS OF THE YEAR
MOIS DE L'ANNÉE

January	janvier
February	février
March	mars
April	avril
May	mai
June	juin
July	juillet
August	août
September	septembre
October	octobre
November	novembre
December	décembre

SEASONS OF THE YEAR
SAISONS DE L'ANNÉE

Spring: summer: fall: winter   printemps: été: automne: hiver

CONVERTING TEMPERATURES

FAHRENHEIT TO CENTIGRADE

Subtract 32° and multiply by 5/9.
50°F = 10°C. −4°F = −20°C.

CENTIGRADE TO FAHRENHEIT

Multiply by 9/5 and add 32°.
40°C = 104°F. −20°C = −4°F.

CONVERTING METRIC MEASURES

AMERICAN TO FRENCH

1 gallon	= 3.785 liters (3.8)
1 pound	= .4536 kilos
1 inch	= 2.54 centimeters (2.5)
1 yard	= .9144 meters (9)
1 mile	= 1.6093 kilometers (1.6)
1 acre	= .4047 hectares (.4)

FRENCH TO AMERICAN

1 liter	= .2642 gallon (.26)
1 kilo	= 2.2046 pounds (2.2)
1 centimeter	= .3937 inches (4)
1 meter	= 1.094 yards (1.1)
1 kilometer	= .6214 miles (.6)
1 hectare	= 2.471 acres (2.5)

Figures in parentheses are approximate equivalences.

To convert American measurements into their approximate French equivalences, or vice versa, multiply as indicated in the examples.

Examples: To determine the approximate number of liters in ten gallons, multiply 10 × 3.8 (approximate liters per gallon) = 38.1.

To determine the approximate number of miles in 14 kilometers, multiply 14 × .6 (miles per kilo) = 8.4 miles.

FRENCH ROAD SIGNS

French traffic signs, like those in the United States, show typical shapes but some bear symbols while others have only words. The most common are shown on the following pages. The three distinct shapes are triangular, circular, and rectangular.

△ — Triangular signs indicate danger ahead.

○ — Circular signs give explicit instructions.

□ — Rectangular signs contain specific information.

French traffic proceeds on the right-hand side of the street.

ROAD SIGNS

LES SIGNAUX DE LA ROUTE

Curve	Tournant
Turn	Virage
Curve to the Right (Left)	Virage à Droite (Gauche)
Winding Road for . . . Kilometers	Virages sur . . . km.
Right of Way	Priorité
Caution	Prudence
Bridge Out	Pont Coupé
Level Crossing	Passage à Niveau
School Exit	Sortie d'École
Slippery Pavement	Chaussée Glissante
Narrowing Pavement	Chaussée Rétrécie
Rough Road, Bumpy Road	Chaussée Déformée
Road Under Repair	Travaux
Slow! Construction	Travaux ralentir
Rock Slide, Fallen-rock Zone	Chute de Pierres
Railroad Crossing	Passage à Niveau
Crossroads, Side Road	Intersection
One-way Street	Sens Unique
One-way Traffic (as indicated)	Sens Obligatoire
Keep to the Right	Serrez à Droite
Speed Limit	Limite de Vitesse
No Passing	Défense de Doubler
No Entry	Entrée Interdite
No Stopping	Interdiction de Stationner, Stationnement Interdit
No Parking	Interdiction de Parquer
Parking Allowed	Parcage Autorisé
Parking on Even (Odd) Calendar Dates .	Stationnement Autorisé Jours Pairs (Impairs)

ROAD SIGNS

LES SIGNAUX DE LA ROUTE

Parking on Even-numbered Side of the Street on Even Calendar Dates: Odd Side on Odd Dates
Stationnement Pair—Impair

Parking Restricted
Stationnement Réglementé

Parking Reserved for Buses (Taxis, Passenger Cars)
Stationnement Réservé aux Cars (Autobus, Taxis, Voitures de Tourisme)

No Thoroughfare
Circulation Interdite

Slow
Ralentissez

Detour
Deviation

Closed to All Motor Vehicles
Interdit à Tous les Véhicules Automobiles

Closed to Heavy Traffic
Interdit aux Poids Lourds

Closed to Cyclists
Interdit aux Cyclistes

End of No Parking Zone
Fin d'Interdiction de Stationner

End of No Passing Zone
Fin d'Interdiction de Dépasser

End of One-way Traffic, Two-way Traffic Begins
Fin de Sens Unique

Use of Horns Forbidden
Signaux Sonores Interdits

Speed Limit
Vitesse Maximum

Low Clearance
Hauteur Limitée

Parking Only with Disk in Window to Indicate Time of Arrival
Dispositif de Contrôle Obligatoire, Disque Obligatoire

Zone in Which Parking Disk Must be Used
Zone Bleue

End of Construction Area
Fin de Chantier

Ferry
Bac

Narrow Bridge
Pont Étroit

Customs
Poste de Douane

Hospital
Hôpital

French Highway Aid, Emergency Telephone
Secours Routier Français

Turn on Headlights
Allumez vos Lanternes

I. DANGER SIGNS

CURVE SIGNS

Curve

Left

Right

Dangerous

S-curve

CROSSING SIGNS

Railroad Signs (guarded)

(unguarded)

Dangerous Crossroad

You Have Priority

Right Has Priority

GENERAL SIGNS

Bump or Dip

Hill

Side Road

Narrow Road

Slippery Pavement

Crosswalk

Cattle Crossing

School

Drawbridge

Stop Ahead

Stop

Yield Ahead

Caution

Yield

Men Working

GENERAL SIGNS

No Left Turn

No Passing

End No Passing Zone

Bicycle Path

50 km. per hr.

cars 50 trucks 30

End Speed Limit

No Horns

No Parking

Traffic Circle

Keep Right

Customs

No Bicycles

One Way

Stop—Police (check-point)

II. DEFINITE INSTRUCTION SIGNS

NO ENTRY SIGNS

Closed to Traffic

No Entry

No Autos

No Motorcycles

No Vehicles

III. INFORMATIVE SIGNS

Parking

Gas Station

Telephone

Garage

Hospital